KU-513-216

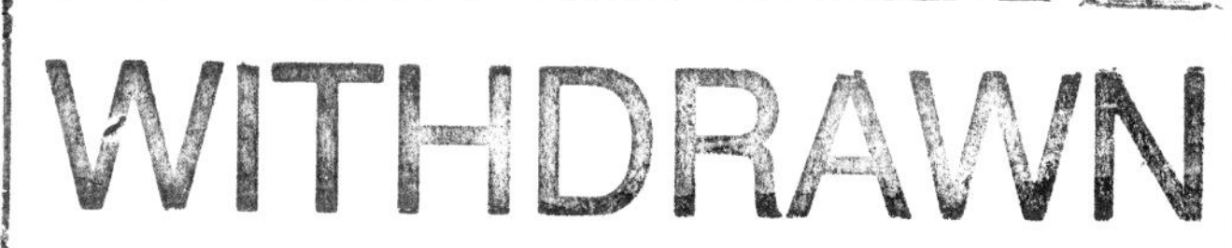
WITHDRAWN

FORENSIC PHOTOGRAPHY

The Importance of Accuracy

Sanford L. Weiss, BCEP, PI

Coordinator of Corporate Communications and Training
Packer Engineering, Inc.
Naperville, IL

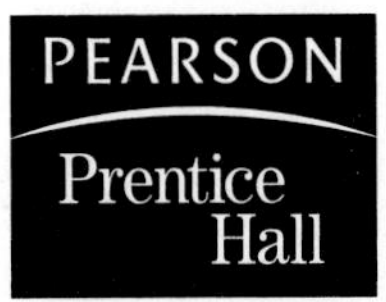

Upper Saddle River, New Jersey
Columbus, Ohio

Library of Congress Cataloging-in-Publication Data
Weiss, Sanford L.
Forensic photography : importance of accuracy / Sanford L. Weiss.— 1st ed.
p. cm.
Includes bibliographical references and index.
ISBN-13: 978-0-13-158286-6
ISBN-10: 0-13-158286-0
1. Legal photography. I. Title.
TR822.W44 2009
363.25—dc22

2008011361

Editor in Chief: Vernon Anthony
Senior Acquisitions Editor: Tim Peyton
Editorial Assistant: Alicia Kelly
Production Coordination: Karen Ettinger, Aptara
Project Manager: Jessica Sykes
Senior Operations Specialist: Pat Tonneman
Art Director: Diane Ernsberger
Cover Designer: Jeff Vanik
Cover Art: Christopher Cali
Director of Marketing: David Gesell
Marketing Manager: Adam Klosa
Marketing Coordinator: Alicia Dysert
Copyeditor: Heath Lynn Silberfeld

This book was set in Janson by Aptara. It was printed and bound by Hamilton Printing Co.
The cover was printed by Phoenix.

Pearson Education Ltd., London
Pearson Education Singapore Pte. Ltd.
Pearson Education Canada, Inc.
Pearson Education—Japan
Pearson Education Australia Pty. Limited
Pearson Education North Asia Ltd, Hong Kong
Pearson Educación de Mexico, S.A. de C.V.
Pearson Education Malaysia Pte. Ltd.

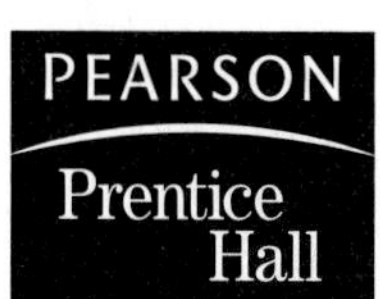

10 9 8 7 6 5 4 3 2 1
ISBN-13: 978-0-13-158286-6
ISBN-10: 0-13-158286-0

Dedication

For his help and understanding, patience and knowledge, encouragement and kindness, I dedicate this work to Dr. Kenneth F. Packer.

Contents

Note: Every effort has been made to provide accurate and current Internet information in this book. However, the Internet and information posted on it are constantly changing, so it is inevitable that some of the Internet addresses listed in this textbook will change.

Preface

Most educational photography books are useful in some way concerning some aspect of photographic practice. However, up-to-date, all-inclusive books designed to educate a practitioner in the field of digital forensic and evidence photography are scarce.

Existing books are often too focused on the "subjective what," rather than the "practicing how." General photography texts, even if they focus on the how, may be inadequate to train photographers in forensics; general texts are off the point. Forensic photography places its importance on the evidence itself and on maximizing the representation of evidential accuracy instead of on aesthetics. Visual quality and optimization of exposure are important to any photography, but where aesthetic photography may concentrate at least in part on composition and visual appeal, evidence photography concentrates on transportation: the transportation of images of something or somewhere, of a place or of an object, to most accurately depict that place or object somewhere else at another time. It's not that aesthetic photographs aren't accurate for this purpose in some ways. Obviously, anyone can recognize certain people, places, and things in a "good" photograph. But just because the viewer can recognize certain things in an image doesn't mean all the necessary information for proper situational analysis can be derived from that same image.

From photography's beginning, technical photographers realized that it was not necessarily a representation of reality. "To nineteenth-century enthusiasts of this new art, the making of a photograph, which fixed forever a moment of time, resembled an act of magic."[1] Photographic images are produced through a mechanical process and have the ability to supply near-perfect representations of reality. Photography, though technically scientific and inherently mysterious, was initially—and is still—considered by many to be artistic. How can a practice conceived as art be accepted as truth? Martin Jay mentions the irony that what denounced photography as art were features that painters of the time thought of as central, describing themselves as passive recorders of what they saw. In fact, he considers painting, in addition to camera obscura, to be predecessors of photography.[2]

Photography becomes less art and more discipline when it can be said that subject content is more important than how the content is arranged in the final representation or composition. In art-form photography, the camera and output are grouped together and considered a media. In aesthetics, a camera and film or memory should be considered tools, grouped together with such items as brushes, paints, and pencils, and the finished photograph should be considered a product of the tools. In evidence photography, the hardware, software, and resultant images *must* be considered an end product.

This product is created with knowledge, all possible skills, and—at the state-of-the-art level—for the ability to relate the images to the subjects. For these reasons, it is critical for the forensic evidence photographer to be at least as well trained in evidence, optics, and human vision as they are in photography.

Most photographers documenting weddings, landscapes, and faces are not properly trained in such subject matter—or for the proper practice of evidence documentation for legal or scientific use (unless they are out-of-work evidence photographers). All photography takes a degree of skill, but—to use an analogy—not everyone who can drive a nail would be safe or skillful as a carpenter.

It would be easier for evidence photographers to compete with portrait and wedding photographers freelancing as evidence photographers if the evidence photographers were properly trained and also educated their clients regarding the subject of proper forensic and evidence documentation. How, then, can trained professional evidence photographers properly educate their clients? They must learn to recognize the difficulties involved in creating images representing reality, within the limitations of the photographic medium, and optimize their photographs within the parameters of realistic possibility. They must be able to properly explain what they are doing both to their clients and in any subsequent legal action. Those evidence photographers and their clients, who are aware of the difficulties involved in proper documentation, stand a better chance of creating images representative of reality in ways less prone to challenge by opposition counsel.

The text and case studies in this book are meant to be read and digested. No two projects are ever exactly alike. Aspects may appear similar, but differences are always inherent. Draw upon the examples in the text for background information in the solution of your own challenges. Performing tasks in ways that are similar to methods that were successful should make your work easier. How can you ever tell if you are doing things in the most accurate and modern manner? Whom should you ask? Positive reinforcement is never easy to find.

The photos in the chapters and case studies were exposed on actual projects, under actual conditions, to be used as evidence in court. They were selected as good or bad examples of what will happen if you make photographs under the conditions described. Most of the photos will be easier to understand when seen in full color. Consult the Companion Website, as most will be there.

It is embarrassing to converse with a client, superior, or attorney and require definitions of terms when you are supposed to be the authority. The learning objectives and key terms in each chapter provide a foundation vocabulary for use in communicating your ideas and understanding your assignments. All the words and terms are in use today and will arise in current projects.

Use or adapt any of the lists and checklists in the chapters as tried methodologies. Many are outlined in the step-by-step sections of the text. The outlines are meant to make the text easier to understand. The lists are not all inclusive but should be useful in constructing a broad-based plan for undertaking any project. If you use an outline and fill in some blanks, save the expanded outline in text or memory to serve as your foundation for the next and any subsequent projects. Discuss and compare your methods with other people in the field. Maintaining a network of friends and coworkers is the most efficient method for keeping up with new advances in equipment and methodologies.

The exercises accompanying each of the chapters require much more than yes or no answers. They are intended to make you think and work and learn. Answering some of the questions may take you an hour, and some may take you a lifetime. They may inspire you to think of more questions to solve on your own. Never hesitate to experiment and solve problems before it becomes necessary to solve them in the field and under pressure.

This book offers a primer on forensic photography that is useful to both the beginner and experienced practitioner. Basic concepts are meant to provide a foundation for proper evidence photography. Learning from my experiences, failures, and successes may make forensic evidence photography easier for others, and that is the objective of this book.

While you develop your technical skills, maintain an open mind. Be careful, diligent, and creative. Be an investigator and a photographer. Use photography as a tool, and use it efficiently.

I have been asked a hundred times how I became involved in forensic photography. I can only say that I was in the right place at the right time. Packer Engineering, Inc., of Naperville, Illinois, was a customer of the commercial photo lab where I worked. I was in charge of the Packer account. It was grueling work but fascinating. I had never before seen such photos—didn't even knew those kinds of photos existed—and I was smitten by the type of work Packer produced. I saw photos of scale model trains crashing into each other, anthropomorphic dummies falling from cranes, automobiles crashing into telephone poles, cracks in materials in places a crack should never be, and a thousand other things, exciting and scary. I called Packer Engineering on a whim one morning and asked for a tour.

While on site I asked why Packer did not do its photo finishing in-house and was answered by a blank stare. I guess nobody had thought of it or that no one had acted upon it if they had. A couple of weeks later, a Packer employee phoned and asked me to come in and tell the company what it would take to set up an on-site processing facility. To make a long story short, I went in full of the confidence and ignorance of the young and got the job. I promised them I was an expert of everything photographic and would not let them down. That was over 27 years ago.

Dr. Packer, the founder of the company and current chairman of the board, gave me my first assignment. A chrome car bumper with a little scuff on it was sitting in the lab. He asked me, "Can you see the mark?" I said, "Yes, I can." He said, "Good, then you can photograph it." I went home frustrated and in tears after each of the first two days of trying. I thought I was going to be fired. I was so scared. I also realized I was not an expert; in fact, I felt I did not know a thing.

I was lucky. Dr. Packer was very patient with me. He and his talented crew taught me skills and how to laugh at my own shortcomings: invaluable lessons. It was a matter of not giving up, not letting anything beat me, and I never have.

I watched, talked, asked, and mostly concentrated on the problems I was asked to solve, and I learned a lot. I learned there were similarities in projects and that experience was a great teacher. I learned to remain openminded and to ask for advice. I learned not to be angry over failures but to minimize them. I learned to be confident but never sure.

I learned that one cannot truly *learn* forensic photography but must *live* it. I also learned I have a passion for figuring out how to most accurately portray evidence photographically. To be successful in this work, you must have that passion, too.

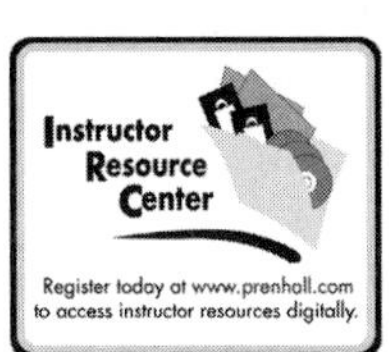

To access supplementary materials online, instructors need to request an instructor access code. Go to **www.pearsonhighered.com/irc,** where you can register for an instructor access code. Within 48 hours after registering, you will receive a confirming e-mail, including an instructor access code. Once you have received your code, go to the site and log on for full instructions on downloading the materials you wish to use.

Supplements:

- Instructor's Manual
- PowerPoint
- Companion Website www.prenhall.com/weiss

ACKNOWLEDGMENTS

I must thank my family, Julie, Stephen, and Jessica, for their patience and support during the many months it took to write this book. I know I have chores to do around the house soon. Special thanks to Jessica for her expertise and imagination in the wonderful illustrations.

Without Packer Engineering, Inc., this book would and could never have been written. Thank you for putting up with me all of these years. I greatly appreciate the time and comments of my coworkers: Ken, Char, Diane H., Penny, Pam, Lynnette, Diane S., Neil, Karl, Noah, Michelle, Tom L., Tom B., Bob, Peter, Jeff, Jane, Anne, Christina, and Kevin.

Aric Dutelle: your time, effort, and expertise are appreciated and were needed so much. Your underwater chapter is great, and your images make the book much better than it would have been without you.

Robert Wyman: you have more patience than I can imagine. Thank you for your time, energy, experience, and ideas.

Karl Fliehler, my good friend: no matter what you say, there is no way I could have done this without you.

Russell Rohde, M.D.: you are the most amazing man. If only I had half your energy. Thank you for your great feedback.

Peter Blackwood, my oldest friend: you make me feel so proud.

John Trimble, Ph.D.: I knew if I could impress you, the book was written properly.

Lou Charbonneau: you are and always will be my inspiration.

Sara Paretsky: I *had* to become an author to know how you must feel.

To the members of the Fire Group, especially Chester Kraus: you made my work so much easier and better.

My friends around the globe who took time from their busy schedules to review this text: I will be forever grateful.

Nikon: you are the greatest.

To all the manufacturers who put their trust in me: I hope you will not be disappointed. Also, you have not heard the last of me.

Last, but certainly not least, thanks to my copyeditor, Heath Lynn Silberfeld, who knows what this book would have been like without her.

Sandy Weiss
Naperville, Illinois

About the Author

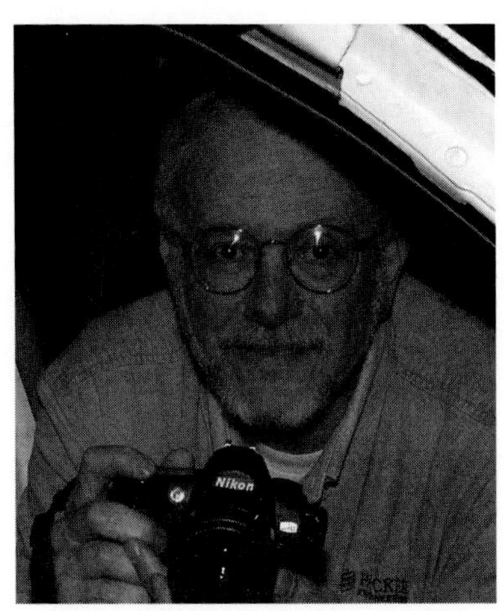

Sanford L. Weiss, BCEP, CI, PI, is an Evidence Photographer's International Council (EPIC) Board Certified Evidence Photographer, a Competitive Intelligence Specialist, and an Illinois State licensed private detective (#115-001807). He works for Packer Engineering, Inc., in Naperville, Illinois, for whom he has documented artifacts and scenes of hundreds of investigations and vision studies over the last 27 years. His work experience includes 17 years managing the Packer photographic laboratory.

Mr. Weiss has a B.S. degree in management from National Louis University. He holds an Illinois State Teaching Certification for Photography and has been teaching for over 27 years. He is regularly published in the *Florida Association of Licensed Investigators (FALI) Newsletter* and has published articles on competitive intelligence and on photography in national periodicals, including *Evidence Technology Magazine.*

In 2003 Mr. Weiss received the R. C. Hakanson, Evidence Photographer of the Year Award from EPIC, and in 2005 he received the Nikon Evidence Photographer of the Year Award. In 2006 he received the Nikon Lifetime Achievement Award.

Chapter 1

Forensic Photography

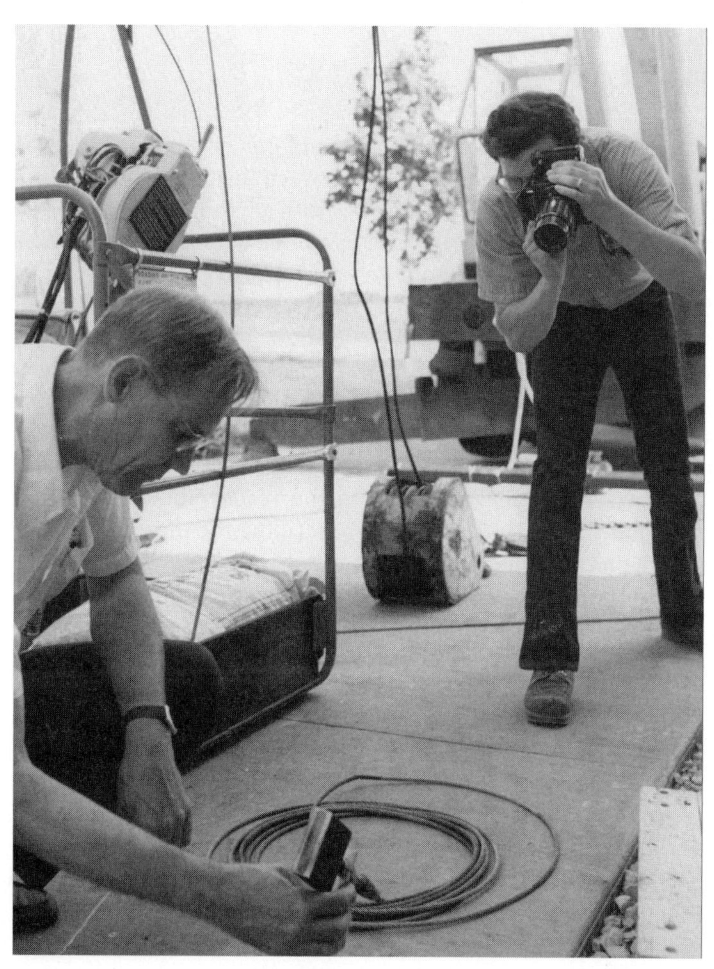

Learning Objectives

AFTER STUDYING THIS CHAPTER, YOU SHOULD BE ABLE TO:

1. Understand the difference between photography and forensic photography
2. Begin to grasp the importance of the "**Fair and Accurate**" standard for evidence photography
3. Understand and minimize the difference between image capture by film and digital means
4. Be familiar with the roadblocks to capturing images representative of reality
5. Understand the importance of observation and visualization
6. Be familiar with the difference between a practice and a protocol
7. Know the difference between enhancement and manipulation
8. Understand the means of image authentication
9. Place proper importance upon the What/Where/Why/and How of evidence photography
10. Place proper importance upon the concept of certification

Digital imaging is the way of today's world. Of course there are still limited uses for traditional, film-based technologies, but they will soon be relegated primarily to the photo-artists.

Anything written regarding image resolution, sensor size, camera size, camera function, camera price, etc., is mostly out of date before the words hit the screen. I have chosen to use mostly the Nikon Digital Single Lens Reflex (**DSLR**s) as the base reference cameras in this book. Some are affordable (pro-sumer) and some are professional and all are certainly adequate for most evidence photography.

Although most of the technological aspects of digital imaging are beyond the scope of this book, the reason for the use of digital technology is the same as it always has been in this discipline. In forensic/evidence/technical photography, it is to capture adequate images for the best possible documentation and reproduction of an accurate version of reality. Whether a person is using film or digital imaging, accuracy is the key.

There are certain fundamental difficulties to attempting this task. The difficulties are due to laws of optics, physics, and physiology. Our brains are the most powerful computers in existence, and our brains can easily discern differences between images and reality. For us to create images with anything other than our eyes, which then say to our brains, "this accurately portrays reality" is daunting.

Some of the major roadblocks to the creation of realistic images are the limitations of photography in capturing the contrast, color, perspective, dimensionality, and resolution of the original scene.

It is the intention of this book to educate the reader about forensic photography, by describing the most up-to-date methods to capture and reproduce images that most accurately represent forensic evidence. It is also necessary for the reader to understand the difficulties in attempting to produce perfection in imaging, and then to explain these difficulties to anyone examining the images or the responsibilities and/or capabilities of the photographer.

The text, case studies, and exercises are meant to be read and then practiced. Of course, no two projects are ever alike. Aspects may seem familiar, but there are always differences. The practitioner must maintain an open mind, be careful, diligent, and creative. The photographer must be an investigator first and a photographer afterward, using photography as a tool.

Above all, there is no way to learn this skill without practice. Trying to be a forensic photographer by practicing what you remember will lead to tragedy; each case is a matter of learning from the beginning.

THE POWERS OF OBSERVATION

Proper use of the basic principle of the **scientific method** not only helps develop solutions to difficult questions, it teaches people who use it to reason analytically in each step of their investigation and/or project. People must use a certain pattern of thought to lead from one step to the next in any endeavor. If they leave out steps due to preconceived notions of results, they are doing a disservice to their work. It is necessary to use good, sound, scientific reasoning to ensure success. Above all else, the powers of **observation** are integral.

American jurist William Wirt once said, "Perhaps there is no property in which men are more distinguished from each other, than in the various degrees in which they possess the faculty of observation. The great herd of mankind pass their lives in listless inattention and indifference as to what is going on around them, while those who are destined to distinction have a lynx-eyed vigilance that nothing can escape."[1]

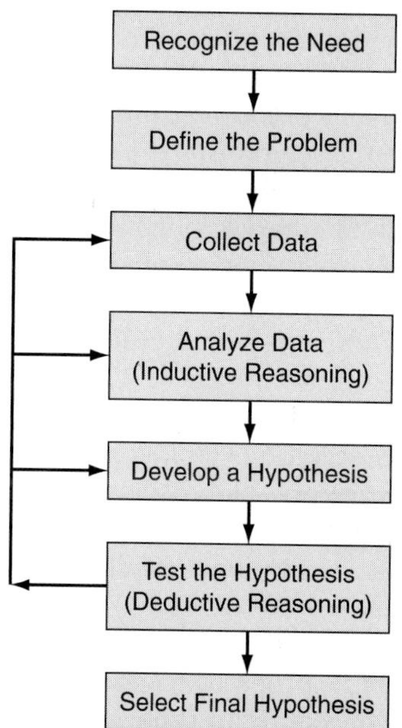

FIGURE 1–1 Scientific Method Flowchar. *Source:* Sandy Weiss.

A familiar fictional character with notoriously astute powers of observation is Sir Arthur Conan Doyle's detective Sherlock Holmes. In the story, *The Red-Headed League*, Holmes states about Jabez Wilson, "Beyond the obvious facts that he has at some time done manual labor, that he takes snuff, that he is a Freemason, that he has been to China, and that he has done a considerable amount of writing lately, I can deduce nothing else."[2] Holmes was able to deduce all these points about the man whom he has just met, after what the untrained observer would classify as a single glance. He stated of his method of detection, "You know my method. It is founded upon the observation of trifles."[3] Holmes also said to Dr. Watson, "Not invisible but unnoticed, Watson. You did not know where to look, and so you missed all that was important. I can never bring you to realize the importance of sleeves, the suggestiveness of thumbnails, or the great issues that may hang from a bootlace."[4] Holmes was a proponent of the basic theorem that everything is significant.

Thomas Edison spent years observing electrical and mechanical phenomena while inventing the electric light bulb. He performed many experiments before he found the correct solution to the problem. He once wrote, "The average person's brain does not observe a thousandth part of what the eye sees. It is almost incredible how poor our powers of observation, genuine observation, are."[5]

The same principles of observation apply in forensics. A good investigator will use their training and intellect to decide what details of a project are truly significant. Missing important details, no matter how small, during an investigation can lead to incomplete or erroneous conclusions.

When photographing evidence, the photographs should substantiate what the investigator can see but not be a substitute for thorough observation. When looking through the camera lens, the photographer should be consciously aware of what story the resultant photographs

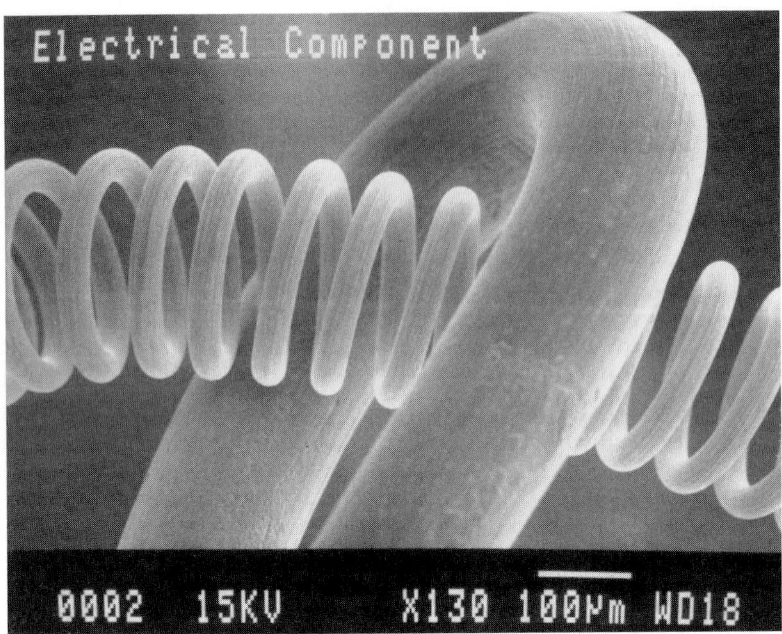

FIGURE 1–2 Electrical contact imaged by scanning electron microscope (SEM). *Source:* Sandy Weiss/Packer Engineering.

will tell and remember the images may be used for multiple scenarios. Each image is a chapter or sub-chapter of the story of the evidence. Photographs must be taken to tell every possible story (storytelling). It takes training and mental discipline to resist telling and illustrating a specific or pre-conceived story, before knowing what the true story is. Once the investigation is completed and an educated conclusion is reached, photographs must be available to substantiate the conclusion. All aspects of the scientific method must be followed and available. Insurance investigators may capture a set of overall photos required by their protocol from each claim. We have all seen those photosets. The problem with performing at that level is the photos are "documentation" without "investigation." It is dangerous when working backwards from a general set of photographs to assume the photographs will, upon later inspection yield the substantiation to prove any concept.

Educators at the Brooklyn Museum of Art originally developed what they call an "Object Observation" exercise as a strategy for honing their skills as careful "lookers" and gallery teachers. NYC Museum School teachers refined the exercise further for use with students. After studying an object for 10–15 minutes, students present their objective and subjective observations and their questions to others in the group as an exercise.[6] In observation, it is necessary to eliminate false assumptions and misleading generalizations. By focusing on the actual rather than the presumed; educated observation leads to proper forensic solutions.

How does a person become an effective observer? The first step is to consciously practice the discipline of looking and remembering. Effective observation depends on a properly trained memory. In science, vision is worthless if what is seen is not retained. The specialists of many forensic disciplines rely heavily on their expertise in observation. Fire, accident and crime scene investigators, blood spatter analysts, anthropologists, archeologists, etc are just a few of the careers relying upon skill in vision and observation.

Photography is a mechanical means of retaining vision. A properly executed photograph is one of the only ways to capture and stop time. Luckily, the camera was never intended to replace vision because it cannot. But, the trained photographer can substantiate and even enhance vision with photographs.

The **photographic go-kit** of required tools will change by specialty. Obviously, the sports photographer will carry different equipment than the portrait or evidence photographer. Evidence photography is its own sub-discipline. The protocol of evidence photography relies upon the documentation of the effect while eventually focusing on the **root cause.** No matter the magnitude of the event, the investigative documentation always tunnels down to the examination of something under magnification.

Forensic photographers specialize in capturing images to accurately preserve forensic evidence. One example is forensic engineering. Forensic engineers apply their knowledge of engineering to the interpretation of the characteristics of physical evidence. For example, a forensic engineer with a background in materials engineering might examine a component of an aircraft engine to reconstruct an accident and determine whether a manufacturer is responsible for the injuries suffered by an owner's family, suing for damages after a crash.

In addition to all the certifications required of an engineer, forensic engineers in an area of specialization such as materials require certification by the American College of Forensic Examiners or the American Board of Forensic Engineers. To qualify as **expert witnesses,** they also need years of experience. Some engineers work full-time in forensics engineering at companies like Packer Engineering; www.packereng.com.

Forensic photographers, like forensic engineers, need proper training, certification and practice to hone their skills and retain their credibility. Any company or institution that uses imaging for evidence documentation must have either an accepted **practice or protocol** to guarantee the authenticity of their images. The practice or protocol must be published, accepted and adhered to in order to guarantee **chain of custody** of the images. It is recommended that the entity do their own image processing and storage.

A brief history of photography follows here to emphasize the acceptability of photographic images in court.

Photography became a reality in 1827 when Joseph Nicephore Niepce, a French lithographer, succeeded in permanently capturing, on a metal plate coated with bitumen, the view outside his window. In 1839 the French government purchased both the patent it had granted to Niepce and the one they had granted to Louis Jacque Mande Daguerre for a process by which he was able to capture images on silver coated copper plates. The French presented both inventions to the world as a gift and news of the discoveries spread rapidly. Within a very few years, photographers were practicing their craft upon architectural subjects, still lifes, portraits and landscapes. On July 5, 1853 George Barnard took one of the first known photographs for journalistic purposes of the fire at the Ames Mill in Oswego, New York.

During the same year, the Crimean War became the first major conflict to be documented photographically. Photography was commonplace by the time the American Civil War was documented in the 1860's. Photography was however, still an awkward discipline to practice as the photographers of the time needed to haul covered wagons which functioned as portable darkrooms, where they could both coat and process their wet-plate collodion images. To avoid some of the battlefield danger, it was standard practice for a photographer to appear onsite after a battle and pose the dead in ways that made for the most graphic compositions, often using the same bodies for many different images.[7] Pre-battle images also exist that depict live soldiers posing as dead.[8] It is an interesting point of discussion to consider if images using those practices should be considered inaccurate or deceptive. The intent of the images at that time, was to inform the viewers of the conditions of the war, not to create a scenario that could not have occurred. "Technical limitations made it necessary to 'enhance' the photographs by staging them, in order to give the public the most accurate depiction of the war."[9]

One of the earliest known forms of photographic deception was spirit or ghost photography. Due to the long exposure times required by early film media, subjects that were not moving in the frame appeared normal or solid in the finished photograph, but subjects who were moving during the exposure were often recorded in a see-through blurry manner.[10] After the discovery of this phenomenon, ghostly images were taken intentionally, intended for amusement and published and distributed to the public. In 1861, a photographer named William H. Mumler from Boston claimed to have photographed real ghosts. His work initiated a wave of international popularity with so-called Spirit Photography and started a scientific controversy that lasted well into the 20th century. It is human nature to practice deception to achieve personal gain. By 1870, Richard Leach Maddox had discovered the process for making dry plate negatives and the "ghosts," who were also part of the scam, were exposed onto the plates ahead of time and the negatives were then double-exposed with the second image. Due to the fuzzy and see-through nature of the would-be ghosts, any person could pose as the ghost and then the photo-salesman would imply the ghost was a part of the departed family. Gullible customers would accept the explanation as the truth. A photo of long dead Aunt Lucy, Uncle Harry or Cousin Earl would compel the family to pay large sums of money for the photographs. In 1872 Mumler himself was put on trial for fraud and his trial became the start of a battle between "Science and the Séance" that lasted for decades.[11] These photographs and the groups formed to study them were afforded a degree of credibility by the people associated with them. Sir Arthur Conan Doyle was vice president of the Society for the Study of Supernatural Pictures and Harry Houdini was later to be a charter member.

Within a very short time after its invention, photography became a standard means of documenting evidence by the police departments of the world. The Belgian police had been using photographs of arrested persons as photographic references (mug shots) since 1843.[12] Photography in any of its forms was then and is now the only way to permanently capture accurate images of an object or event. By written standard, "to be admitted in evidence in a court trial, a photograph must be a fair and reasonably accurate representation of the subject portrayed."[13] This standard has been the major prerequisite for the admissibility of courtroom photographic images since they were first introduced in 1859.[14] Most of the early use for photographs in the courtroom were for the analysis of questioned documents.[15] Photographic evidence has always been challenged by enterprising individuals who find the content of the images in question to be damaging to their side of a case. This statement was entered into evidence in 1899: "It is common knowledge that as to such matters, either through want of skill on the part of the artist, or inadequate instruments or materials, or through intentional and skillful **manipulation,** a photograph may not only be inaccurate but dangerously misleading."[16] It should be remembered that the photograph itself is not the evidence. The testimony of the witness is the evidence and the image is an exhibit to that testimony.[17] "The party seeking to introduce the photograph into evidence must be prepared to present testimony that the photograph is accurate and correct."[18] This rule applies no matter what the media of the photograph.

With regard to forensics, in 1983 John Duckworth wrote that, "We carry photographic evidence into court that tells the story and that is accurate and understandable."[19] The question is, how accurate does a photograph have to be in order for it not to be determined inaccurate? "All 2-Dimensional (2-D) photographs are an abstraction in one way or another. Even if the picture reveals a completely realistic and recognizable subject, it is only a 2-D representation of a 3-D scene, consisting of a pattern of dyes on a piece of chemically treated paper a few millimeters thick."[20] This reasoning does not seem to jeopardize the admissibility in court of 2-D still or motion images. Many factors contribute to the definition of a photograph as an abstraction. Perspective changes through the use of wide-angle and telephoto lenses, differences in magnifications between print and original, variable viewing distances, hardware distortions, film/digital limitations that either expand or contract the contrast range of the scene as compared to human vision, color limitations, etc. are just a few. There is no way for photographers to create artificial images that totally duplicate what humans can see, due to the inherent differences between human vision and the media used to capture the images. Our eyes are very much like cameras except that our eyes are able to adjust to a wider range of brightness than any camera/film/digital combination possibly could. Normal human vision operates at a range between strong sunshine with a light intensity approaching 10,000-**foot candles** (fc) and moonlight at about 1/1,000 of a fc. Night vision after full dilation of the human eye pupil may reach limits of 1/1,000,000 of a fc.[21] The eye cannot see this whole range at one time but it adjusts from one brightness range to another by a dilation and contraction process called adaptation. The maximum brightness ratio that the eye can perceive at any one point is about 1000:1. The camera/film combination or digital camera can capture and reproduce a brightness range of about 300:1. "The intensity level of illumination depicted in a photograph is inferred rather than seen."[22] People with normal color vision can discriminate about 1,000,000 distinct colors. Photo reproduction, either on print or electronic media does not come close to recreating that range, although a computer is able to distinguish more than that number.

One factor that allows us to accept photographs, movies, and television as reasonable facsimiles of reality is that we see what we expect to see. "Photographic identification requires that the pattern in the picture be relatable visually to the image the observer has formed of it, or is expected to form of it, in his mind."[23] "Today's television and video productions have made Americans a truly visually oriented people. Regardless of language differences or degree of literacy, most persons around the world can understand a picture or drawing; hence, visuals can be regarded as a "universal language."[24] People are so used to seeing 2-D representations of 3-D subjects that their minds automatically reconstruct the 3-D image for examination. There was no color in photographic images until well into the 20th century however, black and white photographs were still accepted as representations of reality. Most of the small percentage of people in the world who are color blind are still able to distinguish some colors. Would reality be different for them than it is for people with normal color vision? Obviously, people are able to recreate reality in their minds by viewing images that are only minimal representations of that reality.

Commercial photographers often attempt to enhance certain details of a photograph through the use of special lenses, filters or lighting. However, evidence photographs should be honest and un-enhanced* to most accurately portray the subject photographed.[25] All of the equipment-related limitations that affect the capture of an image are acceptable in the eyes of the court as long as there has been no attempt to consciously deceive the viewer. Only changes in the content of the image should be classified as affecting authenticity. Changes in the elements of contrast, color, density, and enlargement do not necessarily alter the ability of an image to accurately depict the original scene.[26] "Certain procedures for enhancing digital imaging files are analogous to customary basic darkroom techniques for image enhancement. The procedures are normally applied to an entire image. Digital imaging software can, for example, be used to control the contrast of images or to enlarge them.[27] The idea of deception can become an interesting point when the deception is not a conscious effort but instead the limitation in knowledge on the part of the photographer†. For example, the representation of a night scene that is meant to show a jury what the actual scene "looked like" to the original viewer, is a physical impossibility. Given enough exposure a moonlit scene will not only show a normal (daytime-like) brightness range but it will also look like it was taken in bright daylight.[28] Sadly, images of this type often go unchallenged in court.

Most people think it is harder to alter 35-mm film images than it is to alter digital images. This mind-set is worth acknowledging because juries are made up of "most people." Almost everyone has taken conventional film photographs at some point in their lives and they have some prior conception of what a negative is and

*Except for the enhancements acceptable for film images made in the darkroom, including contrast, color, density, enlargement, cropping, etc.

†With "intent," as related to the presentation of evidence: A photographer probably WILL NOT be faulted, censured, held in contempt, or found to have perjured him/herself if the photographer's intent is clearly NOT to deceive.

what it takes to create one. Those same people often think that it would be very difficult to alter or fake a film negative. Film offers a tangible object to study, and after long years of experience, many experts in the field have learned to recognize what an original negative should look like. A reliable expert in conventional photography has an excellent chance of spotting an alteration in film media. The famous "shoes" photographs in the O.J. Simpson civil trial are a perfect example of how hard it may be to get away with 35-mm fakery. They are also a prime example of how different experts perceive the same subject. Photographs of O.J. wearing Bruno Magli designer shoes were put into evidence. Bloody footprints from that type of shoes had been found near the bodies of Nicole Simpson and Ron Goldman. Simpson denied wearing that type of shoes.[29] His less-than-expert comment in rebuttal to the photographs was that they were "ugly suede and that he wouldn't wear them in Buffalo in September."[30] Robert Groden, the man who spent years analyzing the Kennedy assassination photographs, testified for the defense in the trial that the shoes photos were probably forgeries.[31] Groden testified that there were ten separate signs of forgery in the negatives and that one of the easiest of the signs to understand was that the frame of the first shoes photo was physically larger than all of the other negatives on the same roll. He stated that unless the photographer changed cameras between frames; that would be impossible. Gerald Richards, an expert with published credentials, testified for the plaintiff that the images were 100% genuine.[32] The source of the roll of film was the *National Inquirer*. Even with film and film experts, controversy is not an unusual occurrence.

Some people have had experience with digital photography but do not have a clear idea as to what it would take to create a digital image. The inner workings of computers and the methods of image digitization are difficult concepts. "Digital imaging dramatically changes the rules (of photography). It creates a condition in which the image maker may choose among many different devices and procedures for mapping from intensities in a scene to intensities in a display or print, in which image fragments from different sources may quickly and seamlessly be combined, and in which arbitrary interventions in the image-construction process are easy to introduce and difficult to detect."[33] A 1985 article in the *Whole Earth Review* predicted the "end of photography as evidence of anything"[34] due to the ease of manipulation of digital images. As recently as February 2000, digital images were being thrown out of court as being too difficult to defend as tools to properly investigate, evaluate and defend a claim in the insurance industry. As Lee Parker, in *Digital Images Still Don't Hold Up in Court*, said "Good photographs don't lie; people do. And, people can make digital images lie."[35]

One answer to questions about image **authentication** is protocol; another is software. One example is VeriPic™ manufactured by Kwan Software and Engineering of Sunnyvale, California. They make photographic authentication a reality.[36] This software resides within digital cameras and/or computers and locks-in photo contents and is able to prompt the viewer with a message that states if the photograph is or is not in the same state as when it was exposed; when the photo is accessed on a computer within their software. It is possible for anyone with a computer to alter any digital photograph up until the time that the photograph has been subjected to authentication software. It is usually possible to detect the alteration.

W.V. Quine stated that "One way or another, a photograph provides evidence about a scene and about the way things were. Most of us have a strong intuitive feeling that photographs provide better evidence than any other kind of picture. We feel that the evidence presented corresponds in some strong sense to reality, and that it is true because it does so."[37] The issue of choice between film and digital imaging should not be about which media is easiest to fake. The choice between the media should be about which system better suits the purpose of the individual assignment. Both technologies are there for us to use. Both media are currently being accepted into court as the source material for exhibits. As with any other type of evidence, it is the responsibility of the people introducing the evidence to make sure it is a fair and accurate representation of the truth. The job of the person presenting the exhibits is to be able to testify as to how the exhibits were prepared. There have been instances where digital photographs that have been known to be enhanced have been admitted into evidence. In two trials, State of California vs. Phillip Lee Jackson and State of Washington vs. Eric Hayden, enhanced digital images of fingerprints passed Kelly-Frye hearings and were used to convict the accused.[38] Digital imaging is now predominant in legal proceedings. With current digital technology, an attorney is able to go into court with a laptop computer and have access to all documents and images pertinent to the case. All exhibits should be easily found and accessible and able to be projected on a screen in large size for all to see. The era of the reluctance to use digital imaging because of fear of fakery is rapidly closing.

VISUALIZATION

People often ask why it takes a professionally trained and experienced photographer to produce accurate images of evidence. After all, the evidence is just sitting there, the camera is simple to use, and it looks so easy on television.

The truthful answer must be that it looks easy when a talented practitioner does it. It's like watching the Olympics, everyone must think to themselves at least once that all they would have to do is eat right and jog occasionally to win the Decathlon. It looks so simple.

Obviously, the only way to gain experience and build expertise in a skill-based activity is to actually practice. But, there does have to be a place to start for everyone, no matter what their current level. That place must be mental. People must prepare themselves in every possible way to be successful. The evidence photographer MUST be able to see their finished work before they ever touch the camera.

Like any other skill, **visualization** is a discipline that must be nurtured and then practiced. A simple definition of the term is planning ahead. To be successful in this work a photographer must be prepared to take any photograph BEFORE the actual instant of the exposure, and then it is more about seeing than planning. It involves mental training and intelligence.

Most of the variables involved in creating a photograph can be predicted and planned. Some setting up of the photograph can be preset into the camera and eliminated from the "time of exposure thought processes." Some of the environmental aspects of a photo location can also be accounted for in advance, allowing the photographer to be more prepared and comfortable. Upon actually arriving at the time and place of the photograph, more of the photographer's senses will be available to concentrate on the investigation rather than having to worry about mechanics. The setting up can take an instant or hours, depending on the complexity of the photograph and the habitat or location.

Some of the variables that can be planned for are:

What: Have some idea of the subject of the photograph so a selection of the proper equipment and accessories can be made; for example, camera, memory, boots, gloves, umbrella, sun-screen, mosquito-repellent, etc.

Where: Taking photographs indoors requires different preparations than taking photographs outdoors. Is the venue in the daylight or at night? Will it be hot or cold? Will the action be fast or slow?

Why: What is the intended use of the finished photographs? Choose the right equipment and all the other factors that affect the character of the finished images.

How: To make the intended images, will anything unusual be needed? Planning ahead and having forethought of the necessities will afford a better chance for the project to be successful.

The substance of this book will be to educate the forensic photographer in the methods of making the most accurate evidence photos. Proper methods include:

- Make sure to check and double-check everything in your control.

- Have the camera ready to go before arriving at the photographic location.
- Preset any known settings into the camera to save time and effort later.
- Always attempt to visualize the finished photograph in your mind before exposure. This mental exercise will increase the chances of success of the project and it will save time in the long run.

If you say to yourself before you take the photograph, "what is the purpose of capturing this scene or moment," you might prevent yourself from making errors or you may even think twice about clicking the shutter at all. **IT IS NECESSARY TO TRY TO IMPROVE THE QUALITY NOT THE QUANTITY OF EVIDENCE IMAGES.**

SUMMARY

If photography done properly requires art and skill, forensic evidence photography is a subset requiring art, skill, intelligence, and training. There is much more involved than just being present on a scene and taking photographs of anything and everything on hand and hoping for the best. The trained practitioner will understand the what, where, why, and how of the process and visualize the products of the photographic investigation before ever taking the camera out of the bag.

This does not mean that the photographer should be prejudiced about what images to capture. It means the photographer has a grasp of the scientific method and understands what photographs may be necessary to tell the complete story of the evidence presented. Having this understanding, the properly trained forensic photographer will seldom be caught short of proper images by the time a case comes to court.

The means of image capture is not a major issue at the moment. There are still some people refusing to switch to digital technology. It is not necessary to try to convince them otherwise. It is purely a case where they will soon have no choice. Over time the use of film as an image capture device will become impossible to maintain.

The expertly trained evidence photographer will be aware that there is a root-cause/source/heart of every event; whether it is a crime or a crash, a murder or a fire. All photographic investigations should include images that take the observer from the outside in, or from the inside out, in a logical manner, to the heart of the matter.

Images, whether they are film or digital, are eventually going to be questioned for their authenticity. The authentication of evidence photographs must comply with a practice or protocol and be consistent with a chain of custody. The photographer is responsible for the images until they are transferred to the person(s) who, takes the images to the next step. The whole chain must be properly documented to maintain the authenticity of the images to their ultimate end.

There can never be too much education or too much training. The better prepared, smarter, skillful photographer stands a better chance of producing and delivering the images necessary to make the difference in court.

TIP:

Remember, it is seldom, if at all, that the photographer gets a second chance to make the images. EVERYTHING possible must be done to limit error.

CASE STUDY

BACKGROUND

The Evidence Photographers International Council (EPIC) offers **certification** for evidence photographers. The title is Board Certified Evidence Photographer. There are very few individuals certified in the world. These credentialed individuals appear as Certified on the EPIC website[39] and often receive inquiries from perspective clients because of the credential.

The stringent requirements of the certification program are designed to ensure that evidence photographers, whether specializing in civil or law enforcement work, maintain a level of competence and professionalism that maintains the international standard in the field.[40]

The International Association for Identification (IAI) also has a certification board with specific requirements for forensic photographers.

The IAI website also includes a section on ethics for evidence photographers. The certification requirements for both are included in the appendices at the end of this chapter.

Why does anyone need to hire a qualified/certified forensic photographer?

Making well-exposed, sharp, images has never been easier. With recent developments in technology, attorneys, investigators, adjustors, and engineers often take evidence photographs themselves, using everything from advanced DSLRs to cell-phones, without the aid of properly trained photographers.

However, bringing the evidence to a trained photographer or bringing the trained photographer to the scene to capture evidentiary images may make the difference between success and failure in court. Professional photographers "see things differently and document things differently than even experienced attorneys. In one particular case, it was said that "A professional photographer can do things no attorney knows how to do with rulers, macro settings and artwork overlays to vividly demonstrate the ways a stairway violated local building codes."[41]

Also, a trained professional photographer may not be adept at documenting evidence. "(It is) recommended procedure to hire evidence photographers with the best credentials, such as may be found at www.epic-photo.org."[42] Forensic photographers, like properly trained attorneys, investigators, engineers and adjustors, know what is needed to demonstrate evidence in court.

The Standards for Evidence Photography Criminal and Civil, last published in 2002, is available from EPIC Headquarters for $15 and is the only published standard for the field.[43]

CIRCUMSTANCES

In April 2003, a phone call was received at Packer Engineering from a plaintiff's attorney with a job proposal involving a flood and an insurance shortfall regarding a litigation brought by a dentist against the city in which he maintained his office. It was not a project in which Packer's expertise would be called for, so no possible conflict of interest should exist. The project was accepted as a stand-alone photographic project.

The project involved three separate field studies to three different locations. At the time the job was accepted, only one aspect and one location were known. The client was pleased with the work and subsequently rehired Packer twice. The significance of that confidence will be apparent by the end of this section.

As with most accidents, the root cause of this flood was a series of small incidents leading to a disaster. City workers were maintaining the sewers in the alley behind the dentist's office. A spring rainstorm caused a flash-flood, the sewers backed-up, and before receding, several inches of waste-contaminated water flooded the floor of the office.

Scheduled for grand-opening in a matter of weeks, the dentist had spent over $500,000 refurbishing and decorating this location. But sadly, he had very limited flood insurance. The insurance company offered him a $37,000K settlement which he refused, hired a lawyer and sued the city.

LOCATION 1

The interior walls of the building had been covered with custom designed and manufactured water-filled, air-bubbling Plexiglas panels. All had been installed and tested and were free from leaks before the flood. After the flood, they were removed from the walls, packed, and shipped back to the manufacturer for reproduction and/or disposal.

On a visit to the panel factory, the damaged panels were inspected and every aspect was photographed to document the non-removable sewage stains on the inside surfaces. The manufacturer determined it would be cheaper to start from the beginning and re-make everything rather than try to remove the stains and contamination.

The pumps and wiring had also been covered in sewage and were photographed.

The panels were laid out and labeled by the manufacturer by interior wall location, and stacked on pallets on the factory floor in anticipation of the arrival of the photographer. All of the pieces were photographed, pallet by pallet, taking prolific notes to be able to match the photographs to the pieces after processing.

The attorney demanded traditional film-based images rather than digital for this case. 200 ASA Kodak color negative film was used and processed in-house in a roller-transport C-41 processing machine. The prints were made on a RA-4 roller transport mini-lab printer. Only one of four available camera bodies was used; a 50mm macro lens, a Vivitar 283 electronic flash with a Quantum rechargeable battery pack, and a SunPak flash grip. Backups for each piece of hardware were available in the go-kit.

Many special problems were encountered in this phase of the documentation. Of utmost importance was the severity of the sewage contamination. Plastic gloves and a face mask had to be worn when touching the panels. The photo equipment was also packaged, both camera and flash, in plastic bags at all times. Gloves and bags needed to be replaced each time the film was changed. It should be noted that it is very difficult and warm work to spend hours making macro-photographs of evidence under Haz-Mat conditions with camera equipment that does not have a review monitor.

The panels were manufactured from clear Plexiglass about 3/8 inch thick. The water compartments were about 1½ inches front-to-back, 24 inches wide, and 8 feet tall. Only the bottom few inches were contaminated so it was unnecessary to document the upper parts after overall documentation.

A Kodak 18% gray scale card was placed behind each clear section before exposing the photograph so only one panel would be imaged in each photograph.

Each photograph taken contained a Kodak color chart and size scale because there was no other reference for the degree or size of the stains. Photos without the charts and scales were unnecessary in this case because there was no allegation of covered evidence.

All images were printed to be the best possible match of the imaged color charts. All negatives and prints were turned over to the client. Normally, Packer Engineering retains all negatives documenting a project, but in this case no engineering project was forthcoming, so giving the negatives to the client was justified. In a legal sense, the negatives belong to the photographer as protected work product.

LOCATION 2

All the office furniture, including desks, patient examination chairs, cabinetry, appliances, couches, televisions, telephones, computers, and even a pin-ball machine were taken to a warehouse. The pieces were grouped in the warehouse by office location but not individually labeled.

Again, all pieces were Haz-Mat and protective equipment needed to be worn at all times. There was a loft in the warehouse and overall images of each grouping of furniture were taken from an elevated position at the beginning of its documentation. Traditional film-based imaging was again used at the request of the attorney.

Ideally, each piece of furniture would have its own distinct roll of film. However, there were hundreds of pieces and the attorney did not want to pay an individual processing charge for each roll. So, a system of overall images and sketches was used to keep everything in order. Each room grouping was documented by a map and then a piece number. The number was noted on the map and by putting self-adhesive numbers onto the piece (see Fig. 1–3).

Always carry an assortment of number/letter labels in your go-kit (see Fig. 1–4).

In this case, the numbers were left on the pieces after the photo-documentation. In many cases it is necessary to remove the numbers after documentation. It should be noted that spoliation of evidence may be an issue unless specific permission is granted for destructive treatment. Never put markings directly onto evidence unless permission in writing has been obtained in advance.

Appropriate color cards were used at the beginning of each roll of film for color match. The adhesive letters were used for scale in most instances.

All negatives were processed and printed to match color scales and turned over to the client.

LOCATION 3

The office was located in a 1930s, 4000 square foot storefront of brick construction, with some of the original internal and external features intact. There were three entrance/exits,

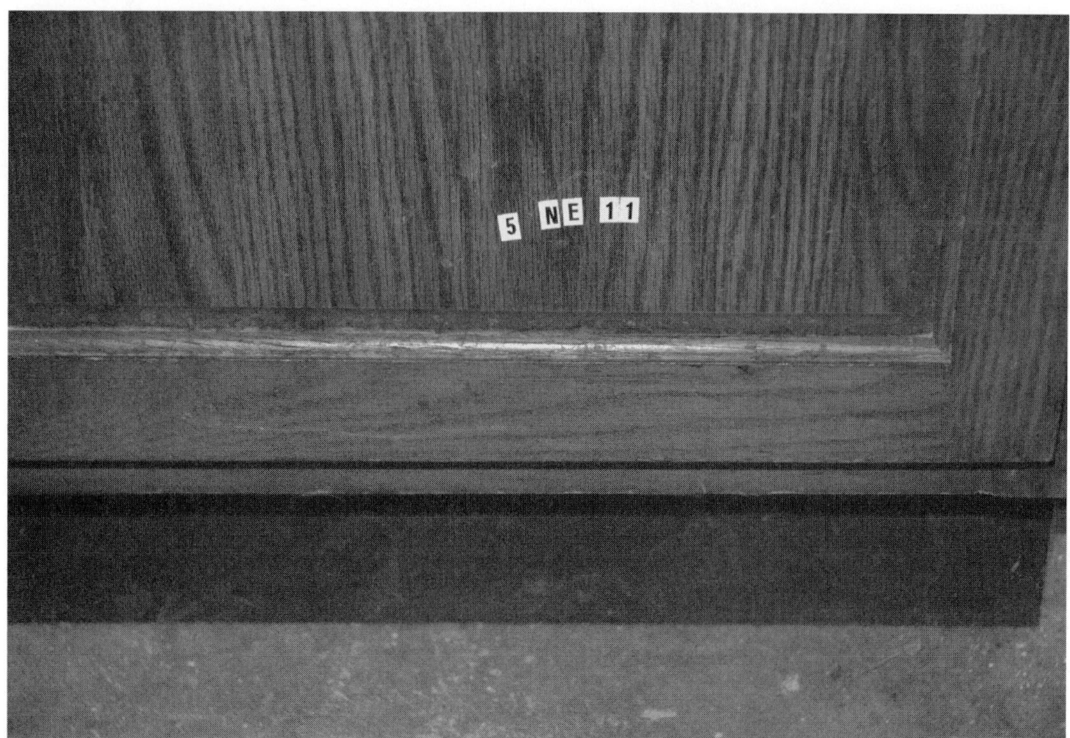

FIGURE 1–3 Location 2, damaged cabinet. *Source:* Sandy Weiss/Packer Engineering.

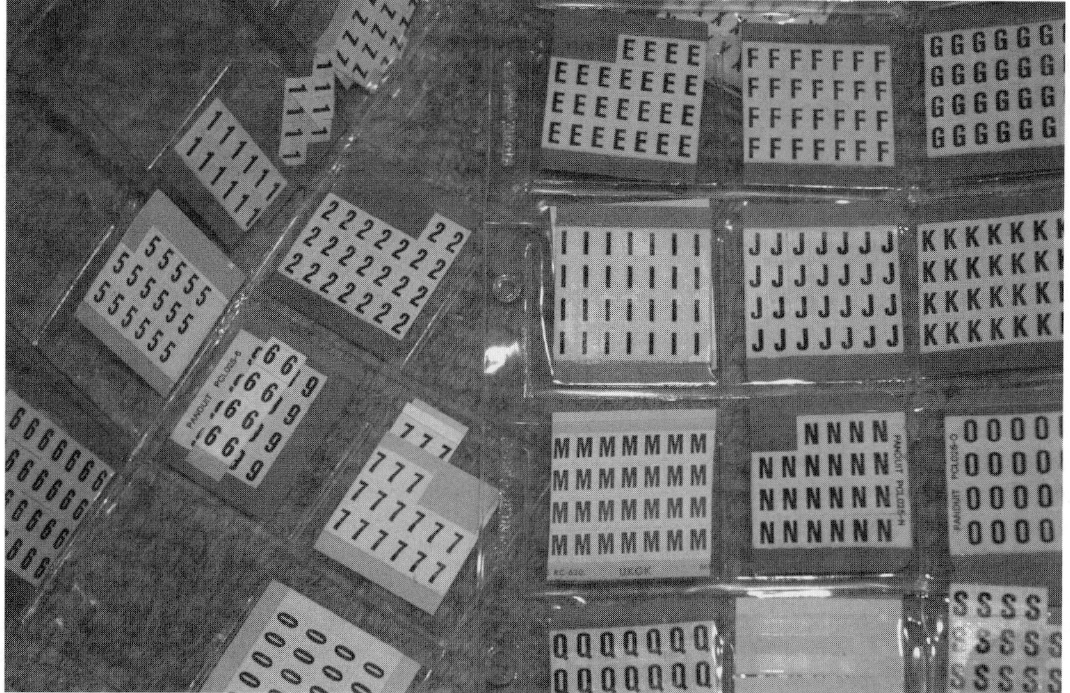

FIGURE 1–4 Self-adhesive labels. *Source:* Sandy Weiss/Packer Engineering.

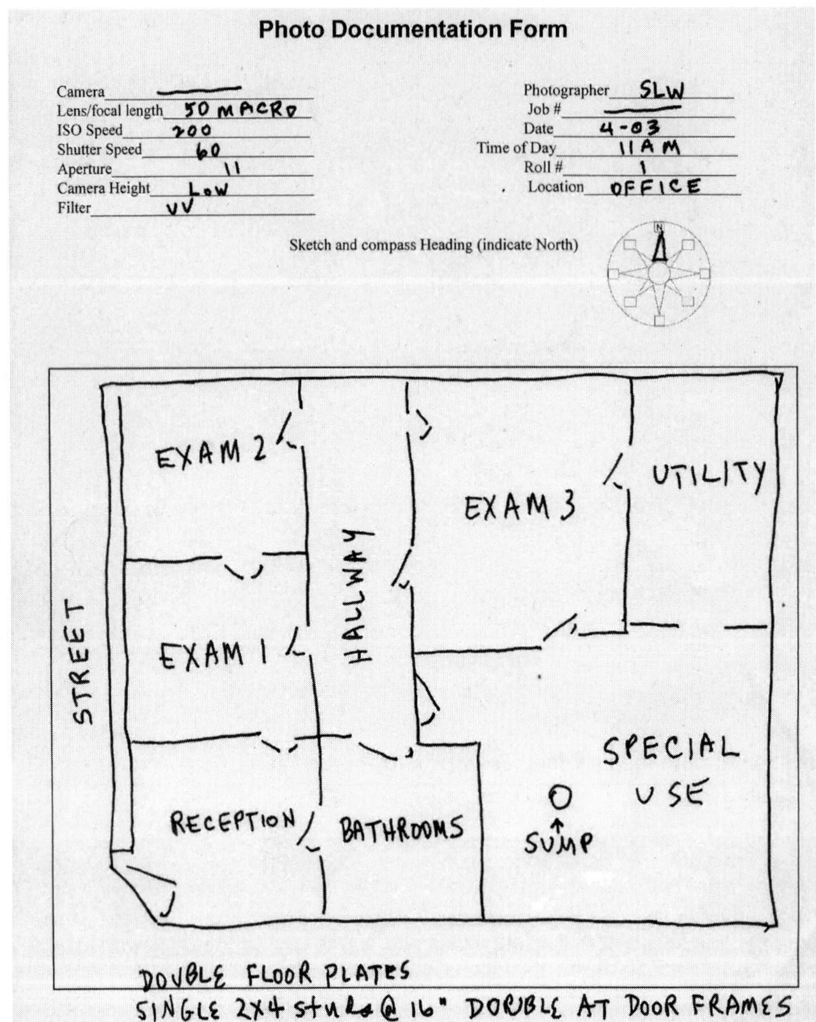

Photo Documentation Form

Camera	——
Lens/focal length	50 MACRO
ISO Speed	200
Shutter Speed	60
Aperture	11
Camera Height	LOW
Filter	UV
Photographer	SLW
Job #	——
Date	4-03
Time of Day	11 AM
Roll #	1
Location	OFFICE

Sketch and compass Heading (indicate North)

FIGURE 1–5 Location 3, Office layout sketch.

two on the west side and a back door on the east (see Fig. 1–5). The main front door was on the southwest corner and opened on to a reception area.

There was a 48-inch tall cement wall along the west interior wall, behind the studs, under high rectangular windows. There was only one main open floor drain besides the sealed ones for the sinks and toilets. The space was divided into a number of rooms with framed 2 × 4 construction; 16-inch on centers, double floor plates and door frames.

Most of the wallboard, paneling, and all the bubbling walls were removed prior to arrival, except on the outside of the studs next to some of the exterior walls. The assignment was to document the water-marks on the bottom of each of the studs, indicating how high the water rose at its maximum depth.

The same unusual imaging circumstances of the previous locations applied to this location as well. All images were made on Kodak, 200 ASA, Color, 35mm, 36-exposure film.

Knowing the stains would be low to the ground, a rolling, one-step footstool was brought to sit on and move from stud to stud. All images were made with the same camera and flash hardware as the first two locations.

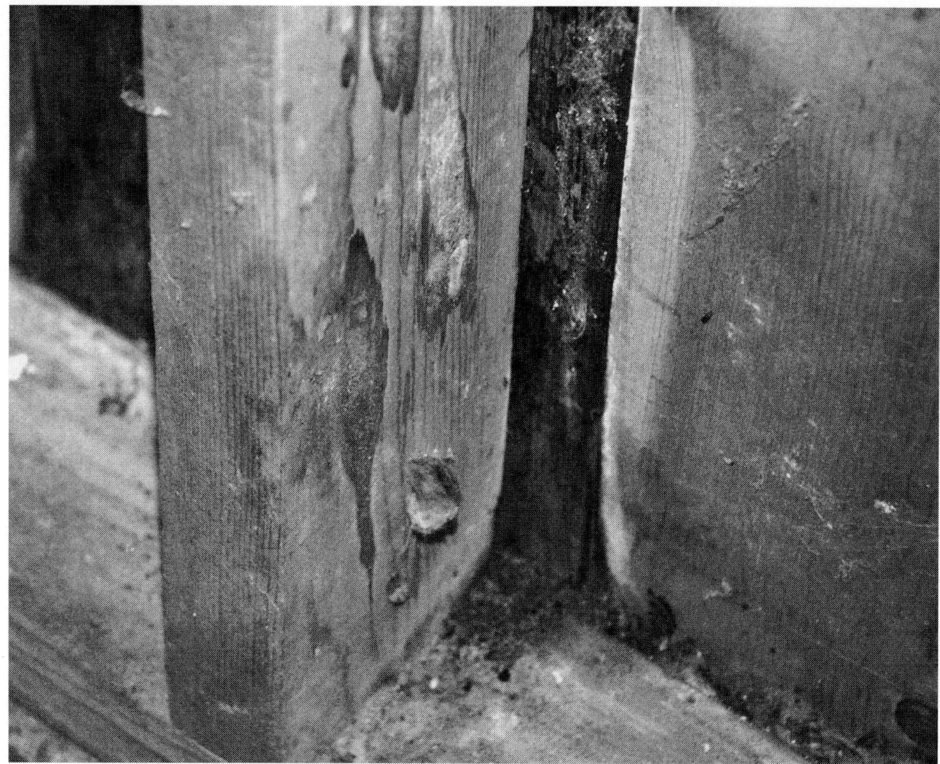

FIGURE 1–6 Location 3, photo 2 (2 N 5), exam room 2, North wall, 5th stud.

Documentation was started in the reception area in the southwest corner and the first stud was labeled R W 1. The sequence continued on to R W 2, R W 3, until the corner and then changes to R N 1, etc. Exam room 1 photos started with the south side of the door frame as 1 E 1, 1E2, etc, until the corner and then 1 S 1, 1 S 2, etc.

Each stud received a label and only macro images were exposed. Normally each stud would have an overall image before a close-up, but they all looked the same and only the water stains were at issue. The tags were left in place after imaging (see Fig. 1–6).

One of the most critical aspects of the project was the documentation of the water testing at the floor drain. As the plastic drain hose was removed from the floor drain in the special use room, the contaminated water that remained was photographed (see Fig. 1–7).

The attorney wanted images to prove chain of evidence of the sample of water removed from the trap, as it had been there since the flood and chemical analysis would show the degree of sewage contamination. The photographs of the collection and packaging of the evidence were critical.

Fourteen (14) 36 exposure rolls of film were exposed on this aspect of the project.

OUTCOME

All film was removed from the premises. A receipt was written for the attorney. The film was taken back to Packer for processing. The usual leader tabs and identification was placed upon the rolls prior to feeding the rolls into the C-41 machine, two by two.

Surprisingly, not one image was exposed by the camera on phase 3 of this case. Obviously, the correct film was put into the machine for processing. Roll after roll came out of the machine totally blank.

The attorney was contacted immediately and, of course, he was unhappy. The studs were

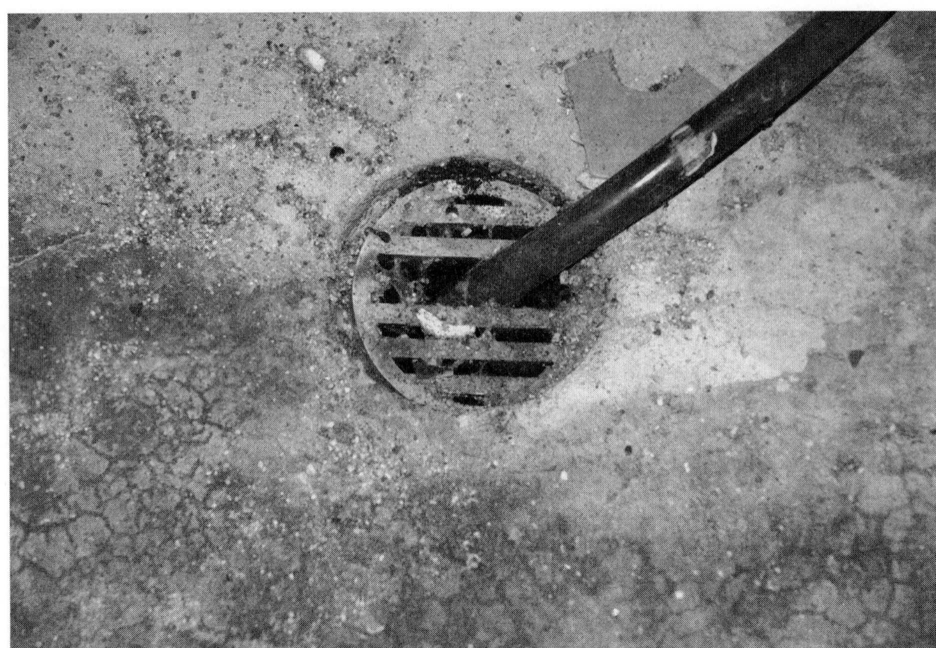

FIGURE 1–7 Location 3, Floor drain.

still in place, so there was just a matter of going back and re-shooting. However, the water evidence collection was now already completed and no images other than a backup videotape of the operation remained, nor could they be re-done.

The scene was revisited with a different camera body and all the studs were re-shot on the next day. The photos were successful on the second attempt.

RATIONALE

Many times, no second chance is afforded the photographer. It is too late. So, a forensic photographer working on critical projects must strive for perfection. Failure of this magnitude is unusual. The attorney did not want to pay the bill. In a higher profile case, the failure could have been catastrophic.

The non-performing camera body was taken in for repair. The shutter speed adjustment had malfunctioned and the 60th second setting was actually firing at about 1/200th of a second; too fast to allow any benefit from the flash. The camera felt fine on location, the flash fired each time, thus there was no easy way to realize it was going to be an issue.

Had this project been undertaken digitally, this failure would not have occurred. It would have been immediately evident that the images were turning out blank. Another camera would have been used.

KEY TERMS

digital imaging, (p. 2)
DSLR, (p. 2)
scientific method, (p. 3)
observation, (p. 3)
photographic go-kit, (p. 5)
root cause, (p. 5)
expert witness, (p. 5)
practice or protocol, (p. 5)
chain of custody, (p. 5)
manipulation, (p. 6)
foot candle, (p. 7)
authentication, (p. 8)
visualization, (p. 9)
certification, (p. 10)

EXERCISES

1. Walk into an unfamiliar room and look at everything for 15–30 seconds, then leave. Write down everything you can remember. Do not forget the space is 3-Dimensional. Practice this exercise on a regular basis and note your progress.
2. Note one car traveling in the opposite direction when you are driving yours. The faster you are going, the less time you will have for details. Imagine the person in the other car is wanted by police and you are the only known witness. Try to recall all possible details, for example, the make, model, and year of the car, tag numbers, condition, and of course, a proper description of the driver.
3. Design an evidence documentation form you think will work well for you in your chosen specialty. The template will be different if you are a medical examiner, odontologist, law enforcement professional, or engineer.
4. With a traditional film camera, devise a method to determine whether the flash is in synchronization with the shutter without exposing and processing a test-roll of film.
5. List ways to explain why a roll of film would come out totally unexposed after using it to take photographs? Partially unexposed?
6. With a digital camera, devise a method to determine if the camera is indeed capturing images besides looking at them on the camera's LCD monitor or opening them on a computer.
7. Create a Go-Kit list for your particular specialty.
8. Create a contract template for a client to sign when hiring you to document evidence. Include a confidentiality agreement, evidence spoliation agreement, statement of ethics, and list of expectations for you and the client.
9. Create a statement of ownership of original images and research its legality.
10. Research spoliation of evidence and make a list of safeguards against this issue.

APPENDIX 1.1

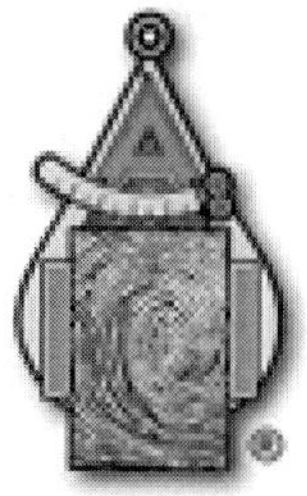

International Association for Identification

Being certified by the International Association for Identification, and being actively engaged in the Forensic Photography profession, I dedicate myself to my work in the forensic community, and respect the constitutional rights of all people to liberty, equality, and justice.

I will never act officiously, and will strive to always make objective decisions in my profession. I will devote myself to unite, promote, and distribute, within the profession, any advancements in my effort too more effectively photograph items of evidentiary value.

I will apply my technical knowledge factually, with perseverance and conviction to preserve the ethical standards of the profession of scientific investigation.

I will constantly strive to achieve these objectives and ideals, dedicating myself to the highest professional ethics in my chosen profession.

For further information, contact:

David T. Gamble
Monmouth County Prosecutor's Office
132 A Jerseyville Ave
Freehold, NJ 07728-8835
Phone: (732) 294-5906
Fax: (732) 409-7521
E-mail: dtg56@aol.com

APPENDIX 1.2

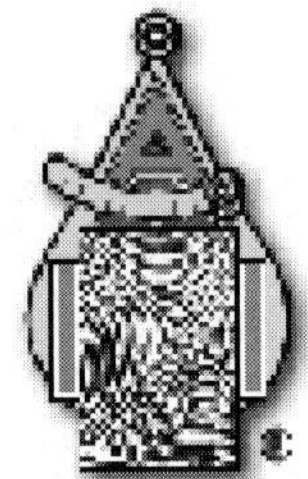

Forensic Photography Certification Requirements of the International Association for Identification

1. General Requirements
   1. An applicant for certification must be of good moral character, high integrity, and good repute and must possess a high ethical and professional standing.
   2. An applicant for certification must be primarily employed in the field of Forensic Science whose duties include forensic photography.
2. Education and Experience Requirements

   An applicant must have a minimum of three (3) years of experience working in the area of photography and/or digital imaging; a law enforcement related field is preferred.
3. Training Requirements

   An applicant must have satisfactorily completed a minimum of forty (40) classroom hours of photography courses, either police or college level.
4. Endorsements

   All applicants must submit two letters of endorsement, one of which must be from an individual actively working in the area of photography and/or digital imaging, and one of which must be from the individual's immediate supervisor.
5. Examinations
   1. Certification shall be determined by testing. The certification test was developed and is maintained by the IAI Forensic Photography Certification Board. Applicants have three (3) hours to complete the written examination and ninety (90) days from receipt of certified mail to work and return the practical test.
      1. The written test shall consist of 100 multiple choice and true/false questions, including, but not limited to, history of photography, cameras, lenses, film, exposure, depth

of field, light and color theory, lighting, filters, close-up photography, presentation and digital imaging. Passing grade 70%. The test questions will be written from three designated texts.

   2. The practical test shall consist of submission of ten (10) assigned images prepared by the applicant, five (5) of which are from a required list and five (5) from a list of optional assignments.
      1. Evaluation of the submitted images are based on a pass/fail basis, using the following factors:
         1. Compliance with requirements
         2. Utilization of proper photographic techniques
         3. Overall image quality
      2. Images are to be submitted as transparencies, 8" × 10" prints, or on a CD-Rom in Tiff format (1,000 ppi with output size of 8" × 10").

6. General Provisions Concerning Certification
   1. The right to deny certification is reserved by the Forensic Photography Certification Board.
   2. Applicants who are denied certification by the Forensic Photography Certification Board may appeal such action in writing to the IAI Board of Directors within sixty (60) days of such notification.
   3. Certificates issued by the IAI are non-transferable. They remain the property of the IAI; but every person to whom a certificates has been issued shall be entitled to its continued possession unless and until such certificate is revoked.
   4. Certificates are issued for a period of five (5) years, subject to renewal upon application by a member. Such application for renewal shall be subject to standards in effect at the time of the request for renewal and payment of the established fee.
   5. Membership in the IAI, or any of its state or regional divisions, is not mandatory for certification.
   6. Certificates may be suspended or revoked by the Forensic Photography Certification Board for any of the following reasons:
      1. Violation of the IAI or Forensic Photography Certification Board code of ethics.
      2. A misstatement, misrepresentation, concealment, or omission of a material fact or facts in an application or any other communication related to certification.
      3. Conviction of an applicant for IAI certification or holder of an IAI certification by a court of competent jurisdiction of a felon or any crime involving moral turpitude.
      4. Issuance of a certificate contrary to or in violation an any of the laws, standards, rules or regulations of the IAI; or determination that the person certified was not in fact eligible to receive such certificate at the time of its issuance.
      5. Unethical conduct or other conduct by a holder of a certificate which brings the specialty of forensic photography into dispute.

7. Certification—Grandfathering

   No waivers or Grandfather provisions are in this program.

Test questions are taken from the following publications:

Photography - 7th Edition, Phil Davis

Police Photography - 4th Edition, Miller (Chapters 1 and 12–18)

Digital Imaging for Photographers - 4th Edition, Davies & Fennessy

For further information, contact:

David T. Gamble

Monmouth County Prosecutor's Office

132 A Jerseyville Ave

Freehold, NJ 07728-8835

Phone: (732) 294-5906

Fax: (732) 409-7521

E-mail: dtg56@aol.com

http://www.theiai.org/certifications/

APPENDIX 1.3

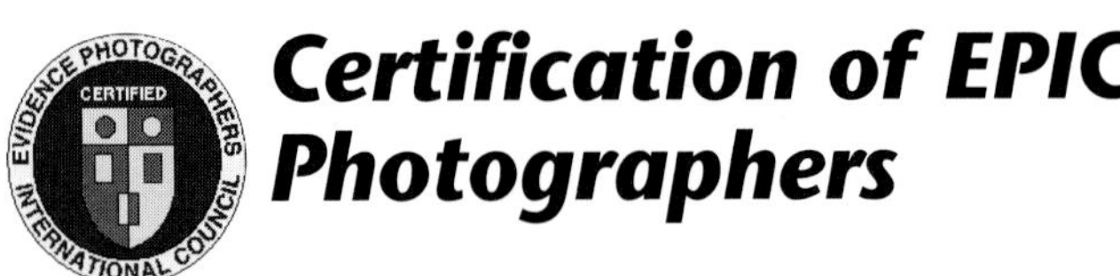

Certification of EPIC Photographers

Board Certification Program Revision of April 1, 2000

HISTORY

The Board of Management of the Evidence Photographers International Council (EPIC) at its July 1985 annual meeting in New York City approved requiring that EPIC members who wish to be acknowledged as "Board Certified Evidence Photographers" meet specific certification criteria through performance, testing, and review. The EPIC Board Certification Program thereby was formed.

The stringent requirements of the program are designed to ensure that evidence photographers, whether specializing in civil or law enforcement/public work, maintain a level of competence and professionalism that will serve as the international standard in the field. The Certification Board updated these rules at the November 1998 Atlanta, GA Annual Board Meeting. Those present were Larry Shavelson, George Pearl, Stephen Appelbaum, Robert Jennings, Jerry Goffe, Joseph Lewko and Marty Coyne.

FOREWORD

All applications for board certification are submitted to the EPIC certification committee (board). The certification board shall consist of 3 board certified members of EPIC who shall be responsible for administering the application process for certification and qualification. The rules and procedures covering certification in either the civil or law enforcement categories are subject to changes as deemed necessary by the certification board. Once a candidate is accepted into the certification program, the rules and procedures in place will bind them at the time of his/her acceptance. Please be certain that you possess a current copy of the requirements, prior to submission.

All applications should be sent to:

Evidence Photographers International Council, Inc.

600 Main Street

Honesdale, PA 18431

Questions concerning certification or qualification may also be submitted to:

CIVIL EVIDENCE PHOTOGRAPHY SECTION:

Frederick H. Bird

P.O. Box 3

67 Hopkins Road

Ellington, Connecticut 06029

Telephone 860-871-0357

email: birdphoto@earthlink.com

LAW ENFORCEMENT/PRIVATE SECTION:

Frederick H. Bird

P.O. Box 3

67 Hopkins Road

Ellington, Connecticut 06029

Telephone 860-871-0357

email: birdphoto@earthlink.com

1. Each applicant must be a member in good standing of the Evidence Photographers International Council for a period of no less than one year and have attended a minimum of one EPIC School on Evidence Photography. The applicant must be experienced in the field of Civil Evidence or Law Enforcement photography.
2. Applicants must pay a nonrefundable $150.00 application fee that is required in advance and before the review of any material, interview and/or written examination. This application fee will cover all administrative, background investigation, professional certificate, and other associated testing costs. For those in the public sector, this fee covers the application/(s) for multiple specializations at time of application. Additional specialization certification may be obtained at a latter date with a nominal fee.
3. The applicant for EPIC Board Certification must pass certain sections of testing which may take up to 24 months to complete as a whole.

   The first step in the certification program is to take a written examination on the basic mechanics of the craft of photography, videography, and imaging. This examination will be worth 25 points toward your total score. This test will be given in the afternoon, prior to the registration and opening of the annual school and meeting or other agreed upon time.

   The second step will be your submission of 10 cases for review by the certification board. These will be color or black & white 8 × 10-inch prints or videotape (or a combination of) produced as applicable to each assignment performed. All assignments must be or represent cases that have been adjudicated or settled prior to certification submission. All prints and videotapes that deal with any manner of perspective will have the correct perspective viewing distance attached. Prints can be made to the correct size for viewing at an average of 14 to 15-inches of viewing distance. Civil Evidence photographers will choose 10 assignments from different areas. A suggestion of 21 areas follows. Those applicants for the public section board certification will produce 10 submissions of their casework from their own direct area/(s) of engagement. This print or videotape case review portion of the program will count 45 points toward your final grade. This submission can be done anytime during a two-year period following the passing of the written examination.

Areas of documentation for civil testing are as follows, but are not limited to:

1. Personal Injury
2. Aerials: Vertical and oblique. (Verticals to scale.)
3. Roadway scenes - Day/Night
4. Auto/vehicle damage
5. Document reproduction: x-rays, signatures, infrared, water marks, etc.
6. Construction problems
7. Fire and arson
8. Macro, Micro, Microscopic, Scanning Macrophotography
9. Night Vision – Low Light Documentation/Perception . . . Conspicuity
10. Video – day-in-the-life
11. Video – Depositions
12. Video – Documentation (acquisition)
13. Video or Still Surveillance (with favorable results demonstrated)
14. Security problems: rape case, break-in, damage, etc., other types of security problems
15. Slip & Fall/Trip & Fall
16. Evidence photography of people places or things that don't fit into these other areas
17. Panoramic evidence of at least 180 degrees coverage angle
18. Painting with light technique of evidence scene or objects
19. Remote sensing evidence including the documentation of your set-up
20. Reverse Projection Photogrammetry
21. Testing/Scientific Documentation

The Third step in the certification process will be an oral board review in person before the certification board. This oral review will be 20 points toward the final total grade. This will be done at the annual school/meeting.

The Fourth and Final step in the certification process will be to help teach others to advance the field of evidence photography by presenting a program, or delivering a paper at the annual school. The submission of an original article with supporting photographs and/or illustrations of professional stature on some aspect of evidence photography, videography, or procedure, which is acceptable with the board, may also serve as a valid presentation. If an article is submitted, EPIC may or may not publish it in the EVIDENCE TECHNOLOGY MAGAZINE. Either the article or speech will count as 10 points toward the total score for certification.

4. Written Test: 25 points

   Print/video submissions: 45 points

   Oral Board Review: 20 points

   Lecture/Article: 10 points

   100 points total

   NOTE: An applicant shall have no less than 80 points total to pass this certification program.

5. For the Civil Evidence Photographer, the certification title will be:

   EPIC Board Certified Evidence Photographer, BCEP.

   For the Law Enforcement or Public area photographer:

   The EPIC Board Certification will be specific as to the specialty area. A total of 10 cases or assignments must be submitted for judging. If actual works from past cases covered by the applicant are not allowed to be reviewed by the EPIC Certification Board due to their department policy, The applicant will be allowed to photograph their own specially set up scenes to demonstrate their abilities. After passing the Board, the applicant will be given the title of EPIC Board Certified Crime Scene Photographer, or EPIC Board Certified Fire and Arson Photographer, or whatever specialty their area of work may be, and what they were certified under.
6. The EPIC certification committee, under the charge and direction of the presiding Board of EPIC, will select and provide additional advisory members, as necessary, consistent with the field or specialty being reviewed.
7. The applicant applying for Board Certification must substantiate that he/she is indeed operating as a practitioner in the evidence photography field. The applicant shall submit relevant representative examples of letterheads, business cards, mail outs, phone book ads, or other promotional materials used. Public sector (law enforcement) applicants may submit letters of recommendation and other documentation from department heads in lieu of promotional materials.
8. Certification shall be recommended by the Certification Board and will be confirmed by the EPIC Board of Directors.
9. The certified member will receive a certificate, EPIC logo for advertisement, a press release from EPIC headquarters, and a photograph of the member receiving the certificate during the awards presentation at the annual meeting.
10. Any and all photographs, videos, articles and other items submitted in connection with the certification process may be published in The EVIDENCE TECHNOLOGY MAGAZINE, with permission, or may be used in organizational advertising and/or for other promotional purposes to benefit EPIC's organization and programs, without compensation. Such use shall be the sole discretion of EPIC. A credit line and copyright recognition will be given to the photographer/author.
11. It is the responsibility of the applicant to properly package, ship and insure all materials when submitting originals for examination. The original submission may be made via USPS, UPS, FedEx, or the like, depending on the applicant's choice. Transfer between committee members shall be via the members' choice, but must be insured. Although every possible care will be taken to return all original materials to the applicant unharmed, EPIC assumes no responsibility for accidental loss or damage to material submitted for review).

CONTINUANCE

Continuance of board certification shall be contingent upon:

1. Maintenance of EPIC's annual membership dues.
2. Participation as a presenter in at least one continuing education seminar given by EPIC in a 36-month period subsequent to certification.

   OR: The submission of a research paper or article directed at the advancement of knowledge in the field of evidence photography is to be presented at an EPIC school of evidence photography in lieu of the presentation requirement. OR: Attending forty hours of continuing education in a related field over the 36-month period.

3. Failure to meet the above requirements may be cause for loss of certification as determined by the certification board.
4. A certified member of EPIC will be notified at least 90 days prior to initiation of any de-certification action.
5. A member may appeal a pending de-certification action to the Certification Board. The Certification Board will decide on the merits of any submission for re-certification. The Committee may choose to either de-certify the individual or allow for a conditional continuance of certification for a period not to exceed two years to meet the requirements lacking. De-certification must be a unanimous decision of the certification board. To grant a continuance, a majority vote is necessary.

http://www.epic-photo.org/epic-certification.htm

Chapter 2

Fair and Accurate Representation

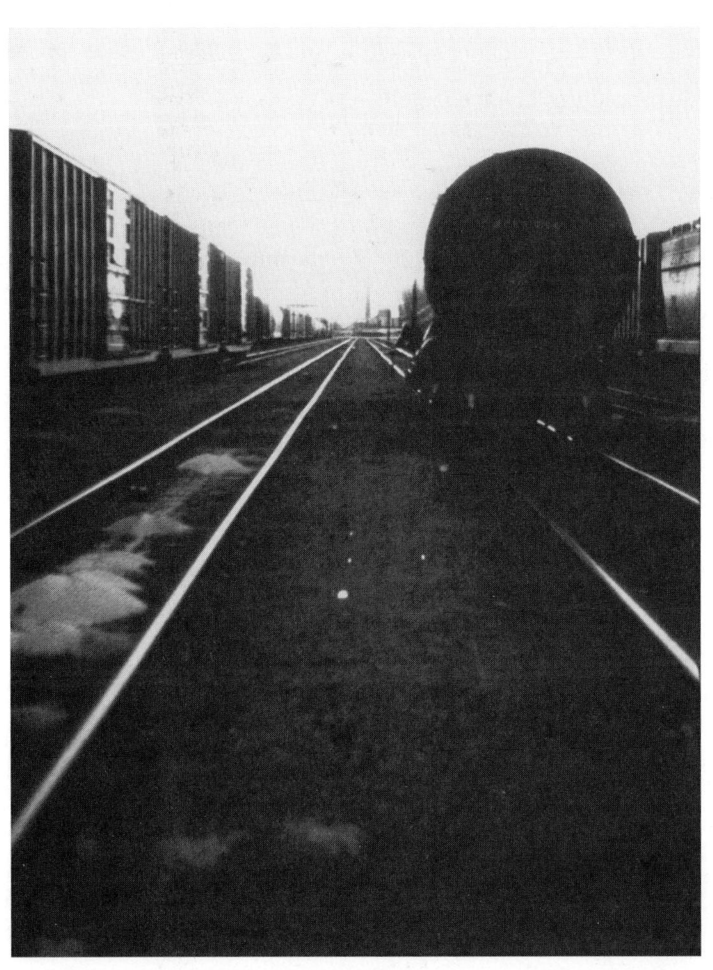

Learning Objectives

AFTER STUDYING THIS CHAPTER, YOU SHOULD BE ABLE TO:

1. To understand the necessity and usefulness of SOPs, protocols, and best practices
2. To become familiar with the Standards of Evidence Photography and understand the difficulties involved with accuracy in making images compared with human vision
3. To understand the parameters of admissibility for images in court
4. To understand the difference between perception and reality
5. To distinguish between point of view and perspective
6. To understand the reasoning behind making 3-D images of every collection of evidence or scene
7. To understand the why and how to authenticate a set of images to be used in court
8. To know the basic parameters for resolution both in input and output of the image construction process
9. To become familiar with the necessity for and availability of the different types of image references
10. To understand the concept of evidence spoliation and be able to prevent its occurrence
11. To know the basic procedures involved in chain of custody

INTRODUCTION

It is understandable that everyone wants to win at trial. People do unusual things to win; they lie, they offer evidence they know is false to save their money and/or their lives. Images, intentionally lacking in accuracy may be manufactured and offered as evidence by parties to substantiate their claims.

The photographs offered as evidence include images of documents, scenes, fires, ashes, scratches, injuries, corpses and/or any number of things. The method of image capture in evidence photographs is irrelevant. Film still has its place, but at some point in the existence of a film image, it will certainly be digitized,* saved, duplicated, and presented in digital form.

In the book *eDiscovery and Digital Evidence,*[1] the author states that "Today, most information is produced in digital format"[2] and it is tantamount to malpractice[3] to not keep current with the impact of technology. However, there are still judges, lawyers, engineers, photographers, and experts in many areas desperately clinging to silver technology. But, the time of such resistence is rapidly coming to a close.

Standard operating procedures (SOPs), i.e. **protocols and best-practices** for imaging to be used in court, are published in many forms on the Internet. It is no longer necessary for anyone to resort to writing these documents to fit a particular endeavor. All one needs to do is download a version for free, and mold it to fit their needs. A generic protocol/practice is attached to the end of this chapter as appendix 1.

A warning: be careful which way the document is handled. If a procedure is adopted as a protocol, it is necessary to follow it to the letter. If that is done, nobody can challenge the presented images. If the procedure is not followed to the letter, the photographer may be in trouble. If the procedure is adopted as a best practice, it will be useful as a framework, but it leaves room for

*Often without the owner's knowledge

errors. It requires more expertise on the part of the person testifying to the images. But normally, witnesses will not be disqualified for an honest mistake. Adopting a procedure as a protocol or as a best practice standard for accuracy is therefore a very serious decision.

Traditional film photographic imaging has these distinct phases:

1. Image capture
2. Negative processing
3. Printing
4. Storage

Digital photography is very similar, with:

1. Image capture
2. Download
3. Processing, including all forms of enhancement and display
4. Storage

In digital photography, all steps are performed by computer and/or electronic means. It is not possible to inspect digital images without the use of an imaging device or printout. A person cannot hold an electronic image in hand and mentally recreate all the steps that have gone into its creation.

Due to the seemingly mysterious operations of computers and their operators upon digital images, it is necessary to handle images using documented best practices and/or protocols, to be able to guarantee the images are un-manipulated at any particular time. Images can and may be changed or enhanced from captured/camera form at any of the download, processing, or storage phases. The techniques involved in these operations must be record-able and reproducible as well as in line with current state-of-the-art.

THE IMPORTANCE OF PROTOCOLS AND SOPS

A one person business/service may be the only type of operation not needing Standard Operating Procedures. A sole owner/operator opens for business when they want, finishes when tired, sells a product or service in which they have personal confidence, and is responsible only to themselves.

On close inspection, it is clear that customers are the most important part of their business. Without sufficient and satisfied customers, the business will fail. If the owner/operator's skill is lacking, they are unpleasant or inept at the job, the prices too high, or if they do not arrive in the right place at the right time, the customers may look elsewhere. Once they go somewhere else, chances are they will not be back, no matter how the owner/operator tries to regain them.

Thus, what at first glance appears a simple business, without following a set of consistent SOPs, may fail. Only by creating and following rigid SOPs, among other related business practices, will the business flourish. If the owner/operator hires help for assistance or to work other shifts, the list of necessary procedures grows. SOPs must be in place and followed to ensure the satisfaction of the customers, and to enumerate the expectations of the employer from the employee and vice versa. As the business succeeds and additional locations are opened and more employees hired, the complexity of the list of SOPs increases proportionally. If the business includes appearances in court, set procedures are mandatory.

Developing a set of SOPs is not an easy project; it must be undertaken with intelligence and the realization that no matter how hard the developer(s) try to anticipate every possible situation, the SOPs must still be dynamic and include the means and mechanisms to accomodate change according to the times and technology.

There are three sources from which a company may draw to produce a set of workable SOPs.

- The adoption of certain company-specific SOPs based on the owner/operator's experience during the normal course of doing business.
- The adoption of Generally Accepted Best Practices (GABP), with or without modifications, learned from the industry or through peer-company publication or interaction.
- The modification of generic industry standards.

In each case, the goals of the SOP's are the same:

1. To guarantee the best possible service to the customer.
2. To specify the level of performance expected of the employee by the company/service
3. To specify the level of performance expected of the company/service by the employee

Learning from experience is a form of **inductive reasoning.** Inductive reasoning is where a conclusion is based on past observation(s). The scientific method is not only used to find answers to scientific problems, but also as an inductive process, as an accepted solution for the development of business-specific SOPs. It is the key for the "acquisition of new knowledge based upon physical evidence"[4] and for an intelligent means of building a supportable, evidenced understanding of a problem. The steps of the scientific method include reasoning through theories, hypotheses, and observations. (see the flowchart in chapter 1) Predictions from theories are tested by experiment. If a prediction turns out correct, the hypothesis is shown to support the theory. If a prediction fails, the theory fails. Repeatability of similar results is not necessarily proof of success or failure, but suggests a supportable opinion.

Once reaching a sufficiently supportable opinion about a procedure, either positively or negatively, the procedure should be adopted or deleted. If adopted, it is mandatory for everyone concerned to adhere to its structure. Deviation from the SOP must be accountable on behalf of the company and/or service and the employee. If the procedure is a best practice rather than a protocol, it allows some room for adjustment.

A good example of a necessarily rigid SOP is provided by the use of digital imaging. Even in litigation-based endeavors, it has been repeatedly shown in trials that adherence to a digital imaging protocol is paramount where authentication of images depends upon both testimony and protocol, and neither is sufficient on its own. GABP leaves options for image capture, but is rigid concerning download, storage, and access to images. To operate a digitally oriented company or service without an adopted and followed SOP is unacceptable and dangerous. One instance of bad practice on behalf of a client is too many.

The major areas of importance in developing a best practice or protocol include:

- Organizational chain of custody
- Evidence handling
- Security
- Filing
- Storage
- Archiving
- Backup

It should be remembered that it is not unusual for companies or services of the same industry to create different SOPs. Therefore, every individual endeavor must provide at least some of the brainwork necessary for the production of the SOP set required. It cannot be expected that the employees or the management of a company will instinctively understand how to act in any particular situation, unless everyone has access to the same set of rules.

How SOPs are written, adopted, and enforced is not the issue. The important point is that once SOPs are published, it is the responsibility of all involved to adhere to them, not because the SOPs are equitable, but because they are what is required to be a successful and ethical business or service.

Fair and Accurate; Qualification of the Standard

For more than a century, photographic representations of visual evidence have been a mainstay in court. **Admissibility** of photographs has always been decided by the judge, who uses the credibility and competency of the witness presenting the images, along with other important factors, as parameters for the decision. Opposing counsel does have the right to challenge the accuracy of the photo(s) according to competency issues and to try to show that the image(s) are not in fact as accurate as the witness attests.

Photographs are generally allowed into evidence irrespective of image quality as long as the images are not inflammatory. It has also not often been necessary for the person who exposed and/or printed the images to testify, unless they are an expert witness, because it is not the images themselves that are evidence.

Black and white or color, reflective print or transparency, offset or letterpress, silver halide or dye-transfer, magazine, newspaper, wallet or mural-size, or in any other of an infinity of forms, all photographic prints used to have at least one thing in common: they were originally captured on film. Most human beings around the world, in this era, are familiar with film-based photographic images, have a basic idea how they are produced, and recognize the images for what they are with nothing more than a glance, with accuracy being unsubstantiated but understood.

Photography has transformed and educated civilized society in many ways. In *On Photography*,[5] Susan Sontag discusses the impact of photography on life in the 20th century. She writes, "The universal presence of the photographic image in our lives, and as something we take for granted, has made the photograph more real than what it represents and has changed irrevocably our notion of reality." However, in court, photographs should not be any more or any less than the best possible representation of a very specific reality.

Professional organizations,[6] in order to promote and guarantee a degree of quality and credibility in photographic images, have written and published photographic **standards** (see Fig. 2–1). All the standards define admissibility, essentially, as a matter of the "**fair and accurate**[7] representation of the subject portrayed." Fair is a relative term and its applicability is always decided by the judge and related to the credibility of the witness. Even poor photographic quality will not necessarily cause an image to be deemed inadmissible if the judge thinks the image is fair and relevant to the proceedings. There is unfortunately, no standard definition and/or set of parameters for the term accurate.

Judge John Panos, a state court Judge in DeKalb County, Georgia says, "I would like to see a standard definition of accurate made and published. This can then be referred to as the standard of the industry." Why is this necessary? For example, in a 1967 Georgia trial,[8] photographs

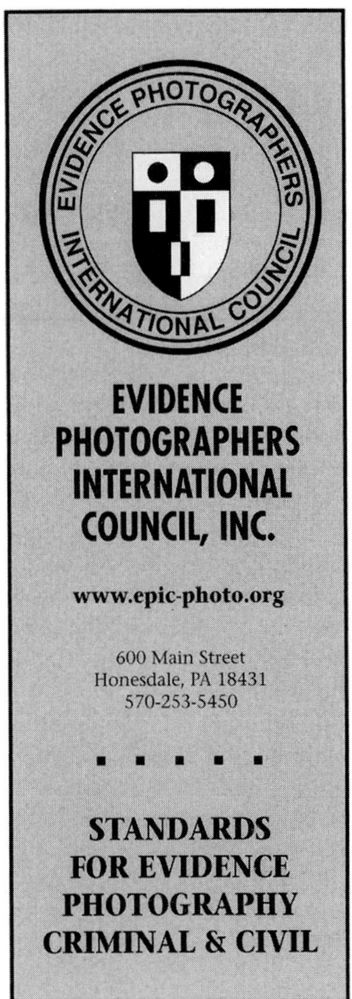

FIGURE 2–1 Cover of the standards published by the Evidence Photographers International Council. *Source:* EPIC Standards.

of a site were excluded on the grounds that they did not accurately portray the site of an accident because they were photographed three years after the accident and the site had changed. It is conceivable that any photographic images in any trial could be excluded because they do not accurately, in someone's view, portray the subject in question.

During testimony, if asked the direct question about a photograph, "Is this image an accurate representation of the subject portrayed," a truthful and educated witness has no choice but to reply "No." Chances are, an astute attorney will not wait for the witness to reply, "No, but." Terms including *color reproduction, dynamic range, resolution, perspective, angle of view, dimensionality,* etc, may not even be fully understood by the professional photographer or the attorney, let alone the juror. How many people can properly define the difference between *vision* and *perception* and understand how it correlates to the accuracy of a photographic representation? Witnesses testifying about images cannot take it for granted that those in the courtroom truly understand photography.

Photographers often attempt to create photographs of objects and/or scenes "as seen" by someone else at the moment in question. Of all the tasks in photography, the most impossible is to create an image of anything as someone else would have seen it. It is, however, possible and appropriate to make images to explain how something looked to the photographer.

Image capture for court is now predominantly digital. Before very long, all forensic images will be produced digitally. This transition has not been without resistance, but that is a separate issue. While the acceptance of film-based images, even by relatively uneducated viewers has been a moot point, digitally produced images are more easily and more often questioned as to their **authentication.** Digital imaging, though in some ways more intrinsically basic than film imaging, will need time, serious education, and the experience of comfortable daily use, for society to grasp a basic understanding of the digital process and workflow.

Judge Panos says, "True and accurate generally means the overall photo showing the questioned area, article, etc. should memorialize it in its most natural state. Typically, if the issue involved is very detail oriented concerning an area, article, etc., then true and accurate will require a stricter scrutiny of that photograph."

For example, in the first instance, if all an attorney wants to show with a photograph is the approximate physical or "general" area of involvement, then chances are a judge will not be too strict in interpreting true and accurate. Thus a photograph of the scene would suffice for the purpose of identifying the location.

In the second instance, however, if an attorney wants to demonstrate in exact detail, the distance between two aspects of a bridge, photographic expertise becomes very important. In this instance, someone cannot give an off the cuff opinion as to distances. Thus, a judge would not allow an attorney who took a photograph showing the bridge to testify that based on the photograph, a specific distance is 25 feet (see Fig. 2–2).

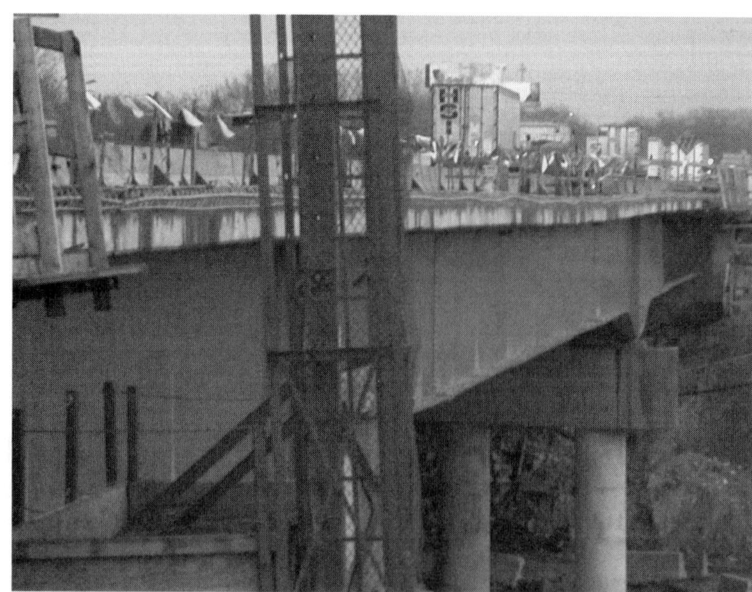

FIGURE 2–2 How would a witness testify about the dimensions of the bridge? *Source:* Sandy Weiss/Packer Engineering.

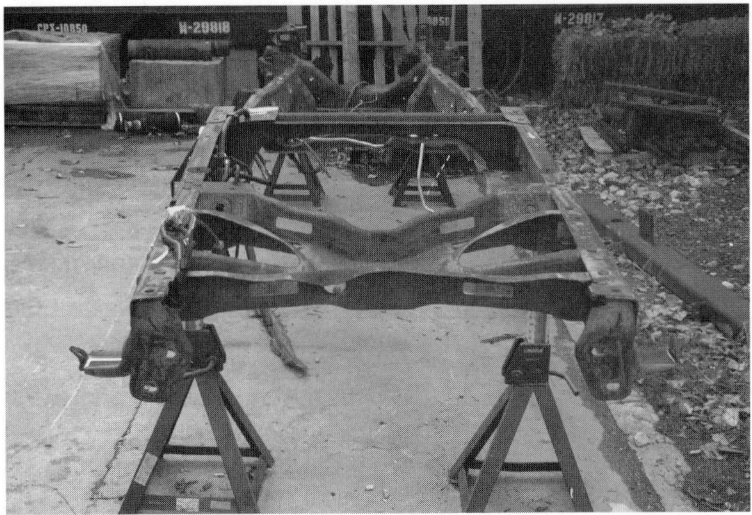

FIGURE 2–3 Automotive chassis. *Source:* Sandy Weiss/Packer Engineering.

Due to the relative ease of digital imaging, many people who require images for trial are making their own. There is no longer a great need for a photo-lab. People who used to make a living in the imaging business are now competing with their past clients. It is very difficult to convince clients to continue to use the services of a professional when they can do things themselves and save money.

How can that be prevented? The photographic skills of a trained forensic photographer will set them above the amateurs who will not be able to compete with their level of expertise. Then if an attorney asks if the images presented are a fair and accurate representation of the subject portrayed, the answer can and should be, yes, they are, and be able to explain why.

Here are two images of the same artifact (see Figs. 2–3 and 2–4). They are both fair representations, but which is more accurate?

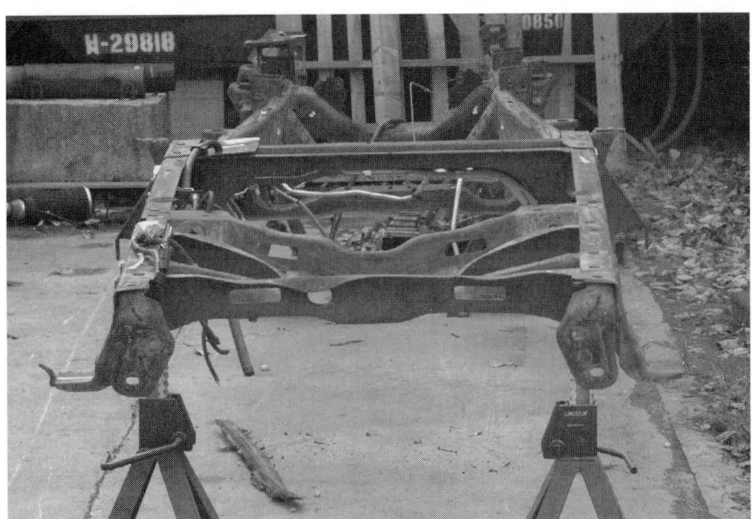

FIGURE 2–4 Automotive chassis. *Source:* Sandy Weiss/Packer Engineering.

VISION, PHOTOGRAPHY, AND PERSPECTIVE

Photography is, "a mechanical process of collecting data for visual purposes."[9]

The inadequacies of an under-trained investigator/photographer may limit the accuracy of evidence documentation, and can be compounded by the inherent limitations of the photographic medium. The properly trained photographer has a better chance to create images more representative of reality, in ways less prone to be challenged, and if challenged, is more likely to be able to properly explain the process and the differences.

In Scientific Evidence In Criminal Cases, the author states, "Photography is the one type of evidence that is best understood by all people, including police officers, lawyers, and judges.[10] Photography's capacity for documenting evidence and its potential in actually uncovering some types of evidence make it an indispensable tool for any detective. Some investigators leave evidence undocumented or impossible to analyze, but it is common knowledge that as to such matters, either through want of skill on the part of the artist (investigator), or inadequate instruments or materials, or through intentional and skillful manipulation, a photograph may not only be inaccurate but dangerously misleading."[11]

At this point, a good description of the process of human vision is necessary, especially to compare vision to photography and explain which shortcomings of photography proper training, thought, and execution should be able to minimize.

Vision/Perception

Vision is one of the tools the human brain uses to experience the world around it. Light rays entering the eye(s) are focused on the surfaces of the retinas and the image information (optical stimuli) are transmitted to the appropriate parts of the brain by means of nerves. The brain processes the information, and the person "sees" what the brain perceives as an appropriate image.[12]

Many physiologists believe that what happens to the optical stimuli in the brain has less to do with the visual information and more to do with the prior experience(s) of the person. **Perception** therefore, is the process of becoming aware of the representation of something in the world through the complex filters of experience. The visual event is a real sensation comprised of a number of activities of the brain, including its immediate analysis of the current image, all other sensory input, and conscious and sub-conscious lessons learned in the past under similar circumstances. The entire process is more or less instantaneous, depending upon the physical condition of the viewer, the number of stimuli, and the amount of stress in the particular situation.

Other factors affecting the mind of the viewer and influencing their particular visual imaging capabilities may include the weight of other tasks/obligations, environmental factors, and possibly emotional reactions to the visual information.

A trained and experienced investigator, who may not necessarily be as accomplished in photography as the trained and experienced photographer, may possess a broader-based level of experience in investigations. For this reason, the investigator may have a better idea of WHAT is pertinent to document in a particular situation while possibly lacking some competence in HOW to do it. It is hoped that with sufficient experience the skill-level of the photographer inside the investigator will be sufficient to enhance and not detract from the essence and quality of the investigation.

Vision and Evidence Photography

One factor that allows people to accept images (photographs, films, television, etc) as reasonable facsimiles of reality in general, is that we often see in the images what we expect to see. The mind applies, to the extent it is capable, what it sees to a standard and analyzes whether or not the sight fits into a past pattern or experience. Each person has his or her own experience-base to use in forming his or her personal standard. In this way, the more experienced the observer, the more accurate their mental analysis of a scene, or object.

The EPIC standard states, "Photographic identification requires that the pattern in the picture be relatable visually to the image the observer has formed of it, or is expected to form of it, in his mind."[13]

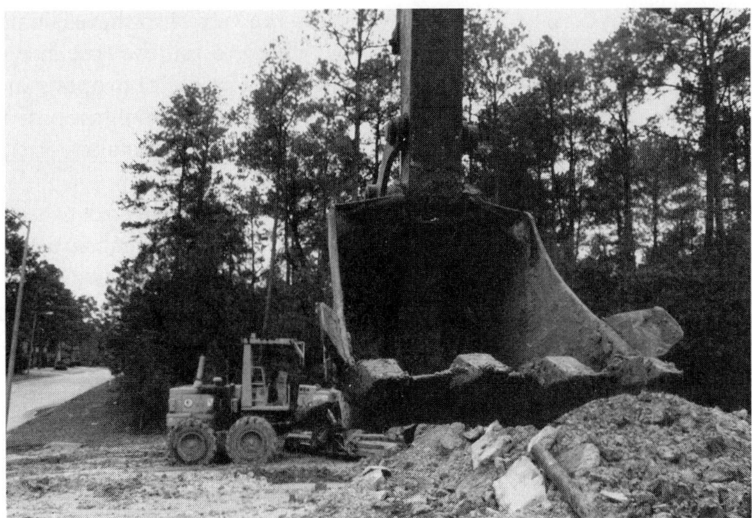

FIGURE 2–5 Is the bucket in front of or behind the tractor? *Source:* Sandy Weiss/Packer Engineering.

So, what does this have to do with the plight of the evidence photographer? The main problem is that when people see photographs, they expect the images to be true and accurate representations. When they expect the truth, the image(s) become the truth, whether they are or not. The challenge is to make photographs the most truthful they can be, and that is not a simple task (see Fig. 2–5).

There are many elements of the human visual process that are difficult or impossible to duplicate photographically and are therefore impediments to the representation of reality in photographic reproduction. Of these elements, proper:

- Perspective
- Dimensionality
- Contrast, and
- Color reproduction

are the most prevalent.

A basic example of one of the differences between vision and photography is the instantaneous sensitivity of the human eye versus the cumulative sensitivity of the photographic light receptor. In other words, the photograph can show less than, similar to, or more than the detail the eye(s) may have seen in the same circumstances, depending upon the lighting and the variables of exposure. For example, it is a simple process to represent a night scene, as if it were broad daylight with a simple camera and long exposure (see chapter 11) Obviously, that is not something the unaided human eye can do, nor is it an accurate representation of any possible reality.

Fig. 2–6 of a railway tank car was taken at a one second exposure and an aperture of *f*1.2 on ASA 1600 film, to illustrate the contrast difference between the blackness of the car and the blackness of the sky after dusk.

The trained photographer will be familiar with the subject of human vision and know how to properly document the evidence to optimize the relationship between how the evidence looks to the photographer and how it will eventually look on the photograph.

Optimization of Perspective

"The intriguing fact that a photographic image is not produced by manual labor, but strictly through a mechanical process, gave way to the conception of photography's ability to give a near perfect representation of the world as we see it."[14] Each technological improvement in photography was seen as one step closer to creating a perfect illusion of the perceptual world. Statements like, now we have perspective, soon we will have reality, are based on the mistaken notion that representation at some point can become nature.

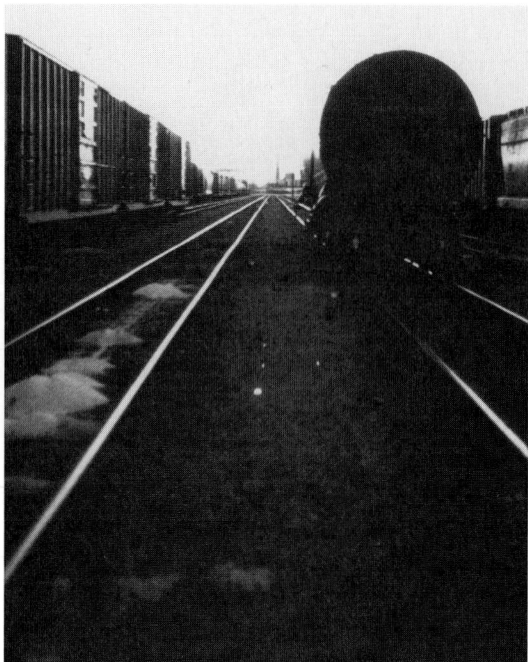

FIGURE 2–6 See hump-yard case study 3 at the end of this chapter. *Source:* Sandy Weiss/Packer Engineering.

Perspective, in this case, is a graphic device used to describe the reproduction of a subject in 3-D space being turned into a 2-D representation. Proper perspective is a representation, either in the brain or in a photograph, of a subject showing spatial relationships corresponding to how the subject looked to the viewer with the un-aided eye. This is often referred to as linear perspective, which is a mathematical system for creating the illusion of space and distance on a flat surface.[15] Linear perspective is a visual clue related to both relative size and depth clues. In linear perspective, parallel lines receding into the distance appear to converge.

Visual clues are important to the perception of correct and appropriate perspective and a correspondingly proper sense of depth and scale. (Consider the tricks played upon the minds of viewers of movies like Titanic, Harry Potter, and The Lord of the Rings. When the cinematographer wants to make a model or person look like a giant, depth-clues are withheld from the viewer so there is nothing in the frame by which to tell the true size of the frame elements.) The use of proper scales and references in a photograph or group of photographs will eliminate most mistakes of size perception by the viewer.

Film (cinema) once existed in a pure, natural state, which is now enhanced by developments in digital technology such as computer-generated imagery (CGI). According to this kind of reasoning, **FILM IS REAL AS LONG AS WE REMEMBER THAT IT IS ARTIFICIAL.**

To view a photograph in proper perspective, the same angular relationship must be maintained between the print and the eye viewing the photograph as occurred between the lens and the image receptor when the image was made. Normal viewing distance for the human eye and a 2-D print is, by definition, about 15 inches. However, the correct viewing distance for a photographic print, in inches, is the focal length of the camera lens used (in inches) multiplied by the number of times the original image is enlarged. To make the calculations simple, suppose a 1-inch lens (25 mm) on a digital camera with a 1-inch wide sensor. The image is enlarged to 8 × 10 inches. The proper viewing distance for this image would be 1 × 10 or 10 inches. It would require an image enlarged to about 12 × 15 to view the print properly at 15 inches.

Using these formulas, consider the correct viewing distance for a 24 × 30 print or, even more to the point, a movie theater screen. Did you ever wonder why the theater puts seats in front, right next to the screen? It can't be for ease of viewing the movie. When you come in late and are forced to sit in front, did you ever notice how much larger the actor's nose appears than when you were sitting in the back row?

The use of a normal focal length lens on any format camera will promote the production of images that look the most natural and have similar visual perspective to those seen by a person with two healthy eyes, when the images are printed at the proper size for viewing at a familiar and comfortable distance. Deviations from normal in lens focal length will produce images with distorted perspective, unless the images are

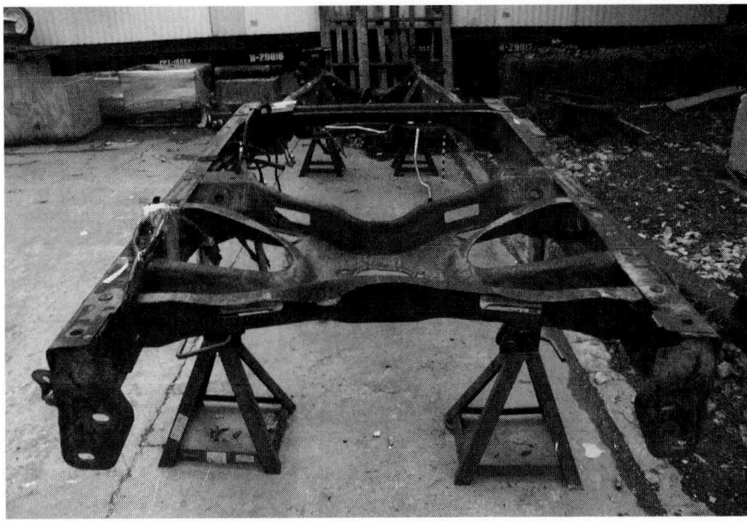

FIGURE 2–7 Automotive chassis. *Source:* Sandy Weiss/Packer Engineering.

printed in the proper size for that focal length and viewed from the appropriate and corresponding viewing distance.

Camera lenses are broadly categorized as normal, telephoto, and wide angle, according to their focal length, and dependent upon the image receptor size in the camera on which they are used. A normal lens is one that yields an image, on the receptor, corresponding approximately to that of normal perspective in human monocular vision†: The focal length of a normal/standard lens producing a 24 X 36 mm (1 × 1.5 inch) image (the length of the diagonal measurement of the image format) with a 35 mm film camera is the familiar 50 mm. The focal length of a normal/standard lens on a digital camera depends on the physical dimensions of the image sensor, and varies according to the proportions of the sensor, width versus height. The "normal" focal length for a particular digital camera should be found in the camera manual or on a website like Digital Photography Review (www.dpreview.com).

Any lens with a focal length shorter or numerically smaller than normal for a given image sensor is considered wide angle. Any lens with a focal length longer or numerically larger than normal for a given sensor is considered telephoto. A wide angle lens shrinks a given subject to a size smaller on sensor than a correspondingly normal lens and a telephoto lens magnifies the subject. For example, a 200 mm telephoto lens yields a 4× magnification on sensor over a 50 mm lens, and a 24 mm lens yields a magnification of .5 times.

Lenses with variable focal length are called zooms. It would seem that a zoom lens would be the answer to every photographer's dream of versatility. The wider the zoom range, the greater the variety and size of subject a camera may capture with the least effort of the photographer. However, if using a zoom lens, consider the confusion you may create if the zoom feature is used for documenting evidence. Switching focal lengths back and forth without warning the viewer may make the images difficult to correlate to each other. It is far more important to represent the image perspective as relatively normal, than to lessen the photographic effort necessary to capture the image. Modern manufacturers are not putting a mark on their zoom lenses to give the photographer a reference for "normal." It is often necessary to determine that focal length and to set the lens there manually.

Fig. 2–3 was taken with a normal lens and Fig. 2–4 was taken with a telephoto. Fig. 2–7 was

†Normal human vision is if the horizontal and vertical fields of view, about 120° horizontally (not including peripheral vision which extends out to about 200°) and 100° vertically. The 50–55 mm lens on a 35 mm camera approximates this field of view without optically distorting (magnifying or reducing) the light transmitted through the lens.

taken with a wide-angle. Use a straight edge to follow the edges of the chassis to the vanishing point to compare the angles formed by the three different lens types.

Perspective Mistakes and Visual Accuracy

The focal length of a lens establishes the field of view of the photographic image. Shorter lenses yield a larger than normal field of view on the image receptor. The magnification factor of the image of an object and the object's actual size can be found by dividing the focal length of the lens used to make the image by the focal length of a standard lens for any given format. The numeric result is then multiplied by the physical size the image would have been if formed by a normal lens. For example, if an object is photographed with a 40 mm lens on a 35 mm camera, the resultant image, on film, will be 40/50× normal. If the subject is 80% of normal, and the image receptor size is constant, the field of view will increase by approximately 20%.

At the time the photograph is taken, the angular placement of the camera governs its **point of view.** (Point of view in this case is the position in space from which something is observed.[16]) The placement of the camera can make a significant difference in the accuracy of the subject depicted.[17] Looking up or down at a subject is not as natural as looking straight ahead, and while making photographs from unusual points of view may be dramatic, it is not recommended when documenting evidence unless the objective is to document evidence which requires a unique angle to best illustrate its features.

No matter what the point of view of the image, no matter what the focal length of the lens, the format of the camera, or the subject, the photograph will contain an inherent vanishing point at the horizon. This is the point to which all parallel lines in the same plane tend (to converge) in the representation.[18] The parallel lines will continue to converge in direct proportion to their distance from the observer within the boundaries of the image. If the point of convergence is outside the image, it will still exist somewhere on the same plane.

The closer the camera is placed to the subject(s), the farther apart the subjects will appear according to the way the perception of depth is perceived in the developed photograph.[19] Even if two objects are in reality the same physical size, the one appearing smaller in the image will be the one farthest from the camera/observer. How much difference in size is visible in the photograph is what supplies the observer with the visual clues to judge their actual separation. The size difference will grow much more quickly when the lens used is shorter in focal length.

The key point is, mistakes made in the representation of proper perspective lead to mistakes in visual accuracy in the analysis of the image(s). What is photographed is, strictly speaking, never the object itself but certain visual properties of the object, that is the light passing through or bouncing off the surface. It is these visual properties the photographer must strengthen

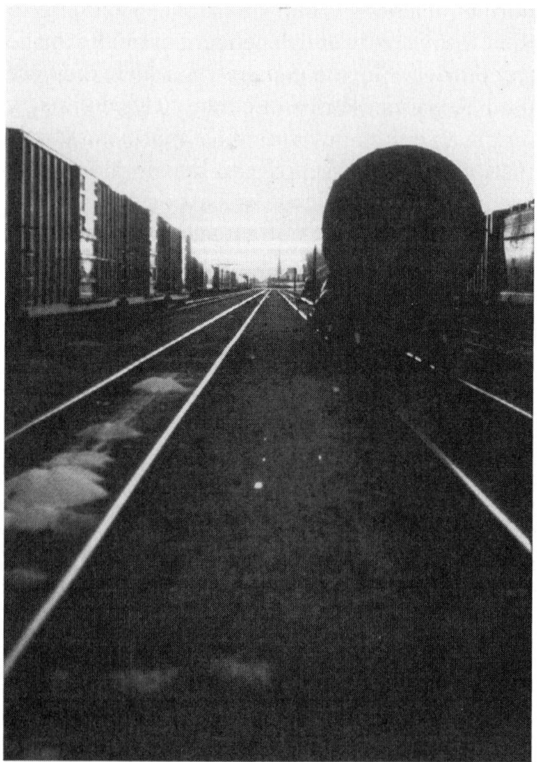

FIGURE 2–8 Perspective of the Hump Yard photograph. *Source:* Sandy Weiss/Packer Engineering.

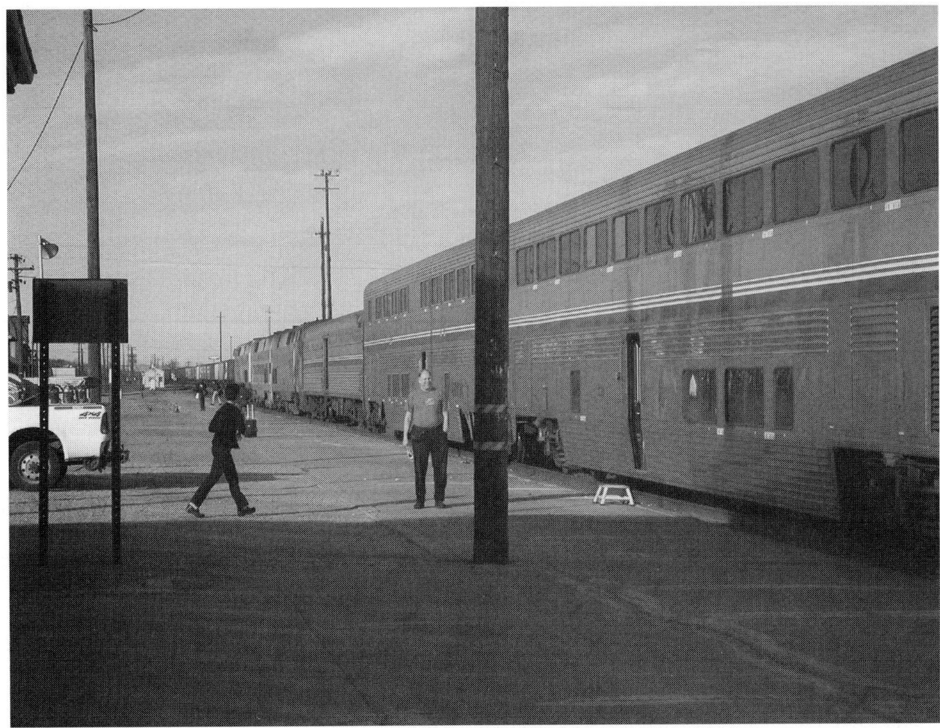

FIGURE 2–9 Wide-angle perspective. *Source:* Sandy Weiss/Packer Engineering.

and sharpen by the choice of the right moment, the control of camera angle, distance, lighting, etc. Nothing in this world is anything but the totality of its properties.[20]

Figs. 2–3 and 2–4 were exposed purposely to make the subject chassis appear to be about the same size in both images. The question asked, which is the more accurate representation of the evidence imaged is a trick question. Both are accurate when viewed separately. Only when the two images are viewed together and compared to each other does the difference in their perspectives become an issue.

Fig. 2–8 was taken with a 55 mm (normal) lens on a 35 mm camera (Olympus OM-4 with 55 mm f1.2). For an exercise, copy this image and make it a bit larger. Place it on a plain piece of paper and draw in a point in front of the image to simulate the point of view of the camera, perpendicular to the frame, and then draw out the angles made by the two sets of tracks. You will see that they converge behind the physical image.

Fig. 2–9 was taken with a wide-angle lens on a digital camera (Nikon 4500 set at 7.85 mm, its widest angle) Perform the same operation on this image and note the difference in angle from a normal image.

Fig. 2–10 is a simple graphic illustration of visual perspective. Foreshorten the horizon or change the size of the object and the angles change accordingly. No matter what the point of view of the image, no matter what the focal length of the lens, the format of the camera, or the subject, the photograph will contain an inherent vanishing point.

USING 3-DIMENSIONAL IMAGING FOR EVIDENCE DOCUMENTATION AND ANALYSIS

Moenssens and Inbau, in their book *Scientific Evidence in Criminal Cases*,[21] a handbook for forensic photography, make no mention of 3-D technologies.[‡] It is a troubling oversight but not unusual. Most books on the subject of evidence and evidence photography skip over 3-D

[‡]Refer to chapter 8 for detailed definitions of 3-D technologies.

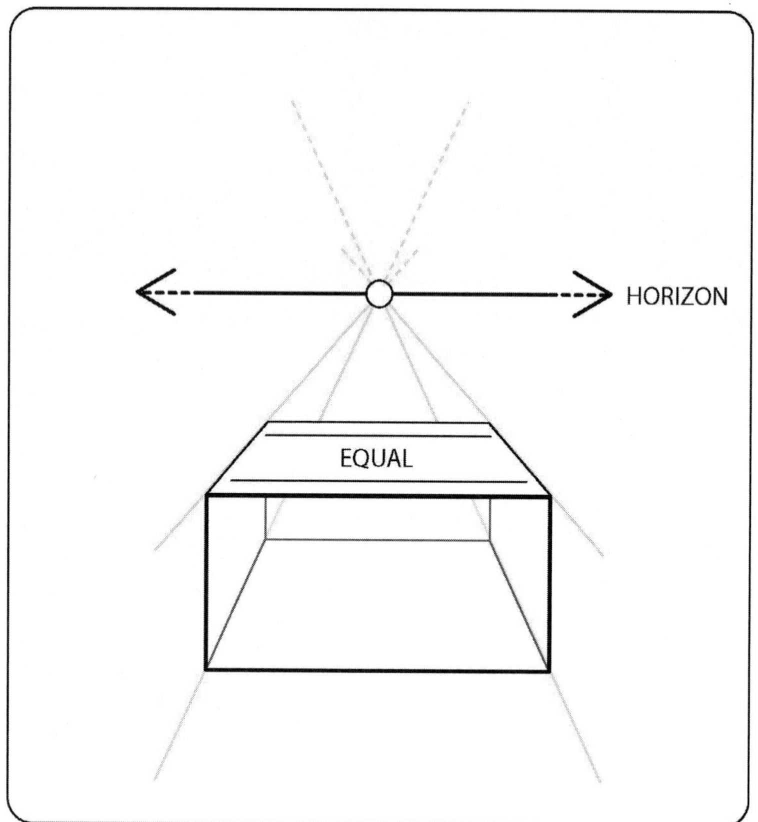

FIGURE 2–10 Visual perspective/vanishing point. *Source:* Jessica Weiss.

material. However, 3-D goes back to the very beginnings of photography, but has since been little used by all but the adventuresome few.

There are reasons to resurrect these practices and use them again as a means of separating the professional forensic photographers from the amateurs.

Photogrammetrists[§] are trained to expose the proper photos for 3-D analysis. It is time that everyone in the evidence photography field started to capture at least some 3-D images on every project they document. All of the technologies mentioned here are applicable to digital as well as film-based photography.

3-Dimensional (3-D) Photography

To reiterate, "To be admitted in evidence in a court trial, a photograph must be **a fair and reasonably accurate representation of the subject portrayed.**"[22] This has been the major prerequisite for the admissibility of courtroom photographic images since they were first used in a case in 1859.[23] However, consider the following theory:

"All (2-D) photographs are an abstraction in one way or another. Even if the picture reveals a completely realistic and recognizable subject, it is only a 2-D representation of a 3-D scene, consisting of a pattern of dyes on a piece of chemically treated paper a few millimeters thick."[24] Is this a paradox? Also, "The conventional 2-D photograph can be and often is an important artistic creation in itself but it is never mistaken for the actual scene."[25]

These are logical statements. How can a photograph be both an accurate representation and also an abstraction that cannot be mistaken for reality? That is where the fair and reasonably accurate standard comes into play.

[§]Refer to chapter 4

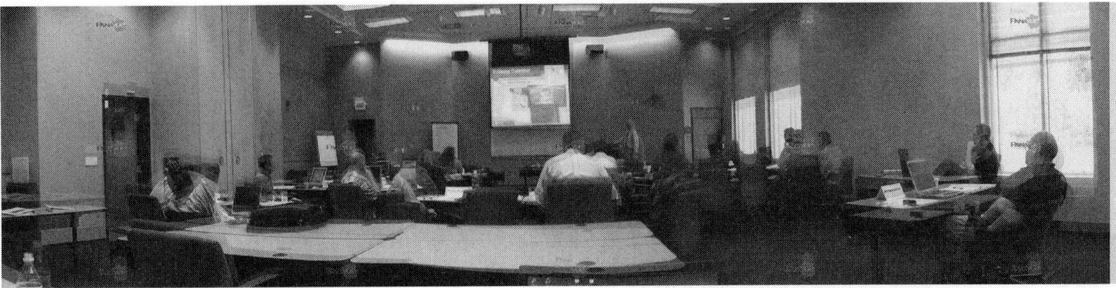

FIGURE 2–11 A 3-D anaglyph image assembled with panorama software and a series of anaglyph still photos. *Source*: Paul Fenoglis/Packer Engineering.

Photographers can only do as well as they can in the depiction of any evidence or scene (see Fig. 2–11). They can only produce images as well as the hardware and photo-receptive material of the day will allow. They can however, address the question of how many dimensions are sufficient to determine that the photographic representation is indeed accurate?

IMAGE MANAGEMENT SOFTWARE

There is software available, that allows users of vast numbers of images the ease of rapid access and strong security. There are many choices but VeriPic®[26] is a tested and mature solution, designed by a pioneer in digital imaging and tested under extreme conditions. Of course, it is not a necessity to purchase security and database software. Large numbers of images can be safely managed and stored using any number of homemade database and protocol applications. However, if your agency, business, or department needs a ready-made package, VeriPic® is one to trust. Here are some of its features:

Benefits of using VeriPic®:

- Automates the process of downloading photos
- Browse thousands of thumbnails in seconds
- Protects copyrights of professional photographers
- Print photos fast
- Find photos by searching titles and notes
- Virtual tours of homes and merchandise
- Share photos with business partners or customers
- Enhancement and Analysis with lossless JPEGs
- **Photo security with multi-level access security and photo authentication.**

Features:

- Authentication (at the pixel level): authenticate that an image has not been altered prior to reaching the software. For example, consider the following image of the tour-ship with another ship. The image was submitted by the National Transportation Safety Board (NTSB) to VeriPic® for authentication of a claim for damages. The software was able to prove that the "phantom" in the distance was an aberration added at a later time.
- Proficient photo management: organize photos by case number, titles and notes. This allows advanced searches by date range, key words, etc.
- High-speed thumbnail processing: the software can extract up to 500 thumbnails per second.
- Audit trail (database only): the database version of VeriPic®, allows the added security of encryption, and activity history to ensure chain of custody. The software is password protected with six

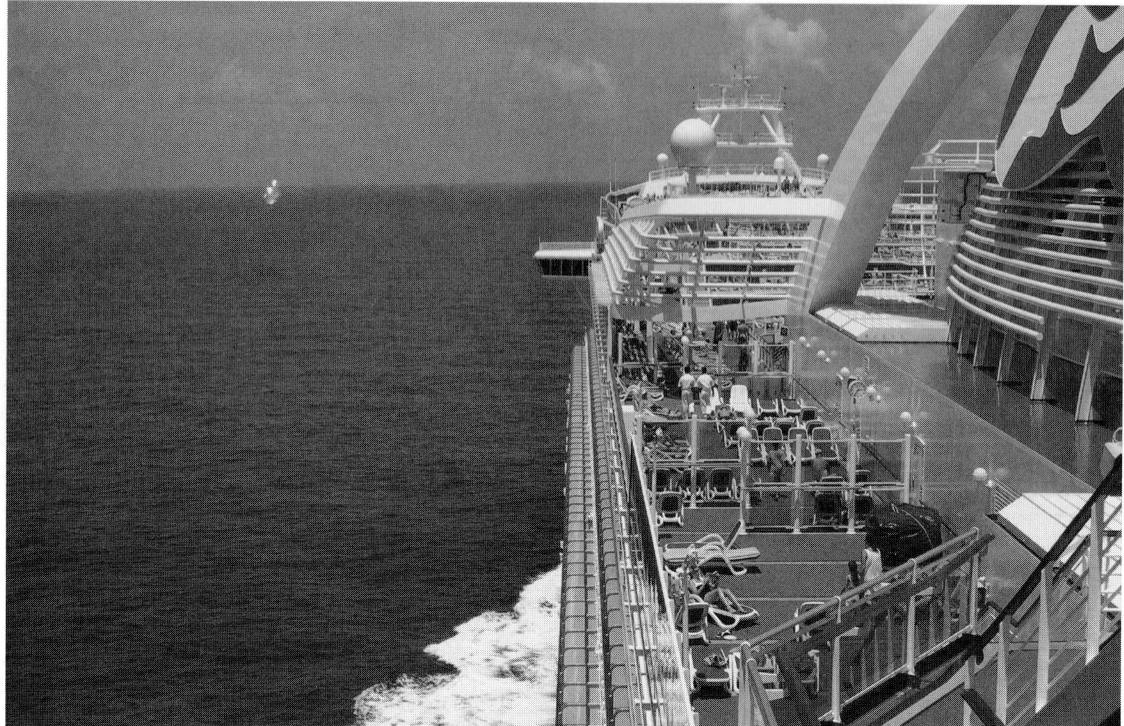

FIGURE 2–12 Image submitted for verification. *Source*: Sandy Weiss/Packer Engineering.

different security levels. This insures that basic users do not see maximum-security photos.

Fig. 2–12 was submitted to VeriPic to determine if the white object at the top-left was another ship or if it was something added to the image. It proved to be an intentional doctoring of the image. Is this image verifiable?

Image (Output) Resolution

Resolution is a measurable characteristic of image accuracy. Printer resolution, scanner resolution and monitor resolution are measured primarily in dots per inch (dpi).** Most scanners default to output 200–300 dpi, which may actually be called pixels per inch (ppi).†† Most printers are optimized, or print their best quality color at 250–300 dpi. Scanner resolution is measured in pixels, and printer resolution is measured in dots. A printer's maximum resolution may be listed at 600–1200 dpi, but pixels are bigger than dots so many dots can be utilized by the printer to create the physical form of every pixel.

If the output resolution is set beyond 300 dpi, the file size increases or the image size decreases, depending upon whether or not the computer is set to **resample** the image.

If the printer resolution is set lower than 300 dpi, it may produce grainy or incomplete-looking images.

Input Resolution

Input resolution from scanning is determined by the final size, in inches, of the necessary image. If the output resolution of the scanner is set to 300 dpi, and the printer requires 300 dpi, it is possible to determine the physical size, in inches, of the necessary scan/final print. Set the scanner output to 300 dpi and set the image size to, for

**Dots per inch; is a standard of measurement for the resolution of images; The higher the DPI, the higher the resolution.
††This is the resolution of an input device. Examples include digital cameras, scanners, and monitors.

example 5 × 7-inches; multiply the 5 × 300 and the 7 × 300 and the products determine the necessary scanned image size. Be sure the output resolution is set to 300 dpi, not 72 dpi monitor resolution before printing.

If a scanned image needs to become a 5 × 7 inch print, the file size will be about 3 MB.

Monitor Resolution

Monitors have a maximum resolution that determines how images look when they are shown full-screen.

> **TIP:**
>
> It is important to remember that what is displayed on the monitor is not necessarily how the image will look when it is printed.

The monitor's resolution is different than the printer's resolution. If the images made are for e-mail or to post on the Internet, monitor resolution may be all that is necessary. However, evidence photographs should always be exposed at a higher resolution to allow in-depth inspection of detail.

Scale Selection

There are many types of scales and references to be used when making evidence photographs. The three main categories are **size, color,** and **positional.** Other scales and references including levels and inclinometers will be discussed in chapters 10 and 13.

When selecting a scale for size documentation, there are several variables to consider, including;

- What type of precision of measurement is required?
- Does the scale need to be flexible or rigid?
- What is the size of the item referenced?
- How many dimensions need to be referenced?
- What type of lighting is to be used?
- Whether a scale is truly needed and for what?

The photographer must supply sufficient size references to achieve necessary accuracy for the needs of the individual case and to satisfy any software requirements.

When selecting a scale, the scale must provide precision in calibration as needed by the system that will be measuring the photographic information. If the system has a precision to one sixteenth of an inch, the scale used must be accurate and precise to at least one sixteenth of an inch.

Be aware of mixing metric or inch scales, in sixteenths or hundredths, if one or the other is not understood or acceptable.

It may be argued by an attorney that the scale used was not "certified" by the International Standards Organization (ISO) or other standards body. To circumvent this argument, use the same scale that is imaged in the photograph to measure the prints or displays and also use the same scale for **rectification** of the images to a particular subsequent scale. Scales should be individually identified and marked so there is no confusion as to which scale was used in the photographs.

If a scale is not totally accurate, using it both in the photographs and in the displays will alleviate any question of possible misrepresentation. Scales that are questionable for accuracy or reliability, including retractable tapes, cloth tapes, wooden and plastic rulers, and folding rules should only be used in emergencies. Also, use of pencils, coins, currency, soda cans, etc. are not recommended BUT, in an emergency, using something is better than using nothing as long as the something is retained for future comparison.

Scale Placement

Consider the item being photographed and the plane upon which the information to be measured is located. The scale should be placed on the same plane as the important information. If the plane runs on an angle in the photograph, that angle must be matched to the scale. The scale does not necessarily need to be physically placed upon the surface of the item, but may be placed alongside the object or photographically suspended in space near the object; as long as it is on the same plane as the information. If there is some thickness to the scale, make sure that the surface that has the ruled markings is on the plane of the information, not the other side of the scale.

Some photographers make the common error of thinking that as long as there is a scale imaged in a photo that the viewer will be able to properly visualize the size of the scale and therefore the evidence (see Fig. 2–13). Because of **parallax** issues, the true size may not be recordable without using **photogrammetry** to extract the dimensions (see chapter 4).

If the scale is to be placed on the same surface as the information being recorded, make sure that the scale does not obscure any important details. If there is a possibility of trace or Haz-Mat evidence being present on the evidence, do not use scales that stick in place. Use another type of scale along-side the surface being photographed.

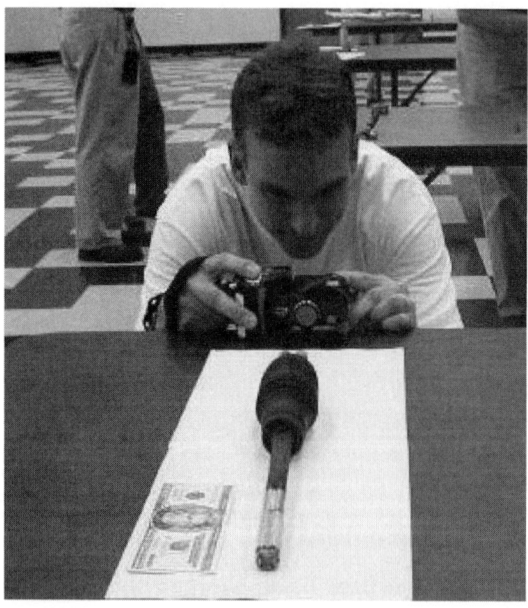

FIGURE 2–13 Is the scale in this photo properly placed? *Source:* Sandy Weiss/Packer Engineering.

Size Scale Types

Machinist scales are expensive but usually accurate. This type of scale comes in a variety of measuring units. Scales may have a non-reflective surface that appears neutral gray when photographed. They are simple to maintain and clean. These scales are made of hardened steel and can either be purchased in flexible or rigid material in varying thicknesses.

Plastic scales are available through medical or forensic catalogs and distributors, including Oregon Rules.[27] This type of scale is useful and will supply any level of precision required. They come in a variety of colors, measuring units, and thicknesses and have many useful features. Color choice may be important depending on lighting selected and the subject tonality. These scales can be obtained with black fields and white units, white field with black units, or gray field with black units to match subject contrast and lighting technique. Sometimes these scales will include circles with cross hairs to indicate any perspective distortion in the image. Alternating contrasting bars of specific lengths are sometimes incorporated into these scales in case photographic exposure makes reading the measuring units difficult. An 18% gray patch might also be present to provide a densitometer/analyzer reference for color printing and sensitometry.

Self-adhesive scales may come in rolls of specific lengths or singly in packages, be marked in inches or metric, and are made to be peeled and stuck to the surface of the evidence. Check the accuracy of the scale prior to use. Some can be fairly accurate, while others may be inaccurate, especially when stretched. These scales can be particularly useful with vertical surfaces and fingerprints.

ABFO #2 were designed by the American Board of Forensic Odontology for use in bite-mark photography and are considered the standard measuring device for this application.

This is an L-shaped scale with measuring units on the inside of the L, and include cross-hair circles, contrasting measuring bars and 18% gray reference patch. The width of the L is one inch to accommodate measuring if exposure errors occur.

There are other L-shaped scales besides the ABFO #2, designed primarily for footwear impressions. Smaller versions, including stick-ons are produced for evidence photography and may be used for fingerprints, but may have limitations depending on physical size and shape of item or surface being photographed (See chapter 10).

Transparent and translucent scales can be used with trans-illumination, dark field, or light field lighting. If light must pass through the scale to observe the measuring units, pick a plastic scale with appropriate units for magnification and appropriate color depending upon necessary contrast. Remember, if a colored scale is used and is the prevalent object in the photograph, the color balance and/or density of the resultant image may be affected (see Fig. 2–14).

COLOR REFERENCES

References for color are needed in evidence photography if the color of the evidence is critical and/or the color needs to be transmitted and represented in a remote location where the color of the evidence is not obvious (see Fig. 2–15).

Color references come in two types. They are either unique or universal. Unique color references are any reference that can be imaged and maintained. Universal references include, but are not limited to, Kodak 18% Gray Scales and Gretag/MacBeth ColorCheckers.

Unique references are always useful as long as the reference is present with the representation of the image. If the reference cannot be retained, change to something that can. If the reference is retained, it must be entered into the evidence system in the same way as the images. Examples include paint chips, carpet samples, plastic cups, stones; anything that can be found and retained.

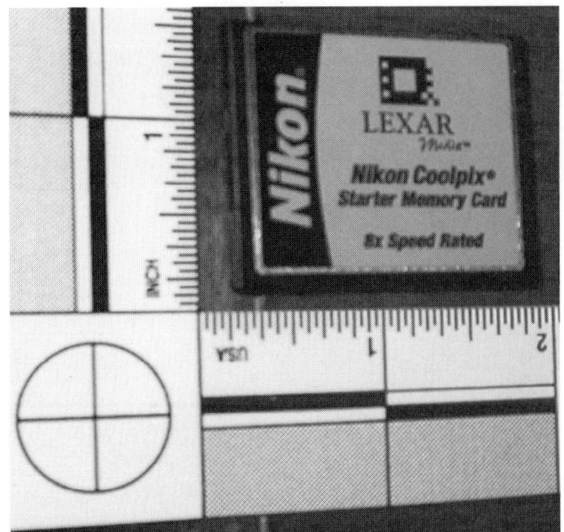

FIGURE 2–14 Example of the need for rectification and the usefulness of the scale. *Source:* Sandy Weiss/Packer Engineering.

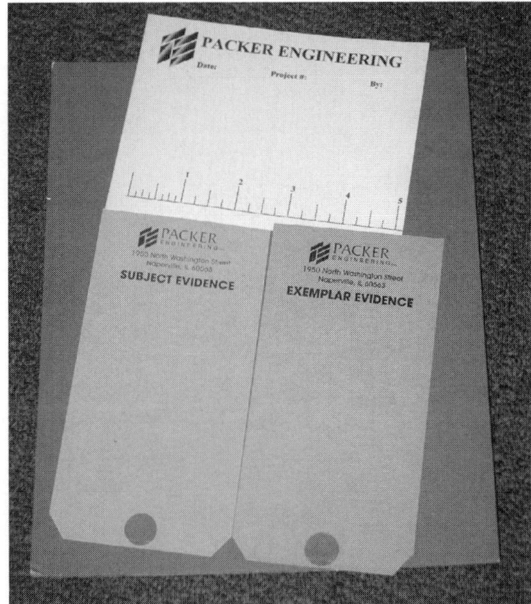

FIGURE 2–15 Color references and evidence tags. *Source:* Sandy Weiss/Packer Engineering.

FIGURE 2–16 Kodak 18% gray card. *Source:* Sandy Weiss/Packer Engineering.

The problem with unique references is that nobody else can share or utilize them unless the reference is sub-dividable into smaller pieces and sent to another location along with duplicate images. If time and convenience are an issue, unique references are not recommended.

Universal references are good for any situation. Each reference is consistent from one to another, universally available around the world, and easily explainable in court. The only problem is that these references are usually expensive so sometimes not budget-able.

The Kodak gray card is a large 18% reflective neutral grey area on one side and a 95% reflective white on the back (see Figs. 2–16 and 2–17). The surface is specially treated to minimize glare. Gray cards are fine for some situations but are susceptible to minor color and density fluctuations in reproduction that are difficult to interpret visually.

GretagMacbeth ColorChecker®[28]

The Macbeth ColorChecker Chart is the industry standard color reference for evidence pho-

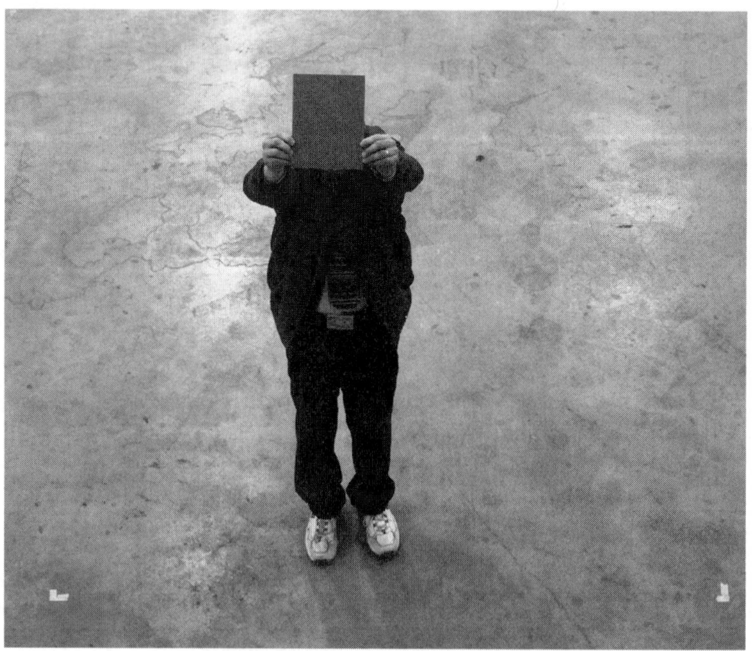

FIGURE 2–17 Author and gray card. *Source:* Sandy Weiss/Packer Engineering.

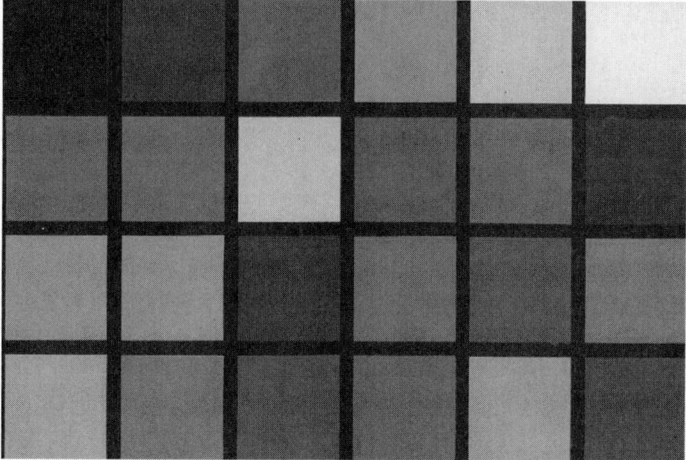

FIGURE 2–18 GretagMacbeth ColorChecker. *Source:* Sandy Weiss/Packer Engineering.

tographers and cinematographers (see Fig. 2–18). The ultimate goal of any process is to reproduce all colors perfectly. To accomplish that, a totally non-subjective standard of comparison is needed. That is why the ColorChecker chart was developed. It provides a scientifically based standard with which to compare, measure, and analyze differences in color reproduction in many processes.

The ColorChecker is designed to help recognize the true color balance of any color image representation. It allows the evidence photographer the best possible chance of accurately reproducing colors.

The ColorChecker consists of an array of 24 scientifically researched colored squares in a wide range of colors. Many of the squares represent natural objects of common use, including human skin, foliage, and blue sky. These squares represent the same color as those objects and also reflect light the same way in all parts of the visible spectrum. Because of this unique feature, the squares should match the colors of natural objects under any illumination and with any color reproduction process.

The ColorChecker chart provides an easy way to recognize and quantitatively evaluate the many factors affecting the final color reproduction. To evaluate the effect of varying any given factor, simply compare the chart's color image (photograph, television picture, computer monitor, or printed sample) with the actual ColorChecker. This comparison may be made visually or with an optical densitometer.

The new Digital ColorChecker Semi Gloss (SG) is designed for digital photography to check and compare the digital reproduction of a real scene or a test pattern, make a white balance with a digital camera, etc.

The digital checker is redesigned to represent more of the colors a person and/or digital camera can see. It has 140 color patches to help the photographer create images capturing the full capabilities of the digital camera and/or scanner (see Fig. 2–19).

It includes all of the usual ColorChecker chart colors and many more. As usual, the gray scale steps are designed to provide accurate control of camera exposure and contrast balance regardless of light source.

GretagMacbeth and the Munsell Color Laboratory manufacture products in conformance to the accreditation practices and procedures set forth by the National Institute of Standards and Technology (NIST). The GretagMacbeth Munsell Color facility is an internationally recognized laboratory holding accreditations from ISO 9001: 2000.

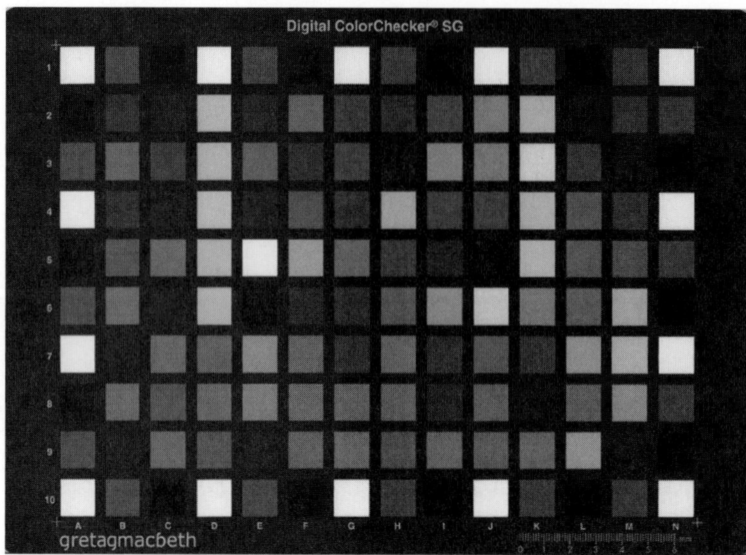

FIGURE 2–19 Digital ColorChecker. *Source:* Sandy Weiss/Packer Engineering.

POSITIONAL REFERENCES

Being able to return at a later date to the exact location of an evidence documentation is often of extreme importance. If a recreation is necessary, the location must be verifiable. If evidence has been moved prior to being photographed, the ability to put it back into the universe becomes non-essential.

Two forms of references are used for referencing a location. Global Positional System (GPS) location/imaging is easily obtainable and relatively inexpensive. Attachments are made to fit onto DSLRs to image the GPS location directly onto the photograph. (Be careful however, to avoid allegations of evidence spoliation by adding data to images) GPS location-finding may be limited by the accuracy of the GPS system. Some GPS locators are intended for forensic imaging, work independently from the camera but in tandem, and are inexpensive and efficient (see the Sony GPS in chapter 14).

The other type of location reference is to record a landmark that does not move. For example, if in a city, the photographer may document the corner of a building, a manhole cover in the street, a fire hydrant, a cable-pole, or any similar immovable object. If outside a city, it may be necessary to travel great distances to find something permanent to document as a reference. It is not possible to put marks on a roadway or in a field and expect the marks will remain there over the years.

Trees can die, foliage trimmed, boulders moved, buildings demolished. Make absolutely certain positional landmarks are PERMANENT.

SPOLIATION OF EVIDENCE[29]

Spoliation is the destruction, significant alteration, or non-preservation of evidence that is relevant to, pending, or reasonably foreseeable in litigation. Often, the critical question is whether the non-spoliating party was deprived of the ability to establish its case.

The Duty to Preserve Evidence

A duty may arise where there exists a potential for litigation and the party knew or reasonably should have known of that potential. Spoliation occurs when crucial evidence is destroyed or altered.

- The physical object itself in the precise condition it was in immediately after an accident or crime may be far more instructive and persuasive to a jury than oral or photographic descriptions.

- Spoliation can also occur when evidentiary items that could shed light on alternative causes of an accident are destroyed. The spoliation for example, may prejudice the manufacturer's efforts to present a causation defense.

Experts may not put themselves in the position of being the only party with first hand knowledge of the evidence in dispute. Parties are **only** required to act "reasonably" in preserving evidence. For example, a party cannot be held responsible for not preserving items that were not relevant to either of the parties at the time they were destroyed.

Consequences of Spoliation: Sanctions and Dismissal

Factors courts apply when considering imposition of discovery[‡‡] sanctions:

1. Surprise to adverse party
2. Prejudicial effect of the proffered evidence
3. The nature of the evidence
4. Diligence of the adverse party seeking discovery
5. The timeliness of the adverse party's objection to the evidence
6. Good faith of the party offering the evidence

Sanctions can include:

Dismissing the action or parts thereof. Courts are reluctant to dismiss a claim, thereby precluding a trial on the merits, unless the defense has incurred prejudice by the alteration or destruction of a crucial piece of evidence or where the party's actions show a deliberate, contumacious[§§] or unwarranted disregard of the court's authority.

[‡‡]In law, discovery is the pre-trial phase in a lawsuit in which each party through the law of civil procedure can request documents and other evidence from other parties or can compel the production of evidence by using a subpoena or through other discovery devices, such as requests for production and depositions.

[§§]willfully obstinate; stubbornly disobedient; "a contumacious witness is subject to punishment."

Evidence should be photographed before the testing or inspection begins and after it is complete so there is a tangible record that the work did not damage the evidence.

- If possible, use exemplars—identical products or components—for the testing instead of the actual evidence.
- Have written agreements with all potentially interested parties (to any extent possible) concerning inspection and/or destruction of evidence.
- Develop and agree to a written protocol for any "destructive testing" of the evidence, including a definition of destructive testing.
- Develop reasonable evidence retention and/or testing policy and follow it. (It may be the responsibility of legal staff to compose the written protocols and releases, not the responsibility of the forensic photographer.)

CHAIN OF CUSTODY

Chain of custody is defined as the set of procedures to account for the integrity of evidence by tracking its handling and storage from point of collection to final disposition. In practical terms, a chain of custody is the documentation and testimony that proves within the limits of probability that the evidence has not been altered or tampered with in any way since it was collected.

The chain of custody*** memorializes the accessibility history of the evidence. It documents the names, positions, dates, times, locations and other data about the handling, transfer, storage and use of the evidence until such time when the evidence is disposed of or returned to its legal owner. In no DIRECT way does chain of custody limit the probability of alteration or tampering; it simply IDENTIFIES who had access to the evidence and thus who had the ABILITY to alter or tamper with it if such individuals chose to do so. Since all individuals are usually unimpeachable, this INDIRECTLY limits the probability of tampering.

***From Robert Wyman, Weyman Enterprises, FL.

"Chain of custody" and "chain of evidence" are often used interchangeably.[30]

A process used to maintain and document the history of evidence, includes;

- Name or initials of the individual collecting the specimen
- Name or initials of each person or entity subsequently taking custody
- The date the specimen was collected or transferred
- Employer or agency
- Specimen number
- Case number
- A brief description of the specimen.

A secure chain of custody, together with the documentation of any practice and/or protocols used by a laboratory for the investigation or analysis of the evidence, leads to the production of defensible evidence.

Many excellent texts, including the *Handbook of Forensic Services*,[31] published by the Federal Bureau of Investigation, are offered free on the Internet and provide information on the proper "marking" and "collection" of various types of evidence (see Fig. 2–20). They should be studied by investigators and photographers having responsibility for the collection of physical evidence.

The basic rule is:

- The item should be "marked" by the investigator placing his/her initials, date, and the case number on the item itself.
- Metallic surfaces should be so "marked" with a machinist's scribe.
- Liquids, soils and small fragments should be placed in a suitable container and sealed.
- The container should be "marked" by scribing the same information on the container, or by using some other permanent form of marking material on the container.[32]

TIP:

Before anything is marked and/or collected it must be assured that the marking and/or collection does not interfere with the pertinent rules for evidence spoliation.

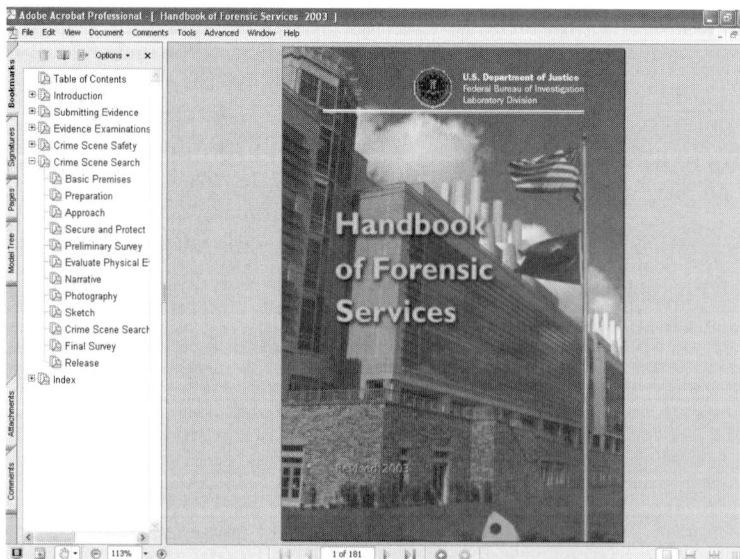

FIGURE 2–20 The *Handbook* of *Forensic Services,* published by the FBI is public domain. *Source:* www.fbi.gov.

A person must be eligible and trustworthy to be a part of the evidence chain and must always have physical custody of a piece of evidence while it is in their care. In practice, this means that an investigator will take charge of a piece of evidence, document its collection, and hand it over to the appropriate person for storage in a secure place. This transfer, and every succeeding transfer of possession between the collection of the evidence and its appearance in court, must be completely documented.[33]

The required proof includes:

1. Testimony by the collector/photographer identifying the item as that which was discovered, collected and documented
2. Testimony by that that collector/photographer that there was no tampering with the item while in his/her custody
3. Testimony regarding delivery of the evidence to the next person who had custody
4. Similar testimony by each subsequent person who had custody until the time of its presentation in court. If the evidence was submitted to a laboratory for analysis or investigation, proof of the chain of custody must include testimony from the person who took the item to the laboratory; proof of the method of reception and storage at the laboratory prior to and after analysis; up to the time of trial.[34]

Insuring that evidence remains admissible into a court of law is a primary responsibility of the forensic investigator. Failure to thoroughly document the possession and transfer of evidence may result in the loss of vital information due to inadmissibility. Anyone having possession of evidence may be called into court to testify about the evidence.

EVIDENCE LOG

All evidence must be documented with photographs. Throughout the process, significant findings will be photographed with references and scales. Any evidence collected must be given its own number and the chain of custody maintained as these subsequent samples are sent to other laboratories or experts. There are numerous guidelines (see the FBI Manual) for packaging and shipping evidence.

Samples must be stored in the proper container and shipped in a secure manner to the appropriate laboratory. All subsequent tests must be performed using methods that are the current standard for a specific field and defensible in court.

SUMMARY

With the state of contemporary digital technology, it is possible for most people to become proficient photographers. The concern in forensics is, some of the same people, newly proficient at photography, also think they can become proficient at forensic evidence photography over-night without proper training. That is not the case. Individuals can make mistakes in investigations and documentations and cost others dearly. The only way to become a proficient evidence photographer is through practice, education, and patience.

As with any other technical endeavor, there are accepted procedures which can be adopted into a service organization as protocols or practices. It is essential that all practitioners be familiar with the procedures, protocols, or practices in use by their department and adhere to their guidelines.

Without proper attention to best practices or protocols, evidence photographs may not be acceptable in court. At the very worst, the person who exposed the photographs, or the client who uses them as displays, can be made to look foolish by an opposing attorney if all rules have not been properly followed.

The SOPs are in place to make photographs verifiable and to provide guidelines for the person responsible for the production of the images. The guidelines are there to make the job easier, not more difficult.

CASE STUDY

On the freeway outside of Newark, New Jersey, a semi tractor and trailer became disabled and the

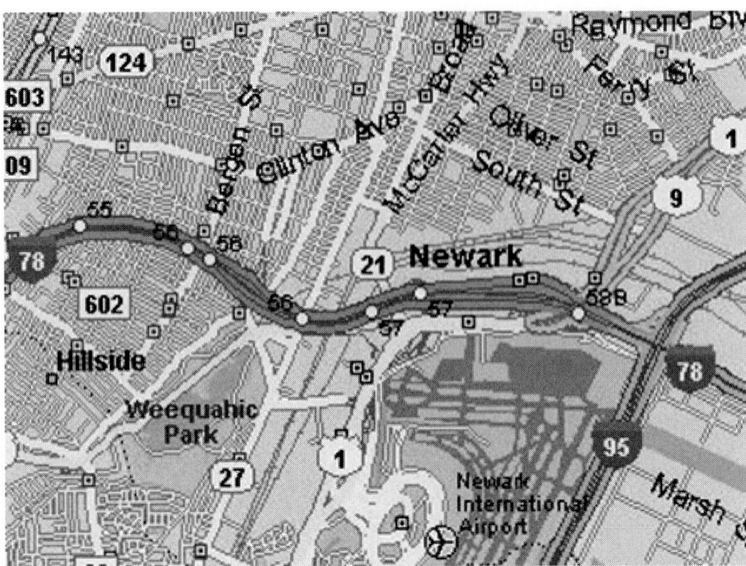

FIGURE 2–21 Map of the location. *Source:* Mapquest.

driver parked it on the right shoulder of the road. A woman with her two children in a car, drove into the back of the trailer at high speed, injuring her and one of the children severely, and killing one child. A lawsuit was filed against the trucking company and the State of New Jersey.

Packer Engineering was hired to investigate the accident and especially to determine how far back from the parked truck the initial point of visibility should have been for the driver of the car and at what point she should have been able to tell the truck was not moving. The re-creation took place one year to the date after the subject accident (see Fig. 2–21).

In any scene reconstruction involving a vision issue, it may be important to proceed on as close as possible to the day of the year of the original occurrence. Even working on the same calendar date is not perfect, but is as good as can be. Try for as close as possible to the subject weather conditions. If there was snow or rain on the day of the occurrence, it would not be as good to recreate the scene on a dry day. It is essential to procure proper vehicles, as close as possible in color and condition to the subject vehicles. Make every attempt to document the subject vehicle's cleanliness of headlights, windshield and mirrors, and the condition, adjustment, and position of the driver's seat before assembling the re-creation.

Many factors were involved in the visual analysis of this case. The truck had been disabled and on the side of the road for some time. A state trooper came to the driver's aid, let him into his car, and drove him to an automotive supply store to purchase repair parts for the truck. The trucker was not present at the time of the accident. The truck driver did claim to have put out the required orange reflective triangles in the positions indicated by the Department of Transportation (DOT) Codes to signal that the truck was disabled. The presence or lack of triangles at the time of the accident was never verified.

At the time of the accident there was an overhead sign at the location of the parked truck, but that had since been removed and there was no way to substitute a temporary sign during the re-creation of the accident (see Fig. 2–22). There were also more trees growing close to the road at this location at the time of the accident, but they had since been trimmed.

Both the plaintiff and an eyewitness who was walking over a nearby bridge allege there were no triangles visible at the time of the accident. Police photos were taken at the scene and measurements from the accident report and the scene photos were used to position the truck for our re-creation. Paint marks applied to the roadway at the time of the accident were obliterated over the elapsed

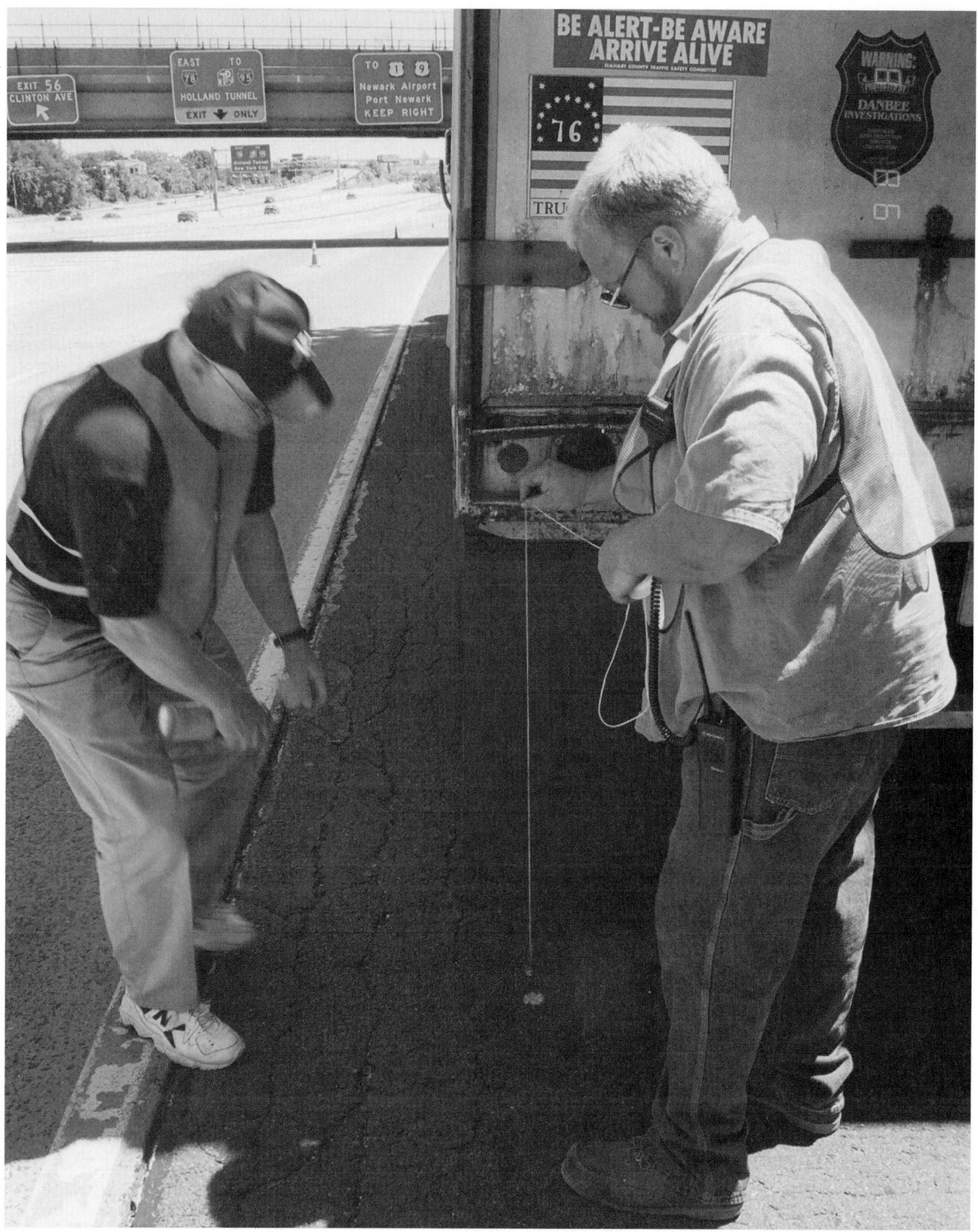

FIGURE 2–22 Using field-notes to pinpoint the location of the truck on the roadway. *Source:* Sandy Weiss/ Packer Engineering.

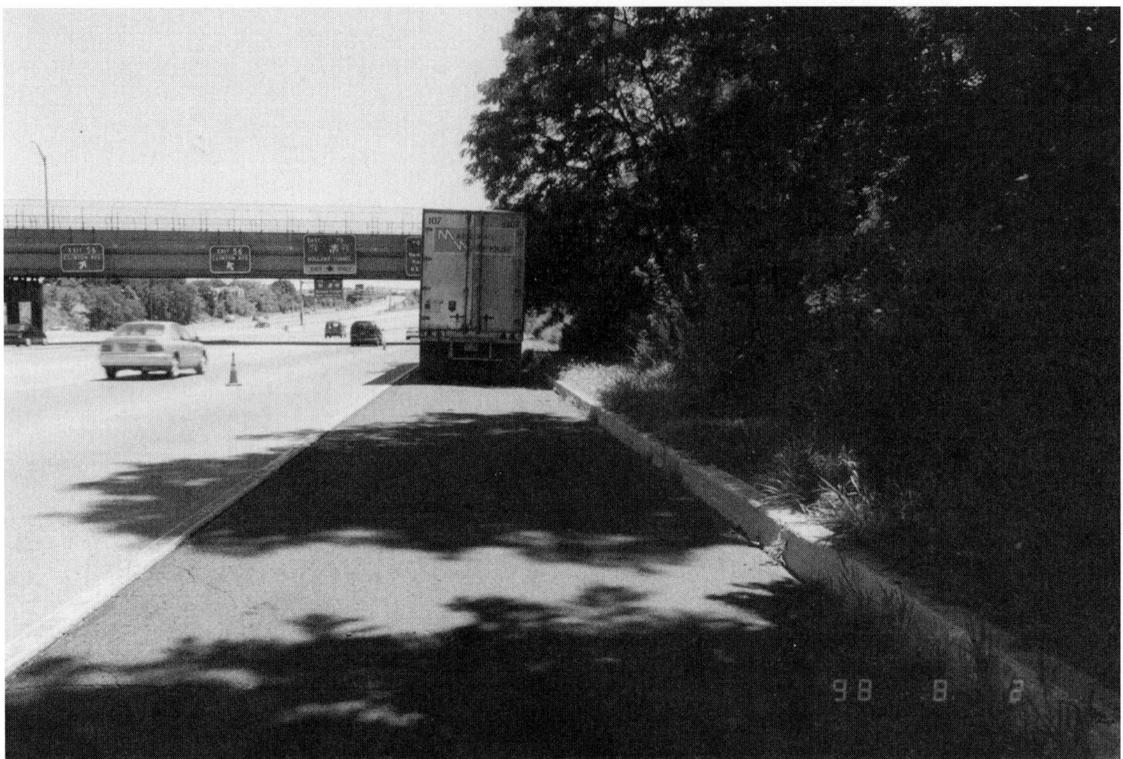

FIGURE 2–23 Location of subject truck on the roadway. *Source:* Sandy Weiss/Packer Engineering.

time. The place where the truck was parked was just west of an exit ramp and the ramp was indicated by appropriate signs. Placement for the recreation was measured from the recorded distance of the next overpass and the trailer position and footage markers placed accordingly.

The subject trailer had been repaired and in use since the accident, but then taken off-line and stored for an extended time (see Figs. 2–23 and 2–24). It was available to use for testing. The recreation was documented with both still photographs and video. An exemplar subject car was purchased in Illinois and prepped before taking it to Newark. It was the same make, model, and color as the subject vehicle. The car was outfitted with custom-built camera mounts inside the passenger compartment so the video camera could be mounted to physically record the footage markers during the drive-through recreation from driver's eye position.

The car was brought to the scene on a flatbed so there was small chance of damages to it on the trip. The state police did close off the outside lane of the freeway for a period of one hour at a non rush time for the testing. The cars going by at 65–80 mph in the next lane were too close for comfort and were a detriment to the photography due to the wind from their motion. Some of the police photos were taken from the inside of the outer lane and the recreation photographs were required to be taken from exactly the same height and angle, so the tripod leg was very close to the passing cars during some of the exposures. The wind shook the tripod so much it had to be weighted with sandbags before each image could be taken. There were six accident scene photographs needing to be duplicated as closely as possible.

After the stills were taken, the video drive-throughs were made. For the videos, a high resolution camera was used for the fixed camera on the bracket inside the car and a helmet mounted ultra-mini-camera was used to record what the driver might see, including the head movements

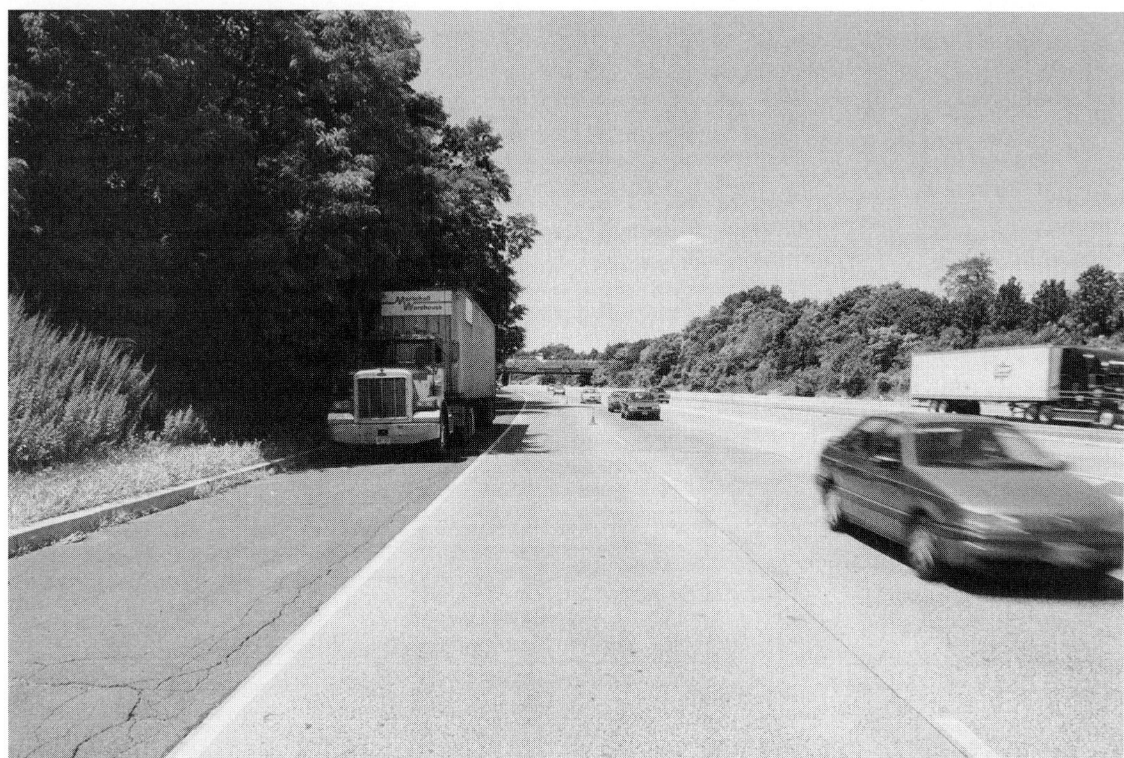

FIGURE 2–24 Location of subject truck on the roadway. *Source:* Sandy Weiss/Packer Engineering.

that the driver could make. The fixed camera was mounted on a bracket directly over the driver's right ear and focused out through the windshield of the car.

Positions were marked on the side of the road in 50-foot increments, on signs that were big enough to be legible in the videos. Orange reflective triangles required by DOT were included, even though they may not have been there (see Fig. 2–25) at the time of the accident.

For the videos, the car was backed to the west, past the 350-foot sign, then accelerated forward; the cameras started and recorded the drive-through and then the tape was reviewed on a monitor in the car before repeating.

The weather conditions were not duplicated in this re-creation. The day of the accident was overcast and the day of the recreation was sunny with deep shadows. The engineers decided to go ahead with the recreation anyway because the shadows provided a worst-case scenario. In other words, it would be easier to see the parked truck on a cloudy day, so the sunny-day shadows would supply conditions making visibility/conspicuity even more difficult (see Fig. 2–26).

The still camera was loaded with 400 ASA color film in order to afford maximum depth of field for the images and to duplicate the sensitivity of the 400 ASA black and white film exposed by the police at the time of the accident. Due to the sunny conditions, the resultant contrast was somewhat high in the finished images.

In conclusion, the truck became visible at a distance of 325 feet after the plaintiff's car came out of a slight curve in the road. That distance is more than sufficient for the car to come to a stop before impact, if traveling at the posted speed limit. It was also found that the truck is obscured by the shadows of the overhanging trees and that the reflective triangles were also shaded by the trees and not highly conspicuous on the roadway.

The plaintiff's lawsuit was not successful.

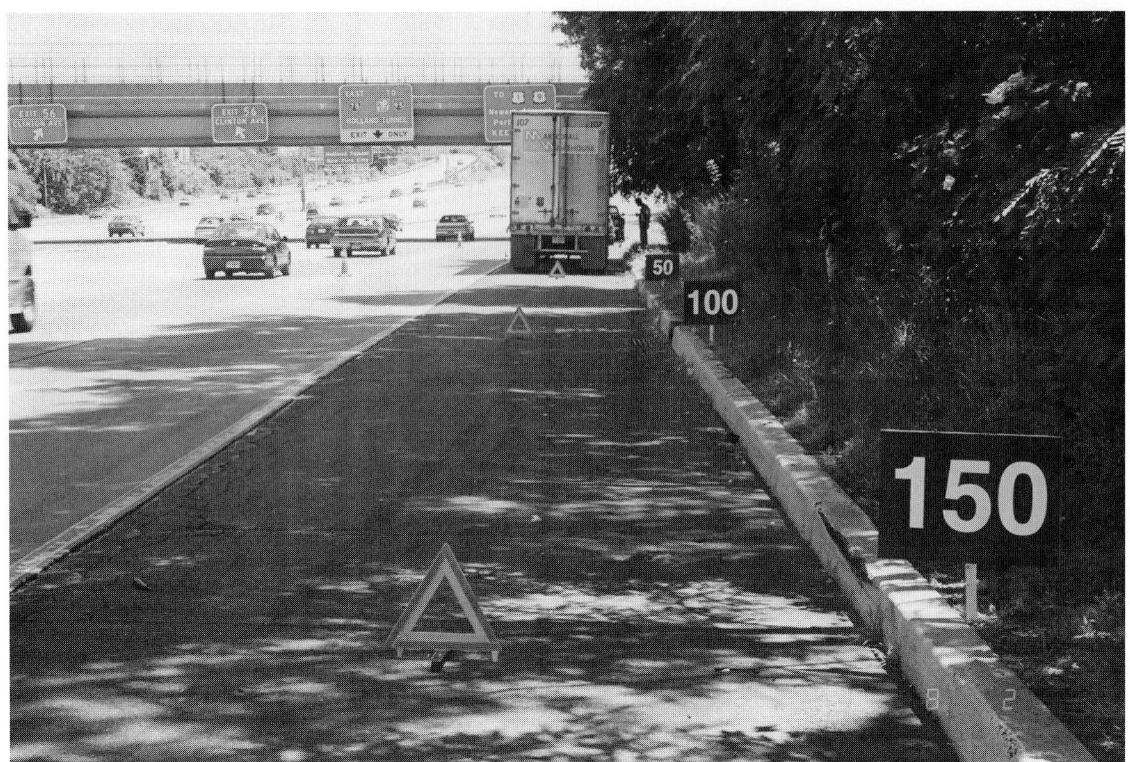

FIGURE 2–25 Orange triangle on the roadway. *Source:* Sandy Weiss/Packer Engineering.

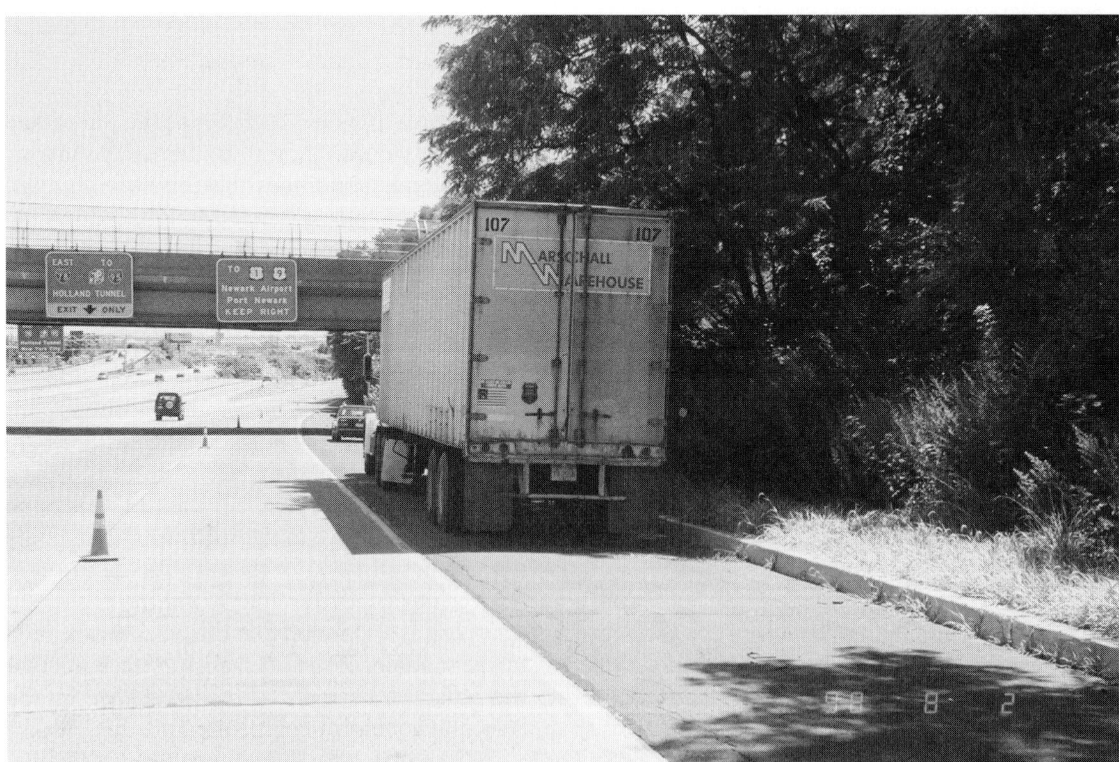

FIGURE 2–26 Truck sitting in the shadows. *Source:* Sandy Weiss/Packer Engineering.

CASE STUDY

A person standing behind a pickup truck was struck, runover, and killed when the truck backed over him. When the driver of the truck was sued, the attorney hired Packer Engineering to do a visibility study to determine how much of the accident victim the driver should have been able to see out the back of the truck through the rear-view mirror and if that was sufficient to meet the code requirements for that type of vehicle (see Fig. 2–27).

At first thought it appeared to be a simple assignment, but this recreation required a large amount of study and preparation. A survey was done of the accident site to determine whether the truck was going uphill or downhill at the time of the accident, or if the ground was level. It was then necessary to survey the areas of land on the grounds of the Packer building to find a spot matching in slope. An identical exemplar truck was rented and placed on the correct spot. Tire inflation was as per tire specs, the truck suspension was stock and as bought, and truck load was empty as per the subject vehicle.

The re-creation scene was then setup with string and stakes. There was one string extending perpendicularly back from the middle of the rear bumper for 100 feet (string A). Another string (string B) was laid out perpendicular to the end of string A and parallel to the rear bumper. The uprights for the limit of view of the rearview mirror were placed along string B (see Fig. 2–28).

A person of the same height as the driver sat in the driver's seat of the truck and, with his eyes centered on the rearview mirror, told us where to put the uprights in the ground for the edges of the visual field possible in the mirror. A cutout 90 percentile man was prepared and pasted on an easel. It was then placed 2 feet to the side of the string A in a placement matching the documented impact point on the subject bumper. It was windy so the cut-out was attached to a heavy tripod with sandbags and the whole apparatus needed to be

FIGURE 2–27 View out the back of the pickup. *Source:* Sandy Weiss/Packer Engineering.

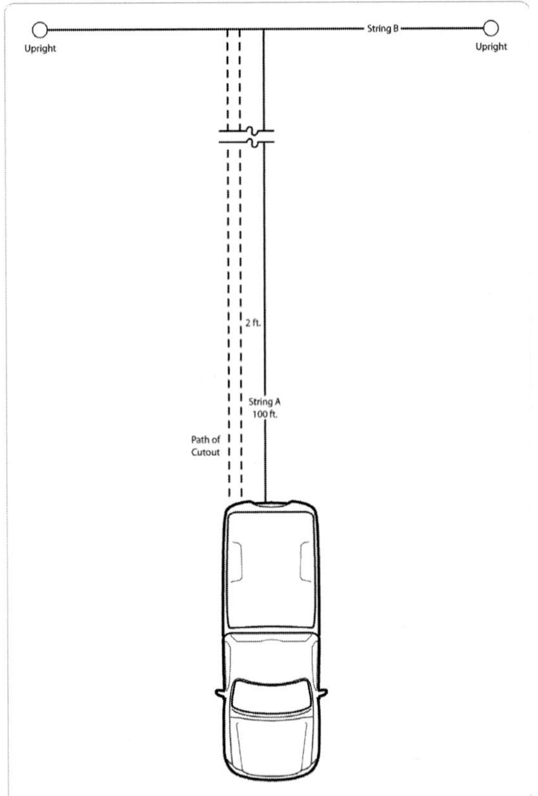

FIGURE 2–28 Plane-view illustration of recreation. *Source:* Jessica Weiss.

moved every time the camera to subject distance was changed.

Lens choice and camera placement were the hardest part of the assignment. Human vision is binocular and normal camera viewing is not. Therefore, the angle of view of the driver could not be duplicated with a camera in the driver's eye position, exposing images off the rearview mirror. The mirror was removed and the photographs were exposed with a camera positioned on the hood of the truck.

The parameters for setting up the camera were:

- The film plane of the camera had to be at the same distance in front of the windshield, (behind the plane of the rearview mirror) as the eye of the driver would have been in front of the rearview mirror.
- Lens focal length was determined by the uprights in the mirror view. The uprights needed to be at the side limits of the field of view of the driver, exactly at the edges of the film-frame. A 100 mm f2.8 telephoto lens was used on a 35 mm camera body.
- The camera was placed on an adjustable elevating stage so it could be raised to the same height as the driver's eyes would have been.
- 50 pounds of bagged lead shot was placed onto the stage and under the camera to keep the camera firm and steady and not be blown by the wind.
- To assure the camera was level to the horizon, levels on the stage were used and both the parallel and perpendicular directions were checked.
- The camera had to be set to shoot down the center line of the truck with the filmplane perpendicular to the string A, and to have the center line of the tailgate in the center of the frame. The vertical upright that was placed at the end of the 100 foot string had to be in line with the mounting bracket for the rearview mirror.
- To compound the difficulty, it was a very expensive truck and as lessee's, we were liable for damages. Therefore, it was impossible to climb onto the hood to set up the camera. It was necessary for the photographer to stand on a ladder and lean over to make all of the adjustments.
- After everything was properly set, the photos were exposed. After each photo, the cutout was moved 10 feet closer to the truck and along the 2-foot-from-center line.
- A radio remote control was used on the camera so the photographer could walk away and out of the field of view before each photo was exposed. As the included photo shows, the accident victim should have been visible from the waist up over the top of the tailgate and the top of the tailgate was visible from the driver's eye position and in the rearview mirror.

The most difficult part of the case study to testify to in court was the use of the 100 mm lens instead of a 50 mm normal lens to represent the vision of the driver of the truck. The answer to the obvious question is that the rearview mirror had a 2× magnification factor.

The blue hue in the included image results from shooting through both the front and rear windows made of tinted glass in the truck.

CASE STUDY

CLASSIFICATION YARDS

A classification yard or hump yard is a railroad yard found at some freight train stations, used to separate railroad cars on to appropriate tracks. Some yards put the cars on a hill or hump to use the force of gravity to propel the cars into place.

In this case, it was post-dusk. A 130 ton black tank-car was rolling silently down the tracks at 6 mph (see Fig. 2–29). Its coupler pointed forward in the darkness, waiting to mate to the back coupler of the next car. Nothing can stop the forward momentum until the cars join; the train assembling in the yard at the bottom of the hill. From total silence to indescribable explosion, the noise the next car makes on contact can only be compared to the report of a canon. On 10:08 p.m. on the night in question, a man got stuck in between the cars.

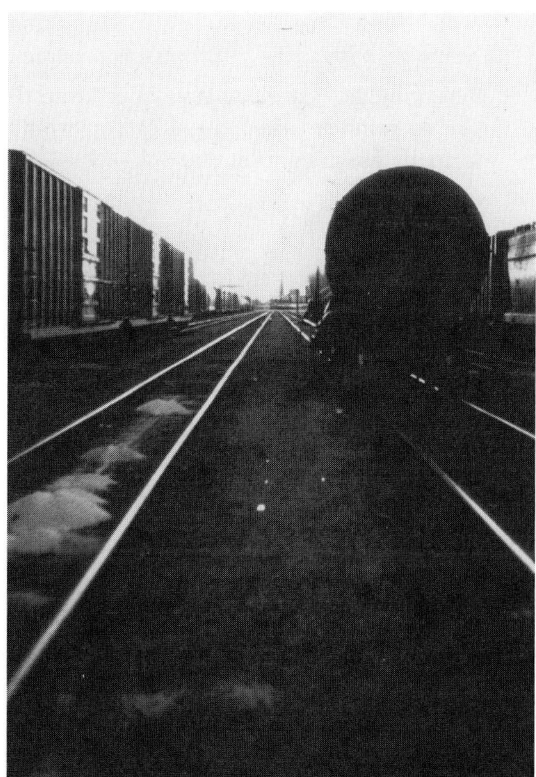

FIGURE 2–29 The tank car approaching at 6 mph. *Source:* Sandy Weiss/Packer Engineering.

The man had been an employee of the yard for 35 years without mishap. On this night he died. His family sued the railroad, contending there was not enough light in the yard to be able to see the approaching black tank car against the blackness of the night sky. Packer Engineering was hired to determine the contrast of the car against the sky as it would have appeared to the man who was killed.

The night of the re-creation, it was very cold and scary at the yard. Tracks are everywhere and cars roll down at a steady rate of one every 30 to 60 seconds. Their momentum is unstoppable, so being careful is a prerequisite.

The camera needed to be able to operate in extreme cold. Snow is visible on the tracks in the photo. An $f1.2$ maximum f-stop lens was purchased specifically for this assignment, to be able to expose film at ASA 1600 and be able to expose it at 1-frame per second. The tank car approaching at 6 mph is in motion so it is not entirely sharp on any of the images. The motor drive of the camera was set at continuous. The camera was kept warm between tests. Communications with the switching supervisor were undertaken by walkie-talkie. It was imperative to let him know when all was ready for him release another car.

There are computerized brakes built into the tracks to maintain the speed of the cars at 6 mph. The brakes work as many times as necessary as the car rolls to its computer determined destination.

The final work-product in this case was a flip-book. The images were printed horizontally across the bottom of a vertical 5 × 7 inch piece of paper, with the selvage at the top, and then connected the photos at the very top so they could be flipped through to give the illusion of movement.

Kodak 2475 Recording film was exposed at ASA 1600 and processed in Kodak HC-110 developer, dilution B, to deliver a density distribution resembling the contrast possibilities of the human eye when accustomed to the level of illumination in the yard.

The resultant images proved there should have been enough illumination in the yard that night for the deceased to see the car coming.

KEY TERMS

Standard Operating Procedures (SOPs), (p. 26)
Protocols and best practices, (p. 26)
Inductive reasoning, (p. 28)
Admissibility, (p. 28)
Standards, (p. 29)
Fair and accurate, (p. 29)
Authentication, (p. 30)
Vision, (p. 32)
Perception, (p. 32)
Perspective, (p. 34)
Point of view, (p. 36)
Resolution, (p. 40)
Size, color and positional scales and references, (p. 41)
Spoliation, (p. 46)
Chain of Custody, (p. 47)

EXERCISES

1. Design and write a protocol/practice in your expertise area and submit it to your coworkers for review.
2. Compare two like items; dollar bills, soda cans, fast food wrappers, coins, business cards, and note the differences in their surface appearance. Make photographs of both and determine if the differences are noticeable in your digital photographs.
3. Expose a digital image of an 18% gray card under as many different light sources as are available, trying to match the camera's built-in white balance settings to the source lighting. Note the difference in the final images and try to make exact matches by re-color balancing the images with an image processing program.
4. Determine how large a file you need to capture to print enlargement sizes you would normally use in court at 300 dpi.

APPENDIX 2.1

Imaging Practice/Protocol

IMAGING PROTOCOL

This *suggested* photographic standard operating procedure (SOP) was developed through research and review of the best silver analog (film-based) and digital imaging procedures currently used for similar applications, capturing and processing images for use in evidence documentation. This SOP is designed to ensure image security. It will also supplement the level of authentication of all captured images.

Purpose

To establish policies and procedures for capture, processing, and storage of images.

Definitions

Definitions abstracted and adopted from Scientific Working Group on Imaging Technologies (www.theiai.org/swgit/ and *Webster's Dictionary*. These definitions are intended to facilitate discussion and any necessary testimony. They are widely accepted and are the recommended definitions.

Analog image file: Non-digital image file (negative or silver-based technology).
Capture: The process of recording an image.
Capture device: A device used in the recording of an image.
Compression: The process of reducing the size of a data file.
Digital image file: A record that includes image data and related data objects in digital form.
File format: The structure by which data is organized in a file.
Grain: The units of density in a negative, causing differences in density in the negative's positive representation.
Graininess: The visibility of individual grains of the negative on the final print.
Image: An imitation or representation of anything, drawn, painted, photographed, etc. (Webster's New World Dictionary, Third College Edition)
Image analysis: The extraction of information from an image beyond that which is readily apparent through visual examination.
Image enhancement: Any process intended to improve the visual appearance of an image.
Image output: The means by which an image is presented for examination or observation.
Image processing: Any activity that transforms an input image into an output image.
Image processing log: A record of the steps used in the processing of an image.
Image transmission: The act of moving images from one location to another.
Image verification: A process by which an individual identifies an image as being an accurate representation.
Imaging technologies: Include systems and/or methods used to capture, store, process, analyze, transmit, or produce an image. Such systems include but are not limited to film, electronic sensors, cameras, video devices, scanners, printers, and computers.
Intermediate storage: Any media or device on which an image is temporarily stored for transfer to permanent or archival storage.
Legacy file management: A methodology for preserving data and images so that they are retrievable as technology changes.
Lossless compression: Compression in which no image data is lost and the image can be retrieved in its original form. Lossless file types include but are not limited to tiff, raw, and psd.
Lossy compression: Compression in which digital image data is lost and the image cannot be retrieved in its original form. Lossy file formats include, but are not limited to, .jpg, tiff
Native file format: The file format of the original image.
Source code: The list of instructions written in a standard programming language used to construct a computer program. This information is not usually provided absent a court order or prior contractual agreement.
Storage: The act of preserving an image.
Storage media: Any object on which an image is preserved.
Original image: An accurate and complete replica of the primary image, irrespective of media. For film and analog video, the primary image is the original image.
Pixel: The basic unit of a digital image. (Acronym for Picture Element)
Pixelate: Through lack of sufficient resolution in a finished image, individual pixels become visible.
Preserving original: Storing and maintaining the original image in an unaltered state. This includes maintaining original digital images in their native file format.
Primary image: The image captured at a scene—of the item being documented. This image is also

called an Original and it is archived without change in content or format as an exact duplicate of the primary image.
Working image: Any image subjected to processing.

POLICY

A. Guidelines for Image Capture

1. Equipment

   Image capture devices should be capable of rendering an accurate representation of the item or items of interest. Different applications will dictate different standards of accuracy. At a minimum, the following should be considered when selecting appropriate devices:

   a. Characteristics (size, movement, location, etc.) of the scene, item, or items of interest
   b. Lighting of the items of interest
   c. Dynamic range of the scene
   d. Time constraints
   e. Required end product(s)

   (When documenting scenes, it is strongly recommended that a camera capable of manual override, with off-camera flash, and a tripod mount be used as the primary capture device. This documentation may be supplemented by video. The camera should be a 35 mm film camera or digital camera in most situations. It is the responsibility of the user to determine that any image capturing equipment is capable to capture an adequate image in particular circumstances.)

2. Personnel

   All personnel utilizing imaging technologies shall be knowledgeable and proficient in accordance with standard operating procedures and the operation of the relevant imaging technologies. No employee shall make use of imaging technology in which they cannot demonstrate proficiency. No employee shall process any image without following the established procedures for documentation and preservation of the processed image. The camera user is responsible for having become sufficiently familiar with the equipment, instruction manuals, and this Imaging Policy to properly utilize the equipment. Photography training is required.

   When a 35 mm camera and film is used for evidence documentation, no options should be used which alter the images in such a way that the images do not accurately represent the subject of the image or some aspect of the subject. If camera options are needed and utilized for a specific purpose, which cause the subject to be distorted in any fashion, that specific purpose and the effect of utilizing the options must be documented. (Such options include utilizing a wide-angle lens, alternate lighting, or any lens option, which may cause the image to degrade and become grainy, decreasing the effective resolution of the image.)

   When a digital camera is used for evidence documentation, no options should be used which alter the images in such a way that the images do not accurately represent the subject of the image or some aspect of the subject. If digital options are needed and utilized for a specific purpose, which cause the subject to be distorted in some fashion, that specific purpose and the effect of utilizing the digital option must be documented. (Such options include utilizing a wide-angle setting, alternate lighting, or a digital zoom option, which may cause the image to degrade and possibly pixilate as the digital zoom increases, decreasing the effective resolution of the image.)

3. Preserving Original: Chain of Custody

   It must be remembered that any images captured in an investigation, with any type of camera, are considered evidence. They must be treated just as any other evidence. Each original image captured of evidence shall be preserved; regardless as to whether an error in procedures may have caused the image to be taken inadvertently or in a manner that causes it to be valueless. A chain of custody must be maintained for the film, memory, or videotape upon which original images are recorded. All scene images will be saved.

For 35 mm images, the chain of custody should document the identity of the individuals who had custody and control of the film/negatives from the point of capture to archiving. An image log and custody information written on the appropriate form should be used with each roll of film (or group on the same project) to record chain of custody information.

For digital images, the chain of custody should document the identity of the individuals who had custody and control of the digital image file from the point of capture to archiving. An image log and custody information written on the appropriate form should be used with each digital media card to record chain of custody information.

When the roll of film is full or no additional images need to be recorded, the film is removed from the camera and placed with the log sheet/custody form in the appropriate location. Only one project should be recorded per roll of film and one form per group of rolls from identical circumstances. The rolls of film should be initialed and then placed in the designated area. Once the film has been processed and archived, the chain of custody should document the identity of the individuals and groups who had custody and control of the archived images.

When digital media is full or no additional images need to be recorded, the media is removed from the camera and placed with the log sheet/custody form in the appropriate location. Allow only one project per media card (or at least, folders on the media, divided by project) and one media card per form. The form with the media card should be initialed then placed in the designated area. Once the file has been archived, the chain of custody should document the identity of the individuals and groups who had custody and control of the archive images.

4. Archive

The original images must be stored and maintained in an unaltered state. Film images must be given to a secure source for printing. Digital images must be maintained in their original native file formats. Duplicates or copies should be used for working digital images when applicable. No original image should ever be altered in any way from how it was captured and must stay in the same image format as it was captured. To keep the images from accidental overwriting or data loss from computer crashes, the data should be backed up daily (or often) and the files should be read-only for all who have access, except for the few individuals trained and authorized to download data to the archives.

If the images are recorded onto media types such as a media card, the authorized personnel should copy the primary images onto the photo server or permanent memory device, after which the media may be reformatted and then reused. An image may be originally captured as a RAW, tiff, or jpg (jpeg) image, depending on the requirements of the end use of the image. An image that will be used for comparison purposes or is expected to undergo image analysis should have minimal artifacts of compression and should be captured in any format and as large a size as found necessary. The average image captured of evidence may be captured as a jpg.

5. Guidelines for Image Compression

It is expected that images captured to undergo image compression should not be compressed to the point that they become too low in resolution to adequately be used for their intended purpose.

6. Documentation of Image Processing

   Techniques common to traditional darkrooms and digital imaging stations, such as cropping, generalized color balancing, and contrast adjustment that are used to achieve an accurate recording of an event or object, are standard processing steps. These steps are visually verifiable, and documentation of such steps is considered mandatory. Manipulation techniques used to increase the visibility of specific details in an image at the expense of other image details are not standard processing steps. The use of such steps should be documented in the image notes in sufficient detail that comparably trained personnel can repeat the steps and produce the same output when the image is subjected to subsequent image analysis.

   Any image enhancement process performed on digital files will always be performed on a copy of the image. Any contemplated enhancement process is more safely done after the original image has been archived, which reduces the possibility that the original will be altered inadvertently. Both the original file and the processed file must be retained. The processed image should be archived with the case photographic images on the network with a file name that indicates the original image and also indicates the image that has been processed.

   No employee should process any image file if they are not sure that the processing and documentation of enhancements are within their competency. The employee should be aware that their competency should extend to testifying about the sequence of alterations on the subsequent image. The processing should be documented in an "Image Processing Log," which is a text file, recorded action, or handwritten report of the sequence of changes to the copy of the file. It should be sufficiently detailed that another person of similar training and experience can take a copy of the original file, make the changes that are noted in the image processing log, and have a resulting image that is essentially the same as the final version of the processed image file. The Image Processing Log should become a part of the records associated with the case and should be filed appropriately.

7. Guidelines for Software

   Software used in processing and analysis of digital images should produce consistent results, permitting comparably trained personnel to achieve similar results.

   If software errors that significantly affect the results of a processing step are detected, corrective actions should be taken.

8. Verification of Original and Processed Images

   Personnel who captured the original image or were present at the time the original image was captured can verify that the image is a true and mostly accurate representation.

   Any processed image subjected to image analysis should be documented with an image processing log. It is necessary that the image processing log document steps such as dodging, burning, color balancing, contrast adjustment, etc. The use of such steps should be documented in the case notes in sufficient detail that comparably trained personnel can repeat the steps and produce similar output.

Section A, Analog Image Procedure

- It is suggested that a card of known color with the inclusion of project identification, date, and photographer's initials be imaged at the beginning of each roll.
- Images captured on analog film must be limited to one project number and one date per roll of film.

- In the case of partially exposed rolls of analog film, the entire roll of processed film will be kept in the visual archive to ensure no images have been lost or discarded.
- Forms for each type of work request must be filled out for analog images to be processed, logged-in and archived. The forms require a project number, date taken, taken by, and date turned in for services. Forms also allow for the ordering of reprints made from the archived originals. A copy of the form will accompany the return of the order.
- All rolls of analog images will be logged-in to the image/media database (if available) as soon as possible after exposure. The database will assign each roll of images a unique number. This will give each individual analog image its own unique image number. The database will track all images for a project and stores information including, photographer's name, date of exposure, image quantity, and descriptive information as needed. The database also allows quantitative information about all images on a project.
- All rolls of original film negatives remain permanently on file. Only prints, or copies made from the original negatives, may be removed from the Visual Services archive.
- Thumbnail gang sheets of all analog film images will be printed and filed in the image archive.

Section B, Digital Still Images

The selection of original still photographic media, digital or analog, or a combination of both, will be determined by the project and personnel.

- It is suggested that a card of known color with the inclusion of project number, date, and photographer's initials be imaged at the beginning of each set of images.
- When digital still images for more than one project or date are captured to a single memory card, folders must be created on the memory card using digital camera menus. Images by project are then captured to those folders and are identified by project number and date captured.
- Digital, still images should be captured at RAW, TIFF or the camera's highest resolution and best quality (least compressed) JPG file format settings.
- It is recommended that no digital image be captured at a resolution lower than the highest resolution jpg available.
- To ensure the primary images on the digital camera's memory card remain unaltered, prior to their log-in and archiving, the images must not be opened on a computer or any other device that supports image editing software. Images may be viewed on camera in order to ascertain whether all necessary images have been successfully captured and are, to the best of the photographer's ability, a true and accurate representation of photographed scenes and subjects. Images must not be deleted from the camera's memory card, just as individual photos cannot be removed or deleted from a roll of analog film.
- Digital cameras or their memory cards containing original digital still images will be submitted for downloading, logging-in, and archiving, as soon as possible and before any images on the card have been opened.
- Forms should be available for each type of work request. These forms must be filled out in order for digital images to be downloaded, logged-in and archived. The forms require a project number, date taken, taken by, and date submitted. Forms also allow for the ordering of prints and/or copies made from the archived originals. A copy of the form will accompany the return of the order.

- Digital still images will be logged-in to a secure image database used for analog images. The image database will assign a sequential set number to the digital image folder and assign unique numbers to the individual images. The database tracks all images for a project and keeps information as to who took the images, on what date, how many were taken, and descriptive information as needed. The database will supply information about all images on a project.
- Before opening, all primary original digital still images will be burned to secure media. This media will contain assigned set and image numbers. Two sets will be recorded for each set of unopened primary original and logged-in numbered images. These copies of original digital images will never be altered, added to, nor have images deleted from them. They will be permanently archived in the appropriate location. These copies of digital original images serve a purpose similar to that of the negatives in traditional analog image capture. They remain, as do the negatives in the case of analog originals, in the permanent archive. Only copies made from the originals may be removed.

  All digital images should have low-resolution copies made and filed by project and image set number. They will reside in the image archives. This is an image database that may be viewed, copied, and e-mailed by personnel. The thumbnail copies on the server image database will be read-only files to ensure they remain unaltered.
- When producing full, high-resolution copies, it is acceptable to use basic image processing techniques including color balancing, exposure, and contrast adjustment. The resultant images should be the best possible, true and accurate representations of the scenes and subjects photographed. These processed copies of digital originals may be delivered using any means requested, including via network, e-mail, on CD-Rs or DVDs, hard printed copies in any size including photo books, thumbnail contact sheets, trial exhibits, over the Internet, e-mailed, or any combination of the above.
- When image analysis involving techniques beyond basic image processing such as, but not limited to, increasing the visibility of specific details in an image at the expense of others, unsharp masking, multi-image averaging, or when measurements are taken, it is required that a detailed record of steps taken and tools used be kept so image analysis is repeatable and verifiable. Image processing and analysis should only be performed on copies of digital original images. This leaves the archived digital camera's originals unaltered.

Original images captured, logged-in, archived, and reproduced following this SOP will guarantee chain of custody and help to ensure the images will remain safe, secure, and unaltered.

Section C, Video Images

- It is suggested that a card of known color with the inclusion of project number, date and photographer's initials will be imaged at the beginning of each reel.
- By request, sound will or will-not be recorded when using video media for documentation. The project leader/manager must decide, prior to the beginning of the project, about any audio recording requirements as well as any post video capture work, requiring effects like picture-in-picture or other editing.
- Only new videotapes or digital media should be used for project documentation. Never reuse or record over previously recorded media.
- Images captured on video media must be limited to one project number and one date each.
- Forms should be available for each type of work request. These forms must be filled out in order for videos to be logged in and archived. The forms require a project number, date taken, taken by, date submitted, and a description of the content of the video. Forms also allow for the

ordering of duplicates made from the archived originals. A copy of the form will accompany the return of the order.

- All videos containing footage will be logged-in to the image/media database as soon as possible after exposure. The database will assign each video a unique sequential number. The database tracks all videos for a project and stores information as to videographer, date produced, how many videos were taken, and descriptive information as needed. The database supplies frequently requested information about all videos on a project.
- All original videos remain on file. Only dubs from the original videos may be removed from the archive.
- Duplicate copies produced directly from the original videos can be made.
- Videos received from outside sources may be logged in and archived into the archive upon request.

Federal Rules of Evidence: Article X (Contents of Writings, Recordings, and Photographs)

Rule 101(1) defines writings and recordings to include magnetic, mechanical, or electronic recordings.

Rule 101(3) states that if data is stored in a computer or similar device, any printout or other output readable by sight, shown to reflect the data accurately, is an "original."

Rule 101(4) states that a duplicate is a counterpart produced by the same impression as the original, by mechanical or electronic re-recording, or by other equivalent techniques which accurately reproduces the original.

Rule 103 (Admissibility of Duplicates) states a duplicate is admissible to the same extent as an original unless (1) a genuine question is raised as to the authenticity of the original or (2) in the circumstances it would be unfair to admit the duplicate in lieu of the original. This means a photograph can be stored digitally in a computer and that a digital photograph stored in a computer is considered an original, and any exact copy of the digital photograph is admissible as evidence.

APPENDIX 2.2

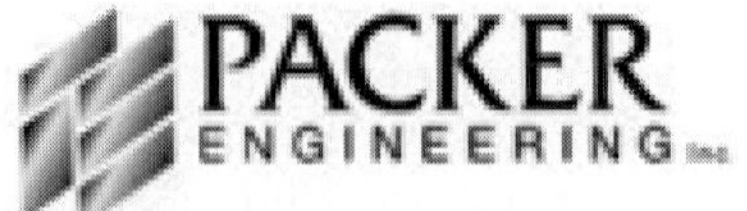

ARTIFACT / CUSTODY RECEIPT

Project No.: ______________ Date: ______________

Project Name: ______________

Received from Packer Engineering, Inc.:

Artifact Type: ______ Subject ______ Exemplar

Description:

Received By:

____
Company Name

____
By: (Signature)

____
Print Name

____
Title

____
Date

Source: Sandy Weiss/Packer Engineering.

Chapter 3

Visual Storytelling

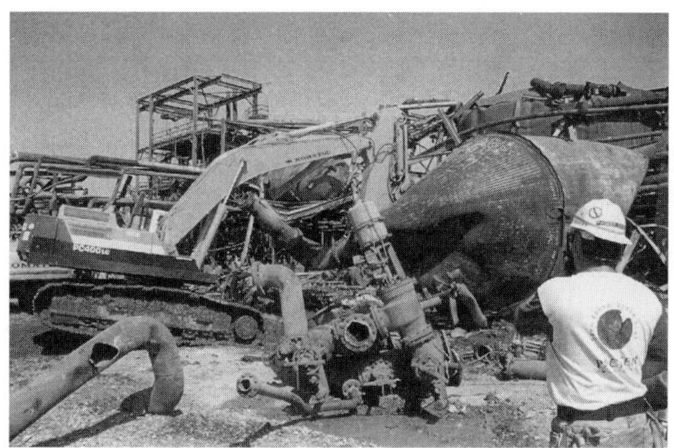

Learning Objectives

AFTER STUDYING THIS CHAPTER, YOU SHOULD BE ABLE TO:

1. Understand the ways humans give visual form to ideas and concepts
2. Understand and use the supplied underlying structure/protocol/best practice for the optimum photographic results
3. Understand why skepticism is heightened among jurors expecting hard forensic evidence
4. Know what images are necessary to visually tell the story of what happened
5. Understand why the photographer cannot enter into a project with visions of conclusions rather than suggestions of hypotheses
6. Understand why it is an error to use a hypothesis for an explanation of a phenomenon, without performing the necessary tests
7. Understand why it is mandatory to capture sufficient images and take specific notes to ensure that the work will tell the whole story
8. Understand the necessary steps for an organized and scientific investigation

Since the dawn of time, humans have left their marks on the world around them. On cave walls, animal tusks, clay pottery, and any available surface, people have drawn, scratched, rubbed, carved, and printed everything from pictures to words. When we see their markings today, we are looking back through time at the way our ancient ancestors lived, hunted, dressed, worshipped, and celebrated life.[1]

Early people constantly searched for ways to give visual form to ideas and concepts, to communicate, to store knowledge, and to bring order and clarity to information.[2] Some images already exist in nature or are generated automatically as the result of experimental procedures.[3] Cave paintings are not the beginning of art as we know it, but rather the dawning of **visual communications**.[4]

The early Egyptians used symbolic objects and pictures to make the transcendental and unseen both immediate and understandable.[5] Aristotle, the acute observer, proposed that we cannot think without images.[6] Observation includes the simplest use of illustration as a device to record vision, with no particular analysis of the thing observed. (I looked, and this is what I saw.)[7]

Photography was invented by nineteenth-century artists for their own purposes. These people were seeking a lasting, literal record of their visual surroundings.[8] Art critics of the time decided that photography was not and could not be an art. The final photograph could be artistic but the technology used to create it was definitely a science: "The world in which we live has a strong grip on photography and pictures are dependent upon mechanical means and are not a part of man's creative imagination."[9] The most important use of photography was in communication. Here the value of photography was seen for its quality of immediacy and the literal description and convincing **presentation of reality**.[10]

Today, a common use for photographs is as memories.[11] Scientists however, use technical images in specific ways to communicate what they have learned.[12] Scientific studies are often published using words indecipherable by the general public. "Images; even complex ones; can however, impart the scientist's objectives in startlingly direct ways."[13] Scientific illustrations and photographs offer an incomparable view of humankind's intellectual evolution. Yet another, quite different,

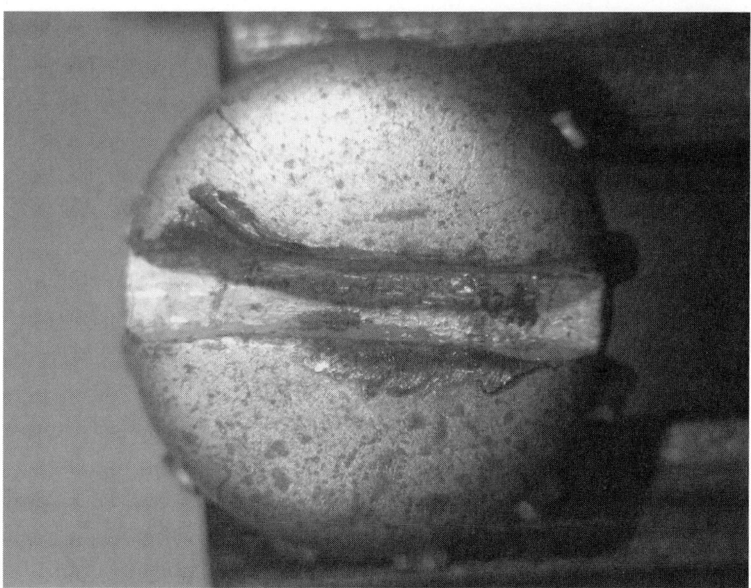

FIGURE 3–1 Deformed screw head. *Source:* Sandy Weiss/Packer Engineering.

experience may be evoked from the contemplation of such images.

The following paragraph is a well-written description of the plastic deformation on the heads of some screws removed from the engine of a small aircraft:

The slotted heads on the screws were plastically deformed (see Fig. 3–1) on the outside edges of the slots. What was initially a rectangular slot is now rounded above and below the original slot centerline on the slot surfaces nearest the outside edge of the screw head.

The slot areas nearest the center of the screw head remain intact. Some screws show some oxidation, and a few also contain obvious tool markings. There is slightly more deformation on the upper right and lower left faces of the slots. The underside of the screw heads are fitted with a lock washer. The washer teeth are angled, creating sharp edges that come in contact with the underside of the screw head when compressed. Teeth marks were observed on the underside of the screw heads with increasing depth in the clockwise direction. The markings on the heads of the screws indicate that torque was applied to the screws in both the clockwise and counterclockwise directions. The magnitude of the moment about the screw head is defined as the product of the magnitude of the force and the perpendicular distance from the line of action of the force to the axis, or center of the screw head. Since a singular amount of force must be applied to the screw slot at any given moment, the amount of torque the slot experiences increases as the radius from the center of the screw head increases. As a result, the screw slot experiences the greatest torques on the outermost surfaces. This is clearly observable on the screw head as the amount of deformation of the slot increases as the radius from the center of the screw head increases. The deformation on the lower right side of the slot and the upper left side of the slot indicate torque being applied in the clockwise direction while deformation on the upper right side of the slot and the lower left side of the slot indicate torque being applied in the counterclockwise direction. Since the upper right side of the slot and the lower left side of the slot were deformed upon receiving the engine, a counterclockwise torque had been applied to the screws, indicating that they had been removed at least one time before we received the engine. There is more deformation in the counterclockwise direction than there is in the clockwise direction, indicating that more force was used to remove the screws than to install them. This asymmetrical torque history could be explained by the resistance to rotate the screw created by the lock washer and minor oxidation of the screw causing it to bind together with surrounding surfaces.[14]

What gives the uninitiated viewer a better idea of the deformation: the preceding paragraph or the accompanying photograph?

At a commission investigating the *Challenger* shuttle accident, a link between the cold weather and the loss of resiliency of O-rings was obvious to engineers, but various officials had camouflaged the issues in the obscurist language of evasive technical jargon.[15] Is it possible that a few photographs of the previously obvious problems observed in O-rings in cold weather conditions could have alleviated the *Challenger* disaster?

Understanding the content of a scientific illustration requires some description of the phenomenon to be studied, as well as an understanding of its labels and terms. "Unlocking the meaning can form a shared intellectual passion, a passion that has animated the scientific community throughout the history of mankind. It may lead to new ways of understanding some aspect of ourselves and the world in which we live."[16]

What is most abstract in nature is, of course, the human mind, which still eludes scientific explanation. Many "realities" exist only in the mind. Mythology, black holes, the structure of the universe, ad infinitum are phenomena that cannot be directly perceived but that we have no trouble imagining and illustrating.[17]

"The **limitations of speech** are the fallibility of human memory and an immediacy of expression that cannot transcend time and place."[18] Images trigger visual motion: the perusal of the elements in the picture. By looking into the picture, the viewer transforms the static image into a dynamic intellectual experience. In some instances this may evoke an aesthetic response or pleasure.[19]

Even though we live in a perceptual world of three spatial dimensions, the world portrayed and accepted by all human observers as reality in our information displays is often the two-dimensionality of paper and video screen.[20]

Categorization, prioritization, and sorting are something people do automatically whenever encountering a set of data. Grouping things forces us to think about why they are the same or different. When showing someone an image, we can say, "Think of it this way."[21] In a technological endeavor, it is necessary for the observer to have an innate underlying structure on which to rely for a basis on which to sort.

THE SCIENTIFIC METHOD

Each photographic project is different from every other one the photographer has ever handled, even though they may be alike in some ways.[22] It is critical to remember the steps taken to add them to your experience database. Experience is a great teacher, but there *must* be an underlying structure for the photographer to follow to furnish a framework upon which to rely so the thought process is free to think of the *what* to photograph rather than the *why* or the *how*. The photographer also needs to furnish straightforward and easily understood work to the client. Initially, it may seem that each project is daunting, but reliance on past experience makes the work easier.

Why jurors in criminal trials behave as they do in voting to acquit or convict has always been a source of bemusement and befuddlement to both watchers and actors at the trial.[23] Looking back, an early forensic education was afforded to jurors from TV and was called "The *Perry Mason* Effect." In the 1950s and 1960s juries were schooled by Perry Mason, as played by Raymond Burr, to expect a full confession in the last act. Later things changed to "The *Quincy M.E.* Effect," when from 1976 to 1983 juries were taught to anticipate that the mystery would be solved by the pathological genius of Jack Klugman portraying Quincy M.E. Today it is "The ***CSI* Effect**," the result of the three popular *CSI* TV programs that participants in the criminal justice system firmly believe are ruling the jury's minds, to the delight of defense attorneys and the dismay of prosecutors watching truly guilty criminals go free.

During interviews with jurors after acquittals, the reasons for their decisions are often found to be a lack of credibility on the part of the prosecution's star eyewitnesses or experts. Reports also attribute some acquittals in part, however, to the

CSI effect and define it as a heightened skepticism among jurors expecting hard forensic evidence that was not observed during the trial. Jurors report, "Eyewitnesses cannot be trusted to be accurate in their recall of the criminal episode under scrutiny."[24]

The people who program *CSI* state, "If it happens on *CSI*, it should happen in a real-life courtroom." In a quote from the newsletter of the American Academy of Forensic Science, "Regardless of the bogus science splayed before the millions who watch and ingest the rubbish displayed on *CSI* some things on the program truly have no scientific value."[25] One of the areas glossed over most often is the methods used by TV investigators making photographs. Apparently, the people who review *CSI* content for accuracy do not think people will notice if the photographic practice is lacking in accuracy.

It may be that part of the *CSI* effect is a change in the burden of proof applied by a jury in deciding on guilt or not. "Reasonable doubt is the legal standard, not scientific doubt, and certainly not beyond *CSI*'s doubt or even no doubt."[26]

> It is not only the attorneys, prosecution and defense, who have been touched by the *CSI* effect. Crime labs, police investigators, legislators and legitimate forensic science and scientists have felt the sting of the *CSI* effect, sometimes to the good and at other times to the bad. Naturally the *CSI* effect can also be seen as a propagation of more, not less, junk science and junk scientists.[27]

Locard's Exchange Principle

The Locard exchange principle, also known as Locard's theory, another well-known aspect of the *CSI* effect, was postulated by twentieth-century forensic scientist Edmond Locard, the director of the very first crime laboratory in existence, in Lyon, France. **Locard's exchange principle** states that "with contact between two items, there will be an exchange."[28] Essentially Locard's principle is applied to crime scenes in which a perpetrator comes into contact with the scene, bringing something into the scene with him or her and leaving with something from the scene. In other words, according to Locard, every contact leaves a trace.

> Wherever he steps, whatever he touches, whatever he leaves, even unconsciously, will serve as a silent witness against him. Not only his fingerprints or his footprints, but his hair, the fibers from his clothes, the glass he breaks, the tool mark he leaves, the paint he scratches, the blood or semen he deposits or collects. All of these and more bear mute witness against him. This is evidence that does not forget. It is not confused by the excitement of the moment. It is not absent because human witnesses are. It is factual evidence. Physical evidence cannot be wrong, it cannot perjure itself, it cannot be wholly absent. Only human failure to find it, study and understand it, can diminish its value.[29]

According to Locard's principle, every crime scene contains evidence of the perpetrator of the crime. **Fragmentary evidence** can consist of any type of material left at or taken from a crime scene, or it can be the result of contact between two surfaces, such as shoes and a floor or soil.

When a crime is committed, fragmentary evidence must be collected from the scene. A team of specialized law enforcement technicians goes to the scene, takes photographs and videos of any victims and items of evidence, checks for shoe and tire-mark impressions, examines any vehicles, and checks for fingerprints, etc. Failure to find evidence or failure to capture sufficient or proper photographs at a scene is often enough to acquit a guilty perpetrator.

Structuring a Forensic Photography Project

Forensic photography encompasses the documentation of a tiny piece of evidence to giant accident scenes, and although every forensic projects is different from all others, the structure of any project must be so basic that it can be used for every project. For example, documenting a scratch on a ball bearing in the laboratory is a different project than in-the-field documentation of the catastrophic collapse of the World Trade Center buildings. What these investigations have in common, however, is the way in which the photographer mentally organizes which images are necessary for **visual storytelling**—in other words, for visually relating the story of what happened to a remote observer. Either of these projects would be daunting to the photographer given the responsibility of doing such work, regardless of their expertise or experience, unless they had some idea of where to start.

The scientific method is the only protocol that will work for any project, of any size, for any purpose, at any time. Knowing the method inside and out before embarking upon a project will help you to achieve success.

Photographic projects, like any other, must have a logical beginning, middle, and conclusion that furnish a direction rather than a rigid delineation of preconceived steps. Entering into a project with conclusions in mind rather than hypotheses leads to backward thinking and the possibility of missing important data. Be assured that downplaying the importance and rigidity of a protocol is not a paradox—rather it is simply the key to the map, and the project is the map itself.

Many practitioners consider the scientific method to be its own branch of science. Others say it is actually more a philosophy of logical thought than a science. Regardless, it has a direct impact on the day-to-day practice of science and law. The **scientific method** depends on observation to properly define the subjects under investigation, to perform reproducible experiments, and to draw viable conclusions.

We often find ourselves in a world that is not readily understandable. We may disagree with others about what we find and see in the world around us, and aspects of some things are beyond our present level of understanding. The scientific method helps to provide a way in which we can reach an understanding with ourselves and our community.

Practically speaking, the scientific method is the normal protocol and best practice of most current scientific investigations and is, by definition, the inductive method of knowledge gathering based upon available evidence. (see Fig. 3–2) Hypotheses, or tentative assumptions, are tested by experiment using the scientific method. If hypotheses are proven true, they are assumed correct; if they are proven false, they are assumed wrong and new hypotheses are tried until they are proven true.

Induction uses a slightly more refined form of imagery: one that incorporates an element of interpretation. The scientist says, in effect, "I looked, and this is what I thought."[30]

Early attempts to delineate an acceptable scientific method met with the problem of justification of the theory of induction. Induction, by definition, does not necessarily lead to the truth, so its results may not necessarily be valid. Inductive reasoning, or inductive logic, is the process of reasoning in which the answer to an argument may be true but depending on the premises also may not be true: it is used to group objects with similar properties or to theorize repetitive performances without the benefit of the time for absolute proof. This difficulty has led to the rejection of the theory that a single scientific method is universally applicable to all sciences.

Thus, the scientific method has been defined and diagrammed in many ways since its appearance in professional literature. For example, H. G. Wells said, "For the true scientific method is this: to trust no statements without verification,

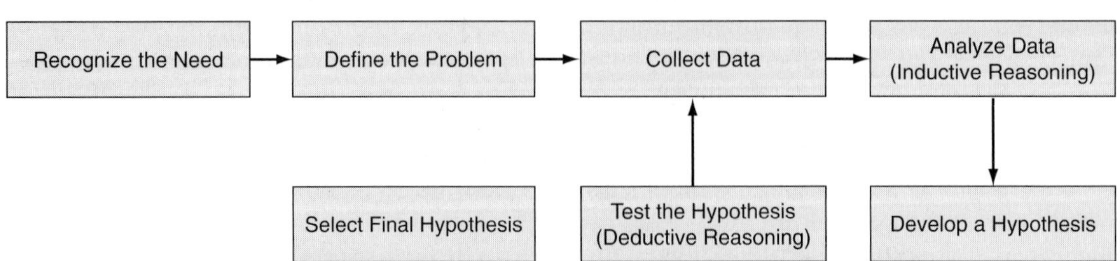

FIGURE 3–2 Flowchart of the basic steps of the scientific method. *Source:* Sandy Weiss.

to test all things as rigorously as possible, to keep no secrets, to attempt no monopolies, to give out one's best modestly and plainly, serving no other end but knowledge."[31] Today, a state-of-the-art definition reads more like this: "A process that is the basis for scientific inquiry. The scientific method follows a series of steps: (1) identify a problem, (2) formulate a hypothesis, (3) test the hypothesis, (4) collect and analyze the data, (5) make conclusions."

It is apparent that some ideas have changed over time but are not entirely different from what they were. In the judicial system, testimony that deviates from accepted scientific practice is grounds for rejection as junk science. **Junk science** is a term used in U.S. political and legal disputes that brands an advocate's claims about scientific data, research, and analyses as spurious.

The type of methodology used in the scientific method is, in fact, a means of communicating understanding; it allows the scientist to say, "This is how I think it works."[32] Then it suggests to the scientist the proper steps to prove the theory.

Current Scientific Method

The steps of the scientific method steps include the following:

- Defining the problem
- Collecting and analyzing data
- Development of a hypothesis
- Testing the hypothesis
- Selecting the final hypothesis

Each step must withstand peer review for verification. Any conclusion becomes accepted only after it is known by others and criticized by publication or review.

DEFINING THE PROBLEM

Defining the problem demands careful preparation and the use of accepted terminology for all relevant concepts. It depends upon a careful characterization of the subject, problem, unknowns, and theories of the investigation.

Collecting and Analyzing Data

If experiments support the hypothesis, it may become a theory or law. If the experiments do not support the hypothesis, it must be rejected or modified. What is key is the predictive power of the hypothesis or theory, as tested by experiment. It is often said in science that theories can never be proved, only disproved. It is always possible that a new observation or a new experiment will conflict with a long-standing theory.

Errors in experiments have several sources. First, an error in measurement is possible. Because this type of error has equal probability of producing a measurement higher or lower numerically than the "true" value, it is called random error. Second, nonrandom or systematic error can occur due to factors that bias the result in one direction or the other. No measurement, and therefore no experiment, can be perfectly precise, but science defines standard ways of estimating, and in some cases reducing, errors. Thus, it is important to determine the accuracy of a particular measurement and, when stating quantitative results, to quote the measurement error, or standard deviation. A measurement without a quoted margin of error is often meaningless. Therefore, any comparisons made between experiment and theory are made within the context of experimental errors.

Developing a Hypothesis

When evaluating a hypothesis, scientists often strive to design theories that are elegant or beautiful because they neatly explain as many of the known facts as possible, as simply as possible, while being aesthetically pleasing. Regardless of the quality of its presentation, any hypothesis must include a basic explanation of its purpose.

Testing the Hypothesis

A hypothesis is a prediction, formulated through deductive reasoning that can be tested experimentally. If results prove that the hypothesis is wrong, then the hypothesis is incorrect or incomplete and requires change. If the hypothesis is proven to be correct, then it can be either correct or complete.

Scientists often use empirical observation to determine the acceptability of hypotheses within a theory. When a researcher makes a hypothesis, it is likely that someone will ask for justification. Thus, once a prediction is made, an experiment must be designed to test it.

Once the steps of an experiment or investigation are complete, the researcher must determine if the results are as predicted. If the experimental conclusions fail to match the predictions or hypotheses, then the next step must be to return to the failed hypothesis and restate or repeat it.

Empirical evidence does not necessarily help a researcher to choose one theory or another, nor does it imply that all theories are equal. Thus, scientific philosophers stress the *necessity* that *scientific* observations *must be* restricted to disciplines in which general agreement on the nature of the observations is involved. It is relatively easy to agree about observations of physical phenomena, *but a record of the results must be maintained and words are often insufficient—thus, well-taken evidence photographs become a necessity.*

Detailed documentation of testing is necessary to record and report the experimental results and to provide evidence of the success of the procedure. This will also guarantee the **reproducibility** of the experimental results.

Part of testing is observation, which involves visual perception and is, therefore, a cognitive process—that is, one does not make observations passively but must be actively and mentally involved in distinguishing the thing being observed. Therefore, observations depend on an underlying understanding of the way in which the world functions, and that understanding may influence what is perceived, noticed, or deemed worthy of consideration.[33] In this way, the scientific method is used to separate science from nonscience, and science from junk science.

Selecting the Final Hypothesis

If the experiment/investigation is successful, then its details are adopted and made available for peer review. After peer review, if no significant discrepancies from acceptable limits of accuracy are found, the hypothesis may be accepted as fact.

USE OF SCIENTIFIC METHOD IN EVIDENCE PHOTOGRAPHY

When testing a hypothesis or a theory, the scientist or investigator may have a preconceived preference for one outcome or another, and it is critical that this preference not bias his or her investigation. The most fundamental error is to use a hypothesis for an explanation of a phenomenon without performing the necessary tests.[34]

It is easy to assume the obvious and totally overlook the truth. If the obvious is accepted in the experimental stage, it is often impossible to return to the time or place of the investigation to capture evidence images that were overlooked or missed in the initial experiment/investigation. It is also easy to prioritize an investigation improperly and to miss information that has disappeared due to the appearance or interference of other investigators or changes in the light or weather.

Scientific Storytelling with Photographs

When photographing an accident, a crime scene, or evidence, it is mandatory to capture sufficient images and take specific notes to ensure that the work will tell the whole story. This documentation must be able to stand alone, without oral explanation to anyone else, at any other location, at any other time—and in front of a jury. Always review your work and how you present it to ensure that everything, including "the story," is easy to decipher.

Steps for Scientific Documentation

The following steps apply to the **scientific documentation** of both digital and film-based photography. It is important to remember that image files and negatives are the raw material of documentation, which makes them a critically important part of the investigation and the results it produces. Neither files nor negatives can be replaced if they are lost or damaged.

- Always properly maintain photographic equipment after it is used and before it is stored.
- Use proper cleaning supplies to ensure that cameras and lenses are clean and dry.
- Store equipment in a temperature-controlled environment. Too much heat will cause damage to camera hardware, lubricants, and media. Too much cold will deplete battery power, stiffen lubricants, and possibly cause problems due to moisture condensation.
- Process exposed film as soon as possible after exposure. When downloading digital images, maintain strict adherence to best practices and be sure the images are as secure as possible before reusing the capture media.
- Avoid taking media and images through multiple passes of airport security X-rays and scanners.
- If possible, record evidence photographically and record all pertinent factual information in notes.
- Record the date and location at the time of photography.
- If the project is located at the scene, be certain to photograph a permanent landmark and connect it through sufficient images so the viewer can place the landmark, and thereby the subject, into the setting. GPS hardware is becoming readily available and affordable. (See Chapters 13, 14, and 15.)
- Always record sufficient photographs to fully document the subject.
- Work within any time constraints set on completion of the documentation. If the scene is subject to change, document the location before photographing subject-specific information. For example, if snow on the ground is going to melt, document the scene before the evidence. If time is limited before the scene is altered, perhaps because evidence must be moved, document its location before it is moved.
- Always avoid taking irrelevant photographs.
- Take the initial photographs with the camera lens at a normal focal length (see Chapter 5) and as close to perpendicular as possible to the front, rear, and sides of the subject to document the magnitude and location of all damage. These photographs may eventually be compared to photographs of an undamaged exemplar to illustrate the magnitude of damage. This comparison may be used to confirm or disprove witness statements or reported data.
- Unless the subject is a sphere, to supply sufficient image information to properly measure the severity of damages directly from the images is necessary to compliment the perpendicular views with photos taken toward the corners of the subject. Corner-view images allow two planes or sides of the subject to be seen in each photo and an accurate depth analysis to be performed photogrammetrically (see Chapter 4).
- Use appropriate scales, and include images of the scales in the photographs.
- Measure and record in writing, sufficient dimensions to enable the re-creation of the damages in 3-D.
- When scales cover damaged areas on the subject, expose images both with and without the scales in the frame.
- Always use universal or retainable color references because color is a factor in the documentation.
- Always perform photographic documentation in an orderly fashion. Start at one position and work around in a single direction.
- If using a zoom lens, try not to use the zoom feature when performing the initial walk-around or view-around of the subject.

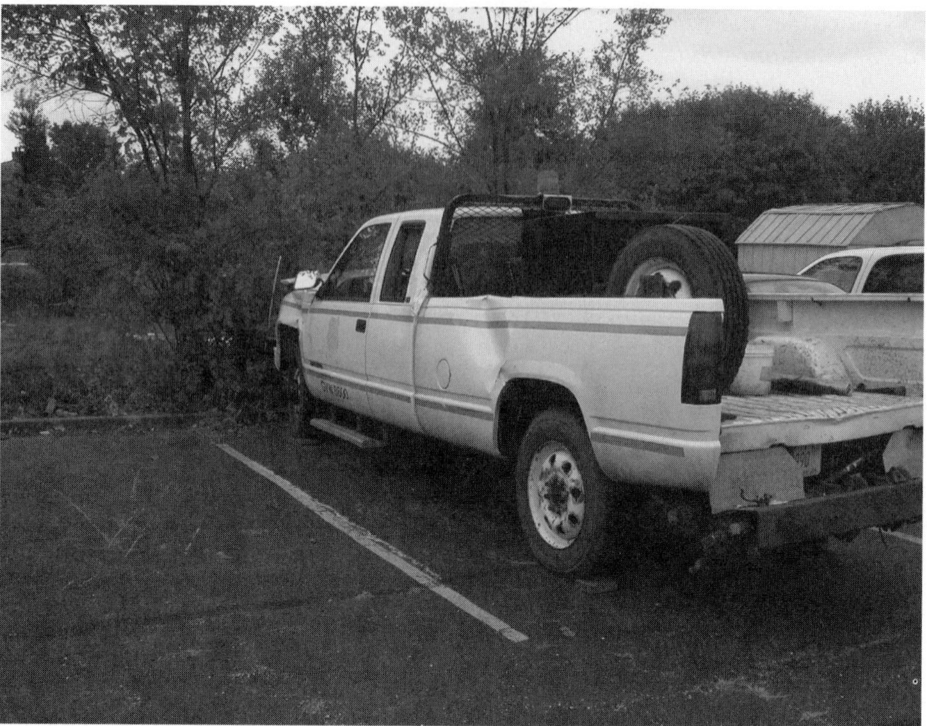

FIGURE 3–3 Overall view of an area of damage. *Source:* Sandy Weiss.

- Always expose an overall image of the area (see Fig. 3–3) before exposing mid-range (see Fig. 3–4) and close-up or macro images (see Fig. 3–5). Make sure the subject area of higher-magnification subject areas is contained within the overall image so it is easy for an observer to determine where the photograph was taken and what part of the subject is documented.
- After overall documentation, take close-up photos of individual areas of damage.
- Always include an image of a scale when changing magnifications.
- Always capture images from relevant points of view. Document both what the victim and witnesses could have seen before the incident. This may help explain why the incident occurred.

By the time the subject is available for documentation, it often has been moved to a remote location where it is difficult, if not impossible, to gain access to all of its aspects. For example, it may be in a salvage yard, warehouse, garage, or attorney's office, where ambient illumination is often poor. In such cases, it is vital to photograph as much detail of damages as possible, using whatever means are at your disposal. Carry enough accessories in your go-kit to make your work easier—but not so much that the kit becomes unwieldy.

Take photographs of the subject from different points of view. If all the images are exposed from eye level, valuable information may be missed. Bend down, lie on the ground, stand on a ladder or any other nearby elevated surface, and generate images of surfaces missed by documenting in only one plane.

Carry convenient gadgets. A small mirror may be the handiest thing a photographer could carry. It can be mounted on a tripod to reflect the sun onto small details under a vehicle where a flash will not reach. Photos also can be taken off the mirror if the subject is close to an obstruction and the camera cannot be maneuvered

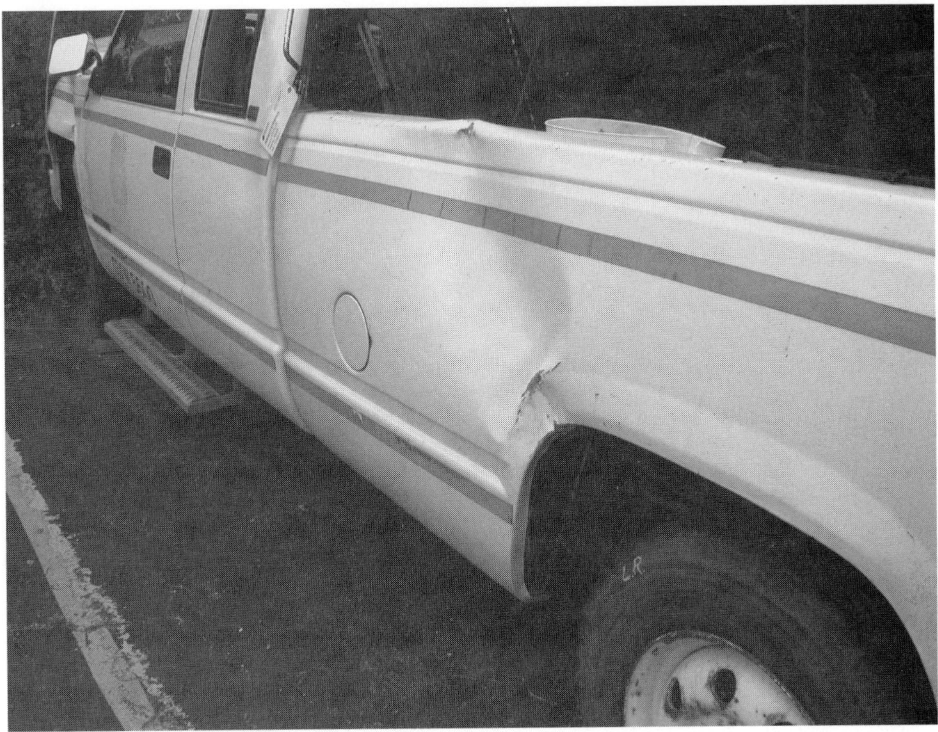

FIGURE 3–4 Midrange view of an area of damage. *Source:* Sandy Weiss.

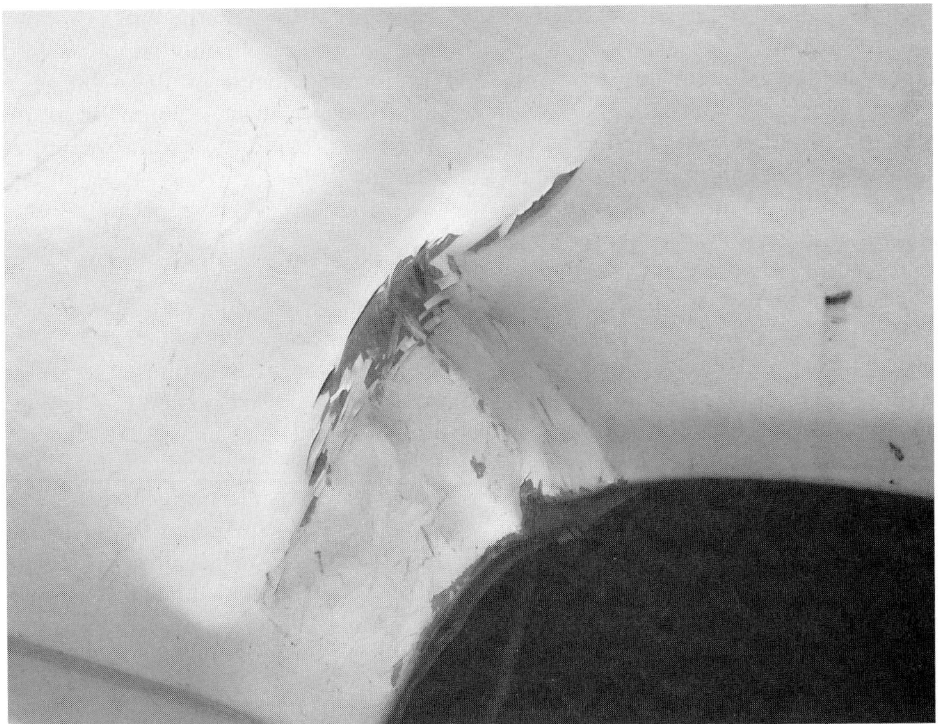

FIGURE 3–5 Close-up view of an area of damage. *Source:* Sandy Weiss.

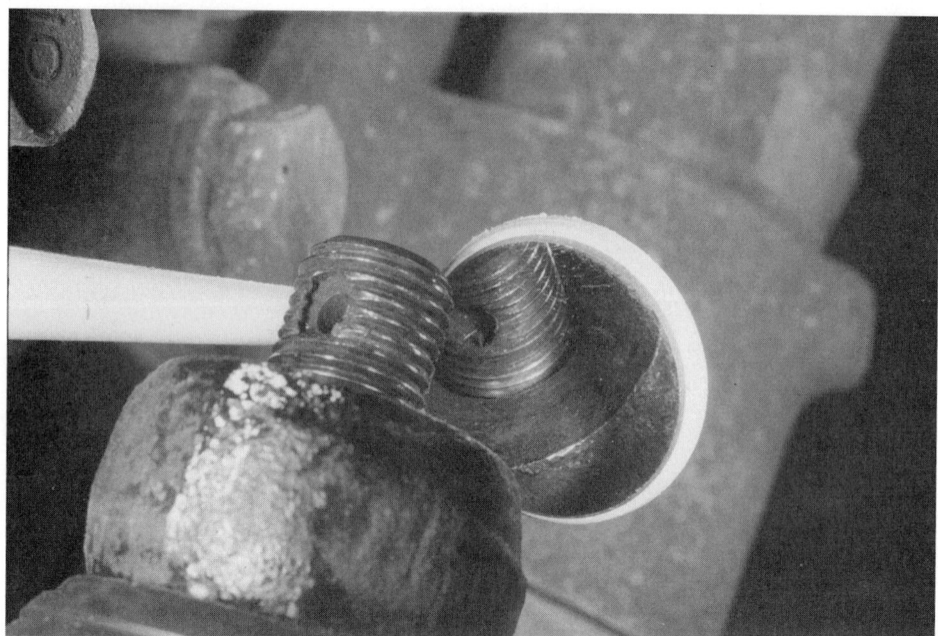

FIGURE 3–6 Using a mirror to show both sides of threads in the same image. *Source:* Sandy Weiss.

to the desired location, or the mirror can be used to document multiple aspects of the same subject that are best imaged in the same frame (see Fig. 3–6).

Bright sunny days are the best time to use fill-flash (see Chapter 9) for outdoor photography. The coverage distance is limited by the size of the flash, but the light the flash provides, within its suggested parameters of use, will lighten the shadows caused by the high-contrast lighting of the sun. This is especially useful in recessed areas of a subject, such as the wheel well of a vehicle. Photos taken without flash show nothing but blackness in the shadows. Photos taken with flash show details inside recesses. Be sure to account for the added exposure of flash, and set the proper exposure if the camera does not do it automatically. Be sure to set the correct shutter speed for flash if the camera does not do that, too. If possible, remove the flash from the camera and hold it at an angle to properly illuminate the detail important for documenting without reflections.

If it is possible to set the camera manually, expose the photographs at a shutter speed fast enough to avoid blurry images from camera movement but slow enough to allow proper exposures while using smaller lens apertures (see Chapter 7) Use of the smallest possible lens apertures will yield photographs with the greatest possible depth of field. Images with extended depth of field will be easier to analyze and will provide the greatest detail of imaged objects.

Photographing Fractures

When material failure ends in breakage, fractography may identify the fracture origin, direction of crack propagation, failure mechanism, material defects, environmental interaction, and nature of stresses (see Fractography).

Many forensic photography assignments will range from overall documentation to macrophotographs. No matter how large the catastrophe (see Fig. 3–7), usually something small has been broken (see Fig. 3–8). The break may even be the root cause. When the project originates at a fracture, the project becomes a matter of **failure analysis.**

Properly trained observers may be able to deduce the nature of the failure from the obser-

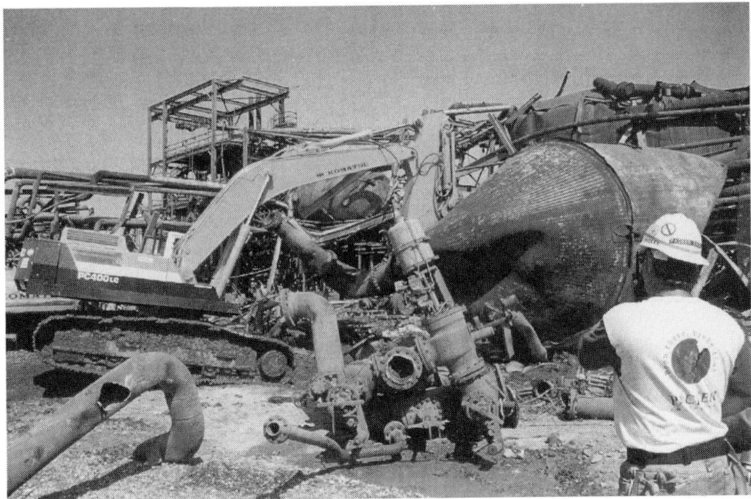

FIGURE 3–7 Scene of a catastrophic refinery explosion. *Source:* Sandy Weiss/Packer Engineering.

vation of the fracture or from its facsimile. It is a fact of life that engineered materials fail, often with catastrophic results.[35] For example, consider the sinking of the *Titanic.*

The Titanic sank in the North Atlantic on April 14, 1912, after a glancing collision with a large iceberg. In 1996, metallurgists from University of Missouri-Rolla, Bethlehem Steel, and the National Institute of Standards and Technology (NIST) performed a study on a piece of the *Titanic's* hull retrieved from the wreck site in 1991. The steel was 1 inch thick and had three rivet holes and traces of the original paint. "The steel edges appeared jagged, shattered like broken glass, and displayed no evidence of bending." Chemical, stress, and charpy impact tests performed on appropriate samples of the steel show it was approximately 10 times more brittle than modern steel when tested at freezing temperatures, as the water and the steel would have been at the time of the collision. When Titanic was built, shipbuilders used the best available steel, but at the time they were more concerned about tensile strength than toughness. The steel used was high in oxygen and sulfur: key ingredients for brittleness.

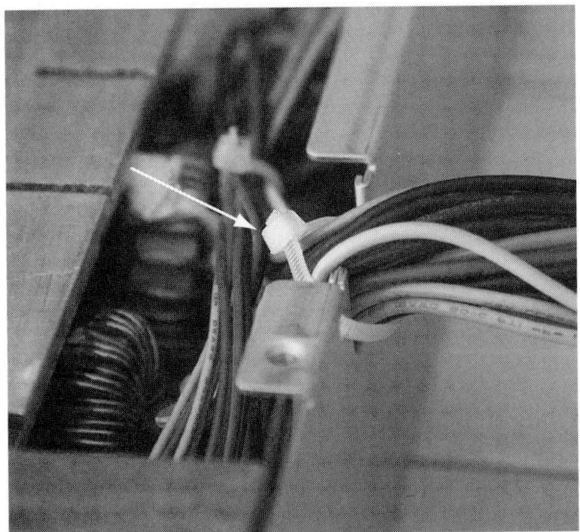

FIGURE 3–8 Root cause of the catastrophic refinery explosion: a fractured wire tie (exemplar). *Source:* Sandy Weiss/Packer Engineering.

Titanic's rivets were wrought iron and different in composition from the hull plates, but they also failed in a brittle manner due to high-impact energy and low temperature.

The iron rivets along plate seams were sheared off when the ship hit the iceberg. The brittleness of the steel caused the plates to shatter and split. The splits allowed enough water to enter at the bow and sink the ship.

In a failure analysis, proper photographs to accompany intelligent testing and observations should tell the whole story of the event. Without documented evidence of each stage, the story must remain a hypothesis rather than become an educated conclusion.

Historically, material failures provide the impetus for the development of comprehensive failure analysis methods, including photography. It is important to note that many of the established techniques used for the failure evaluation of metals are also applied to plastics, composites, glass, and other materials, with minor modifications.

Fractography

Fractography is a descriptive treatment of fractures of materials, particularly of metals, specifically through photographing the fracture surface. The primary objective of a material failure analysis is to determine the root cause of failure. Whether dealing with metallic or nonmetallic materials, normally the root cause of failure can be assigned to one or more of four categories: design, manufacturing, service, or material. Fractography is important in its ability to identify and document unanticipated stresses and catastrophic failures arising from any of the four categories. Fractography is also used to reconstruct material information, through the documentation of the topography of the fracture-generated surfaces. These investigations provide engineers with the opportunity to recognize and interpret the various features of a fracture and add to the knowledge base regarding failure analyses and how to better determine the relationship of the fracture mode to the microstructure of the material. Fractographic investigations usually start with documentary photographs proceed to optical microscopy at lower magnifications, and finish with scanning electron microscopy (SEM) for topographic studies at higher magnifications and also for the microanalysis of the material.

FAILURE MECHANISMS AND CAUSES

On a macroscopic scale, most fractures fall into one of two categories: overload and time- dependent processes. Subcategories of overload include ductile and brittle; time- dependent processes include fatigue, corrosion, and wear.

Reading Fractures Through Witness Marks

Materials must be subjected to load prior to failure. A load is produced by energy, energy creates forces, and forces leave traces to be read on the faces of the resultant fractures. The failure analyst must be able to read the resultant fractures to understand the clues presented.

Ductile fractures exhibit plastic deformation and are characterized by material tearing. **Brittle fractures** display little or no macroscopically visible plastic deformation. Whether a material is *brittle* or *ductile* often depends on temperature, strain rates, and other environmental conditions. At moderate temperatures, materials may exhibit characteristics of both types of fracture. Materials with greater elongation can be considered ductile, and those with less elongation can be considered brittle.

Brittle fracture is the end product of rapid cracking with little plastic deformation through a stressed material, with the failure zone perpendicular to the direction of the applied stress. The cracks usually travel at a high rate of speed, and the fracture appears instantaneously. In most cases, this type of fracture allows no repair of the material before failure because no sign of damage is visible before the breakage.

Brittle fractures leave a relatively flat surface at the break and often display a pattern on fracture surfaces. Some brittle fractures have lines and ridges beginning at the origin of the crack and spreading out across the fracture surface. The surface of such fractures may appear crystalline, and some display continuous V-shaped markings, **chevrons,** pointing to the origin of the fracture. Very hard or fine-grained materials may not display a pattern on their fracture surfaces, and amorphous (without crystallization in a solid) materials may have shiny and smooth fracture surfaces.

Some materials fail from fatigue. The origin of the fracture; the appearance of the fracture

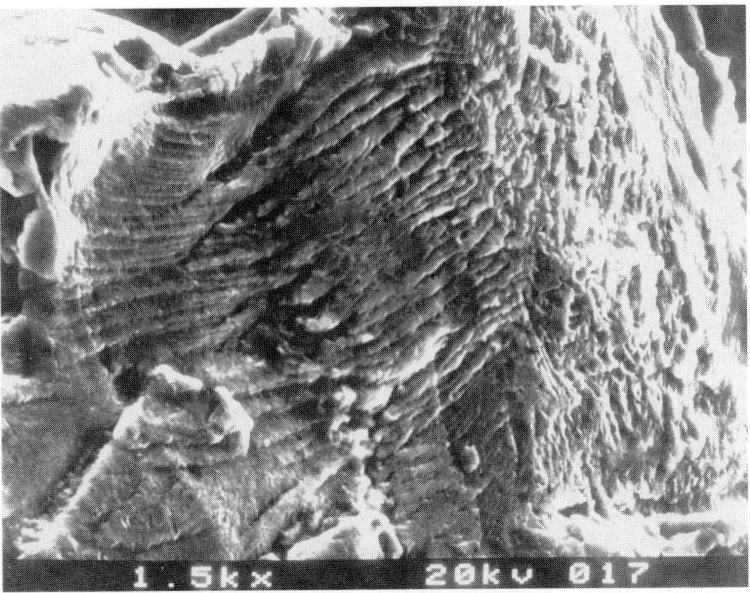

FIGURE 3–9 A fatigue fracture image from a scanning electron microscope (SEM). *Source:* Sandy Weiss/Packer Engineering.

face; the shape of the **beach marks** (see Fig. 3–9) (if any); the location, shape, and size of the fast failure zone; and the direction of the failure propagation tell how the fracture occurred. In some situations, high-powered microscopy is required, but most of the time careful observation with proper lighting and low power (5× to 25×) magnification is all that is needed.

SUMMARY

Normally, forensic documentation requires many photographs to fully illustrate the subject. It is the unusual case for which several or even one photo will show enough information that more is not required. The photographer must take enough photos, and in the proper order, to relate to the viewer the whole story behind the work. Tell the story correctly, the documentation must follow an accepted and understandable structure.

It is a mistake to approach a project with preconceived ideas of what happened or how and to make photographs that illustrate only that particular mental process. It is never simple, and most of the time it is impossible, to get another chance to document the evidence. The forensic photographer is responsible for capturing all the relevant images in the least number possible to relate every aspect of the story visually in the least time.

CASE STUDY

BRIDGE PHOTOGRAPHY

The outside (both northbound and southbound) lanes of the Interstate 294 bridge over the Cal-Sag Channel near Alsip, Illinois, were under construction for many months, causing extreme traffic problems, but they were improperly built. Packer Engineering was called and contracted at 5:00 A.M. to photographically document the bridge problems made evident by the bridge sagging near the supports. The new construction, having cost many millions of dollars, was going to be removed and redone, but the state of Illinois wanted documentary images taken before demolition was begun. Demolition was scheduled to begin at 6:30 A.M. on the day Packer was contacted, so it was necessary to arrive at the site before dawn (officially 6:09 A.M.) to wait for the sun to rise and supply the

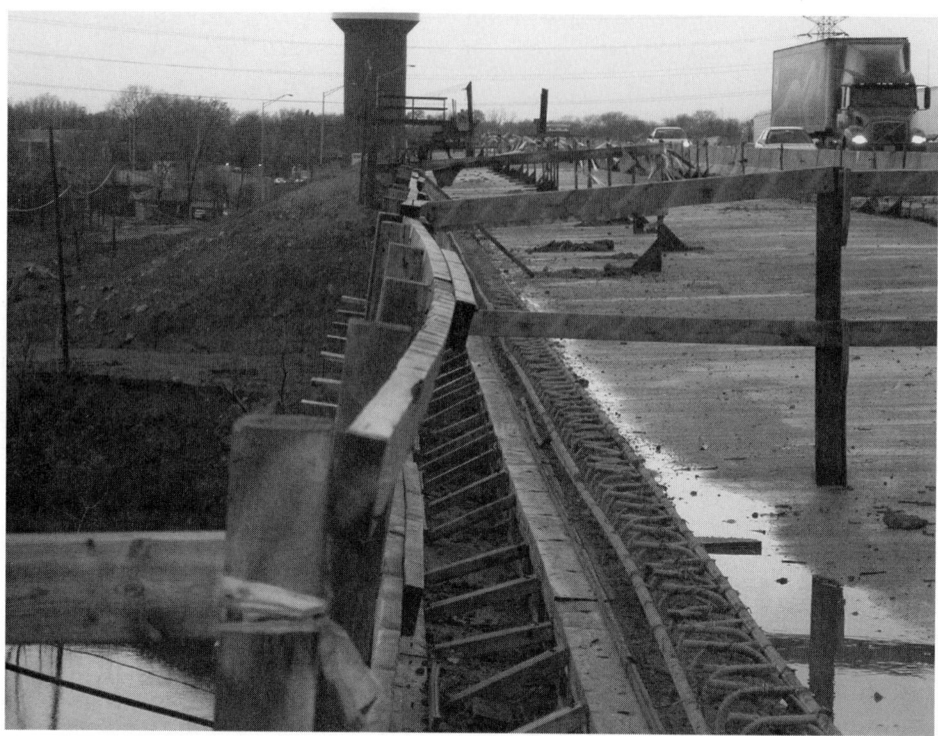

FIGURE 3–10 Bridge photograph taken without a tripod and with the camera set on telephoto zoom and fully automatic exposure. *Source:* Sandy Weiss/Packer Engineering.

illumination necessary for photography. It was also necessary to procure the proper images on the first try.

The state requested that the images be taken with film rather than digitally. Three different focal length lenses were used (50, 210, and 500 mm) to document the appropriate parts of the bridge using a conventional film camera and backing up with digital images. For all film work, the official camera was on a heavy tripod, leveled using a bullet level in the tripod head for side-to-side orientation and a torpedo level on the camera for proper vertical orientation.

The sky was light before sunrise, but no direct lighting was on the bridge until after official sunrise. After sunrise, the sun shone more brightly on the east side (northbound lanes) than the west side of the bridge. Because of this high contrast, using automatic light metering would be an error.

Both properly and improperly exposed digital photographs were knowingly made with a second camera set on variables of automatic operation to illustrate the possible problems associated with automatic metering under these conditions. As intended, the digital images were created for insurance in case anything went amiss with the film images.

The photos included here appear as exposed, not adjusted for exposure, contrast, or sharpness, were taken without a tripod and with the camera pointing north/northwest along the side of the southbound lanes (see Fig. 3–10).

The camera was set on telephoto zoom and fully automatic exposure. The built-in flash fired, and the camera chose an appropriate exposure for flash under the ambient lighting conditions. Outdoor firing of a built-in flash on this particular camera covers a maximum distance of 12 to 20 feet. The wooden barrier with orange paint in the lower left corner of the frame is approximately 20 feet from the camera. The image is nearly properly exposed because the ambient lighting and the exposure-for-flash

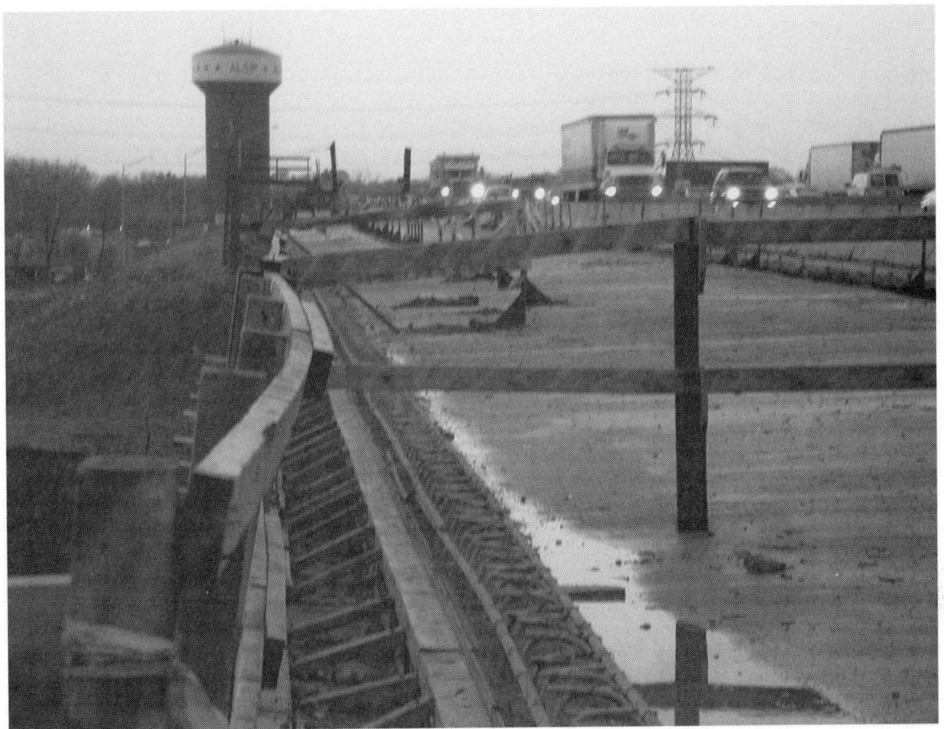

FIGURE 3–11 Camera set on manual, with flash turned off. *Source:* Sandy Weiss/Packer Engineering.

setting were approximately the same. The image lacks overall sharpness and has insufficient depth of field, evidenced by the lack of sharpness in the green tie-rods along the pavement.

When using a fully automatic camera in this type of marginal lighting, the built-in flash will always fire unless it is purposely turned off. If the flash is allowed to fire, the camera circuitry will set the internal exposure systems as if the flash would be sufficient to illuminate the entire frame. The outcome is a photo exposed at a shutter speed too fast for adequate overall exposure, too slow for hand-held sharpness, and with an aperture too large for adequate depth of field.

Figure 3–11 was exposed shortly after Figure 3–10.

The camera was set on manual, and the flash was turned off (see Fig. 3–11). A small lens aperture was chosen to supply adequate depth of field for front-to-back sharpness and a slow shutter speed to supply adequate exposure. The camera was not on a tripod, and therefore the images suffered from camera movement during the long exposure. The traffic was moving slowly, but the headlights are still blurred. This setting did not allow sufficient exposure, extended depth of field, or maximum detail in the shadows.

See Fig. 3–12 was exposed with the flash turned off but with the camera set on fully automatic exposure.

Inclusion of the sunrise-bright sky in the image caused the camera to compute the scene as brighter than would be appropriate for a proper exposure of the side of the bridge. Shooting at a physically lower point of view and eliminating most of the sky from the composition would have resulted in a better exposure. The image is not usable even if printed lighter, as it is not sharp and is missing information in the shadows due to underexposure. The shutter speed and lens aperture picked by the camera are not appropriate in this image for stopping motion or capturing sufficient depth of field.

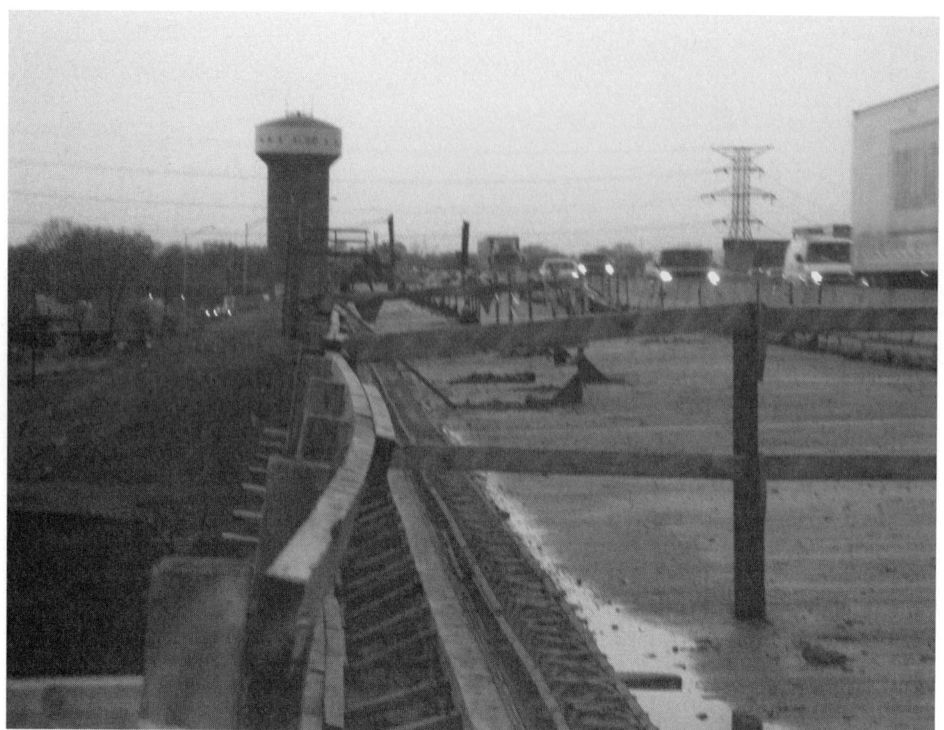

FIGURE 3–12 Inclusion of the sunrise-bright sky in the image caused the camera to compute the scene as brighter than would be appropriate for a proper exposure of the side of the bridge. *Source:* Sandy Weiss/Packer Engineering.

You can see the view north/northwest along the side of the northbound lanes of the bridge in Fig. 3–13.

The camera was again set on fully automatic with the flash turned off. This image exhibits the most appropriate of the auto exposures. The visible part of the sky and the bridge are both subject to the same intensity of illumination from the rising sun. The dynamic range (contrast) of the scene is somewhat wider than the capabilities of the camera to handle at the default settings, but in this case the area under the bridge is not the area in question.

Figure 3–13 was actually the first frame exposed. It displays the sagging concrete between the supports. The bridge could not be used in this form and had to be totally re-done.

Automatic exposure and no flash produced a finished image (see Fig. 3–14) with good contrast and density, but the auto-focus reacted to the closer parts of the bridge, and the large lens aperture necessary for proper exposure limited the depth of field.

In many cases, a specific part of the resultant photograph is the area needed for documentation. Therefore, it is necessary to expose proper exposures of every scene in order to capture the most detail. Following standard procedure, multiple combinations of shutter speeds and lens apertures are taken to ensure proper exposure for the final image. For optimum sharpness and contrast in difficult lighting situations, it is advisable to manually determine the intensity of the light reflected from, or falling upon, the subject area and to set the camera to the best speed/aperture combination to either stop the action or supply sufficient depth of field, or both.

Multiple photographs and views were recorded because in many cases, a specific part of a photograph will be the area needed for documentation.

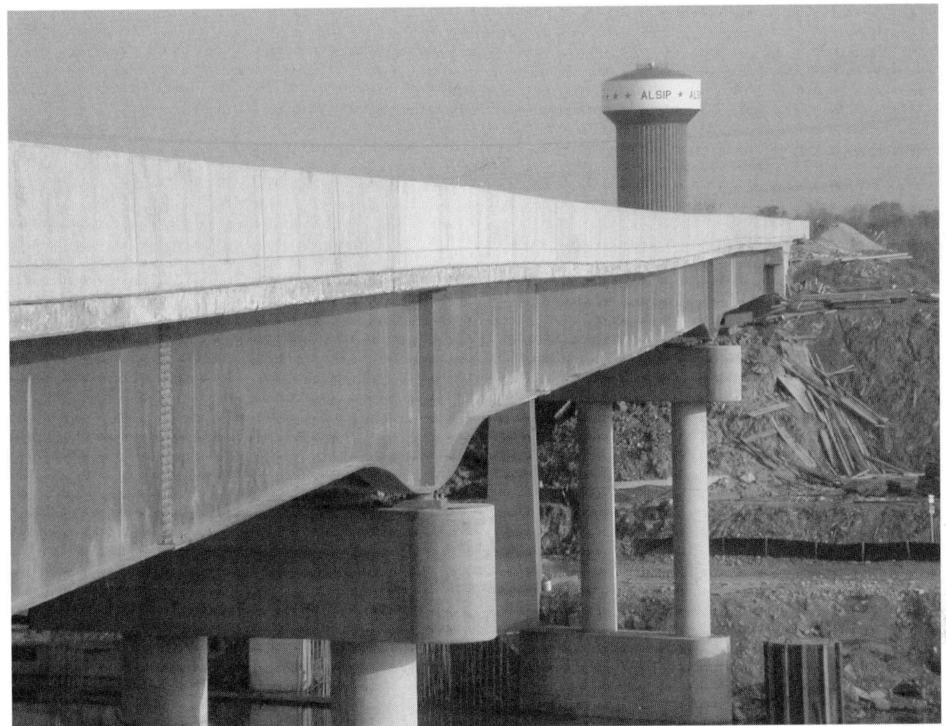

FIGURE 3–13 Northbound view of bridge. *Source:* Sandy Weiss/Packer Engineering.

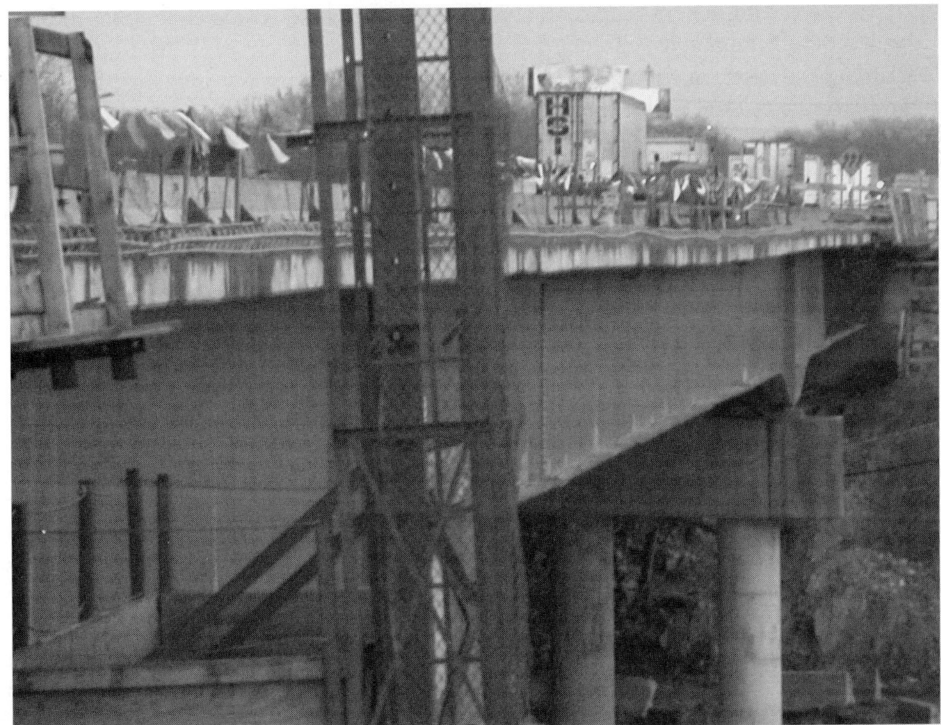

FIGURE 3–14 Properly exposed photograph of bridge. *Source:* Sandy Weiss/Packer Engineering.

CASE STUDY

TEXAS A&M BONFIRE COLLAPSE

The headlines read, "Bonfire Stack Collapse Kills Nine Texas A&M Students."[36] And it was true. Nine students at Texas A&M University had been killed early on Thursday, November 18, 1999, in the collapse of a 40-foot-high stack of heavy logs that was to have been set ablaze before the school's annual football game with rival University of Texas. Nearly 30 students were injured in the accident, some critically. The final death toll was 12.

> In a tragedy that marred a nearly century-old tradition at Texas A&M, the huge bonfire stack, under construction by trained students and others since mid-October, came crashing down about 2:30 A.M. CST while 60 to 70 students were standing atop it. The accident occurred on a field northeast of the campus in College Station, about 80 miles east of Austin.[37]

The collapse of the bonfire stack was the second in recent years. A collapse in 1994, in which no one was hurt, was blamed on wet ground. Rescuers with saws, heavy equipment, and listening devices searched for survivors in a pile of about 4,000 logs, many of them 10 to 12 feet long, while officials said that the accident investigation would be led by the campus police. Tura King, a university spokeswoman stated that students, with volunteer help from construction engineers and heavy-equipment operators, had cut the logs in Texas forests, hauled them to a field near campus, and spent weeks erecting the teepee-shaped pile.

Investigators looked closely at the 100-foot center support pole. Rusty Thompson, the faculty adviser to the bonfire event, said the pole was cracked above and below the center point, where two timbers were joined. Layers of logs were wired to the 100-foot-long pole. The pole, actually two long telephone poles that had been fused together with bolts, wire, and metal plates, served as the chief support for the structure. One end of the pole had been driven about 10 feet into the ground.

Investigators stated that the center pole may have snapped in two or that one of the wires attached to the center pole may have broken. According to the Texas A&M student newspaper, *The Battalion*, some witnesses claimed that a crane used to build the pyramid may have cracked the center pole. However, other witnesses claimed that the pole showed no signs of problems.[38]

Witnesses and some survivors said they heard the center pole crack, perhaps under the crush of timber. However, university officials cautioned that it could be weeks before a final determination could be made on what had caused the collapse.[39]

INVESTIGATION

A design/forensics team was tasked with determining the physical causes of the accident. The project was divided into four areas:

- Building process overview
- Collapse mechanisms
- Causal factors
- Collapse sequence

Because so much media and witness attention was focused on the center pole, it became a priority for investigation. By the time Packer Engineering arrived, the logs had all been moved and sorted and the majority of the center pole had been removed from the scene and taken to a local warehouse. The only part of the pole left behind was a 10-foot broken section. It was the part that had been buried in the ground during the pole's erection. It had been excavated only enough so that most of its fracture surface was visible inside the hole, and a tent had been put over the area to protect it from the weather.

The photographic documentation was, therefore, undertaken at two locations. The above-ground sections were photographed first, then the part in the ground was photographed. A full-time forklift operator was on site at the warehouse (see Fig. 3–15) to lift and roll the sections so all surfaces were available for documentation.

The photography was started at the fracture surface that matched the section left in the ground (see Fig. 3–16) and continued in a logical

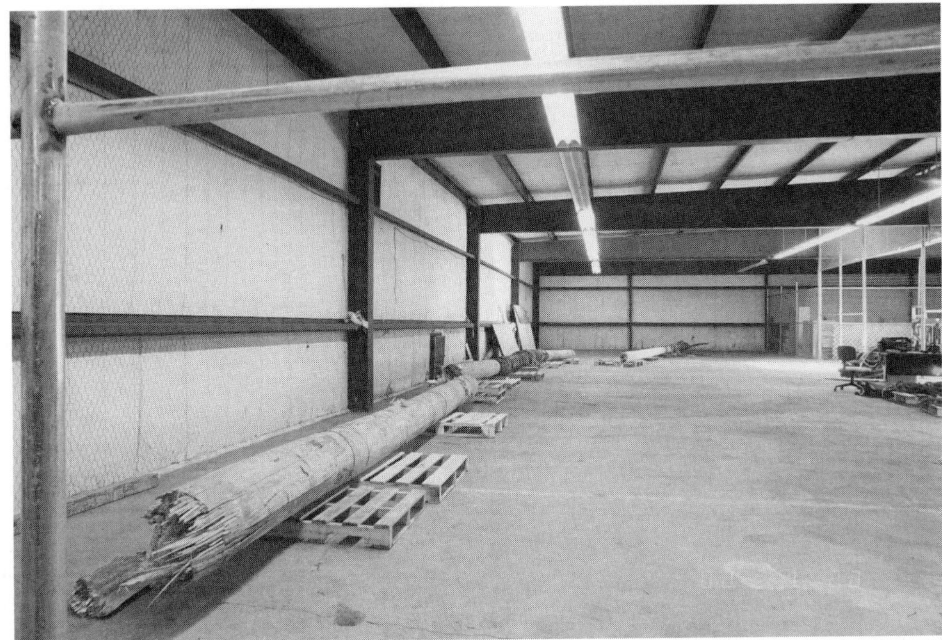

FIGURE 3–15 Warehouse where the center pole was stored. *Source:* Sandy Weiss/Packer Engineering.

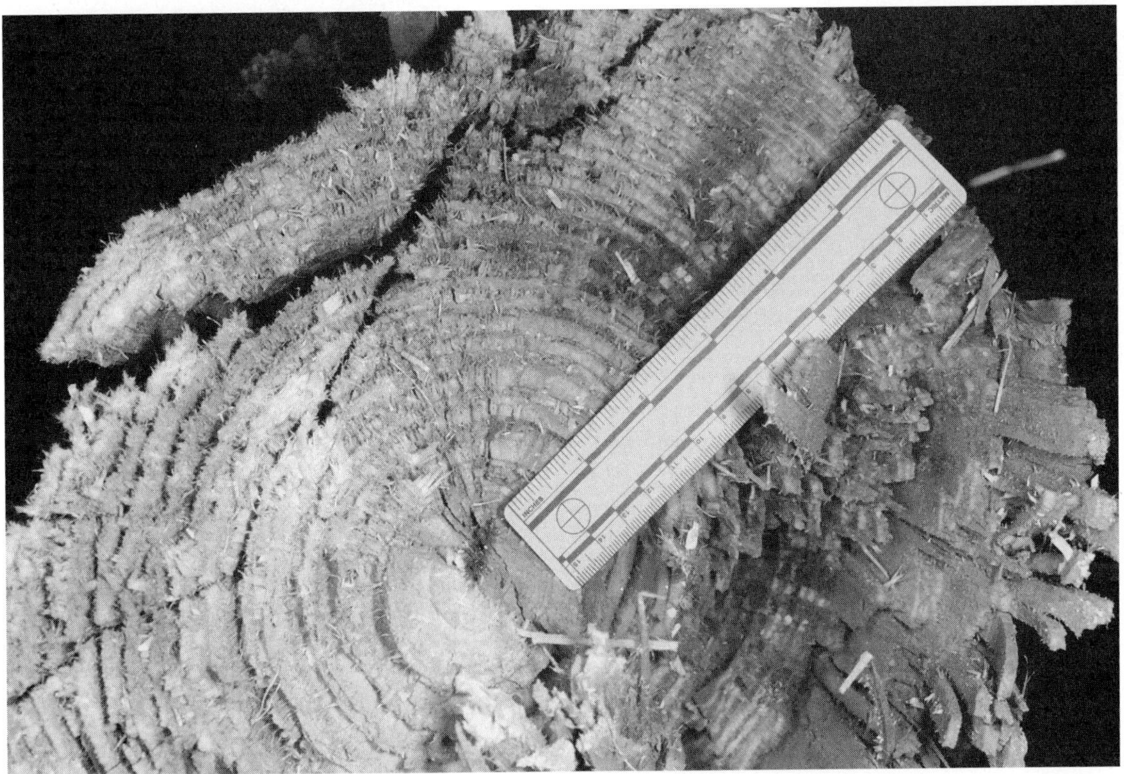

FIGURE 3–16 Fracture surface of center pole. *Source:* Sandy Weiss/Packer Engineering.

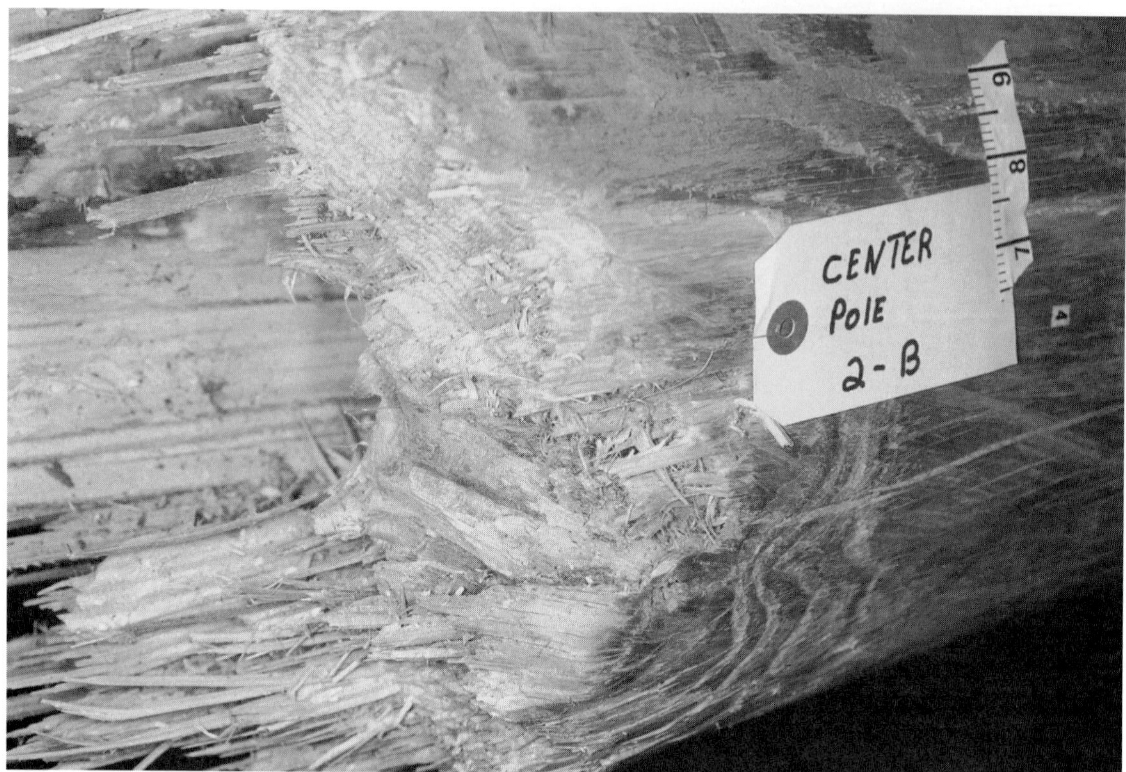

FIGURE 3–17 Tagging method performed on pole. *Source:* Sandy Weiss/Packer Engineering.

manner up the pole, including fracture surfaces, until the part that would have been at the top was reached.

The pole was labeled numerically by section, left to right, and white cards and small yellow cloth letters were used to label areas by sectors (see Fig. 3–17).

The pole was revolved counterclockwise after reaching the right-hand termination of each piece so that documentation could proceed in a clockwise orientation.

Areas of specific interest, including fractures (see Fig. 3–18), splices (see Fig. 3–19), and damages were given extra coverage. Each time magnification changed, a scale was included in the frame for sizing.

A Canon MacroLite ML-1 (see Fig. 3–20) was used for all supplementary illumination (see Chapter 10) Many alternative flash units are currently available on the market to fit modern digital cameras.

The reason for choosing this particular kind of flash was so the images could be spliced into full-length montages without dark to light banding being an issue. To get enough contrast on the surface of the pole to determine if a landmark was depressed or raised, one diffuser was used on one side of the flash. The diffuser decreases the output of that side of the unit by one half f-stop (25%). This variance is enough for surface modeling but reduces the dark to light banding normally found on montages taken with a single flash unit aimed at the surface at a 45-degree angle (see Fig. 3–21 and 3–22).

The MacroLite has three automatic ranges. The depth of field increases as the camera-to-subject distance decreases, and the f-stop number increases as the diaphragm opening decreases in size. This became important where the relief of the subject increased. The fracture surfaces were documented to show where the cracks in the wood appeared to be new and where they had weathered.

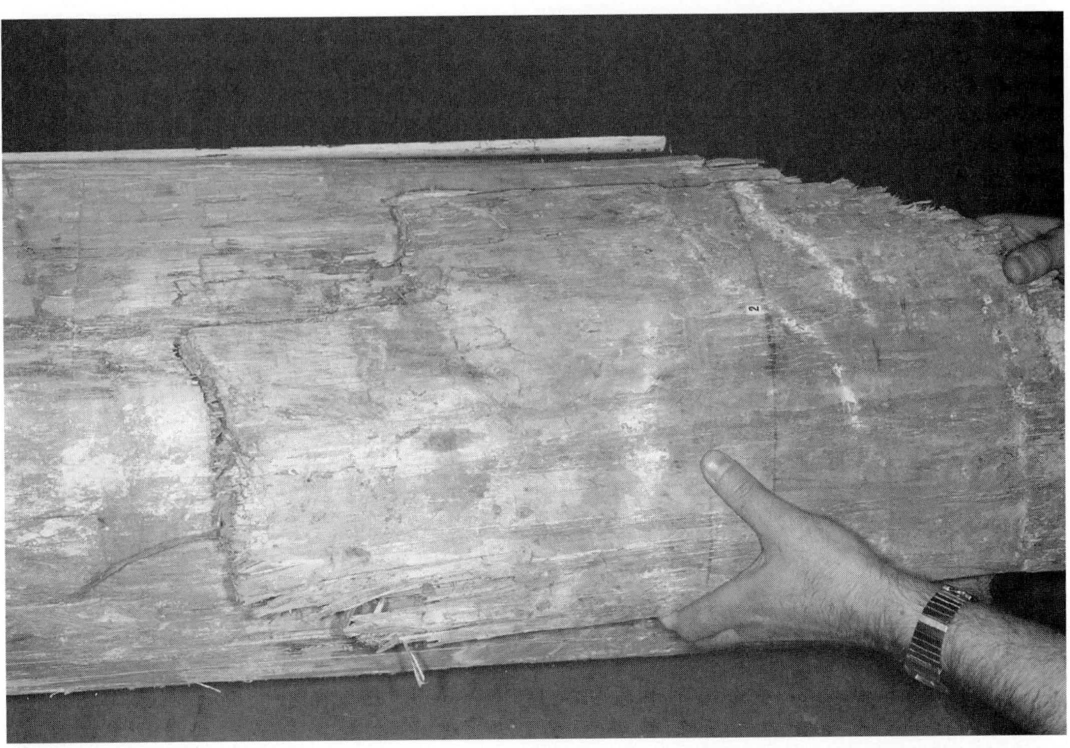

FIGURE 3–18 Typical documentary image, first section of center pole. *Source:* Sandy Weiss/Packer Engineering.

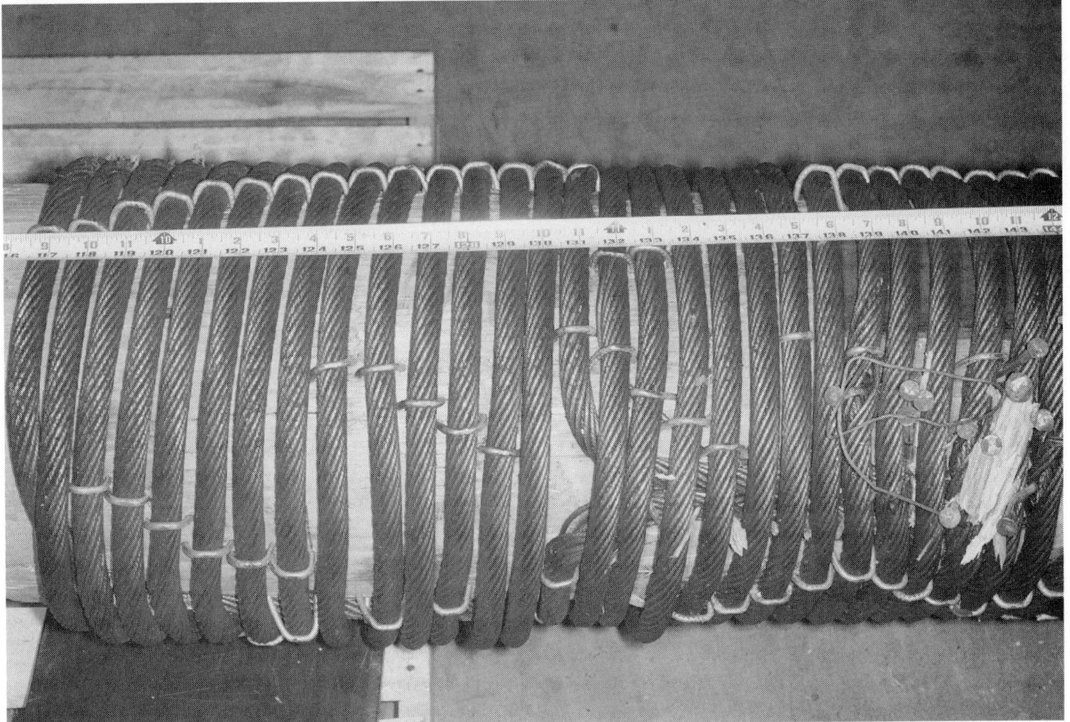

FIGURE 3–19 A splice from the center pole. *Source:* Sandy Weiss/Packer Engineering.

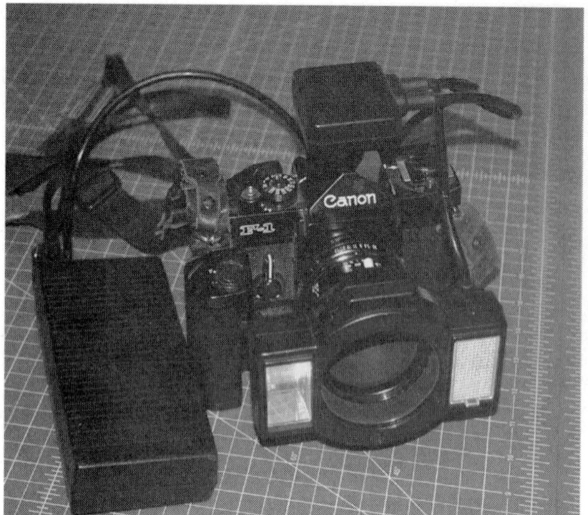

FIGURE 3–20 A Canon Macro flash system. *Source:* Sandy Weiss/Packer Engineering.

The project was completed in a very logical order. Hundreds of images were taken so that every inch of the pole was captured on film. If the documentation had been undertaken in anything but the most logical manner, sorting the images and correlating them to their proper positions would have been impossible.

Had all written documentation been lost or separated from the images at a later date, it would have been very simple for anyone viewing the images to place any image in its proper place on the pole. This is what is meant by **photographic storytelling.**

AUTHORITY

It is of utmost importance for the forensic photographer to understand the chain of command for site documentation. Regarding the methodology used for storytelling/documentation, it is proper and accepted protocol for the photographer to defer to the person of highest rank on site. If the photographer is alone, he or she is the authority in charge. Thus, project design is the responsibility and duty of the ranking officer or client in attendance.

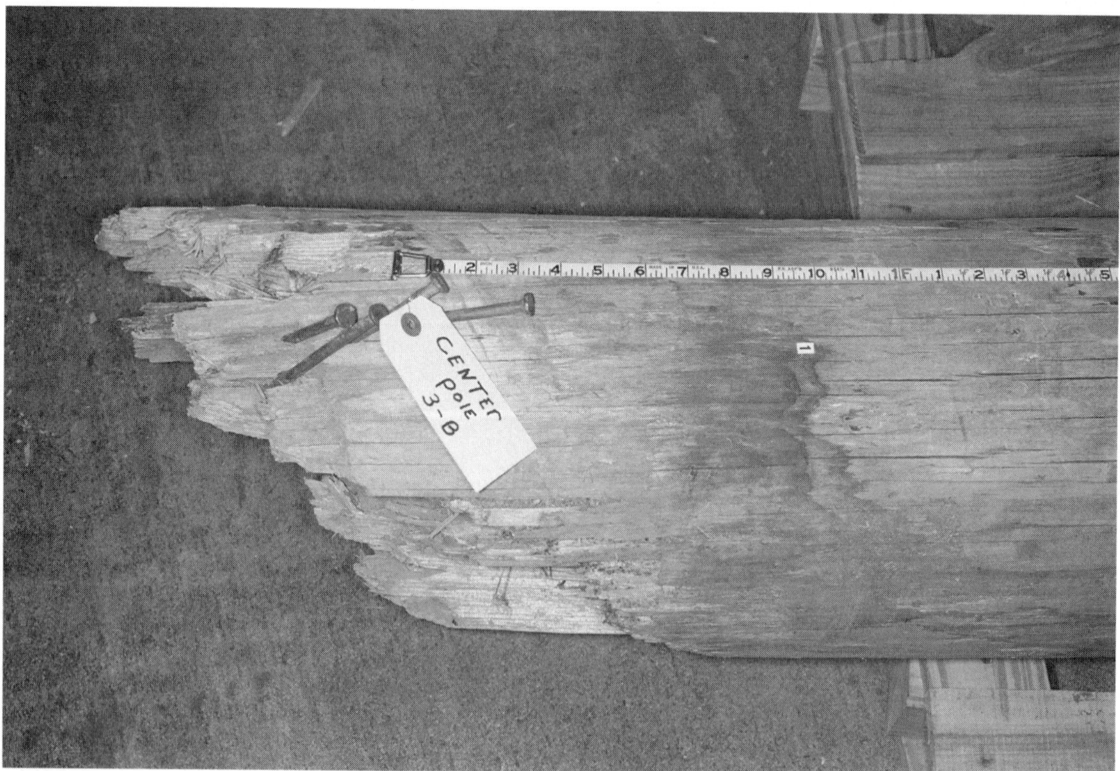

FIGURE 3–21 A typical montage. *Source:* Sandy Weiss/Packer Engineering.

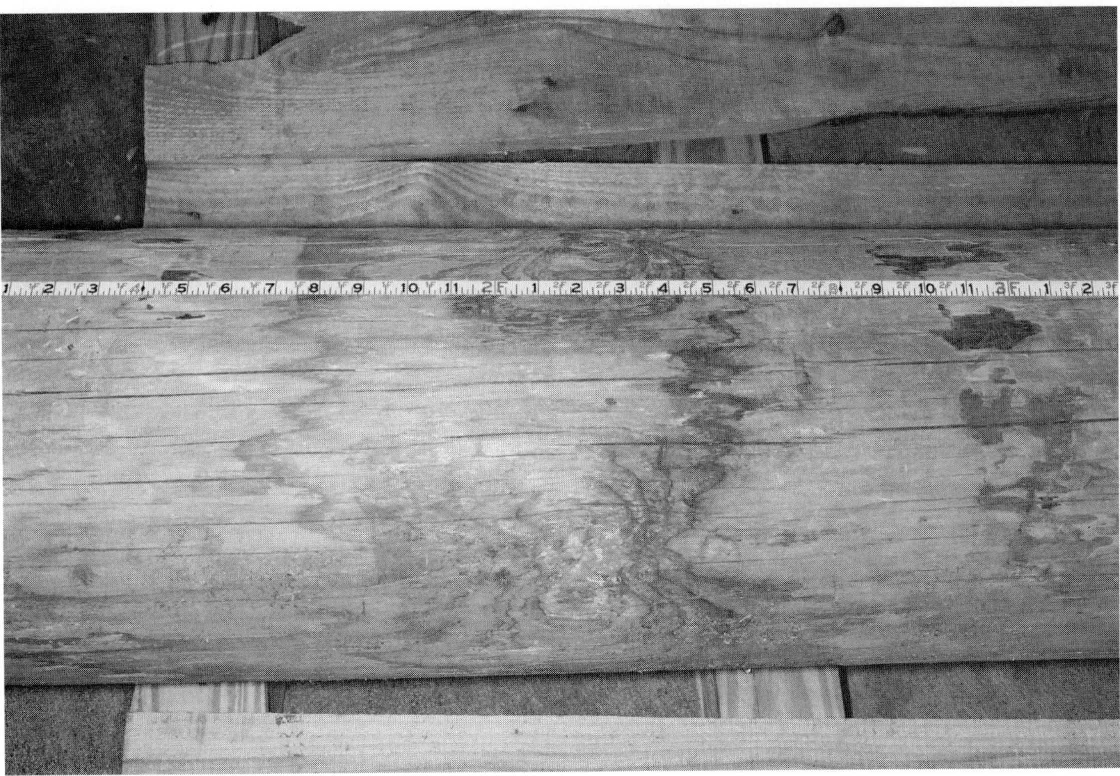

FIGURE 3–22 A typical montage. *Source:* Sandy Weiss/Packer Engineering.

Naturally, the photographer is the expert on hardware, media, technique, and such, and that authority is never deferred. The photographer may make suggestions about doing things the client may not know can be done or would have forgotten. However, how the story is ultimately told should be determined by the person who is eventually going to be writing the report or testifying in court. This is a concern in many investigations, so it is always important for the photographer to concentrate on creating a logical and analytical collection of images for every project. It is also important to understand that the photographer owns and is responsible for all original photographic images, until such time as that ownership is relinquished to the client.

COMPLETING THE PICTURE

The following morning, examination was undertaken of the fracture surface of the part of the pole still in the ground. (see Fig. 3–23, 3–24, and 3–25) This part of the pole also was photographed so the images proceeded in a clockwise manner and could be assembled into a montage if necessary.

A detailed examination of the extent of the visible fracture was performed by an engineer after the documentation. While the examination was being performed, a separate roll of film was exposed to capture an outward-looking panorama of the site from the outside of the tent (see Fig. 3–26). This was done to place the location of the accident in context.

The camera was placed on a tripod raised to convenient eye-level height. A mental note was made of the landmarks in the viewfinder at the side of the frame from each image, and the next image overlapped the previous one by at least 15%. The camera and tripod were physically moved for each frame. Had there been no tent, the tripod could have been put over the pole with only the pan head rotated for each image.

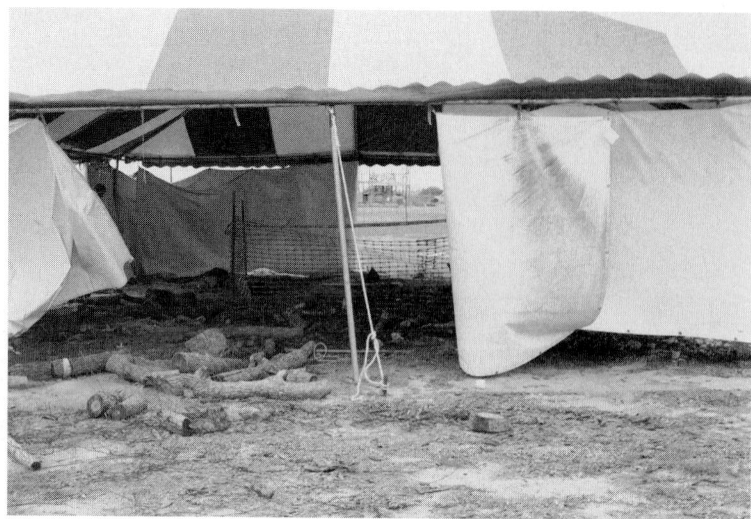

FIGURE 3–23 Tent over the center pole. *Source:* Sandy Weiss/Packer Engineering.

OUTCOME

Upon examination, an expert in wood fractures determined that the center pole itself was not the origin of the collapse. An assortment of small problems, each exacerbating the other, had led to the catastrophic collapse of the bonfire stack.

All the images that were made of the center pole proved to be essentially useless. The outward-looking panorama images were of tremendous value, and an additional trip to the site would have been necessary to create them if that had not already been done (see Fig. 3–27, 3–28, and 3–29).

The individual 4 × 6 images were joined into a 360-degree montage and formed into an inward-looking ring about 24 inches in diameter. Compass headings were added to the images. This ring of images was then mounted inside a Plexiglas ring that was attached by a revolving frame to a typical safety helmet (see Fig. 3–30).

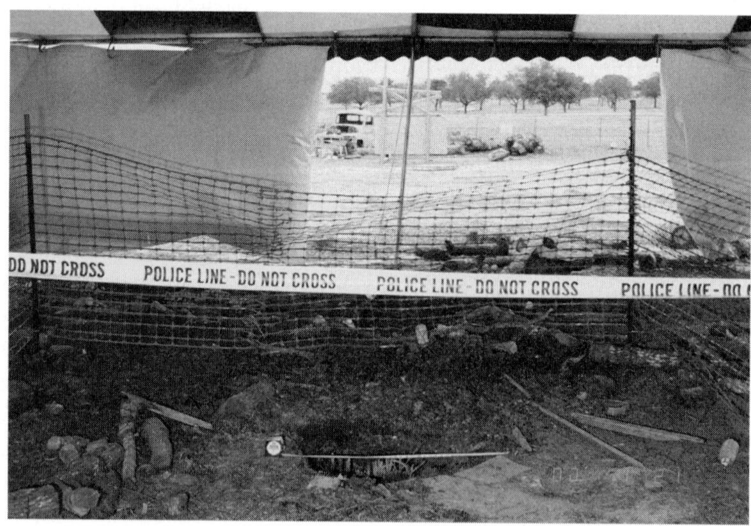

FIGURE 3–24 Inside the tent. *Source:* Sandy Weiss/Packer Engineering.

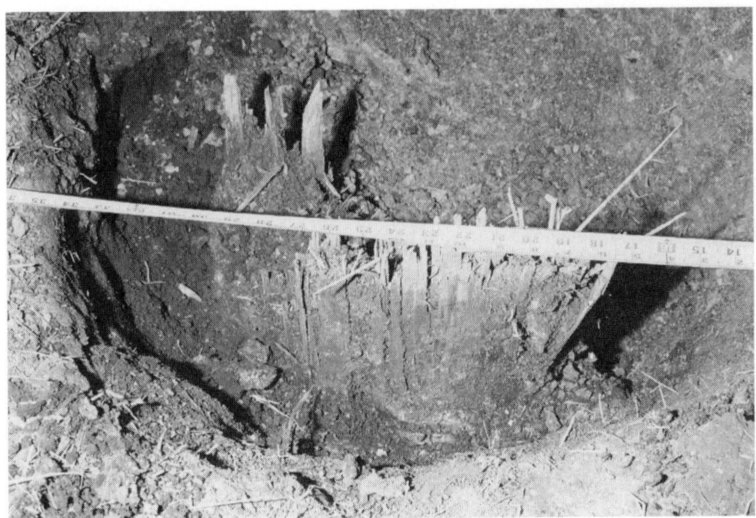

FIGURE 3–25 Section of the center pole remaining in the ground. *Source:* Sandy Weiss/Packer Engineering.

Hundreds of individual images were collected from onlookers who had taken photographs at various stages of construction. The dates could not be positively determined at first, but the stage of construction was always obvious, making it possible to sort and date the images later. The direction in which the camera was pointed for each of the onlookers' photographs

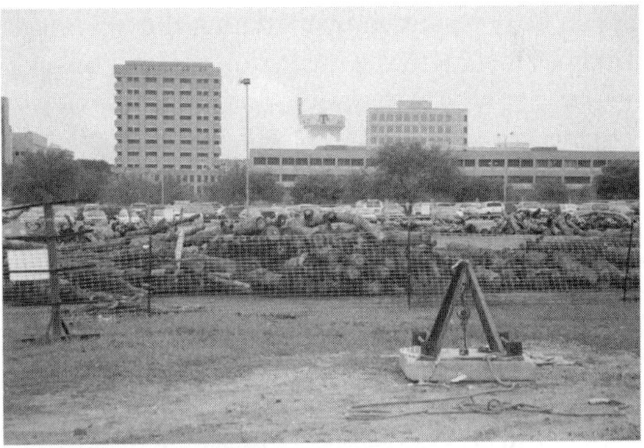

FIGURE 3–27 Montage images of the bonfire stack location. *Source:* Sandy Weiss/Packer Engineering.

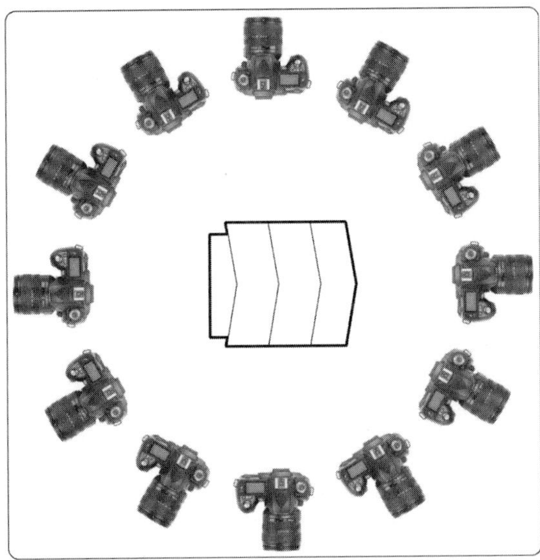

FIGURE 3–26 Diagram of camera setup for outward-looking 360-degree montage. *Source:* Jessica Weiss.

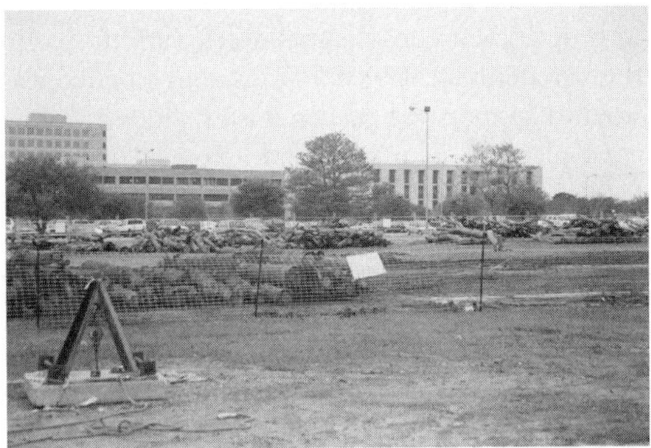

FIGURE 3–28 Montage images of the bonfire stack location. *Source:* Sandy Weiss/Packer Engineering.

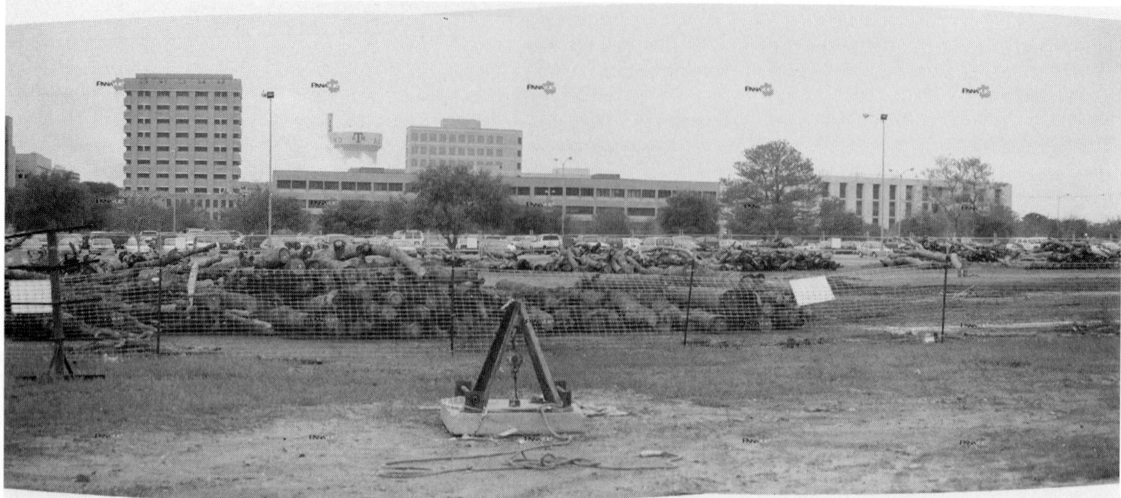

FIGURE 3–29 Spliced montage of the bonfire stack location. *Source:* Sandy Weiss/Packer Engineering.

could be determined by matching the landmarks in those images to the images on the ring of background photos. This yielded a time-lapse view of construction, and many of the theories proposed to explain the eventual collapse could be accurately documented, assessed, and substantiated.

CASE STUDY

SHOTGUN EXPLOSION

An exploded shotgun arrived at the lab as a large assortment of miscellaneous parts. It took the better part of a day to sort and reassemble them into their appropriate positions. Pieces of 2 × 4 lumber were cut to proper sizes and painted a flat gray to reduce their conspicuity. Holes were drilled in the wooden blocks to hold pins, and a pencil was used to support the pieces. Also included were a clear-plastic 6-inch scale and a couple of rubber bands to hold the grip section in place.

The only serious injury incurred at the time of the accident, although the shooter also received a cut on the hand, was the shooter being struck in the eye by a small piece of barrel when the gun exploded.

With the pieces assembled, (see Fig. 3–31), it was simple to recreate the accident. A shell was overloaded and exploded instead of firing when the trigger was pulled. The barrel peeled like a banana. If the small piece had not detached and lodged in the shooter's eye, the accident probably would not have been reported.

The majority of time spent on the photo documentation was used to reassemble the pieces. The photography took only moments. A single photograph adequately tells the story of the mechanics of the accident. Sometimes this is the way a scenario will best be exhibited.

The shooter claimed that the weapon was faulty and sued the manufacturer. Close inspec-

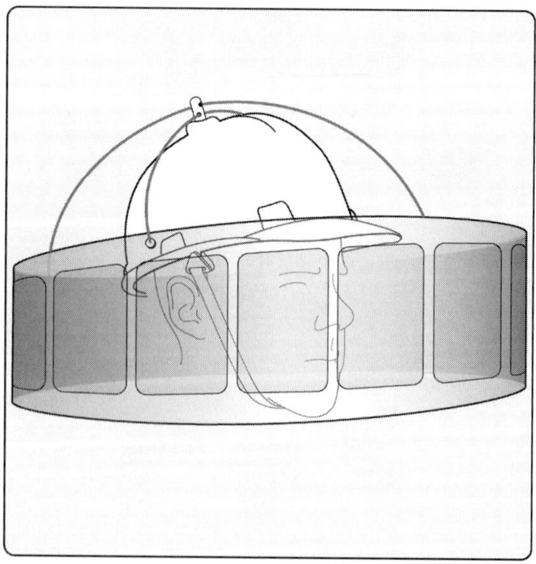

FIGURE 3–30 Helmet-mounted 360-degree panorama of accident site. *Source:* Jessica Weiss.

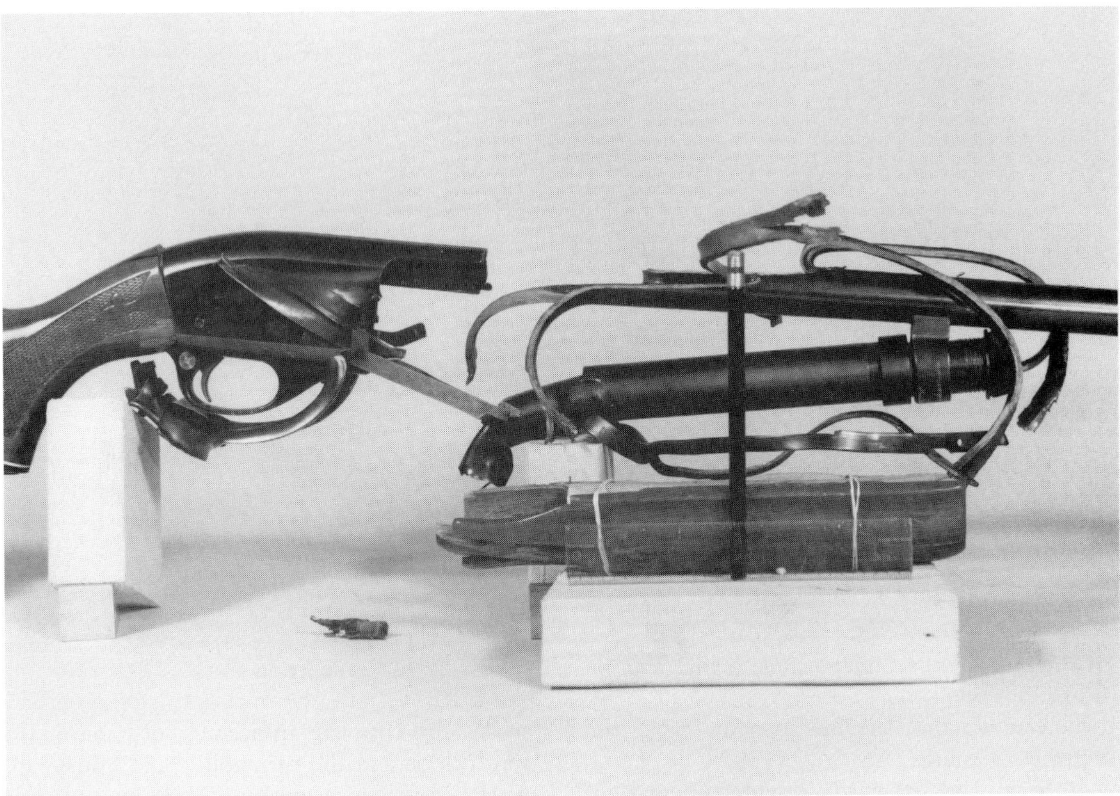

FIGURE 3–31 The exploded shotgun. *Source:* Sandy Weiss/Packer Engineering.

tion of the fracture surfaces in the scanning electron microscope showed no unusual faults in the metal, and the accident was attributed to an improperly loaded shell.

CASE STUDY

CRANE FAILURE

Early one snowy, windy, winter morning, a phone call was received informing of a crane failure in the middle of the Loop in downtown Chicago. Traffic was snarled for miles after police blocked the street where part of the evidence had landed. The police wanted an investigative team on site immediately to document the artifacts in situ so the street could be reopened for rush-hour traffic (see Fig. 3–32). Two engineers, a technologist, and a photographer were dispatched in all possible haste.

Upon arrival, we found that the accident scene was distributed into three distinct zones. Pieces of the crane were located across the street, in the street, hanging onto the front of the building, and on the highest existing (ninth) floor of the building under construction. Everything was covered with snow.

The priority was obvious: the parts in the street had to be documented and moved so the traffic could flow normally. The police allowed us 30 minutes to accomplish what we needed to do. Knowing that an accident reconstruction would be needed, it was important to determine a location for each of the pieces. We made drawings and took measurements. We took photographs of the pieces as they were found and before they were moved. We took more detailed photographs of each piece after all were shipped back to the lab.

The fractured bolts from the turntable were the hardest items to find. The catastrophic failure of that part of the crane launched the head and body sections of most of the bolts to places beyond where our search could cover. Most were never found. That made it doubly important to document the fracture surfaces of the parts of the bolts remaining in the turntable. It was possible

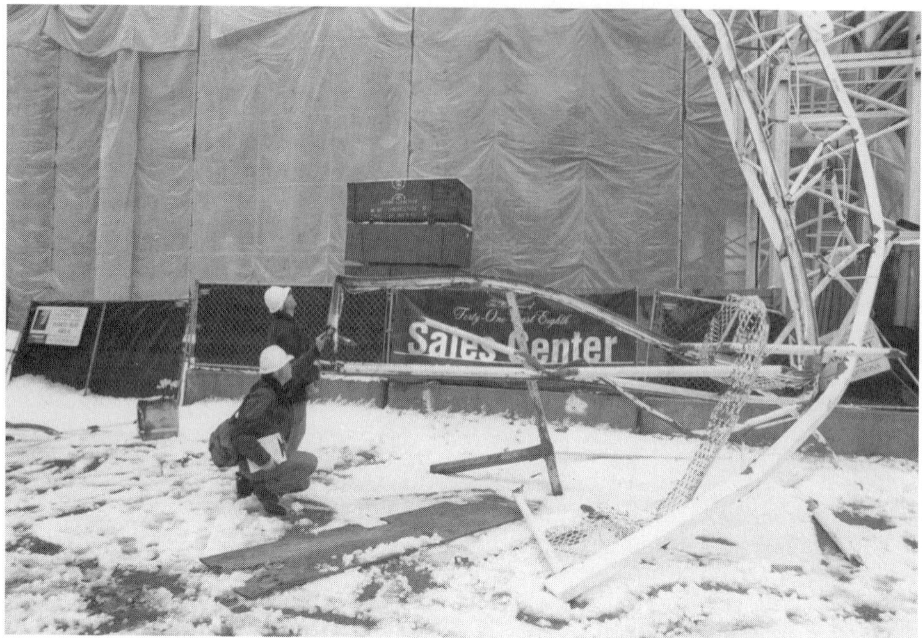

FIGURE 3–32 Inspecting the crane failure. *Source:* Sandy Weiss/Packer Engineering.

to determine from the fractures the type and sequence of failure.

From the street, on-site documentation moved to the top of the ninth floor. All the photographic equipment had to be carried up manually because the building had not yet been fitted with a working elevator. The turntable had landed upside down on the concrete surface, had broken through it, and was perched at about a 45-degree angle, with fracture surfaces underneath. The concrete surface was not stable on the ninth floor and the turntable could not be approached for close-up study. A telephoto macro lens had to be used to acquire any usable images.

A total of 36 fractured bolts had to be documented in the field before the turntable was moved, in case any of the bolts were lost or damaged when the turntable was lifted out by another crane.

The hardest part of the project was dealing with snowmelt on the surface of the metal. The

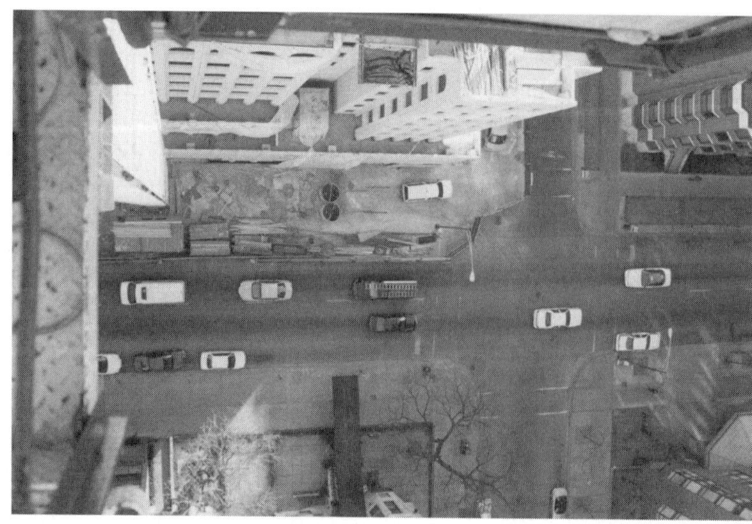

FIGURE 3–33 View from the ninth floor and down to the street. *Source:* Sandy Weiss/Packer Engineering.

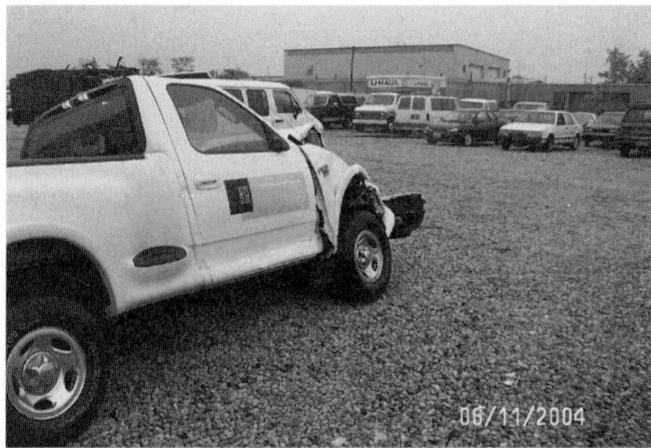

FIGURE 3–34 Adjuster photos. *Source:* Packer Engineering.

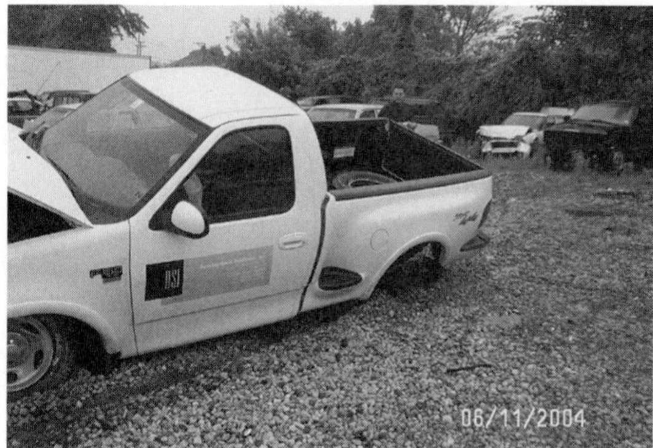

FIGURE 3–35 Adjuster photos. *Source:* Packer Engineering.

temperature had gone above freezing, as can be seen in the photo taken from the ninth floor and down to the street (see Fig. 3–33).

A great deal of water dripped from the turntable and interfered with the photo equipment. In addition, a lot of rubble on the eighth floor was in the way, and so it became a project in itself to set up for every one of the fracture photos. Many needed to be shot off mirrors. Many fractures were recessed into the metal of the turntable. In most of the photos, the photographer had to be on his back, in the rubble, in the dripping water, and in an overall dangerous environment.

The boom was not photographed in detail until it was removed from the edge of the building.

The fracture surfaces of the bolts were the most important evidence for telling the story of this accident visually. It would have been much easier to expose the images early, before the snow started to melt, but triage of the accident had prevented the photographs from being taken in the most expeditious manner. As long as the whole story was told, however, the documentation was a success.

It is not always possible to take all photographs in what would be considered a logical order. It is also not possible for the photographer to have the subject of the documentation brought to a place with a controlled environment and lighting. This type of work is very difficult and requires the photographer to be ingenious and flexible. It is also extremely important to carry a go-kit with enough gadgets so you can create complex documentation with what you have—not just what you may be able to get if you have time.

CASE STUDY

INSURANCE ADJUSTER

Packer received six photographs (See Figures 3–34 through 3–39) from a company that wanted us to determine if the wheel fell off the truck and

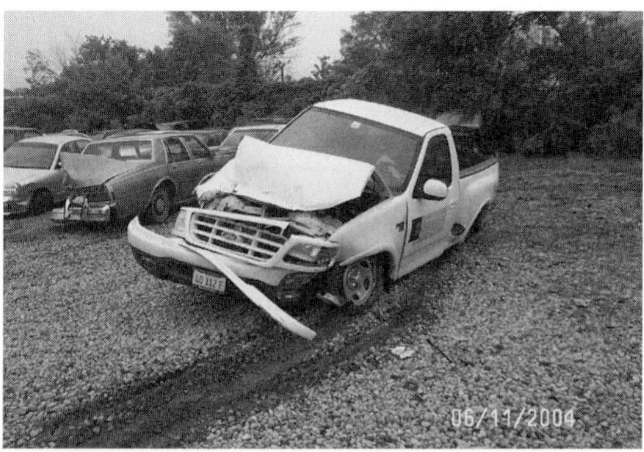

FIGURE 3–36 Adjuster photos. *Source:* Packer Engineering.

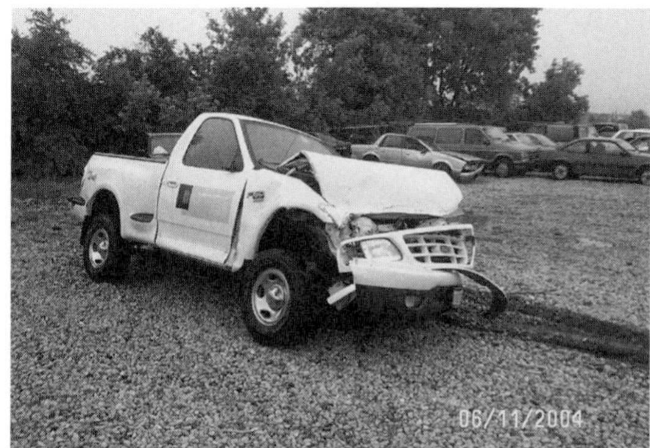

FIGURE 3–37 Adjuster photos. *Source:* Packer Engineering.

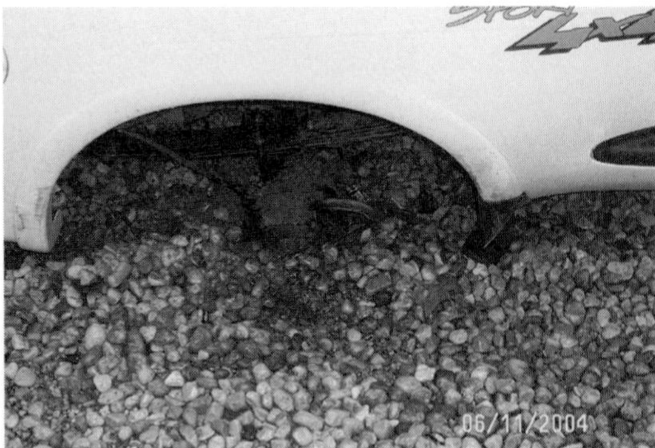

FIGURE 3–38 Adjuster photos. *Source:* Packer Engineering.

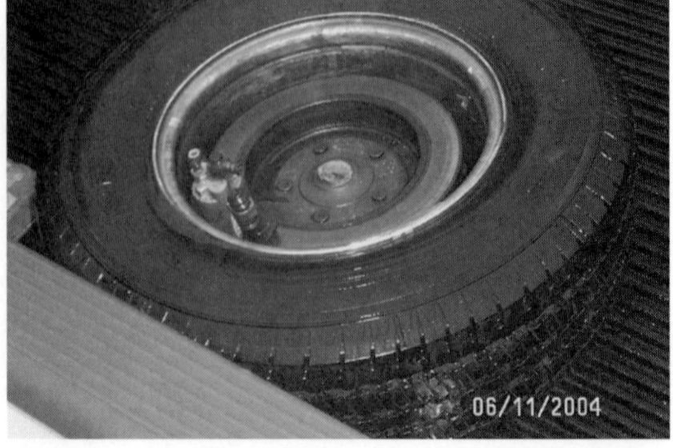

FIGURE 3–39 Adjuster photos. *Source:* Packer Engineering.

caused the accident or if the accident caused the wheel to fall off the truck.

It had been a while since the accident and the truck had been crushed and removed. The adjuster did not make a detailed study of the axle fracture, and no notes about its appearance were available. The police photos were of no further help.

In this case, the adjuster thought the photos that were taken were sufficient to document the state of the vehicle after the accident. They were certainly enough to substantiate the decision to call the truck a total loss, but they were not sufficient to tell the story of how the accident occurred and in what sequence the damages were sustained.

This misassumption provides a perfect example of how an inexperienced photographer can tell a visual story of an investigation but not tell enough to allow the viewer to form an opinion.

KEY TERMS

visual communications, (p. 68)
presentation of reality, (p. 68)
limitations of speech, (p. 70)
CSI effect, (p. 70)
Locard's exchange principle, (p. 71)
fragmentary evidence, (p. 71)
visual storytelling, (p. 72)
scientific method, (p. 72)
induction, (p. 72)
junk science, (p. 73)
reproducibility, (p. 74)
scientific documentation, (p. 74)
failure analysis, (p. 78)
fractography, (p. 80)
ductile fracture, (p. 80)
brittle fracture, (p. 80)
chevron, (p. 80)
beach mark, (p. 81)
photographic storytelling, (p. 90)

EXERCISES

1. Design and create a visual story in as few images as possible of an object or situation. When completed, allow someone to tell you what he or she thinks the story tells. If he or she does not understand the story correctly, add to or change the images until he or she can.
2. Compare the visual storytelling tasks necessary to document the ball bearing example and the World Trade Center project, and discuss their similarities and differences.
3. Pick a Pulitzer Prize–winning image of the last few decades and explain why that single image was strong enough to convey to the world the story the photographer was trying to tell.

Chapter 4

Photogrammetry

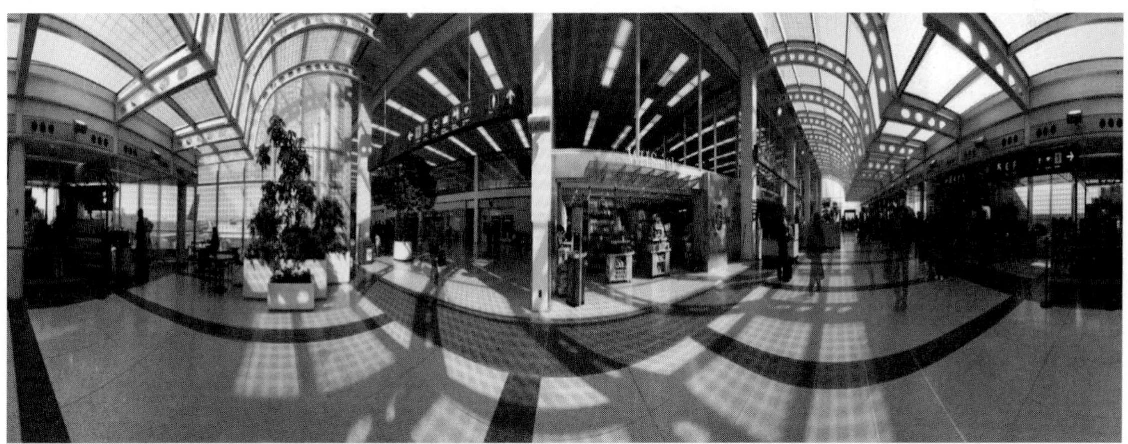

Learning Objectives

AFTER STUDYING THIS CHAPTER, YOU SHOULD BE ABLE TO:

1. Understand the necessity and usefulness of a photogrammetric examination
2. Understand the different types of photogrammetry
3. Recognize the various types of data-gathering tools for a photogrammetric project
4. Understand perspective and to be able to use its properties to derive measurements from basic photographs
5. Be familiar with various software used for photogrammetric analysis when the available photographs contain the necessary information
6. Recognize the different types of modern photographic hardware used to document images with directly readable dimensions
7. Recognize the types of projects to which photogrammetric analysis may be applied

PHOTOGRAMMETRY

Photogrammetry, as defined by Paul Wolf in his book entitled *Elements of Photogrammetry*, is "the art, science and technology of obtaining reliable information about physical objects and the environment through processes of recording, measuring and interpreting photographic images."[1] As the name implies, photogrammetry is a three-dimensional coordinate-measuring technique that uses photographs as the fundamental medium for **metrology.** Photography describes the photographic principles involved in photogrammetry, while metrology describes the techniques for producing three-dimensional coordinates from two-dimensional photographs.

To reconstruct an accident or crime, it is often necessary to make a map of the scene.[2] For example, sometimes a measurement was not made at the time of an occurrence and the investigator needs to know how long a skid mark is so the speed of an approaching vehicle can be calculated. Sometimes it is critical to calculate the distance between a gun and the hand of a body. Sometimes all the necessary photographs exist and just the data are missing. Sometimes not enough photographs exist and more have to be taken to ensure a successful study.

Of course, many sources of data are used to produce a scene map. Some of the normal sources include the following:

- Verbal reports of on-site investigators
- Measurements from field notes
- Roadway or building construction plans
- Published dimensions
- Photographs

Checking the accuracy of all input is of critical importance. It is not a good idea to assume that all input data are correct. Under stress, investigators have been known to document things incorrectly or incompletely. Even if the occurrence took place years before, it is often possible to go back and gather quantitative data at the scene if the original documentation was complete enough to place the contemporary investigator correctly into the universe.

With the power of current computer technology, even photographs that were not taken properly will yield invaluable data to the trained analyst for a precise **photogrammetric examination.** Information that went unnoticed or was not intended to be documented is contained in the photographs, and those images become the only source of information that can be utilized in a reconstruction.

The two distinct types of photogrammetry are (1) metric photogrammetry, involving precise measurements and computations to determine sizes and shapes of objects, and (2) interpretative photogrammetry, involving the recognition and identification of objects. Metric photogrammetry includes applications for (a) aerial photogrammetry and the generation of aerial maps, and (b) terrestrial (close-range) photogrammetry and the generation of ground-to-ground measurements and **orthogonal (right angle) maps.**

Architects, civil engineers, and archaeologists use photogrammetric techniques for construction, excavation, deviation, and deviation from plans. Accident reconstructionists and law enforcement personnel use photogrammetry to document and quantify accident and crime scenes. Gathering photogrammetric data is one of the most important tasks of forensic photography.

Photogrammetric Practice, Tools, and Techniques

If a person wishes to perform photogrammetry the way it has been done for over a century, the following information must be established.

A photographic image (subject) is, for photogrammetric purposes, considered a **central perspective.** Every **light ray** passing through or bouncing off the subject before reaching the image receptor passes through the camera lens during exposure. In this case, the lens is mathematically considered to be a single point: the image/perspective center. To take measurements of objects from the photograph, the pertinent light rays must be quantified.

The internal geometry of the camera must be precisely known, including the following:

- *The lens focal length*, also called the **principal distance,** which is the distance of the projection center from the image plane's **principal point** (the location in the camera where the optical axis of the lens intersects the image receptor)
- *Position of the principal point*, which is the projection of the point of sight upon the image plane
- *Total lens distortion* (barrel or pincushion)

As the reader can see, the old-fashioned way is daunting.

PHOTOGRAPHIC DEVICES

Fortunately, it is no longer necessary to learn this technology the old-fashioned way. If the images for a photogrammetric project are properly gathered, software programs can be used to perform the mathematics. First, it is wise to be familiar with the equipment necessary to expose the images.

Metric Cameras

Metric cameras (see Fig. 4–1), by design and construction, have stable and precisely known internal geometries and minimal lens **distortion.** The principal distance is constant, which means that the lens cannot be focused when taking photographs. As a result, metric cameras are only usable within the limited range of distances from the camera to the object, which is determined by the depth of field. The image coordinate system (object data) is defined by **fiducial marks,** which are permanent markings within the frame of the camera. (The marks also appear on the photographs because the film is held against the glass plate with the marks during exposure.) **Terrestrial cameras** are often used with theodolites (for example, a **total station,** a combination electronic transit and electronic distance-measuring device) to extract base measurements from which to derive unknown dimensions. A transit is an instrument used by a surveyor to derive measurements of landforms for map-making. With a total station, as with a transit and tape, the operator can determine angles and distances from the instrument to points being surveyed. With the aid of trigonometry, the angles and distances can be used to calculate the actual 3-D positions in space using the x, y, and z coordinates of surveyed points.

A standard transit is basically a telescope with crosshairs for sighting a target; the telescope is

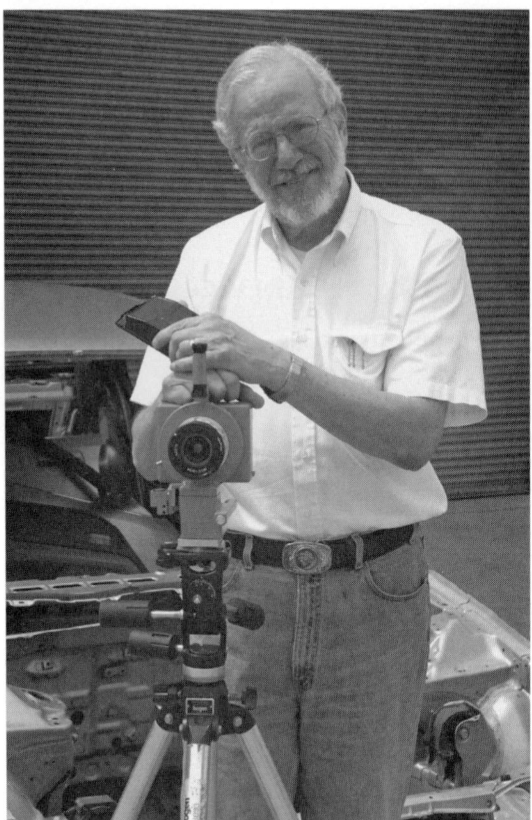

FIGURE 4–1 Author and Wild metric terrestrial camera. *Source:* Karl Fliehler/Packer Engineering.

attached to scales for measuring the angle of rotation of the telescope (normally relative to north as 0 degrees) and the angle of inclination of the telescope (relative to the horizontal as 0 degrees). After rotating the telescope to aim at a target, one may read the angle of rotation and the angle of inclination from a scale. An electronic transit provides a digital readout of those angles instead of resorting to a scale. The other part of a total station—the electronic distance measuring device or EDM—measures the distance from the instrument to its target.

Stereometric Cameras

If an object is photographed from two different positions, the distance between the two projection centers is called the **base.** If both photographs have viewing directions that are parallel to each other and in a right angle (theoretically) to the base, then they have properties similar to those of the two images perceived by a human's eyes. Therefore, the overlapping area of these two photographs (a **stereo-pair**) can be viewed in 3-D, simulating stereoscopic vision. In practice, a stereo-pair can be produced with a single camera by exposing images from two distinct (and proper) positions or by using a stereo camera. (See Chapter 8)

Normal Cameras

In a **normal camera,** the internal geometry is not stable and is unknown, as is the case with any commercially available film or digital camera. By photographing a test field with multiple control points, at a fixed distance setting (for example, at infinity), any necessary calibration of the camera can be calculated.

PHOTOGRAMMETRIC TECHNIQUES

Mapping from a single photograph can be accurately accomplished if sufficient known values (control points) exist. The photo must be clear and sharp to yield dimensions with accuracy. Single photographs are also useful for **reverse photogrammetry** (Inverse Camera), where sufficient measurable points exist in both the photograph and current reality. This procedure is explained elsewhere in this chapter.

Recommended Software

PhotoModeler Pro is a Windows-based software program from Eos Systems. It makes possible the creation of accurate, high-quality 3-D models and measurements from photographs. The new release, PhotoModeler Pro 5, offers fully automated camera calibration, support for a variety of file export formats, enhanced photo texturing, and multimedia tutorials for learning to use PhotoModeler more efficiently.

PhotoModeler Pro also has features for extracting data from a single photograph. The features work well even when the camera type or model is unknown, making it useful for forensic applications and accident scene reconstruction.

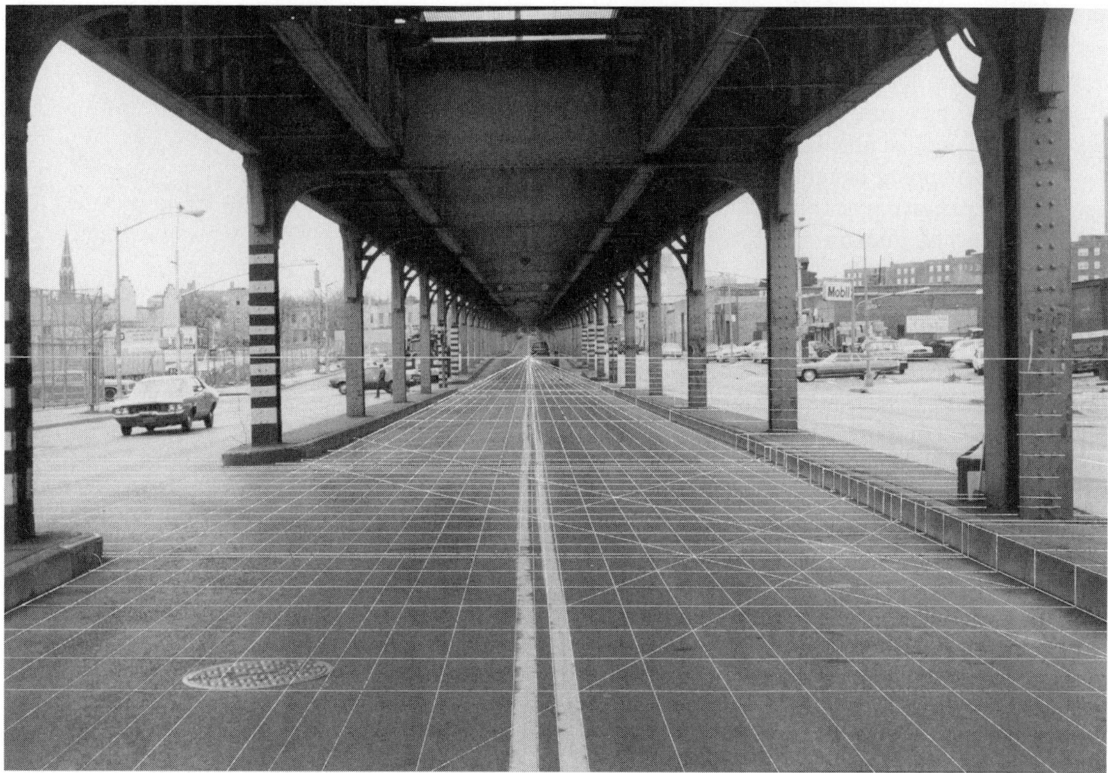

FIGURE 4–2 Perspective grid inscribed on photograph and used to derive measurements from a known scale: in this case, the man hole cover. *Source:* Sandy Weiss/Packer Engineering.

Perspective

Due to the effects of perspective, it is not possible to extract measurements of 3-D objects directly by taking measurements from 2-D photographs. Near objects appear larger than far objects in the image, even when they are actually the same size. An ordinary 2-D photo can be used to extract 3-D information by changing the perspective to an **orthogonal view.**

In each 2-D photograph, it should be possible to find a measurement that is known or that can be very closely approximated. In Fig. 4–2 the width of the man hole cover in the left foreground was used as the known. If there is nothing in the photo that can be quantified, it may be possible to go back to the scene and procure a useful dimension.

Using the known dimensions and the vanishing point, of which there should be at least one in any photo, grid lines can be drawn to cover the areas of interest in the image. Objects can then be placed within the grid lines in a plan view (overhead) to rectify the perspective effect and create a 2-D view from which it is simple to extract fairly accurate map data.

When only one vanishing point is available in a photograph and only one photo is being used, it may be easier to do a simple perspective analysis than an Inverse Camera analysis with PhotoModeler.

Stereo Photogrammetry

In **stereo photogrammetry,** stereo-pairs are used as input data. If a single camera is used, two photographs are made from different positions, in an attempt to match the conditions of human vision. Vertical aerial photographs are an example. They are made using metric cameras that are built into airplanes, and their aspect, by definition, looks straight down. While taking such photographs, the airplane flies over a certain area in a specific way, so the whole area is covered by overlapping photographs. The overlapping part of each stereo-pair can be viewed in 3-D and consequently mapped in 3-D.

Digital mapping assigns each picture element (pixel) a known position and measured intensity value. The dimensions are gathered for quantitative information.

Mapping from Several Photographs

Plotting in 3-D can be done with multiple photographs and a computer. The 3-D objects are photographed from several positions around them, with a chosen object point visible on at least two, and hopefully three or more, distinct photographs.

Using known control points and triangulation points, the geometry of the whole group of photographs can be reconstructed with high precision. Then the image coordinates of any desired object point measured in at least two photographs can be intersected. The results are the coordinates of the required points. In this way, a 3-D object can be digitally reconstructed.

Using PhotoModeler Software

Using the PhotoModeler software, one or more views of the object are captured as an image on film or on a digital image sensor (see Figs. 4–3, 4–4, 4–5, and 4–6) re-marked and referenced as a, b, c, and so on at distinct features on the object.

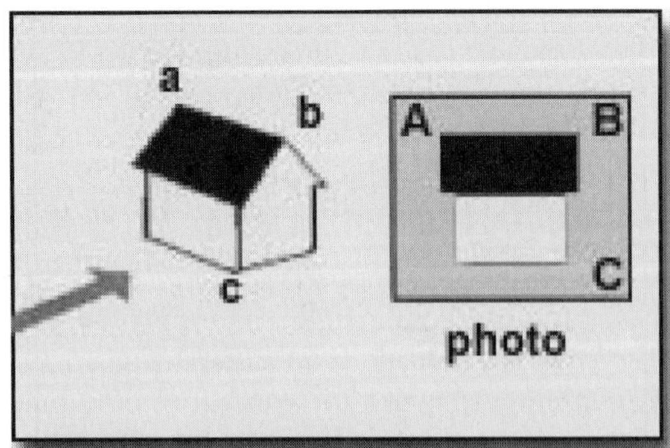

FIGURE 4–3 PhotoModeler is used to calculate the position of the camera station for each photo. *Source:* Image courtesy of EOS Systems, Inc.

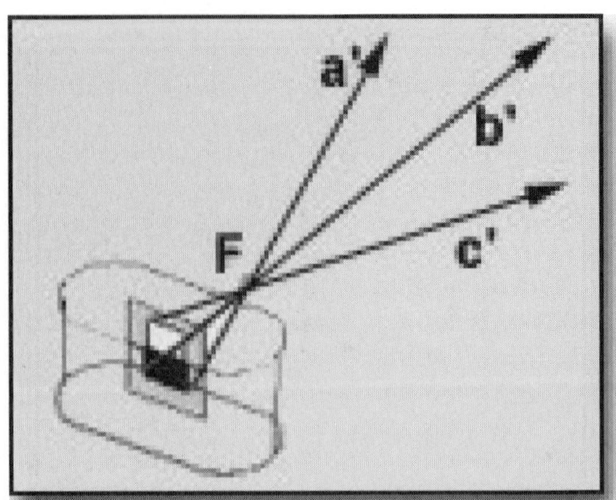

FIGURE 4–4 PhotoModeler is used to calculate the intersection of light rays from each photo position and out into 3-D space. *Source:* Image courtesy of EOS Systems, Inc.

Crime Scene Measurement with PhotoModeler

It is best to include every point of the subject in at least two photographs to produce a project with good accuracy. It is even better to include

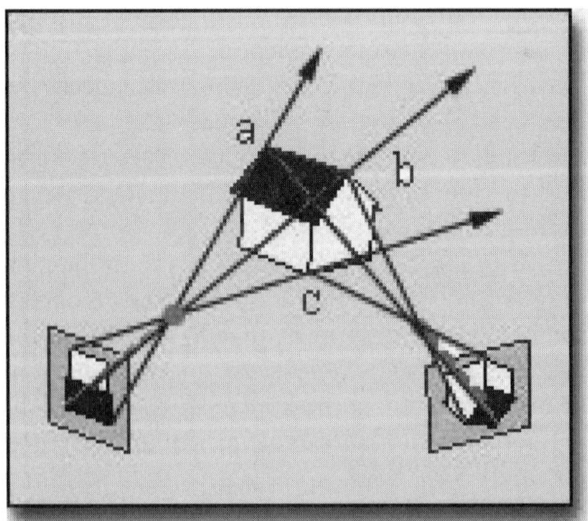

FIGURE 4–5 By using multiple photographs, the whole object or scene can be captured. *Source:* Image courtesy of EOS Systems, Inc.

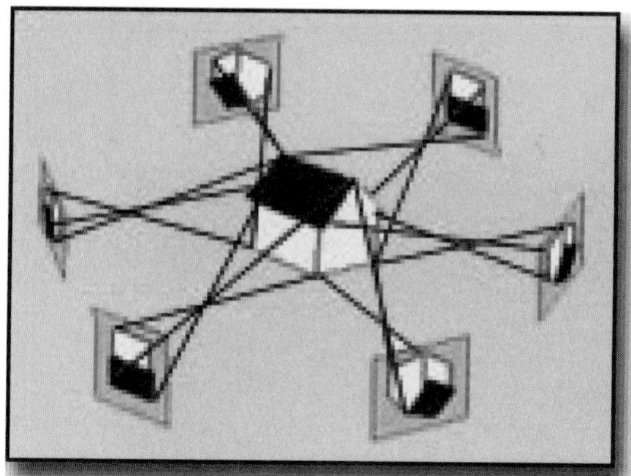

FIGURE 4–6 Multiple views of the object are captured as an image on film or on a digital image sensor. *Source:* Image courtesy of EOS Systems, Inc.

every point in at least three photographs (see Figs. 4–5 and 4–6) The more shared points used in the project, the higher the degree of accuracy yielded in the final solution.

PhotoModeler may also be used for diagramming a crime or accident scene where the only remaining evidence is a single photograph or video frame. With PhotoModeler's tools designed for this work, measurements can be extracted long after the evidence within a scene has been collected and removed (see Fig. 4–7).

The parameters of this camera were not known so it was necessary to use the **Inverse Camera** process (See Fig. 4–8).

When the project was solved, the camera parameters (including its position, angles, and focal length) were solved along with the positions of the lines in 3-D space. Additional detail was then added to the model using **Surfaces and Surface Draw.** After adding scale to the model, it was ready for measurement and for export to a diagramming package, such as Crime Zone, for further enhancement.

Using Inverse Camera

PhotoModeler can often be used to model objects and/or scenes from a single photograph. Strict requirements apply though, and many photographs cannot be used.

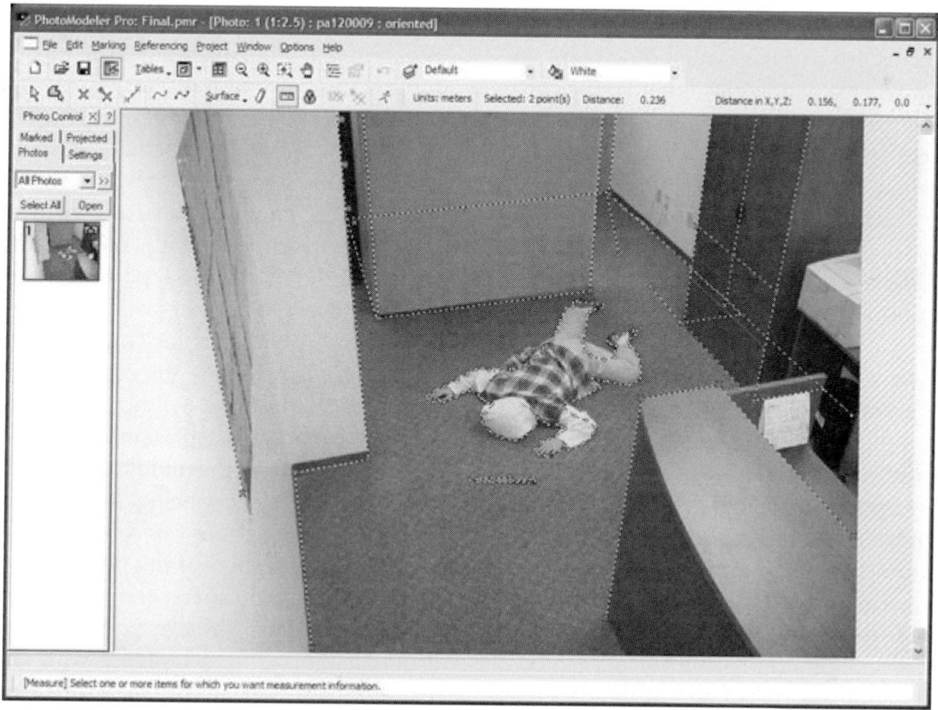

FIGURE 4–7 A single image from a surveillance camera was used for this crime scene project. *Source:* Image courtesy of EOS Systems, Inc.

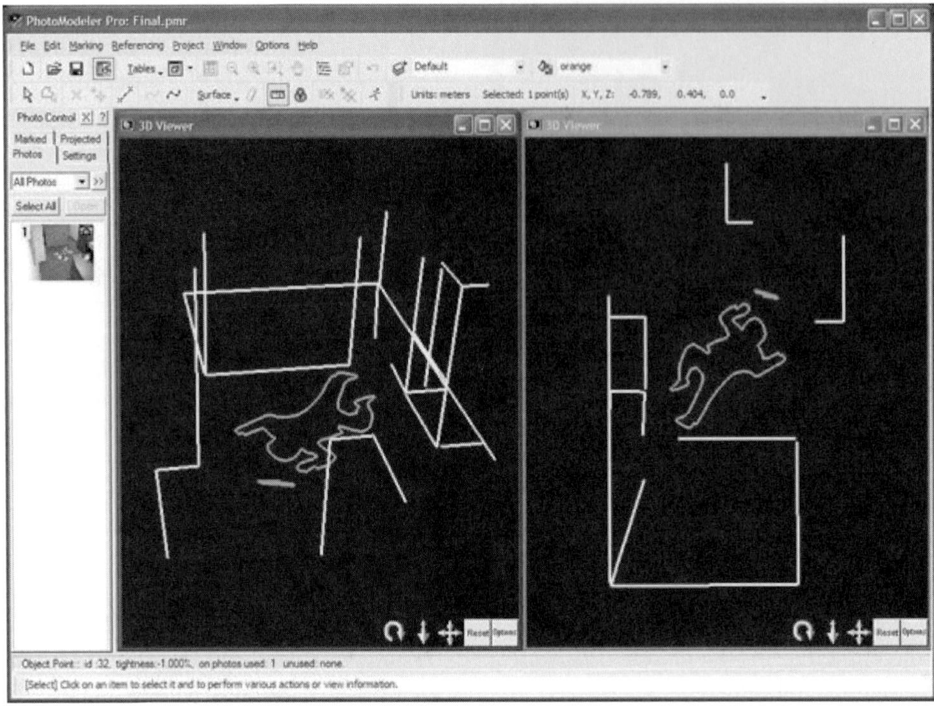

FIGURE 4–8 This is a crime scene diagram created using the Inverse Camera function of PhotoModeler. *Source:* Image courtesy of EOS Systems, Inc.

In the fields of forensics and archaeology, measurements from unknown photographs are often required. These unknown photographs may come from archives, historical files, police, bystanders, and so on. In such cases, little or nothing is known about the camera used to create the photographs. PhotoModeler normally requires information about the camera (focal length, principal point, and format size) before photographs taken with it can be used. PhotoModeler's Inverse Camera feature overcomes this problem.

To use Inverse Camera, some information about the scene or object is required. This information is called a **constraint.** Inverse Camera can use known 3-D points or **axes constraints.** When some points or shapes in the photographs are known but the information necessary for the investigation is not, PhotoModeler can calculate what is needed. For example, it may be necessary to determine the relative position of two cars that appear in several photographs from an unknown camera. The dimensions of one of the cars may be known but the dimensions of the other car, or their relative positions, are not. Inverse Camera is executed using constraints, the most common form being **control points.**

If axes constraints are used, the photo must have the correct perspective. With axes constraints, it is possible to solve for the lens focal length if the photo has a strong **two- or three-point perspective,** and it is possible to solve for focal length and principal point if the photo has a strong three-point perspective. A single-point perspective photo has just one vanishing point and the horizon is near the center of the photo.

Inverse Camera will not work for a single-perspective photo, such as one in which the photographer stood in the middle of a pair of railroad tracks, took a photo looking down the tracks, and the tracks in the photo vanish in the distance to a point near the center of the photo.

A two-point perspective photo has two vanishing points. A photo exposed at 45 degrees from the corner of a building with the camera parallel to the ground plane (which makes the vertical edges of the building appear vertical in

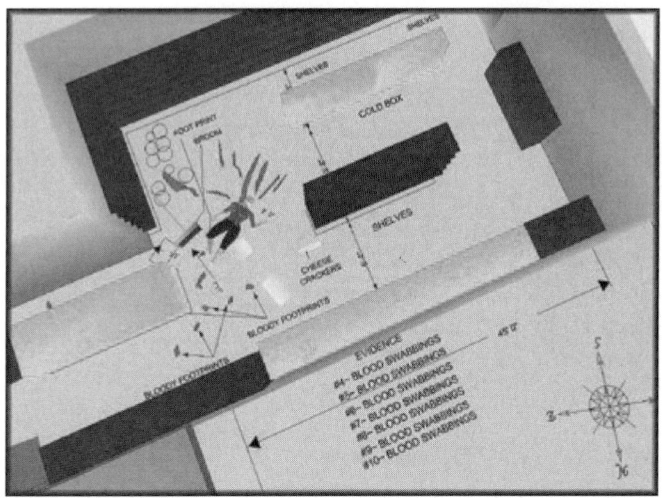

FIGURE 4–9 Crime Zone software–generated scene diagram. *Source:* Images published with permission of The CAD Zone, Inc.

the photo) is a two-point perspective photo. If the perspective is strong enough, PhotoModeler can solve for the camera position and focal length. The operator would mark two sets of lines or edges and set up two axes constraints.

A three-point perspective photo has three vanishing points. A photo taken at 45 degrees to the corner of a building with the camera pointed toward the top of the building (which makes the vertical edges of the building appear to vanish to a point near the top of the photo) is a three-point perspective photo. If the perspective is strong enough, PhotoModeler can solve for the camera position, focal length, and principal point for this photo. The operator would mark three sets of lines or edges and set up three axes constraints.

Using Crime Zone Software

Crime Zone (Version 8) software is for investigators needing to create 2-D and 3-D crime scene diagrams. It creates accurate, realistic, 3-D views of any scene ideal for courtroom presentations. Thousands of predrawn symbols are included, and its Symbol Manager feature helps users find the right symbol and place it perfectly.

Among other Crime Zone tools are Body Poser for exactly posing body symbols and Easy Builder for automatically drawing complex floor plans.

Crime Zone (Version 8) also allows users to do the following (see Figs. 4–9 and 4–10):

- Use Easy Tools for drawing complex intersections, streets, and buildings
- Select predrawn symbols and intersection templates
- Draw 3-D surfaces and bullet trajectories, calculate slopes, place symbols on slopes, assign exact heights, generate profiles
- Enter measurements in the Coordinate Data Entry Table
- Import and export AutoCAD .dwg and .dxf files

Using MapScenes PRO Software

MapScenes Pro 2006 is forensic mapping software. It provides law enforcement professionals and accident reconstruction specialists with precise, compelling, and irrefutable evidence through the production of scaled diagrams that can be used in court.

Evidence collected at a crash or crime scene is entered as data into the MapScenes Evidence Recorder software. Using these products ensures accurate diagrams that enable investigators to testify on specific conditions and effects of an incident.

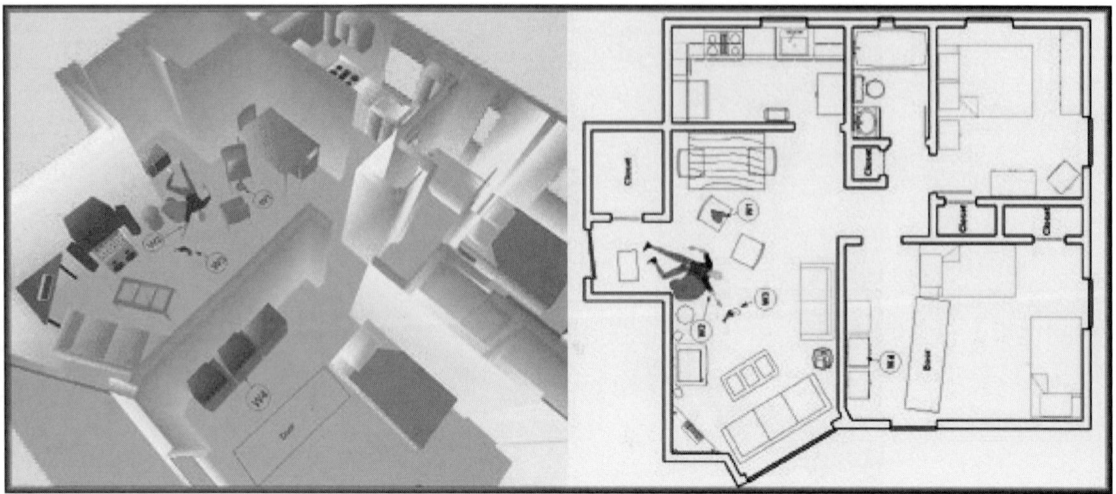

FIGURE 4–10 Crime Zone software–generated floor plan. *Source:* Images published with permission of The CAD Zone, Inc.

Accident Reconstruction with PhotoModeler

The accident reconstruction project presented here demonstrates PhotoModeler's ability to produce accurate crush measurements by comparing a damaged vehicle against an undamaged vehicle. The screenshot in Fig. 4–11 shows two cropped photographs of a crushed 1997 Toyota Corolla.

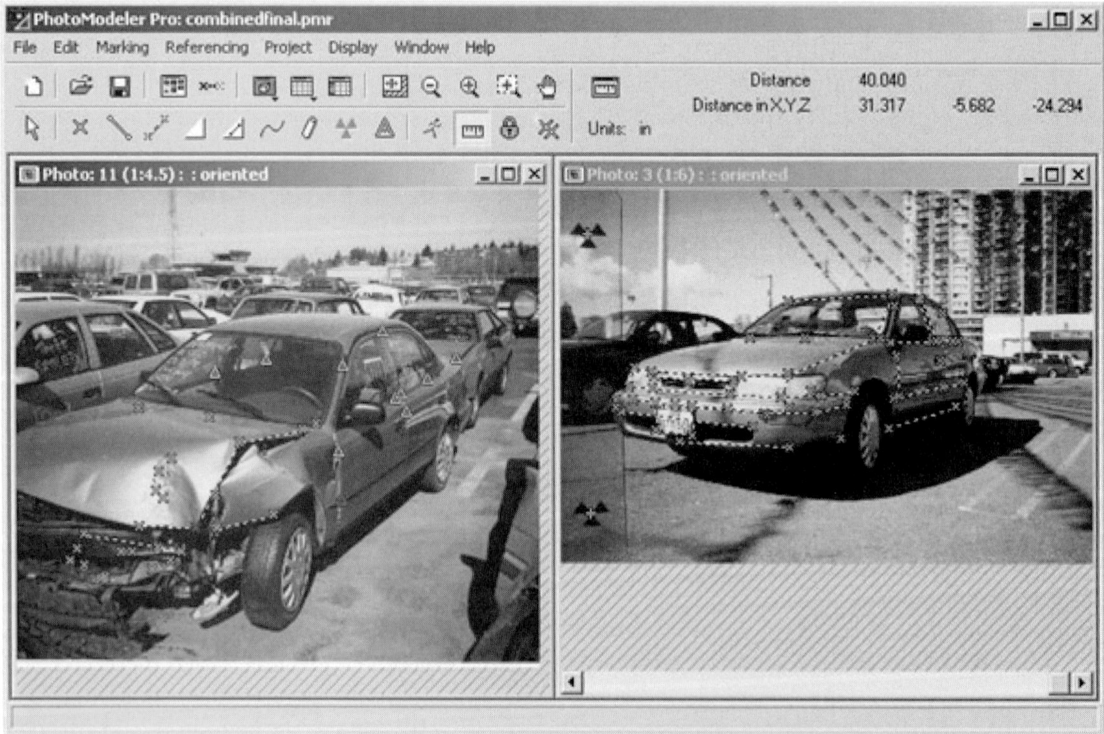

FIGURE 4–11 Two cropped photographs of a crushed 1997 Toyota Corolla. *Source:* Image courtesy of EOS Systems, Inc.

Using an exemplar undamaged vehicle, photos were exposed using a calibrated camera. PhotoModeler was then used to model the exemplar vehicle, paying special attention to the area around the front bumper. To help link the two computer models, special attention was paid to the undamaged areas of the crushed-vehicle.

Using the exemplar vehicle model, PhotoModeler's **Point Properties** feature was used to freeze the 3-D points on the exemplar model as control points. Then the crushed vehicle images were imported into the same project and set for Inverse Camera processing in PhotoModeler. Then points were marked and referenced from the exemplar vehicle to matching points on the crushed vehicle photos. Next Inverse Camera was performed, the images were oriented, and marking was continued on the crushed vehicle images. To complete the project, distance and comparison measurements were used to calculate crush displacements. These measurements were all made within PhotoModeler, thus eliminating the need for an external CAD program.

Skid Mark Mapping Project with PhotoModeler

The skid mark mapping project presented here demonstrates PhotoModeler's ability to extract information from a single photo of a skid mark from an unknown source. Using only a photo (see Fig. 4–12) and some control points, the length and shape of the skid mark were measured.

The first step in this project was to gather some known 3-D information from the existing scene that also appeared in the photo. The scene was surveyed to generate control point information. Then control points were marked on the single photo, and Inverse Camera, which uses the control points to determine the characteristics of the unknown camera, was performed. These control points were not on the skid mark itself as the skid mark would normally be gone by the time of the survey. Instead, the control points were on features that existed in the photo and the scene as it stood when the photo was taken, with emphasis on extracting the surface of the road. Items such as divider lines, sidewalk

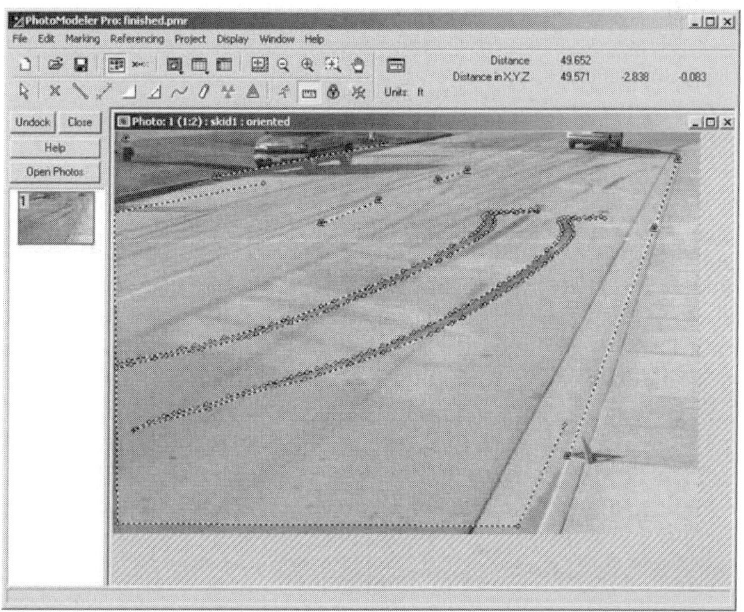

FIGURE 4–12 Note the skid marks in this photo. *Source:* Image courtesy of EOS Systems, Inc.

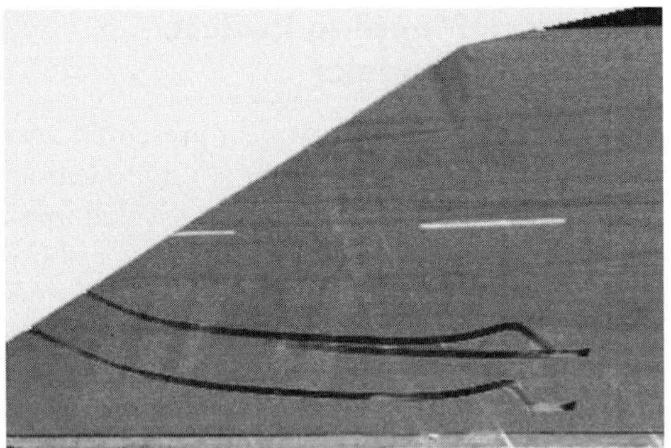

FIGURE 4–13 Skid marks represented in an orthographic view. *Source:* Image courtesy of EOS Systems, Inc.

cracks, and road or street signs are typically used for control points.

With the camera parameters determined, work on the project continued. Various control points were connected by using Surface Draw, another feature of the software. Surface Draw was also used to trace the shape of the skid mark. It allowed the surface of an oriented photo to be marked properly, and 3-D point locations were then calculated. This enabled calculation of the length of the skid marks using PhotoModeler's Measure Tool.

The final step of this project involved exporting the surface information as an **orthographic photo** (see Fig. 4–13). PhotoModeler's Ortho Photo Export removes perspective and shape distortion from an image. This allows an image to be made of the true shape of the skid mark.

Using Panoscan Software

Panoscan Inc. manufactures fast digital panoramic cameras. Their unique, rotating camera scans 360 degree images in a single pass so no image stitching is required. The images are high in resolution and dynamic range. The captured images can be viewed as flat panoramas or as virtual reality movies using players like Apple QuickTime VR. Scanning allows instant viewing with no post-processing (see Fig. 4–14).

Panoscan software contains an accurate application for measuring panoramic images.

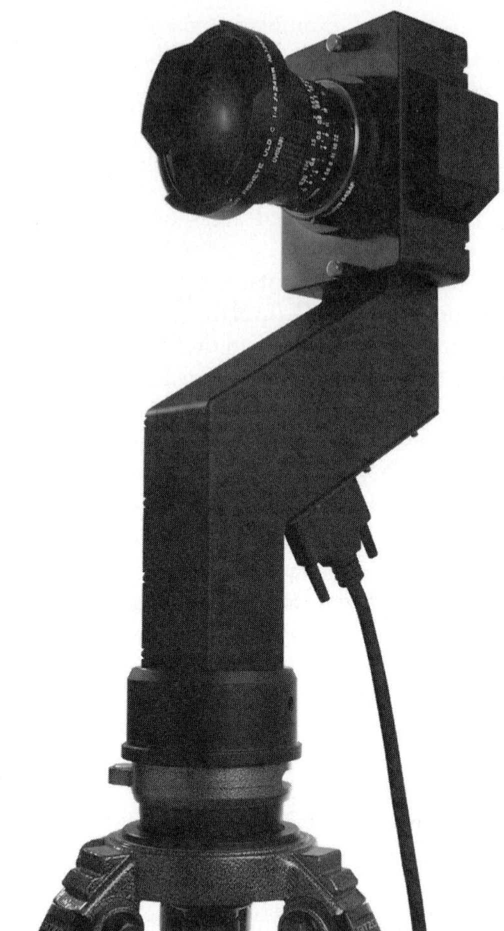

FIGURE 4–14 Panoscan panoramic camera. *Source:* Panoscan.

PanoMetric software allows users to take accurate measurements from panoramic images of any scene, indoors or outdoors.

To create a metric panorama (see Fig. 4–15), the camera is set up on a special tripod and two panoramas are scanned (see Fig. 4–16). Next, the images are processed to ensure geometric accuracy. To conclude the process, the images are loaded into PanoMetric to be measured. The user simply points to any pixel in the scene and accurate distance and spatial data will be displayed. Point-to-point measurement is easy and accurate.

Once the points and measurements have been collected, the results can be saved in DXF

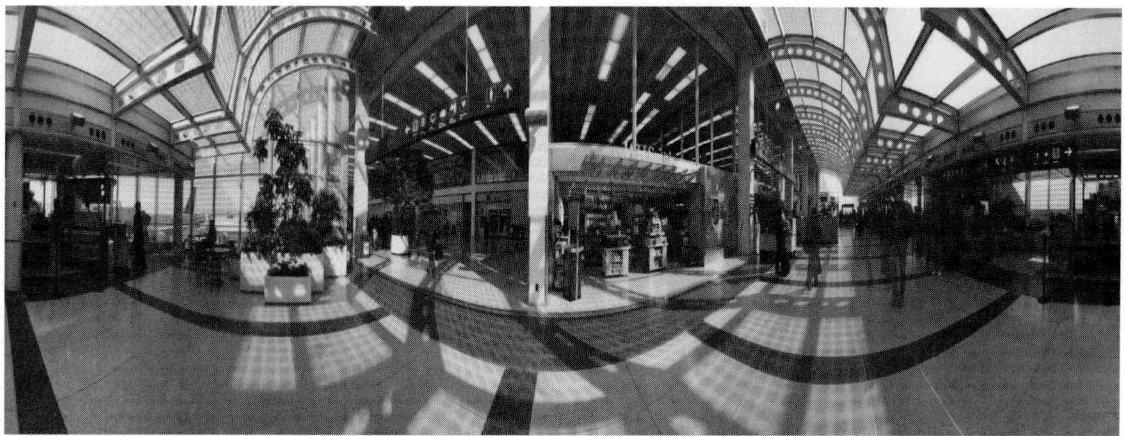

FIGURE 4–15 A panoramic image of an airport concourse. *Source:* Sandy Weiss/Packer Engineering.

format for use with popular CAD programs and 3-D modeling applications such as Cad Zone, AutoCAD, Maya, Lightwave 3-D, and such.

PanoMetric is accurate to fractions of an inch over a 25-foot radius. The high resolution and repeatability that are achievable with the Panoscan system supply excellent accuracy to spatial measurement. Since the PanoMetric application is based on image data, measurements of surface details, such as skid marks or blood spatter, can be measured accurately where laser scanners may be less useful.

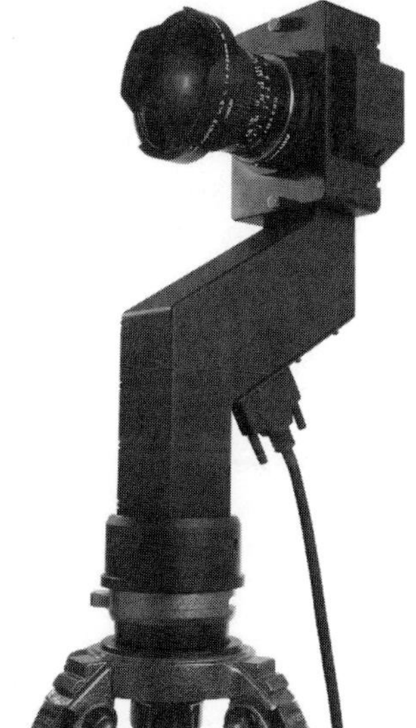

FIGURE 4–16 PanoMetric camera setup. *Source:* PanoScan.

An entire 360-degree scene can be captured in the field and brought to the lab for measurements. New measurements can be added at any time, and users need not return to the scene to take more measurements.

Laser Scanning

Of course, a **laser scanner** is the ultimate data-gathering tool for the extraction of 3-D data from a site or an object. Major factors in **digitization** of an accident or incident scene are the speed and quality of the scan. Digitization in mapping is the process of encoding geographic features in digital form as x, y, and z coordinates. The process involves the use of a digitizer to encode the locations of geographic features by converting their map positions to a series of x, y, and z coordinates stored in computer files.

Many users now utilize *line-of-sight* scanning devices. New laser scanners using phase shift technology (see Fig. 4–17) are exponentially faster than traditional *time-of-flight* scanners. The speed of point capture is 120,000 points per second, compared to time-of-flight technology at only 4,000 points per second.

The scanning device documents the necessary area as **point cloud data.** The scanner recognizes the shade of a reflective surface and builds a 360-degree point cloud with grey scale

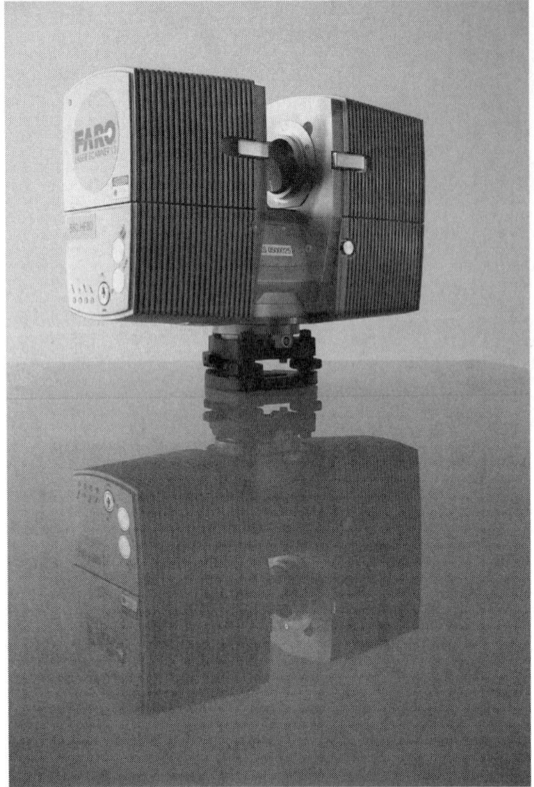

FIGURE 4–17 Faro phase shift laser scanner. *Source:* Photo courtesy FARO Technologies, Inc. © 2007.

(see Figs. 4–18 and 4–19), which results in a black-and-white image similar to a 3-D photograph. This gives the user perspective that cannot be achieved through conventional methods, such as traditional digital photography. With year 2007 updates, the scanner images can also be combined with full-color digital images to produce color point cloud data.

Line-of-sight laser scanners do not interfere with the object being scanned, making them ideal for evidence preservation at the scene of the accident or incident. They can be used indoors and outdoors, during day or night, with little concern for weather and lighting conditions.

When using a camera and total station or theodolite for data gathering, the investigator must know exactly what must be documented, and he or she must record the precise information at the time of documentation. Fortunately, the line-of-sight scanner documents all of this automatically. Unfortunately, most people do not have a laser scanner in their go-kit. Lacking this state-of-the-art technology, use of a camera as a data input device allows the capture of extensive detail in a short time, and that is what is necessary in investigations.

The FARO LS880 laser scanner is a medium-range, phase-shift type of scanner, capable of 120,000 line-of-sight measurements per second. It can scan a typical room with 7 to 8 million data points in 60 seconds. Its practical range is approximately 100 feet, with a maximum of 200 feet in certain situations. Due to the unit's construction, however, the only segment that cannot be scanned from a single location is a 12-degree cone below the scanner, (under the tripod) which is due to the unit's construction. Entire coverage of objects blocked by other objects can be accomplished by moving the scanner to different locations and connecting together the scans. Larger areas are may be scanned using the same leapfrog method.

A 3-D point cloud is generated and exported to CAD programs for analysis or to surface modeling packages for the construction of 3-D models. Along with the actual data, a black-and-white representative image is created to help identify objects in the point cloud.

Examples of representative projects that can be accomplished with a laser scan include the following:

1. *Instant response to railroad accident scenes.* Scanning is an effective way to preserve evidence that might be overlooked or unavailable at a later date. Line of sight is a major concern for such accidents. By scanning the scene, details such as trees and building locations, condition, and size can be preserved.
2. *Scanning vehicles for deformation used for accident reconstruction.* This process preserves deformation for energy and directionality calculations. It is possible to compare exemplar vehicles to subject vehicles to evaluate, for example, any twisting of door openings that might have caused door unlatching during a rollover. Scanning the interior of a vehicle for roof crush also is possible

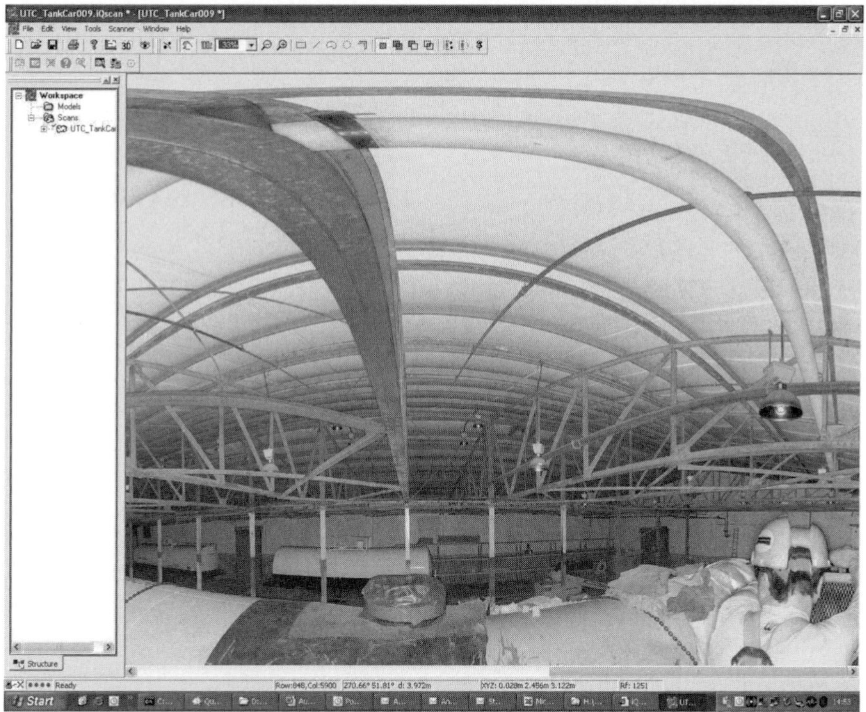

FIGURE 4–18 Point cloud data constructed into a gray scale image. *Source:* Photo courtesy FARO Technologies, Inc. © 2007.

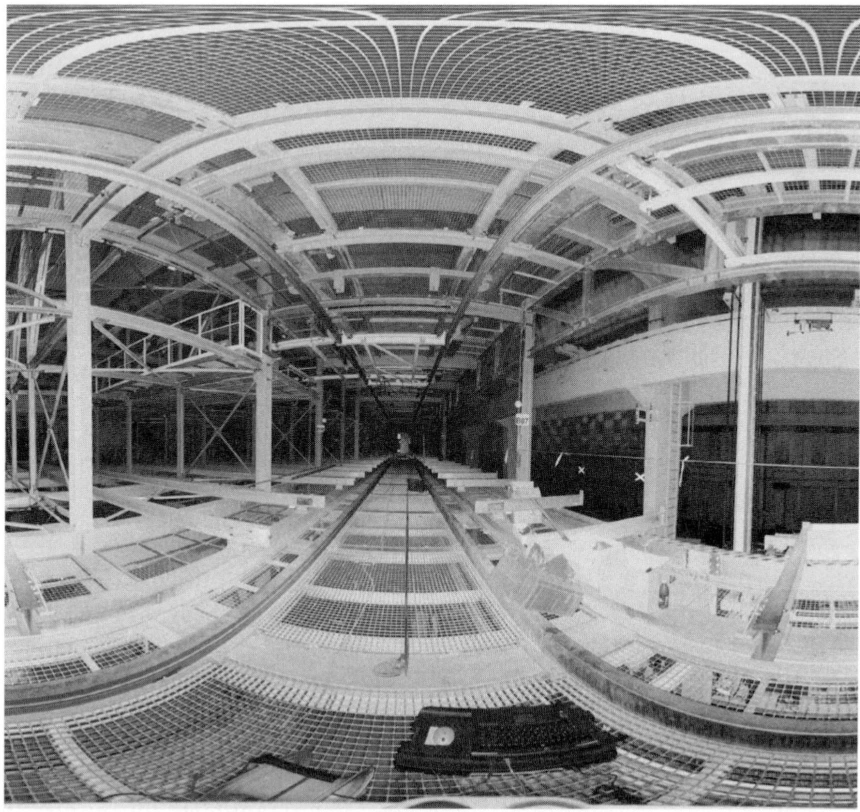

FIGURE 4–19 Point cloud data constructed into a gray scale image. *Source:* Photo courtesy FARO Technologies, Inc. © 2007.

because the scanner can scan in any position, including upside down. In one application, a fuel tank was scanned to determine its volume after it was crushed in a two-vehicle accident.

3. *Scanning large buildings for permanent records of their existing condition, and using the data for future improvements.* In one application, the building was a cast-in-place concrete structure for which no as-built drawings were available. New windows needed to be designed to fit all the existing window openings, and a scan provide the necessary measurements.
4. *Documenting the debris field at a power plant explosion.* A scanner can document much faster than a total station. Days can be saved, and objects that might be missed can be measured at a later time.
5. *Documenting fire damage and smoke patterns.* The scanner captures smoke patterns by measuring the reflectivity of the objects, as well as their positions in space.

SUMMARY

It is often necessary to extract measurements from existing photographs or to make photographs with the express purpose of extracting dimensions. In all cases, the higher the resolution of the images, the more the known data, the higher the accuracy of the derived measurements. Both film and digital image capture cameras are appropriate for use in such photogrammetric projects.

Modern hardware solutions are available for almost every type of photogrammetric project, if the time and budget are available to get them on site. If existing or multipurpose images are to be used, modern software packages are available that can diminish how much mathematics the analyst must know to perform the work.

However, hardware and software by no means diminish the amount of training and skill the analyst must have to be able to gather accurate data. In addition, the limitations of the project must be recognized before work begins so that disappointment and unneeded expenditures may be avoided.

CASE STUDY

CLOSE-RANGE PHOTOGRAMMETRIC ASSIGNMENT IN A SUBMARINE

Retrofitting nuclear submarines is an endeavor the U.S. navy undertakes with regularity. When the navy redecorates with new bulkheads, it uses three-inch-thick steel plate that must be cut to size and then fit into the appropriate locations within the ships. The locations that the bulkheads fit into can be very irregular in shape. A multitude of pipes and other surface-mounted structures must be accommodated. When the steel is cut too small, it must be scrapped, which costs a great deal of time and money, and the process must begin again from scratch. When the steel is cut too large, crews of grinders must resize the piece laboriously until it fits into the opening. This operation can take a crew many days to complete. In an attempt to find a better way to cut the bulkheads to the right size the first time, the navy hired Packer Engineering to devise a solution.

The particular submarine at issue was in dry dock in Charleston Naval Shipyards, South Carolina. The boat was not only receiving a new bulkhead but also was being outfitted with two 40-ton diesel generators intended to be backups to the nuclear reactor. Packer's project was to supply dimensional data for the new bulkhead that could then be fed into a computerized torch that would cut the steel plate to the perfect size to fit the opening. We also supplied a map of the bolt posts that had to be installed in the floor of the generator room to fit the holes in the bottoms of the generators.

The requirements of this project could have been accomplished in an assortment of ways, but only one of the ways would work under the imposed time constraints. We were allowed only one 16-hour day to obtain all of the required images necessary to derive measurements. We could not be on the base before 8:00 A.M., and we had to be off the base by midnight, due to naval regulations. The bulkhead location was deep inside the ship, below too many decks and through too many hatches to bring in any kind of lift. The ceiling was too high to use a digitizing arm, portable coordinate-measuring machine for data acquisition without building a scaffold. The bulkhead location was very irregular in shape and

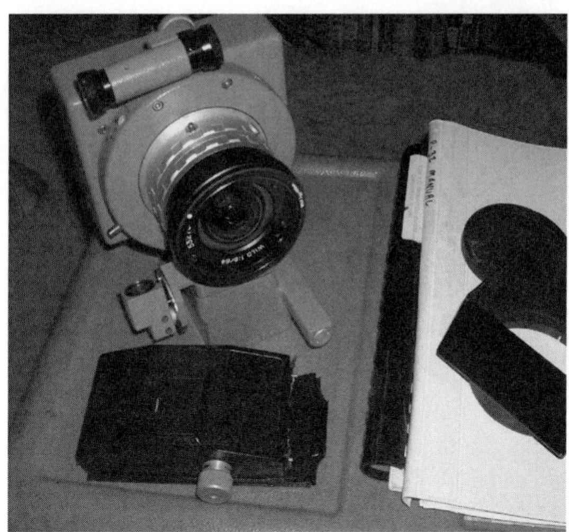

FIGURE 4–20 Wild-Heerbrugg P-32 terrestrial metric camera. *Source:* Sandy Weiss/ Packer Engineering.

would require too many sightings with a total station to acquire enough information to use it as the only means of data acquisition. A laser scanner would have been a good choice but was not available at the time of the project. We decided to solve the problem photogrammetrically.

For this project, we used a Wild-Heerbrugg P-32 terrestrial metric camera (see Fig. 4–20). This camera uses 120 roll film and flattens the film against a glass plate at the time of exposure. The glass plate has six fiducial reference marks etched into it. These cameras were distributed in North America, until recently, by Leica. Leica has now ceased distribution, but the cameras can still be rented from some large surveying companies. The only comparable camera currently sold in the United States is the Rolleiflex 6008, whose metric has a number of advantages over the Wild, including interchangeable lenses, through-the-lens metering, motor drive, and an 11 × 11 built-in grid plate (Reseau plate). The Rolleiflex is, however, a 6 × 6 cm format, while the Wild is a 6 × 9 cm format. For the ultimate in measuring precision, we use the older camera with the larger format. For more information about the Rolleiflex 6008 and the new Rollei digital metric cameras, log onto the Rollei web site at www.rollei.com.

We used Kodak technical pan film for the ultimate in both sharpness and contrast. To shoot the intended bulkhead location, we first had to grind, stripe, and target the entire circumference (see Fig. 4–21). Then we brought in four 1,200-watt photoflood reflectors so that we would have enough light to shoot at a small aperture setting. We had to shoot at a distance closer than the minimum focusing requirements of the camera and rely on depth of field to supply the required sharpness. We used a total station to record sufficient reference control points, some of which would be contained in each of the photographic images. We then shot sufficient overlapping stereo pairs to cover the whole opening into which the bulkhead was to fit.

After shooting the required photos inside the ship, we went on shore to a nearby hangar-type building where the generators to be installed were located. To shoot photos of the holes in the bottom of the generators, the naval personnel hoisted one of the generators up to the roof of the hangar, where it was held steadily while the camera was positioned on the floor below and pointed straight up (see Fig. 4–22). This would have been a scary undertaking under the best of conditions but was scarier yet when we learned the crane that was lifting the generator was rated for only 30 tons. Luckily, the cables held and we only had to take photos of one unit because the two generators were identical.

The navy requires that all film shot at its classified installations be processed and inspected before leaving the base. We knew this before leaving our lab and brought along a portable darkroom and set it up in the men's locker room. We had a changing bag, developing tank, developer, fixer, and alcohol for drying the film. The film was developed in Kodak Technidol. The pressure to have the film developed successfully was intense. A crew of 11 naval personnel awaited the results with the generator still hoisted in the air. The film came out perfectly, and the generator was lowered to the ground without mishap.

Back at our office, the data were compiled. Highly trained specialists performed the data acquisition task, using an analytical stereo compiler to extract the necessary data directly from the negatives. They converted radial angle and distance measurements to the XYZ 3-D Cartesian coordinates associated with each control point in the stereo model. They were able then to successfully interpolate the unknown points that we

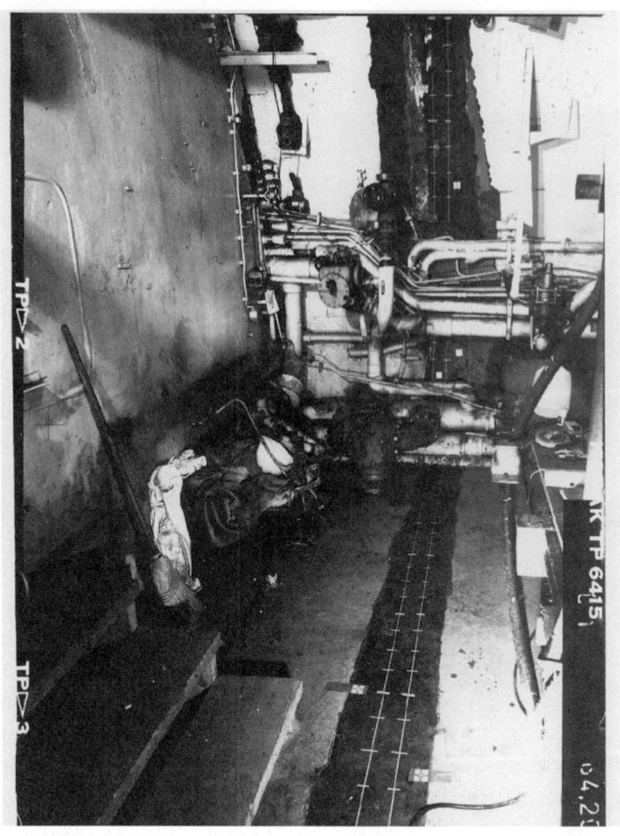

FIGURE 4–21 Inside submarine; ground and striped bulkhead location. *Source:* Sandy Weiss/Packer Engineering.

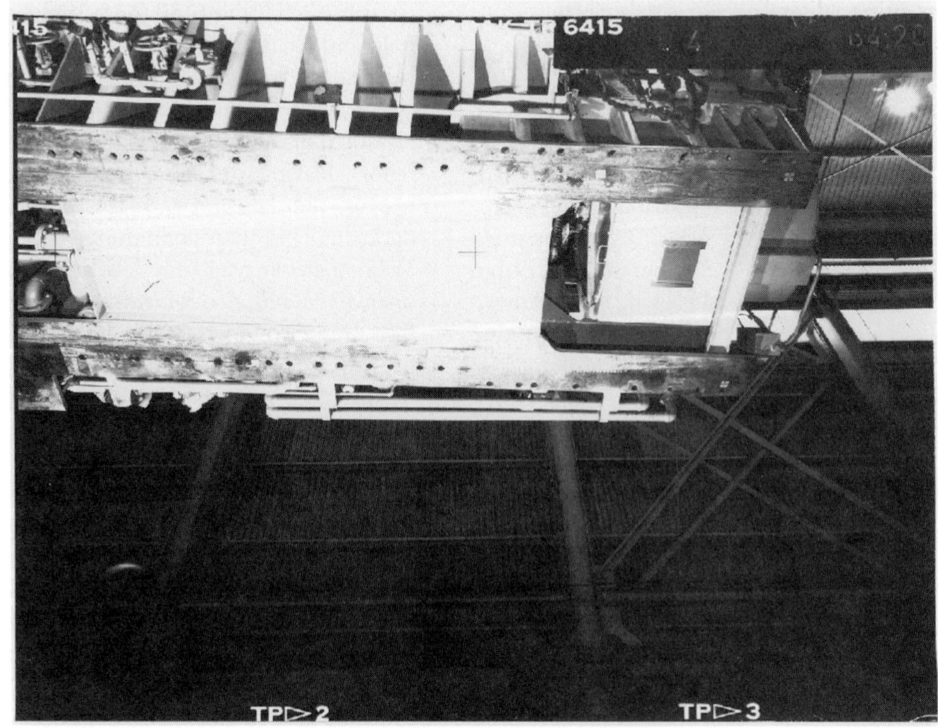

FIGURE 4–22 Under 40-ton generator. *Source:* Sandy Weiss/Packer Engineering.

did not have time to physically measure and to develop data from the internal geometry of the camera and the measured control points.

Software solutions also could have been applied to this aspect of the project. For example, PhotoModeler can be used for data acquisition from photogrammetric images. PhotoModeler utilizes a wide variety of photographs, from any type of camera, and supplies dimensions of the visualized subject. The accuracy of the measurements obtained is directly proportional to the type of camera used to take the photographs and the skill of the person doing the work. The person using a compiler should be highly skilled and well trained if the resultant measurements are to be accurate. The average accuracy obtainable with a 35 mm or small digital camera is in the range of 1:1700 of the object size, and with a P32 is 1:6500 of the object size. In the case of the submarine project, the required accuracy could have been achieved using either size of camera system. (For more information on PhotoModeler, consult the Web site at www.photomodeler.com.)

Considering that the negatives from the P32 needed to be digitized to be used by the software, using a digital camera for data acquisition is possible and advisable. Eos Systems recognizes this as a viable option but warns that the resultant measurements might suffer in accuracy if the resolution of the digital camera is insufficient. The use of proper targets on the subject will help to foster the accuracy of measurements.

The finished product for both the bulkhead and the generator base was a mathematical model of 3-D space with dimensions accurate to less than one-eighth of an inch. This degree of error was within the parameters specified by the navy. The mathematical model was then transferred to Pro-Engineer software by way of a DXF file. The computerized torch used for cutting out the bulkhead had a CAD-generated map capability. The project was successful, and the navy adopted this protocol for similar applications.

A version of this case study first appeared in the *EPIC Journal: The Official Publication of the Evidence Photographers International Council* (Honesdale, PA), Spring/Summer 2000: 15–17. The study was authored and edited by Sandy Weiss.

CASE STUDY

PHOTOMODELER

The accident presented in this case study occurred on a rural roadway, and no eyewitnesses were identified to testify about the accident scenario (see Fig. 4–23). Only the skid marks

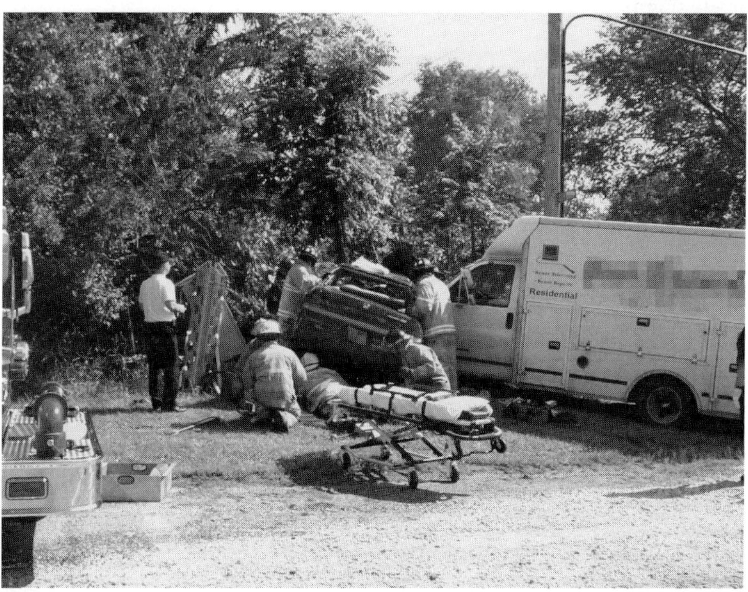

FIGURE 4–23 PhotoModeler accident reconstruction project. *Source:* Tom Bundorf/Packer Engineering.

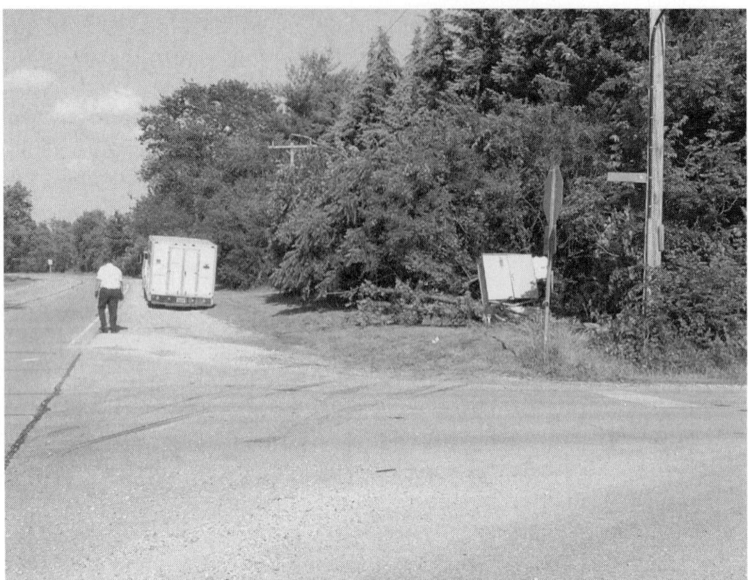

FIGURE 4–24 Subject accident scene. *Source:* Tom Bundorf/Packer Engineering.

on the roadway and the crush damages to the vehicles were available to determine impact speeds and which driver was the cause of the crash.

The driver of the red car was coming out onto the state highway from a road controlled by a stop sign (see Fig. 4–24). The panel truck did not have to stop or yield and had a speed limit of 55 miles per hour.

The questions to be answered were these:

- What were the pre-impact trajectories of the vehicles?
- What was the area of impact?
- What were the post-impact trajectories?
- Could the car have reached the speed at which impact occurred if it had stopped at the sign and then progressed into the intersection?
- Was the truck traveling in excess of the speed limit?

Using the photographs provided by the police and a number of landmarks (see Figs. 4–25 and 4–26) surveyed after the accident by a team with a total station, an orthogonal map (see Fig. 4–27) was prepared and the impact speeds were determined. It was concluded that in no way could the car have reached impact speed had it stopped at the sign prior to the accident (see Fig. 4–28).

CASE STUDY

REVERSE PHOTOGRAMMETRY

A railroad company retained a photographer/engineer two years after a collision involving its train. The plaintiff (the motorist) alleged that a large pile of dirt, deposited by the railroad near its tracks, blocked his view of an approaching train, causing him to be struck by the train while attempting to cross the intersection. The defendant (the railroad) countered that the plaintiff should have seen the train's headlight, which was indicative of an approaching train.

The task was to render a view of the scene as it would have appeared to a motorist stopped at the grade crossing on that date, just at that moment, when deciding if it was safe to proceed into the intersection.

THE BACKGROUND

Ballast cleaning is a routine maintenance task for the railroad. A machine gathers ballast from the track bed, separates it from accumulated dirt

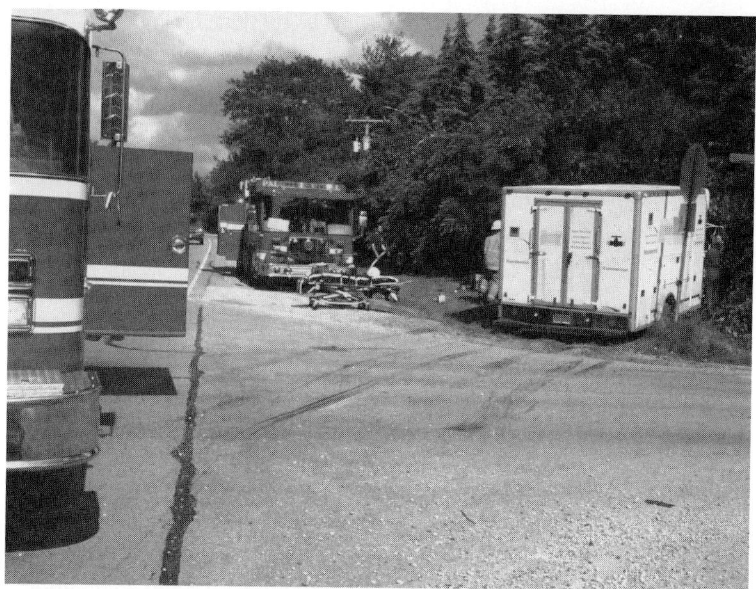

FIGURE 4–25 Skid marks left on the roadway. *Source:* Tom Bundorf/Packer Engineering.

and mud, returns the cleaned ballast to the track bed, and conveys the waste material to gondola cars. The waste material is taken to a location where it is stored until it can be transported to a proper waste disposal station. Unfortunately, the location the defendant chose to store the pile of refuse was in the line of sight of motorists using this particular grade crossing.

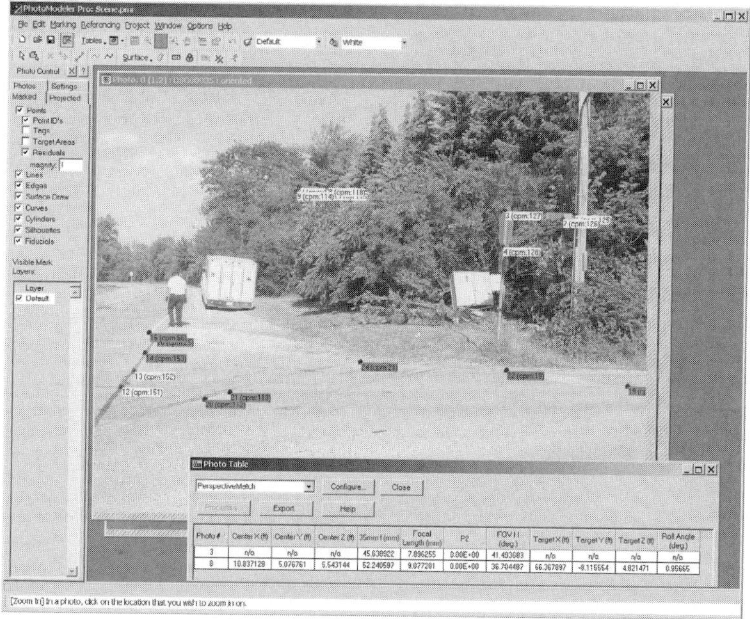

FIGURE 4–26 PhotoModeler screen grab. *Source:* Tom Bundorf/Packer Engineering.

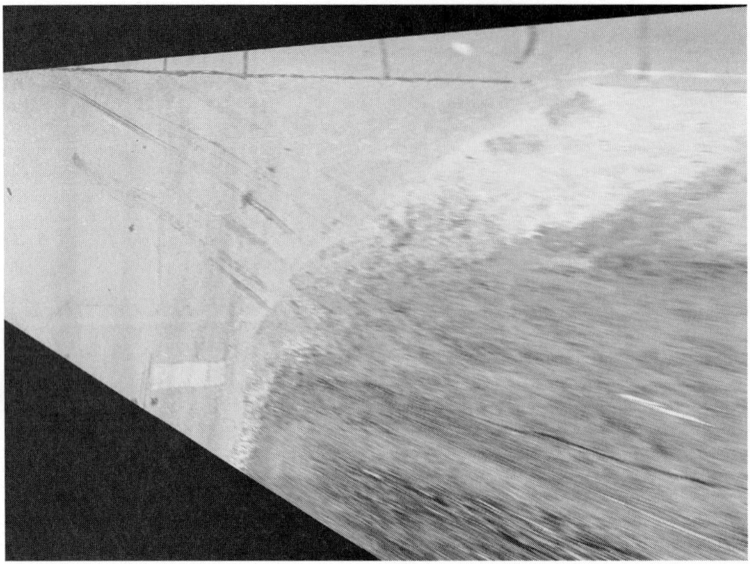

FIGURE 4–27 Orthogonal map of skid marks. *Source:* Tom Bundorf/Packer Engineering.

THE FACTS

The defendant furnished fact data from multiple sources, including police investigation records, eyewitness accounts, and, post-event photographs taken at the time of the collision. Among the post-event photos was one of the dirt pile taken from about 20 feet east of the nearest rail of track.

The 20-foot distance was a good choice for the photo. Motorists are required to yield at a crossbuck sign, with the words "RAILROAD" and "CROSSING" in black and white assembled in a large × configuration, at the grade crossing. If a motorist must stop his or her vehicle to determine that a railroad grade crossing intersection can be entered safely, the motorist must stop not less than 15 feet from the nearest rail of track. Allowing 5 to 8 feet for driver setback from the front bumper, a driver stopped 15 feet from the track is actually viewing the intersection from a point 20 to 23 feet from the nearest track.

From furnished data, the primary collision scenario and vehicle dynamics were computed to place the train in relation to any position the plaintiff's vehicle occupied during the last few moments

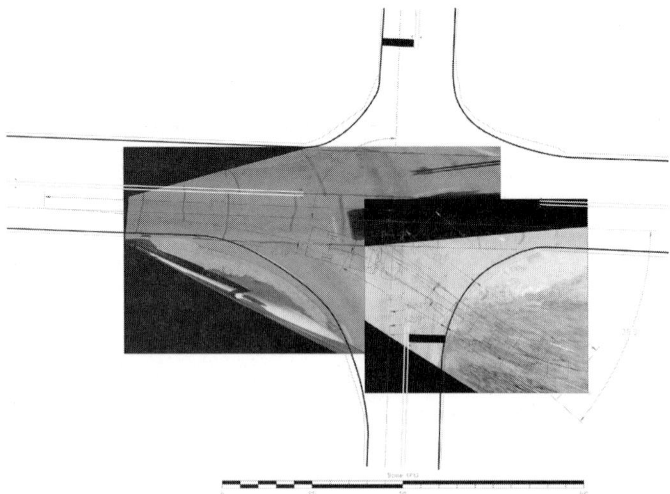

FIGURE 4–28 PhotoModeler mapping image. *Source:* Tom Bundorf/Packer Engineering.

before collision. The plaintiff testified that he stopped about 15 feet east of the tracks to look and listen for a train, then accelerated past the crossbuck sign to enter the intersection. When the plaintiff made his decision to go, a freight train moving 38 miles per hour was about 300 feet south of the intersection and approaching at constant speed.

THE FIELD INSPECTION

Essential to a crash investigation is a visit to the crash site. Before visiting this site, the engineer arranged with the defendant for a train and crew to be made available for vehicle-in-view photographs. Once at the site, a standard field site inspection was performed to measure and record the locations of relevant landmarks and to set flags for positioning the train for photos.

A reference point was established at the nearest rail of track and landmarks were located, including the intersection's traffic control devices, signs, trees, and major objects observed in furnished photographs. Photos were taken of the site with no train or motor vehicles present.

DAYTIME VEHICLE-IN-VIEW PHOTOGRAPHY

Although the collision event occurred after sunset, the vehicle-in-view photos were taken during daylight hours. It is easier and faster to set flags and mark the site when well lit, and daylight photos give the litigants, court, and jury the opportunity to better characterize the night view of the site under investigation. Panned photographs were exposed with a normal lens and stitched together to produce a seamless panorama at a good approximation of the field of view available to the plaintiff at the time of the accident.

Figure 4–29 shows the original photograph of the dirt pile, furnished by the defendant. The landmarks in this view—the street sign and phone poles—are essential elements utilized to align this photo within another of the same scene. The photo was analyzed at the site to determine exactly where the defendant's photographer was located when the photograph was taken. By aligning landmarks, the camera's position could be determined, recorded, and marked at the site. This position was 20 feet east of the nearest rail of three tracks, at a height of 5 feet, 1 inch (photographer's eye height). The train was placed 300 feet south of the intersection (in accordance with computations) with the locomotive headlights on bright (in accordance with fact testimony), and four overlapping images were exposed. The resulting stitched view of the scene in daylight is shown in Figure 4–30.

By aligning the street sign and the pair of telephone poles of the new photograph with the railroad's original photograph, the dirt pile could

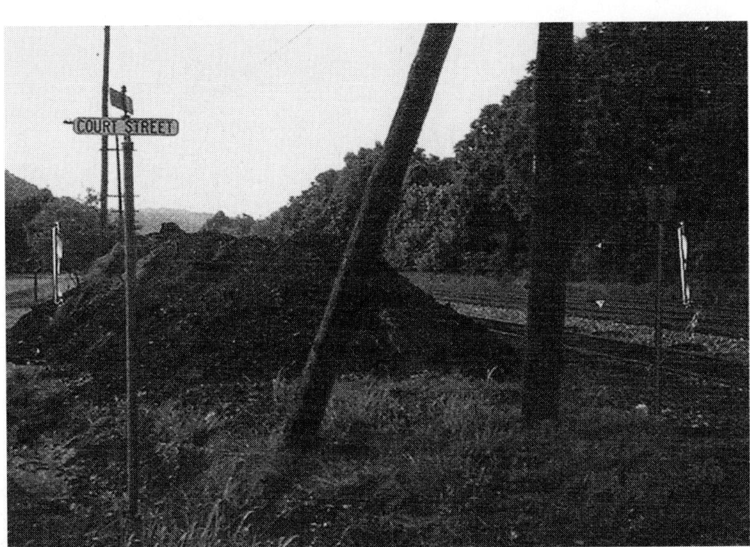

FIGURE 4–29 The original dirt pile photograph taken by the railroad at the time of the collision. *Source: EPIC Journal,* Fall 2003.

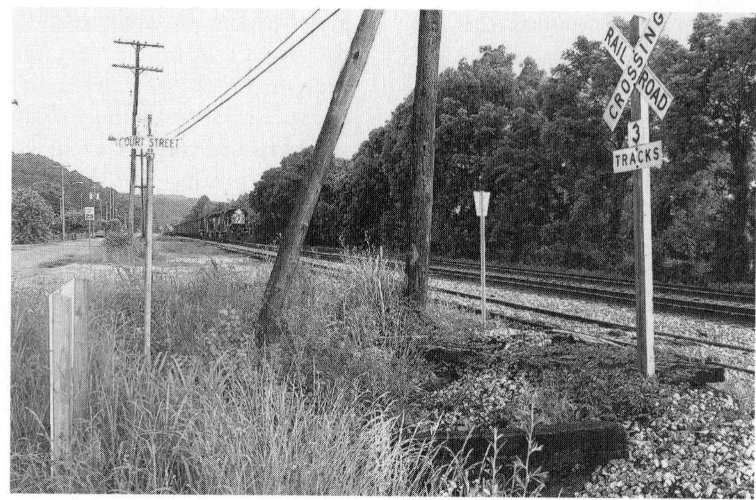

FIGURE 4–30 An analysis of the dirt pile photograph showed it was taken 20 feet east of the nearest rail of track, at the left-wheel path of Court Street, at a height above road surface of 5 feet, 1 inch. Computations of vehicle dynamics showed that the northbound train was 300 feet south of the intersection, approaching on the east main track, when the motorist was 20 feet east of the nearest rail of all tracks. This photograph, with a train in view, was taken at the same camera location on the anniversary date, two years later. *Source: EPIC Journal,* Fall 2003.

be, as was, superimposed into the scene. The interim composite view is shown in Figure 4–31. A span of two years separates the photos shown in this composite view.

The collision took place at about 9:20 P.M. Witnesses stated that the sky had some residual daylight at the time. The same tripod and camera setup used for daylight exposures was used for the nighttime images. They were placed 20 feet east of the nearest rail of track, as previously marked. The lighting of the scene was based on fact data and limited to only the approximate lighting exist-

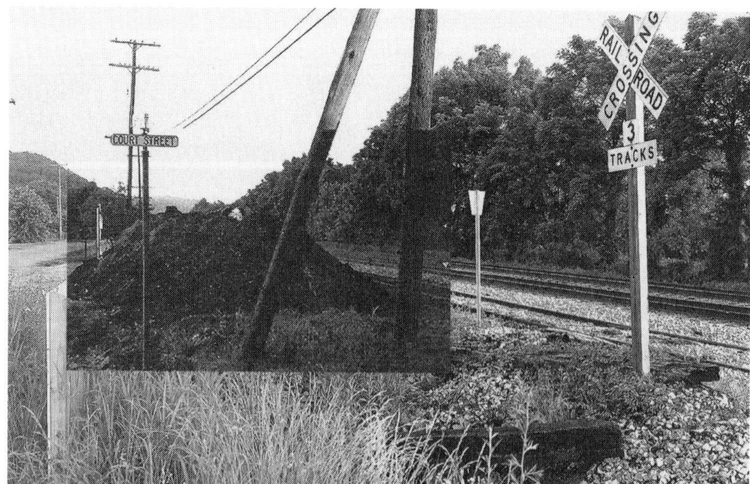

FIGURE 4–31 In this view, the photograph of the dirt pile has been superimposed onto the later view by aligning similar landmarks. Once the night view was ready, the dirt pile from this view was selected and superimposed onto the night photo, then darkened and nestled into the view until it became part of its surroundings. *Source: EPIC Journal,* Fall 2003.

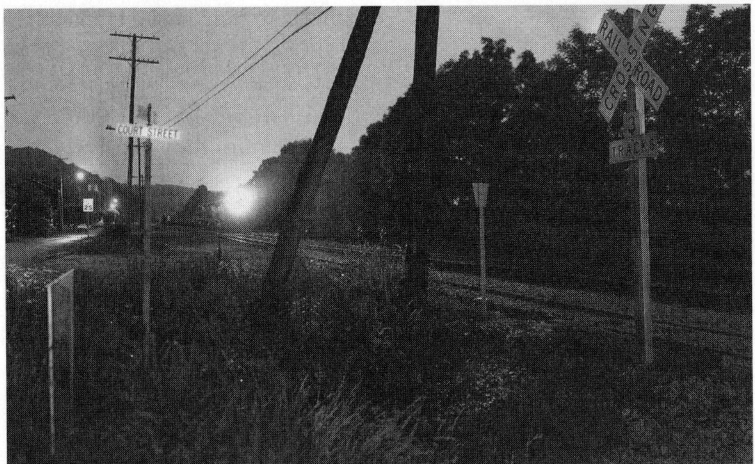

FIGURE 4–32 Since the collision took place at 9:20 P.M., at about twilight, the same train-in-view scene was photographed at 9:20 P.M. on the anniversary date two years later. The train was spotted 300 feet south of the intersection, on the east main track, its apparent location at that moment when the driver was 20 feet east of the track. All lighting of the scene was set up in accordance with fact testimony: no flashbulbs, electronic flash, or other additional lighting were used to illuminate the scene. *Source: EPIC Journal,* Fall 2003.

ing on the night of the collision. The panoramic nighttime scene of the train 300 feet south of the grade crossing is shown in Figure 4–32.

The final step in the production of the composite exhibit was to superimpose the dirt pile photograph onto the night scene. Once superimposed, the luminance and color saturation of the original photo were adjusted to accommodate nighttime illumination, making the overlay fit naturally into its surroundings.

THE OUTCOME

The locomotive's twin 200-watt headlights flared over the top of the dirt pile (see Fig. 4–33) as the photograph was exposed. The light from the locomotive's headlights was plainly visible viewing from the camera location 20 feet east of the track, with and without the dirt pile in place.

Was the dirt pile located directly in the sight line of the motorist? Yes. Did the dirt pile mask all clues of the, train's approach? No. Litigants made their arguments in a settlement conference, viewed the composite photographs, and concluded that negligence was shared. A fair and reasonable apportionment of blame was assigned and the matter concluded.

COMMENTS

Most of this study was done well. The investigator failed to mention that the driver's eye height might have been considerably lower than the 5 foot-plus height of the photographer. That could have become an issue at the trial.

This study also shows the usefulness of working backward from existing photographs to recreate an accident from years past. It does not however, explain how difficult it is to go back to the scene with old photos and find the correct location for the unknown camera and to duplicate the image it had exposed when its focal length is not known.

A version of this study appeared in the *EPIC Journal of Evidence Photography,* Fall 2003, written by Deane H. Ellsworth and edited by Sandy Weiss.

CASE STUDY

WRONGFUL DEATH

A motorist was involved in a high-speed chase on a toll road in a northeastern state. The car was being chased by multiple state interceptors and was finally brought to a stop at a toll booth. The officers left their cars, guns drawn, and told the driver to turn off the motor and get out of the car.

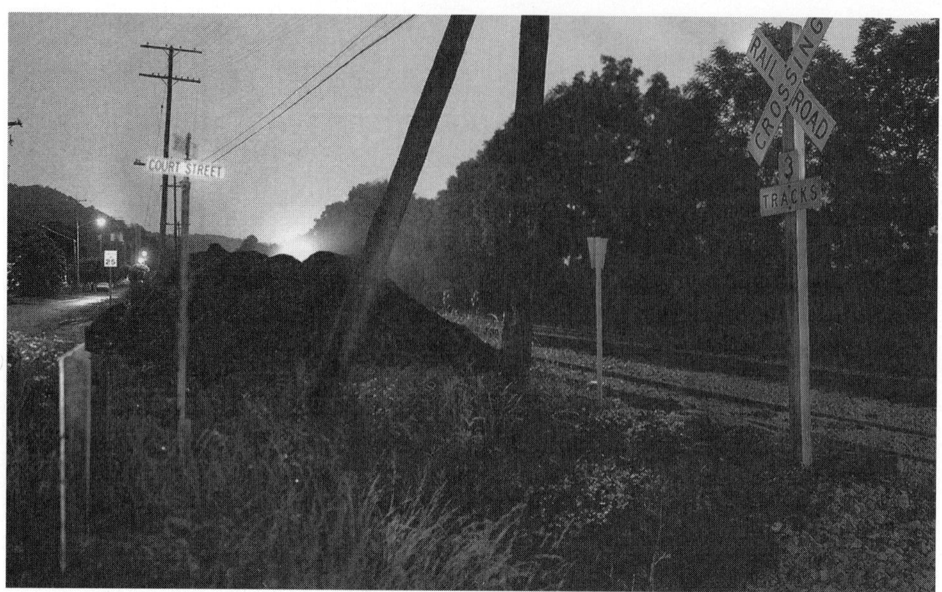

FIGURE 4–33 This is the final composite, with the dirt pile restored and in place as it was on the night of the collision. It is clear that the dirt pile was in the line of sight of the motorist, but it is also clear that something on the tracks behind it is backlighting the dirt pile with a brilliant light. Litigants concluded, during settlement negotiations, that a careful and prudent motorist would recognize that as a clue that something was on the tracks and might be approaching this grade crossing. *Source: EPIC Journal,* Fall 2003.

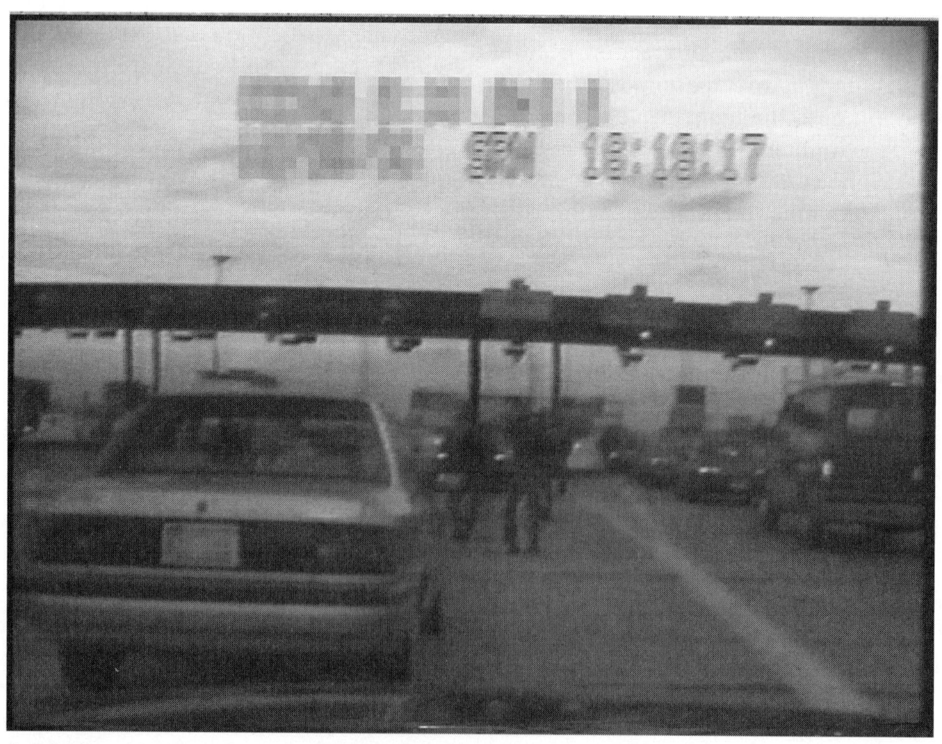

FIGURE 4–34 View from patrol car dash-cam used to analyze scene dimensions. *Source:* Tom Bundorf/Packer Engineering.

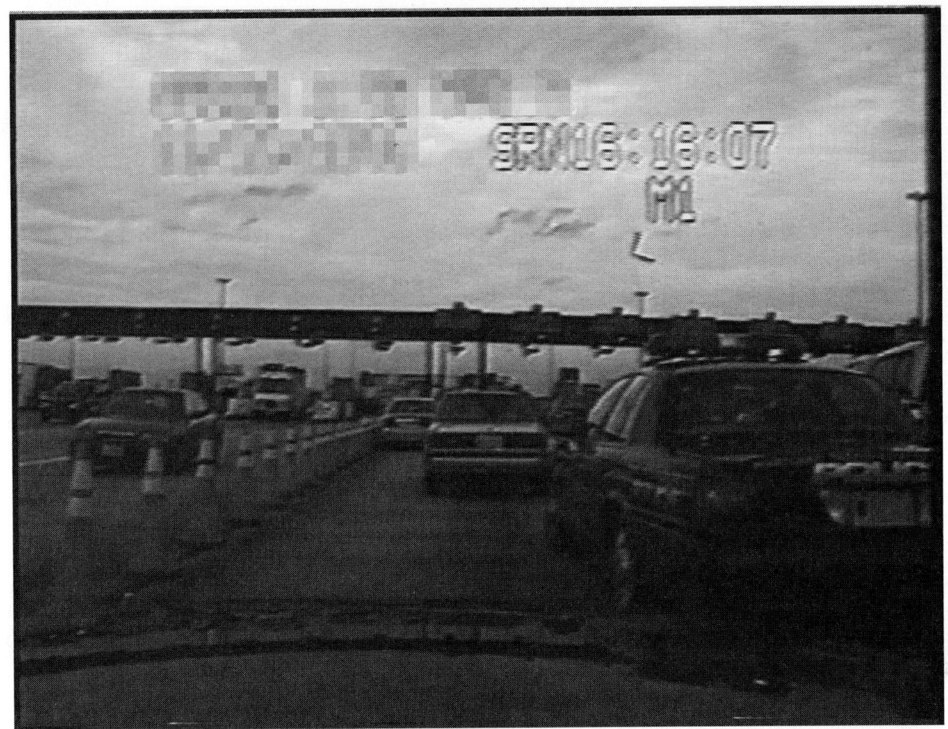

FIGURE 4–35 View from patrol car dash-cam used to analyze scene dimensions. *Source:* Tom Bundorf/Packer Engineering.

The driver instead put the car into gear and proceeded to try to elude the police and get back onto the road. The officers shot the driver fatally. The officers said that the car was heading in a path to hit one of the officers and that they had shot in self-defense. The family of the driver filed a wrongful death suit against the state claiming excessive force and that the car was not in a trajectory to impact the officer.

The only photographic evidence in existence were the videotapes that were being exposed by the interceptors' in-car cameras during the incident. (see Figs. 4–34 and 4–35) The video frames were not of the best quality, and very few landmarks in the frames could be used for scale from which to draw dimensions. Accuracy, though not great in the video evidence, was not of the utmost importance in this case.

It was determined that a single-point perspective photogrammetric analysis should be performed. The resulting plan-view aerial map (see Fig. 4–36) shows plainly that the car was proceeding on a path that would impact Officer A. The images and map were used in court during testimony, and the plaintiffs lost the suit.

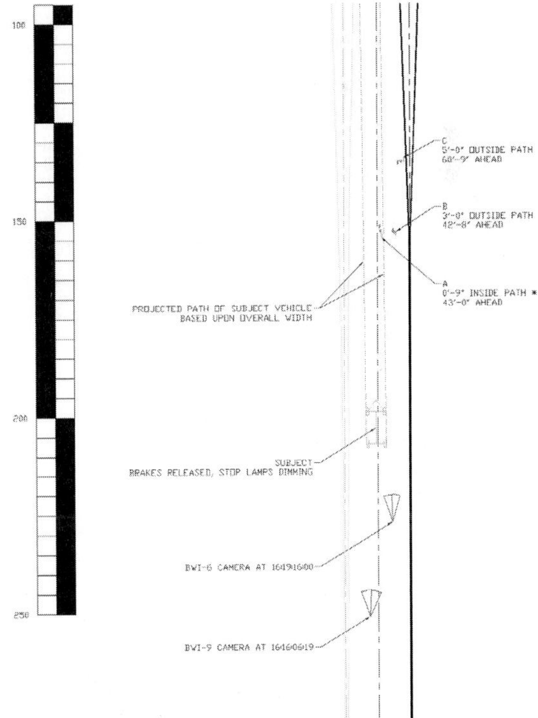

FIGURE 4–36 Plan-view aerial map of the scene. *Source:* Tom Bundorf/Packer Engineering.

KEY TERMS

photogrammetry, (p. 100)
metrology, (p. 100)
photogrammetric examination, (p. 100)
orthogonal (right angle) map, (p. 101)
central perspective, (p. 101)
light ray, (p. 101)
principal distance, (p. 101)
principal point, (p. 101)
distortion, (p. 101)
fiducial mark, (p. 101)
terrestrial camera, (p. 101)
total station, (p. 101)
base, (p. 102)
stereo-pair, (p. 102)
normal camera, (p. 102)
reverse photogrammetry, (p. 102)
PhotoModeler Pro, (p. 102)
orthogonal view, (p. 103)
stereo photogrammetry, (p. 103)
inverse camera, (p. 105)
Surfaces and Surface Draw, (p. 105)
constraint, (p. 106)
axis constraint, (p. 106)
control points, (p. 106)
two- or three-point perspective, (p. 106)
Point Properties, (p. 109)
orthographic photo, (p. 110)
Panoscan, (p. 110)
PanoMetric, (p. 110)
laser scanner, (p. 111)
digitization, (p. 111)
point cloud data, (p. 111)

EXERCISES

1. Select a vehicle and move it to a location where all four sides are accessible. Expose minimum but sufficient images in which every point on the vehicle is visible in at least three images, without zooming the lens or refocusing. Record control points so you can use the images for a future photogrammetric project.
2. Expose and print an image with an obvious vanishing point and enough control points to mark a perspective grid on its surface. Make an orthogonal map of at least one of the landmarks on the original photograph. Check the accuracy of your map by physically measuring the imaged and mapped landmark.
3. Download a photogrammetric software sample package from the Internet, work on the example projects, and watch the sample videos.
4. Find any photograph of a recognizable and available view. The newspaper or a friend are good sources. Make sure the image is from an unknown camera. Take the image and your camera and tripod to the imaged scene. Set up your camera to exactly match the supplied image.

Chapter 5

Getting Started

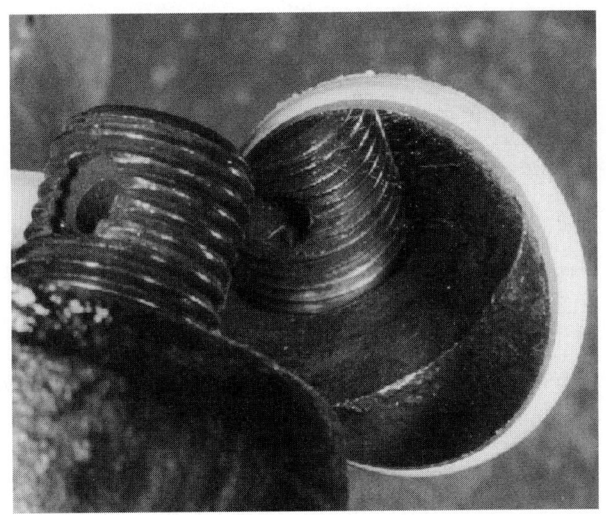

Learning Objectives

AFTER STUDYING THIS CHAPTER, YOU SHOULD BE ABLE TO:

1. Understand how to pick an appropriate camera for your work
2. Understand how many pixels are needed to appropriately create the required image
3. Understand the relationship between camera image size and printer image size
4. Understand how to set up, use, and care for a new camera and protect it in inclement conditions
5. Understand the usefulness of the LCD monitor
6. Understand the importance of camera defaults
7. Know the different types of camera batteries and how to care for them
8. Understand when and why to turn the camera off when changing accessories
9. Understand how, why, and when to format memory cards
10. Understand the difference between types of lenses
11. Determine when an image is acceptably focused
12. Understand the dangers of airport security to photographic media
13. Know how to assemble an appropriate go-kit

CHOOSING A DIGITAL CAMERA

What to Buy?

With the wide-ranging differences in prices and styles, and the diverse needs of the photographer, picking the right camera is often fraught with confusion. By staying within the boundaries of cameras manufactured by reputable companies, buying a "good" camera is guaranteed. Using cost, size, brand, and features as parameters will normally yield hardware with capabilities appropriate for the task and furnish reliability and durability for the circumstances of use.

Photographic hardware is divided by features, style, and price into amateur and professional by style and price. However, a great deal of crossover occurs within those groupings, and it is difficult to determine a choice for forensic applications when using only those parameters.

What Is the Perfect Camera?

No one brand or type of camera is going to be the perfect choice for every forensic photographer. The best method for determining which camera to buy is to examine a checklist of relevant features and to make a choice that best fulfills the need.

Many photographers will already own an array of photographic hardware and may wonder if what they have is sufficient for entering into this field. If the equipment is good quality and reliable, it will probably be suitable. It is, however, better to buy digital equipment if the photographer is currently using film-based equipment.

It is a good idea to browse through consumer guides to discern what brand of equipment is currently receiving accolades for value and reliability. Every current still and video digital camera is reviewed in detail at the outstanding Digital Photography Review Web site at www.

dpreview.com. The information on that site is current, well presented, easy to understand, and reliable.

A trip to a local retailer of electronic equipment should allow the potential buyer to examine an array of cameras and to decide if any particular one feels better in their hands. It is never a good idea to buy a camera that feels too heavy or does not feel comfortable at eye level or in the hand because it is never likely to feel any better.

Anything bought today will rapidly become obsolete and considered "out of date" due to continually new improvements made by the manufacturer. Many users do not buy expensive cameras, even if the equipment is affordable, because they do not want to endure the disappointment caused by finding the same equipment selling for hundreds of dollars less in a matter of months, or even weeks.

One useful purchasing parameter is to decide on the proper maximum **image resolution** to satisfy the requirements of the project. If the photographer or client routinely requires images to be enlarged to 24 × 30 inches, a 2-megapixel camera will not suffice. If the photographer or client only needs 2 × 3-inch images for reports to be published on the Internet, an 11-megapixel camera is not necessary. However, the resolution parameter alone is not enough to determine the right choice of camera. A high- and low-resolution camera will expose images of comparable quality at a smaller size and price.

Consider the following questions (some of which will have more meaning after you read other sections of this chapter) and answer them honestly and fairly before selecting a camera to purchase:

- What type of photographer are you most likely to be, and what type of projects will you undertake?
- How many megapixels will you routinely need for each exposed image?
- How important are camera size and weight?
- Is it going to be necessary to have a range of lenses?
- Is one type of camera memory more appropriate or reliable for your use?
- Will a particular brand or type of camera be more appropriate for the type of photos you normally take?
- How much money can you afford to spend?

Analyzing Your Needs

The next step in the selection process should be to correlate the answers to the preceding questions with hardware that is currently on the market. If the choice is too confusing, take your list to a reliable dealer and ask for assistance. Buying mail-order equipment is often a way to save money, but do not be surprised if what arrives is a surprise. Photos in camera catalogs do not lie, but they may be confusing to the inexperienced buyer.

A wealth of information about currently available cameras is available on the Internet. Special-interest groups are often free to join, and a question posted to the group usually brings an array of well-conceived and informative answers to questions unanswerable anywhere else, by people who are already using the equipment you are considering for the work you are attempting.

Understanding Megapixels

Digital camera images are composed of rows of colored dots, captured by an image sensor, that form a rectangular grid and become a photograph. These dots are called **pixels.** An image on a Web page might be composed of 500 rows with 400 pixels per row. The total number of pixels in the image would then be 500 × 400, for a total of 200,000 pixels. In digital images, pixels are red, green, or blue (**RGB**), with twice as many green pixels as red and blue ones.) The pixels are assigned a **brightness value** within a standard range. The number of pixels per image is determined by the overall size and receptor density of the camera image sensor.

A **megapixel** (Mp) is equal to 1 million pixels. Digital camera images generally contain multiple Mp. An image containing 200,000 pixels is equal to 0.2 Mp.

Reducing or Increasing Megapixels

It is common practice to reduce the number of pixels in a digital image to create a smaller-size file. This is done to save space during storage or because a larger file size is not needed due to the parameters of use. If a small file size is what is available and a larger file is needed for a particular purpose, the image software can be used to interpolate the image information of the extra pixels. Different methods of making these guesses are called **interpolation algorithms**. Interpolation is usually unreliable and results in the creation of images with limited detail and insufficient contrast.

Pixels and Usage

The number of pixels needed in any situation depends on the intended use of the image. For viewing on a computer screen (or TV), fewer pixels (lower resolution) are required than when the image will be printed. The larger the prints will be, the greater the number of pixels needed for satisfactory results.

Usage	**Typical Image Dimensions**	**Image Size**
Web site	450×350 pixels	0.05–0.25 Mp
Onscreen viewing	800×600 pixels	0.5–1.5 Mp
4×6 print	1,200×1,800 pixels	1.5–2.5 Mp
8×10 enlargement	2,400×3,000 pixels	5–7 Mp

Printers and Pixels

Whether printing on a desktop printer or one owned and operated by a magazine or newspaper, the number of pixels needed per inch of the output (print size) is dependent on the technology used. If the software and hardware for image reproduction are properly designed and matched, the minimum pixel density needed to supply a reasonably resolved image is defined by the ability of the eye to resolve detail within the image, and that is usually about 200 to 300 pixels per inch.

To make use of the 256 different color shades within the capabilities of each screen pixel may require a pixel grouping (**matrix**), which contains a number of colored dots. A simple color matrix may use a 16×16 cell design that may contain from 0 to 256 dots, with each pixel requiring 16 dots. This would require a printer resolution of around 3,000 dots per inch.

If the camera images are intended solely for viewing on the Web or on screen, images larger than 1.5 Mp are not needed. If the largest print needed is a 4×6, a 2 Mp camera image will be sufficient. If 8×10 prints are needed, it is necessary to use a camera with 4 or 5 Mp. For professional quality prints up to 11×14, a 6 or 7 Mp camera is necessary, and for results that will compare in image quality to medium-format film images, 11 Mp or more are required.

Camera Size

Size is certainly an issue with digital cameras. Whatever its size, the camera must be comfortable to use and convenient to carry. Sometimes, the smaller the camera, the better it is. However, it must never be too small to hold securely or too large that it becomes unwieldy or inconvenient.

When carrying an array of lenses is necessary, size also becomes a limiting factor. The interchangeable lenses of **digital single-lens reflex cameras (DSLRs)** are as large as their film-based kin, and perhaps even larger. If a very large sensor size or image resolution or both are needed, the DSLR is going to be the best choice. The smaller-size point-and-shoot cameras not limited to 8 Mp are priced nearly as high as their DSLR equivalents.

Many of the smaller cameras do not offer through-the-lens viewing, except on liquid crystal display (LCD) monitors, and that may be an issue if macrophotography is required, especially on bright days when LCD images are difficult to see.

Nobody wants to carry more equipment than needed, and it is always inconvenient to carry extra weight. A good rule to follow may be to pick the smallest available camera that has the required features and image quality necessary for the photographer's typical investigation.

A number of classes of digital cameras are denoted by size:

- **Miniature/small** cameras may be so small that they are not easily recognizable as cameras. These cameras are useful for photographers who are satisfied with lower quality images for their projects and are hampered by limitations on the size or weight of their kits. It should be recognized that there are some extremely fine cameras available in very small sizes.
- **Compact** cameras are about the same size as film-based point-and-shoot models. These cameras may be too large for the average pocket but will fit inside larger pockets or briefcases.
- **Medium** cameras are too large to be called compact and are normally carried on a neck strap. These include the cameras that are about the size of small film-based SLRs and weigh up to around 700 grams, including lens.
- **Large** cameras include the interchangeable lens models, from the relatively light Nikon D80, Canon Rebel, to heavier professional models such as the Nikon D2Xs which, including a lens, may weigh over 1000 grams.

The shape of small- and medium-size cameras is important to consider, as it can make a difference as to how portable the camera is. Cameras with lenses that retract into the body are helpful and may also automatically cover the lens to protect it from damage.

The following subsections present examples of representative cameras in the more popular sizes.

Small Cameras

The Fuji SlimShot (see Fig. 5-1), which is as small as any camera a photographer might use, measures 85.6 × 54 × 6 mm and weighs 35 grams (1.25 oz.). It is about the size of a credit card and

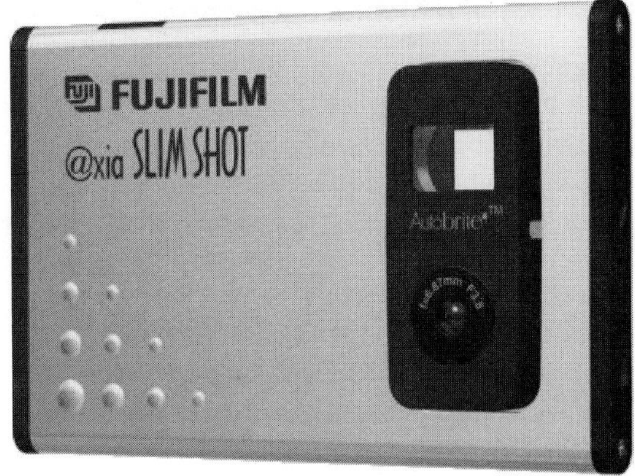

FIGURE 5–1 The Fuji SlimShot, a representative small, point-and-shoot digital camera. *Source:* Sandy Weiss.

.25 inch thick. It makes 0.31 Mp images, and the built-in memory will hold 26 exposures or just over a hundred exposures at the smaller default size of 320 × 240 pixels:

- Sensor: 0.31 Mp
- Resolution: 640 × 480, 320 × 240
- File format: JPEG after software conversion
- Internal memory: 8 MB
- Focal length: 6.87mm (equivalent to 47mm on a 35mm camera)
- Aperture: 3.8
- Shooting distance: 60 cm to infinity
- Focusing: Fixed
- Battery: Internal Lithium-Polymer
- Shutter speed: Auto (1/30 to 1/15000)

The Fuji SlimShot has a fixed focus lens, which is an advantage for ease of documentation, but its close focus capability is an unreasonable 14 inches. That limits this type of camera to making photographs of vehicles or similar subjects, and the image size is only satisfactory for e-mailing or for small prints and reports. Most miniature to medium-size digital cameras have built-in zoom lenses.

DSLR cameras usually allow any lens to be attached with a suitable mount. The cost of lenses should be added to the estimated price of any camera, unless the user already owns the lenses.

Compact and Medium Cameras

The Canon PowerShot A710 IS (see Fig. 5-2) includes optical image stabilization, it has a resolution of 7 Mp and a reasonable mixture of manual and automatic features, including the following:

- 7.1 Mp 3,072 × 2,304
- 6× optical zoom with optical Image Stabilizer (35–210mm equivalent)
- 9-point AutoFocus and AutoExposure
- Digital Tele-Converter and Safety Zoom
- 2.5-inch LCD with wide viewing angle and real-image optical viewfinder
- 20 shooting modes
- Movie clips 640 × 480 @ 15/30 fps; up to 1 GB or 1 hour
- 1cm macro mode
- Shutter speeds of 15–1/2000 sec
- Apertures F2.8 - 8 (Wide) F4.8 - 8 (Tele)
- ISO 80, 100, 200, 400, 800
- White Balance
- Weight with batteries about 210 grams
- Dimensions 97.5 × 66.5 × 41.2

Point-and-shoot cameras will be priced lower than DSLRs, and that is an important aspect to consider. They are also self-contained and the lens does not come off, so dirt will never get on the sensor when the lens is off, which is a common problem with DSLRs. Image quality is good, ease of operation is simple, and quality and features are high. It may be a good idea to carry a camera like this in your go-kit as either a main camera or as a full-featured backup.

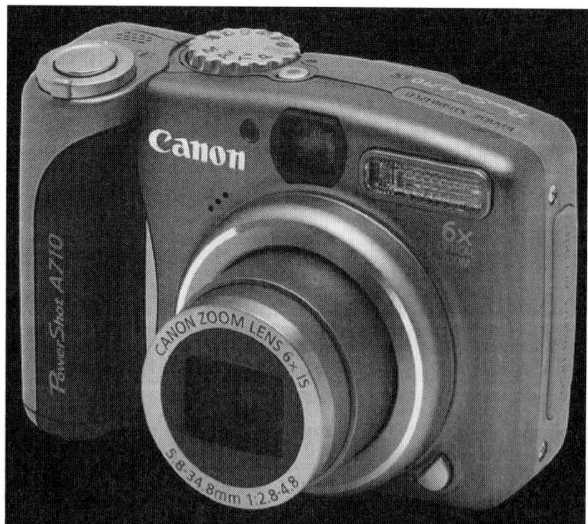

FIGURE 5–2 The Canon PowerShot A710 IS, a representative medium, point-and-shoot digital camera. *Source:* Sandy Weiss.

Sometimes it is beyond the limitations of a departmental budget to purchase a large, impressive, professional camera. The smaller cameras produce respectable images. It should be remembered, though, that a small and inexpensive camera is available to any attorney or private party who wishes to own one. If a forensic photographer is planning to earn a living wage by producing photographs as a person for hire, it must be known that camera size plays a role in terms of credibility. For example, a client may not realize that a little camera may be totally appropriate for his or her project and, based on the size of the camera, may assume that the photographer is not properly equipped. *Never* underestimate the importance of the photographer's credibility. How does it look if a client hires a forensic photography specialist and that person appears at the project with a $200, palm-size camera? Keep that in mind before traveling light!

Large Cameras

The Nikon D80 (see Fig. 5-3) is featured between the entry-level D40 and the semiprofessional/professional D200 and D300. It is based on the established D70 design but is different enough to be considered a completely new model. It features a 10 Mp DX format CCD (one of the two main types of image sensors used in digital cameras), the metering sensor from the D50, and numerous other items taken or modified from the D200. The features include the following:

- 10.2 Mp 3,872 × 2,592
- 11 area Through The Lens (TTL) Autofocus
- 420 pixel RGB sensor metering
- ISO 100 to 1600

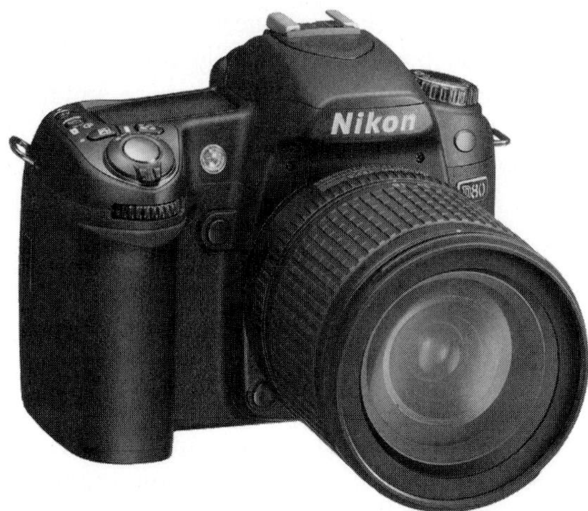

FIGURE 5–3 The Nikon D-80, a representative DSLR camera. *Source:* Sandy Weiss.

- 6 auto white-balance presets + manual
- 95% viewfinder
- 2.5-inch TFT LCD monitor
- Luminance and RGB histogram
- SD/SD-HC memory
- Dimensions 132×103×77 mm
- Weighs 668 grams with battery
- In-camera retouching

The larger and more professional the camera, the more and wider ranging are the built-in features. If the photographer really needs features and that are only contained on the larger and more professional camera, it makes the decision of which camera to purchase much simpler to make.

DSLRs usually contain a larger imaging sensor, which contributes to higher-quality images. A larger image sensor produces images with a better "feel" and "look" and images that are less susceptible to the problems of **visual noise**.

Most DSLRs record images using a 12-bit sensor—that is, they can discriminate and record between 4,096 different (black to white) tonal values. Point-and-shoot cameras may use an 8-bit sensor that can only discriminate and record between 256 different tonal values. Therefore, DSLRs may capture images with more fidelity and can more easily handle difficult lighting situations.

Larger sensors require larger lenses. Larger lenses have larger maximum apertures, which restrict the diameter of the beams of light striking the image plane and allow more light into the camera. Larger apertures also allow the use of faster shutter speeds in low-light situations without the necessity of setting the camera to a higher ISO and sacrificing image quality. DSLRs utilize high-speed circuits that respond immediately when the shutter release is pressed, in contrast to the delays often experienced in shutter reaction with point-and-shoot cameras.

Small and medium DSLR cameras have small in-camera flash units that only work properly to a distance of about 15 feet. They cannot match the illuminating power of larger, detachable flash units.

The effects of a **polarizing filter** can be seen through the lens on a DSLR camera. When using a polarizer on a point-and-shoot camera, the results can only be seen on the LCD or in the finished photograph.

Large DSLRs have batteries that deliver longer life than the batteries used in smaller cameras.

THE NEW CAMERA

When opening the box of a new camera, a large percentage of users will charge the battery, insert a memory card, set the camera on its most automatic setting, and start taking photographs. These users may not know the settings of the factory defaults and may not care. They will not have set the built-in clock and calendar. Having mastered the basics of operation, they may never go back to the instruction manual but will continue to expose all of their photographs with the camera set as it came out of the box. In many cases, the state of sophistication of contemporary technology allows these users to expose relatively adequate images. And seeing the images immediately on the LCD provides instant gratification, so the user is assured that the photographs taken are essentially well exposed and relatively in focus.

As implausible as this may sound, it is the truth. A medical examiner's office in Wisconsin bought new cameras for all of the staff and distributed them without supplying specific instructions or training. The new director was supplied with multiple images labeled *P000101.jpg.* Trying to associate the images with the office's various cases, and having all of the images labeled as having been taken at 12:00 on 1/1/01 was an insoluble problem. As sophisticated as new cameras are, only human input can maximize their functionality.

The instruction manuals supplied with new cameras are often confusing. Most of them are either translated from a foreign language or written by someone whose first language is not English. The manuals are also organized in a manner that does not directly conform to normal use and may lead to more confusion. Two solutions to the instruction manual problem are recommended. First, use the quick-start menu usually included as an addition to the manual. Second, buy an aftermarket publication (see Figs. 5-4 and 5-5) written about your camera by someone proficient in the language with which you are familiar. Such books are usually affordable and readily available for almost any camera, and they include useful information beyond what may be included in the original equipment manufacturer's (OEM) manual.

GETTING STARTED

How much information is needed to comfortably use a new camera on a forensic assignment and make use of a significant number of its capabilities?

The Nikon D70 manual supplied with the camera leads the user through the important initial setup. It tells how to select a default language, set the correct date and time, attach a lens, insert a memory card, and format the card, and then it explains the basics of taking photographs.

The *D70 Field Guide* (see Figs. 5–4 and 5–5) includes a quick tour that starts after the

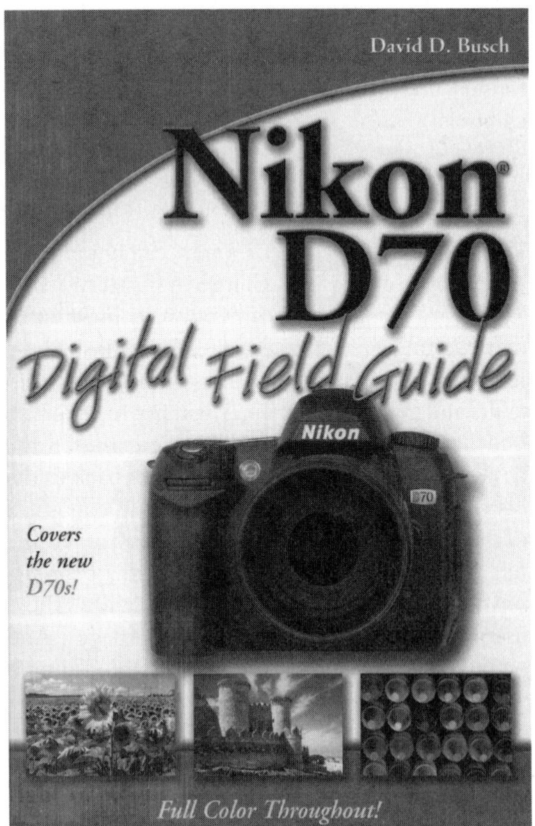

FIGURE 5–4 Front page of the *Nikon D70 Field Guide* user's manual. *Source:* Sandy Weiss.

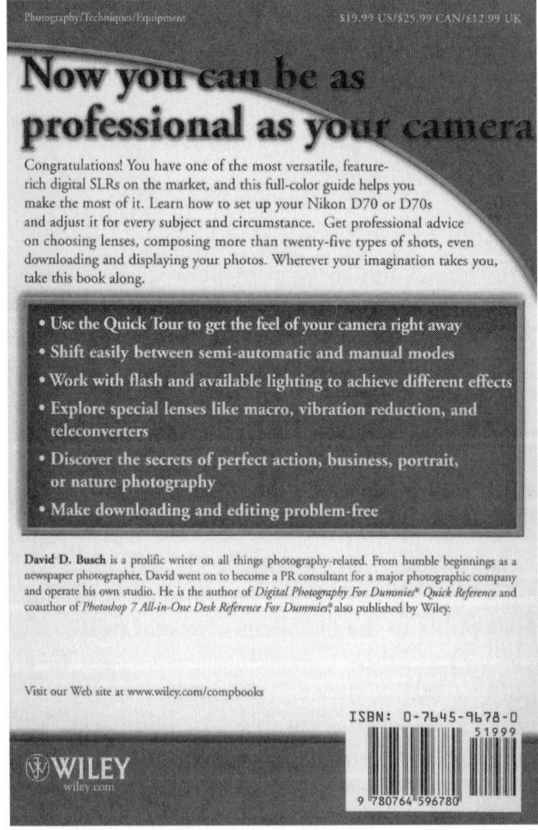

FIGURE 5–5 Back cover of the *Nikon D70 Field Guide* user's manual. *Source:* Sandy Weiss.

photographer has "Mounted a lens, charged and installed a battery, and inserted a memory card. It assumes a previous knowledge of focusing, shutter speeds, and apertures."[1] Every camera/instruction manual/guidebook combination you purchase will start exactly the same way unless the camera referenced has a fixed lens, in which case one will not have to be attached.

The next step is to select a picture-taking mode. All better-quality cameras will include a choice of automatic settings. To start, most users select an auto-everything setting. After acquiring some experience, it may be advisable to pick a type of automation that allows the user to set a lens aperture and the camera picks an appropriate matching shutter speed. This type of automation is called **aperture priority** and is suggested for most forensic photography because it allows the user to maximize the depth of field (discussed in depth in Chapter 7).

Setting the lens focus on automatic or manual is dictated by the situation. If the lens aperture is wide and the depth of field limited, or if numerous objects are in the viewfinder and the camera's digital computer may need to make decisions about what to focus on, setting the camera on manual focus may be the right choice. If the lens aperture is small, the depth of field will be wide and, even if the camera has many objects on which to focus, automatic focus may supply well-focused images throughout the image frame. When exposing macrophotographs, manual focus is always recommended due to the inherently shallow depth of field when focusing close up.

It is usually difficult to judge if a photo is properly focused by inspecting the small image displayed on the LCD. It may be necessary to zoom in on the display or to inspect the image on a computer monitor to ensure that all is functioning properly.

> **TIP:**
>
> If the image on the LCD is not to your liking, determine the problem and fix it before continuing with the project. Never assume that the problem is simply an issue with the LCD.

DEFAULTS AND MENUS

Your new camera left the factory with some settings programmed into its memory. These are referred to as its **default settings**. Many of the settings may never be adjusted because there will be no reason during the course of normal photography to make a change. Some of the settings will be adjusted by the user at certain times. Whether or not the settings will be changed, it is important for the user to be familiar with everything the camera is doing. Eventually the user may find himself or herself in a situation in which they *must* consult the camera manual to determine what the camera is going to do if it is left on its own to make a decision.

The factory default settings are listed in a Technical Notes appendix at the back of the Nikon D80 user's manual. Every function of the camera that can be set has a default. In many cases, the camera defaults change when the camera system is reset to a mode that differs from the factory default. Find and study the appropriate section of the manual for any camera that is going to be a part of your kit, or run the camera through all of its menu settings after doing a system reset to determine all the default settings.

Following are some of the important questions users should ask about any camera they will be using:

- If the user changes a setting during operation, will the camera retain that new setting after it has been turned off and then back on?
- Is there more than one way to insert an exposure correction into the camera meter system, and how is the user notified if a manual correction is in use?
- Does the built-in flash mode revert to the default setting after use, or does it stay at the new setting?
- Does the white balance reset to default if it has been reset to anything other than auto?
- Does the ISO setting remain at a number other than the default setting after

the camera has been turned off and then back on?

- What happens if the user programs for a focus area other than the default?
- Will the camera shutter release if it has no memory card inserted in the slot?
- What is the default image quality?

The list is not endless, but it is extensive. At this time, no industry standards have been established to apply to all of these functions. Every one of these questions, and many more, may be answered by studying the menus on the camera's LCD display. Familiarize yourself with the menus and learn the factory settings. If a visual services department has distributed the camera to you, learn whatever settings were programmed. If the department is adhering to an imaging protocol, it may be important for the user *not* to change some of the set defaults, including image quality.

Camera functions can be changed or adjusted using buttons or menus that are included on the camera for that express purpose. Menu options will allow users to do everything that can be done with a button, but the buttons will not allow users to do everything that can be done with the menus. It is important to remember that using the menu options and reviewing settings and images on the LCD are a drain on battery power.

CAMERA HANDLING

To ensure that you are comfortable with the camera you choose, consider the following specifics:

- Check how comfortable the camera is to hold in your hands.
- Put your eye to the viewfinder, and look through it to see how easily you can compose an image.
- How good is the image on the LCD? Does it show roughly the same view as you saw in the viewfinder?
- Having taken one picture, how much time is necessary before you can take the next?
- Are the autofocus and autoexposure rapid, or do you get a noticeable delay between pressing the shutter and the picture being taken?
- How easily and quickly can the zoom setting be altered?
- Can you lock the focus and the exposure?
- Can you set the focus or the exposure manually?
- How sharp is the image?
- How good is the color reproduction?

CAMERA BATTERIES

Rechargeable Battery Care and Maintenance

Three types of rechargeable batteries are used in digital cameras:

- Nickel Cadmium (NiCad)
- Nickel Metal Hydride (NiMH)
- Lithium Ion (Li-ion)

NiCad Batteries

NiCad batteries have good capacity characteristics and maintain stable voltage throughout their discharge cycle. The stable voltage discharge allows electronic devices using NiCad batteries to operate properly until the batteries are depleted. NiCad batteries have a reasonable shelf life between charges.

One NiCad battery problem is the **battery memory** effect, in which the batteries operate properly for less and less time as the battery ages. This is because most people use their NiCad batteries in a device and then place the batteries or device into a battery charger. Over time, NiCad batteries develop crystals in the unused portions of the battery material, and those prohibit the chemical reaction that produces electricity. If the NiCad battery is used for 30 minutes, and only 30 minutes, although it has a longer capacity before needing to be recharged, over time the battery will only be capable of operating for 30 minutes.

Two simple steps can be taken to minimize NiCad battery memory effect. Always use NiCad battery–operated devices until the batteries are completely drained. This will minimize crystal buildup and will extend battery life. Perform a deep discharge cycle about once a month by operating the NiCad-powered device until it stops operating completely.

NiCad batteries usually require replacement every year or two.

NiMH Batteries

NiMH batteries have the same power advantages as NiCad batteries, but they do not have the same battery memory problems, which may be why they are more expensive. They also have a longer useful life cycle: three or four years before requiring replacement. NiMH batteries have a fairly fast discharge rate while in storage. A fully charged NiMH battery left unattended for a week will lose about 20% of its charge. Keep them in a battery charger when not in use.

Li-ion Batteries

Li-ion batteries have all the advantages of NiCad and NiMH batteries, plus they have a longer useful life. The main disadvantage of Li-ion batteries is that they lose about 10% of their useable capacity each year due to chemical breakdown within the cells. Nothing can be done to prevent this condition.

Li-ion batteries have a typical useful life of between 300 and 500 discharge cycles, or about four or five years. Maximize the useful life of Li-ion batteries by always keeping them on a charger—during use (e.g., laptop computer) and when not in use. Because these batteries are "smart," they cannot be overcharged. It is advisable to charge Li-ion batteries every night.

TIP:

Alternate continually between two batteries. Keep one in the camera and keep the second fully charged in a go-kit for a spare. That way each battery is used only half the time.

TIP:

Li-ion batteries are usually dedicated and operate only in the device for which they were designed.

Battery Tips

- Always use batteries that are manufactured by the manufacturer of the camera.
- To maximize battery life, use the camera LCD as little as possible and turn it OFF when possible while making photographs.

TIP:

To avoid causing problems to the camera circuitry or memory, always turn off the camera before removing and replacing batteries.

Cold Weather and Batteries

Little condensation will occur when a camera is taken from a warm place to a cold one, but battery power may be lost. This can be a serious problem with modern electronic cameras, so the photographer must anticipate a loss of power and plan for it by carrying spare batteries and keeping them warm.

To keep the camera and accessories as warm as possible, carry them close to your body, even under your coat, except when you are actually using them. When using a tripod, keep the camera warm until you need it, and then put it on the tripod quickly.

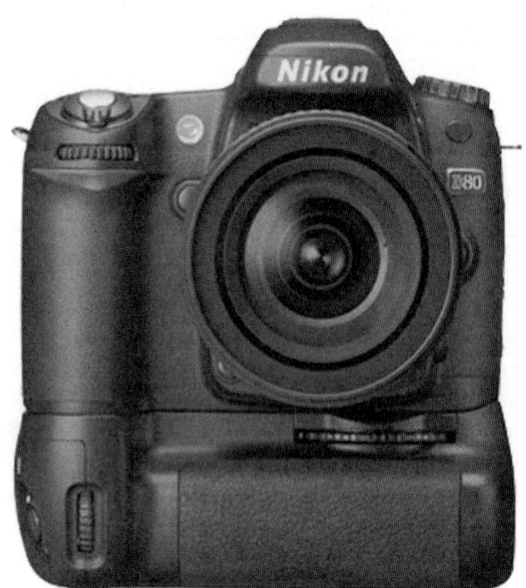

FIGURE 5–6 Nikon D80 with battery grip. *Source:* Sandy Weiss.

Battery Grip

An excellent gadget to buy with a DSLR is a battery grip (see Fig. 5-6), if one is available. It will connect through the camera's battery compartment and screw into the camera's bottom tripod mount.

A battery grip enhances the stability of handheld cameras, and it provides a convenient shutter release button for vertical exposures. In the case of the Nikon D80, the battery grip includes an AA adapter magazine that allows the placement of six AA batteries for extended shooting time. It also holds two Nikon ENEL3 or ENEL3A OEM batteries for twice the power. Since one ENEL3a provides for 2,500 exposures, with a battery grip the photographer may safely expect 5,000 (nonflash) exposures.

The battery grip is a good choice for cold weather because it increases the amount of power inherent to the camera.

CAMERA MEMORY

A digital camera needs digital memory. An image size of 1,600 × 1,200 pixels, as produced by a 2 Mp camera, will take up less memory than an image of 2,592 × 1,944 pixels produced by a 5 Mp camera.

Most cameras now have removable memory devices. Remove the memory, replace it with another if all the space on the device is filled, and continue shooting. Always purchase an extra memory card or two. Most digital cameras come from the factory with a small card containing a small amount of memory, and buying an extra memory card when purchasing a camera always proves to be a good idea.

Many types of memory cards are available, so it is important to check the memory options of the camera you are buying. If the camera resolution is high, it is necessary to use high-capacity memory cards.

TIP:

No predetermined number of images can be stored on a particular memory card. The number depends on the kind of images, the file type of the images, and the compression rate per photograph.

Many kinds of memory cards are available. The following are some of the more common ones:

- *CompactFlash (CF) Memory Card*[2]: **CompactFlash (CF)** is available almost everywhere and is compatible with many digital cameras and devices. These cards have a built-in controller that allows for fast data transfer speeds.
  - Lack of battery power is a major cause of card lockups.
  - After long periods of use, fragments from past use may remain on CF cards. This happens because the camera performs only minimal formats that do not completely remove old images. To improve CF card performance, reformat them in the camera every six to eight weeks, and before each new project, to ensure their freshness.
  - Keep the same group of CF cards with one camera system. It is not a good idea to switch CF cards between different camera systems, although it can be done if the card is first

reformatted in the camera system in which it will be used.

- Do not shoot beyond the capacity of a CF card.
- Do not overshoot a CF card by trying to put a few extra images on it because it may cause the card to overwrite and corrupt the last images. This may lead to CF card lockup. The card can be salvaged using a recovery utility as long as the user has not tried to reformat the card.
- Purchase image recovery utility software so you can recover images if a CF card locks up due to overshooting or shooting with a low battery.
- Do not remove CF cards before the camera has completed data writing.
- Do not remove CF cards from readers until the computer accessory is properly shut off.
- Wait several seconds before removing CF cards from readers after use.
- Do not launder, freeze, expose to large magnetic fields, or otherwise mistreat CF cards.
- Do not put a CF card into your pocket unless it is in its plastic case.

- **Secure Digital and Multimedia Cards: Secure Digital (SD)** and multimedia cards are some of the smallest cards available today. They can be used in different types of equipment, including digital still cameras, phones, MP3 players, and video cameras. The difference between SD cards and multimedia cards is that SD cards come with an additional write-protect switch for data security.
- **Memory Stick: Memory sticks** are made by Sony. If you have a Sony digital camera and another brand of computer, you will need a card reader to download images efficiently.
- **Card Reader:** You will probably need a card reader to transfer images to a computer. Card readers are usually attached to a computer via a Universal Serial Bus (USB) port. Card readers do not require battery power.

Erasing Images from a Memory Card

When images are erased from a memory card, either individually or all at once, space becomes available on the media for more photos. The camera will allow you to erase image and video files but not other data on the card.

Formatting a Memory Card

Formatting a memory card in the camera ensures that it is going to work properly in that camera. Like computers, memory cards have filing systems, folders, and so on. By formatting the card in the camera, the card is set up in the way the camera needs to function properly.

If you put an unformatted memory card into a camera, it will usually function properly. Most cameras will automatically program the card appropriately regardless of whether it has been formatted or not. However, formatting a card is a quick and simple procedure and good operational insurance, so programming is recommended before using it any camera for the first time. Consult the owner's manual for specific formatting instructions.

Formatting in a computer overwrites everything on a card, including images, directories, and camera data, and it sets up new folders and data on the card. In addition to getting the card ready to use with the camera, formatting can fix minor problems. If a card and camera are not working properly, try reformatting the card to erase error message and bad writes.

TIP:

Format a card only after transferring all photos to permanent computer memory or another storage device.

Formatting is a quick way to delete all the images from a memory card. It is quicker than erasing them one at a time with a camera or computer.

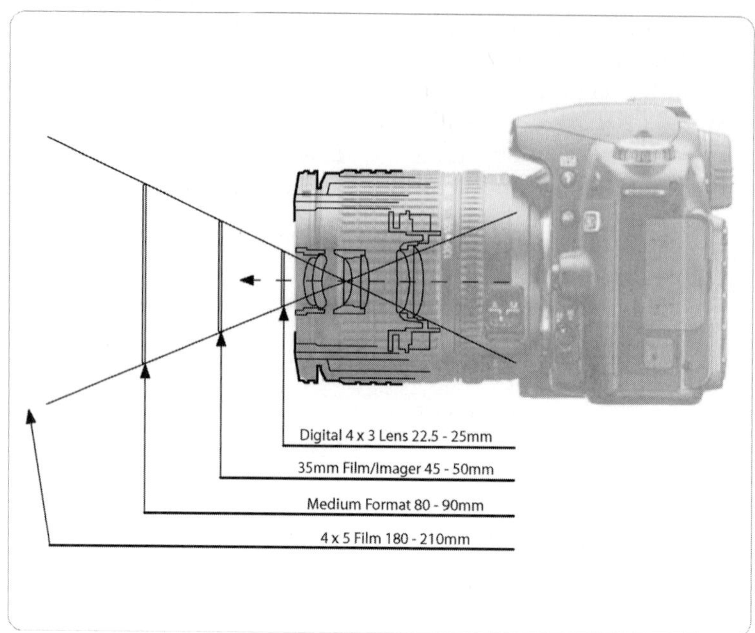

FIGURE 5–7 Normal focal length is determined by format. *Source:* Jessica Weiss.

> **TIP:**
>
> If you have formatted a card by mistake, do not panic and do not use it. Software solutions are available for retrieving the images that have been deleted.

CAMERA LENSES

Focal Length

Camera lenses are broadly categorized as normal, telephoto, and wide-angle, according to their **focal length,** which is dependent upon the image receptor size in the camera they are used on. Lenses with variable focal lengths are called **zoom lenses.** A normal lens is one that yields an image, on the receptor, corresponding approximately to that of normal perspective in human monocular vision.* The focal length of a normal/standard lens producing a 24 × 36 mm (1 × 1.5 inch) image with a 35mm film camera is approximately 50mm. The focal length of a normal/standard lens on a digital camera depends upon the physical dimensions of the image receptor, and it varies according to the proportions of the width and height of the receptor (see Fig. 5-7).

*Perspective in photography is defined as the spatial relationship between objects as they relate to one another in the image. A telephoto lens reduces and a wide-angle lens increases the perceived distance between objects in a photograph.

What Is Normal?

The image sensor in a digital camera is usually smaller than the physical dimensions of a 35mm negative. Therefore, a 50mm lens is not necessarily the normal field of view lens on a digital camera.

To find the size of the sensor in any camera, look it up in the camera's user manual. For example, the Nikon D200 has a 23.6 × 15.8 mm CCD (DX).

Most interchangeable-lens digital cameras physically resemble 35mm cameras. However, most of these cameras have photo-sensors that are smaller than 35mm full-frame negatives. The dimensions of digital photo-sensors are similar to the APS-C image frame size, for example, the 24 × 16mm. Therefore, the angle of view for any given focal length lens will be narrower than it would be when used on a full-frame 35mm camera because the smaller sensor captures less of the image projected by the lens. The camera manufacturers provide a crop factor (sometimes called a field-of-view factor or a focal-length multiplier) to explain how much smaller the sensor is than a full-frame 35mm film. A common crop factor is 1.5 (Nikon DX format and some others), although many cameras have crop factors of 1.6 (most Canon DSLRs), 1.7 (the Sigma DSLRs), and 2 (the Four Thirds–format cameras). The 1.5 indicates that the angle of view of a lens on the digital camera is the same as a 35mm full-frame camera with a lens focal length 1.5 times longer, which explains why the crop factor is also known as a focal-length multiplier. For example, a lens with a focal length of 42mm on a DSLR actually images the angle of view of a 28mm lens on a full-frame 35mm camera. So, to determine the focal length of a lens for a digital camera that will give the equivalent angle of view as one on a full-frame camera, the full-frame lens focal length must be multiplied by the crop factor. For example, to get the equivalent angle of view of a 28mm lens on a full-frame 35mm camera, from a digital camera with a 1.5 crop factor, one would use an 18mm lens.

To respond to this problem, lens manufacturers are making wide-angle lenses of shorter focal lengths for DSLRs. At the same time, they limit the diameter of the image projected through the lens to slightly more than the diagonal measurement of the photo-sensor. This gives the designers the ability to provide the necessary optical corrections while economically producing high-quality images at short focal lengths, especially for zoom lenses. Examples include 10mm minimum focal length zoom lenses from several manufacturers. At 10mm, these lenses provide the angle of view of a 15mm lens on a full-frame 35mm camera when the crop factor is 1.5.

Any lens with a focal length shorter or numerically smaller than normal for a given image receptor size is considered a **wide-angle lens**. Any lens with a focal length longer or numerically larger than normal for a given image receptor size is considered a **telephoto lens**. A wide-angle lens shrinks a given subject to a size smaller on the receptor than a corresponding normal lens, and a telephoto lens magnifies the subject. For example, a 200mm telephoto lens used with a 35mm camera yields a 4× magnification on film over the normal 50mm lens, and a 24 mm lens yields a magnification of .5 times.

The focal length of a lens also establishes the **field of view** of the photographic image. Shorter lenses yield a larger-than-normal field of view on the image receptor. The magnification factor of the image of an object and the object's actual size can be found by dividing the focal length of the lens used to make the image by the focal length of a standard lens for any given format. Then multiply the numeric result times the physical size the image would have been if formed by a normal lens. For example, if an object is photographed with a 40mm lens on a full-frame 35mm camera, the resultant image, on film, will be 40/50×normal, or 80%. When the subject is 80% of normal, and the image receptor size is constant, the field of view will increase by approximately 20%.

It would seem that a zoom lens would be the answer to every photographer's dream of versatility. The wider the zoom range, the greater the variety and size of subject a camera may capture with the least effort of the photographer. However, wide-angle and telephoto lenses may distort the photographic perspective of objects in the finished photograph. It is more important to represent the image perspective as relatively normal than it is to lessen the photographer's effort necessary to capture the image.

Fixed Focal Length Lenses

In photography, a **prime lens** is a lens whose focal length is fixed, as opposed to a zoom lens, which has a variable focal length. Prime lenses are not as versatile as their zoom counterparts but are often of superior optical quality, higher speed (have a larger maximum aperture), and lower cost. This is because the designs are less complicated by having fewer moving parts, and these lenses can be optimized for one particular focal length. They also produce images with a perspective that is the closest to matching the angle of view of monocular human vision.

When the lenses built into digital cameras have a fixed focal length, they are usually a moderate wide-angle, the equivalent of a 35mm lens on a 35mm camera. Compared to zoom lenses, a fixed lens will normally be smaller and lighter and will have a larger maximum aperture. This makes fixed lenses a good choice for exposing photographs in low light. Fixed focal length lenses are normally higher in resolution and contain fewer aberrations than do zoom lenses.

The disadvantage of wide-angle lenses is that the subject may appear smaller in the photograph than it would appear to normal vision unless the camera is close to the subject at the time of exposure. Moving closer to the subject is not always possible for obvious reasons. The closer proximity may also cause problems in perspective. Some photographers prefer to work with fixed focal length lenses because all the photos taken with the same lens can be grouped and used together if photogrammetry is being used to derive measurements. Also, the visual perspective of all the images will be the same.

Zoom Lenses

A zoom lens is a mechanical assembly of lens elements with the ability to vary its focal length, as opposed to a prime lens, which has a fixed focal length. Zooms are commonly used with still, video, and motion picture cameras, some binoculars, microscopes and telescopes, and other optical instruments.[3]

Photographic zoom lenses should not be confused with telephoto lenses. Some zoom lenses are telephoto, some are wide-angle, and others cover a range from wide-angle to telephoto. Lenses in the latter group, sometimes referred to as "normal" zooms, have displaced the fixed prime lens as the popular one-lens selection on many contemporary cameras.[4]

The major advantage of a zoom lens is its versatility. A photographer using a zoom lens can quickly change framing and more easily photograph a moving subject while keeping the size of the object constant. Zooms may also capture many different compositions of the same subject in less time than it would take for the photographer to physically move.

A camera with a fixed focal length lens must move to the proper distance when the subject moves to maintain a consistently sized image. Most forensic photographers capture photographs of objects that are not moving, so attempting to maintain a fixed subject size is not normally an issue.

The typical inexpensive zoom lens on a digital camera is manufactured to yield images with angles of view equivalent to about a 35mm to a 105mm lens on a 35mm camera, representing approximately a 3:1 zoom ratio.

Optical zoom and digital zoom differ in a fundamental way. In **optical zoom** the lens has moving elements that change relative position to change the physical focal length of the lens. In **digital zoom** the camera computer crops the image to a smaller size so that the image appears as if it were taken with a telephoto lens. The difference between the two lens types is that the optical zoom yields maximum resolution throughout its focal length. The digital zoom depreciates images whenever it is engaged because it limits the number of effective pixels involved in creating the image.

Zoom lenses often have relatively small maximum apertures—usually about *f*3.5 to *f*5.6—which makes the lenses difficult to use without a slower shutter speed or higher ISO when the light level is marginal or low. One of the more popular methods enabling the use of zoom lenses in low light is the use of a flash. However, many flashes may not be powerful enough to illuminate a large scene and may also cause problems with reflections or the darkening of shadows.

Modern optical design techniques have enabled the construction of zoom lenses with good aberration correction over widely variable focal lengths and apertures.[5]

DSLR Lenses

DSLR cameras designed for professional use always allow the use of interchangeable lenses. If the photographer already owns a Nikon, Canon, or other similar brand of SLR film-based camera, it will be an advantage to buy a digital camera that uses the same lenses. Nikon lenses will also work on Fuji DSLRs.

Image Sensors

The CCD or CMOS (the two main types of image sensors used in digital cameras) sensor used to detect the image in DSLRs is usually smaller than the film frame in a 35mm camera. Using the lenses from a film camera on a digital camera will result in images with a narrower field of view because the same lens is now effectively longer. This means that any lens that is considered normal on a film camera will yield images corresponding to a telephoto lens when attached to a digital camera. The difference is expressed as a "multiplication factor" that calculates the digital equivalent of a 35mm format lens equivalent on a digital camera. The Nikon D100 has a multiplication factor of 1.5. This means that when a film-standard 50mm lens is attached to the D100, it produces images with the same angle of view as a 75mm telephoto lens on a 35mm camera.

When using longer lenses, the multiplication effect grows larger. A 200mm lens on a digital camera will yield images that appear as if they were exposed with a 300mm lens. A 24mm lens creates images that appear as if they were exposed with a 36mm lens.

Angle of View

The **angle of view** is the measure in degrees of the coverage of a given lens for a given film format. For example, a 50mm lens covers a 47° view on a 35mm camera, and an 81° view on a 6×6cm camera.

The angle of view is the angle at which light rays pass through the lens to form an image on the film. Although this angle is often defined as the angle across the film diagonal, the dimensions across the width and height of the film are generally of more practical interest because they define the physical format of the resultant image.

The **point of view** of an image is the aspect from which a particular scene or object is seen or imaged. The image exposed from a particular point of view is variable only by changing the focal length of the imaging lens.

Lens Equivalents

DSLR manufacturers supply low-priced zoom lenses to use with their cameras to match the focal lengths of the popular and familiar zooms that had been used for years with film. A 12–24mm zoom lens on a digital camera produces images equivalent to an 18–36mm in film, thus covering virtually the full wide-angle range. A digital sensor roughly two-thirds the size of a normal 35mm film frame (about 24×16mm) provides about the same image quality yielded by normal 35mm film.

Some digital camera manufacturers are marketing full-frame cameras, the size of 35mm film, with sensors. These cameras are meant to equal the quality of medium-format film cameras and are priced accordingly.

Accessory Lenses

Some manufacturers of noninterchangeable-lens digital cameras market optional accessory lens converters that fit onto the front of the camera lens to alter the focal length. The wide-angle adapter provides a wide-angle effect, in some cases yielding an angle of view equivalent to a 24mm lens on a 35mm camera.

Although the increase in angle of view may be useful, front-of-lens converters may yield relatively poor image quality and should not be relied upon when high-quality images are desired. Lens adapters also reduce the effective aperture of the lens, increasing exposure times.

Macrophotography is close-up photography in which the image projected on the sensor or film is either about the same physical size as the subject or even larger. Another definition of a macro image is that when a 4×6-inch print is made from the image file, the subject is rendered life size or larger. This requires a magnification ratio in the file of approximately 1:4, which is easily attainable by most macro lenses.

Macro lenses are constructed with a long barrel designed for close focusing. A macro lens may be optimized to provide its best performance at a magnification of 1:1. Some macro lenses can achieve magnifications up to 5:1.

Other accessories for macrophotography include extension tubes, bellows, auxiliary close-up lenses, and reversing rings (see Chapter 10).

APERTURE AND DEPTH OF FIELD

Only one actual plane of focus is in front of the camera, at the distance where the lens is set. Any other part of the image is increasingly blurred by a factor equivalent to its distance from the plane of focus. Actually, the plane of focus is not a plane, but part of the surface of a sphere whose radius is the distance of the focus point from the camera.

> **TIP:**
>
> No distinct boundary exists when an image is within depth of field and when it is outside the limits of acceptable depth of field. It amounts to whether an image appears acceptably sharp in the finished image.

Depth of field is defined as the region within which the level of blur will be undetectable to most people under normal viewing conditions. The farther away an object is from the plane of focus, the more blurred it will be.

If the image of a subject is focused perfectly on the image plane, then a small point on the image plane will represent a small point on the subject. However, if the precise point of focus lies in front of or behind the image plane, then each point of the subject will be represented by a circle on the film plane. This is termed the **circle of confusion**.

People have varying abilities to detect fuzziness within an image. Viewing conditions also will have an effect on this ability. For example, the farther away the viewer is from an image, the harder it will be to detect blur. Therefore, conventions exist that define maximum circle of confusion size for adequate viewing.

Acceptable focus by definition, is the largest circle in an image that the eye cannot differentiate from a dot. In 35mm format cameras, a 0.03mm-diameter circle of confusion is considered acceptable. The larger the image, the larger the circle is allowed to be because larger images tend to be viewed at greater distances. If 2,000 pixels are distributed across the diagonal of a digital image, the circle of confusion must be slightly smaller than a single pixel.

Under optimum viewing conditions, a person with good vision may resolve objects whose diameter is 1/3,000 of the viewing distance. This means that lines 1 mm across can be distinguished at a viewing distance of 3 meters. Photographic convention assumes that at 10 inches the eye cannot separate image patches less than .001 inch across. Therefore, image patches less than .001 inch in diameter will be perceived as sharp. Hence, an acceptable circle of confusion in these circumstances is deemed to be .001 inch.

The Effect of Aperture on Depth of Field

Aperture restricts the diameter of the beams of light striking the image plane. This means that, for the same subject distance and focus point, the circles of confusion are smaller if the aperture is smaller.

DISTORTION CORRECTION

A perfect lens would yield even illumination across the entire image, would yield excellent image sharpness for all colors of light across the entire image, and would yield acceptable linearity, meaning that if the lens was rectilinear, it would represent any straight line in reality by a straight line in the image. No such thing as a perfect lens exists. All lenses have defects, or *aberrations*. All photographic lenses contain multiple elements, usually combining converging and diverging lenses made of different glasses to cancel out some of the inherent problems.

Today most images are captured by digital technology, and most imaging is performed digitally. In fact, film is often scanned into a digital format, and film-based printing methods are becoming increasingly obsolete.

Following exposure, digital images may be corrected in various ways. Digital cameras often incorporate lens-specific algorithms to correct some inherent lens faults. This increases the necessity of using OEM lenses, rather than aftermarket accessories, for forensic photography.

Almost all lenses show some distortion from a perfectly rectilinear shape. When photographed, a rectangle may bulge out in the middle into a barrel shape or bulge in to create a pincushion effect. It is not uncommon for zoom lenses to show both effects, often with pincushion effects at wide-angle focal lengths and barrel effects at telephoto lengths. Prime lenses also suffer from pincushion or barrel distortion, although it is usually less noticeable.

CAMERA MAINTENANCE

Taking photographs in the field is difficult under the best of conditions (see Fig. 5–8). The sites of accidents, explosions, fires, and crimes are hard on the equipment and hard on the photographer. The temperature range may be very hot to very cold. The air may be damp. The atmosphere may be dusty and polluted with dirt and ash. Use of a camera protected from the elements with some type of weatherproof housing to prevent inevitable and expensive damage, if only a plastic bag, is recommended.

> **TIP:**
>
> The environment where you take your camera will not always be sterile.

A good camera, like any other fine mechanical device, will maintain operational status if it is used regularly. Normal use prevents lubricants from becoming stiff and gummy. If the camera in use has been dormant for a while, do not be surprised if it has developed mechanical problems, no matter how much it cost.

Impact damage from being dropped is the worst problem for a camera. In addition, blowing dirt, dust, and sand can enter the camera's mechanisms and cause problems that can only be repaired by a trained technician. If your camera gets rained on, dry it with lint-free materials as soon as possible. Remove surface dirt and dust with a lint-free cloth, a camera brush, or compressed air before changing lenses, batteries, or memory media. If the dirt on the camera is not easily removed, a cotton swab moistened in alcohol is an acceptable cleaning tool.

Avoid leaving cameras and film in closed areas at high temperatures. Heat can damage media, melt plastics, and cause lubricants in the camera and lenses to melt and run onto surfaces where lubricant was unintended. This will cause problems.

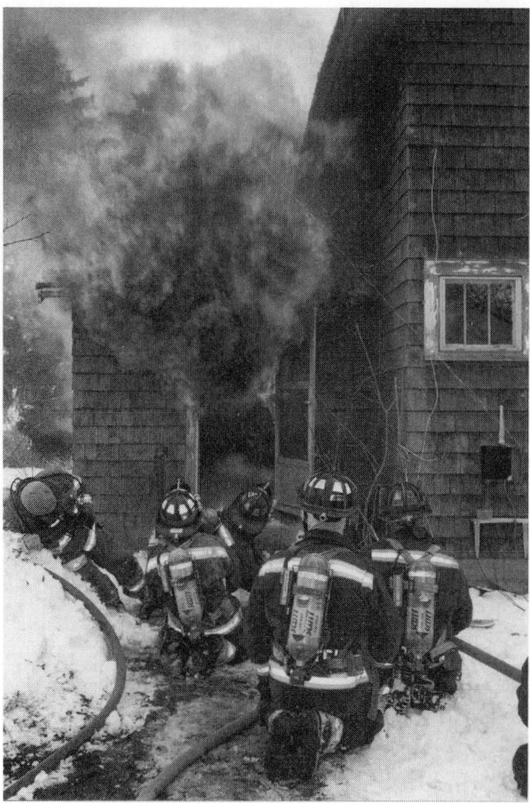

FIGURE 5–8 Fire scenes are always damp and dirty, so use utmost care to protect photographic equipment at all times. *Source:* Packer Engineering.

A hot and damp environment (see Fig. 5–9) is as difficult for the photographer as it is for the equipment. When the relative humidity is over 65%, moisture may condense on the inside surfaces of the camera and short-circuit the electronics. It may also form cloudy deposits on interior lens surfaces. This may happen to new cameras, and if it does, the damages will not be covered under warranty.

Never leave a camera in a sealed bag in direct sunlight. Condensation that forms inside the bag may penetrate the camera and lenses, causing interior mechanisms to rust.

Check your camera's strap and strap lanyards periodically. If any part is worn or loose, tighten or replace it.

Keep photographic optics clean. Dirt, dust, and fingerprints on lenses will cause the degradation of images. Lenses can be cleaned with lens

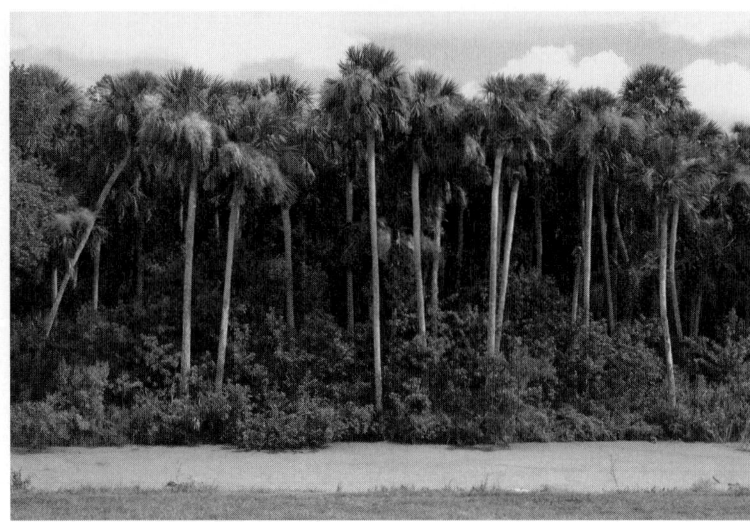

FIGURE 5–9 A swamp is an example of a moist and warm environment that could harm a camera. *Source:* Jimmy Brown.

tissues or any soft, absorbent, lint-free cloth. Anything safe for use on eyeglasses is appropriate. Do not use facial tissues, which are soft on your face but not lint free; if used repeatedly on coated optics, they may scratch off the lens coating.

DSLR Sensor Cleaning

DSLRs that produce images with small white spots may have dust on the sensor. In its E1 model, Olympus has added an ultrasonic vibrator that shakes the dust off before each image is exposed. No other manufacturers have developed similar technology.

Image sensors attract dust. Even a new camera may leave the factory with a dusty sensor. Some cameras are less prone to this problem than others. One possible reason for this problem is that CMOS sensors display less attraction for dust than CCDs.

DSLR camera manuals may not offer practical solutions for the dust problem. Nikon DSLR manuals state that the actual CCDs in their cameras are protected from dust by a low pass filter, present in front of the CCD to reduce **moiré effects**, which are interference patterns caused when regular patterns in the subject interact with the regular array of the image sensor. What looks like dust on the sensor may actually be dust on the filter. Most dust particles are too small to be visible with the naked eye. Many attempts to remove dust result in the filter gathering even more dust. Unless you use a camera with a self-cleaning sensor, the equipment may require professional maintenance.

Recommendations and Warnings

Major camera manufacturers recommend that their equipment be cleaned by factory-authorized service personnel. The cost, inconvenience, and time involved may make that an impractical solution. As previously noted, it is possible to damage the filter (and possibly also the sensor) by either excessive force, scratching with hard materials, or using excessive or unsuitable liquids.

TIP:

Any work photographers perform on their own cameras is undertaken entirely at their own risk—and may invalidate the camera warranty.

Before cleaning a camera sensor, be sure that the mirror chamber, mirror, and back of the lens are clean. Be sure to work in the cleanest and most dust-free area available.

TIP:

Read the camera's instruction manual to determine how to lock the mirror safely for cleaning.

TIP:

Do not use canned air around a camera mirror because the some propellants may damage the camera.

Use a large rubber bulb blower-brush with the brush removed to blow dust out of the inside of a camera. Do not touch the filter or sensor with anything but air. After cleaning, replace the lens on the camera body and take a test exposure of a sheet of paper or a similar clean, detail-free surface, using even lighting and a high number (small) aperture using auto-exposure. Inspect the resultant image on a computer monitor and any remaining dust will be clearly visible. If dust is still an issue, go through the cleaning procedure again.

Kits and gadgets are available at most photo shops for cleaning digital cameras, but be very careful when doing your own maintenance.

SPECIAL SITUATIONS

Inclement Weather Photography

Forensic photographers will be forced to work outdoors under every type of weather condition. Living and working in a warm climate may eliminate the need to prepare for cold weather, just as living and working in Alaska may eliminate the need to prepare for excessive heat. Yet everyone must prepare for moisture in the form of rain or high humidity.

Unless photographic hardware is waterproof, it must be protected from rain. Another concern for the forensic photographer is that rain creates shiny surfaces on most materials. Thus, the photographer working in overcast or rainy conditions that block direct sunlight may need to use longer shutter speeds, wider apertures, or higher ISO settings. To be properly prepared for rain, always carry some type of waterproof bag for camera equipment, as well as an umbrella to shield the top and front of the lens so water does not reach the lens elements and diminish clarity. Carrying and using a tripod on overcast and rainy days may be a necessity.

Snow Photography

The whiteness of snow adds contrast to the normal colors of a scene and can cause difficulties when using a light meter. The light meter's built-into cameras see snow as a very bright object, which causes the camera to set the exposure for the brightness of the snow and to create underexposed images. Most experienced photographers routinely overexpose snow photos to make the snow appear as bright as it actually is and to properly expose the rest of the frame.

The presence of snow may disrupt the camera's automatic white balance sensor. In such cases, the photographer should either adjust the white balance to suit the snow or switch to automatic.

Dew Point

All air contains water vapor. The amount varies. The *dew point* is an indication of the amount of moisture in the air. A higher dew point indicates greater moisture content at a given temperature. The dew point of humid air always will be higher than the dew point of dry air.

Air is *saturated* when it is holding the most water vapor possible at the existing temperature and pressure. *Dew point temperature* is defined as the temperature to which the air would need to cool (at constant pressure and constant water vapor content) to reach saturation.

Condensation of water vapor begins when the temperature of air is lowered to its dew point and beyond. For this reason, never bring a camera that is cold into a warm and damp environment. Moisture will immediately condense on the camera surfaces and may cause electrical and eventually oxidation problems.

The camera manufacturer does not warranty its equipment against short circuits caused by moisture. Use of a plastic bag over the camera is a very inexpensive but satisfactory solution to the moisture problem. Position the lens so it protrudes through an opening in the bag. Clean off water droplets on the front of the lens with a lint-free cleaning cloth.

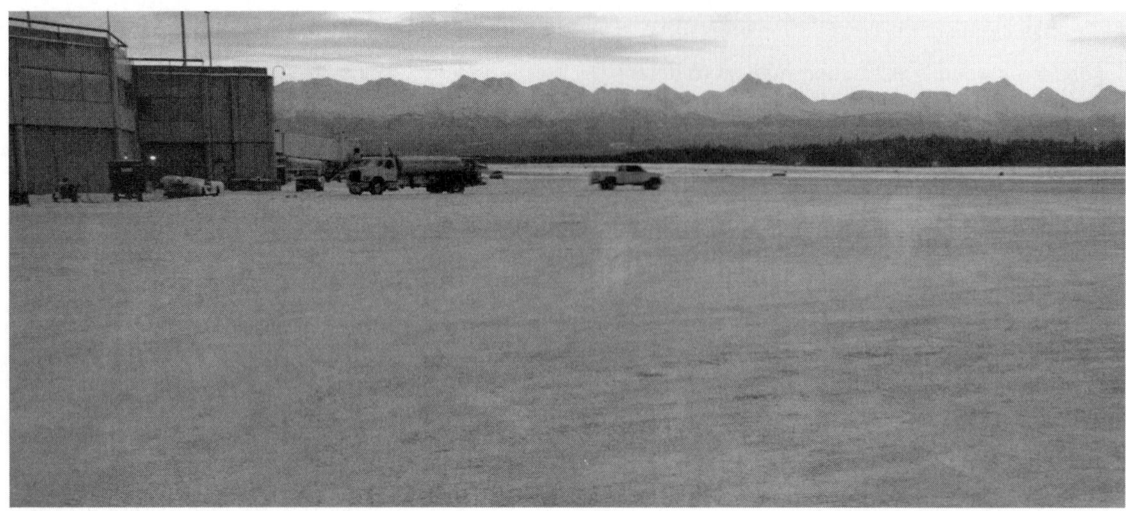

FIGURE 5–10 Outside Anchorage, Alaska (January 2006). The camera was being used on a weeklong project, and the temperature never rose above –10° F. Even at the very low temperature, the humidity was relatively high. The camera could only be taken outside of the photographer's jacket for the brief moments required to make the photographs. To prevent condensation, the camera had to be placed into a sealable plastic bag every time it was brought into a warm environment. *Source:* Sandy Weiss.

Preventing and Managing Condensation

If the camera does get cold, allow it to warm slowly. Several hours may be required for the camera to gradually and safely rise to room temperature. You also may enclose a cold camera in a sealed plastic bag, in which case the moisture will condense on the outside of the bag rather than on the camera (see Fig. 5–10).

Airport Security

When comparing digital technology to the older and more established conventional film technology, much is published on the subjects of acceptability in court, archival characteristics, resolution, quality, cost, ease of manipulation, versatility, reliability and durability of cameras, and, of course, the susceptibility of images to airport scanners and X-rays.

Over time, airport security equipment has often been detrimental to exposed and unexposed, unprocessed camera film. Depending upon the type of X-ray machine, the level to which it has been set, the number of passes through, the degree of protection of the film, and the factory-produced light sensitivity (ASA) of the film, X-rays have been the cause of fogging, lowering the contrast of exposed/unprocessed film and essentially raising the ASA of unexposed/unprocessed film. These effects have not been consistent from airport to airport, country to country, or carry-on to checked baggage. Authorities report that the latest high-intensity X-ray scanners *will damage* unprocessed film.

Not so long ago, many photographers routinely carried their film in lead-foil pouches to protect it from X-rays. Those pouches are no longer recommended. In fact, they may cause more severe damage to film, in carry-on as well as checked baggage, because the inspector may increase the X-ray intensity when inspecting baggage containing lead pouches to enable inspection of the contents of the pouch. The decision to install new, more powerful X-ray scanning equipment at United States airports is intended to make air travel safer, but it also means anyone carrying unprocessed film must take steps to safeguard film when traveling by air.

Are airport scanning and X-ray inspection as harmful to digital equipment and image files as it is to unprocessed film? According to most current authorities, digital cameras, memory cards, and exposed images will not be adversely affected by airport scanners or X-rays. However, even the authorities leave room for doubt. A major manufacturer of digital memory has stated that a possible cause of damaged digital files could be airport X-ray machines, and it recommends carrying cards through the scanner rather than packing them in luggage. It is not certain how the newer security screening devices will affect digital cameras or memory cards. For this reason, it may be best to request that these items be hand inspected to avoid any possibility of damage to the images they contain.

It is a known fact that radiation exposures in repeated doses can visibly fog unexposed camera film. I3A's Committee for Integrity in Transportation of Imaging states, "X-ray exposures and the new high-intensity scanning devices pose a considerable risk to film. The scanners are now being used on checked luggage and randomly selected carry-on items. The tests showed damaging streaks and fogging of film."[6] It would be best practice with unprocessed film to minimize scans and X-rays. If you have unused film left in your kit, do not take it through scanners again. Rather, use that film when traveling by car and take fresh film on your next trip through airport scanners.

The semiconductors used in electronic systems, including CompactFlash (and other memory), may be irreparably damaged if subjected to the irradiation process being used by the U.S. Postal Service (USPS) to sanitize the mail[7] (during anthrax inspections). Such damage will not only cause loss of data stored on the cards, but the cards will no longer be operable. It is not advisable to send image media by USPS because carriers, including UPS and FedEx, may be safer. Many articles and discussion forums address the subject of X-rays and scanners in relation to digital memory and hardware. Some people state they have sustained damage to their cameras and camera memory when transporting them through X-ray exposure. The only factor all the claims have in common is the lack of substantiated proof.

You may ask, "What is the bottom line? Should I worry?" To this question it seems best to respond yes, always worry; use good sense when it comes to irreplaceable images.

TAKING BETTER EVIDENCE PHOTOGRAPHS: A CHECKLIST

The following parameters are relevant to creating better evidence photographs:

1. Your digital or film camera is available and ready for use.
2. It contains an empty and appropriately sized image storage card or new roll of film.
3. The camera and lens are clean, dust free, and unsmudged, inside and out.
4. All camera batteries are charged to maximum power.
5. An appropriate situation needing forensic photographs occurs.

What more can a photographer do to prepare for the successful capture, storage, and transportation of appropriate images for evidence documentation? The next recommended step is to *stop and think*, if only for a moment, about the current project and any similarity it may have to previous evidence documentation experiences. Before commencing photography, mentally compare the current and planned documentation with prior experiences. Follow your mental roadmap to the current documentation that you used successfully for previous projects. The more practiced and automatic the steps the photographer takes to accomplish the photographic documentation, the more capacity the photographer will have for other means documentation and data collection. If the photographer must think about every step taken to produce the photographs, it is probable that photography is the only part of the investigation that will be successfully accomplished. For all projects, always follow established and appropriate documentation protocols—both physically and mentally.

For every project, ensure that the following are in place:

1. A reason for the documentation
2. A plan for the steps of the documentation
3. A vision of the end-product and eventual use of the images

The preceding quantifiers, properly used, should promote sound photographic decisions regarding the following:

1. Choosing the right images to expose
2. Setting the correct resolution, compression, format, lens focal length, sensor sensitivity, metering mode, and so on.
3. Elimination of the practice of exposing photographs for the sake of exposing photographs—that is, shooting just to shoot

Learning to make well-exposed and properly inclusive photographs in evidence situations and environments is a learning process that takes a lifetime for some people. The point is that photography, taken seriously, is like any other discipline: creating outstanding work requires focused and persistent effort, the correct equipment, and the appropriate mindset.

Follow these 10 basic steps to promote photographic quality:

1. Use Lighting Properly. When exposing photographs outdoors, the ambient lighting conditions present minimal and maximal opportunities for achieving the desired effect. In evidence work, two additional qualifiers apply to opportune timing: (1) the specific time the photographer has with the evidence and (2) when the photographer chooses to be with the evidence to characterize the situation as it appeared at a specific time in the past.

In either case, the ambient lighting will be used to greatest advantage by exposing the photographs with the sun or other light source illuminating the subject at the most appropriate angle. Proper light metering procedures must always be performed. Camera automation should be used only in situations in which the camera's internal metering systems are not easily confused. If the photographer is utilizing auxiliary lighting of any type, exposure must be adjusted to take proper advantage of the additional lighting.

If the scene being photographed is the subject of a vision study intended to portray what someone could have seen at the same place but at another time, lighting to approximate the situation at a specific time in the past must be used. If the photography is performed in low light with no supplementary lighting added, the following must be in place:

- A tripod must be used to hold the camera steady during exposure.
- Proper metering must be performed to expose the film or digital image for the desired effect.
- If the scene is to be measured for the quantity of light and/or compared to human vision, luminance or illuminance metering must be performed.
- Camera f-stops must never be compared to an amount of illumination enabling human vision.

2. Determine the appropriate composition. Good composition is desired and even mandated in aesthetic photography. In evidence photography, composition is not as important as content. Photographs must portray a reasonable representation of the evidence to be meaningful. Making the composition of evidence photographs pleasing to the eye is unnecessary.

3. Expose images from an appropriate point of view. Taking photographs with the camera at the photographer's eye level (5 to 6 feet above ground) is common practice, and that vantage point represents the way most people are accustomed to seeing the world. It may be useful to expose photographs from a higher or lower vantage point to document aspects of a subject that would be invisible from eye-level height.

When photographing an accident or crime scene, it is necessary to expose photographs from the angle and height occupied by a possible eyewitness. It is then necessary to document the position from which the eyewitness images were captured.

4. Maximize the depth of field. Use the smallest appropriate lens aperture (highest number) when exposing each image to maximize depth of field. Use the slowest appropriate shutter speed to maximize lens aperture.

With most photographic systems, depth of field may be predetermined before exposure to determine whether the whole subject will be in focus in the finished image. If the depth of field will be insufficient, you may do the following:

- Expose multiple images at various depths closer and farther from the subject.
- Adjust the camera-to-subject angle (perspective) to minimize subject relief.
- Add supplementary light to the subject to allow the use of smaller lens apertures.

5. Use light metering accurately. Camera meters are preset at the factory to register scene reflectance at a level of 18% of the light falling upon it. If the reflectance of the scene is greater than 18%, the camera will still calculate the reflectance at 18%, and if the camera meter is set on automatic, the resulting image will be underexposed. If the reflectance of the scene is less than 18%, the camera will still calculate the scene at 18%, and if the meter is set on automatic the resulting image will be overexposed. In-camera metering systems that are weighted in particular patterns and set properly will yield more accurate exposures than camera meters with automatic averaging systems.

The most accurate light metering methods require the acquisition of exposure information from the most important part of the scene. Using exposure information obtained in either of the following ways will yield properly exposed and more consistent images:

- A handheld light meter with an appropriate measurement angle
- The camera's built-in meter, and moving close to the important area of the scene until that area fills the camera viewfinder

6. Optimize contrast. Unless appropriate for a visual situation, avoid placing the light source behind the subject. If the source must be behind the subject, use extra care to meter properly on the subject. On bright, sunny days, expose images for the best detail in the shadows or use supplementary lighting to minimize the darkness of the shadows. Use of an appropriate lens filter will minimize contrast.

7. Use appropriate references. Visual references are necessary to best approximate, within the capabilities of the media, the following:

- Color
- Dimensions
- Location

Use any appropriate object of known color, size, or location as an in-image references. If the reference blocks any part of the subject evidence, expose a second photograph without the reference in the image.

8. Choose the proper focal length. Wide-angle and telephoto lenses should be used minimally for evidence photographs because they may exaggerate image perspective. If a normal lens is not sufficiently wide- angle to document entire scene from the photographer's position, expose overlapping photographs that can be assembled into a montage. Do not refocus the lens when exposing a series of photographs of a single object or scene.

9. Compromise as needed. Control of the visual depth of field, or the area of the finished photograph that is in acceptable focus, is valuable to most evidence photographs. It requires practice and an understanding of optics to properly capture optimum depth of field photographically. The lens aperture used to expose a photograph is the variable that controls the finished depth of field in the photograph.

Controlling shutter speed is necessary to minimize camera and subject movement. The relationship between lens aperture and shutter speed is what governs proper exposure. Every photograph involves some degree of compromise between the two exposure variables for image optimization.

10. Optimize perspective. *Perspective* is a graphic device used to describe the reproduction of a three-dimensional subject in a two-dimensional representation. *Proper perspective* is a representation of a subject with spatial relationships corresponding to how the subject appears with the unaided eye. Using sufficient visual clues is important to the capture of appropriate perspective and a correspondingly proper visual sense of depth. The use on any format camera of a lens with a normal focal length will promote the production of images with similar visual perspective to what is seen by a person with two healthy eyes. In general, a normal focal length lens approximates the diagonal measurement of the image format. Deviations from normal lens focal length will produce images with distorted perspective, unless the images are printed in an appropriate size and viewed from an appropriate distance to minimize the distortion.

Remember, photographs should tell as much as possible of the story of the evidence, and notes, drawings, and human testimony will substantiate the images.

USING A TRIPOD

A tripod can either be a great advantage to the photographer or the photographer's worst enemy. When going on a long field assignment—for example, when performing surveillance—a photographer should always bring a tripod. If the assignment requires photography in low light, a tripod is also essential. However, carrying a heavy tripod to every job site may not be practical. To bring a tripod or not becomes a question only the photographer can answer by assessing the situation.

Blurring is especially noticeable in photographs exposed at slow shutter speeds and becomes more apparent when photographs are enlarged. The use of a tripod minimizes movement caused by shaky hands. Most people cannot hand-hold a camera with a normal lens at a shutter speed under 1/30 of a second. A good rule is to use a tripod if the camera must be set at a shutter speed slower than the reciprocal of the focal length of the lens being used for the photograph. For example, if a 200mm lens is used, the shutter speed is slower than 1/250 second, and the lens is not stabilized, a steady hand or a tripod is required to avoid blurry images.

The camera attaches to the tripod head, which allows the camera to swivel and move up and down. Two basic types of head are available: the three-way pan tilt head and the ball head. Three-way heads have three different axes of movement, and each is controlled with its own mechanism and lock. The mechanisms allow the camera to be leveled and turned vertically. A ball head tripod is more expensive and usually used for videography because of its ease of positioning and fluidity of motion.

Types of Tripods

The type of tripod the photographer uses depends on the weight of the camera being supported. Lighter-weight, digital, 35mm, medium-format rangefinders and camcorders may be properly supported on lightweight tripods. Heavy medium- and large-format cameras, longer lenses, and video cameras require heavier tripods. Tripods are rated by on the weight they can properly support. The stiffest and lightest tripods are constructed with fewer sections. For most purposes, the maximum height should allow the photographer to use the camera at a comfortable standing position. (A tripod higher than this is rarely needed; however, see Case Study: Rail Yard for an exception.) Monopods are suitable in situations where tripods are either too heavy or too cumbersome.

The most expensive tripods are constructed of composite materials, including carbon fiber, which is lighter and more durable than either aluminum or steel. Expensive tripods are usually equipped with quick-release mechanisms for adjusting the legs and camera mount.

Tripods usually have a center column on which to attach the tripod head. This center column may also be used for fine height adjustment. Some tripod models allow the camera to be tilted down toward the ground for close-up work.

GO-KITS FOR THE FORENSIC PHOTOGRAPHER[8]

Whether it is called a go team, emergency response team, special response team, special operations group, multidisciplinary investigation team, special weapons and tactics (SWAT) team, or anything else, the unit represents a focused approach to problem solving and situational response.

A forensic photographer may be part of such a squad or may operate independently. In some circumstances, and often dependent upon whether the photographer is a government employee or private-sector practitioner, the photographer's participation in a team may be dictated by the size and scope of the situation to which the team is responding.

Specialized knowledge and equipment are required of any go team and its go-kit.

The photographic equipment contained in any go-kit may be dictated by the composition of the go team and the type(s) of situations to which the team is dispatched. In addition to a typical camera bag, a photographer attached to a SWAT team may need personal protective equipment and possibly the same armament worn by other team members. A photographer attached to a medical examiner's unit may require an entirely different style of personal protective equipment.

Photography at traffic and industrial accidents and other catastrophic events require another set of tools. Larger scenes require the use of larger scales to properly measure the location of artifacts. Larger scenes may also require the use of aerial photography and all of the equipment necessary for that discipline. The accepted protocol dictated by the needs of these types of situations will dictate the types of images necessary for the documentation of injury causation, component failure, compliance with legal standards, and other related issues.

It is always necessary to address the weather conditions on site. A photographer working in snowy mountains requires different equipment than a photographer working in a swamp.

Photography with Mirrors

One of the most important categories of gadgets to keep in a go-kit is a selection of mirrors. Mirrors are used to add light to an area otherwise difficult or impossible to illuminate in other ways. Mirrors may be used to reflect the image of an object that is then photographed. Mirrors come in different sizes and are made of different materials.

The reflective surface of *rear-surfaced reflectors* is on the back of a piece of glass. These mirrors should be used only for reflecting a light source onto another surface. Using a camera to photograph images on rear-surfaced reflectors will produce photographs with double images (see Fig. 5–17). Most common household, hardware, and automotive mirrors are rear surfaced. These mirrors are easily identified by the gray surface on the opposite side of the reflector.

Front-surfaced reflectors are constructed of glass, plastic, or metal. All reflectors intended for photography are front surfaced and must be purchased from medical/dental/scientific supply companies (see Fig. 5–11). Many have specialized purposes, such as the stainless-steel reflectors designed to be placed by a dentist (or photographer) in a person's mouth to view upper and lower teeth without having to bend over or stand on a ladder.

Mirrors may be the only tool that makes it possible to tell multiple aspects of the same visual story in single photographs. Mirrors are also use-

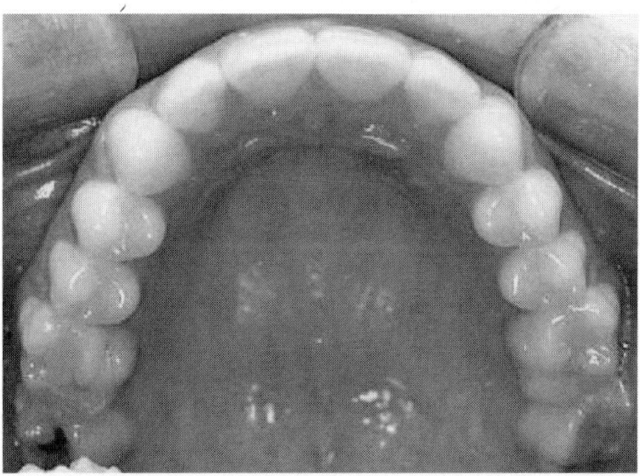

FIGURE 5–11 Intra-oral imaging with a dental mirror. *Source:* Dr. Warren Wakerlin.

ful for making photographs of aspects of objects where it is impossible to physically place the camera. It may be necessary to photograph aspects of mechanisms where disassembly would be the cause of evidence spoliation.* It is necessary to maintain a selection of front-surfaced reflectors of different sizes in a go-kit. Front-surfaced reflectors are fragile and expensive. Dentists who routinely use disposable plastic front-surfaced mirrors on patients may be a good source of supply for mirrors of that size.

What to Pack in a Go-Kit

Only the photographer can decide, based on the types of situations and locations to be encountered, what equipment is necessary. Forensic photographers realize their go-kits will change and grow as they encounter new situations and new equipment is becomes available.

The go-kit list in the following section is a small sample based on traffic accident experience.

A Typical Go-Kit for Traffic Accidents

Vehicle Equipment

Emergency beacons (LED or halogen flashers, strobes, etc.)

Work zone lights, tripods, power supplies, extension cords, etc.

Flares or portable electronic strobes/flashers

Traffic cones and traffic barriers (MUTCD compliant)*

Portable advance warning signs (MUTCD compliant)

Other equipment as needed

Personal Safety Equipment

Traffic safety vests (ANSI Class 3) and personal conspicuity lighting (portable electronic strobe/flasher)

Traffic control flags and traffic baton lights

Hard hat

Safety Glasses

Respirator

Gloves

Safety-toe shoes

Safety harness, etc.

Specialized personal protective equipment for hazardous duty, environmental contamination, etc.

Other equipment as needed

Personal Health Items

First-aid kit

Ice chest

Drink cooler

Portable refrigerator or personal hydration system

Skin protection items, such as sunscreen and insect repellent

Coveralls or other work clothes

Other items as needed

Site and Component Documentation Equipment

GPS navigation system

GPS measuring/surveying system

Laser measuring/surveying system

Optical measuring equipment

Measure wheels and tapes

Contour gauges, depth gauges, and calipers

Macro measuring tapes and scales

Optical and radar vehicle-speed measuring guns

Roadway traffic volume counting system

Vehicle acceleration and braking force measurement systems

Evidence markers and survey flags

Aerial photo target equipment

Other equipment as needed

*Lawyers and courts use the term *spoliation* to refer to the withholding, hiding, or destruction of evidence relevant to a legal proceeding. It is a criminal act in the United States under federal and most state law.

**Manual on Uniform Traffic Control Devices*, Federal Highway Administration, http://mutcd.fhwa.dot.gov.

Photography Equipment

Cameras

Camera memory cards or film

Lenses

Filters

Batteries

Power supplies

Cables

Cases and accessories applicable to the camera brand(s) and model(s) being used

Electronic flash units, macro flash units, axial lighting devices, flash cables, or wireless flash modules

Shades, reflectors, mirrors, gray cards, color-checker cards, and other illumination and electrical accessories

Tripods, monopods, tabletop mini-pods

Copy stands

Clamps and specialized mounting equipment (such as suction cup mounts for vehicle interior or exterior camera mounting)

Portable computer, with photo-management software, computer cables, and power supplies

Other equipment as needed

SUMMARY

A camera system for forensic photography may be assembled in many ways. It is best to consider many issues before spending a lot of money on a system you are going to use for a long time. Most important, the equipment must be appropriate for the type of work it is expected to perform.

One of the most confusing issues in digital photography is attempting to understand the significance of the number of pixels a camera has available and how that relates to the ultimate print quality. Always select an image resolution large enough to satisfy the needs of the largest print it is necessary to produce.

Weather is an issue when making photographs outdoors. It is critical to understand how to care for a camera system in all conditions and keep the equipment in proper working order. No camera manufacturers will warranty a camera against moisture, and moisture is the most common problem a photographer will face in either heat or cold.

A new camera will arrive from the factory with predetermined default settings. Always consult reference material to understand how the camera you buy has been preset and to determine which of those settings you will want to use and which you will want to change.

It is critical to understand the differences among camera batteries and how to care for each type. Without battery power, modern cameras will not operate.

Photographers must care for and respect the memory media in their cameras to ensure the capture of images. If the camera memory has problems, irreplaceable images may be lost.

Understanding the various types of lenses and what they do is fundamental for good photography. One of the hardest things to explain in court is how to correlate a camera image with what a person sees. The photographer should be properly prepared to address this issue.

Assembling a go-kit is a lifetime endeavor. The most valuable and useful gadgets for fieldwork may be items bought at a hardware store or automotive supply. Always design your kit for usefulness and portability, and always keep the kit together and ready to go for any eventuality.

CASE STUDY

RAIL YARD

A man driving a specially designed freight-moving truck drove into a heavy cart parked on the asphalt near the railroad tracks and was fatally injured. His family sued the railroad, claiming there was insufficient illumination to see the parked cart (see Fig. 5–12).

The preparation for the vision study/re-creation of this accident was extensive. Many hours of depositions were studied to enable, as closely as possible, the duplication of the lighting conditions as they existed on the night of the accident.

It was exactly a year after the occurrence that we had access to the scene. It was a rainy night on both nights. (It should be remembered that, although the study was performed on the

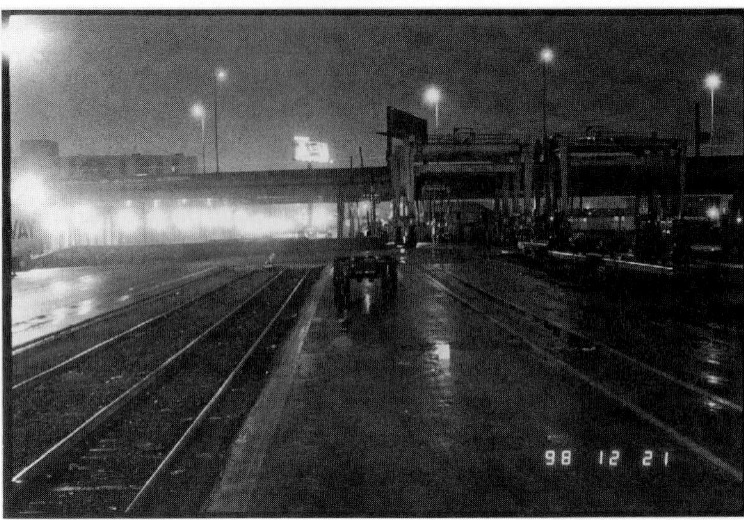

FIGURE 5-12 On location at the South-side Chicago rail yard where this project was performed. *Source:* Sandy Weiss/Packer Engineering.

same calendar date as that of the accident, the lighting would not necessarily be exactly the same on both nights). The assignment was to set up the scene as closely as possible to the conditions as they were the night of the accident and to take luminance and illuminance readings of the scene and to make photographs.

Several of the streetlights to the west (left side) of the scene were not lit the night of the accident, so we had the city remove the bulbs from the same lamps during our study. The time window was short. We had only limited access to the scene, limited time with the streetlights out, and limited time after moonset and before dawn. The actual project work was undertaken between midnight and 4:00 a.m.

Special meters are available for reading luminance and illuminance. The ones we used were manufactured by Minolta. *Illuminance* is the light falling on the subject. The whole scene was divided into a grid of 2-foot squares, and a reading was taken at every square. Those readings were recorded onto a predrawn survey and later analyzed, averaged, and mapped. Standards have been set for illumination of workplaces, and it was necessary to determine if the site met code. The *luminance* is the light reflecting off the objects in the scene. Luminance readings were taken of both the asphalt and the cart. A step wedge was placed in the illuminance of both, and the relative contrast of each was determined. The conspicuity of the cart was determined by comparing the contrast of the cart against the contrast of the asphalt/site.

The illumination from the headlight of the truck the man was driving when he was killed was a factor needing to be addressed. According to testimony and testing, the headlight on the truck was lit at the time of the accident. Headlight alignment must be assumed because the accident would make the alignment of the subject vehicle indeterminable.

The plan was to take photographs from the truck driver's point of view, through the windshield of an exemplar truck, to represent the view of the deceased driver as closely as possible. The cleanliness of the windshield had to be assumed. The seat height and eye level of the driver were calculated from the subject vehicle and the actual height of the driver.

One unusual problem was not foreseen. The truck headlight was inoperable unless the truck motor was running. The motor caused heavy vibrations inside the truck. The lighting was low enough that the images required long exposures to produce images with reasonable contrast. A tripod was brought to the scene to support the camera in the driver's seat. The driver's eye height was approximately 10 feet above the ground.

Making the photographs with the headlight turned on was critical. Taking the photographs from the cab of the truck with the motor running was not possible. The compromise was to make the exposures from the driver's eye height but outside the truck. This required a tripod that would extend to 10 feet to support the camera.

Not many photographers carry a tripod that tall in their go-kit. And we had no other time when we could come back and start over. A solution had to be found.

We drove back to our office and cut three lengths of iron pipe, large enough to fit over the tripod legs and long enough to raise the camera to the desired height. Then we went back to the scene, assembled the gear, and made the photographs. The only factor varying from the actual accident scenario needing to be explained in court was the difference the lack of the windshield made to the vision of the driver.

Conclusion: The photographs showed that the conspicuity of the cart was sufficient that the truck driver should have been able to see it under normal conditions.

This case illustrates the need to carry and use a tripod. Although no one expects photographers to carry leg extensions in their go-kits, ingenuity is always a good ability to have.

CASE STUDY

REFINERY

An explosion and resultant fire caused by a malfunctioning pressure relief valve differentially damaged a large section of a central Illinois refinery (see Fig. 5–13). One of the pressure tanks exploded, became ballistic, and landed several hundred yards from where it originally stood. Many pieces of wreckage were scattered over an area of acres, some of it in a grassy area to the west of the plant and some among the piping and tanks still standing.

The project in this case was to document the extent of the damage with both still and video photography and to map the wreckage to

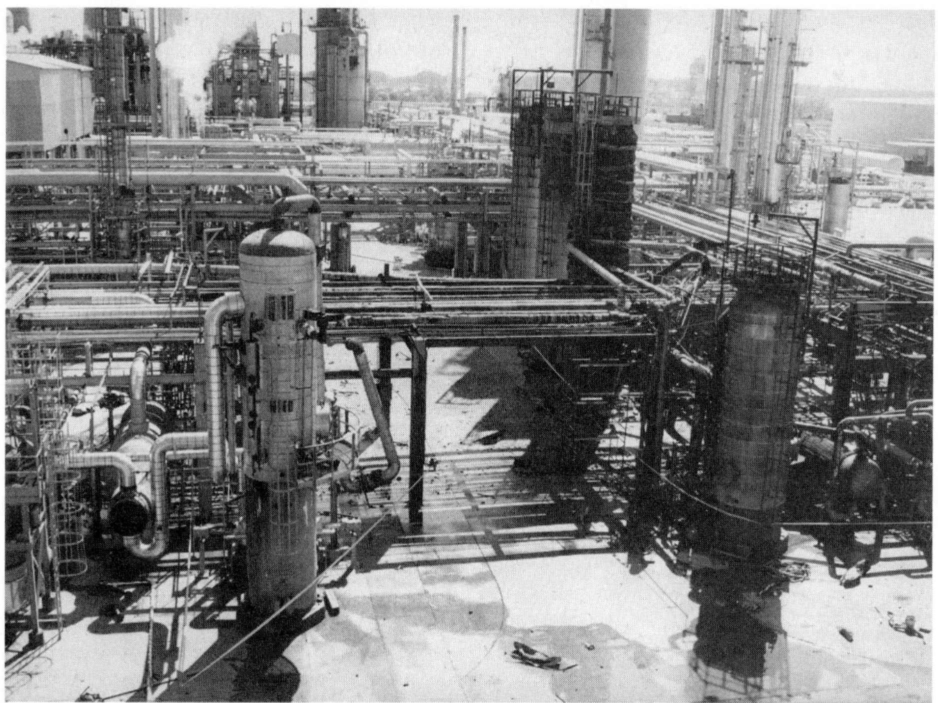

FIGURE 5-13 Overall image of the damage to the refinery, taken from an adjacent tower. *Source:* Sandy Weiss/Packer Engineering.

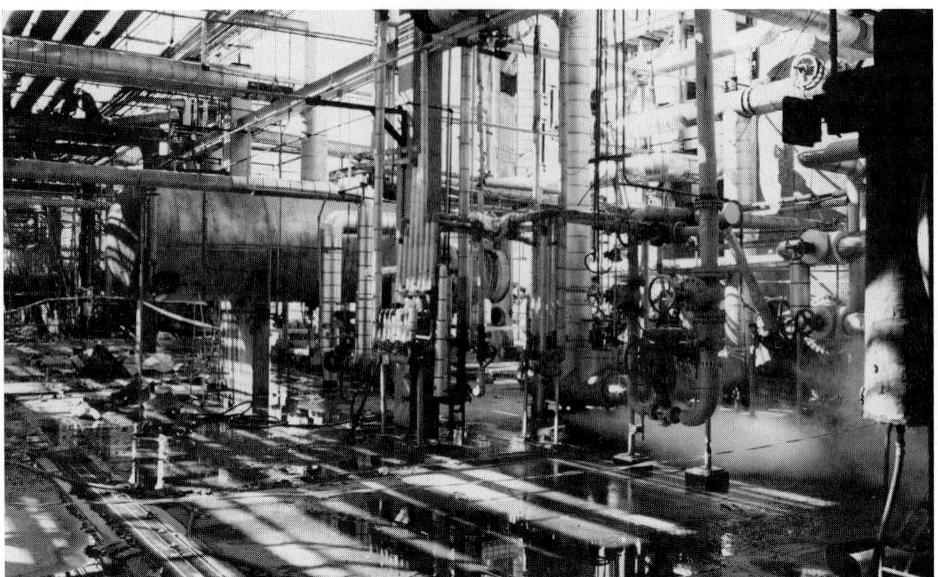

FIGURE 5-14 Medium-range photo of damage to the refinery. *Source:* Sandy Weiss/Packer Engineering.

reconstruct the sequence of the explosion by showing where everything had landed.

We were there the day after the fire. Nothing had been moved. The police and fire departments had strung yellow tape around the damaged areas and around any wreckage that happened to fall to the ground inside the boundaries of the burned sections.

That day's rainy conditions caused two distinct problems. The first was the protection of our gear from the falling water. We put plastic bags over all the equipment, with the lenses sticking out through holes in the plastic, to protect the cameras from the rain. The second problem involved photographing while the evidence was wet. The reflections of the wet surfaces added to the confusion (see Fig. 5–14). When a flash was used, it was necessary to hold the flash away from the camera at a large angle so the reflections would not bounce the light directly back into the camera lens. It was also necessary to minimize the contrast of the resultant images. In this case, it was accomplished by using low-contrast film and, if the project was performed digitally, by setting the contrast to a lower setting within the camera.

Another issue was the danger inherent in the slippery metal. It was necessary to climb ladders to the top of nearby metal tanks to expose overall images of the damages. It is difficult to climb ladders in the best of conditions while carrying heavy equipment, and these ladders were slippery. Such situations are typical of the kinds of situations forensic photographers must be prepared to endure.

CASE STUDY

STEERING ARM

A sports car allegedly went out of control while an elderly man was driving in a crowded city. The car struck multiple pedestrians; some were killed and many were injured.

It was necessary for the manufacturer of the car to determine the accident scenario, and we inspected the car to recreate the event. The car was brought to our laboratory for careful disassembly and study. We took photographs of each step.

The car manufacturer was content to place the blame on the driver. The driver testified that he was unable to steer when the car accelerated. The car had been damaged on impact, which made it critical to determine if any of the problems with the steering gear were extant before the accident.

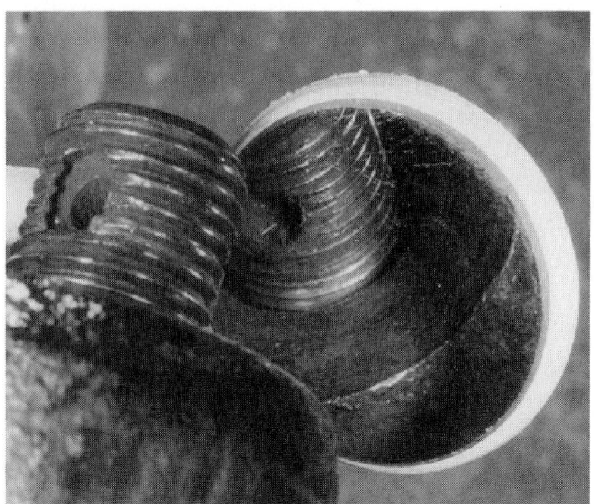

FIGURE 5–15 Both sides of the threads of a steering arm, shown by using a front-surfaced dental mirror. *Source:* Sandy Weiss/Packer Engineering.

The driver's-side steering arm was disconnected when the car was received and became a subject of close scrutiny. An engineer determined that a cotter pin that should have held the arm to the wheel had fallen out at some time prior to the accident. The photographic challenge was to illustrate the findings in as few photographs as possible to provide visual simplicity in the report.

Using a front-surfaced dental mirror (see Fig. 5–15), both sides of the hole where the cotter key was supposed to be could be shown in one photo. There was damage to one side of the hole and not to the other. Obvious wear also could be seen on the flat machined surface of the face of the arm below the threaded part. The clean threads at the root show the key was not missing for long.

Documenting all these factors in the single photograph made it easier for the engineer to explain the series of events leading to the accident.

CASE STUDY

DOOR LATCH

The door of a station wagon opened while the car was in motion. A passenger fell out and was injured. The owner of the vehicle claimed faulty design and sued the manufacturer. The manufacturer hired us to investigate.

The car was brought to the laboratory for inspection. We were ordered not to disassemble the door. Using mirrors for inspection, we found the door latch had scratches on the edge of the metal where there would be nothing on the mating surfaces to cause the damage.

The depositions of the car owner disclosed that he felt the door latch had been giving him problems for some time. He had taken the car to a repair service to have the door adjusted. While at the repair shop, a technician inserted a screwdriver into a hole in the door and bent the latch, leaving tool marks on the tongue. This is not a method authorized by the manufacturer for proper adjustment.

It was necessary to insert a front-surfaced mirror into the door, behind the latch, and take a photograph of the damage off the mirror (see Fig. 5–16). It was also necessary to shine appropriate flash illumination into another opening. It took hours to devise an appropriate shooting arrangement.

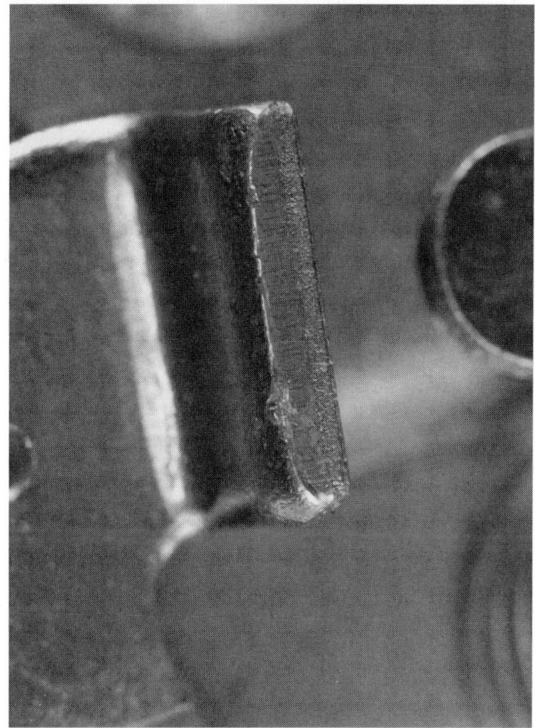

FIGURE 5-16 Subject door latch showing tool marks. *Source:* Sandy Weiss/Packer Engineering.

A medium-format camera was used. A bellows for magnification, a homemade adapter, and a 105mm lens from an enlarger (acting as a macro lens) were mounted on the camera. The advantage of using enlarging lenses for macrophotography is that they are sharp and small so they can be used in tight quarters. The 105mm length was used to provide added working distance between the camera and the latch (see Chapter 10).

Rear-surfaced mirrors (see Fig. 5–17) sold in hardware stores, intended to be used for inspecting remote parts of an automobile, yield photographs in which each landmark is doubled. The mirror displays one image off the front of the glass and one image off the mirrored surface on the back. These mirrors are not intended to be used for photography.

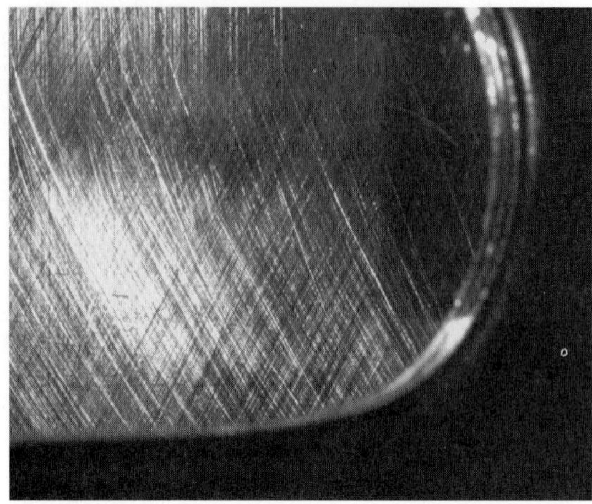

FIGURE 5–17 The inside of an aircraft engine cylinder, exposed with a rear-surfaced mirror. *Source:* Sandy Weiss/Packer Engineering.

KEY TERMS

image resolution, (p. 129)
pixels, (p. 129)
RGB, (p. 129)
brightness value, (p. 129)
megapixel, (p. 129)
interpolation algorithm, (p. 130)
matrix, (p. 130)
digital single-lens reflex camera (DSLR) (p. 130)
visual noise, (p. 133)
polarizing filter, (p. 133)
aperture priority, (p. 135)
default setting, (p. 135)
NiCad, 000 (p. 136)
battery memory, (p. 136)
NiMH, (p. 137)
Li-ion, (p. 137)
CompactFlash (CF) card, (p. 138)
Single Digital (SD) card, (p. 139)
memory stick, (p. 139)
focal length, (p. 140)
zoom lens, (p. 140)
wide-angle lens, (p. 141)
telephoto lens, (p. 141)
field of view, (p. 141)
prime lens, (p. 141)
optical zoom, (p. 142)
digital zoom, (p. 142)
angle of view, (p. 143)
point of view, (p. 143)
macrophotography, (p. 143)
depth of field, (p. 144)
circle of confusion, (p. 144)
aperture, (p. 144)
moiré effect, (p. 146)

EXERCISES

Choose any object of a reasonable size and interest as your subject. A sunny day is preferable, but a cloudy day is okay for some subjects and creates different problems.

1. Expose images of a subject (perhaps a vehicle), aiming at the narrow end, using a range of shutter speed and aperture combinations. Start at 1/30 second and proceed in logical steps to 1/500 second, using corresponding apertures to yield a satisfactory exposure.
2. Starting at ISO 200, expose one image of the subject at each higher ISO until you reach the camera's limitations. Record exposure information for review. Compare depth of field and image quality.

3. Set the default color balance to automatic and record a base exposure. Change the color balance to all possible combinations, including flash. Use flash where appropriate.
4. Create a composition of the subject with the zoom lens set at a normal focal length. Expose a series of images at wide-angle and telephoto settings on the zoom lens, keeping the short end of the subject the same size in the frame.
5. Expose a macro image of a selected area of the subject at the camera's closest focus distance. Expose a series of images of the same area, while zooming through the lens focal lengths, from telephoto to wide-angle. Compare the quality of the first image to the quality of the others. Remember to use appropriate scales.
6. Expose a bracketed series of overall exposures of the subject, running through very dark, to normal, to very light.
7. On a very sunny day, expose various images of the subject with and without flash fill.
8. Expose a photo story of the subject, starting with appropriate overall images and working your way in to close-ups, to explain any aspect of the subject to another person or a jury. Use appropriate scales and placements for each image.
9. Expose overlapping close-up images of the long side of the subject, appropriate for stitching into a panorama.
10. Record in a logical manner everything you do.

Chapter 6

The Image

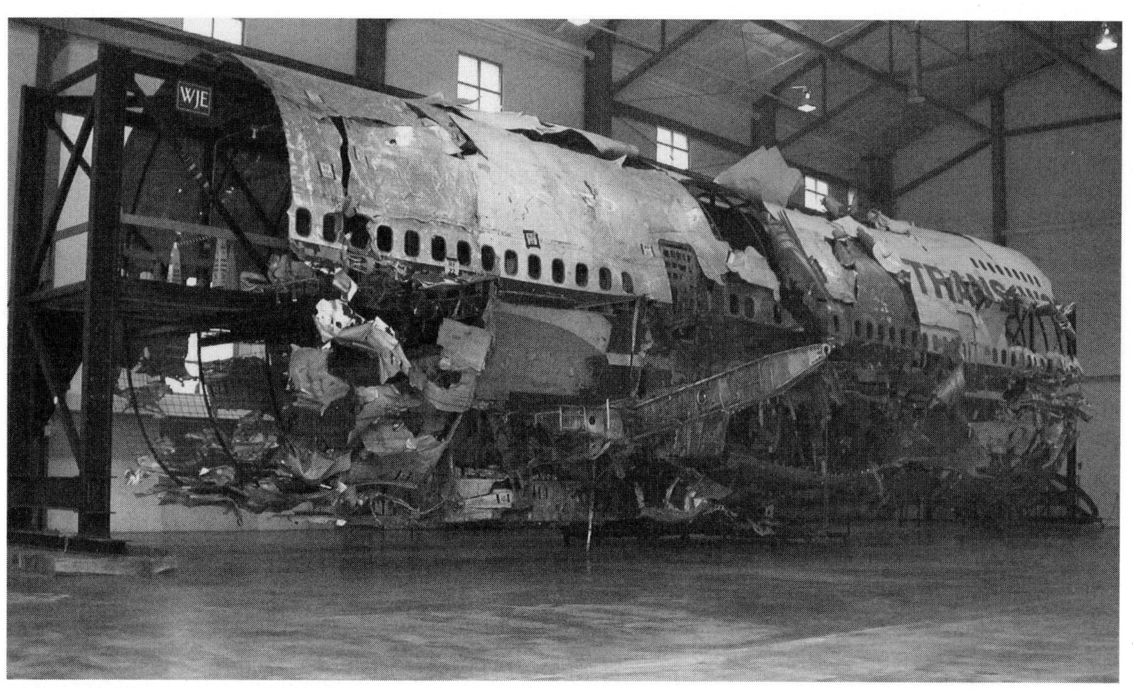

Learning Objectives

AFTER STUDYING THIS CHAPTER, YOU SHOULD BE ABLE TO:

1. Understand the similarities and differences between film and digital images
2. Understand what happens to the image receptor after it is exposed to light
3. Understand the differences among types of image receptors
4. Understand how a digital image is formed
5. Understand how to handle exposure for the optimum image
6. Understand the differences among both film and digital image formats
7. Understand the differences among light sensitivities in different speed receptors
8. Understand how to use, control, and manage both film and digital color
9. Understand how to use lens filtration properly

PHOTOGRAPHY

For over a hundred years, all photographic images were exposed onto light-sensitive material called *film*. The emergence of digital imaging has caused film photography to become less viable for evidence documentation. An understanding of the film process is still useful and essential for comparing and contrasting it to the digital process.

Film was not without its advantages. Images could be produced with a certain character representative of the media and a comfortable familiarity to the viewer's eye. Digital images may never replace that character. The popularity of digital imaging is due to several advantages, including speed of turnaround at every stage of the process, the lack of reliance upon silver, and lessened negative impact on the environment.

BLACK-AND-WHITE PHOTOGRAPHIC FILM

A camera is a tool for exposing film to light in measured quantities in order to record images. Black and white photographic film consists of a plasticized base thinly coated with a gelatin **emulsion** of light-sensitive silver halide salts of variable crystal sizes. The crystal sizes determine the film's sensitivity and, ultimately, its resolution. When the ionic (electrically charged) silver in the emulsion is subjected to an exposure of light (or other form of radiation, such as X-rays), it forms a latent (and invisible) image of metallic silver. Black and white camera film is typically **panchromatic,** meaning that the silver salts are sensitive to all colors of light. Some special-purpose **monochromatic** films are more limited in their sensitivity to light.

In black-and-white photography, the chemical process of **development** is used to amplify the latent image to create a visible one. After proper development, a fixing bath removes the remaining ionic silver from the emulsion and leaves behind a layer of metallic silver in varying densities directly proportional, if well exposed and processed, to the amount of the film's exposure to light. In a negative, the brighter areas of the subject retain the most dense layer of silver, and the dimmer areas retain the thinnest. If the film has been developed to a positive, the result is exactly opposite. Black-and-white photographic film usually contains only one layer of silver salts.

C-41 COLOR NEGATIVE PROCESS FILM

Film Layers

C-41 film consists of a plasticized (acetate) base onto which three color-sensitive emulsion layers are coated. Each emulsion layer contains colloidal silver halides and is sensitive to a different color light. In Kodak films, the top layer is blue sensitive, and beneath the blue is a yellow filter, made of special dyes, which traps all extraneous blue light that would fog the subsequent layers because they are also sensitive to blue light. The second layer is green sensitive, and the third is red sensitive.

Each layer, in addition to its light-sensitive components, contains dye couplers. These couplers, located in the blue-, green-, and red-sensitive layers will produce yellow, magenta, and cyan dyes, respectively, when developed.

Process

After exposure, film is developed in a **paraphenylene diamine** developer, which creates visible dyes from the embedded couplers. The developer creates both a silver and dye image on the film.

Development is followed by treatment in a combined bleach and fixer (bleach-fix), which dissolves the metallic silver generated during development and also removes all undeveloped silver halides.

The Negative

The resulting C-41 film is now a negative. The densest areas on film are those that were brightest in the subject. The negative image occurs because exposure to light and development converts the photographic silver halides into metallic silver. Dye couplers tied to the silver create colored dye layers in densities directly proportional to the film exposure. Then the bleach converts the silver back to its ionic form, and the fixer removes it from the film.

FILM BASICS

Traditional color silver photographic imaging has distinct phases:

1. Image capture
2. Negative processing
3. Printing
4. Negative and print storage

Two primary types of photographic film are available:

1. *Negative film*, when developed, turns into a negative with the colors (or black and white values) reversed from the imaged subject. This type of film must be printed, either projected through a lens or placed in contact with light-sensitive media, in order to be viewed as intended to represent the original subject.
2. *Positive or reversal film*, after development, is called a **transparency** and can be viewed directly using transmitted light or projected. Reversal film in various sizes, mounted with rigid plastic, cardboard, metal, or glass frames for projection, is often called **slides.**

Some professional photographers prefer reversal films because they are generally higher in resolution than negative films of comparable ISO. Color reproduction may also be more accurate if the film was properly exposed, because the final product of the photography is the original film rather than the film being an intermediate step needed for the creation of a print.

To produce the most accurate image, film must be properly exposed. The amount of exposure variation a given film will be able to tolerate and still produce an acceptable level of image quality is called its **exposure latitude.** Transparency film has less inherent latitude than negative film.

LATITUDE

Dynamic range is the measurable difference between the brightest highlight value and the darkest shadow value. Some parts of any subject may be dark, and some parts may be bright. The range of lightness and darkness between what the human eye perceives as totally black and what it perceives as totally white is the eye's dynamic range, and the human eye has a wide dynamic range. The ability to resolve a wide range of simultaneous detail in shadow areas and highlight areas is a characteristic of a wide dynamic range. If a subject is very bright without appreciable shadows or very dark without appreciable highlights, the human eye can also adjust to those conditions.

Emulsions vary in dynamic range, but all films have a much narrower dynamic range than healthy human eyes. If the recorded image retains detail in both shadows and highlights at the same time, the image possesses a wide dynamic range and will have very small latitude for mistakes in exposure.

Positive films display less inherent latitude than negative films. Slide films in general have about one-third the latitude of negative films. Any film is more limited in dynamic range than human vision.

When a film has limited latitude, scenes with high dynamic range may often cause exposure problems. When the shadows are properly exposed, the highlights may wash out; if the highlights are properly exposed, the shadow areas may block and look flat black.

When printing from negative film, even if the final image appears to possess a full range of tones representative of the original subject, the media used to make the final print have less dynamic range capability than the negative used to record the image.

DIGITAL IMAGING

The phases of digital photographic imaging are similar to those of film:

1. Image capture
2. Image download
3. Image processing, including enhancement
4. Storage

In digital photography, all steps are performed electronically, and digital images are visible only by display.

The film process, though complicated, is familiar to most laypersons, and negatives and prints are easily recognizable products. Computers operate covertly on digital images, using methods not easily understood by anyone other than computer experts. Thus, it is necessary to handle digital images using best practices and protocols, in order to be able to explain every step and to create unmanipulated images that can be presented in testimony. Images can be altered from their captured form at any phase of download, processing, or storage, either intentionally or by accident. The techniques involved in forensic digital image processing must be recordable and reproducible, as well as in line with current state-of-the-art practices.

Digital images exist as a set of bytes in a computer's random access memory (RAM) or as files on memory cards, hard drives, CDs, or DVDs. Digital images are obtained from digital cameras or input devices, including scanners, using film or prints as sources.

Digital cameras utilize solid-state devices (image sensors), usually of CCD or CMOS design. The sensor is a silicon chip containing millions of light-sensitive diodes called **photosites.** Each photosite corresponds to a **picture element (pixel)** of an image. A *pixel* is the smallest individual unit used to construct a digital image. Each pixel contains information concerning the color and tone of that particular section of the image, as well as its precise location stated in **Cartesian coordinates** on the *x* and *y* axes of the sensor matrix. The matrix or grid on which pixels exist is called a **bitmap.**

When the camera shutter opens, each photosite of the sensor accumulates a charge directly proportional to the amount of light falling onto it. When the lens focuses the subject on the sensor, some photosites record highlights, some record shadows, and others record the levels of brightness in between. The brightness recorded by each photosite is then stored as a set of numbers used to represent the brightness of the pixel in that space on the displayed image and to accurately reconstruct the original subject.

The computer uses the values stored in the digital image file to specify the brightness and color of each pixel in the grid. The layout of the photosites can be a collection of squares or a honeycomb, depending on the sensor design and manufacture.

Once the sensor has captured an image, the file must be read, have its charge information converted to digital information, and then be stored. The charges stored on the sensor are read a row at a time, not all at once. The reading can be accomplished by using interlaced scans or progressive scans. On an interlaced scan sensor (CMOS), the image is first processed by reading the odd-numbered lines, and then the even-numbered lines. On a progressive scan sensor (CCD), the rows are processed one after another in sequence.

FILM EXPOSURE

The concentration of dyes in color negatives or silver in black and white negatives remaining on the film after development is referred to as optical density, or **density.** The optical density is directly proportional to the logarithm of the optical transmission coefficient of the developed film. A dense area of the negative is higher in density than a light image.

Most films are affected by the physics of silver grain activation, which determines the minimum amount of light required to expose a single grain, and by the statistics of random grain activation by photons. The film must be struck by at least its minimum amount of light before it begins to expose. The film then responds by progressively darkening according to its dynamic range, until all the necessary grains are affected and the film achieves, after proper development, its maximum appropriate optical density. The density of the film can be quantified by using a transmission densitometer (see Fig. 6–1).

To enable the construction of a graph representing the exposure and development characteristics of a given film and developer combination, an image must be exposed and processed of a commercially available step wedge (see Fig. 6–2). Over the dynamic range capability of most films, the density of the developed film is proportional to the logarithm of the total amount of light to which the film was exposed. A plot of the measured optical density versus the exposure value creating the density is called the *D log E curve.* It is characteristic and unique for every film and developer combination (see Fig. 6–3).

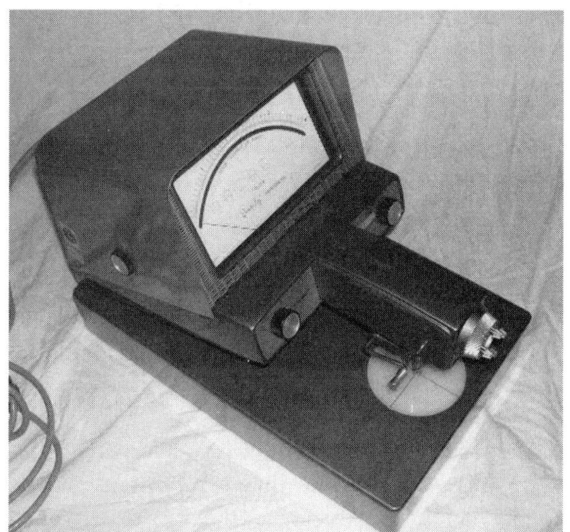

FIGURE 6–1 Macbeth Transmission Densitometer, for reading and recording the transmission optical density of exposed and processed film in color or black and white. *Source:* Sandy Weiss.

FIGURE 6–2 An image of a step wedge is exposed and processed, and then the resultant densities of each portion of the image are plotted to make the curve. *Source:* Sandy Weiss.

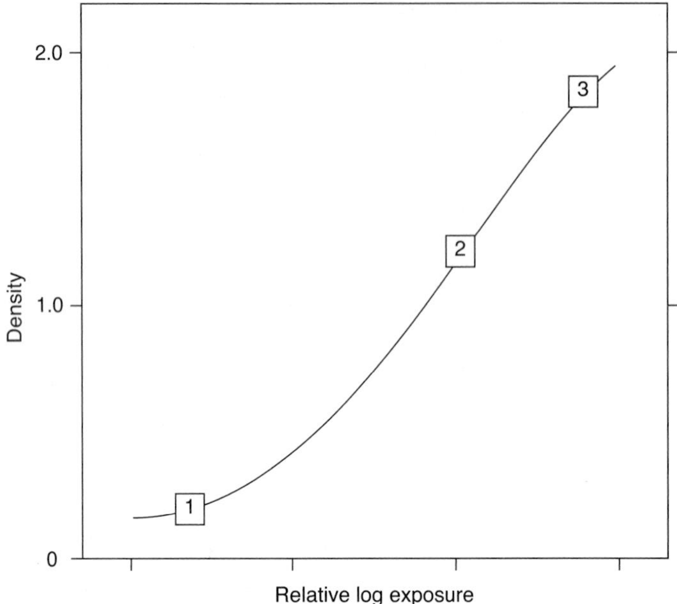

FIGURE 6–3 D log E curve for a theoretical film and developer combination. *Source:* Sandy Weiss.

The slope of the central part of the curve (the area of the curve labeled #2) represents the degree to which the film and developer combination react like human vision, yielding a 1:1 ratio of density versus exposure (light to visibility).

If areas of an image are exposed sufficiently to approach the maximum density possible after normal development for a negative, those areas will lose the ability to display tonal variations in the final print. Those areas are termed *overexposed* and will appear as detail-free white on the print or transparent in a positive. (The overexposed areas will record in the area of the curve labeled #3).

If areas of an image receive less than the beginning threshold level of exposure, which depends upon the film's sensitivity to light (**ISO**), the film will have no image density greater than the inherent density of the film base in those areas and will appear on the print as detail-free black. (The underexposed areas will record in the area on the curve labeled #1).

Using the limitations of the over- and underexposure capabilities of the film to determine the optimum exposure for a photograph is a skill demanding proper light-metering techniques. The goal of most in-camera exposure meters is to achieve an average density on the final negative that exhibits detail in both the bright and dark areas of the displayed image (see Chapter 7).

CONTRAST AND RESOLUTION

Inexperienced photographers may operate under the misconception that bright sunshine is the best illumination in which to expose photographs. Bright sunlight will produce dynamic scenic images, but it is the most difficult lighting to use for the creation of accurate evidence images. High-contrast lighting, including bright sunlight, direct electronic flash, and/or undiffused incandescent lighting, may produce images with shadows too dark or highlights too bright to yield proper detail. This is due to the image capture device or media being incapable of producing detail in such a wide range of illumination. Detail lost in the shadows or highlights of an image may be irretrievable and could make the difference between success and failure in the courtroom.

In film-based photography, the ratio between the brightest and darkest parts of an image that the film exposure and processing procedure of choice can record is directly proportional to the brightness range (inherent contrast) of the subject. The contrast of the finished representation of the image, if everything in the photographic process is done properly, will also be directly proportional to the subject brightness range.

In digital photography, the ratio between the maximum recordable signal strength (highest brightness capability) and the camera noise of a captured image is called the **dynamic range** of the camera sensor or the **signal-to-noise ratio (SNR).*** Signal strength is limited by the maximum sensing capacity of the individual pixel. Noise in general is the sum of the dark and read noises. **Dark noise** is the image degradation caused by the image sensor's inability to discern detail in low light. As the light level decreases, dark noise increases, due to either the lack of visible detail in the subject or the time duration necessary to capture the image when the light level is sufficiently low. The lower the overall light level, the longer the exposure, resulting in greater dark noise. Noise also increases proportionally with higher sensor temperature. Longer exposures raise the temperature of the sensor due to the duration of work. **Read noise** is the image degradation arising from the limitations of individual pixel amplifiers during signal processing. Cameras contain built-in signal amplifiers in their on-board software. Again, the longer it takes to process the image, the more the read noise. A subject and its representation that vary from brightly lit to deeply shadowed (see Fig. 6–4) are said to have a high dynamic range. Indoor,

*Camera noise is the ratio between the signal's maximum peak-to-peak signal voltage and the measured voltage of what remains when the signal is removed. In a digital image, noise is visible as pixels of the wrong density in various parts of the image.

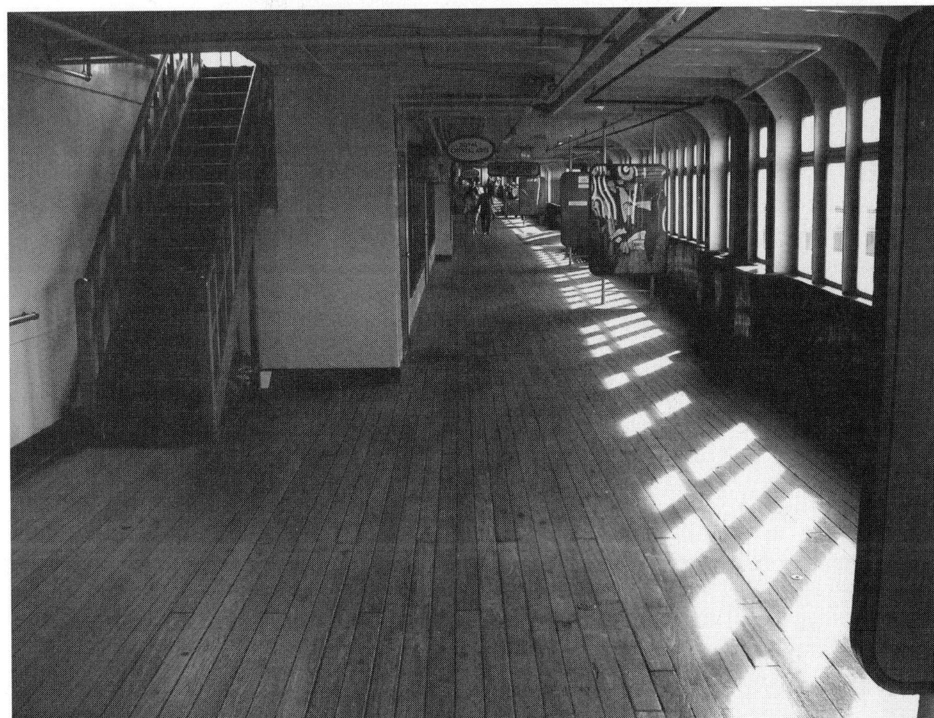

FIGURE 6–4 The deck of the *Queen Mary* in an exposure taken on the automatic setting of a digital camera on a sunny day lacks detail in the staircase. A photo taken on manual exposure, set properly for the shadows, yields full shadow detail without loss of highlight detail. *Source:* Sandy Weiss.

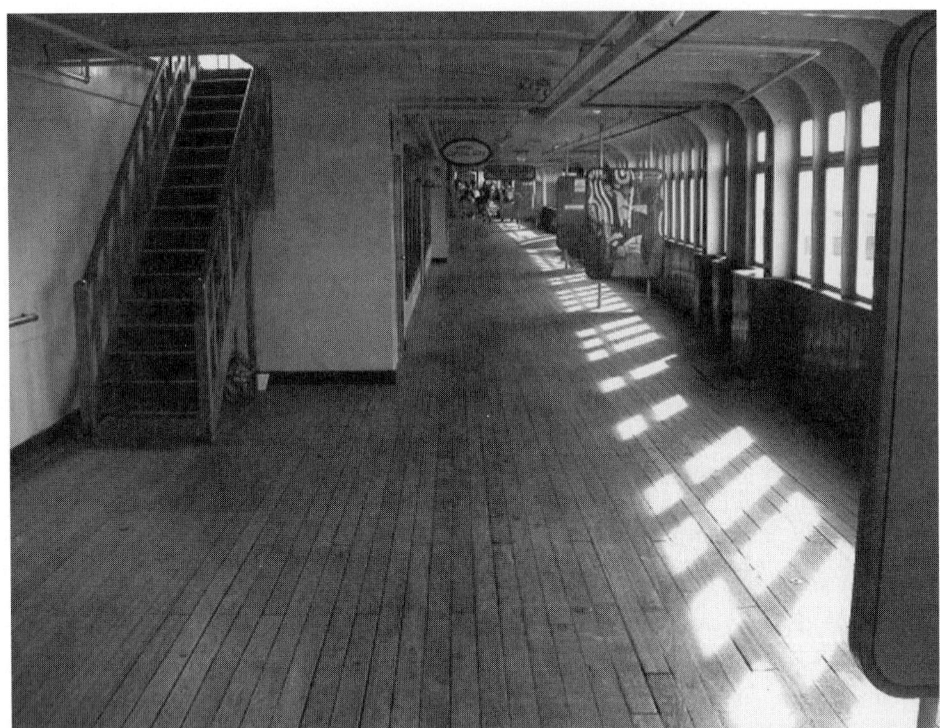

FIGURE 6–5 The deck of the *Queen Mary* in an exposure taken on manual setting of a digital camera on a sunny day, exposed for the shadows, shows detail in the staircase. A photo exposed with manual exposure, set properly for the shadows, yields full shadow detail without loss of highlight detail. *Source:* Sandy Weiss.

dimly lit, or other low-contrast subjects will have a low dynamic range.

As noise decreases, dynamic range increases. As dynamic range increases, the ability of the device to differentiate between the light and dark areas of the subject increases (see Fig. 6–5). A digital image, when viewed on a monitor or reproduced in printed form, will only reproduce image contrast information within the capabilities of the capture device, and within the ultimate capabilities of the display and printing output. As in human vision, the lower the inherent contrast of certain aspects of the subject, the more difficult it will be for the camera sensor to resolve the differences in the subject features. Therefore, the higher the dynamic range or contrast of the subject, the better the perceived resolution of the resultant image. Some camera manufacturers use image-optimizing software while processing captured images to bring the dynamic range of the subject into what the camera senses as ideal parameters. Some manufacturers also optimize the size and design of the individual pixels in an attempt to widen the dynamic range capabilities of the pixels.

In film-based photography, several methods are commonly used by photographers to optimize the subject brightness range for successful capture and reproduction of the widest possible range of existing tones. However, this capture and reproduction may constitute a condensed version of reality. As in film-based photography, digital technology may or may not allow the capture of the entire existing dynamic range of the subject When recording subjects with very high dynamic range, digital cameras will of necessity make compromises, allowing the capture of only the parts of the subject the camera decides are most important, or the parts of the range the operator has set by choice for the camera's capture parameters. These compromises are necessary because no camera or output device (including even the unadapted human eye) can reproduce in an instant the very broad dynamic range and contrast of many subjects. The normal, healthy, and young human eye is able to discern a dynamic range or contrast ratio somewhere between 10,000:1 and 30,000:1 at any one time and under regular adapted visual conditions. This corresponds photographically to a range of at minimum about 13½ camera f-stops.

The necessity for compromise in image capture, when using either traditional or digital photographic hardware, becomes understandable when considering the photographic limitations compared to what exists in reality or what most humans can truly see. Traditional black-and-white silver-based film, exposed and processed under the most exacting conditions, is capable of a contrast capture ratio of about 256:1 or 8 f-stops. When the negative is converted to a reflective print, the ratio falls to about 100:1 or 5 f-stops. Color glossies from color negatives will yield a maximum of about 50:1 or 4½ f-stops. Some digital cameras set at normal ISO display a dynamic range capture capability of about 500:1, which means that the camera is capable of handling all the detail in an image comprised of about 9 f-stops of brightness.

Digital Photography Review (www.dpreview.com) divides the dynamic range capture capabilities of a digital camera into these categories:

1. *Noise:* a calculated figure that represents the average noise level in the image (using standard deviation from averages)
2. *Range:* the dynamic range (based on signal-versus-noise levels) of the sensor system represented as a magnitude ratio
3. *Bits:* the number of digital bits required to store the resultant dynamic range (thus a result of 7.8 bits would require 8 bits to store the data)
4. *Density:* a figure more commonly used in film and film scanners for reference (log10 at a density of 2 is 10^2 or 100:1)5. *dB:* the dynamic range in decibels; a measure often used in describing signal-to-noise ratio in capture devices.

www.dpreview.com published these results for the Nikon D1: "At ISO 200, a noise level of 0.09, dynamic range capability of 470:1, bit density of 8.9, maximum density of 2.7 and total noise of 53 Decibels (Db)."[1]

Most monitor images cannot be reproduced with a contrast in that ratio. Depending upon technology, digitally produced color prints are a reasonable match with glossies printed from color negatives. It has been demonstrated that no existent digital capture device, capture method, film, monitor, or hard copy can properly reproduce the range of illumination existing in some normally lit subjects. (It is important to remember that, as in conventional photography when using slow-speed film, the light sensitivity [ISO] of the digital camera should be set at the lowest practical level to capture the broadest sampling of the subject brightness/dynamic/contrast range of the subject.)

Some practitioners have developed state-of-the-art practices for using combinations or layers of multiple images of the same subject, recombined to increase the details discernible in the finished contrast or dynamic range of the representation. These multiple images must be captured specifically to contain image information elements from the light, normal, and dark parts of the subject brightness or dynamic ranges, while not changing the inherent content of the image. Multiple images must be captured at varying exposures of the same scene. Some cameras have built-in settings to capture the appropriately bracketed images.

FILM SPEED

Film speed is an indicator of a film's sensitivity to light. The international standard for rating film speed is now the ISO scale, which replaces the older ASA speed. **ASA** is often used interchangeably, though mistakenly, with the term ISO. ASA is still printed on film packaging along with the ISO speed, which is always printed in smaller type.

Common film speeds range between ISO 25 and 3200. Consumer films are usually in the ISO 100 to ISO 800 range. Some films, such as Kodak's Technical Pan (sadly discontinued), are not ISO rated because their sensitivity is variable depending on development. These types of media require knowledge of the film's properties before exposure and development.

ISO 25 is a slow-speed film and requires more extensive exposure to light to produce a satisfactory image than does faster film, such as ISO 800. Faster films are designed for low-light situations, and their inherent contrast enhancement for those conditions is manufactured into the film. Conversely, slow-speed films are lower contrast and more suitable for situations where light is plentiful. Slower-speed films may display finer grain and better color rendition than faster-speed films.

Digital photography has induced the obsolescence of film and the manufacture and popularity of most film-based photographic hardware. Some companies, including Kodak and Fuji, have recognized the need for the continued manufacture of transparency film in the professional market and continue to manufacture a supply. Many types and brands of films are no longer produced.

DIGITAL LIGHT SENSITIVITY

Digital cameras have a built-in ISO range that indicates their level of sensitivity to light. ISO 100 is the normal (default) setting for most cameras, although some may default as low as ISO 50. The sensitivities may range up to 200, 400, 800, 1600, or even 3200 in some DSLRs. When the ISO goes up, the sensitivity of the image sensor increases.

ISO Speed and Exposure

When making digital exposures in low light or when the subject is too far away to be properly illuminated by electronic flash, it may be necessary for the photographer to select and program a higher ISO setting into the camera. If the camera is set at automatic ISO mode, the camera will set a higher ISO automatically. Once the camera is set to a higher ISO, it becomes necessary to determine if the correction is sufficient to create an image with sufficient quality or depth of field.

The ISO speed will affect the shutter speed and aperture combination used to expose an image with what the camera determines are appropriate density and contrast. (See Chapter 7)

Unfortunately, higher ISO speeds also amplify noise, which is undesirable, where noise is any signal captured by the image and not attributed to light from the subject. An image sensor inherently generates noise. The increased sensitivity of higher ISOs allows the image sensor to record more signal and, at the same time, more noise. The signal to noise ratio (SNR) determines the total noise in the resultant image.

An image sensor is usually calibrated to deliver the best image quality (greatest SNR) at its lowest possible ISO speed. As with film, an image sensor will exhibit more noise (comparable to graininess in film) at higher ISO speeds. Noise produced by an image sensor appears as patches of distracting color in the image.

Improvements in sensor technology are steadily reducing the noise levels at higher ISOs in more professional cameras. Unlike film cameras, which require a change of film or the use of multiple bodies, digital cameras allow instant change of the ISO sensitivity, depending on lighting conditions.

TIPS:

Remember to reset the ISO to default after using a higher speed for a low-light situation. Using a higher ISO speed unnecessarily in normal lighting produces images of lower quality.

ISO Speed and Image Sensor Size

The physical size of the image sensor determines the ISO speed range that a digital camera can use without suffering from undue noise. Pixels on a larger image sensor are larger and capture more light than smaller pixels, which generates a higher SNR. Given two image sensors of different size, each with a resolution of 4 Mp, the 4 Mp sensor with the smaller dimensions will exhibit more noise at higher ISOs than the larger one.

COLOR TEMPERATURE

Color temperature (T) is a characteristic of visible light. The color temperature of a light source is determined by comparing its hue with a theoretical, heated **blackbody** radiator. (A *blackbody* is an object that absorbs all incident light—neither reflecting it nor allowing it to pass through.) The Kelvin (K) temperature at which the heated blackbody radiator matches the hue of the light source is that source's color temperature.

Color temperature is of critical importance in both film photography and digital imaging. A lack of proper color balance between the light source and the film or image sensor causes color shifts in the resultant image, which sometimes cannot be fully rectified during printing or image processing and display.

If the color temperature of the light source is too low for the film, the images will have a warm yellow or red cast. If the color temperature of the light source is too high for the film, the images will have a cool blue cast. The degree of mismatch determines the extent of the color shifts.

LIGHT SOURCES

Nature supplies only one main, natural light source for everything the human eye sees and transmits to the brain for analysis and recognition. If nature's light source is diminished at sunset or by entry into an enclosure, vision and photography must often be reinforced and enabled by the use of supplementary light sources. Accomplished portrait photographers realize that, as in nature, for a portrait to represent a visual possibility of how the same face would appear to the human eye, only one main light source can illuminate the subject. Use of an infinite number of secondary light sources depends upon the effect or detail the viewer is attempting to see or the photographer is attempting to reproduce. Other light sources will cause no visual confusion to the viewer of the scene or image as long as they remain secondary to the main light source.

Imagine a group of people on stage in front of an audience. The stage lighting often consists of multiple light sources of the same intensity. The lighting is projected from above, and each object on the stage generates a shadow as it blocks each light. On the stage floor, a viewer in the audience will observe multiple shadows emanating from each member of the cast. This situation is impossible in nature, but it is not confusing to the viewer in the audience because the effect is expected. However, images of the cast's faces exposed by a photographer in the audience will be evenly illuminated from all sides. The images have no shadows and, therefore, will appear unnatural and flat in the finished images. The detrimental effects of multiple main light sources may be less noticeable when observing objects less familiar to humans than another human face, and in some cases multiple main lights may even be an advantage as long as they are properly documented.

In low-light vision, the eye observes the subject and relays a message to the brain. The brain assists the person attempting to observe and recognize the subject. Adaptation of the eye to the low light level, given sufficient time and the use of the supplementary senses of hearing and smell, may also be helpful in the visual identification process. In any attempt at visual recognition, it must be remembered, the contrast between an object and its background is what affords recognition, no matter what the level of illumination. For example, camouflage clothing allows a hunter to disappear in the forest in broad daylight, and a red tomato may be difficult to see when it is placed upon a red background if it generates no shadows.

In low and marginal levels of illumination, the receptors in the human eye are unable to discern color. Even easily recognizable colors such as safety-yellow appear gray to the observer when the level of ambient light is sufficiently low. The visual contrast of different colors or tones, and not ambient light level alone, is the factor a vision expert will attempt to determine when analyzing the cause of a vision-related incident.

The same rules of lighting apply to evidence photography. The subject must have sufficient contrast to allow identification, but too much contrast in an image is more often the problem than not enough. No films or sensors currently are being manufactured that are able to capture the wide range of contrast often encountered in natural situations. Photographers must use many devices and methods to reduce the effects of too much contrast in their subjects so they can capture the optimum range of subject brightness. Digital imaging is the technology of today and the future. The days of exposing and

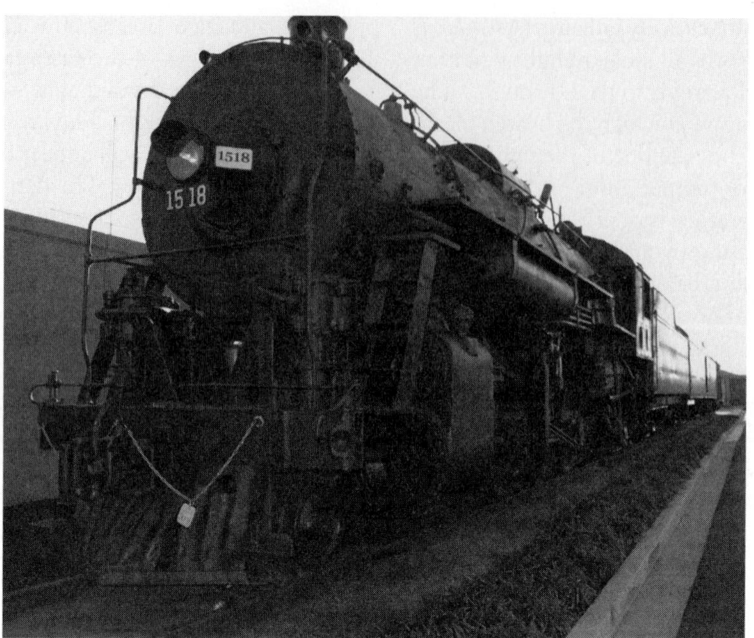

FIGURE 6–6 This image of a locomotive was exposed on a very bright day using an automatic exposure. The resultant image is underexposed and its contrast representation is lacking in necessary detail. *Source:* Sandy Weiss.

processing film, by special methods designed to capture the optimum subject contrast range, are drawing to a close.

The lighting on bright sunny days produces images with high contrast and dark shadows (see Fig. 6–6). Using artificially generated fill lighting for subjects of high contrast is recommended as a way to increase detail in otherwise impenetrable shadows. For any chance at a representative version of accuracy, image detail in dark shadows must be visible to the observer of the finished images (see Fig. 6–7).

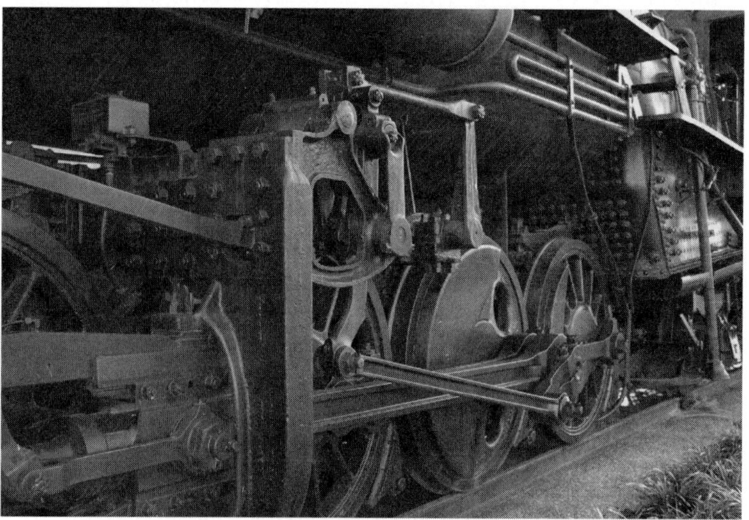

FIGURE 6–7 This close-up image was exposed with a flash. Although the flash makes the black paint appear gray, the image has good detail in the shadows. *Source:* Sandy Weiss.

TYPES OF LIGHTING

Daylight may appear red, orange, yellow, or white in a finished image, depending on the position of the sun at the time of the exposure relative to the condition of the atmosphere and the type of camera. The color of the sun changes during the day due to refraction and the scattering of light in the atmosphere.

When the sun is low on the horizon it appears red and measures about 2,500 K. However, it always measures about 5,770 K outside the atmosphere (see Fig. 6–8).

Some Common Temperatures of Light

1,700 K	Fire
2,800 K	Incandescent bulbs
3,400 K	Studio photofloods
5,000 K	Daylight (U.S. standard)
5,500 K	Average daylight and electronic flash
5,770 K	Effective sun temperature
6,420 K	Xenon arc lamp
6,500 K	Daylight (European standard)

Reminder

Red is the coolest in temperature of the visible colors and is by definition a warm color.

MIREDS

In film photography, an alternative numerical measure to color temperature is the **micro reciprocal degree (mired).** Color temperature and mireds are convertible to each other via mathematical formulae. The mired temperature scale corresponds to the appropriate color-correcting filters used for specific film and light source combinations.

The mired (M) is a unit of measurement equal to 1,000,000 divided by the color temperature (degrees K), per the following formula (decamireds, or dM, are 10 mireds):

$$M = 1{,}000{,}000 / K$$

A standard electronic flash, with a color temperature 5,000 K, has a mired value of M = 200 mireds (20 dM).

FILM PHOTOGRAPHY: COLOR TEMPERATURE APPLICATIONS

Film sometimes exaggerates the color of the light. An object that appears illuminated by white light to the human eye may yield a blue- or yellow-hued print in a final photograph. It is useful to correct the color balance of the light while exposing the image to make it easier to achieve color prints representative of what the normal human eye can see.

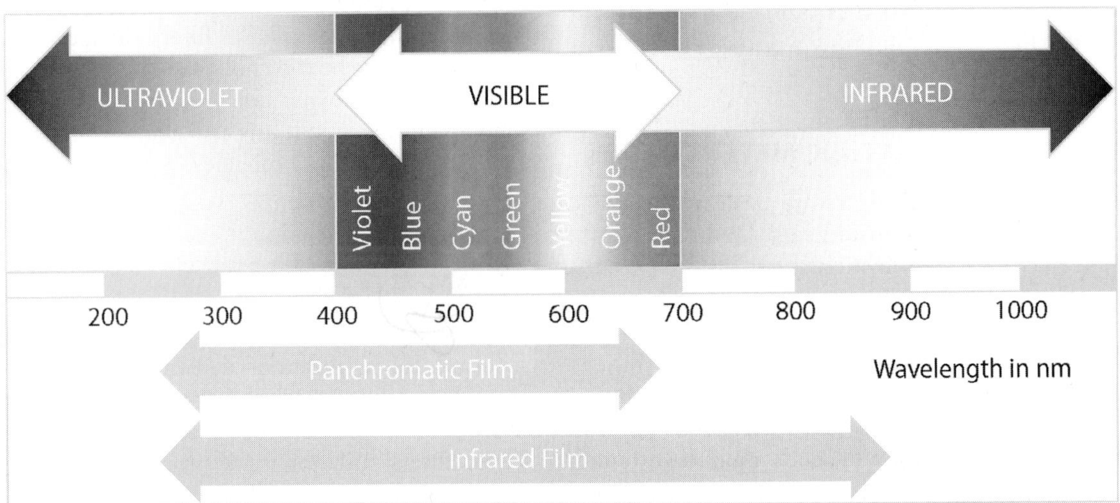

FIGURE 6–8 Visual table showing the different colors of visual and invisible light. *Source:* Jessica Weiss.

Film is balanced at the factory for specific colored light sources (for example, daylight and tungsten lamplight). If the proper film is paired with the matching lighting, it will yield neutral color prints, and there will be no need to remove unnatural casts in the printing stage. Matching the color sensitivity of the film to the color temperature of the light source is highly recommended. If tungsten film is used with incandescent lamps, the yellow–orange light of the tungsten bulbs (3,200 K) will appear white in the photographs.

Of course, it is possible to filter out some unnatural color cast during printing by using the appropriate **filtration** if the wrong film is exposed with the wrong light. Problems may occur, though, when parts of the image retain an unnatural look or when lighting is mixed.

Filters placed over camera lenses or light sources may be used to correct color balance. If using daylight film under tungsten light sources, different degrees of blue filters can be used to adjust any light source to the film. To accentuate the warm look when the color of the sun is red to yellow, landscape photographers may use daylight film specifically for sunrise and sunset photos. That practice is fine for scenic photography but not recommended for evidence photography.

Fluorescent lights vary in color, and it may be useful to identify the tint of the light tubes in order to use the appropriate fluorescent correcting filter. No film is made to be used under fluorescent lighting without corrective filtration.

COLOR TEMPERATURE METERS

As long as a person's eyes are healthy and the level of illumination is sufficient, the human eye perceives most illumination as primarily neutral in color balance. No matter what color the light source, the human brain automatically color corrects for what it thinks is the correct color of the subject. If the eyes are older, vision tends to shift toward yellow. If a person is color blind, his or her perception of color depends upon the extent of the problem. Older eyes always require a higher level of illumination for proper color differentiation.

Photographic film does not automatically correct for different colors of illumination, so it is necessary for the photographer to perform the necessary adjustments. Some color casts in negative images can be corrected during printing. It is not critical to balance color negative film when exposing the image. It is critical to balance the light when exposing color positive film. A transparency that is color balanced improperly is always going to appear wrong. The only way to fix an improperly color-balanced transparency is to create duplicate transparencies, utilizing the proper color correction during duplication. Remember, the duplication of film images causes depreciation of image quality.

Three-Color Meters

An exemplar, state-of-the-art, three-color meter is the Gossen 3F Color Temperature Meter. Once it is set for a type of film, it will determine which light-balancing filter—mired, Wratten (see Appendix 6–1), or CC—value is needed.

Two-Color Meters

The Gossen Sixticolor Meter is an established hardware solution used to determine if the light being used with a particular film is too blue or too yellow to create an appropriately colored image. By using a set of dM filters, images that would otherwise be too cool or too warm may be corrected during exposure. The Sixticolor meter is no longer made, but it is available secondhand and is inexpensive and reliable (see Figs. 6–9 and 6–10).

DECAMIRED FILTERS

Decamired (dM) filters (see Figs. 6–11 and 6–12) are available in different densities of red and blue. They are appropriate for use when lighting is too cool or too warm for any type of film. These filters will not work properly for color correction of fluorescent lighting.

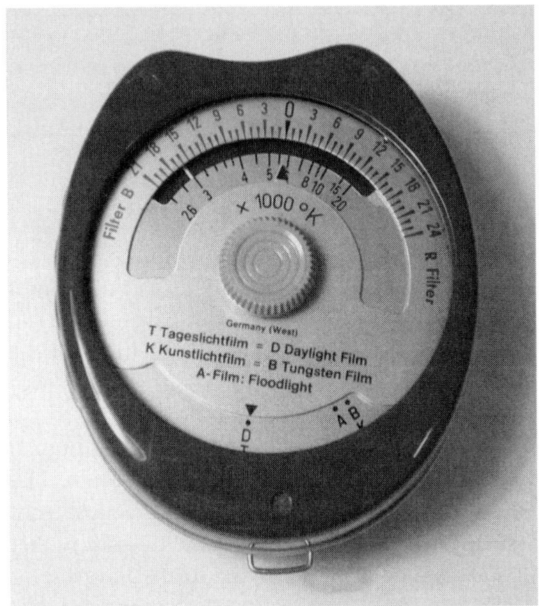

FIGURE 6–9 Front side of a Gossen Sixticolor Meter. *Source:* Sandy Weiss.

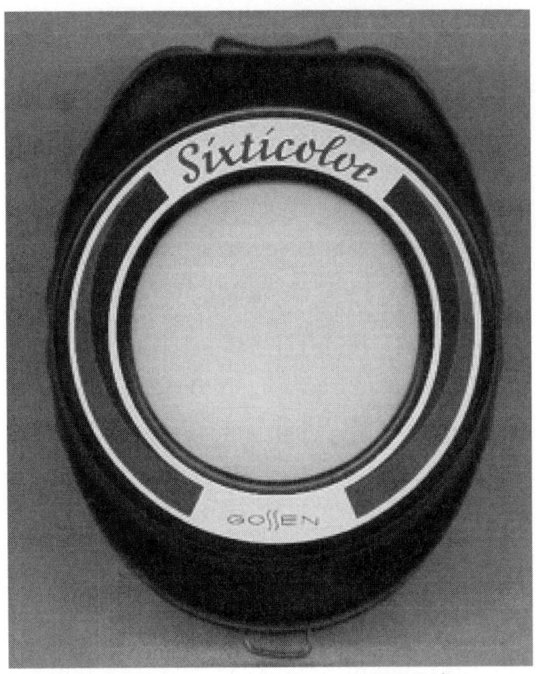

FIGURE 6–10 Back side of a Gossen Sixticolor Meter. *Source:* Sandy Weiss.

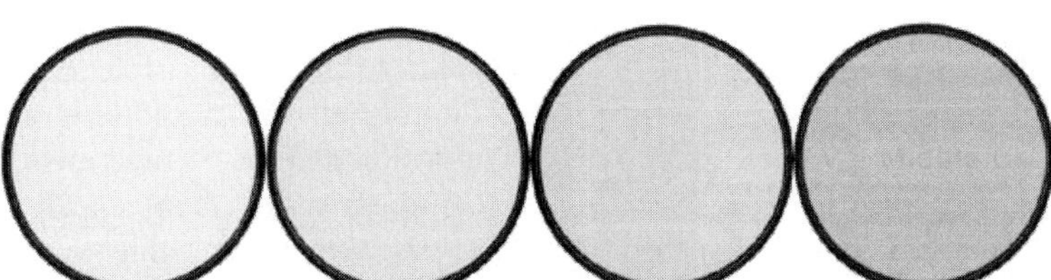

FIGURE 6–11 Gossen Decamired filters in the red range for warming an image. *Source:* Sandy Weiss.

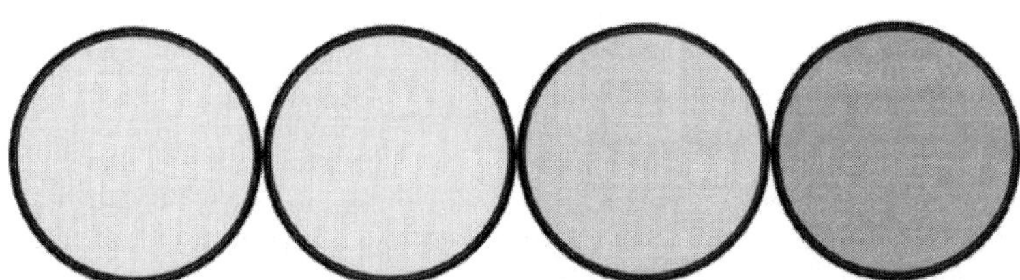

FIGURE 6–12 Gossen Decamired filters in the blue range for cooling an image. *Source:* Sandy Weiss.

COLOR TEMPERATURE AND MICRO RECIPROCAL DEGREE

The micro reciprocal degree value, or mired value, of any light source is the reciprocal of its actual color temperature multiplied by 1,000,000.

Example

Daylight = 5,500 K

The reciprocal (1/5,500) equals .00018181.

Multiply by 1,000,000 = 180

The decamired value is the mired value divided by 10 or = 18.

If the dM value of the film and light source are known:

dM value (light source) − dM value (film) = dM value of the filter required

dM value (light source) $<$ dM value (film) = a red (R) filter is necessary

dM value (light source) $>$ dM value (film) = a blue (B) filter is necessary

Example

Quartz lamp at 3,200 K = dM 31

Daylight film dM value = dM 18

31 − 18 = 13

dM shift = +13

Since the dM value of the light source is higher than the dM value of the film, a B12 filter must be used.

> **TIP:**
>
> If the dM value cannot be achieved exactly because the exact filter value is not available, use the closest lower number.

> **TIP:**
>
> Avoid using multiple filters attached to the lens at the same time as each glass-to-air-to-glass interface diminishes image resolution. Instead, use the next *lower-numbered* filter.

> **TIP:**
>
> Color temperature for film correlates to white balance in digital imaging.

COLOR

Color is the visual appearance of different wavelengths of electromagnetic energy in the form of light. For example, consider a grapefruit. The sun or an artificial light provides illumination for the yellow object. The grapefruit absorbs some wavelengths of light and reflects others. Some of the reflected light reaches the retinas of the human eye, which then stimulates the viewer's brain. The brain relates a perception of the color yellow from the optic nerves to the part of the brain that processes the information and forms an image.

The **visible spectrum** is the range of colors of light that can be seen with the unaided eye. Wavelengths above the visible spectrum include infrared (heat). The wavelengths below the visible spectrum include ultraviolet, X-rays, and gamma rays.

The visible spectrum and the colors that can be reproduced on a computer screen or printed by an output device are different. The total number of colors that a device can produce is called its color **gamut.** The visible spectrum is wider than the color gamut of a color monitor, which in turn is wider than the gamut of a color printer. No computer system is capable of reproducing all the colors humans are able to perceive, unless the health and age of the human's eyes create limits.

Tone

The most visible wavelengths of the visible spectrum are red, orange, yellow, green, blue, indigo, and violet—the same colors contained in a rainbow. **Tone** is the lightness or darkness of the color in an image as it relates to other colors in the image.

Color defines what a human sees, and tone is what gives color its depth and form. Tone has depth even without color, as in the range of grays in a black-and-white continuous tone image. As the tonal range of an imaging system increases, so do the breadth of tone and ultimate image quality.

If an image is copied from one device to another and the second device has limited tonal capacity, the tonal range of the image must be compressed before it is displayed. Tonal compression causes the image to lose tonal values. The appearance of the image should still be satisfactory, unless it is compressed enough to lose detail through the subsequent loss of tones.

Hue, Saturation, and Value

All colors and tones have a specific hue, saturation, and value. **Hue** is the description of the color, with words such as orange, purple, and blue. **Saturation** is the intensity or purity of the color. For example, 100% red appears vivid red, and 10% red appears light pink. **Value** is the relative lightness or darkness of the color.

Digital Color

Image sensor pixels record gray scale values only, in a series of increasingly darker tones ranging from pure white to pure black, and corresponding to brightness in the imaged areas of the original scene. To capture colors in each pixel, the individual pixels have red, green, and blue filters to separate the red, green, and blue components of the light reflected by the subject.

Each pixel typically consists of 8 bits in black and white (1 byte) if in JPEG format; or 24 bits (3 bytes) for color images, 1 byte each for red, green, and blue (RGB). 8 bits are able to represent 256 tonal levels, numbered 0 to 255.

Usually, filters in a repetitive red–green–blue–green pattern, called a **Bayer mosaic,** are installed over the individual pixels so that each pixel can capture only one of the three colors. In this way, one-quarter of the image is captured by red light, one-quarter by blue, and one-half by green. The higher amount of green is appropriate because the human eye is most sensitive to green light and more green information is required to yield visually accurate images. The Bayer mosaic is named after its inventor, Dr. Bryce E. Bayer of Eastman Kodak, and refers to a particular arrangement of color filters used in most single-chip digital image sensors built into digital cameras, camcorders, and scanners.

Each pixel records only its captured color. To instill all color values onto each pixel, interpolation algorithms are used. **Interpolation** utilizes the colors of neighboring pixels in the matrix to calculate the values of the two colors each pixel is missing. By combining the two interpolated color values with the color actually measured by the pixel, the original color of every pixel is calculated. Dr. Bayer termed the green photosensors *luminance-sensitive elements* and the red and blue ones *chrominance-sensitive elements.*

Different interpolation algorithms result in varying quality final images. The interpolation occurs either in-camera or in-computer to produce the finished RAW or JPEG images.

Some resolution is lost by using the Bayer filter matrix, and other side effects occur, including moiré fringing. The red and blue pixels are spaced twice as far apart as the green pixels, making their intrinsic resolution only half that of the green. Sophisticated reconstruction algorithms routinely recover most of the lost resolution as long as some green is present in the original subject.

THE FOVEON X3 DIRECT IMAGE SENSOR

One manufactured image sensor incorporates a pixel for every color at every position of the imaging sensor matrix. The major camera manufacturers have not adopted this technology. The Foveon X3 Direct Image Sensor captures red, green, and blue light at each point in an image during a single exposure. CCD image sensors record only one color at each point in the captured image.

The Foveon X3 sensor is similar to the layers of color film in construction. The image sensor has three layers of pixels. The layers of pixels are embedded in silicon to take advantage of the fact that red, green, and blue light penetrates silicon to different depths, allowing full-color capture at every point in the image.

BINARY NUMERIC SYSTEM

The **binary numeric system** is the basis of traditional digital computing. The simplest pixel has two choices: it can be either black or white. A pixel with two choices is known as a one-bit image. The more the bit information, the higher the number of color choices. Color bit depth is the number of binary bits that define the shade or color of a pixel in a digital image. For example, each pixel in a black-and-white image has a depth of 1 bit because it can only be black or white. The number of color values that a given bit depth can produce is equal to two to the power of the bit depth.

The color choices in bits per pixel include the following:

1 bit = 2 colors	6 bits = 64 colors
2 bits = 4 colors	7 bits = 128 colors
3 bits = 8 colors	8 bits = 256 colors
4 bits = 16 colors	16 bits = 32,768 colors
5 bits = 32 colors	24 bits = 16,777,216 colors

A pixel with 8 bits per color defines a 24-bit image (8 bits × 3 colors = 24 bits.)

ADDITIVE COLOR

Colors in a digital photographic image are formed by varying amounts of the three primary colors—red, green, and blue (RGB)—to form **additive colors**. When the three primary colors are combined in equal quantities, they form white. This occurs whenever light is perceived or projected to form colors. On a computer monitor, each pixel is comprised of a group of three dots: one for red, one for green, and one for blue. Differing amounts of these colors are used to represent different hues. The absence of all RGB light results in black.

SUBTRACTIVE COLOR

Most digital cameras use the additive RGB color system. Printers use the **CMYK**—cyan, magenta, yellow, and key (black)—**subtractive color** system. When cyan, magenta, and yellow are blended at 100%, they produce black. Deeper black tones are created by adding more black. The absence of CMY pigments forms white.

On a photographic print made from a digital image, each pixel is represented by dots of cyan, magenta, yellow, and black ink. Where and how these dots overlap forms all the necessary colors.

WHITE BALANCING

Most digital cameras adjust for color temperature by focusing on a white object and setting the **white balance (WB)** from that reference under that particular lighting, basically informing the camera of what is truly white. Unnatural color casts should then be removed so that subjects appearing a certain color in reality appear the same color in the finished image. The camera retains a corrected white memory and makes all other color balance adjustments accordingly.

WB is totally dependent upon the color temperature of the light source. Setting the WB is especially necessary when exposing images under fluorescent or incandescent lighting or when changing lighting during a project.

Remember

Using the automatic white balance setting is not a foolproof approach (see Figs. 6–13 and 6–14).

WB is a nonissue with black-and-white (B&W) photography because light is simply illumination with B&W. WB with color negative film is not as difficult or critical as it is with color positives. For example, daylight film exposed under fluorescent lighting produces negatives that will print with a green cast if uncorrected. If the printing machine or enlarger is calibrated properly, the green cast will be removed by using appropriate printing color correction (CC) filtration.

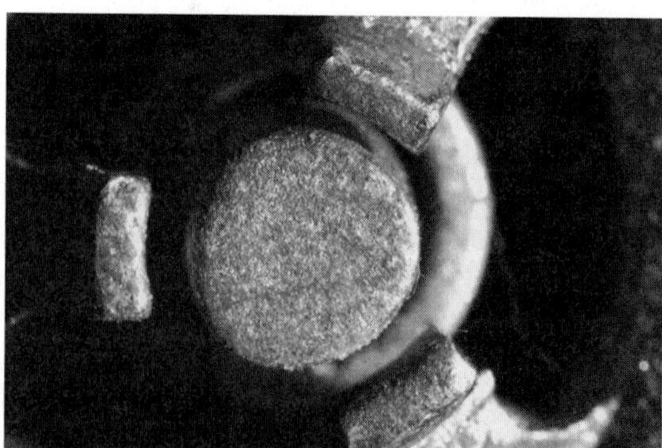

FIGURE 6–13 Image exposed on auto color balance with no reference included shows the steel with a slight yellow/red cast. *Source:* Sandy Weiss.

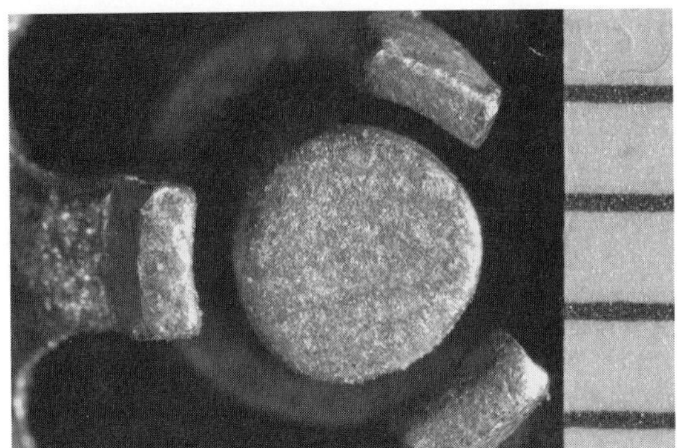

FIGURE 6–14 Image exposed with a neutral gray reference shows the steel as it appeared to the human eye. *Source:* Sandy Weiss.

WB with color positive film is more critical because the resultant positive may be the final image, and if it is tinted green or yellow it will not accurately represent the subject. The appropriate film and lighting combination must be used or filtration must be added in front of the lens or the lighting to adjust the lighting to match the color balance of the film. If tungsten lighting is used, tungsten film is appropriate. Tungsten film used in daylight will yield blue images. Daylight film used in tungsten lighting will yield yellow images.

With digital photography, the camera has built-in calibrations to allow the use of any color of light and yield a well-balanced image. When digital images are exposed under mixed lighting (see Figs. 6–15 and 6–16), the images may have areas where the color balance is not accurate.

Most digital cameras have a number of WB settings. These will often include default settings for the following options:

- tungsten
- fluorescent
- daylight
- flash
- cloudy
- shade
- automatic
- custom

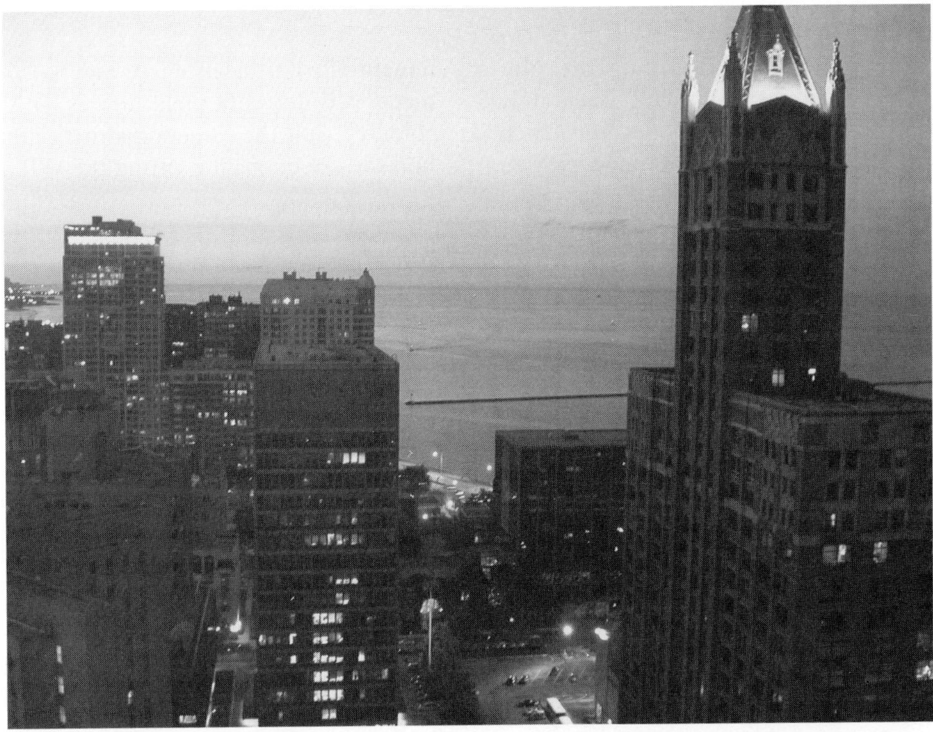

FIGURE 6–15 Multiple color temperatures at the Chicago lakeshore, with lighting of five different color temperatures. *Source:* Sandy Weiss.

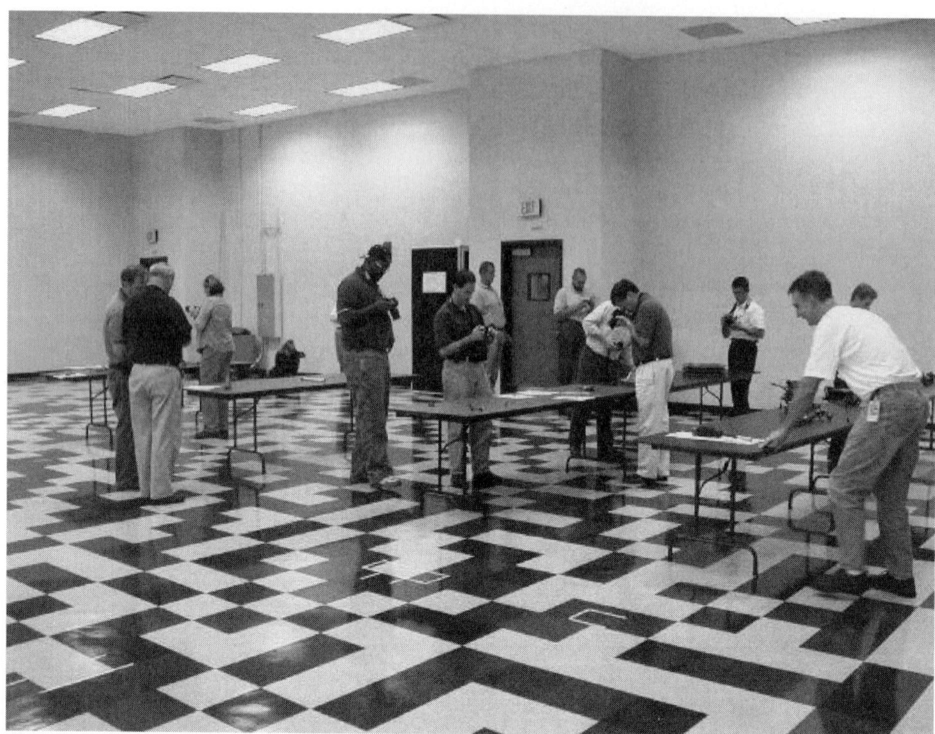

FIGURE 6–16 This image was exposed with flash to compensate for the mixture of overhead fluorescent light and daylight from the large windows. *Source:* Sandy Weiss.

When the lighting matches the setting, the color of the subject should reproduce accurately (see Fig. 6–17). If the lighting does not match the setting, the subject will reproduce with an unnatural color balance (see Fig. 6–18). If automatic WB does not yield images with accurate color, consult the camera instruction manual to find the directions for setting the WB manually.

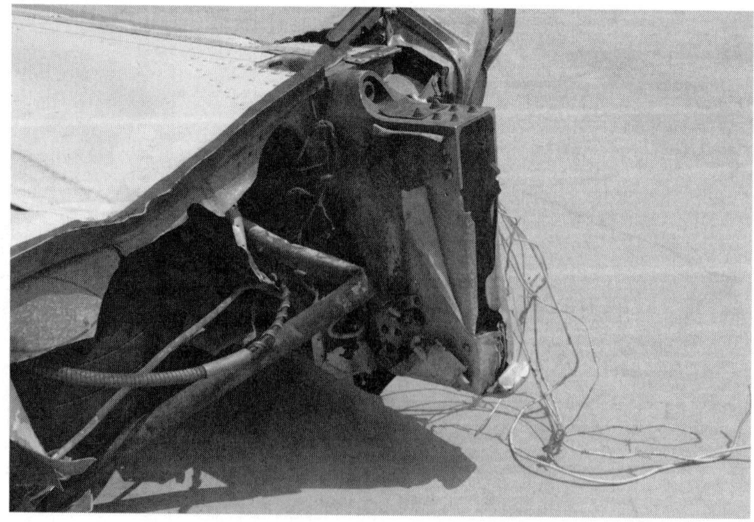

FIGURE 6–17 Image exposed in daylight on a daylight setting. *Source:* Sandy Weiss.

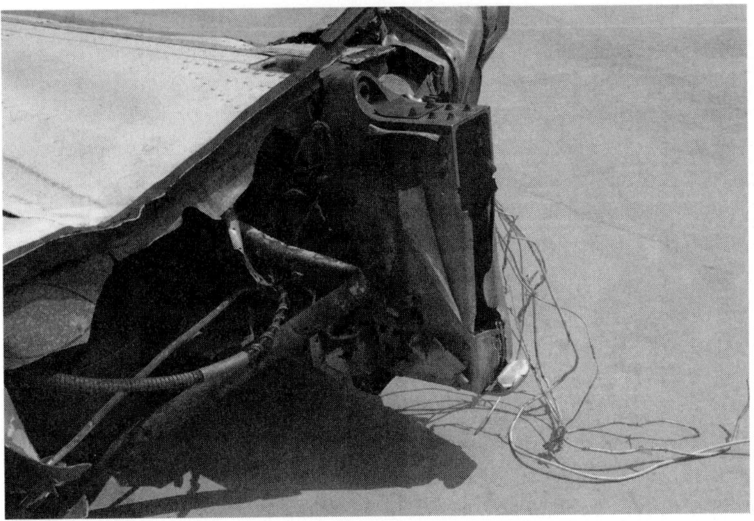

FIGURE 6–18 Image exposed in daylight on a tungsten setting appears blue. *Source:* Sandy Weiss.

After it has been set manually, do not forget to change it back to the default after the lighting changes.

Use an 18% gray card, available at any photographic supply, for a perfect neutral reference. Exposing an image of a gray card with every project is recommended. The gray image may be consulted when attempting to color balance a group of images when the lighting does not exactly match the color balance set on the camera and produces images with unnatural colors. The custom WB setting on the camera uses a built-in 18% gray neutral reference.

Auto WB averages the color temperature for the entire scene and uses the result as the white balance. This works adequately in some situations; however, some light sources may affect the image more strongly than others and will be visible in the finished image (see Fig. 6–16). If the image was exposed on auto WB, the color balance may have matched the daylight coming in the window and the people may have looked purple or green due to the presence of the fluorescent lighting.

Calibrating for WB with RAW files can be accomplished either by adjusting the color temperature and green-to-magenta adjustment of the image files until unnatural color casts are removed or by selecting a neutral reference within the image on which to balance the entire image. If only one photo of a set contains a neutral reference, it can be used to white balance the whole set exposed on the same project as long as the color of the lighting was constant.

FILM FORMATS

The most popular format film for evidence photography is 35mm camera film. This film is 35mm wide and has perforations along the edges used for advancing the film at a fixed rate through the transport system of the camera. The film is enclosed in a light-tight cassette (see Fig. 6–19) to allow loading of the camera in daylight. The

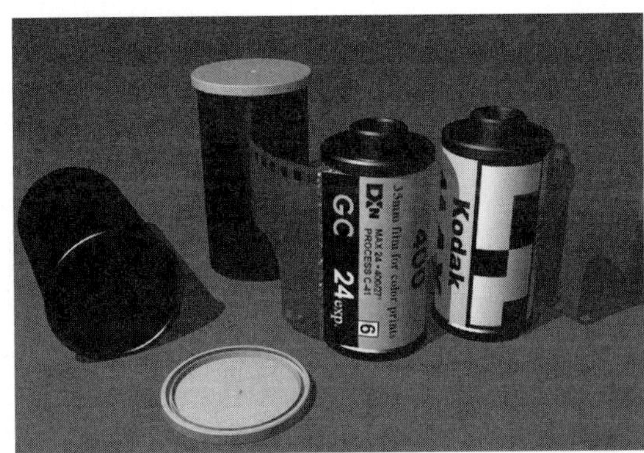

FIGURE 6–19 Cassettes of 35 mm color negative film. *Source:* Sandy Weiss.

standard image format is 24 × 36 mm. Some panoramic cameras create wider images on the same film.

Varying roll lengths of 35mm film allow the creation of different numbers of exposures per roll. The standard-size roll contains 36 exposures if the images are 24 × 36 mm. Also available in some film varieties are film rolls with 8, 12, 15, 20, 24, and 27 exposures. Bulk rolls of 100 feet of film allow photographers to load the length of film they choose but not more than 36 to 40 exposures per cassette, unless a thinner emulsion film is being used or the camera has a special back that will accommodate longer rolls.

In most cameras the film must be rewound before the camera can safely be opened. Some cameras unwind the film fully upon loading and then expose the images in reverse order while returning the film to its cassette.

For most forensic purposes, 35mm is a useful format because the film is sufficiently fine grained to allow enlargement up to courtroom-size displays without suffering extensive loss of image quality. Also, 35mm camera hardware is small enough to allow the photographer to carry a selection of bodies and lenses into the field. Prices of hardware, though expensive for top quality, are within the budgets of most evidence photographers and departments.

Medium-Format Film

Film rolls for 120-size film (see Fig. 6–20) are 72 cm (28.3 inches) long. 120 is the only medium-format film width currently being manufactured. It is still popular with serious professionals. In construction, it is a roll of film with a paper backing on a plastic spool. Rolls of 220-size film are twice as long and contain no paper backing, although they are the same width as 120. Depending on the format of the camera, different numbers of exposures are made on the same-size roll.

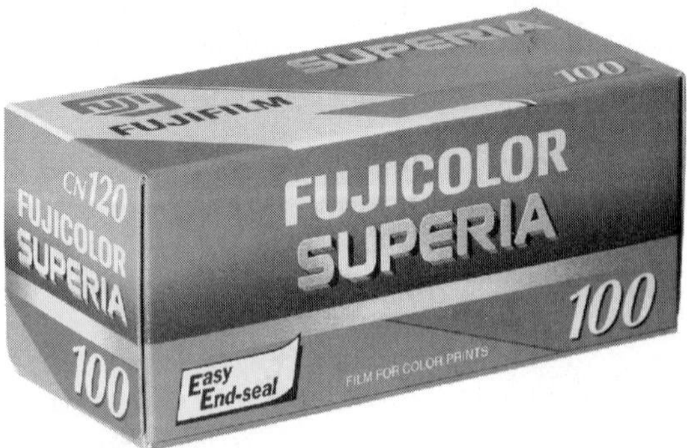

FIGURE 6–20 120 color film. *Source:* Sandy Weiss.

120 frame size in cm	Exposures per roll
6 × 4.5	15 or 16
6 × 6	12
6 × 7	10
6 × 8	9
6 × 9	8
6 × 12	6
6 × 17	4
6 × 24	3

Because they have the same proportions as 8 × 10-inch photographic paper, 6 × 7 and 6 × 4.5 are considered to be the ideal format. Since 35mm film in 24 × 36 mm format does not match 8 × 10-inch paper, to make full-frame enlargements onto 8 × 10-inch paper the images must be made in a shape similar to wide-screen or letter-boxed movies, which have blank areas above and below the images.

Large-Format Film

Sheet film (see Figs. 6–21 and 6–22), constructed on a plastic base, replaced the use of glass negatives. It is considered large format unless it is the same size as medium format.

The sheet of film is placed into a light-tight holder, emulsion side out, and the holder is inserted into a large-format camera. The dark slide, a thin piece of metal that fits into the film holder, is removed and the exposure is made. Then the dark slide is replaced and the film is ready to be removed for processing in a zero-light or film-safe lighted darkroom. When the ultimate color image quality is needed, the film photographer should use the size of film that will

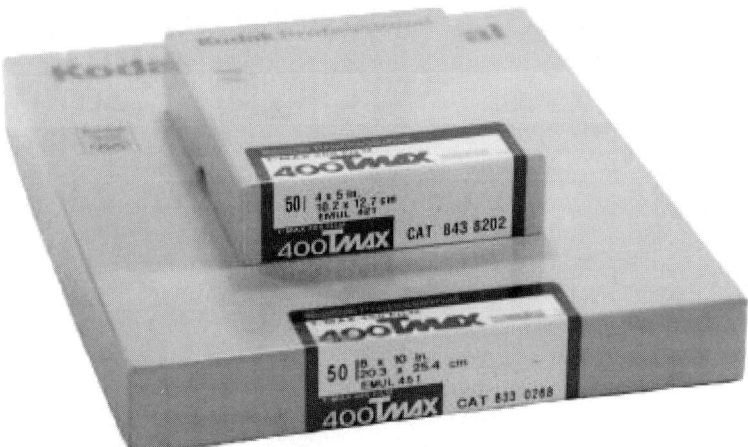

FIGURE 6–21 Boxes of sheet film. *Source:* Sandy Weiss.

make the necessary enlargement with minimal loss in image quality.

DIGITAL RESOLUTION

Resolution is defined as the number of pixels displayed per unit of printed length in a digital image and is usually measured in pixels per inch (ppi) or dots per inch (dpi). An image will appear more or less grainy based upon its pixel count or resolution. For an image to appear smooth, the individual pixels that were used in its creation must not be visible. If the resolution of an image is lower than that required by an output device, individual pixels' edges will be visible and will yield objects with jagged edges.

The optical resolution of a digital camera is a finite number because an image sensor's photosites/pixels are a finite number. Enlarging any digital image to extreme sizes may make individual pixels visible. This is called **pixelization** and is similar in character to the graininess displayed in silver-based prints after sufficient enlargement. The higher the resolution of a digital image, the more it can be enlarged before pixelization occurs.

A sensor's resolution is determined by how many photosites it contains. This resolution is usually specified in one of two ways: by the sensor's dimensions in pixels or by its total number of pixels. For example, the Nikon D80 maximum resolution is 3,872 × 2,592 or just over 10 Mp.

An image's resolution is the total number of pixels—for example, 1,600 × 2,000 = 3.2 Mp, corresponding to 3.2 MB in a computer for an 8-bit

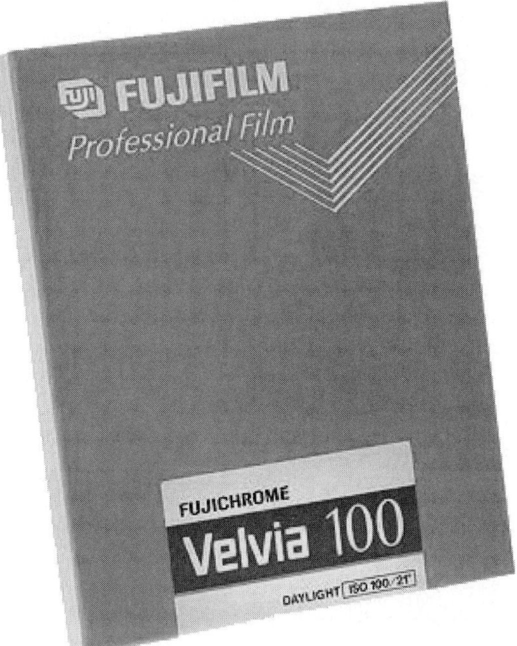

FIGURE 6–22 A box of color sheet film. *Source:* Sandy Weiss.

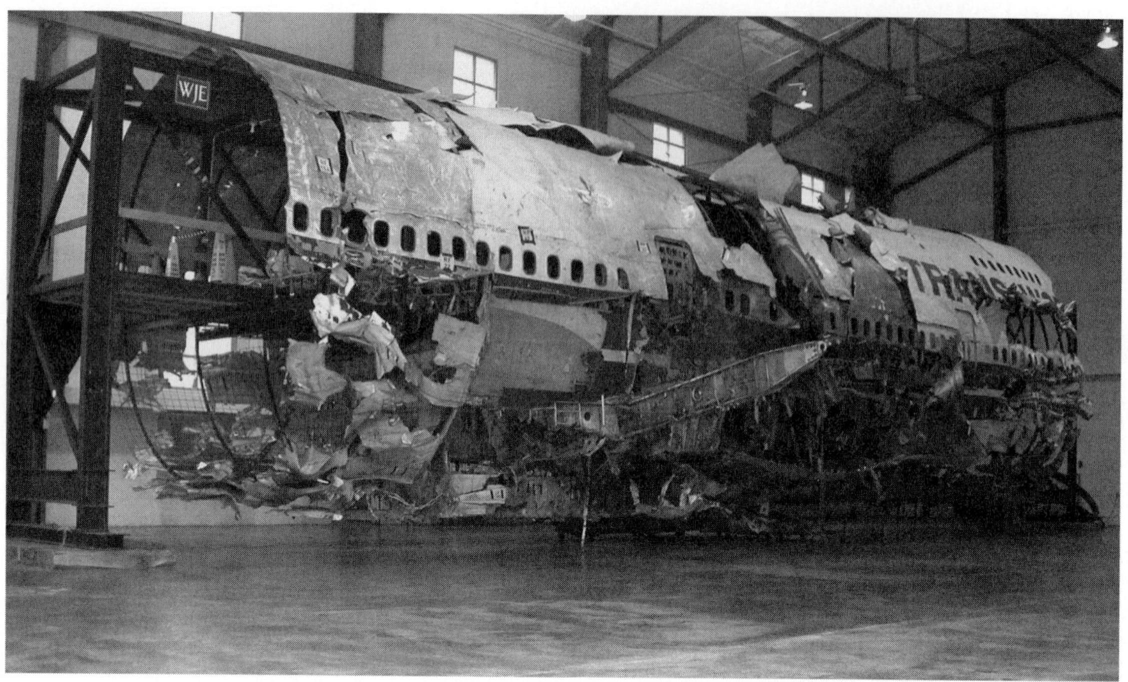

FIGURE 6–23 An original exposed image of the reconstruction of TWA Flight 800, which exploded in midair and crashed off the coast of New York. This image was presized in pixels per inch (ppi) to 300 from the capture resolution of 72 ppi. This procedure yielded an image with smaller physical dimensions but identical resolution. If a section of this image is cropped tightly, the resolution remains at 300 ppi and the image is sharp and clear. *Source:* Sandy Weiss.

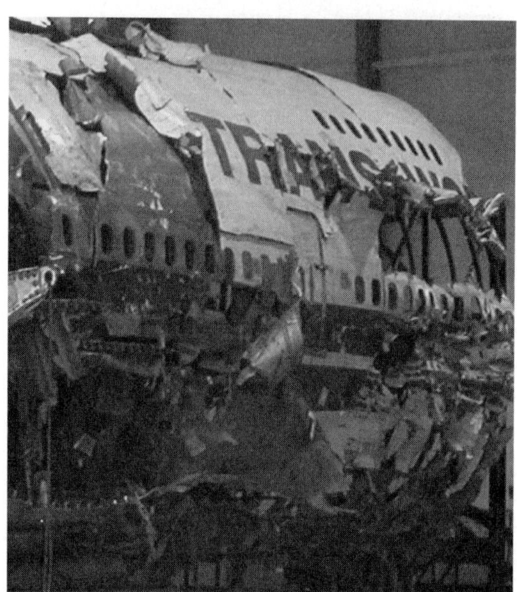

FIGURE 6–24 TWA Flight 800 reconstruction in the hangar at the NTSB Academy in Virginia at 300 dpi and cropped. *Source:* Sandy Weiss.

black-and-white image or 9.6 MB for a 24-bit (3 bytes/pixel) color image.

In general, the larger the digital file, the higher the resolution of the image. In some cases, use of the maximum file size is unnecessary. If the image is going to be placed on the Internet or printed small, a smaller file may be captured. However, if the image captured must be made larger at some point, the small captured file may be insufficient in resolution. A useful practice is to work backward from the desired print size to determine the size of the digital file needed to produce an image of sufficient resolution.

Interpolation for full RGB color triples the finished file size (for a given bit depth) of an image. For example, a 7-Mp RAW file (one pixel per color, bit depth = 12, compressed without loss) is transformed into an 18.9 MB 24-bit file (8 bits per color, which sacrifices some tonal detail) or a 37.8 MB 48-bit file (16 bits per color, which keeps the full tonal detail).

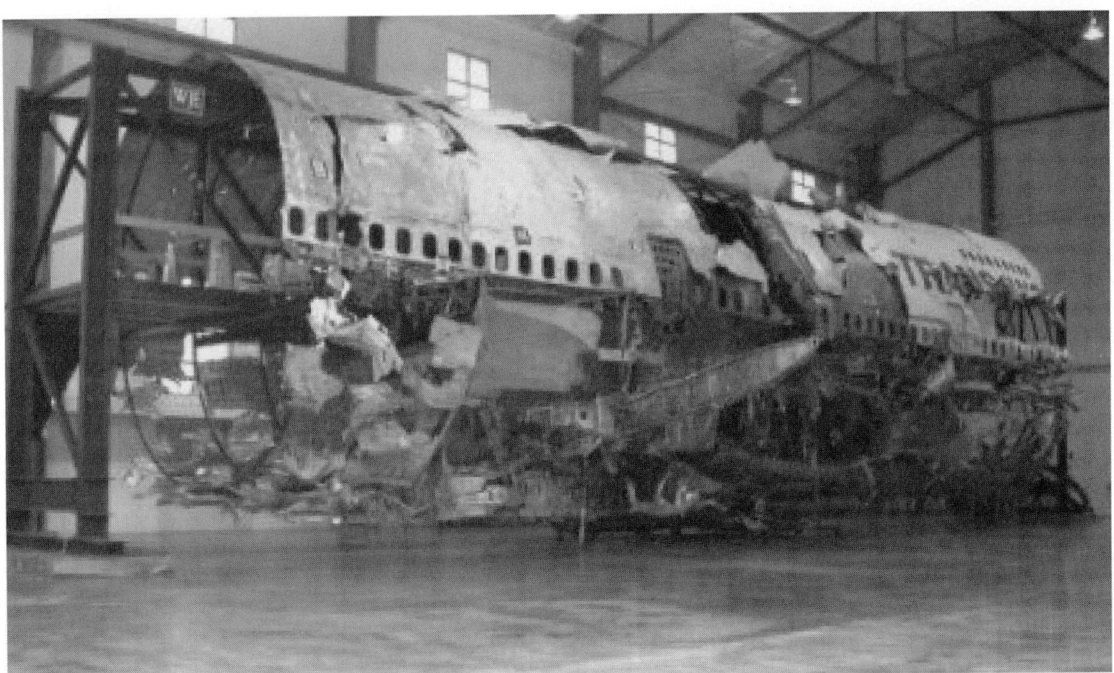

FIGURE 6–25 This is the same original image as Figure 6–23 but shown at capture resolution of 72 ppi. If a section of this image is cropped tightly, and the resolution remains at 72 ppi, the image will appear blurred and pixelated. *Source:* Sandy Weiss.

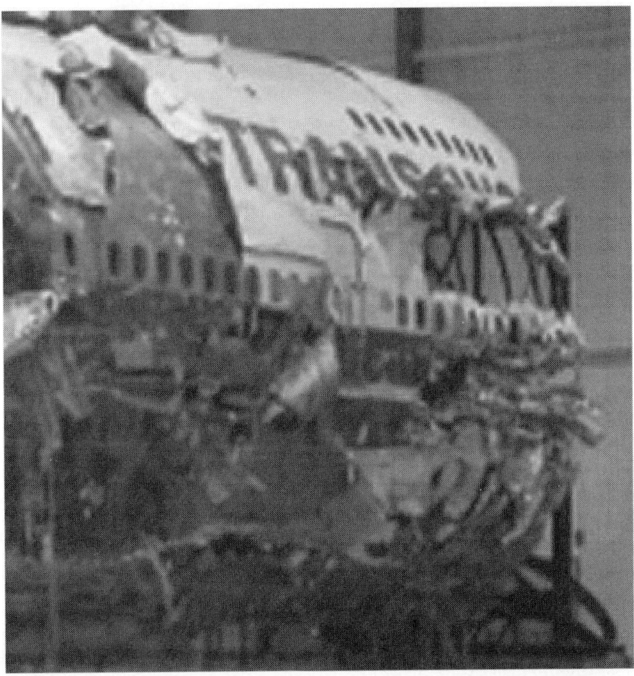

FIGURE 6–26 TWA Flight 800 reconstruction in the hangar at the NTSB Academy in Virginia at 72 dpi and cropped. *Source:* Sandy Weiss.

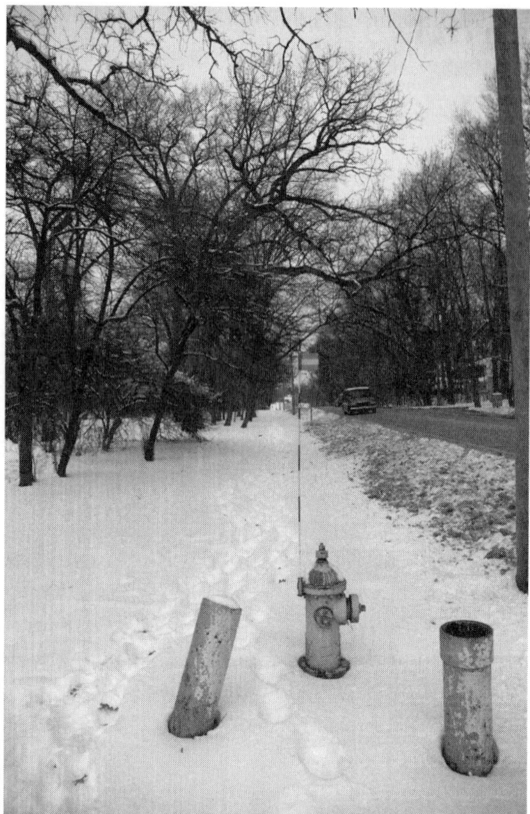

FIGURE 6–27 This image, in the same physical size and resolution as Figure 6–28, will compress to a smaller JPEG file because the contrast is lower. *Source:* Sandy Weiss.

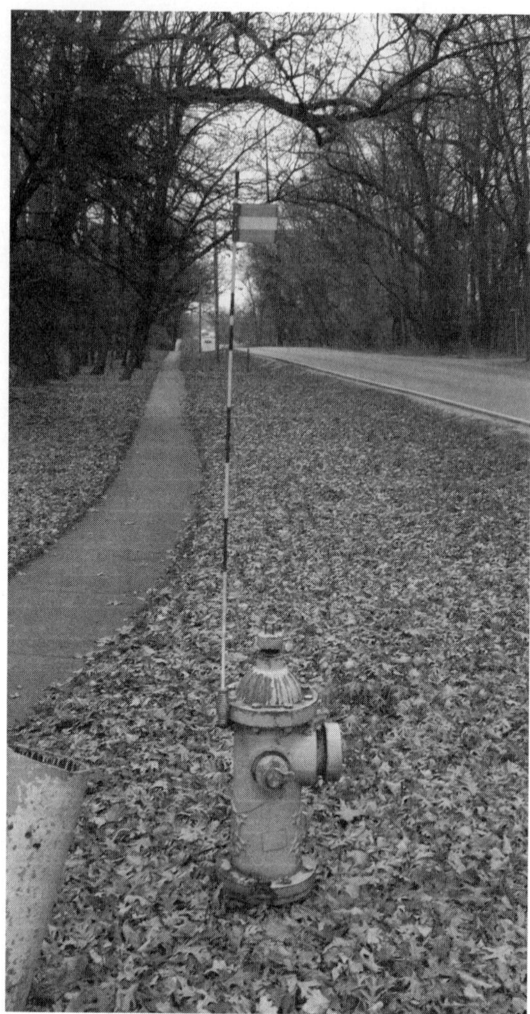

FIGURE 6–28 This image, in the same size and resolution as Figure 6–27, will compress to a larger JPEG file because the contrast is higher. *Source:* Sandy Weiss.

IMAGE FILE FORMATS

JPEG Files

Several file formats are available for image capture and storage. Currently, the most popular are RAW, JPEG, and TIFF. **JPEG** is a usually a compressed* file, while **RAW** and **TIFF** files are uncompressed. RAW is the whole file in colored layers as captured in the camera. Compression reduces the amount of storage space required for an image. For example, a 1,600 × 2,000 pixel 24-bit color image (3 bytes per pixel) requires 9.6 MB of memory to store without compression; it requires less with compression. The exact amount of storage size depends on certain factors, including the contrast and color range of the image (see Figs. 6–27 and 6–28).

*A scheme that, after decompression, does not produce exactly the same data that were given to the compressor. Due to the nature of image data, the losses are often imperceptible to the human eye. Although image quality may suffer, many experts believe that up to 95% of the data in a typical image may be discarded without a noticeable loss in apparent resolution.

Saving JPEG Files

The digital image sensor itself does not record color. It only records the intensity of illumination in its sector. A Bayer matrix or color filter array placed over the sensor supplies red, blue, and green information to each photosite by taking image information from the neighboring sites and interpolating it.

JPEG images utilize **unsharp masking (USM)** applied by the camera, which enhances the junctions between light and dark areas in the image by raising the contrast. Halos may be produced around the edges if the sharpening is set too high. If set too low, sharpening may be insufficient. Contrast can be set on some cameras to a selection of different levels to most accurately reproduce images under different contrast-lighting situations.

The camera captures JPEGs in 12- or 14-bit mode and then converts the files to 8-bit mode. **Lossy compression,** which sacrifices detail to achieve higher compression ratios, is then applied. By making the files smaller, some data are discarded, but the images are more convenient to store and process and are sufficiently accurate in subject reproduction for most forensic purposes.

JPEG is by far the most popular format for storage and display of photographic images. The loss in quality and stored image size depends on the quality setting used to save the image. The higher the quality setting of the JPEG compression is, the larger will be the file size and the amount of detail saved. The more detail and contrast in the camera captured image, the more information will be saved. Higher-quality JPEGs exhibit fewer **compression artifacts,** data errors that are typically the result of quantization in lossy data compression.

JPEG image quality may deteriorate when images are opened, saved, and reopened in JPEG format. The deterioration is minimal when files are saved at the highest-possible JPEG quality but may be noticeable if the files are saved at less than maximum. JPEGs saved on write-only media, including CDs and DVDs, cannot be compressed. Consult the protocol section in Chapter 2 for details.

Some reasons to save camera files as JPEGs include the following:

- Files are smaller.
- Image quality is sufficient in most applications.
- The files do not have to be converted to be used.
- White balance and other functions are performed by the camera.
- Images can be exposed faster in the camera.
- It is simpler to share images with other users.

TIFF Files

Tagged Image File Format (TIFF) is another digital format for capturing and storing images. Adobe Systems now controls the TIFF specification.

TIFF stores image data in a lossless format. Unlike JPEG, TIFF files can be edited and resaved without compression loss. Other TIFF options include the ability to save multiple layers within an image. TIFF provides an option to use lossless data compression for reducing file size during storage.

RAW Files

A photographer needing the highest-quality digital images may wish to expose images in RAW format, which consists of data copied directly from the image sensor. All newer professional digital cameras will produce RAW images, and many other digital cameras now include an option to store images in this format.

The information in RAW files conforms to the mosaic pattern of the Bayer filter array. RAW files do not meet any industrywide standard and are unique to each camera and manufacturer. They must be converted to a standard format by a RAW converter (or a de-mosaicing program) before they can be opened by some generic image editors. Some software will work with any RAW file.

Saving image files as RAW is synonymous to retaining the latent images formed on exposed, undeveloped film. RAW images retain what the image sensor recorded. The saved image will yield the maximum image quality for any end purpose.

RAW files are not white balanced in the camera. Color temperature and white balance can and should be set after download. RAW file capture inherently allows for a broader range of color temperature and color shifts.

Color conversion in RAW is performed on a computer, which always contains a microprocessor superior to any found in cameras. The RAW file is tagged with contrast and saturation information as set in the camera by the user, but the actual image data have not been processed or changed by the camera.

RAW files include 16-bit information. This is important when editing an image, particularly if the user is attempting to show detail in shadow areas or alter brightness in any part of an image in any significant way.

A digital sensor records the amount of light hitting each photosite (pixel) during exposure. The exposure is recorded as a level of voltage, photosite by photosite. The voltage signal is converted into a digital representation. The camera circuitry records either 12- or 14-bit data. If 12 bits of data are used, each pixel can differentiate between 4,096 levels of brightness. If 14 bits are used, 16,384 levels of brightness will be discernible.

Image files saved in RAW mode will be converted to TIFFs or PhotoShop documents (PSDs) and then exported in 16-bit mode. If the camera is simultaneously saving JPEGs, they will be converted to 8-bit mode with only 256 brightness levels per pixel.

Each of the green photosites in the sensor has two nearby red sites and two nearby blue sites (see Fig. 6–29). An averaging interpolation of their intensity values would yield reasonably accurate results. The red and blue sites have four nearby green sites. Averaging and interpolating these will furnish a nearly accurate green value. A missing red or blue value for these sites can be overcome by averaging the four diagonal sites of the appropriate color. Higher color accuracy is gained from more complex interpolation methods.

Interpolation is more inaccurate at the outer edges of the sensor as fewer site values need to be averaged. Most TIFF and JPEG images are cropped in from the edges by several pixels, whereas RAW images are not.

An advantage of RAW format over TIFF is that the finished images are only about one-fourth the size of a comparable file. With RAW images, the full original image can be archived and processed again at a later time.

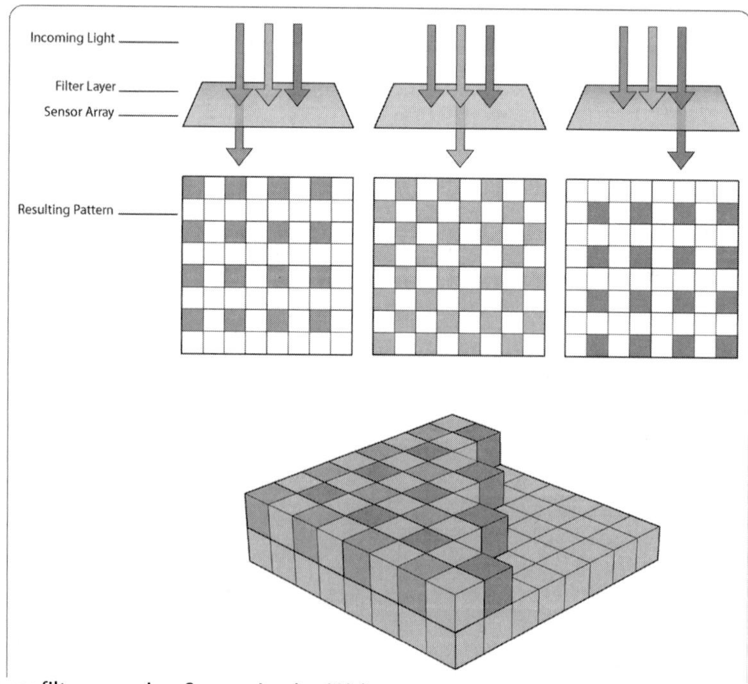

FIGURE 6–29 Bayer filter mosaic. *Source:* Jessica Weiss.

Suggested Basic RAW Protocol

1. Capture images in RAW format.
2. Set the camera for sequential numbering.
3. Archive the files.
4. Batch process to produce JPEG images.
5. Use Adobe Photoshop to edit the RAW files to produce new files in any format (TIFF, JPEG, etc.).

Remember

Some cameras simultaneously save both RAW and JPEG files so the photographer does not have to make a choice at the time of capture.

MONITOR RESOLUTION

Monitor resolution is almost always denoted as a pair of numbers indicating the screen's width and height in pixels. For example, a monitor may be specified as being 800 (horizontal) × 600 (vertical), 1,024 × 768, and so on. Monitor images are low-resolution, usually 72 pixels per inch (ppi).

MONITOR CALIBRATION

To calibrate a monitor, find a high-resolution image of a gray-scale step wedge on the Internet and display it on the monitor. The important sectors for calibration are the white and black at the opposite ends and the adjoining densities. If the pair of white rectangles appears visually the same, the *white point* of the monitor is out of adjustment. If the pair of black rectangles appears the same, the *black point* of the monitor is out of adjustment. If the white rectangles have a tint of color, the middle tones, or *gamma*, of the monitor need to be calibrated for R, G, and B.

Monitor black and white points may be calibrated without any special software. Monitor brightness and contrast controls are the only tools needed for calibration. However, to adjust monitor gamma, special software, such as Adobe Gamma, is required. Adobe Gamma is packaged with Photoshop and Photoshop Elements software.

Once calibrated, a monitor will display images as they are intended to look using the parameters of the image file. If the images viewed are shared with other people using other computers, it is critical for both monitors to be calibrated to a standard. In many cases, the **sRGB** standard, a third method of handling color in the operating systems, is recommended.

Proper calibration is intended to yield the RGB values (0, 0, 0) that correspond to 0% brightness, or black point. When adjusting contrast, the goal is to make RGB values (255, 255, 255) correspond to 100% brightness, or white point.

The sRGB standard uses a color temperature of 6,500 K. Most monitors have provisions for setting color temperature using on-screen menus. *Be sure to set the monitor color temperature before calibrating with Adobe Gamma.*

Also be sure the display is configured for 24-bit color. With 16-bit color, not enough color depth is available for proper calibration. Let the monitor warm up adequately before calibration.

Calibration Theory

When adjusting monitor gamma, the tonal value of mid-tones of the display are changed. Gamma relates pixel values to brightness according to the following formula:

Brightness = C × (pixel value) gamma,
where C is a constant

Macintosh computers and monitors operate at a gamma of 1.8; PC monitors operate at a gamma of 2.5. Popular demand is calling for standardization of monitor display parameters to the sRGB standard with a gamma of 2.2.

PRINTER AND SCANNER RESOLUTION

Printer and scanner resolutions are usually specified by the number of dots per inch (dpi) that they print or scan.* Pixels per inch refer to the image and display, dots per inch refer to the printer and printed image, but in most cases the two terms are used interchangeably. Monitors usually display at

*Printer resolution is typically 720, 1,440, or 2,880 dpi. This number is the stepper motor pitch, not the actual visual resolution. It typically requires several printer dots to represent one image pixel.

72 ppi for text and images; inkjet printers will yield up to about 1,500 to 2,000 dpi, and commercial printers operate at a range between 1,000 and 2,400 dpi.

Meeting the resolution requirements of the output device is critical to the ultimate quality of the displayed or printed image. The number of pixels an image needs to conform to the visual quality requirements of a device is directly proportional to its chosen output. When the resolution of the digital image is the same as the needed resolution of the device, individual pixels will not be seen in the display or image.

Print Resolution Rules

- Images should be sized at about 300 dpi at the final size at which they will be printed. Lower resolution may be used in some situations, but a test should be done to ensure a lack of pixelization.
- Resolution and size (dimensions) are inversely proportional to each other. When an image is enlarged, its resolution is reduced. When an image is made smaller, its resolution is increased.
- The original size of an image will determine its resolution, and thus the maximum size it can be printed before deterioration.
- Low-resolution images print with jagged edges and fuzzy appearance.

Up-sampling happens when a low-resolution image is taken to a higher resolution with no changes in dimensions. This will add more pixels per inch (dpi) but does not increase sharpness.

If an image must be made physically larger than the original when scanning, increase the scanning resolution above 300 dpi by the same percentage used to enlarge the finished image. The human eye can detect about 300 pixels per inch (ppi) on an inkjet print, which is more than sufficient in a print from a sharp image file.

If the original photo size is 4 × 5 inches and the new size is to be 8 × 10 inches:

> 8/4 = 2, so enlarge the photo 2 times, or 200% and scan the photo at 2 × 300 dpi, or 600 dpi

The pixel dimensions of an image limit its usable resolution. Divide the pixel width and height by 300 to determine the dpi:

> Image = 1,200 × 1,600 dpi
>
> 1,200/300 = 4
>
> 1,600/300 = 5.33
>
> Thus, maximum print size for this image is 4 inches × 5.33 inches

The lower limit on resolution to produce a print without pixelization is 150 ppi. In many cases, a print made at 150 ppi will look identical to one made at 300 dpi on the same printer. When an image is sent to the printer, the image editor or printer driver resizes it to the printer's **native resolution,** the actual number of physical pixels on the display device, whatever that happens to be. Thus, the printer may not use all of the 300 ppi information it is sent. These numbers correspond to the actual pixels per inch on the print, not the ppi setting of the image file.

THE FUTURE OF FILM

Film still has a market and uses, especially large format. Eastman Kodak, Ilford, and others still manufacture black-and-white and color sheet films to meet the needs of working professionals. Digital imaging will totally replace the need for film for forensic applications over the coming years.

FACTORS AFFECTING COLOR PERCEPTION

Paper

Colors created by identical inks may look different to the human eye when printed on different colors, finishes, and weights of paper stock.

Viewing Conditions

Different lighting will affect the human perception of reflective color. A color viewed under fluorescent light will look different from the same color viewed under incandescent light. The printing industry uses a standard viewing light color temperature of 5,000 K. This color light is very close to normal daylight.

Digital Values for Color

The most widely used color system for digital imaging is the 24-bit color system. A 24-bit continuous tone system allows for 16.7 million colors. 24-bit RGB color images are comprised of 8 bits each of the colors red, green, and blue. CMYK color uses 32-bit color, with 8-bits for each color.

Color Space

Color space is a term used to describe the organization of all available colors on a set of axes. This organization allows the colors to be communicated from person to person or device to device. Color is influenced by lighting conditions, personal psychology, and personal physiology. Therefore, a way is needed to describe color accurately and across all platforms.

For example, a blue sky may be represented by a combination of 100% cyan and 50% magenta. Color can be quantified, measured, and translated from a computer to a printer. The translation must be correct; if not, the color created may not be accurate. The color reproduction process involves the transition from the view on a monitor to the creation of a product from a printer. The two devices utilize different color spaces. Monitors are based on RGB color, and printers are based on CMYK. Therefore, it is difficult to match colors on a monitor to colors produced by a printer.

Reminder

All color images printed for reflective viewing must be translated from RGB color to CMYK color.

The International Commission on Illumination (CIE) develops standard methods for measuring color. Their standards of **colorimetry** are internationally accepted specifications for the mathematical definition of color values. CIE color models do not vary by device because the colors should theoretically be constant from one output device to another if everything is properly calibrated.

Because RGB digital images must enter CMYK color space to be printed, the accurate translation from one to the other is critical. RGB can be translated to CMYK in an infinite number of ways because different software programs use different formulae that yield different results. The color gamut of RGB is also larger than that of CMYK, so some colors will not translate properly, no matter how close the systems are to proper calibration.

Color Management

In many cases the photographer's computer, monitor, scanner, and printer are made by different manufacturers, so they may communicate in different color languages. No color language is standard for all the different hardware and software a photographer may use.

The color spaces of monitors and printers are also different from each other. Each has a finite number of colors—its color gamut—that it can produce or recognize. The human visible spectrum is broader than any color monitor can display, and the monitor's color gamut is larger than a color printer can print. The color information sent from the computer to the printer is converted from RGB space to CMYK space. Some colors visible on the monitor are outside the printer's gamut, so another similar color must be substituted for the end product.

Color management systems are programs that manage and match color between devices. As hardware and software become more sophisticated, the images produced become more accurate. Color management systems are still necessary, and they require information on device profiles, device calibration, and color gamut.

A *device profile* defines the color capabilities of the device, including gamut, production method, and mode of operation. The device profile is based upon original defaults and will vary over time. Calibration is needed to properly monitor variations and make changes to bring the device back to standard after it starts to be innacurate.

Hopefully, the software in use will allow for consistent communication among devices over the useful operating ages of the hardware. All light sources change over their useful life and require constant recalibration. Also, it is always impossible for a printer to perfectly match the image visible on a monitor. Another issue that cannot ever be fully addressed is the variation between transmitted and reflected light, as well as variations in paper stock.

Standards for color profiles are defined by the International Color Consortium (ICC). Its published standard profiles are available to all hardware and software developers. The goal is to provide true color communications that will work properly in all hardware and software.

CAMERA FILTERS

Clear and Ultraviolet Filters

Ultraviolet (UV) filters are essentially clear and are used primarily to protect the front of a lens. Other useful applications for UV filters are to diminish the effects of atmospheric haze and to reduce the overabundance of bluish highlights on white subjects, accentuated by the UV output of many electronic flash units.

Color Correction Filters

Color correction (CC) filters are used to compensate for lighting not balanced for a particular film's color temperature. The use of CC filters for light balancing is unnecessary in digital photography because color balance problems are mostly compensated for with by options inside the camera or by processing software subsequent to image capture.

Color Subtraction Filters

Color subtraction filters work by absorbing certain colors of light and letting the remaining colors through. These filters are useful when attempting to separate images of objects of different colors. Another use is in fingerprint photography, where a print is powdered and located on a colored substrate. Using the appropriate filter may lighten the substrate while making the fingerprint more visible, or it may lighten the fingerprint against the background.

The use of colored filters for normal color evidence documentation purposes is not recommended because the color of the image will be permanently changed when it passes through the colored filter.

Contrast Enhancement Filters

Colored filters may be used in black-and-white photography to change the contrast of the negative. Using yellow, orange, red, and green filters will markedly affect the contrast of finished images.

Polarizing Filters

A polarizing filter may be used in documentary photography to darken light skies. The whiteness of the clouds is not appreciably affected, so the contrast between the clouds and the sky is increased.

In evidence work, the primary uses for a polarizer are for the ultimate reduction of atmospheric haze and reflected sunlight. In color photography, the overall color saturation of an image may be increased. Polarizers are often used to diminish reflections off shiny and reflective surfaces, and they may add to the transparency of glass.

Polarizers are often used in digital photography. The effects of polarization at the time of capture cannot be replicated by image processing.

The two types of polarizing filters are linear and circular. Circular polarizers will perform properly with all types of cameras, while linear polarizers will not perform properly with DSLRs.

Filter Factors

Compensation for filter density is unnecessary with cameras having through-the-lens metering. Light from the subject passes through the filter, and the built-in meter compensates automatically for the light absorption. It is important, however, to remember that any density added to the light path absorbs light and necessitates compensation by exposure, requiring the use of slower shutter speeds or larger lens apertures. If this is an issue, try another way of accomplishing the affect of the filter in use.

SUMMARY

Most people are somewhat familiar with the intricacies of traditional film photography but are baffled by the mysteries of digital imaging. Many of the features of both are similar, and it is useful to compare and contrast the two to gain understanding.

The first true step in creating an image is the exposure of light-sensitive material to light. Whether using film or a digital sensor, the importance of good exposure is integral to capturing the ultimate image detail.

The image sensor is the heart of the digital camera. Cameras are capable of using the information gathered by the sensor in several ways to create an image. The various formats have advantages and disadvantages over one another. To gather the most accurate images, it is important to understand the intrinsic differences and to make the proper choices.

In some cases, the default settings of the digital camera will not work properly to create the necessary images. In these cases, it is important to know how to set the camera to take advantage of its full capabilities in adjusting to difficult conditions. It is also critical to understand why settings must be set back to default once the difficult situation is ended.

Although the camera often compensates for differences automatically, color is an important factor in most evidence documentations. It is one of the most difficult factors to capture accurately in digital imaging. Understanding the difference in the colors of light sources and being able to take advantage of all lighting are most useful in the creation of evidence images representing the best possible reality.

Filters screw onto the threads at the front end of all camera lenses. Filters are mostly inexpensive and possibly useful for more than lens protection.

This chapter, beyond its inherent importance in understanding digital imaging, is an introduction to Chapter 7, in which are described methods of proper exposure for creating the best possible and most accurate images under any lighting conditions.

CASE STUDY

WHAT COLOR WAS THE MONTE CARLO?

A fatal traffic accident occurred in 1981, involving a 1972 Monte Carlo struck by another vehicle that trapped the occupants inside while the Monte Carlo was consumed by fire. It was a difficult accident to reconstruct from the existing evidence, as the car rolled several times before coming to rest and the scratch patterns in the paint overlapped and changed directions. There were no living witnesses.

Packer Engineering was hired to reconstruct the accident and investigate the reasons for the post-collision fuel-fed fire. Engineers and technologists visited the site and mapped the evidence remaining in the roadway. A careful study was made of the remains of the vehicle. Displays for court were made of the dynamics of the accident, along with many images of the accident vehicle.

All the photographs were made on Kodak color negative film. Many images were exposed with size scales for future photogrammetric reconstruction of crush. No color control images were exposed.

Many large enlargements were made from the negatives, using only the common sense and visual color perception of the laboratory personnel for density and color balance of the images.

After all the images were printed and mounted, the technologist who did the photography inspected the work. He was certain the vehicle was blue, while all the images printed showed the vehicle as green (see Fig. 6–30). Blue and green are very close to one another in color balance, with just a small amount of yellow CC filtration setting them apart. How is a situation like this resolved?

In truth, the actual color was not an issue. However, if all the images shown in court were totally the wrong color, it would be an issue for the opposition attorney to use as ammunition for discrediting the defense.

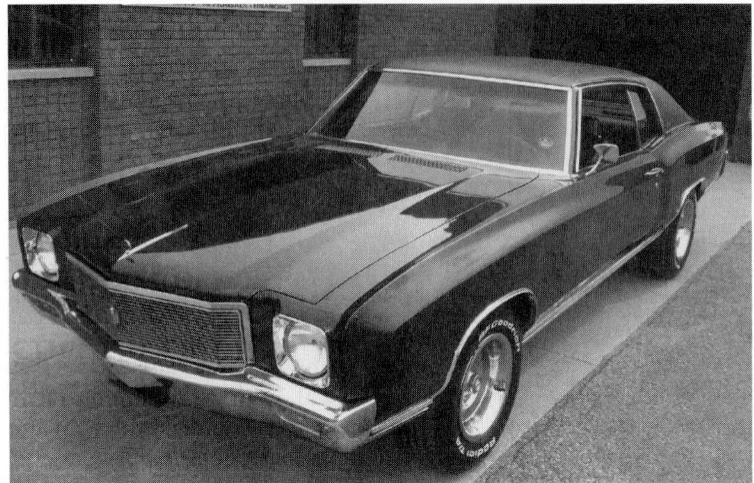

FIGURE 6–30 Exemplar Monte Carlo. *Source:* Sandy Weiss/Packer Engineering

The easiest, if not the most expeditious, way to resolve the issue would be to go back to the vehicle and make a color control image using a color card and then make a print with the color card and see what car color appeared. In this case, that was impossible as the vehicle had been crushed since the initial inspection.

No paint chips had been collected. It would have been simple to send the vehicle identification number (VIN) to General Motors and ask what the color of the vehicle was when it came off the line. However, that was not done because the technologist was sure he was correct and refused to make the inquiry.

The issue was finally solved by procuring a copy of the 1972 Monte Carlo color selector. No stock cars ever left the production line painted the color of blue that the technologist described. The actual stock color of the vehicle is the same as in Figure 6–30, dark green.

KEY TERMS

emulsion, (p. 164)
panchromatic, (p. 164)
monochromatic, (p. 164)
development, (p. 164)
paraphenylene diamine, (p. 165)
transparency, (p. 165)
slide, (p. 165)
exposure latitude, (p. 165)
photosite, (p. 166)
picture element (pixel), (p. 166)
Cartesian coordinates, (p. 166)
bitmap, (p. 166)
density, (p. 167)
ISO, (p. 168)
dynamic range, (p. 169)
signal-to-noise ratio, (p. 169)
dark noise, (p. 169)
read noise, (p. 169)
ASA, (p. 171)
color temperature, (p. 172)
blackbody, (p. 173)
micro reciprocal degree (mired), (p. 175)
filtration, (p. 176)
visible spectrum, (p. 178)
gamut, (p. 178)
tone, (p. 178)
hue, (p. 179)
saturation, (p. 179)
value, (p. 179)
Bayer mosaic, (p. 179)
interpolation, (p. 179)
binary numeric system, (p. 179)
additive color, (p. 180)
CMYK, (p. 180)

subtractive color, (p. 180)
white balance (WB), (p. 180)
resolution, (p. 185)
pixelization, (p. 185)
JPEG file, (p. 188)
RAW file, (p. 188)
TIFF file, (p. 188)
unsharp masking, (p. 189)
lossy compression, (p. 189)
compression artifact, (p. 189)
sRGB, (p. 191)
up-sampling, (p. 192)
native resolution, (p. 192)
color space, (p. 193)
colorimetry, (p. 193)
color management, (p. 193)

EXERCISES

1. Are black, white, and gray colors, or are they the absence of colors?
2. Research and prepare a paper about the mentality behind retaining 72 dpi as the default resolution of all digital cameras.
3. On a bright, sunny day, with a digital camera on a tripod, expose the same high-contrast image in both RAW format and the highest resolution JPEG offered by the camera. Process both to 300 dpi at their maximum size. Determine which image retains the better shadow and highlight detail.
4. With the camera on a tripod and in a safely guarded location, expose a photo of the same scene in the early morning and in the middle of the day, using both automatic and manual white balancing. Compare the images to determine the competence of the camera working on automatic.
5. Send a well-balanced digital image to a color printer and compare what is seen on the monitor to what is printed. If the colors are radically different, devise a way to better control the results.

APPENDIX 6.1

Kodak Technical Filter Data

Consult the chart at www.kodak.com/global/en/professional/support/techPubs/b3akic/b3akic.pdf for a published list of Kodak filters for any color correction application.

APPENDIX 6.2

Color Temperature Conversion Factors

Value = Equation

Decamired = mired / 10

Decamired = 100,000 / Kelvin

Mired = 10 decamired

Mired = 1,000,000 / Kelvin

Kelvin = 100,000 / decamired

Kelvin = 1,000,000 / mired

DAYLIGHT COLOR TEMPERATURES

Description	Degrees Kelvin
Clear blue sky	8,000 to 27,000
Rainy, misty daylight	7,200 to 8,500
Overcast daylight	6,500 to 7,200
Direct sun + clear blue sky	5,700 to 6,500
Summer sunlight	5,400 to 5,700
Summer sunlight (early/late)	4,900 to 5,600
Electronic flash (typical)	6,200 to 6,800

ARC LAMP COLOR TEMPERATURES

Description	Degrees Kelvin
Xenon arc (unfiltered)	6,000
White flame carbon arc	5,000
Yellow flame carbon arc	3,200

FLUORESCENT LAMP COLOR TEMPERATURES

Description	Degrees Kelvin
True daylight	6,500
Cool white	4,300
Warm white	3,000

TUNGSTEN LAMP COLOR TEMPERATURES

Description	Degrees Kelvin
Photoflood tungsten–halogen	3,400
Photoflood	3,200
Projection lamps (500 to 1,000 watts)	2,900 to 3,000
General-purpose lamps (200 to 500 watts)	2,900
Household lamps (100 to 150 watts)	2,850
Household lamps (60 watts)	2,800
Household lamps (40 watts)	2,750

Chapter 7

Operating Hardware: Holding, Focusing, and Metering

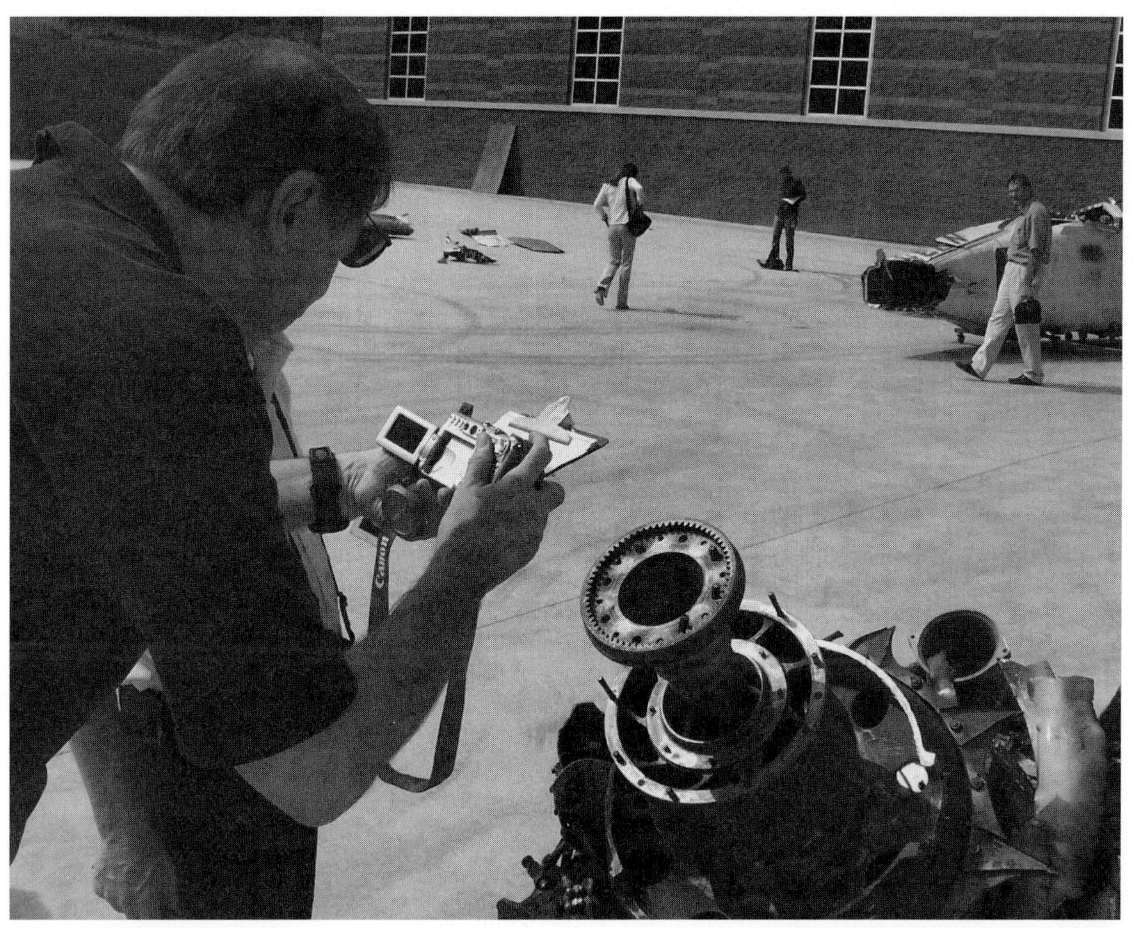

Learning Objectives

AFTER STUDYING THIS CHAPTER, YOU SHOULD BE ABLE TO:

1. Master the best methods for holding and operating a camera
2. Utilize the optimum methods for focusing a camera
3. Maximize depth of field in all photographs
4. Understand and compute the digital focal length multiplier and crop factor
5. Calculate the correct distance for viewing a print of any size
6. Focus any lens by setting its hyperfocal distance
7. Select the most appropriate automatic focus setting
8. Understand light meters and metering
9. Select the optimum shutter speeds and lens apertures
10. Understand and use image histograms
11. To understand and use the Zone System

HAND-HOLDING THE CAMERA

When photography was new, cameras were physically large and light-sensitive media took a long time to expose. At that time, use of a tripod was always necessary to produce images undistorted by camera movement. Over time, cameras became smaller, media became faster, and tripods became less of a necessity. Currently, tripods are used for low-light photography; sports and action photography with long telephoto lenses; and time lapse, surveillance, copy-stand, and other related disciplines—but most general photography is accomplished with the camera hand-held. This has not necessarily been a good change.

Lightweight cameras are convenient to carry but are easily moved during exposure. Some of the newer point-and-shoot cameras focus by viewing an image on the LCD preview/review panel and must be held away from the body during exposure (see Fig. 7–1), often with one hand. The farther away from the photographer's body the camera is held, the more significant the chance of moving the camera during exposure. It may be impossible to discern that an image is out of focus when reviewing it on such a tiny monitor. A small amount of camera movement will create a blurry image.

Some method must be practiced to hold the camera sufficiently still during exposure. Assuming a constant sensitivity of media, camera shutters stay open longer to achieve proper exposure when the light level is low in intensity. When the shutter is open for an extended period, camera movement is more likely to occur unless the camera has been placed on a stable platform. The use of a telephoto lens or the telephoto position of a zoom lens also may require the use of a stable camera platform due to the magnification factor of the image. The magnification and narrower field of a telephoto lens make it more difficult to hold the camera steady during exposure. The same thing happens when a viewer looks through a telescope or binoculars.

Using a tripod is one way to diminish camera movement if the tripod is sufficiently heavy to support the weight of the camera and its accessories. Extra-heavy tripods should be used on windy days.

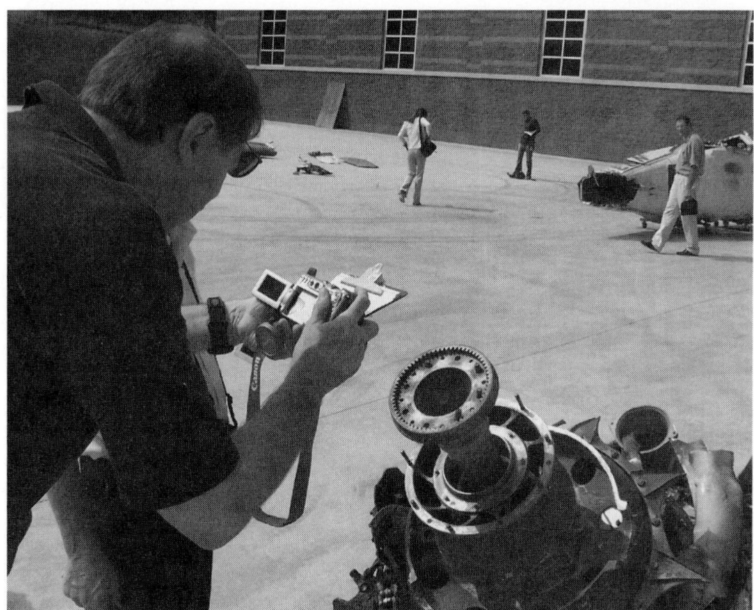

FIGURE 7–1 This is the way many point-and-shoot cameras are held during normal photography. *Source:* Sandy Weiss/Packer Engineering.

All modern cameras are designed to be held primarily in the photographer's right hand. The forefinger should be positioned above the shutter release and the other three fingers should wrap around and hold the front of the camera. The right thumb should be placed firmly on the top of the back of the camera. Many cameras have a rubberized grip to indicate where the photographer's fingers should rest for maximum efficiency. The thumb should be positioned to easily operate the camera's rear dial. If this orientation is difficult for left-handed photographers, they may consider performing right-hand exercises to strengthen hand muscles.

TIPS:

Always hold a camera firmly—but not so firmly that the muscles of the hand jerk during shutter release.

The positioning of the left hand depends upon the camera. The wrist should be flexed with the palm up to support the weight of the lens or the camera (see Fig. 7–2), depending upon which is heavier. The left hand is used for focusing and for zooming the lens when necessary. A DSLR camera should never be held by putting both hands on the sides of the camera body during exposure (see Fig. 7–3).

When using the viewfinder of a point-and-shoot camera, keep the camera close to your eye

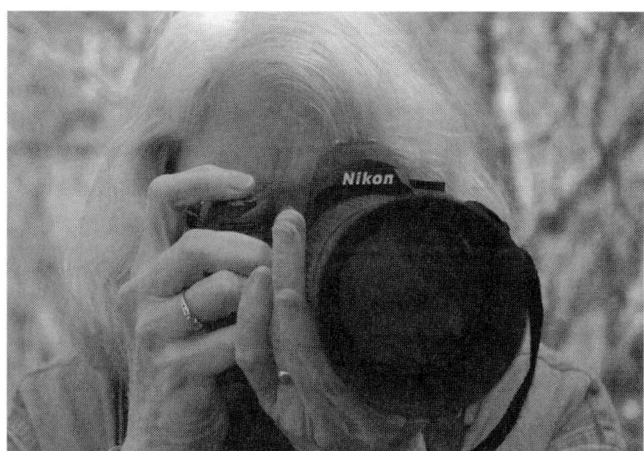

FIGURE 7–2 This is a *proper* hand-holding method to support and operate a DSLR camera. *Source:* Sandy Weiss/Packer Engineering.

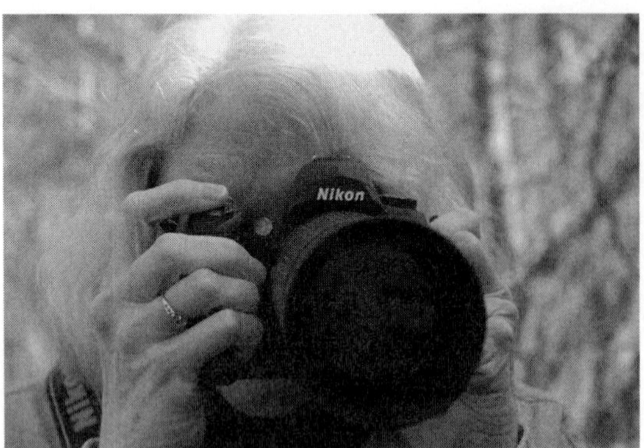

FIGURE 7–3 This is an *improper* hand-holding method to support and operate a DSLR camera. *Source:* Sandy Weiss/ Packer Engineering.

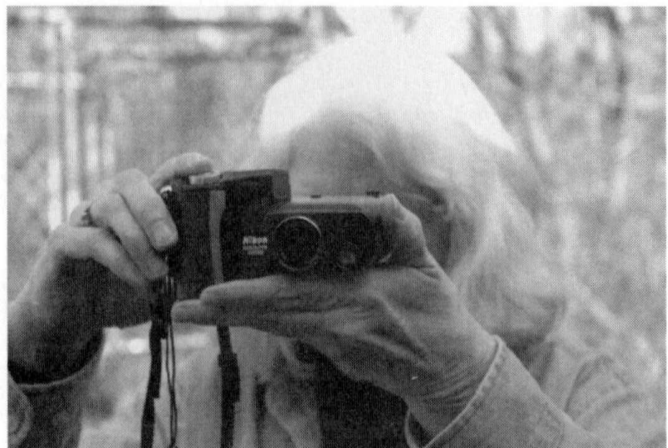

FIGURE 7–4 This is a *proper* hand-holding method to support and operate a point-and-shoot camera when focusing through the viewfinder. *Source:* Sandy Weiss/ Packer Engineering.

during exposure so you can utilize the additional stability of your arms and legs (see Fig. 7–4). If using the LCD panel to focus, keep the camera as close as possible to the eye to enable review of the image display on the LCD (usually 10 to 12 inches) (see Fig. 7–5). It may be difficult to hold very small cameras and keep your fingers out of the way of the lens, flash, and sensors during exposure. Be careful.

Some point-and-shoot cameras have built-in electronic anti-shake or **image stabilization (IS)** systems. Consider the purchase of a camera with one of these systems if your point-and-shoot photographs are often blurry. IS in cameras or lenses enables sharper photographs by damping vibration.

When using a slower shutter speed, if possible, lean against a solid object when making exposures. Take a deep breath, hold it, let some of the air out, and then release the shutter. The photographer must concentrate on keeping his or her body as still as possible when releasing the shutter of a camera. Maintaining the proper body position can make a positive difference. Keep your elbows tucked in and either lie down with your elbows resting on the ground or sit up with your elbows resting on the knees. Make a tripod out of your body using your elbows as two legs. Keeping your muscles relaxed is necessary to reduce camera movement during exposure.

> The choice of shutter speed must be made with consideration for the subject, whether moving or stationery. Sharpness may be increased in any case by using faster shutter speeds. With a normal lens and a handheld camera, a shutter speed slower than 1/250th second may produce (surprisingly) less than a completely sharp image.[1]

The photographer's heart is always beating and may contribute to camera movement, especially during extended hand-held exposures. Use of the optimum shutter speed and aperture combination allows the use of the shortest shutter speed.

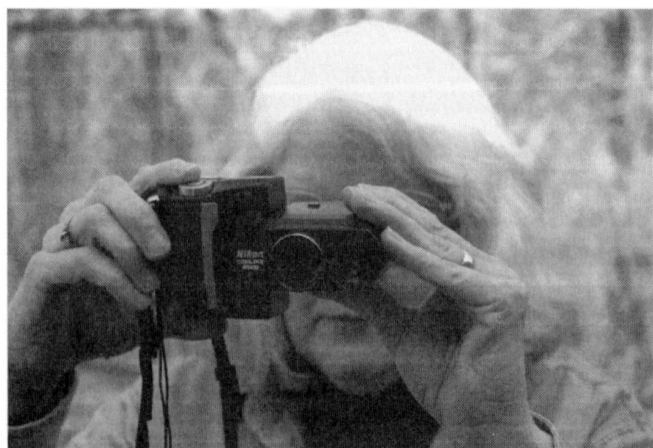

FIGURE 7–5 This is a proper hand-holding method to support and operate a point-and-shoot camera when focusing on the LCD. *Source:* Sandy Weiss/Packer Engineering.

TIPS:

For practice, tape the switch of a laser pointer in the on position and tape the pointer on a camera. Point the camera at a wall and try to hold the camera as steady as possible during an exposure. With practice, the movement of the bright dot should define smaller and smaller circles of movement.

Always wear a camera strap on the neck or the wrist. This may not help to keep images in focus, but it will prevent the camera from being dropped and damaged.

If possible, obtain a rubber eyecup for the viewfinder of the DSLR. This will make the camera more comfortable to use, especially for eyeglass wearers. Also, by pressing the camera against your eye during exposure, you will have an extra point of contact, which will provide additional support and steadiness.

TIP:

When pressing the shutter release, squeeze it smoothly and do not jerk the camera.

TIP:

When hand-holding the camera, select a shutter speed that is approximately the reciprocal of the focal length of the lens in use. This will help to prevent blurring due to camera movement. For example, when using a 300 mm lens, the shutter speed should be set no slower than 1/250 second. Always set the next speed faster, not slower, than the numeric value of the focal length.

Lenses are effectively longer in focal length and narrower in **field of view,** to the extent of the observable world at any given moment, when used on digital cameras than they would be when used on film cameras. This is due to the crop factor of the smaller digital image sensors. Inherently, the same lens is more difficult to hand-hold and use to capture sharp images on a digital camera than it would be on a film camera.

These holding recommendations are pertinent only if the photographer is making the decisions about the shutter speed used to expose the photographs. Keeping the camera set on fully automatic is convenient but may yield improperly focused photographs if the subject or camera is moving during exposure.

Aerial Photography

When taking photographs from an aircraft, it is important to adhere to the following guidelines:

- Do not let the camera touch the aircraft during exposure.
- To prevent Plexiglas aircraft windows from being scratched, do not let the camera touch the windows.
- Keep the camera out of the wind and weather.
- Sit on a cushion, if possible, to isolate the camera from aircraft vibrations.
- Expose images along the same plane as the aircraft is traveling, not perpendicular to it.
- Use the fastest possible shutter speed allowable for the lighting conditions.
- If resolution is not an issue, utilize a higher-than-normal ISO setting to allow faster shutter speeds.
- Use an image stabilized camera and/or lens whenever possible.
- Use an ultraviolet (UV) filter on the lens to reduce atmospheric haze.

FOCUSING

Manual Focus

Until recently professional cameras, both range finder and SLR, primarily utilized manual focusing. The design and operation of their focusing systems were designed to optimize fast and accurate operation. In manual focusing range-finder cameras, the image of the subject is normally seen through two separate windows on the top of the camera. When the lens is properly focused, the two images are superimposed.

In manual focusing SLR cameras, a mirror behind the lens reflects the image of the subject to a pentaprism. The pentaprism rectifies and intensifies the image before it is projected onto a focusing screen. The screen is often made of ground glass or ground glass with a focusing aid, such as a microprism or split image.

Focusing aids are used to improve the accuracy of focusing and to generate sharper images. They are useful only with lenses of large maximum aperture. They may appear black to the photographer's eye and be useless or detrimental if the lens used has a small maximum aperture or if lens attachments are used that diminish the quantity of transmitted light.

As a lens turns, the beam of light it transmits is focused and judged in the viewfinder by the photographer. The SLR design allows the camera to focus through any lens attached to it. This design has been used in film cameras for many years, and most photographers are experienced and comfortable with its use.

Depth of Field

In evidence photography, there is never a good reason to minimize the depth of field (DoF) of an image. The range of distances over which an image is acceptably sharp is one of the most important factors for the evidence photographer to learn to maximize for accurate evidence documentation.

Consider a circle to be a point with an opening in the center. If a point is not in sharp focus, the open center will be visible to the viewer. The **circle of confusion (CoC)** is the fuzziest a point can be and still be called "in focus." CoC quantified is the largest circle in an image that will be perceived as a point rather than a circle when the image is enlarged to 8 × 10 inches and viewed from a distance of 2 to 3 feet.

If quantification of the DoF is necessary, the photographer must be able to calculate the largest circle of confusion that is perceived as a dot, or in acceptable focus, in the finished image. The circle of least confusion also is the smallest dot a lens is capable of producing.

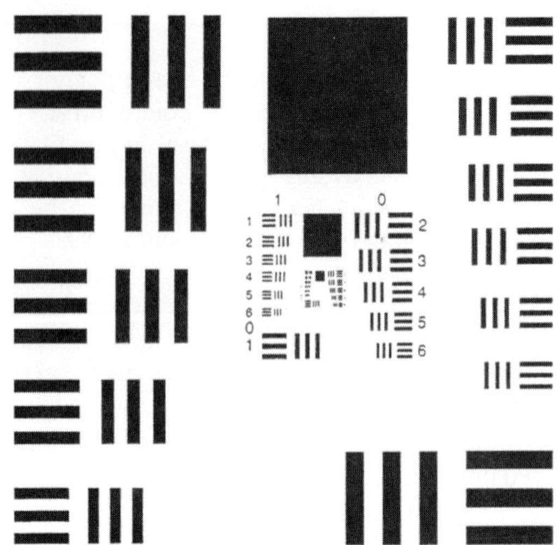

FIGURE 7–6 A chart of line pairs of different sizes. *Source:* Sandy Weiss/Packer Engineering.

Visual Acuity

For most people with reasonable uncorrected or corrected vision, the closest comfortable distance for viewing a printed image is approximately 10 inches (25 cm). At that distance, a person can normally resolve an image of 5 **line pairs** per millimeter (lp/mm) (see Fig. 7–6), which equates to a CoC of 0.2 mm on a printed image.

RULE:

The maximum CoC size at which a printed image will be perceived as sharp overall, when viewed at about 10 inches, is 0.2 mm.

Sensor Size

Using the image sensor size of a digital camera as a parameter when choosing which to buy is a decision filled with trade-offs. The **focal length multiplier** is a mathematical term that relates the focal length of a lens used on a sub-35 mm digital sensor to the focal length lens that will produce an equivalent **angle of view** on a full-size 35 mm sensor or film. This multiplier is equal to the **crop factor.**

For example, the Nikon D70s has an image sensor with the physical dimensions of 23.7 mm × 15.6 mm (3,008 × 2,000 pixels). Its crop factor is

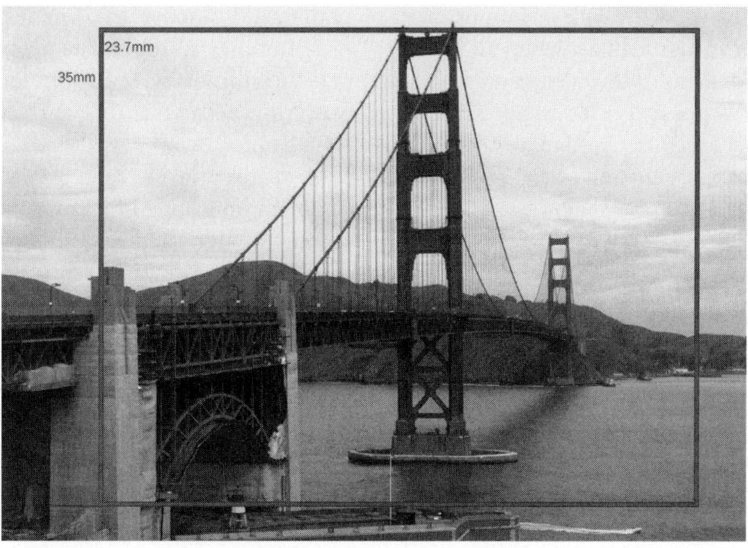

FIGURE 7–7 The same focal length lens captures two different fields of view as the sensor size changes. *Source:* Sandy Weiss/Packer Engineering.

1.5x compared to a full-frame 35 mm sensor or film.

A 50mm lens used on an image sensor with a 1.6x crop factor, such as the Canon Rebel XT, will capture an image with the same field of view as an 80mm lens (1.6 × 50) used on a 35 mm full-frame sensor (see Fig. 7–7).

RULE:

The focal length of a lens does not change when it is used on cameras with different size sensors, but its angle of view does.

If the same lens is used on a DSLR with a sub-35 mm sensor and a 35 mm film camera body, and the resultant 35 mm film image is cropped to yield the same field of view as the digital image, the DoF in the two images will be identical.

If the same lens is used on a DSLR with a sub-35 mm sensor and a 35 mm film camera body and the same subject is photographed from two different distances so that the field of view is the same in both images, the DSLR image will exhibit 1.6x more DoF than the film image.

When photographing the same subject, filling the frame, and using the same aperture on the same lens, DoF decreases as sensor size increases. The larger the sensor, the closer the camera must be to the subject to fill the frame with the subject when using the same lens. If the distance from camera to subject is constant, a lens with a longer focal length must be used on a camera with a larger sensor to fill the frame with the subject.

When using the same lens on cameras with larger sensors and the field of view is constant, a higher-number (smaller) lens aperture must be used to maintain the same DoF.

On a DSLR with an image sensor having a 1.5x crop factor, a lens of 1.5x the focal length and 1.5x the aperture number must be used to capture an image with the same visual perspective and DoF on a camera with a full-frame 35 mm sensor. For example, an image taken with a Nikon D70s and a 20 mm lens set *f*/8 must be exposed on a 35 mm film camera with a 35 mm lens set at *f*/11 (the next available aperture).

Larger image sensors are usually constructed with physically larger pixels. Due to their higher capacity for the capture of light, sensors with larger pixels may produce images with less noise and greater dynamic range than sensors with smaller pixels.

DoF is reduced when photographs are made using sensors of larger size, when all other factors remain constant. However, the use of smaller apertures is possible with larger sensors without the image reaching sufficient CoC size and subsequently appearing and out of focus.

TIP:

DoF is inversely proportional to format size. Format size is inversely proportional to the focal length multiplier. The higher the multiplier, the smaller the format and the greater the DoF.

RULE:

If print size is constant, angle of view is constant, lens aperture is constant, and the image sensor size is halved, DoF will be doubled.

Print Viewing Distance

Human eyes do not zoom. Humans perceive the perspective of a scene at only one magnification unless they move physically closer or farther away. It is not reasonable to assume that camera lenses will capture images of a visual scene at the same magnification as human vision. The magnification of a given scene will also change when the image is printed in different sizes.

The most comfortable distance for the viewing of printed images is 14 to 15 inches from the eye. This is considered the **normal viewing distance** of prints for people with reasonable uncorrected or corrected vision. To ensure that images are viewed without **perspective distortion,** divide 14 by the focal length (in inches) of the lens used to make the image, then multiply the result by the crop factor for the sensor, and then enlarge the image to the resultant number. This formula works only when the image file is not cropped, as in the following example for a 50 mm lens on a Nikon D70s:

50 mm = 2 inches
2 × 1.5 = 3
14/3 = about 5

Enlarge the image to 5 inches wide and view it at 14 inches to represent proper perspective. If the viewing distance is doubled, the dimensions are doubled and the surface area must be quadrupled.

A print larger than 8 × 10 inches, enlarged from an uncropped file, must be viewed at a distance greater than 25 cm to represent proper perspective. When viewing prints from farther than optimum distances, it may be possible to use an image file yielding CoC values larger than 0.2 mm because the human eye is unable to differentiate the circle from a dot at the larger distance.

When printing from a digital image file, if the file measures 8 × 10 inches at any resolution, and the final print measures 8 × 10 inches, there is no enlargement. The CoC requirement for this print is, therefore, the same as the original image file. If a 35 mm image is enlarged to 8 × 10 inches, the enlargement factor is 8×, making the CoC requirement for the original image on the negative 0.2 mm divided by 8, or 0.025 mm.

How sharp does an 8 ×10 print need to be to look sharp at a viewing distance of 14 inches? How large can a point on the print be before it looks like a small disk rather than a point? A typical value is about 250 microns, .25 mm, or .001 inch.

Conversions

1 micron = 0.001 millimeter

1 millimeter = 0.0393700787 inch

Question: Assume the diameter of a dot is a 250-micron spot on an 8 × 10 print. What size is the dot in the original image (negative or digital file)? *Answer:* It depends on the final magnification needed of the original image to achieve the 8 × 10 print.

For example, when enlarging a 35 mm negative (24 mm × 36 mm) to an 8 × 10, the file must be magnified by a factor of about 8. The size dot on the negative that would yield a 250-micron spot on the print is 250/8 microns, or about 30 microns. This is the **circle of confusion value** for this print. It is the largest spot in the original image file that looks like a point in the print. The minimum requirement for the quantification of acceptable 35 mm DoF calcu-

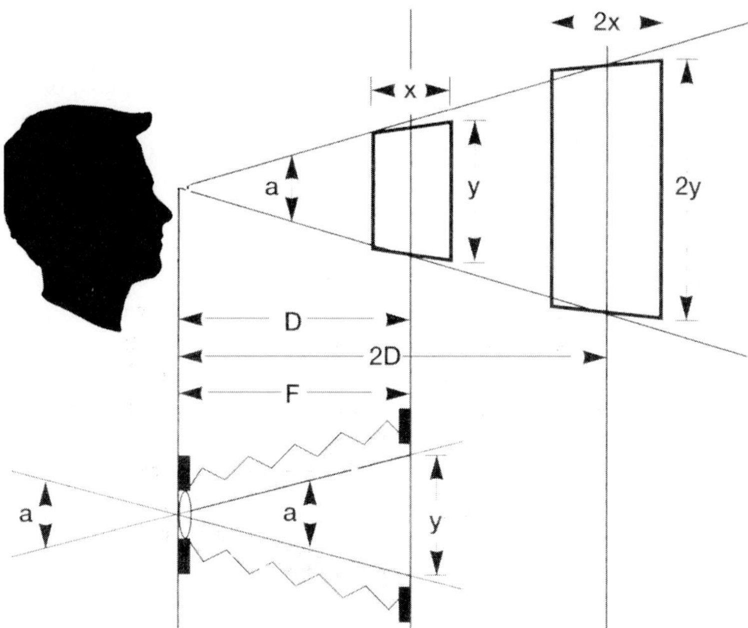

FIGURE 7–8 The ideal distance for viewing a print made with a lens with a normal focal length is the focal length of the lens times the degree of enlargement of the image file. *Source:* Sandy Weiss/Packer Engineering.

lations is often 30 to 35 microns. Any DoF larger than 35 microns in any area of a finished print made from a 35 mm negative will be considered out of acceptable focus.

RULE:

Proper viewing distance in inches for any print is equal to the focal length of the camera lens in inches times the enlargement factor of the print.

If the print is then enlarged to a larger size, or is viewed at a shorter (closer) distance, a proportionally smaller CoC is necessary for the appearance of sharpness (see Fig. 7–8).

Hyperfocal Focusing

If a lens has manual focusing controls, it may include DoF indicator points or lines to calculate the approximate range in which the subject and its surroundings will appear acceptably sharp when the lens is focused at a given distance and set at a given aperture. In the image of the older zoom lens (see Fig. 7–9), the lines that slant in toward the center above the aperture ring are the **hyperfocal focus** indicator lines. On a fixed focal length lens, the slanting lines are absent. On a zoom lens, DoF varies with focal length, so the lines need to vary as the lens is zoomed. When the lens is set at a longer (telephoto) position, DoF is narrower or compressed.

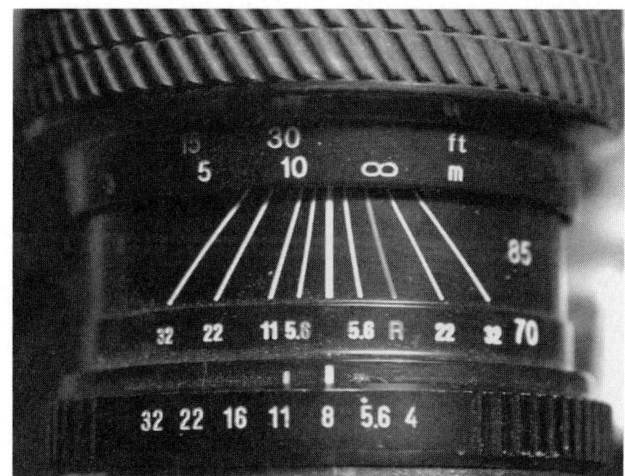

FIGURE 7–9 A manual focusing zoom lens from a 35 mm camera. *Source:* Sandy Weiss/Packer Engineering.

To judge the DoF of the finished photograph before exposing the image, do the following:

- Determine the lens aperture appropriate for a given exposure. In this case, the lens was set at *f*/8).
- On the DoF ring, each aperture number appears twice, once on either side of center. In this case the *f*/8 indicators are interpolated because not enough room was available to stencil them in.
- Left of center, the *f*/8 line would appear between *f*/5.6 and *f*/11. Right of center, the line would be about where the red R appears. If the following are true:
  - The image was exposed at *f*/8.
  - The focal length was set at about 95 mm.
  - The lens was focused sharply on the subject.

The indicators show that everything in the image between about 35 feet and almost to infinity should appear sharp (with sufficiently small CoC) in the finished image.

In a situation where the field of view is the same, a Canon EOS 10D will produce images with 1.6 times greater DoF than a full-frame 35 mm film camera would produce using the same lens.

Computerized Active Auto-Focus

Some auto-focus point-and-shoot cameras have eliminated controls to allow convenient manual focus or manual focus altogether, and that has made manual focus difficult, inaccurate, or impossible. Some manufacturers have substituted scrolling devices for lens focusing that are usually controlled by switches on the back or top of the camera. Optical viewfinders are usually small and do not include such focus aids as split images or microprisms. In most cases, the camera allows the photographer to preview the image on an LCD preview/review panel, essentially making these cameras true through-the-lens (TTL) focusing cameras. LCD panels are difficult or impossible to see under many conditions, especially when the ambient lighting is bright. Also, the display image is small and may lead to a misleading impression of sharpness.

The inexpensive point-and-shoot digital cameras usually have active auto-focus systems. The correct focusing distance is determined when the camera projects a beam of light, usually infrared, onto the subject. Some systems measure the distance to the subject by quantifying the reflectivity of the returning beam, others calculate the lag time before its return, and others rely simply on triangulation.

If the camera has an infrared focusing system, it is critical to keep the emitter/sensor clean and unobstructed during exposure. Exposing photographs through glass (windows, windshields, and display cases) is difficult with this system, and sharper images may be obtained under these conditions if the cameras are focused manually.

Extraneous objects in the frame may cause the camera to focus in the wrong place or in the wrong plane. Consider the image of the goat in the bushes in Figure 7–10. An active auto-focus system may focus on the bushes rather than the goat. This would cause the goat to be either out of focus or improperly exposed if the focus controls the flash. If the camera has a spot-focusing capability, set the spot on the part of the image that is of utmost importance before exposing the image. Insufficient lighting or lack of image contrast is not a problem with this type of focusing system.

> **TIP:**
>
> Some lenses on point-and-shoot cameras do not maintain focus when zoomed and must be refocused before exposure and after zooming.

Computerized Passive Auto-Focus

The passive auto-focus system that is used in DSLR cameras judges the camera-to-subject distance by analyzing the contrast of the image. Before the camera will make an exposure, the onboard computer examines the scene and signals a small motor to focus the lens until the scene is determined to be focused optimally. Some lenses are built with manual focus overrides so the photographer is able to focus manually.

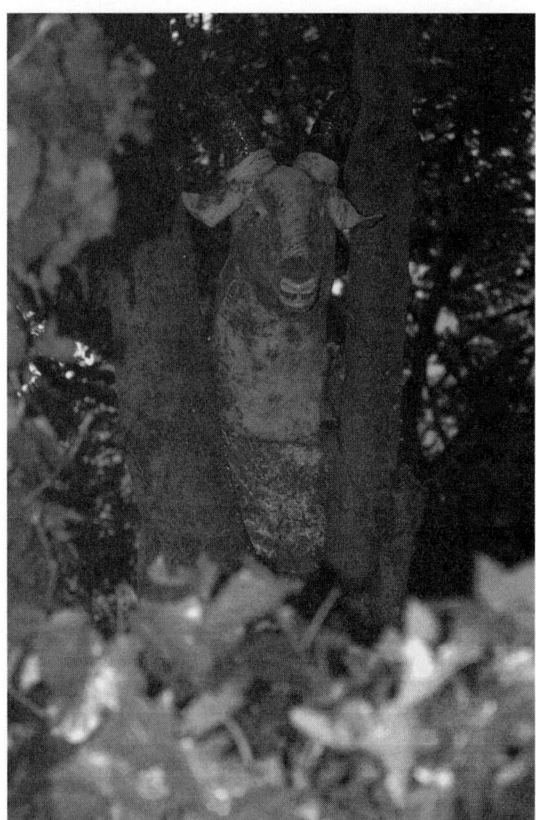

FIGURE 7–10 An underexposure caused by an auto-focus camera focusing on the wrong part of the subject. The head of the goat was the intended subject, but the camera focused on the bushes, yielding the underexposed image. *Source:* Sandy Weiss/Packer Engineering.

The auto-focus sensors are located on the camera's image sensor. They provide the necessary data to compute the contrast of adjacent pixels in the image. The auto-focus section of the sensor is usually a strip of specialized pixels, whose location is selected by the photographer when setting the area of auto-focus for the image. Light from the scene is evaluated by the auto-focus strip, and the onboard computer compares the values, pixel to pixel.

The computer examines the pixel values and judges the difference in intensity between adjacent pixels. If the scene is out of focus (see Fig. 7–11), adjacent pixels will have similar intensities. The computer then refocuses the lens, reevaluates the strip and determines if the difference in intensity between adjacent pixels is now higher or lower. The computer calculates the point where the difference between adjacent pixels is the greatest (see Fig. 7–12). This is considered to be the point of best focus.

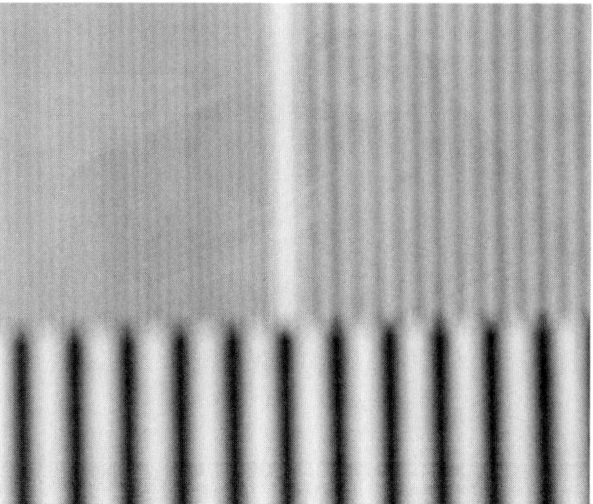

FIGURE 7–11 This image of a test strip is out of focus. Pixel intensities will be similar across the strip. *Source:* Sandy Weiss/Packer Engineering.

Accurate passive focus requires sufficient ambient lighting and image contrast. If the camera attempts to focus on a scene that is all one

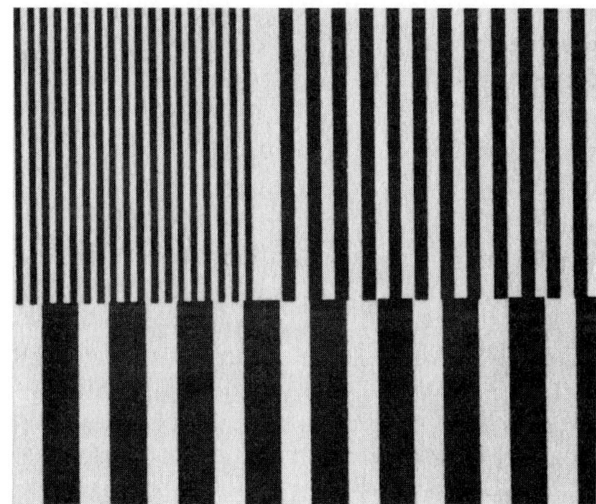

FIGURE 7–12 This image of a test strip is in focus. Pixel intensities will be different from pixel to pixel across the strip. *Source:* Sandy Weiss/Packer Engineering.

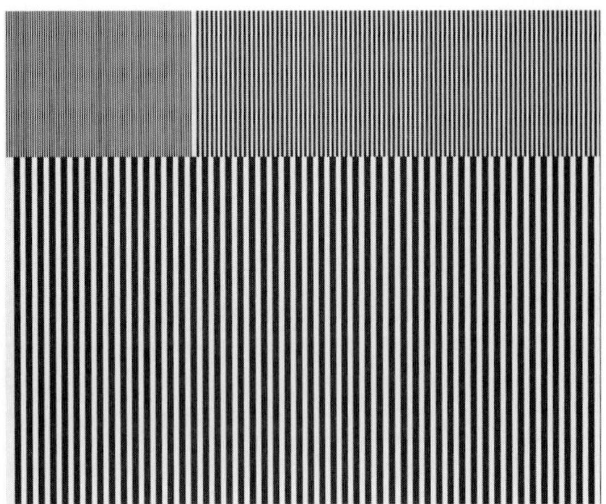

FIGURE 7–13 Representative test target with its bars in a vertical orientation. *Source:* Sandy Weiss/Packer Engineering.

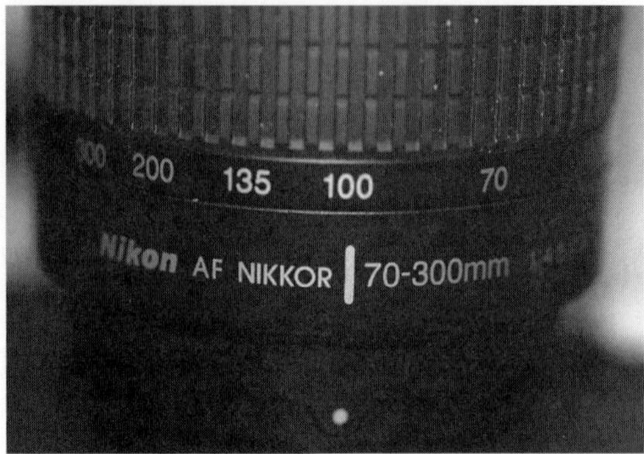

FIGURE 7–14 This Nikkor 70-300G zoom lens has no manual focus control. *Source:* Sandy Weiss/Packer Engineering.

color or low in intensity (low in contrast or dark), the camera may not focus and will refuse to expose an image if it is set on auto-focus. Some cameras contain and utilize auto-focus assist lamps that illuminate the subject in low light. These lamps can help if the subject is close to the camera. (In the Nikon D70s, the beam works up to a distance of 3 meters). The minimum and maximum auto-focus distance limits for passive auto-focus are determined by the choice of lens, not by any limitations inherent in the computer system.

Passive focusing works best when scenes include vertical detail, like the vertical focusing target pictured in Figure 7–13. If the camera is turned in a vertical orientation, making the vertical detail horizontal, the camera may be more challenged to determine the proper focus. Some cameras contain both vertical and horizontal focus sensors to alleviate this difficulty.

TIP:

If focus accuracy is in question in any digital camera focusing situation, check the image on the LCD panel after exposure. If the camera has an LCD magnification option, zoom in to magnify the image. This will enable finer evaluation of the small test image.

When using passive auto-focus with a DSLR, the onboard computer evaluates the focus of the scene and then sends a signal to the lens motor, telling it which way and how much to turn. If the scene is then evaluated as sharp, the camera will expose the image. If the scene is evaluated as not sharp, the computer will make the lens focus again. Some auto-focus lenses have manual focus rings and some do not. The Nikon 70-300G zoom (see Fig. 7–14) is strictly auto-focus. OEMs market lenses of this type to allow photographers the option of purchasing medium-length zoom lenses for very low prices. The Nikkor 18-70 zoom (see Fig. 7–15)

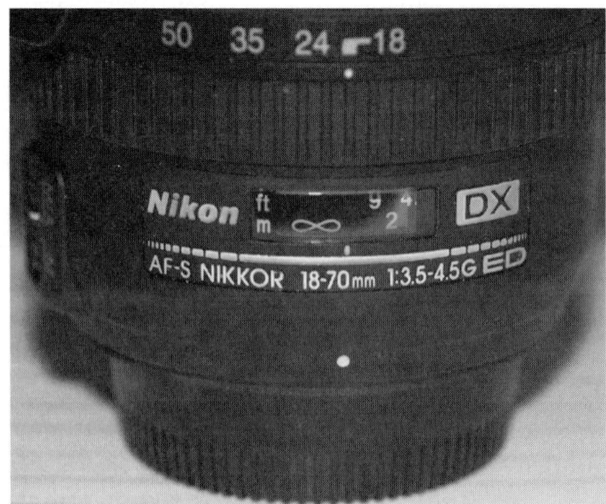

FIGURE 7–15 This Nikkor 18-70 zoom lens has manual focus override. *Source:* Sandy Weiss/Packer Engineering.

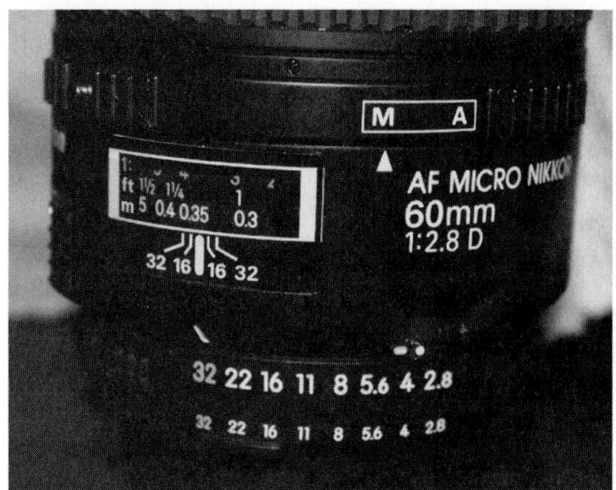

FIGURE 7–16 This Nikkor 60 mm Micro lens has full manual override, including settable lens apertures equivalent to a 90 mm Micro lens on a Nikon DSLR. *Source:* Sandy Weiss/Packer Engineering.

was the default on the D70 and D70s. It was low priced, sharp, and efficient for many situations. It has manual override of the focus but not of the apertures. The Nikkor 60 mm Micro lens (see Fig. 7–16) is intended for professional use. The price is expensive, but the lens is high quality in every way. Because it is designed for critical professional use, and DoF is an important factor during macrophotography, both the focus and aperture controls can be overridden manually.

LIGHT METERING

Light metering involves using a device to determine the optimum amount of light, utilized as media exposure, necessary for the photographic equipment to capture an image of a given subject with the qualities of reasonable and appropriate contrast and density. Understanding light metering is a necessary and recommended practice that will improve photographic results.

Hand-held photographic meters used for judging exposure perform metering by measuring reflected or incident light. The intensity of the reflected light is defined as the subject luminance.

The earliest light meters were **extinction meters.** They used a series of neutral-density filters of increasing densities as a reference for judging appropriate exposure. The meters were not very accurate, but the media was very slow and mistakes in light determination were compensated by long exposures. These meters depended on the light sensitivity of the photographer's eye to determine which was the proper filter reference.

Later meters were developed using selenium, cadmium sulfide (CdS), and silicon **photosensitive sensors.** In time, the meters were miniaturized sufficiently to allow them to be added to small cameras.

Selenium and silicon photovoltaic sensors generate a voltage proportional to the amount of light affecting them. CdS light meters use a sensor based on photo resistance, and they require a battery. Most modern hand-held and built-in light meters use silicon or CdS sensors. They indicate the suggested correct exposure either by the deflection of a needle galvanometer or by digital readout on an LCD screen. Point-and-shoot camera meters judge the exposure through the use of an onboard sensor.

The major breakthrough of metering accuracy was the ability of meters to measure the subject luminance through the camera lens. All modern DSLR cameras use TTL metering. Some TTL meters determine exposure automatically and some work manually, suggesting the intensity of the subject luminance to the photographer. Automatic metering cameras set either the lens aperture or the shutter speed, or both. The meters that set both adjust to programmed parameters; setting the variables to where the onboard computer judges correct exposure for the image.

All current in-camera meters measure reflected light as subject luminance. Reflected-light meters are designed and calibrated to yield the appropriate exposure for the luminance of "average" scenes. Difficult scenes with high or low contrast may yield either under- or overexposed images due to the camera meter being affected by large areas of too-bright highlights or too-dark shadows (see Fig. 7–17). It is recommended to meter high contrast scenes off an 18% gray card placed in the same illumination as the subject. This will yield an

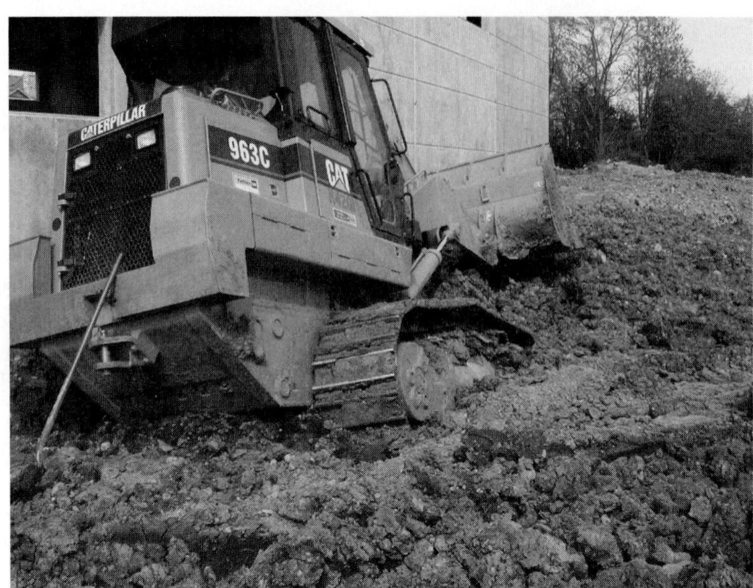

FIGURE 7–17 This image was metered using the overall luminance of the scene and was exposed improperly because of the high-contrast lighting. This resulted in a photograph with underexposed, flat shadows. *Source:* Sandy Weiss/Packer Engineering.

exposure very close to average for the scene and should place the highlights and shadows safely within the imaging capabilities of the camera sensor.

For safety and accuracy, many experienced photographers and motion picture cinematographers use hand-held incident-light meters to measure the light falling on various parts of the scene (illuminance), thus avoiding the exposure mistakes that can easily be made by inappropriate luminance readings on subject scene sections. Making incident-light readings entails placing the meter at the subject's position and pointing the meter in the direction of the camera. If in doubt, exposing an image using the reading from the placement of the shadows (see Fig. 7–18) is one possible way to produce an image with reasonable detail from its entire brightness range.

Spot Metering

Spot meters measure light reflected from subjects at a small angle (usually 1 to 10^{j} degrees). Using a spot meter is one way to avoid under- or overexposure of images with high contrast. Sampling multiple light readings from the shadow, mid-tone, and highlight areas of a scene, a photographer combines the readings and uses that information to determine optimal exposure. The zone system developed by Ansel Adams is the seminal work on this metering method.

The photographer may also pick a tone in the subject that is similar to the tone of a gray card, determine its exposure with the meter, and use it to expose the whole image. This re-creates an 18% reflectance tone from that surface area. This exposure is then used as the correct exposure for a whole scene. This practice has a high probability of exposing images that capture reasonable highlight and shadow area details of almost any scene.

The Pentax spot meter was introduced in 1961 (see Fig. 7–19). In-camera spot meters were introduced in 35 mm cameras in the 1980s. Most current professional-quality DSLRs include a spot metering option.

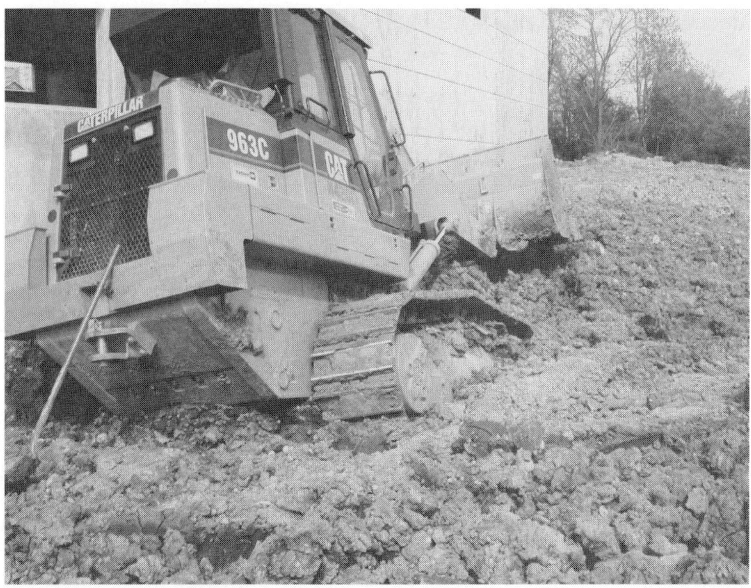

FIGURE 7–18 This image was metered only from the shadows of the scene and was exposed accordingly, yielding a photograph with good detail in the shadows and in the highlights. *Source:* Sandy Weiss/Packer Engineering.

Matrix Metering

Most newer digital cameras have multisegment or matrix-metering system options that measure the luminance of different parts of a scene and use computer algorithms to combine the readings and determine optimal exposure.

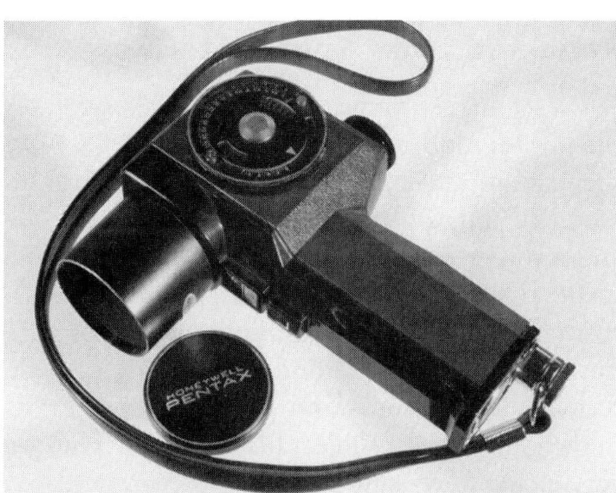

FIGURE 7–19 An early Pentax 1 degree spot meter. *Source:* Sandy Weiss/Packer Engineering.

TIP:

It is easy to fool the light-metering computers of automatic cameras. Even cameras that meter manually can be fooled if the photographer reads the luminance of the wrong portion of the subject. The photographer must watch for conditions where error is most likely to occur and learn how to prevent the occurrence of common exposure problems. If an automatic camera is allowed to function without input from the photographer, certain scenes may create exposures that are difficult or impossible to process and accurately represent the original scene.

TIP:

Exposure is less critical when using color or black-and-white negative film, as compared to positive film or digital imaging, because of film's wider inherent tolerance to over- and underexposure.

The following are the different methods of TTL light metering:

- Reflected light averaging
- Reflected light spot
- Matrix

Reflected Light Averaging Metering

The amount of light admitted to the camera is controlled by two settings: shutter speed and lens aperture. The combination of these two settings determines how much light reaches the image sensor, and setting these variables correctly is the intended function of the camera metering system.

When metering a scene manually—and after setting the shutter speed of the camera at a level appropriate for the action of the subject or setting the lens aperture to predetermine the DoF—a light meter (see Fig. 7–20) reading taken off a gray card or an appropriate area of the scene supplies the other variable. Then the photo is exposed.

A gray card reflects 18% of its luminance. All camera manufacturers calibrate their built-in light meters as if every scene reflected 18% of its luminance. When taking photos in the snow, for example, or where a large proportion of the scene is in shade, the scene does not reflect 18% of the light. Most scenes reflect more or less than 18%, and 18% is just an accepted average.

Using a Gray Card

1. Place the gray card in the same intensity of light that is falling on the main subject.
2. Meter off the card and use the shutter speed and lens aperture reading information the card yields to expose the photograph of the subject. This will guarantee that at least the main subject of the photograph will be properly exposed. If no gray card is available, meter off a part of the scene that appears gray and use that information for the exposure of the whole scene.

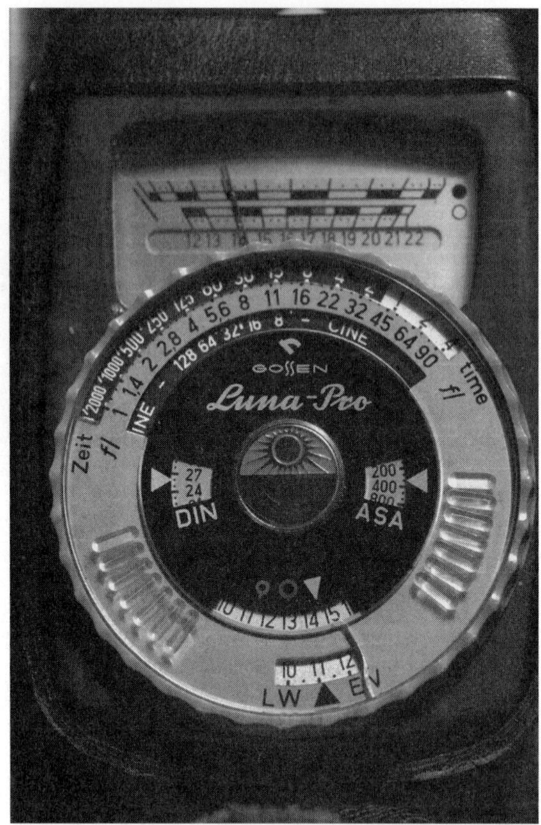

FIGURE 7–20 Luna-pro exposure meter for reflected and incident light metering. Shutter speed and aperture combinations appear in exposure value (EV) numbers. *Source:* Sandy Weiss/Packer Engineering.

Reflected Light Spot Metering

Some scenes do not have an illuminated area that the photographer would call normal or 18%. In such situations, take a narrow angle or close-up meter reading off the brightest part of the scene and a meter reading off the darkest part of the scene. Then set the camera for an exposure directly between the two readings and expose the image there. This method will usually provide reasonable exposures and usable images across the whole range of subject brightnesses. This is a very elementary zone system.

If the camera meter is allowed to register the entire scene when making photographs of interiors where the room is dark and the doors and

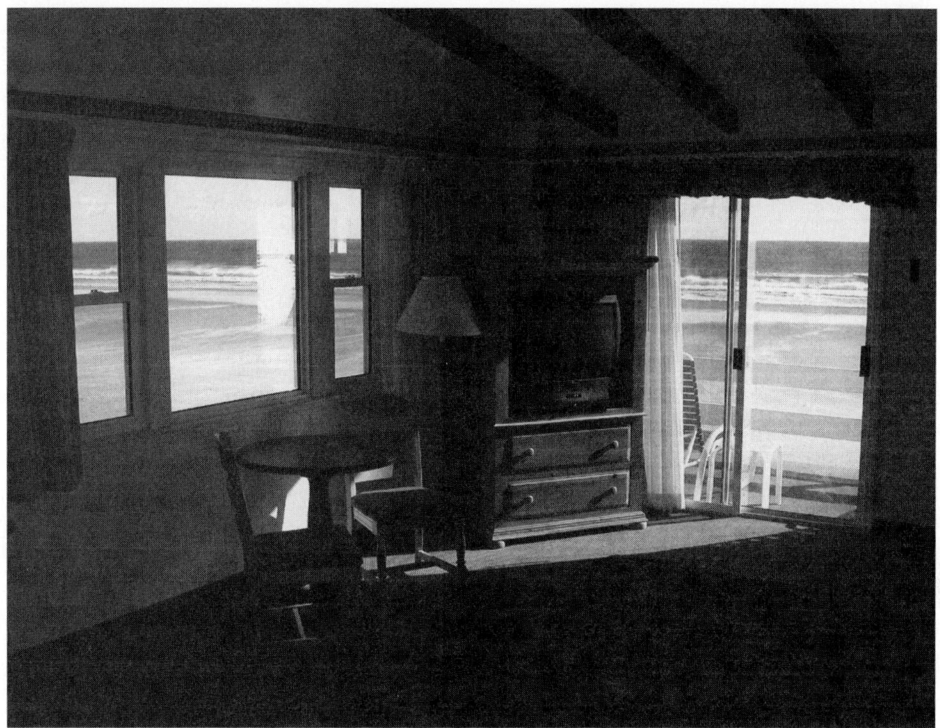

FIGURE 7–21 Interior of a room, illuminated only by exterior daylight and metered for the exterior. *Source:* Sandy Weiss/Packer Engineering.

windows are bright, the resultant image will be properly exposed for the windows and doors but not for the interior of the room (see Fig. 7–21). If the important part of the image is the room and not the windows, as it would be at a crime scene, allow the camera meter to register off an interior wall that does not have a window. Maintain that exposure reading to make the subject photographs. The windows and doors will be overly bright, but the room will be properly exposed (see Fig. 7–22).

Incident Light Metering

Exposures may be metered by measuring the light falling onto the subject rather than the light reflected off it. This can be done by the use of an incident hand-held meter with a translucent spherical attachment covering the meter cell. Incident-light meters have some distinct advantages. The amount of light incident upon a scene is normally greater than the amount reflected from it. Therefore, incident-light meters have a greater amount of light to measure, making the measurement more accurate in low ambient lighting. Incident meters have a wide **acceptance angle**—the maximum cone half-angle for which incident light is captured by and will travel through the optical fiber—so the light does not have to be measured off a specific surface.

Matrix or Multizone Metering

The default on many newer cameras is a multizone setting, where light is measured across the entire subject and averaged, regardless of the subject brightness range. This system produces reasonable images under most conditions.

When digital cameras set both the aperture and shutter speed automatically, the most common metering formula is matrix. The **matrix** is a collection of areas in the scene that the camera measures and averages to calculate appropriate

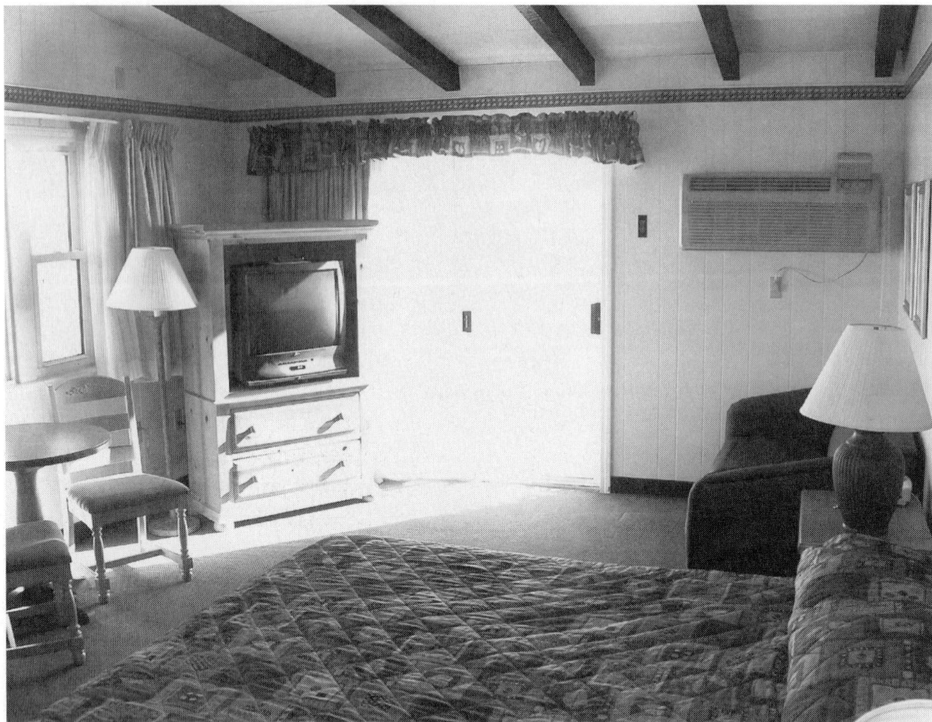

FIGURE 7–22 Interior of a room, metered for the interior. *Source:* Sandy Weiss/Packer Engineering.

aperture and shutter speed settings. Sometimes the matrix is weighted at the center, and sometimes it is weighted at the bottom. In many cases, modern cameras maintain a library of sample images and successful exposures in its memory, and it compares the imaged scene to the image library and meters accordingly.

ISO

The light sensitivity of the imaging sensor is designated by its ISO number. Less light is necessary for proper exposure when higher ISO sensitivity is used. Higher ISO numbers are associated with low-light conditions, or when action needs to be stopped by a short exposure.

> **RULE:**
>
> Images exposed at higher ISO numbers will generally exhibit coarser grain than those with lower ISO numbers.

LENS APERTURE

The *lens aperture* is the diameter of the opening through which light is admitted to the image sensor. Aperture is expressed as an *f-number* or *f-stop*. The lower the f-stop number, the larger the lens opening and the greater the amount of light admitted to the image sensor within a specific amount of time. Releasing the camera shutter allows light to pass through the lens aperture and expose the sensor, which creates an image.

> **RULE:**
>
> Each consecutive f-value represents double or half the amount of light.

MATHEMATICS OF F-NUMBERS

> **RULE:**
>
> The f-number (f) is the ratio of the focal length (f) of the lens to the diameter of the aperture (D).

Thus, a lens with a focal length of 50 mm and an aperture with a diameter of 25 mm, has an f-number of 2.0, usually written as "*f*/2."

$$f = \frac{\mathrm{f}}{D}$$

The largest possible aperture for a lens is observed when

$$D = \mathrm{f} = f/1.0$$

It is common terminology to refer to the *speed* of a lens in terms of its *maximum* aperture. Thus, a 50 mm lens with a maximum aperture of *f*/1.4 would be a full f-stop faster than a 50 mm lens with a maximum aperture of *f*/2. That lens would be described as a 50 mm *f*/1.4 lens. A lens *two* full stops faster than an *f*/2 lens would be rated at *f*/1, the fastest possible lens speed for that focal length.

> **TIP:**
>
> Aperture affects DoF. If the goal of the image is to achieve the ultimate DoF in a photograph, it is best to use a slower shutter speed that will adequately capture the action in front of the camera and allow, dependent on the amount of illumination, the use of the smallest possible lens aperture.

Elements of Depth of Field

- The lens opening: the bigger the apertures, the shallower the DoF
- The focal length of the lens: the wider angle, the greater the DoF)
- The lens to subject distance: the nearer the subject, the shallower the DoF

For times when it is necessary to visualize the DoF that will exist in the final image before the image is exposed, some cameras have a DoF preview button that allows the photographer to see the image through the lens at the aperture the camera will use to expose the image. (see Fig. 7–23). The use of *aperture priority* automation entails selecting the aperture for a given exposure while allowing the camera to set the appropriate shutter speeds for optimum exposure.

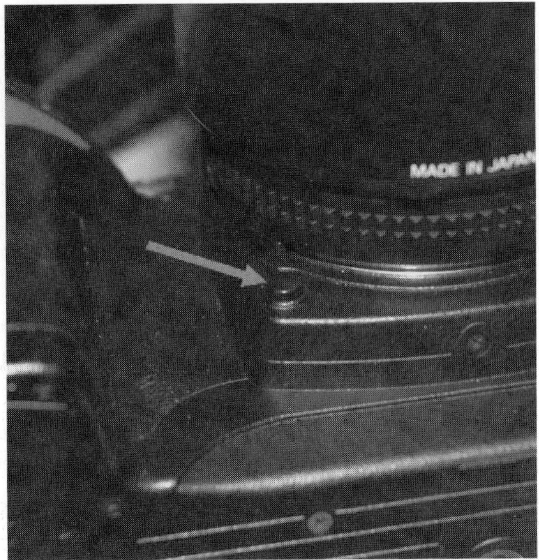

FIGURE 7–23 The DoF preview button on a Nikon D70s. *Source:* Sandy Weiss/Packer Engineering.

When the focal length of a lens is divided by the f-stop number, the result is the diameter of the aperture. Lenses with longer focal lengths admit less light at the same aperture size than do shorter lenses. For example, a 50 mm lens using a 14.3 mm aperture diameter (*f*/3.5) will admit more light (*f*/5.6) than an 80 mm lens using the same 14.3 mm aperture diameter.

Optimizing DoF.

- The same f-stop number will admit the same amount of light, regardless of the focal length of the lens.
- Where the axis of the object is parallel with the axis of the image plane (see Fig. 7–24), exposed images will display the greatest overall sharpness by utilizing the existent DoF.
- Where the axis of the object is perpendicular to the axis of the image plane (see Fig. 7–25), exposed images will display the least DoF.
- The closer the camera is to the subject, the less the DoF (see Fig. 7–26).

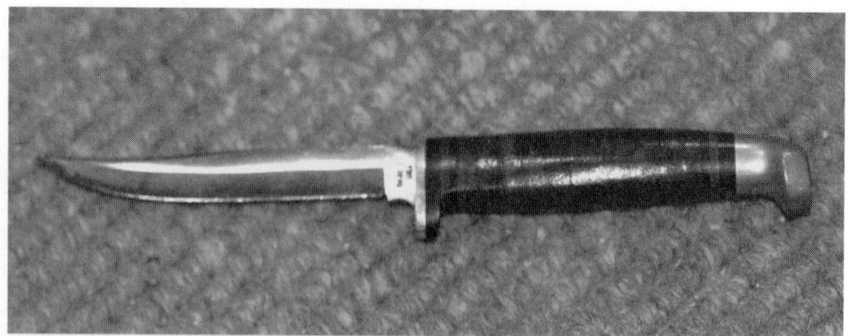

FIGURE 7–24 An exposed image in which the axis of the object is parallel with the axis of the image plane. *Source:* Sandy Weiss/Packer Engineering.

Shutter Speed

The shutter speed should be set to stop the action as required by the situation. The higher the number set, the faster (the smaller part of a second) the shutter speed will be. The lower the number set, the slower the shutter speed. The numbers on the shutter speed dial are the denominator of a fraction—for example 500 stands for 1/500 second.

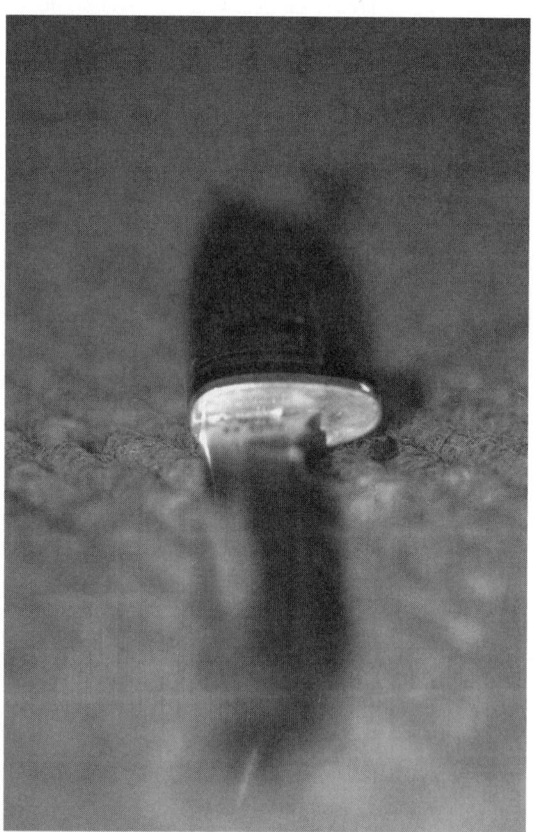

FIGURE 7–25 An exposed image in which the axis of the object is perpendicular to the axis of the image plane. *Source:* Sandy Weiss/Packer Engineering.

Shutter Speed Rules

- Most human motion can be stopped with a shutter speed of 1/250 of a second.
- Speeds faster than 1/250 second may be necessary to freeze the motion of fast-moving vehicles in a perpendicular plane.
- Speeds as slow as necessary for proper exposure may be used for subjects that do not move.

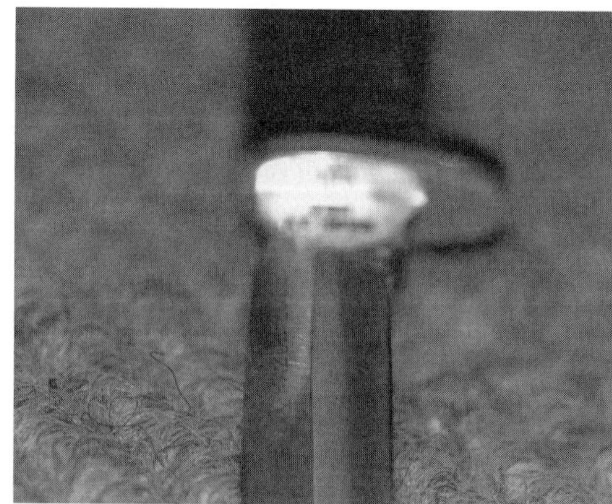

FIGURE 7–26 Close-up image with shallow DoF. *Source:* Sandy Weiss/Packer Engineering.

TIP:

A camera support to reduce movement of the image will be needed at speeds of 1/30 of a second or less.

Some cameras have shutter speed and aperture units referred to as *stops* or **exposure values.** Changing the exposure value by one stop will either double or halve the amount of light exposing the media. The pair of values (shutter speed/aperture) used for correct exposure of any scene is infinitely variable.

Shutter priority automation entails selecting the shutter speed for a given exposure while allowing the camera to select the appropriate aperture for optimum exposure. Fully automatic and program automatic exposure entail allowing the camera to select both the aperture and the shutter speed for what it computes as the optimum exposure.

TIP:

A relationship exists between f-numbers, shutter speeds, and ISO. A change of ISO by a factor of 2 corresponds to a change in the f-number of one full stop. Therefore, doubling the film speed (in ISO units), decreases the necessary lens aperture or shortens the necessary shutter speed by one unit for an equivalent exposure.

EXPOSURE COMPENSATION

Many photographers desire to maintain camera meter automation while programming for intentional over- or underexposure in a particular photograph or group of photographs, due to the contrast of the lighting. This meter adjustment may be accomplished by using the exposure compensation program of the camera. **Exposure compensation** allows all camera functions to operate as originally automated, while a selected amount of exposure change is programmed into the metering system. This feature is usually available within all camera metering modes. If a particular metering mode or lighting situation consistently yields under- or overexposed images, an over- or underexposure compensation factor may be programmed into the exposure process. Most cameras allow up to two stops of exposure compensation in quarter- or third-stop increments.

TIP:

Zero compensation is the default compensation setting in all cameras.

IMAGE HISTOGRAM

Most digital cameras include an optional histogram display either in capture mode or in playback mode on the rear LCD screen. A **histogram** is a graphic representation used to judge the brightness range of an image. The graph includes a quantification of all the pixels in a digital image. The left side of the histogram shows how many dark pixels were captured, the right side shows how many light pixels, and the center shows the mid-tones. A total of 256 brightness levels exist between black (0) and white (255), and 18% gray has a numeric value of about 128. The vertical axis, the height of points on the graph, indicates how much of the image was exposed at any particular brightness level. Using an 18% gray card as a reference, and exposing the image of a scene where the luminance value of the card is found in about the center of the histogram, should assist the camera to capture the maximum dynamic range for any subject.

An accurate light-meter reading suggests an exposure that will reproduce an 18% gray card as a mid-tone in the image. In reality, this setting is a compromise. The calculated exposure is intended to place the subject brightness range safely within the dynamic range capability of the image sensor. If the mid-tone values in the image fall about halfway between the darkest and the lightest values of the normal scene, all the values should be differentiable. This practice only works properly if the scene or object has a full range of tones. If the image is intended to be bright or

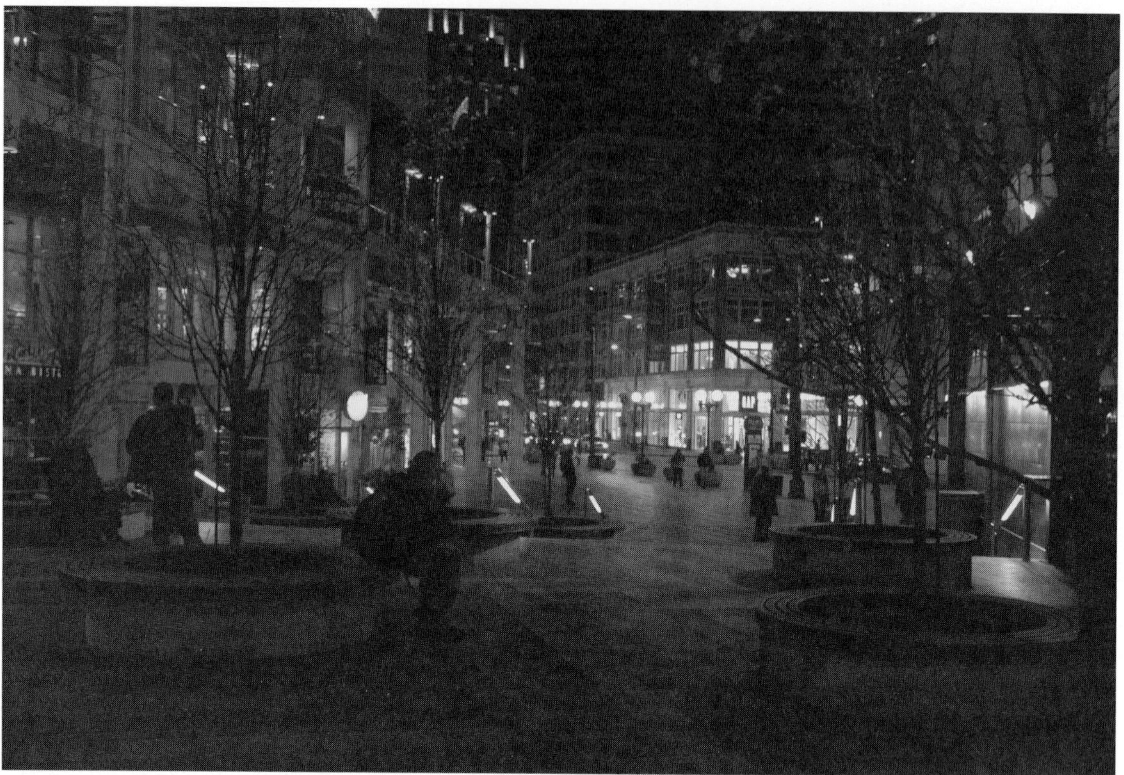

FIGURE 7–27 An intentionally dark image of an outside mall at night. *Source:* Sandy Weiss/Packer Engineering.

dark for a particular reason, the position of the gray card on the histogram must be adjusted to the right or the left.

If a histogram indicates that most of the pixels are in the dark zone, it is a bad exposure unless the subject was primarily dark. If the dark pixel peak is cut by the left edge of the graph, it indicates that the image may be underexposed.

A histogram that tends toward the left side of the graph does not necessarily indicate an underexposed image. The night image of the mall (see Fig. 7–27) exposed with only a few point-light sources displays a histogram that tends toward the left, but it is properly exposed. The dark peak does not touch the left side of the graph (see Fig. 7–28).

The locomotive (see Fig. 7–29) is a high-contrast scene with very few mid-tones. Its histogram display (see Fig. 7–30) contains only two distinct peaks, one for the highlights and one for the shadows.

If a histogram indicates most of the pixels are in the highlight zone, it may be a bad exposure, unless the scene contains primarily bright subjects (see Figs. 7–31 and 7–32). If the pixel peak on the right is cut by the edge of the graph, it indicates hat the image may be overexposed.

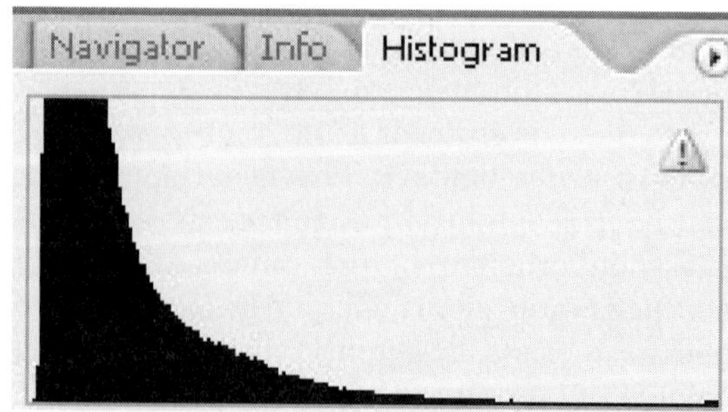

FIGURE 7–28 Histogram of the mall image in Figure 7–27. *Source:* Sandy Weiss/Packer Engineering.

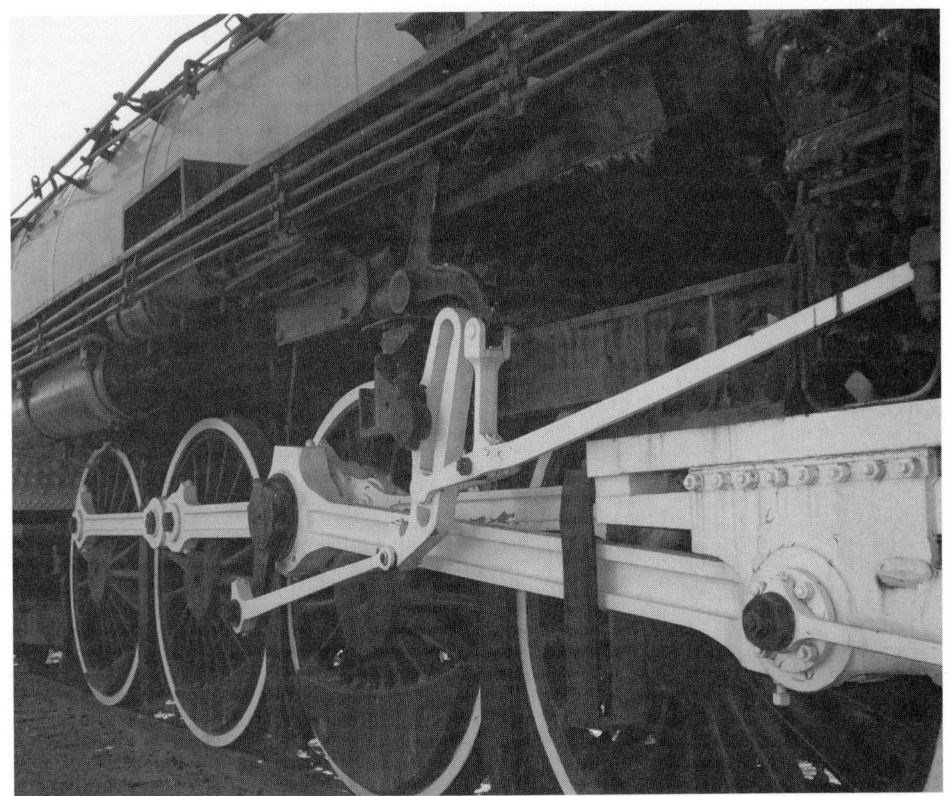

FIGURE 7–29 An image of a steam locomotive exposed with the camera set on automatic exposure. *Source:* Sandy Weiss/Packer Engineering.

If a histogram display shows that most of the pixels are in the middle zone of the graph, it is only a proper exposure if it was a low contrast scene (see Figs. 7–33 and 7–34).

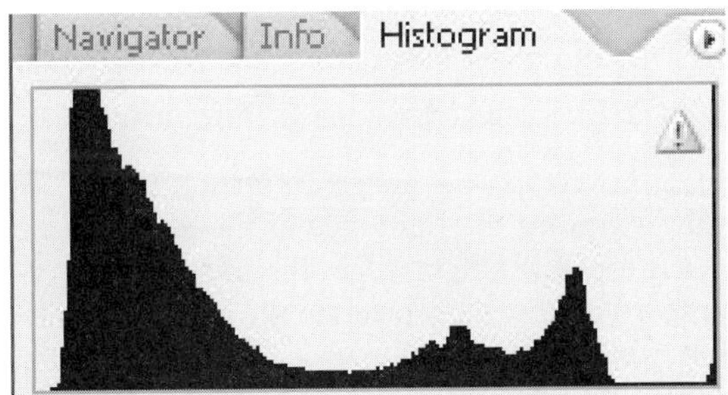

FIGURE 7–30 Histogram of a steam locomotive exposed with the camera set on automatic exposure. *Source:* Sandy Weiss/Packer Engineering.

If the histogram indicates three distinct peaks, all inside the edges of the graph, that was probably what the camera would consider a normally illuminated scene (see Figs. 7–35 and 7–36).

> **TIP:**
>
> If the camera does not include a histogram display, or the one in the camera is insufficient for detailed evaluation, a program such as Photoshop or Photoshop Elements can provide a more detailed version.

If the Exposed Image Is Too Dark

In an underexposed image, most of the pixels will be toward the left side of the graph. If the pixels touch the left edge, the image is underexposed,

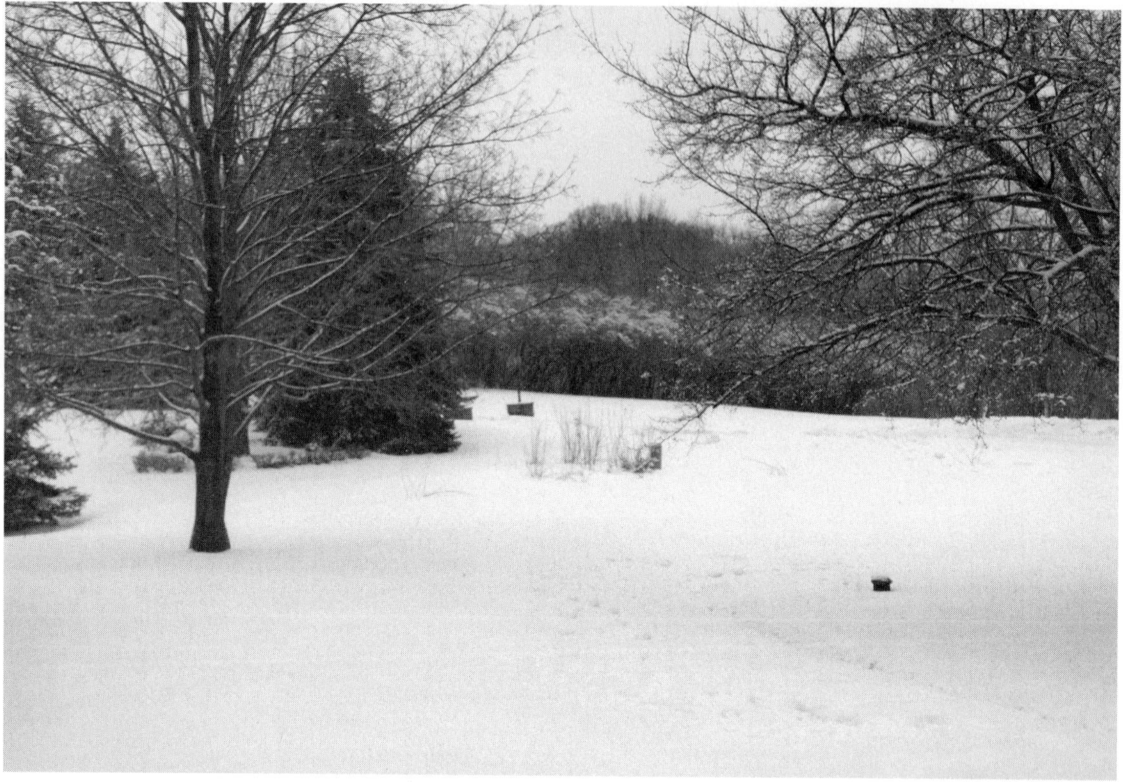

FIGURE 7–31 An image of a snow scene. *Source:* Sandy Weiss/Packer Engineering.

with too many pixels in the shadows. The following should help you to correct the exposure:

- *If the camera is set on fully automatic*, set a + (positive) exposure compensation.
- *If the camera is set in manual mode*, set a slower shutter speed and keep the same aperture, *or* set a larger aperture and keep the same shutter speed.
- *If the aperture is already at maximum*, set a higher ISO.

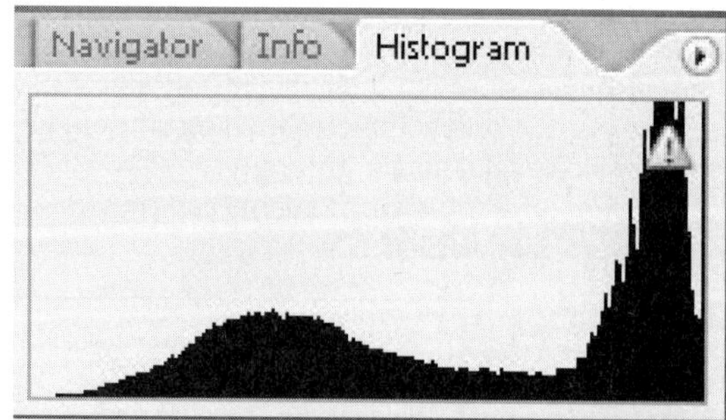

FIGURE 7–32 Histogram of the snow scene in Figure 7–31, another example of only two peaks. *Source:* Sandy Weiss/Packer Engineering.

These operations instruct the camera to ignore the recommendations of the light meter and allow more light to reach the image sensor. The histogram must shift to the right.

If the Exposed Image Is Too Light

In an overexposed image, most of the pixels will be toward the right side of the graph. If the pixels touch the right edge, the image is overexposed, with too many pixels in the highlights. The following should help you to correct that exposure:

- *If the camera is set on fully automatic*, set a – (negative) exposure compensation.
- *If the camera is set in manual mode*, set a faster shutter speed and keep the same

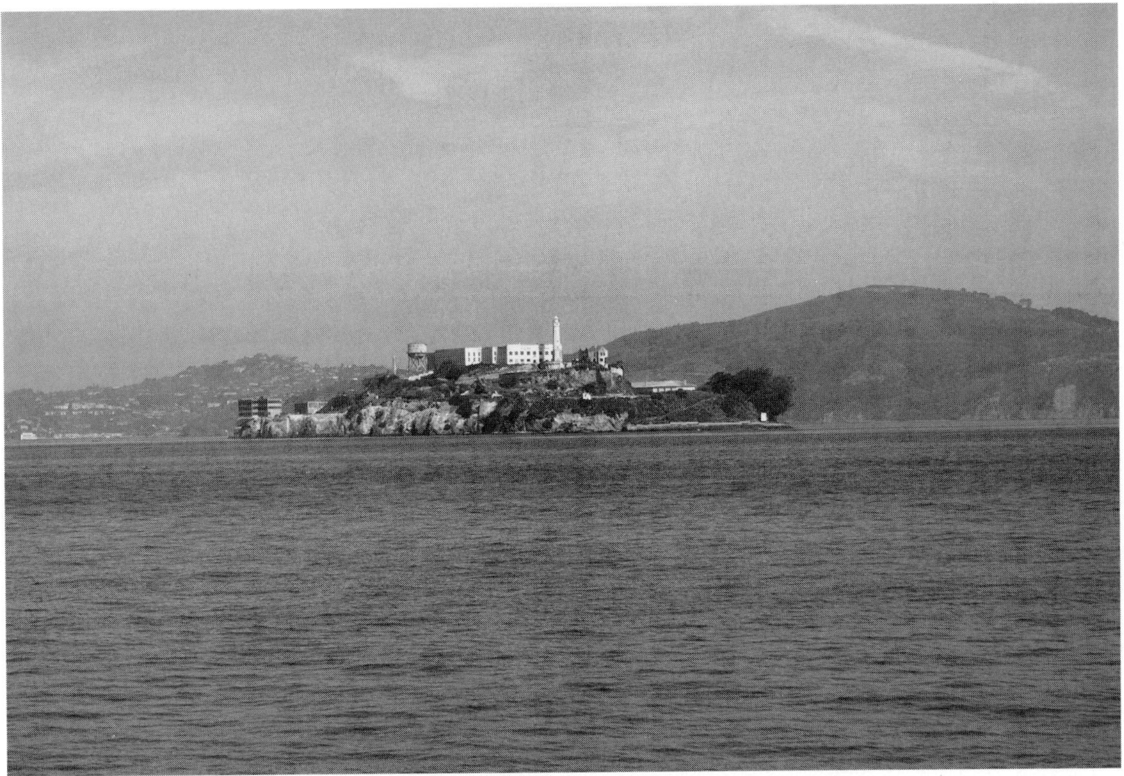

FIGURE 7–33 An image of Alcatraz Island. *Source:* Sandy Weiss/Packer Engineering.

aperture, or set a smaller aperture and keep the same shutter speed.

- *If the aperture is already at minimum*, set a higher ISO or use a polarizer or other neutral density filtration to reduce the quantity of light impacting the image sensor.

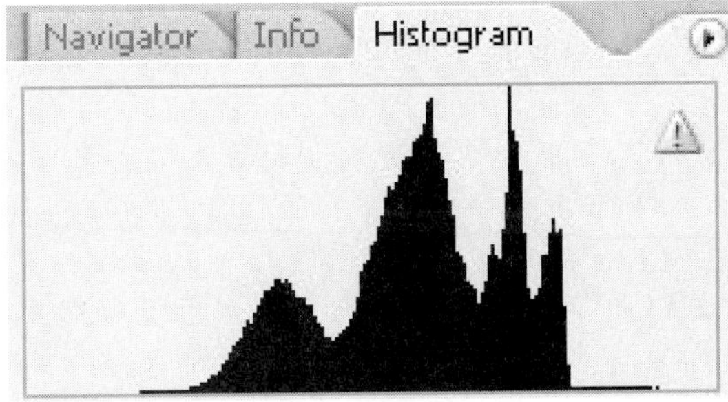

FIGURE 7–34 A histogram of the Alcatraz Island image in Figure 7–33, a low-contrast scene with peaks bunched in the center of the graph. *Source:* Sandy Weiss/Packer Engineering.

These operations instruct the camera to ignore the light meter and allow less light to reach the image sensor. The histogram must shift to the left.

RGB HISTOGRAMS

LCD image replays are often insufficient to properly evaluate exposure, especially in bright ambient illumination. With cameras that can display an image histogram along with the thumbnail review image, the histogram may be the better choice for image evaluation.

In some newer cameras, especially DSLRs, a three-channel (RGB) histogram, showing a graph for each of the three colors, is available (see Fig. 7–37). A three-channel histogram displays the full range of luminance values, from 0 to 255, for each color channel. RGB histograms are a more precise indicator of exposure because they show if the photograph is clipping any of the color channels at either end of the graph.

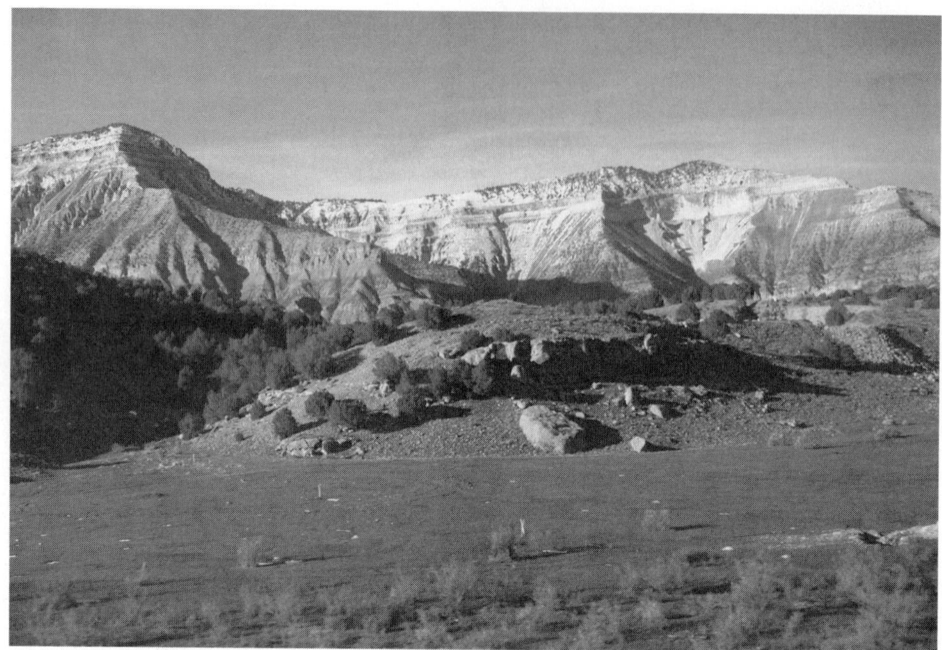

FIGURE 7–35 What the camera would consider a normal photo with a full range of tones. *Source:* Sandy Weiss/Packer Engineering.

Clipping, or placing under- or overexposed pixels at the 0 or 255 levels on a color channel, may provide overexposed, flat highlights or shadows that are nearly flat black.

When exposing RAW files, the camera's built-in software must set a white point, black point, and midpoint to display the in-camera histogram for that image. RAW images have no white, black, or midpoint setting until they are opened in a RAW converter. Therefore, the camera builds the in-camera histogram for RAW images based on the parameters already set for JPEG images. When exposing in RAW, and using an aftermarket RAW converter, check the in-camera histograms against the

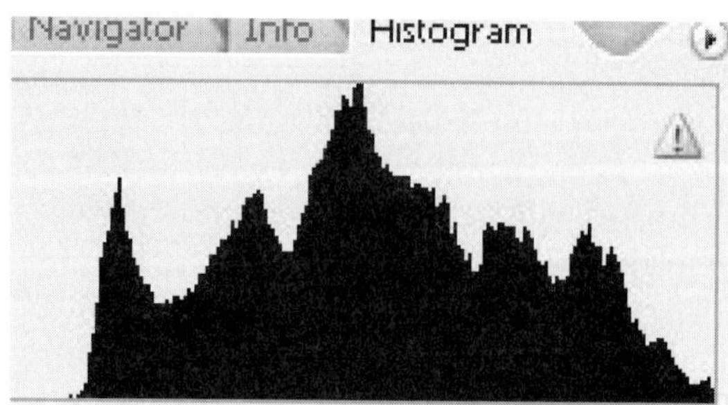

FIGURE 7–36 A histogram of a normal photo, indicating peaks for shadows, highlights, and midtones. *Source:* Sandy Weiss/Packer Engineering.

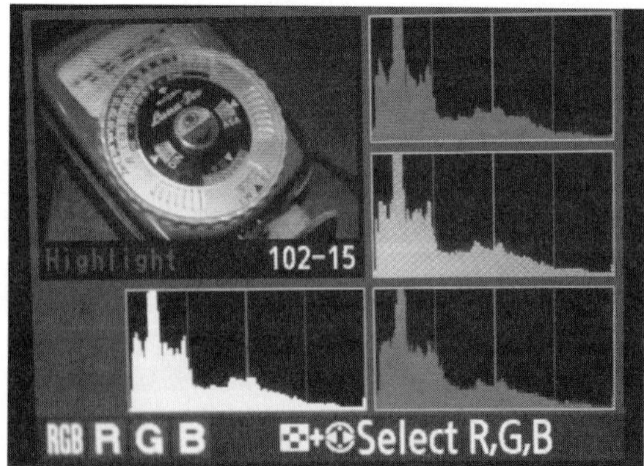

FIGURE 7–37 RGB histogram representation of image of Luna-pro exposure meter. *Source:* Sandy Weiss/Packer Engineering.

histograms for the same images in the RAW converter to see if they are the same. If not, a manual change may be programmed into the converter.

THE ZONE SYSTEM FOR FILM

Modern black-and-white photographic papers have a tonal range ratio capacity of not more than about 500:1, or 9 f-stops. However, the dynamic range of the human eye is approximately 1,000,000:1, or about 20 stops. For the sake of accuracy, the photographer is required to make final prints match as closely as possible the amount and differences of tonality seen by the human eye. The **zone system** is a method used to help control the contrast of film negatives to create prints of higher accuracy by indicating a wider range of tones. (It is notable that the inherent accuracy of black-and-white images for evidence photography is more convention than science.)

Principles of the Zone System for Film

Contrast control in negative film involves the following:

- Allowing the film sufficient exposure to capture details in the shadows
- Utilizing proper development time to manage the density of the highlights

Professional photographers practiced these principles before the zone system was formulated. Ansel Adams and his colleagues created the latter for photographers to translate the range of tones they could see into a "visual ruler" to measure subject brightness range in a predictable and practical way. This process is known as "**previsualization**" and includes several types of exposure zones:

- *Zone IX* is pure white, and *Zone 0* is featureless black; no texture or detail will appear in these areas.
- *Zone VIII* is near white, and *Zone I* is near black, and they may display some texture but no real detail. These zones represent extremely dark or extremely bright objects in the photograph.
- *Zones VII and II* may display minor texture and detail, and they represent very dark or very bright objects in the photograph.
- *Zone VII* may be textured white, and Zone III may be textured black.
- *Zones VII, VI, V, IV, and III* are capable of full texture and comprise the majority of detail in most photographs (see Fig. 7–38).

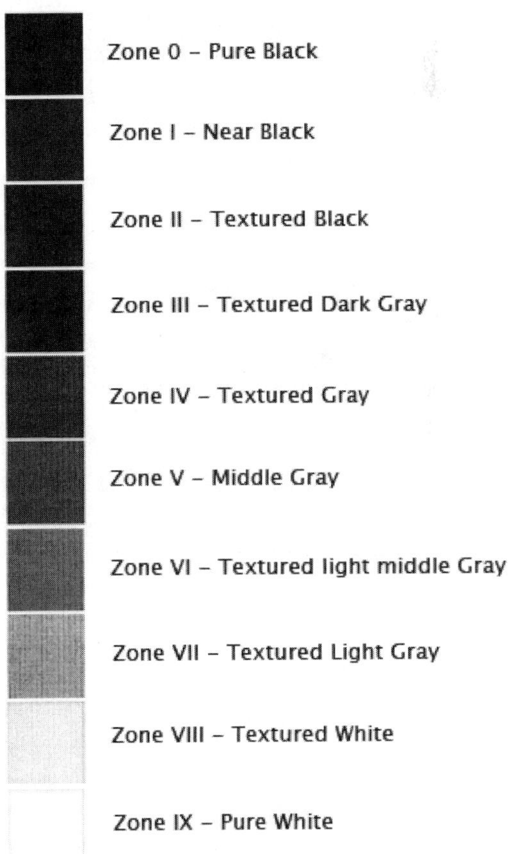

FIGURE 7–38 Tonal zones of a photograph. The amount of light necessary to indicate a zone on a print doubles as the zones go lighter (higher number) and halves as they go darker (lower number). *Source:* Sandy Weiss.

Zones are like stops (one stop for each doubling/halving of contrast resolution possible on the print):

- One zone equals one stop.
- One zone equals one exposure value (EV) number. (Each EV number indicates a constant exposure obtained by utilizing an appropriate pair of shutter speeds and apertures. If the shutter speed is slower, the aperture is smaller. If the shutter speed is faster, the aperture is larger.)
- One zone equals double or half the ISO number.

According to the zone system, the image of a dark area of a scene that was in full light should reflect the same amount of illumination as a light area in minimal light. All light meters should measure both areas with the same result. For this reason, light meters read 18% reflectance in the middle of Zone V.

The steps for creating negatives in the zone system are as follows:

1. The photographer first previsualizes the area of the subject needing to be a dark value with full texture and detail (Zone III) in the final print.
2. Then the photographer takes a meter reading off that particular area of the scene and records that as Zone III, remembering the recommended exposure supplied by the meter.
3. The recommended exposure of the meter would create that area as Zone V on the negative, not Zone III. To correct for this discrepancy, the photographer must expose the subject two f-stops less than the recommended meter reading.

The Zone System of Development for Film

Every combination of film and developer has a normal or recommended development time, temperature, and agitation that should result in a negative that displays contrast equal, but reversed, to that of the subject. Consult the published D log E curve for any film and developer combination you want to use. Normal development should yield low-contrast negatives when photographing low-contrast subjects, and high-contrast negatives when photographing high-contrast subjects. Variations in time, concentration, temperature, and/or agitation, may increase or decrease the development of a roll of film. By increasing or decreasing development, low- or high-contrast subjects may be adjusted to print on normal contrast photographic print media.

The zone system quantifies the contrast of subjects correlating to a zone scale, thus suggesting to the photographer the need to use either more or less than normal development in a particular situation. This is what Ansel Adams designated as either "Normal Minus" or "Normal Plus" development times.[2] The specific times for plus or minus developments are determined by using tables and performing tests.

Digital Zone System

The zone system also applies to digital photography. The computer used for processing the images must meet the following criteria:

- It must be calibrated for black level, brightness, and contrast.
- The gamma of the monitor must be properly set. (Changing the value of the gamma affects the middle tones while leaving the white and black areas of the image unaltered. Gamma should be set to 2.2 for Windows.)
- Color temperature should be set at 6,500 K.
- Color quality should be 24 or 32 bits.
- Color balance should be set so that a gray image looks gray and does not have a pink or yellow cast.
- Color space should be set at sRGB.

DSLRs may create images with dynamic ranges up to 9 or 10 f-stops, which is comparable to film negatives and better than film positives.

Exposure meters are calibrated to set all scenes with a middle gray tonal value of about Zone V. When a scene is bright—for example, a snow scene—and the suggested meter reading is used, the snow will appear middle gray in the unprocessed image and will be underexposed. If the scene is very dark—for example, a night scene—and the suggested meter reading is used, the unprocessed image will be overexposed, making the night look brighter.

Ansel Adams's zone system, if properly used, helps the photographer to visualize the final image by determination of a correlation between portions of the scene and tones in its representation. Adams would meter, expose, and develop a negative according to how he visualized it would eventually look. His basic rule was "Expose for the shadows; develop for the highlights," which works for negatives but not very well for digital imaging. Digital images are essentially positives, so they must be exposed like film positives, not negatives, to avoid losing detail in the image highlights.

In the digital zone system, the photographer is not required to process film. Exposure with the camera is the variable factor for capturing images with extended tonality.

The Digital Zone System

- The eight steps between the nine zones represent a luminance range of 256.
- Zone V corresponds to middle gray of 18% reflectance.
- As with film positives, overexposure in digital files results in images with flat white highlights.

In digital photography, the photographer is able to do the following:

- Correct color
- Adjust contrast in the camera

Determining Exposure

The first step of the digital zone system is to visualize how specific areas of the scene should appear in the final image; Select an area of the scene, meter it, then adjust the exposure by the difference between the zone you want that area to occupy in the final image and Zone V (middle gray).

The second step is to figure out how to determine the region to meter. The correct choice should be the light shadows, not the deep ones. Make a test exposure and look at its histogram to be sure its highlights are not touching the edge of its graph.

The third step is setting the proper exposure.

The final step is to examine the histogram of the image, both in and out of the camera. If the images are underexposed, it may be necessary to decrease the ISO speed setting. If they are overexposed, it may be necessary to increase the ISO setting. If the histogram looks proper for the imaged scene, the result will contain the maximum possible dynamic range of the subject.

Adding Dynamic Range

Digital images may be produced with too many pixels in the highlights or shadows when they are exposed in less than optimum lighting. Some cameras provide the option to display the highlights that are overexposed in the image by blinking on the LCD. Even if an exposure is correct and not overexposed, blinking highlights may be displayed, depending on the situation. It may mean the highlights in those areas will not contain any noticeable texture. That particular area will have a pixel value greater than or equal to 255.

At times, a pure white area (Zone IX or X) is proper. The evidence photographer should always attempt to create exposures with a dynamic range as close as possible to fitting within the dynamic range capability of the camera sensor. In some situations, that is not possible. Ansel Adams mentions full-range prints that have areas of shadow and highlight with no detail—but only when they should be that way. Having a pure black and a pure white in an image may be absolutely accurate (see Fig. 7–39).

A print may exhibit a complete range of tones, as well as the extremes of black and white, to properly display a scene. The amounts of pure white and solid black may be small, but when

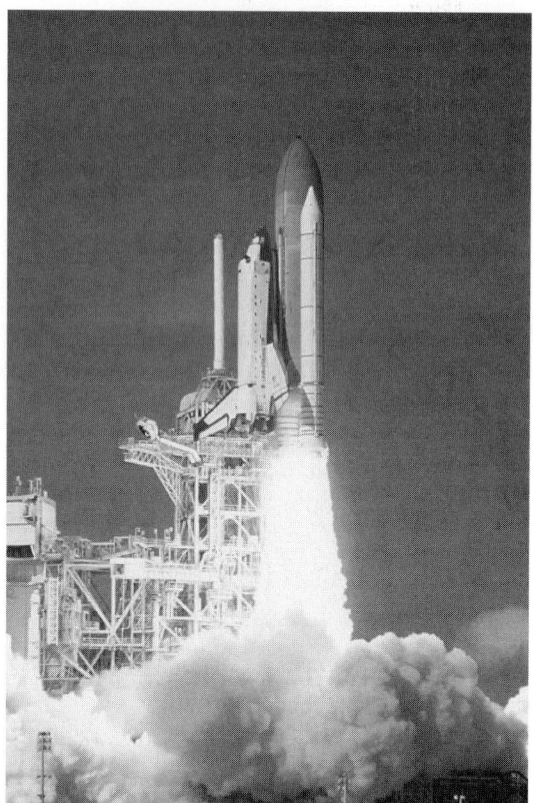

FIGURE 7–39 An image of a shuttle launch. This scene has totally flat white highlights, but that is the way it actually looked. *Source:* Jimmy Brown.

either one or both of these extremes appear, they are used to provide the viewer with a visual key to the dynamic range of the representation.

In digital images, the highlights can reach a value of 255 and can never become any brighter. An overexposed digital image has a peak on the right side of its histogram, with the peak touching the right edge of the graph.

The R, G, and B channels in a digital image are exposed independently unless the subject is neutral gray, white, or black. This means that one color channel may maximize before the others. This makes single-channel histograms difficult to read when color issues are present. When one channel has maximized at 255, the other channels may retain contrast capability. In cameras with differences among the capabilities of the R, G, and B channels, that may lead to hue shifts in the final captured image.

Retaining Highlight Detail

If highlight detail is being lost, set the exposure compensation in the camera for intentional underexposure and lighten the image in post-processing. If desired, expose a series of images of the same scene with the camera on a tripod. One exposure should be at –2.0 EV, then one at normal, and then one at +2.0 EV. The images must stack perfectly on top of each other. Combine the images in Photoshop to bring the best parts of each exposure into the final result. When the processing is completed, the resultant image will display lower contrast but higher dynamic range than the image exposed at normal. This process is widely accepted by digital photographers. However, it may be difficult to explain in court, so be extra careful to document all steps and save all original image files.

> **TIP:**
>
> Digital images display wider dynamic range in the shadows than film images do. If setting the camera to overexpose, shutter speeds or aperture settings allowing wider DoF may be gained.

Other techniques may be used to expand the dynamic range of images when that range is insufficient in nature.

Minilab Processing

Most minilabs are now digitally based. Due to the popularity of digital imaging, the amount of film being processed and printed has declined. Many of the larger traditional photo labs are going out of business. Small department-store minilabs have taken over the processing market niche.

Digital Minilab

A **digital minilab** is a computerized printer that uses traditional chemical photographic processes to make prints of digital images. Photographs are input using a built-in film scanner that captures images from negative films, positive films, and any digital media. The operator makes necessary corrections, including brightness, color saturation, contrast, scene lighting color correction, sharpness, and cropping. Photographic paper is exposed from the digital image, which is then processed by the minilab just as if it had been exposed from a negative. The resulting photographs have the same durability as traditional photographs from negatives, since the same chemical processes are used.

FILM QUALITY VERSUS DIGITAL QUALITY

The dynamic range capability of an image from a modern professional DSLR is equal to or better than that made from scans of ISO 100 transparencies on a Nikon Super Coolscan 4000 ED. A 6 Mp DSLR image file can equal or exceed scan quality of 4,000 dpi 35 mm film. The Nikon Coolscan has a high level of scan quality, color rendition, dynamic range, and control.

Remember, a film scanner creates a second-generation image. The first generation is the film image created by the camera. The second generation is the image being reproduced on the scanner CCD. With each succeeding generation, the possibility and probability exist of noticeable depreciation of image quality. Digital camera images are always first generation, no matter how many times the digital file is duplicated.

Factors causing image depreciation include the following:

- Light dispersion in the film emulsion during exposure
- Blurred effect at the edges of a highlight area of a photograph caused by reflection of light that passed through the film (**halation**)
- Lack of critical film plane flatness in the camera or film scanner
- Film grain aliasing during scanning
- Digital noise incurred during scanning
- Scanner lens and focusing issues
- Inaccurate color interpretation by the film dyes or by the scanner

RULE:

Film has low resolving power in low contrast situations.

Modern digital camera technology has nearly eliminated noise artifacts in DSLRs. ISO 400 and 800 images are very comparable to the same ISO images on film.

SUMMARY

A camera, like any other tool, must be properly used to yield optimum results. Many modern cameras are electronic, automatic, and user friendly. In most cases, that is a very good thing, but it also may lead to complacence from the photographer. The camera is purchased and the box opened, battery and memory are installed, and when the camera is switched on it accompanies the photographer into the field and immediately yields decent images. It is far easier today to go from absolutely nothing to a reasonable something without reading instructions or asking for help. When this happens, the level of competence of the user immediately levels at a plateau of adequacy and will stay there until a situation arises that cannot be handled by the user's level of education or experience.

This is never more evident than when it involves intuitive actions such as holding, focusing, and metering with a camera. The manufacturer designs the camera to be ergonomically comfortable, so why should the user need to concentrate on a specific protocol for best results? Focusing is done automatically, so why should the user need to learn how to do that manually? Handholding a camera to capture images that are in focus may be compared to the operation of a high-powered rifle. Without using appropriate precautions and accessories, it is difficult or impossible to achieve accuracy.

Metering is the easiest photographic operation of all. Just turn on the camera, set it at fully automatic, and the camera takes care of everything, doesn't it? This chapter takes those incredibly simple, intuitive operations of our modern do-everything automatic cameras and makes them more difficult. It instructs the user about how to take the camera off automatic and do the settings manually to improve the finished images.

CASE STUDY

NEVER TAKE ANYTHING FOR GRANTED

This actually happened to me. I taught photography at West Chicago High School for five wonderful years. For those of you who have not taught, I highly recommend it. It is the ultimate learning experience and one of the best possible ways to make a lasting impression upon the world.

My classes were limited to 25 students per semester because our darkroom only contained five enlargers and class was five days a week. Everyone had one hour per week of darkroom time in which to complete their assignments.

The pedagogy was to teach *everything* the students needed to progress from the idea of an image to a finished image. The curriculum started with photographic history and ended with theory. Everyone who did not own their own camera was loaned a 35 mm camera to use for the whole semester. The students viewed demonstrations of loading film in cassettes, loading film on reels, processing, enlarging, and image presentation. Everyone loaded their own film from bulk loaders.

Each student prepared a weekly assignment that involved locating, planning, photographing, processing, and printing a single image of a subject of their choosing to fulfill the assignment. A written paper explaining their image and how their idea evolved, what they think they did right or wrong, and what they learned was also required. *There were no right or wrong answers or ideas.*

Normally, the semester's work started slowly but gained speed as proficiency increased. Usually, by the second week nobody ended up with a blank roll of film. All necessary adjustments were routinely made, and the students' first images were produced. By the end of the semester, the submitted images were well exposed and printed, and the explanatory papers were well written and intelligent.

One young lady experienced failure after failure, week after week, with her photographs. I watched her film processing and printing, and her technique was fine. Her camera exposures were fine. The main problem with her work was that all her images were consistently out of focus. I checked her camera and exposed and processed a test roll myself, and it was fine. I let her try again, only to see her again disappointed.

I decided to accompany her on an excursion to make images. We did everything together; I was hoping to determine the problem through observation. We loaded the film together. We loaded the camera together. We walked the school grounds together. I watched her make exposures. Her stance was fine. Her shutter release was smooth and comfortable. We took the film into the lab and processed it. Again, it was hopelessly out of focus.

I was stumped. I sat and discussed all the steps and conditions with her until we finally solved the problem: she was neglecting to focus the lens before she exposed her photographs. I asked her, "Why have you been making photographs without focusing?" Her answer was simply, "Well, you never told us to!"

The truth of the matter is that she was absolutely right. After all my years teaching and all the students I'd taught, it never occurred to me that anyone would not know they had to focus the lens.

I learned a lesson from this event. Since then I have never taken *anything* for granted. Now I try to put myself into my students' position and ask myself, when writing instructions, "Have I included enough information to curtail any possible confusion?" That event made me a better teacher.

You, too, can learn from your mistakes. Each should occur only once.

KEY TERMS

image stabilization, (p. 202)
field of view, (p. 203)
circle of confusion, (p. 204)
line pair, (p. 204)
focal length multiplier, (p. 204)
angle of view, (p. 204)
crop factor, (p. 204)
normal viewing distance, (p. 206)
perspective distortion, (p. 206)
circle of confusion value, (p. 206)
hyperfocal focus, (p. 207)
light metering, (p. 211)
extinction meter, (p. 211)
photosensitive sensor, (p. 211)
acceptance angle, (p. 215)
matrix, (p. 215)
exposure value, (p. 219)
shutter priority automation, (p. 219)
exposure compensation, (p. 219)
histogram, (p. 219)
clipping, (p. 224)
zone system, (p. 225)
previsualization, (p. 225)
digital minilab, (p. 228)
halation, (p. 229)

EXERCISES

1. In daylight, select a scene and make an exposure with a normal lens using every possible shutter speed, fastest to slowest. Do the same with a telephoto lens. Inspect the images closely and record your threshold for handholding without camera movement.
2. In daylight, select a scene and make an exposure with a normal lens using every possible lens aperture. Do the same with a telephoto lens. Inspect the images closely and make note of the differences in DoF. Perform the same exercise while exposing close-up images of a subject.
3. Using the sharpest and best-exposed images from exercise 2, make a print of the appropriate size to be viewed at the normal distance of 14 inches.
4. Figure the focal length multiplier for the size of the sensor in your camera.
5. Compute the hyperfocal distance for your camera and lens, expose an image at the precise distance, and examine the DoF.
6. Use each of the metering patterns and systems of your camera on the same scene and determine which is best for both a stationary subject and a moving subject. Do the same with a subject of high and low contrast.
7. In a low-light situation, attempt to use your auto-focus setting on a subject with no contrast and determine how low the light must be before the camera will not fire.
8. Create a low-contrast, medium-contrast, and high-contrast image of subjects of your choice. Inspect and compare their histograms.
9. Use the spot meter in your camera (if available) to meter a scene. Using the principles of the zone system, make an exposure and compare it to the exposure the camera would make when set on automatic.

Chapter 8

Three-Dimensional Imaging

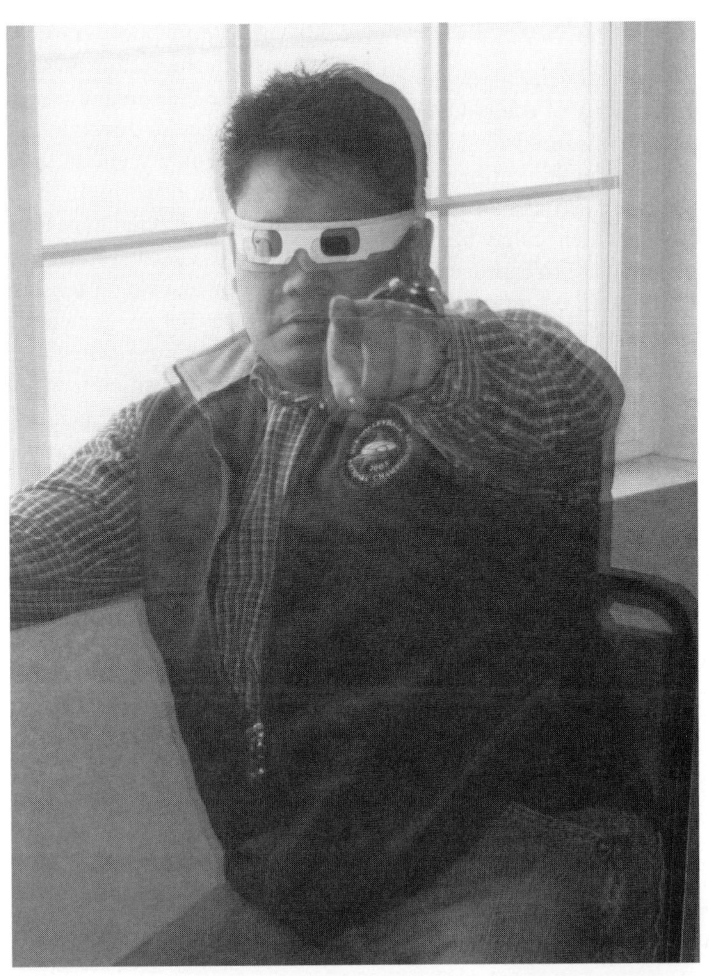

Learning Objectives

AFTER STUDYING THIS CHAPTER, YOU SHOULD BE ABLE TO:

1. Understand the importance of 3-D documentation
2. Differentiate the means and methods for capturing and producing 3-D photographs
3. Discuss the methods of scanning photography for micro and macro documentation
4. Understand and be able to create panoramic images with normal cameras and lenses
5. Understand the basics of laser scanning technologies and determine when they would be appropriate for evidence documentation
6. Recognize the situations and choose the appropriate procedures to capture images for quantitative analysis through photogrammetry

INTRODUCTION

Photographers are able to document evidence only as well as the limitations of their medium will allow. Does the practicing forensic evidence photographer understand the limitations self-imposed by capturing images strictly in two dimensions? In many cases, evidence may be more accurately documented in 3-D. To capture accurate photographic representations, it is necessary to understand when and how to properly create 3-D images and to be able to explain them in court.

Forensic and 3-D photography are synonymous in many ways, as others have noted: "Stereo (3-D) photography can provide valuable records of subjects where an accurate indication of depth is important"[1] and "In photographing the crime or accident scene, and many types of evidence, the investigator should attempt to provide a series of images supplying a maximum of useful information. This may enable the viewer to better understand how the crime or accident was committed or occurred. The photographs should demonstrate the relationships of the various important objects to one another in space. Locations of articles should be clearly seen with reference to recognizable backgrounds."[2]

Henny and Dudley, and others, have noted the differences between 2- and 3-D as it relates to vision and photography: "Monocular vision consists in the reception on a surface (the retina) of a single 2-D image (see Fig. 8–1), which has been projected through the crystalline lens of one eye from a scene in space, and the resultant interpretation by the brain of this image. Disregarding the anomalies of the photoreceptor, such an image is closely reproduced on the film or image sensor of a single-lens camera. The resultant print from that image, when properly viewed, reproduces an image on the retina of the viewer similar to that which it would have received had the eye occupied the position of the camera lens when the picture was taken. From this 2-D image, the brain infers the original 3-D space scene."[3]

This inference of 3-D information justifies the use of 2-D photographs that are only reasonably accurate in the depiction of the evidence. When interpreting 2-D images "we rely entirely on what might be called depth clues (cues), and where some or all of these are absent we are left to draw conclusions, sometimes completely wrong, of the distance to and hence the true size of an object. In general, we assume that the size of an object, in the absence of other clues, bears some relation to the amount of space it occupies in the picture area."[4]

The importance of recognizable depth in images is the reason to include references of

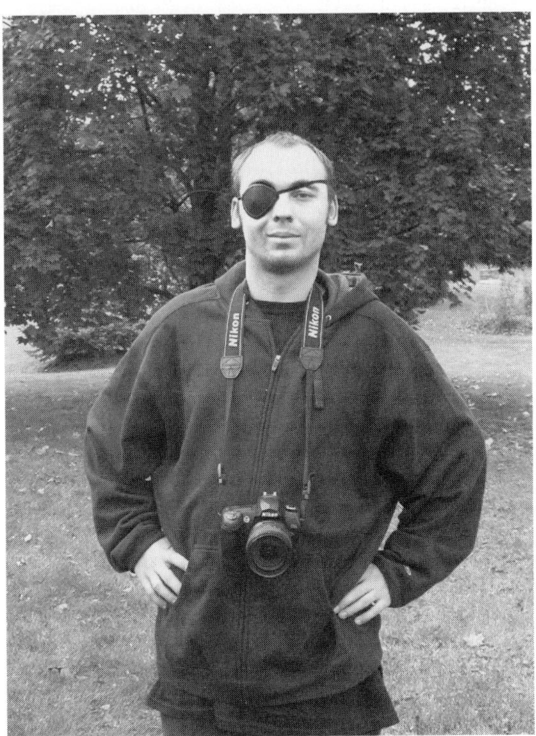

FIGURE 8–1 A person with only one eye has monocular vision. *Source:* Sandy Weiss.

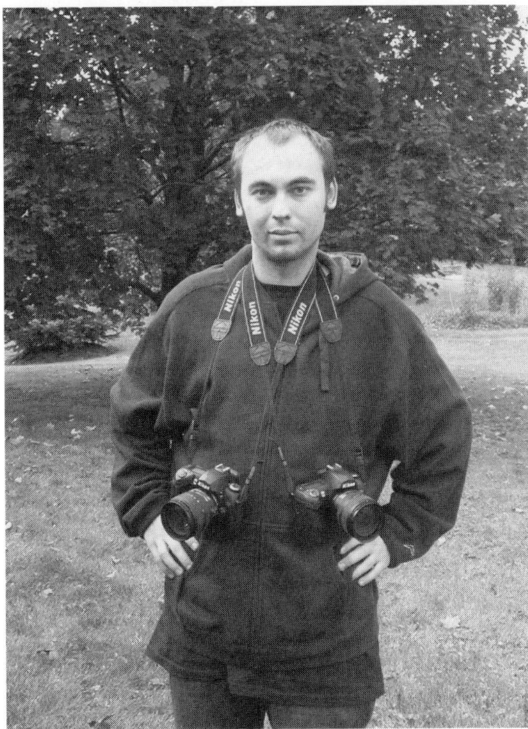

FIGURE 8–2 A person with two eyes has binocular vision. *Source:* Sandy Weiss.

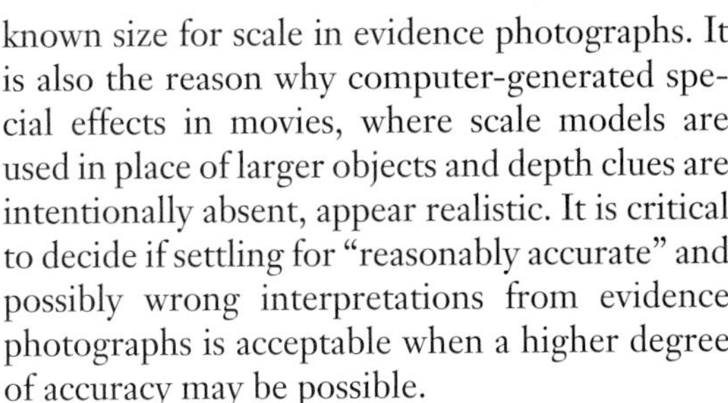

known size for scale in evidence photographs. It is also the reason why computer-generated special effects in movies, where scale models are used in place of larger objects and depth clues are intentionally absent, appear realistic. It is critical to decide if settling for "reasonably accurate" and possibly wrong interpretations from evidence photographs is acceptable when a higher degree of accuracy may be possible.

> Binocular vision consists in the reception on the two retinas of two images of a single scene in space and the resultant fusion and interpretation by the brain of these images (see Fig. 8–2). Since the position of the two eyes is not the same, different portions of objects are visible and near objects obscure different areas of far objects. Thus the two retinal images are not identical. The brain fuses these two different 2-D images and interprets them as a single 3-D space scene in which depth appears to exist as a definite reality. If two photographs are taken from positions occupied by the two eyes and the resultant prints are properly viewed, two retinal images are produced which correspond to those which would have been formed, had the eyes occupied the positions of the camera lenses. With proper viewing aids the resultant fusion and interpretation is substantially the same as that of binocular vision including the sense of the reality of depth.[5]

When viewing images, the left eye sees the image taken from the left side of the subject and the right eye sees the image taken from the right side. Photographically speaking, this reproduction of binocular vision by the use of two 2-D images is called **stereoscopic or 3-D photography.**

Perspective is a term often confused with 3-D, but in perspective the third dimension is only simulated by objects appearing to be smaller and smaller the farther they are from the camera.

True 3-D viewing of a subject can only be accomplished by the use of a minimum of two appropriate images. The 3-D information can be retrieved photogrammetrically from a single photograph by using perspective analysis (see Chapter 4, but true 3-D viewing of that same image will never be possible.

After considering the appropriate standards and intended goals of modern evidence photography, one wonders why a larger number of evidence photographers do not regularly produce true 3-D photographs and displays. It could be that the inference of 3-D is sufficient to satisfy most viewers, or that the production, viewing, and understanding of 3-D images are daunting for some people. It may be argued that the image ceases to be 3-D when a 3-D scene is represented on 2-D media, such as paper or a computer monitor. That is absolutely true, but some 2-D images appear more 3-D than others. That is why a photographer should capture 3-D information even if the representation is going to be in 2-D.

> **RULE:**
>
> If a representation is perceived by the viewer as 3-D, it is 3-D.

Regardless of the medium of the representation, if the viewer is able to visualize some 3-D aspect of the subject or is able to quantitatively extract 3-D information, the representation may be considered 3-D. Therefore, all 2-D images, except images of a flat plane, are essentially 3-D in some way. In some cases, additional dimensionality is needed for proper visualization and a true 3-D representation of a subject may be the only practical solution. A true 3-D representation may be easier for the observer to understand than a verbal explanation of the photogrammetry necessary to extract 3-D information from a 2-D image.

In the early days of photography, most photographers thought all their photographs needed to be 3-D to be accurate. As late as 1936, Morgan and Lester wrote this:

> 3-D photography is the only method of rendering pictures so that the subject looks round and plastic. It is unfortunate that at the present time we are unable to lend this plasticity to single picture views obtained by ordinary 2-D photography, which always has and still is endeavoring to assist our imagination to see things in pictures as we are accustomed to seeing them in life.[6]

It is not now and never has been necessary to produce all evidence photographs in 3-D, but when the extra dimensions would be useful for the sake of accurate representation, it is important for the photographer to understand the methods and the hardware necessary to create and display 3-D images.

Historically, photography became a reality in 1827 when Joseph Nicéphore Niépce succeeded in permanently capturing the view outside his window. He used a **camera obscura** combined with a light-sensitive silver-based material of his invention that hardened after exposure to light. This was before the days of chemical image amplification, and his initial exposure took eight hours to complete.

In contrast, stereoscopy was being used long before photography. Around 350 B.C., Euclid theorized that each of a person's two eyes perceived a different scene. In 1519, Leonardo da Vinci stated that binocular vision added relief to the perception of objects. In 1838, Sir Charles Wheatstone invented the first practical stereoscope, using a mirror system to view specially prepared drawings and yielding 3-D images. By 1845 William Henry Fox Talbot, the man who later invented chemical film developer, was supplying Wheatstone with stereo photographs to view in his stereoscope.

By the 1850s, the production and distribution of stereo images had become a popular commercial venture, due to the simple reproduction of original photographic images. Soon competition in the stereoscope field was evident, with further inventions by Sir Oliver Wendell Holmes and by David Brewster, who was the first to incorporate lenses instead of mirrors in a commercial stereoscope (see Figs. 8–3 and 8–4).

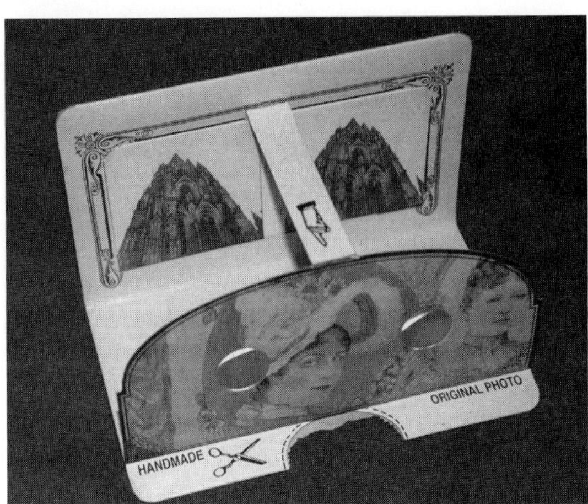

FIGURE 8–3 An inexpensive instrument for viewing stereo photographs in 3-D. *Source:* Sandy Weiss.

The sudden popularity of stereo systems made a tremendous impact on the nation's viewing habits. Stereo images were mass produced and sold by the millions. It is a little-known fact that "virtually all of the original (photographic) images made of the Civil War were taken as stereoscopic views" because most books about the Civil War reproduce only one-half of each stereo pair.[7]

An 1870 edition of the *Philadelphia Photographer* states, "There is no parlor in America where there is not a stereoscope."[8] The popularity of stereoscopes and cards lasted into the 1940s. At that point in the timeline of photography, cameras were getting smaller, and the 35mm format was gaining in popularity. Photographers were able to take small cameras into the field and return with very good-quality images.

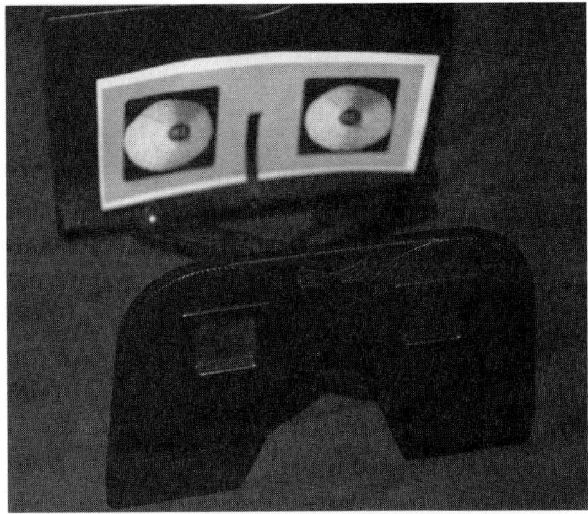

FIGURE 8–4 A folding, pocket-size stereo print viewer. *Source:* Sandy Weiss.

During the 1930s, Leica invented a beam splitter to attach to the front of the lenses of their 35mm cameras to enable simple stereo photography. In 1936 Ihagee of Dresden, Germany, introduced the first 35mm single lens reflex (SLR) camera.[9] Shortly afterward Ihagee also introduced a beam splitter for its SLR that actually allowed the photographer to view the intended subject in 3-D at the time of exposure. The same viewing device used in the optics of the camera doubled as a viewer for the finished slides. Beam splitters for modern cameras continue to be available in the used market on the Internet and are very practical tools (see Fig. 8–5).

During the 1950's there was a short lived but widespread public interest in (do-it-yourself) stereo-photography that resulted in a temporary proliferation of equipment and literature; but this passed, as most fads do."[10] *Life* magazine experimented with the addition of 3-D images in its publication, and a brief but popular trend was explored by some major Hollywood studios in the production of 3-D feature films. "Despite the (theater) critics, it's clear the public wants 3-D, and Warner's *House of Wax* (1953, its first effort) is a major crowd pleaser."[11] The studios produced 3-D movies with outlandish effects meant

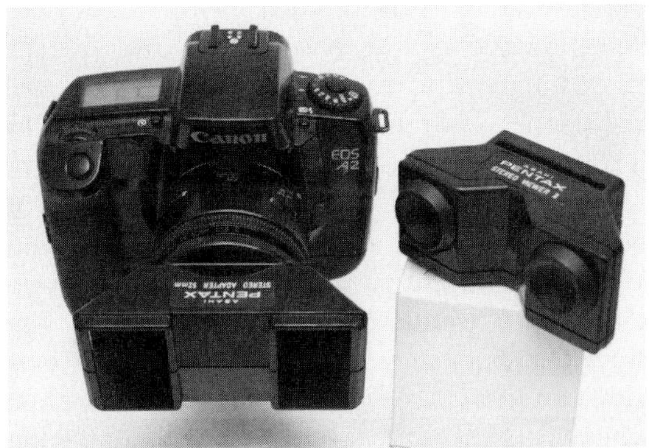

FIGURE 8–5 A beam splitter manufactured by Pentax. *Source:* Dan Rose.

to awe and startle the viewing audiences. It is interesting and a little-known fact that the director of *House of Wax*, Andre de Toth, was hired for the job specifically because he had only one eye and the studio wanted an edge to ensure that the movie would be equally viewable in 2-D as in 3-D, just in case the new effect was a flop.

So why did the popularity of 3-D movies wane? One possible explanation suggested that "3-D is proving a problem with audiences. Many viewers are complaining of headaches."[12] The red and green glasses that the viewers were forced to wear were uncomfortable and felt unusual. Also, a long time delay occurred between reels, caused by the projectionist changing two film reels at a time instead of just one. Sometimes the two reels would slip out of synchronization, producing effects reminiscent of the sound and image problems of early sound films.

After the early 1950s, the popularity of the 3-D effect in both movies and still photography rapidly came to an end, possibly because some people cannot under any circumstances resolve a pair of 2-D images in any media into one 3-D representation: "Imperfect fusion reflects a failure of the eyes to coordinate. Even perfect fusion is not perfect all the time; heavy drinking, fatigue, emotional upset, or even illness will impair it."[13]

In addition, two landmark inventions encouraged the end of 3-D popularity. The first was the availability, starting about 1935, of economical color photography. The use of color in and of itself brought to the photo viewer a sense of pseudo 3-D reality. "Photographers who used color film, had to overcome the idea that their pictures were somehow too explicit to be art, and too literal a representation of reality."[14] Even so, "there are few people now remaining who would not prefer a color print to one in black and white."[15]

Even more destructive to the practice of 3-D photography was an invention that changed the twentieth century. In 1932, Vladimir Kosma Zworykin's iconoscope began to imitate the ways that human eyes viewed images for television broadcast.[16] When television went public after World War II, it changed the way people looked at the world. Even though early television was essentially a 2-D, black-and-white medium, it has always had an inherent three-dimensionality because the objects on the screen move and appear superimposed over other objects. The impression of depth is afforded the viewer through the use of changeable viewpoints and constant motion.

"Virtually all Hollywood movies of the period were shot in color using Cinerama, Vista Vision, Cinema Scope and 3-D" to have an advantage over television being only a black-and-white medium.[17] Due to these modern technologies, 3-D still photography was forgotten by most photographers. The ones who continued its use were enthralled by the true perception of depth of the 3-D effect. Even today, many stereo photography clubs and societies around the world with hundreds of members work on their own to keep the media alive. The New York Stereoscopic Society, a large group, still meets quarterly at the American Museum of Natural History in New York City. The *Reel 3-D Catalog* of February 1, 2000, had a circulation of 42,000 subscribers.[18]

Photogrammetrists also capture some images in 3-D for mapping and for quantification. Today, the number of people involved in 3-D imaging is growing due to the capabilities of the computer. New technologies killed the mass popularity of 3-D, and now different technologies are bringing it back.

The 3-D movies shown at Imax and other theaters around the world are extremely popular. "Some television programs and feature films are also being produced specifically in 3-D."[19]

The obvious difficulties associated with 3-D photography should not dissuade today's forensic evidence photographers from the production of 3-D images. Given the state of modern technology, many useful things can be done with 3-D images, both qualitatively and quantitatively, and their routine capture should be part of every forensic investigation. Fortunately, 3-D images are easy to convert to 2-D displays.

METHODS OF 3-D PHOTOGRAPHY

The method chosen for the capture of 3-D information from any particular subject is dependent on the nature of the subject and the purpose of the information. Some of the techniques are basically the same as for normal 2-D photography, except that extra photos of given subjects must be captured and then appropriate combinations of those photos must be used for the construction of the 3-D images. Some of the methods involve the use of specialized and often expensive equipment. If the need is great enough, the specific equipment can be rented or bought.

Images for Documentation and Display

The accuracy of any 3-D representation is directly proportional to the ease of its visualization, and 3-D images make an impression on the viewer. It may be impossible for the viewer of a 2-D representation to accurately visualize the degree of slope of a landscape feature, the dip in a roadway, or the severity of a dent in an artifact. It may even be impossible to judge if a particular formation is a dip or a rise.

As plentiful as the reasons for working in 3-D are the types of subjects that can be documented three-dimensionally. Fortunately, the list of possible subjects is easily organized into a few groups:

- Static or dynamic
- Small or large
- Close or distant

It is the job of the photographer to assess the purpose of the final images, to choose the subject, and to select the proper method to capture the necessary images. The simpler the subject, the greater the number of methods available to create the images needed for 3-D viewing. A breadbox-size object sitting on a solid table in good light is easier to document than a single human hair, a building with 20 rooms and three floors, a person running at full speed, a battleship, or a wad of chewing gum stuck to the bottom of a trash can. Numerous methods are available for documenting any of these cases, but some will be easier and more appropriate to document.

The following subsections present some of the types of hardware and software used for this purpose, along with examples of the typical subject type for each.

Stereo Cameras

Cameras with two lenses (**stereo cameras**) for exposing stereo pairs have been manufactured since the early days of photography. In contrast to twin-lens cameras, where one lens is used for viewing the subject and one lens is used for exposing the film, twin-lens (3-D) cameras expose two images at the same time from slightly different points of view.

In the 1950s, during the height of 3-D mania, many companies, including Kodak, Revere, Realist (see Fig. 8–6), and Wollensak, manufactured cameras of this design. The two lenses of 35mm stereo cameras are separated by about 2½ inches (65 mm) to expose two photos from angles resembling the angles of view of a person's eyes. These cameras can be used to take photos of subjects that are either static or dynamic because both images are exposed simultaneously. The cameras can be focused down to a few feet and then to infinity. At infinity the 3-D effect is practically nonexistent because at that distance from the camera, any difference between the two captured images is insignificant.

Stereo 35mm cameras can be used with negative film but are most often used for exposing positive transparencies (slides), which are then viewed in a handheld viewer (see Fig. 8–7) or used for projection. The handheld viewers are small and inexpensive and the slides are easily duplicated, which means a viewer and full set of slides can be given to each member of a jury if desired. The most useful purpose for this type of

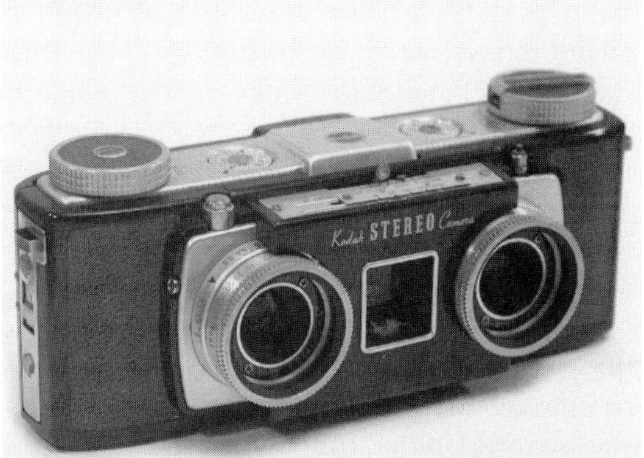

FIGURE 8–6 A Realist stereo camera manufactured in the 1950s. *Source:* Sandy Weiss.

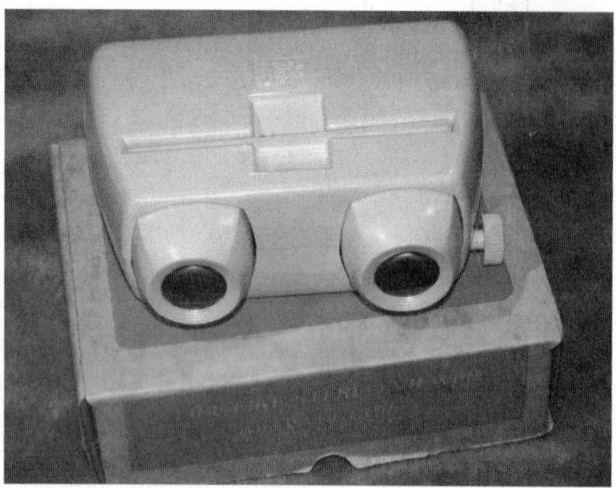

FIGURE 8–7 A stereo slide viewer, such as this one, is used to view slides taken with the stereo camera. Each eye sees only one of the two images. The brain sees this as true 3-D. *Source:* Sandy Weiss.

slides is to illustrate, in great detail, the relief of landforms or relative positions of objects in a particular location.

It is important to hold the stereo camera as level as possible during the exposure to allow the person viewing the image to resolve the image into its three dimensions. The format of stereo cameras is slightly vertical. The camera cannot be used in a fully vertical orientation when taking photos.

Stereo cameras are currently available on the used camera market in good condition and at reasonable prices. Several repair services in the United States still repair them, and instruction manuals can be found on the Internet. The slides process conventionally, but the photographer may have to do his or her own mounting. Handheld viewers are still available new.

Beam Splitter

Beam splitters expose stereo pairs with standard 35mm or DSLR cameras and/or cameras up to and including 4 × 5 inches, as long as the camera can focus through the lens. These devices screw onto the front of the existing normal lens. Wide-angle and telephoto lenses will not work properly.

Leica invented the beam splitter in the 1930s, and similar equipment has been made and marketed ever since. Pentax manufactured a similar device of very high quality (see Fig. 8–5). The devices produce a stereo pair within the normal single frame limitations of any camera on which they are mounted. If 35mm positives are exposed, any processor will be able to process, mount, and duplicate the slides as if they were normal single-frame images. These devices are supplied with a matched, drop-in, 35mm viewer. If the photographer exposes negative film, any conventional lab can print the stereo-pair images from the frames. If the images are digital, they can be printed on any desktop printer. Many styles of 3-D print viewers are available and inexpensive (see Figs. 8–3 and 8–4).

Beam splitters are usually available in only one threaded accessory size but can be adapted to almost any other accessory size by the use of step-up or step-down rings. Beam splitters will allow closer focusing distances than a twin-lens stereo camera, but the fixed separation dimensions of the images prohibits the use of the devices for macrophotography. Ihagee manufactured a special splitter for macrophotography with a reduced separation between the images, but that item is no longer available and is quite scarce.

Because both exposures are made at the same time, dynamic subjects can be captured. One of the greatest advantages of these devices is that the photographer can use a normal camera for both 2-D and 3-D image capture on the same roll of film or digital file and can switch back and forth whenever desired. Normal light-metering capabilities and the full range of the camera's shutter speeds are retained. If a through-the-lens meter is not used for image capture with a beam splitter, the device itself may absorb some light, so experiment before exposing anything important in case underexposure is a problem.

As with the twin-lens stereo cameras, the format of the images is slightly vertical and the camera cannot be turned to capture vertical subjects due to the inability of the viewer to resolve the image from that orientation.

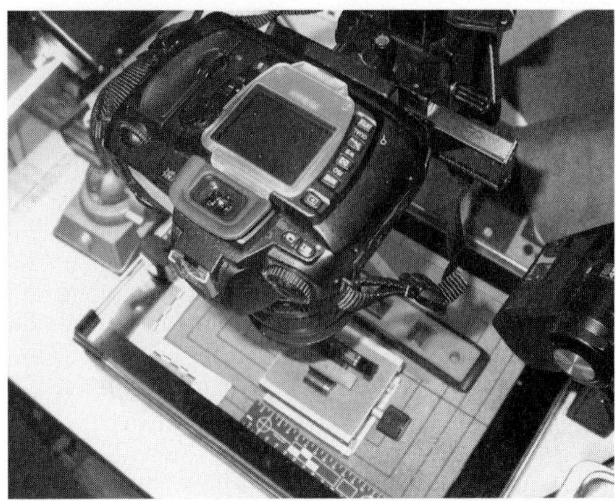

FIGURE 8–8 Digital camera mounted on a slide rail and used for macrophotography. *Source:* Sandy Weiss.

Slide Rails

Any camera and any focal length lens can be used to photograph two successive images of a static subject, separated by the correct dimensions. This is the simplest form of 3-D image capture to understand and execute. For best results, the camera must be mounted on a device called a **slide rail,** either bought or manufactured by the user, and then moved approximately 2½ inches side to side between each exposure for normal subjects (see Fig. 8–8). These devices are called **slide rails.** An excellent rail system known as the 3-D ImageTrack was manufactured in the 1990s by Image Tech of Norris, Georgia. The price for a new ImageTrack rail was then about $250, and it had excellent scales and an assortment of other deluxe features. Sadly, these are no longer manufactured.

This method of image capture has some disadvantages. First, because the two images are captured at different times, any movement of the subject will cause the two resultant images to be unresolvable into 3-D. Second, this method requires extra thought and planning to capture each image, because the photographer must determine the appropriate separation between the images.

Although difficulties exist, the use of the same camera for the capture of both halves of 3-D images does have certain advantages. The images can be captured with a lens of any focal length and from any camera-to-subject distance. Since the same camera and lens are used for both exposures, no hardware-matching difficulties are evident unless the photographer changes shutter speed, aperture, or focus between exposures. In some instances, when the stereo-pair will be used for measurement and not strictly for viewing, the camera may be moved up and down rather than side to side for the two exposures.

Macro, telephoto, and wide-angle lenses are all suitable for this work. Wide-angle lenses are preferred for some subjects because they have inherently greater DoF at the same working distance. Also, the distance beyond which everything is in focus to infinity is closer to the camera with wide-angle lenses. Images can be captured in vertical, horizontal, or even square format if desired.

Table 8–1 lists the suggested starting points for lens separations (interocular distances) for

TABLE 8–1 Interocular Distances (Separation Between Camera Lenses)

Camera-to-Subject Distance	Camera Separation
Infinity to 10 feet	1/50 of the camera-to-subject distance
10 feet to 3 feet	2½ inches
30 inches	2 inches
24 inches	1.6 inches
18 inches	1.2 inches
12 inches	0.8 inch
6 inches	0.4 inch

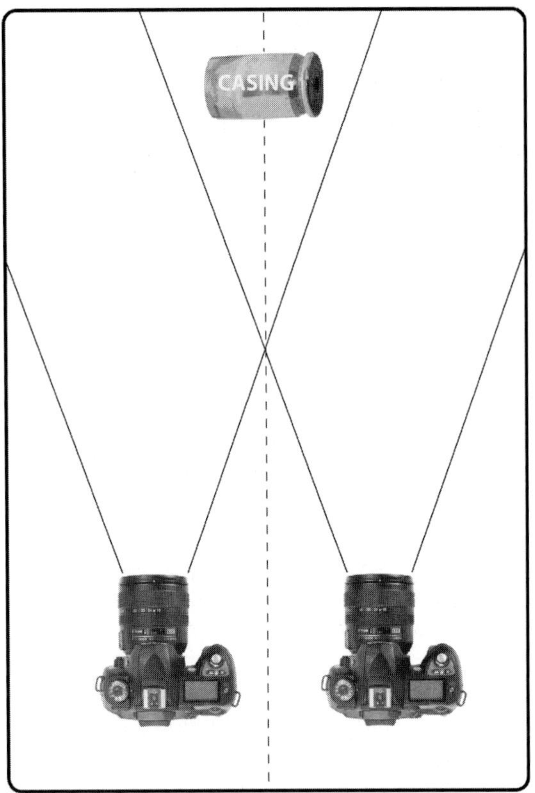

FIGURE 8–9 The correct orientation for the proper capture of two images in 3-D photography. *Source:* Jessica Weiss.

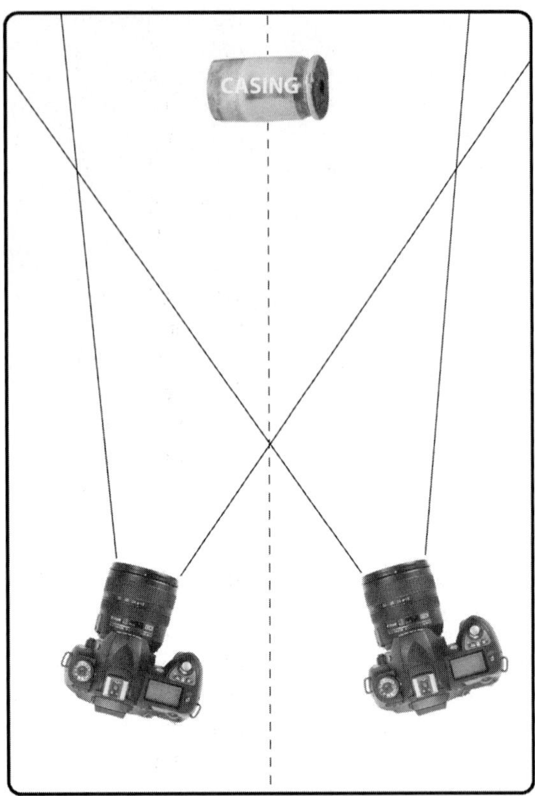

FIGURE 8–10 An incorrect orientation for the proper capture of two images in 3-D photography, unless the subject is at close camera-to-subject distances. *Source:* Jessica Weiss.

the capture of stereo pairs when using a single camera. The photographer may need to adjust the separation under certain circumstances (see Figs. 8–9 and 8–10).

Somewhere between 200 and 1,000 feet, depending upon the subject, and using a lens separation of 2½ inches between the lenses for the exposure of the two images, the subject will become identical and the 3-D effect will be negligible. When this occurs, it is an acceptable practice to use a larger distance between the two exposure positions. The same principle applies in aerial photography, where stereo pairs are captured from flying airplanes. The stereo effect will be resolvable with separations of hundreds of feet between images. The extra separation is often an aid to the photogrammetrist doing aerial mapping from the resultant stereo pairs.

It is acceptable to point the camera slightly inward when exposing 3-D photos at macro camera-to-subject distances and high magnifications, or to roll the subject slightly between exposures. For example, if a person attempts to look with both eyes at a fly that landed on the tip of his or her nose, the eyes must slightly cross in order to focus on the fly.

RULE:

At normal camera to subject distances, the following are true.

- Both images must be exposed with the camera and lens in parallel orientation.
- The camera must be level, at the same height, and at the same focus and exposure settings, for both exposures.

Two Matched Cameras

Two identical cameras may be physically joined together and used for simultaneous 3-D image capture. The separation between the two lenses must remain at 2½ inches for most normal subjects. Lens separation may be adjusted, depending on the focal length of the lenses used on the cameras. The lenses and cameras must be especially well matched; otherwise the resultant images will be difficult to resolve. The cameras also must be well matched mechanically, so that the exposures are close to identical. In addition, the two shutters must work simultaneously if the subject is dynamic. A double cable or electronic release may be used.

SCANNING ELECTRON MICROSCOPE

Most evidence photographers do not utilize the capabilities of a **scanning electron microscope** (SEM). The images an SEM produces cannot be gathered using any other technology. Specifically, an SEM can expose images at much higher magnifications and DoF than is possible with light microscopy (see Fig. 8–11). The SEM performs as well at lower macro magnifications as it does at higher magnifications.

The limitation of magnification with light microscopy is the wavelength of light itself (about 1/50,000 inch). When using light microscopes, it is not possible to observe subjects smaller than the amplitude of the light. The SEM uses a stream of electrons for imaging that impacts and reflects from the surface of a sample and is then viewed on a monitor or sent for capture. Samples must be sufficiently small to fit into the SEM vacuum chamber.

Because the SEM views the surface of a sample with extended DoF, its images appear as if the viewer had been shrunk to the same size as the sample and was standing next to it. "By restoring three dimensions to our view of the microscopic world, it has given it reality."[20]

That reality is the illusion of 3-D reality when viewing SEM images that have been exposed individually. For realistic 3-D images, stereo pairs can be exposed and then viewed with appropriate print viewing devices. SEM stereo pairs are useful in cases where the contrast alone is insufficient to allow the viewer to optically resolve the relief of the subject from

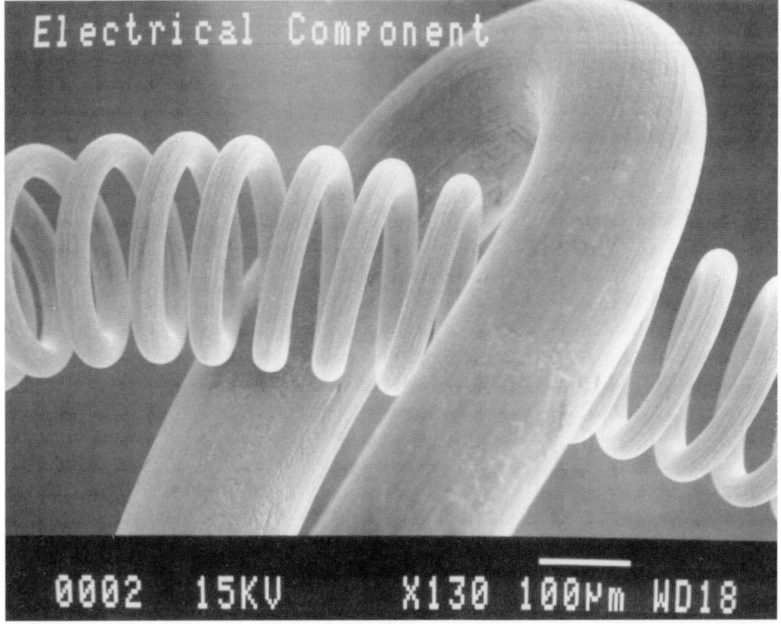

FIGURE 8–11 Scanning electron micrograph of the filament of an electric light. *Source:* Sandy Weiss/Packer Engineering.

the image. The SEM is especially useful in fractography, in which the detail of the subject fracture is instrumental in the determination of the fracture mechanics.

Commercial SEM services are available for hire when needed.

3-D LIGHT SCANNING PHOTOMACROGRAPHY (OR DEEP FIELD PHOTOMACROGRAPHY OR ZERO-PERSPECTIVE IMAGING)

Scanning photomacrography was first mentioned in print in 1964.[21] This technique "enables the photographer to obtain a photograph in which all parts of the subject are in sharp focus without regard to the depth or shape of the object."[22] It is a technology, practiced by few people, but fills a niche and yields images unavailable through any other method.

One of the reasons for scanning photomacrography's lack of popularity is that only one commercially available apparatus was ever produced. The Dynaphot was produced by Irvine Optical of Burbank, California, for a short time and in limited quantities. It was an expensive apparatus. Finding a used example is difficult. However, a number of articles have been published that include instructions on the manufacture of homemade versions.[23]

With the Dynaphot, stereo macrophotographs may be exposed of subjects that retain color, texture, and transparency at magnifications up to about 200x on film or sensor, with no limitations in DoF (see Figs. 8–12 and 8–13). Subjects that cannot be put into a SEM vacuum chamber, are good candidates for this technique. Any format of film or digital camera can be used.

With this technology, the subject is raised or lowered through a very thin slit of light during the exposure. The camera is focused on the same plane as the slit of light and exposes only the illuminated part of the subject. As the subject travels through the light, the image of the subject is applied to the image sensor. The image is usually high in contrast because of the lighting formula, but simple methods can be used to reduce the contrast, including the use of multiple light sources or pre- or post-flashing of the subject.

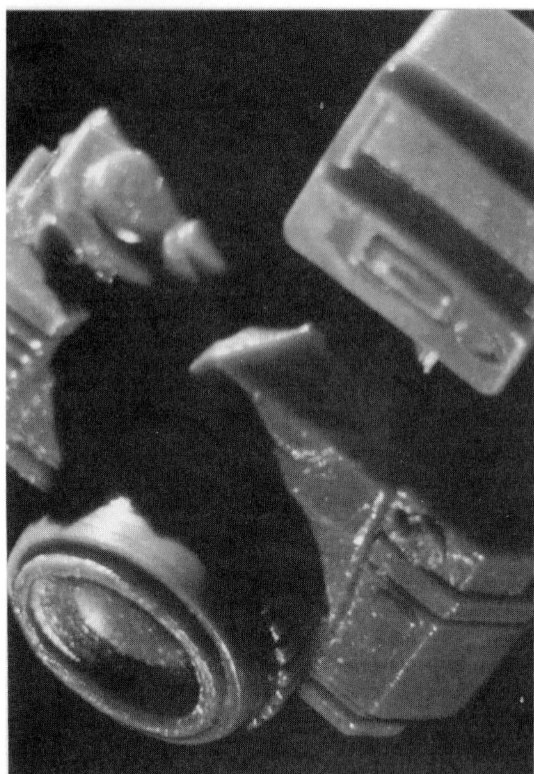

FIGURE 8–12 Scanning macrophotography result. *Source:* Sandy Weiss/Packer Engineering.

The DoF achievable by this technique will be up to 200 times greater than it would be if using conventional macrophotography.[24] The depth creates a sense of 3-D in the resultant images.

When created in stereo, the resultant images may be viewed in a conventional 3-D print viewer. The separation between the two images must be less as the magnification increases. The objects photographed by this technique will be in total focus. The complete imaged object is the same distance from the camera lens, which results in images in true axonometric form.[25]

A number of articles describe the construction and use of this type of system (see Fig. 8–13). Anyone with basic mechanical and electrical talents and access to a Radio Shack should have no problem following the instructions. (If instructions prove difficult to obtain, please contact the author of this book at sweiss@packereng.com for all necessary literature and tips far too extensive for inclusion here.)

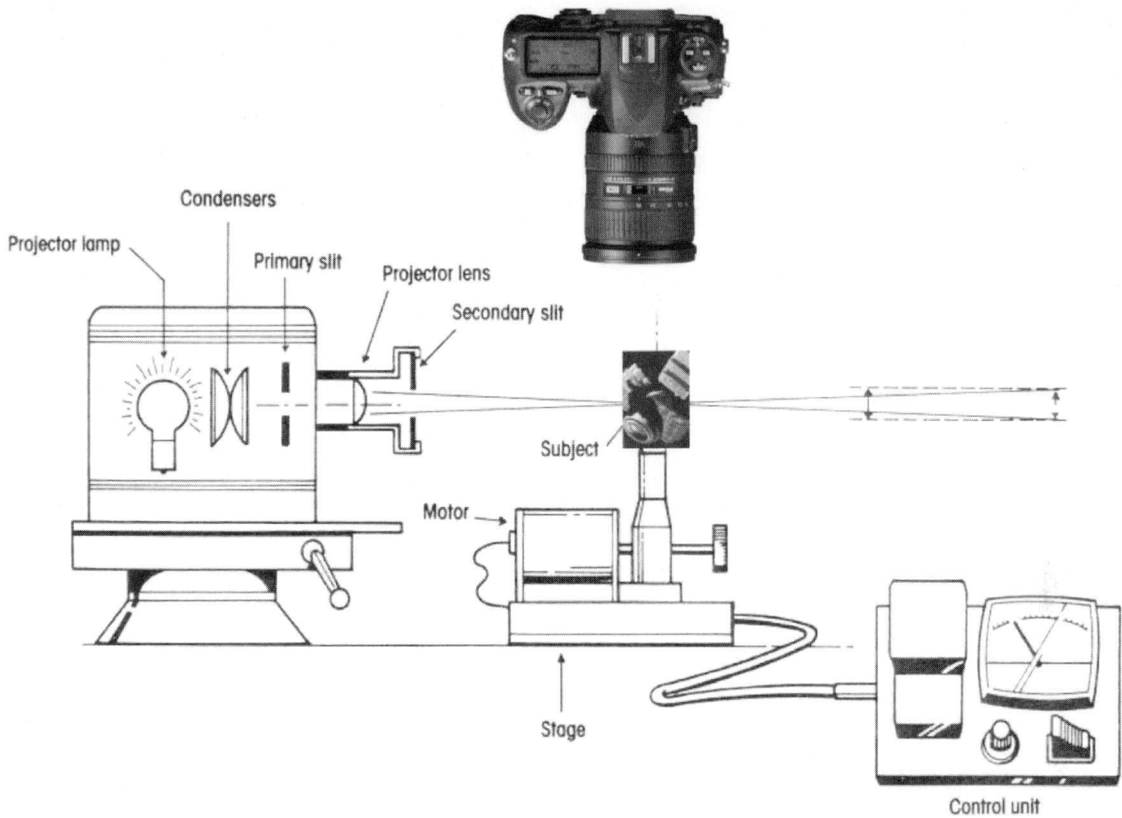

FIGURE 8–13 Diagram of a homemade scanning macrophotography system. *Source:* Sandy Weiss/Packer Engineering.

(This system was discussed in this chapter rather than in Chapter 10 because it is a truly 3-D method of macrophotography. See Chapter 10 for photographic technique information.)

LENTICULAR TECHNOLOGIES

"Douglas F. Winnek invented lenticular technology in the 1940s. Lenticular allows 3-D viewing without special apparatus. The U.S. Navy helped perfect the process for both B&W and color images in 1947."[26] The current version uses a cylindrical lenticular screen, which is built into the back of a camera, just in front of the film plane. The images recorded with **lenticular** technology are a series of narrow interlaced strips of left- and right-eye viewpoints.[27]

The popularity of lenticular technology received a boost in the 1970s when Nimslo introduced and marketed a quad-lens lenticular camera. Photographers used Nimslo cameras for general documentation purposes, mailed the film to Nimslo for processing, and received in return snapshot-size lenticular 3-D prints. The four images exposed simultaneously are separated into individual layers in the prints, giving the prints their 3-D quality.

Lenticular images are popular but used mostly for novelty and marketing purposes. The images appear to be 3-D when viewed from different angles (see Fig. 8–14) and are used as evidence photography in large court displays and small images for report covers. The images are not useful for quantitative analysis.

ANAGLYPH IMAGING

"The principal of 3-D anaglyph images was first proposed in 1853 by Rollmann, and then adapted to practical use by Ducos du Hauron in France

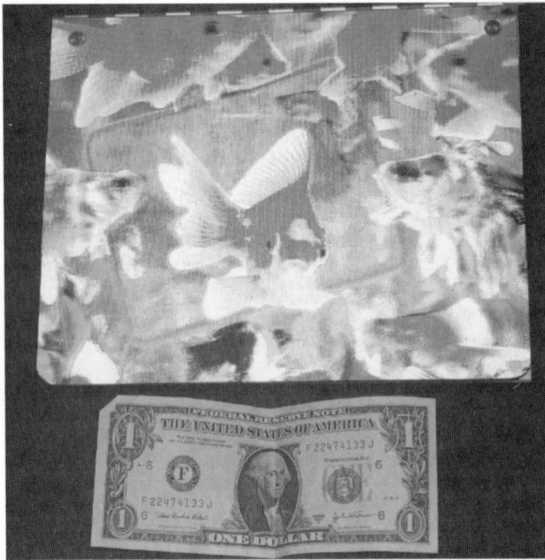

FIGURE 8–14 The aquarium effect is seen in a print made with lenticular technology. *Source:* Sandy Weiss/Packer Engineering.

in 1891."[28] **Anaglyphs** are generated by superimposing into one new image a pair of stereo images that are printed in two different colors. The images are usually red for the left eye and blue for the right eye. When viewed with special glasses that have the corresponding lens colors (see Fig. 8–15), the 2-D anaglyph images look like a 3-D object.

Anaglyph technology works by allowing only red image information to pass through the glasses to the left eye of the viewer and only blue image information to pass through to the right. In this way, each eye sees only the part of the image information that would have been seen when viewing the original 3-D object.

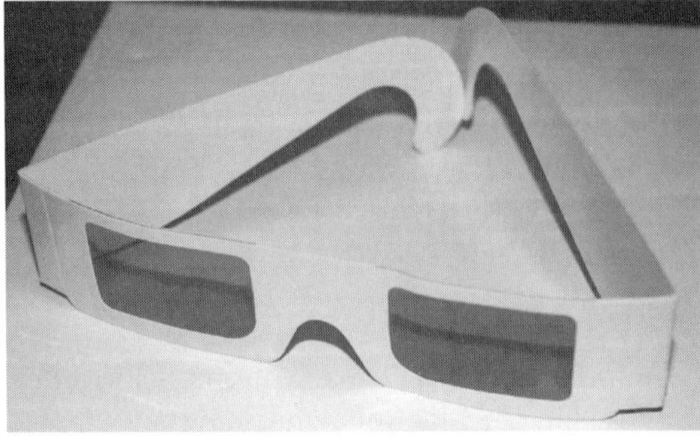

FIGURE 8–15 Red and blue 3-D glasses. *Source:* Sandy Weiss/Packer Engineering.

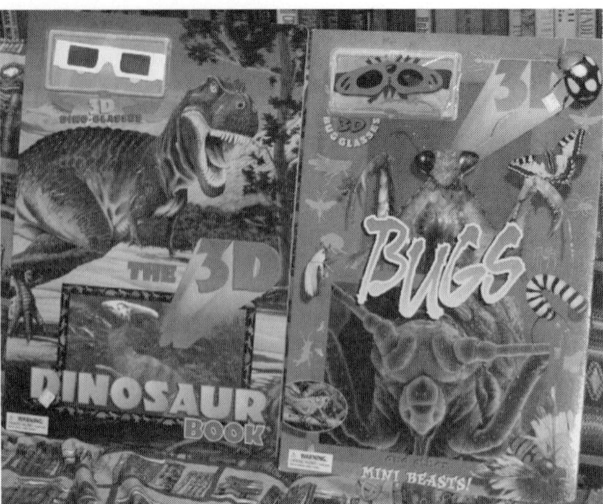

FIGURE 8–16 Anaglyph children's books. *Source:* Sandy Weiss/Packer Engineering.

Anaglyph technology has been popular for over a hundred years. Many children's books are printed in anaglyph for educational purposes (see Fig. 8–16). In the 2000 *Sports Illustrated Swimsuit Edition* and *Olympics 2000 Edition*, the magazine publisher included a pair of red/blue glasses and anaglyph 3-D photos of the models in their swimsuits and the Olympic athletes in their respective competitions. Such 3-D anaglyph images are accurate and descriptive. When used as evidence photographs, the viewers of the images can differentiate the camera-to-subject depth of various features.

Many anaglyph creation programs are available on the Internet. One can be downloaded for free from www.stereoscopy.com/downloads. It creates anaglyphs in JPEG format that can be viewed on a computer monitor, projected on a screen, or printed on paper.

It should be noted that some LCD projectors work better than others for anaglyph projection and viewing. If your results on screen are difficult to distinguish in 3-D, try using a different projector.

The images needed to create anaglyphs can be captured by any of the types of cameras and techniques that have been described previously in this chapter; digital photography works perfectly. Anaglyph technology can be combined with other technologies, including panoramas and virtual reality tours. NASA regularly publishes anaglyph images of objects in space, including many of the planet Mars. Forensic

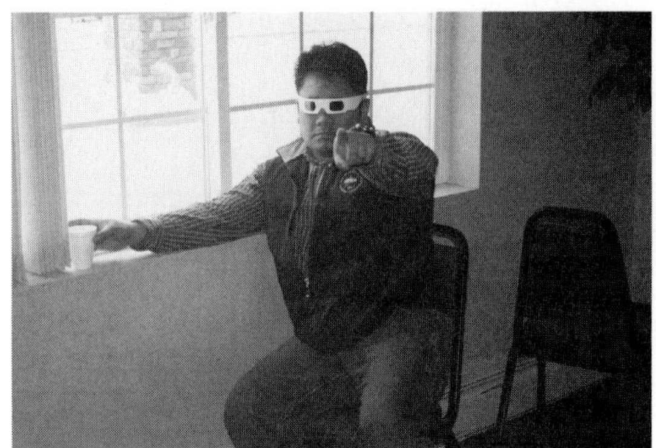

FIGURE 8–17 The left-eye component view used to create the 3-D image in Figure 8–19. *Source:* Sandy Weiss/Packer Engineering.

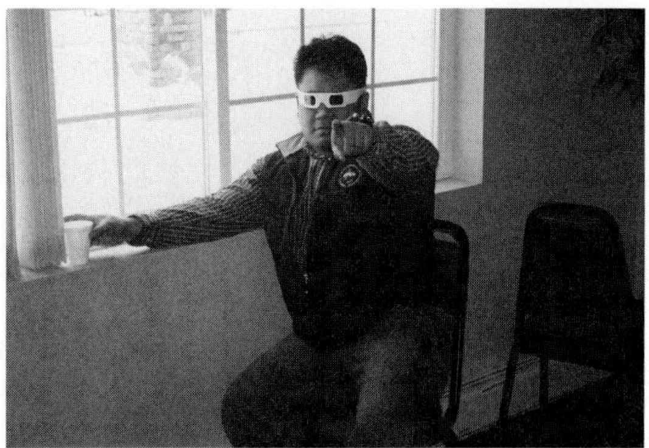

FIGURE 8–18 The right-eye component view used to create the 3-D image in Figure 8–19. *Source:* Sandy Weiss/Packer Engineering.

photographers should note that anaglyphs have been used successfully in court.

In Figures 8–17 and 8–18, the left and right components were separated by 2½ inches and exposed by the same camera and lens. The two images were incorporated into the 3-D anaglyph image in Figure 8–19 with software downloaded from the Internet.

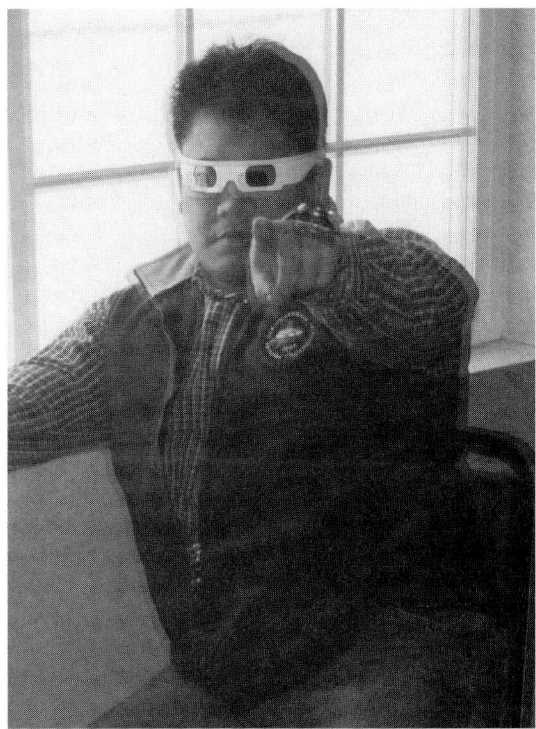

FIGURE 8–19 Assembled anaglyph, 3-D. *Source:* Sandy Weiss/Packer Engineering.

IMMERSIVE AND VIRTUAL REALITY TECHNOLOGIES

Immersive and virtual reality (VR) technologies provide the viewer with a feeling of actually being somewhere they are not. VR uses computers to generate virtual artificial spaces and objects from photographs of the actual space or object. This technique is useful for the creation of computer-generated **virtual tours,** in which the viewer gets the sense of actually walking through the space or of being at the scene where the images were exposed. It is also practical for people removed by distance or time from an actual occurrence. Some law enforcement departments use this technique to walk witnesses and jurors virtually through crime and accident scenes.

By definition, true virtual reality is immersive in that the viewer participates in the image and is an active part of the space. A participant may wear special headgear and gloves and feel as if he or she is participating in the action by opening doors, moving through the scene, and such. Even pseudo-VR, including Apple QuickTime, gives the viewer a sense of being on the outside of the scene while looking in. QuickTime is a type of VR that the forensic photographer can create using a regular camera and personal computer. (The QuickTime player is downloadable for free at www.apple.com/ quicktime/download.)

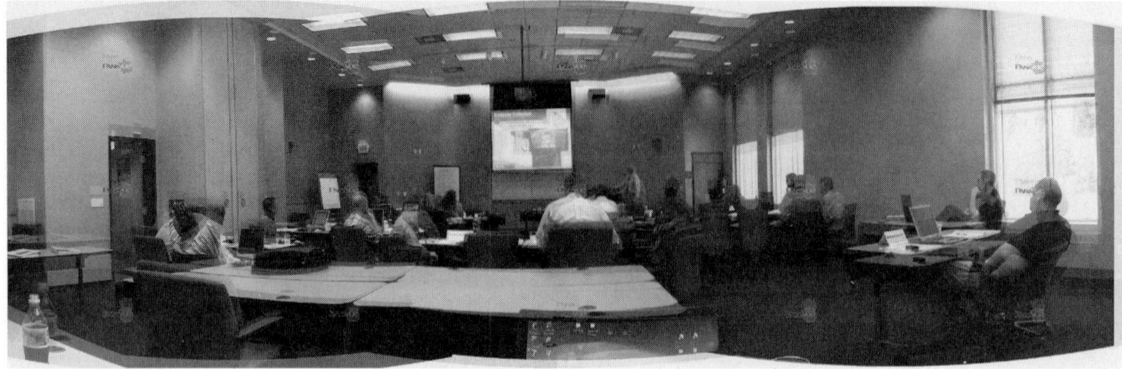

FIGURE 8–20 Anaglyph panorama, created by exposing a succession of stereo pairs, converting them to 3-D anaglyphs, and then stitching them together with panorama software into the 300-degree image. *Source:* Paul Fenoglio/Packer Engineering.

The forensic possibilities of these applications are virtually infinite. Three-dimensional panoramas, 360-degree VR panoramas, and object images can be created for many demonstrative purposes in litigation. Each additional depth cue adds to the ability of humans to comprehend complex 3-D objects. VR supplies more cues than any of the other 3-D techniques that are easily accomplished.

In 360-degree panoramic movies, the viewer uses peripheral vision and normal vision for visual cues to correctly place objects in the visual field. Panoramic movies allow viewers to stand in one place and revolve the visual field around them so they can observe a full 360 degrees of a room or scene (see Fig. 8–21). The image can be zoomed in and out to study small details. The image clarity is dependent upon the resolution of the original photographs and the amount of compression of the files when the software stitches the images. The images must be produced with a camera that is leveled to the horizon and is set to overlap from image to image at exactly the right spacing.

Some VR technologies will allow the viewer to move the view up and down to 360 degrees in the vertical axis. The PanoMetric camera (www.panoscan.com/PanoMetric) allows the user to take accurate measurements of any scene, indoors or out.

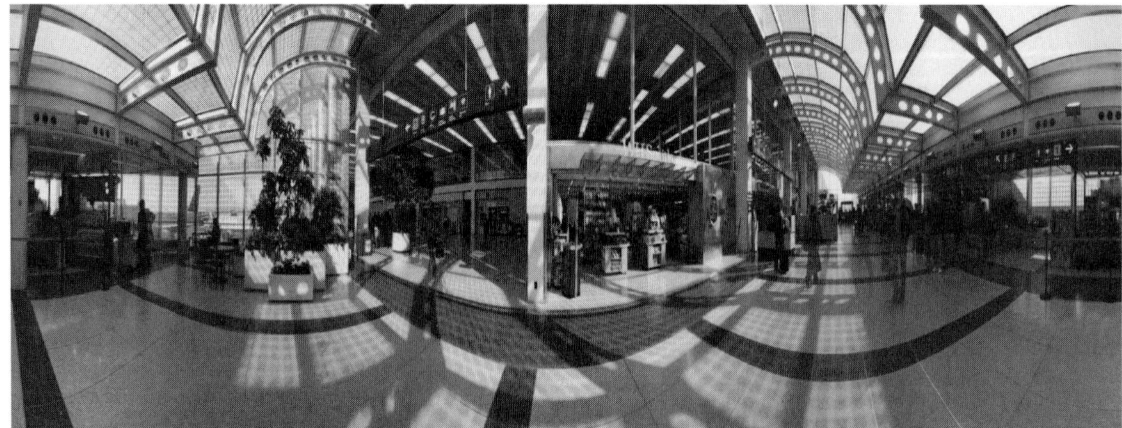

FIGURE 8–21 This VR panorama was made from 16 wide-angle images taken at one of the concourses of O'Hare Airport near Chicago. *Source:* Sandy Weiss/Packer Engineering.

Tactical VR studies for malls, schools, office buildings, hospitals, and so on are produced commercially. Police and fire department personnel use these to see the actual places they have to reach before entering the facilities. If a VR study of a facility or scene is done at the time of an accident or crime, people will be able to see and walk through the location the way it appeared at the time the images were taken, no matter what changes occur at a later date.

VR tours of any 3-D object can be produced. The tours can be as simple as one row of images around a subject, or they can be multilevel to show a subject from different elevations.

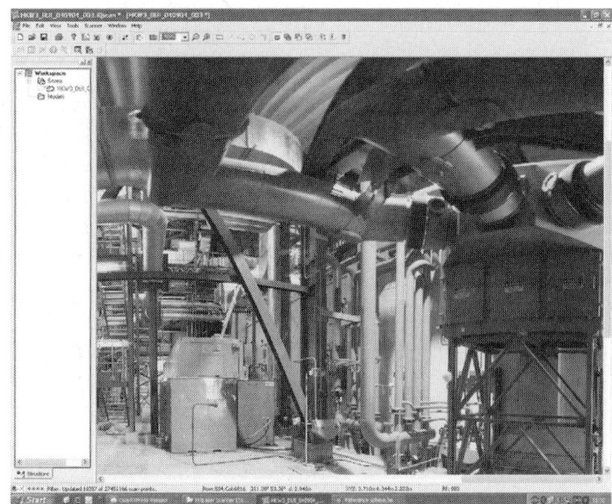

FIGURE 8–23 Color point cloud. *Source:* Faro.

LASER SCANNING

A 3-D laser scanner documents and analyzes objects or scenes and collects data on their shape and size. The FARO Laser Scanner (see Fig. 8–22) uses phase-shift technology in the creation of photorealistic 3-D images. The scanner produces 3-D black-and-white images where every pixel has an X, Y, and Z coordinate in space. For enhanced realism, it is also possible to add color (see Fig. 8–23) to the pixels by exposing simultaneous digital images with a Nikon DSLR camera and ultrawide-angle lens. Measurements can be made directly in the point cloud and 3-D objects can be generated, creating dimensionally accurate CAD models.

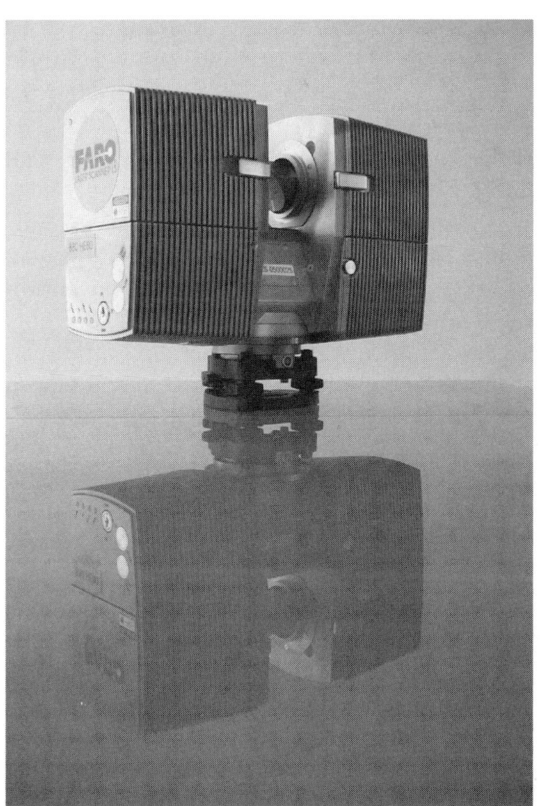

FIGURE 8–22 Faro phase-shift laser scanner. *Source:* Faro.

In less than 60 seconds, the scanner can take an 8 Mp scan of a scene. This is more than a hundred times faster than conventional scanners, which dramatically reduces the time needed for capturing data on site.

With some measurement technologies, it is necessary for an operator to enter the scene to take measurements. In some cases, evidence may be accidentally touched or moved. Laser scanners are non-contact devices, working totally from outside the scene, and do not interfere with the object(s) being scanned. This makes the technology ideal for evidence preservation. Another of their assets is that they can be used indoors as well as outdoors, day or night, in marginal lighting conditions.

Line-of-sight scanners document everything (see Fig. 8–24), in contrast to mechanical measuring devices that require the investigator to know exactly what needs to be documented and measured.

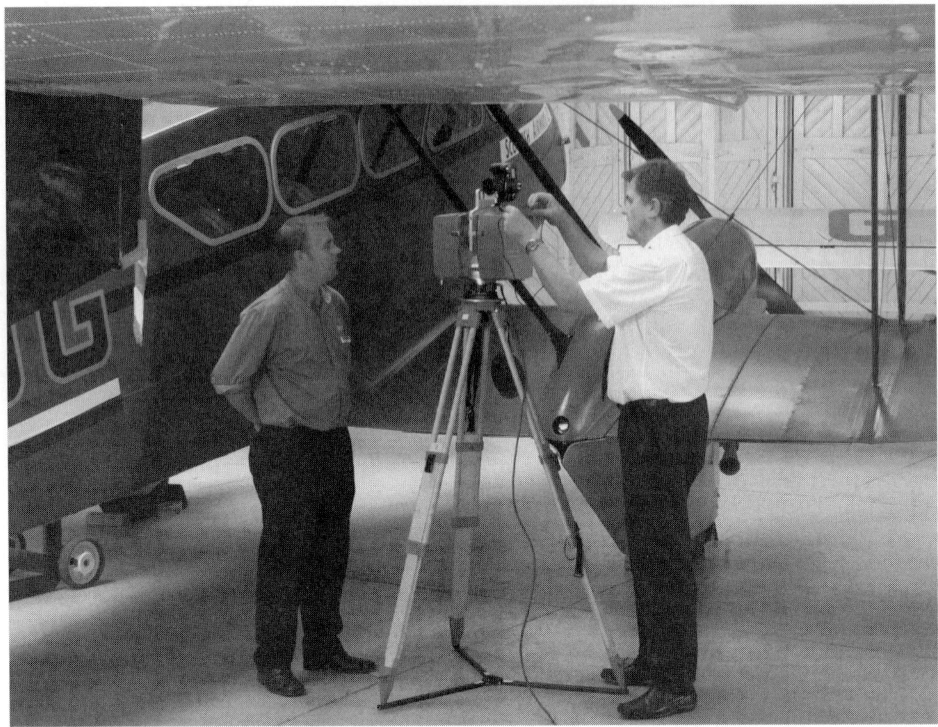

FIGURE 8–24 Setting up a laser scanner. *Source:* Faro.

3-D INFORMATION FOR ANALYSIS

Most 3-D images may be used for display or analysis. Most images captured for 3-D display will yield some quantitative data when subjected to analysis. It is also possible to use 3-D images that are captured for analysis for different types of display. The 3-D images that are captured specifically for analysis will yield the best accuracy if they are captured correctly for a specific purpose.

See "Photogrammetry" in Chapter 4.

SKETCHES IN 3-D DOCUMENTATION

In *Techniques of Crime Scene Investigation*, Dr. Barry A. J. Fisher talks about the use of sketches for the documentation of crime scenes.[29] Crime scene sketches, which require skill on the part of the investigator, are illustrative diagrams that more or less accurately depict the appearance of the scene. They are usually drawn by the same person doing the scene photography but often require more than one person to create them, with one person doing the actual drawing and one person taking measurements.

Sketches are meant to supplement photographs. Items must be located within the sketch, and measurements must be taken from known reference points. All evidence manual authors agree that an investigator must be careful and patient to create an accurate sketch. It is also absolutely critical to be sure to document references and measurements in 3-D space. Absolutely no crime or accident scene is two-dimensional.

Sketches and notes must be preserved for documentation and location of reference points and base measurements. If sufficient references and measurements exist, the analysis of the scene image may be performed photogrammetrically and can also be proven in court to be more accurate than handmade measurements. Handmade measurements are subject to human error, but the demonstration of mathematical principles and the production of reference items that are both measured from the photos and measured from the actual scene cannot be found to be in error.

Prior to the invention of photogrammetric software, it was necessary to use the perspective method of photogrammetry to derive measurements when only a single photograph of something existed (see Fig. 4–2). If stereo pairs of images were available, an analytical plotter could be used to derive quantitative information. With a computer and the proper software, it is now possible to derive accurate measurements from single or multiple photographs. (See Chapter 4 for instructions about proper image capture.)

SUMMARY

There can never be too much data. All 3-D information yields more data than does 2-D information. In many cases, 3-D imaging is as simple to accomplish as 2-D. Capturing only 2-D information for documentation amounts to leaving useable evidence behind.

All forensic disciplines have been impacted by 3-D technologies. Forensic photographers should be familiar and comfortable with the opportunities 3-D technologies offer for evidence documentation. Imaging in 3-D is necessary because it is expected, and 3-D documentation brought into the courtroom will find a willing audience.

CASE STUDY

ATV Accident on the Illinois Prairie Path

The Illinois Prairie Path is a network of approximately 61 miles of bicycle and pedestrian trails, predominantly in DuPage County, Illinois. Most of the route is built on the raised track-bed of the abandoned Chicago Aurora and Elgin Railroad right of way. The ties and rails have been removed and the bed is now a wide path of crushed limestone gravel of various sizes. Although the path is intended for non-motorized vehicles, the rules are easily and often broken by riders of motorized cycles, many of whom speed through sections late at night, lit only by their headlamps.

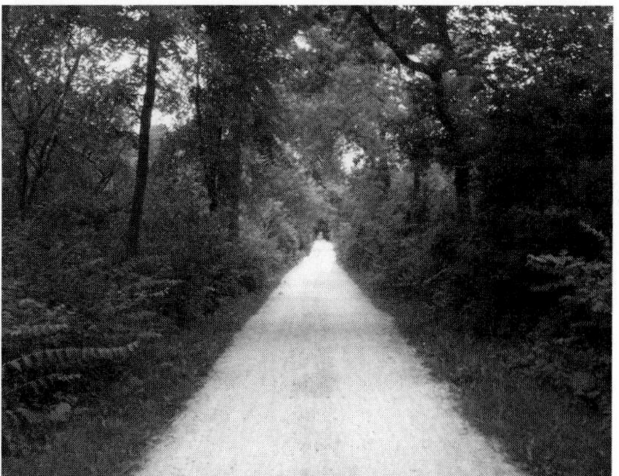

FIGURE 8–25 Prairie path and overhanging foliage. *Source:* Sandy Weiss.

An All-Terrain Vehicle (ATV) is a small, open, three or four wheeled, motorized cycle designed for off-road use. The Wisconsin Statutes, 1997–98, Volume 4, Chapter 340.01[2g], defines ATVs as engine-driven devices with a net weight of 650 pounds or less, a width of 48 inches or less, equipped with a seat designed to be straddled by the operator, steered with handlebars, and designed to travel on three or more low-pressure tires. The extra wheels, compared to standard two-wheeled motorcycles, are intended to provide enhanced stability at slow speeds.

On a bright, sunny, summer afternoon, a man riding an ATV sustained a permanently disabling injury when he drove off the side of a section of the path and his vehicle overturned. He filed suit against the manufacturer of the ATV, claiming the vehicle displayed a lack of suitable stability under normal operating conditions. The project assignment for me included the survey and photo-documentation of the scene of the accident to enable the accurate representation of the conditions of the location to the judge and jury at the ensuing trial.

In many places, the path is closely bordered on both sides with foliage (see Fig. 8–25) and the terrain profile is difficult to visualize and document. Accomplishing the scene survey was not an extraordinary problem, but photographs from ground level failed to display the magnitude of the dip from the old track-bed with sufficient detail to demonstrate why the vehicle may be

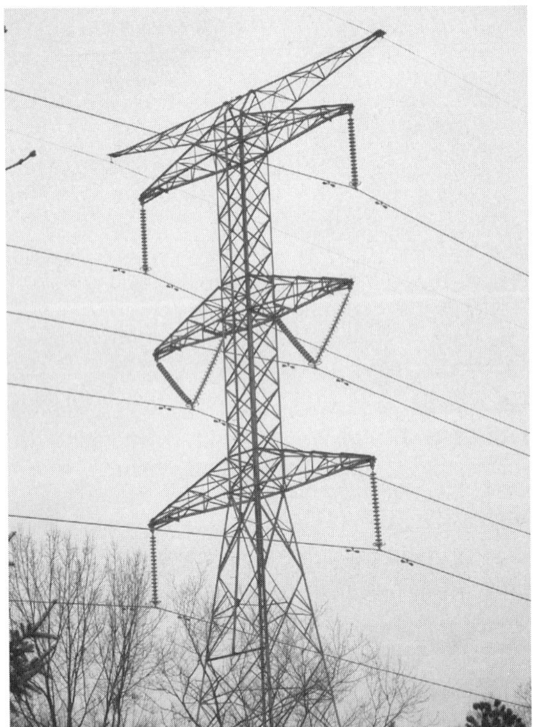

FIGURE 8–26 Commonwealth Edison Company high-tension towers. *Source:* Sandy Weiss.

expected to overturn. The decision was made to perform an aerial flyover with a light fixed-wing aircraft to expose stereo images of the scene to use in court.

The Commonwealth Edison Company maintains a network of high-tension power lines adjacent to the path at the location of the accident (see Fig. 8–26). The proximity of the lines prohibited the use of a low-altitude unmanned aircraft for the capture of the images.

The combination of the velocity of the moving aircraft and the use of a high-speed motor driven SLR camera provided a series of overlapping stereo-pair images of the scene. The viewer of the images is easily able to discern the severity of the terrain contour.

The aircraft used was a Cessna Cardinal (see Fig. 8–27). The choice of this aircraft is due to the high wing configuration, keeping the field of view unobstructed during oblique photography. In this case, however, the images needed to be exposed in plane view, from directly overhead. The aircraft was not fitted with a transparent window in the belly, and the windows could not be opened.

The photography was planned for summer, midafternoon on a partially overcast day. At that time of day the sunshine illuminated the area down the path from an approximately 45 degree angle and was the most advantageous lighting for the enhancement of the terrain contour. A Canon F1 camera with a 100 mm *f*/2.8 lens was used. The camera was fitted with an MD motor drive that exposed frames at a speed of 3.5 per second when set in continuous mode and the shutter speed was at 1/1000th of a second. The lens was fitted with an ultraviolet filter to eliminate any possible haze from the working altitude. Kodak Ektachrome, ASA 400 film was used as the media.

It was necessary for the pilot to locate the appropriate section of the path and then stand the plane on the starboard wingtip for the flyby, while keeping the flight-path directly over the section of the prairie path in question. The pilot was skillful. A rubber lens hood was placed on the UV filter on the lens to prevent the filter from directly contacting the Plexiglass window. The rubber hood ensured that the camera did not scratch the inside of the window during shooting.

Multiple flybys were performed, shooting only from west to east down the path. The consistent direction was used so the slides could be interchanged in the viewer in a fixed order to maintain the stereo viewing effect. Each member of the court was given a viewer and a set of slides. The slides were placed in the viewer in consecutive order. Slide 1 went into the left side and slide 2 went into the right side (see Fig. 8–28). After sufficient inspection, slide 1 was discarded and slide 2 was placed in the left side and slide 3 was placed in the right side. This system of viewing afforded the judge and jurors with a virtual tour in 3-D of the section of path where the accident occurred.

For those photographers who will be exposing images from a moving aircraft while

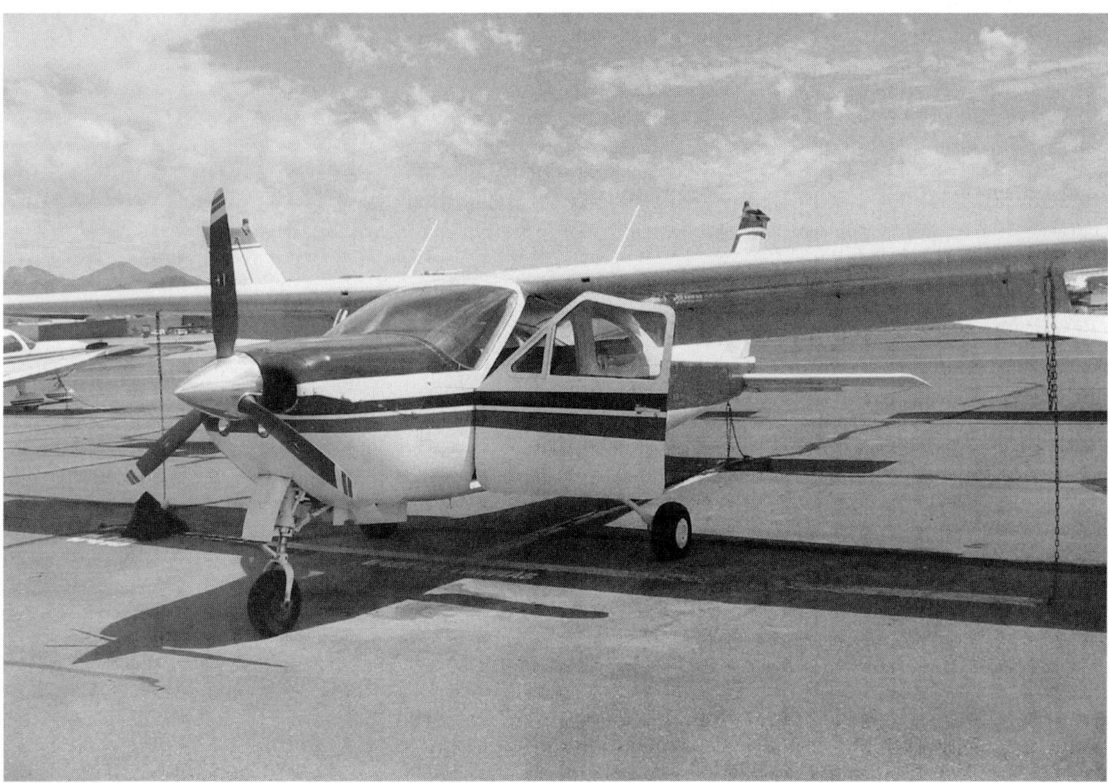

FIGURE 8–27 Cessna Cardinal used for aerial photography. *Source:* Sandy Weiss.

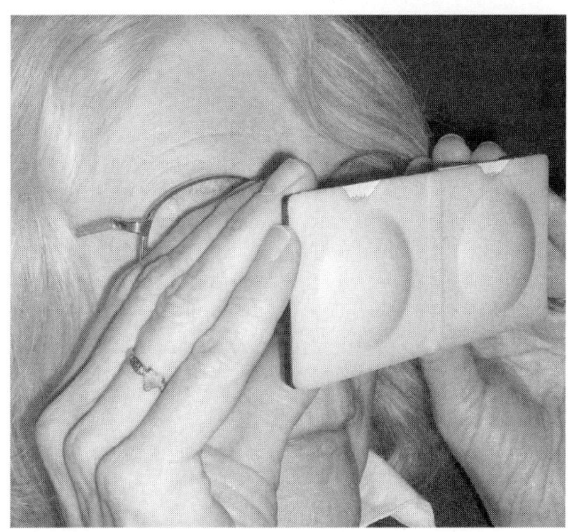

FIGURE 8–28 Stereo viewer for the viewing of individual slides into stereo-pairs. *Source:* Sandy Weiss.

looking through the viewfinder of a camera at a moving landscape, please be prepared for the feeling of nausea that will overcome you. It took me totally by surprise but I have found it to be a common malady among photographers performing this type of project.

From the results of the survey, an exemplar accident scene was constructed and stability testing was performed with different types of similar vehicles and anthropomorphic dummies for simulated riders. No vehicle and rider combination was able to traverse the accident terrain without turning over. The judge and jury were well educated. The plaintiff suit was lost.

KEY TERMS

stereoscopic/3-D photography, (p. 235)
camera obscura, (p. 236)
stereo camera, (p. 239)
beam splitter, (p. 240)
slide-rail, (p. 241)
scanning electron microscope (SEM), (p. 243)
scanning photomacrography, (p. 244)
lenticular, (p. 245)
anaglyph, (p. 245)
immersive and virtual reality, (p. 247)
virtual tour, (p. 247)

EXERCISES

1. Develop and maintain a list of networked contacts to help you during the documentation of evidence. Concentrate on skills you do not have. Maintain a list by expertise, location, availability, competence, and so on.
2. Download anaglyph software and practice constructing 3-D anaglyph images. Study the table of interocular separations and make necessary adjustments for the ease of image viewing.
3. Simulate a crime or accident scene in a location with hilly terrain and expose photographs in both 2-D and 3-D. Compare and contrast the results.
4. Find a reliable source and establish a collection of 3-D equipment.
5. For practice, expose stereo pairs of subject or exemplar evidence, scenes, macro images, and anything else relevant to your work. View the images with the proper viewing equipment to check your success.
6. Procure or assemble a slide rail for your camera.
7. Find and read articles about scanning macrophotography and decide if the technology would be useful in your work. Formulate a list of possible questions and/or problems.
8. Expose a series of images for the construction of a 360-degree panorama and stitch them together with available software.
9. Select a small object, for example a child's toy, that has a high relief to surface area ratio. The blue plastic camera and sheet-metal screw in Photo 8–29 are excellent choices.

   Support the subject under the camera lens at a 45-degree angle and expose a series of macrophotographs, using various focus depths, shutter speeds, and lens aperture combinations. Determine which image yields the best DoF (see Fig. 8–12 for a comparison). If none of your photos is an accurate representation of the subject, consider scanning.

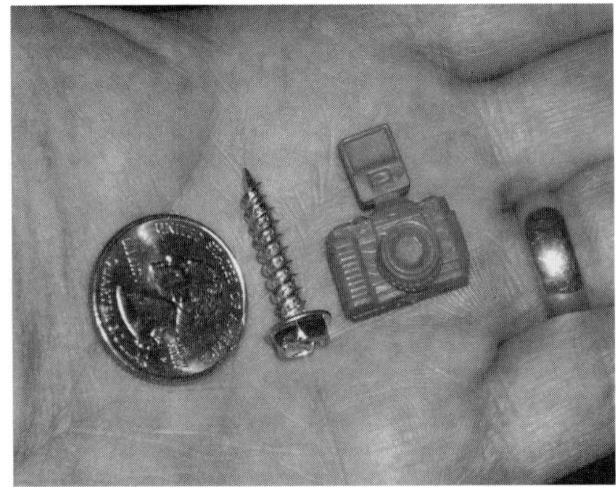

FIGURE 8–29 When photographed at oblique angles, photographs that are made by conventional methods of subjects with high relief-to-surface-area ratios will yield images with limited depth DoF. Scanning macrophotography provides unlimited DoF and is an appropriate option. *Source:* Sandy Weiss/Packer Engineering.

Chapter 9

Supplementary Lighting

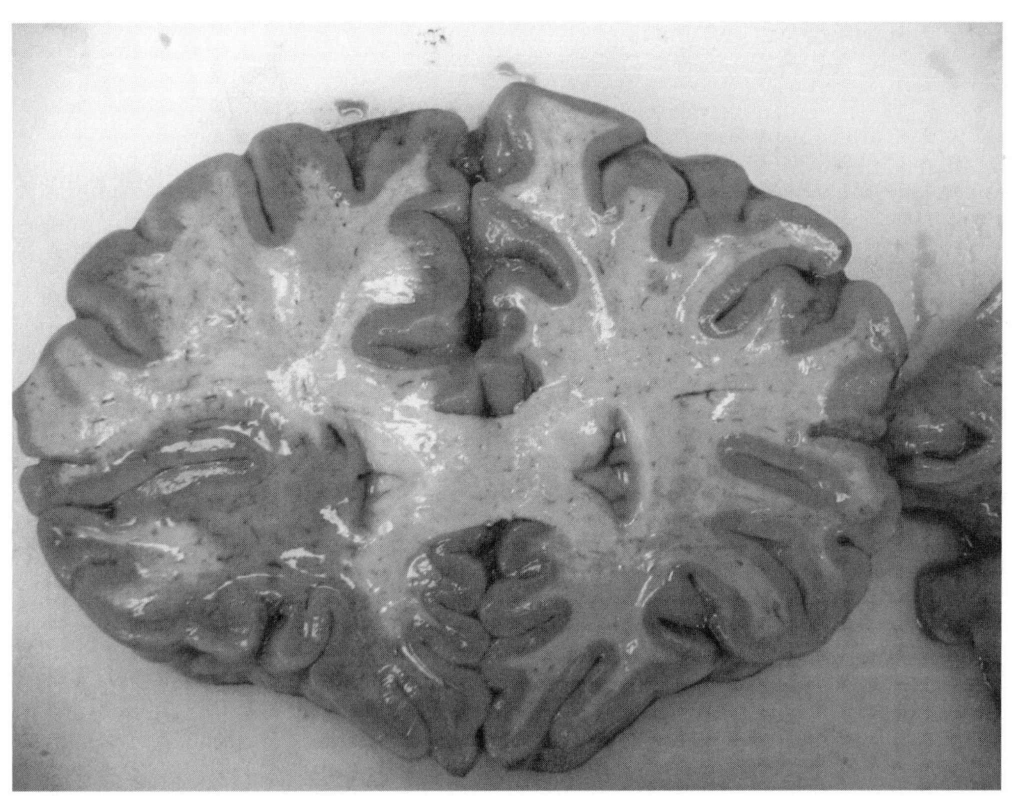

Learning Objectives

AFTER STUDYING THIS CHAPTER, YOU SHOULD BE ABLE TO:

1. Understand the different types of lighting available for photography
2. Understand the limitations and possibilities of supplementary lighting
3. Understand the need, use, and types of electronic flash
4. Understand and properly use the automation options of electronic flash
5. Properly set the camera to synchronize with the flash
6. Utilize a meter for flash
7. Differentiate the uses and limitations of built-in flashes
8. Minimize the limitations of flashes with digital cameras
9. Paint with light in large areas of low ambient light
10. Understand the types and uses of alternate light sources (ALS)
11. Properly use ultraviolet (UV) and infrared (IR) light sources

SUPPLEMENTARY PHOTOGRAPHIC LIGHTING

Instantaneous flash is a commonly used device to generate extra lighting for the exposure of photographs.

Flashbulbs

The earliest flashes were made from **flash powder**, ignited by hand while the camera shutter was held open. When magnesium foil **flashbulbs** were invented, they provided a safer replacement for powder. Bulbs are ignited at the time of the exposure when a contact in the camera shutter closes and a small electrical current is sent to the bulb. The foil ignites and creates a controlled flash. Bulbs can be used only once and then must be thrown away.

Flashbulbs have been used since the 1920s. The size of the bulb is proportional to its light output. Some bulbs have a blue coating on the glass (see Fig. 9–1). The coating provides explosion prevention, as well as lighting that is properly color balanced for color negative film. IR bulbs that create a flash that is invisible to the human eye are available for surveillance and wildlife photography.

Flashbulbs continue to be readily available and are used for some specialized purposes when other light sources are unavailable. The light output from flashbulbs is considerably longer in duration than from electronic flash. The longer burn duration may make images easier to see on

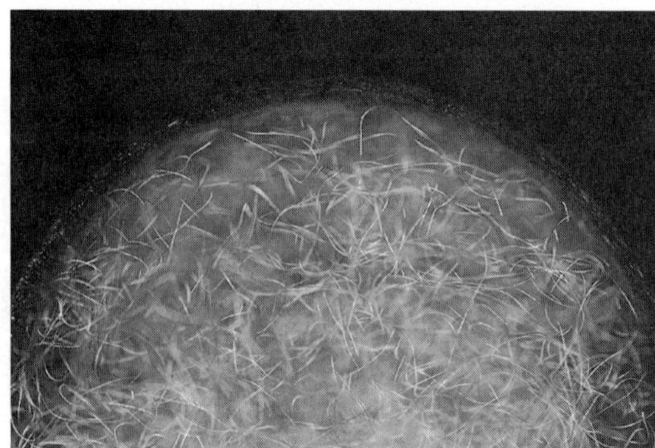

FIGURE 9–1 Blue flashbulbs are properly color balanced for use with color negative film. *Source:* Sandy Weiss/Packer Engineering.

a video when a burst of light is needed to key the start of a reconstructed event. When properly linked, a flashbulb array will produce the huge amount of light necessary for the proper exposure of extensive fire and accident scenes at night.

Electronic Flash

Today's electronic flash units (see Fig. 9–2) often contain a glass tube filled with xenon gas. Electricity of high voltage is discharged to generate an arc that emits a brief flash of light. Typical duration of the light burst is 1/1000 second or less. Electronic flashes are color balanced at 5,500 to 6,000 K, allowing their use with color media without a color correction filter.

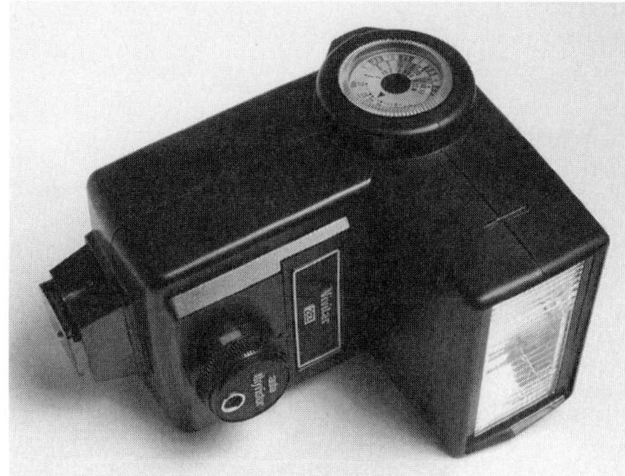

FIGURE 9–2 The ever-popular Vivitar 283 electronic flash unit. *Source:* Sandy Weiss/Packer Engineering.

INVERSE-SQUARE LAW

The intensity (or illuminance) of light from a point source is inversely proportional to the square of the distance from the source. An object of the same size, illuminated by the same lighting but twice as far from the source, receives only one-fourth the amount of light in the same time period (see Figs. 9–3 and 9–4).

Photographers use the **inverse-square law** to determine the optimal distance and location of flash units for proper illumination of a subject.

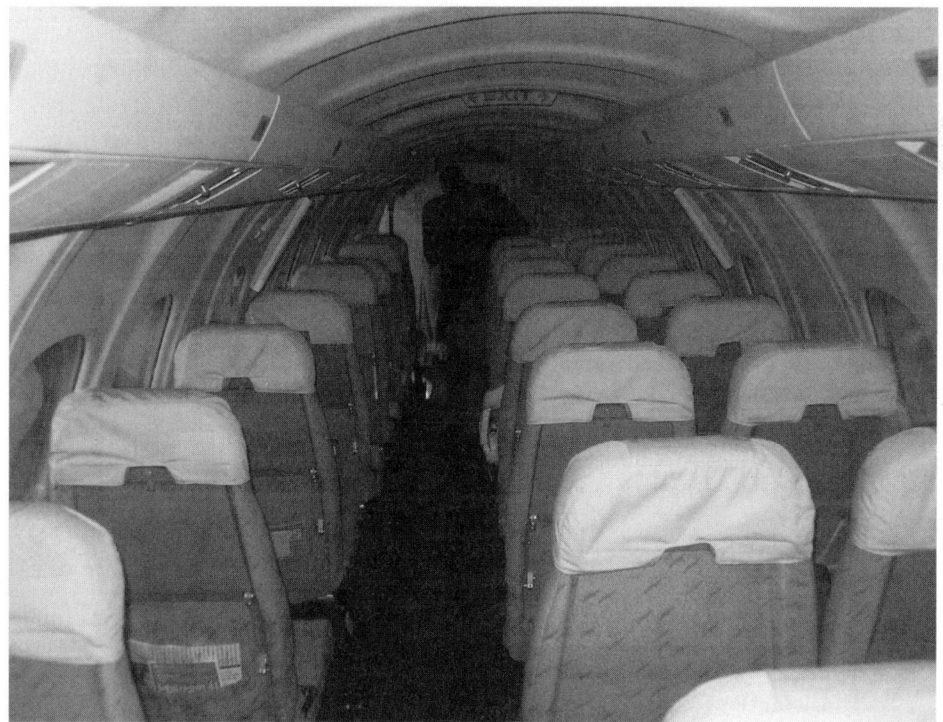

FIGURE 9–3 Flash fall-off inside a jet fuselage illustrates the inverse-square law. *Source:* Sandy Weiss/Packer Engineering.

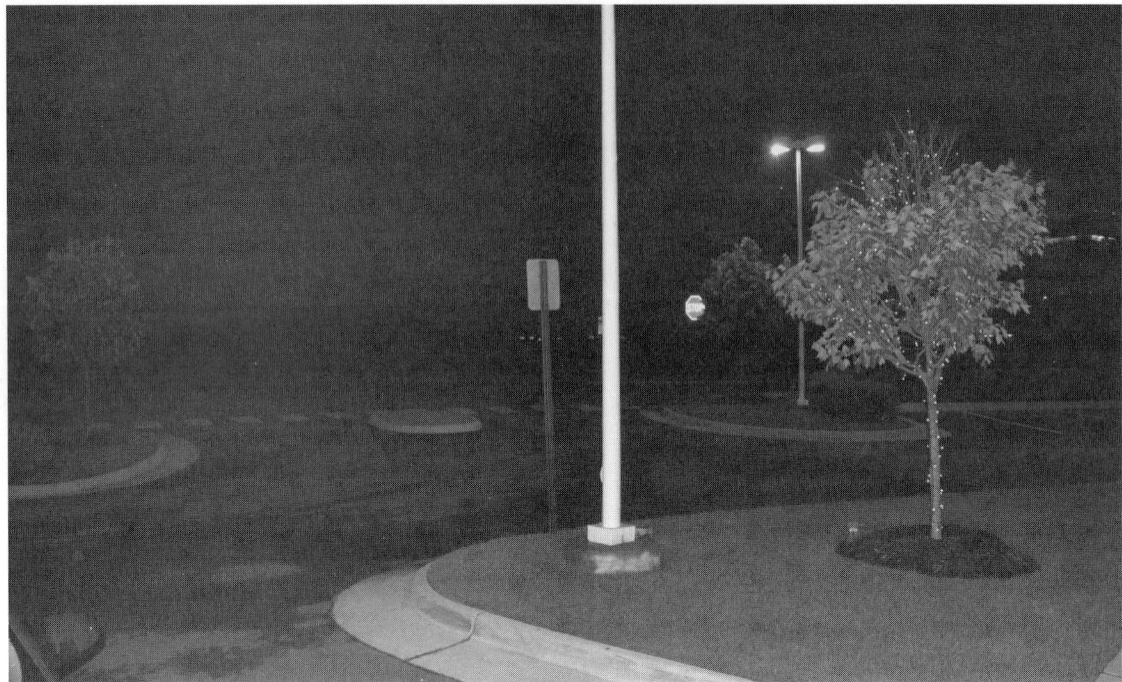

FIGURE 9–4 Flash fall-off outside at night. *Source:* Sandy Weiss/Packer Engineering.

The farther a subject is from a flash, the less exposure it will receive.

As for all forms of supplementary lighting, the most common use for electronic flash is to add to the illumination of subjects where the ambient lighting is insufficient to adequately expose the camera media in a reasonable length of time.

Flash circuitry is powered by a battery or alternate power source. The electricity is converted to high voltage (about 300 V) to charge a *capacitor*. This conversion makes the characteristic high-pitched whining noise when an electronic flash unit (EFU) is charging. The capacitor is connected to electrodes in the gas-filled glass tube. When the EFU fires, the capacitor discharges through the gas, emitting a bright light. After the flash event, the charging operation starts again, unless the EFU has been turned off.

CONTROLLING FLASH OUTPUT

In "automatic" flash units, the electrical discharge may be turned off before the point of maximum illumination. The flash emission is reduced either by electrical program or by a circuit that measures the light reflected back from the subject. If the subject is close to the flash, the EFU turns off quickly because it does not usually need all its power to create adequate illumination. In some flashes, the remaining capacity of the circuitry is dumped and the flash must recharge from the beginning before it can fire again.

Some modern automatic EFUs, include a thyristor in their discharge circuit. The **thyristor** switches off the discharge current when sufficient light has been emitted for the subject. Energy left in the capacitor is recycled and used for the next emission. This efficient power utilization conserves batteries and allows extended use of the EFU before power sources must be changed or recharged.

Some EFUs have variable power settings to limit the output power to one-half, one-quarter, one-eighth, and so on of maximum. These settings are used to vary the power output when the EFU is used on manual rather than automatic exposure.

In through-the-lens (TTL) camera systems, the photocell for measuring flash output, is located inside the camera, behind the lens. In film cameras, the TTL sensor measures the light that comes back from the subject and is reflected off the film. In digital cameras, the TTL circuitry is included on the image sensor. When sufficient light has been registered by the sensor, a signal is sent from the camera to the EFU to terminate the discharge. The advantage of TTL flash systems is that they are affected by the focal length of the lens used on the camera to make the exposure.

Built-in Electronic Flash Units

A small EFU is often built into modern digital cameras. Professional digital cameras also have a built-in capability for using a supplementary EFU when more light output is necessary. Supplementary EFUs may be mounted on a camera's accessory shoe (see Fig. 9–5), on a standard flash bracket, or in some other convenient way. The camera-to-flash communication method used to trigger and synchronize the flash event is dependent upon the type and brand of the camera and EFU.

Some **accessory shoes** are nothing more than a secure point of attachment for an EFU or other camera accessory. Some have an electrical contact in the center (hot shoe) that will trigger a flash event during a camera exposure if the EFU has a matching contact on the bottom and the EFU is charged and ready to fire. The most sophisticated hot shoes are dedicated to the brand and model of the camera. They have extra contacts, in addition to the firing contact, that allow communication between the camera and EFU.

Synchronization Speed

Leaf shutters are found in many point-and-shoot cameras. With leaf-shutter cameras, the built-in flash will fire and synchronize with the camera exposure at almost any shutter speed. Most SLR and DSLR cameras have focal-plane shutters. Flash synchronization with focal-plane shutters has a distinct speed limit for proper utilization of the flash lighting. If the shutter speed is set too high, the shutter will open and close before or during the flash event. This will yield images that are either totally or partially unexposed.

The EFU must be fired at a sufficiently slow shutter speed to include a period of time during which the whole image is open to the flash. The highest speed at which this is possible is referred to as the **synchronization speed** of the camera.

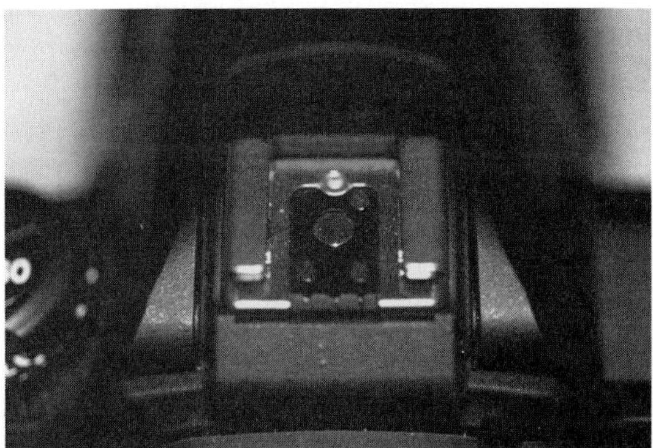

FIGURE 9–5 Dedicated hot accessory shoe on the top of a Nikon D-70S. *Source:* Sandy Weiss/Packer Engineering.

Studio Lighting

Studio lighting may be *continuous incandescent or instantaneous flash.*

Continuous Incandescent Studio Lighting

With incandescent photo-flood lighting, the photographer is able to see the result of the lighting before the time of the exposure. It is possible to re-arrange the lighting to eliminate distracting shadows and highlights before exposing images.

One drawback to photo-flood lighting is that it produces heat that can be detrimental to the subject and the photographer. When making videos, continuous lighting is usually the only practical supplementary lighting solution. When making videos at high frame-rates for motion analysis, more light is necessary for proper exposure. With high- speed video (HSV) cameras, the light must often be close to the camera and subject. When the lighting is close, the heat may be an issue. Remember to keep backgrounds and diffusers a reasonable distance from the lighting. The photographer's clothing and skin may also be at risk to the heat.

Most incandescent (tungsten) lighting is NOT balanced to daylight color temperature. Some blue (daylight corrected) photo-flood lighting is available, but only in limited sizes and intensities. Remember to use the proper color correction filtration to match the media or to set the media at the temperature of the lighting.

Tungsten filaments have a color temperature of about 3200 degrees K. When film or sensor is daylight balanced, and the lighting is 3200, a blue filter must be used on the camera. The filtration absorbs much of the light and makes focusing difficult. It also requires the lens aperture to be opened 2 full stops, or the shutter speed or frame rate to be reduced by 2 stops.

One possible solution to the color match issue is to use tungsten balanced color film or set the camera sensor to 3200 with tungsten lighting. Digital still or video cameras may also be white balanced for a specific lighting. Situational white balancing is the best solution because the color of incandescent lighting changes gradually, becoming warmer through use and age. Only automated white balancing will track the changes and maintain accuracy.

Instantaneous Flash Studio Lighting

Studio flashes are often large, free-standing units, used two or three at a time for the exposure of large areas. They are powered by electric current (AC) or battery packs (DC). Multiple flashes are synchronized with the camera shutter by cable, radio transmitter, or light-sensitive slave unit. One of the main advantages of studio flashes over the use of multiple, camera-size EFUs, is the availability of a modeling lamp. Many high-end OEM EFUs are designed to operate in tandem for the exposure of large areas. This solution is often expensive to buy and possibly complicated to set up and compute exposure. **Slave flash units** fire remotely, by registering the light from another flash. Slave flashes are synchronized at the speed of light to the camera. The use of slaves is often useful in macrophotography (see Chapter 10).

Modeling Lamp

A continuously illuminated modeling lamp built into studio flash units remains illuminated until or even during the flash exposure. Because of the position of the modeling lamp, it delivers an accurate indication of the angle and quality that the flash(es) will produce when fired. Modeling lights help during lighting setup because unwanted reflections and shadows are obvious and may be eliminated.

Studio Flash Power

Modern studio flash units have very high power output, far higher than the built-in or top-mounted EFUs available for modern cameras. The power of an EFU is measured in watt/seconds (w/s) or joules and is usually indicated within the name or classification of the flash. A 500 w/s unit is half the power of a 1,000 w/s unit. An increase from 500 to 1,000 w/s is equivalent to an increase of one f-stop in exposure. Using the mathematics of the inverse-square law, if a flash head is 1 meter from the subject, the imaging sensor sensitivity is ISO 100, and the lens aperture is *f*/11; moving the head to 2 meters will take the exposure to *f*/5.6, or two f-stops less lighting.

Consumer-grade studio flashes usually include built-in synchronization circuitry in each of the flash heads. Larger, more professional units usually have the circuitry built into a controller or power-pack component.

Flash Techniques

Many photographic situations require the use of supplementary lighting. EFUs are the most common, convenient, and color-accurate types of lighting available to the forensic photographer. Once the photographer learns the advantages and limitations of a built-in or accessory EFU, the range of lighting situations for successfully illuminated images increases markedly.

A mistake often made by inexperienced evidence photographers is to rely too heavily on flash power and camera exposure automation. Judging the exposure in a flash event is no simpler than judging the exposure in ambient lighting. If the extra darkness of a fire scene is not correctly compensated for and programmed into the equipment by the photographer, the camera and flash may yield underexposed images (see Fig. 9–6).

Bright sunshine is high in contrast and will often produce photographs with dark shadows. Thus, the use of an EFU outdoors on sunny days is a normal and recommended procedure. Be sure to use the EFU at a range within which it has sufficient power to affect the subject (see Fig. 9–7).

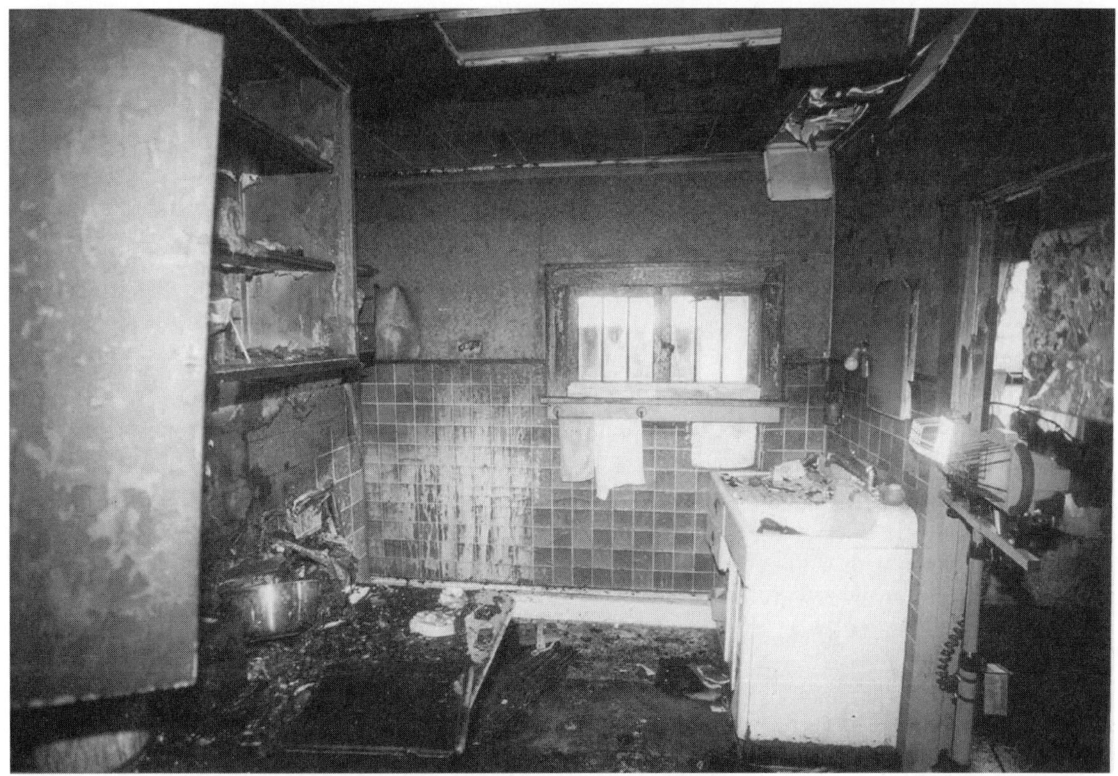

FIGURE 9–6 This underexposure occurred when using an EFU on automatic setting in a fire-darkened room. *Source:* Robert Russell/Packer Engineering.

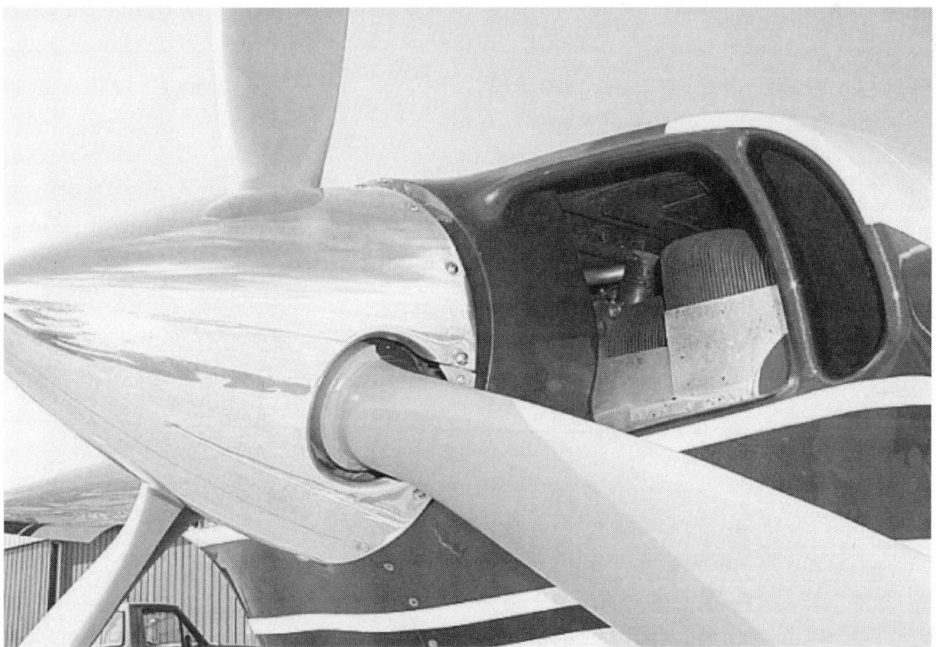

FIGURE 9–7 EFU used on sunny day showing detail in a deeply shadowed area. *Source:* Sandy Weiss/Packer Engineering.

FLASH METERS

Flash meters (see Figs. 9–8 and 9–9) measure light emitted from EFUs in a manner similar to the way in which ambient meters measure ambient light. All modern flash meters can also be used to measure the intensity of ambient lighting. Some flash meters have a place to plug in the EFU trigger cable so the flash can be triggered when a firing button is pushed on the meter. This allows the photographer to place the meter close to the subject and measure the flash output from the subject position.

Sekonic L508 II

The Sekonic L508 II is a popular example of a modern flash meter with a built-in spot meter and incident meter (see Fig. 9–8).

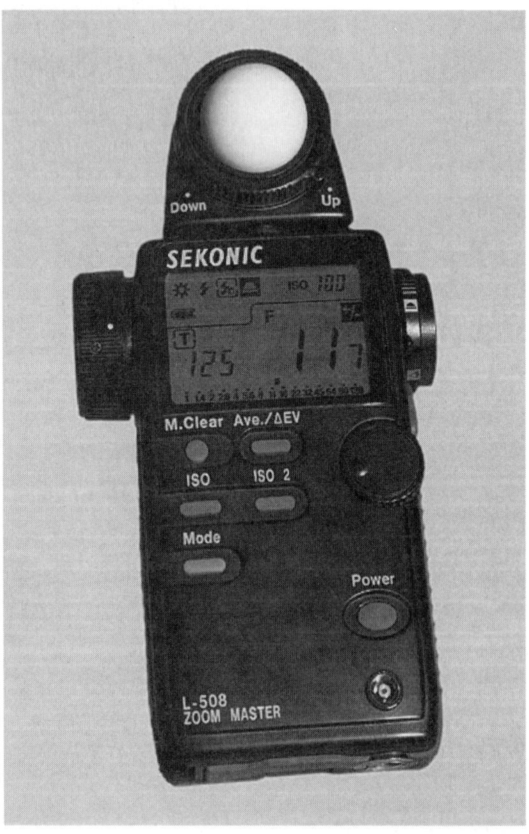

FIGURE 9–8 The Sekonic L508 II combination flash and ambient meter. *Source:* Sandy Weiss/Packer Engineering.

The L508 includes the following:

- A 1-degree reflective spot meter that can be widened continuously to 4 degrees
- A lever to change the meter to incident reading
- Corded or cordless flash meter function, in reflective or incident modes
- Cumulative measurements of up to nine flash events
- LCD readout that auto-illuminates when ambient light level is low
- Display including f-stops from *f*/1 to *f*/128 and shutter speeds from 30 minutes to 1/8,000 second
- Frame speeds from 2 to 360 frames per second (fps) for cinematographers and videographers
- ISO range from 3 to 8,000

Sekonic L-308S Flashmate

The Sekonic L-308S (see Fig. 9–9) is a less-expensive, lighter-weight meter than the L-508. It measures ambient light or flash exposure by incident or reflective metering modes.

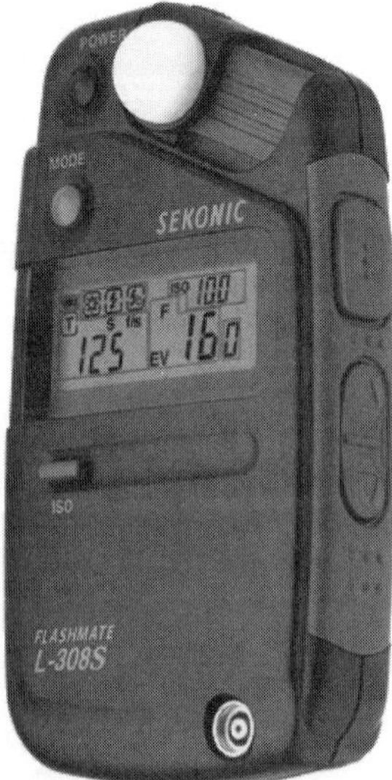

FIGURE 9–9 The Sekonic L-308S Flashmate, with combination flash and ambient meter. *Source:* Sandy Weiss/Packer Engineering.

The L-308 includes the following:

- Built-in sliding lumisphere for selection of incident or reflected light measurements
- Corded or cordless flash meter function, in reflective or incident modes
- Mode selector button for flash or ambient mode setting
- Full, one-half, and one-third stop settings
- Frame speeds from 8 to 128 fps for cinematographers and videographers

FLASH GUIDE NUMBERS

The light burst from an EFU is short in duration, usually lasting about 1/500 to 1/50,000 second. **Guide numbers (GNs)** describe the power of the light output. The higher the GN, the greater the light output.

Because of the inverse-square rule, the farther the subject is from the EFU, the higher the necessary level of illumination for proper exposure. If the power of the flash is constant, it is necessary to use larger and smaller lens apertures as the distance between the EFU and the subject changes. The shutter speed of the camera should always be set at the fastest possible speed for proper synchronization. This will limit the effect of ambient illumination during the flash event. It will then limit the problems caused by exposure from variable light sources.

GNs are derived from the ratio of the output of the EFU to the ISO speed of the media. The higher the GN, the higher the quantity of light the EFU produces. GNs are used to calculate lens apertures when using EFUs in manual exposure mode. When making images of subjects with average reflectance, dividing the flash-to-subject distance into the GN indicates the correct aperture. For example, a flash with a GN of 80 with ISO 100 will produce a correct exposure at 10 feet at an aperture of *f*/8.

All flashes indicate a GN that is used for assessment of their relative power. By convention, the GN for any particular flash is computed for ISO 100. GN is determined by multiplying the flash-to-subject distance by the f-stop required for a correct exposure of the subject at that distance. By convention, 10 feet is the normal distance.

A flash meter is used for calculations. If the meter is positioned 10 feet from the flash, the meter is set at ISO 100 and *f*/8 is indicated from a flash event:

$$\text{GN} = \text{f-stop} \times \text{distance},$$
$$\text{so GN} = 8 \times 10 \text{ feet},$$
$$\text{or GN} = 80$$

GNs have two uses:

1. If the flash is in manual mode, a subject is a particular number (X) feet from the flash, and ISO 100 is being used, divide the distance X into the GN to determine an appropriate aperture for a trial exposure.
2. If you are considering the purchase of a flash and want to know how powerful it will be, the GN allows a comparison of one flash to another.

FILL FLASH

Fill flash is used to fill in a subject's shadow area with light, thereby reducing contrast. When the main light illuminating a scene is the sun, or any other bright light source, the dark shadows produced may often be lightened and the image contrast reduced by using an EFU for fill flash lighting (see Fig. 9–10).

When using an EFU for fill lighting, the flash should normally be set on manual exposure mode. When filling shadows, the EFU should supply enough illumination to lighten the shadows but not add further noticeable illumination to the highlights. This technique is one of the best, easiest, and safest ways to increase the dynamic range of an image. If the EFU only outputs its maximum illumination when it is set on manual, the output may possibly overexpose the highlights or the whole image. In general, it is suggested to reduce the flash output by 50% to 75% from maximum, depending upon the situation.

In some situations, it may be possible to set the EFU on automatic exposure and allow the camera meter and flash circuitry to assess and set the proper exposure. If using automatic exposure

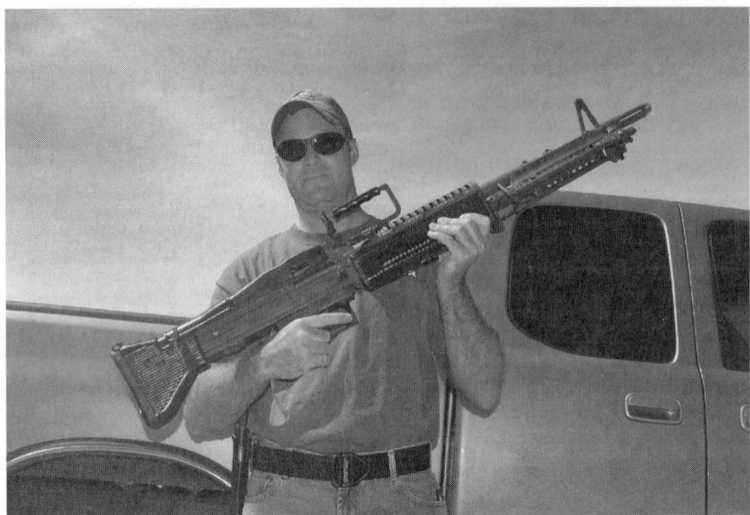

FIGURE 9–10 Fill flash on sunny day showing overall lightening of a back-lit scene. *Source:* Constance Rohrer, Evidence Forensics Photography.

and flash, the flash must be sufficiently close to the subject to allow the camera or flash-sensing circuitry to read the exposure and properly terminate the flash event before the highlights become overexposed.

Exposure Settings for Fill Flash

With point-and-shoot cameras, the flash menu may contain a dedicated fill flash mode. With DSLRs that have built-in pop-up flash, the instruction manual may explain the correct method for setting the mode and power of the flash.

> **TIP:**
>
> When using an EFU for fill, remember to adjust the flash exposure, not the camera meter exposure. Fill flash should do nothing to change the overall exposure. It is intended only to lighten the shadows and reduce the subject brightness range.

In-Camera Flash Problems

The EFUs built into digital cameras often have the following characteristics:

- They are inflexible in output and directionality.
- They are low in output and insufficient for subjects more than 10 feet away, especially when outdoors or in large rooms.
- They are often placed in the wrong position for optimum lighting.
- They cause glare and subsequent underexposure of reflective surfaces (see Fig. 9–11).
- They cause red eye (see "Red Eye") in living subjects because the flash is in close proximity to the camera lens. The illumination bounces off the retinas of the subject and makes the eyes look red in the resultant image.
- They drain battery power.
- They fire when unwanted.

The small flash built into most digital cameras (see Fig. 9–12) is always situated too close to the camera lens. This creates disadvantages for the built-in flash as a light source in evidence photography. Although the built-in may be too small for many normal subjects, it can be useful for close-up subjects. Be aware that the built-in flash may produces flat lighting from highly reflective, shiny surfaces (see Fig. 9–13 and 9–14). The lens or lens hood may get in the way of the flash and create a

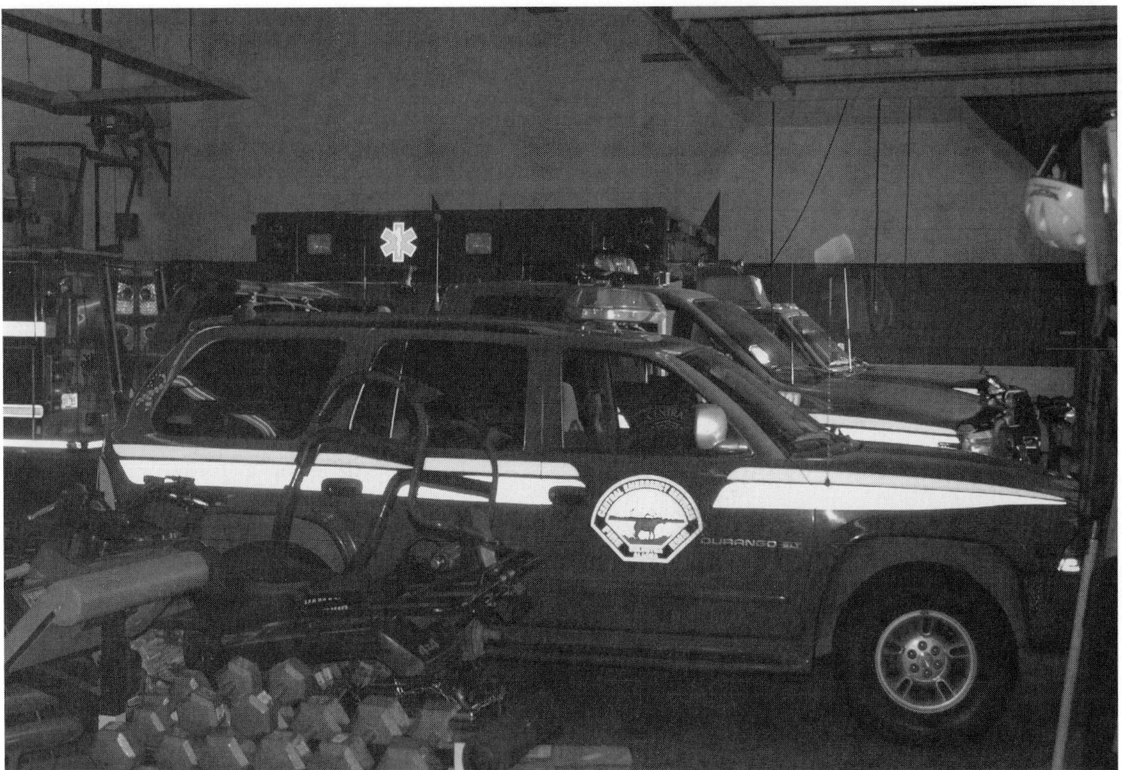

FIGURE 9–11 Underexposure due to the reflective subject. *Source:* Sandy Weiss/Packer Engineering.

shadow. The top of an image may be brighter than the bottom because the flash is situated high on the camera (see Fig. 9–15) This occurs especially often in close-up photographs.

If a subject is highly reflective, the camera should be held at a slightly oblique angle to the subject when using the built-in flash illumination for the main light source. This will

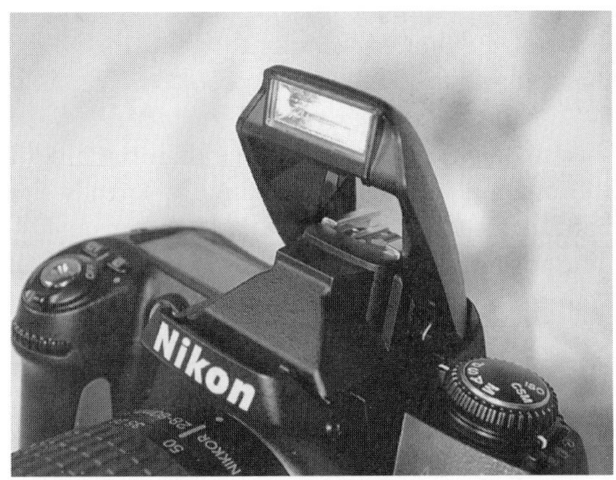

FIGURE 9–12 Built-in pop-up flash. *Source:* Sandy Weiss/Packer Engineering.

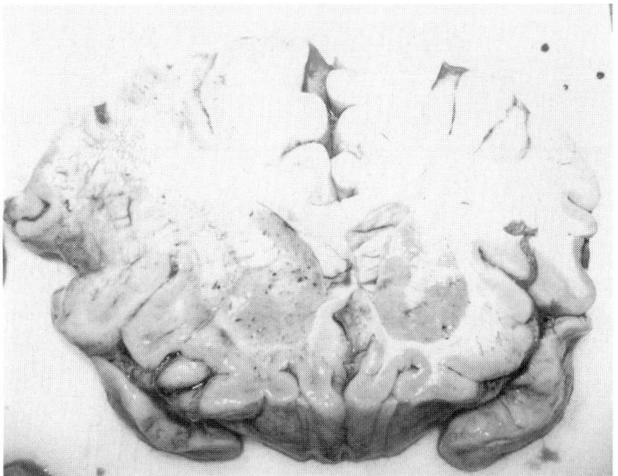

FIGURE 9–13 Overexposed image of a brain caused by light reflected from direct, built-in flash. *Source:* Dodge County, Wisconsin, Medical Examiner's Office.

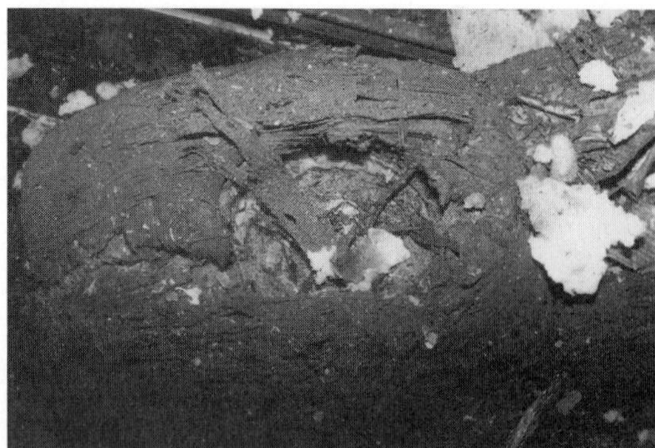

FIGURE 9–14 Inconsistently exposed image due to top-mounted flash. *Source:* Sandy Weiss/Packer Engineering.

eliminate most of the problems of reflection (see Fig. 9–16).

Deflecting the Built-in Flash

If the photographer uses the built-in flash to trigger other flashes, the flash must fire to be of any use. If the subject is close to the camera position, the built-in flash may improperly illuminate and adversely affect the image.

The built-in flash output can be deflected by using a piece of opaque cardboard or plastic attached to the front of the flash at an angle with tape or Velcro. The light output can then be used only to trigger the slave. The camera's accessory shoe often makes a good anchoring device for the deflector. Some deflectors are marketed as ready-made gadgets for this purpose. It may be necessary to purchase an extrasensitive flash slave sensor for this purpose if the slave flash is being used in bright ambient lighting.

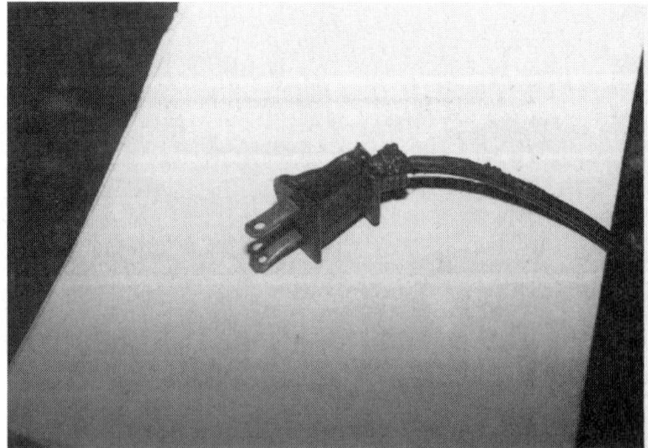

FIGURE 9–15 Underexposed and inconsistently exposed image due to light, reflective background, and built-in flash. *Source:* Sandy Weiss/Packer Engineering.

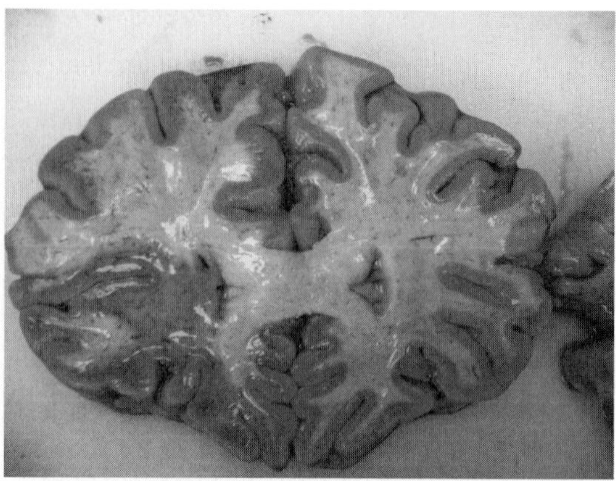

FIGURE 9–16 Properly exposed (with oblique flash) image of a brain. *Source:* Dodge County, Wisconsin, Medical Examiner's Office.

Diffusing the Built-in Flash

The small flash built in to most digital cameras is placed close to the camera lens. This often creates disadvantages for its use as a technical light source. The flash may be too small for normal photography. It may be useful for close-up work, but it can produce a flat light that is highly reflective from shiny surfaces. The flash is also badly placed because the lens or hood may get in the way and, because of the limited working distance, the image may be brighter on top than on bottom.

A **flash diffuser** is used to shine the light forward but off a larger surface than the one in the built-in flash. The attachment spreads the light so it is lower in contrast and softer in quality. The advantages include the following:

- Lightening of dark shadows
- Reduction of bright reflections
- Easily used, transportable, inexpensive
- Interchangeable from camera to camera if properly made
- Easily replaceable if lost or damaged

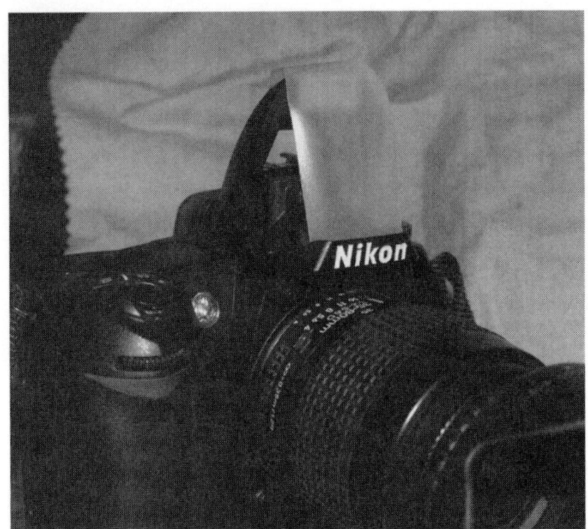

FIGURE 9–17 Flash diffuser made from a plastic milk jug. *Source:* Sandy Weiss/Packer Engineering.

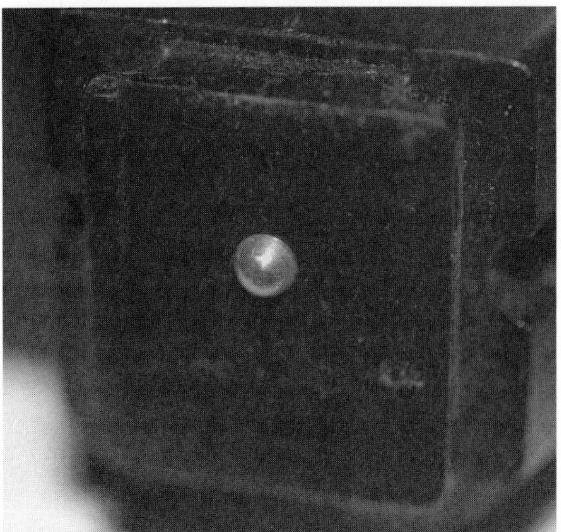

FIGURE 9–18 Contact on the bottom of a Vivitar 283. *Source:* Sandy Weiss/Packer Engineering.

It is simple to create a flash diffuser from a variety of materials. The flash diffuser in Figure 9–17 was cut from a plastic milk jug. A small, inexpensive, lightweight, and convenient piece of plastic can make a large difference in the quality of close-up photos.

Electronic Flash Trigger Voltage

Most digital cameras have a hot accessory shoe, but some have no other synchronization outlet to connect the camera to an accessory EFU. Before connecting an EFU onto the shoe of a modern digital camera, it is necessary to determine if the EFU has a safe **trigger voltage** (internal voltage the flash generates before it flashes) for the camera.

Some older EFUs have trigger voltages between 200 and 400 volts in their hot shoe or synchronization socket. If applied to a DSLR's flash synchronization socket, that level of voltage may damage the camera circuitry.

> **TIP:**
>
> The maximum safe trigger voltage for most modern digital cameras is 6 volts.

Checking Trigger Voltage

If possible, consult the EFU manufacturer to determine the trigger voltage. If that is not possible, use a voltmeter with an input impedance of 10 megohms or greater and check the voltage yourself. With the EFU turned on, the voltage is read by putting the voltmeter leads onto the two contacts of the hot shoe section of the flash. The center pin on the bottom (see Fig. 9–18) is usually the positive contact and the contact on the side (see Fig. 9–19) is negative. The voltmeter contacts are red for positive and black for negative.

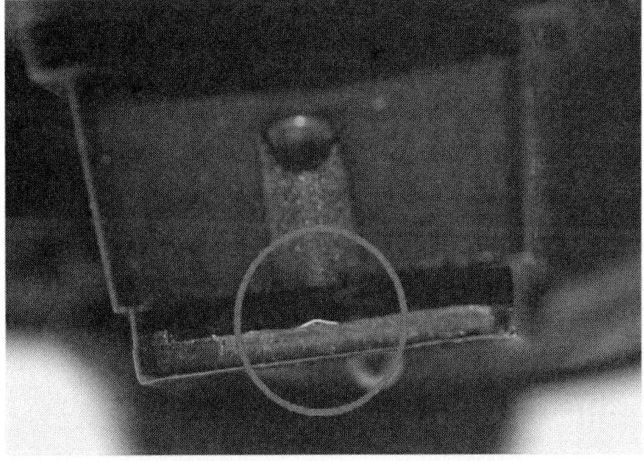

FIGURE 9–19 Contact on the side of a Vivitar 283. *Source:* Sandy Weiss/Packer Engineering.

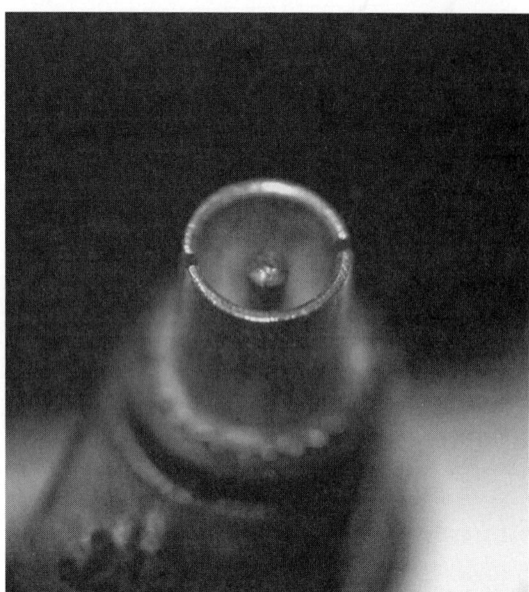

FIGURE 9–20 A PC connector contact. *Source:* Sandy Weiss/Packer Engineering.

If the negative contact of the flash is difficult to access, the voltage can be measured from the pin on the end of the PC synchronization cord. The outer part of the PC connector is negative, and the center pin is positive (see Fig. 9–20).

When the meter touches both contacts, the trigger voltage can be read on the meter. If the voltage is more than 6 volts, the flash must not be connected directly to the camera. One solution to the voltage problem is to trigger the flash without connecting it to the camera. This can be accomplished by using a photoelectric slave. Attach a slave to the synchronization of the EFU, and it will trigger the flash when another flash fires.

Some after-market adapters mount onto most digital camera hot shoes, connect to the flash, and bring the trigger voltage to a safe level.

Built-in Flash for Macrophotography

If the built-in flash is too bright for close-up photography, using a diffuser may bring the output down to a tolerable range. High flash output requires small lens apertures, which are necessary to maximize DoF.

Ring Flash or Macro Flash

A **ring flash** or **macro flash** attaches to the front of the lens and is intended strictly for close-up photography. These may consist of one or more flash tubes. If it has multiple tubes, some may be turned on or off or reduced in power individually. Some ring flashes have modeling lights to aid in low-light focusing. The light from these units is multidirectional and low contrast.

Painting with Light

Some scenes and/or objects are too large to be illuminated by a single flash event. If a photographer is working alone and has only one flash for the project, and the ambient light level is low, it may be possible to use the single flash for multiple exposures of the large subject. Painting with light may be used outdoors (see Fig. 9–21) and in large interior areas, such as parking garages, gymnasiums, and theaters (see Fig. 9–22).

The technique of **painting with light** involves mounting a camera on a tripod, focusing on the subject or area, and opening the shutter of the camera for as long as it takes to walk the entire object or scene while firing a handheld flash unit multiple times to illuminate the entire object or scene sufficiently for a proper exposure. Using multiple flash exposures allows the use of small apertures, making the DoF sufficient for the entire scene.

Steps for Painting with Light

1. Mount the camera on a tripod.
2. Use a relatively high ISO setting (400 to 800).
3. Use a normal or wide lens. Field-of-view is controlled by the angle of view of the lens.
4. Position the camera to yield a natural-looking image. If a very wide-angle lens is used, make note of the resultant change in perspective.

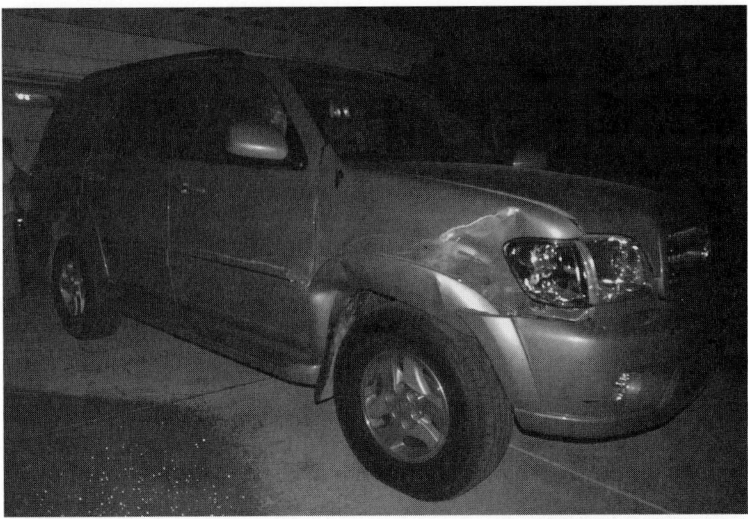

FIGURE 9–21 Painting with light outdoors at night. The flash will illuminate a limited area with each exposure. *Source:* Constance Rohrer, Evidence Forensics Photography.

5. Maintain the camera at the normal eye height of the photographer.
6. Photograph the object or scene from the closest point of view at which it is possible to visualize the complete scene, but at a reasonable distance back from the closest object of importance.
7. Set the camera to the manual mode.
8. Set the shutter speed to "B."
9. Set the camera f-stop. The setting can be determined by trial and error. A reasonable starting point is the aperture recommended by the flash, for the ISO in use, and the flash set at its most distant automatic range. If the exposure is wrong, adjust it and try again.
10. Fire the flash at a constant flash-to-subject distance, or sections of the subject may be over- or underexposed.
11. Set the flash in manual mode if necessary. Set the lens aperture at the recommended aperture for the flash-to-subject distance.
12. Focus the lens using the hyperfocal focusing technique presented in Chapter 7. If it is too dark to see at all, use a flashlight beam or the low-light focusing aid in the camera.
13. When the camera is level on the tripod, the bottom edge of the viewfinder should be aligned with a point about 10 to 15 feet away from the camera. If not, use a wider-angle lens.
14. Stand in safe locations. Be aware of the danger of moving vehicles.
15. If the scene is marginally lit, the flash operator should remain out of the field of view of the camera. If the scene is dark, the flash operator may safely walk through the scene during exposure, as long as the flash does not backlight the operator during any part of the exposure. (The photographer appears as multiple shadows in Figure 9–22.
16. Overlap the flash exposures.
17. Repeat the procedure with the camera in multiple positions.

TIP:

Hold a gray card over the lens between flashes if stray light is an issue.

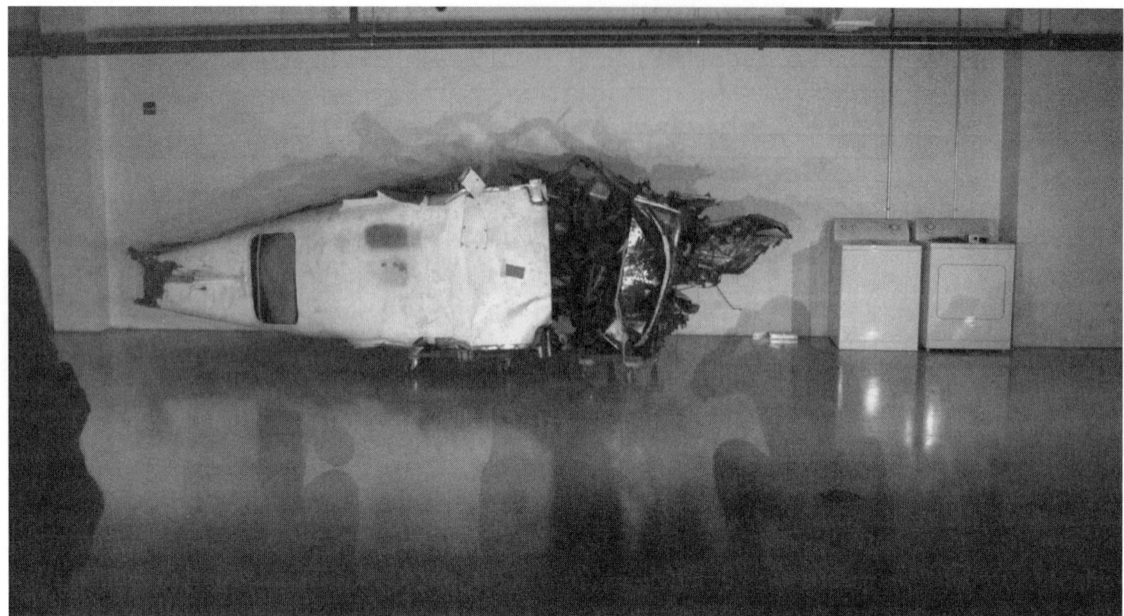

FIGURE 9–22 Painting with light indoors. *Source:* Sandy Weiss/Packer Engineering.

Red Eye

Red eye is a common issue in photographs of living creatures and a camera with a built-in flash. The retina(s) of the eye(s) reflect(s) the flash illumination straight back to the flash (see Fig. 9–23). When the flash is close to the lens, the image(s) of the retina(s) is captured with the reflection highlighted.

This problem can be partially solved by use of the "red eye reduction" setting built into many cameras. It is a blinking preflash that makes the subject's irises contract, yielding a smaller area of red eye. The only way red eye can be totally removed is to position the EFU at a farther distance from the camera lens during exposure. This makes the light reflected off the retina(s) come back to the camera at an angle at which it does not register in the camera image (see Fig. 9–24).

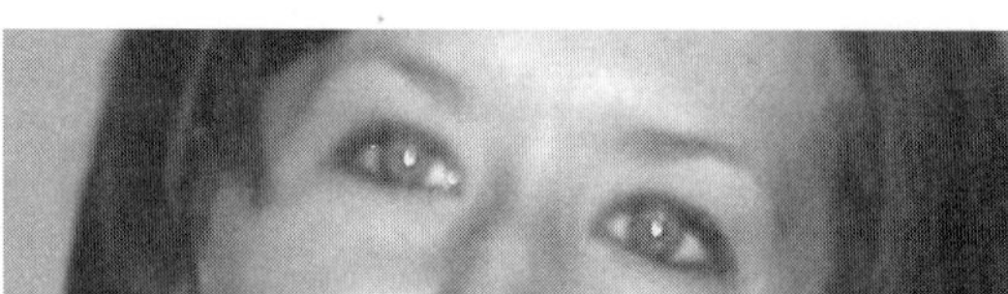

FIGURE 9–23 Red eye effect. *Source:* Constance Rohrer, Evidence Forensics Photography.

Bare Bulb Flash

Most flashes have a limited angle of output. Adding a diffuser will make the angle wider but not universal. A **bare bulb flash** or attachment creates diffused lighting in a 360-degree pattern. It is especially useful when it is necessary to illuminate a large area in tight quarters or at close working distances.

A bare bulb flash may be used on any camera. The units may have a variable reflector to change the angle of the illumination between 45 and 360 degrees. Some bare bulb EFUs screw into a standard lightbulb socket. They synchronize through the use of an add-on or built-in slave circuit.

A basic bare bulb effect can be created by placing a clean, white, Styrofoam coffee cup over the end of a normal EFU. *Remember:* The cup

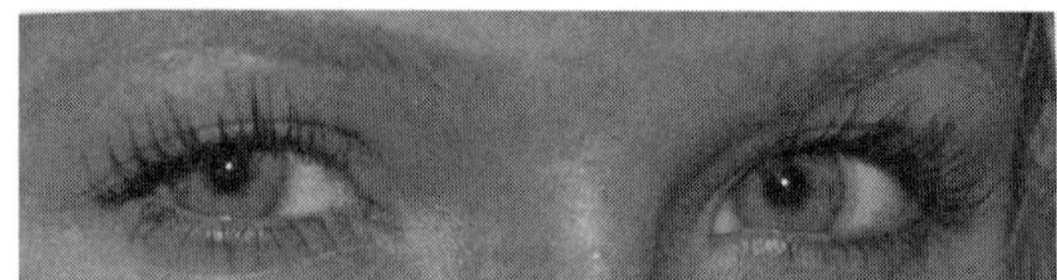

FIGURE 9–24 Eyes without red eye. *Source:* Constance Rohrer, Evidence Forensics Photography.

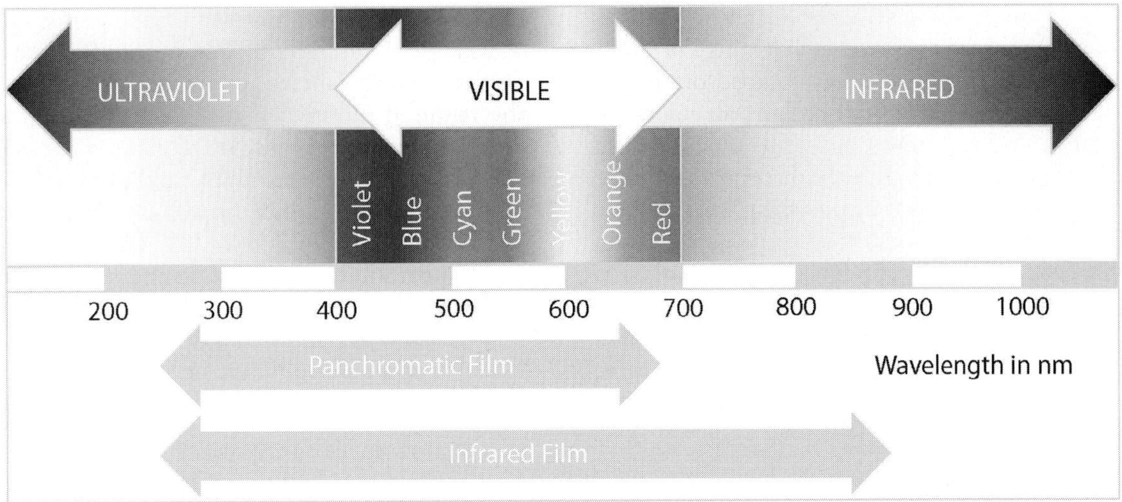

FIGURE 9–25 At either end of the visible spectrum are two "invisible" spectra. The UV extends from X-rays to the blue end of the visible spectrum, and the IR extends beyond the red and into heat. *Source:* Jessica Weiss.

will spread the light but will also reduce the effective GN of the EFU output.

Bounce Flash

When an EFU is aimed to reflect (bounce) off another surface, like the ceiling of a room, it produces diffused lighting and covers a wider angle. Bouncing the light makes it very soft and low contrast, and it reduces glare and reflections. *Remember:* Bouncing will spread the light but will also reduce the effective GN of the EFU output.

> **TIP:**
>
> If using the ceiling of a room for a bounce reflector, the ceiling must be white. If the ceiling is any other color, the light reflecting to the subject will be changed to the color of the ceiling and cause color shifts of the subject.

ALTERNATE LIGHT SOURCES

Use of an **alternate light source (ALS)** is often important for crime scene searches and evidence collection. The normal uses in forensic photography include the detection of latent fingerprints, study of forged or questioned documents, and inspection of counterfeit money. In biology and serology, the uses include the detection of semen, blood, saliva, vaginal fluids, sweat, feces, footprints, gun shot residues, bruises, bite marks, fibers, hairs, bone fragments, and so on.

Color Vision

To understand the use of ALS, it is critical to understand the physiology of human color vision. Humans are able to detect light in the range of about 400 nanometers (violet) to about 700 nanometers (red) (see Fig. 9–25). This is referred to as the **visible spectrum.** Light that is sufficient to allow normal levels of illumination appears to the human eye simply as "light." Incandescent light, fluorescent light, daylight, or light consisting of a mixture of colors is difficult for the human brain to differentiate. The normal brain does not find the differentiation of color-specific information important enough to calculate.

The human eye can detect colors only if the level of illumination is sufficiently high. Color vision does not exist in low light. The rod cells of the eye, used for black-and-white vision, detect the luminance of images at all levels. The cone cells in the eyes are used only for color vision. The range of wavelengths of "visible light" from 400 to 700 nanometers is considered to be the range of human visual **spectral sensitivity.**

Human vision senses and identifies images of objects and scenes over a wide range of ambient illumination. The cones do not work in low light, but the rods do. In low light, all colors appear as shades of gray.

The cone cells sense the three portions of the visible spectrum equivalent to the primary colors: red, green, and blue. Normal human color vision has peak sensitivities at frequencies relating to red (580 nm), green (540 nm), and blue (450 nm). Light at any wavelength in the visual spectrum range will register on one or more of these three sensors.

Selective Sensing

Different wavelengths of light allow human vision to perceive color. Some people have trouble distinguishing among certain colors and are referred to as "color blind." Red–green color blindness may occur if the R and G sensor response curves in their brains overlap excessively or if an insufficient number of either R or G sensors are present. A person with this problem may have extra difficulty at lower levels of illumination.

Spectral Selectivity

Spectral selectivity involves the creation of images using intentionally limited ranges of light radiation in the UV, visible, or IR portions of the spectrum. Photographic materials are available with specific sensitivities to limited portions of the spectrum from 250 nanometers (UV) to 925 nanometers (IR). Specific characteristics of a subject can be enhanced or selected for viewing by limiting the range of spectrum used to create an image.

Spectral selectivity is created by the use of specially colored lights or by the use of colored filters.

Built-in Flash for Ultraviolet and Infrared Photography

Evidence photographers in the fields of law enforcement, the military, surveillance, medicine, research, art history, and biology often require the use of UV and IR (UVIR) lighting to visualize evidence that would normally be invisible to human eyes. Until recently, all UV and IR photography was only captured on film. UV photography required filtration that was almost opaque and long exposure times. IR required a special film that was sensitive to all radiation and had to be loaded into the camera in absolute darkness. Normal digital cameras have UV and IR cutoff filters incorporated in their image sensors to promote color accuracy in visible light.

UV and IR photography may show the following that would normally be invisible to the human eye:

- Presence of gunpowder residue
- Altered writing on documents
- Different inks on a document
- Bone fragments
- Injuries below the skin
- Old bite marks that are no longer visible to the eye

Ultraviolet Lighting

The UV spectrum includes the following:

- Near UV (NUV): 380–200 nm
- Far or Vacuum UV (FUV or VUV): 200–10 nm
- Extreme UV (EUV or XUV): 1–31 nm

NUV is divided into the following wavelengths:

- Long wave UV: 320 to 400 nm (black-light bulbs emit long wave UV radiation)
- Medium wave UV: 280 to 320 nm
- Short wave UV: 200 to 280 nm

UV light may be used for either reflectance or fluorescence imaging.

Reflected Ultraviolet Photography

Reflected UV light may reveal hidden cracks in materials, work or restoration performed on an artifact, as well as many other types of evidence that are not visible in normal lighting. UV radiation is present in sunlight. On sunny, clear days,

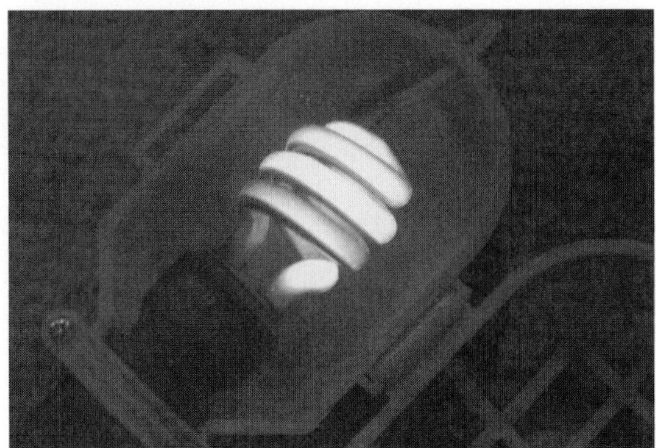

FIGURE 9–26 A UV light source. *Source:* Sandy Weiss/ Packer Engineering.

the level of UV radiation increases EFUs often generate a high level of UV output. Some UV light sources may be purchased at hardware stores, and others are available from scientific supply companies.

If the subject is illuminated by a UV light source (see Fig. 9–26) and a UV transmittance filter (e.g., Kodak Wratten 18A, generally referred to as a "Woods filter") is placed on the camera lens, the filter will absorb all visible light and allow only the invisible long wave UV light reflecting off the subject to pass through and expose an image.

A combination of UV and ambient lighting may be used to illuminate the subject so that it is shown in a more photorealistic image. If using both UV and ambient light, use a deep yellow filter on the front of the lens. Work in subdued ambient illumination, and judge exposure by trial and error.

Reflected Ultraviolet Photography for Bruise Documentation

Long wave UV light penetrates deeper into the skin than visible light. Use a Kodak Wratten 18A filter on the camera lens to expose images of subject skin. The UV light penetrates to document images of bruises and bite marks that have been absorbed into the skin over time and are invisible in normal light. This light may reveal bruises for months after the injury. (See Chapter 16 for in-depth instructions.)

Tattoos, birthmarks, and other discolorations may be located deeper in the skin than UV light can penetrate. They cannot be imaged with this technique. Bruising that would otherwise be hidden by these markings may be made visible and documented by UV imaging.

The following are the steps for reflective UV imaging of bruises:

- Focus the camera lens on the subject.
- Expose a visible-light photo of the skin area first.
- Be sure the camera and subject do not move.
- Place an 18A filter on the camera lens.
- Use a camera that is sensitive to long wave UV lighting.
- Use an appropriate UV light source for illumination.
- Use an appropriate scale for dimensions.
- Expose the image with the UV illumination.
- Change the directionality of the illumination until the best image of the bruise appears in the image.

Ultraviolet Fluorescence Photography

Many substances fluoresce when illuminated by UV light. For best results, visible light must be subdued during fluorescence photography because the visible light will reduce the fluorescence effects.

Use the same light source as in reflected UV photography, but place the filter in front of the light source instead of on the lens of the camera. This absorbs the visible light and allows only the UV light to pass. The same type of UV filters are made for EFUs; they are called *exciter filters* because they excite fluorescence from the subject. Another filter must be placed on the camera lens to exclude residual UV and image only the fluorescence. This is called the *barrier filter*. A Kodak Wratten 2A or 2B is usually used. Such photography is performed in low ambient illumination. Older digital cameras, with less sophisticated UV reduction systems, perform better than many newer cameras.

When focusing the camera with UV illumination, it may be necessary to focus into the subject rather than at the subject surface. This step may be eliminated with adequate DoF.

Infrared Photography

IR photography is used to photograph evidence in the same manner as UV. Some substances display enhanced visibility when illuminated by IR lighting.

IR film is sensitive to visible and IR light so it must be handled, loaded into the camera, and processed in total darkness. Digital IR photography is easier. It is possible to digitally photograph subjects illuminated by light in the near infrared (NIR) part of the spectrum at 700 to 1200 nanometers.

Because living vegetation reflects almost all IR light, it will appear lighter in IR images than it does to the eye. The sky appears darker than normal in IR images because it reflects very limited amounts of IR illumination. Human skin often appears lighter in IR images than it will to the eye in visible light.

Some digital image sensors are sensitive to NIR unless the camera has a built-in IR reduction filter. Some digital cameras with IR cutoff filters will allow enough IR light to pass and create images. Another effective method is to place a filter on the camera lens that blocks visible light and allows NIR to pass. Light sources for NIR photography include incandescent lamps and the sun. (See Fig. 9–27.)

> **TIP:**
>
> Digital camera sensors are not sensitive to far IR wavelengths: the heat emitted by objects at high temperatures. Objects at body temperature and above do not glow in NIR or in visible light. IR energy above 1,350 nanometers can be imaged with thermographic equipment.

> **TIP:**
>
> Digital cameras with CCD sensors normally have greater IR sensitivity than cameras with CMOS sensors.

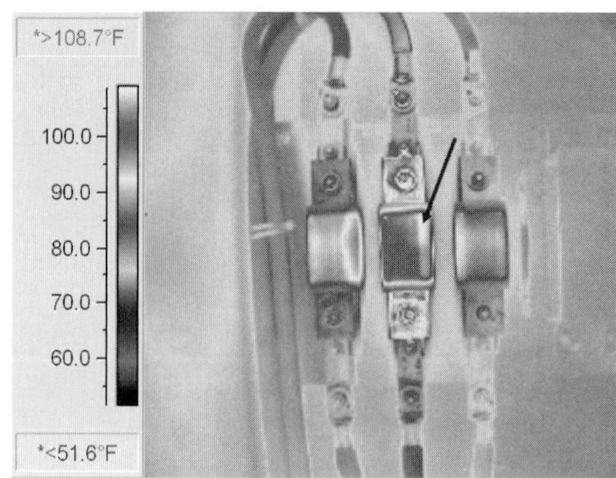

FIGURE 9–27 IR thermograph of an electrical circuit. *Source:* Sandy Weiss/Packer Engineering.

Digital Hardware Appropriate or IR Photography

- Use an older digital camera with less or no anti-IR filtration, or
- Have the anti-IR filter removed from a new camera, or
- Use a camera designed for IR photography.

Infrared Filters

Two types of filters are used for IR photography

- Red filters, including #25, #29, #70
- Opaque filters, including #87, #87B, #87C, #88A, #89B

The following steps describe how to make IR images:

- Attach a filter to the camera.
- Turn off the built-in flash.
- Set the camera to a high ISO rating.
- Expose a test.
- If the image is dark, it is underexposed; set the aperture and/or shutter speed to overexposure.

Most photographic lenses are designed to retain the same focal length in all colors of the visual spectrum. Photographic lenses are not designed to focus correctly in IR. IR has a longer wavelength and focuses at a slightly different point than visible light does. Many older lenses have a red IR focus reference offset from the regular focus reference. The photographer must move the focus ring of the lens to align the proper focus point of a visible light image to the IR focus reference. (See Chapter 7.)

INFRARED PHOTOGRAPHY FOR BIOMEDICAL USE

IR lighting penetrates the top layers of the skin, is able to make images of what lies beneath, and may document the following:

- The healing process under deep bruises
- Hair stubble in shaved areas
- Removed or obliterated tattoos
- Various layers of tooth composition
- Varicose veins and blood clots

FORENSIC OR ALTERNATIVE LIGHT SOURCES

Forensic examinations conducted in visible light wavelengths may not reveal all the existent evidence. Depending on the chemical composition of the evidence or the material it is on, its presence may be camouflaged in conventional light. The use of alternate light sources of different colors may increase evidence visibility. Portable ALS help investigators to find more evidence in less time and generate higher-quality data, including better photographs of trace evidence and latent prints.

Forensic light sources or **alternative light sources (ALS)** are used for the observation, photographing, and collection of evidence. Newer ALSs are constructed with light-emitting diodes (LEDs). LEDs deliver exact ALS wavelengths for specific purposes and emit single colors from green at 540 nanometers through blue at 470 nanometers. Some LEDs emit long wave UV at 365 nanometers.

LEDs are convenient and efficient light sources. Laser and filtered incandescent ALS are also used.

ALSs are used to locate and identify the following:

- Latent fingerprints (green and blue)
- Body fluids (blue)
- Hairs and fibers
- Bruises (purple)
- Bite marks (purple)
- Wound patterns
- Shoe and foot imprints
- Gunshot residue
- Drug traces
- bone fragments

TIP:

Many substances fluoresce under different wavelengths of ALS. It is difficult to identify a substance by its fluorescence.

Latent Fingerprint Detection

Fingerprint recording and identification are accomplished through contrast enhancement. In order to be studied, compared, and identified, fingerprint ridges must stand out from what they are on (see Fig. 9–28). Fingerprints can sometimes

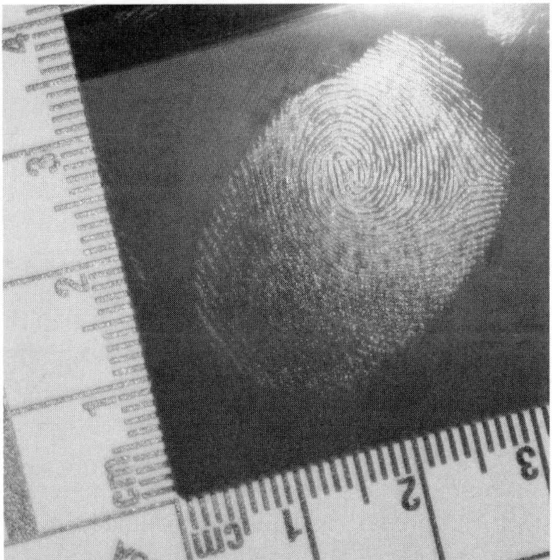

FIGURE 9–28 Fingerprint on a cell phone. *Source:* Sandy Weiss/Packer Engineering.

be located by their absorption of UV illumination. The skin oils and amino acids in fingerprints absorb short wave UV at 240 to 320 nanometers. When fingerprints on smooth surfaces are illuminated in short wave UV, they may be visible in the light reflectance. For successful photography, it is necessary to use a camera that is sensitive to UV lighting.

Different wavelengths may be used for inspecting different surfaces. ALSs with multiple wavelengths are desirable. Fluorescent powders should be used with an ALS when dusting a scene for prints. Conventional black print powder does not fluoresce.

Body Fluid Detection

Some body fluids, including semen, saliva, and vaginal fluids, are naturally fluorescent. Specific locations of stains for collection and documentation are found under ALS illumination. Both dried and wet body fluids fluoresce. Body fluids fluoresce under UV black light. The materials the fluids are on may also glow. ALSs can be tuned to most adequately assess the fluids. Bloodstains appear slightly darker under ALS and may be easier to locate and photograph.

Hairs and Fibers

Processing crime scenes for forensic evidence takes time, and most scenes degrade over time, particularly in exposed or highly trafficked locations or where evidence is chemically or physically unstable. Visual and photographic scene processing with an ALS may involve multiple sweeps with different colored filters. Portable lasers may help visualize a wider range of trace evidence with less time in the scene. Lasers may visualize evidence that is chemical, biological, serological, print, fiber, accelerant, and so on.

ALS may be used to photograph evidence or locate it for collection. Light sources may be used to reveal the evidence by fluorescence or by contrast. In both cases, photographic documentation is enabled by the enhanced visibility.

Fluorescence occurs when a material absorbs light of one color and re-emits it as another color. The new color is usually higher in wavelength than the illumination. Materials may be illuminated with blue or green light and then viewed through goggles that pass orange or red.

Modern ALS systems are often LEDs that emit light over a specific color band. The popularity of LED systems may be overshadowed by the efficiency of lasers. Laser ALS produce light in one color. Laser power may reveal evidence that LEDs cannot find. The latest versions of forensic green lasers use OPS (optically pumped semiconductor) technology.[1] These produce intense green light, are hands-free, battery-powered, and simple to operate.

Sexual Assault

ALS may help to locate hair and semen evidence in sexual assault cases. A brown hair on a brown carpet will fluoresce by ALS and collection will be enabled. Modern DNA amplification and identification techniques (mitochondrial DNA: mtDNA) may identify an individual from a part of a human hair, even without the root.

Bruises, Bite Marks, and Pattern Wounds

It is useful to assess the effects of various wavelengths of ALS for visualizing markings on skin. Some wavelengths penetrate skin to different depths, and some wounds and bruises require different wavelengths to display contrast sufficient for marks to be seen. (See Chapter 16 for detailed information.)

Questioned Documents

Indented writing on a pad of paper is difficult to see and photograph. Oblique or side lighting may be useful. Some government or other official documents include hidden images or security features that must be documented for authentication. ALS may be useful as tools to reveal some of the latent images.

The use of various colors of ALS may help to distinguish different inks and to visualize changed text in questioned documents.

SUMMARY

Photography is the art or process of producing images by the action of light on the surfaces of objects. Light is required to produce a photograph. In some cases, ambient illumination is sufficient and appropriate to create the necessary images. Evidence photography often requires light supplied by artificial means.

The light may be instantaneous or continuous, defined by the situation and subject. Consistency and rules are nonexistent. The subject may be the head of a pin, the head of a person, or the scene of a crime, accident, or mass disaster. Having a suitable camera is only part of the issue. Having the necessary lighting equipment and knowledge to document a scene outside at night, in a place that is difficult to access, of a reflective surface or of a subject that is invisible to the eye may be the most difficult aspect of a project. Proper lighting is often the issue when the knowledge and ingenuity of the evidence photographer becomes challenged.

CASE STUDY

HELICOPTER INSPECTION

Nondestructive testing (NDT) is a method used in failure analysis for the inspection of evidence that may not be altered. NDT does not disturb the structural or surface integrity of evidence. It has specific techniques, protocols, and materials for use.

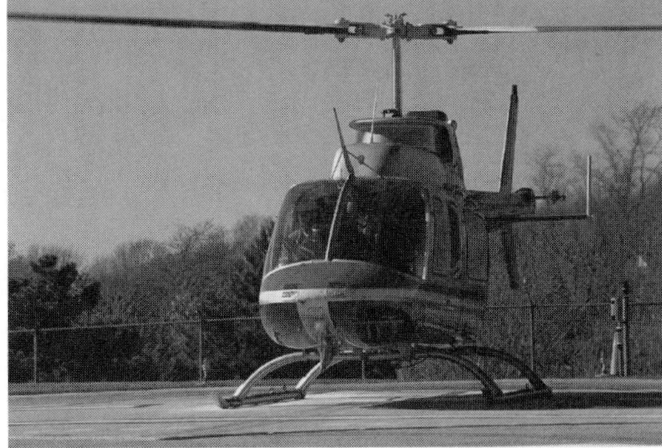

FIGURE 9–29 Helicopter before crash. *Source:* Sandy Weiss/Packer Engineering.

In a specific helicopter crash (see Fig. 9–29), the rotor continued to turn despite the failure of several integral bearings at the base of its shaft (see Fig. 9–30). Great heat was generated through friction, and some of the bearings were melted into an indistinguishable lump of metal. The problem was to visually distinguish and separate the bushings. The lump of metal was too large to fit into the SEM for inspection and analysis.

The parts were taken into a room where the lighting could be controlled and subdued. A light source was utilized for inspection and photography.

The materials fluoresced under the UV lighting in ways specific to their composition. Photography of the parts under the UV lighting showed how one type of material was smeared

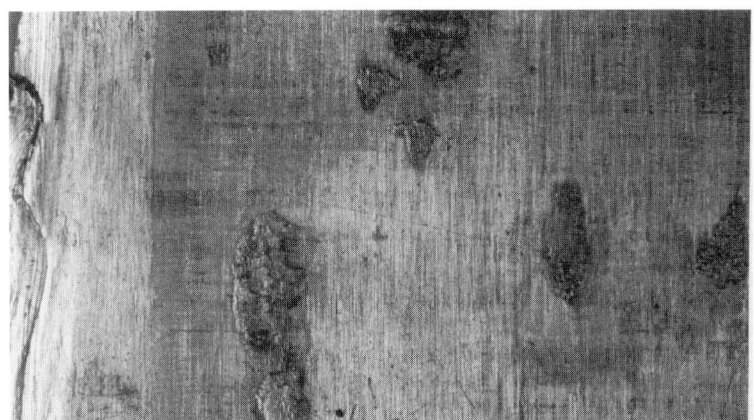

FIGURE 9–30 Close-up of a bearing from a crashed helicopter. *Source:* Sandy Weiss/Packer Engineering.

onto the other. This demonstrated the type and degree of destruction of one material over the other.

CASE STUDY

SHOTGUN INSPECTION

When subjected to sufficient pressure to cause failure, the barrels of shotguns may explode when fired. The catastrophic destruction may injure the operator. To determine the reason for the failure, it is necessary to reconstruct the event. The owner of the weapon may file suit against the manufacturer by claiming a material failure rather than an operator error.

In this case, the explosion of the barrel caused severe personal injury to the operator. The inspection and reconstruction were court ordered to be performed under the principles of NDT, so pieces of the barrel could not be sectioned and placed in appropriate microscopes for inspection.

The images illustrate two types of NDT testing. The first was a dye penetrant inspection (see Fig. 9–31). The barrel was sprayed with a red dye that was subsequently wiped off. The only dye remaining on the metal was what was in the subsurface cracks. When the developer powder was sprayed onto the metal, the dye that was in the cracks was absorbed into the developer and colored it red. This indicated the location and severity of the cracks. The images were exposed with ordinary film and EFU.

Another method of crack documentation is the UV fluorescence method (see Fig. 9–32). A petroleum-based fluid was sprayed onto the metal. The metal was then subjected to a strong magnetic field, in this case a large magnet. The fluorescent fluid aligned itself into the cracks of the metal and fluoresced brightly for inspection and documentation under UV lighting. This image was exposed through a dark yellow filter for extra contrast.

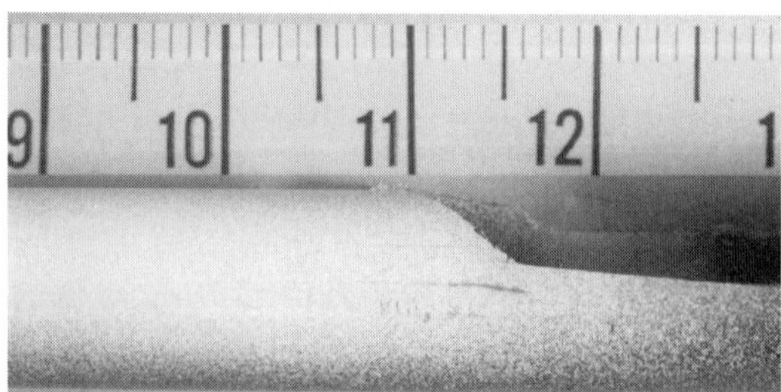

FIGURE 9–31 Dye penetrant testing. *Source:* Sandy Weiss/Packer Engineering.

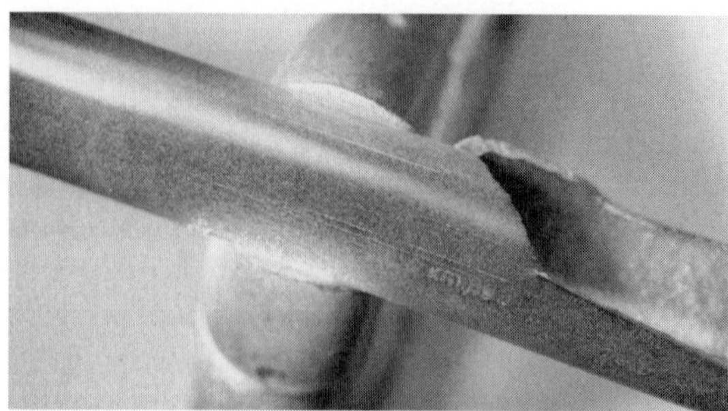

FIGURE 9–32 UV fluorescence. *Source:* Sandy Weiss/Packer Engineering.

CASE STUDY

BALL BEARING

Reflective surfaces are the most difficult subjects to illuminate by EFU. Wherever the flash is placed, the light reflects off the surface of the subject and creates a hot spot that yields no useful image information in the finished photograph.

Many reflective surfaces are curved or multifaceted and add difficulty by reflecting light back to the camera from multiple directions. Bearings are common and very difficult subjects in evidence photography (see Fig. 9–33).

I purchase and distribute ball bearings to each student in my macrophotography classes. I make a mark on each bearing by touching it on a spinning grindstone. The students use any methods they may devise to create photographs with good detail of the grinding spot on the bearing (see Fig. 9–34 and end-of-chapter exercise 2).

This is a difficult assignment and usually requires many attempts before each student figures a way to produce a useable image. In many cases, the final result is a variation of a light tent or flash diffuser (see Chapter 10).

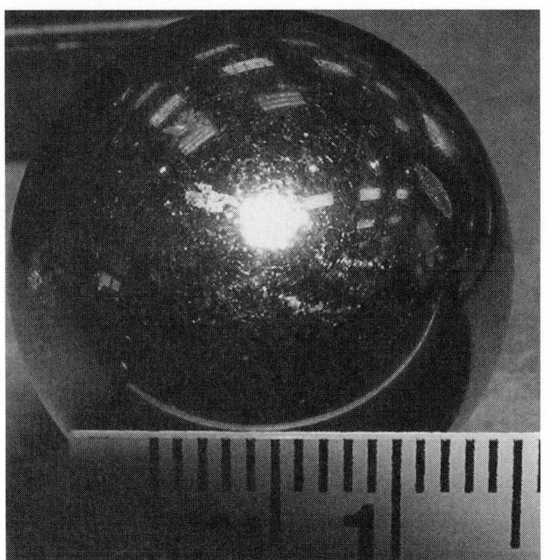

FIGURE 9–33 Ball bearing with hot spot illuminated by direct flash. *Source:* Sandy Weiss/Packer Engineering.

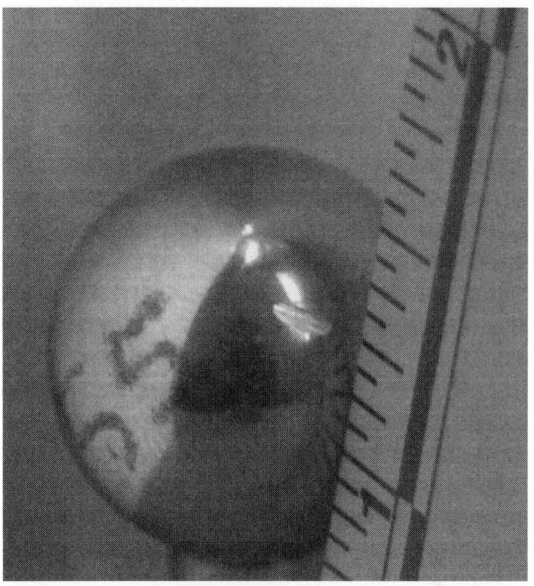

FIGURE 9–34 Ball bearing with diffused flash showing grinding mark. *Source:* Sandy Weiss/Packer Engineering.

KEY TERMS

flash powder, (p. 256)
flash bulb, (p. 256)
inverse-square law, (p. 257)
thyristor, (p. 258)
accessory shoe, (p. 259)
synchronization speed, (p. 259)
studio flash, (p. 260)
slave flash unit, (p. 260)
flash meter, (p. 262)
guide number, (p. 263)
fill flash, (p. 263)
flash diffuser, (p. 266)
trigger voltage, (p. 267)
ring flash, (p. 268)
macro flash, (p. 268)
painting with light, (p. 268)
red eye, (p. 270)
bare bulb flash, (p. 270)
visible spectrum, (p. 271)
spectral sensitivity, (p. 271)
spectral selectivity, (p. 272)
forensic light source, (p. 275)
alternate light source, (p. 275)

EXERCISES

1. Devise a method for testing the maximum synchronization speed for flash of a film camera (if one is available) without physically processing the film to check if it is properly working.
2. Procure a ball bearing or other highly reflective metallic object and photo-document a surface irregularity without the problem of hot spots.
3. Make a set of reflective sheets of cardboard with the numbers 5, 10, 15, 20, 25, 30, 35, and 40 written onto them in bold, large characters to designate distance in feet. Set up the cards outdoors at night at the appropriate distances from the flash in a darkened environment, expose a series of images, and determine how far the flash you are using will illuminate your subject under those conditions.
4. Procure a slave unit of some type and attach it to a flash that will fire when the built-in flash of your camera fires. Use the slave flash in different situations to both illuminate and fill in difficult lighting situations. Be aware of how high the slave will register in an ambient lighting situation.

5. Use fill flash in a bright, sunny situation and compare the images taken both with and without the flash.
6. Practice painting with light in an appropriate situation.
7. Use appropriate materials and construct a set of flash diffusers for the EFU you use. (These will be used in an exercise in Chapter 10, too.)
8. Determine the exact GN for the built-in flash on your camera.
9. Think of as many reasons as you can for being able to set an EFU on variable power with manual exposure.

APPENDIX 9.1

Nikon Speedlight SB-800

The Nikon Speedlight SB-800 is the state-of-the-art EFU, and in some ways it is more complicated than any camera on which it is used. In fact, the instruction manual for the flash is longer and more detailed than the one for the camera. Many other OEM EFUs have similar features, but the SB-800 is the best example to study as a modern EFU.

Wireless operation with the SB-800 allows the flash or flashes to be placed at a reasonable distance and in any appropriate position, and the camera will control the flash(es) remotely. The camera computes appropriate exposure no matter how many flashes are used in an array. Wireless features are included in all of the Nikon DSLR cameras, including the SB-600.

The Nikon camera's built-in flash, when it has one, is used as the controller and trigger for the other units. The photographer can control the output level of any of the flash(es) from the controller flash at the camera position.

FLASH COLOR INFORMATION

The color of light emitted by an automatic EFU may change in relation to the length of the burst of light. With the Nikon Speedlight SB-800 (see Fig. A9.1–1), the auto white balance (AWB) in the camera works properly, irrespective of flash duration.

FLASH VALUE LOCK

The SB-800 enables the user to Flash Value Lock (FV-Lock) the flash output over a sequence of exposures, using the same camera body button as the AE-Lock (AE-L) function used for ambient exposure locking.

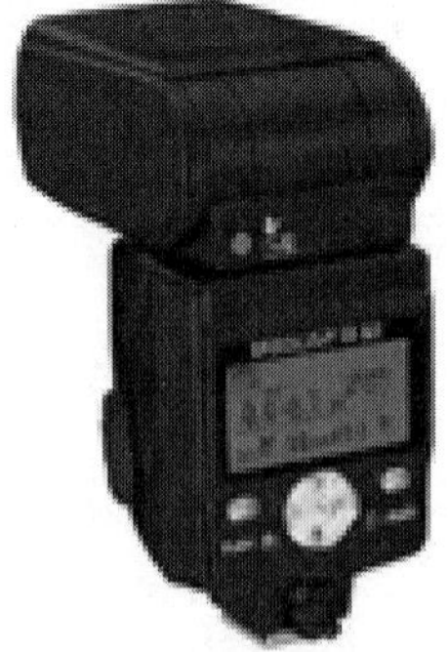
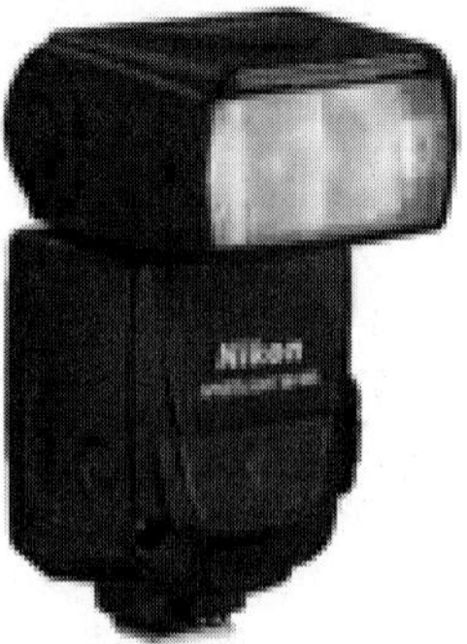

FIGURE A9.1–1 Nikon Speedlight SB-800 *Source:* Sandy Weiss/Packer Engineering.

AUTO FP HIGH-SPEED SYNC

The SB-800 can automatically set itself to focal plane (FP) flash mode if the shutter speed is above the standard flash sync speed for balanced fill flash in bright ambient light while using fast shutter speeds.

APPENDIX 9.2

The Foster and Freeman DCS-3 Latent Fingerprint Enhancement and Recording System

The Foster and Freeman DCS-3 Latent Fingerprint Enhancement and Recording System (see Fig. A9.2–1 and www.fosterfreeman.com/products/fingerprints/dcs3/dcs3.html) includes the following components:

- 6 MP camera
- Image enhancement software
- High-intensity LED ring light
- Image validation software
- Software interface for camera
- Photographic quality prints
- Battery pack for scenes of crime
- Image archiving
- National Fingerprint Archive Database interface

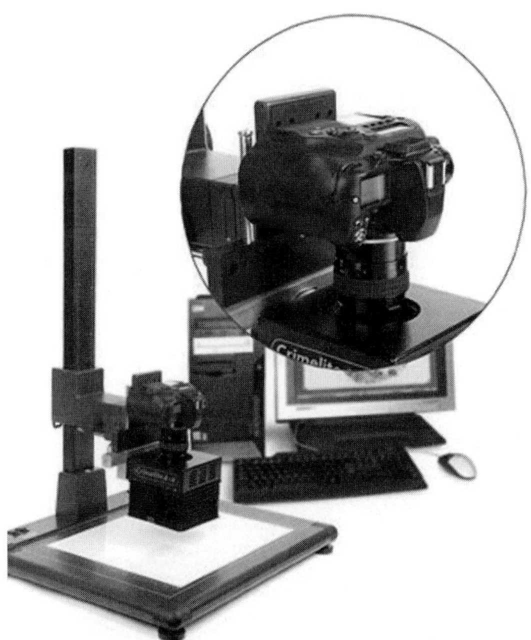

FIGURE A9.2–1 The Foster and Freeman DCS-3 fingerprint camera system. *Source:* Photograph courtesy of Foster & Freeman Limited.

The DCS-3 is a complete system for the capture, enhancement, and printing of latent fingerprints. It includes a high-resolution digital camera, high-intensity LED illumination, and unique software programs for image enhancement. The software allows the enhancement of fingerprint images on patterned, colored, and uneven backgrounds; on images treated with a variety of developers; and on images found in blood, grease, or dust. The high-intensity LED ring light provides narrow band illumination for fluorescence photography and white light, a polarizing filter, and a filter slot for color correction.

APPENDIX 9.3

Fujifilm FinePix S3 Pro UVIR

The FinePix S3 (or S5 in the near future) Pro UVIR (see Fig. A9.3–1) is a production DSLR capable of making photographs using the illumination available in the UV and IR light spectrums. The Super CCD image sensor in the Fuji camera can image invisible, UV, and IR spectrums continuously. Filters of specific colors allow only the desired wavelengths of light to create the image. All modern digital cameras—except the Fuji—have UV and IR protection filters built into their optical systems. The filters enable accurate color rendition of the digital image unaffected by detrimental radiation. The filters effectively disable all of the other cameras as instruments designed to capture images by utilizing UV/IR radiation. Other DSLRs must be customized to offer imaging at these spectral values. Once the cameras are customized, their factory warranties are negated.

The camera has a double-photodiode (6.17 million S-pixels and 6.17 million R-pixels) for increased dynamic range. Fully automatic operations are not suitable for work outside the visible spectrum, so manual focusing and exposure control are required and their controls are optimized. The camera allows a 30-second live preview mode to verify images before capture and to allow direct manual focusing from the LCD before exposure. Most DSLRs have no live preview capability. The S3 Pro UVIR camera can be focused by viewing on the LCD with dark IR or UV filters over the lens. This allows the photographer to judge which filter is most effective in specific applications.

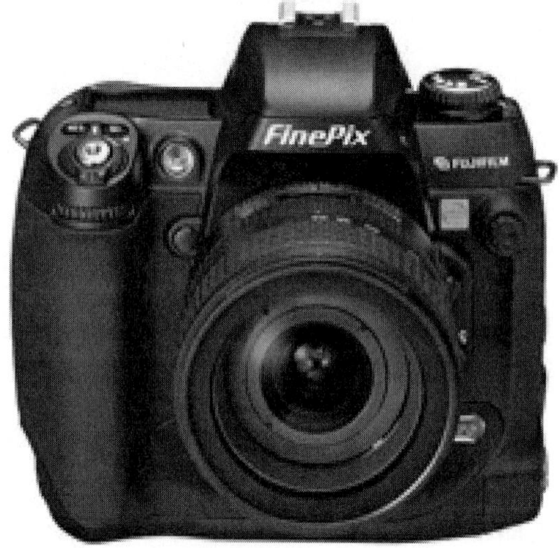

FIGURE A9.3–1 The Fuji S3 Pro UVIR. *Source:* Sandy Weiss/Packer Engineering.

Chapter 10

Macrophotography

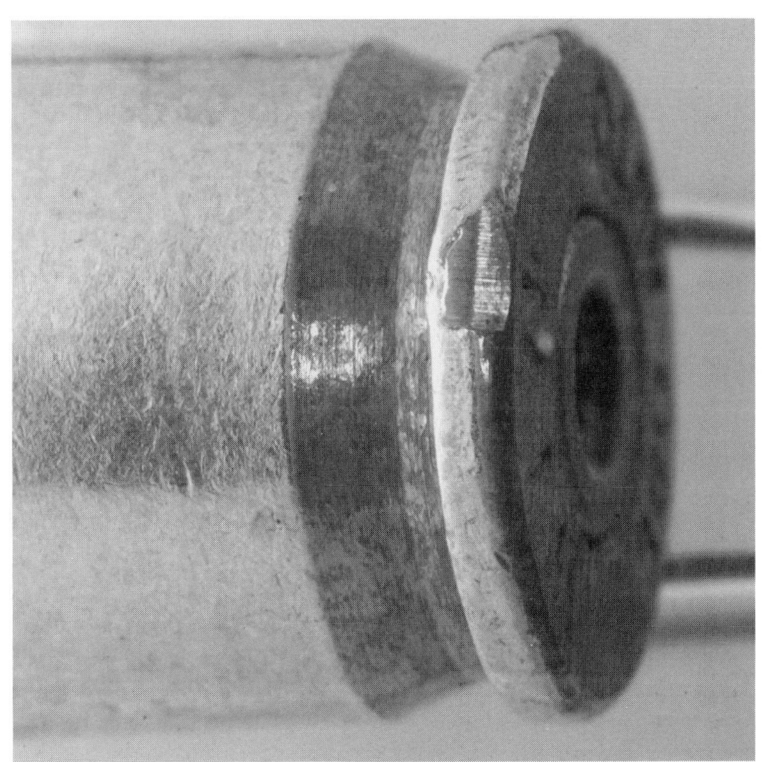

Learning Objectives

AFTER STUDYING THIS CHAPTER, YOU SHOULD BE ABLE TO:

1. Be comfortable with the concepts and practices of close-up and macrophotography
2. Understand the methods and means for gaining magnification
3. Master the steps for the quantification of the reproduction ratio of an image
4. Understand the use and importance of the proper type and placement of references and scales
5. Differentiate various lighting techniques
6. Calculate the ratios involved with magnification to exposure
7. Comprehend the basics and the importance of evidence images for comparison with original evidence

INTRODUCTION

Macrophotography is the type of close-up photography in which the final magnification of the image of the subject is anywhere from about .5 times (×) to about 25× the **life size** (1:1) on the image sensor. This type of photography is useful for the documentation of small objects and small parts of large objects that require close inspection or ease of demonstration. Macrophotography fits the niche between normal photography and microphotography.

In forensic evidence documentation, it is often necessary to photograph subjects that are sections of twisted metal, hunks of charred ash, or pieces of broken bodies. The documentary images must be technically accurate and not necessarily aesthetically pleasing. To illustrate the characteristics of subjects, the forensic photographer must be able to create accurate representations of evidence by the selection and use of the most appropriate hardware and lighting, even if the finished photographs are not technically works of art. Macrophotography is often required to capture images of small scratches and other **witness marks** (punch marks or scratches used to position or locate characteristics for comparison) on shiny surfaces or in difficult locations where reflections are common and shadows from other parts of the subject are troublesome.

Every evidence photography project may require macrophotographs. Something small may need to be documented in the largest disasters. Macrophotography may be performed in the field, where the evidence photographer must use close-up accessories and an EFU to document the evidence in situ. In many cases, it is not appropriate to move the evidence until after it has been documented.

Sometimes macrophotography must be undertaken in a laboratory, studio, warehouse, morgue, home, or some other place to which the evidence has been moved. In these cases, the evidence must be properly protected but may be handled, set up, lit for proper exposure, put in front of a suitable background, and subjected to inspection and documentation, using all available equipment and techniques. In any case, the photography may be tedious, exacting, and require skill and experience of the photographer.

Macro images may be the most important aspect of the documentation. Small marks and colorations may be the key to an accident reconstruction. Always use the proper scales and references. The type of lighting used is extremely important, as well as how the lighting is utilized.

Working in the field with a minimum of accessories, the evidence photographer must create accurate macrophotographs. If the subject is simple, lighting is sufficient, extreme DoF is not necessary, and high magnification is not required, the work should not be too complicated. However, "simple" subjects, conditions, and parameters do not normally exist.

The following are the greatest challenges in macrophotography:

- The inherent lack of DoF when the camera and lens are close to the subject
- Proper lighting to either avoid or create shadows

TIP:

At one-tenth life size (1:1) on the image sensor, an area about 7 by 10 inches imaged onto a Nikon D70s digital sensor will have approximately 1.5 inches of DoF at *f*/5.6 with a 35 mm focal length lens, or it will have 6 inches at *f*/22. At 1:1, a subject .66 inch × 1 inch will have DoF less than 1 mm at *f*/5.6 or 3 mm at *f*/22. At 6x life size, DoF will be .25 mm at *f*/22.

TIP:

Due to the shallow DoF in macrophotography, the film plane or image sensor of the camera should always be as close as possible to parallel with the most predominant plane of the subject.

It is possible to utilize a variety of lighting techniques and formulas to properly illuminate macro subjects. Light must reflect off or pass through a subject to capture its image. In either case, the light must be controlled to limit shadows, emphasize textures and landmarks, and achieve proper exposure to supply the most accurate images.

Several kinds of equipment are commonly used for creating the required magnification and exposure, including the following:

- Close-up (diopter) lenses
- Extension tubes
- Bellows
- Reversing rings
- Macro lenses
- Appropriate lighting
- Appropriate references

TIP:

Focus the camera manually when making macrophotographs.

CLOSE-UP LENSES

Placing **close-up lenses** in front of the cameras lens is a simple means to accomplish low magnification. Screw-in (see Fig. 10–1) or slip-on lens attachments provide close focusing at low cost. The quality is variable, with some brands being higher in resolution. This type of close-up system works well on cameras having built-in and noninterchangeable lenses.

Screw-in lenses fit into the filter threads on the front of camera lenses and allow a reduction in the minimum lens-to-subject distance. The magnification of a close-up lens is specified in **diopters,** with the higher numbers providing higher magnification. The maximum focusing distance of the lens is reduced when diopter lenses are applied.

The lenses of digital cameras are shorter in focal lengths than those on 35 mm cameras and will need close-up lenses with higher numbers to

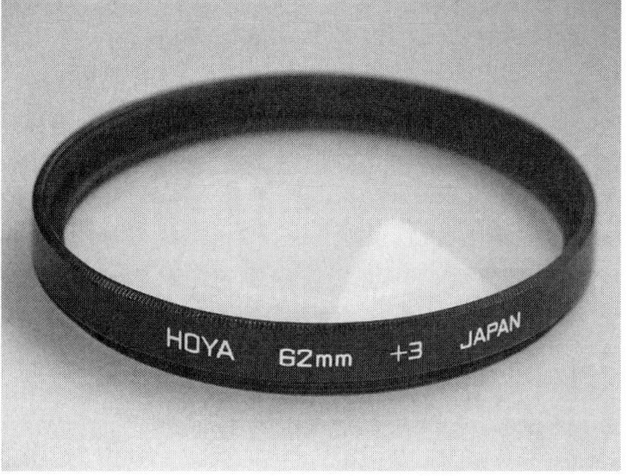

FIGURE 10–1 A screw-in type of close-up lens. *Source:* Sandy Weiss/Packer Engineering.

accomplish the same magnification. It is possible to use close-up lenses in combinations of two or three at a time. Always put the lens with the highest number closer to the camera. Adding a +1 and a +2 lens yields the same magnification as a +3.

TIP:

When using close-up lenses in tandem, use the smallest possible lens aperture to minimize lens aberrations caused by inferior optics.

Some advantages of close-up lenses include the following:

- They do not affect exposure.
- They do not make the image more difficult to see on the LCD screen.
- They do not interfere with auto-focus.

EXTENSION TUBES

Extension tubes (see Fig. 10–2) are used on SLRs between the camera body and the lens to move the lens farther from the film or digital sensor. With tubes attached, the camera will focus at a closer distance to the subject but will not focus to infinity. Extension tubes contain no optical elements, so they will not depreciate image resolution.

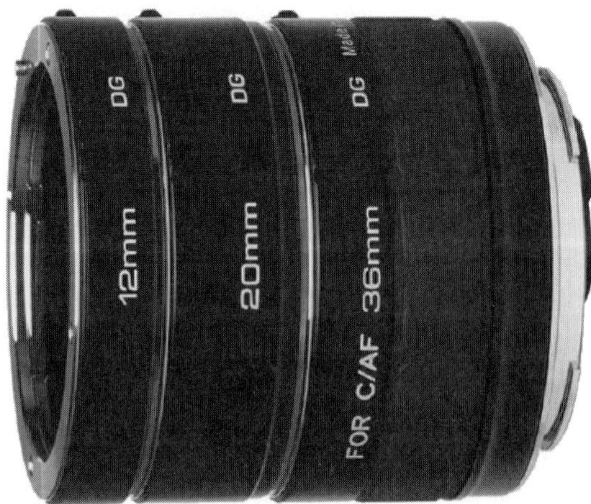

FIGURE 10–2 Set of extension tubes. *Source:* Sandy Weiss/Packer Engineering.

Extension tubes are available for every brand of SLR with interchangeable lenses. They may be used on lenses of any focal length but are recommended for normal and longer lens lengths. If a tube is used on a short focal length lens, the minimum focal distance may be behind the front lens element. To retain automatic operations of the camera, it is necessary to use tubes manufactured specifically for the brand of camera on which they are used. Many tubes will eliminate automatic focusing. Manual tubes will cancel automatic metering.

Tubes can be used individually or in combination. The longer the extension used, the greater the magnification gained. Longer extensions require extra light to create the same exposure. When using tubes, the subject image will appear darker in the viewfinder and on the LCD.

Extension tubes reduce the minimum focal distance of the lens and increase the lens magnification, which enlarges the size of the subject in the image. When using longer lenses with the same size tube, the tube will create less magnification. The longer the lens, the greater the minimum focusing distance, lens to subject.

REMEMBER:

DoF is reduced as the lens moves closer to the subject.

MAGNIFICATION

Magnification (M) is the relationship of subject size to its image size on the sensor and may be expressed in three ways:

1. As a *ratio*, image size to object size: for example, 2:1)
2. As a *multiple:* for example, $\times$ 4, $\times$ 1.0 or $\times$ 0.5
3. As *lens-to-subject distance* (u) and lens-to-image distance (v): for example,

M = v/u = image distance/subject distance

1/u + 1/v = 1/F

where F is the focal length of the lens.

Or

v = (M + 1) F

Magnification will change when the focal length of the lens or the lens-to-image distance changes. Therefore, magnification can change by adding extension tubes or diopters.

> **TIP:**
>
> Using sufficient extension to raise the magnification to life size (1:1 magnification) requires two extra stops of light.

Magnification may be mathematically calculated by dividing the focal length of the lens into the length of the extension.

Magnification = extension/focal length

For example, when using a 50 mm lens on a 40 mm tube, the magnification will be .8 × life size.

When adding close-up lenses to alter focal length:

Magnification = focal length of lens/focal length of diopter

Reproduction Ratio (RR) = the size of the image/the size of the subject.

For example, if an image of a 4-inch subject is .5 inch on sensor, the RR is 1:8

RR = .5 inch/4 inch = 1:8

If an image of a .5 inch subject is .5 inch on sensor,

RR = .5 inch/.5 inch = 1:1

Scale = linear size of image/linear size of subject

For example, if an image is 8 inches wide and the subject is 1 inch wide, the scale of the image is 8/1 = 8× = 8:1.

For another example, if an image is 1 inch wide and the subject is 1 mile wide, the scale of the image is 1 inch = 1 mile.

Lens Extension:RR:Magnification

Magnification = extension/focal length

For example,

RR for a 50 mm lens and 10 mm extension is 1:5, or .2×.

RR for a 50 mm lens and 20 mm extension is 1:2.5, or .4×.

RR for a 50 mm lens and 50 mm extension is 1:1, or 1×.

RR of 50 mm Lens with Close-Up Lencses

50 mm with +1 lens = 1:20

50 mm with +2 lens = 1:10

50 mm with +3 lens = 1:6

50 mm with +4 lens = 1:5

Exposure Increase (EI) for Lens Extension

EI = (lens focal length + extension/lens focal length)^2

For example, a 50 mm lens with a 25 mm extension:

$$EI = (50 + 25/50)^2$$

$(75/50)^2 = 2.25 \times E = 1⅓$ f-stops increase

$1.4 \times E = ½$ f-stop

$2 \times E = 1$ f-stop

$2.9 \times E = 1½$ f-stop

$4 \times E = 2$ f-stop

EXTENSION BELLOWS

Using **extension bellows** (see Fig. 10–3) between the camera body and the lens is another way to gain magnification by extending the distance between the sensor and the lens. Bellows are similar in purpose and operation to extension tubes.

Bellows provide variable extension and, therefore, variable magnification. They are available for any interchangeable-lens SLR camera. The minimum and maximum extensions are determined by the construction of the bellows. The magnification is computed by dividing the lens focal length into the extension.

For example, if using a 50 mm lens on a 200 mm bellows, the magnification will be 4:1 on the image plane.

200/50 = 4

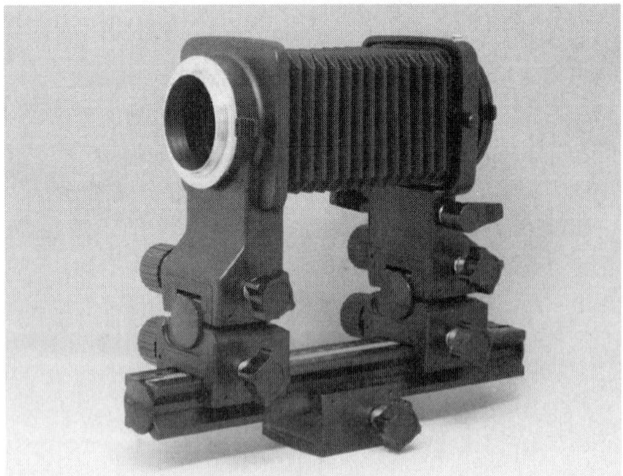

FIGURE 10–3 An extension bellows. *Source:* Sandy Weiss/Packer Engineering.

Special **bellows lenses** are available through some OEMs. Such lenses are designed for use only on a bellows and contain no built-in focusing mechanisms, relying on the bellows or a change of lens-to-subject distance for focusing. Bellows lenses are available over a range of focal lengths between about 10 mm and 135 mm. Some contain automatic lens diaphragms, but most do not. Bellows lenses of some focal lengths will focus to infinity when on the bellows.

All lenses manufactured for use on photographic enlargers and many lenses manufactured for use on motion picture cameras provide excellent results for macrophotography when used on a bellows. All these lenses must be used in manual mode. Calculations of extension divided by focal length provide magnification figures. The advantages of using these lenses for macrophotography are that they are readily available, normally inexpensive, optically sound, and physically small, so when in proximity to the subject they do not block the illumination source.

It may be necessary to manufacture an appropriate **lens mount** adapter to affix the special lenses to the bellows or extension tubes. Camera body caps may often be milled to the proper size and then threaded to fit the lens. If threading is not possible, it may be possible to mill a hole and then glue on a part that is already threaded to fit the lens.

TIP:

Use of a focal length lens that is longer than considered normal for the image format will increase the working distance between the lens and the subject.

Exposure must be adjusted for extension and magnification: the longer the extension, the more light is needed for a comparable exposure. When a camera's built-in light meter performs wide-aperture exposure metering, the lens aperture is not reduced to the size of its setting until the time of the exposure. When a camera's built-in light meter performs **stopped-down mode** exposure metering, the lens aperture is reduced to the size of its setting before the time of the exposure, while the photographer is viewing and composing the image. If the camera's built-in meter contains stopped-down metering capability, it may be possible to meter through the lens, even if the lens does not contain automatic meter-coupling hardware. Some bellows have an integral focusing rail, so the magnification may be set at the desired ratio and the whole camera unit may be focused by moving closer and farther from the subject on the rail.

All the necessary parts are readily available for the attachment of Nikkor enlarging lenses to Nikon bellows. Do the following to fit an El-Nikkor enlarging lens onto a Nikon bellows:

1. Obtain a lens between 50 mm and 135 mm.
2. Purchase a 42 mm-to-39 mm adapter ring (many are available on the Internet). A 42 mm fits screw-mount Pentax lenses. A 39 mm fits the enlarging lens.
3. Attach the 42 mm-to-39 mm ring onto the lens (see Fig. 10–4).
4. Purchase a 42 mm-to-Nikon-bayonet ring (many are available on the Internet).
5. Screw the lens and ring into the 42 mm to bayonet ring (see Figs. 10–5 and 10–6).

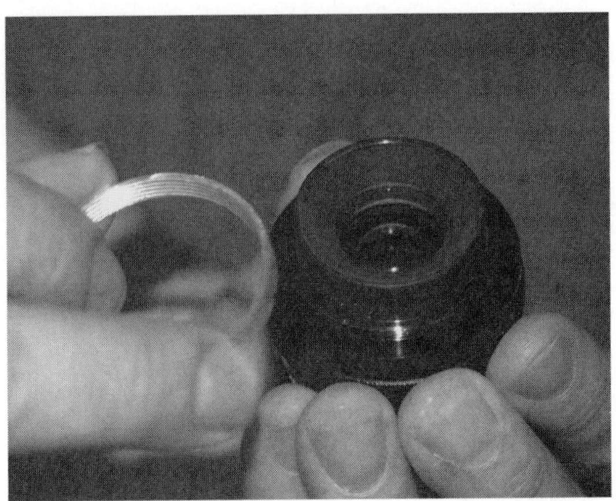

FIGURE 10–4 A 42 mm-to-39 mm adapter. *Source:* Sandy Weiss/Packer Engineering.

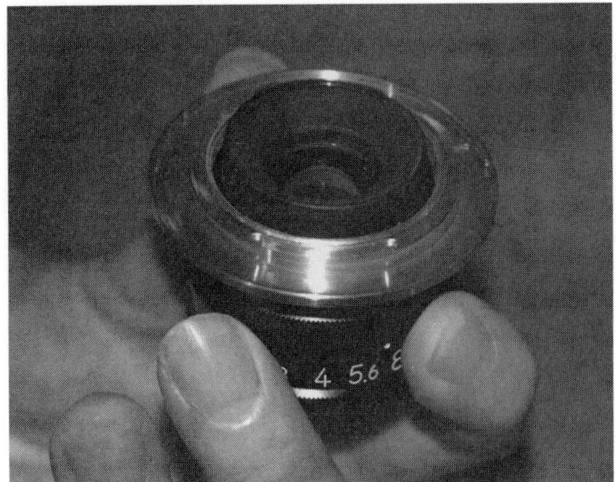

FIGURE 10–6 An El-Nikkor lens with a Nikon bayonet. *Source:* Sandy Weiss/Packer Engineering.

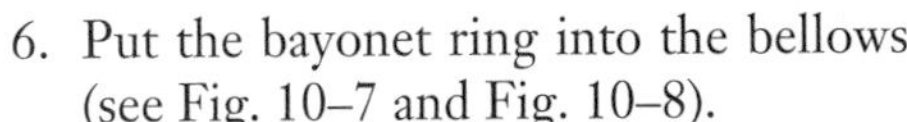

6. Put the bayonet ring into the bellows (see Fig. 10–7 and Fig. 10–8).

These images illustrate the use of a Nikon bellows with an El-Nikkor 75 mm enlarging lens. Three flashes are used and two are fired by photo-optical slaves. The subject is a 4 mm kidney stone produced by the author during the writing of this chapter. The stone is placed on an elevating stage, and a U.S. nickel and stainless steel mechanic's rule are used for scale. In this case, the copy stand is an old unit manufactured by Polaroid and contains two fluorescent tubes used for focusing lights (see Figs. 10–9 thru 10–13).

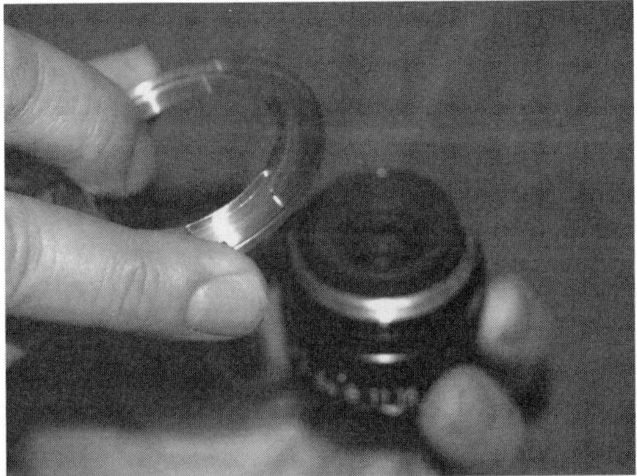

FIGURE 10–5 A 42 mm-to-Nikon-bayonet adapter. *Source:* Sandy Weiss/Packer Engineering.

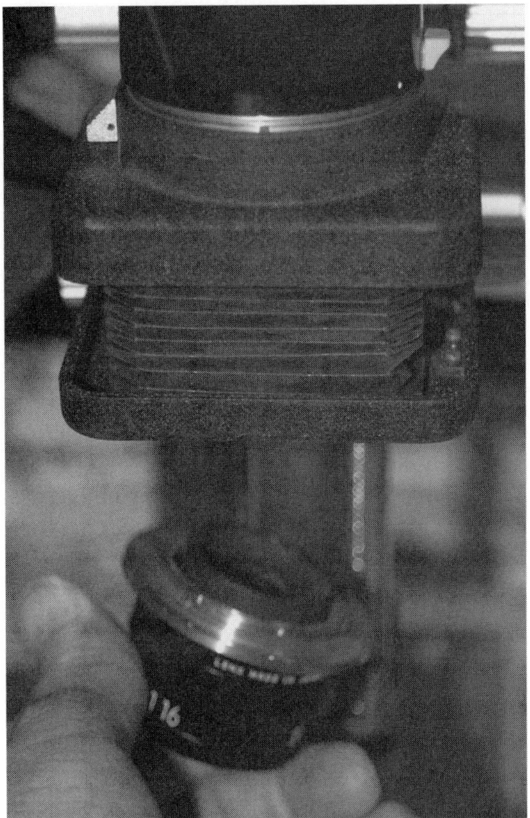

FIGURE 10–7 Connecting the bayonet to the bellows. *Source:* Sandy Weiss/Packer Engineering.

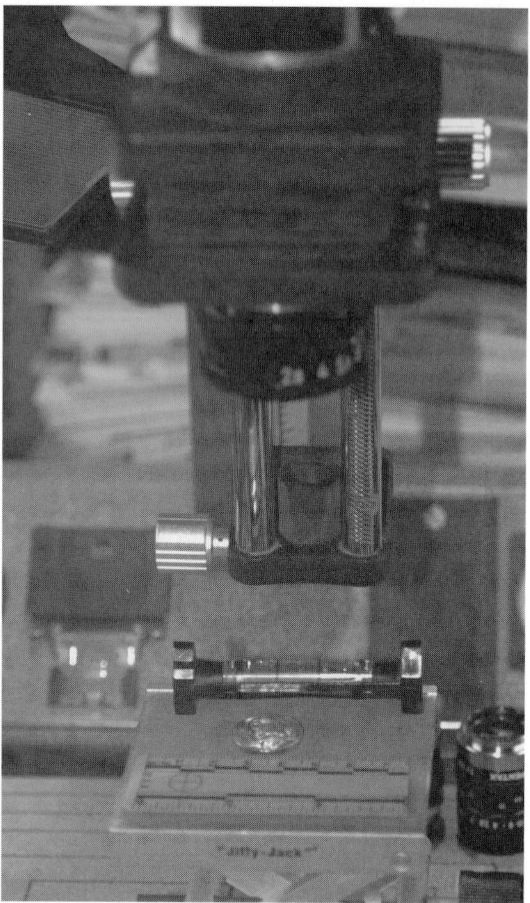

FIGURE 10–8 Completed assembly for macrophotography with a digital camera, bellows, and enlarging lens. *Source:* Sandy Weiss/Packer Engineering.

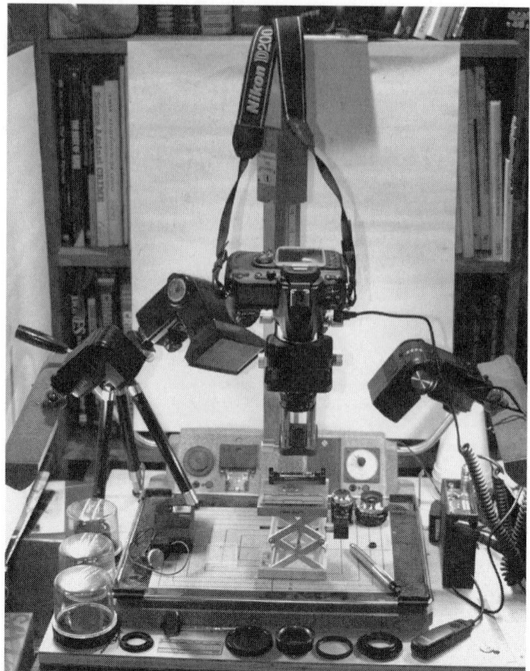

FIGURE 10–9 Nikon bellows with an El-Nikkor 75 mm enlarging lens, and three flashes, in use for photography of kidney stone. *Source:* Sandy Weiss/Packer Engineering.

REVERSING RINGS

Lenses intended for normal photography may provide increased resolution if mounted backward on the bellows with a **reversing ring** (see Fig. 10–14). For best resolution, focus the lens at infinity. Very little additional magnification is gained by focusing the lens at any other distance.

Reversing rings attach to the filter thread on the front of a lens. The appropriate mount for the camera lens is on the other side of the ring. This makes it possible to attach the lens to the camera body in reverse. Rings may produce magnifications up to 4x life size using normal lenses not designed for macrophotography.

MACROPHOTOGRAPHY LIGHTING

Ring flashes are designed for photographing subjects in fine detail with shadowless, low-contrast illumination. Ring flashes work well only at macro range. Many ring flashes have a full array of flash tubes arranged around the front of the lens. Some modern ring lights have white LEDs to provide continuous light sources for aiming and focusing.

Nikon SB-29S Speedlight

The Nikon SB-29S Speedlight (see Fig. 10–15) is a double flash designed specifically for macrophotography, and is not actually a ring light. The two flashes are positioned on either side of the detachable unit. The SB-29S works TTL with Nikon film cameras but not Nikon DSLRs. Both or only one of the flashes may be fired. The ring revolves around the front of the lens to enable the light to originate at any angle appropriate for the subject. The unit has a built-in

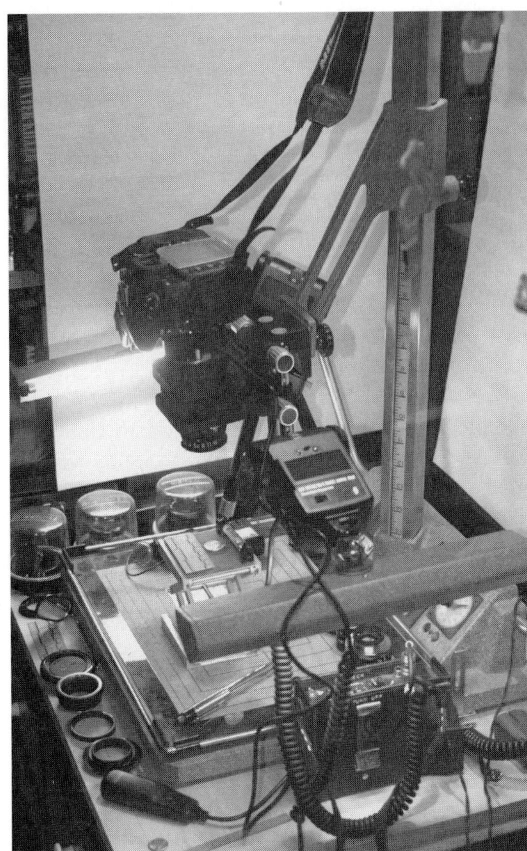

FIGURE 10–10 Side view of the Nikon bellows with an El-Nikkor 75 mm enlarging lens, and three flashes, in use for photography of kidney stone. *Source:* Sandy Weiss/Packer Engineering.

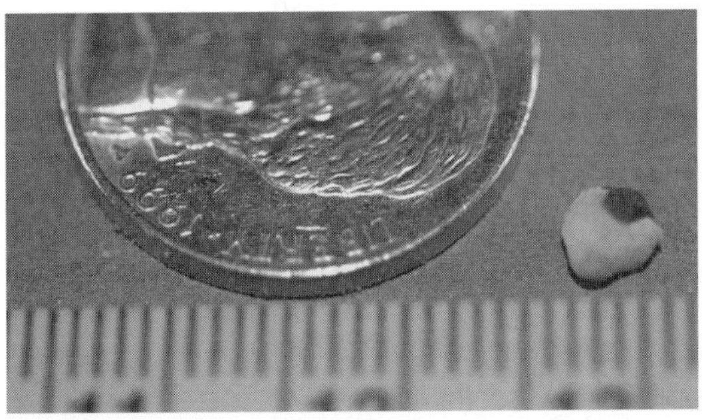

FIGURE 10–11 Size comparison of a nickel and a kidney stone, with appropriate scale. *Source:* Sandy Weiss/Packer Engineering.

FIGURE 10–12 Nickel only, to demonstrate the macro capability of a Nikon bellows with an El-Nikkor 75 mm enlarging lens. *Source:* Sandy Weiss/Packer Engineering.

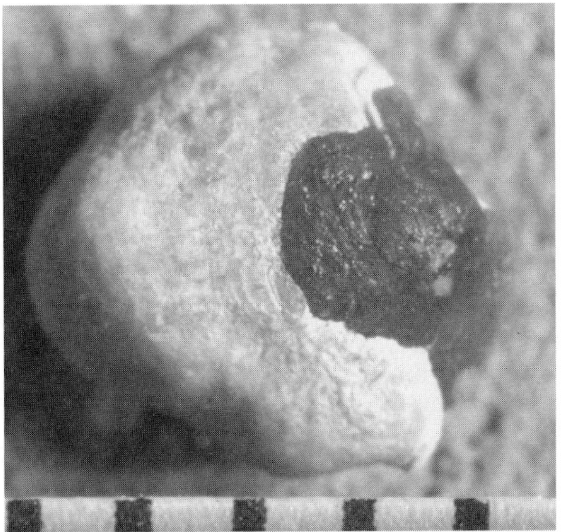

FIGURE 10–13 A kidney stone, 4.06 mm. *Source:* Sandy Weiss/Packer Engineering.

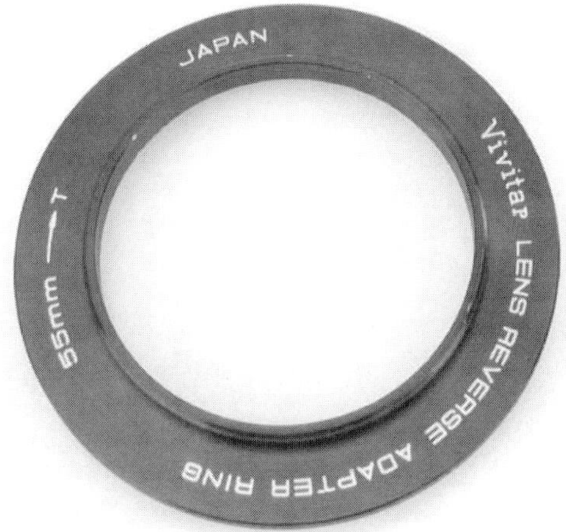

FIGURE 10–14 Reversing ring adapter. *Source:* Sandy Weiss/Packer Engineering.

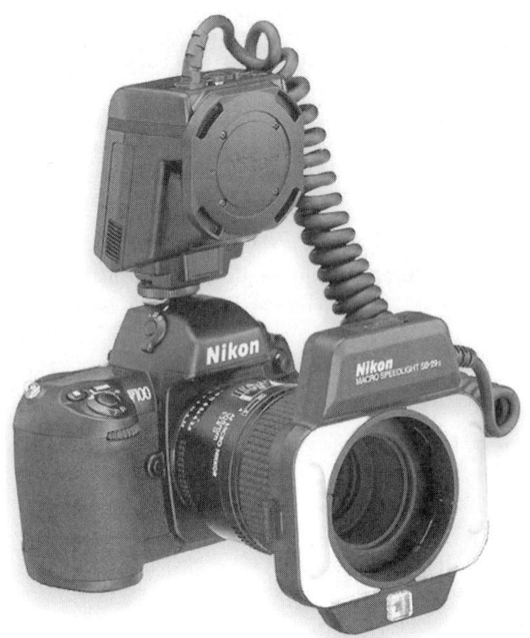

FIGURE 10–15 Nikon SB-29S. *Source:* Sandy Weiss/ Packer Engineering.

modeling light to preview the lighting effect or to help focusing.

Nikon SB-R200 Remote Macro Flash

The Nikon SB-R200 Remote Macro Flash units are shown on each side of the lens in Figure 10–16. The flashes are wirelessly controlled, mastered

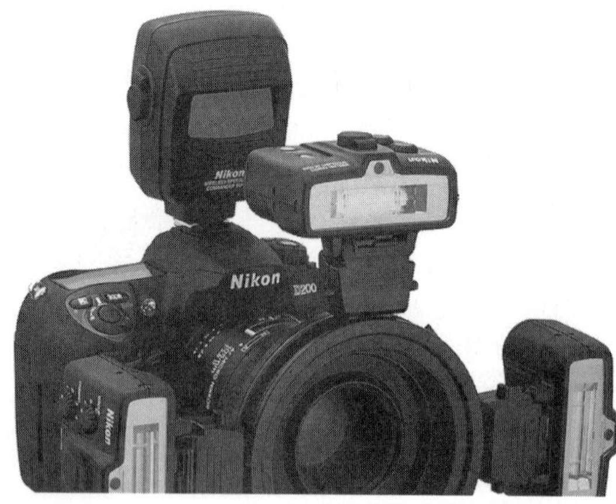

FIGURE 10–16 Nikon SB-R200 Remote Macro Flash on a camera. *Source:* Sandy Weiss/Packer Engineering.

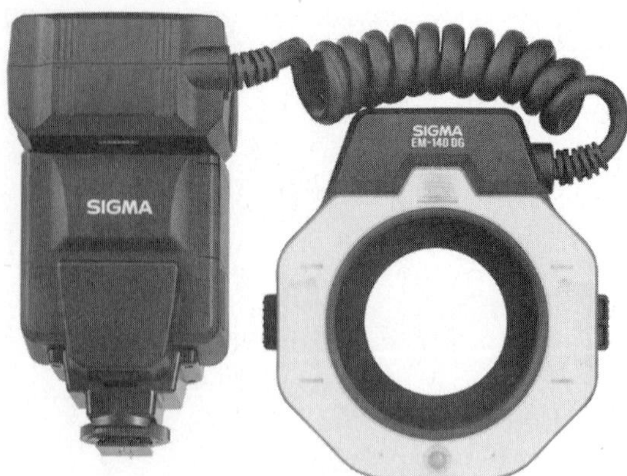

FIGURE 10–17 Sigma Electronic Macro Flash EM-140 DG. *Source:* Sandy Weiss/ Packer Engineering.

by the built-in flash of some Nikon DSLRs or by an SU-800 remote commander. The flashes are adjustable in all directions from the optical axis. They contain white LEDs for accurate positioning. Up to four units may be used at once.

Sigma Macro Flash

Sigma Corporation manufactures the Electronic Macro Flash EM-140 DG (see Figs. 10–17 and 10–18). It works with auto-focus 35 mm and

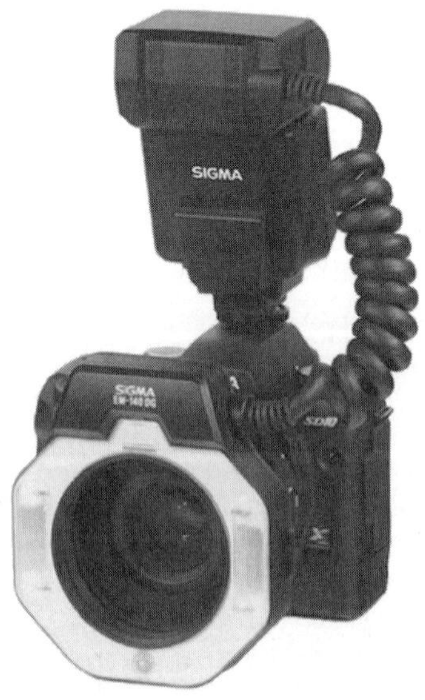

FIGURE 10–18 Sigma Electronic Macro Flash EM-140 DG on a camera. *Source:* Sandy Weiss/Packer Engineering.

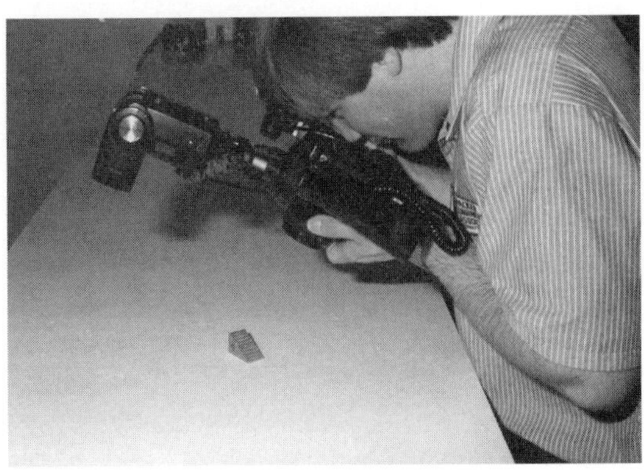

FIGURE 10–19 Flash aimed too high. *Source:* Sandy Weiss/Packer Engineering.

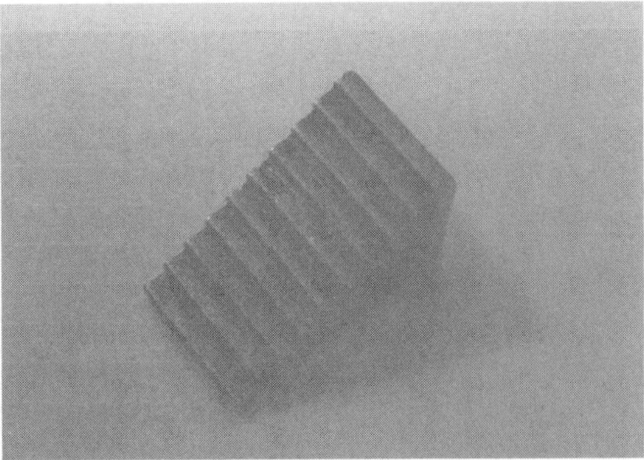

FIGURE 10–20 The image will be underexposed when the flash is aimed too high. *Source:* Sandy Weiss/Packer Engineering.

DSLR cameras. It operates properly with all OEM-dedicated TTL auto-exposure systems. Its dual flash tubes may be fired simultaneously or separately. The GN of the unit is 14 with an ISO sensitivity of 100. It has a built-in modeling light to check for reflections and shadows before exposing the flash image. The unit is supplied with 55 mm and 58mm adapter rings, and 52 mm, 62 mm, 67 mm, 72 mm, and 77 mm adapters are also available to adapt the flash to all lenses.

Oblique Flash and Auto-Exposure

In situations where the evidence photographer does not have a ring flash, it may be necessary to use a built-in or accessory EFU for macro lighting. If using the built-in flash and no diffuser, the lighting will illuminate the subject from the lens axis and may display bright reflections or deep shadows. If an accessory EFU is available, the most commonly used technique used for illuminating the subject is to hold the EFU off to the side of the camera and subject so the reflections will bounce past the camera and not be an issue. This technique is called **oblique lighting.** One EFU or continuous light source is held at about a 45-degree angle to the side of the subject. In macrophotography, it is critical to aim the flash directly at the subject. If the flash is set on automatic exposure and aimed anywhere but at the subject (see Fig. 10–19), the image will be underexposed (see Fig. 10–20).

In Figure 10–21, the flash is aimed at the proper place and the subject will receive sufficient illumination. However, the subject is again underexposed because it was photographed against a white background (see Fig. 10–22).

In Figure 10–23, the subject is placed on an 18% gray background and the flash is properly aimed. The resultant exposure is proper for the subject (see Fig. 10–24).

In Figure 10–24, the exposure for the subject is correct; however, the front and right sides of the subject are underexposed because of the deep shadows. To reduce the density of the shadows, a reflector may be used.

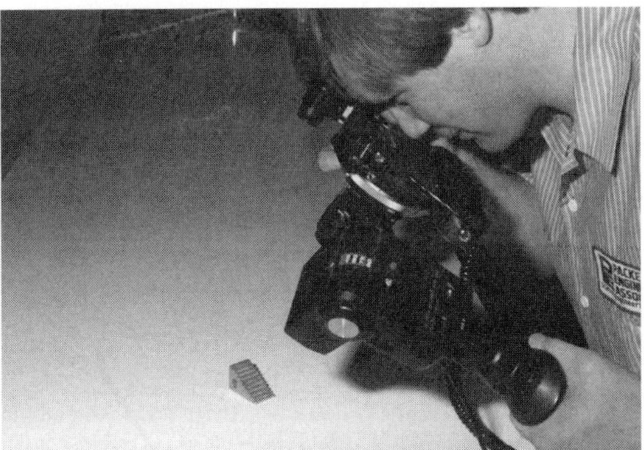

FIGURE 10–21 Flash aimed at the right place. *Source:* Sandy Weiss/Packer Engineering.

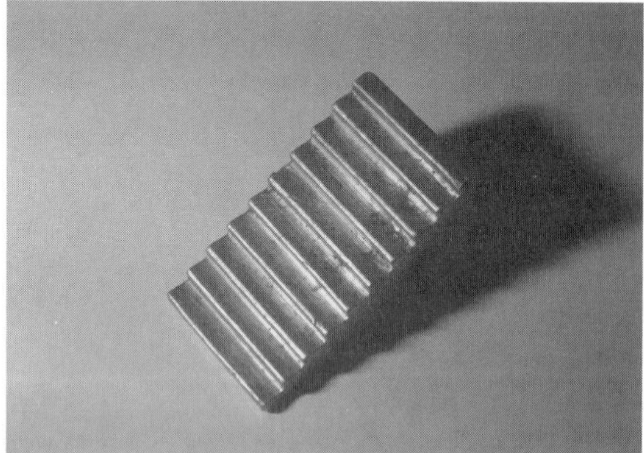

FIGURE 10–22 Subject underexposed because the background was too light. *Source:* Sandy Weiss/Packer Engineering.

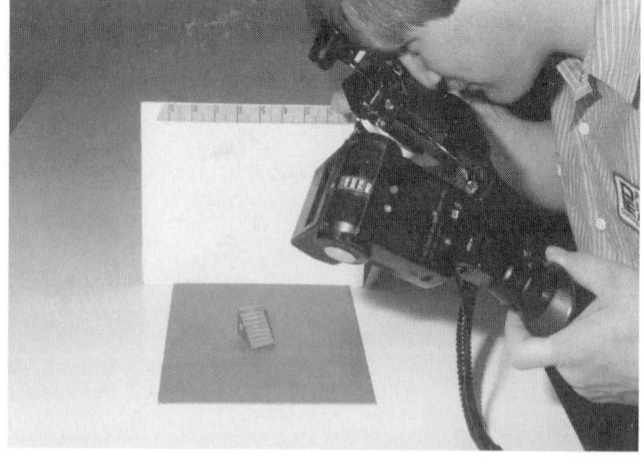

FIGURE 10–25 A white reflector illuminates the right and front sides of the subject. *Source:* Sandy Weiss/Packer Engineering.

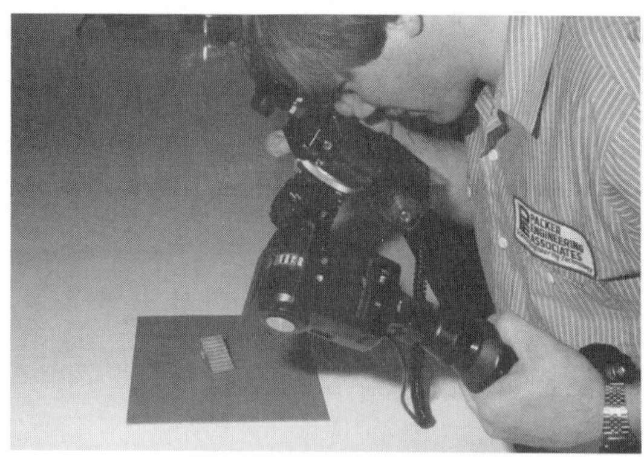

FIGURE 10–23 The subject is photographed against an 18% gray background. *Source:* Sandy Weiss/Packer Engineering.

In Figure 10–25, the front and right sides of the subject are illuminated by reflected light bouncing off the white card (the reverse of the 18% gray card) held to the right of the subject. This is a reasonable overall exposure of the subject (see Fig. 10–26).

To eliminate the shadows from the front and right side of the subject in Figures 10–25 and 10–26, the subject may be supported on a piece of glass with the 18% gray card beneath (see Fig. 10–27). The shadows will appear far enough to the side of the subject to be separated. The subject appears suspended in space (see Fig. 10–28), and the exposure of the subject remains correct.

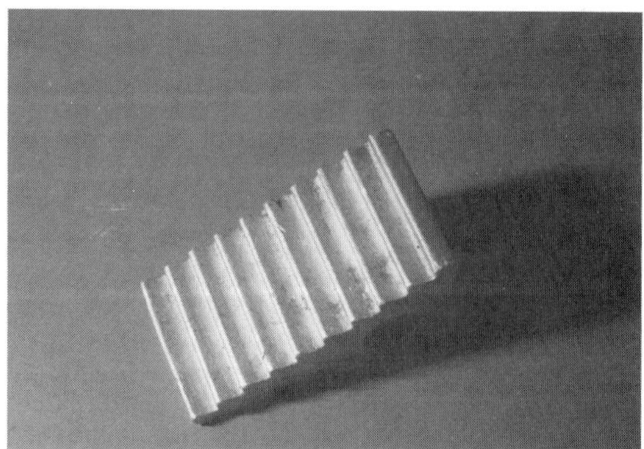

FIGURE 10–24 The exposure is correct for the subject due to the neutral background. *Source:* Sandy Weiss/Packer Engineering.

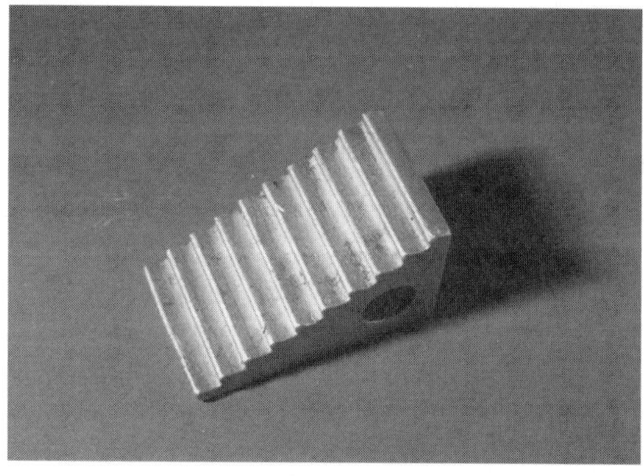

FIGURE 10–26 A properly exposed macrophotograph. *Source:* Sandy Weiss/Packer Engineering.

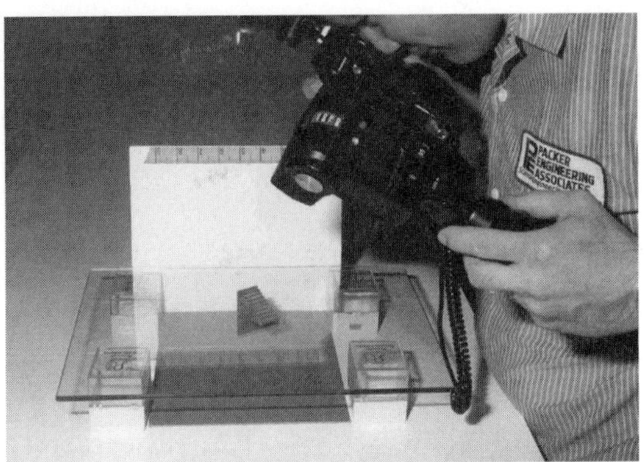

FIGURE 10–27 Subject supported on a glass stage. *Source:* Sandy Weiss/Packer Engineering.

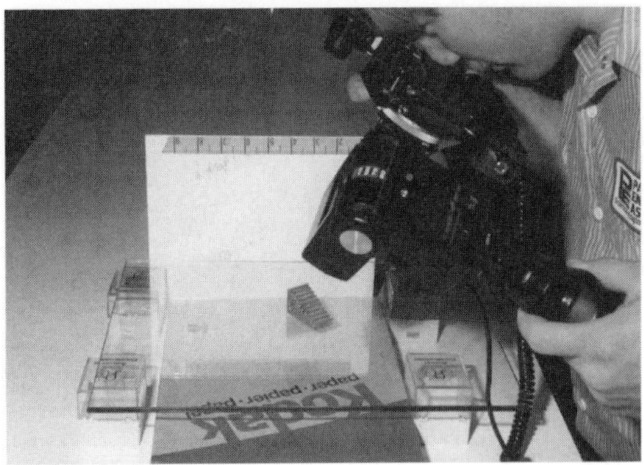

FIGURE 10–29 Using a brightly colored background for contrast. *Source:* Sandy Weiss/Packer Engineering.

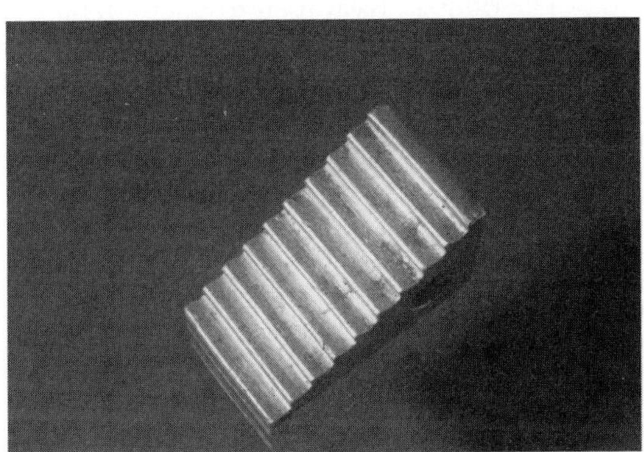

FIGURE 10–28 The shadows are separated from the subject. *Source:* Sandy Weiss/Packer Engineering.

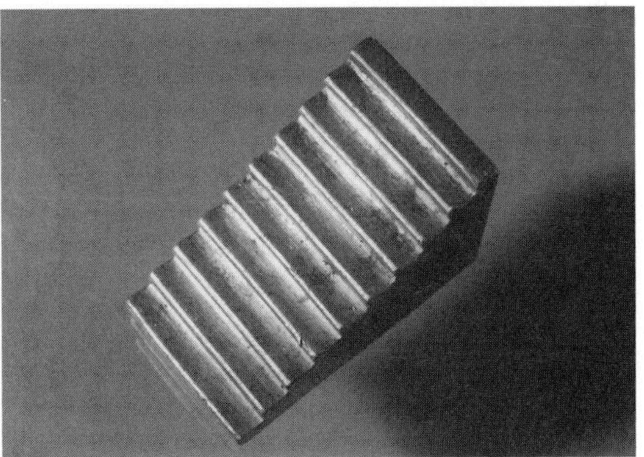

FIGURE 10–30 A yellow background gives the subject a cool blue appearance. *Source:* Sandy Weiss/Packer Engineering.

In Figure 10–29 the photographer used a background of a contrasting color so the subject would be rendered in higher contrast and stand out from the background. The yellow background provides some relief for the subject but also causes the color balance of the neutral metal subject to look excessively cool/blue in the resultant image (see Fig. 10–30).

In Figure 10–31, the photographer used a black background behind the subject and under the glass. The subject is well exposed, but it is difficult to see where the subject stops and the background starts (see Fig. 10–32), although the contrast is high between their tones.

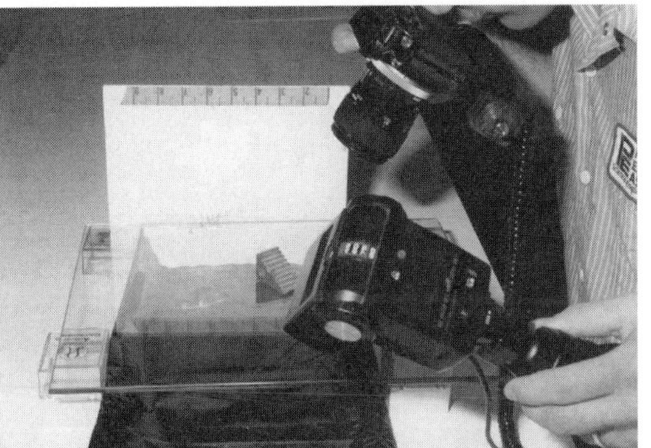

FIGURE 10–31 A dark background can be used for contrast, but it may be difficult to see the boundaries of the subject and the background. *Source:* Sandy Weiss/Packer Engineering.

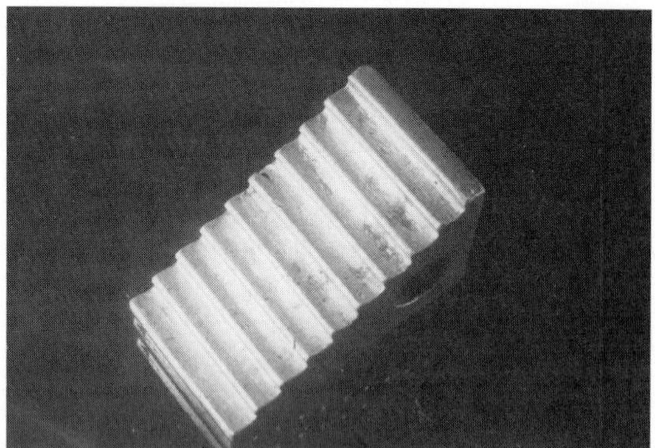

FIGURE 10–32 This well-exposed subject is difficult to differentiate from the background. *Source:* Sandy Weiss/Packer Engineering.

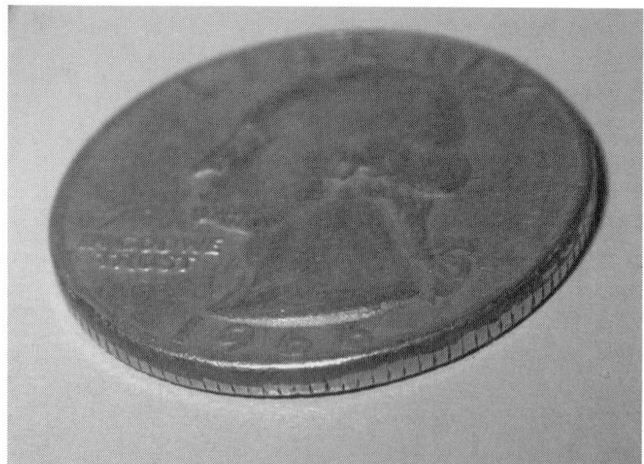

FIGURE 10–33 A U.S. quarter exposed with a point-and-shoot digital camera and a built-in flash. *Source:* Sandy Weiss/Packer Engineering.

When using an EFU on automatic exposure for macrophotography, it is advantageous to use reflectors or multiple flashes to evenly illuminate all sides of the subject. Use neutral backgrounds of approximately 18% reflectance to promote proper exposures.

Using Built-in Flash and Auto-Exposure

When using only the built-in flash, some cameras will produce acceptable macrophotographs of small subjects. Figure 10–33 is an image of a U.S. quarter exposed with a point-and-shoot digital camera and a built-in flash.

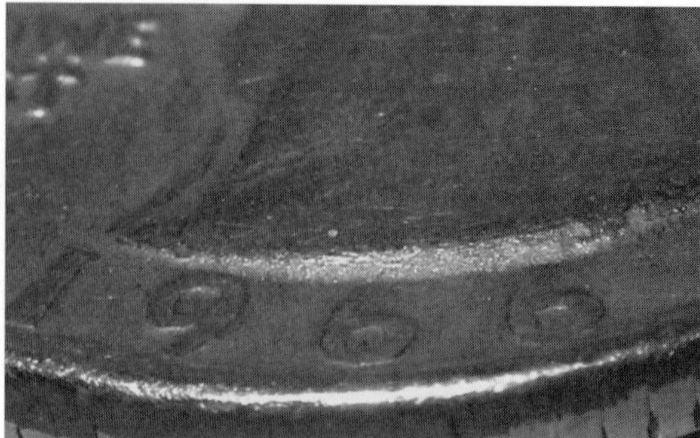

FIGURE 10–34 A close-up of a U.S. quarter exposed with a point-and-shoot digital camera and a built-in flash. It is difficult to differentiate between raised and recessed features. *Source:* Sandy Weiss/Packer Engineering.

The built-in flash used to photograph the coin provides adequate lighting, but the flatness of the lighting produces an image with minimal **relief** contours (see Fig. 10–34). It may not be possible to differentiate between raised and recessed features on the surface of the subject. In Figurs 10–35 and 10–36, an accessory EFU held to the side at a 45-degree angle was triggered by the deflected illumination of the built-in flash. Note the shadow to the right side of the quarter. The shadow indicates the position of the main illumination. (See the explanation of flash deflectors in Chapter 9.) A small EFU was about 8 inches from the subject. In this image, the

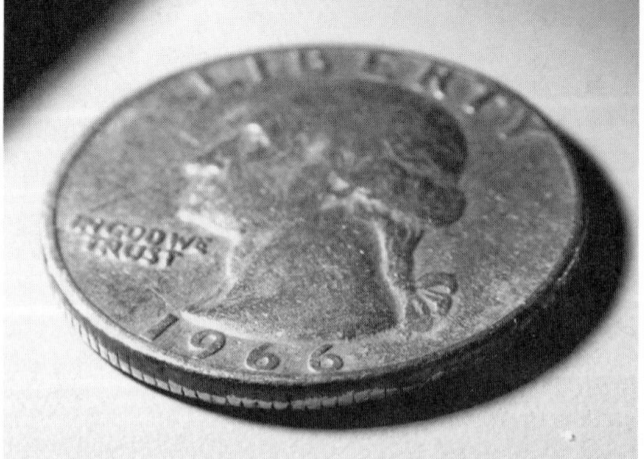

FIGURE 10–35 U.S. quarter exposed with a point-and-shoot digital camera and camera flash triggered by the built-in flash. *Source:* Sandy Weiss/Packer Engineering.

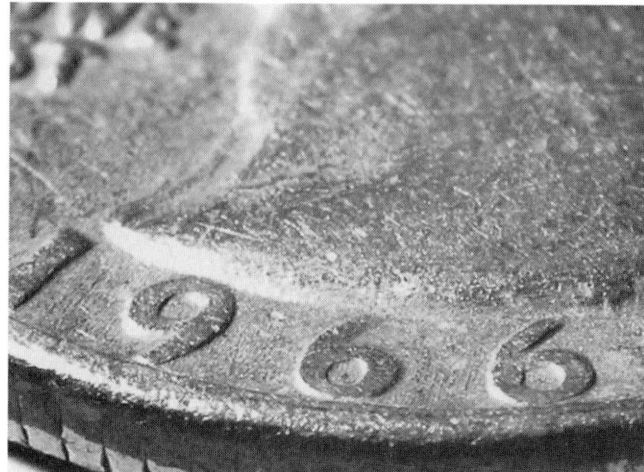

FIGURE 10–36 Close-up of U.S. quarter exposed with a point-and-shoot digital camera and off-camera flash, showing the raised details of the subject. *Source:* Sandy Weiss/Packer Engineering.

landmarks on the surface of the coin are easily identified as raised.

In Figure 10–37, the fracture surface of a broken bolt was exposed with only a built-in flash. The image displays good quality and exposure, but the character of the fracture is impossible to analyze when the image is exposed with lighting from the axis of the lens. The same fracture surface exposed with oblique flash (see Fig. 10–38) yields information about the mechanics of the failure.

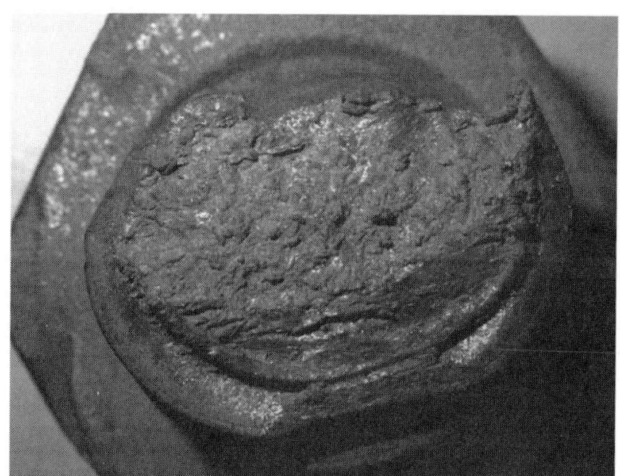

FIGURE 10–37 Fracture surface of a broken bolt exposed with built-in flash. *Source:* Sandy Weiss/Packer Engineering.

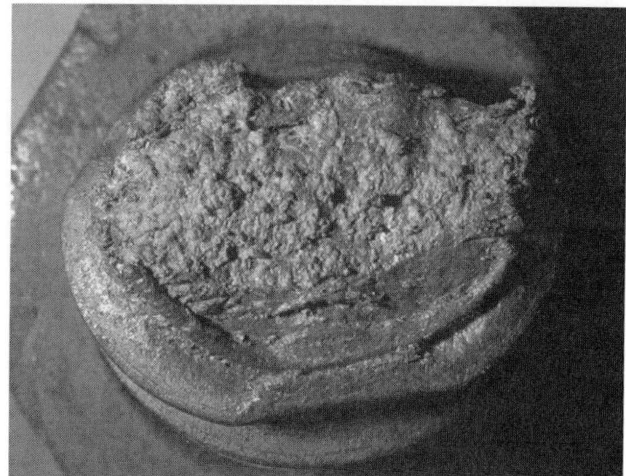

FIGURE 10–38 Fracture surface of a broken bolt exposed with oblique flash. *Source:* Sandy Weiss/Packer Engineering.

Proper Exposure of Small Subjects with Auto-Exposure EFU

When small objects are free standing in space and the flash is set for automatic exposure, the subject must be large enough to reflect sufficient light back to the flash and camera to prevent overexposure. If the free-standing subject is small, the subject (the top of the threaded rod in Fig. 10–39) will yield an image that is overexposed (see Fig. 10–40).

An 18% gray card, or other suitable object, may be placed behind the subject to

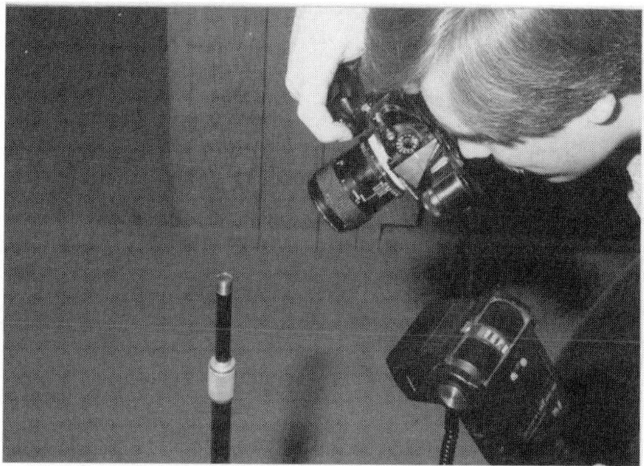

FIGURE 10–39 Flash exposure of a small, free-standing object. *Source:* Sandy Weiss/Packer Engineering.

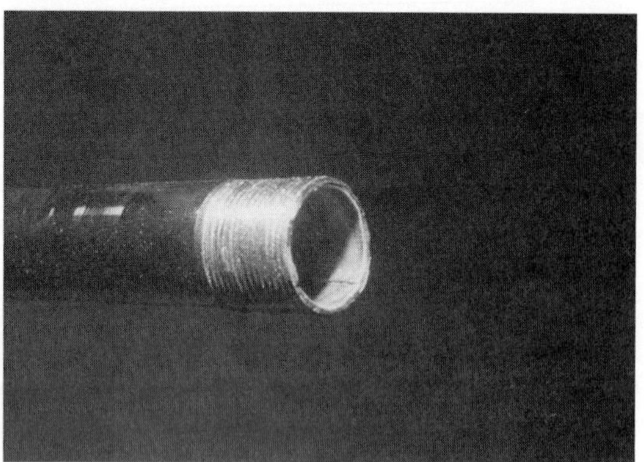

FIGURE 10–40 Overexposure of a small, free-standing object. *Source:* Sandy Weiss/ Packer Engineering.

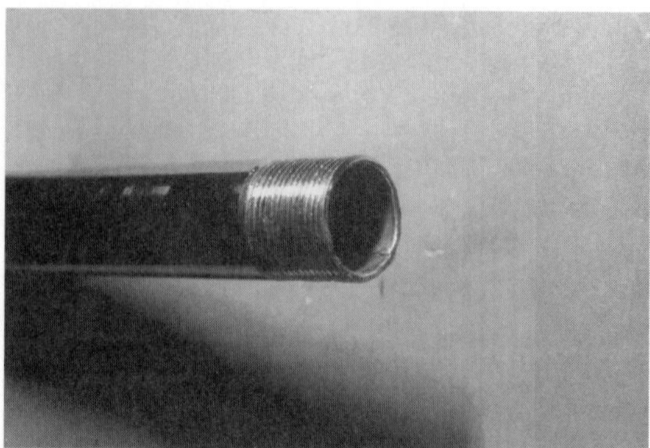

FIGURE 10–42 A gray card placed behind the free-standing subject results in proper exposure. *Source:* Sandy Weiss/ Packer Engineering.

produce an image that is properly exposed (see Fig. 10–41). The gray card reflects enough light back to the flash to create a proper exposure (see Fig. 10–42).

Axial Lighting

Direct lighting from an EFU creates an image that is high in contrast. When lower-contrast illumination is necessary due to the nature of the subject, axial lighting (see Fig. 10–43) and tent lighting formulas may be used.

By definition, **axial lighting** is derived from a lighting formula that is used to provide illumination to the subject with the light emanating from the same axis as the lens of the camera.

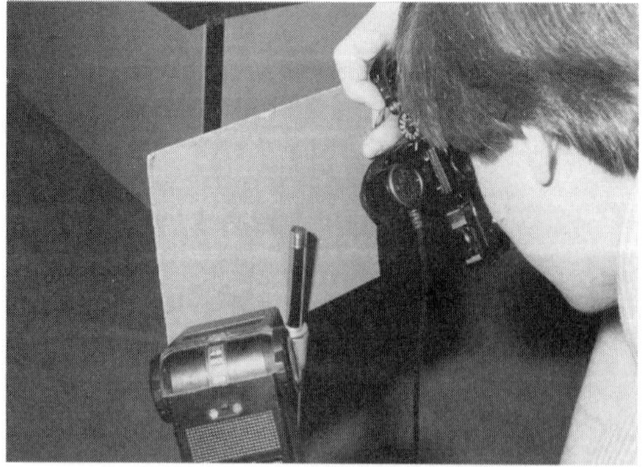

FIGURE 10–41 A gray card placed behind the subject for background. *Source:* Sandy Weiss/Packer Engineering.

Ring and built-in flash are low contrast, but not truly axial, because they are offset slightly to the side of the lens. Axial lighting is achieved by bouncing the source light off a piece of glass and exposing the image through the same glass (see Fig. 10–43). This lighting formula is useful when photographing highly reflective surfaces or small objects with a high relief-to-size ratio (for example, printed circuit boards).

All other types of lighting used for general macrophotography may cause unwanted reflections or deeper shadows (higher contrast) on parts of the subject. The reflections and shadows may necessitate exposing extra images of the same subject with lighting at various angles to capture all the aspects of the subject. The lower contrast of axial lighting allows wide latitude for exposure error.

The shell casing shown in Figure 10–44 is an easily photographed subject with any type of lighting. Oblique lighting will display surface landmarks but will also create dense shadows. Axial lighting will display the surface characteristics and detail of the recessed surfaces in the same image.

Creating Axial Lighting

It is often necessary to photograph details on shiny objects. Oblique lighting is practical, but the oblique lighting angle may create unwanted

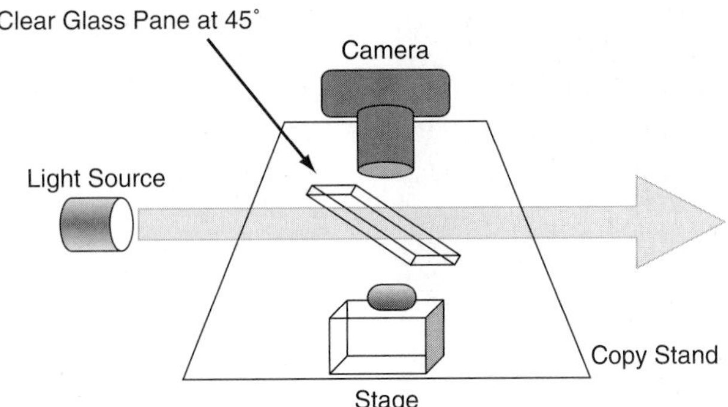

FIGURE 10–43 Axial lighting set-up. *Source:* Sandy Weiss/Packer Engineering.

shadows. At high magnifications, if a shiny subject must be photographed at an angle to the lens, limited DoF may also be an issue. Axial lighting facilitates the imaging of shiny subjects, without the problem of reflective highlights, when the subjects are arranged in a parallel plane to the light sensor of the camera.

Figure 10–45 was exposed with an axial apparatus and a Nikon D1-X with a 60 mm macro lens and a Vivitar 283 EFU. The sensitivity was set at ISO 100, the lens aperture at *f*/36, and the shutter speed at 1/400 second. The EFU was set on automatic exposure. The flash must always be left far enough outside the apparatus for the sensor to register the reflected light.

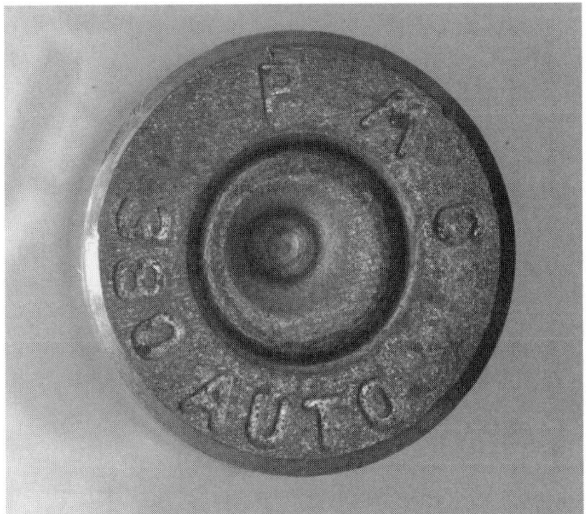

FIGURE 10–44 Axially illuminated shell casing. *Source:* Sandy Weiss/Packer Engineering.

Trial and error is the best method for the determination of the proper exposure settings for axial lighting. Experience will eventually allow the photographer to select an exposure setting that is close to correct, before exposing an image. When compared to a macro lens, the physical size of an enlarging lens makes it a practical choice for axial set-ups.

REMEMBER:

It is important to factor for extra exposure when using a bellows or extension tubes.

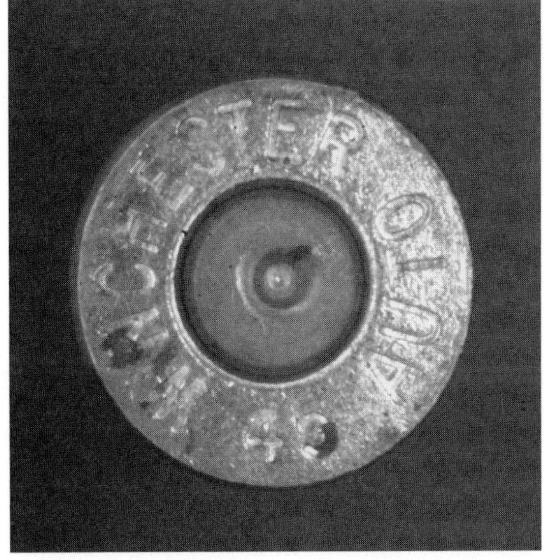

FIGURE 10–45 Another axially illuminated shell casing. *Source:* Sandy Weiss/Packer Engineering.

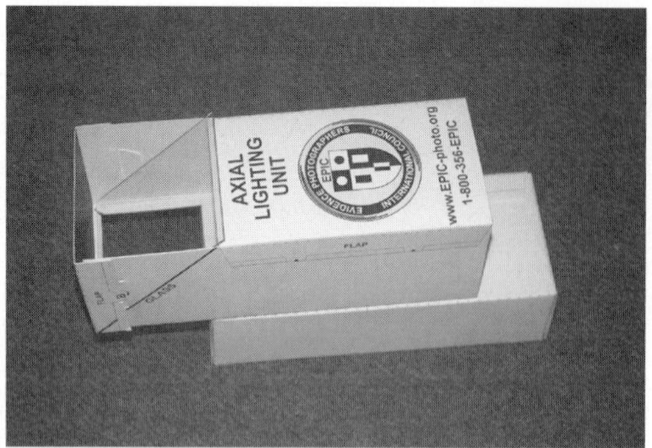

FIGURE 10–46 EPIC axial lighting apparatus. *Source:* Sandy Weiss/Packer Engineering.

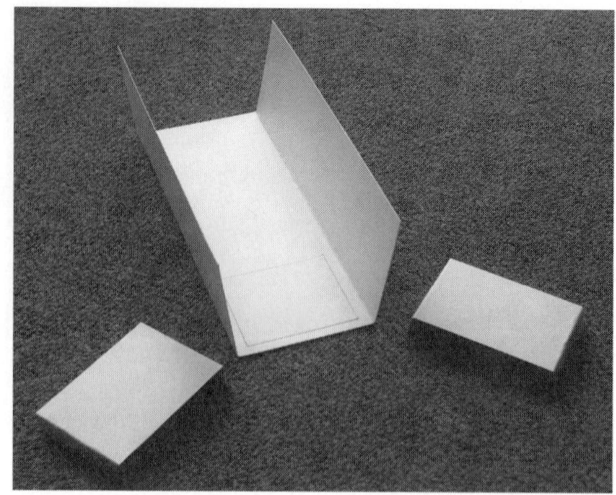

FIGURE 10–48 Assembly of an axial lighting apparatus: folded cardboard. *Source:* Sandy Weiss/Packer Engineering.

Building an Axial Lighting Apparatus

The Evidence Photographers International Council markets ready-made axial lighting kits (of my design) (see Fig. 10–46; for current information and prices, go to www.evidencephotographers.com). For photographers who wish to save the money and build their own axial lighting kits, use the following instructions. You can vary the contrast of an axial lighting assembly by changing the color of the mirror chamber or the terminal wall. White provides the lowest-contrast light, brown/gray provides medium contrast, and black provides the highest contrast.

Instructions for Assembly of an Axial Lighting Apparatus

To build your own axial lighting apparatus, gather the supplies and instructions that follow (see Figures 10–47 through 10–52).

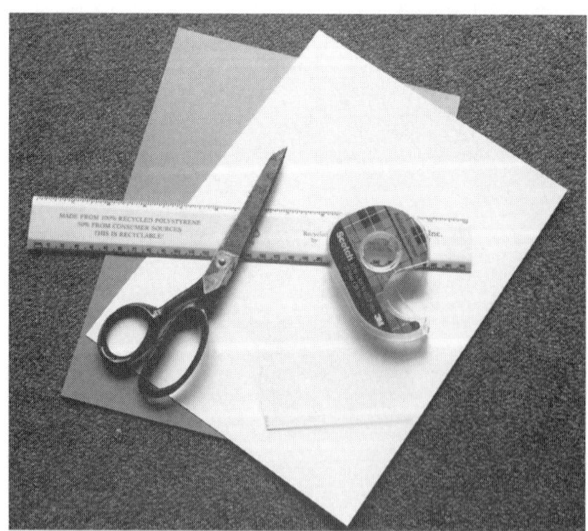

FIGURE 10–47 Supplies for building an axial lighting apparatus. *Source:* Sandy Weiss/Packer Engineering.

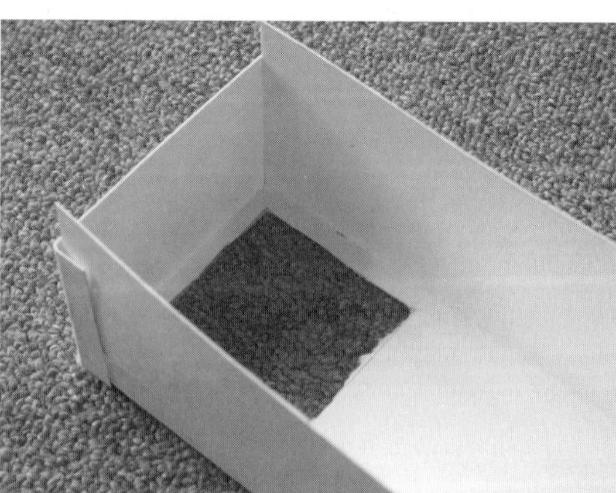

FIGURE 10–49 Assembly of an axial lighting apparatus: partial assembly 1. *Source:* Sandy Weiss/Packer Engineering.

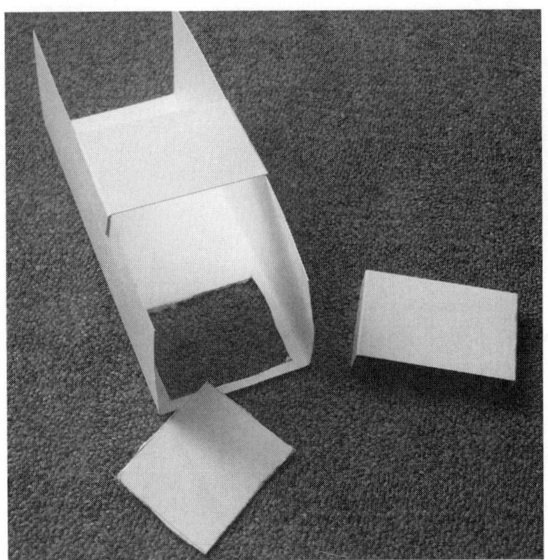

FIGURE 10–50 Assembly of an axial lighting apparatus: partial assembly 2. *Source:* Sandy Weiss/Packer Engineering.

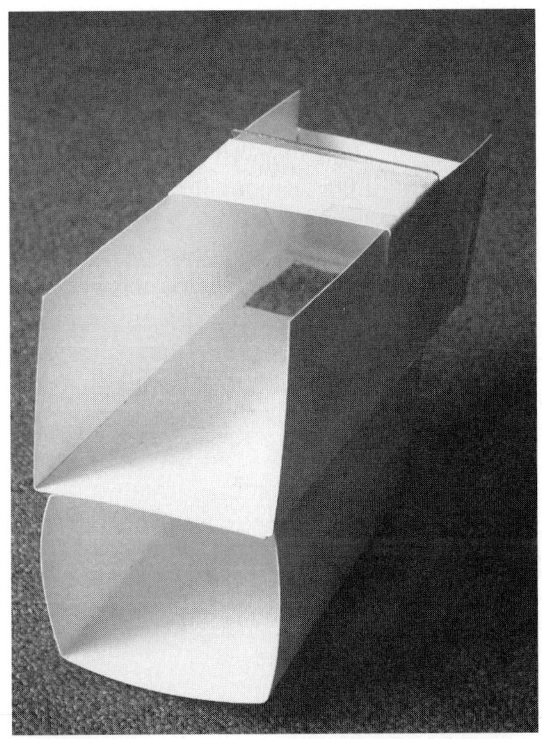

FIGURE 10–51 Assembly of an axial lighting apparatus: base assembly. *Source:* Sandy Weiss/Packer Engineering.

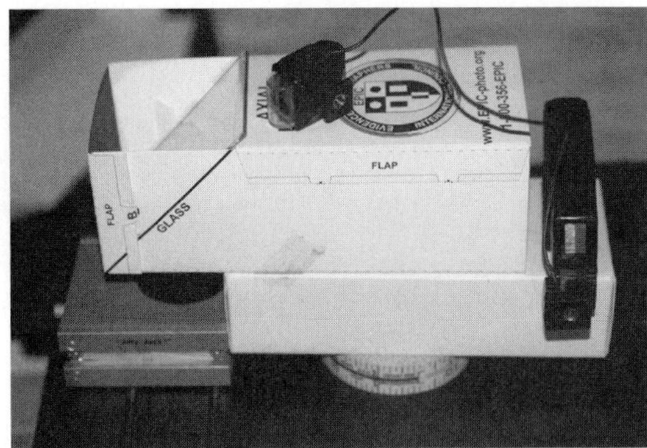

FIGURE 10–52 Assembly of an axial lighting apparatus: completed assembly in use to photograph a shell casing. *Source:* Sandy Weiss/Packer Engineering.

Supplies

- 2 sheets of thin 8½; × 11-inch white cardboard
- Scissors
- Razor knife
- Ruler
- Tape
- A piece of thin glass, such as Kodak projector slide cover glass 3¼ × 4 inches (Cat. No. 140 2130)

Assembly (see Fig. 10–47)

- Measure and cut a strip 2¼ × 8½ inches off the narrow side of one of the 8½ × 11-inch sheets of cardboard.
- Fold the remaining 8½ × 8¾-inch sheet into three sections: 2¾ × 3¼ × 2¾ × 8½ inches.
- Mark a 2¼ × 2¾-inch rectangle on the 3¼-inch section, ¼ inch from the end.
- Cut and remove the section.
- Cut the 2¼ × 8½-inch section in half on the long end.
- Fold up the edges of the two small pieces, ½ inch from either end.

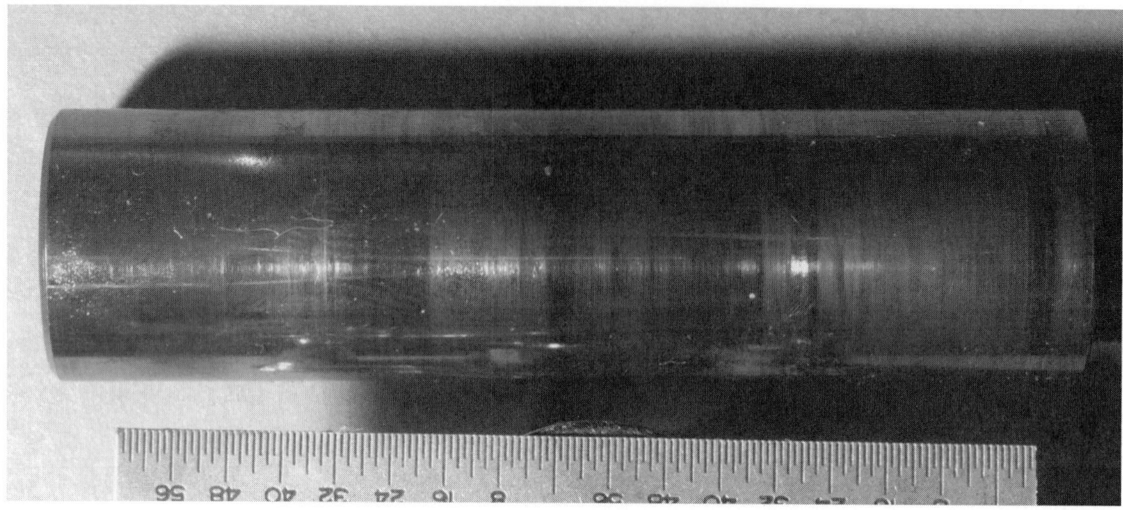

FIGURE 10–53 Direct lighting on a highly reflective bearing yields little surface detail. *Source:* Sandy Weiss/Packer Engineering.

- Tape one small section on the end of the channel with the cutout.
- Tape the other section on top of the channel, 2¾ inches from the end with the cutout.
- Assemble a base by taking a full 8½ × 11-inch sheet and measuring 2½-inch, 3-inch, 2½-inch, and 3-inch divisions on the board. Cut four slits along the measured lines, 2½ inches into the board.
- Fold along lines into a rectangular box.
- Fold in and tape the flaps. Tape the channel to the box.
- Put the glass into the channel above the cutout so that it is at a 45-degree angle when nested into the front guide and supported by the upper guide.

Tent Lighting

Some highly reflective objects are too large to be illuminated axially. Direct flash yields images with no surface detail (see Fig. 10–53). Diffusing the light from an EFU is necessary to produce photographs where the objects exhibit their surface detail (see Fig. 10–54). The lighting must be very low in contrast, so bare-bulb flash is not an option.

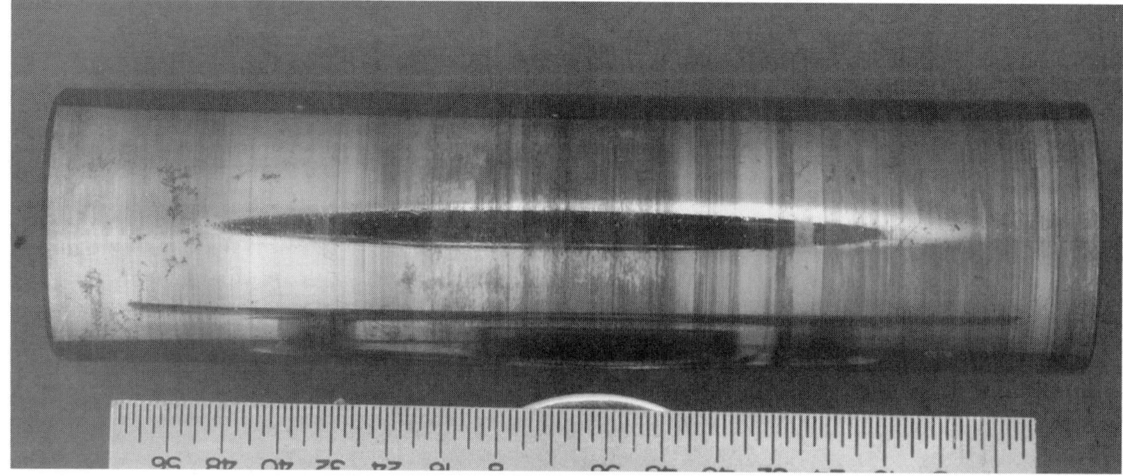

FIGURE 10–54 Diffuse lighting on a highly reflective bearing reveals banding. *Source:* Sandy Weiss/Packer Engineering.

Bearings are difficult to photograph because they reflect the illumination back into the camera lens. They also reflect the camera, the photographer, the walls and ceilings of the room, and anything else around them. The bearing from an aircraft engine shown in Figure 10–54 shows banding caused by extreme heat during operation.

Figure 10–53 was exposed with a Vivitar 283 EFU set on automatic and held to the left of the subject at a 45-degree angle. The flash placement is inferred by the position of the shadow. The banding is barely visible through the reflections.

Figure 10–54 was exposed with the same camera, lens, and flash, except the bearing was encased by a foam coffee cup. The bottom of the cup was cut out to provide an opening for the camera to focus and expose through. The flash was aimed at the side of the cup. The dark oval on the bearing is the reflection of the opening in the cup. The flash was diffused by a tent of foam that converted the image from dark to light and provided a better view of the banding.

If foam is not available or the subject is too large, you can roll semitransparent white material, such as thin white paper, into a cylinder, fasten it with transparent tape, and place it around the subject. Use one or more EFUs flashed at the cylinder for illumination. Evaluate exposure by trial and error.

REFERENCES AND SCALES IN MACROPHOTOGRAPHY

When exposing macrophotographs, it is often necessary to include in the image a scale for size reference.

Three Rules of Scales

- Use a scale manufactured to be accurate.
- Place the scale in the same plane as the subject, or part of the subject, being photographed.
- Include an image of the subject without the scale, so nothing in the image is hidden from view.

Use specific forensic or machinist type scales whenever possible for the best accuracy. The most commonly used scale type and size for normal macrophotography are provided by a 6-inch straight scale (see Fig. 10–55). If possible, use a scale with a dull gray or other neutral-colored finish.

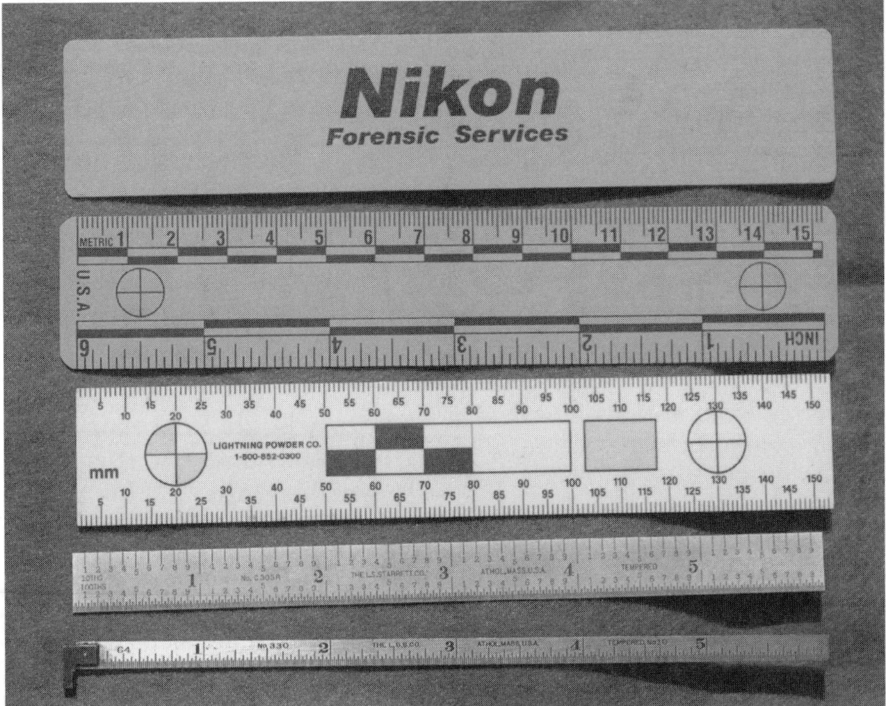

FIGURE 10–55 Samples of 6-inch scales for evidence photography. *Source:* Sandy Weiss/Packer Engineering.

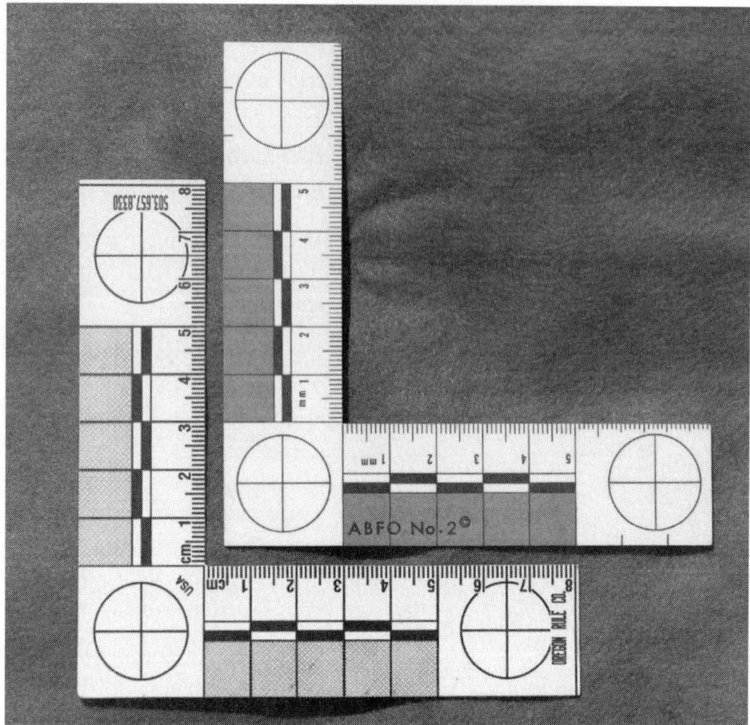

FIGURE 10–56 ABFO No. 2 Scales. *Source:* Sandy Weiss/Packer Engineering.

The ABFO No. 2 Bite Mark Standard Reference Scale

The ABFO No. 2 is a standard scale of spatial reference, designed by the American Board of Forensic Odontology (ABFO) for use with bite-mark photography. The scale has linear and circular graduations to satisfy the requirements of **forensic odontologists** (dentists who specialize in proper examination, handling, and presentation of dental evidence in a court of law) in the rectification and measurement of photographs of bite marks. Photographic distortion is shown when the scale's markings are not parallel or are not shaped uniformly. **Rectification** of the photographed evidence, the process by which an image or grid is converted from image coordinates to real-world coordinates, is necessary for an accurate representation of the shape and dimension of the evidence. The ABFO No. 2's L-shaped scale, or an adequate substitute, enables accurate measurements in two directions to facilitate the rectification of distortional errors created by oblique camera angles.

The scales shown in Figure 10–56 and many similar versions are commonly used by law enforcement photographers when measurements must be made from objects in evidence photographs. (See the cover of this book and Fig. 10–57, 16–4, and 16–10.)

Forensic protocol demands that a linear scale be placed next to the evidence during photography to enable an accurate size comparison. The ABFO No. 2 dimensional reference allows the photographer and investigator to re-create accurate life-size reproductions.

Photographic Protocol for Rectifying Distortion and Creating Life-Size Reproductions

Bite-mark evidence found with skin injuries, or other objects, are photographed for documentation, preservation, and analysis. Inaccurate positioning of the evidence, camera, or scale creates perspective and parallax distortion of the images. The distortion must be corrected to ensure that

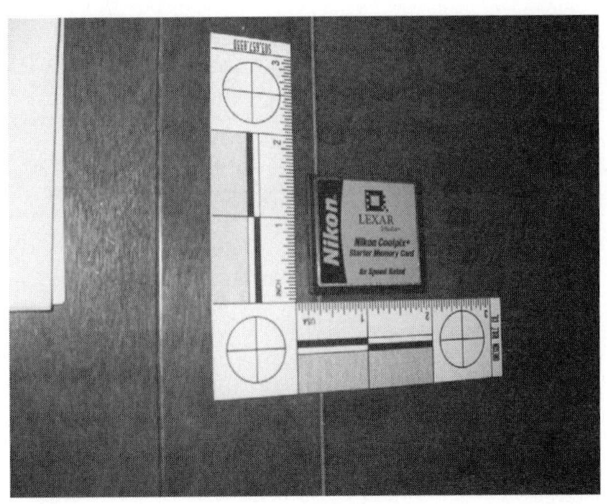

FIGURE 10–57 Scales are used for images needing rectification. *Source:* Sandy Weiss/ Packer Engineering.

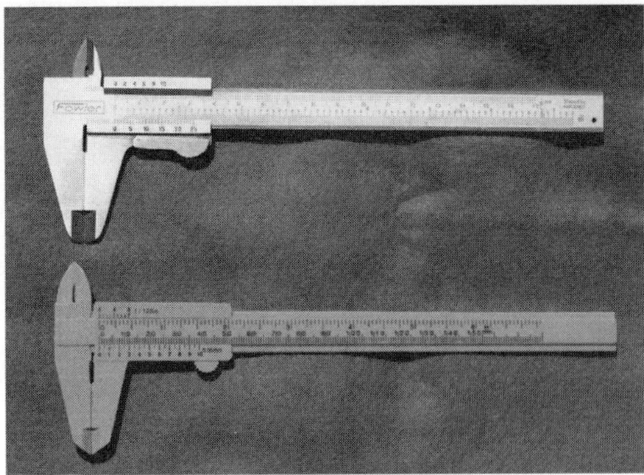

FIGURE 10–58 Large calipers. *Source:* Sandy Weiss/ Packer Engineering.

reliable results are derived from comparison of the evidence and the image—for example, a suspect's teeth and a bite mark. Quantification of camera, evidence, and scale misalignment in evidence photographs is enabled by digital imaging techniques contained in recognized software. Adobe Photoshop is a valid software program to use to correct certain types of distortion.

Useful Scales for Evidence Photography

Calipers (see Figs. 10–58 and 10–59) are used to measure the diameter of round objects, such as bolts and rods, and the depth of depressions and dents (see Fig. 14–49). Machinist tools may cost \$80 to \$100 for a standard-size tool. It is not necessary to have a tool's accuracy certified. The use of plastic, \$1-per-pair calipers requires the photographer to retain the tools with the photographs for subsequent comparison to the photographs. This will enable the accurate sizing of objects in images. Plastic tools are also useful because they are easily passed through airport scanners.

In some cases, the use of a 6-inch scale is not possible because the scale must be placed into a position where 6 inches will not fit. Keep a

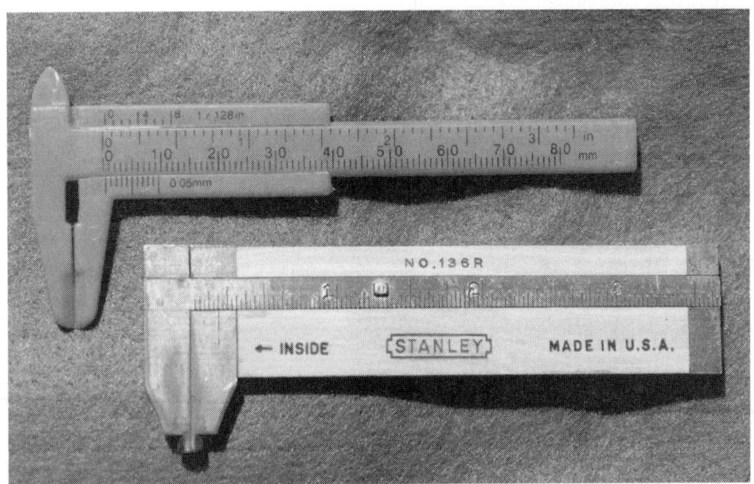

FIGURE 10–59 Small calipers. *Source:* Sandy Weiss/Packer Engineering.

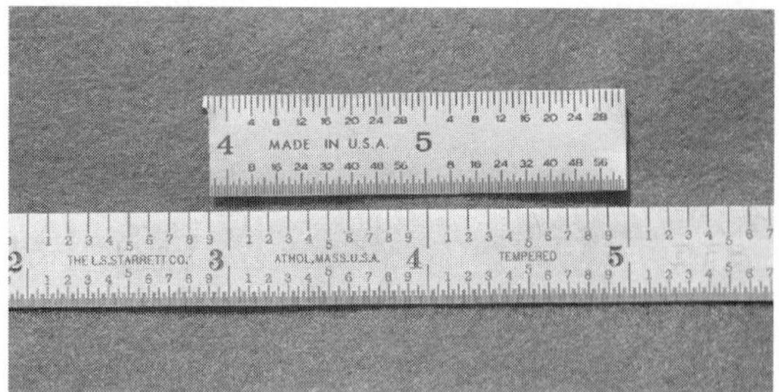

FIGURE 10–60 Small scales. *Source:* Sandy Weiss/Packer Engineering.

selection of scales that have been cut down from 6 inches to an inch or two (see Fig. 10–60) to fit into small or confined spaces.

Never trust or testify to a scale's accuracy until it has been verified. The Home-Cad scale shown in Figure 10–61 was produced from dull aluminum with a cork backing and was intended to be used for accurate sizing of drawings and plans. It was manufactured 1/16 inch too long over its 6-inch length.

REMEMBER:

Never trust or testify to a scale's accuracy until it has been verified.

The 12-inch green plastic school ruler shown in Figure 10–62 is an accurate scale. However, its markings are indistinct and its color distracting for a photographic reference. If such a ruler is used for photography, it must be retained and included in the case file for future verification.

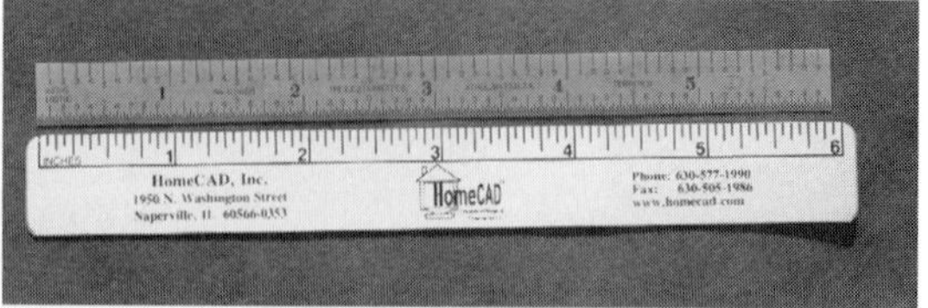

FIGURE 10–61 Inaccurate scale. *Source:* Sandy Weiss/Packer Engineering.

Paper cards, like the one shown in Figure 10–63 were made specifically for tagging evidence. The size and color are a good color for inclusion in evidence photographs. They are also convenient and accurate.

Always place the scale in the same plane as the significant evidence (see Fig. 10–64). Inaccurate positioning of the scale (see Fig. 10–65) creates perspective and parallax distortion of the images. If the scale is misplaced, it is difficult to use for measurements from the images.

In Figure 10–65, the photographer put the scale behind the subject. From behind, the scale is out of the plane of focus and would require photogrammetric analysis to recover dimensions.

TIP:

Fill the frame! Use a scale!

Focus carefully and fill the frame. The closer the camera and lens are to the subject, the shallower

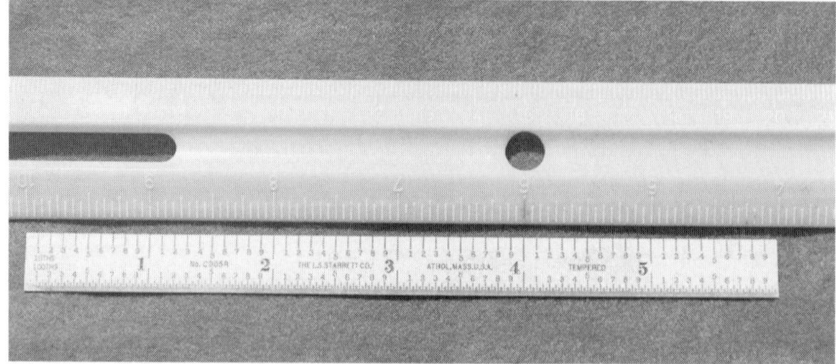

FIGURE 10–62 A common school ruler. *Source:* Sandy Weiss/Packer Engineering.

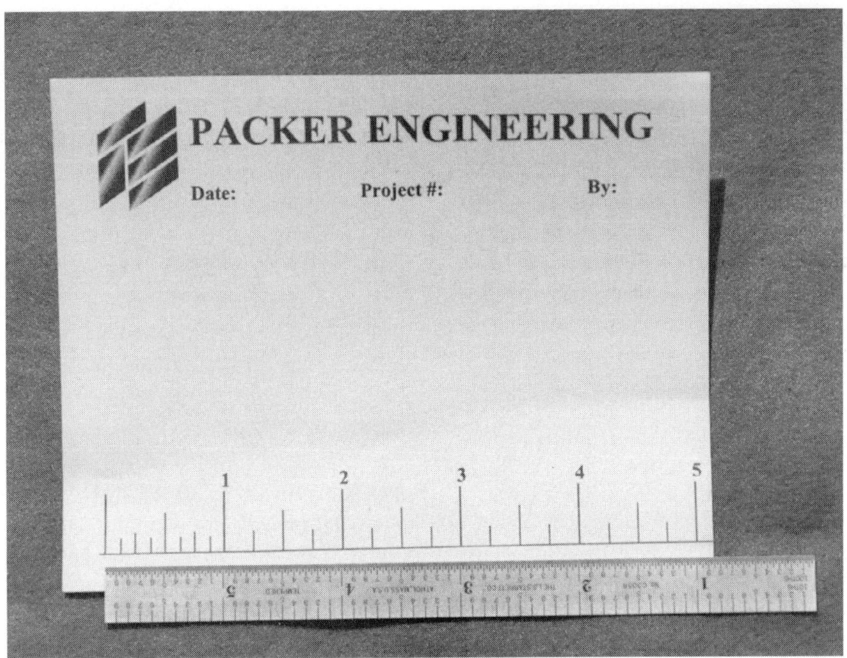

FIGURE 10–63 A color card with scale. *Source:* Sandy Weiss/Packer Engineering.

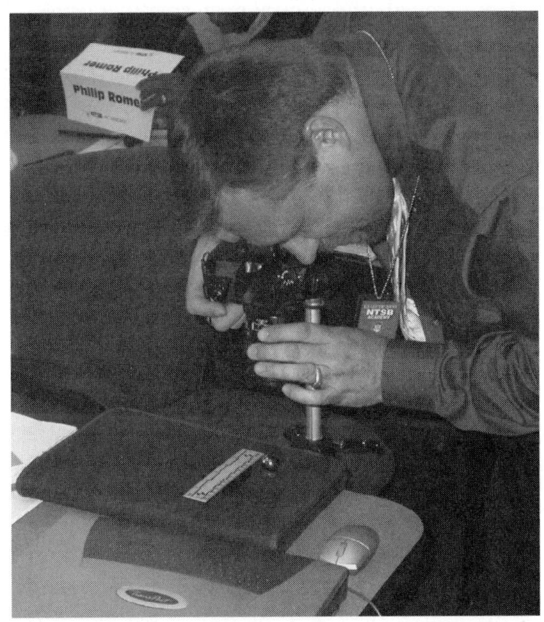

FIGURE 10–64 Proper use of a scale. *Source:* Sandy Weiss/Packer Engineering.

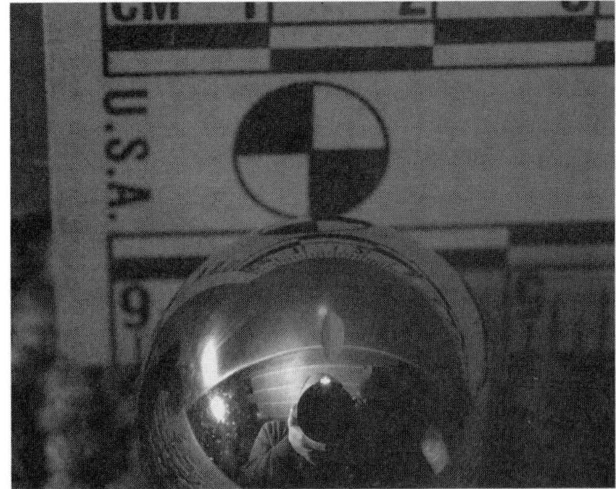

FIGURE 10–65 Improper use of a scale. *Source:* Sandy Weiss/Packer Engineering.

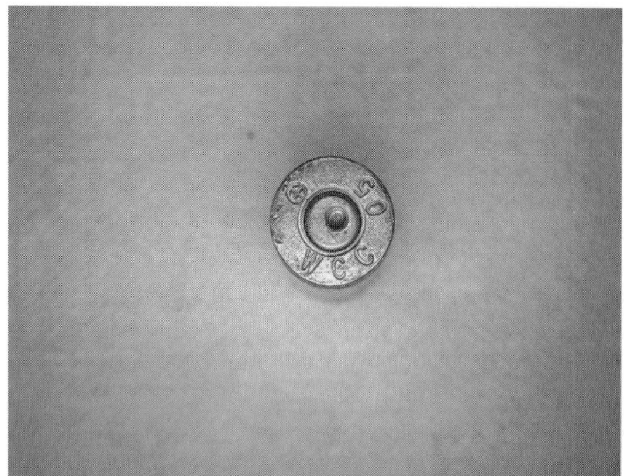

FIGURE 10–66 Fill the frame. *Source:* Sandy Weiss/ Packer Engineering.

the DoF will be. The higher the magnification of the photograph, the easier it will be to move the camera during exposure. In macrophotography, use a tripod, cable release, and lens hood when possible. (See Figs. 10–66, 10–67, and 10–68.)

REMEMBER:

Focus carefully. Fill the frame. Use a tripod, cable release, and lens hood when possible.

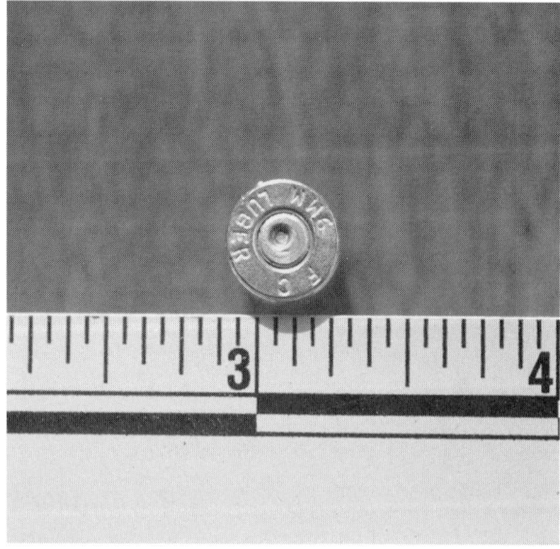

FIGURE 10–67 Focus carefully. *Source:* Sandy Weiss/ Packer Engineering.

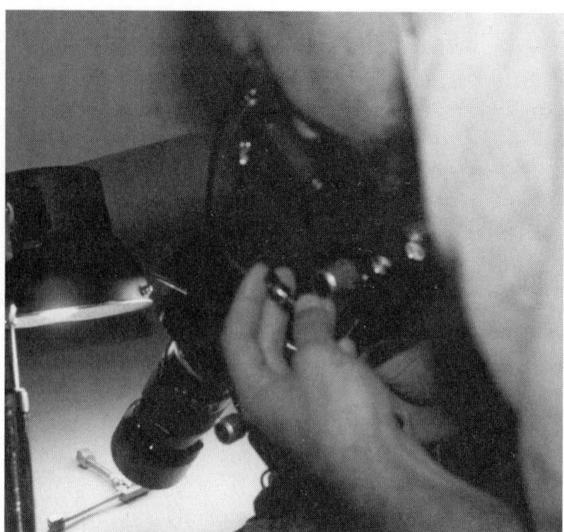

FIGURE 10–68 Use a cable release. *Source:* Sandy Weiss/Packer Engineering.

SUMMARY

Macrophotography is a skill all forensic photographers must master. Every investigation probably will need photographs of small objects or small aspects of large objects.

The photographer must be prepared in the field and the lab with adequate hardware, lighting, and references to capture photographs to accurately tell the story of the evidence. The photographer must be able to determine the magnification of the finished photographs and correlate that to the evidence.

Modern cameras perform much of the focusing and metering automatically, even at macro distances. It remains important to be able to figure out what settings must be made manually to obtain proper focus and exposure. It is necessary to operate the camera properly to gain DoF through the use of the optimum lens apertures.

Many inexpensive gadgets may be used to aid in the practice of macrophotography. Do not be afraid to experiment. Be sure to practice sufficiently before working in the field. Create a go-kit that is sufficient to create any necessary images.

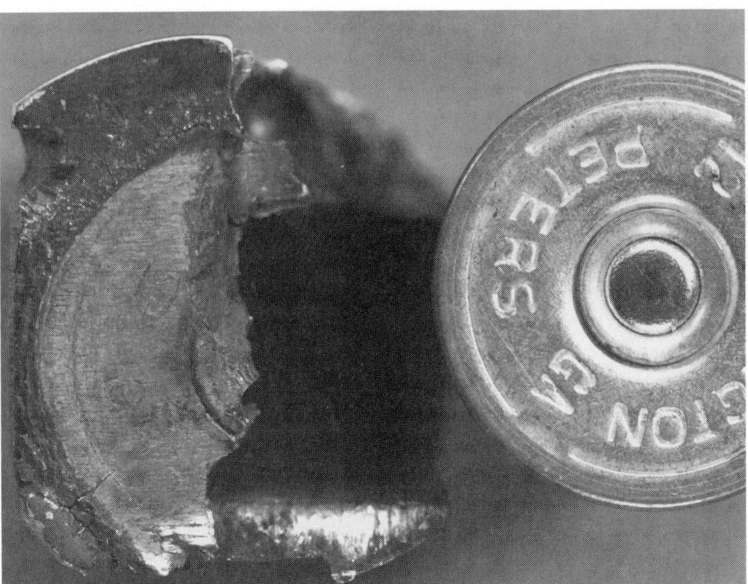

FIGURE 10–69 Exploded shotgun receiver part and exemplar shell. *Source:* Sandy Weiss/Packer Engineering.

CASE STUDY

EXPLODED SHOTGUN

A shotgun exploded when fired and severed some fingers from the hand of the man who pulled the trigger. He sued the manufacturer of the shotgun, claiming the weapon was defective. Packer Engineering was hired to investigate the accident. All the remaining pieces of the gun were inspected and photographed. The area of concentration for the investigation was the receiver, which on close examination was found to have the imprint of the back of a shell burned into it (see Fig. 10–69).

No factory-loaded shell would burn with enough heat to transfer the printing. In the plaintiff's deposition, he admitted that he customarily did his own reloading. Some of his other shells were inspected, and it was determined that he was reloading with the wrong powder to increase the power of the shells. Through experimentation, the force and heat needed to destroy the subject weapon were duplicated under controlled conditions. The explosion was sufficiently violent to explode the metal used to manufacture the subject weapon. The explosion was not the fault of the shotgun manufacturer or the ammunition manufacturer—it was the fault of the overpowered shell constructed by the shooter.

A 6 × 7 Pentax with a Pentax auto-bellows and Pentax 6 × 7 135mm macro lens was used for the photography. The photo depicted in Figure 10–69 was illuminated with a Novotron studio flash system and three flash heads. One flash head had a directional snout attachment. It was aimed at a low angle to the subject to make the faint lettering visible and legible in the final photograph. The other two flash heads were held farther from the subject and were used for fill lighting.

The undamaged shell casing was included in the photograph to allow the viewer to see exactly what was imprinted on a new shell and what was transferred in part to the receiver of the shotgun. The "ERS" and "GA" are easily recognizable on the gray metal.

CASE STUDY

HANDGUN CASING MARKINGS

Two small boys were playing with a semiautomatic handgun. When the gun fired, one of the boys was fatally wounded by a gunshot to the head. The other boy testified that no magazine was in the weapon at the time of the incident, so he thought it was not loaded. The assignment was to fire the weapon with and without a magazine

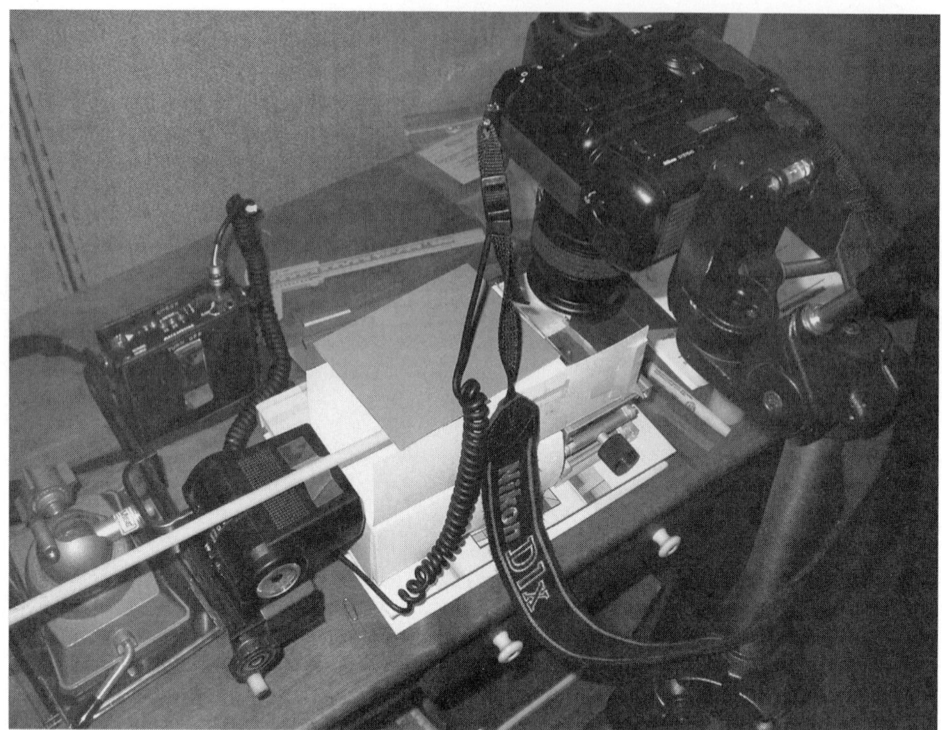

FIGURE 10–70 Axial photographic project with handgun shell casing. *Source:* Sandy Weiss/Packer Engineering.

to inspect and photograph the markings left on the exemplar casings.

A Nikon DSLR and micro lens was used with an axial lighting set-up to minimize reflections from the brass. The images were exposed with the axial lighting apparatus described in this chapter. In Figure 10–70, a dowel rod supports the shell casing. The rod fits loosely inside the casing and is also loosely taped to the top of the electronic flash. This enables the casing to revolve with the rod and under the lens. Notice the separation between the flash and the base of the axial apparatus. The flash must remain a few inches away from the light tunnel to allow sufficient bounced lighting to impact the flash sensor and turn off the flash after a small exposure. If the flash were slid forward into the light tunnel, the flash would fire as if it were set on manual exposure and would severely overexpose the subject. It is advisable to place a small gray card on top of the light tunnel to concentrate the light. It may also be necessary to position a neutral-colored umbrella over the whole set-up during photography of very reflective subjects to eliminate reflections from ceiling illumination.

Figure 10–71 shows the mark left on the side of the casing when the weapon was fired without a magazine. The weapon was loaded

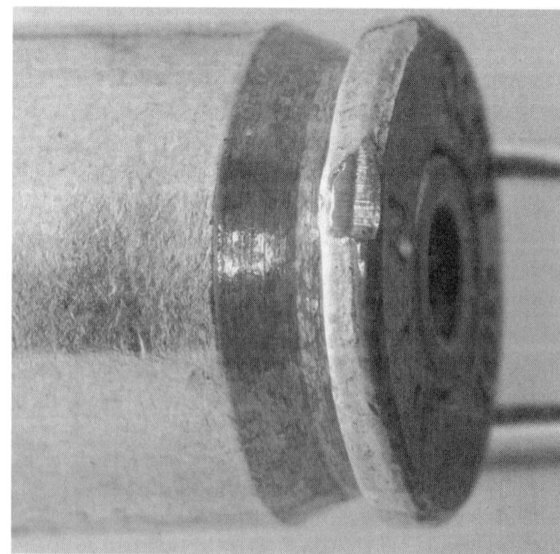

FIGURE 10–71 Ejector mark on the edge of the casing. *Source:* Sandy Weiss/Packer Engineering.

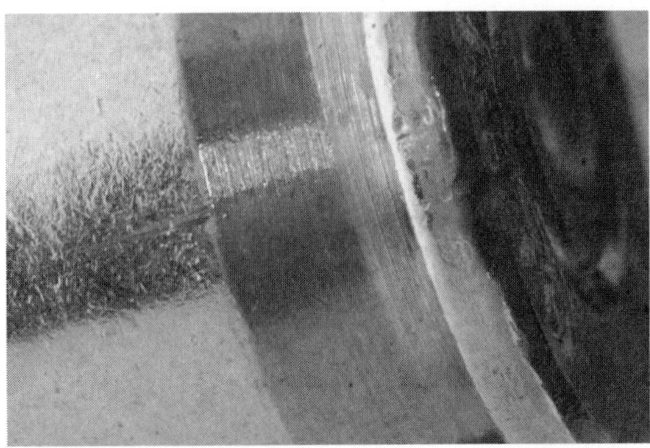

FIGURE 10–72 Markings left on an exemplar casing. *Source:* Sandy Weiss/Packer Engineering.

by placing a round in the chamber. The casing was then fired and ejected. The mark is thus significant.

Figure 10–72 shows the markings left on an exemplar casing when the round was fired from a magazine and ejected. The rim was not significantly dented, and fine scratches can be seen down the side matching the condition of the subject casing (see Fig. 10–73).

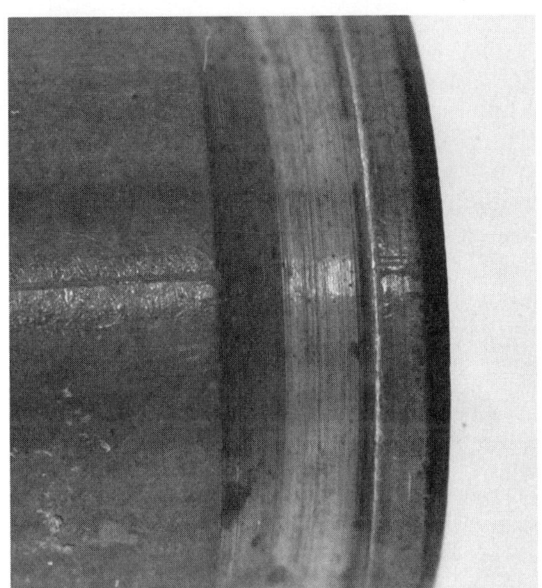

FIGURE 10–73 Fine scratches down the side match the condition of the subject casing. *Source:* Sandy Weiss/Packer Engineering.

CASE STUDY

AIRCRAFT CRASH

A lawsuit was filed against the manufacturer of a small aircraft when the pilot was killed in a crash. After inspecting the wreckage, a plaintiff's expert testified that the throttle control cable displayed a fatigue fracture and broke when it was pulled by the pilot. This would have caused an out-of-control situation leading to the crash.

Packer Engineering represented the manufacturer of the aircraft and performed another inspection of the wreckage. The fractured throttle control cable would normally have been put into the SEM to inspect, characterize, and photograph the fracture surfaces of the individual wire elements. In this case, the cable was still attached to a large piece of wreckage (see Fig. 10–74), making it too large to fit into the SEM vacuum chamber. By court order, destructive inspection was not allowed, so the cable could not be cut from the wreckage to reduce its size. An attempt was made to replicate the cable elements with plastic replica material, but the fractures were too fine to yield adequate replicas (.015 inch in diameter)

The solution was to make photographs of the individual fractured wires to characterize the fractures. Ordinary low-magnification macrophotography was not appropriate. It was necessary to design a specific apparatus to achieve enough

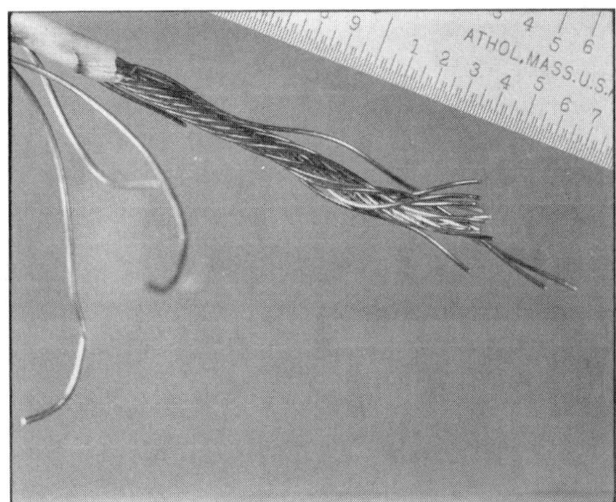

FIGURE 10–74 Throttle cable with fractured ends. *Source:* Sandy Weiss/Packer Engineering.

magnification for the study. A Pentax 6 × 7 camera was used and attached to a Pentax auto-bellows. A custom-built Canon adapter was attached to the front of the 6 × 7 bellows and a Canon 35 mm bellows was added for additional extension. Another custom adapter and a 1-inch C-mount cine-lens from a 16 mm movie camera was added to the front of the Canon bellows. The resultant magnification was about 25× at the film plane. The coverage of the lens, along with the length of the fully extended bellows, would not allow the 6 × 7 image area to be exposed without cutting off the corners of the image. The corners were not the area of main interest. An adjustable height elevator with a fine thread was used to raise and lower the subject cable under the camera for focusing. Illumination of the subject was accomplished with a three-head Novotron studio flash system: one head with a snout for aiming the light at a specific area and the other two heads for fill. Exposure was done by trial and error due to the extreme length of extension from the camera body.

The photographs taken successfully display the deformation on the individual cable ends, which is characteristic of a one-time ductile overload failure (see Fig. 10–75). This type of failure would only be possible if the engine was ripped out of the plane on impact with the ground. The engine would have been thrown clear of the wreckage, and its weight would pull the cable apart, causing the overload. No human would have had sufficient strength to fracture the cable in the manner documented. The ductile fracture would not have been in evidence if the cable failed in fatigue. The evidence photographs were used to successfully characterize the failure and defend the manufacturer.

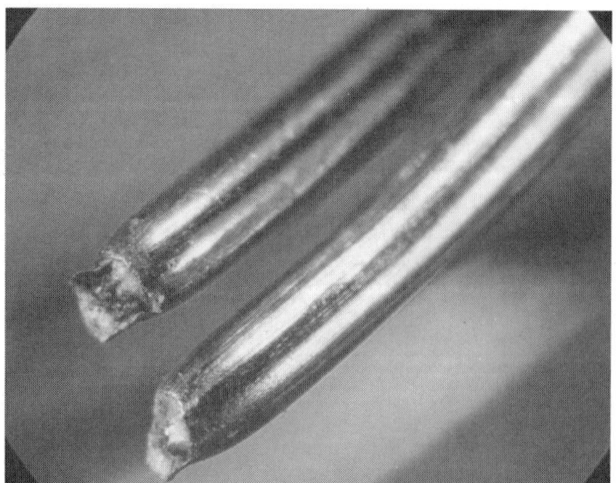

FIGURE 10–75 Macrophotograph of the throttle cable at 25× on film. *Source:* Sandy Weiss/Packer Engineering.

CASE STUDY

BROKEN CHAIR

A cast-aluminum flange was used to attach the legs to a fiberglass chair (see Fig. 10–76). The chair collapsed under the weight of a person, and the person was injured. The chair was brought to the laboratory for inspection and testing. One aspect of the study was to determine if the chair was assembled according to factory specifications.

The specifications for the assembly of the chair stated that a specific washer must be used under the head of the bolt. The washer was larger in diameter than the head of the bolt. Upon

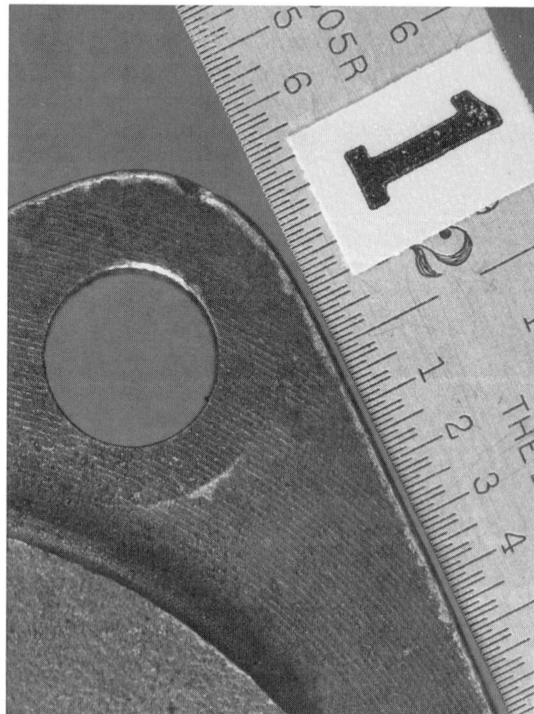

FIGURE 10–76 Flange from bottom of chair. *Source:* Sandy Weiss/Packer Engineering.

inspection, a witness mark left by a bolt head or washer was found on the surface of the aluminum flange. The photographic assignment was to document the mark on the flange with a scale, assess the diameter of the mark with accuracy, and determine if the mark was left by the washer or the bolt head.

A machinist scale graduated in hundredths of an inch was used in the images. The flange was placed parallel to the image plane of the camera. The scale was placed in precisely the same plane as the marking on the flange so there would be no parallax problems and a size could be measured directly from the photograph, if the flange was reproduced at life size. Yellow cloth numbers were used to mark the position of the hole on the flange.

Machinist scales are manufactured to precise tolerances, and their accuracy can be attested in court. The diameter of the hole in the flange was precisely .25 inch. The diameter of the round mark around the hole was exactly the size that would have been left if the washer had been applied to the bolt during assembly.

CASE STUDY

SEALED BEAM

It is often necessary to determine if a lamp was lit to reconstruct a crash. A sealed beam headlight from a light truck (see Fig. 10–77) was inspected after a crash.

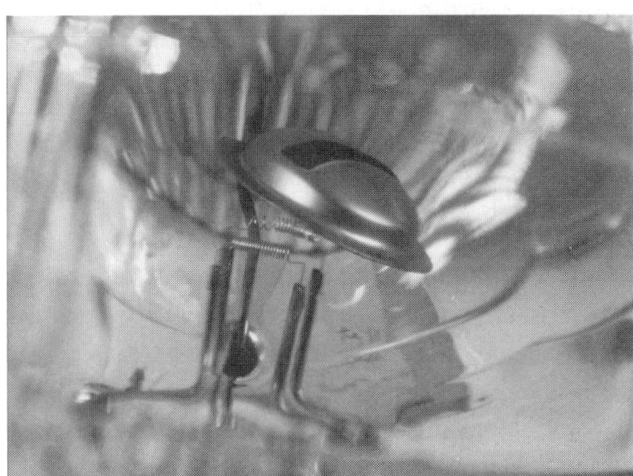

FIGURE 10–77 Sealed beam headlight filament. *Source:* Sandy Weiss/Packer Engineering.

Bulb filaments are brittle when they are not powered up or are cold and will break upon impact. Warm filaments will distort at impact. In this case, the low beam was distended and the high beam was not, indicating that the low beam was on at the time of the vehicle crash.

The exterior glass of the sealed beam was not broken, so the image had to be exposed through the heavy glass. A 35mm Canon F1 camera with a 50mm Canon macro lens on a bellows were used for the exposure. The lens was fitted with a collapsible rubber lens hood that was placed directly onto the glass of the sealed beam. This kept the light from the flash illumination from creating a flare on the image during exposure. Illumination was from one Vivitar 283 EFU set on automatic exposure and its closest range. It was not possible or necessary to use a scale during the exposure.

CASE STUDY

AIRCRAFT OIL PUMP

An oil pump (see Fig. 10–78) was recovered postcrash from a small aircraft. The plaintiff's expert contended that the oil pump failed in flight, causing the engine to fail and the aircraft to crash. If the pump had failed in flight, the engine would have seized and the prop would have ceased turning, or the prop would have been turning powered only by air turbulence.

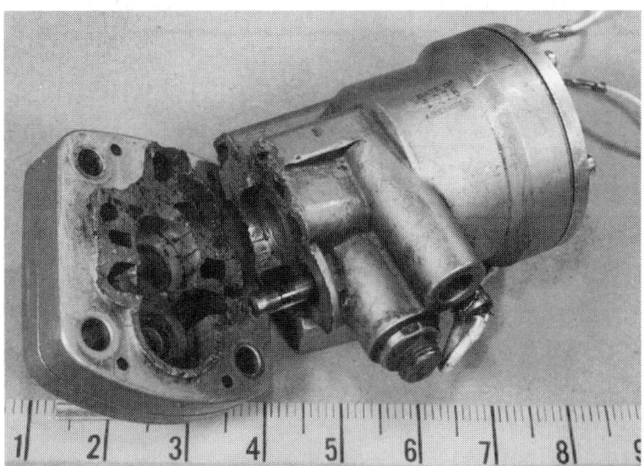

FIGURE 10–78 Oil pump. *Source:* Sandy Weiss/Packer Engineering.

When the prop is turning, the oil impeller is turning. Upon inspection, witness marks made by the oil impeller were found inside the circumference of the chamber in the middle of the flat broken section. These marks show that the prop was turning with great force at the moment the aircraft crashed and that the impeller dug into the sides of the chamber and shaved off pieces of the aluminum.

Figure 10–78 shows the condition of the pump as it was received. The scale indicates the overall size of the unit. The pump was placed on a plain background of brown paper with about 18% reflectance. Yellow plastic inch-tape, graduated in inches like a ruler, is available in rolls from any forensic supply. A piece of the tape was used in the overall image for scale because the size of the pump was not an issue.

The pump chamber measured about 1 inch in diameter. The area with the witness marks was too small to have a scale placed inside it for photography (see Fig. 10–79). The size of the chamber was not the issue. The flakes of aluminum dug out of the side of the chamber during the crash were the issue, and that is what was being photographed.

The camera was a 6 × 7 Pentax with a Pentax auto-bellows and 135mm Pentax auto macro lens. A Novotron studio flash system with two heads provided lighting. One head had a snout to provide directional lighting onto the shaving, and the other head was diffused to provide background and fill illumination.

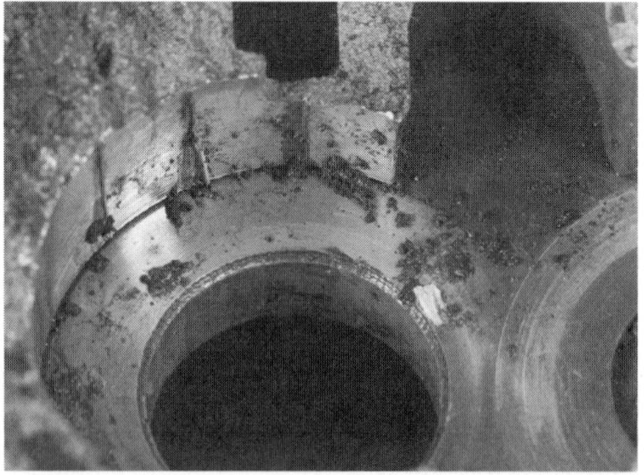

FIGURE 10–79 Oil pump macro. *Source:* Sandy Weiss/Packer Engineering.

CASE STUDY

AIRCRAFT ENGINE DOCUMENTATION PROJECT

A small aircraft engine (described at the beginning of Chapter 3) was brought to the lab for the purpose of examining its wear and to determine its previous operating conditions. The engine had been used as a classroom demonstration project, and was disassembled and reassembled at a local university.

It was disassembled in the lab, down to individual components, with the intention of macrophotographic documentation. The wear patterns were closely examined and photographed to determine the wear of each component.

The spark plugs were unusual. One was missing entirely. Two were two-prong plugs, although the specifications called for three-prong plugs. The wear of aircraft spark plugs is demonstrated by a flattening of the material opposite the prongs. A Nikon D1-X camera, with a 25mm extension tube, a Nikon bellows, and a Nikkor 60mm micro lens were used. Twin, small EFUs were used, one to each side of the subject (see Fig. 10–80). One was attached to the camera by a synchronization cable and the other was fired photoelectrically as a slave.

The images show that the two-prong plugs were not worn (see Fig. 10–81) and were probably not used in flight operation. The three-prong plugs display normal wear (see Fig. 10–82).

The three-prong plugs were exposed with the same equipment and set-up as the two-prong plugs. The camera was set on auto white balance. A gray scale provided the camera with reference for color balance, and the color of the material is normal (see Fig. 10–83).

The engine cylinders were inspected individually. The machining lines on the inside walls of the cylinders started and stopped abruptly at the limits of the piston strokes.

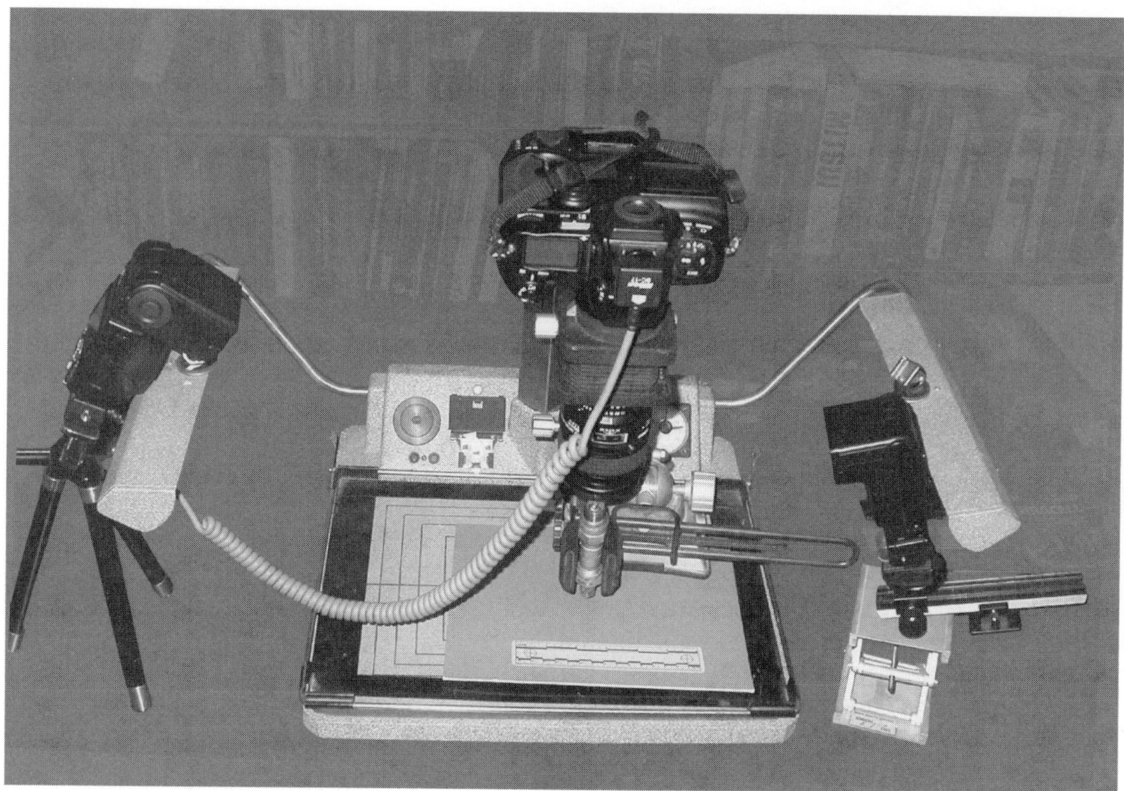

FIGURE 10–80 Macro set-up with camera, extension tube, bellows, and micro lens. *Source:* Sandy Weiss/Packer Engineering.

It was important to document the texture of the metal on the insides of the cylinders to illustrate that wear aspect in the report, even though it is difficult to make photographs of the inside of a cylinder (see Fig. 10–84). Because of the physical restrictions of the metal and because of the shiny surfaces, it is often necessary to expose the photographs off mirrors

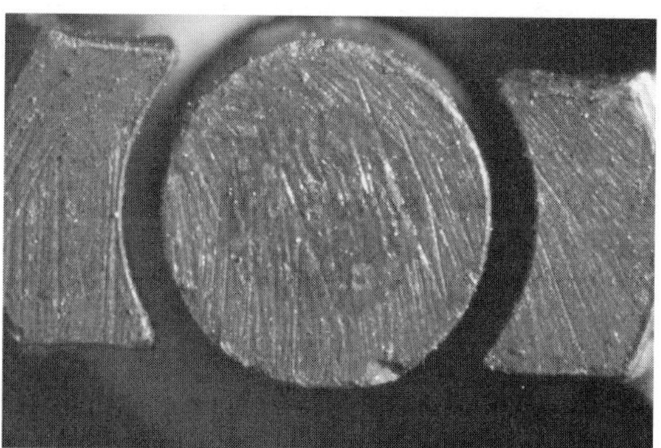

FIGURE 10–81 Two-prong spark plug. *Source:* Sandy Weiss/Packer Engineering.

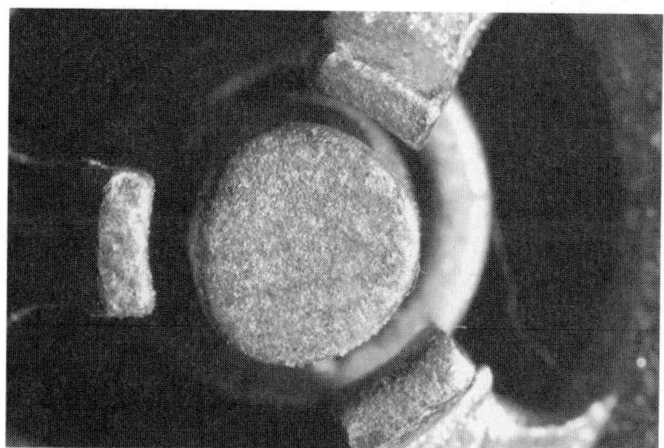

FIGURE 10–82 Three-prong spark plug. *Source:* Sandy Weiss/Packer Engineering.

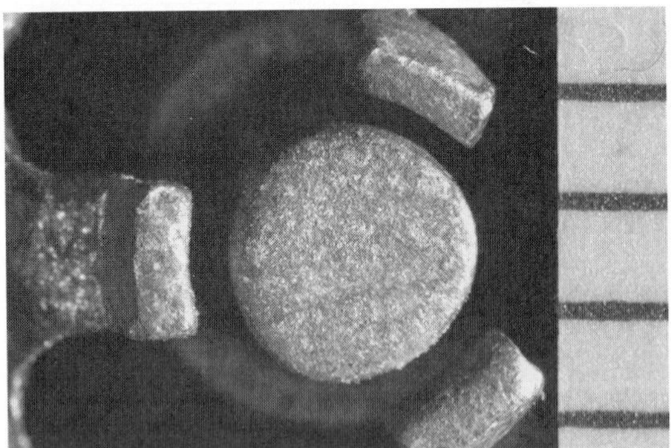

FIGURE 10–83 Spark plug and gray scale. *Source:* Sandy Weiss/Packer Engineering.

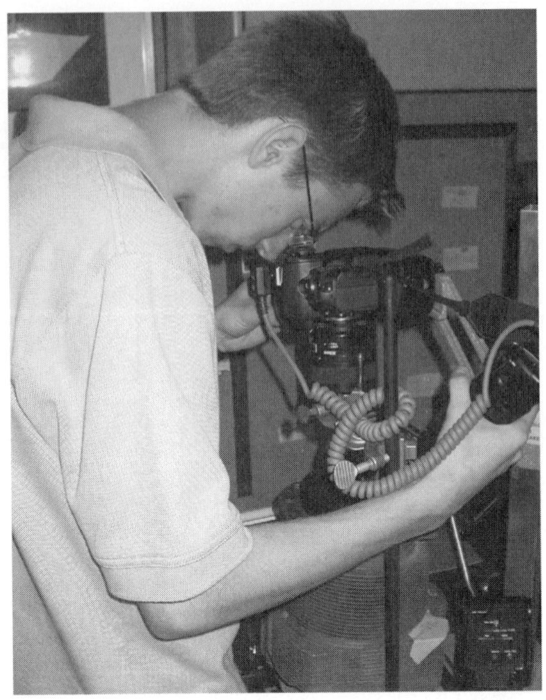

FIGURE 10–84 Making photographs of the inside of a cylinder. *Source:* Sandy Weiss/Packer Engineering.

inserted into the space (see Fig. 10–85), angled to bounce the light of the flash against the subject, and serving as a surface from which to expose the images. In this case the mirror is inside the cylinder and invisible in the overall photo.

Rear-surfaced mirrors have a reflective coating on the back surface of the glass. When rear-surfaced reflectors are used for photography, the images will be doubled, due to one reflection from each surface of the glass being recorded (see Fig. 10–86).

A hardware store automotive inspection mirror (see Fig. 10–85) was used in this case. It is shown firmly attached to a test-tube stand and lowered into the circumference of the cylinder.

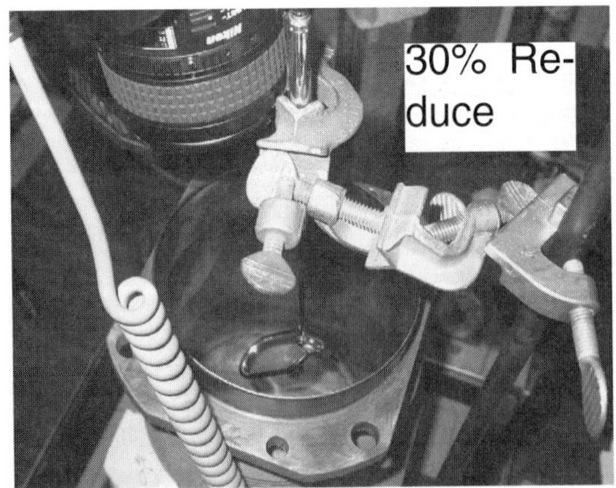

FIGURE 10–85 Cylinder photography using mirrors. *Source:* Sandy Weiss/Packer Engineering.

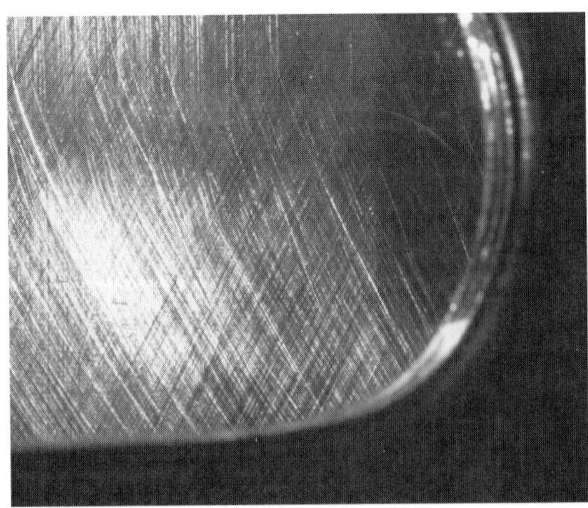

FIGURE 10–86 Rear-surfaced reflector. *Source:* Sandy Weiss/Packer Engineering.

KEY TERMS

macrophotography, (p. 284)
life size, (p. 284)
witness mark, (p. 284)
close-up lenses, (p. 285)
diopter, (p. 285)
extension tubes, (p. 286)
magnification, (p. 286)
reproduction ratio, (p. 287)
scale, (p. 287)
exposure increase, (p. 287)
extension bellows, (p. 287)
bellows lens, (p. 288)
lens mount, (p. 288)
stopped-down mode, (p. 288)
reversing ring, (p. 290)
ring flash, (p. 290)
oblique lighting, (p. 293)
relief, (p. 296)
axial lighting, (p. 298)
forensic odontologist, (p. 304)
rectification, (p. 304)

EXERCISES

1. Determine the actual diameter of the fractured bolt in Fig. 10–87.
2. Determine the scale of the fractured bolt in Figure 10–87.
3. If PhotoShop is available, rectify Figure 10–88 to life size.
4. Construct an axial lighting apparatus and use it for photographing a small metallic object or an electronic printed circuit board.
5. Using any available apparatus, expose a macrophotograph of an object and determine the magnification on the sensor.
6. Carefully break a piece of window glass and photograph the fracture surfaces lit to illustrate the direction of the fracture.
7. Photograph a metallic object on six different colored and contrasting backgrounds, without adjusting the camera exposure. Compare the results.
8. Place a coin in the bottom of a foam coffee cup and, without taking the coin from the cup, expose the highest magnification macrophotograph your equipment will allow.
9. Place a coin in the bottom of an opaque coffee cup or mug and, without taking it from the cup, expose the highest magnification macrophotograph your equipment will allow.
10. Expose an image of the vehicle identification number (VIN) through the windshield glass of an automobile at optimum magnification.

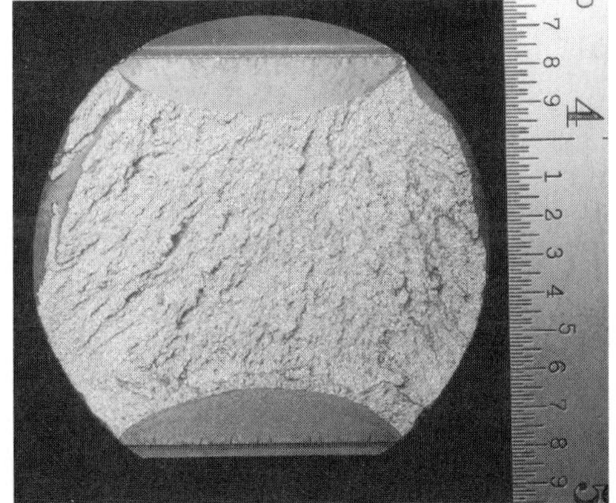

FIGURE 10–87 Surface of a fractured bolt. *Source:* Sandy Weiss/Packer Engineering.

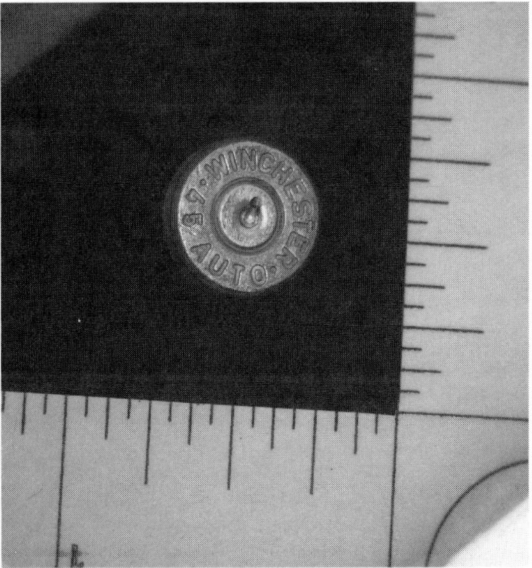

FIGURE 10–88 Image of a shell casing needing rectification. *Source:* Sandy Weiss/Packer Engineering.

Chapter 11

Low-Light Photography

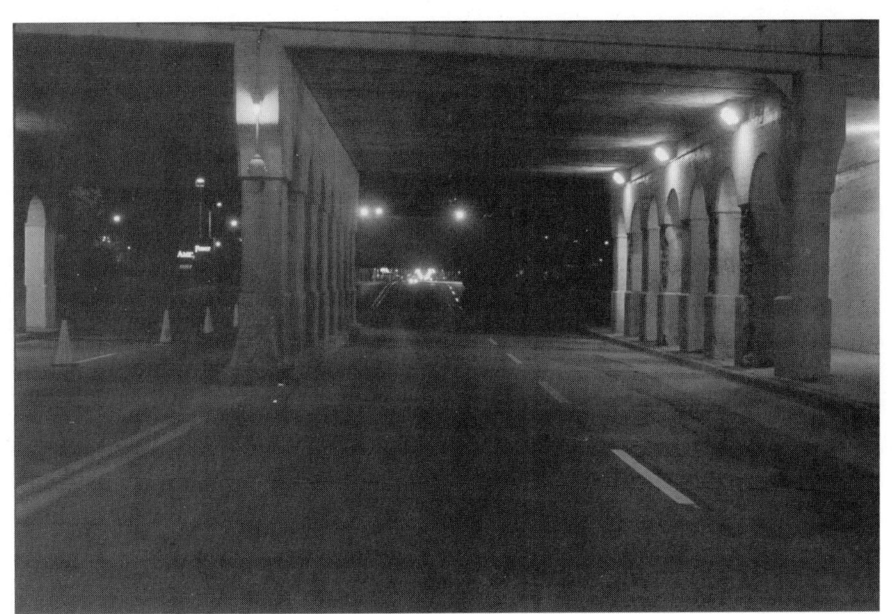

Learning Objectives

AFTER STUDYING THIS CHAPTER, YOU SHOULD BE ABLE TO:

1. Comprehend the challenges and understand the methods for making images of accident and crime scenes at nighttime with low-light illumination
2. Understand how contrast affects conspicuity and visibility
3. Know the differences between using film and digital imaging when making low-light exposures
4. Recognize the differences between exposure meters and meters that measure luminance and illuminance
5. Understand and quantify luminance and illuminance
6. Know the difference between low-light and daylight vision and understand low-light limitations
7. Plan and execute a successful nighttime/low-light photography project
8. Explain how the means and methods of nighttime/low-light photography have evolved over the last 25 years

LOW-LIGHT AND NIGHTTIME PHOTOGRAPHY

Exposing photographs in normal light levels is routine and uses lens aperture and shutter speed combinations recommended by a built-in meter. When ambient light levels are low, creating good exposure becomes more difficult. Forensic evidence photographers are often required to document large indoor or outdoor scenes at night, when supplementary lighting may be insufficient or inappropriate.

> If the scene is to be realistically portrayed for the observer, the limiting resolution should be that associated with the visual acuity of the observer of the photograph, and not the resolution of the photograph itself.[1]

The addition of electronic flash or other supplementary lighting to a scene may achieve sufficient exposure, but in-camera and portable electronic flash may create its own inaccuracies. EFUs are limited in effective range by their size. Most small units will illuminate a small area within 15 to 25 feet from the camera, depending upon the environmental situation. To accurately resemble the scene, images created with electronic flash or other supplementary lighting may be inappropriate because the lighting covers unevenly (see Fig. 11–1).

Sometimes electronic flash is the logical and expected choice because it is the only alternative. For example, law enforcement officers and evidence photographers would not be able to work outdoors at night at accident or crime scenes without EFUs (see Fig. 11–2).

Action photos exposed with low ambient illumination often exhibit blurred details due to the use of slow shutter speeds (see Fig. 11–3). When the subject is moving or long shutter speeds cause the movement of the photographer or the camera, electronic flash is the recommended form of supplementary lighting.

TIP:

When using electronic flash in dark areas for images of objects with reflective markings, you must intentionally overexpose the images or they will appear too dark. This happens because the high reflectivity of the subject causes more than the normal amount of light to bounce back to the flash, which causes the EFU to turn off too quickly.

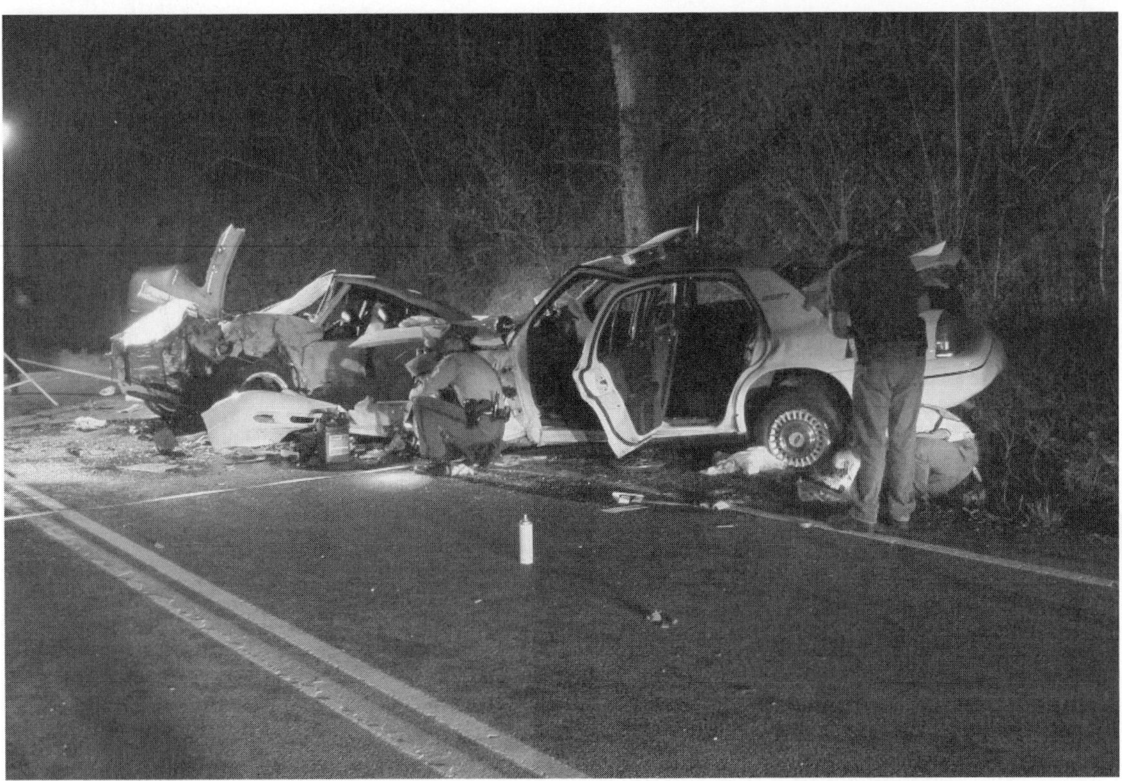

FIGURE 11–1 Wreck at night illuminated by the concentrated lighting of squad car spotlights. *Source:* Sandy Weiss/Packer Engineering.

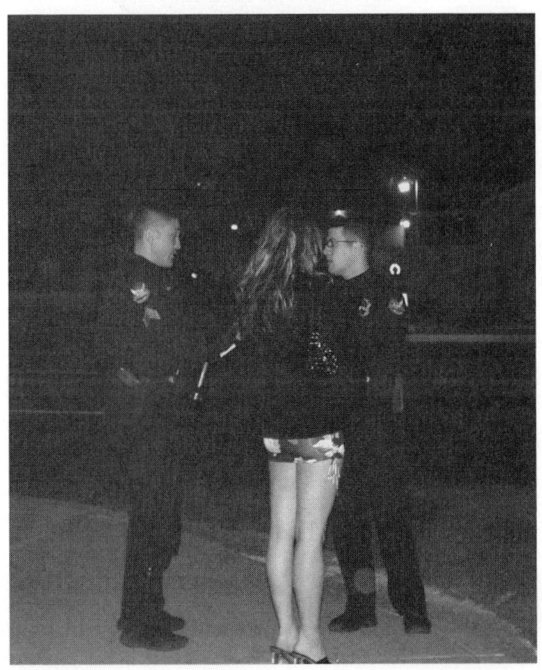

It is necessary to use electronic flash for macrophotography of evidence in most ambient light levels because the flash enables the use of small lens apertures necessary for critical DoF. When the subject is normal or large in size and static, methods are available that will achieve exposures of accurate appearance in any ambient level of illumination.

When using electronic flash in dark areas for images of objects with reflective markings, you must intentionally overexpose the images or they will appear too dark. This happens because the high reflectivity of the subject causes more than the normal amount of light to bounce back to the flash, which causes the EFU to turn off too quickly (see Fig. 11–4).

FIGURE 11–2 Handheld exposure with electronic flash. *Source:* Constance Rohrer, Evidence Forensics Photography.

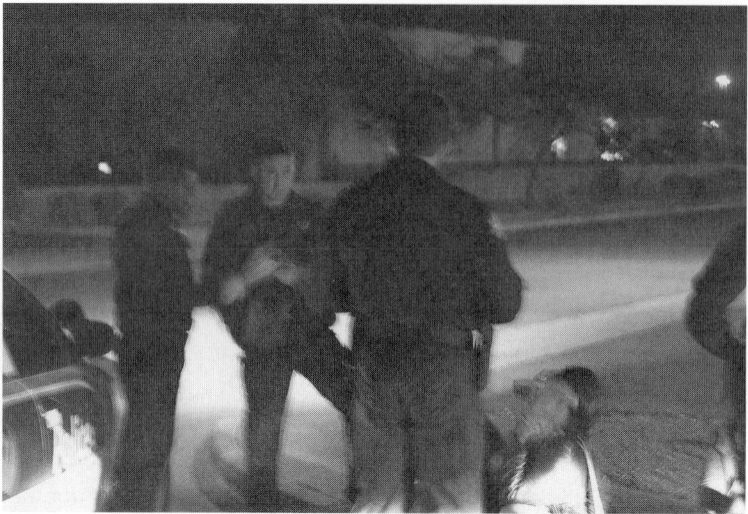

FIGURE 11–3 Handheld exposure by headlight illumination. *Source:* Constance Rohrer, Evidence Forensics Photography.

Contrast

The contrast between objects is what allows the brain to differentiate among the various things it perceives. If an object is conspicuous against its background, it will be easily noticed. The contrast can be perceived as differences in tone or color, depending upon the level of ambient illumination. To photographically produce images that a viewer will perceive as accurate representations of the subject, the **subject brightness range/contrast** may of necessity be exposed only by the ambient illumination.

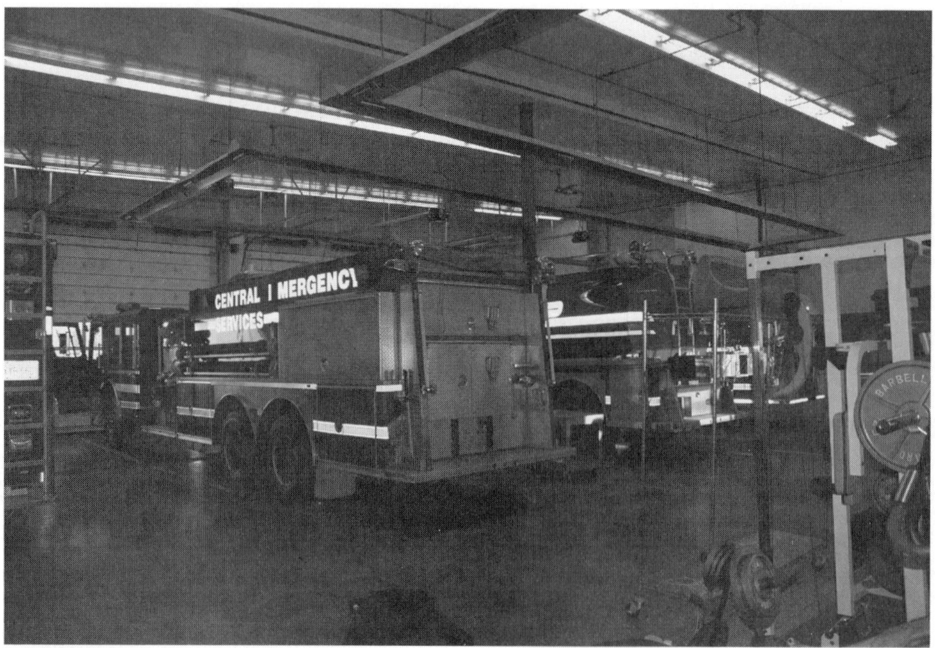

FIGURE 11–4 Underexposure due to reflectivity. *Source:* Sandy Weiss/Packer Engineering.

If a subject is inconspicuous against its background, the subject will be difficult for the viewer to perceive. A black car parked in front of a black tree at night may be difficult to see and to photograph. A white car parked in front of a snowdrift in the moonlight is another challenging composition. These subjects are difficult to photograph in black-and-white or color photography, film or digital.

Contrast is determined by the level and angle of illumination. As the light level decreases, the perception of colors, shapes, and forms decreases. If the angle of the illumination approaches zero, shadows cease to exist and subjects become less conspicuous. Color vision does not exist in low light where black and white vision remains. Due to the fact that humans lack color vision in low light, a person with normal color vision may perceive a subject wearing a red coat in low light as appearing identical to a subject wearing a gray coat.

RULE:

If the ambient illumination level is greater than nil, it is possible to properly expose a photograph to accurately represent the scene if sufficient exposure is used. It may not be simple or feasible, but it is possible.

TIP:

In total darkness (of the visible spectrum), a sufficient level of exposure to form an image on sensor or film cannot be achieved. Monochrome images may be exposed using infrared light, if an infrared light source exists and the camera is sensitive to that wavelength.

After sufficient exposure in low light, an image may or may not be a reasonable representation of what the viewer perceived with his or her eyes, depending upon how the image was created.

Night Photography

Night photography is accomplished using the same equipment and exposure factors as daylight photography. To accomplish sufficient exposure, the aperture and shutter speed must be properly set. They are dependant on the ISO of the media, the level of ambient illumination, and the contrast desired in the final image.

Reciprocity failure (RF) occurs when film requires extra light and exposure time increases. When film is exposed outside the range of exposure times considered normal—for example, at times longer than one second—the film may display a loss of sensitivity. The contrast may appear incorrect, and color shifts may occur. Digital sensors are not subject to RF but may create images with elevated noise at low ambient illumination. While RF is a common problem with film photography, it is not an issue with digital photography.

The high range of ISOs available in modern digital cameras allows OEMs to supply relatively slow-speed normal lenses as the default with new cameras. Many of the new default lenses are zoom lenses. Higher ISOs allow conventional photography to be undertaken in lower levels of ambient illumination without the necessity of supplementary lighting.

TIP:

A slow normal lens, with a maximum aperture of *f*/3.5 requires 8 to 16 times more light to properly expose an image in the same, low level of ambient illumination as a lens with a maximum aperture of *f*/l.4. Consider this fact when choosing lenses to purchase with a new camera.

When exposing photographs in marginal and low-light conditions, lenses of higher speed, lower number, and larger maximum aperture, if available, are recommended. In many cases, it may also be necessary to set the camera at a higher ISO, including 400, 800, 1,600 or higher.

It is not practical to hand-hold a camera at shutter speeds slower than about 1/30 second. If it is necessary to go below 1/30, use of a tripod or other stable support for the camera is recommended. If a tripod is unavailable, put the camera on a steady support and use a cable release or the

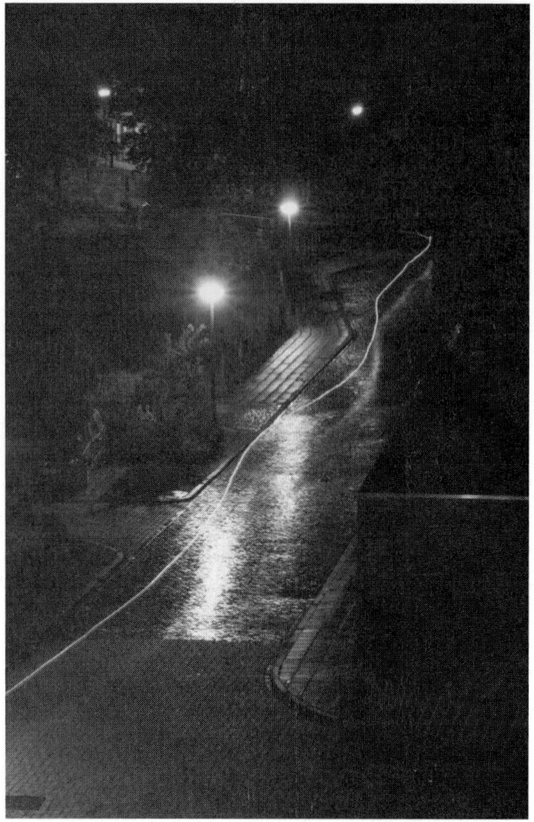

FIGURE 11–5 Timed exposure at night. *Source:* W. Thomas Miles.

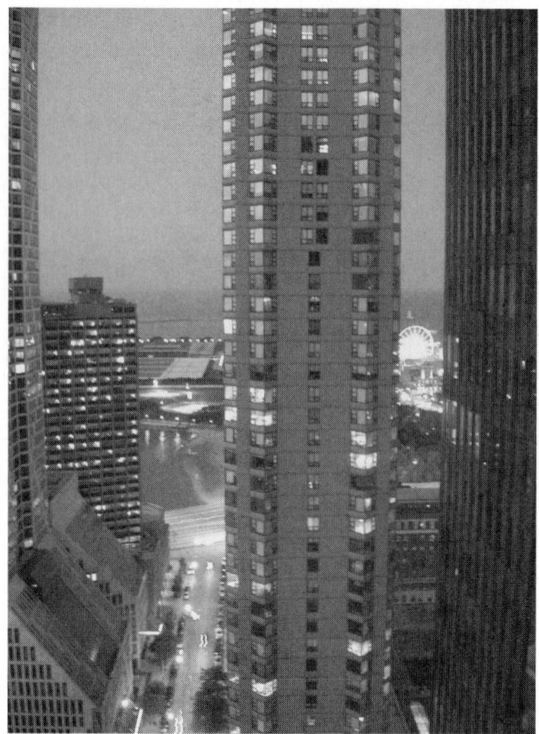

FIGURE 11–6 Night scene in Chicago. Image exposed with a Nikon D200 and 18-70 zoom lens, set at 18 mm and *f*/8, 0.5 second on a tripod. Image shows the variety of colors supplied by different types of lighting. *Source:* Sandy Weiss/Packer Engineering.

built-in self-timer to release the shutter (see Fig. 11–5; see Appendix 11.1 for all data on this image).

Most night scenes consist predominantly of darkness with small areas of illumination from windows, signs, headlights, reflections, and streetlights. Aesthetically pleasing photographs may be exposed with a variety of techniques over a wide range of exposures. Short exposures will enhance the well-lit areas by preserving highlight detail. The shadows will appear dark due to underexposure. Longer exposures enhance detail in the shadows, while highlight detail may be lost due to overexposure.

Night scenes that are predominantly dark are difficult to meter accurately with the built-in camera meter and from the camera position. It is often necessary to perform light-meter readings from the position of the subject using a sensitive, handheld meter with spot or incident capabilities. (See Fig. 11–6.)

Tips for Low-Light Photography

- Carry a small flashlight to see the settings on the camera.
- Make multiple exposures over a wide range. (Use the camera's built-in autobracketing capabilities, if available. If not, expose images over- and underexposed from the built-in meter recommendation.)
- Focus carefully. (Depth of field is shallow at wide apertures.)

- Use the appropriate light-balance setting for the predominant light source.
- Use electronic flash or other supplementary lighting when it is unavoidable.

Metering at Night

The most difficult question to answer about night exposures is "How long is long enough?" That question has no specific answer. The image must display reasonable contrast and density in the areas of importance. So, how is exposure properly determined? Two conventional methods follow:

1. Trial and error, or bracketing
2. Using the recommendation of the camera's built-in meter

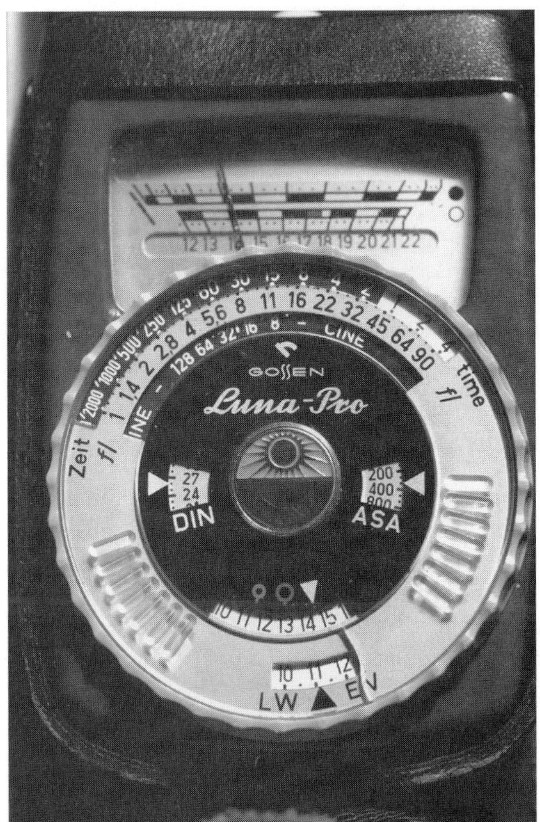

FIGURE 11–7 Gossen Luna-Pro handheld exposure meter. *Source:* Sandy Weiss/Packer Engineering.

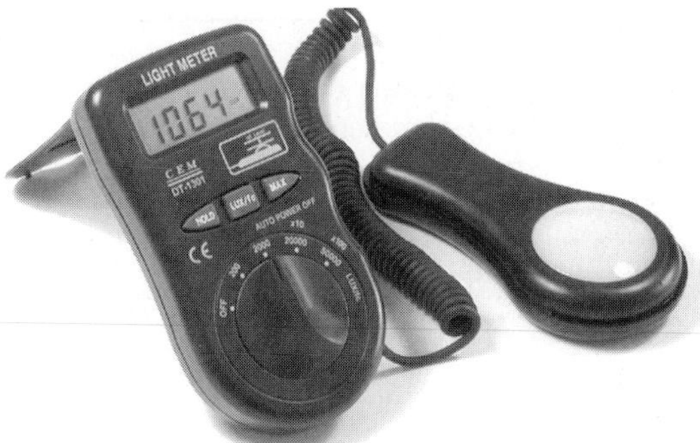

FIGURE 11–8 CEM digital DT-1301 dual function digital Lux foot candle meter. *Source:* Sandy Weiss/Packer Engineering.

In the first case, trial and error is time consuming and cumbersome. In the second case, the camera meter is not designed to "know" how the image is supposed to appear. The camera may expose the scene as it would appear in normal daylight. This result is fine if the images are meant to be aesthetically pleasing. If the images are intended to be an accurate representation of how the scene appeared to the photographer, light metering should be performed manually to enable the photographer to decide on the appropriate rendition.

In some cases, manual metering may be accomplished with the camera's built-in meter. It is usually more accurate to read exposure with a handheld exposure meter. Contemporary meters, including the pre-digital Gossen Luna-Pro (see Fig. 11–7), can calculate the recommended exposure of a scene in exposure times of minutes and hours, over a wide range of sensor sensitivities, and by either reflected or incident lighting. Modern meters, including the digital Luna-Pro or the CEM DT-1301 dual function digital Lux foot candle meter (see Fig. 11–8), have increased sensitivity and a more reliable power source, enabling accurate metering in a wide range of weather conditions. The acceptance angles of some meters may be varied by using appropriate sensor attachments.

> **TIP:**
>
> Use the exposure information suggested by the meter, but review test exposures to ensure the captured images appear as intended.

TIP:

Inspect the image after capture to assess if it is an accurate representation of the scene. Check the image histogram to assess if the exposure lies within the dynamic range of the camera sensor.

TIP:

When making images in low light, expose in RAW format whenever possible and process the images on the computer. JPEG images are processed in the camera and will not yield image detail comparable to RAW files in low light.

Digital Night Photography

No inherent difficulties prevent the use of digital imaging for low-light photography. Digital cameras provide instant feedback, enabling the inspection and assessment of captured images. The correlation of apertures, shutter speeds, and sensor sensitivities work identically in digital and film technology.

Depending on its stage and the condition of the atmosphere, the moon provides varying intensities of illumination. During daylight photography, the sun may create dark shadows. Moonlit exposures are usually of long duration. In some cases, the movement of the moon may fill and soften the shadows the moon creates. This is not normally an issue with photos of evidence.

TIP:

Use a lens with a large maximum aperture to increase viewfinder and/or LCD brightness.

TIP:

Larger format sensors may produce brighter viewfinder and/or LCD images

TIP:

When working in low light, the photographer should allow sufficient time for his or her eyes to adapt to the darkness, which will allow for proper focus and image composition in the viewfinder or on the LCD.

Mirror Lock-Up

Mirror lock-up (MLU) may be helpful for image resolution during night photography. In some DSLR cameras, the reflex viewing mirror can be locked in the up position after focusing. This eliminates the vibration caused by the operation of the mirror. Consider that the time it takes for a camera to self-dampen vibration after mirror operation may be incidental compared to the length of the exposure.

TIP:

Performing hyperfocal focusing may be simpler than visually determining DoF in low light.

TIP:

Low-light scenes are usually low in contrast. The absence of contrast may disable the camera's auto-focus systems. Use manual focus whenever possible.

HUMAN VISION IN LOW LIGHT

Human eyes work differently in different levels of light. In dim light, the eye sees only **monochrome,** usually black and white, that is called **scotopic vision.** Scotopic vision occurs at luminance levels of 10^{-2} to 10^{-6} candles per square meter (cd/m^2). **Mesopic vision** occurs in intermediate levels of lighting (luminance level 10^{-2} to 1 cd/m^2) and is a combination of scotopic and photopic vision. **Photopic vision** occurs in normal light (luminance level 1 to10^6 cd/m^2). Color vision is best in the photopic range. Visual acuity increases after full adaptation to low levels of illumination, but colors may remain absent.

The healthy human eye can perceive images in an illumination range ratio of over nine orders of magnitude. An amount of light equal to 10 times a given amount is one order of magnitude greater. Two orders of magnitude equals 100 times greater, 10 × 10. Human vision is possible in lighting 100 million times brighter than its darkest capability. But, healthy eyes are able to perceive a contrast ratio of only up to one thousand times, at one particular time. When the light levels change, the eyes adapt and shift the perception of brightness and darkness. The light level that was interpreted as black or white before may be moved through a range of six orders of magnitude (1,000,000 : 1).

Healthy eyes fully adapt from bright sunlight to complete darkness in approximately 30 minutes. It takes approximately 5 minutes for the same healthy eyes to adapt to bright sunlight after total darkness. The perception of color changes during adaptation.

Spectral Sensitivity of the Eye

Human eyes are sensitive to light in the wavelengths between 400 and 700 nanometers (nm). In the eyes, the cone cells are sensitive to three wavelength ranges. The brain interprets these as blue (with a peak near 419 nm), green (with a peak near 531 nm), and red (with a peak near 558 nm). All the colors that healthy human eyes may see are composed of combinations of intensities of red, green, and blue. In low-light/scotopic vision, the rod cell peak sensitivity is about 500 nm.

Quantifying Spectral Sensitivity

Human eyes perceive two main features about any object. The features are color and brightness. The relative brightness of different colors is not easily quantifiable. To most people with healthy vision, red objects appear brighter than blue ones under normal illumination. When the level of illumination is lower, blue objects appear brighter than red ones.

In many cases, it is necessary to quantify the luminosity—the amount of light energy output in a unit of time—of different colored light sources. For example, it is important to ensure that traffic signals are sufficiently bright at night and in bright daylight so that motorists can distinguish between green and red. Quantification of luminosity is performed with light-measuring instruments called radiometers or photometers.

Radiometers measure radiance, the energy emitted or reflected by a source. Radiance does not represent what people see. For example, if red, yellow, and green traffic signals were adjusted so that they emitted equal radiance, they would by definition be radiometrically equal. To healthy eyes, the yellow light would appear brighter than the red and the green. The green would appear brighter than the red. Radiometry does not adequately specify a method to make all three colors appear the same intensity. Radiometry is inadequate for measuring the perception of **luminous intensity** or relative brightness.

Photometers measure luminance and consider the spectral sensitivity of human eyes. Photometers are similar to radiometers that are scaled to the wavelength response of the human eye.

Luminance

Luminance is a measure of the brightness or luminous intensity of light, usually expressed in units of candelas per square meter. The candela is the current standard unit of luminous intensity. In **photometry,** which deals with the measurement of the intensity of light as perceived by human eyes, luminous intensity is the measure of the power emitted by a light source in a particular direction. The intensity is based on the **luminosity function,** which describes the average sensitivity of the human eye to light of different wavelengths.

The human eye sees light with wavelengths only in the visible spectrum. In photopic vision, the human eye is most sensitive to greenish-yellow light at about 555 nm, which is why the Bayer filter array has been designed to supply more green information than each of the other colors. In forensic photography, this additional green information is necessary for the accurate representation of evidence in imaging.

Originally, luminous intensity was measured in candles. One candle represented approximately

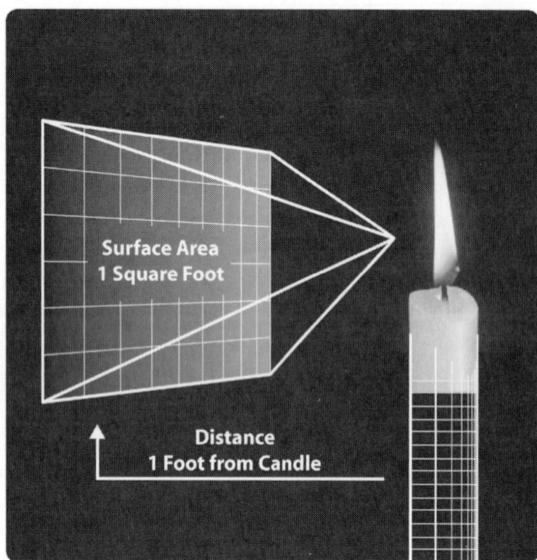

FIGURE 11–9 Visual definition of 1 foot candle. *Source:* Jessica Weiss.

the same amount of visible radiation emitted by the flame of a standard candle (see Fig. 11–9 and physics.nist.gov/cuu/Units/candela.html). This was not an exact specification. The units of luminous intensity, based before 1948 on flames or incandescent filaments, were later replaced by a newer definition of candle based on the luminance of a blackbody radiator at the temperature of freezing platinum. The difficulties in construction of blackbody radiators at high temperatures and the capabilities of modern radiometry prompted the 16th Conférence Générale des Poids et Mesures (CGPM) to adopt a new definition of the candle in 1979. The term *candle* was changed to *candela.* A **candela** is the luminous intensity, in a given direction, of a source that emits monochromatic radiation at 540×10^{12} hertz frequency and that has a radiant intensity in that direction of 1/683 watt per **steradian** (see the Glossary). A typical candle produces approximately 1 candela of luminous intensity.

Illuminance

The International System of Units (SI) is the modern metric system and is the world's most widely used system of units. In 1960, the SI was developed from the meter–kilogram–second (mks) system. SI is nearly universally used, except in the United States of America.

In photometry, **illuminance** is the total luminous flux incident on a surface, per unit area. **Luminous flux** or **luminous power** is the measure of the human eye's perception of the power of light. **Radiant flux** is the measure of the total power of light emitted from a source. Luminous flux of a light source is adjusted by the manufacturer to reflect the varying sensitivity of the human eye to different wavelengths of light. **Luminous emittance** is the luminous flux per unit area emitted from a surface. Luminous emittance is also known as **luminous exitance.** In SI units, these are both measured in **Lux (lx)** or lumens per square meter (1 FC = 1 Lumen per square foot, and 1 Lux = 1 Lumen per square meter). In the **CGS system,** the unit of illuminance is the phot. One **phot** is equal to 10,000 Lux. Illuminance was formerly called *brightness.* It is not possible to quantify the concept of brightness. Brightness is only an individual perception.

The human eye is capable of identification of a contrast range of more than 100 million to 1. It is possible to see white objects by starlight illumination at 5×10^{-5} Lux and to read large text at 108 Lux, or about 1,000 times the intensity of direct sunlight. Using your vision in high-intensity lighting is not recommended.

CAPTURING THE SCENE IN LOW LIGHT

To determine what a person may have seen in a limited light situation, the photographer may be required to create a **vision study,** which is the most difficult type of low-light photography.

> **RULE:**
>
> Nothing is more photographically impossible to achieve than images that accurately portray what a person may have seen at the time of an event.

Nothing is more photographically impossible to achieve than making images that accurately portray what a person may have seen at the time of an event for the following four reasons:

1. The scene can never again be exactly the same. Even on the same calendar day of another year, some factors are variable, including the weather, moon phase, street and advertisement lights, new construction, foliage, and so on.
2. It is impossible to know all the factors involved with a specific person's vision at the time of an occurrence. Factors include a person's physical condition, age, stage of adaptation, eyeglass correction and cleanliness, windshield condition, headlight condition, other headlights at the scene, and so on, ad infinitum.
3. Too many factors prevent a photograph from accurately representing reality in any lighting conditions. Accuracy problems include the recreation of contrast, color, dimensionality, DoF, field of view, perspective, general impression of the actual scene, and so on, ad infinitum.
4. A photograph captures a moment in time and a specific angular view. It is impossible to recreate the events from both a specific view and the full viewpoint of the person being represented.

It is critical at trial to demonstrate to the judge and jury, *approximately* what a scene looked like to a specific person at a specific time. It may be the part of the presentation on which everything else will rely. The best a photographer may achieve is to capture photographs of the way the scene looked to the photographer. The photographer must make every effort to recreate the scene photographically, to look as much as possible as it looked to the photographer.

E. S. Bomback: 1966

In 1966, E. S. Bomback said, in the *Manual of Colour Photography* that "in spite of every kind of exposure aid yet made available to the photographer, there remain certain kinds of subject or lighting conditions which can only be satisfactorily resolved by the time honored method of trial-and-error."[2] He suggested making three separate bracketed exposures at night to facilitate making one that was adequate to illustrate the character of the scene. The lack of advanced technology at that time was the primary reason for the absence of nighttime/low-light photographs being used routinely in court.

Little documentation exists of forensic procedures for low-light photography before the early 1980s. Over the last 25 years, ingenious methods have evolved to create images in low light with enhanced accuracy. Some of the methods follow in chronological order.

Most forensic evidence photographers will adapt a proven method or various parts of several to use as their own system. They find something that works for them that they are comfortable explaining in court and that makes sense to interested parties. Any system that works is fine, as long as they understand and are able to explain to their audience the inherent difficulties and shortcomings of reproducing the nighttime/low-light scene photographically.

John Duckworth: 1983

In 1983, John Duckworth suggested in *Forensic Photography* that "recreating what a driver could see at a later date becomes a bit sticky."[3] He states it is important to duplicate the car that was being driven. He checks the weather and phase of the moon for the date of the incident. He ensures that the scene photographs are exposed from proper viewpoint in the lane the car was using and that it is critical not to use a lens that distorts perspective. He suggests bracketing exposures to yield darker and lighter images from which to select one that looks the most like the original scene.

Stannard Baker and Lynn Fricke: 1986

In *The Traffic Accident Investigation Manual*, Baker and Fricke state, "It is sometimes important to have a record to explain what a driver or pedestrian could have seen at night with the light available to him/her at that time."[4] Photographic representations may easily be made to show more or less than a person with normal vision might see at any given time. For the nighttime visibility photography to be of use, the images must be as close an approximation as possible of what the person did actually see at the time of the incident.

The differences in the abilities of various persons to see things in low light must be considered. Adaptation level is very important, and often there is no way for that to be determined. The photos must be exposed under conditions as close as possible to those in place at the time of the incident. In many situations, this involves exposing photographs using the headlights of the subject or exemplar vehicles.

Because variations in processing may make a huge difference in the final result of the image (film or digital), the images must be processed to a standard. Baker and Fricke recommend making at least three bracketed exposures of every image so a range of images is available from which to choose. Viewing conditions must also be standardized and similar to the lighting conditions in which the images were exposed. This is true for slides and prints.

The use of test targets (see Fig. 11–10) is a method to make the images more "accurate and credible."[5] The targets must be equally recognizable in both the scene and the image. A target must be placed in the scene at a point where it is just discernible. The final images must also produce the target as just discernible. Then the image and the scene should match.

This procedure is not without problems, but it is widely used. It is a recognized and useful system if the photographer is able to adequately explain the disparities between the resultant images and the actual scene.

William Hyzer: 1988

In 1988, William G. Hyzer wrote in *An Extinction-Type Photometering Technique for Low-Light Luminance Measurements in Accident Investigations* that several aspects of human vision are impaired at low light levels.[6] These include the following:

- Acuity
- Color discrimination
- Depth perception
- Contrast sensitivity

Photometric analyses are necessary in investigations at crime and accident scenes where low-light levels may have been contributing factors in an accident or crime. It is necessary to make luminance and illuminance measurements of critical areas of the scene.

A common cause of nighttime accidents is low **conspicuity,** the inability of a driver to discriminate an object against its background. There is a contrast threshold level at which an object should be barely discernible. This contrast is determined by the following formula:

C = contrast

L_1 = subject/target luminance

L_2 = background luminance

$C = L_2 - L_1$ divided by L_2

The threshold value varies by the ambient lighting conditions and the visual abilities of the viewer.

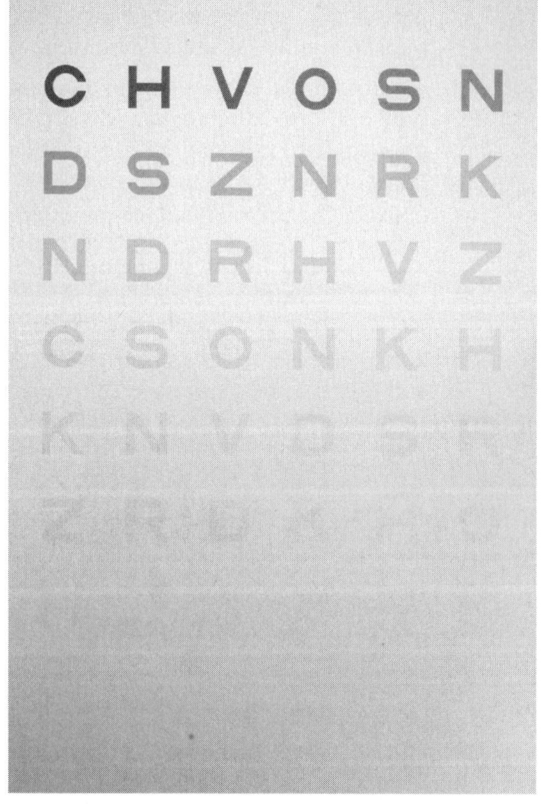

FIGURE 11–10 Exemplar test target. *Source:* Sandy Weiss/Packer Engineering.

Robert Holohan: 1989

In *Nighttime Photography: Show It Like It Is*, Robert D. Holohan suggests a technique for the production of "a photograph that accurately illustrates the limits of perception for an observer's view of objects under night lighting."[7] The photograph may be used in court to illustrate the visibility issues of a nighttime accident.

Holohan says that one solution to the problem of low-light photography is to make images at different bracketed exposures and select the one that looks the most like the scene. This requires a second trip to the scene on a different night, unless it is possible to create positive images at the scene. He did not suggest the use of Polaroid cameras and knew nothing of digital imaging at the time.

The photographs must be viewed in approximately the same lighting conditions as existed at the scene, and that is not often possible because the scene is too dark to illuminate the photographs properly. The adaptation level of the eyes of the viewer must be considered, and a standard must be established and used to assess the final prints.

Using test targets at varying distances from the camera is recommended to assess the threshold density that allows recognition of the characters in the target, as is using the same threshold density as a standard for making the prints. Holohan states that a search of the contemporary literature "identified little other work that specifically addressed techniques to provide photographs corresponding to an observer's nighttime perception."[8]

Ernest Klein and Gregory Stephens: 1992

In 1992, Ernest Klein and Gregory Stephens wrote in *Visibility Study: Methodologies and Reconstruction* that it is crucial to pick a future date and time with similar lighting conditions upon which to perform any vision study of an incident.[9] Photographic factors of importance include the following:

- Media speed
- Aperture
- Shutter speed
- Appropriate processing
- Appropriate printing

The ultimate goal was to ensure that the final photographs depicted the objects as they were seen under the actual illumination. Remember, the limiting factor affecting visibility is the conspicuity of the subject. In the early 1990s, digital photography was not available. Photographers routinely used 4 × 5-inch press or view cameras fitted with 4 × 5-inch Polaroid backs to expose instant images of scenes and evidence to judge exposure factors and composition. The authors recommend using that technology here. They say to expose Polaroid images at bracketed exposures. Use the image that most accurately portrays the scene, mark it with its exposure information, and retain it as a reference for the final prints made from the actual camera images. The images exposed at the scene must be printed at bracketed exposures. The one that most closely resembles the reference Polaroid image is considered the most accurate.

James Harris, Sr., and James Harris, II: 1992

In July 1992, James Harris, Sr., and James Harris, II, wrote in *Forensic Photography and Nighttime Visibility Issues* that low-light incidents regard the failure of people to react to a danger.[10] The argument at a trial will be the difficulty of performing in the existing light a **visual task** to designate those details and objects that must be seen for the performance of a given activity and include the immediate background of the details or objects.

> There are some very specific requirements that must be satisfied if photographs are to truly represent how things looked at the scene. Nighttime situations impose additional difficulties and many nighttime photographs are frequently not a legitimate representation of the level of difficulty associated with visual tasks.[11]

The most important factor for capturing accurate nighttime photographs is that, at the time of the photography, the scene "lighting conditions should be sufficiently similar" to the way they were at the time of the subject incident.[12] The lens of the camera must be placed at the eye location and height of the observer.

Consider these factors when exposing the images:

- Moon phase
- Cloud cover
- Changes, additions, and/or deletions of artificial lighting
- Painting of buildings
- Road resurfacing
- Lane line painting
- Moisture on roadways and vehicles
- Window and windshield cleanliness
- Headlight condition and alignment

It is essential to assess the possible differences and be aware of how they may alter results. Because of its contrast linearity, and luminance range, Harris and Harris recommend the use of Kodak slide-duplicating film SO366 for capturing low-light scene images. The current replacement for SO366 is EDUPE (see www.kodak.com/global/en/professional/support/techPubs/e2529/e2529.pdf for further information).

The variables that determine conspicuity include the following:

- contrast
- **Angular size** (the size of an object as viewed from Earth)
- Adaptation level of the eye
- Duration of stimulus

The objective of a photograph is to demonstrate the difficulty or ease with which objects can be detected or recognized.[13]

To be accurate, the measured contrast ratio between two different objects in a scene must exhibit the same ratio in the photograph. The media must display contrast linearity, and the ratio between exposure and density must be as close as possible to 1:1. In Fig. 11–11, the slope of the characteristic curve of the film is roughly equal to 1 in the straight-line portion (area 2) between the shoulder (area 3) and the toe (area 1).

For every film and development combination, there is a **characteristic curve** that illustrates the relationship between the logarithm of exposure (log K), and the optical density of the film after processing (D). (See Chapter 6 for more information.)

After processing, the slides are projected on a screen, using a projector with neutral density filters on its lens to limit the output of the lamp. When projected, the images produce the same luminance measurements as were taken at the scene. Luminance readings of the images are made with a spot meter, directly from the screen.

The processed film may be used as a photometer. "When a piece of film such as SO366 is exposed with a specified light energy (the product of illumination and time), and developed under standard conditions, the processed film will have a transmittance or density as predicted by the characteristic curve."[14] In this way, the density of the processed film may be related to the luminance of the actual scene. The difficulty of the visual task may be assessed by measuring the luminance of the scene from the slides and comparing the readings to accepted standards. "Since the projected slide cannot be a 'perfect' representation of the original scene, it is important to have some means of quantifying the accuracy with which courtroom observers can draw visibility conclusions."[15]

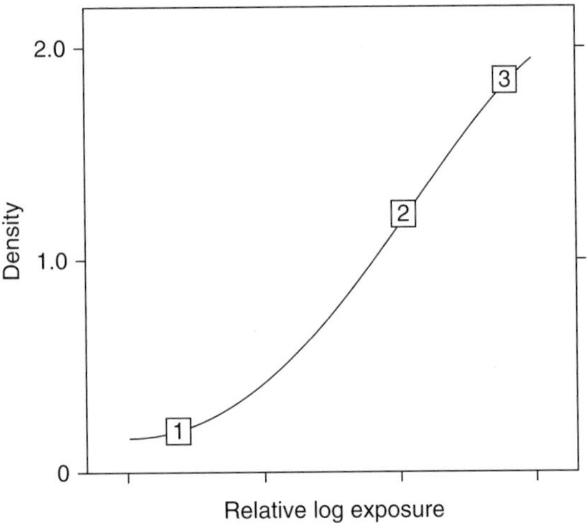

FIGURE 11–11 D log E curve of a typical film. *Source:* Sandy Weiss/Packer Engineering.

William Hyzer: 1993

In February 1993, William Hyzer wrote in *The Eye, Brain, and Camera in Nighttime Accident Reconstruction*, "The most important low-light-level visual degradation contributing to nighttime accidents is the failure to see an object against its background, because the contrast sensitivity of the eye is reduced to the point where it can no longer discriminate between the luminance levels of the object and its background."[16]

Hyzer also notes differences between visual images and camera images (still and video), but the camera images are being used regularly in courtrooms to demonstrate "what an observer was able or not able to see under low-light conditions."[17] He recommends two different methods for the presentation of nighttime images in the courtroom:

1. View the photographs under normal room-light conditions
2. View the photographs at low-light levels similar to those existing at the scene in the photograph

The first method is not realistic because it fails to address the inherent difficulties the human eye has in differentiating objects in the scotopic and mesopic ranges of vision.

The second method is more accurate. The images "must be rendered in the full tonal scale and color (if possible) as they would naturally appear under the extant viewing conditions, so that both the judge and the jury, whose visual processes are intentionally impaired by low-light-level mesopic or scotopic viewing conditions, perceive the scene as a human observer would under the actual low-light-level conditions that existed at the scene."[18]

Hyzer points out that the human eye is capable of vision in a luminance ratio at any one time of 10,000:1, or 13½ camera stops, and that all of the following media are incapable of creating accurate photographic representations of scenes with luminance ratios in that range.

- Black-and-white film, exposed and processed properly, is capable of a ratio of 256:1 (8 stops).
- Black-and-white prints, printed properly from good negatives, are capable of a ratio of 100:1.
- Color glossy prints from negative film are capable of a ratio of 50:1.
- Color matte prints from negative film are capable of a ratio of 20:1.

To create images with a full tonal scale (and color, if possible) as they would appear at a scene, Hyzer recommends the use of Kodak SO366 Ektachrome color slide duplicating film.

SO366 color slide duplicating film has a maximum transmittance ratio of 300:1 and good linearity between transmittance and scene luminance, through an exposure range of 5 stops in area #2 of the D log E curve. SO366 is a good choice, but can a film that produces a ratio of only 300:1 produce images to accurately represent the range of human vision at 10,000:1?

The slides are projected in court with a projector fitted with appropriate neutral density filters over the lens. This reduces the luminance of the projected image to the approximate luminance of the original scene. The courtroom must be totally darkened to resemble nighttime. This practice contains inherent difficulties. Reflectance from the screen of the projected image adds light to the room. Light also leaks from the air vents of the projector.

He concludes that, "Forensic photographers seriously contemplating the use of photography or videography in order to 'truly and accurately' represent a nighttime scene, need to be ever mindful of the numerous physical, physiological, and psychological pitfalls, waiting to frustrate their honest efforts."[19]

T. J. Ayres: 1996

In *Psychophysical Validation of Photographic Representation*, T. J. Ayres writes, "In order to represent how a scene would appear to a typical observer, a photographic print can be calibrated based on careful observation."[20]

Photographs are routinely produced under specific conditions of illumination from the points of view of the participants in an incident. Many attorneys attempt to use the photographs to explain to jurors and judges the features of a scene without the necessity of explanations of the science involved in luminance and vision. Many people think that doing a vision study will in some way validate the nighttime images to "Establish that the image faithfully represents some aspect of the visual experience that an observer would have at the actual scene."[21]

Ayres says that much research has been performed about the role of visibility issues in incidents, but very little has been done on the accuracy of photographic representations of low-visibility conditions. "Most books on photography or on accident reconstruction do not discuss the problems of portraying night visibility conditions, or else note that a low-light photograph can be exposed to yield an arbitrarily dark or light image."[22]

The evaluation of a photograph must be performed by the use of actual observations made at the scene. The procedure for test targets discussed in *The Traffic Accident Investigation Manual* places the targets at specific points in the scene, where they are just barely discernible.[23] Photographs must be exposed to duplicate the same quality of the targets. In an identical image exposed without targets, under the same circumstances, lighting, camera settings, developing, and so on may be represented as a validated, accurate, representation of the scene. When viewing the image, the illumination must be a reasonable approximation of the illumination at the scene. "It is essential to note that the validated image does not necessarily show the scene as it appeared to the investigating observer. The validation procedure is tied to accurately representing featural detectability."[24]

This procedure has been adopted and adapted by many modern forensic photographers making nighttime photographs of scenes. The question of contrast linearity throughout the range of luminance is a subject that must be technically addressed. Ayres states that if luminance measurements are made of various elements at the scene, then the objects may be correlated to the resultant images by comparison readings. This method does not work well if the characteristic curve of the media is not a linear ratio of 1:1.

Paul Olson: 1996

Paul Olson references both Harris and Hyzer in *Forensic Aspects of Driver Perception and Response.*[25] He writes, "Jurors tend to believe that what they see in a photograph is what they would have seen had they been there themselves at the time the photograph was taken."[26] In truth, most jurors are not well educated regarding the technical aspects of photography and have little idea of the limitations of the media.

Photographs of objects are normally exposed in daylight conditions. These images are automatically accepted as accurate if the color and exposure appear correct and the subject is not outrageous, like people floating in space. Normal skills are needed to make daylight photographs. Specialized skills are needed for evidence photographs, even in daylight. Many attorneys expose their own evidence images with their own cameras. Nighttime images that are exposed by attorneys and amateurs are commonly entered into evidence to show "the visibility available to an individual in a particular situation."[27] The person(s) who made the images and the attorney using the images, may have little idea of the particular shortcomings of the images.

Nighttime photographs "must depict with great accuracy the luminance levels and contrast present in the scene. They must cause the perceptions of the jurors to reasonably duplicate that of the person or persons whose perceptions are at issue."[28] When showing these photographs in court, it must be assumed that the camera and accessories used were capable of accurately duplicating human vision in images. It must be assumed that the judge and jury are seeing what the person(s) in question must have seen. *These premises are faulty.*

Olson offers a list of possible problems with nighttime photographic images:[29]

- The field of view commonly created in photographs is limited when compared with actual vision, and there may have been important factors involved outside the frame limits of the images.
- A photograph is static, and at the time of an incident the vision of the individual was dynamic. Making videos or animations is a partial answer to address this issue. (See Chapter 12.)
- Static photographs can be studied for any length of time, but the scene was instantaneous to the person involved.

- The level of adaptation of the person involved cannot be assessed.
- Images are often enlarged for ease of viewing in court, while the person involved could not see at that magnification at that time.
- The person involved had certain expectations of what may have been seen before the instant in question, but expectation cannot be shown in a photograph.

Olson recommends the use of Polaroid images to make nighttime photographs more fair and accurate. He suggests exposing a series of Polaroid images at bracketed exposures, to be viewed and compared at the scene to the scene. The exposure that most closely resembles what the people at the scene could see becomes the reference for the preparation of conventional images. He recommends, as Harris and Hyzer do, the use of SO366 and says it is an improvement over many methods performed in court, but the practice is not without issues.

J. B. Hyzer: 2002

J. B. Hyzer states in *Photographically Maximizing the Information Recorded in Forensic Images* that the reason photographs of nighttime scenes can never be totally accurate is that color negative film, like Kodak Gold 200, captures an extensive subject brightness range of up to 10,000:1.[30] It has a linear portion of its D log E curve of about 300:1. Prints made from the resultant negatives decrease in dynamic range to about 100:1 with a linear range of only 4:1. Due to this issue, it is necessary to produce a range of prints of varying densities and to inspect different aspects of each to relate to different parts of the scene. This is a time-consuming and confusing method.

Paul Olson and Eugene Farber: 2003

In 2003, Paul Olson teamed with Eugene Farber to release the 2nd edition of *Forensic Aspects of Driver Perception and Response*, in which they state, "If the individual presenting the images can testify that the image(s) depict exactly what he or she could see, the photographs are likely to be accepted as exhibits and the jurors will probably assume that they truly represent the object or scene depicted."[31]

RULE:

Never state that the images are what another person involved in an incident could see. At best, the images should represent what the photographer, investigator, or attorney could see at a similar time. This is the highest level of achievable accuracy.

The production of Polaroid images is deleted in Olson and Farber's second edition. This is most likely because of the availability of digital technology. Digital cameras will automatically adjust exposure to make nighttime images appear however the photographer wants them to appear. Instant replay of the images on the LCD, or even on a computer monitor, determines if the exposure was successful. Bracketing can be performed in the camera or in post-processing.

Boyd Allin, Kurt Isling, and David King: 2007

In 2007, Allin, Isling, and King, presented a paper entitled, "Digital Camera Calibration for Luminance Estimation in Nighttime Visibility Studies."[32] This paper is the door to the digital future for nighttime photography and vision studies. The authors' premise is that a digital camera can be calibrated so that any pixel in any image exposed by the camera may be quantified for luminance. This enables the luminance ratios between any two pixels to be calculated, and it allows contrast to be determined to define conspicuity between any objects imaged in a scene under any illumination.

The forensic photographer may document any scene, in any lighting, and then use his or her computer to accurately calculate the contrast of any objects. It is no longer necessary to make photographs that accurately depict a scene as someone else would have seen it. The process is to make images that display the scene as the photographer saw it. The photographer may testify that the images are exposed to the best of their ability. Then, the visibility, contrast, and conspicuity of an object may be computed and presented with reasonable accuracy.

Proper calibration is not an easy process. If the calibration of cameras becomes a regularly requested function, software may become available to perform the procedure. Metering of luminance and illuminance is still necessary for a base reference.

HARDWARE FOR MEASURING LUMINANCE AND ILLUMINANCE

Meters are specifically designed to read the illumination of a scene or an object. These meters are not designed for photographic purposes. They do not suggest shutter speeds and lens apertures. They measure the intensity of light falling onto, emitted by, or reflected from a subject. Such meters are more expensive than photographic meters and are built for precision and accuracy.

> **TIP:**
>
> When measuring the intensity of light for non-photographic purposes, never use a photographic light meter.

Konica-Minolta Luminance Meter LS-100

The Konica-Minolta Luminance Meter LS-100 (see Fig. 11–12) is useful for measuring the luminance of light sources or reflective surfaces. The meter incorporates a TTL viewing system to enable accurate metering from a specific aspect of a subject.

Features

- Measurement angle 1 degree, for measurements of small areas
- Measuring range: 0.01 to 999,900 cd/m^2
- 2-Way RS-232, via USB, communication to a computer for remote operation and for direct download
- Multicoated optics for flare-free and accurate measurements

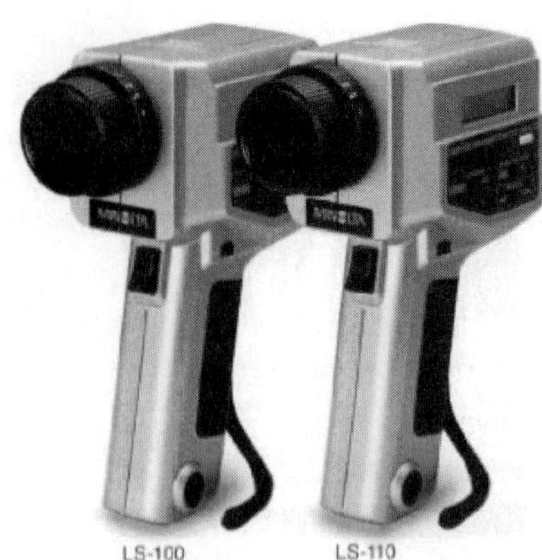

FIGURE 11–12 Konica-Minolta luminance meters. *Source:* Sandy Weiss/Packer Engineering.

- Simple calibration and color-correction functions
- Luminance ratio and peak luminance measurement capabilities
- Measures luminous intensity of backlit sources

Gossen Mavolux 5032 USB Luxmeter/Footcandle Illuminance Meter

The Gossen Mavolux 5032 USB Luxmeter/ Footcandle Illuminance Meter (see Fig. 11–13) is useful for measuring the illuminance of ambient lighting.

Features

- Illuminance can be measured in Lux or foot-candles.
- Luminance may also be measured in candles per square meter (cd/m^2) or foot-Lamberts.
- The meter conforms to standards DIN 5032-7 and CIE No. 69.
- The silicon photo diode is color corrected, and the spectral responsitivity is matched to the spectral phototic vision of the human eye.
- A USB interface is available for remote operation by computer and for direct download.

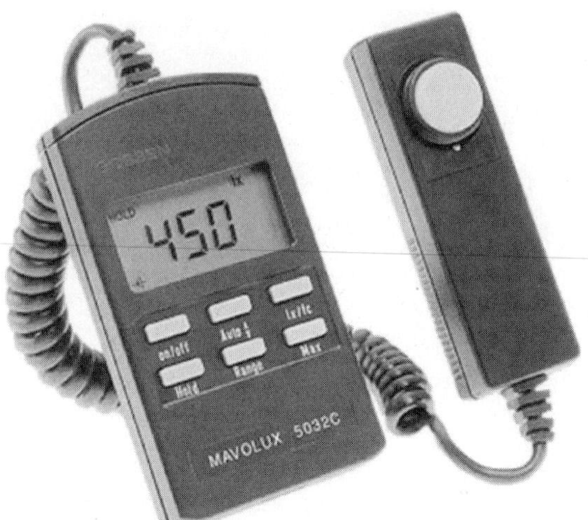

FIGURE 11–13 Gossen Mavilux 5032 USB Luxmeter/Footcandle Illuminance Meter. *Source:* Sandy Weiss/Packer Engineering.

Meter Applications

The representative Konica-Minolta and Gossen meters depicted in Figures 11–12 and 11–13 have a wide range of applications, including the control of light sources, adjustment of streetlights, and lighting of workplaces, public buildings, and sports facilities. Lighting designers and architects use these meters for quality control and quality assurance in the manufacture of lamps and light sources. They make possible the measurement of light over a wide range of intensities and may be certified when calibrated for inspection procedures.

SUMMARY

In the years of slow-speed film, slow lenses, large cameras, and long time delays in film processing, nighttime images were not used extensively in court. About 25 years ago, for a number of reasons—including high-speed film, lenses, processing, and changes in the legal system—nighttime images became more commonly used. Initially it was thought that images could be produced photographically that would duplicate what a person could have seen at the time of an incident. That theory was disproved.

Due to the complex differences between vision and photography, it is now known to be impossible to accurately represent photographically the vision of a victim. But photographs can be made by evidence photographers that supply to judges and jurors an idea of what a scene looked like. The subtle difference between definitions of accuracy have led to a steady progression of updated practices in nighttime forensic photography.

This chapter enumerates and illustrates the progress made in the nighttime techniques and offers a selection of techniques for use in contemporary cases. If the photographer is aware of the limitations, the benefits of making nighttime photographs are obvious.

Digital imaging is the current technology for this endeavor. Photographers may enter the field equipped with a camera and computer and expose images and view them at the scene. In this way the images may be compared to the scene and exposed as close as possible to what is seen at the time.

Digital imaging offers breakthroughs in data acquisition regarding the inherent contrast of scenes. Nighttime digital photographs afford more quantitative information than was ever available when using film.

CASE STUDY

Vision Study of Traffic Fatality

A young man was killed when he drove his car underneath the side of a semitrailer on his way home from a Chicago Cubs night baseball game at Wrigley Field. His vehicle had just passed under a dark railroad bridge (see Fig. 11–14). At the time of the accident, the trailer was blocking all four lanes of a state route while the truck driver was backing out of a loading dock at a retail superstore. The young man's family sued the trucking company, the store chain, and the city. The suit against the trucking company alleged improper street blockage (against the trucking company), improper safety practices (against the store), and lack of visibility of the truck due to insufficient street lighting (against the city). The deceased was above the legal limit of intoxication

FIGURE 11–14 Looking north under the bridge. The trailer is blocking the street past the bridge. *Source:* Sandy Weiss/Packer Engineering.

at the time of the accident, but that was not considered an issue during the case. The issue was that all the streetlights on the east side of the road were inoperative at the time of the accident. The family members and their expert claimed that contrast between the truck and the bridge was insufficient, making them inconspicuous.

A visibility study of the scene was performed, and an opinion was reached about the conditions on the night of the accident. The most significant issue was whether or not the truck should have been visible to the automobile driver at the time of the incident.

To prepare for the reconstruction, the weather conditions on the night of the accident were checked. The conditions were comparable a year later on the same night of the year. Lunar conditions were also similar on the same day and at the same time of night.

The police were able to block the traffic on the road from 1:00 a.m., at moonset, until 5:00 a.m., the start of rush hour. At the time of the test, the city turned off all the lights that were not lit at the time of the accident. A thorough investigation involving a study of the photographs taken by the police at the scene on the night of the accident determined that no other significant conditional changes had occurred between the time of the accident and the time of the testing.

The subject trailer was brought to the scene. This made the reflectance of the side of the trailer as identical as possible to the reflectance at the time of the accident The trailer had been placed in storage and had remained in the same condition since the time of the accident. An exemplar car was purchased and used for the re-creation. Photographs were exposed from a position directly in front of the car's front bumper, at driver's eye height, with the car headlights both on and off. The reason for the headlights being both on and off is that the precrash alignment of the headlights in the subject vehicle could not be determined after the vehicle was damaged. Because the front end of the car was crushed on impact and the subject headlights were shattered, it also could not be determined if the lights were turned on at the time of the incident. After careful study of the illumination pattern of headlights similar to the subject headlights, the illumination of properly adjusted headlights was determined to be a nonissue in this case, due to the configuration of the roadway.

The roadway was marked in 25-foot increments from 300 feet south of the position of impact to 50 feet from the position of impact. It was not necessary to document closer than 50 feet from the trailer because that was the minimum stopping distance of the vehicle at its velocity at the time of the accident.

Three types of photographs were exposed from each position, and three cameras were used. The two 35mm camera bodies were identical and had the same focal length lenses. The images exposed included the following:

- 35mm color negatives
- 35mm Ektachrome SO366 slides
- 4 × 5-inch color Polaroids

The color negative images were intended for documentation of the reconstruction. The slides were to be used in court to present an idea of the visibility issues. Because the scene could not be reset again and only one chance was allowed for this recreation, the Polaroids were intended for instant confirmation that useable images had been captured. Luminance and illuminance readings were measured from the scene, and the subject trailer was also measured for reflectance to correlate to the measured projected values of the slides in court.

The Harris and Harris article from *The Journal of Forensic Sciences* provided the guidelines for the exposure of the slides.[33] Kodak SO366 slide duplicating film was used. A gray scale was included in each photograph, and the luminance for each exposure of the scale was recorded at the scene. The intent was to take the slides into court and reproduce the same luminance on the screen as was found at the scene. This would illustrate to the judge and jury approximately what the scene looked like to us. All the images were successfully processed with excellent results.

At every step of the procedure and from each camera location 4 × 5-inch black-and-white Polaroids were taken. Each was shown to the attorney at the time of exposure and then adjusted for density and contrast until the attorney said, "Yes, that looks just like what I see right now." When the case was tried, enlargements of the Polaroids were used as exhibits. The slides were not used. The attorney said, "It was just less work than lugging in all of the projection equipment and trying to explain to the judge and jury what luminance was."

This case settled against the plaintiff.

CASE STUDY

Injury at a House Party

A party in a private home led to an injury when an intoxicated woman fell down a stairway. The woman was too drunk to drive. Out of concern and courtesy, the woman was invited to spend the night at the home. The woman was to spend the night on a couch near the kitchen. During the night, she awakened with a need to use the bathroom. The guest bathroom in the house is located through the kitchen, down a hallway, and to the left. The only light illuminating the area was over the sink in the kitchen. The woman arose from the couch, walked toward the kitchen, made the left turn in the wrong place, and fell down the basement steps. (The steps to the basement are to the left of the half-wall pictured at the bottom left of Fig. 11–15.) A serious injury resulted, and the woman filed suit against the homeowners, claiming the area was insufficiently illuminated for her to see the stairway.

On a subsequent night I went to assess and photograph the scene in the same illumination as existed at the time of the incident and to form an opinion about what the woman could and should have been able to see. The night visit was necessary to make photographs that were not affected by daylight entering the windows.

The homeowner was consulted, and the lights in the house were on or off, the same as they were on the night of the accident. Light readings

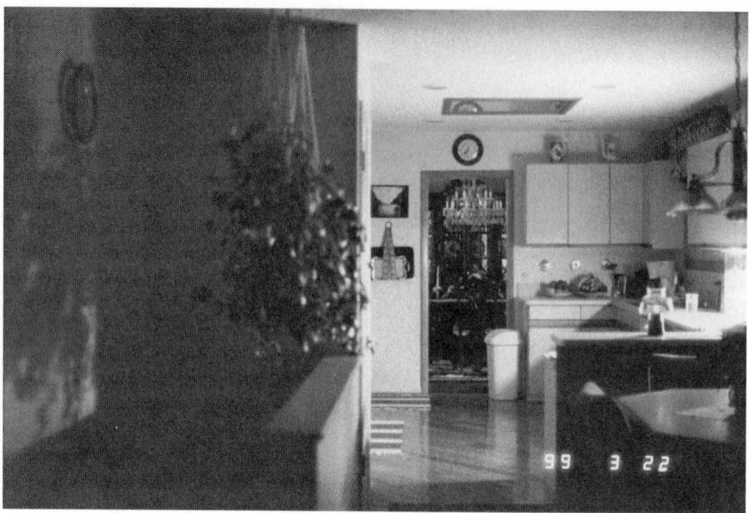

FIGURE 11–15 How the subject kitchen appeared. The steps to the basement are to the left of the half-wall at the bottom left in the image. *Source:* Sandy Weiss/Packer Engineering.

were obtained with an illuminance meter to ascertain the level of illumination.

A local code of illumination exists and must be met. The pertinent code section reads as follows:

> Normal intensity of lighting shall be not less than one foot candle per square foot on the floor surfaces of vertical exits and not less than one half foot candle per square foot on the floors of other exits.[34]

I exposed photographs of the scene on Kodak 2475 Recording Film (see Fig. 11–16) rated at 1,000 ASA. The 2475 film has a linear D log E curve when processed in HC110-B developer. It was the appropriate black-and-white film for making images to represent a vision study. (Study the D log E curve of the film and developer used for determination of linearity.) (The 2475 film is no longer manufactured by Kodak. The appropriate substitute is a high ISO black-and-white film of any brand.)

I used an Olympus OM-2 camera with a 50 mm *f*/1.4 lens. The height of the camera was set at the carefully measured eye height of the plaintiff. The image sequence commenced at the point where she would have been standing when she arose from the couch and continued every 2 feet to the point where she fell down the stairs. The angle of view of the 50mm lens used for the photograph is not the same as for a person with binocular vision, but the relative perspective in a photograph is similar to human vision. It was determined that the lighting at the top of the stairs did meet the minimum code requirements of 1 foot candle per square foot.

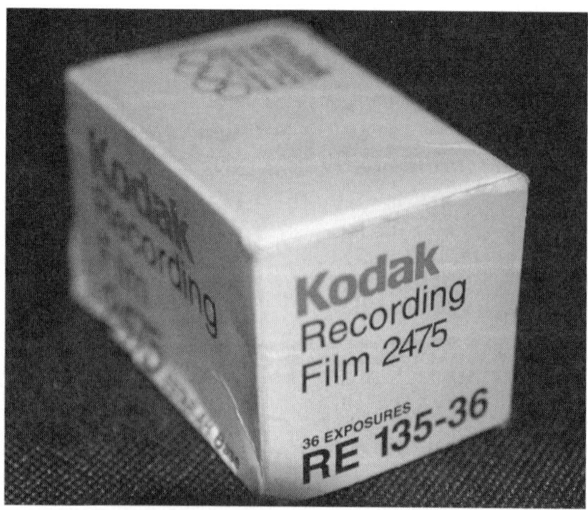

FIGURE 11–16 Kodak 2475 Recording Film. *Source:* Sandy Weiss/Packer Engineering.

KEY TERMS

subject brightness range/contrast, (p. 322)
reciprocity failure, (p. 323)
mirror lock-up, (p. 326)
monochrome, (p. 326)
scotopic vision, (p. 326)
mesopic vision, (p. 326)
photopic vision, (p. 326)
radiometer, (p. 327)
luminous intensity, (p. 327)
photometer, (p. 327)
photometry, (p. 327)
luminosity function, (p. 327)
candela, (p. 328)
steradian, (p. 328)
illuminance (p. 328)
luminous flux, (p. 328)
luminous power, (p. 328)
radiant flux, (p. 328)
luminous emittance, (p. 328)
luminous exitance, (p. 328)
Lux, (p. 328)
CGS system, (p. 328)
phot, (p. 328)
vision study, (p. 328)
conspicuity, (p. 330)
visual task, (p. 331)
angular size, (p. 332)
characteristic curve, (p. 332)

EXERCISES

1. Document a nighttime scene with a camera on a tripod, using the light meter on automatic for one exposure and on manual for another. Compare the results and examine the differences in detail.
2. Complete a visual story of walk-through of a nighttime outdoor scene. Develop a hypothetical incident, and then plan and execute all the necessary images to tell the whole story at trial.
3. Complete a visual story of a walk-through of a nighttime or daytime, but low-light, indoor scene. Develop a hypothetical incident, and then plan and execute all the necessary images to tell the whole story at trial.
4. Assemble a nighttime go-kit with everything that would be needed to be conveniently equipped.
5. Do an actual nighttime documentation under inclement conditions, protecting the camera equipment against the elements.
6. Develop a collection of nighttime visibility targets for placing at and in the scene.
7. Research and record the appropriate illumination standards for your geographic area so you will be prepared to measure a scene for conformance.
8. **ONLY FOR THE DARING:** Procure a copy of SAE 2007-01-0718 and follow the steps to achieve a calibrated camera, and then document a scene for a visibility study and determine the contrast among appropriate objects.

APPENDIX 11.1

Technical Specifications for Figure 11–5

Camera Model	Canon EOS XTi (400D)
Shooting Date/Time	5/9/2007 0:24:22 AM
Shooting Mode	Aperture-Priority AE
Tv (Shutter Speed)	30 seconds
Av (Aperture Value)	13.0
Metering Mode	Partial Metering
Exposure Compensation	+1
ISO Speed	100
Lens	EF75-300mm *f*/4–5.6
Focal Length	85.0 mm
Image Size	2,592 × 3,888
Image Quality	Fine
Flash	Off
White Balance Mode	Auto
AF Mode	AI Focus AF
Picture Style	Landscape
Sharpness	4
Contrast	0
Saturation	0
Color Tone	0
Color Space	sRGB
Noise Reduction	Off
File Size	1,643 KB
Drive Mode	Single-frame shooting

Location: Steenwijk, The Netherlands

The photo was made from a fourth-floor window looking out on a small street between two apartment houses. The image was exposed just after midnight during a light rain. The only ambient lighting was from the small streetlights along the sidewalk. The streak of light evident in the frame, running from top to bottom, was from the headlight of a bicycle that started down the street the instant the shutter was released for the photo.

The camera was placed on a small cardboard box on the windowsill. No tripod was available.

W. Thomas Miles, Lakeland, FL, e-mail:
Thomas@wthomasmiles.com, Web site: wthomasmiles.com.

Chapter 12

Videography

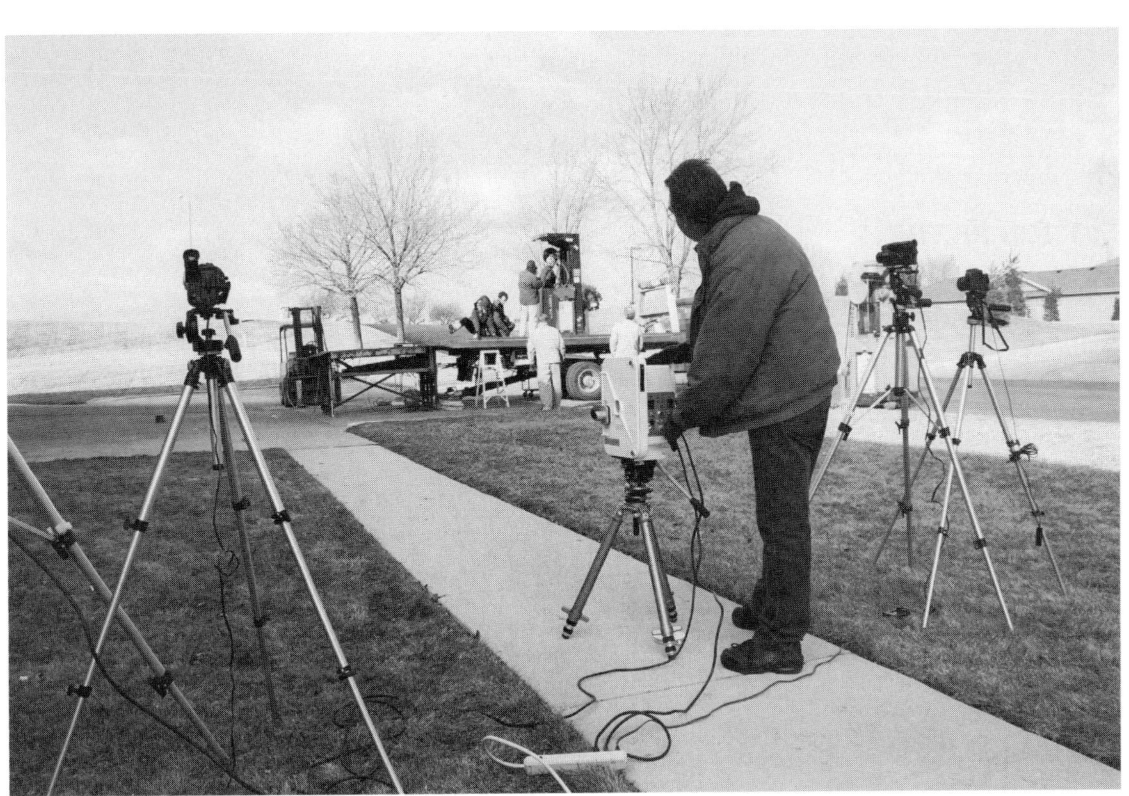

Learning Objectives

AFTER STUDYING THIS CHAPTER, YOU SHOULD BE ABLE TO:

1. Know when it is appropriate to use motion pictures or videos in cases where still images will not accurately document evidence
2. Understand the role of the forensic cinematographer in creating motion pictures and videos for use in the courtroom
3. Identify the different types of hardware and software involved in the creation and postproduction of forensic motion pictures and videos
4. Understand the differences and know when to select film or electronic motion picture production for various purposes
5. Be familiar and comfortable with the steps required to produce motion pictures or videos under various conditions
6. Undertake surveillance and high-speed video technology
7. Perceive and utilize the proper steps and requirements for video documentation of depositions
8. Understand the concepts of multimedia and virtual reality

MOTION PICTURES

The earliest recorded use of motion pictures for law enforcement was for a case in Fresno, California, in 1945. An amateur 8mm movie camera was used to document a person arrested for driving under the influence (DUI).[1] The practice became popular with departments around the country and world that were at the cutting edge of advances in technology. The use of color and sound in motion pictures became standard for the recording of the demeanor of DUI suspects. This evidence-gathering technique raised conviction rates from a level between 5% and 30% to one between 85% and 95% in most jurisdictions.[2]

FORENSIC CINEMATOGRAPHY

Video recordings are used for evidence documentation in numerous situations, including the following:

- Scene walk-throughs
- Incident recreations
- Testing documentation
- Inspections
- Surveillance
- Deposition testimony

Various types of video cameras are available, including the following:

- Standard-speed video camcorders
- High-speed video recorders
- Surveillance cameras

EXAMINATION AND VIDEO DOCUMENTATION OF A SCENE

When static images are insufficient to accurately document and explain certain evidence, film or video motion pictures may be required. Some viewers are able to comprehend a visual story more easily when the images move, the way they do in normal human vision. Motion pictures and videos are not used for the high-resolution documentation of small items of evidence, but they are often used for systematic and sequential tours through scenes and for the documentation of reconstructions. Most law enforcement departments have switched from film to video, due to its availability, low cost, and instant turnaround.

Steps for Video Documentations

Evidence videos should have a logical beginning, middle, and conclusion. It is often useful to include computer-generated titles or footage captured from storyboards to explain the action and to inform the viewers of important data, including location, date, time, and case title. A logical and systematic sequence of steps for the creation of a forensic video may include the following:

- Formulate a plan about how the scene is to be processed, examined, and documented.
- Perform a careful examination for fragile, trace evidence.
- Place markers at evidence locations.
- Document evidence first that is in danger of being destroyed.
- Remember that the scene is three-dimensional.
- Document the floor or ground before walking on it.
- If indoors, examine and document the point of entry into the scene.
- Document a walk-through of the event.
- Examine and document the location of the incident to place it in the context of the scene and the world.
- Examine and document areas of other activity.
- Examine and document the point of exit.
- Write notes to accompany the videos, including recording times and locations.

Video Documentation

Video provides a different perspective of evidence and events and may be simpler to record than a series of static images for the viewer to understand. A logical sequence of video images allows the viewer to correlate the evidence to the scene, just as a logical sequence of preparation will ensure proper and complete documentation:

- Document evidence before it is collected.
- Check the availability of sufficient charged batteries and media for the camera.
- Check that the date and time are correctly set in the camera.
- Ensure that the condition of the scene is as close as possible to the way it was found. Exceptions include the following:
  - Evidence markers placed at the locations of evidence.
  - If a victim was checked for vital signs, the scene may look different than when it was discovered. Record this in your notes.
- If allowed by departmental protocol, record pertinent observations by voice onto the audio track of the video, as it is being made.
- Try to avoid documenting personnel or equipment that have been brought to the scene and were not part of the original scene.
- If the video cannot be recorded without distracting and extraneous sounds, consider disabling the sound capability of the camera.
- Once the video commences, keep the camera running until the documentation is completed or you have to do one of the following:
  - Pause while recording
  - Change the media if it ends
  - Change discharged batteries
- Move the camera slowly during documentation. Slower is better when panning a scene.
- Begin the documentation sequence with a general wide-angle overview of the scene.
- Pan the camera—always—in a clockwise direction. (In countries where the language is written left to right, panning the camera clockwise enables long blocks of text to be read as they were written.)

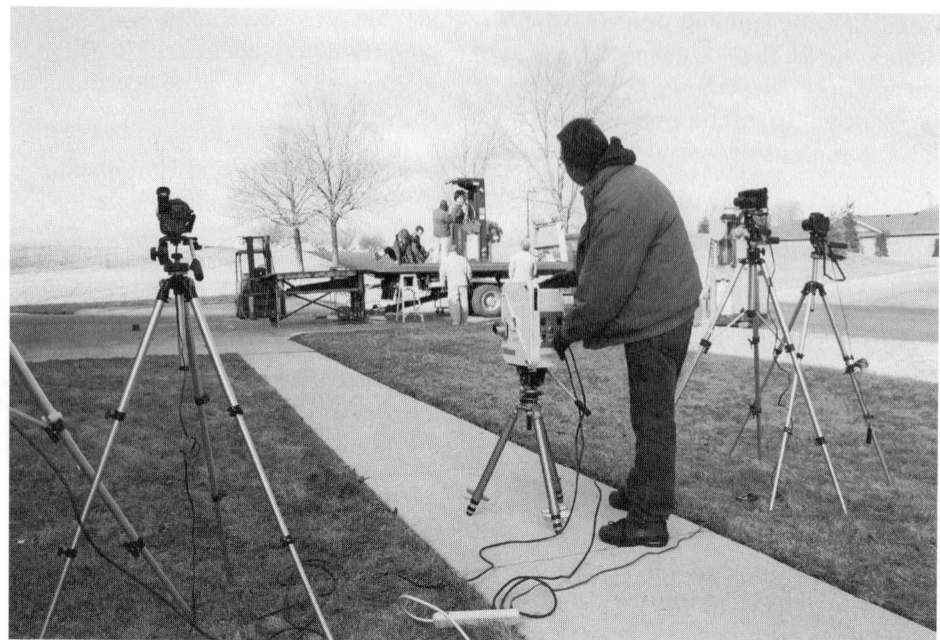

FIGURE 12–1 Incident recreation using multiple, stationary video and film cameras. *Source:* Sandy Weiss/ Packer Engineering.

- Use a wide-angle, medium, and then close-up sequence to document the scene and the evidence in relation to the scene.
- When zooming in for a close-up of a specific area, do the following:
  - Stop panning first.
  - Zoom in slowly to document the evidence.
  - Zoom back out to the original focal length before continuing the pan.
- The scene consists of 3-D space (x-y-z coordinates). When panning horizontally in x-y space:
  - Stop panning before moving the camera to view in the z direction.
  - Return to the location where the camera was stopped before continuing the horizontal pan.
- Once the video has been completed, it should be:
  - Transferred to the media used for permanent storage.
  - Filed as per departmental procedure or protocol.
  - Recorded on appropriate forms, along with all the steps of the documentation.

Video Recreations, Documentations, and Inspections

You may have to record significant action with stationary cameras (see Fig. 12–1). Follow these steps to do so:

- Place the camera(s) in the proper location(s) to capture the action.
- To avoid unnecessary camera movement, put the camera(s) on a tripod and allow everything to run without operator contact.
- Move the camera closer to the subject when the action becomes too small in the frame, using close-up detail as necessary.

Two types of tripods are available. The one intended for still cameras has one handle to control horizontal movement and another to control the vertical. Video tripods have a **fluid head** so the camera may be panned and tilted smoothly in any direction, using only one control. The tripod controls are properly placed to promote convenient operation of the camera. Fluid heads may fit on the same legs as still camera tripods.

Heavy-duty fluid heads cost more than light-duty ones. To minimize extraneous camera movements, heavy-duty tripods are required when using high-definition cameras. Fluid heads dampen vibrations and facilitate smooth movements.

TIP:

Level the tripod and camera to the horizon to avoid adding distracting tilt errors while creating the video. High-quality tripods usually have built-in bubble levels. If not, be sure to have one available.

INSPECTION AND VIDEO DOCUMENTATION OF OBJECTS

The video documentation of evidence may include weapons, personal property, clothing, electronic devices, vehicles, etc. It is important to use an established, practiced, and systematic approach when processing and documenting evidence, regardless of conditions. Think ahead and prepare mentally for the sequence of necessary steps to successfully document the object(s) and tell the whole story.

TIP:

Application of a practiced and systematic approach to video documentation of all evidence will limit mistakes and allow you to concentrate on the evidence, rather than on the process.

To fully process and document all evidence, the following sequence of steps should be used as a guide:

- Document any serial numbers, tags, or aspects of the evidence that make it unique.
- Include the following in the overall documentation:
  - Complete coverage of the exterior, going around the object in a clockwise direction
  - Appropriate references for size, color, and location
  - Images of the object from above and below, if possible
  - Open flaps, doors, pockets, compartments, or other hidden areas, documented in a clockwise orientation
- Expose extra video where unusual evidence is encountered.
- Start with wide views to establish a point of view, and then zoom to close-up, detailed coverage.
- Always return to the wide-angle, overall view before proceeding to different aspects of an object.
- If documenting a vehicle, provide detailed coverage of the driver's area.

After completion of the video documentation, stop the camera and perform a detailed visual inspection of the same areas. Look closely for anything that may have been overlooked previously. If you find anything new, turn the camera back on and perform a complete video documentation of the new area.

Look inside pockets, behind flaps, under carpeting, at seams, and anywhere that may easily be overlooked; someone may have attempted to clean the object to eliminate trace evidence.

TIP:

Only after the evidence has been completely documented in still photographs and video, should it be collected.

Collect evidence that is most fragile first. Always use the appropriate container for each item of evidence. Video document the evidence collection and its marking process.

VIDEO SURVEILLANCE

In many cases, people will realize they are being surveilled. Overt surveillance equipment is common and expected in all security locations. The equipment should be as visible and obvious as possible to discourage breaches in security. Some locations install mock security equipment that is inexpensive and requires no maintenance, in low-security areas.

Covert surveillance is performed to ensure safety and as a detriment to crime. In many situations the surveillance will be expected, but the surveillance equipment will be hidden and difficult to observe. Miniature covert video cameras may be hidden inside clocks, smoke detectors, flowerpots; behind one-way mirrors; or in a multitude of other locations. Cameras may be attached to wireless or conventional video recorders. Wireless surveillance camera systems are easily installed and moved. Video quality of such systems is adequate for law enforcement to identify individuals. Covert surveillance is well documented in modern professional literature.[3]

Remote Surveillance Videography Equipment

Remote surveillance videography may be covert or overt and is overseen by individuals in centralized locations. Many locations of the same business may be surveilled by one person. Companies exist that specialize in supplying remote surveillance for a fee. These operations are usually hard-wired into law enforcement located near remote cameras. (Remote equipment has features inherent to the discipline, plus the ability to be controlled from a location separated from the camera.) Examples of state-of-the-art equipment are discussed in the following paragraphs.

The *Samsung Mini Surveillance Camera* (see Fig. 12–2) is easy to disguise and provides high-resolution video images. The following are some of its key features:

- Day and night, 32x optical zoom lens
- Wide Dynamic Range (WDR) for well-exposed images under a wide range of lighting conditions

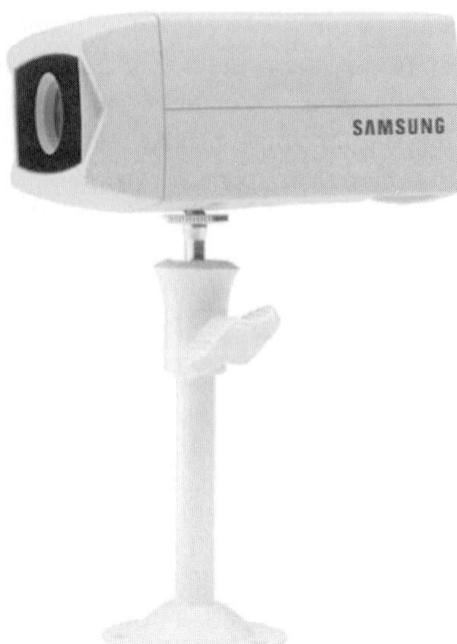

FIGURE 12–2 Samsung Mini Surveillance Camera. *Source:* Sandy Weiss/Packer Engineering.

- Automatic switching from color in daylight to black-and-white at night
- Auto-focus and exposure
- RS-485 for wireless communications, or for hard-wiring to a computer

A high-quality covert surveillance camera disguised as a motion sensor is illustrated in Figure 12–3.

Dome security cameras (see Fig. 12–4) are available in small or large sizes. They usually contain a mini or compact video camera, and the domes conceal the camera to camouflage the focal direction. The domes are high impact plastic for vandal resistance. They are water resistant but not waterproof.

Different types of dome cameras expose subjects in color or in black and white. Some of them switch automatically from day to night modes. Some have fixed focal length or variable focal length lenses that are adjustable remotely. Some versions operate under infrared illumination. Some have motion detection circuitry for automatic image capture when a scene changes. These cameras run on AC24V or DC12V power.

Infrared illuminators (see Fig. 12–5) are used with infrared cameras to acquire nighttime

FIGURE 12–3 Samsung motion detector camera. *Source:* Sandy Weiss/Packer Engineering.

surveillance images by invisible lighting, above 900 nanometers. Most illuminators are weatherproof and can be used indoors or outdoors. They have built in cadmium-sulfide sensors that turn the illuminator on at night and off in daylight.

IR illuminator light sources illuminate large areas. The area surveilled is limited by angle of the camera. Applications for nighttime surveillance include criminal investigations, border patrol, coast patrol, and surveillance of industrial facilities, including power plants, chemical plants, and public areas such as dams and reservoirs.

Night Vision

Night vision technology allows viewers to see in wavelengths of light that would be invisible to the unaided eye. Human vision is normally restricted to visible light (see Chapter 9). To see in what would normally be called darkness, human viewers may use nonvisible, near-infrared, or ultraviolet radiation for image enhancement. With those aids, small amounts of ambient light are collected and amplified to allow observation of an image.

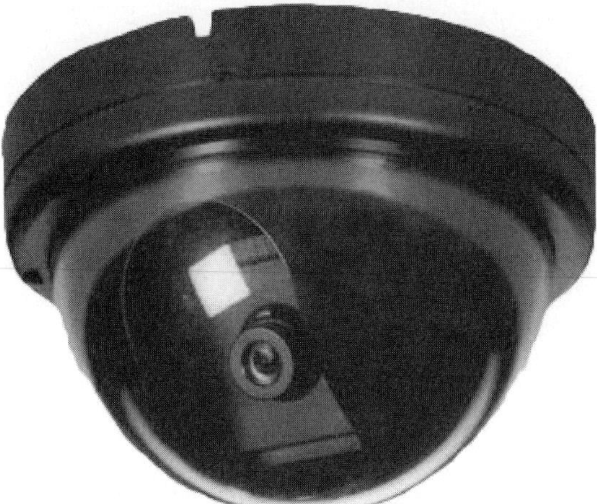

FIGURE 12–4 A Samsung camera dome. *Source:* Sandy Weiss/Packer Engineering.

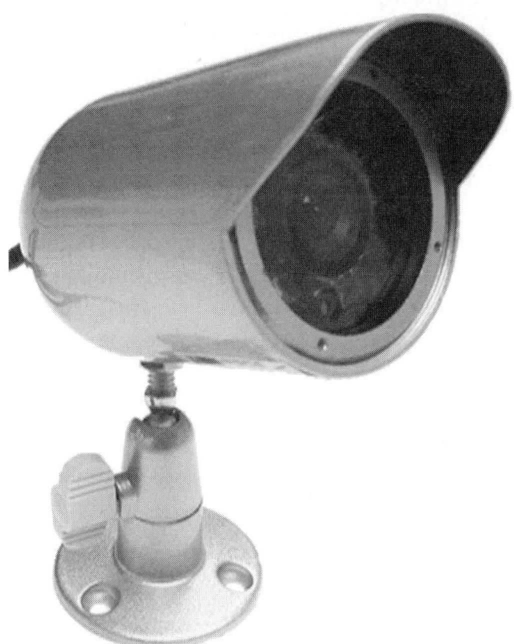

FIGURE 12–5 The Electrophysics ALS-20 Laser infrared illuminator. *Source:* Sandy Weiss/Packer Engineering.

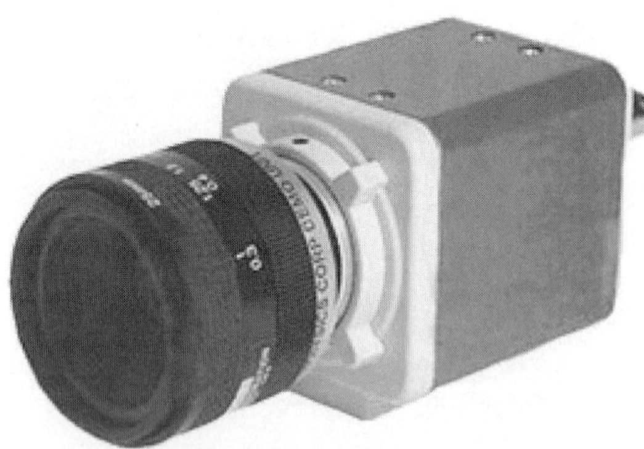

FIGURE 12–6 The SunStar 300 has ultra-low light sensitivity to 0.00005 Lux and a CCD sensor with advanced optics that boosts a signal to view images in nearly total darkness. *Source:* Sandy Weiss/Packer Engineering.

Some cameras are manufactured especially for night vision (see Fig. 12–6). Accessories are available for nighttime use that can enhance what is seen and captured with the human eye, as well as on film, digital, or video media. This technology expands the capabilities of law enforcement and surveillance photographers, enabling them to capture high-contrast and high-resolution images in light levels that allow facial recognition and vehicle registration identification.

Thermal Imaging

Thermal imaging technology operates by utilizing the high wavelengths of the infrared light spectrum for imaging. This radiation is emitted as heat instead of light. Hot objects, including living bodies, emit a higher quantity of this radiation than do cold objects. Thermal imaging cameras capture still and/or video images and are quantifiable for temperature. (See also Fig. 9–30).

VIDEO DEPOSITIONS

Depositions are statements collected from parties who are subject to legal proceedings. The two major reasons for deposition testimony are the following:

- To discover information relevant to a litigation
- To preserve testimony for trial

Deposition testimony is presented in several ways:

- An attorney may read a transcript at another deposition or in a courtroom.
- Deposition testimony may be presented as a video.
- Deposition testimony may be presented using specialized litigation software.

When recording videos of depositions, the following aspects are the most important to document:

- The witness must be clearly seen; the face and hands are important to document.
- The attorneys and the deponent must be clearly heard.
- Plain, undistracting backgrounds are best.
- No supplementary lighting should be used.
- The white balance of the camera should be properly set.
- The camera should remain still while recording, unless a pan of an exhibit is necessary.
- A microphone should be worn by everyone in the recording area.
- To avoid frequent changes, media with extended recording times are best.
- The original videos should not be edited but, rather, copied directly to the permanent storage media.
- Depositions may be edited from copies to present at trial.

Video Camcorders

A **camcorder** (see Fig. 12–7) is a portable electronic device for recording video images and audio onto an internal storage device. The camcorder contains a video camera and a video recorder in one unit.

Early camcorders used analog videotape. Since the introduction of miniaturized digital video (**MiniDV**) in the mid-1990s, most camcorders have used digital technology. MiniDV

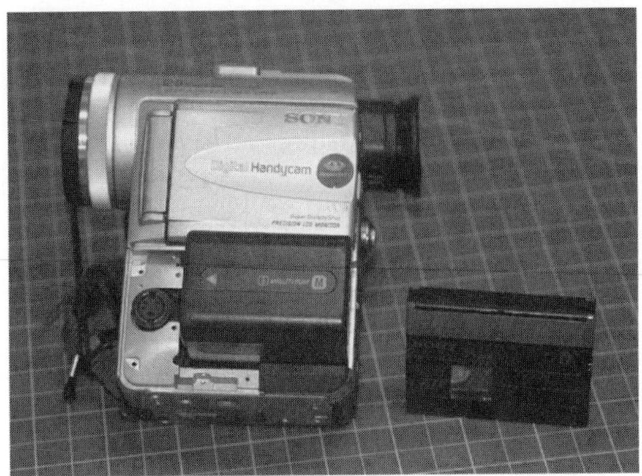

FIGURE 12–7 Sony Digital HandyCam and media. *Source:* Sandy Weiss/Packer Engineering.

has improved audio and video quality over all the preceding analog camcorders.

The following are the components of a camcorder:

- A lens to gather and focus light on the imager
- An imager (a CCD or CMOS sensor)
- A recorder to encode the video signal into memory

Extra capabilities incorporated into some cameras may include the following:

- Time and date stamping
- Car or badge number of the operator
- Compass direction at the time of recording
- Geographical (GPS) coordinates

> **TIP:**
>
> MiniDV displays little or no quality loss during duplication and editing.

Original analog and digital video tape recordings may deteriorate over time, but digital information may be stored indefinitely, with no deterioration, on computer disk. Although video-capture capability is now available in some cell phones, digital still cameras, and other portable consumer electronic devices, only digital camcorders capture videos that are sufficiently high in quality for most forensic purposes.

MOTION PICTURES AS EVIDENCE

It is possible to alter the appearance of evidence through motion picture and video representations by changing camera frame rates and by manipulations during editing or postprocessing. Courts minimize the possibility of alterations by the maintenance of specific protocols, including the following:

1. The motion pictures must be captured by a competent videographer.
2. The video must be a fair and accurate representation of the evidence.
3. The media, camera, lens, and frame rate must be appropriate.
4. The circumstances of the documentation must approximate the actual event, including weather conditions and lighting arrangements, or the reason for any variance must be documented.
5. Media must be properly developed.
6. The proper chain of custody must be followed for all documentation.
7. Media must be projected appropriately, including frame rate and distance between the projector and the screen.
8. To establish the degree of accuracy of the depiction of the subject event, corroborative testimony must be obtained from a person who was present at the time the media was captured.

Admissibility of Films

Motion pictures are commonly used as representations of evidence.[4] It does not matter if they are color or black and white, sound or silent, as long as they are relevant to the proceedings.[5] Motion pictures are exhibits of the person presenting them in court, to aid in testimony, but they are not usually considered to be evidence.[6]

It is a matter of the judge's discretion if motion pictures are admissible and provided they may be correctly authenticated.[7] Authentication is usually established through testimony by the cinematographer, but any competent witness to the capture of the film may testify to the fact that they accurately portray the action captured.[8]

The visual part of the film is normally treated as a series of still images; therefore, the rules for still photographs are applied to the motion pictures.[9] When motion pictures include audio, the audio portion requires a separate foundation.

If the foundation is satisfied, motion pictures may be permitted into evidence as substantiation of chain of evidence, to substantiate confessions, to show the robbing of a bank and identify the robber, document the reenactment of a crime, or to illustrate the nature and extent of wounds inflicted onto a murder victim.[10] Motion pictures of DUI suspects are admissible, to document the demeanor, appearance, and mannerisms, of defendants upon arrest.[11]

Admissibility of Videos

In general, the same rules apply to videos as to photographs and motion pictures.[12] Videos are commonly used for the documentation of depositions and the videos are admissible to be shown in court.[13]

Digital video (DV) uses a digital, rather than an analog representation of the video signal. DV is captured in a camera and then archived for permanent storage, review, and editing. DV may be recorded on any of the following media:

- Tape
- Disk drive
- DVD (the most convenient and common method for most purposes)

DV was introduced in 1983. At first it was too expensive to be widely used. It recorded uncompressed image data. The consumer version of DV followed shortly. The Sony Digital Betacam used compressed data. Apple's QuickTime system for capturing streaming data followed in 1990.

The first versions of DV captured an analog video source that was later digitized and converted to a format that a computer could read. At first the resolution was low in quality. Image quality was improved with the development of playback standards, including **MPEG-1** and **MPEG-2**. DV tape format came next. It allowed for direct digital recording and simplified the editing process, using nonlinear editing systems on personal computers.

Linear editing is an old-fashioned system that is simple to understand. A user cuts and splices pieces of film or video together, end to end, to create a new sequence of recorded events. This process used chemical or tape splices with film of any format. Digital images may be edited in a linear sequence, but modern software contains a higher level of sophistication.

Nonlinear editing uses a computer for the editing process. The nonlinear process is digital, with film-based or digital images. The only mechanical aspects of the process include the input of the videos to the computer and the final output to storage. Nonlinear editing is simply a virtual cut-and-paste process.

Image Capture

DV cameras are available in two distinct image capture formats:

- Interlaced
- Progressive scan

Interlaced digital cameras (IDV) record the image in a series of alternating sets of lines. **Progressive scanning (PSDV)** records each frame individually. When operating at the same number of **frames per second (fps)**, IDV records twice the number of images per second as PSDV. This is one reason for the enhanced image quality of IDV. IDV creates new frames at 60 fps; PSDV records 24 or 25 fps.

PSDV is similar in image quality to motion pictures captured on 16mm and 35mm film. PS and film record frames progressively.

Video is commonly recorded in two different **frame rate** standards:

- NTSC at 30 fps
- PAL at 25 fps

The recorded electronic signal of video varies from country to country. The two most common video standards are NTSC and PAL. **NTSC** is the video standard in North America, and **PAL** is used in Europe. DVDs are the most common media. U.S. (Region 1) DVD players cannot play PAL DVDs. Their PAL playback ability is disabled. Most NTSC display devices cannot display PAL images.

DVDs contain data files of compressed audiovisual information. This information may be recorded on the DVD with either of two resolutions:

- 720 × 576 pixels resolution (PAL)
- 720 × 480 pixels (NTSC)

PAL DVDs are 20% higher in resolution than NTSC DVDs. Frame rates include the following:

- 24 fps
- 25 fps
- 30 fps

PAL is higher in resolution than NTSC. NTSC updates the image faster (30 fps) than PAL (25 fps). Motion is rendered more accurately in NTSC than in PAL.

DVDs contain images with various aspect ratios. The image resolution is defined by the number of active pixels on the DVD. Widescreen images do not use all the pixels available on a DVD and have black bars above and below the image on a monitor. The image format that provides the highest number of active pixels on a given monitor is the monitor's optimum format.

The quality of motion picture images is increasing through developments in **High-Definition (HD)** technology. Many videos are being captured in HD video. HD may be copied down to PAL or NTSC formats with a loss of quality. Broadcast television will convert to HD in 2009, and higher-resolution formats are now in development. As of 2008, the highest-resolution DV is 33 megapixels (7,680 × 4,320) at 60 frames per second (**UHDV**).

Digital video is processed and edited on nonlinear editing devices (NLEs). NLEs edit video and audio imported from analog and digital sources. NLEs may change video sequences to follow a specific order of events. This type of manipulation is an acceptable forensic practice with appropriate documentation.

DV must be edited on equipment with sufficient disk space. DV with standard compression requires up to 250 megabytes of memory per minute of images or 13 gigabytes per hour of playing time.

DV is available in some mobile phones and video conferencing systems, and it is also used for distribution of media on the Internet. **Video compression** is necessary to create DV in practical formats for Internet usage and for DVDs. **MPEG-4** and **Windows Media** are the most commonly used contemporary formats for video on the Internet. MPEG-2 is used for DVDs.

EDITING SOFTWARE

Software for editing video footage is manufactured by many companies. Adobe manufactures and markets a package of applications that is complete and versatile for every situation and application. The applications in the Adobe Production Studio Premium package include all of the following programs.

Adobe Production Studio Premium

Adobe Production Studio Premium is a highly recommended and widely used postproduction package for film, video, DVD, and Internet production. It is available for both Intel-based Mac and Windows systems. The package includes Adobe After Effects CS3 Professional, Adobe Premiere Pro CS3, Adobe Photoshop CS3, Adobe Audition, Adobe Encore CS3, Adobe Illustrator CS3, Adobe Dynamic Link, and Adobe Bridge.

Adobe After Effects CS3 Professional

Adobe After Effects CS3 Professional software is used to create motion graphics (animations) and visual effects. It enables the design of vector graphics, for realistic motion. The software combines moving images, still images, graphics, text, and sound, in 2-D or 3-D space, and then animates any aspect of each element, separately or in tandem.

Adobe Premiere Pro CS3

Adobe Premiere Pro CS3 software enables capture, editing, and delivery of video to disk, Internet, and mobile devices. An entry-level version, Adobe Premiere Elements, is available for the consumer market.

The software is a real-time, timeline-based video editing application, often included as an OEM package with video editing cards, such as the Matrox RT.X2. A **timeline** is an editing interface that sorts a video project in a linear display, horizontally across a monitor. This is the normal design used by video and audio editing software. Multiple formats, including AVI, WMV, MP3, MPEG, MOV, JPEG, and so on, may be combined on the same timeline.

Steps for using this software include the following:

- Capture video and audio footage.
- Plan scene transitions.
- Lay out the sections.
- Assemble the sections.
- Add necessary titles.

Adobe Photoshop CS3

Adobe Photoshop CS3 is used for editing images. It changes image sizes and colors, converts formats, repairs problems, combines and compares images, and edits in 2-D and 3-D. It can be used to paint and clone over multiple video frames, measure sizes, count features, and supply quantitative and qualitative information down to individual pixels.

Adobe Audition

Adobe Audition audio production software is used to record, mix, edit, and master audio tracks. It can be used for musical composition and the creation and compilation of audio for production videos.

Adobe Encore CS3

Adobe Encore CS3 software is used for DVD and Blu-ray Disc authoring and Internet export as an .SWF file. When a Macromedia Flash (.FLA) file is published for the Web, it adopts an .SWF extension. Macromedia Flash MX is a vector graphics and audio program for the creation of videos, demos, and Web components. Flash works in 2-D and 3-D for live images, drawings, and text.

Adobe Illustrator CS3

Adobe Illustrator CS3 software is a vector tool to make drawings and artwork for print, Web, mobile, and video use.

Adobe Dynamic Link

Adobe Dynamic Link eliminates the need to re-render compositions when moving from Adobe After Effects to Adobe Premiere Pro and Adobe Encore software.

Adobe Bridge

Adobe Bridge CS3 is a media manager for organization, browsing, locating, and viewing creative assets. It provides centralized access to project files, applications, and settings, as well as metadata tagging and searching capabilities.

QuickTime Pro

QuickTime Pro, available for PC and Mac, is software intended for watching, recording, creating, or sharing **multimedia**, the combination of multiple art formats, including the following:

- Text
- Multichannel audio
- Still images
- Video
- Graphics

All elements must be saved in digitized form before use in a computer application. QuickTime Pro allows export of any playable QuickTime Player file to a format optimized for iPod, iPhone, or Apple TV.

Multichannel Audio

Multichannel audio expands and enriches the sound quality of audio playback by recording multiple sound channels that are subsequently replayed on multiple speakers. **Surround sound,**

which uses a system of speakers placed throughout a space, is one application of multichannel audio. Built-in surround sound hardware is available on some consumer camcorders, and it is also available as an add-on.

HIGH-SPEED PHOTOGRAPHY

High-speed photography captures images for slow-motion playback and the study of industrial and scientific applications. Normal motion pictures are captured and replayed at 24 to 30 fps. The speed of high-speed cameras depends on format, resolution, and duration. Some **high-speed digital (HSD) cameras** are capable of filming 1024 × 1024 resolution video at more than 1 million fps in short bursts.

To capture frames rapidly in film cameras, the film is transported past a rotating prism or mirror instead of a shutter. This process may record 1 second of actual motion as more than 10 minutes of playback for observation.

One familiar example of an industrial application utilizing high-speed motion analysis is crash testing of vehicles (see Fig. 12–8). Crash testing is often performed to study cases where a vehicle's gas tank ruptures from impact and the fuel causes a post-collision fire.

In the reconstruction illustrated in Figure 12–8, four high-speed motion picture cameras were in operation during the event. One was located to each side, one was in the basket of an overhead crane, and one was behind glass in a pit under the point of impact. High-intensity photoflood lighting was used to illuminate the underside of the vehicles and was turned on remotely, prior to the crash event, while the cameras were being run up to speed. At the subject speed, the collision was too severe to allow the use of an onboard **high-G camera**. This image was captured by one of the observers who displayed an excellent sense of timing with a Nikon 35mm camera and an 85mm lens. It was so cold when this work was done that the film became brittle and would have frozen if left in the camera too long before running the test (see Fig. 12–9).

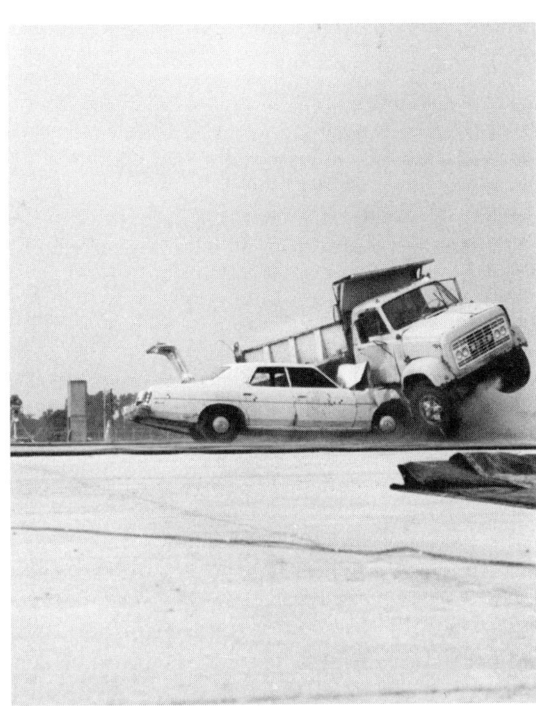

FIGURE 12–8 Crash test documentation. *Source:* Sandy Weiss/Packer Engineering.

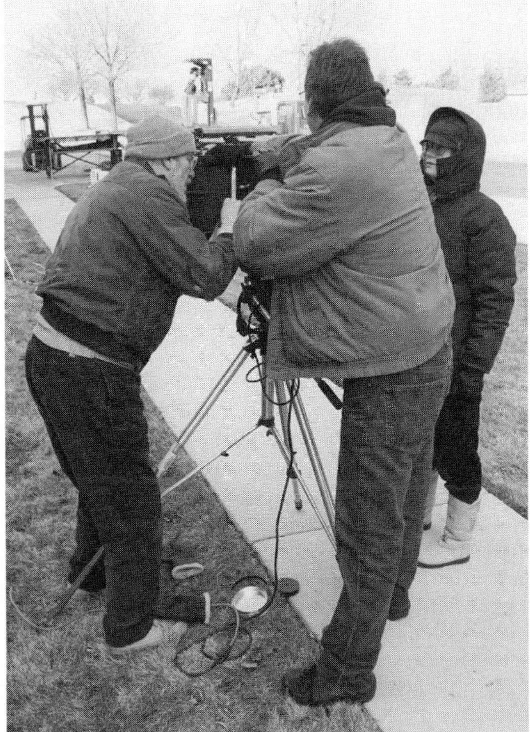

FIGURE 12–9 Testing in cold weather. *Source:* Sandy Weiss/Packer Engineering.

REMEMBER:

Have appropriate clothing available for surprise assignments.

TIP:

A major requirement for high-speed photography is the high level of illumination needed for proper exposure of the film at high frame rates. If the subject under examination is susceptible to heat, it may be damaged or destroyed by the heat of the lighting.

TIP:

The closer the camera is to the action, the more illumination is needed.

High-Speed Film

To enable faster frame rates, Kodak changed its film base from acetate to Estar for enhanced strength. Estar is difficult to tear and may be pulled through the camera faster than acetate. Estar also stretches less than acetate, enabling increased accuracy of time measurement.

High-Speed Video

CCD technology improved sufficiently in the 1980s to enable **high-speed video** that could capture NTSC video at frame rates up to 60 fps. The Kodak HG2000 was a later invention. It had a variable fps rate up to 1,000 fps in 2-second bursts with a 512 × 384 pixel sensor resolution.

CMOS

CMOS sensor technology was incorporated into high-speed video in the late 1990s. Based on the same process and materials as computer memory, CMOS technology proved superior to CCD technology for camera design, but it is similar in image quality and efficiency.

HIGH-SPEED DIGITAL IMAGING CONSIDERATIONS

To obtain proper motion analysis data, always compute the following:

- Frame rate necessary to properly study the motion
- Image resolution necessary for the desired display
- Necessary light level for optimum exposure

Digital high-speed imaging has the advantage of immediate playback. If the frame rate used was too slow, it may be increased. If the light level was too low, more can be added or the lens aperture can be opened if DoF is sufficient.

Photron USA, Inc.

Photron USA, Inc., supplies photo-instrumentation, high-speed image processing systems, and photo optical technologies for the automotive, industrial manufacturing, film, television, medical, and military markets. The company's products are excellent examples of state-of-the-art technology.

Photron Fastcam 1024 PCI Camera

The Fastcam 1024 PCI (see Fig. 12–10) is a PC-based, high-resolution at 1,000 frames per second (fps), high-speed video camera, with resolution greater than 1 megapixel per frame. Recorded images are stored in the PCI memory and then downloaded to a computer for display and/or analysis. Images may be transferred to permanent media for archiving. The camera uses CMOS technology and creates 10-bit images up to a top speed of over 100,000 fps.

The camera head is compact and works well in difficult and hazardous locations. It uses either *C mount* (see Fig. 12–11) or *Nikon F mount* lenses with the proper adapters. A 16-foot cable connects the camera head to the PCI card, which fits in either a desktop PC or a more portable PCI cradle connected to a laptop.

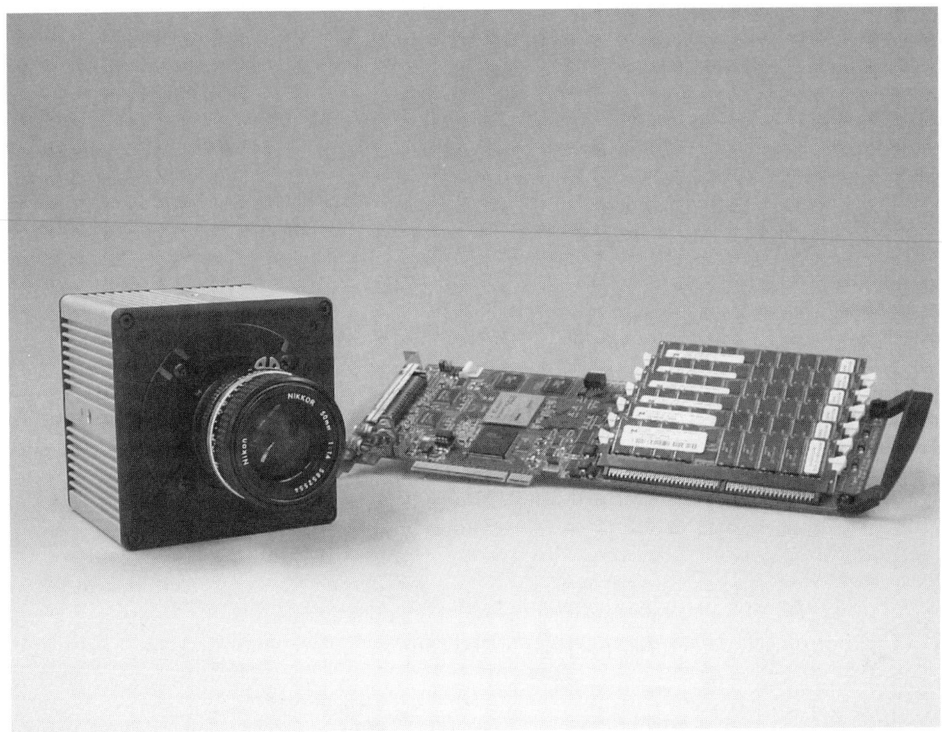

FIGURE 12–10 The Photron Fastcam 1024 high-speed video camera and PCI card. *Source:* Photron USA.

Memory Options for the *Fastcam* 1024

- **Standard speed:** 1.54 seconds record time at 1,000 fps 2 gigabyte files
- **Enhanced image:** 4.61 seconds record time at 1,000 fps, 6 gigabyte files
- **Expanded time:** 9.22 seconds record time at 1,000 fps, 12 gigabyte files
- **Maximum image:** 18.44 seconds record time at 1,000 fps, 24 gigabyte files

Four 1024 PCI cameras may be operated simultaneously from one PC. Live images may be viewed on a monitor with or without recording.

Photron Ultima APX-RS High-Speed Camera

The Photron Ultima APX-RS high-speed camera (see Fig. 12–12) contains features unavailable in most high-speed DV cameras. It is a CMOS sensor camera, capturing 10-bit monochrome

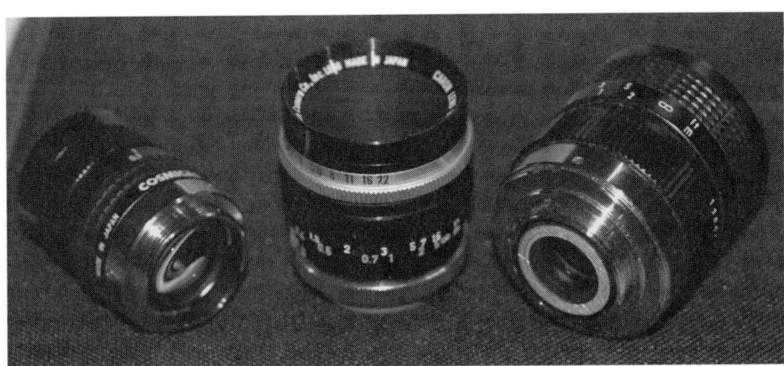

FIGURE 12–11 C-mount lenses. *Source:* Sandy Weiss/Packer Engineering.

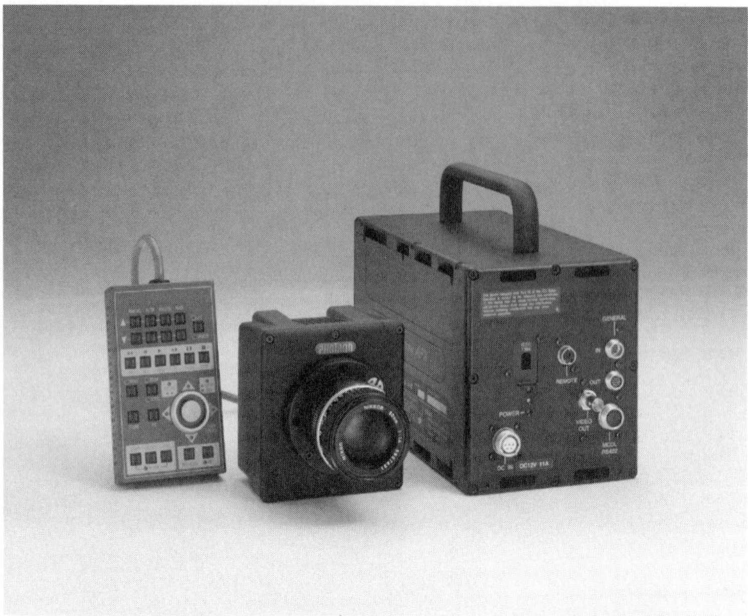

FIGURE 12–12 Photron Ultima APX APX-RS high-Speed camera. *Source:* Photron USA.

and 30-bit color image files. It exposes images with square or rectangular aspect ratios. It has one-piece construction and will operate in inclement weather and under high g-forces. It captures the following resolutions:

- 3000 fps at 1,024 × 1,024 pixels
- 10,000 fps at 512 × 512 pixels
- 250,000 fps at low resolution
- 6-second recording duration at 1,000 fps

The Ultima is available with multiple forms of computer communication and is operable in the field without an attached computer. The shutter speed operates as fast as 2 microseconds. Exposure is automatic. The camera has built-in remote capabilities. Multiple cameras may be synchronized when they are attached to a computer. The low-light capabilities of this camera are exceptional, with light sensitivity available to ISO 4,800. Frame rates may be changed during recording.

Photron Fastcam MH-4

The Photron Fastcam MH-4 (see Fig. 12–13) is a miniature high-speed video system that uses up to four detachable camera heads at one time (see Fig. 12–14). Each head measures 35 mm × 35 mm × 35 mm, without lens, and weighs less than 100 grams. The system has excellent low-light capabilities. It has an 8-bit monochrome and 24-bit color CMOS sensor. It has 1 gigabyte of memory per camera:

- Resolution up to 512 × 512 pixels at 60 to 2,000 fps
- Reduced resolution up to 10,000 fps

The Fastcam camera heads may be mounted in confined areas and at any orientation. They are attached to the system with a flexible 10-meter

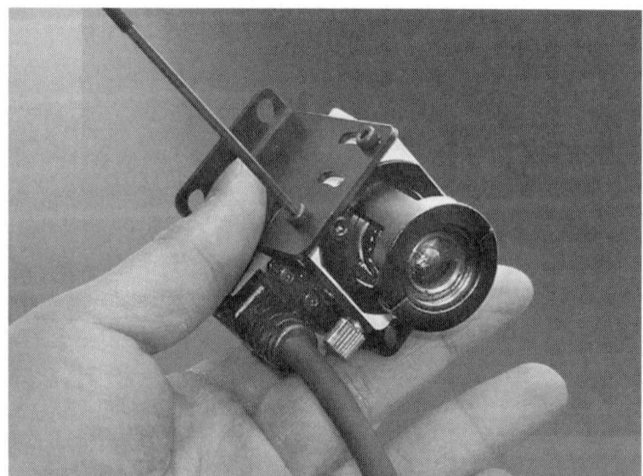

FIGURE 12–13 Photron Fastcam MH-4 miniature high-speed video camera. *Source:* Photron USA.

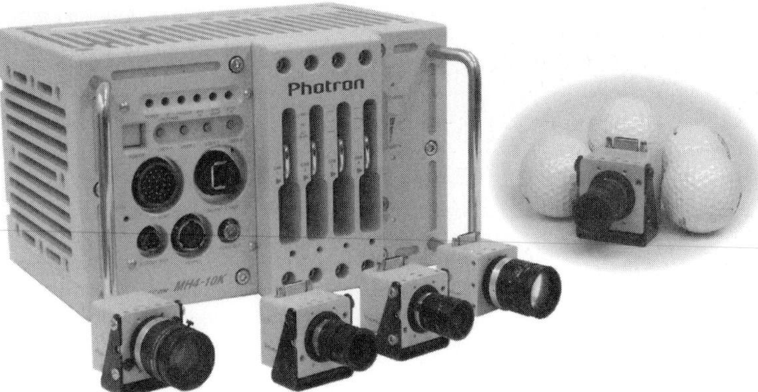

FIGURE 12–14 Ultima Fastcam MH-4 miniature camera system. *Source:* Photron USA.

cable. The camera has an adjustable lens mount, accepting Nikon F-mount and C-mount lenses. The MH-4 withstands high levels of shock, vibration, and g-ratings up to 100 g's. It may be used for recording and motion analysis of high-impact testing.

VIRTUAL REALITY

Virtual reality (VR) is a technology that allows a person to interact with a real or imagined, computer-simulated environment. Virtual reality environments may include visual and audio information displayed on computer screens or through special stereoscopic equipment.

Some advanced haptic VR environments include tactile information. In medical and gaming applications, this is known as **force feedback.** Users may interact with a virtual environment by using a keyboard or mouse, or through devices like a wired glove. The simulated environment may be like the real world, or it may be different, as in VR fantasy games.

Nonimmersive Virtual Reality

Immersive virtual reality is a hypothetical technology of the future. It is where a user becomes part of a virtual reality, an artificial environment. Today's VR is not fully immersive, even though a person may navigate through a 3-D environment while wearing red–green stereo glasses or by stereo projection systems. Apple's QuickTime VR is a **nonimmersive virtual reality** that uses a series of still photographs, captured in a specific way, to model and re-create a three-dimensional space on a computer monitor. (See further information in Chapter 8.)

SUMMARY

Forensic photography includes the capture of still and motion picture images for the accurate documentation of evidence in court. Video is often used when it is difficult to document the motion in still images. The hardware and media limitations are similar in still and video cameras. It is always necessary to conform to the rules of photography and the rules of evidence during documentation.

Industry practices and protocols are established for the proper capture of clear, demonstrative videos. The best way to become proficient at this discipline is to practice and plan: practice mentally, and plan each assignment before picking up a camera.

Some types of video equipment are specialized and easily leased if not owned. It is imperative to select the right equipment for its current use.

CASE STUDY

TREADMILL PATENT INFRINGEMENT

A series of in-field tests of different treadmills were performed in a patent infringement suit against the manufacturer of a treadmill. It was necessary to determine how the machine reacted

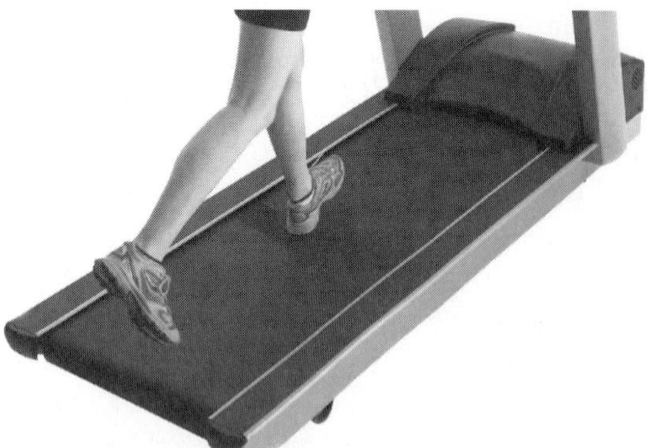

FIGURE 12–15 Treadmill testing. *Source:* Sandy Weiss/Packer Engineering.

to the impact of people of different heights and weights when they were running on the base.

People of various sizes were recruited to perform a set of programmed exercises on a number of treadmills from different manufacturers. High-speed videos were exposed from several angles of certain aspects of each test. The subjects ran at a set speed for a short time. The treadmill was adjusted for base stiffness to a predetermined level.

The videos were analyzed photogrammetrically to determine the deflection of the base, affected by people of different weight and stride. It would have been impossible to properly analyze the deflection of the base of the treadmill on video footage exposed at 24 fps. Greater accuracy was extracted from the data at 250 fps.

The infringement claim was denied.

CASE STUDY

FORKLIFT SEAT BELT

A study was performed to determine if seat belts were a help or a hazard to the operators of forklifts involved in tip-overs (see Fig. 12–16).This testing procedure required a dedicated space with controlled conditions. The testing could not be performed outdoors due to changes in weather.

A warehouse was outfitted specifically for this project. Large floodlights were installed on tracks suspended from the ceiling. To assist in the analysis of the images, a grid of lines was painted on the concrete floor.

Large pieces of canvas were suspended to surround the test floor and provide a background

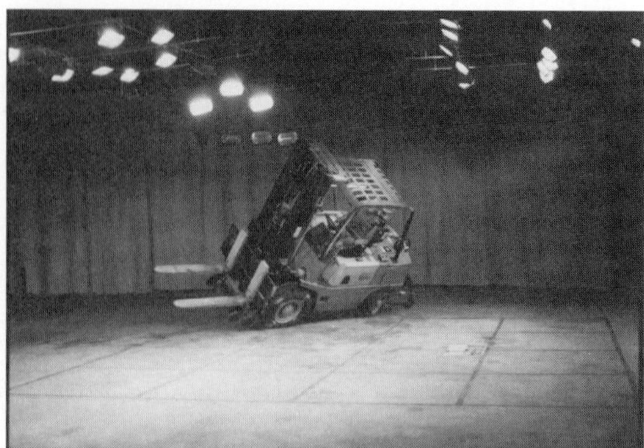

FIGURE 12–16 Tip-over testing of a forklift. *Source:* Sandy Weiss/Packer Engineering.

for the photography. The testing was documented on video and high-speed still photographs. A Canon high-speed motor drive (HSMD) camera (see Figs. 12–17 and 12–18), which exposes photographs at 9 fps, was used to expose the still photos.

The camera exposes images in rapid sequence through a **pellicle mirror,** rather than off a movable mirror, in its viewing system. Most cameras have mirrors that flip up and out of the way before each exposure. Cameras with pellicle mirrors have fixed half-silvered mirrors that direct light to the viewfinder for focusing and to the image sensor or film.

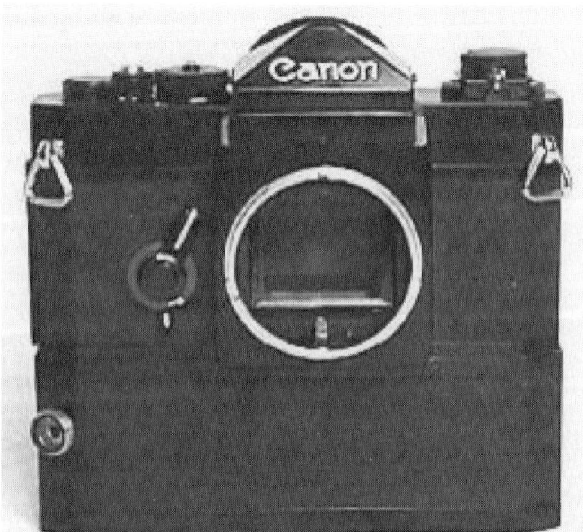

FIGURE 12–17 Canon high-speed motor drive camera. *Source:* Sandy Weiss/Packer Engineering.

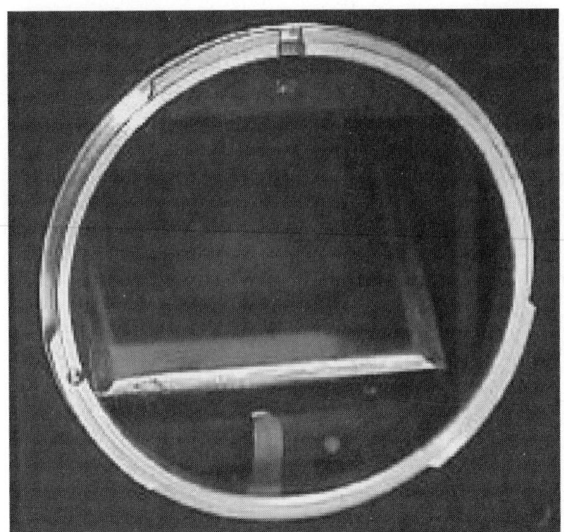

FIGURE 12–18 A pellicle mirror inside the Canon HSMD camera. *Source:* Sandy Weiss/Packer Engineering.

Standard SLR cameras have a period of image blackout, when the mirror is out of the light path during media exposure. During that time, nothing can be seen through the viewfinder. Mirror blackout can be a problem for action photography.

Pellicle cameras are quieter than standard cameras and add less blur through vibration. Pellicle mirror cameras allow semi-instant exposure because the mirror does not have to change positions. The drawbacks of pellicles include a higher susceptibility to image degradation because of dirty surfaces, lower resolution because of the extra air-to-glass interface, and loss of light due to the transfer of some of the light to the focusing screen.

A 400 ASA film was used without flash, at a shutter speed of 1/500 second, with an 85 mm *f*/1.8 lens set at 1.8. The yellow color balance caused by exposing daylight film under flood lighting was filtered out during printing. At the time, Kodak produced a 35 mm, floodlight (tungsten) balanced, color negative film (Vericolor Professional type L (VPL), but its ASA was too low for practical use in this case.

An instrumented anthropomorphic dummy was used as a model in each of the tests. The test number was indicated on a large, numbered placard that was placed on the floor in view of the cameras during each test. The forklift was run by remote control over a predetermined route, to a predetermined speed, to a predetermined spot, so that it would tip over on the correct part of the grid. The crash effects on the model were recorded by all the cameras.

Crash test dummies behave very similarly to human beings. In each case, the head of the dummy would impact the floor whether seat belts were used or not. OSHA standard 29 CFR 1910.178 covers powered industrial vehicles, including forklifts.[14] The compliance directive, CPL 2-1.28A of 29 CFR 1910.178, Compliance Assistance for the Powered Industrial Truck Operator Training Standard states that OSHA enforcement policy relative to the use of seat belts on powered industrial trucks is that employers are obligated to require operators of powered industrial trucks that are equipped with operator-restraint devices or seat belts to use the devices.[15] OSHA enforces the use of such devices under Section 5(a)(1) of the Occupational Health and Safety (OSH) Act. OSHA may cite an employer if it has not taken advantage of a manufacturer's operator-restraint system or seat belt retrofit program.[16] In the "General Duty Clause," it states that employers "shall furnish to each of his employees employment and a place of employment which are free from recognized hazards that are causing or are likely to cause death or serious physical harm to his employees.[17]

CASE STUDY

CHICAGO FREIGHT TUNNEL FLOOD

At 5:57 a.m. on April 13, 1992, the Merchandise Mart in the Chicago Loop had two inches of water in the sub-basement. The water level rose quickly to nearly 2 feet. Within several hours, over 17 feet of standing water were in the basement. Many other downtown buildings reported similar flooding.

Emergency response personnel traced the source of the water to Chicago's abandoned 50-mile system of freight tunnels, whose construction had begun in 1899. The system was used for underground freight delivery service to downtown

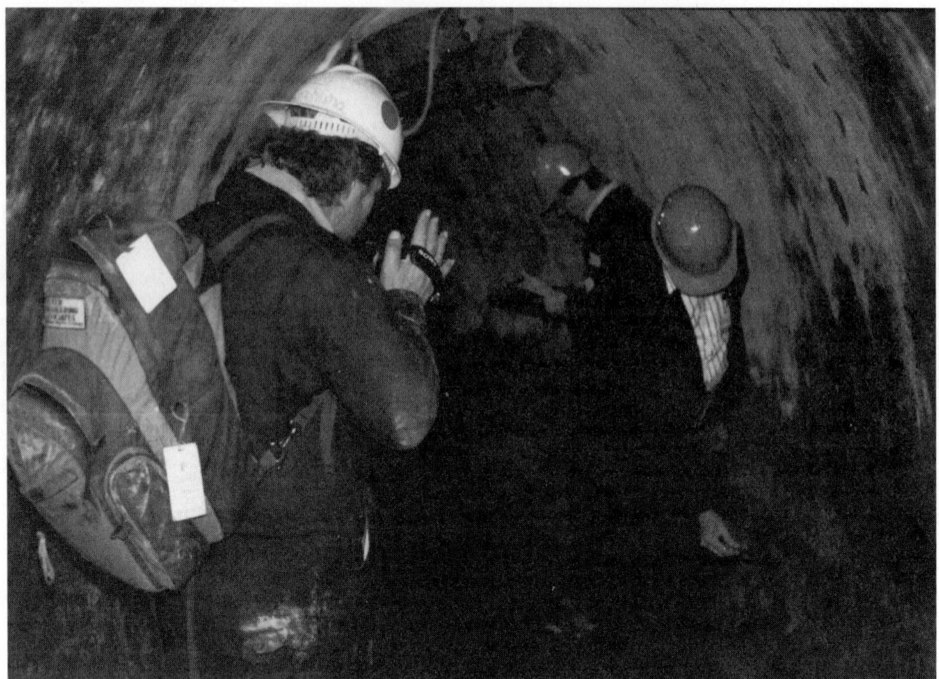

FIGURE 12–19 Chicago tunnel documentation. *Source:* Sandy Weiss/Packer Engineering.

businesses. Many Loop buildings were connected by the tunnels to ports and railroad terminals. The tunnels had an electric railway. The freight service was eventually abandoned.

Water from the Chicago River was flooding the system from an opening near the Kinzie Street Bridge. The installation of an underwater support piling cracked the tunnel at that location. City, state, and federal emergency officials worked to find a way to plug the large hole. Sandbags, rubber bladders, steel plates, and other materials did not work. The city dumped 65 truckloads of concrete, gravel, and stones into the river in another unsuccessful attempt to solve the problem. The Army Corps of Engineers pumped fast-drying cement into the tunnel to effectively seal the hole.

Over the next month, the Chicago Fire Department supervised the removal of over 134 million gallons of water from basements and tunnels in the Loop. Engineers believed that the tunnel system might collapse and cause more damage if the water level dropped too quickly. The pumping was limited to 1 or 2 inches per hour.

To seal the tunnels for protection against another flood, city personnel worked over the subsequent months with construction companies, engineers, and contractors to drain and reinforce the tunnels and to install bulkhead-style doors, like those inside submarines, in the tunnels near the rivers.

Packer engineers inspected and documented the tunnels (see Fig. 12–19) to form an opinion regarding how to best preserve the tunnels for the future. Videotapes of the inspection process were made to share among experts.

CASE STUDY

O'Hare Airport Trip and Fall

A woman was fatally injured when she tripped and fell down a set of movable stairs at O'Hare Airport in Chicago. Her family sued the subject airline and the airport authority for failure to provide a safe route from the terminal to the tarmac so she could board her plane.

To illustrate the routes that were not used, the plaintiff's attorney requested a virtual tour of all the routes from the concourse to the gate, in case a safer route might have protected the deceased.

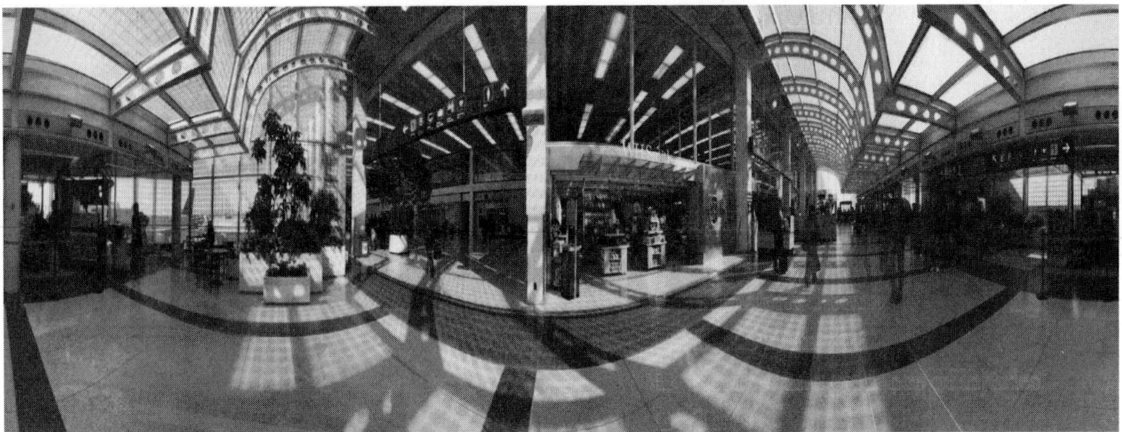

FIGURE 12–20 A still image of the first node of the tour of O'Hare Airport. *Source:* Sandy Weiss/Packer Engineering.

The woman had been escorted from the concourse by an airline employee, who passed several elevators and interior stairways on the way to the gate. A VR tour was more useful in court than a video walk-through. A video would have been difficult to run backward and forward and to move quickly from one location to another. Since VR is higher resolution than video, it allowed the attorney to zoom into doorways and down stairs.

Permission from airport security is always required to expose images near baggage scanning equipment, so we obtained permission. A Nikon camera with a 15mm wide-angle lens was used for capturing the images at the airport. The camera was mounted on a specially designed VR tripod head on a heavy tripod. A 360-degree panorama of each location was captured in 16 exposures at 14 locations (nodes). The images were stitched into nodes at the lab. All the nodes were assembled into one virtual tour. A series of still photographs was added to the tour to illustrate the various stairs and elevators that were seen en route. Sound was not used in this case.

Figure. 12–20 is a still image of the first node of the tour. (Also see Figure 8–23).

The final tour was used in court, and depositions were taken as to the method of its creation. The suit was eventually settled out of court.

CASE STUDY

1903 WRIGHT FLYER

To commemorate the 100th anniversary in 2003 of the Wright Brothers first powered flight on December 17, 1903, four separate groups (including NASA) built flight-worthy reproductions of the first airplane. One group, the Wright Redux Association (WRA) of Glen Ellyn, Illinois, built a plane named *The Spirit of Glen Ellyn* (see Fig. 12–21). Packer Engineering built a replica of the original gasoline engine to power the airplane. It is the only one of the replicas to actually fly.

The flight took place at Clow Airport in Aurora, Illinois. In this photograph, it appears

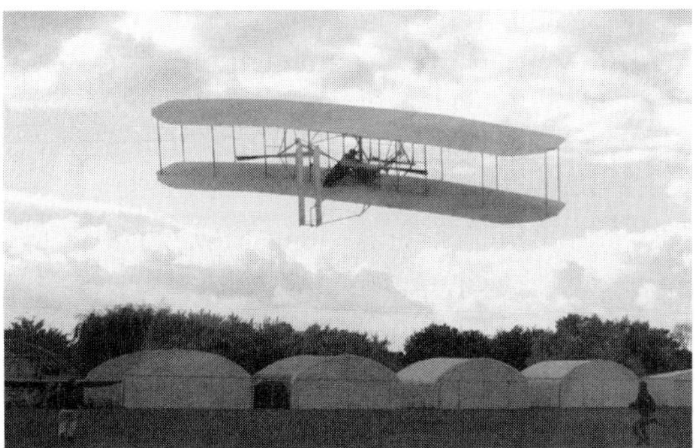

FIGURE 12–21 *The Spirit of Glen Ellyn* in flight. *Source:* Sandy Weiss/Packer Engineering.

that the airplane is flying smoothly and at a level attitude. It actually had a very short flight. The path was up and then down. This image captured it at the apex of its motion. A video of the flight lacks the same resolution but more accurately describes the motion.

KEY TERMS

fluid head, (p. 346)
covert surveillance, (p. 348)
night vision, (p. 349)
thermal imaging, (p. 350)
deposition, (p. 350)
camcorder, (p. 350)
MiniDV, (p. 350)
MPEG-1, (p. 352)
MPEG-2, (p. 352)
nonlinear editing, (p. 352)
interlaced digital camera (IDV), (p. 352)
progressive scanning (PSDV), (p. 352)
frames per second (fps), (p. 352)
frame rate, (p. 352)
NTSC, (p. 353)
PAL, (p. 353)
High-Definition (HD), (p. 353)
UHDV, (p. 353)
video compression, (p. 353)
MPEG-4, (p. 353)
Windows Media, (p. 353)
timeline, (p. 354)
multimedia, (p. 354)
multichannel audio, (p. 354)
surround sound, (p. 354)
high-speed photography, (p. 355)
high-speed digital (HSD) camera, (p. 355)
high-G camera, (p. 355)
high-speed video, (p. 356)
virtual reality (VR), (p. 359)
force feedback, (p. 359)
immersive virtual reality, (p. 359)
nonimmersive virtual reality, (p. 359)
pellicle mirror, (p. 360)

EXERCISES

1. Design a multicamera video coverage of a familiar project, including the following details:
   - Number of cameras
   - Type of cameras
   - Number of people needed
   - Necessary accessories and lighting
2. If a camcorder is available, perform an overall, 360-degree documentation on specific items of evidence, including macros. If a camcorder is not available, a digital still camera may be used in continuous mode.
3. Set up a mock video deposition. Plan all the necessary equipment and techniques.
4. Research the current state-of-the-art video equipment used in covert surveillance, and make a list of what is necessary with prices for a budget.
5. Expose sufficient still images with a digital camera to stitch together into a 360-degree panorama of an interior space. Attempt the stitching using available software, and evaluate the results.
6. Make a list of local dealerships where specialized video equipment can be leased, and keep it current.

APPENDIX 12-1

Matrox Realtime DV and HDV Editing Platforms

The Matrox Realtime DV and HDV Editing Platforms (see Fig. 12–22 are specifically designed for compatibility with Adobe Production Studio software.

Matrox AXIO LE features include the following:

- Adobe Premiere Pro CS3
- Full-resolution, multilayer, real-time editing of HD and SD video, graphics, and effects
- Color correction, speed changes, and chroma/luma keying
- 2-D and 3-D digital effects
- Real-time mixing on a timeline
- Real-time playback of clips in HD
- Real-time downscaling from HD to SD
- Export to DVD and multimedia formats, including Flash and Adobe Clip Notes
- Compatibility with Adobe After Effects and Adobe Photoshop

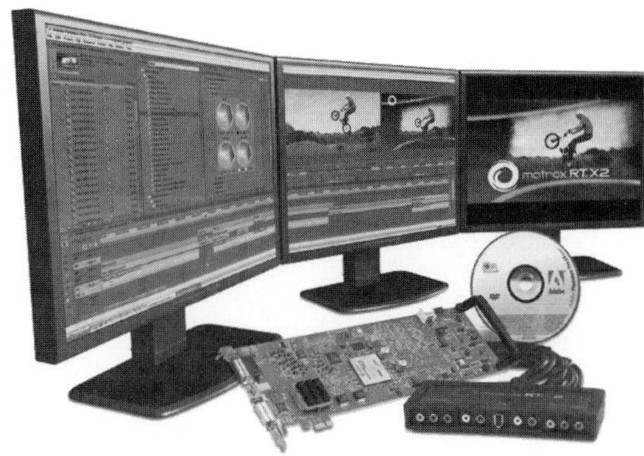

FIGURE 12–22 The Matrox editing system. *Source:* Matrox.

Chapter 13

Photographing Fires

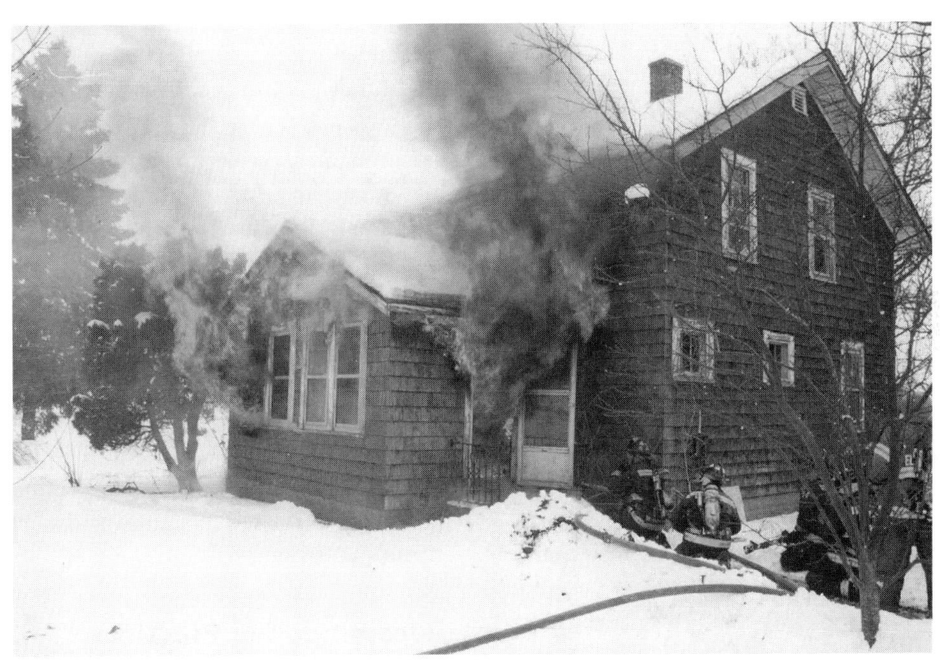

Learning Objectives

AFTER STUDYING THIS CHAPTER, YOU SHOULD BE ABLE TO:

1. Understand the difference between fire photography and fire investigation
2. Understand what is necessary to perform competent and accurate fire scene photography
3. Capture photographs with correct references for their placement in the scene and in the world
4. Understand the functions of the forensic specialists involved in fire investigation
5. Be aware of the differences between the manner, cause, and mechanism of death
6. Recognize and accurately document signs of arson
7. Understand the concept of an autopsy and be able to accurately document the procedure and subject
8. Understand and appreciate the correct methods for documenting and identifying victims of fire

INVESTIGATING FIRES

Fire investigation is often called **origin and cause investigation**. It involves the processing and documentation of fire-related incidents. An investigation begins after firefighters extinguish a fire and is conducted using a systematic approach and knowledge of fire science to determine the origin and the cause. The series of steps always includes, but is not limited to, photography.

Among the forensic sciences, fire investigation is one of the more difficult undertakings. In most forensic disciplines, an investigation is conducted due to the commission of a crime, and in many instances the results of the crime are readily obvious. A fire, however, may or may not be the result of a crime, and the fire event may hide or destroy the evidence of a crime.

Fire investigators inspect the results of a fire and gather information to reconstruct the events that occurred before and during the incident. They must determine if an incident involves arson. Since **arson** is the *willful* or *malicious* burning or attempt to burn property, if a person dies it changes the manner of death from accidental to murder. A determination of arson will govern the type and direction of the ensuing investigation.

Fire investigations require multidisciplinary knowledge of the following:

- Fire science
- Construction
- Materials
- Electricity
- Human factors
- Vehicles
- Chemistry

Fire investigators often work with forensic engineers when examining appliances, wiring, lighting, lightning strikes, computer failures, gas-related incidents, and so on at a fire scene.

Recommended Practices

In the United States, fire investigators use the National Fire Protection Association's publication entitled *NFPA 921: Guide for Fire and Explosion Investigations* for codes, standards, and suggested practices regarding fire investigations.[1] This publication is considered the essential reference for conducting fire investigations. The photography section of *NFPA 921* is due for revision at next publication.

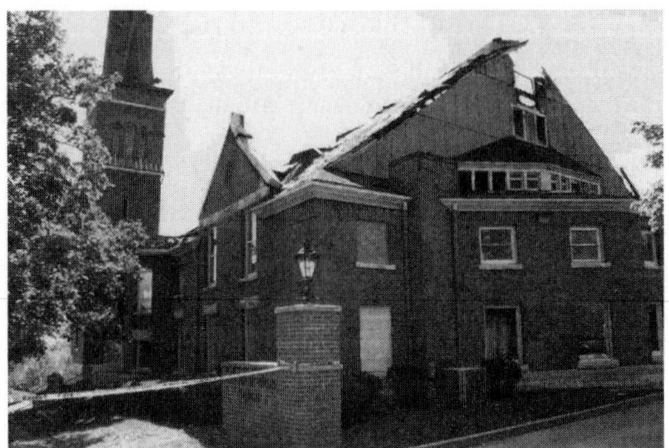

FIGURE 13–1 Outside view of a burned church. *Source:* Sandy Weiss/Packer Engineering.

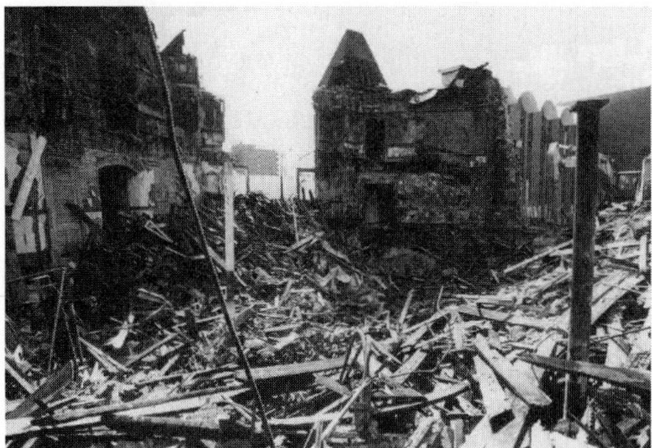

FIGURE 13–2 Inside view of a burned church. *Source:* Sandy Weiss/Packer Engineering.

Conducting Investigations

Fire investigators rely on the scientific method for a systematic approach. The basic steps to investigations include the following:

- An incident occurs and an investigator is notified of the assignment.
- The investigator plans the work and assembles the necessary equipment and personnel.
- The scene is examined and photographed, and evidence is noted.
- Physical evidence is documented, collected, tested, and evaluated.
- The proper forms for chain of custody are provided (see Appendix 13.1).
- The scientific method is used to analyze the investigation.

Photographing the Fire Scene

Photographs are an excellent medium for documenting evidence and supporting the observations, opinions, and conclusions of the investigator. Most people, including judges and jurors, are not experienced fire investigators. It is up to the investigator and photographer to construct a photographic essay that tells the whole story of the incident and provides an accurate representation of the scene and the evidence. This story must be easily understood and evaluated by the general public. When the images are presented logically and chronologically, they also must illustrate how and why they were taken.

If the fire occurred in a structure, the photographer *must* start the documentation outside and proceed toward the inside. This sequence is the easiest for the viewer to understand because the outside of the structure may remain recognizable (see Fig. 13–1), and the inside may be a blackened disaster (see Fig. 13–2). The average person who is untrained in fire science may find it difficult to correlate the interior images to what was once a home, business, barn, factory, and so on.

The Importance of Accurate Documentation

The fire photographer should follow an industry-accepted practice that is logical and systematic for the proper and accurate documentation of a scene. The basic outline in this chapter conforms to *NFPA 921* but is more complete. It is intended as a starting point for the development of a practice satisfying the prerequisites of any department or agency. It includes steps for setting up, equipping, and completing accurate fire-scene documentations.

The accurate documentation of a fire scene should include the following:

- Personnel responsibilities
  - Who is in charge?

- Who does what?
- Coordination of activities

- Concentration on safety of the investigator, bystanders, and equipment
  - Use of appropriate personal protection equipment (PPE) (see Chapter 14)

- Optimization of exposure
  - For contrast
  - Bracketing, if necessary
  - Auto or manual metering
  - Inspection of image histograms
  - Color or black and white
  - ISO

- Imaging protocol
  - Training of all participants
  - Adherence to accepted industry standards and practices
  - Who will have access to the original images?
  - Use of appropriate software (for file type, size, processing, and storage)

- Storytelling
  - Scene coverage
    - Scene assessment
    - Selected layout method for documentation
    - Evidence marking
    - Logical and systematic presentation (in sequence from overall views to close-ups, with high and low viewpoints of all victims and witnesses)
  - Position the scene in the world
    - Global Positioning System, if available
    - Compass headings
    - Aerial views from a neighboring building, platform, or aircraft
  - Position of victims and other evidence in the scene
  - Every possible story told photographically
    - References for size
    - References for color
    - Notes
    - Sketches
    - Audio recordings

- Triage of the scene and the preservation of evidence
  - Document from most fragile to most permanent
    - Victims
    - Injuries
    - Footprints and tire marks
    - Snow or dirt impressions
    - Evaporating liquids
    - Fire patterns
  - Lab work
    - Evidence documentation
    - Evidence analysis

- **Forensic archaeology**
  - Photographs of scene as layers are uncovered
  - Appropriate references for size, color, and location

- Photographic Hardware
  - Camera
    - Still
    - Video
  - Lenses
    - Lens filtration for protection
    - Lens filtration for color correction
    - Appropriate focal length
    - Proper perspective
    - Optimization of DoF

- Macro accessories

- Batteries

- Lighting
  - Electronic flash
    - Painting with light
  - Daylight
  - Flood light
  - Alternate light sources (ALS)

- Media

- Barrier tape

- Evidence-gathering supplies

- Hand tools

- Markers and flags

- Writing supplies

- Communications devices: radios, cell phones, Internet

- Dimensionality
  - 2-D imaging
  - 3-D imaging
  - Photo montage
  - Panorama
- Quantification of data
  - Photogrammetry
  - Scene mapping
  - Laser scanning
  - Presentation
- Courtroom presentation
  - Certification

Documentation of Fire Scene Evidence

To properly and completely document a fire scene, the following protocols should be followed:

- Work through the scene in a systematic and logical manner.
- Expose overall images that place the evidence in the scene.
- Photograph the evidence from multiple perspectives and varying distances, including but not limited to the following:
  - Broken locks due to forced entry
  - All windows
  - All doors
  - Small evidence
  - Tool marks
  - Vandalism
  - Evidence of accelerant
  - Melted objects
  - Suspected points of origin
  - Discovery of evidence
  - Examination of evidence
  - Collection of evidence

TIP:

For reference, obtain photographs that were exposed before the fire.

When collecting evidence, develop the following documentation:

- The evidence items in chronological order of collection
- A complete description of the evidence submitted, including, date, time, location, and name of recoverer
- The history and possession of a sample from the time of collection, through analysis and data reporting, to its final disposition, as well as who will remain responsible and who will testify in court about the specific evidence (**chain of custody**)

SAFETY AT THE FIRE SCENE

Safety is always a primary concern. It is easy to forget where you are, what you are walking on, and what is over your head. The scene may be chaotic. It is impossible to concentrate on everything at once. Vehicles will be entering and leaving the scene. If possible, eliminate safety hazards before someone is injured. To ensure that you are seen by others working in the field, wear conspicuous, brightly colored clothing.

Flames and smoke are not usually a major problem for the scene investigator and photographer because that part of the event is over before photography starts, but many other hazards may be present, including the following:

- Sharp objects
- Broken glass
- Chemicals
- Biohazards
- Weakened construction
- Dirt, dust, ash, water, humidity, cold, heat, and related hazards

Wear heavy shoes and other personal protective equipment, as dictated by conditions. If the floor is unstable, wear a safety harness and lines that conform to applicable codes.

After you have minimized safety concerns, you should define the extent of the scene, then proceed in a logical and systematic manner to perform the documentation.

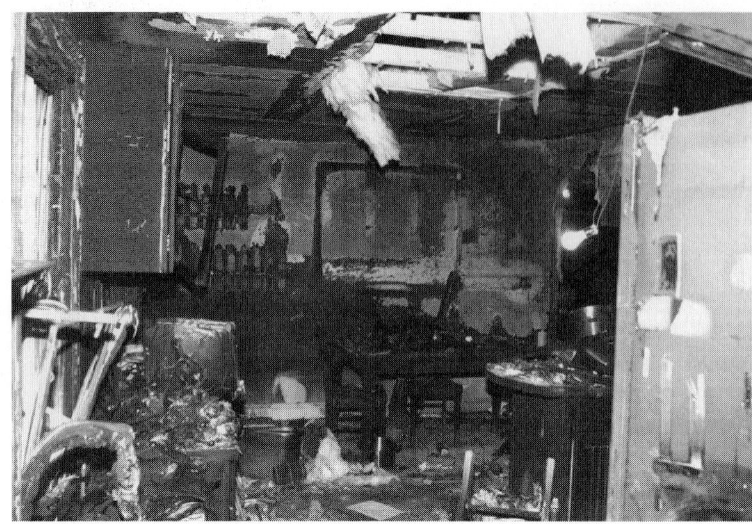

FIGURE 13–3 Representative fire scene with charred surfaces and reflective objects. The shadows are very dark, and the highlights are very bright. *Source:* Sandy Weiss/Packer Engineering.

PROPER EXPOSURE AND LIGHTING

Fire scene photography requires special attention to proper exposure because of the nature of exposure in darkened conditions. When the photography is being performed in daylight, use of a gray card for metering will alleviate some underexposure problems.

When the project takes place indoors, electric power is usually disabled. The photographer must provide sufficient illumination for the proper exposure of black, charred surfaces. Providing sufficient illumination for large areas is difficult. Even with sufficient illumination, the contrast range of the scene will be extensive, between the blackness of char and the whiteness of reflective surfaces (see Fig. 13–3). The high contrast range means limited latitude is available for exposure mistakes.

DoF is critical in all forensic images. To capture deep depth, small lens apertures must be used. To use small apertures, light levels must be high. Due to the potential for camera or subject movement, the shutter speed of the camera cannot be set slow for long exposures. In addition, it is not practical to use a tripod and slow shutter speeds at most fire scenes because extended exposures require time that the photographer will not have. Image resolution will be sacrificed if the ISO sensitivity of the camera is set too high.

This combination of difficulties makes fire scene photography a difficult pursuit. Experiment with your camera and determine the upper limits of its ISO capabilities before ending up with depreciated images. Bring the highest-output flash that is convenient to carry. To optimize DoF, be certain that overexposure is never allowed in your photographs. Visually examine image histograms for elimination of under- and overexposure issues.

Histograms at the Fire Scene

No histograms will be available during capture of fire scene images on film. Exposure errors with film media may be mediated in the darkroom but will be irreversible if image data are lost. If you are exposing with a digital camera, it may have histogram display capabilities; if it does, watch the image histograms carefully for proper placement of the subject's contrast range within the limitations of the camera and the media. Figure 13–4 provides an example of a basic black-and-white histogram of a color digital image. (Refer back to Chapter 7 for further information.

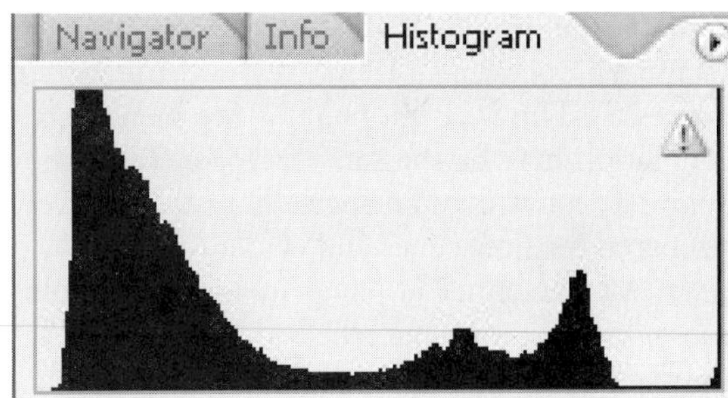

FIGURE 13–4 A digital image histogram. *Source:* Sandy Weiss/Packer Engineering.

TIP:

If your camera does not have built-in histogram capability, inspect your images on a computer or sufficiently bracket all exposures.

Image information on a histogram is read left to right, from darkness at the left to brightness at the right. Luminance values range from 0 to 255, for a total of 256 different values. An image pixel that is fully black (no exposure) is 0. An image pixel that is fully white (overexposure) is 255. The histogram shown in Figure 13–4 is from the exposure shown in Figure 13–5.

Correlate the locomotive image (Fig. 13–5) to its histogram (Fig. 13–4). Most of the pixels in the image are black or very dark gray, and their values peak at the left side of the histogram. No appreciable mid-tones are present, leaving that section of the histogram very low.

Fire photographs will display histograms similar to this image if they are properly exposed. Most of the pixel values in a fire scene image are black, very dark gray, or white. Within the limitations of the contrast capabilities of digital cameras, high-contrast subjects are more difficult to properly document than low-contrast subjects.

The histogram for the fire scene exposed in Figure 13–3 is shown in Figure 13–6.

The shape of the histogram graph in Figure 13–6 is similar to the shape of the locomotive image histogram in Figure 13–4. One obvious difference between the two graphs is that the image information on the right of Figure 13–6 is cut off: the histogram does not go down to zero before it ends against the right side of the frame. The highlights in Figure 13–3 are overexposed and contain no image detail, which may be due to

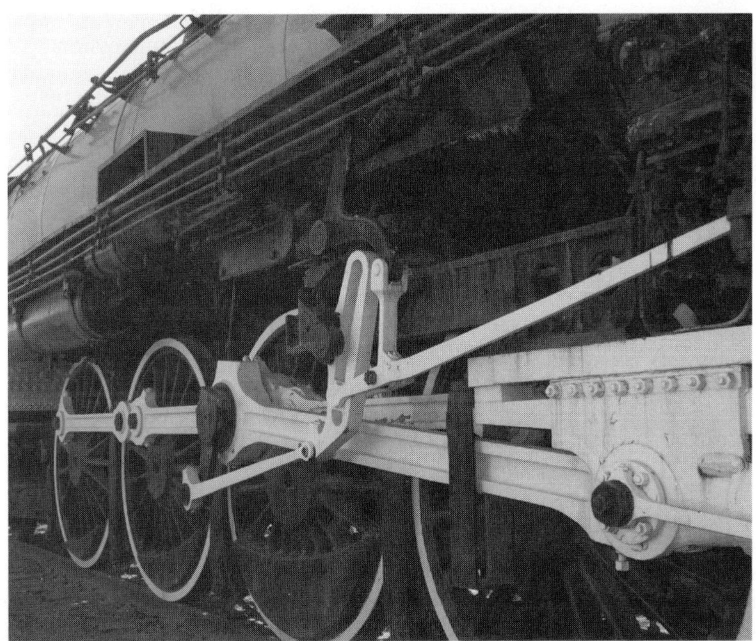

FIGURE 13–5 A locomotive in daylight. *Source:* Sandy Weiss/Packer Engineering.

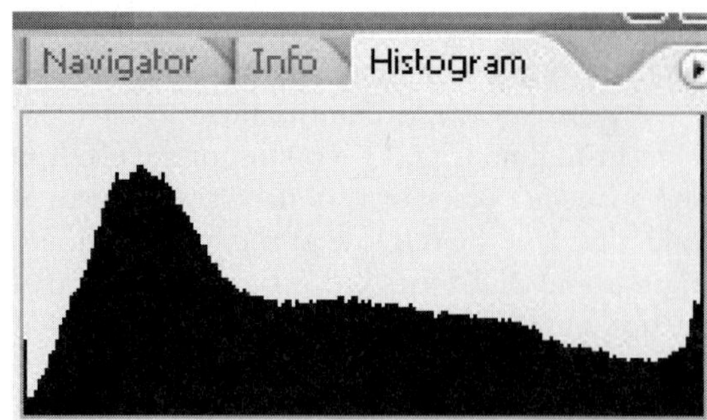

FIGURE 13–6 Histogram for fire scene depicted in Figure 13–3. *Source:* Sandy Weiss.

the reflectivity of the materials in the scene or improper setting of the camera. One possible method for minimizing high-contrast problems and subsequent improper exposures is to manually set the contrast control of the camera to a lower level.

TIP:

Experiment with the contrast setting on your camera before using a low setting on project photographs.

Photographers who use black-and-white film may expose and process the media specifically to yield low-contrast images and avoid detail-poor shadows and highlights. Low contrast is accomplished by overexposure and underdevelopment. Black-and-white photography is not popularly used for fire scene photography anymore because it provides no useful color information.

Bracketing exposures is another possibility for generating detail in the highlights and shadows for film and digital imaging. The benefit of bracketing is minimized by the availability of histograms.

FIRE SCENE IMAGING PROTOCOL

Before exposing images at a fire scene, it is highly recommended that you be familiar with the imaging practices or protocols used by your agency or department. The FBI laboratory says, "SOP's [standard operating procedures] are the key to success."[2] The SOP adopted for fire scene documentation may be the same as for general photography, or it may be specially and exclusively prepared for fire scenes and evidence.

All personnel utilizing imaging technologies must be knowledgeable and proficient in accordance with the SOP and the relevant imaging technologies. No personnel should use imaging technologies for which they cannot demonstrate proficiency. No personnel should process an image without following the established SOP for documentation and preservation of the processed image. The camera user is responsible for being familiar with the equipment, instruction manuals, and the SOP for operating the equipment.

Consider the development of an SOP if none exists. SOPs for fire documentation purposes should include the following:

- Assessment of proper equipment for projects
  - See previous bulleted list
- Image Capture
  - Standard for image capture file formats
  - JPEG
  - Resolution
    - Compression
  - RAW
- Image Processing
- Image Storage
  - Choice of format for stored images
    - CD
    - DVD
    - Disc drive
- Use of appropriate forms
- Organizational chain of custody
- Security
  - Access
- Backups
  - Keeping up with technology
  - Digitizing negatives

Only individuals listed in the SOP should be able to access original archived images, and only people with access should be able to copy the original images for distribution. In addition, only people performing actions on the images should have access to the necessary software.

STORYTELLING

When photographs of a scene are exposed in a logical and systematic sequence, a person viewing the photographs should be able to progress through the images and have a reasonable idea of where each photograph was taken.

When capturing documentation, perform the following specific tasks:

- Expose overall photos of the scene.
  - Approach
  - Street signs
  - Streetlights
  - Street addresses
  - Identifying objects
  - Outside the structure from every possible angle
- Photograph the scene in a clockwise direction.
- Document evidence.
- Photograph each room from all four corners.
- If a victim is present, photograph the corpse and its immediate vicinity.
- If possible, expose photographs looking down from ceiling height.
- Document suspected points of origin.
- Document ignition sources.
- Take photographs of spectators.
- Avoid taking photographs of other personnel.
- Take notes.
- Make sketches.

Photographing Exteriors

To document the amount of fire damage and the locations of entrances and windows, photograph the exterior of a structure from all available sides (see Fig. 13–7). The proximity of neighboring buildings should be easily derived from the images. Document any objects that may have contributed to the fire. Document any objects that may have been a detriment to the suppression of the fire.

Images of exteriors should include exposures of the following physical features:

- Structural construction methods and materials
- Locations of chimneys

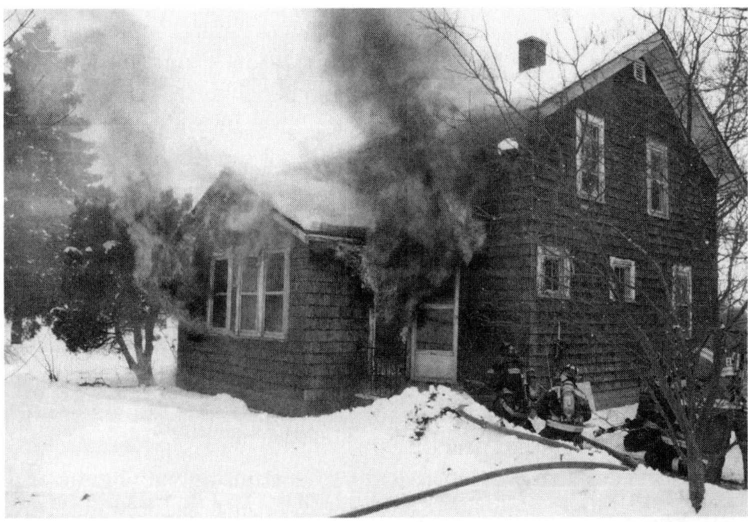

FIGURE 13–7 Exterior view of a burning house, two sides exposed. *Source:* Sandy Weiss/Packer Engineering.

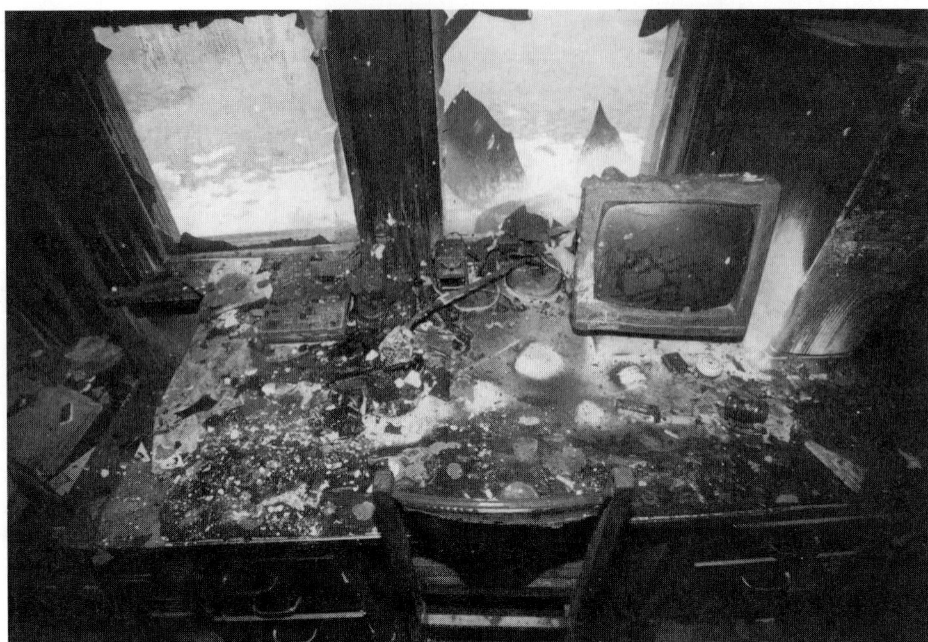

FIGURE 13–8 Burned interior of a house, illuminated with an electronic flash unit. *Source:* Sandy Weiss/Packer Engineering.

- Power poles
- Power lines
- Service boxes or connections
- Gas meters
- Hydrants
- Vegetation
- Vehicles
- Dumpsters
- Security devices
- Footprints
- Tire tracks
- Evidence of explosion
- Anything unusual

Document openings where the fire vented and scorched the exterior materials. The origin of the fire may be determined from studying the heat and burn patterns on the exterior of window frames, walls, or roofs if the fire started near an exterior wall. Use a ladder, elevated work platform, aircraft, or nearby building to obtain the proper vantage for exposing overhead images.

Photographing Interiors

Use accessory lighting for interior fire scene photos. The directional lighting provided by an electronic flash unit (EFU) or other concentrated source will illuminate details in dark corners and under debris (see Fig. 13–8).

A fire scene may be equipped with emergency lighting during investigation and documentation. Emergency lighting affords safety and benefits to the investigators and the photographers. Incandescent lighting (see Fig. 13–9) will not cause a yellow color cast in the images if the photographer is using an EFU sufficiently large to overpower the color of the light bulbs. Digital cameras should be set on automatic or EFU color balance if flash is in use with emergency lighting. If the images are being exposed by incandescent lighting only, the color balance should be set to incandescent. Color correction filters should not be used at fire scenes unless absolutely necessary.

Painting with light (see Chapter 9) may be of value at fire scenes for exposing images of objects and areas too large for a single flash. It

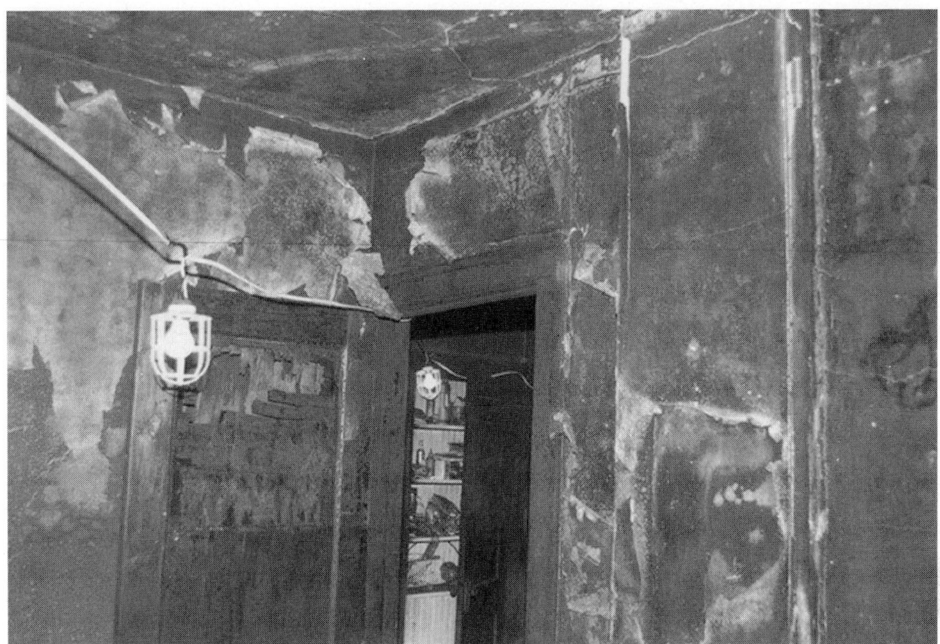

FIGURE 13–9 Incandescent emergency lighting. *Source:* Sandy Weiss/Packer Engineering.

requires the use of a tripod, which may not be available at a fire scene. Use the same steps listed in Chapter 9 but use a larger lens aperture, due to the dark subject, than you would use normally for single exposures.

All areas of a structure affected by fire should be photographed, including peripheral sites, even if they seem undamaged within a fire-damaged structure. Follow a logical route, starting with areas where the fire had the least effect, and work toward the areas where it had the most effect. Expose extra images at doorways, air vents, and interior windows, where burn patterns may indicate the mode of fire spread from room to room. The burn patterns on the walls, ceilings, and floors may indicate where the fire originated and how it spread.

> **REMEMBER:**
>
> All scenes are three-dimensional. Document the floors, walls, ceilings, and contents.

Use the focal length lens considered normal for the format of the camera for photographs of fire scenes. On most 35mm cameras, a 50mm lens would be appropriate. On a Nikon DSLR, it might be a 35mm lens. Normal lenses are not the most convenient ones to use, but they cause the least distortion to perspective. Many photographers use a wide-angle lens for interior photographs because they capture the subject in fewer images, but the walls may slant and the apparent distance between objects in a room may appear larger than they are. If many photos are exposed with a normal focal length lens, they may be assembled into a **photomontage**, or even **digitally stitched** together to a panorama.

> **TIP:**
>
> When photographing fire scenes, *always* use an ultraviolet filter or clear glass filter on the camera lens to protect the front lens element from the dirt inherent in such locations.

When switching between locations, use appropriate scales and references in the initial photographs. For visual references, use recognizable objects, including furniture, flooring, doorways, light fixtures, and so on. The person

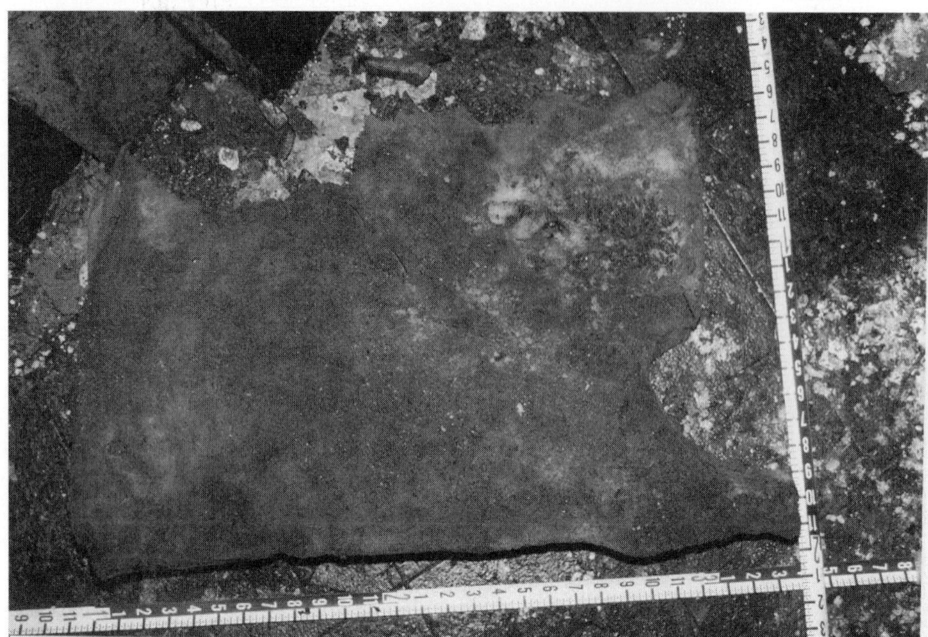

FIGURE 13–10 Use of a two-dimensional scale for image rectification. *Source:* Sandy Weiss/Packer Engineering.

viewing the photographs should be able to correlate the references to a tour through the area. If objects or markings are flat (see Fig. 13–10), use sufficient references to allow rectification to actual size.

Using a single 2-D scale in an image of 3-D space will afford the viewer only an idea of size (see Fig. 13–11). If quantitative data are going to be derived from the image, use extra scales. Accuracy of quantification depends on

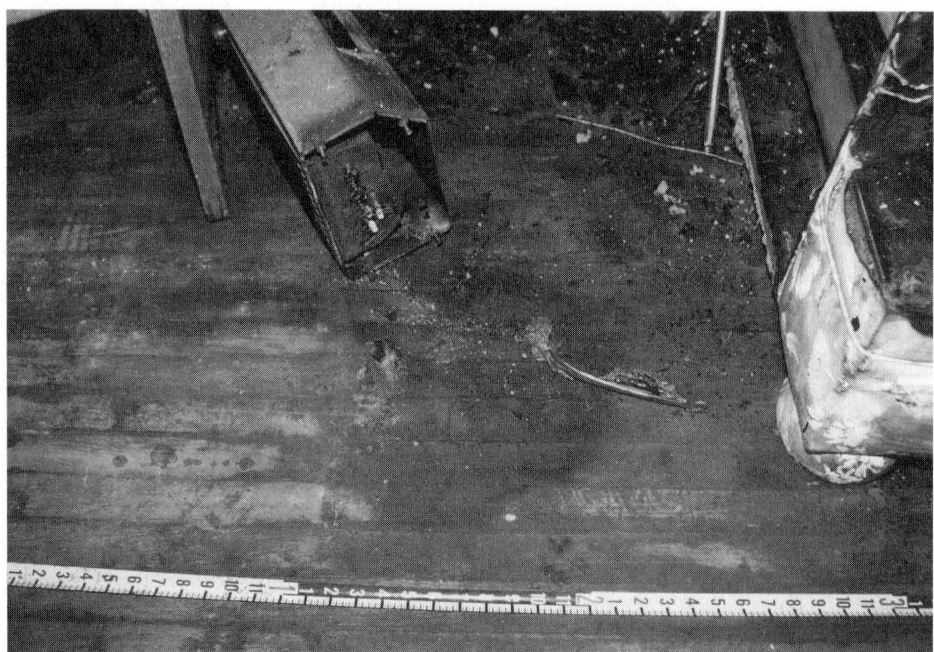

FIGURE 13–11 Use of a single reference for size in a 3-D space. *Source:* Packer Engineering.

the amount of information contained in the images.

If the origin of a fire is determined during documentation, it should be photographed thoroughly before the removal of any evidence or the beginning of any excavation. The site of origin also should be heavily documented during excavation. After properly documenting any fire damage in the area, it should be cleaned and photographed to record the composition of flooring layers and materials.

Photographing Doors and Windows

If possible, locate, document, and photograph the position of all doors and windows as they were before the fire. The position of broken glass may indicate the position of a window or if the window was broken from the inside or the outside. The smoke and heat patterns above windows may indicate if the window was open or closed at the time of the fire.

LOCATION OF EVIDENCE

When evidence is discovered, it should be marked with an appropriate locator and documented prior to collection and removal. This will facilitate chain of custody.

REMEMBER:

If possible, photograph the evidence before it is moved.

The use of a recognized system for notation of evidence location is recommended in all documentations. In grid notation, if an item is found

	A	B	C	D	E	F	G	H	I
1									
2									
3									
4									
5									
6									
7									
8									
9									

in the north-center of a room, or three squares from one wall and four squares from the other wall on the grid, it may be recorded as at D3, rather than at the north-central part of the room.

Some photographers and investigators use spirals, squares, and any other simple pattern appropriate to the scene. The shape of the pattern does not matter as long as it is logical.

Global Positioning Systems

A **Global Positioning System (GPS)** is a system of satellite-based navigation. GPS works in any weather, everywhere in the world, 24/7. GPS satellites circle Earth in precise orbits and transmit signal information to Earth, while GPS receivers use the information for triangulation to calculate a user's location.

A GPS receiver must have the signals of three satellites to calculate a 2-D position in latitude and longitude. It can also be used to track movement. With four or more satellites in view, a receiver may determine a 3-D position of latitude, longitude, and altitude.

Newer GPS receivers may pinpoint an object in space to within 3 meters of its true location. The relative positions of multiple objects provide sufficient accuracy for maps and charts to be developed from such information.

Sony GPS-CS1

Sony manufactures a GPS device designed specifically for evidence photographers. It records the sequence of positions where photographs were exposed. The GPS-CS1 is 3.5 inches long and weighs 2 ounces (see Fig. 13–12). If it is carried by the photographer during a project, it records GPS locations in a continuous stream to match everywhere the photographer travels, night and day, indoors and out. To arrange pictures geographically, the data from the GPS device are imported to a computer. After all the images are downloaded, the software synchronizes the images from the camera to the latitude and longitude where they were exposed. It operates by comparing the time of exposure to the time of the GPS reading. If the camera's clock has been properly set, the actual time of exposure is recorded in the image metadata.

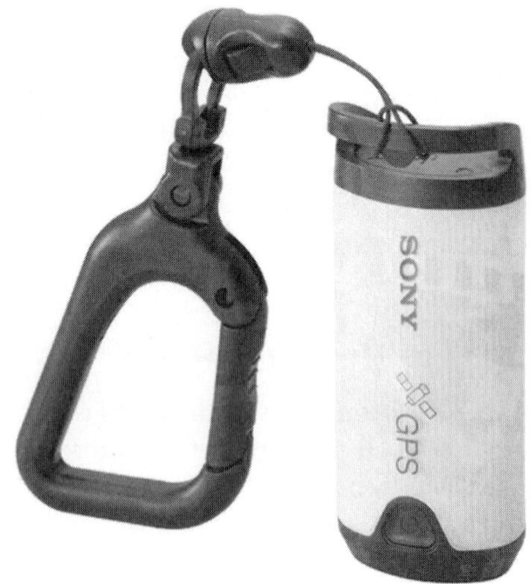

FIGURE 13–12 Sony GPS-CS1 compact recording device. *Source:* Sandy Weiss/Packer Engineering.

MOTOR VEHICLE FIRES

Guidelines for fires involving automobiles, trucks, and recreational vehicles (but not aircraft, boats, or trains) are included in *NFPA 921*. Many factors in all vehicle fires are similar, including fuels, ignition sources, and ignition scenarios.

> **TIP:**
>
> The burn or damage patterns found on various body parts and in the interior of a vehicle, are often used to locate the point(s) of origin and for determination of the cause.

The type and quantity of combustible materials built into modern vehicles may burn and cause extensive damage, without the presence of gasoline. Interpretations drawn from damage patterns may be verified by witness accounts, laboratory analyses, service records, electrical faults, or factory recall notices.

Photographing Vehicle Fires

Vehicle fire documentations use the same techniques and SOPs as structural fire projects do. The vehicle should be photographed at the scene whenever possible (see Fig. 13–13).

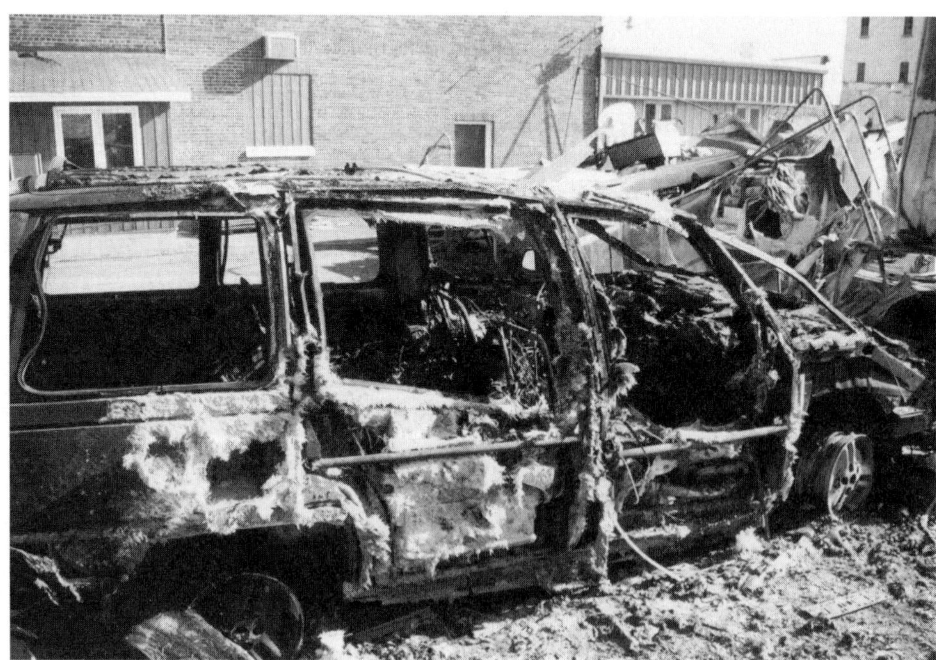

FIGURE 13–13 Exterior view of burned van. *Source:* Sandy Weiss/Packer Engineering.

If working at the scene, prepare the following:

- Diagram/sketch
    - Reference locations and distances
- Photographs
    - Make
    - Model
    - Year
    - License plate
    - Vehicle identification number (VIN)
    - Vehicle sides, top, bottom, interior, cargo spaces and cargo, tires
    - Path of fire spread
    - Surrounding structures
    - Vegetation
    - Other vehicles
    - Footprints
    - Tire prints
    - Damages
    - Debris
    - Fuel spills
    - Scene after vehicle removal
    - Vehicle damages caused by removal

If the vehicle has been moved, placing the vehicle into the scene is not necessary, but the photographs should include the following:

- Make
- Model
- Year
- License plate
- Vehicle identification number (VIN)
- Vehicle sides, top, bottom, interior, cargo spaces and cargo, tires

TIP:

Document the condition of the window glass and door hinges. They may establish the open or closed status of the windows and doors at the time of the fire.

FATALITIES AND INJURIES AT A FIRE SCENE

When the fire scene involves the recovery of human remains, a team of specialists may be required. The team may include the following:

- First responder
- Crime scene investigator
- Coroner/medical examiner
- Forensic pathologist
- Photographer

When they are available, consult other specialists, including the following:

- Forensic anthropologist
- Forensic entomologist
- Forensic odontologist
- Surveyor

Manner of Death

The **manner of death** explains how the cause of death occurred. For example, was it a natural death or a violent death? Natural deaths are caused by disease or old age, rather than an accident or act of violence. An injury may cause or contribute to death. In that case, the fatality will be classified as nonnatural. The following are subclasses of the manner of death:

- Natural
- Accident
- Homicide
- Suicide
- Undetermined

Forensic pathologists investigate the manner of death through **autopsy.** The information found during an autopsy may reveal the following, within a reasonable certainty:

- Cause of death
    - How
    - When
    - Where
- Manner of death

Natural Death

The mechanisms of natural death include these:

- Heart failure
- Disease

- Death while sleeping
- Brain death

The autopsy should reveal if death was sudden or unexpected or if the person was ill. **Accidental death** results during an accident from injury sufficient to end life. The mechanisms of accidental death include these:

- Vehicle crashes
- Falls
- Fires
- Drowning
- And so on

Homicide

Homicide is the killing of one human by another. Some examples include these:

- Shooting
- Stabbing
- Strangling
- Bludgeoning
- Burning

All murders are homicides, but not all homicides are murders. **Murder** is the unlawful taking of one human life by another. This may include premeditation. If a police officer takes a life in the line of duty, it is homicide, not murder.

Every type of weapon leaves distinct marks on a corpse. A pathologist may be able to identify whether an injury was caused by a certain type of weapon.

Suicide

When a person terminates his or her own life, it is called **suicide**. The manners of death by suicide include these:

- Gunshot
- Stabbing
- Incision
- Poisoning
- Hanging
- Falls
- Entrance into an unsurvivable situation
- And so on

Undetermined Manner of Death

The manner of death is undetermined when the conclusion concerning a particular manner of death cannot be determined after all the available information has been considered.

Cause of Death

National mortality statistics are gathered by classifying each and every death as due to one specific condition. This is based on the information reported on the death certificate and using international rules for categorizing the **cause of death** from reported conditions. The *ICD-10: International Statistical Classification of Diseases and Related Health Problems* is used for coding cause of death.[3]

Mechanism of Death

The **mechanism of death** consists of the physiological or biochemical events that end life. The mechanism is determined by the cause—for example, cardiac arrest or respiratory arrest—due to, but not limited to, any of the following:

- Gunshot wounds
- Stabbing
- Smoke inhalation
- Assault
- Arson
- Vehicular accident

Burn Injuries

The investigator may determine information about various aspects of the fire by examining the effects of fire on a victim's body. The injuries may also help to develop the timeline of the fire. This information may be crucial to the determination of the origin and cause. The injuries may also provide information regarding the occurrence of arson.

Many deaths and injuries are caused by fire, heat, and smoke. Burn injuries occur when the skin of a victim receives more heat than can be absorbed by the body. The common types of burns include the following:

- Thermal, from high temperatures
- Flame, from direct contact with fire
- Radiation, from close exposure to heat or radiation
- Scalds, from hot liquids or steam
- Contact, from touching hot objects
- Chemical, from contact with corrosive chemicals
- Ultraviolet, from overexposure to solar radiation or sun lamps
- Electrical, from contact with live conductors

Burns are seen in the following types of crime scenes:

- Arson
- Insurance fraud
- Drug abuse
- Child/elder abuse
- Domestic violence
- Suicide
- Homicide

Failure to use proper SOPs when examining and processing burn victim evidence may compromise the admissibility of the evidence at trial. It may also lead to inaccurate conclusions regarding the origin and cause of the burns and the possibility of arson. It is critical to process fire victims properly to preserve any evidence of value.

Use the same SOPs, if possible, with living victims at the scene, following these steps:

- Collect clothing, shoes, and personal effects.
- Collect other evidence.
- Document injuries.
- Record your observations of medical personnel.

Regardless of whether the victim is alive or deceased, fire suppression activities should have been minimized at their location. It is SOP to use the minimum of destructive procedures during fire suppression in the location of victims. Excess water may wash away evidence. The utmost care and common sense must be used to preserve the scene. As soon as it is safe to enter the area where the victim is located, that area should be given the highest priority for investigation and documentation. Foot traffic in the area should be minimized until after documentation is completed.

TIP:

The position and condition of the body may supply the medical examiner and fire investigator with crucial information. The body should not be moved until it has been fully documented in writing, sketches, and photographs.

When exposing photographs, strive to answer the following questions:

- Who is the victim?
- What are the cause and manner of death?
- What injuries did the victim sustain?
- Was the victim alive or conscious at the time of the fire?
- What is the victim's relationship to the scene?
- What is the timeline of the fire events?

Photographing Fire Survivors

Victims who survive a fire will not be part of the scene for long because they will require immediate and intensive medical care. It is, however, a priority to photograph the victim in situ if possible. Whenever possible, photograph the following:

- Where the victim was found
- The victim's wounds before treatment

Document and collect samples of debris for analysis. When the victim is removed from the scene, photograph and then collect all debris on, near, and under the victim. Search and sift as required, and handle everything with care and caution.

SKETCHING AT THE FIRE SCENE

To supplement photographs, a sketch of the fire scene should include a record of the objects, conditions, distances, and positional relationships of the evidence found in the scene. Use coded numbers to correlate the evidence to the sketches.

Sketches do not have to be drawn to scale but should include enough accurate measurements and details to correlate the sketch to the scene. The detail will be used for subsequent diagrams.

A sketch should always include the following:

- Case number
- Date
- Time
- Location
- Key
- Legend
- Compass orientation
- Scale
- Weather conditions
- Lighting conditions
- Personnel and their assignments
- Dimensions of rooms, furniture, doors, and windows
- Distances between objects, victims, entrances, and exits

Every object in a sketch should be located by making and indicating at least two measurements from the object to other objects. This process is called **triangulation.**

FORENSIC ARCHAEOLOGY

Forensic archaeology is a discipline that combines archaeological techniques and forensic science. *Forensic archaeologists* work with law enforcement agencies to excavate death locations and gravesites to reconstruct the events that took place prior to and during the burial of victims. The person may have been a victim of homicide, and the murderer may have attempted to hide the evidence. Layers of debris often fall on top of fire victims and require excavation. Excavation of a scene, using proper archaeological SOP, may provide the following data:

- Time of burial
- Circumstances of burial
- Timetable of burial
- Manner of death
- If homicide, the techniques and tools used for burial
- Peripheral evidence

Forensic archaeologists may recover any of the following evidence:

- Human remains
- Personal effects
- Weapons
- Stolen property
- Peripheral evidence of a crime or accident

To explain the pattern and timing of the evidence, the forensic archaeologist examines any objects that were buried with the victim. Human remains may yield valuable evidence after fires and long after burial. Evidence may include the following:

- Fingerprints
- Hair
- DNA
- Teeth
- Paint flakes
- Pollen
- Chemicals

Forensic archaeologists employ technologies common to surveyors. The use of grids and references is SOP. All evidence is labeled with 3-D coordinates for reconstruction. Archaeological methods assist with accurately identifying bodies and body parts at mass disasters and in subsequent investigations.

Interpol Disaster Victim Identification Guide

The **Interpol** (an international intelligence agency) "Disaster Victim Identification (DVI) Guide" was developed using the tools and techniques of forensic archaeology.[4] The current edition is used in all Interpol member countries to facilitate efficient and accurate disaster management and victim identification, as well as compatible international SOPs.

Body Recovery and Evidence Collection

Interpol provides a series of excellent forms and suggested SOPs for use in mass disasters. See the Interpol Web site at www.interpol.int/public/DisasterVictim/guide/chapitre4.asp.

Identification of Fire Victims

All photographs of fire fatalities should be accompanied by a form that includes the following information:

- Photographer's name and/or initials
- Agency name
- Date
- Time
- Description
- Location
- File number

Appropriate forms must be procured or produced, completed, and retained. They must be available to accompany the photographic documentation of victims in the field and in the lab. In cases of individual fatalities, the corpse is usually relocated to a morgue. In the case of multiple fatalities, a staging and autopsy area may be positioned near the location of the incident.

Photographic documentation of fatalities in the field includes the following information:

- Overall photographs of the body, including position
- Record of the collection and removal of the body
- Location of the body after removal
  - Body fluid patterns
  - Blood spatters
  - Stains

Photographic documentation in the lab of fatalities includes the following information:

- Body clothed, including all surfaces of clothing
- Body unclothed, including clothing matches to injuries
- Photographs enumerated in autopsy SOP
  - Impact markings
  - Body areas burned
  - Body areas not burned
  - Bruising
  - Bruise aging

Fatalities with injuries and in various states of decomposition must be examined and documented. If the body is intact, photographic documentation may be used for identification based on the following:

- Visual recognition
- Hair color
- Effects (personal possessions found with the body)
  - Wallet
  - ID
  - Jewelry
  - Eyeglasses
- Fingerprints
- Fingernails
- Tattoos
- Birthmarks
- Scars

If the body is damaged and fingerprints are unavailable, a preliminary identification will be undertaken through reconstruction of the circumstances of recovery and the effects found with the body. Definitive identification may be made in various ways:

- Biological methods (DNA)
- Identification by dentition
- Identification by radiographs
  - Skull
  - Chest

- Arms
- Legs

If the body is in skeletal form:

- Biological methods (DNA)
- Physical anthropology
  - Height
  - Musculature
  - Race
  - Healed fracture or bone malformation
  - Wounds or injuries
- Dentition
  - Photographs of the inside tooth surfaces (intra-oral) and the outside surfaces (extra-oral)
  - Use of dental charts for comparison
- Site archaeology
  - Determination of scene boundaries
  - Location of fatality within the scene
  - The layer of debris in which the evidence was found

Always document fatalities in relationship to the center of the scene, disturbing as little as possible. Photograph only the surfaces of the body unobstructed by the surroundings:

- When photographing a fatality, use a SOP sequence.
  - Start at the top of the head.
  - Expose overlapping images from the top down.
  - Expose extra images of any obvious injuries.
  - Expose extra images of any burn pattern.
- After initial external examination, document aspects of the victim that were previously hidden.
  - Patterns and injuries
  - Hands and held objects
  - Personal effects
- Photograph everything done at the autopsy, according to the SOP in use.

Postmortem Dental Evidence

The American Board of Forensic Odontology (ABFO) has an SOP guideline for body identification through forensic dentistry, which is completely accurate for the identification of fatalities in mass disasters and in many types of routine cases.[5]

Postmortem dental examinations are conducted under the direction of a coroner, medical examiner, or forensic pathologist. The SOP in this specialty should include chain of authority for the decision to cut facial tissues for access to the teeth. Removal of the larynx and tongue at autopsy may facilitate the visual and photographic examination of the teeth and allow placement of intra-oral (inside the mouth) films for radiographs.

Antemortem information, including dental and medical records, should be collected and then transcribed on the appropriate Interpol disaster victim identification form. The ante- and postmortem information are then compared to properly identify the victim.

Scale Selection and Placement

Scale selection for documentation of victims is determined by the following:

- Type of lighting
- Accuracy required
- Rigidity necessary
- Dimensions of subject

Choose scales that provide measurement graduations that satisfy the requirements of the subject and situation. If the image requires accuracy to 1 millimeter, use a scale that is accurate to at least 1 millimeter across the entire scale.

> **TIP:**
>
> If the scale in use is not certified, use the same scale for measurements of the photograph and the subject.

Place the scale along the edge of the object or suspend it near the object, in the same plane. If the scale is placed on the same surface as the information being photographed, be sure the scale does not hide any information.

Forensic Odontology

A forensic odontologist may be able to approximately calculate the age of a victim. More accurate identification may be made if sufficient antemortem information exists.

A universal numbering system is in use for dental notation. It facilitates the association of specific information to specific teeth. The same system is used by forensic odontologists and by dentists. The uppercase letters A through T are used for primary (baby) teeth, and the numbers 1 through 32 are used for permanent teeth. Tooth 1 is the right maxillary third molar, and the sequence continues along the upper teeth, right to left. Tooth 17 is the left mandibular third molar. The numbers continue along the bottom teeth, left to right.

External Images of the Teeth

External images of teeth require no special equipment or methods. A camera with a macro lens, and a reliable EFU, are sufficient. Appropriate scales should be used. A normal sequence of images typically includes the following:

- Full facial anterior view
- Left and right lateral facial views

Intra-Oral Images

Intra-oral images require extra equipment and expertise. A normal sequence of images usually includes the following:

- Full face, lips retracted
- *Occlusal* views, upper and lower teeth
- Close-up view, *anterior* teeth
- *Palatal* surfaces
- *Lingual* surfaces
- *Lateral* views of teeth in slightly open position and in *occlusion*
- Left and right *buccal* views
- Left and right *lingual* views

Equipment for Intra-Oral Photography

The camera system for intra-oral photography consists of the following equipment:

- Single lens reflex camera (DSLR)
- Macro lens(es)
- Close-up accessories
- Electronic flash
- Mirrors (see Fig. 13–14)
- Retractors
- Scales

Macro lenses, including those used for intra-oral photography, are often inscribed with numbers designating magnification ratios. The inscriptions facilitate standardization of images, including magnifications and exposure information. For magnifications greater than 1:1, close-up accessories besides the macro lens are needed.

Intra-oral photography requires extreme DoF to ensure that the entire tooth array is in focus. Long focal length macro lenses add working distance and DoF in most situations.

Mirrors for dental photography are constructed from polished metal or front-surface glass. They must be purchased from dental or forensic supply companies.

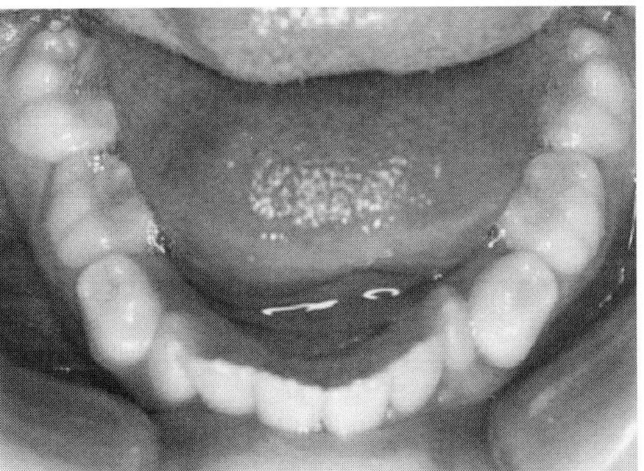

FIGURE 13–14 Teeth photographed with an intra-oral front-surfaced mirror. *Source:* Dr. Warren Wakerlin.

Three shapes of mirrors are suitable for dental photography:

- Palatal
- Buccal
- Lingual

Mirrors for use in intra-oral photography are available in various child and adult sizes. These mirrors are fragile and easily scratched. To facilitate photography with them, retraction of the lips may need to be necessary. Non-reflective retractors are best for this use.

Lighting for Dental Photography

Electronic flash is the only practical light source for dental photography. Automatic flashes may produce satisfactory exposures, but manual capabilities should be on hand. The face and lips of the subject are situated between the flash and the teeth. Brightly illuminated facial skin is a common cause of underexposure of teeth.

Ring-Light Versus Standard Flash

Ring-lights are a good choice of equipment for intra-oral, intra-oral mirror, pathology, and wound photos. If extra shadows are needed to differentiate the contours and shape of subjects, turn off part of the ring-light or use a standard EFU.

TIP:

Full-mouth photographs should be exposed at a perpendicular perspective for accurate viewing and quantification. This will show the teeth in a spatial relationship that is effective with minimal distortion for comparison to earlier images.

AUTOPSY PHOTOGRAPHY

Autopsies are performed to determine the cause of death. Forensic pathologists are experts in **medicolegal** autopsies that relate to both medicine and law, criminal investigation, judicial testimony, toxicology, and other forensic sciences.[6]

Medicolegal Autopsy in the United States

REMEMBER:

No standardized national system of death investigation exists in the United States, so it falls under the authority of state and local officials.

The steps for autopsy are followed in this manner:

1. Examine the exterior of the corpse.
2. Open the chest and abdomen.
3. Remove the organs for further examination and dissection.
4. Open the skull and examine the brain.
5. Examine areas with specific injuries.
6. Examine tissue and fluid samples.

Autopsy photographs, with and without reference scales, should include the following (see Fig. 13–15 for one example):

- The body clothed and unclothed
- All sides from various angles
- Close-ups of burns and other injuries
- Imbedded fire and explosion debris
  - Blast injuries
  - Shrapnel injuries
  - Thermal injuries
  - Building collapse injuries
- Condition of the victim's airways
- Injuries not caused by the fire
- Representative images of each step and sample

Collection of Autopsy Evidence

Evidence collected from an autopsy will help to determine the scientific factors that led to the death. All autopsy SOPs should include, at a minimum, the following steps:

- Collect trace evidence from the clothing and body.
- Brush all hair over clean paper.

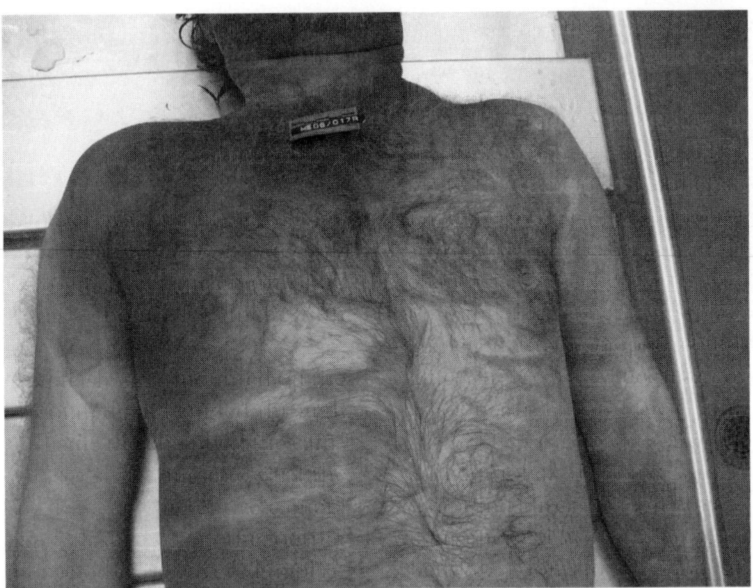

FIGURE 13–15 A decomposing body at autopsy. *Source:* Dodge County, Wisconsin, Medical Examiner's Office.

- Remove trace evidence from skin and clothing.
- Collect samples of pooled blood.
  - Collect blood samples for controls
- Collect exemplar material
  - From environment (vegetation, soil, insects)
  - From structure (carpet, paint, fibers)
  - From vehicle (carpet, seats, tires)
  - From animals (hair, bedding)
- Collect fingernail clippings
- Swab bite marks.
- Swab cavities.
- Collect exemplar hairs.

SUMMARY

Fire investigation is one of the most difficult aspects of the forensic sciences because the evidence often destroys itself before it can be documented and investigated. Fire scenes are operational challenges because they are dirty, cold, damp, dangerous, and dark places where everything looks the same and is piled in layers, one on top of another. Normal objects are unrecognizable because they are melted into an assortment of unusual shapes that are deformed from the heat.

People are often killed or injured in fires, and that compounds the difficulty of investigation and documentation. Still, the photographer must conform to rigid SOPs when documenting the victims and the scene. Fire-related projects are hard on the photographers and the equipment.

In most fire investigations, the origin and cause will be determined. The debris will be shoveled and sifted, analyzed for accelerants, examined, photographed, and swept away, leaving patterns from the heat, smoke, and flames.

It is critical to determine if the incident was accidental or arson. The determination is important and must be ascertained by trained investigators and photographers.

Images of the scene and evidence must be exposed systematically and logically to allow viewers to make sense out of confusion. Following the scientific method in the investigation is essential.

CASE STUDY

MCCORMICK PLACE FIRE

The original McCormick Place of Chicago was only six years old when it was severely damaged by fire on January 16, 1967 (see Fig. 13–16) during the National Housewares Manufacturer Association 46th Semi-Annual Exhibition. One security guard was killed.

Smoke was seen near a display booth at about 2:00 a.m. Within five minutes, the entire booth was in flames. The fire department was called at 2:11 a.m. Firefighters arrived, entered the building, and immediately ordered a second alarm at 2:16 a.m. Nine alarms were eventually struck. A total of 500 firefighters and 94 pieces of fire equipment were used. Suppression was complicated by failure of the water supply. At 2:53 a.m., firefighters completed a relay from hydrants a quarter mile away. Fireboats arrived next. By 3:00 a.m. the whole building was involved and the roof was collapsing.

The fire was struck out at 9:46 a.m. Part of the lower level and the theater were saved.

A number of factors contributed to the severe destruction. For example, the 1,250 exhibits were constructed of wood, paper, and plastic. In addition, the wiring used for exhibit power was temporary and did not necessarily conform to the Chicago Building Code. No sprinklers were installed in 92% of the building, including the main exhibition hall. Although McCormick Place had private hydrants, they had been closed for a construction project on the Stevenson Expressway and not reopened afterward. The pumping system was inadequate. An overall lack of compartmentalization, a large amount of fuel, and little water for suppression added to the difficulties.

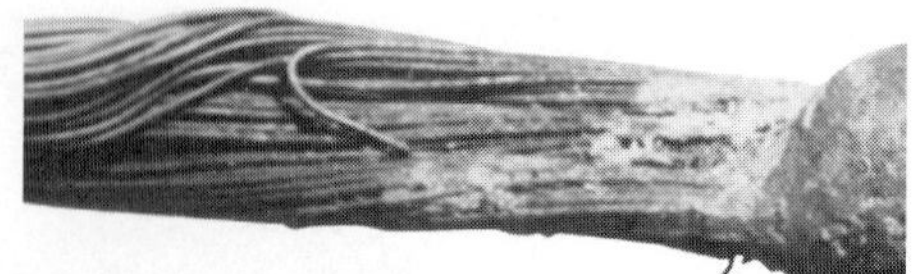

FIGURE 13–17 McCormick Place Fire evidence. This piece of electric wiring is melted and is thought to be from the location of the origin of the fire. *Source:* Sandy Weiss/Packer Engineering.

Packer Engineering investigated the fire and traced the origin to a section of the temporary wiring that was found during the excavation of the rubble near the former location of the booth in question (see Fig. 13–17). Several thousand photographs were taken to tell the story of the investigation and enable reconstruction of the event.

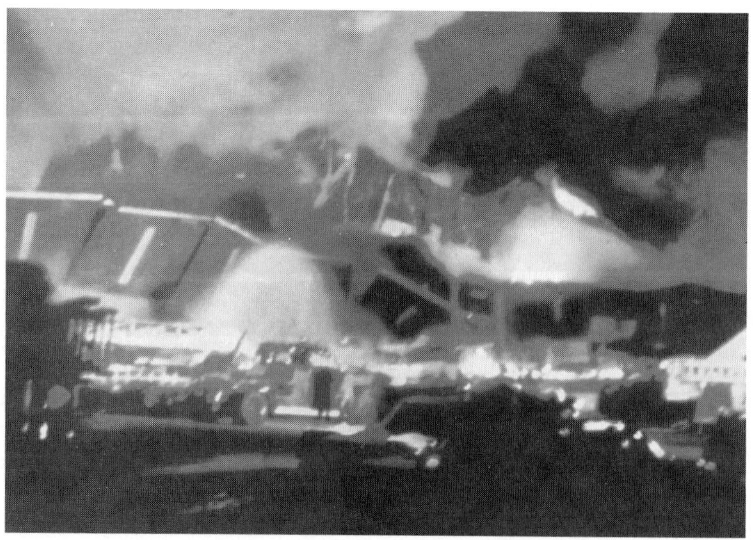

FIGURE 13–16 McCormick Place fire. *Source:* Sandy Weiss/Packer Engineering.

CASE STUDY

VEHICLE FIRE

This actual case was investigated and documented by Chester Kraus, communications officer and fire investigator for the local fire department of Roselle, Illinois.

A car fire occurred in June 2007. A 77-year-old female had been driving for approximately 45 minutes when she realized she was lost. She pulled into an office complex (see Fig. 13–18) to ask for directions. When she returned to her 2003 Ford Focus, she observed smoke and flames coming from both sides of the hood nearest the windshield. She went inside one of the offices for help. Shortly after, the vehicle was almost fully involved.

To accurately tell the story of this incident, 48 photos were exposed, and 10 are included here.

All projects documented by the Roselle Fire Department include a case identifier (see Fig. 13–19). Documentation of a vehicle begins by exposing overall photographs of all four sides (see Fig. 13–20). After the overall photographs have been made, mid-range photos, from various angles are exposed of areas of specific interest (see Figs. 13–21 and 13–22). Fire patterns may indicate an area of origin (see Fig. 13–23), and in this case the fire origin was located in the engine compartment. Mid-range and close-up photographs were exposed of heavily burned areas (see Figs. 13–24 and 13–25). Vehicle identification photos are always exposed, including license plates and the VIN (see Fig. 13–26). The passenger compartment also is an area of interest for every vehicle fire investigation and documentation (see Fig. 13–27).

This incident is still under investigation to determine the cause.

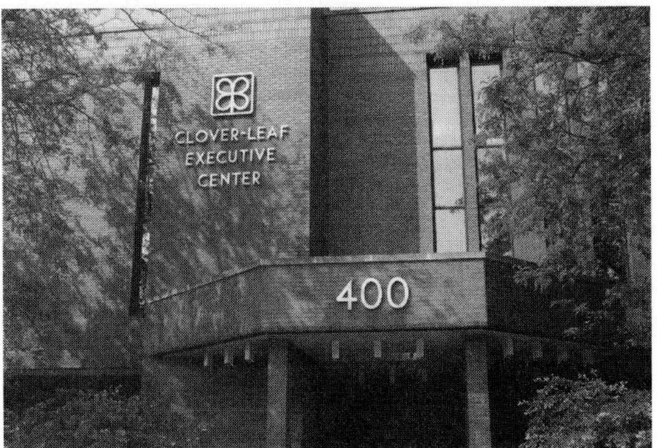

FIGURE 13–18 Office Complex, scene of the fire. *Source:* Chester Kraus, Roselle, Illinois, Fire Department.

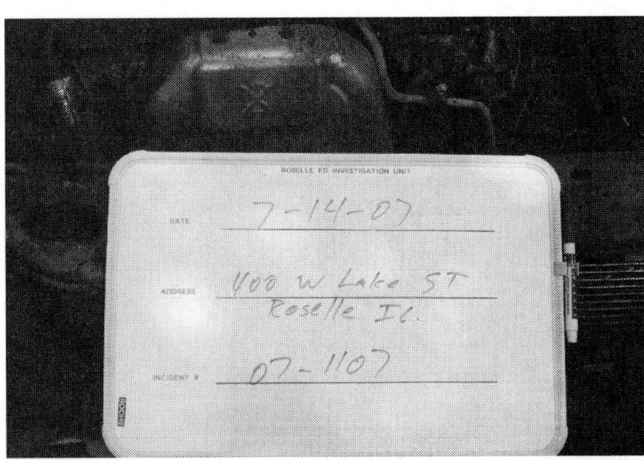

FIGURE 13–19 Case identifier. *Source:* Chester Kraus, Roselle, Illinois, Fire Department.

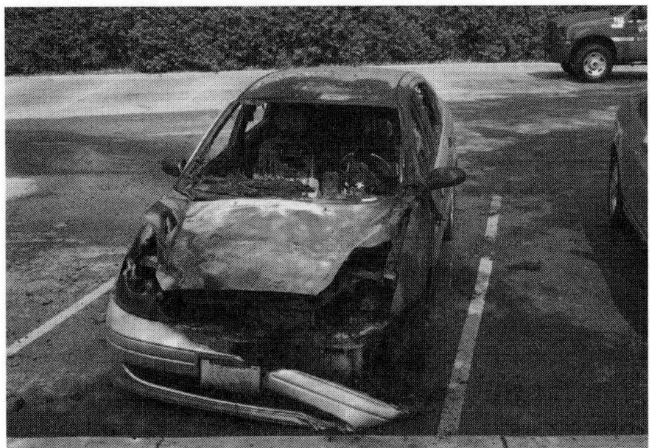

FIGURE 13–20 Overall image of front side of vehicle. *Source:* Chester Kraus, Roselle, Illinois, Fire Department.

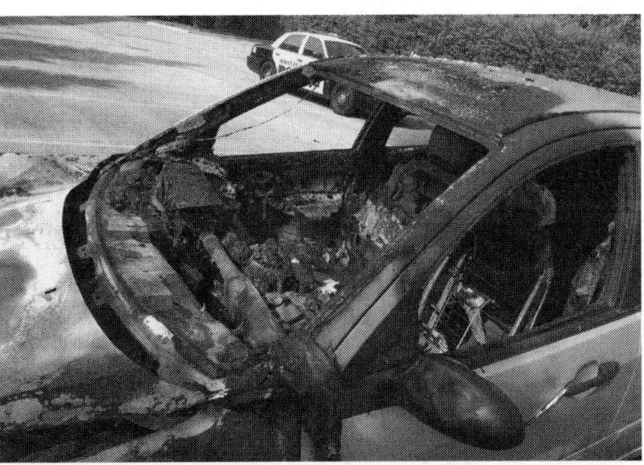

FIGURE 13–21 Mid-range photograph of area of damage. *Source:* Chester Kraus, Roselle, Illinois, Fire Department.

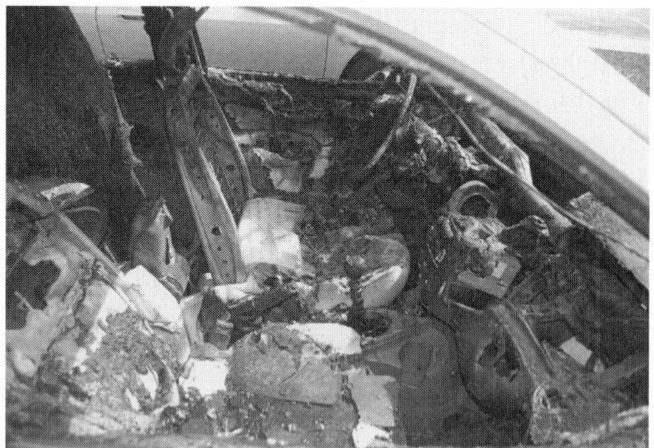

FIGURE 13–22 Mid-range photograph of area of damage from opposite angle. *Source:* Chester Kraus, Roselle, Illinois, Fire Department.

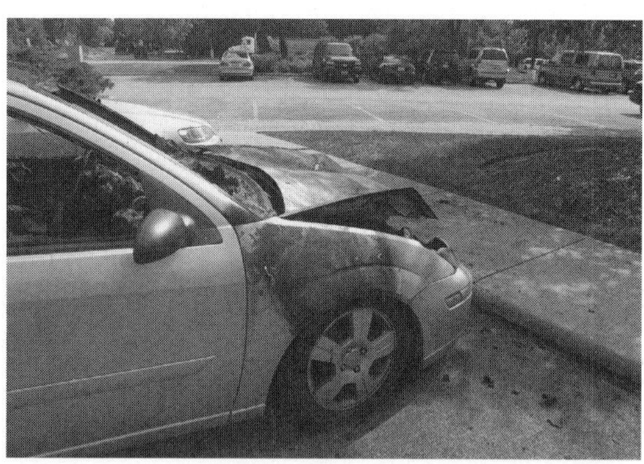

FIGURE 13–23 Mid-range photograph of fire pattern. *Source:* Chester Kraus, Roselle, Illinois, Fire Department.

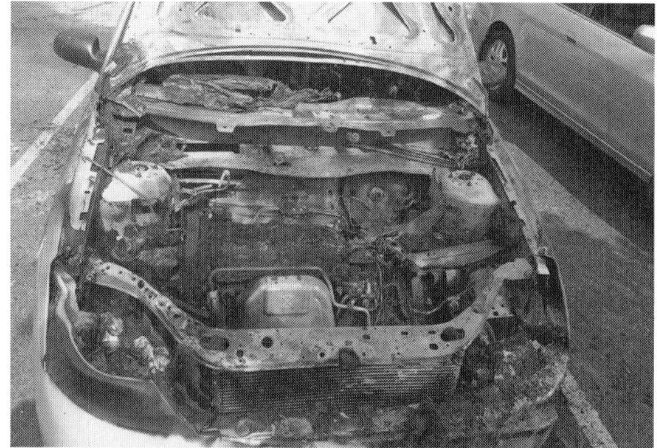

FIGURE 13–24 Burned-out engine compartment. *Source:* Chester Kraus, Roselle, Illinois, Fire Department.

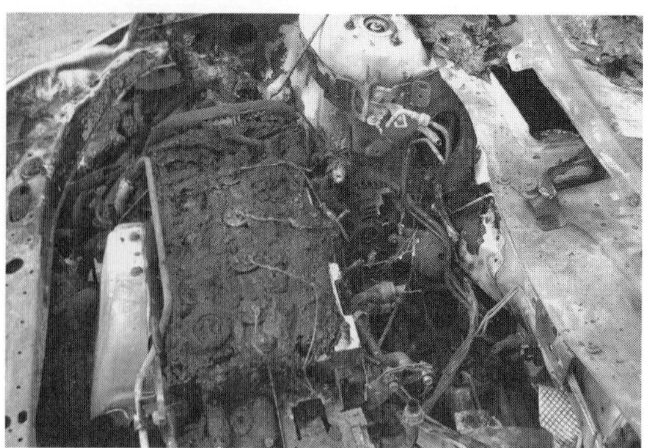

FIGURE 13–25 Burned-out engine com-partment from another angle. *Source:* Chester Kraus, Roselle, Illinois, Fire Department.

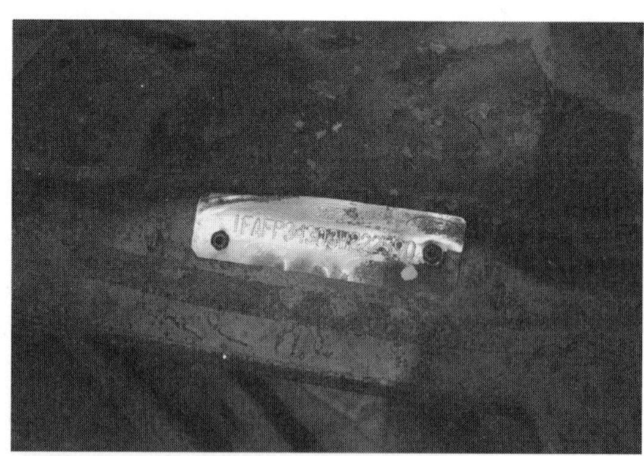

FIGURE 13–26 VIN after cleaning. *Source:* Chester Kraus, Roselle, Illinois, Fire Department.

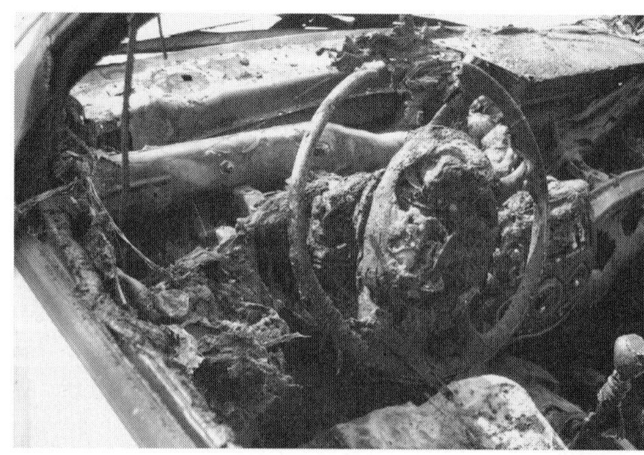

FIGURE 13–27 Study 2, Photo 10. *Source:* Chester Kraus, Roselle, Illinois, Fire Department.

CASE STUDY

TOWNHOUSE FIRE

This is another actual case investigated and documented by Chester Kraus, communications officer and fire investigator of the Roselle, Illinois, Fire Department.

In June 2007, an 85-year-old resident of a multifamily townhouse was at home but unaware of the fire. He was living by himself, asleep at around 7:00 p.m. His neighbor noticed smoke and called 911. The resident awoke and opened the front door while fire personnel were in the process of forced entry. The occupant's home was equipped with smoke detectors, but because the batteries were not connected properly they

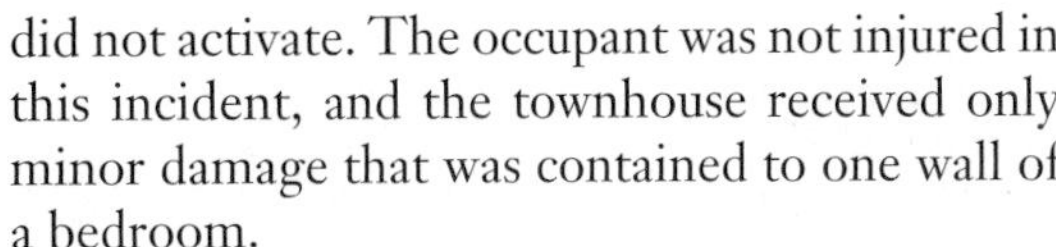

did not activate. The occupant was not injured in this incident, and the townhouse received only minor damage that was contained to one wall of a bedroom.

To accurately tell the story of this incident, 182 photos were exposed, and 18 of them are included here as Figs. 13–28 through 13–45:

- All projects documented by the Roselle Fire Department include a case identifier (see Fig. 13–29).
- Overall images of the outside of the townhouse were exposed to document the type and construction of the structure (see Fig. 13–30).
- Next, mid-range images were captured to lead the viewer to the area of origin (see Fig. 13–31).

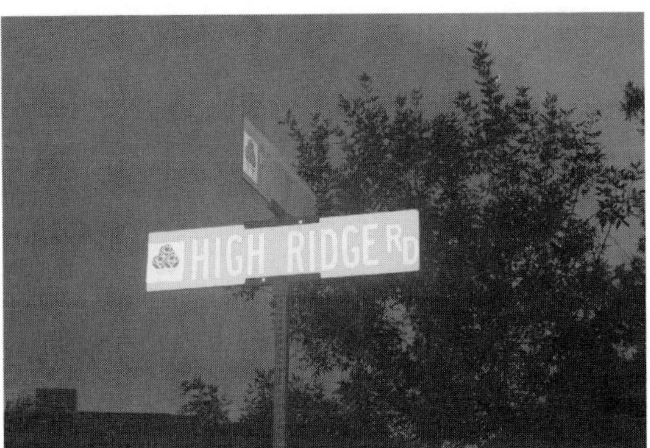

FIGURE 13–28 Street sign on outside corner nearest the structure. *Source:* Chester Kraus, Roselle, Illinois, Fire Department.

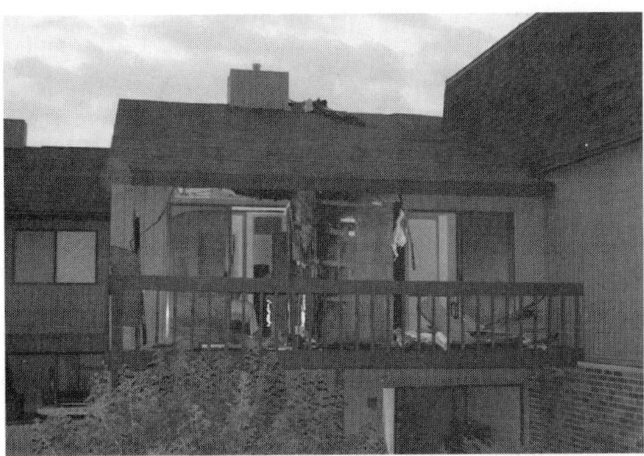

FIGURE 13–30 Overall image of the scene. *Source:* Chester Kraus, Roselle, Illinois, Fire Department.

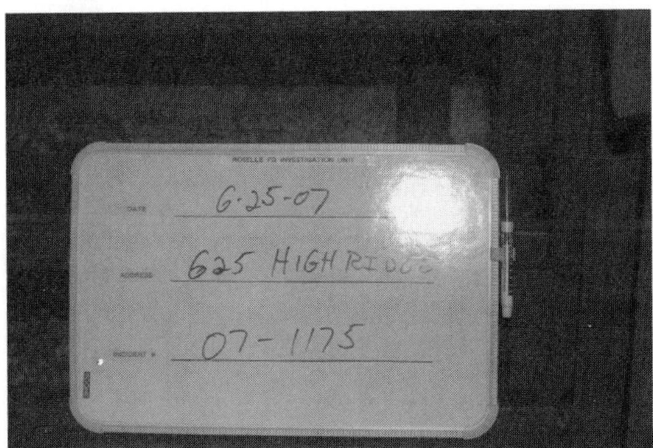

FIGURE 13–29 Case identifier. *Source:* Chester Kraus, Roselle, Illinois, Fire Department.

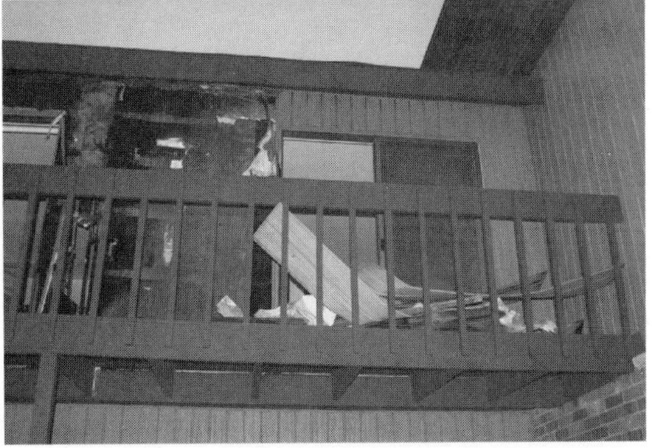

FIGURE 13–31 Mid-range image of the scene. *Source:* Chester Kraus, Roselle, Illinois, Fire Department.

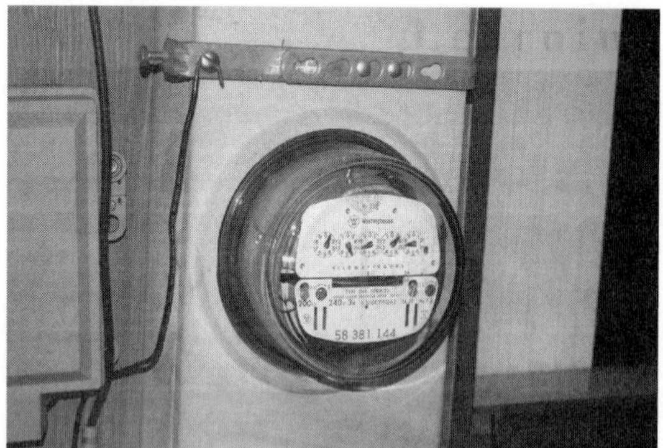

FIGURE 13–32 The electric meter inside the townhouse. *Source:* Chester Kraus, Roselle, Illinois, Fire Department.

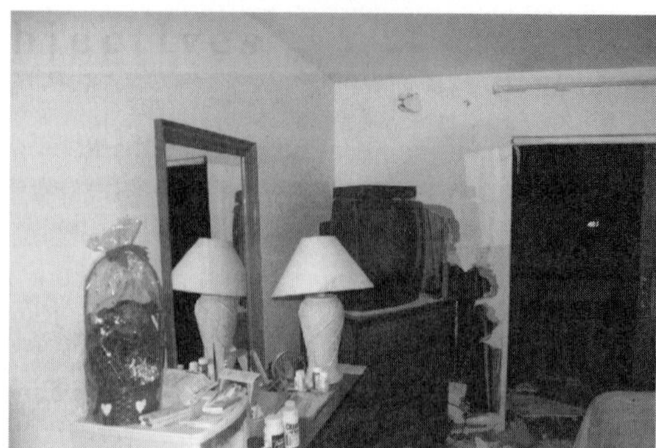

FIGURE 13–35 Overall view of interior of the townhouse bedroom. *Source:* Chester Kraus, Roselle, Illinois, Fire Department.

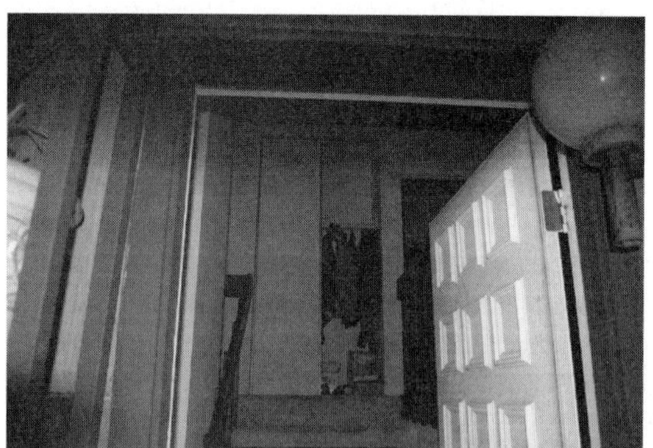

FIGURE 13–33 The front door of the townhouse. *Source:* Chester Kraus, Roselle, Illinois, Fire Department.

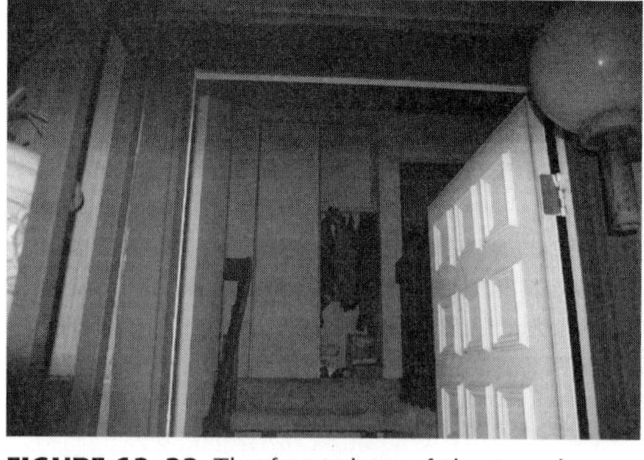

FIGURE 13–34 Circuit breaker panel in the townhouse. *Source:* Chester Kraus, Roselle, Illinois, Fire Department.

- SOP requires the documentation of all service meters (see Fig. 13–32).
- The photographic walk-through of the townhouse was begun at the front door (see Fig. 13–33). Images proceeded into the structure in a logical manner, always including a reference for point of view.
- After structural fires, it is always necessary to document the condition of the electrical circuit breaker or fuse panel (see Fig. 13–34).
- The bedroom, at the area of the origin, was documented with a series of images, starting with overall views (see Fig. 13–35).
- Mid-range photographs were taken to lead the viewer to the area of interest (see Fig. 13–36).The origin of the fire appeared to be in the area of an electrical box, located in the bedroom wall (see Figs. 13–37 and 13–38).
- Close-up images of the debris in the wall near the electrical box are important for the analysis of the incident (see Fig. 13–39).
- Close-up images were exposed of all cord ends plugged into the subject electrical outlet at the time of the fire (see Fig. 13–40).
- After removal of the wallboard in the area of the electrical box, mid-range and close-up images were exposed to document the extent of the charred materials (see Figs. 13–41 and 13–42).

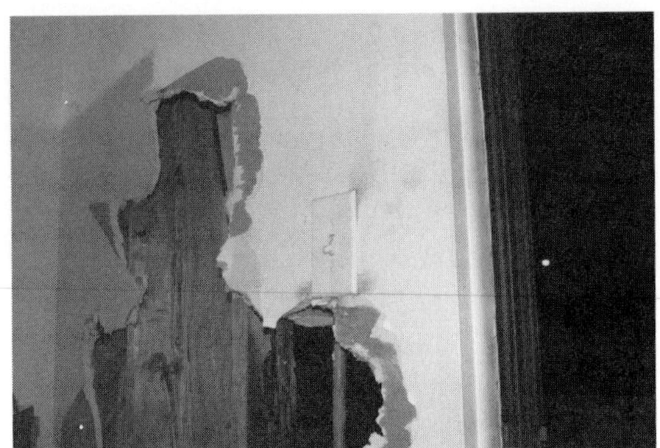

FIGURE 13–36 Mid-range view of area of origin. *Source:* Chester Kraus, Roselle, Illinois, Fire Department.

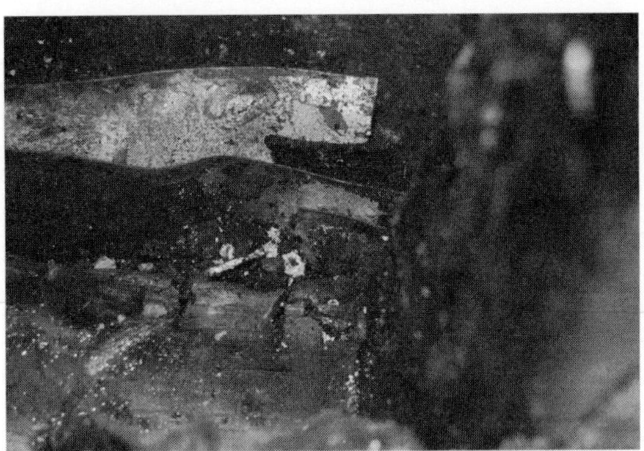

FIGURE 13–39 Debris inside the townhouse wall. *Source:* Chester Kraus, Roselle, Illinois, Fire Department.

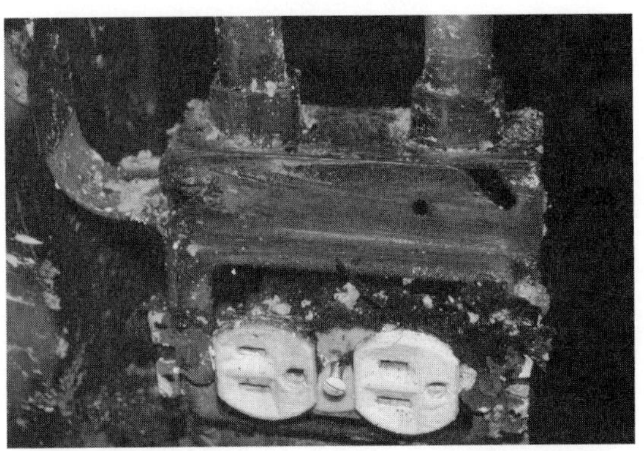

FIGURE 13–37 Duplex receptacle and electrical box in the townhouse. *Source:* Chester Kraus, Roselle, Illinois, Fire Department.

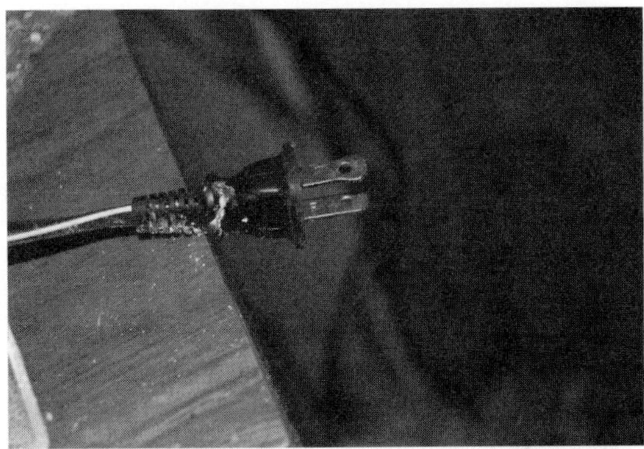

FIGURE 13–40 The condition and type of cord end plugged into the townhouse electrical box. *Source:* Chester Kraus, Roselle, Illinois, Fire Department.

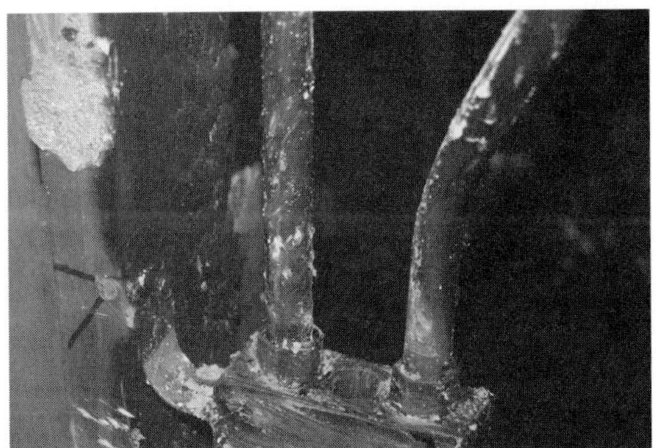

FIGURE 13–38 Another view of the townhouse's electrical box. *Source:* Chester Kraus, Roselle, Illinois, Fire Department.

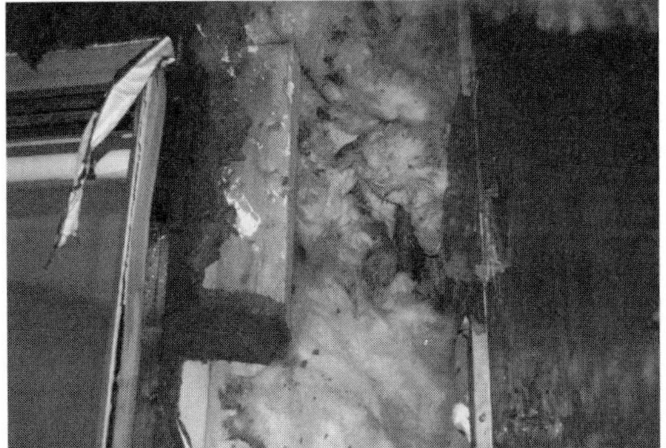

FIGURE 13–41 Mid-range view after wallboard removal. *Source:* Chester Kraus, Roselle, Illinois, Fire Department.

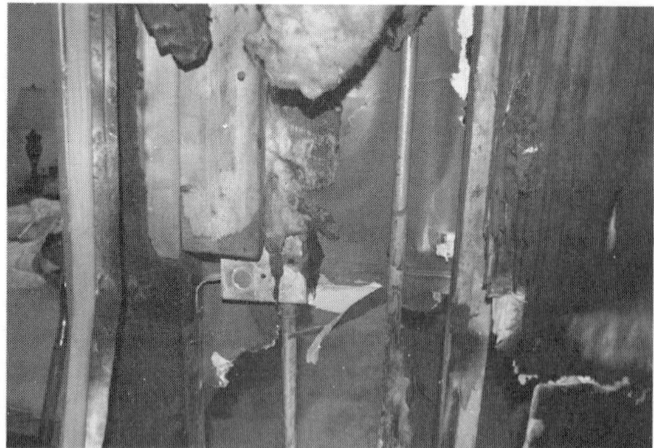

FIGURE 13–42 Mid-range view after wallboard removal. *Source:* Chester Kraus, Roselle, Illinois, Fire Department.

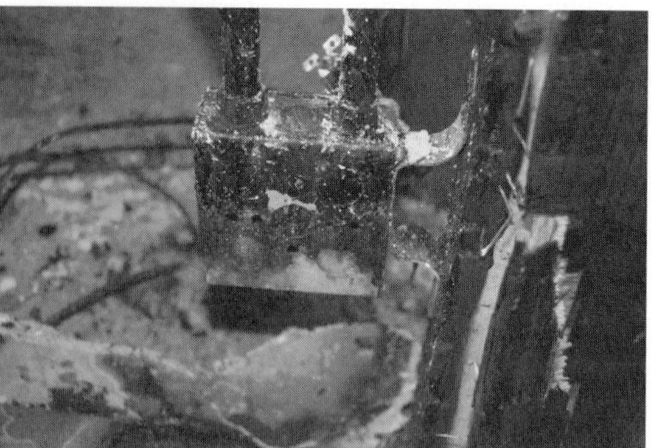

FIGURE 13–44 The back side of the electrical box displays representative fire patterns. *Source:* Chester Kraus, Roselle, Illinois, Fire Department.

- The effect of the fire on the wall studs resembles alligator skin and is called *alligatoring*; it will supply information to the investigator about the severity of the fire and the direction of spread (see Fig. 13–43).
- The reverse side of the electrical box at the origin of the fire displays representative fire patterns (see Fig. 13–44).
- Overall, mid-range, and close-up images were exposed of the television that was plugged into the electrical box at the time of the fire (see Fig. 13–45).

The cause of the fire is suspected to be electrical, pending an electrical engineer's evaluation.

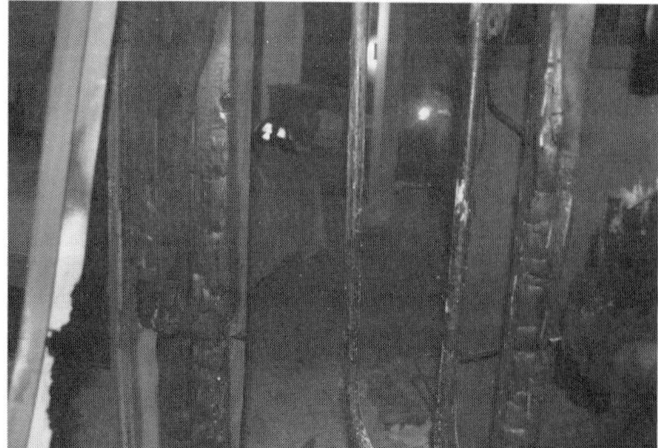

FIGURE 13–43 Charred studs in the townhouse wall. *Source:* Chester Kraus, Roselle, Illinois, Fire Department.

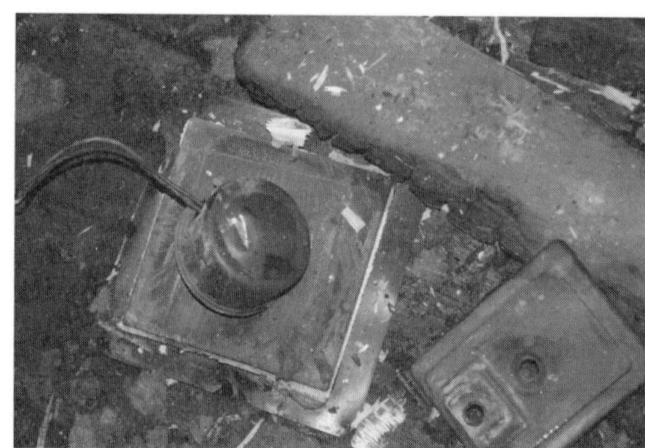

FIGURE 13–45 Back of burned television. *Source:* Chester Kraus, Roselle, Illinois, Fire Department.

KEY TERMS

origin and cause investigation, (p. 368)
arson, (p. 368)
chain of custody, (p. 371)
photomontage, (p. 377)
digital stitching, (p. 377)
Global Positioning System, (p. 379)
manner of death, (p. 381)
forensic pathologist, (p. 381)
autopsy, (p. 381)
accidental death, (p. 382)
homicide, (p. 382)
murder, (p. 382)
suicide, (p. 382)
cause of death, (p. 382)
mechanism of death, (p. 382)
triangulation, (p. 384)
forensic archaeology (p. 384)
Interpol, (p. 385)
intra-oral, (p. 387)
medicolegal, (p. 388)

EXERCISES

1. Research the scientific literature regarding the use of alternative lighting for the documentation of accelerants at fire scenes. Develop a protocol for the use of alternative lighting for the documentation of accelerants at the fire scene.
2. Perform a documentation of a vehicle as if it had been burned by a fire. Assume it is still in the location where it burned. Write a concise report to accompany the photographs to explain the content of the images.
3. Perform a documentation of a room in a house, at night, as if the room had been damaged by a fire. Work in a systematic manner, starting with the outside of the house and finishing with the area of possible origin. Overcome each problem as it is encountered. Select the proper equipment for each aspect of the project. Write a concise report to accompany the photographs and explain the content of the images.
4. Perform a documentation of an outdoor fire, at night. Work in a systematic and logical manner, starting with a reference for the location of the fire and finishing with the area of possible origin. Overcome each problem as it is encountered. Select the proper equipment for each aspect of the project. Write a concise report to accompany the photographs to explain the content of the images.
5. Find and interview a local fireperson who performs investigations. Use a set of prepared questions regarding his or her methods of documentation. What kind of equipment does he or she use and why? Does his or her department have an accepted SOP or not, and why or why not?
6. Critique the documentation contained in the vehicle fire case study. What images would you add?
7. Critique the documentation contained in the townhouse fire case study. What images would you add?

APPENDIX 13.1

Chain of Custody Receipt

This Chain of Custody Receipt is an example of a form that is simple and effective. Use it as a model to construct a similar form that will suit your organization.

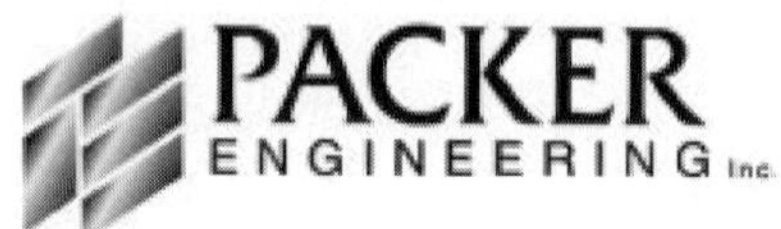

ARTIFACT / CUSTODY RECEIPT

Project No.: ____________ Date: ____________

Project Name: ____________

Received By Packer Engineering, Inc.:

Artifact Type: ____ Subject ____ Exemplar

Description:

Received By:

Packer Engineering, Inc.

____

____
By: (Signature)

____
Print Name

____
Date

Received From:

____
Company Name

____
By: (Signature)

____
Print Name

____
Title

____
Date

FIGURE A13.1–1 Exemplar artifact/custody receipt form for the documentation of chain of custody. *Source:* Sandy Weiss/Packer Engineering.

APPENDIX 13.2

U.S. Department of Defense Forms Management Program

The U.S. Department of Defense (DOD) Forms Management Program (www.dtic.mil/whs/directives/infomgt/forms/formsprogram.htm) provides a number of public-use forms in Adobe Acrobat format. The program is intended to make important forms accessible to the public for enhanced capabilities in situations where victims have been injured or killed.

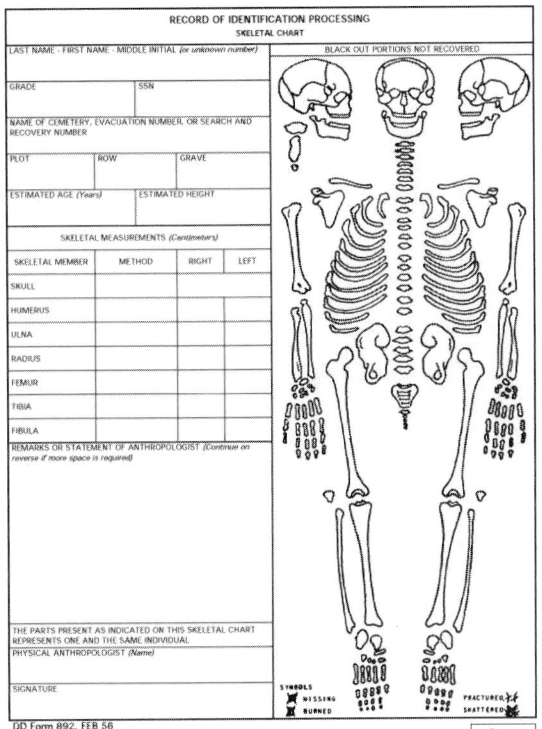

RECORD OF IDENTIFICATION PROCESSING
SKELETAL CHART

LAST NAME - FIRST NAME - MIDDLE INITIAL *(or unknown number)*

GRADE | SSN

NAME OF CEMETERY, EVACUATION NUMBER, OR SEARCH AND RECOVERY NUMBER

PLOT | ROW | GRAVE

ESTIMATED AGE *(Years)* | ESTIMATED HEIGHT

SKELETAL MEASUREMENTS *(Centimeters)*

SKELETAL MEMBER	METHOD	RIGHT	LEFT
SKULL			
HUMERUS			
ULNA			
RADIUS			
FEMUR			
TIBIA			
FIBULA			

REMARKS OR STATEMENT OF ANTHROPOLOGIST *(Continue on reverse if more space is required)*

THE PARTS PRESENT AS INDICATED ON THIS SKELETAL CHART REPRESENTS ONE AND THE SAME INDIVIDUAL

PHYSICAL ANTHROPOLOGIST *(Name)*

SIGNATURE

BLACK OUT PORTIONS NOT RECOVERED

SYMBOLS
MISSING
BURNED
FRACTURED
SHATTERED

DD Form 892, FEB 56

FIGURE A13.2–1 An exemplar DoD form for skeletal documentation, available from the DoD Forms Program. *Source:* Department of Defense Public-Use Forms Program.

APPENDIX 13.3

Documentation Forms for Injuries in the Field or Lab

Making custom forms is highly recommended for special needs. They save time when sketching in the field. Figure A13.3–1 illustrates a custom-made injury documentation form.

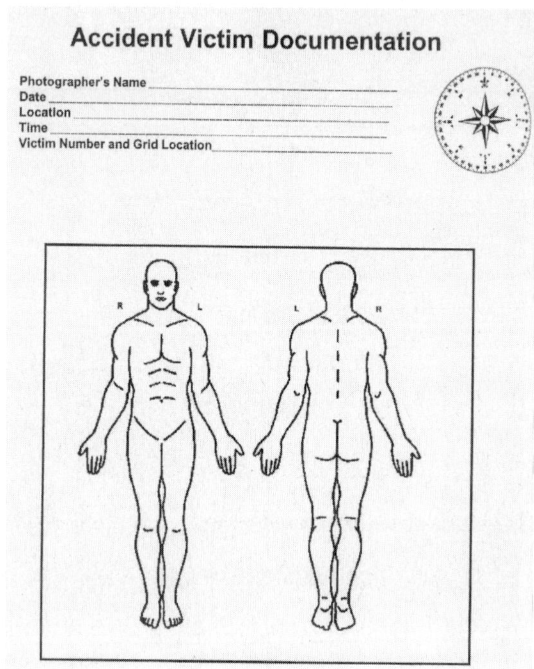

Accident Victim Documentation

Photographer's Name __________
Date __________
Location __________
Time __________
Victim Number and Grid Location __________

FIGURE A13.3–1 A custom-made injury documentation form. *Source:* Sandy Weiss/Packer Engineering.

Chapter 14

Photographing Accident Scenes and Evidence

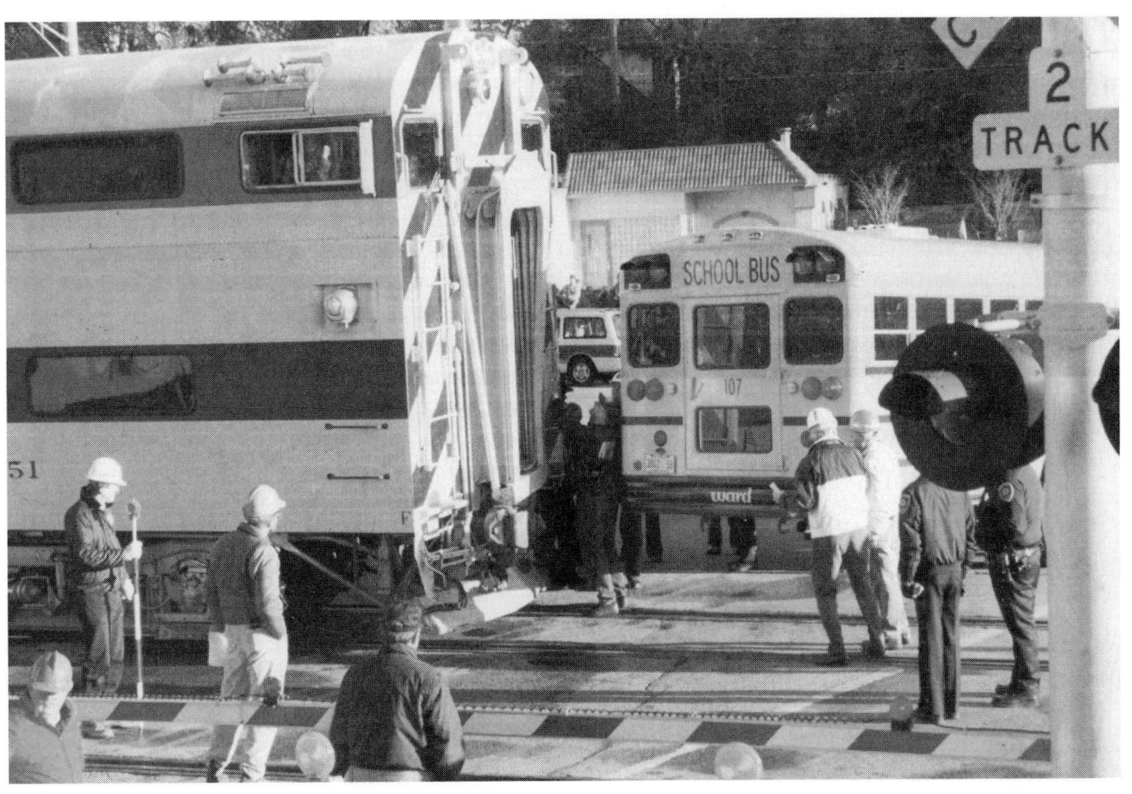

Learning Objectives

AFTER STUDYING THIS CHAPTER, YOU SHOULD BE ABLE TO:

1. Understand the common risk factors contributing to personal injury accidents
2. Select the equipment necessary for photographic projects of accident scenes and evidence
3. Photograph the effects of mass disasters
4. Know which government agencies assist with mass disaster projects
5. Understand and use the standards and protocols available for dealing with accidents and mass disasters
6. Know which personal protection equipment (PPE) is appropriate for various levels of Haz-Mat exposure
7. Properly protect photographic equipment from various levels of Haz-Mat exposure
8. Adhere to the methods for photographic documentation of accident scenes of different sizes and in any environment
9. Properly collect and label data and evidence for the forensic investigation of accidents and disasters

PREPARING TO PHOTOGRAPH ACCIDENT SCENES AND EVIDENCE

Photographic documentation of accident scenes, victims, and peripheral evidence is within the normal scope of activities of the forensic photographer. Mental and physical preparations should be considered and made before going to a scene. The following lists include examples of the information that must be gathered and the types of questions that must be answered. Many processes should be undertaken and completed as an accident investigation, inspection, or reconstruction project begins. Be familiar with the person or agency commissioning the assignment. They may supply specific preferences for SOPs. Open lines of communication are essential.

Scope of Use for the Photographs

- What is the ultimate purpose of the images?
- Who will use the images?
- Are any uses of the images permitted or restricted?
- How will the images be archived?
- Who will have access to the images?
- What types of presentations will the images be used to create?

Delivery and Communication

- What is the timetable for each stage of the project?
- When and where will meetings take place?
- Will e-mail, postal mail, or fax be used to deliver images?

Status of Images

- In what form are images to be delivered?
- Does the photographer retain the original media?
- What material is to be delivered to the client?

The Scene

- Where will you be photographing?
- How is the scene described?

- Can you do a walk-through?
- What kinds of sketches (with necessary references) can you provide?
- What progress is expected?
  - When are photographs due?
  - What is the method of delivery?
- What are your goals?
  - What areas need to be photographed?
  - How many photographs must be exposed?
  - What views and angles must be exposed?
  - Where will the photographs be exposed?
- What details are relevant to this shoot?
  - Light sources?
  - Personal protective equipment?
  - Communications?
  - Food and water?
  - Facilities?
  - Backups?

ISSUES RELATED TO THE SCENE

Communication is essential for describing and resolving questions and problems before they become issues. The photographer must know how to contact various personnel who are involved in the investigation:

- Client or supervisor
- Security personnel
- Law enforcement
- Maintenance
- Electric service
- Natural or bottled gas service
- Water service
- Computer operator

It is also necessary for you to know how to access the site:

- Has access been granted to the site?
- Is parking available?
- Is access (in and out) available after hours?
- Do you need keys or security codes?
- Are the elevators working?
- Are windows and blinds adjustable?

The time of year and the weather will also have bearing on your photography:

- Is natural light available, and what is the angle of the sun?
- In which direction is the scene oriented?
- Does sunlight fall on the façade?

Consider the season, too. Do any of the following impact the scene?

- Foliage
- Snow
- Rain
- Mud

Even the day of the week can have impact on your work:

- Are moving automobiles or parked cars present?
- Are pedestrians, office workers, service providers, or delivery personnel present?

Consider the time of day and how it relates to the lighting of the scene:

- Is the scene interior, exterior, or both?
- Is the natural light sufficient?
- Can access to circuit breakers or computer controlled lighting be arranged?
- Is the lighting mixed?
  - What is the color temperature of light sources?
  - Are the light sources in working order?
  - Are spares available?
- Will you be working at night?

PERSONAL INJURY: SLIPS, TRIPS, AND FALLS

Children and adults have accidents involving personal injuries in every environment, season, and geographical location. Some accidents involve the documentation of injuries (see Chapter 16), and most require documentation of the scene.

Many causal factors contribute to personal injuries. It may be necessary to photograph the location and any object that obstructs a floor, makes a dip in concrete, or causes a person to lose traction, fall, and be injured. It is up to an expert to decide which factors are pertinent to an incident. The scene is always an area of prime interest.

The fact that an injured party was intoxicated, nearsighted, preoccupied, or known to be clumsy could be a factor argued in court. The physical condition and mental competence of the injured party are not issues during documentation, unless a particular tie exists between the condition and the incident.

If a person is intoxicated and chokes on something that was accidentally included in a bottle of liquor, the intoxication and the liquor are relevant factors. If a person is intoxicated and trips on a walkway and breaks a leg, the intoxication is not a factor affecting the technique used to document the walkway. No matter what the conditions leading to the incident, photographic documentation of personal-injury accident scenes should always be undertaken following the SOP adopted by the photographer or the agency of employ.

If the accident is vision related, the scene may require the following two forms of documentation:

1. Photographs exposed in lighting and physical conditions to recreate the scene at the time of the incident
2. Photographs exposed in sufficient lighting to properly and sufficiently document the physical attributes of the scene that constitute the suspected cause

If the accident is not vision-related, only the full-light documentation is necessary.

Always undertake the documentation of a scene in a logical and systematic manner, telling the whole story of the incident from the time the injured party entered the area until the subject incident occurred. Include images exposed from the viewpoints of witnesses and exposed from witness eye height. Be sure to include references to place the scene into the world. Perform, record, and document, all pertinent measurements. (If the intensity of lighting is a factor, refer to Chapter 11 regarding how to accurately create documentary photographs of the scene in low light.)

The following lists are representative issues that may be factors in an incident. Consult with the client or supervisor for instructions, and read any available deposition testimony or reports regarding the scene and incident.

Slips

Floor surfaces may be slippery when wet. Shoes may supply inadequate traction for the situation and increase the risk of a mishap. The following are some of the common risk factors involved in slips:

- Floor surface friction levels
- Variation in friction level between adjacent areas
- Inappropriate or movable carpeting or rugs
- Inclined surfaces
- Low-friction footwear or uneven wear of soles or heels

Published standards provide a reference for determining acceptable levels of friction. Levels are determined through the use of specially designed meters.

Trips

Surface variations or obstructions may occur unexpectedly. Excessive friction between shoes and floor surfaces also increase the risk of trips. Risk factors include the following:

- Improper floor maintenance
- Variation in floor surface levels
- Ground-level obstructions
- Improperly fitting clothing or footwear
- Improper floor design
- Low, unexpected, or hidden steps
- Loose rugs, mats, and carpeting
- Insufficient lighting

Falls

Falls occur on level flooring or from uneven heights. The injured party experiences low stability, concentration, or balance. Factors that may result in a fall include the following:

- Unstable surfaces
- Structural collapse
- Gaps between surfaces
- Absence of suitable safety equipment, including railings
- Inadequate traction
- Structural design
- Improperly fitting clothing or footwear

TIP:

If necessary, recruit people to use as exemplar subjects during inspection and documentation. To provide an accurate sense of scale, exemplar subjects must be similar in stature to the injured party and must be photographed at the location of the incident, within safety limitations.

VEHICULAR ACCIDENT SCENE PHOTOGRAPHY

Law enforcement and other emergency personnel require photographs of vehicular accident scenes and vehicles (see Fig. 14–1). If the accident occurred on a public roadway, it will always be necessary to work at increased speed to remove the evidence and reopen the roadway to traffic. Other emergency personnel may be at the scene, in the way, or obscuring the evidence. At most accident scenes, the roadway must be examined and documented quickly. Measurements may be taken at a later time, unless fragile evidence will be obliterated through use. At fatal accidents in many states, the roadway may be closed for an extended period.

If a public roadway is photographed after it has reopened, only local law enforcement may divert traffic during the project. Time limitations will always be a factor in road closures.

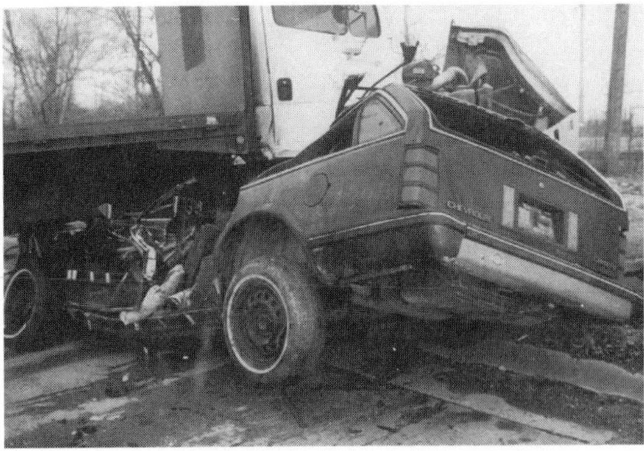

FIGURE 14–1 Vehicular accident scene. *Source:* Sandy Weiss/Packer Engineering.

Weather and Vehicular Accidents

Inclement weather conditions may contribute to the cause of an accident and be a problem during scene documentation. Nighttime is not a favorable time for outdoor photography. Skid marks and other evidence are often spread or scattered over a large area. The photographer must think and act quickly to accurately document all the necessary aspects of the scene. It is usually not possible to ask for a second chance if mistakes were made.

TIP:

If it is raining or snowing, photography should be accomplished by available light, or by using an EFU at an extremely oblique angle. Do not use direct flash as it will illuminate the drops or flakes in front of the camera and cause underexposure of the main subject.

Consult Chapter 9 for a review of painting with light. This procedure may be an option for extensive photography of nighttime scenes.

Go-Kit for Vehicular Accident Photography

Chapter 7 contains a comprehensive list of items to include in a vehicular accident go-kit. The basic items must include the following:

- Camera
- Extra batteries for everything you may use

- Media
- Lens(es)
- Tripod
- Shutter release
- Reliable and large EFU
- References
  - Cones
  - Evidence flags and tags
  - Scales
- Flashlight
- Writing materials
- Tools for communication

References should include scales for macrophotography and scales for measurement of the scene. Retain an assortment of long tape measures, from 25-foot lengths to walking **measuring wheels** (see Fig. 14–2). Certification of the scales is not necessary if they are available for inspection if questioned.

If equipment is shared person to person, it is especially critical to make certain that the go-kit is complete, accessible, clean, and ready to go at all times. Remember to charge sufficient batteries and keep enough empty media on hand for large assignments. If the environment is severe, remember to protect the equipment from the elements for optimum performance.

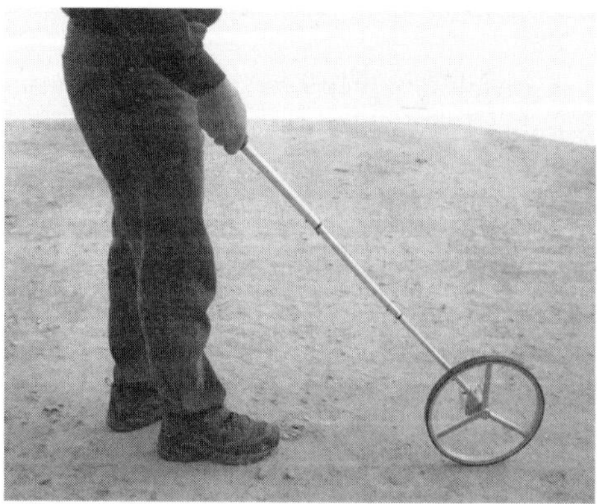

FIGURE 14–2 A measuring wheel. *Source:* Sandy Weiss/Packer Engineering.

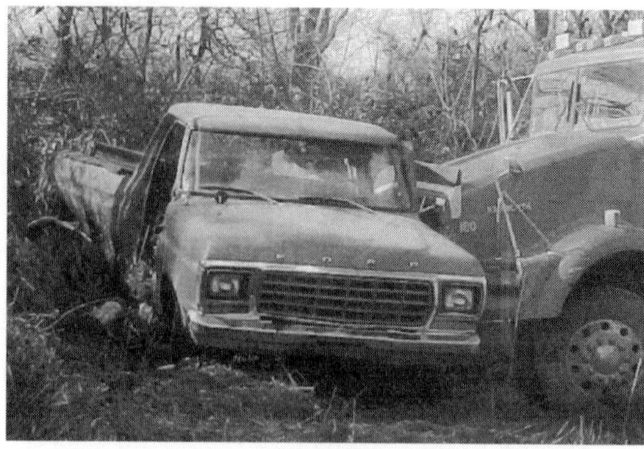

FIGURE 14–3 Documentation of a vehicle accident involving two trucks. *Source:* Sandy Weiss/Packer Engineering.

Standard Operating Procedures at the Scene

RULE:

Always complete the documentation of victims first.

After all victims are properly treated, begin your photographic documentation of the scene, including the following:

- Final positions of the vehicle(s) or other accident related equipment (see Fig. 14–3
- Landmarks to place the scene into the larger context
- Roadway, shoulder, skid marks (see Fig. 14–4)

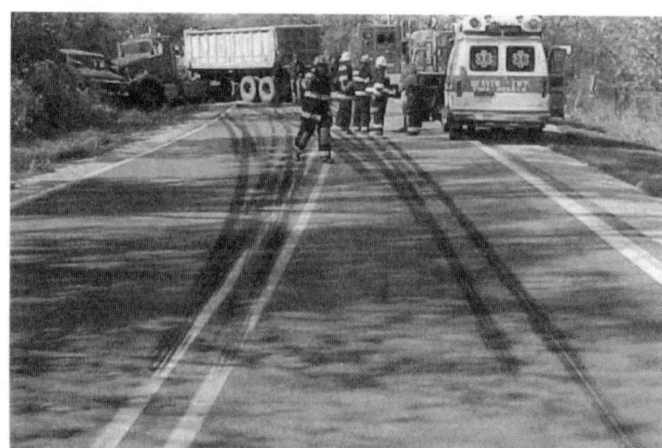

FIGURE 14–4 Documentation of skid marks at a vehicle accident. *Source:* Sandy Weiss/Packer Engineering.

- Debris in situ
- Necessary measurements

Photographing Vehicles at the Scene

The following steps are a guide to photographing vehicle at the scene:

- ID vehicle(s) photographically (plates, VIN).
- Photograph damages to vehicle.
  - Use appropriate scales.
  - Exposes images of all damages so that at least three distinct images are available.
  - Do not zoom the lens.
  - Use available structure(s) for high vantage points.
- Document vehicle interior(s).
- Expose images from the point of view of witnesses.

In multiple vehicle accidents, one vehicle may obstruct the view of another. Expose images from various heights and angles to capture the greatest detail. *Never* climb on top of accident vehicles.

Photograph skid marks in the direction of travel, as well as in the opposite direction. Capturing extra detail of the marks will aid in the accurate calculation of pre-crash speed. An excellent perspective on skid marks can be exposed by photographing them from the top of emergency vehicles that are conveniently placed and accessible at the time.

Reconstruction of Vehicular Accidents

Reconstructions are deliberate re-creations of crimes or accidents. The events are used by law enforcement and other investigators to demonstrate a catastrophic event under controlled conditions. Documentation of a reconstruction is often used in court to illustrate the sequence of events to the judge and jury. Accidents may be replayed in slow motion or stopped motion to analyze critical moments.

When it is necessary or advantageous to reconstruct a vehicular accident, during preparations pay close attention to accurate detail. Reconstructions are expensive and time consuming, and it is never a good idea to go through the process more than once. Use the actual scene photographs to extract data. Plan the reconstruction to represent the subject accident and tell an accurate and complete story. Work as closely as possible to re-create the following attributes:

- The same day of the year
- The same weather conditions
- The same specifics of the subject vehicles
  - Make
  - Model
  - Year
  - VIN
  - Condition
    - Windshield
    - Headlights
- Placement of vehicles to coincide with the accident report and photographs

> **TIP:**
>
> Expose images of the reconstructed accident and scene from the eye height at the time of the accident of the person whose vision is being demonstrated.

Vehicle Documentation Sequence

Figures 14–5 through 14–13 represent a logical and systematic sequence for the documentation of a vehicle. In every case of evidence documentation, either turn the subject clockwise or walk around the subject counterclockwise to capture the consecutive images from a clockwise orientation (see Figs. 14–5 to 14–13). Before changing the point of view, complete all the clock angles using the same lens focal length and camera-to-subject distance. It is best not to refocus the lens. If the sun is being used for illumination, it may be necessary to change the exposure in outdoor sequences, depending on the angle of the sun.

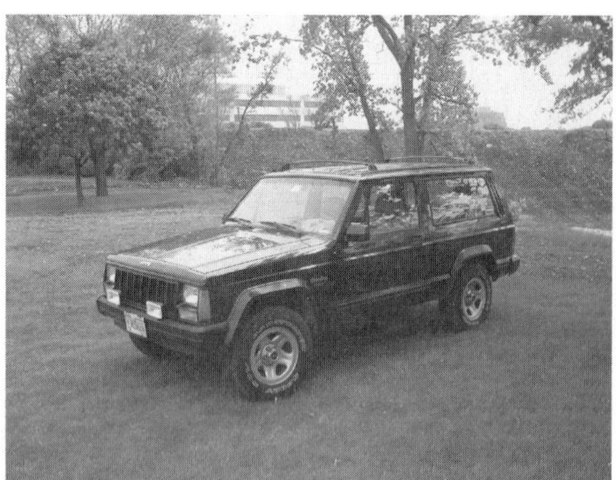

FIGURE 14–5 First image in an exemplar vehicle sequence. *Source:* Sandy Weiss/Packer Engineering.

> **TIP:**
>
> Capture an image of a color reference in at least one of the photographs in the sequence for comparison to the final displays.

Start the documentation sequence with an image that identifies the vehicle and captures the license plate if one is present (see Fig. 14–5). The same view also provides a reasonable view of the driver's compartment from the outside.

If the photographer walks around the vehicle in a counterclockwise direction to expose the images, the vehicle will appear to revolve in a clockwise direction (see Fig. 14–6)

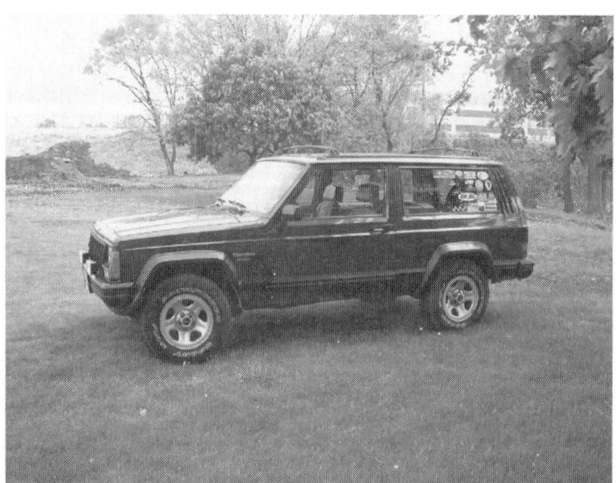

FIGURE 14–6 Second image in an exemplar vehicle sequence. *Source:* Sandy Weiss/ PackerEngineering.

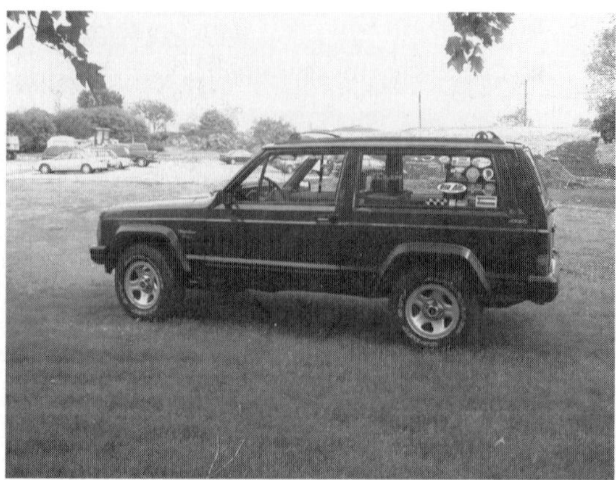

FIGURE 14–7 View of the driver's side in an exemplar vehicle sequence. *Source:* Sandy Weiss/Packer Engineering.

Images should be exposed of each corner and each face of the vehicle. (see Fig. 14–7) If the background is excessively bright, it may be necessary to overexpose the image to maintain the proper exposure of the vehicle.

Maintain the same camera-to-subject distance for each of the overall walkaround images (see Fig. 14–8).

Be certain the license number is legible in the image if it is still attached to the vehicle (see Fig. 14–9).

Expose the same sequence of images of the passenger side as were done of the driver's side (see Fig. 14–10).

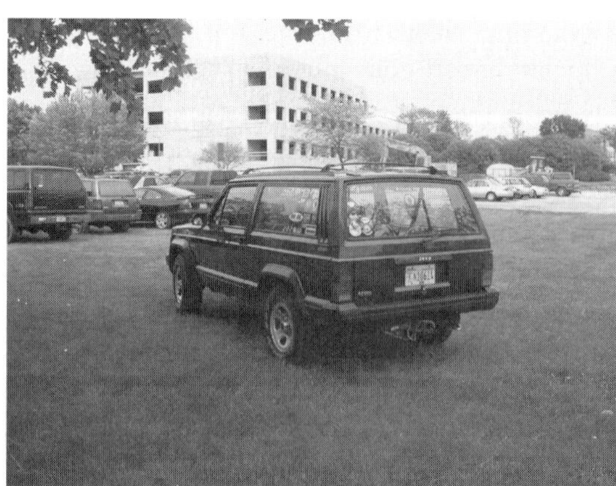

FIGURE 14–8 View of the driver's rear corner in an exemplar vehicle sequence. *Source:* Sandy Weiss/Packer Engineering.

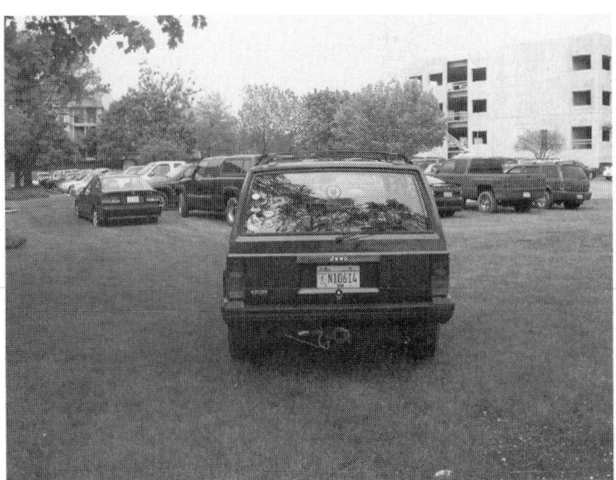

FIGURE 14–9 View of the rear face of the vehicle in an exemplar vehicle sequence. *Source:* Sandy Weiss/Packer Engineering.

Do not move closer to document damages until the overall image of the section of the vehicle has been captured (see Fig. 14–11). Capture a mid-range image before the close-up to reference locations.

If the background is excessively dark, it may be necessary to underexpose the image to maintain the proper exposure of the vehicle (see Fig. 14–12).

If the license number is still attached to the vehicle, ensure that it is legible in the image (see Fig. 14–13).

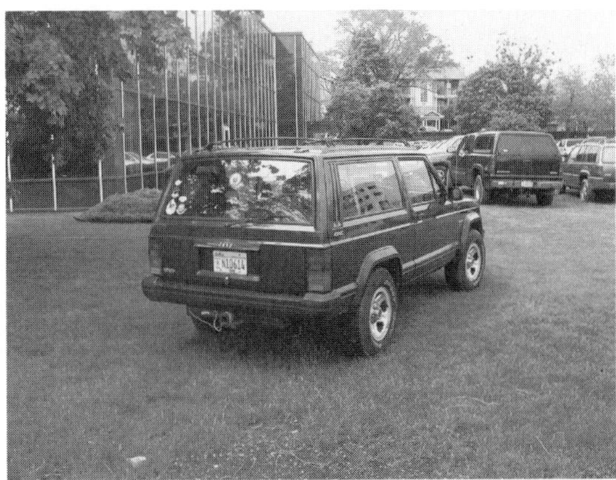

FIGURE 14–10 Start of the passenger side sequence in an exemplar vehicle sequence. *Source:* Sandy Weiss/Packer Engineering.

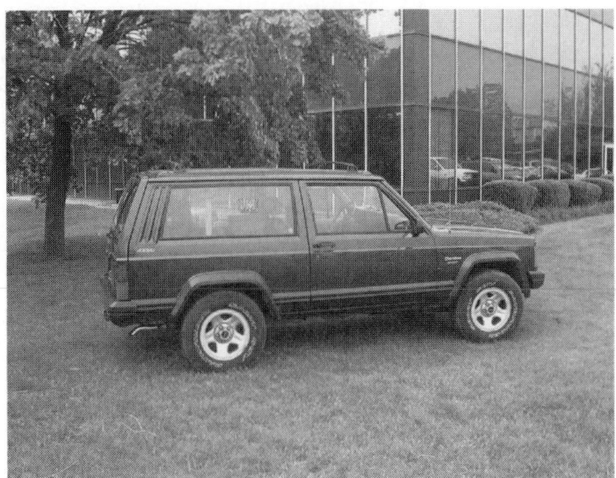

FIGURE 14–11 Passenger side in an exemplar vehicle sequence. *Source:* Sandy Weiss/Packer Engineering.

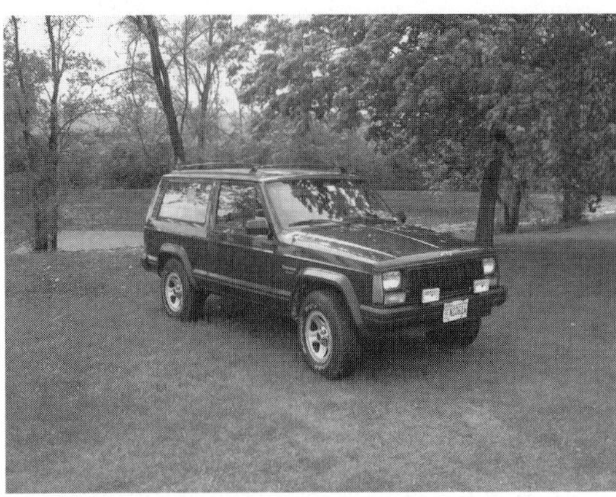

FIGURE 14–12 Passenger front corner in an exemplar vehicle sequence. *Source:* Sandy Weiss/Packer Engineering.

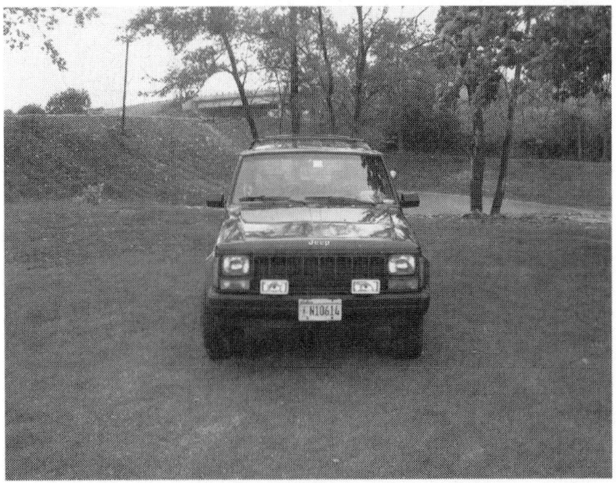

FIGURE 14–13 Front side in an exemplar vehicle sequence. *Source:* Sandy Weiss/Packer Engineering.

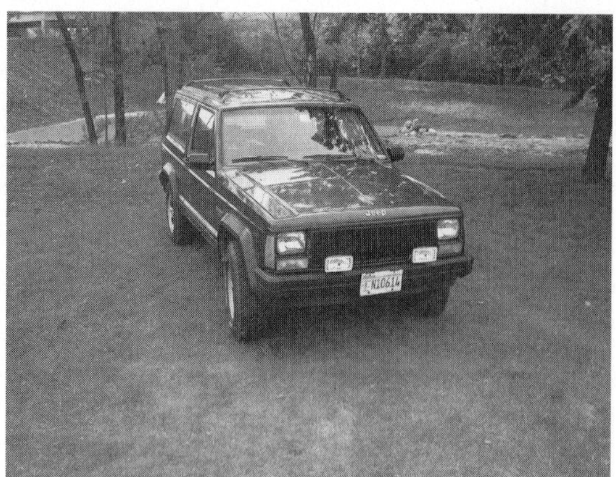

FIGURE 14–14 High-level view in an exemplar vehicle sequence. *Source:* Sandy Weiss/Packer Engineering.

The 360-degree coverage of the vehicle in Figures 14–5 through 14–13 shows each part of the vehicle in at least three distinct images. If a photogrammetric analysis is necessary for damage documentation and reconstruction, the photogrammetric project should yield excellent accuracy.

To further increase accuracy, include images from as high as the camera or photographer will allow (see Fig. 14–14).

To further increase accuracy, include images from as low as the camera or photographer will allow (see Fig. 14–15).

Extension jibs or **camera booms** (see Figs. 14–16 and 14–17) are useful accessories for high-aspect photography or for when the camera must be inserted into small openings or hazardous conditions. Consider the purchase or manufacture of a similar accessory.

Remember to include all appropriate scales and references for measurements, color, and location.

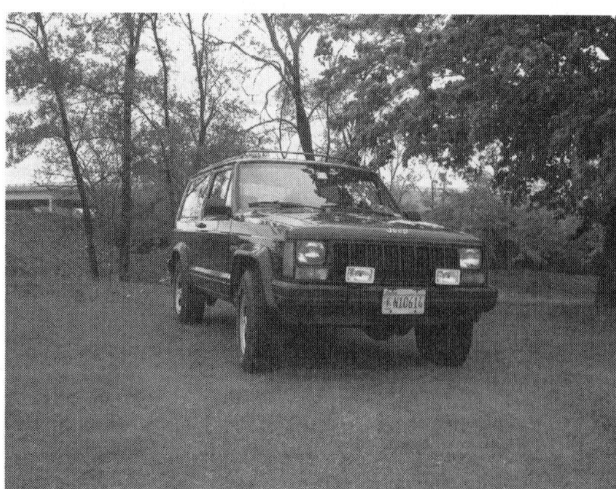

FIGURE 14–15 Low-level view in an exemplar vehicle sequence. *Source:* Sandy Weiss/Packer Engineering.

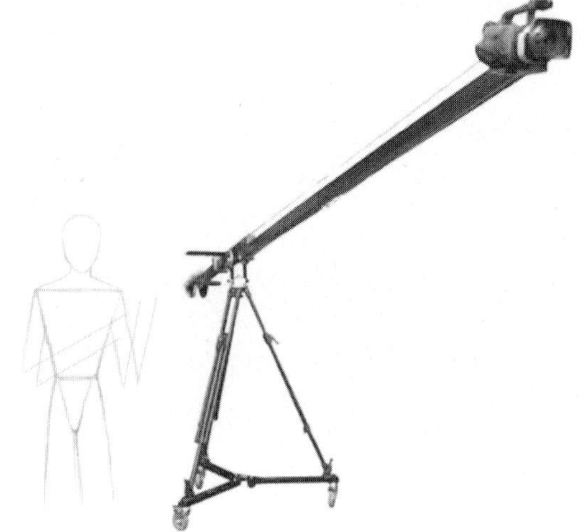

FIGURE 14–16 Camera jib arm for tripod mounting. *Source:* Sandy Weiss/Packer Engineering.

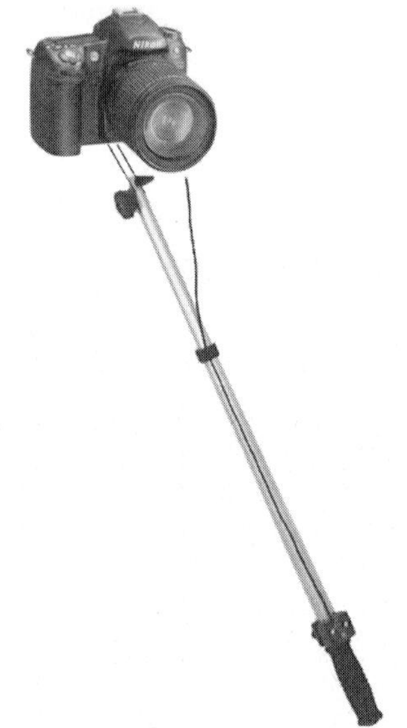

FIGURE 14–17 Camera boom for hand-holding. *Source:* Sandy Weiss/Packer Engineering.

When photographing vehicles after they have been moved from the scene, it is not necessary to document the new location or include references for determination of where the vehicle was photographed (see Figs. 14–18, 14–19 and 14–20).

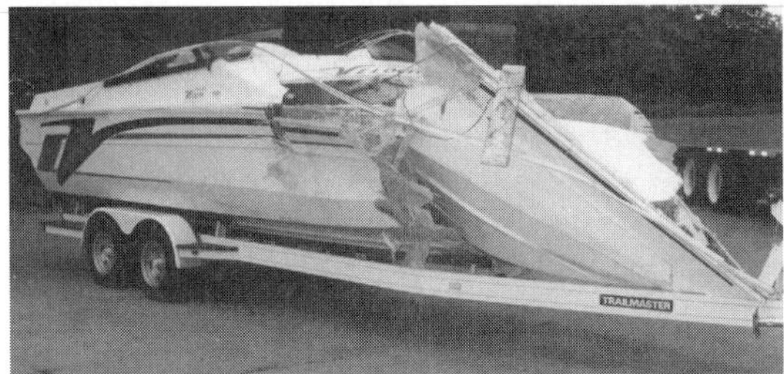

FIGURE 14–18 A fiberglass boat after collision. *Source:* Sandy Weiss/Packer Engineering.

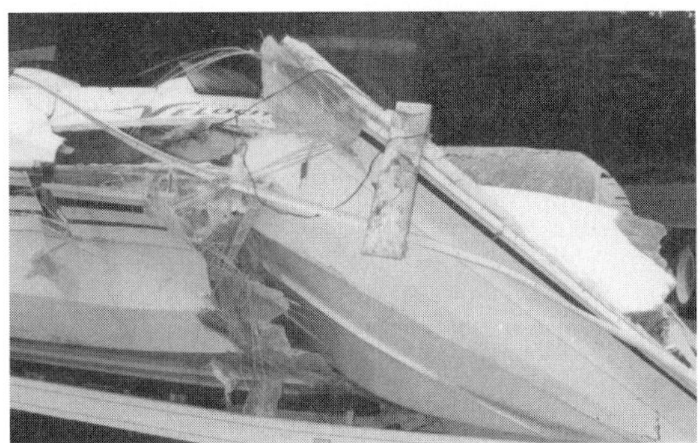

FIGURE 14–19 A mid-range view of a fiberglass boat after collision. *Source:* Sandy Weiss/Packer Engineering.

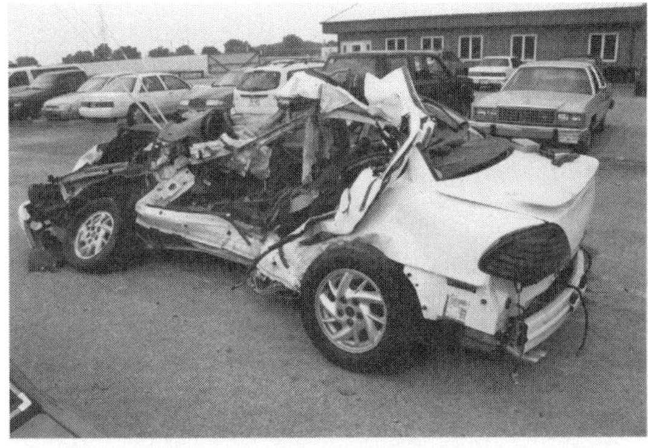

FIGURE 14–20 A relocated wreck. *Source:* Sandy Weiss/Packer Engineering.

MACROPHOTOGRAPHY AND VEHICLES

Areas of specific concentration for macrophotography of vehicles include the following:

- Marks from other vehicles
- Marks from obstructions
- Abrasions
- Transferred paint
- Lamp filaments
- Sources and evidence of injuries
- Tires
- Wheels
- Vehicle identification

Document all observations and testing procedures performed on subject vehicles (see Figs. 14–21 and 14–22).

MASS DISASTER PHOTOGRAPHY

Recognized and practical SOPs for rescuing people and recovering remains from mass disasters have been developed by forensic anthropologists, law enforcement agencies, firefighters, emergency response personnel, and public health officials, including the following events:

- Airplane crashes
- Structural collapses

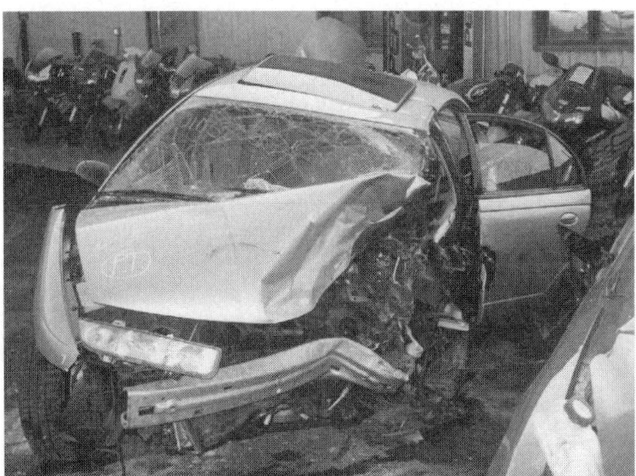

FIGURE 14–21 A wrecked car at a scrap yard. *Source:* Sandy Weiss/Packer Engineering.

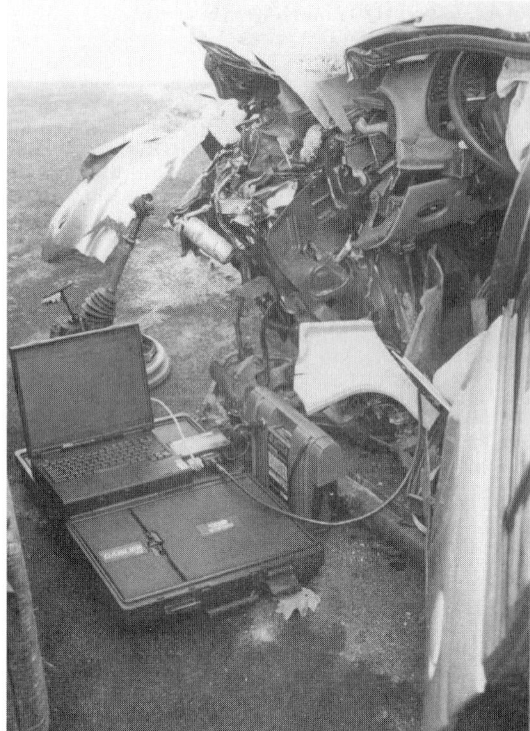

FIGURE 14–22 A vehicle computer being downloaded for analysis of pre-crash and crash data. *Source:* Sandy Weiss/ Packer Engineering.

- Fires
- Earthquakes
- Hurricanes

Scenes may include aspects of hazardous materials (**Haz-Mat**) or may be the result of terrorism or **weapons of mass destruction (WMD)**. In the event of a mass disaster, the recovery of living victims is undertaken first, before anything else is done. The next priority is the recovery of human remains. The final stage includes the observation, investigation, documentation, and recovery of accident-related evidence.

Disasters and mass disasters are classified as natural, transportation, or man-made:

Natural Disasters

- Flood
- Hurricane (see Fig. 14–23)
- Earthquake
- Tornado
- Fire
- Drought

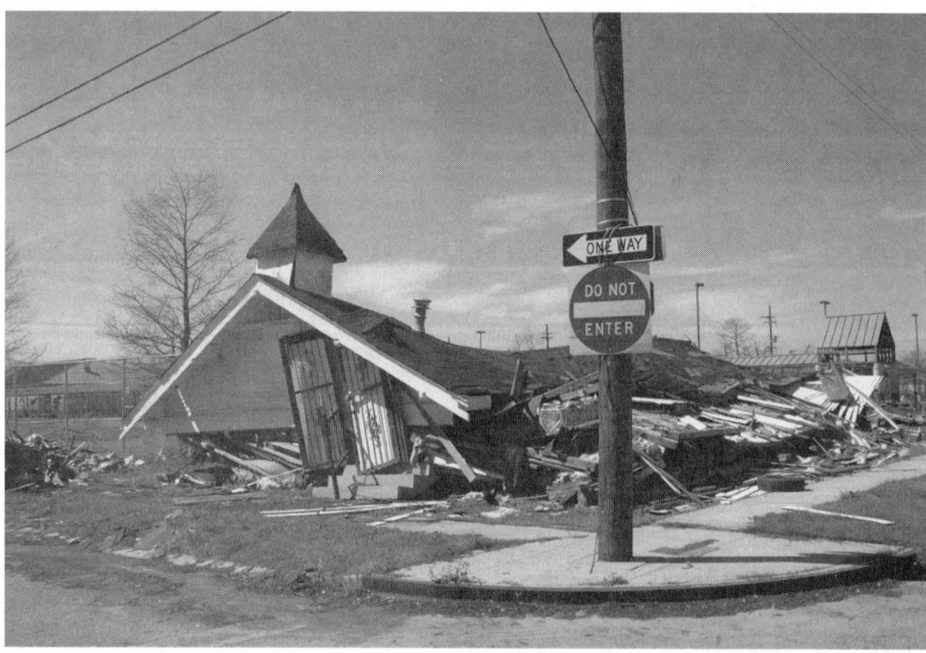

FIGURE 14–23 Damage from Hurricane Andrew in 1992. *Source:* Sandy Weiss/Packer Engineering.

Transportation Disasters

- Airplane crash
- Vehicular accident
  - Automobile
  - Truck
  - Bus
  - Train
  - Boat
  - Shipwreck
  - Train crash (see Fig. 14–24)

Man-made Disasters

- Fire
- Explosion (see Fig. 14–25)
- Mass suicide or mass murder
- Civil unrest
- Power plant, chemical plant, manufacturing center, or other industrial mishap
- Terrorism (including WMD)

The National Transportation and Safety Board (NTSB)

The **National Transportation and Safety Board (NTSB)** is an independent federal, congressionally designated agency assigned to investigate in the United States, every civil aviation accident and most other significant accidents in other modes of transportation, including railroad, highway, marine, and pipeline. The NTSB issues safety recommendations intended to discourage and prevent similar occurrences in the future.

The NTSB determines the probable cause of the following types of events:

- All U.S. civil aviation accidents and some public-use aircraft accidents
- Some vehicular accidents
- Railroad accidents involving passenger trains or other train accidents resulting in at least one fatality or major property damage

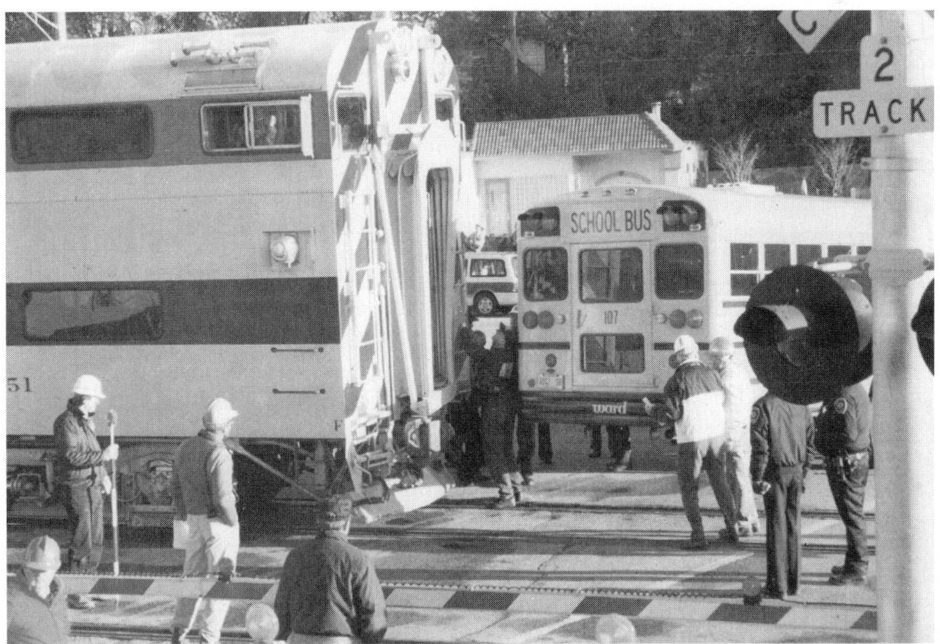

FIGURE 14–24 Reconstruction of a train and bus crash involving fatalities. *Source:* Sandy Weiss/Packer Engineering.

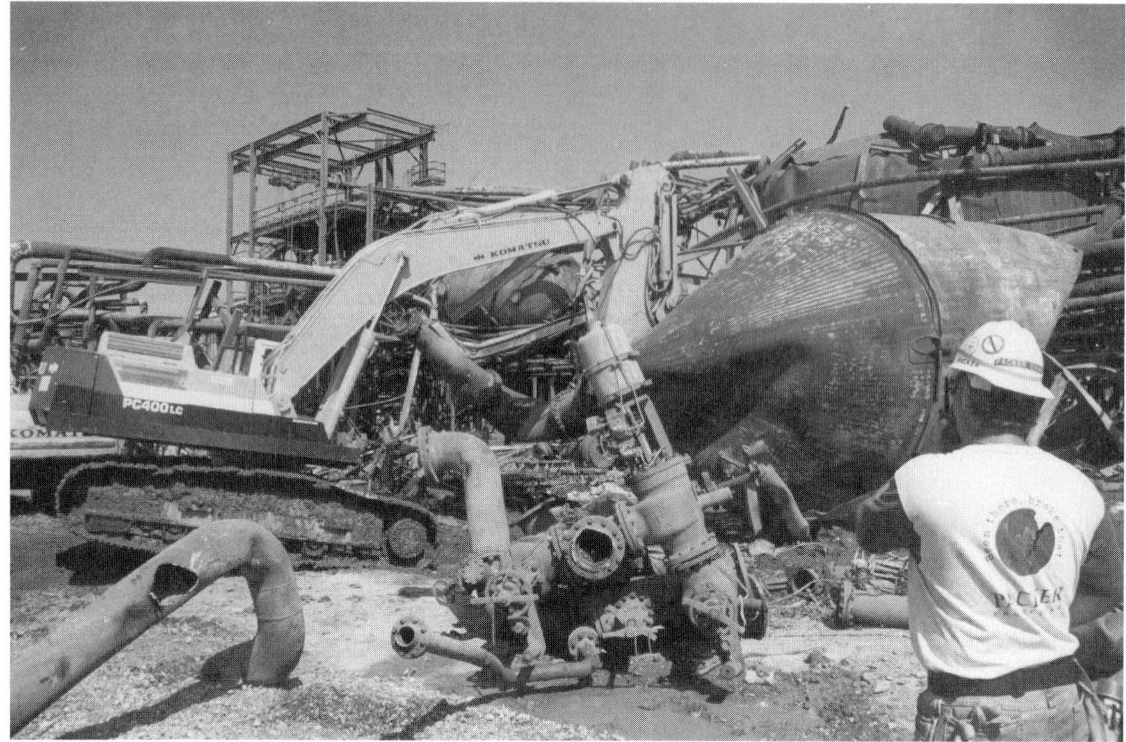

FIGURE 14–25 Explosion at a refinery. *Source:* Sandy Weiss/Packer Engineering.

- Any marine accident involving a public and a nonpublic vessel
- Pipeline accidents involving at least one fatality or major property damage
- Releases of hazardous materials in any type of transportation
- Some transportation accidents involving issues that reoccur

The rules of the NTSB are found in the **Code of Federal Regulations (CFR)**, Chapter 8, Title 49. The authority of the NTSB is found in Chapter 11, Title 49 of the CFR.

The NTSB must answer two questions regarding every incident investigation:

- How did the incident occur?
- What can be done to prevent similar incidents from occurring in the future?

Hazards at Disasters

The most commonly occurring major hazards at disaster scenes, include these:

- Biohazards
- Chemical hazards (Haz-Mat)
- Physical hazards
- A combination of all three

Disaster Scene Standard Operating Procedures

Training information regarding recommended SOPs for all disasters is formulated and distributed to the public by the following agencies:

- National Incident Management System (NIMS)
- Federal Emergency Management Agency (FEMA)

- National Response Plan (NRP)
- Occupational Safety & Health Administration (OSHA)

The **National Integration Center (NIC)** was established by the U. S. Secretary of Homeland Security to provide strategic direction and oversight of the **National Incident Management Systems (NIMS)** Integration Division. The NIC supports routine maintenance and continuous refinement of the system and its components over time. The center oversees all aspects of NIMS, including the development of compliance criteria and implementation activities at federal, state, and local levels. It provides guidance and support to jurisdictions, incident management, and responder organizations within the system.

The **Federal Emergency Management Agency (FEMA)** became part of the U.S. **Department of Homeland Security (DHS)** on March 1, 2003. The primary mission of FEMA is to reduce the loss of life and property and protect the nation from all hazards, including natural disasters, acts of terrorism, and other man-made disasters, by leading and supporting the nation in a risk-based, comprehensive emergency management system of preparedness, protection, response, recovery, and mitigation.

The **National Response Framework (NRF),** effective March 22, 2008, is a comprehensive all-hazards approach to enable national management of domestic incidents.[1] It is the basis for incident coordination between federal and state, local, and tribal governments and the private sector.

The National Response Plan establishes incident SOPs for all of the following:

- Saving lives and protecting the health and safety of the public, responders, and recovery workers
- Security of the nation
- Prevention of imminent incidents, including acts of terrorism
- Protecting and restoring critical infrastructure and key resources
- Conducting law enforcement investigations to resolve an incident, apprehend the perpetrators, and collect and preserve evidence for prosecution and attribution
- Protecting property and mitigating damages to individuals, communities, and the environment
- Facilitating recovery of individuals, families, businesses, governments, and the environment

The **Occupational Safety and Health Administration (OSHA)** is the government agency that ensures the safety and health of the workers of the United States. It places and enforces standards; provides training, outreach, and education; establishes partnerships; and encourages continual improvement in workplace safety and health. (OSHA standards may be downloaded for free at www.osha.gov.)

Most workers in the United States are under the jurisdiction of OSHA, including the following:

- Occupational safety and health professionals
- Educators
- Lawyers
- Journalists
- Government personnel

OSHA does not cover miners, transportation workers, public employees, or the self-employed.

Safety Procedures and Equipment

Safety SOPs for photographic projects involving Haz-Mat conditions, concern exposure due to any of the following:

- Inhalation
- Ingestion
- Mucous membrane contact
  - Skin
  - Eyes
  - Nose

Personal protective equipment (PPE) (see Fig. 14–26) may be required during photographic assignments involving chemical and

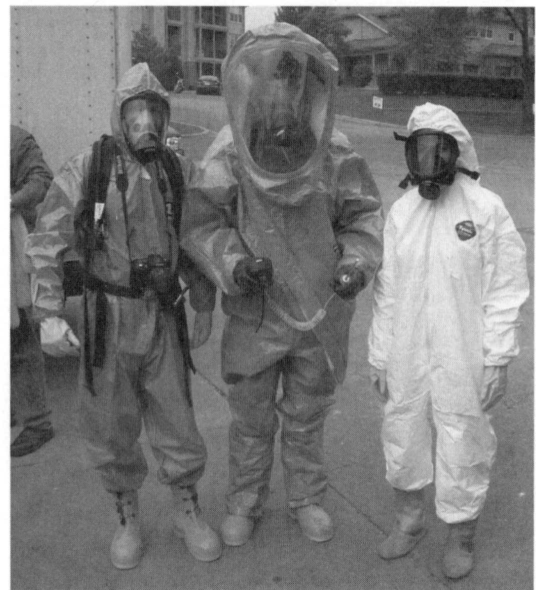

FIGURE 14–26 Some examples of personal protective equipment (PPE). *Source:* Sandy Weiss/Packer Engineering.

Haz-Mat conditions. All PPE must be approved by the **National Institute for Occupational Safety and Health (NIOSH**, www.cdc.gov/niosh), a department of the Center for Disease Control and Prevention (CDC), which is part of the U.S. Department of Health and Human Services. Photographic equipment may also require protective covering. PPE must be available by departmental SOP and by OSHA for the photographer. Protective covering for photographic equipment may be available or may be improvised for temporary use from plastic wrap or other types of bags. The photographer must maintain the functionality and dexterity needed to operate the protected camera equipment while wearing gloves, masks, and other PPE.

> **TIP:**
>
> Before attempting to expose photographs in Haz-Mat conditions, make certain it is possible to operate the camera and flash with protective equipment in place.

The four categories of PPE are as follows:

Level A (the highest level of personal protection from all types of exposure)

- Totally-encapsulating, chemical-protective suit
  - Positive pressure
  - Full face piece
  - Self-contained breathing apparatus (SCBA)
  - Chemical-resistant outer gloves
  - Chemical-resistant inner gloves
  - Overalls under suit if necessary
  - Chemical-resistant boots, steel toe and shank
  - Hard hat if necessary, under suit
  - Disposable outer suit worn sometimes over the encapsulating suit

Level B (the second level of personal protection from all types of exposure)

- Full respiratory protection
- Lower level of skin protection
- Plus Level A

Level C (used when the concentration and type of airborne substance is known)

- OSHA's full-face or half-face mask, air-purifying respirator criteria must be met/
  - Hooded chemical-resistant clothing
  - Chemical-splash suit, two-piece
  - Escape mask, if needed
  - Face shield, if needed

Level D (a work uniform, affording minimal protection in low levels of contamination)

- Coveralls
- Gloves, if needed
- Chemical-resistant safety shoes
- Safety glasses or goggles
- Hard hat, if necessary
- Face shield, if necessary

Decontamination

All Haz-Mat scenes must include a special area for decontamination. All disposable protective garments should be removed and then packaged in biohazard-labeled containers for safe disposal. All reusable garments are washed and dried.

Protective Housings for Cameras

Cameras may be protected from adverse exposure by use of plastic **camera housings.** Such camera containers are available in an array of styles, similar in degrees of protection to the PPE available for photographers. Numerous types are available.

Thick-wall, hard-plastic housings are manufactured by companies including Ikelite (see Fig. 14–27) (www.ikelite.com). These offer the highest degree of protection in underwater (see Chapter 15 for further information) and Haz-Mat conditions for point-and-shoot, SLR, and video digital cameras. An assortment of different-size lens ports are available for SLRs with lens interchangeability. A full range of accessories are also available for use with EFUs and other accessories. Manufacture of these housings for film-based cameras is essentially discontinued, but some can still be found on the used market.

Thin-walled, soft-plastic housings are manufactured by companies including Ewa-Marine (www.ewa-marine.de) (see Fig. 14–28). These housings offer the next-best protection for any type of camera in underwater and Haz-Mat conditions. The camera, components, buttons, and switches may be operated through the bag.

Any camera may be protected by placing it inside a disposable plastic bag, such as those available in almost any food store or pharmacy. This will not be chemical- or waterproof, but it will be better than using nothing when the environment is dirty, corrosive, or dangerous. Make a hole in the bag for the lens to go through and fasten the bag to the lens with a rubber band. Plastic wrap may also be used in conditions where the equipment is too large or oddly shaped for conventional bags.

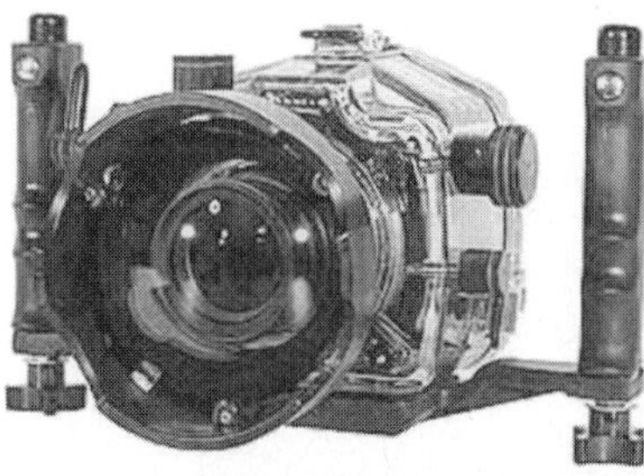

FIGURE 14–27 Ikelite housing for Nikon D80. *Source:* Sandy Weiss/Packer Engineering.

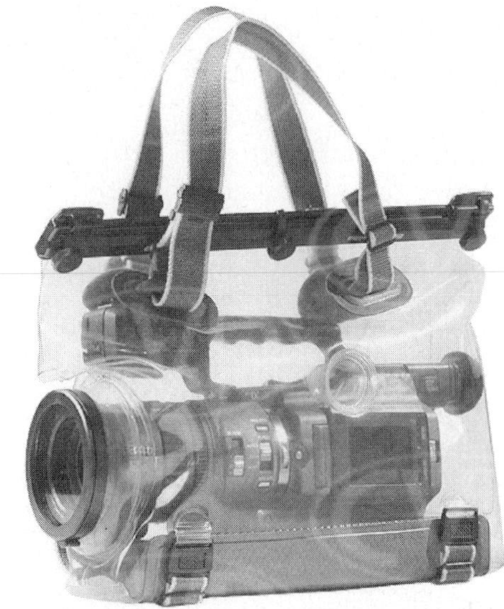

FIGURE 14–28 Ewa-Marine DSLR Camera Housing. *Source:* Sandy Weiss/Packer Engineering.

For protection from rain and snow, consider the use of the Popabrella Camera Umbrella (www.popabrella.com), which may also be useful for blocking direct sunlight in certain conditions.

AERIAL SCENE PHOTOGRAPHY

It may be necessary to photograph the extent of accident and crime scenes from the air (see Figs. 14–29 and 14–30) and from various altitudes. Light aircraft, helicopters, hot air balloons, and unmanned aircraft may be used for this type of aerial photography. Photographs exposed this way may be considered to be overall views and are useful for annotating the locations of photographs exposed from the ground.

In urban areas, especially near airports, full-size aircraft are usually forbidden clearance to fly through restricted airspace. In such situations, aerial photography is now being accomplished with **aerial drones,** unmanned aircraft

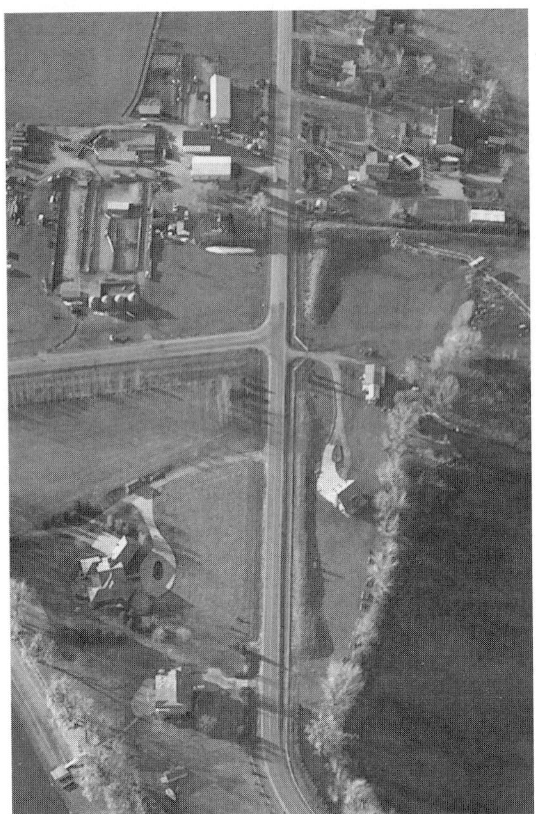

FIGURE 14–29 An aerial view from a manned balloon. *Source:* Aric Dutelle, University of Wisconsin-Platteville.

weighing up to 50 pounds. The **Federal Aviation Administration (FAA,** www.faa.gov) allows these instruments to fly in any airspace. Slow-flying drones containing high-resolution, remote-controlled, digital cameras; operate in most weather conditions; and, from sufficient altitude, can capture overall images of any scene. Fixed-wing model aircraft may glide while exposing photographs to minimize vibration. The SOPs usually specify oblique and plane views of a scene. Standards for drone aircraft technology are published by the **Academy of Model Aeronautics** (**AMA**, www.modelaircraft.org).

Use of Accessory Lighting for Accident Scenes

> **TIP:**
>
> To reduce the adverse affects of atmospheric haze when exposing photographs from an aircraft, always use an ultraviolet filter on the camera lens when exposing photographs.

Infrared film was formerly used to detect fresh soil **disruption** at aircraft accident scenes. Infrared photography from moving aircraft is

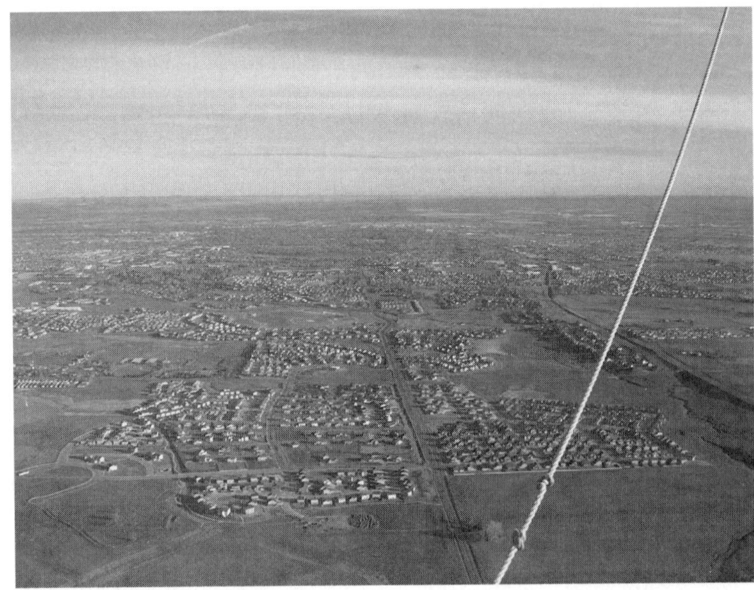

FIGURE 14–30 Oblique aerial view from a manned balloon. *Source:* Aric Dutelle, University of Wisconsin-Platteville.

more difficult to accomplish digitally. Some cameras have extended sensitivity in the near infrared range, but a high level of infrared lighting must be available for the camera to create an image. In daytime, ambient light overcomes most infrared. It may be possible to use an infrared light source at night when making photographs from a helicopter, but little has been done in this area.

Soil disruption patterns at an aircraft accident's area of impact may provide information about the aircraft configuration, attitude, and angle of impact. This information could help to reconstruct the accident.

Consider infrared photography to improve scene contrast and aid in recognition of patterns. Subsoil on top of surface soil may be visible in infrared images because of its difference in moisture content.

Aircraft fuel kills vegetation. The change in colors between living and dead vegetation may be visible in aerial photographs. Infrared photographs may differentiate vegetation while it is dying, even before it is apparent visually.

REMEMBER:

Documentation of the distribution of aircraft wreckage, which may be larger than the burn area, will help to re-create the breakup of the aircraft and the sequence of the accident.

ACCIDENT VICTIM IDENTIFICATION STANDARD OPERATING PROCEDURES

The initial purpose of a forensic investigation of an accident scene involving victims is to document and analyze the injury data. Medical, forensic, and biomechanical injury analysis data are used to reconstruct the events that occurred to cause the injuries during an accident.

The National Transportation Safety Board (NTSB) used its standard accident victim identification SOP in the investigation of the crash of TWA 800 in 1996. This SOP covers mass casualties in accidents that occur on land or in water. The following outline was derived from the complete report published by the NTSB regarding the incident. It is adaptable to documentations and investigations of any vehicle in any conditions. Patterns of damage or injuries assist in the reconstruction of an event.

An aviation accident injury sequence may include the following:

Circumstances of the Crash

- Explosion
  - Fire
  - No Fire
    - Explosive device
- Breakup
- Impact
  - Water
  - Land

Victim Disposition

- Alive: aided or sent for aid
- Dead: placed in body bags
  - Intact bodies
  - Body parts
  - Effects
- Each bag assigned an accession number by the medical examiner
- Photography
  - Victims photographed with clothing
  - Victims photographed without clothing
  - Clothing documented
    - Clothing damage related to wounds on bodies
    - Personal effects cataloged and cross-referenced to bodies, using the bag number
- Data recorded on recovery location
- Circumstances of recovery recorded
- Radiography
  - Skeletal
  - Dental
- Fingerprinting
- Bodies refrigerated and stored
- Dentition photographed
  - Use the American Board of Forensic Odontology (ABFO) Body Identification Guidelines (www.abfo.org/ID.htm)

- Photographs labeled with bag number
  - Include preliminary ID information, if available
  - Name of photographer
  - Date and location of photography
  - Documentation of all relevant photographic information should be documented
- Photograph views of the body (see Chapter 13)

Autopsy

- Detailed forensic autopsy and photography (see Chapter 13)
  - Done
  - Not done

Identification

- Methods
  - Visual
  - Fingerprint
  - Forensic odontology
  - DNA
  - Forensic radiography
  - Forensic anthropology

Foreign Materials

- Removed from bodies and sent to FBI lab
  - Location of materials recorded
  - Trajectory information recorded

Medical Data (reviewed and abstracted into summary data for each victim)

- Autopsy protocol
- Photographs
- Radiographs
- Recovery information
- Identification information

Database

- Demographics
- Injury data
  - Autopsy SOP
    - Aspect
    - Object
    - Injury
    - Location
  - External
  - Internal
  - Fractures
- Recovery data
- Assigned seating information

Database Reviewed and Produced for Each Victim

- Summary data sheet
  - Autopsy protocol
  - Body diagrams
  - Photographs
  - Radiographs

The existence of a detonated explosive device in proximity to passengers or crewmembers may be determined by the study of the remains of the accident victims. They will display burn and breakup patterns to determine injury sequences.

All data are reviewed by a team from the **Armed Forces Institute of Pathology (AFIP)**[2] to relate seating information to physical evidence of seat restraint and other factors, including the following:

- **Geographical Information System (GIS)**
  - Technology used for investigations, management, and planning
- Cabin seating arrangement
- Seating coded to victim, enabling search for injury or combination of injuries
- Comparison of recovered and unrecovered seats to victims
- Location of fire-damaged seats
- Bodies coded for fragmentation or loss of extremities
  - Color coded (for example),
    - Green = body intact
    - Yellow = crushed head and loss of one extremity
    - Blue = loss of two extremities, with or without crushed head
    - Red = loss of three extremities or complete transection
- Seats coded for damage

- Victims with foreign bodies
    - Radiographs
    - CT scans

For Land-Based Accident Scene

- Recovery information
    - Location information
    - Injuries
        - Burns
        - Bruises
        - Fractures
        - Dismemberment

For Water-Based Accident Scene

- Recovery information
    - Floating body
    - Burns on floating bodies
        - Floating bodies burned on backs, from burning fuel
        - Bodies burned on front, from fuel fire in plane, backs protected by seats
        - Injury predominance (left/right) (anterior/posterior)
        - Seat deformation (left/right) (front/back)
        - Trauma severity
            - Severe
            - Moderate
            - Minimal
    - Sunken bodies
        - Injury predominance (left/right) (anterior/posterior)
        - Seat deformation (left/right) (front/back)
        - Trauma severity
            - Severe
            - Moderate
            - Minimal

SUMMARY

The photography of accident scenes is another challenging aspect of forensic photography. Accidents can be as small as a cut finger or as large as an airliner crash or hurricane that devastates an entire region. Each photographic project involves telling as much of the story as possible regarding how the accident occurred, the results, and possibly the re-creation.

Most of the time, an accident involves litigation. This makes accuracy essential. The proper equipment and references must be available to the photographer to properly complete the photographic task. After the accident occurs, it is usually too late to gather equipment and knowledge about how to undertake the photography.

Government agencies have been established for every accident eventuality. These agencies publish SOPs for investigation and documentation. If the photographer is involved in a certain type of accident, it is essential they be familiar with the correct SOPs and how to properly use them. This will add credibility to their work.

Be aware of what type of personal protective equipment may be needed in Haz-Mat situations and what should be done to protect camera equipment. Be sure the equipment is operable when the photographer is wearing gloves, face masks, and so on.

To be able to properly document victims and provide the information necessary to enable proper identification, it is essential for the photographer also to be versed in victim inspection and autopsy protocols in the case of fatalities.

CASE STUDY

TRIP AND FALL ACCIDENT DOCUMENTATION

A section of walkway with a variation in surface levels between sections, adjacent to a public building, was the scene and alleged cause of a trip-and-fall incident. The plaintiff sustained personal injury. An attorney contracted an accident reconstructionist/forensic photographer to document the scene.

The incident occurred at night, but the case was not vision related, so the documentation was undertaken on a bright sunny morning. The walkway was in the same condition as at the time of the incident. The only change was that the property owner had placed three 5-gallon plastic pails of water on the walkway at the point of the incident, to discourage subsequent foot traffic.

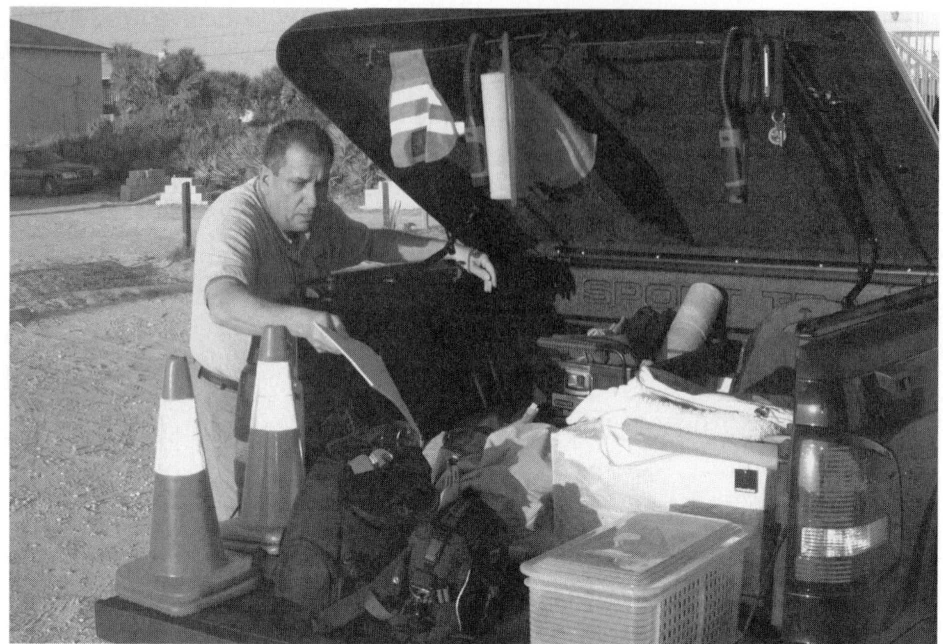

FIGURE 14–31 All equipment contained and organized in the back of a truck for easy access. *Source:* Robert Wyman, Wyman Enterprises.

The go-kit used for this documentation consisted of the following:

- Digital camera
- Metal rule of sufficient length to measure the width of the walkway
- Plastic triangle for determining 90-degree angles
- **Profilometer** to accurately document the disparity between the adjacent sections of the walkway
- Paper and pen
- Caliper to measure the disparity
- Rigid plastic sections to place on the rough concrete for use with the caliper
- Smart-level with digital readout for measuring inclination
- Cell phone for conversing with the client

Other optional accessories that were available but not used included these:

- Reflective cones to warn traffic and pedestrians
- Personal protective devices, including gloves and knee pads
- Tape recorder to document the proceedings

The documentation proceeded in a logical manner.[3] All necessary tools were made ready to use. (see Fig. 14–31). Overall photographs were exposed from different angles as the scene was found on the day of the documentation (see Figs. 14–32,

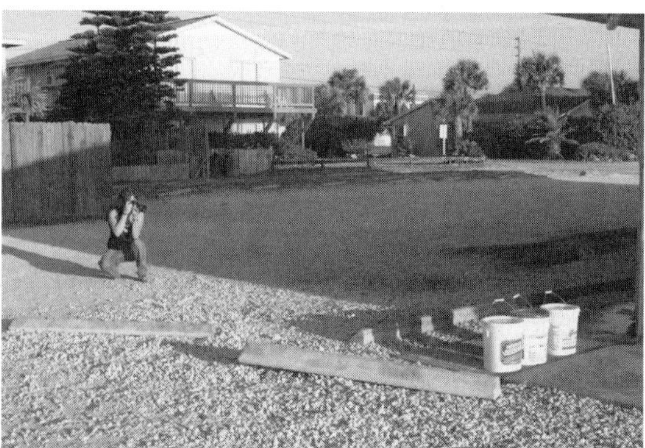

FIGURE 14–32 Overall documentation from west to east. *Source:* Robert Wyman, Wyman Enterprises.

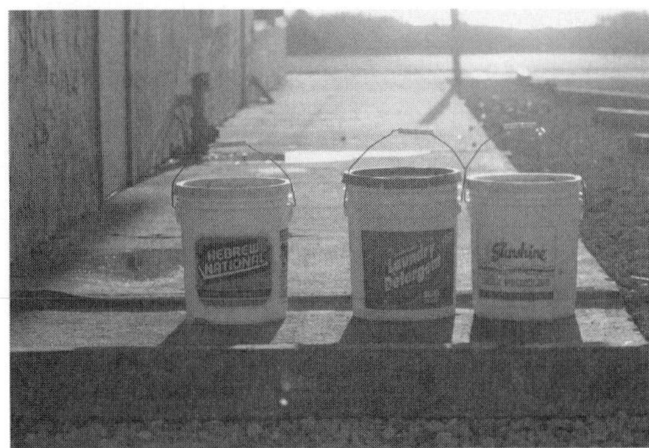

FIGURE 14–33 Resultant image. *Source:* Robert Wyman, Wyman Enterprises.

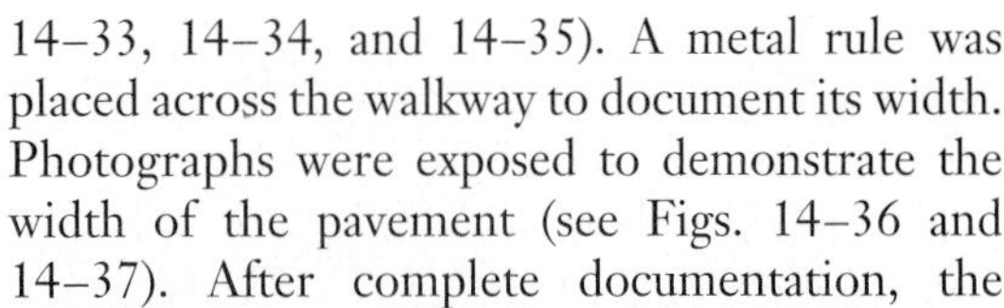

14–33, 14–34, and 14–35). A metal rule was placed across the walkway to document its width. Photographs were exposed to demonstrate the width of the pavement (see Figs. 14–36 and 14–37). After complete documentation, the

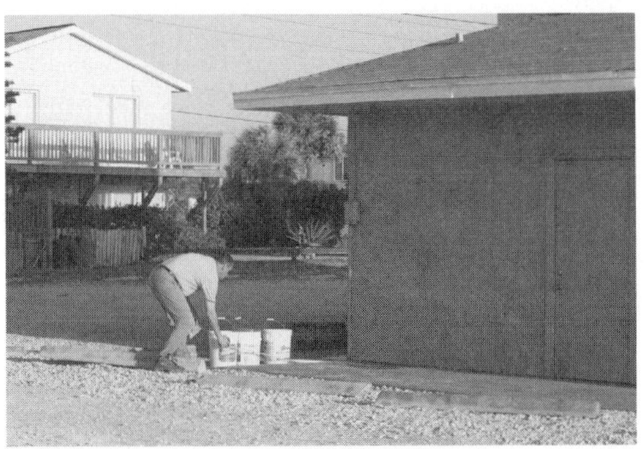

FIGURE 14–34 Another angle on the 5-gallon buckets. *Source:* Robert Wyman, Wyman Enterprises.

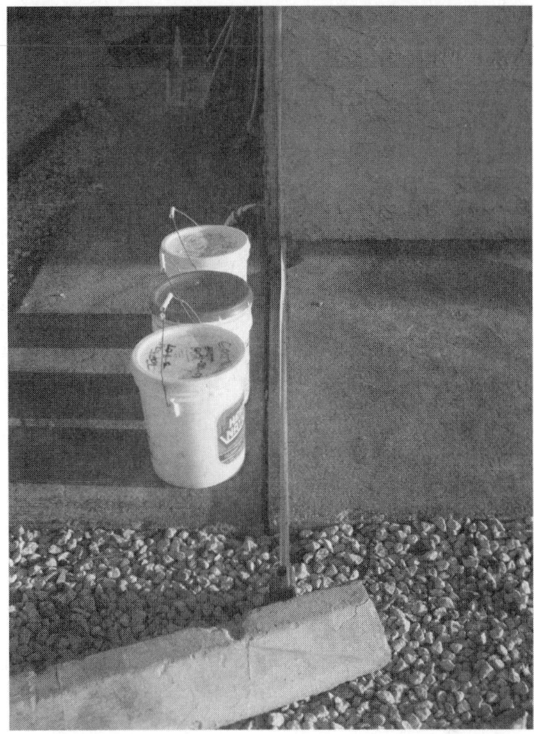

FIGURE 14–36 Metal ruler to measure the width of the walkway. *Source:* Robert Wyman, Wyman Enterprises.

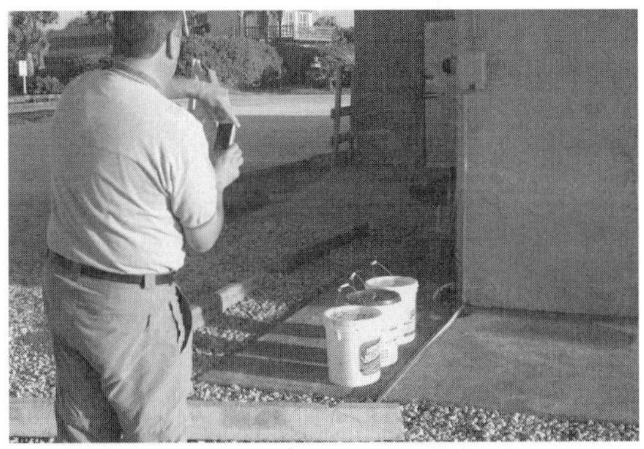

FIGURE 14–35 View to the north. *Source:* Robert Wyman, Wyman Enterprises.

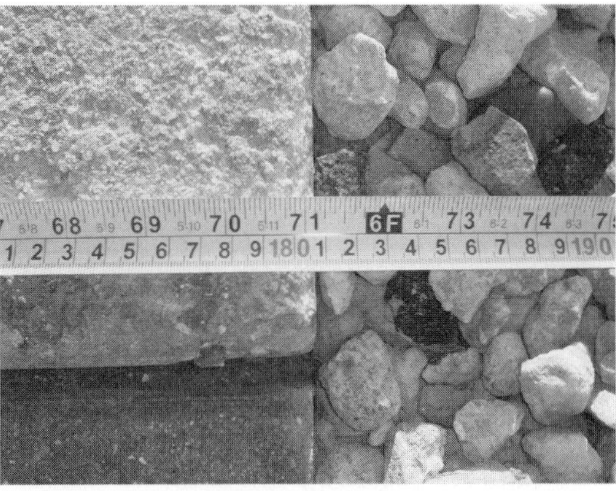

FIGURE 14–37 Close-up of measurement. *Source:* Robert Wyman, Wyman Enterprises.

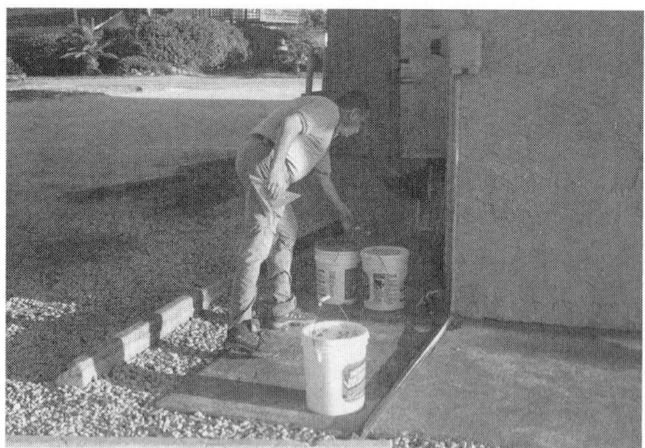

FIGURE 14–38 Moving the buckets out of the way. *Source:* Robert Wyman, Wyman Enterprises.

plastic buckets were moved out of the way (see Fig. 14–38). To enable visualization and documentation of the disparity, a plastic triangle was placed on the lower section, and a level was placed parallel to the triangle on the upper section of the walkway (see Figs. 14–39 and 14–40). The disparity was measured and photographed at several locations (see Figs. 14–41 and 14–42). A profilometer/contour gauge was used to document the contour of the disparity at five locations across the pavement, starting at the side closest to the building (see Figs. 14–43 and 14–44). The contour taken at each position was permanently recorded on paper (see Figs. 14–45, 14–46, and 14–47). A smart-level was used to document the

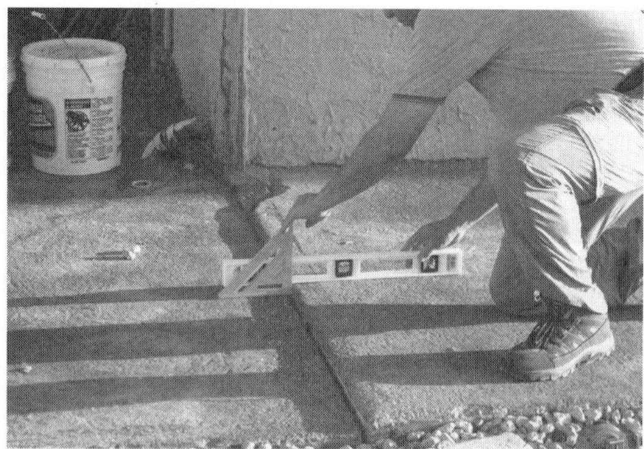

FIGURE 14–39 Measuring the disparity between sections of the walkway. *Source:* Robert Wyman, Wyman Enterprise.

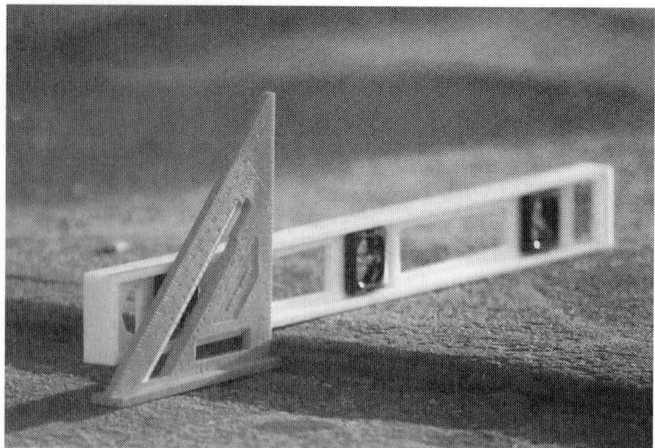

FIGURE 14–40 Close-up view: measuring the disparity between sections of the walkway. *Source:* Robert Wyman, Wyman Enterprises.

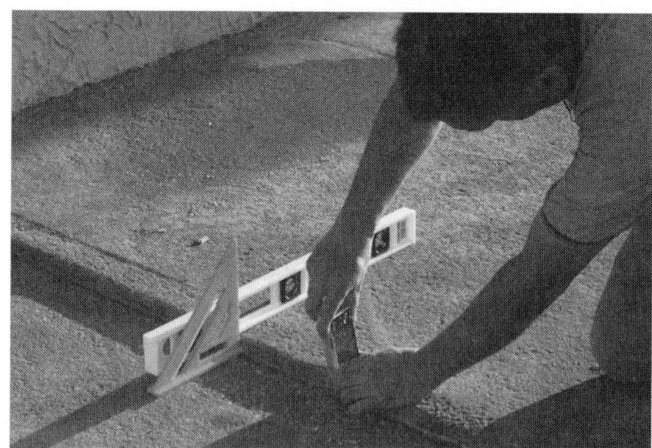

FIGURE 14–41 Another view: measuring the disparity between sections of the walkway. *Source:* Robert Wyman, Wyman Enterprises.

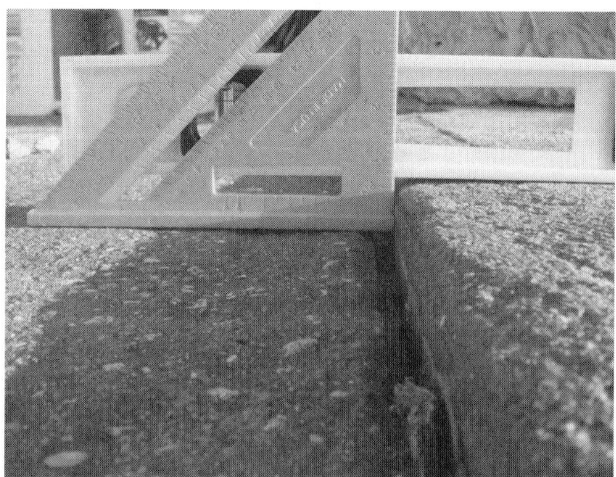

FIGURE 14–42 Another close-up: measuring the disparity between sections of the walkway. *Source:* Robert Wyman, Wyman Enterprises.

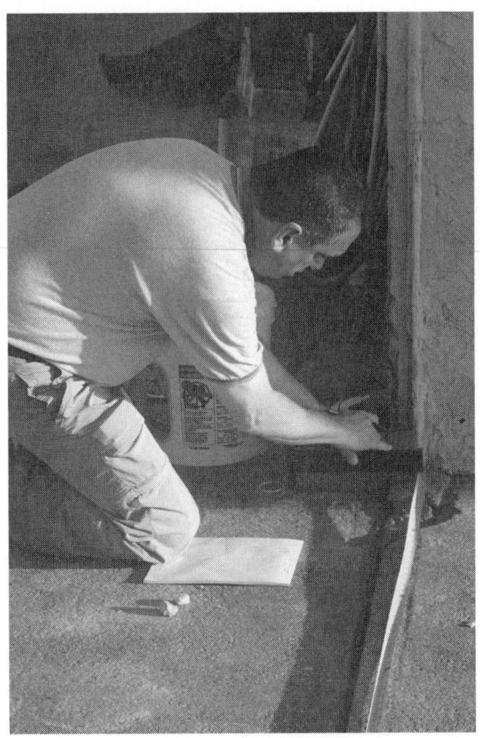

FIGURE 14–43 Using a profilometer/contour gauge. *Source:* Robert Wyman, Wyman Enterprises.

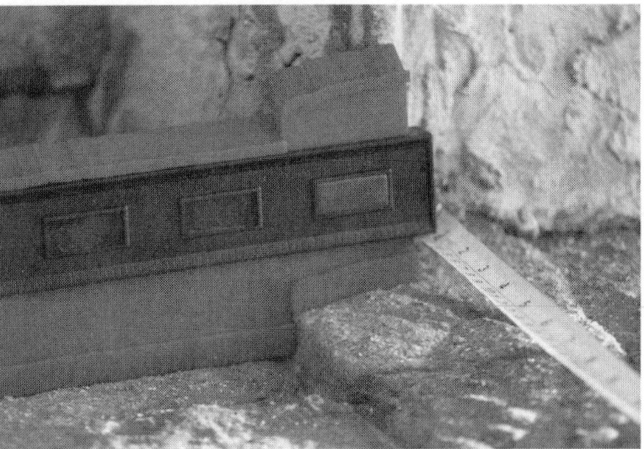

FIGURE 14–44 Close-up: using a profilometer/contour gauge. *Source:* Robert Wyman, Wyman Enterprises.

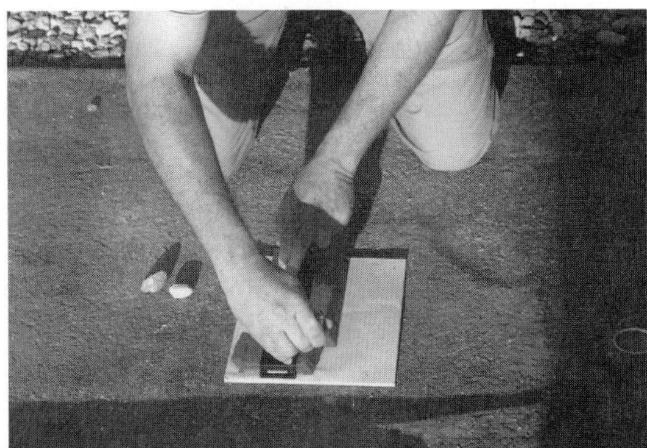

FIGURE 14–45 Tracing the contour onto paper. *Source:* Robert Wyman, Wyman Enterprises.

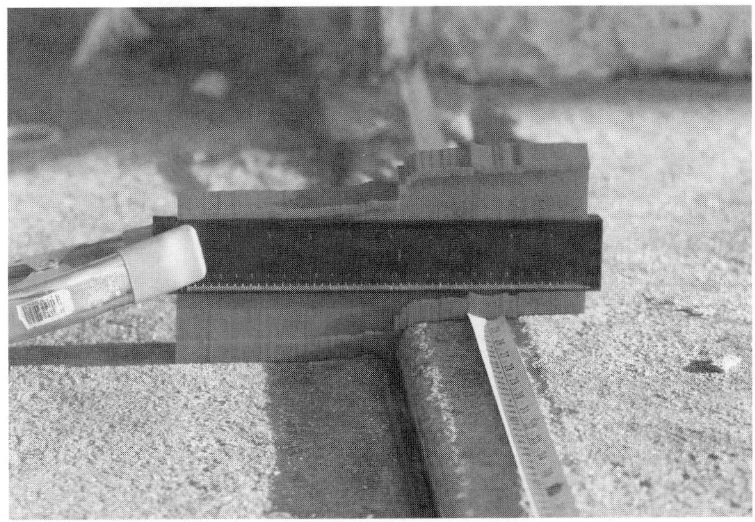

FIGURE 14–46 Profilometer at position 3. *Source:* Robert Wyman, Wyman Enterprises.

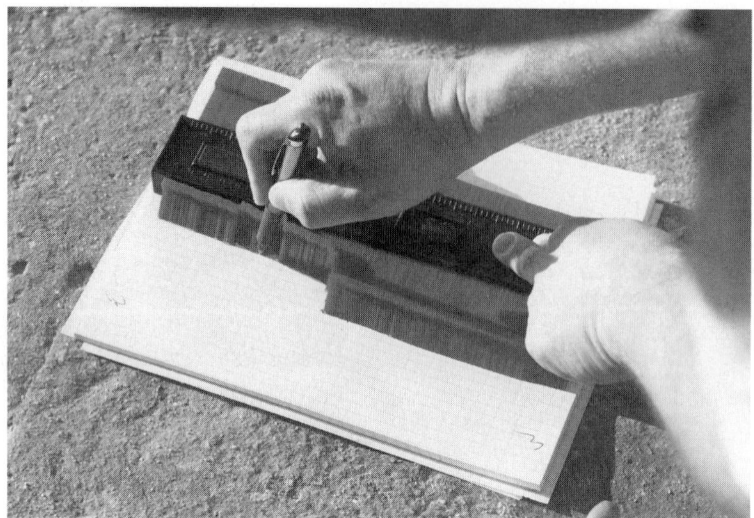

FIGURE 14–47 Tracing the contour onto paper. *Source:* Robert Wyman, Wyman Enterprises.

pitch of the concrete, perpendicular to and on both sides of the disparity and parallel to the disparity (see Fig. 14–48). A digital caliper was used to take detailed measurements of the disparity and to double-check the measurements derived from the profiles. Small sheets of rigid plastic were placed on both surfaces of the concrete to prevent the caliper from penetrating into the concrete. Both sheets were the same thickness, so they did not change the disparity between the measurements. This procedure allows extra accuracy of readings (see Fig. 14–49). Distant overall photos of the location of the walkway

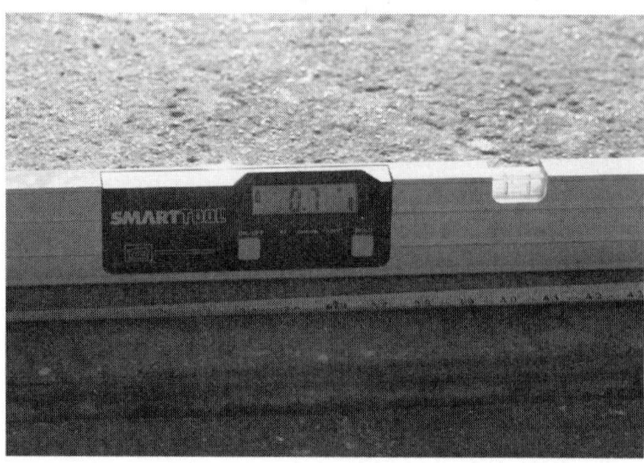

FIGURE 14–48 Using a smart-level. *Source:* Robert Wyman, Wyman Enterprises.

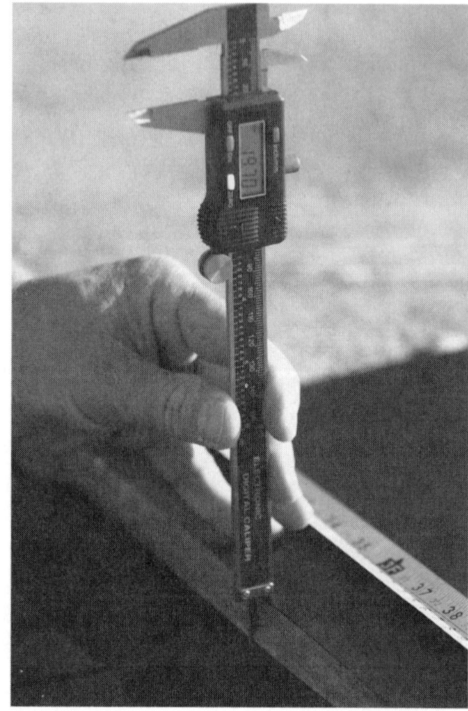

FIGURE 14–49 Using a caliper for measurement. *Source:* Robert Wyman, Wyman Enterprises.

were taken after all measurements were completed (see Fig. 14–50). The drawings made of the contours were used in a CAD application to construct a 3-D model of the walkway (see Fig. 14–51). The images were used to document the findings of the inspection and to substantiate the report furnished by the reconstructionist. The finished report was sent to the attorney, and it was used as an exhibit at trial.

The average vertical displacement of 0.78 inch between the sections of the walkway exceeds the vertical elevation change allowable by the Americans with Disabilities Act (ADA) of 1994 and the Florida Building Code.

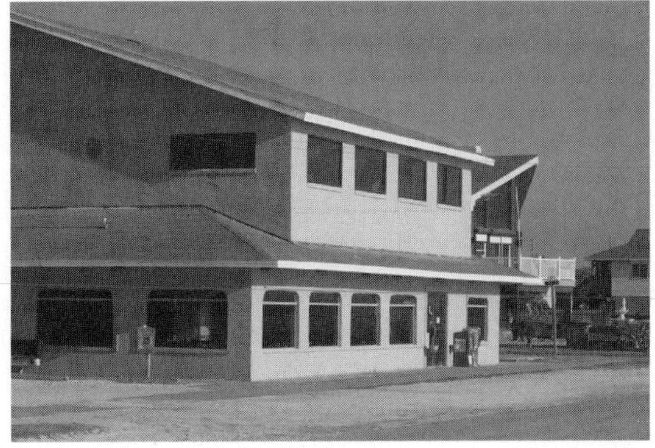

FIGURE 14–50 Distant overall view of location. *Source:* Robert Wyman, Wyman Enterprises.

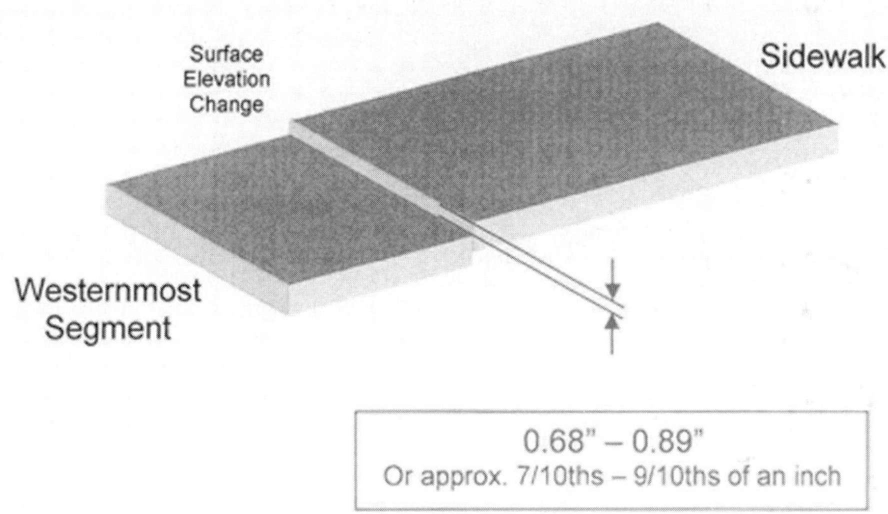

FIGURE 14–51 CAD drawing of walkway. *Source:* Robert Wyman, Wyman Enterprises.

CASE STUDY

TWA FLIGHT 800

The Accident docket is coded: DCA-96-MA-070. The accident occurred July 17, 1996, at the Atlantic Ocean, located at 72:37.46 North Latitude, 40:39.52 West Longitude, near East Moriches, New York. The aircraft involved was a Boeing 747-131, number N93 119 operated by Trans World Airlines, Inc. (TWA) Accident time is recorded as 2031 Eastern Daylight Time (EDT). The wreckage was salvaged over time and reconstructed (see Fig. 14–52) to enable the analysis of the crash scenario.

On July 17, 1996, TWA Flight 800 was en route from John F. Kennedy International Airport (JFK), New York, NY, to Paris Charles de Gaulle International Airport, France. Shortly after departure from JFK and while gaining altitude, the aircraft exploded and broke-up in flight near the southern coast of Long Island, NY, and crashed into the Atlantic Ocean near East Moriches, NY.

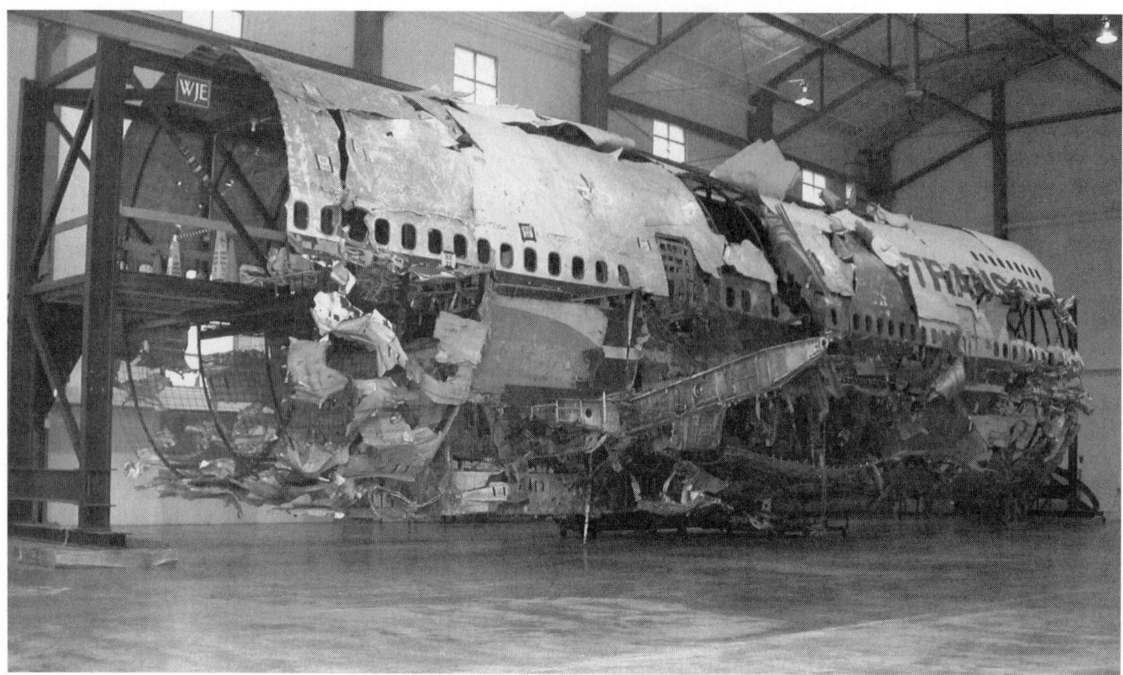

FIGURE 14–52 The TWA 800 reconstruction. *Source:* Sandy Weiss/Packer Engineering.

Flight 800 was a scheduled air carrier flight, operated and conducted under Title 14, Code of Federal Regulations (CFR), part 121. The weather was visual conditions at the time of the crash and an Instrument Flight Rules (IFR) plan had also been filed. All 18 crewmembers and 212 passengers aboard the aircraft were fatally injured and the airplane was destroyed.[4]

DETAILS OF THE INVESTIGATION: VICTIM RECOVERY, EXAMINATION, AND IDENTIFICATION

The remains of all 230 victims were recovered and identified. The remains were recovered at sea and taken to a temporary morgue at the Coast Guard station at East Moriches, NY. The first 99 bodies were found floating on the surface of the ocean and were recovered by civilian, military, and police vessels during the night of July 17, 1996, and the day of July 18, 1996. The majority of the remaining victims were recovered by U. S. Navy divers and local police divers during the next 96 days. Trawling operations were subsequently utilized for the recovery of most of the wreckage and some remains, until April 30, 1997. The last remains were recovered by a fishing trawler on May 22, 1997 and subsequently identified.

The reconstruction is now housed at the NTSB Academy, training facility in Virginia (see Fig. 14–53).

The preceding **Accident Victim Identification Protocol**, is a condensed version of the steps taken for the documentation and investigation of the incident. Most of the seats were recovered, examined and photographed (see Figs. 14–54 and 14–55). The victims were photographed for injuries and burns, after recovery. The location of the recovery of each victim was carefully documented and was cross checked against the seating assignment. The pattern of the explosion, breakup, and eventual crash, was determined by the damages to the seats, locations of recovery, and the injuries to the victims.

The accident is now attributed to the explosion of fumes collected in the nearly empty center-wing fuel tank as a direct result of a long wait on the tarmac prior to take-off. With the

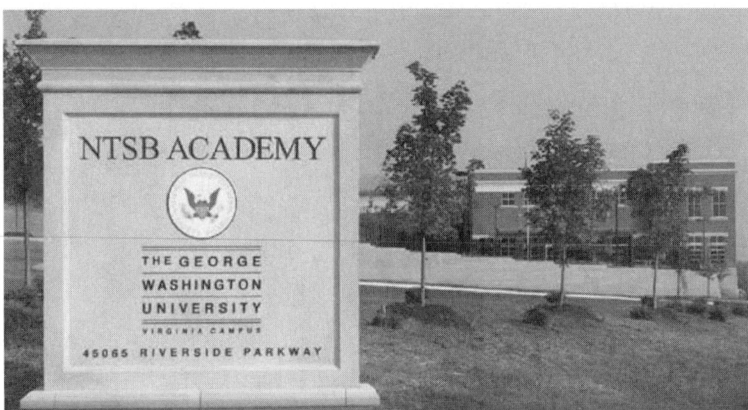

FIGURE 14–53 Academy sign. *Source:* Sandy Weiss/Packer Engineering.

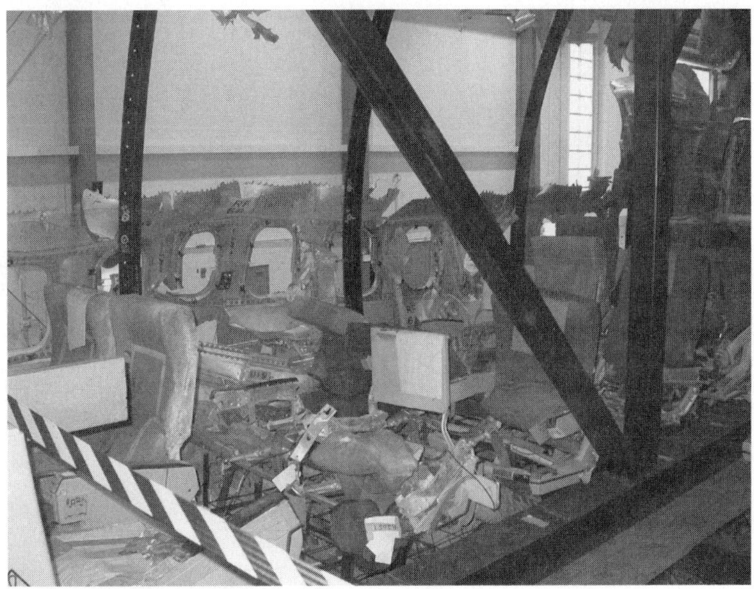

FIGURE 14–54 Seating. *Source:* Sandy Weiss/Packer Engineering.

engines running on a hot day, the heat from the cabin air-conditioning unit below the fuel tank vaporized the fuel and a very-small discharge from electric wiring in the area was the ignition source. The explosion blew out the skin of the aircraft (see Fig. 14–56) causing a catastrophic in-flight separation and crash.

The photographs of the recovered seats and victims, and the location of recovery data, were used to calculate the origin, direction, and severity of the explosion to reconstruct the sequence of the incident.

A number of eye-witnesses to the crash stated that they thought they saw a missile come up from the ground, impact the aircraft, and cause the explosion and crash. The wreckage did not support those observations.

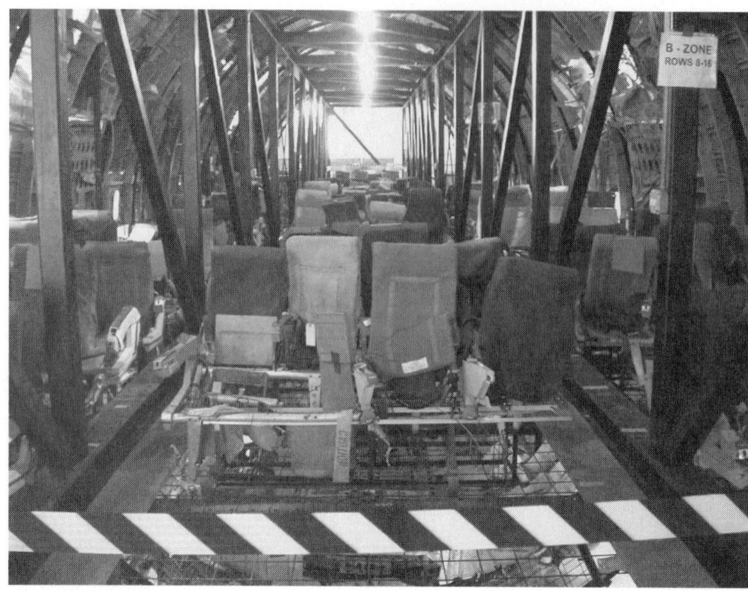

FIGURE 14–55 Seating 2. *Source:* Sandy Weiss/Packer Engineering.

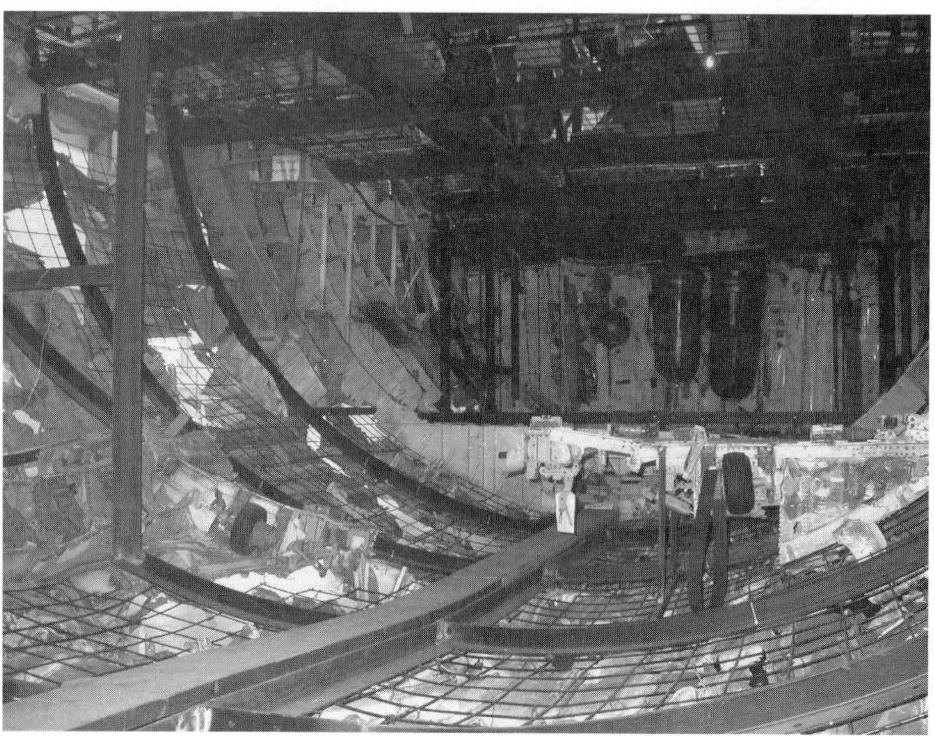

FIGURE 14–56 Blown-out section. *Source:* Sandy Weiss/Packer Engineering.

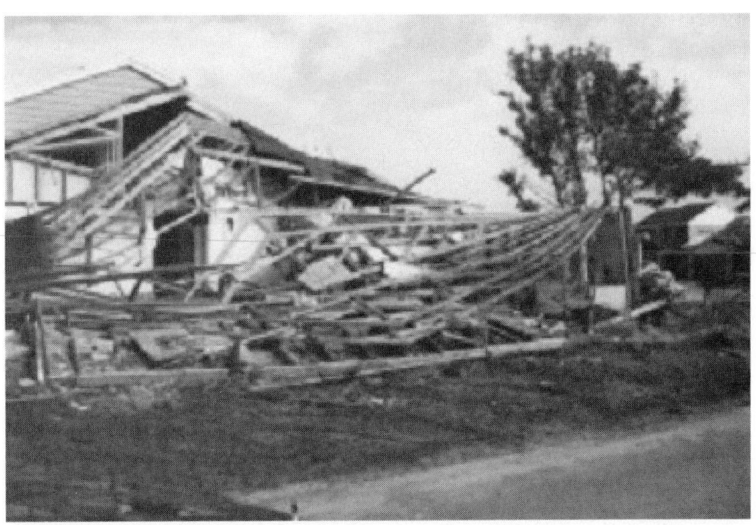

FIGURE 14–57 Damage from Hurricane Andrew. *Source:* Sandy Weiss/Packer Engineering.

CASE STUDY

HURRICANE ANDREW, AUGUST 1992

Hurricane Andrew was the first named storm of the 1992 Atlantic hurricane season. The Category 5 storm hit southern Florida near Homestead and hit southwest Louisiana near Morgan City. Andrew caused $26.5 billion in damages, mostly in south Florida, and was the most catastrophic natural disaster in U.S. history until Hurricane Katrina in 2005.

Andrew had recorded average winds of 142 miles per hour with peak gusts of 177 miles per hour. The storm damaged or destroyed every building in its path, including most of the Homestead area. In Dade County, 90% of the structures had major roof damage and another 117,000 homes had major or total destruction (see Figs. 14–57, 14–58, and 14–59).

Insurance claims caused the bankruptcy of 11 insurance companies and the serious damage of 30 more. After the bankruptcies, nearly 1,000,000 homes were no longer insured.

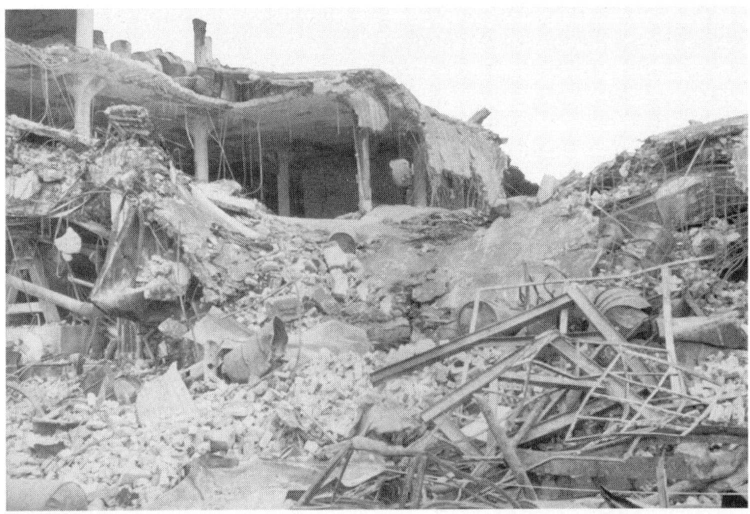

FIGURE 14–58 Along the path of Hurricane Andrew. *Source:* Sandy Weiss/Packer Engineering.

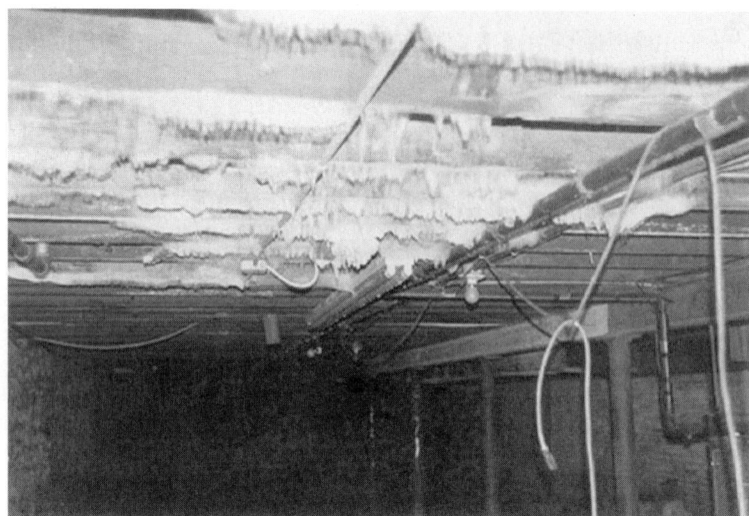

FIGURE 14–59 More damage from Hurricane Andrew. *Source:* Sandy Weiss/Packer Engineering.

Homeowners and government criticized developers and contractors for inadequate building practices and lax building codes. An inquiry after the storm concluded that there may have been some construction flaws in some buildings.

The photographic documentation of the damaged residences was an enormous undertaking. The photographs served multiple purposes:

- Documentation of the residential damages for a decision about whether the structure was a total loss or could/should be repaired
- Documentation of any obvious remaining building code violations so the contractor/builder could be held responsible for some of the damages

The region was designated a federal disaster area, as well as a state disaster area. Road signs had been almost totally obliterated. The destroyed structures held little in the way of clues to their identification. Government agencies spray-painted addresses on the structures that remained. A major part of the project was locating the correct structure to assess the damages.

Each structure was photographed systematically:

- Identification by address
- All sides of the exterior
- If walls still stood, each room of the interior
- Details within the rooms
- Services (gas, electric, etc.)
- Any obvious building faults

Sorting and archiving the images was a cumbersome task. The project had an assigned number. Each structure was a distinct file within the file. Each photograph was marked with a negative number within the structure file and within the project file.

Teamwork and communications were essential to discourage repetition of work. HazMat precautions were mostly unnecessary due to the lack of fatalities.

CASE STUDY

FOUNDRY ROOF COLLAPSE

In a foundry (a facility where iron and steel are made into useable items) on the west side of Chicago, a roof collapsed over a production area. The collapse was due to the weight of sand that had leaked out onto the roof of the building over time. One worker was killed; he was working directly under the part of the roof that collapsed.

In some foundries, molten iron is formed by casting, a process by which the molten material is introduced into a mold (see Fig. 14–60), allowed to solidify in the shape of the inside of

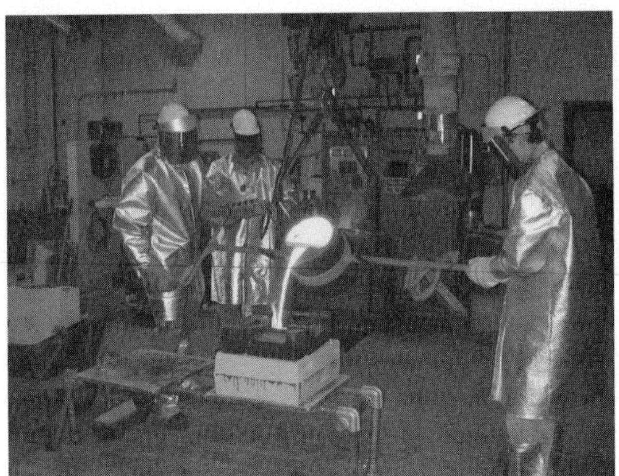

FIGURE 14–60 Pouring parts for the Wright Flyer engine. *Source:* Sandy Weiss/Packer Engineering.

the mold, and then removed. Sand casting produces rough metal castings using a mold usually made from sand, formed around a replica of the object to be cast. Castings made by this process are then further refined by peripheral processes. (see Fig. 14–61).

The cast is filled with properly prepared casting sand or green sand, a slightly moist mixture of sand and clay. The sand is packed into the mold by vibration. Sand may also be bonded with chemicals, including resins. Foundries purchase sand in large quantities and store it in elevated tall tanks (see Fig. 14–62). The sand is fed through a system of pipes that lie on top, across, through, and under the ceilings of the foundry

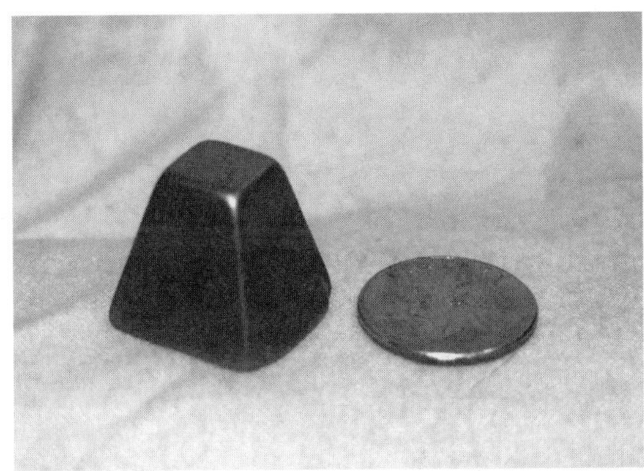

FIGURE 14–61 A rough casting out of the mold and a coin for scale. *Source:* Sandy Weiss/Packer Engineering.

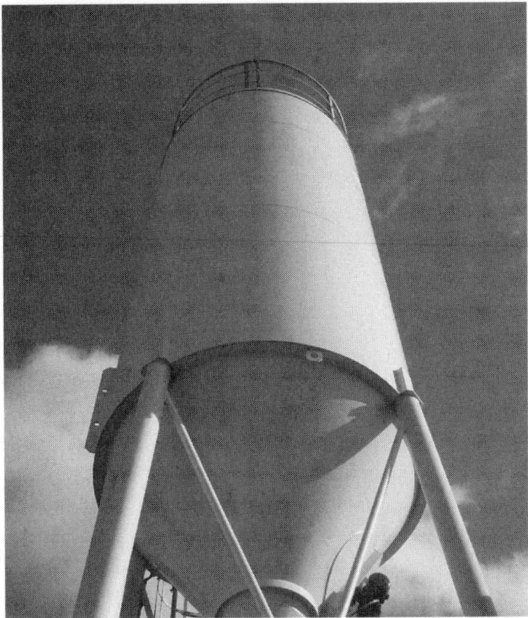

FIGURE 14–62 Sand Storage. *Source:* Sandy Weiss/Packer Engineering.

buildings. Each position in the foundry requiring sand has an outlet from the feed system.

The photographic project included documentation of the sand feed system (see Fig. 14–63) from the tank to the building that collapsed. Special attention was directed to leaks. The amount of sand could determine how long it had been leaking and who was to blame for the leaks.

The photographs were assembled into a long montage of images, showing every foot of the run. The project was complicated by the

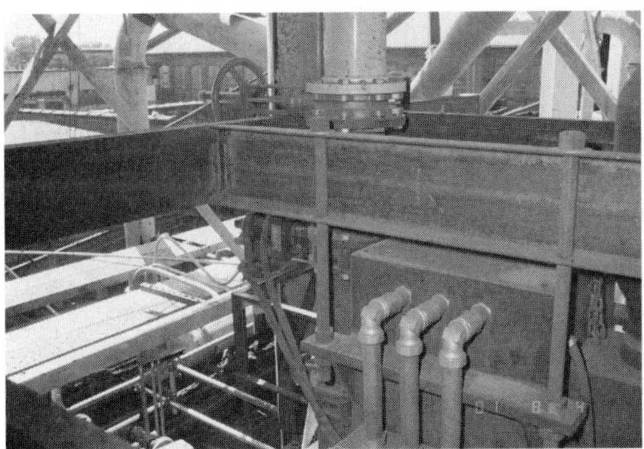

FIGURE 14–63 Sand system piping. *Source:* Sandy Weiss/Packer Engineering.

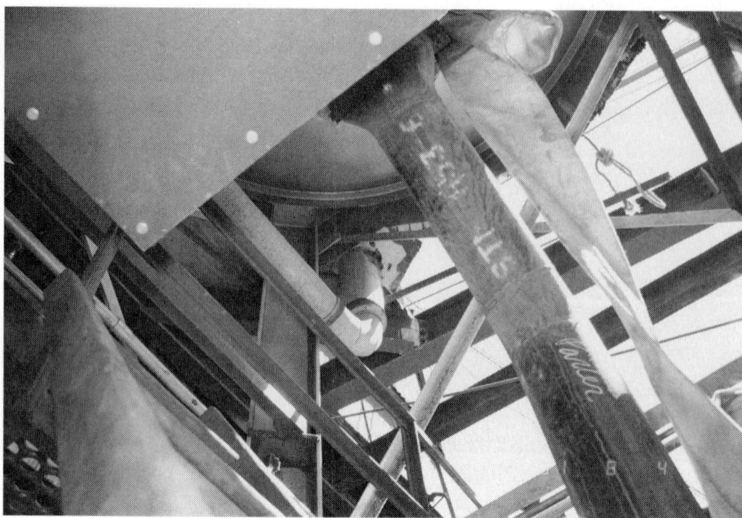

FIGURE 14–64 Vertical run of sand system. Source: Sandy Weiss/Packer Engineering.

route of the piping. In some places it was outside, on top of the roof. In some places it was inside, hung from the roof. When it was inside, it was criss-crossed with air ducting, electrical service, sprinkler piping, and lighting. To document the full run in a way that allowed all the photos to fit together, the magnification of all the photos needed to be essentially the same. Some of the photos were exposed from the ground, looking up, and some from the roof, looking down. The buildings had 16-foot tall ceilings. Lenses were interchanged, depending on the camera-to-subject distance, to create images with constant pipe dimensions (see Fig. 14–64).

Telephoto lenses were used in images made from the floor. Wide-angle lenses were used on the roof. Some of the angles were nearly impossible to document, due to obstructions (see Fig. 14–65). Heavy bags of equipment were carried up ladders to roofs. The length of the run was over 200 yards. Eventually, all the images were captured.

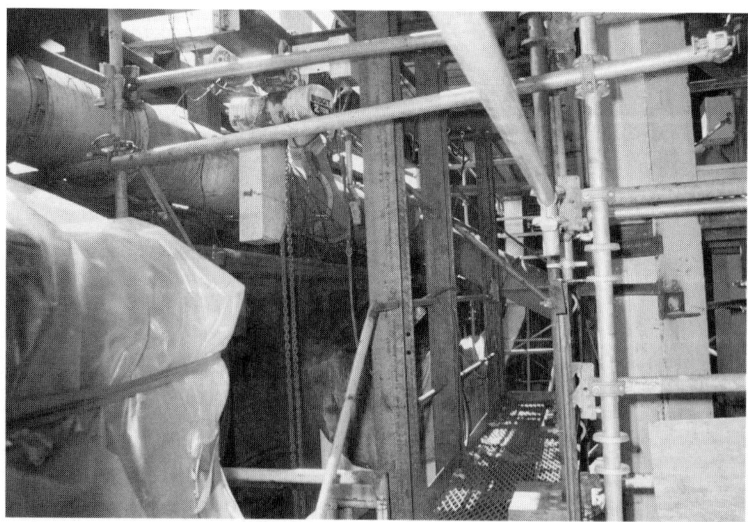

FIGURE 14–65 Following the pipes. *Source:* Sandy Weiss/Packer Engineering.

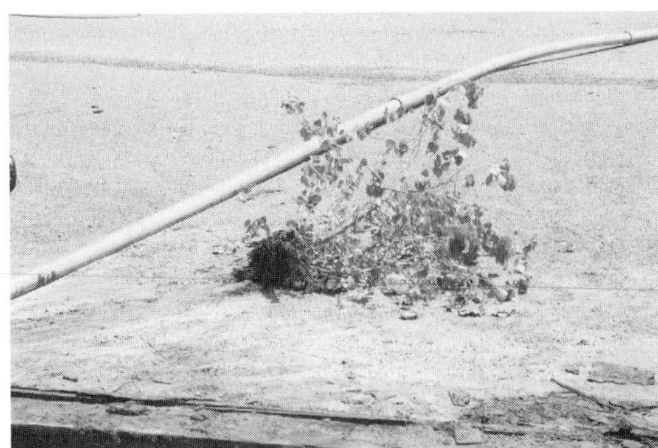

FIGURE 14–66 Mulberry tree growing out of the sand on the roof. *Source:* Sandy Weiss/Packer Engineering.

One particular image turned out to be a key. On top of the building that collapsed, a 6-foot-tall mulberry tree was growing out of the sand (see Fig. 14–66). Nobody planted it there full grown. It grew there from a seed and into a seedling. This clue demonstrated that the leaked sand on that roof was not a new issue.

> **TIP:**
>
> Clean all safety equipment, including shoes, after use and before storage. Contact with chemicals may cause serious deterioration of the equipment.

CASE STUDY

ROCK CRUSHER*

The documentation of inspections for accident prevention and/or insurance claims, studies, research, or future reference are very similar to accident scene and evidence photography. In this case, the project involved a large rock-crushing apparatus (see Fig. 14–67) used by a company dealing in quarry stone, crushed rock, and concrete.

The rock-crushing apparatus transfers energy from a horizontal pinion gear to a vertical shaft inside a sealed, pressurized gear chamber. The issue was that pressure and friction sensors indicated abnormalities in the pinion gear rotation. The company believed the abnormalities were due to manufacturing defects, not wear. At the time of the project, the pinion gear that was documented was new.

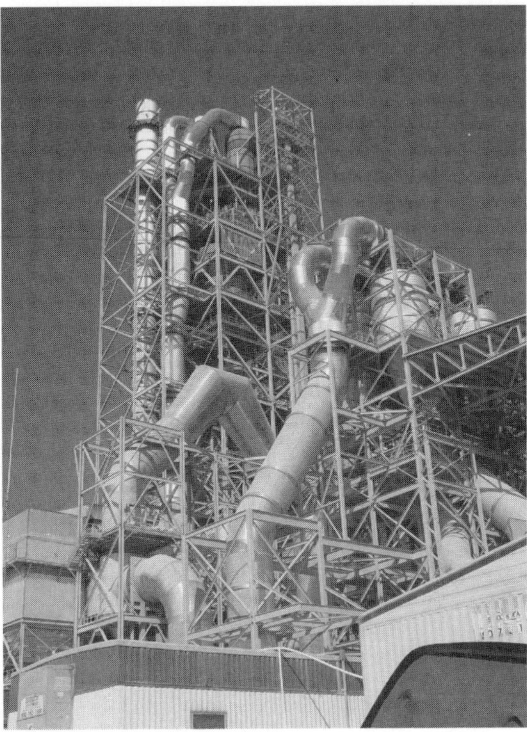

FIGURE 14–67 Stone quarry equipment. *Source:* Robert Wyman, Wyman Enterprises.

The most difficult part of the assignment was to physically insert a camera into the chamber. The chamber mechanism was stopped and the chamber depressurized. Close-up photos of the pinion gear teeth were needed by the engineers to determine if wear patterns were abnormal.

An inspection port was removed to allow observation (see Fig. 14–68). Photographs were exposed through the inspection port with an off-camera flash aimed through the port (see Fig. 14–69). The images were taken during a walk-though and familiarization/evaluation visit prior to the actual assignment. The company required verification that the technique proposed would fulfill it requirements for inspection.

*This case study was submitted by Robert Wyman, Wyman Enterprises.

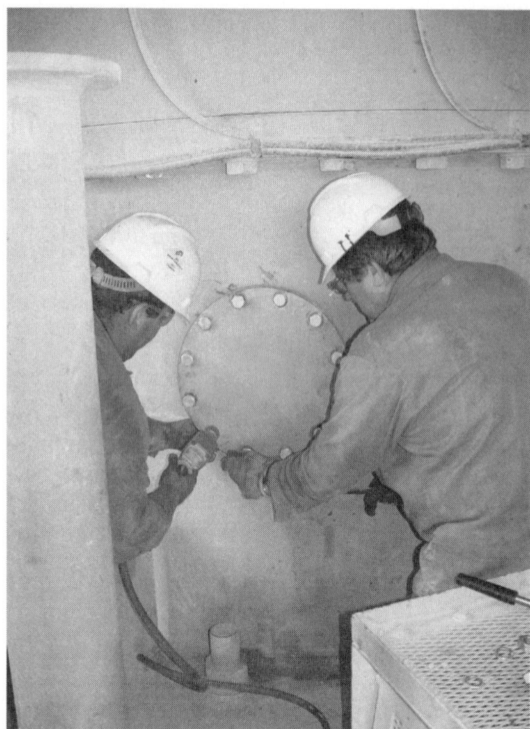

FIGURE 14–68 Opening an inspection port. *Source:* Robert Wyman, Wyman Enterprises.

A 10-foot monopod was used to elevate the camera above the pinion gear and other parts of the mechanism. The parts obstructed a direct view of the gear from the inspection port (see Figs. 14–70 and 14–71).

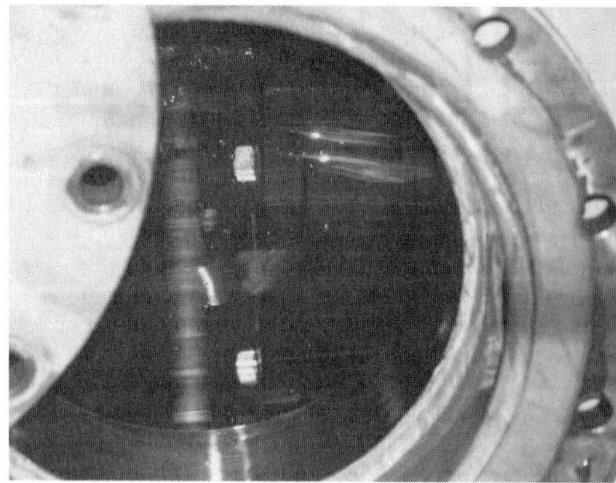

FIGURE 14–69 A view into the inspection port. *Source:* Robert Wyman, Wyman Enterprises.

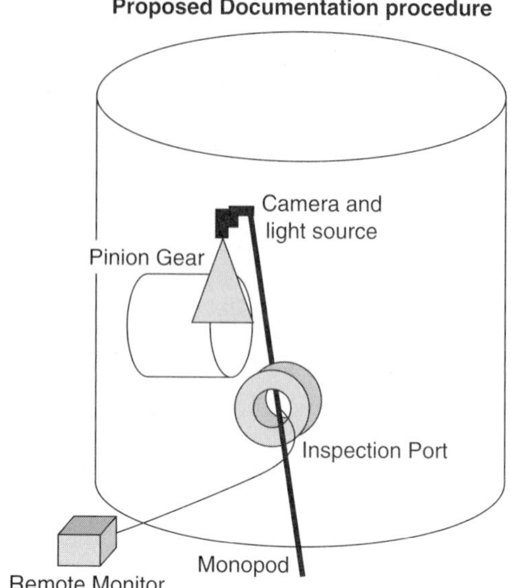

FIGURE 14–70 Apparatus used for the study of the pinion gear. *Source:* Robert Wyman, Wyman Enterprises.

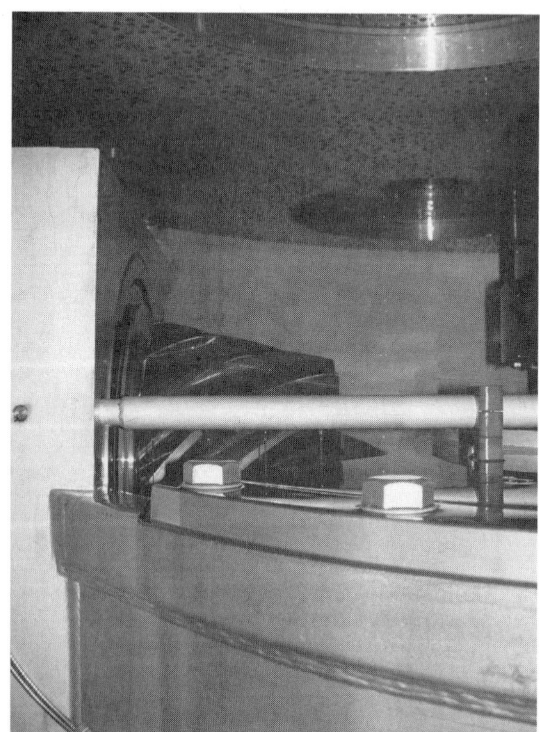

FIGURE 14–71 Gear. *Source:* Robert Wyman, Wyman Enterprises.

The yellow-orange and red-orange liquids and droplets are condensed lubricant. During use, the entire chamber housing the gearing is pressurized and has a lubricant-mist atmosphere to reduce friction and heat of the pinion gear.

The gear chamber was about 12 feet in diameter. The pinion gear was about 4 feet in diameter and also about 4 feet in length. The inspection port was about 18 inches in diameter.

The camera and flash were mounted on the monopod and held, rotated, and angled through the inspection port. Inside the chamber, the camera was aimed down at a slight angle toward the pinion gear (see Fig. 14–72). The entire camera (except the lens) and flash (except the output window) and the monopod were covered in plastic wrap to protect them from the dripping lubricant environment. The camera lens was kept in a downward-facing position to avoid ruining the lens and contaminating the camera with dripping lubricant.

The monopod was fed toward the gear at an angle from the port. There was no way to bring the camera to parallel along the length or width of the gear. The monopod head was adjusted by sight estimate and then fed into the chamber. Once the plastic wrap was on the system and the camera was placed, the mounting angle on the monopod could not be changed. The whole system became covered in lubricant as soon as it entered the chamber.

The assignment was completed. It required an additional 30 minutes to remove the plastic wrap and discard it without contaminating the equipment. The results were perfect. No damage had been done to the photographic equipment, and the images were used effectively to evaluate the gear (see Fig. 14–73).

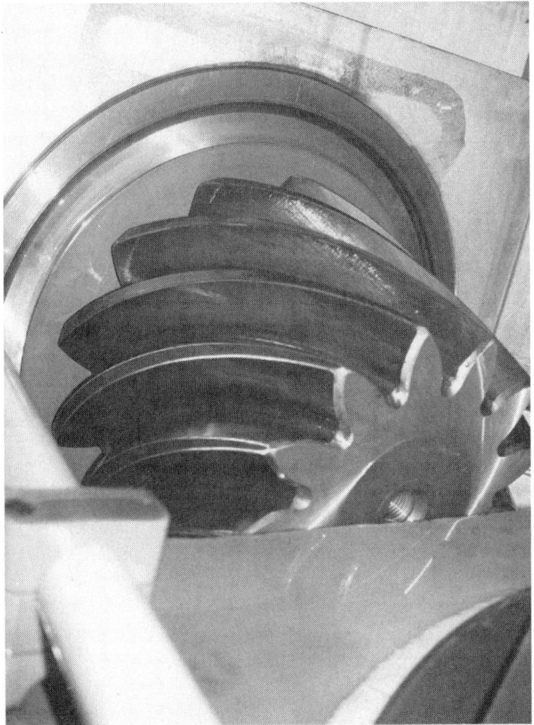

FIGURE 14–72 The pinion gear. *Source:* Robert Wyman, Wyman Enterprises.

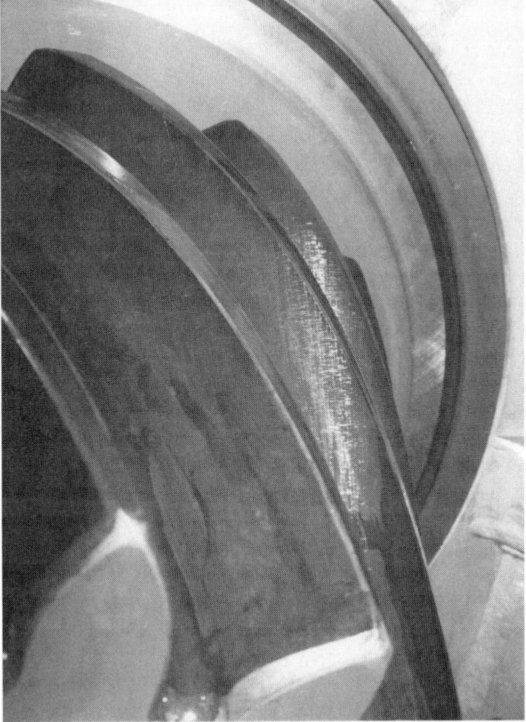

FIGURE 14–73 Gear close-up. *Source:* Robert Wyman, Wyman Enterprises.

KEY TERMS

measuring wheel, (p. 406)
camera boom, (p. 410)
Haz-Mat, (p. 412)
weapons of mass disaster (WMD), (p. 412)
National Transportation and Safety Board (NTSB), (p. 413)
Code of Federal Regulations (CFR), (p. 414)
National Integration Center (NIC), (p. 415)
National Incident Management System (NIMS), (p. 415)
Federal Emergency Management Agency (FEMA), (p. 415)
Department of Homeland Security (DHS), (p. 415)
National Response Framework (NRF), (p. 415)
Occupational Safety and Health Administration (OSHA), (p. 415)
personal protective equipment (PPE), (p. 415)
National Institute for Occupational Safety and Health (NIOSH), (p. 416)
camera housing, (p. 417)
aerial drone, (p. 417)
Federal Aviation Administration (FAA), (p. 418)
Academy of Model Aeronautics (AMA), (p. 418)
disruption, (p. 418)
Armed Forces Institute of Pathology (AFIP), (p. 420)
Geographical Information System (GIS), (p. 420)
profilometer, (p. 422)

EXERCISES

TRAFFIC ACCIDENT DOCUMENTATION EXERCISES

Figure 14–74 is an adaptation of an illustration of a scene sketch that appeared in J. Stannard Baker and Lynn B. Fricke, *The Traffic-Accident Investigation Manual* 9th ed. (Evanston, IL: Northwestern University Traffic Institute, 1993), 36–37. This type of illustration may be drawn by hand or developed on a computer, using any available software package designed for the purpose. It places suggested locations A through F for the exposure of *some* of the essential images in an accident scenario, as follows:

1. *Position A:* Directly down the roadway, showing the vehicles and the roadway and the stop sign at the NW section of the intersection

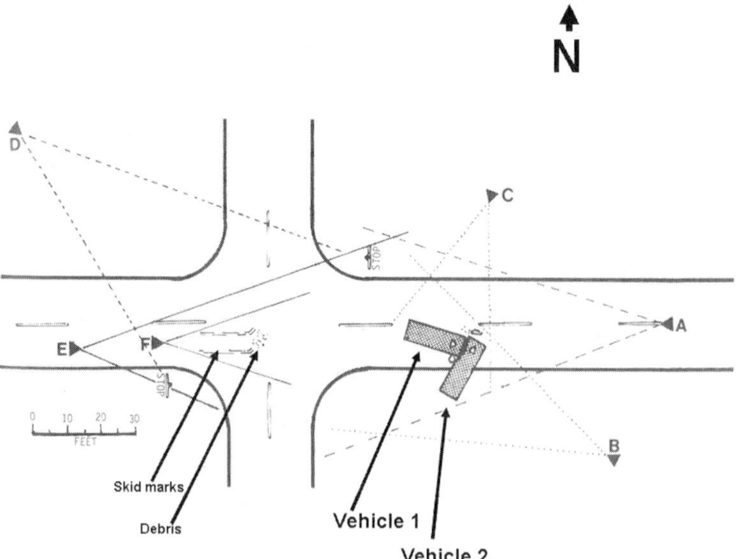

FIGURE 14–74 Suggested locations A through F in a roadway drawing. *Source:* Sandy Weiss/Packer Engineering.

2. *Position B:* One side of the vehicles, the position relative to the roadway, skid marks, and stop sign
3. *Position C:* Vehicles only, and their positions relative to each other
4. *Position D:* Overall of the intersection, skid marks, and stop signs
5. *Position E:* Closer view of D, the debris field, skid marks, vehicles, and damages
6. *Position F:* Closer view of E

1. Using this sketch and exposure list, complete the list of essential images necessary to properly document this accident. Don't forget that the scene is three-dimensional.
2. List the necessary dimensions to be gathered and the best tools for each purpose.
3. List the photographic equipment necessary for proper documentation.
4. If the accident happened at night, what would be the differences in necessary equipment?
5. Create a set of overlapping images of a vehicle that could be stitched together into a total-vehicle montage.
6. Interview a law-enforcement officer about the SOP used in his or her department for the documentation of accident scenes, then write a report that reconstructs the SOP into a set of steps.
7. Attempt to arrange a ride-along with a law enforcement officer, and write a report covering what you learned.

Chapter 15

Photographing Underwater

Aric Dutelle, University of Wisconsin-Platteville

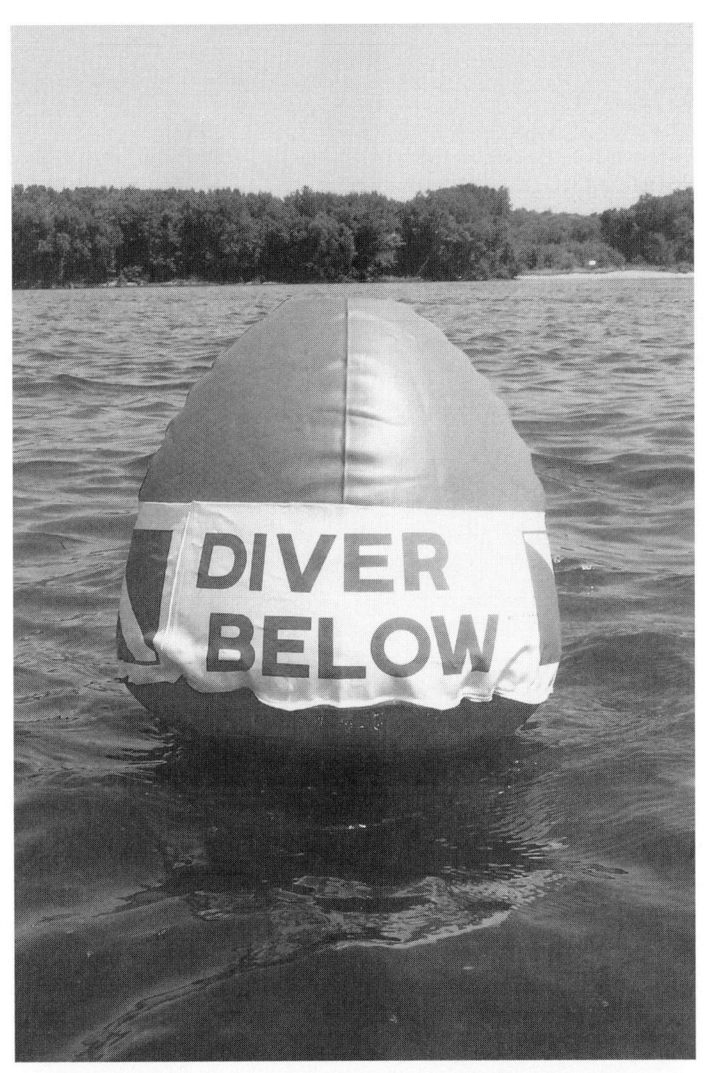

Learning Objectives

AFTER STUDYING THIS CHAPTER, YOU SHOULD BE ABLE TO:

1. Understand the safety concerns that apply whenever taking underwater photographs
2. Differentiate reflection and refraction and their effects on underwater photography
3. Minimize backscatter in underwater photographs
4. Explain how color is absorbed by water at different depths and some ways to reduce or eliminate this problem
5. Understand "black water" diving and what causes it
6. Explain the general pre-dive and post-dive care and maintenance required for photography equipment

WHY UNDERWATER PHOTOGRAPHY?

The number of people making use of recreational waterways across the United States has increased dramatically in recent years. Not unrelated are the number of violent crimes and accidents, including drownings, that occur in such settings. Criminals have found these watery estuaries useful for attempting to conceal evidence of their crimes. These increases have caused law enforcement agencies to become more involved in underwater recovery operations.

When an investigation leads to an underwater environment, it becomes an underwater criminal investigation (see Fig. 15–1). The process should be as forensically thorough and systematic as any process conducted out of water.[1] However, unlike the separation of duties often found in land-based investigations, underwater scenes typically call for the investigator to become the crime scene photographer, fingerprint specialist, and evidence recovery specialist. They also call for the investigator to be a skilled diver. This is a position that demands very specialized training and equipment (see Fig. 15–2).[2]

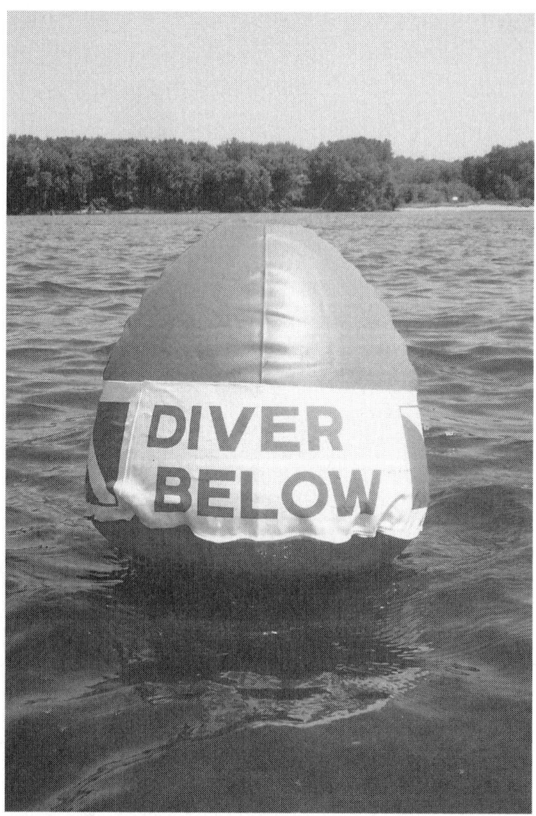

FIGURE 15–1 Diver buoy. *Source:* Aric Dutelle, University of Wisconsin-Platteville.

Today's forensic photographer is well versed in the methodology and logistics associated with above-water photography. A great deal of emphasis and training have been dedicated to ensuring that proper viewing angles, distances, and

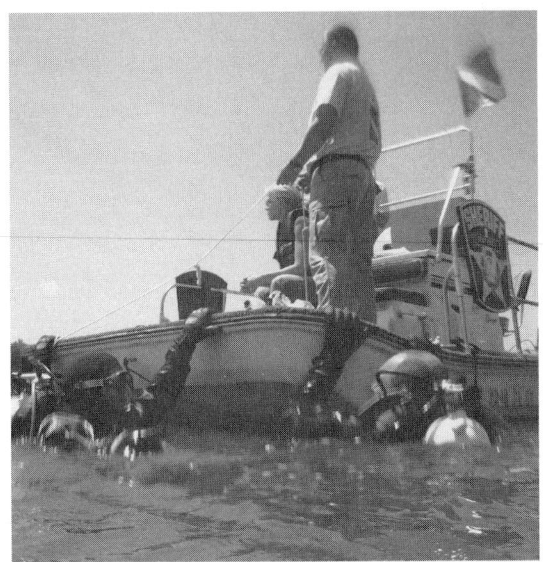

FIGURE 15–2 Grant County Sheriff's dive team members involved in an underwater investigation. *Source:* Aric Dutelle, University of Wisconsin-Platteville.

subject matter are captured as they were, in a fair and accurate representation of the scene. What if the crime scene in question is located underwater? Would the same practices and methodologies apply? Would the same equipment and personnel be appropriate (see Fig. 15–3)?

The SOPs associated with processing aboveground crime scenes may be forgotten or ignored when an underwater crime scene is encountered. The reasons for this disparity include differences in equipment, personnel, or environmental issues. Sometimes, it results from improperly trained or equipped personnel, or the impatience or lack of forethought of the investigator who thinks quality does not really matter as long as the assignment is completed in some manner. It must be remembered that underwater scenes and evidence are equally important and subject to the same scrutiny and legal considerations as land-based scenes, and thus they should be processed in an equally thorough and competent manner.[3]

PERSONNEL REQUIREMENTS AND TRAINING

The first challenge in underwater projects requires the photographer to submerge to document the scene, unless the project is in very shallow water and can be accomplished by wading or making photographs from a boat or other floating object.

Underwater investigators must be physically and mentally capable of venturing into and working within the hazards, risks, and restrictions involved when their bodies enter an environment in which they were not meant to live (see Fig. 15–4).

It is important that underwater forensic photographers be certified, comfortable, and competent divers. Several professional organizations certify divers. Some are dedicated to recreational divers and the civilian population, including the

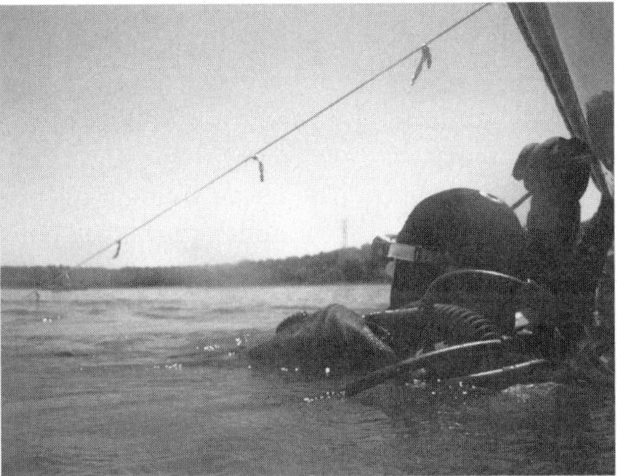

FIGURE 15–3 Grant County Sheriff's dive team member involved in an underwater investigation. *Source:* Aric Dutelle, University of Wisconsin-Platteville.

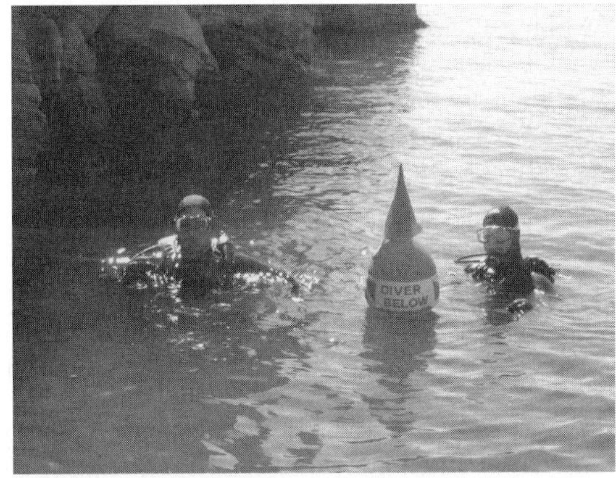

FIGURE 15–4 Divers and buoy. *Source:* Aric Dutelle, University of Wisconsin-Platteville.

Professional Association of Diving Instructors (PADI), National Association of Underwater Instructors (NAUI), and Scuba Schools International (SSI). Others are specifically geared for public safety professionals (e.g., Dive Rescue International, Miami-Dade).

Underwater documentation typically involves photography by moving photographers of moving subjects in moving environments. The photographer must be properly trained and proficient with all equipment to capture sharp images.

The diver must maintain proper buoyancy or attitude. **Buoyancy** is the upward force exerted on any object placed in a fluid. In underwater photography, it refers to how the forces affect the attitude of the diver.[4] Attitude is dependent on how a diver breathes, how his or her weight and equipment are distributed, and the current of the surrounding environment. Proper attention to buoyancy control and attitude will result in less diver movement, resulting in better photographs. Underwater photographers cannot typically use a tripod, therefore, they must control their breathing and body movements to capture sharp photos.

To aid the diver in controlling buoyancy, a **buoyancy control device (BCD),** such as an inflatable jacket, may be worn by the diver. Scuba systems are attached to the BCDs. The BCD adds or releases air to control buoyancy.[5]

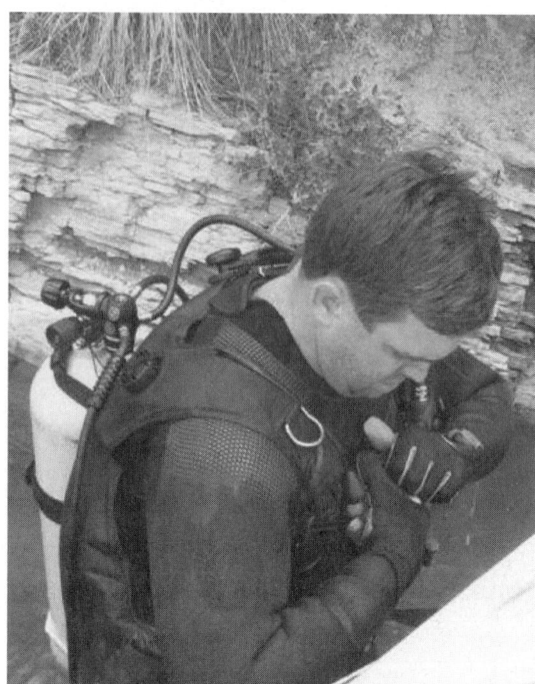

FIGURE 15–5 A diver in a wet suit prepares to enter the water. *Source:* Aric Dutelle, University of Wisconsin-Platteville.

PREPARING FOR THE UNDERWATER ENVIRONMENT

In addition to a BCD, the diver will also require various degrees of exposure protection, depending upon the marine environment encountered. Similar to normal PPEs, underwater exposure gear varies in thickness and style for heat retention and in function and type to prohibit environmental contact with the diver.

The basic level of protection is an **exposure suit,** sometimes called a **skin suit.** These provide little thermal protection and minimal abrasion protection. **Wet suits** are available in varying thicknesses and provide more insulation than body suits (see Fig. 15–5). Full-body suits are lightweight, flexible, nylon or neoprene clothing for warm water environments or as a layered under-suit for extremely cold conditions. Wet suits are suited to longer dive times in cooler temperatures. Wet suits allow the surrounding water to slowly creep inside the suit. The diver's body heats the trapped water between the skin and the wet suit. This provides thermal benefits, as opposed to diving in a body suit or with no exposure gear. However, a wet suit will not protect the diver from the environment. **Dry suits** provide the most insulation and protect the diver from the surrounding marine environment (see Fig. 15–6).

The diver requires proper training regarding how an in-water scene affects the human body and how the underwater environment affects photography. Above-water photographic training is helpful but insufficient to prepare for underwater photography. Underwater challenges include the following:

- Equipment
- Visibility
- Lighting
- Color

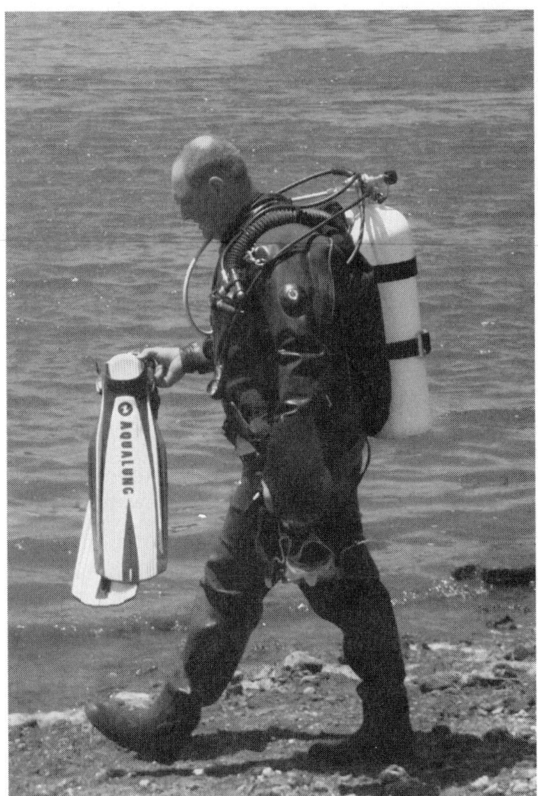

FIGURE 15–6 A diver in a dry suit prepares to enter the water. *Source:* Aric Dutelle, University of Wisconsin-Platteville.

Equipment

Photography underwater may not be compatible with the same equipment used for land-based scenes. Special marine or underwater cameras must be used, or underwater housings must be utilized to encapsulate the equipment. Previously, only a small number of camera models and manufacturers of underwater photography equipment were available. Today, a diver has a wider selection. The photographer must make the choice between the use of underwater cameras or compatible waterproof housings for their aboveground equipment.

Underwater Cameras

Cameras designed to be used underwater are common. Some manufacturers, such as Sea & Sea, advertise the utility of their cameras designed for use above *and* below water. Until recently, the most common underwater camera in the world was Nikon's Nikonos.[6] Nikon's commitment to underwater photography was solid for many years but has faded recently. Users of Canon and other brands found it difficult to find compatible gear. The Nikonos sustains a faithful following, but many current professionals are adapting their land-based equipment to underwater use.

Adapting Camera Equipment Using Housings

When contained in underwater housings, modern digital cameras have a wide range of technical capabilities. The majority of film-based SLR housings were made for Nikon cameras. Modern, major camera manufacturers, including Canon, Sony, and Nikon, produce waterproof housings for their OEM equipment. Underwater housings are not available for some cameras.[7] Ikelite manufactures aftermarket housings compatible with many brands of still and video cameras.

Using above-ground camera equipment in a housing for underwater use, instead of purchasing an underwater camera, has some benefits:

- It allows the photographer to use the camera equipment that he or she is comfortable and experienced with above water.
- It gives the photographer extended choices of camera type, model, manufacturer, accessories, and lenses.

Purchasing New Underwater Equipment

Digital underwater systems should be chosen based on budget and capability. Point-and-shoot, video, and DSLR systems are available. Underwater imaging is technologically dynamic. Due to the possibilities of obsolescence and lack of interchangeability, it is usually best to purchase underwater equipment as a system.

Water is 600 times denser than air and creates high pressure even at shallow depths.

For every 33 feet a diver descends, one atmosphere of pressure is added. This pressure affects both the diver and the camera equipment. For example, an inflatable ball under 33 feet of water would be half its original size, and it halves for every successive atmosphere. Water pressure exerts force on cameras and/or housings, so camera housings must be built to withstand the pressure and to minimize water leakage.[8]

Still and video cameras used underwater require appropriate light sources. EFUs that operate TTL are the best choice because they are controlled by the camera and are more reliable underwater. Several aftermarket manufacturers supply underwater EFUs with TTL control for specific cameras and housings.

MAINTAINING UNDERWATER PHOTOGRAPHY EQUIPMENT

Water and chemicals, including salt, are detrimental to electronic equipment. Therefore, it is important to practice proper pre-dive and post-dive maintenance to avoid expensive accidents. Every camera, housing, and accessory has specific care requirements. Consult the manufacturer's recommendations for specifics.

Basic maintenance guidelines include the following:

Pre-Dive Maintenance

- Thoroughly inspect and clean O-rings and contact surfaces.
  - Use a soft, lint-free cloth for cleaning O-rings.
  - Use cotton swabs to clean O-ring grooves and channels.
  - Replace damaged or worn O-rings.
  - Have spare O-rings available, and replace them if their integrity is at all in doubt.
- Apply a thin coating of silicone to O-rings.
  - Distribute silicone evenly. O-rings should appear wet, without globs.
  - Replace O-rings into their grooves, taking care to keep them clean.
  - Do not overstretch O-rings.
- Inspect and clean O-rings prior to each day of use.
  - Clean O-rings if the housing is opened to change batteries or media.
  - Inspect the surface contacts before sealing the housing.
  - If in doubt, clean the O-rings.[9]

Post-Dive Maintenance

- Immerse the completely assembled camera system in fresh water.
  - Agitate gently for approximately one minute to flush out contaminated water and debris from tight areas.
  - If an immersion tank is not available, rinse with flowing fresh water.
- If time permits and additional dives are not imminent, do the following:
  - Soak the system for about 30 minutes in fresh water.
  - Follow the soak with a gentle drying of the system, being careful not to scratch the optical surfaces.
- Disassemble the system.
- Download the acquired images.
- Recharge or replace the batteries.
- Clean the O-rings.
- If additional dives are not imminent, leave the system disassembled and store the O-rings separately in plastic bags.[10]

Condensation on the inside of the camera housing is a common problem. Place the assembled housing in an air-conditioned room or other low-moisture location. Another option is to insert silica packets inside the housing, in an unobtrusive location. After a few uses, silica packets become moist, and can no longer dehumidify the air. To recondition them, place them in a moderate temperature oven (approximately 200 degrees F) for one hour. Store them in a sealed plastic bag between uses. Some camera housings are supplied with anti-fog solution. Put some on the inside of the lens port to reduce the effects of condensation.

Handling Suggestions

- Keep wet to dry cycles to a minimum during use.

- Keep equipment cool prior to submersion.
- Do not put cold equipment into a warm environment.

Large changes in temperature increase the formation of condensation.[11] Equipment should be placed in a transition tank prior to submersion. Transition tanks should contain water from the dive location at dive temperature. This will allow the equipment to acclimate to the dive temperature. The transition tank also allows the user to check for proper watertight sealing of the equipment. Be sure to visually inspect the equipment for leaks when it is removed from the transition tank.

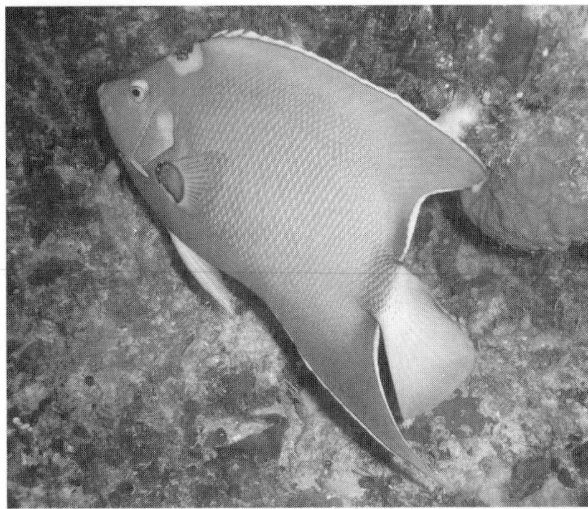

FIGURE 15–8 Underwater wildlife. *Source:* Aric Dutelle, University of Wisconsin-Platteville.

ACCLIMATING TO THE UNDERWATER ENVIRONMENT

After preparing the equipment, the photographer must acclimate to the necessary environmental conditions involved with the project. When most people think about underwater photography, they visualize beautiful photos of underwater creatures and scenery (see Figs. 15–7, 15–8, 15–9 and 15–10). However, underwater forensic evidence photographers rarely require images of the beauty

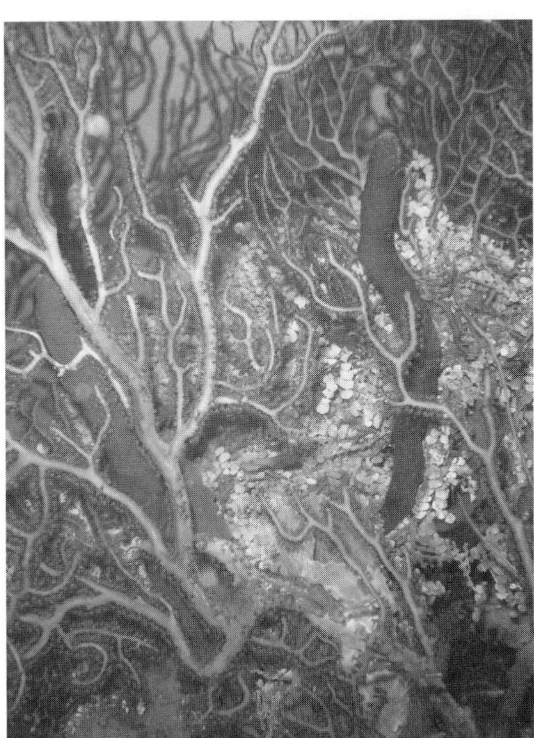

FIGURE 15–7 Underwater wildlife. *Source:* Aric Dutelle, University of Wisconsin-Platteville.

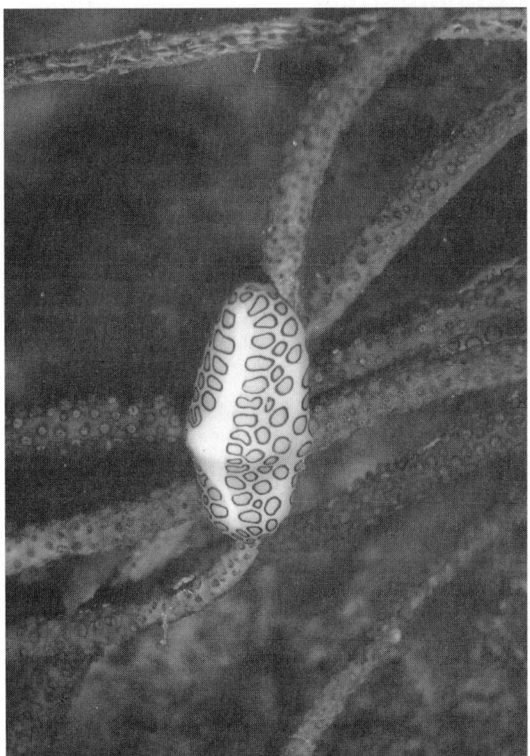

FIGURE 15–9 Underwater wildlife. *Source:* Aric Dutelle, University of Wisconsin-Platteville.

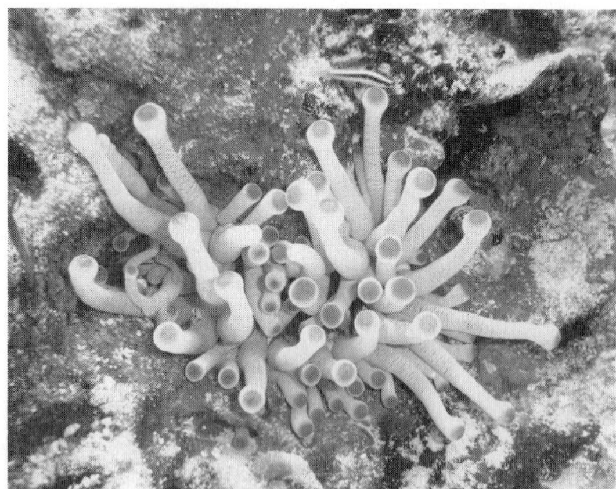

FIGURE 15–10 Underwater wildlife. *Source:* Aric Dutelle, University of Wisconsin-Platteville.

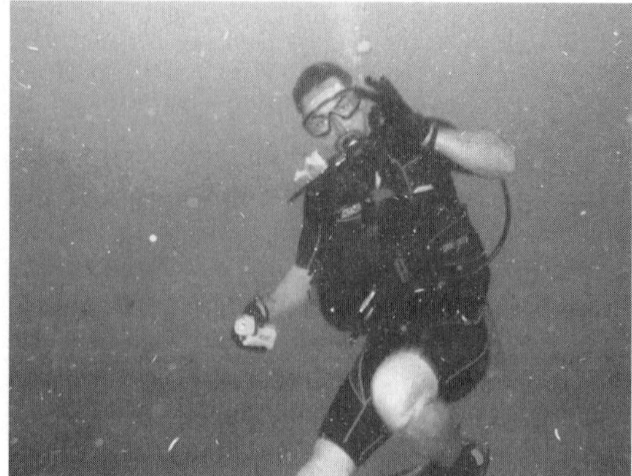

FIGURE 15–11 Example of backscatter from an EFU placed close to the camera lens. *Source:* Aric Dutelle, University of Wisconsin-Platteville.

of the scene. The waters of the Caribbean and South Pacific are warm and clear, but forensic assignments often occur in water with low visibility and temperatures.

Visibility Issues

The most obvious difference between underwater and land-based photography is the lack of visibility (**viz**) underwater,[12] and a major obstacle to image clarity underwater is the presence of small suspended particles. The relative concentration of suspended particles is defined as **turbidity. Suspended particles** may be organic, as in plankton, or inorganic, as in sediment (silt). Turbidity may result from healthy and natural phenomena, including rainwater runoff, or artificial, unhealthy phenomena, including pollution.[13] In both cases, the higher the turbidity, the less light penetrates the water and the less visibility. The more the particles between the viewer and the object being viewed, the less the image quality of photographs will be in direct proportion to the degree of turbidity. The **reflection** of light from turbidity is called **backscatter.** Backscatter is more visible when a flash is used (see Fig. 15–11).

Backscatter is minimized by moving the flash away from the lens, if possible. If the In-camera flash is close to the camera lens, it illuminates the particles directly in front of the camera, the same way a flash will light rain or snow above ground. If the EFU is located to the side of the camera or above the camera, the light bouncing off the particles will be reflected more toward the flash and less toward the lens.[14] (See "Using Underwater EFUs" in this chapter.)

The amount of water between the flash and the subject also influences the amount of backscatter. More particles are suspended in a larger amount of water. Exposing images close to the subject is an effective method to reduce backscatter. If the water is very turbid, it may be better to use only **ambient light** or available light.[15]

Silt, sediment, algae, and pollution may cause "black" or "brown" diving conditions. In these conditions, visibility may be less than 2 feet. Use utmost care and diving skills to ensure proper buoyancy and to avoid extra disturbance to the environment, which will diminish photo quality.

Light Properties and Coloration

Digital cameras create images by converting light to electrical energy in pixel form. The behavior of light changes significantly as it passes through water, affecting what the photographer and the camera may see and image. To take proper underwater photographs, the underwater properties of light must be understood by the photographer.

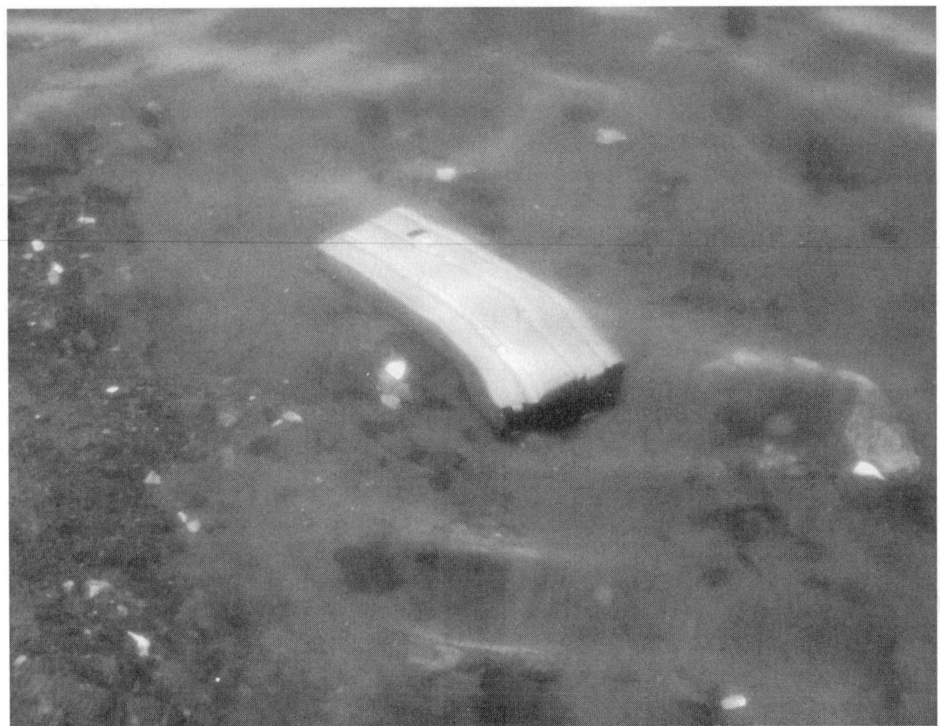

FIGURE 15–12 An example of light refraction and how it distorts the image of an object's shape. *Source:* Aric Dutelle, University of Wisconsin-Platteville.

A phenomenon evident in underwater photography is **refraction**, the tendency of light to change direction when it passes from a medium of one density to a medium of another density, including from air to water, or water to air (see Fig. 15–12). This happens because the speed of light changes proportional to the density of the medium it illuminates, which causes shifts in the light's path. Images are magnified underwater due to light refraction (see Fig. 15–13). To see this phenomenon, put a pencil in a glass of water and look at the pencil from the side of the glass (see Fig. 15–14) The pencil appears to be bent where it meets the water. It also looks thicker underwater than above water.

One particular concern in underwater photography is the refraction that results when an image passing through water, glass, or air interfaces with a diver's mask, camera lens, or camera housing. Light refraction causes these objects to appear magnified, and their distance becomes distorted. Objects that are magnified underwater appear closer by a ratio of about 4 (actual distance) to 3 (apparent distance), so an object that is four yards away will appear to be three yards away. In other words, objects appear 25% closer than they are, or are 33% farther than they look.[16] Thus, it is extremely important to include a scaled object for size and distance reference in underwater images. The scale will also be magnified, but

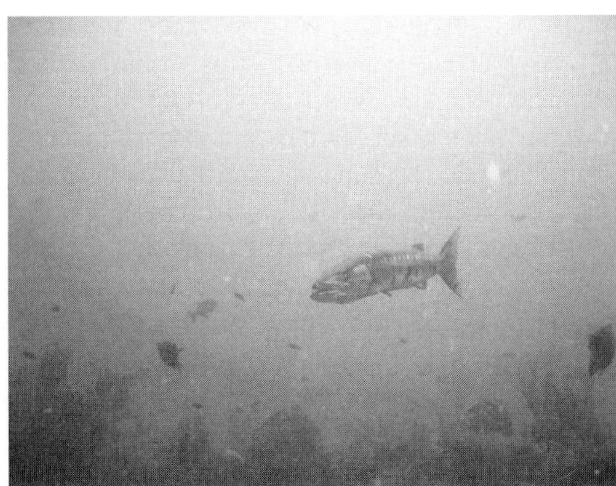

FIGURE 15–13 How far away is the barracuda? *Source:* Aric Dutelle, University of Wisconsin-Platteville.

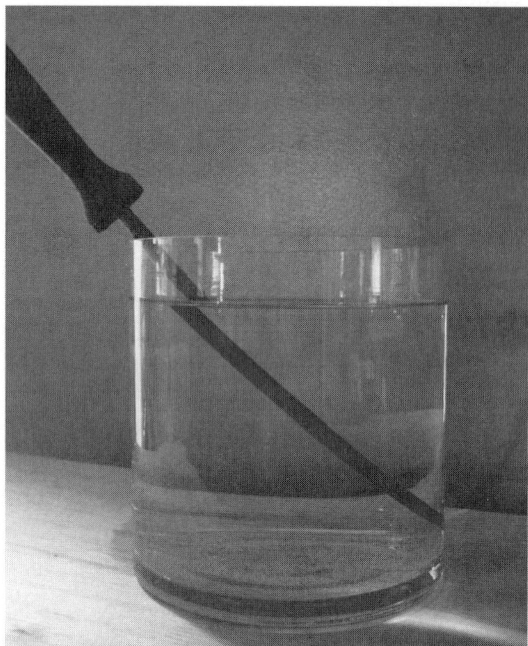

FIGURE 15–14 Example of refraction bending and magnifying a partially submerged object. *Source:* Aric Dutelle, University of Wisconsin-Platteville.

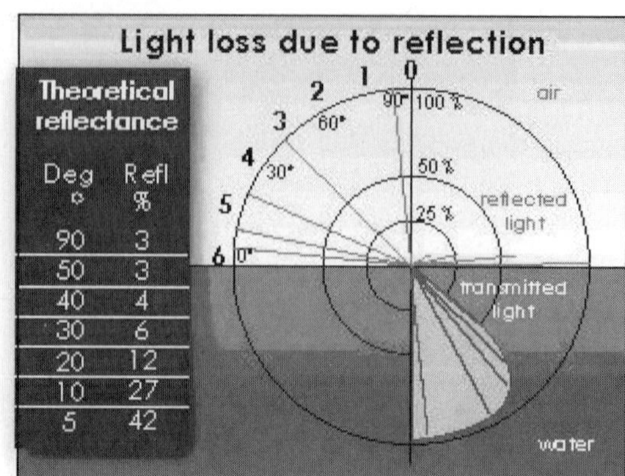

FIGURE 15–15 Light loss due to reflection. *Source:* Aric Dutelle, University of Wisconsin-Platteville.

it will be magnified in direct proportion to the object depicted. This helps the viewer to interpret the true size and dimension of the subject.[17]

LCD Screens

The underwater camera system visualizes the object in the same way the diver does through his or her mask. Digital cameras allow the photographer to review images on the LCD screen. When photographing underwater, it is important to focus the camera on the apparent subject distance, not the actual subject distance (if the photographer uses an auto-focus system, it will do this automatically), then review the image on the LCD for composition and clarity. The magnification caused by refraction reduces the visual angle between the camera and the subject. This causes a slight telephoto effect in the images. For this reason, shorter focal length lenses may be used to image what a longer focal length lens would image above water, without refraction.[18]

A domed lens port may be used to minimize distortion, but this method of changing the view of the subject may not be an accurate representation.

Besides bending, water also **scatters** and **deflects** light (see Figs. 15–15 and 15–16). This is called **diffusion**. Even totally clear water reduces the amount of penetrating light. Light will deflect or scatter particles as it travels through water. This spreads the light and reduces or eliminates shadows underwater. In above-water photography, shadows must be reduced by using special techniques. Underwater, shadow reduction is a gift of physics. However, the lack of contrast makes distant objects appear less distinct. This is an environmental phenomenon, not a result of poor focus. The light traveling from the object to the lens deflects slightly out of line, or diffuses. The higher the amount of turbidity, the more the image will be diffused.

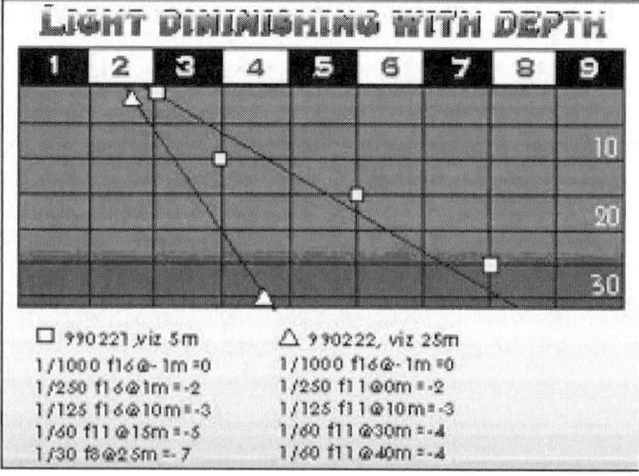

FIGURE 15–16 Light loss due to depth. *Source:* Aric Dutelle, University of Wisconsin-Platteville.

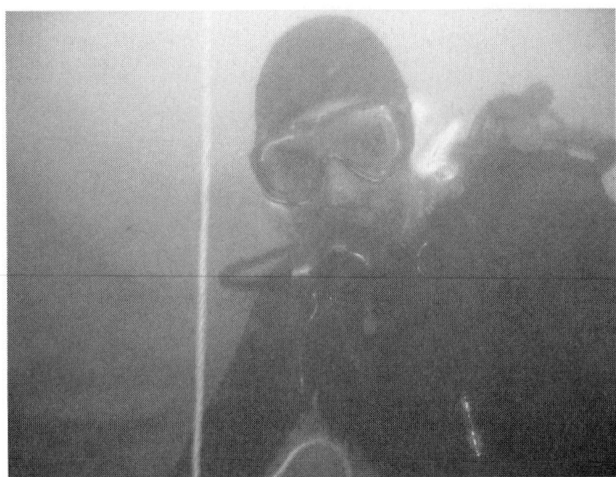

FIGURE 15–17 The environment affects color in underwater photographs. *Source:* Aric Dutelle, University of Wisconsin-Platteville.

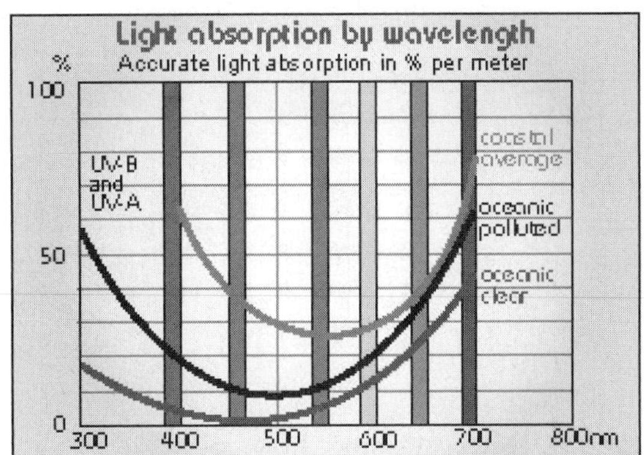

FIGURE 15–18 Light absorption by wavelength. *Source:* Aric Dutelle, University of Wisconsin-Platteville.

Another concern with underwater photography is the accurate depiction of subject coloration (see Fig. 15–17). When sunlight strikes the surface of water, it may be comprised of all the colors of the spectrum. As the depth of the water increases, red, orange, and yellow wavelengths are absorbed by the water. This occurs in all water, no matter how clear. Only blue and green wavelengths typically penetrate to a depth of 30 feet. If the water is polluted or murky, this level is significantly reduced. Bodies of water appear visually blue because water reflects that wavelength of light.

Clear water transmits high levels of light at wavelengths around 480 nanometers, or what the human eye perceives as blue. In higher levels of turbidity, the maximum transparency shifts to yellow-green wavelengths.[19] Turbid water appears more yellow-green than blue, from above and below (see Figs. 15–18 and 15–19).

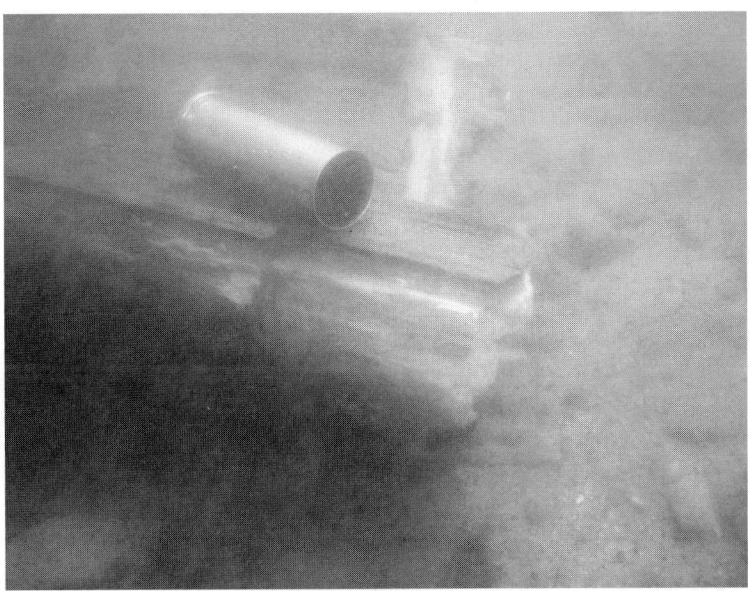

FIGURE 15–19 The underwater environment affects the colors of underwater photographs. This image displays the typical yellow-green of turbid water below the depth where other colors have been absorbed by the water. *Source:* Aric Dutelle, University of Wisconsin-Platteville.

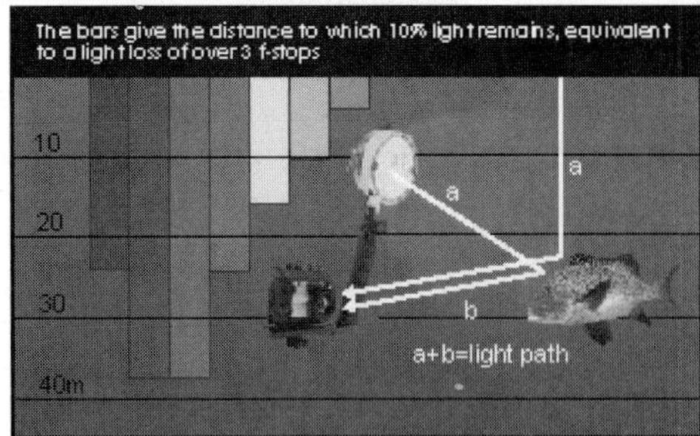

FIGURE 15–20 Keep the EFU to the side to reduce or eliminate backscatter. Warm-colored light from the EFU penetrates the water for short distances. *Source:* Aric Dutelle, University of Wisconsin-Platteville.

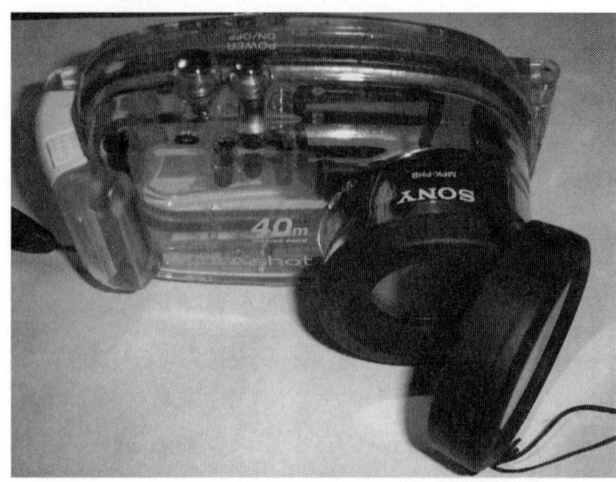

FIGURE 15–22 Color correction (CC) filter and housing. *Source:* Aric Dutelle, University of Wisconsin-Platteville.

The photographer has assorted options with which to compensate for the loss of warm colors underwater.

To illuminate subjects and capture their images in the most accurate colors, in most photographic situations the majority of the natural light is absorbed or scattered by the water. Supplemental lighting is usually introduced by using a built-in or accessory flash with the camera EFUs used underwater. Most EFUs will not illuminate objects in a full range of color wavelengths farther than six to eight feet, depending on the power of the flash (see Fig. 15–20).

Color correction filters may be used underwater without flash. When photographing underwater with natural light, use a red (CC30R) filter to minimize blue, or a magenta (CC30M) filter to minimize the green (see Figs. 15–21, 15–22, and 15–23). Color casts are a more serious problem when exposing images of distant objects.[20]

Record the use of the color correction filtration in the notes for the photographs. Filtration creates images of what the subject would or should look like, except for the environmental abnormalities associated with being underwater. Filters also reduce the amount of light impacting the camera sensor. Thus, the use of filtration may

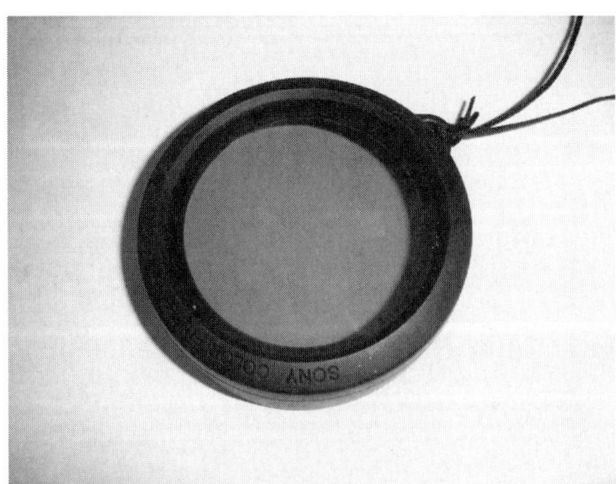

FIGURE 15–21 Color correction (CC) filter for a camera housing. *Source:* Aric Dutelle, University of Wisconsin-Platteville.

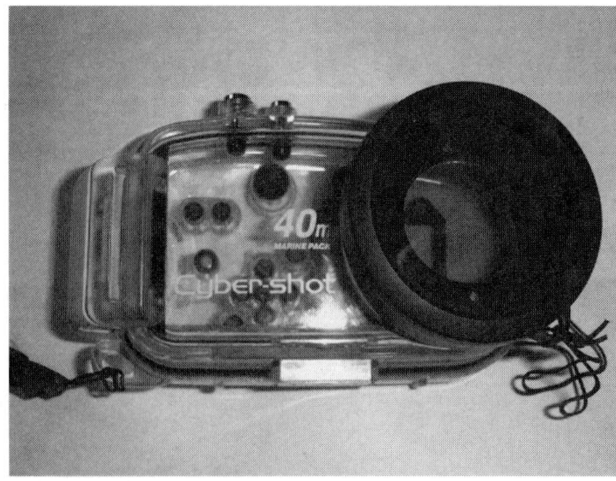

FIGURE 15–23 Color correction (CC) filter on housing. *Source:* Aric Dutelle, University of Wisconsin-Platteville.

necessitate longer shutter speeds or larger lens apertures, which may reduce ultimate image quality. If possible, use flash.[21]

REMEMBER:

Remember, the photographer sees the scene in unnatural colors—shades of green and blue—not in the true colors created by the filtration.

The photographer may point the camera upward toward the surface to take full advantage of the ambient illumination. Color absorption affects conspicuity by altering the contrast and color of the subject. It is easier to see something that stands out against its background. Turbidity, depth, salinity, particle size, and pollution all affect light absorption by water, and they also affect contrast. Anything that affects the apparent color of a subject affects the apparent contrast too.[22] A red object displays high contrast against a dark green background above water, but at a depth of 100 feet both may appear the same color.

Using Underwater EFUs

Underwater EFUs (see Fig. 15–24) may yield the most accurate images. The factors affecting their effectiveness include the following:

- Type and size
- Aiming to avoid backscatter
- Setting the camera for proper exposure

Underwater EFUs with TTL capabilities are widely available. They are similar to those used above water. The basic operation and functionality remain the same as above water (see Chapter 9).

When an underwater flash is imaged by the camera, it overexposes part of the image, just as it would on the surface (see Fig. 15–25). Be sure to

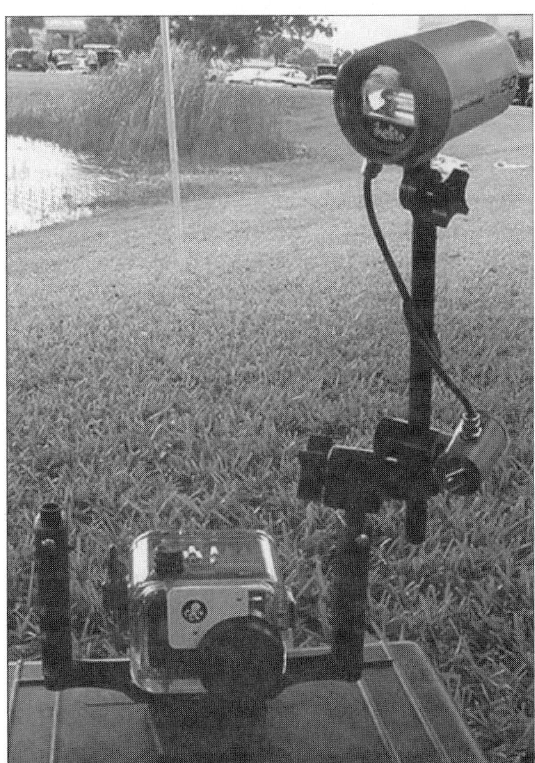

FIGURE 15–24 Underwater camera system with EFU. *Source:* Aric Dutelle, University of Wisconsin-Platteville.

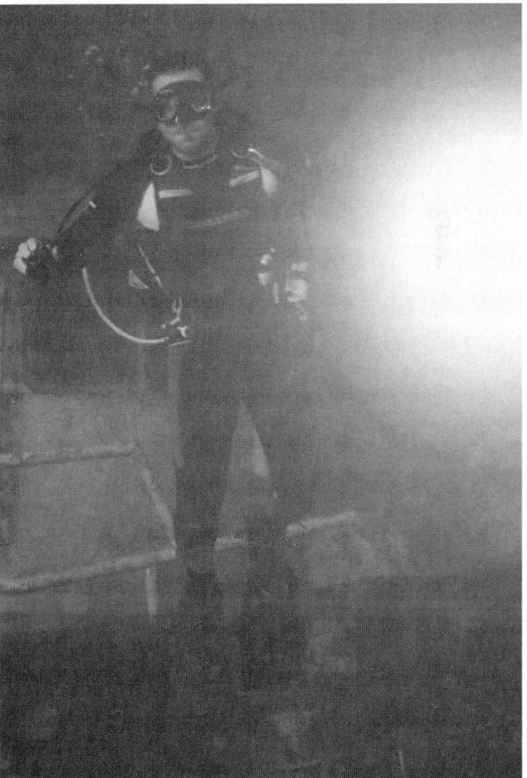

FIGURE 15–25 A diver utilizing a strobe underwater. *Source:* Aric Dutelle, University of Wisconsin-Platteville.

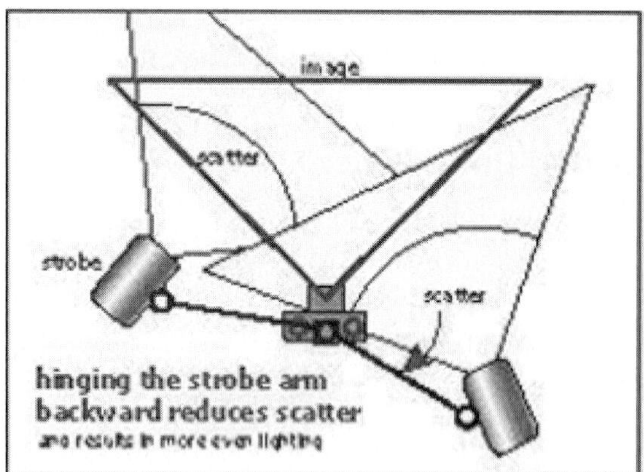

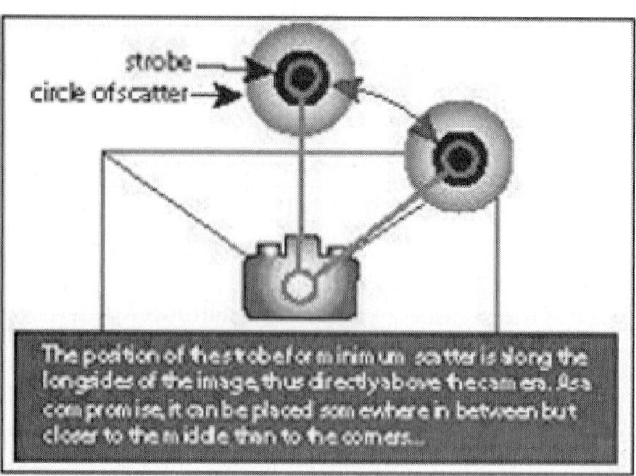

FIGURE 15–26 EFU adjustment. *Source:* Aric Dutelle, University of Wisconsin-Platteville.

aim the flash in the optimum direction to illuminate the subject without interfering with what the camera is imaging (see Fig. 15–26).

EFU usage and handling may differ underwater. Ideally, the strobe should be positioned to the side of the camera and aimed at the subject at an oblique 45-degree angle.[23] In certain situations, dual strobes are used, positioned on each side of the camera, at 45-degree angles to the subject. The angling reduces backscatter.[24] When aiming the flash, remember refraction: the subject is farther from the camera than it appears, so the flash must be aimed behind the apparent location to provide proper illumination.[25]

LENSES FOR UNDERWATER PHOTOGRAPHY

A normal lens will have perceived telephoto properties when used underwater. A wide-angle lens may create images as if it were a normal lens. A lens with a shorter focal length will capture the same area underwater as a lens with a longer focal length above water.[26]

Most photographers use a wide-angle lens as the normal lens for underwater photography because it compensates for the changes caused by the effects of water. Capturing the increased subject size in the image also decreases the amount of water between the camera and the subject. This reduces the amount of particulates softening the image between the subject and the camera, and it reduces backscatter. Wide-angle lenses reduce the amount of light and color loss due to distance. Wide-angle lenses also maximize DoF compared to other lenses.[27]

FILM VERSUS DIGITAL

Digital photography is an easier media to use for the capture of underwater photographs. One advantage is that digital systems capture more than 36 photos before needing to be reloaded. In addition, digital media allows the capture of hundreds of photographs at high resolution, and it provides image review while underwater.

In addition, digital photography simplifies problems related to color in underwater images. Some photographers prefer images captured with an underwater flash, and some use the automatic white balance capability and ambient illumination. The white balance function partially compensates for the absorption of color by water. This improves color accuracy with or without use of a flash.

COLD WEATHER UNDERWATER PHOTOGRAPHY

It may be necessary to submerge and photograph during cold weather, perhaps in water that is iced over. The cold climate will not harm the equipment, or the properly prepared photographer, although it may result in slower functioning of both. It is suggested that the underwater photographer obtain proper training and certification prior to submersion in cold environments. The photographic equipment used will not change, but the photographer's attire may differ greatly.

Consult local divers or dive professionals regarding the recommended attire for the body of water and conditions involved.

Camera operation and control may be slow and labored, as will the movements and actions of the photographer. Use photographic equipment chosen specifically with large, workable buttons and features so you can control operations through the bulk of gloves and other exposure equipment.

Pre-submersion of the camera equipment into cold water may not be necessary. If possible, place the camera equipment out of the sun, in a dry area of similar temperature to the water, for temperature transition. The cold may deplete battery power. Have extra batteries on hand, and place a fresh battery in the camera immediately prior to submersion to prolong battery life.

UNDERWATER VIDEO

Consumer digital video systems may rival or exceed the image quality of professional cameras used 10 years ago. Cameras are also smaller and ideal for placement in underwater housings. The same environmental factors and problems with still photography apply to underwater video. One major difference is the use of underwater continuous lighting, rather than instantaneous flashes. Video results benefit from artificial lighting by improving color and the use of optimum camera settings. Quartz-halogen lamps were once standard. Modern underwater sources are **high-intensity discharge (HID) lighting.** HIDs are more efficient systems. A 10 watt HID bulb emits about the same intensity lighting as a 50 watt quartz-halogen bulb.[28] In addition, HIDs are more efficient in power drain. Since the underwater white balance of some digital video systems is not completely accurate, color correction filters may be used with and without supplementary lighting.

PROCESSING AND DOCUMENTING THE UNDERWATER SCENE

When investigating an underwater crime scene (see Fig. 15–27) the team members must be prepared to document multiple scenes and levels of scenes. Multiple methods of documentation will be appropriate.

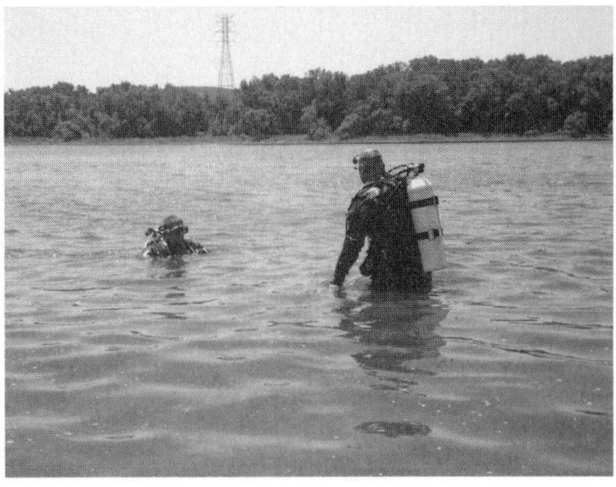

FIGURE 15–27 Underwater incident: Grant County Sheriff's dive team members involved in an underwater investigation. *Source:* Aric Dutelle, University of Wisconsin-Platteville.

Underwater Investigation and documentation will include all of the following:

- Still photography
- Videography
- Sketching
- Mapping
- Written report

There are two basic types of scenes with varying locales:

- Surface scenes
  - Water access points
  - Piers
  - Shorelines
  - Waterfronts
- Submerged scenes
  - Added difficulty of depth
  - Environmental issues
  - Visibility issues

Submerged scenes are three-dimensional, including objects at various depths. Fixed markers and items to aid in reference are always absent. As for surface scenes, underwater scenes must be thoroughly searched. Items of evidence must be photographed, marked, and their positions and depths noted on a sketch. It is suggested that the diver or dive team assemble a diver's slate, made specifically for the purpose of annotating underwater scene information.[29] (Consult the author of this book for assistance in the design and production of slates.)

Evidence recovered from water requires special handling and packaging. It may be necessary to package the evidence underwater to ensure the collection of trace evidence that may have adhered to the item. It also is often necessary to package the evidence in the water in which it was found to slow environmental deterioration that may be caused by removing the item from the water. Consult published SOPs and standards for the collection and preservation of underwater evidence.

Above-Water Evidence

Not all evidence associated with an event is submerged. And investigative personnel may encounter black water or other environmental conditions that make underwater photography impossible. Remember to photograph the following aspects of the scene above water:

- Object or subject entry point or route
- Object or subject exit point or route
- Overall photographs of geographical area adjacent to the water
- Personnel and equipment utilized in the operation (if appropriate for liability reasons)
- Staged equipment and personnel not utilized in the operation (If appropriate for liability reasons)[30]

Underwater Safety

The goal of any criminal investigation is to determine whether or not a crime has been committed. If it has, the goal is to document and collect evidence to identify and prosecute the guilty. During this process, the safety of all personnel involved in the investigation process is paramount. Underwater photography is dangerous, and the underwater environment may cause fatigue, entanglement, and other safety issues.

The photographer should ensure that all of his or her equipment is connected properly and does not present any entanglement threat. A neck strap should never be used. Instead, equipment should be affixed to the wrist or BCD.

It is extremely important for forensic photographers to learn dive-related skills from a certified professional and to participate in ongoing education and training related to the underwater environment. That will help ensure the safety and competency of the photographer.

SUMMARY

Underwater crime scenes, and the evidence contained therein, are not always properly documented or processed. This failure can result in the loss, contamination, or inadmissibility of the evidence. Proper underwater crime scene processing and documentation methods will ensure that the evidence is located, properly documented, preserved, and admissible, in subsequent litigation. The underwater investigation team must be properly trained and take part in ongoing training, specifically relating to crime scene documentation and processing methods involving the underwater environment. What is not looked for will not be found. What is not found cannot be analyzed to uncover the truth.

To overcome the difficulties encountered when photographing an underwater scene, several basic methods can be employed. Some of these may not be viable, depending on the environments requiring documentation.

- If possible, stay shallow. This will reduce the color loss from the limited wavelengths of light reaching the subject. If the crime scene is deep and photographs must be taken at that depth, use an EFU or color correction filter.
- Stay close to the subject. Underwater distortion, coloration issues, and environmental haze will be minimized.
- Maintain proper buoyancy. If a diver-photographer can maintain his or her proper attitude, it will reduce or eliminate distortion and obliteration caused by stirring up environmental elements.
- Photographs are enhanced when the sky is sunny and clear.

- If possible, photograph when the sun is highest, between 10:00 am and 2:00 p.m., to reduce light loss due to reflection.
- Photograph when the water is calm.
- In some cases it may be possible to increase image detail by using a plastic bag of clear water pressed between the object and the camera lens to provide extra clarity in close-up photographs.

CASE STUDY

BANK ROBBERY

Two men armed with a semi-automatic assault rifle and a handgun allegedly held up a local branch bank. They fired one shot, doing no harm, and made off with approximately $110,000. An off-duty firefighter saw the suspects wearing ski masks as they left the bank. He called police dispatch on his cell phone to report the violation. The firefighter followed the two men in his vehicle as they left the bank and drove away. The firefighter's descriptions and real-time information updates allowed police officers to intercept the vehicle prior to its leaving the area. A 13-mile high-speed pursuit ensued. Three law enforcement agencies participated. At one point, several objects were observed being thrown from the passenger window of the suspect vehicle as it crossed a highway viaduct over a lake. While the vehicle was moving, the passenger exited, and the suspects split up. The passenger was pursued by police while he ran through several houses in an attempt to elude them. The passenger was observed carrying a semi-automatic rifle during the pursuit. The suspect on foot evaded officers and was not found for several hours prior to arrest. The suspect did not have a firearm in his possession at the time of his arrest. The driver continued, and the vehicle pursuit terminated when the suspect vehicle disregarded a traffic control device and collided with another passenger vehicle. The suspect driver was injured, and the other driver died.

Crime scene investigators found one spent .40 caliber (.40 cal) shell casing in the lobby of the bank. One AR-15 assault rifle (see Fig. 15–28) was located in the living room of a home in which the passenger was seen. No additional firearms were located in the vicinity of the foot pursuit, nor in the vehicle of the suspect driver. The assault rifle was missing its magazine. The bag containing the money was found in the vehicle.

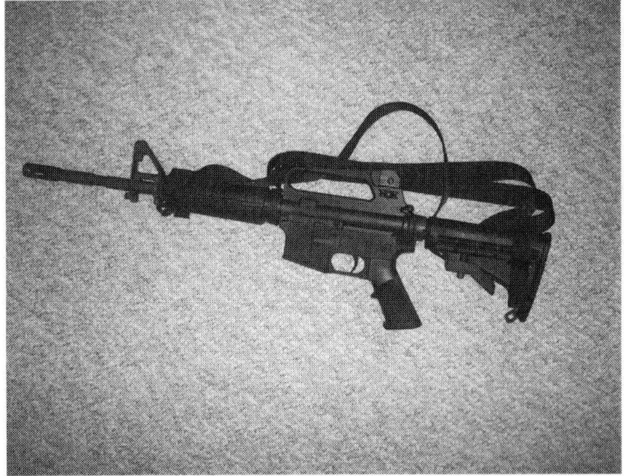

FIGURE 15–28 AR-15 assault rifle. *Source:* Aric Dutelle, University of Wisconsin-Platteville.

The money found in the vehicle was considered a "smoking gun" in this case. Since the possession of semi-automatic weapons and their use in federal offenses carries additional penalties, it was especially imperative that all firearm evidence be located and recovered.

The firearm located in the house, on the living room floor, was photographed and collected for evidence. Pursuing officers recalled the passenger throwing something out his window while the vehicle traversed the viaduct over the lake. Investigators were dispatched to the location to determine if an attempt had been made to destroy or ditch evidence. When investigators arrived, they recognized that it would not be possible to conduct a thorough investigation without the use of divers. A dive team was mobilized and responded to the location. The dive team included a crime scene technician, whose duty was the documentation of the scene and the collection of all discovered evidence.

The crime scene technician had recently been issued a Sony DSC-P200, 7.2 Mp, point-and-shoot camera, with compatible underwater housing and flash for use in underwater environments.

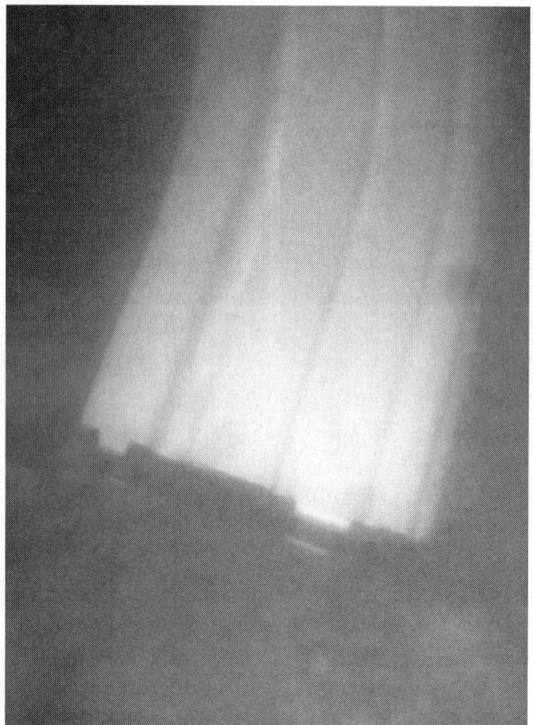

FIGURE 15–29 Rifle magazine 1. *Source:* Aric Dutelle, University of Wisconsin-Platteville.

The equipment conformed to the agency budget considerations for the purchase of limited-use equipment.

The crime scene technician was tasked with the documentation of the submerged and surface scenes. He photographed the suspected entry area of the unknown objects from numerous angles, including from the position of the viaduct, from which they were believed to have been thrown. The technician also photographed the presence of the dive team while conducting the search and all equipment associated with the effort.

The dive team entered the water and subsequently found one high-capacity magazine for a .223 cal rifle, the same caliber as the assault rifle that was located in the living room (see Figs. 15–29, 15–30, and 15–31). The team also discovered a magazine for a .40 cal semi-automatic handgun (see Figs. 15–32, 15–33, and 15–34), the same caliber as the expended cartridge found in the bank. Nothing else was located that was

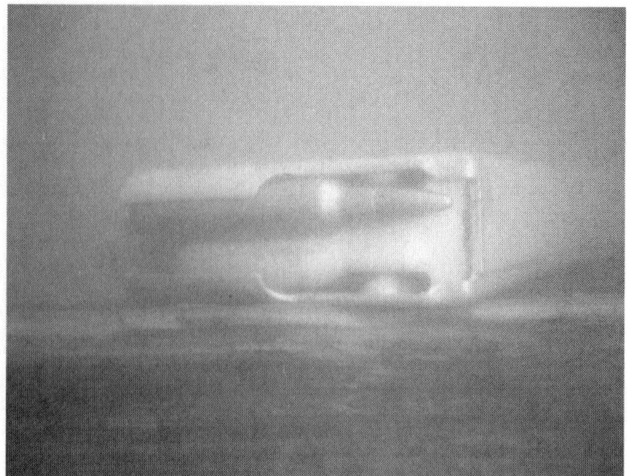

FIGURE 15–30 Rifle magazine 2. *Source:* Aric Dutelle, University of Wisconsin-Platteville.

believed to be associated with the alleged crime. The magazines were photographed in situ by the crime scene technician, utilizing the underwater system he was assigned.

Visibility in the dive area was less than two feet. Photography was difficult. The level of environmental debris was high, and visibility had been further diminished as a result of the search activity. The severe turbidity and added backscatter prompted the photographer to photograph the scene using available light. A fast shutter speed was used to minimize the movement of the diver and the water around the subject. The items were photographed with and without scales of reference. The overall coloration was

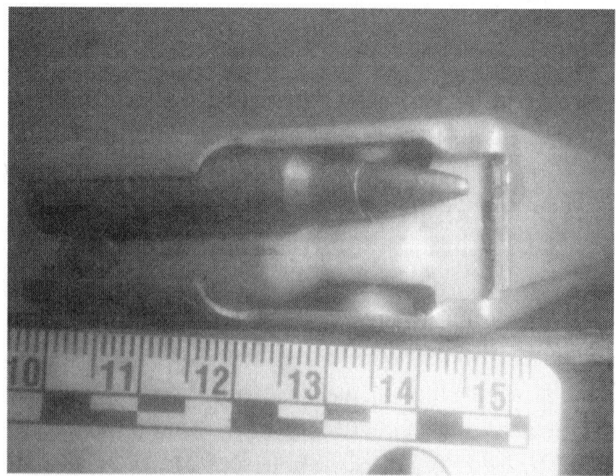

FIGURE 15–31 Rifle magazine 3. *Source:* Aric Dutelle, University of Wisconsin-Platteville.

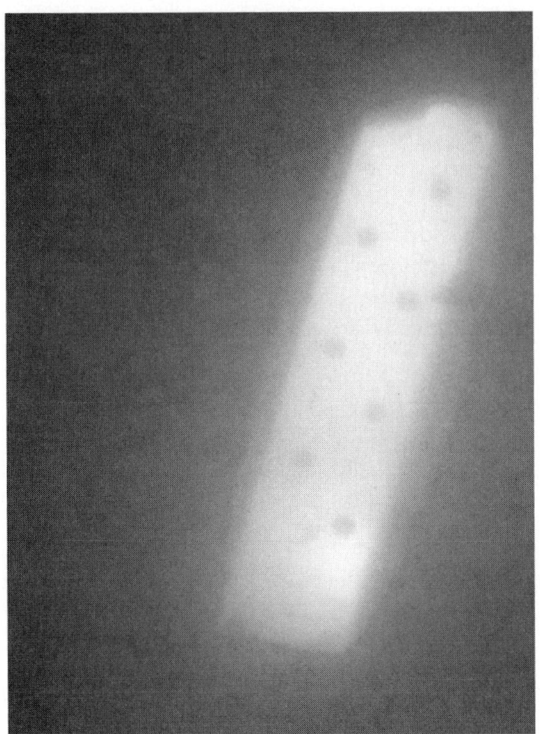

FIGURE 15–32 Magazine for handgun. *Source:* Aric Dutelle, University of Wisconsin-Platteville.

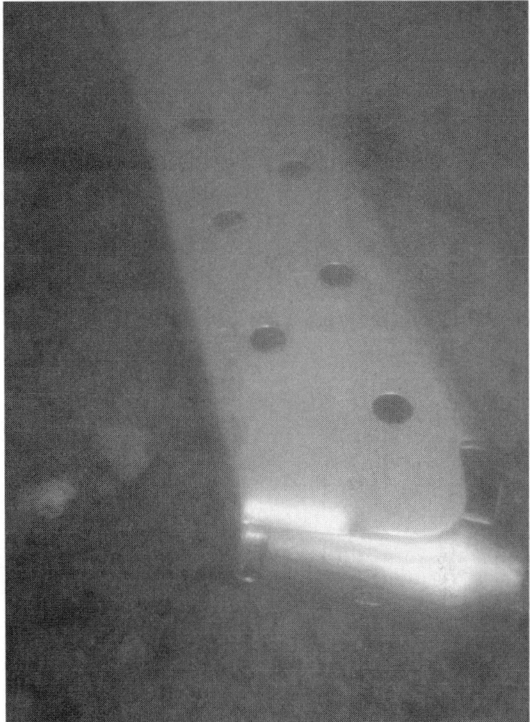

FIGURE 15–33 Handgun Magazine 2. *Source:* Aric Dutelle, University of Wisconsin-Platteville.

yellow-green, due to the heavy level of algal growth. A color correction filter was not used. Underwater video was also exposed.

The underwater photographs were a major part of this investigation. They documented the attempt to disguise evidence associated with criminal activity. The evidence helped tie the expended round in the bank to the suspected individuals. The round did not match the firearm located in the living room. The round did match one of the magazines found and photographed in the lake. Despite the assistance of the public and numerous police searchers, the semi-automatic handgun was never located.

At several points during the vehicular pursuit, the subject vehicle was out of the line of sight of law enforcement. The missing firearm possibly had been discarded during one of those moments. Still, the located evidence was sufficient to convict both men of federal charges for bank robbery, possession of illegal firearms, use of a firearm to commit a felony, and first-degree murder for the death of the driver of the passenger vehicle.

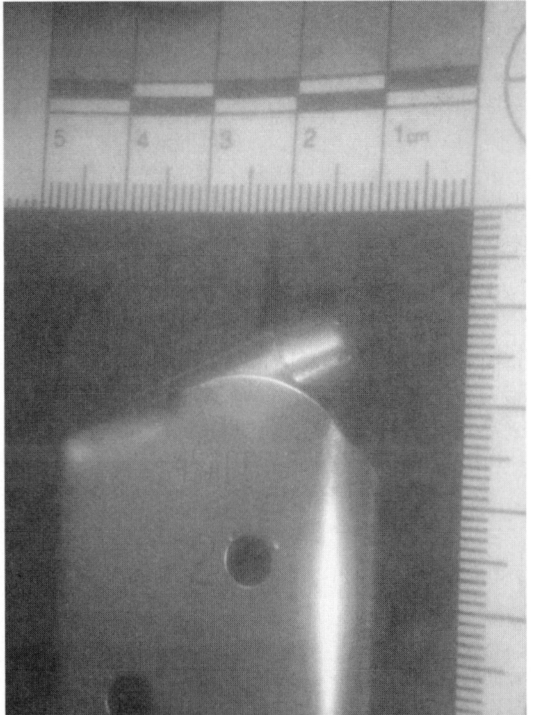

FIGURE 15–34 Handgun magazine 3. *Source:* Aric Dutelle, University of Wisconsin-Platteville.

KEY TERMS

buoyancy, (p. 444)
buoyancy control device (BCD), (p. 444)
exposure suit, (p. 444)
skin suit, (p. 444)
wet suit, (p. 444)
dry suit, (p. 444)
viz, (p. 448)
turbidity, (p. 448)
suspended particles, (p. 448)
reflection, (p. 448)
backscatter, (p. 448)
ambient light, (p. 448)
refraction, (p. 449)
scatter, (p. 450)
deflect, (p. 450)
diffusion, (p. 450)
color correction filter, (p. 452)
high-intensity discharge (HID) lighting, (p. 455)

EXERCISES

1. Locate a clear glass cylindrical container. Fill the container three-quarters full with water. Take photographs of a pencil, and note the differing affects that refraction has on the images when the pencil is:
   a. Immersed totally in the water
   b. Half in and half out
   c. Standing straight up (with a portion sticking out of the water)
   d. At an angle (with a portion out of the water)
2. Place an object in shallow water (if no other sources are available, use the sink or tub). Expose a photo of the object in the water. Fill a gallon-size zip-seal bag and place it over the object (breaking the surface of the water) between the object and the camera lens. Be sure to keep the lens dry. Be sure the lens is tight against the bag. Take various photographs of the object, noting how the bag allows the camera to get close to the object, while never entering the water environment, and improves visibility.
3. If you do not have one, locate an underwater camera from a local dive shop or use a disposable one. In a pool, expose photographs of yellow, red, green, and blue objects in depths of 1, 5, 10, and 12 feet, as your breath and pool depth allows. Note the differences in coloration.
4. Using the same pool and camera as in exercise 3, expose photographs of objects 3, 6, 12, and 24 feet away from you. Note how distance, refraction, and the medium affect clarity, size, and perceived distance.
5. Research the first recorded use of underwater photography.

Chapter 16

Photographing Crime Scenes

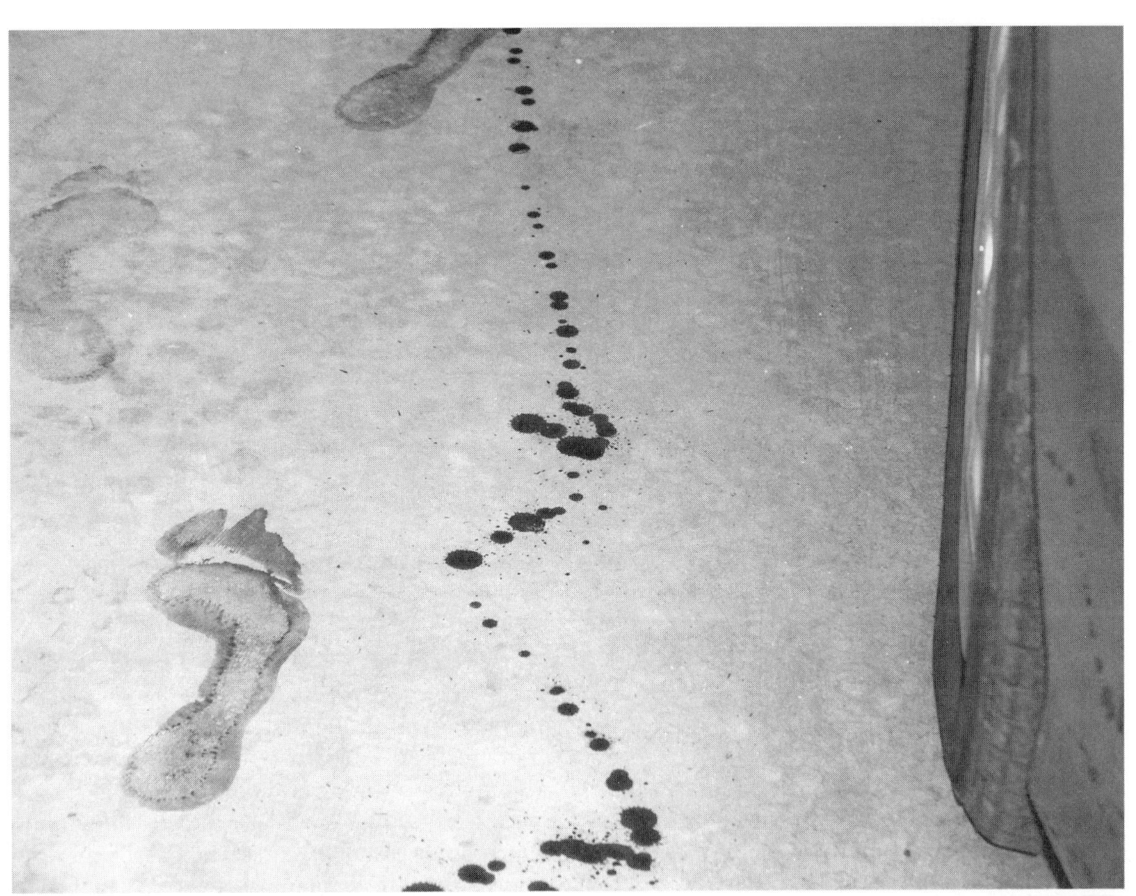

Learning Objectives

AFTER STUDYING THIS CHAPTER, YOU SHOULD BE ABLE TO:

1. Differentiate the types of evidence found at a crime scene
2. Plan how to expose, process, and archive crime scene photographs to withstand challenge in a courtroom
3. Follow the guidelines of the scientific method for the accurate processing and documentation of crime scenes
4. Match the appropriate photographic process to the particular crime scene and evidence
5. Describe the most appropriate methods for the documentation of shoe prints and tire tracks at the crime scene under all conditions
6. Differentiate types of bruises and wounds, along with the most accurate methods for their documentation
7. Describe the most appropriate methods for the documentation of a corpse at a crime scene
8. Describe the appropriate methods for the documentation of different categories of evidence at a crime scene

PHOTOGRAPHS AS EVIDENCE

The intention behind exposing crime scene photographs is to accurately and systematically document the scene and evidence of a crime. Physical evidence has the potential to play a key role in the overall investigation and resolution of a suspected criminal act.[1] Photographs taken at a crime scene are critical to the investigation and resolution of the case.

When photographs are judged to be fair and accurate representations of evidence, they are admissible in evidence for a variety of purposes:

- The identification and documentation of
  - Persons
  - Places
  - Things
- Relative locations of objects
- Better or clearer understanding of testimony
- Detection of forgeries
- Representation of documents for which the original cannot be readily produced[2]

In some cases, crime photographs may be considered to be **primary evidence,** such as the following three examples:

- When a suspect is arrested for creating and/or selling pornographic photographs[3]
- When a burglar breaks and enters a residence and steals a valuable photograph
- When the original evidence is no longer in existence and only the photographs remain[4]

In these particular cases, the photographs *are* the evidence.

In most other cases, when photographs are taken of primary evidence and the photographs are used at trial, the photographs are **secondary or supporting evidence.** A person may use photographs as exhibits in testimony, but only the testimony is primary evidence.

The testifier must substantiate exhibit photographs as accurate representations of the evidence, within the limitations of the media. A judge decides if the photographs are fair and admissible as evidence. The testifier may or may not be the person who exposed the photographs.[5] If the testifier understands how the photographs were made and can testify that the photographs have not been altered, and the images are not inflammatory, the photographs will usually be allowed. The competency of the photographer may be questioned at trial, and the perceived accuracy of the photographs as representations of the evidence will depend on the skills and qualifications of the photographer.

Before photographs can be introduced in evidence, they must be properly identified.[6] The use of an imaging SOP is important for the testifier. The judge must rely on the character of the testifier to relate the circumstances of the documentation, in order to pass judgment on image admissibility. The character of the testifier may be reflected in the way the photographs are identified and used.

Metadata

Metadata consist of the electronic information about the creation of an image. The metadata stored in JPEG and RAW photographic files include the following:

- Date and time information
- Camera settings
- Camera model and make
- Aperture
- Shutter speed
- Focal length
- Metering mode
- ISO speed
- Descriptions and copyright information

Federal Rules of Evidence

Under Federal Rule of Evidence 901 and its state analogues, photographs are typically admitted as secondary evidence to support testimony. Videos are authenticated in the same manner as still photographs.[7]

Under Federal Rules of Evidence 1001 through 1004 (see Appendix 16.2), original documents (including photographs) are required to prove the truth of the facts for which the documents are offered. Duplicates, including electronically made prints or digitally identical electronic files, are also admissible as evidence to the same degree as originals, unless the duplicate is inaccurate or unfair.

The inherent inaccuracies of photographs do not necessarily lead to their inadmissibility, as long as they are explainable.[8]

The Federal Rules of Evidence require that all discoverable electronic information be produced upon request in the proprietary file format of the application that was used, often referred to as its **native format.** Production of photographic images must include digitally identical copies of original JPEG or other format files.

The Federal Rules of Evidence may also require the production of the metadata of image files. All native format files will include accurate metadata, unless the metadata have been intentionally altered or removed. The importance of accurate metadata stresses the importance of proper setting up of the camera.

REMEMBER:

Always make sure the camera is set for the right time, day, and date and that it is correct for daylight saving time, leap years, and such.

Original Files

RULE:

Keep each original photograph in its unaltered state. Never modify an original file. Make any corrections and/or adjustments to copies.

TIP:

Most digital cameras number each photograph sequentially. Deleting images on memory media will result in numbering gaps. Gaps may cause problems in court. It is always best to retain all exposures and, if necessary, to classify them as photographer errors.

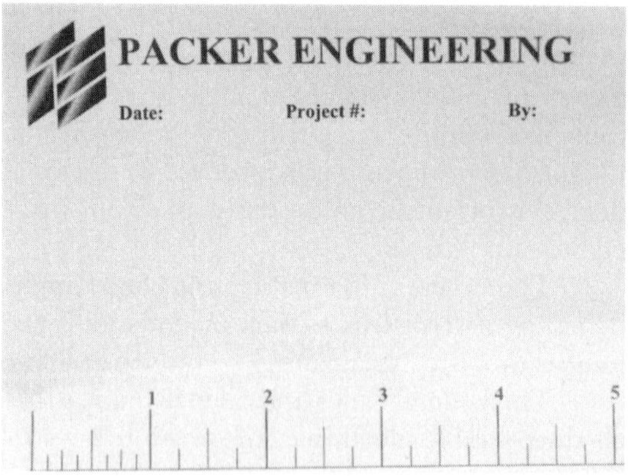

PACKER ENGINEERING

Date: Project #: By:

1 2 3 4 5

FIGURE 16–1 Case/project photo identifier. *Source:* Sandy Weiss/Packer Engineering.

In many jurisdictions, SOP requires a case identifier (see Fig. 16–1) and photo log (see Fig. 16–2) to accompany images for the following reasons:

- **Case identifiers** provide correlation between the image files and the case in question.
- The time lag between the documentation and the trial may be prolonged.
- Written information accompanying the photographs may aid the testifier.
- The person who exposed the photographs may not necessarily be the person presenting them in court.
- Having the written documentation of the images may enhance their admissibility.

It is normal to record the time, date, location, photographer, and other pertinent information into the case report. The information in the photographs and accompanying them should match the report for continuity.

The absence of a case identifier or log document will not necessarily lead to inadmissibility. It is likely that the evidence photographer will make errors when completing the log. The most that should be required is best possible effort to remain complete and accurate.

Crime Scene Imaging Sequence

Each image should be exposed in a systematic, methodical, and logical manner. Each photograph should be substantiated by its predecessor. A logical sequence of images at a scene may include the following:

- Location in the world, establishing photograph of a recognizable and immovable landmark
- Overall images showing where the evidence lies within the scene
- Mid-range images to identify the evidence
- Close-up images to characterize the evidence

Photo Sheet **Site**__________

Date_____ **Job**_____ **Roll letter**_____ **Person**_____

Photo	Location	Description
1		
2		
3		
4		
5		
6		
7		
8		
9		
10		
11		
12		
13		
14		
15		
16		
17		

FIGURE 16–2 Photo log sheet. *Source:* Sandy Weiss/Packer Engineering.

RULE:

Each time the photographer changes position or subject, new overall images must be exposed.

It is necessary for the testifier to establish that no material change in the scene of an accident or crime occurred for any reason during the interval that elapsed between the time of the event, and the time of the documentation.[9]

Scientific Method

When using the scientific method for crime scene organization and documentation, *never assume anything*.[10] Keep an open mind and attempt to tell every possible story with the photographs.

Timing is crucial. Photography should begin as soon as possible after arrival at the scene, even if the scene is still active. If the photographer has the opportunity to capture images of the crime in progress, those images may be critically useful for event reconstruction (see Fig. 16–3). After the event is concluded, fragile evidence should be documented first because it may be destroyed unintentionally over time. Use a systematic approach in the documentation to keep the story of the photographs cohesive and logical. The photographs must be accurate representations of the conditions and locations of the evidence, as it was found. Nothing should be touched, moved, or added into the scene until it has been thoroughly photographed.

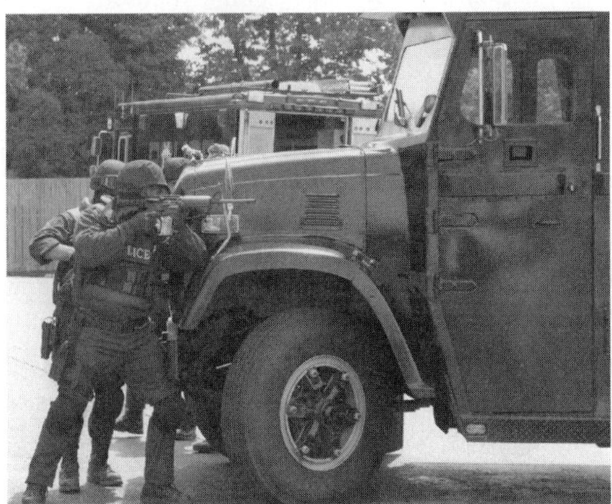

FIGURE 16–3 Special response team training. *Source:* Christopher Cali, CSI, Naperville, IL PD.

TIP:

Photographs are critical for recording the condition of the scene and the scene evidence as closely as possible to their original condition at the time of the crime.

TIP:

Organize the photography to correspond with and compliment the sketch and notes.

TIP:

Do not place the camera bag or evidence kit where it will be imaged in subsequent photographs.

SCIENTIFIC CRIME SCENE PROCESSING

Crime scene processing is a multi-task function involving, at a minimum, the following steps:

1. *Interviews* to develop a hypothesis of the case and determine if any changes have been made to the scene before your arrival. This includes opening doors and windows, turning on lights, and approaching the victim(s) to check for life signs.
   a. Witness(es)
   b. Suspect(s)
   c. Victim(s)
   d. First responder(s)
2. *Examination* of the scene.
   a. Is the hypothesis substantiated by the evidence?
   b. What should you search?
3. *Photograph* the scene and the evidence.
   a. Photograph the entire scene.
   b. Tell the story with the images.
   c. Examine and photograph the evidence on the floor or ground around the victim(s).

d. Use a systematic search and documentation method.
   i. Photograph overall images of the scene from 12:00, 3:00, 6:00, and 9:00 positions.
   ii. Photograph outward overall images of the scene, working through a structure or area to a stationary landmark.
   iii. Overlap photographs when possible, to allow the photographs to be assembled into a panorama or montage.
e. Remember that the scene is three-dimensional.
f. Photograph with and without scales (see Fig. 16–4).
g. Document all shoe prints and tire tracks.

4. Sketch
   a. To document the layout
   b. To identify the position of evidence and victims within the scene
      i. Document only essential elements.
      ii. Include name, date, location, compass direction, landmarks, scale, legend, color references.
      iii. Use the same system of designation of evidence in all documentation.
      iv. Use appropriate forms.
      v. Use templates for shapes and curves.

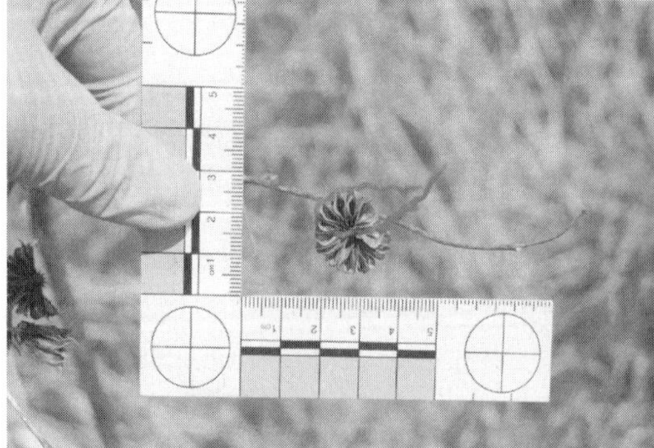

FIGURE 16–4 Use of two-dimensional scale. *Source:* Christopher Cali.

5. Process
   A. The scene for evidence
   a. Identify
   b. Document
   c. Collect subject evidence[11]
      i. Keep complete inventory
      ii. Chain of Custody
   d. Collect exemplar evidence
      i. From environment (vegetation, soil)
      ii. From structure (carpet fibers, paint, fibers, other)
      iii. From vehicle (carpet fibers, seat fibers, tires)
      iv. From animals (hairs, bedding)
      v. Blood samples from victim
      vi. Fingernail clippings
      vii. Swab from bite mark areas
      viii. Exemplar hairs
   B. Follow local, state, and federal laws for collection and admissibility.
      i. Physical
      ii. Testimonial

REMEMBER:

Each step leads logically into the next when the investigation follows the scientific method.

TIP:

Communication and teamwork are indispensable for proper crime scene processing.

TYPES OF SCENES

Scenes are classified by type of crime, including the following:

- Homicide
- Assault
- Rape and sexual assault

- Arson/bombing
- Robbery
- And so on

Crime scenes are also classified as primary or secondary. A primary scene is where the crime occurred or the victim was found. Secondary scenes include the victim's or suspect's home or vehicle, as well as any other related indoor or outdoor area. Most secondary scenes are not processed as thoroughly as primary scenes, unless peripheral reasons are discovered.

TYPES OF FRAGILE EVIDENCE

Shoe Prints

Evidence of the presence of certain persons or vehicles may be critical to a case and are critical to document properly. This evidence is very fragile and should be given highest priority. Shoe print photography and identification constitute a technique that requires specialized training and has been the subject of many studies in forensic literature. The subject is covered here in basic form. For more extensive instructions, search the literature by situation and specialty.

The basic steps for the processing of shoe print evidence include these:

- Examination
- Recovery
- Identification

In many criminal investigations, it may be necessary to determine if a particular person was present at the scene at some time. Shoe prints exist at most crime scenes but may easily be overlooked. They are among the most fragile types of evidence and may be obliterated by subsequent traffic. Shoe prints may be crucial to an investigation, and they necessitate following specific criteria for accurate inspection and photographic documentation (see Figs. 16–5, 16–6, 16–7, and 16–8).

Shoe print evidence may show any of the following:

- Brand of shoes
- Type of sole
- Wear patterns

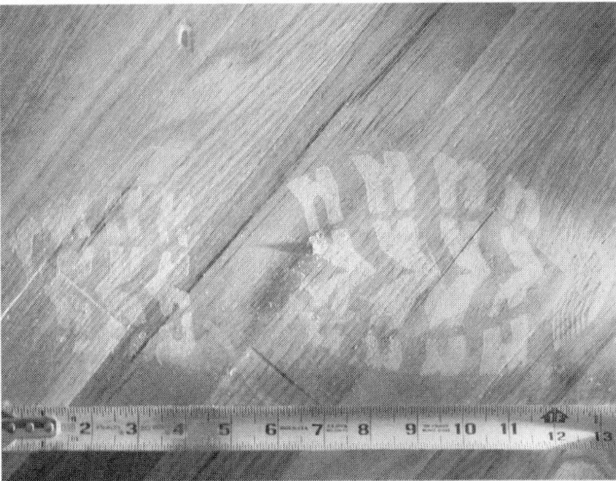

FIGURE 16–5 Muddy suspect shoe print on wooden floor, with scale. *Source:* Aric Dutelle, University of Wisconsin-Platteville.

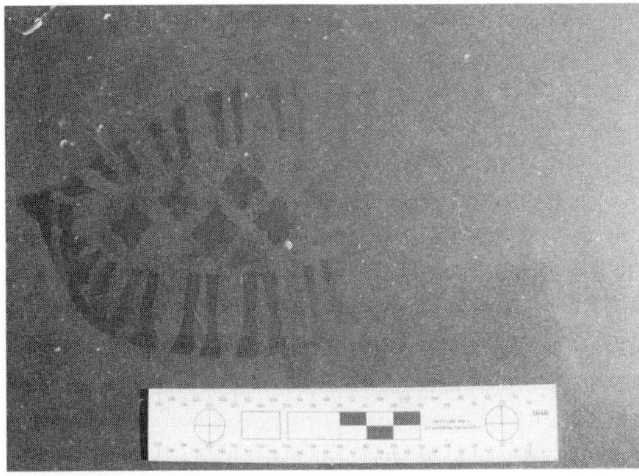

FIGURE 16–6 Suspect shoe print in the dust on a tile floor, with scale. *Source:* Aric Dutelle, University of Wisconsin-Platteville.

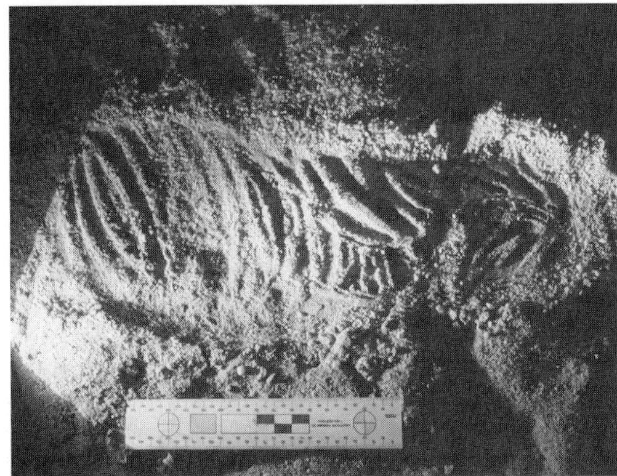

FIGURE 16–7 Suspect shoe print in soft dirt, with scale. *Source:* Aric Dutelle, University of Wisconsin-Platteville.

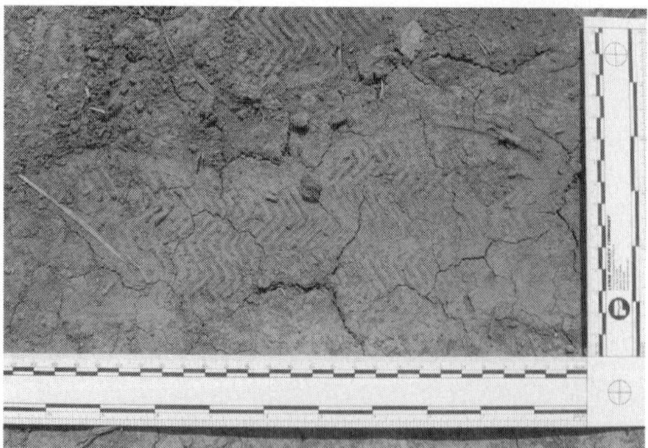

FIGURE 16–8 Suspect shoe print in hardened mud, with L-shaped, 2-D scale. *Source:* Aric Dutelle, University of Wisconsin-Platteville.

- Approximate shoe size
- Size and weight of person(s)
- Number of persons at the scene
- Paths of travel
- Sequence of events

After the processing of any victims, conduct a complete search and marking for shoe prints, within a logical perimeter. The documentation and collection of the prints should be completed after the search and marking are completed (see Fig. 16–9). Once a location is marked, remember to correlate it to the scene and to the other prints, through a logical and systematic set of consecutive images.

If the scene is complex, or requires extensive foot traffic from emergency medical services (EMS) personnel, protection may be placed over the shoe prints (cardboard box, cone, bag, and such) until the scene is available for processing. Investigators and EMS personnel should always mark their shoes for easy identification and elimination from the subject evidence. Common methods of such identification include the use of disposable shoe covers or rubber bands wrapped around the shoes.

FIGURE 16–9 Evidence markers. *Source:* Sandy Weiss/Packer Engineering.

Weather conditions at an outdoor scene are always a factor but should never rule out a search for shoe prints. Snow, rain, ice, and fire after the crime may obliterate the markings.

Steps for shoe print photography include the following:

- Set the camera for sufficient image resolution.
- Use a camera and lens with macro capabilities.
- Use an appropriate scale, next to and on the same plane as the evidence. Right-angle scales (see Fig. 16–10) are recommended because they make it possible to successfully rectify the image to life size during image processing.
- Focus the camera on the evidence, not on the scale.
- Photograph each shoe print with a positional reference
- Position the camera directly over the print with the image sensor parallel to the evidence.
- Use a tripod if one is available
- Crop the image in the camera view finder to include only the evidence, scale, and label.
- Use a flash and position it obliquely to the print.
- Photograph each shoe print with the flash set at various aspects to the evidence.
- If the substrate of the shoe print is very dark or very light, bracket exposures.
- Block distracting ambient illumination.

The flash will be more effective if taken off the camera. It should be positioned obliquely, to the side of the subject. Experiment by moving

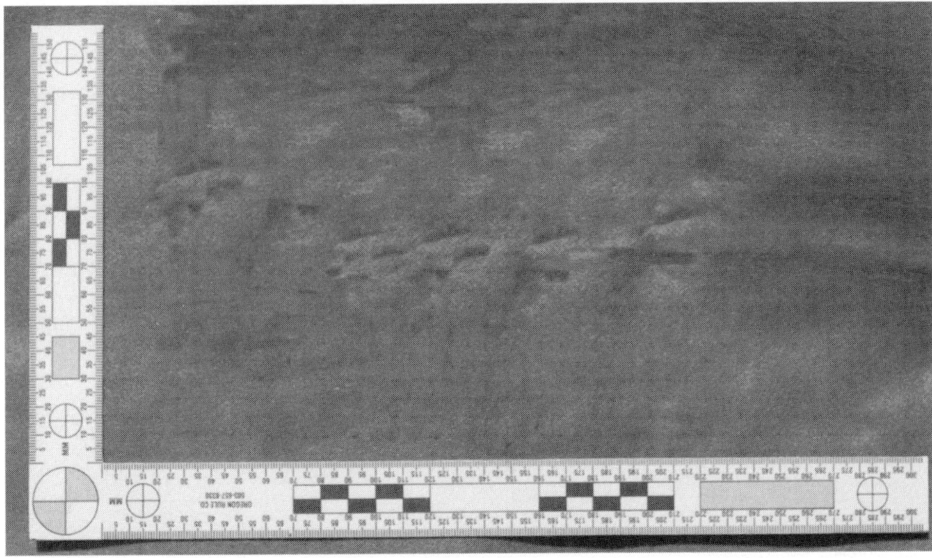

FIGURE 16–10 Right angle 2-D scale manufactured in the proper size for ease in documentation of shoe prints. *Source:* Sandy Weiss/Packer Engineering.

the flash to various sides of the shoe print to capture optimum detail. Areas that are shadowed in one image may be visible in another. When the prints are on reflective surfaces, a top-mounted or built-in flash may cause reflections or uneven exposures that hinder visibility. If the shoe prints are three-dimensional, they should be cast as well as photographed.

When shoe prints are located on smooth interior surfaces, such as linoleum and tile, they may be difficult to find and see. If possible, darken the room and use a directional light source, such as a flashlight, from a very low angle to illuminate and inspect the suspected surfaces. If a shoe print is found, for best results use the same angle of directional lighting for the camera exposure as the angle that made the print visible to the eye.

Even when it is not possible to definitively match a suspect to a shoe print, the evidence is admissible as evidence under the guidelines established by the Supreme Court.[12]

> **TIP:**
>
> Expose shoe print photographs with and without scales, and possibly with and without flash.

> **TIP:**
>
> If possible, photograph as many examples of the same subject's prints as are necessary for complete left and right foot impressions.

Tire Tracks

A suspect may be associated to a crime scene by the impressions left by vehicle tires. This is another area that is heavily documented in the forensic literature.

Steps for Tire Track Photography

1. If possible, mount the camera on a tripod.
2. Adjust the camera to bring the image plane into a parallel orientation with the marking. If the track is on an inclined surface, adjust the camera to the same angle.
3. Expose photographs with a detached EFU placed about 45 degrees obliquely to the track and from both sides.
4. Vary the angle of the EFU to create the most usable relief view of the markings (see Fig. 16–11).

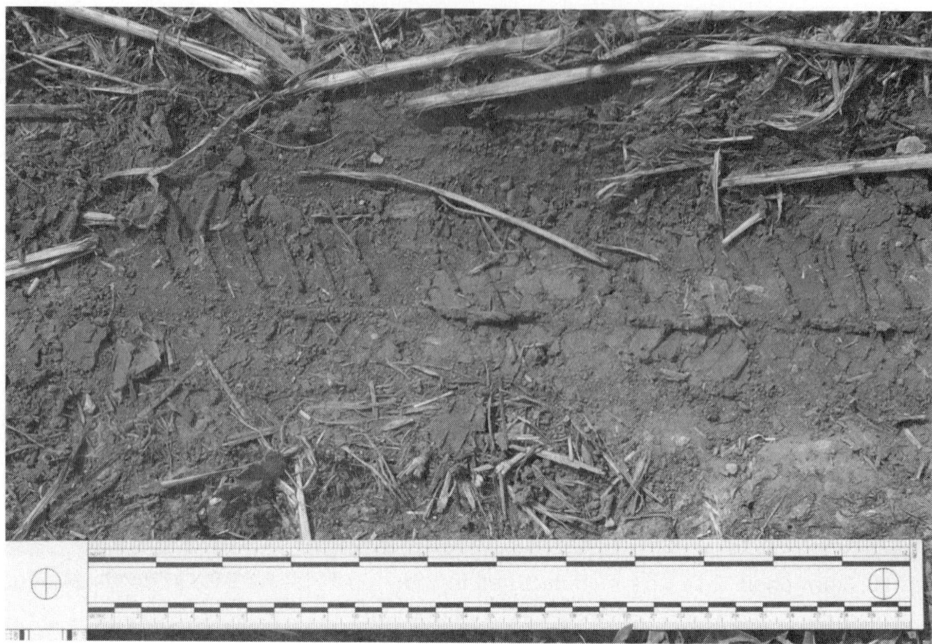

FIGURE 16–11 Tire track on soft dirt. *Source:* Aric Dutelle, University of Wisconsin-Platteville.

5. Use a scale next to the marking and in the same plane.
6. Continue to make exposures until one complete circumference of the tire has been captured, if possible.
7. Overlap the images sufficiently so they can be successfully stitched together into a montage or panorama.
8. Concentrate on specific tire characteristics that make the tire unique.

As with shoe print evidence, overall photographs should be taken using a macro lens, showing the impressions in relation to the other features of the scene.[13] Take physical measurements of the dimensions of the tracks and any separation between them.

A vehicle's **track width** is the distance between the center of the tire of one side of the vehicle to the center of the tire on the opposite side. Front and rear track width may be different on some vehicles. The measured track width may be used to provide a list of possible vehicles matching the tire impressions.

The **wheelbase** of a vehicle is the measured distance between the center of the front axle and the center of the rear axle. This is a useful measurement, but it is often difficult to compute from tire tracks.

VICTIMS: INJURIES AND CORPSES

Photographic images are the best means for the documentation and preservation of the physical evidence of injuries, bruises, and general condition of the skin of victims of crimes and accidents. Visual, ultraviolet, and infrared illumination may be used under various conditions and circumstances. The techniques and equipment are similar whether the victim is alive or deceased.

Photographing Bruises

Bruises are discolored areas on the skin that form due to the rupture of capillaries and veins after injuries (see Fig. 16–12). This causes the **extravasation** of blood into the tissues, called **ecchymosis.**

Bruising is normally caused by a blunt-force trauma injury. It occurs when a body part strikes objects during a fall, is hit by a fist or club, is crushed in a closing door, and hundreds of other

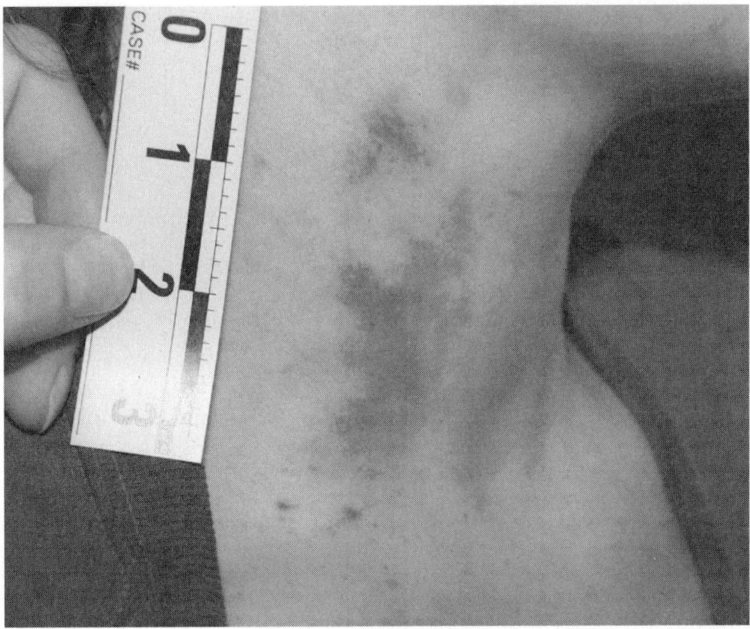

FIGURE 16–12 Example of a bruise. *Source:* Dodge County, WI, Medical Examiner's Office, P. J. Schoebel.

scenarios. Bruises may also occur on internal organs from vehicular and other accidents and from any severe blunt-force trauma, as during an assault.

Bruise Timetable

Bruises appear as a result of injuries after variable amounts of time. The chronology may include the following characteristics:

1. Swelling
2. Discoloration
3. Color changes

It is necessary to reexamine bruise victims 24 hours after an injury because bruises may become more visible over time. A mark that looks red or sore on one day may be a bruise the next day.

Bruises produced **perimortem** (at the time of death) will normally not swell, and bruises will be more distinct in victims who survive for any length of time after the bruise injury.

Deep Bruises

Deep bruises may be difficult to see and/or photograph. At **postmortem** (after death) examination, incisions at suspected bruise sites may be made to find and document ecchymosis.

TIP:

The shape and severity of a bruise are directly proportional to the object that caused the injury and the amount of force used.

Factors Affecting Bruises

The extent and severity of bruises caused by injuries may vary due to a number of factors:

- The condition and type of tissue
  - Bruising will be more extensive and severe at places on the victim where the skin is loose and has many blood vessels.
  - Bruising will be less extensive and severe in places on the victim where the skin is tough and has fewer blood vessels.
  - Bruising may not appear on certain parts of the body or internal organs even though the trauma may be the cause of death.

- The age of the victim
  - The young and the old bruise more easily and extensively than adults.
- The sex of the victim
  - Women may bruise more extensively and severely than men.
- The skin color of the victim
  - Bruises are more visible when skin is light colored.
- The health of the victim
  - High blood pressure and some circulatory diseases may cause extensive bruising.
  - Ill health may delay the reabsorption of extravasated blood. This will shift the bruise timetable.
  - Good health reduces the severity of bruises.
- Other causes
  - Changes in climate
  - Personal traits

Color Changes of Bruises Over Time

Victims who do not die will exhibit a sequence of bruise color changes over time. The blood collected under the skin is gradually reabsorbed into the body. The color changes begin at the outside edges of the bruise and travel inward to the center (see Fig. 16–13).

- The color of bruises is variable:
  - New bruises may appear red.
  - Up to 3 days, the color may be blue, blue-black, brown, or red.
  - By the fifth or sixth day, bruises are often green.
  - Between the seventh and twelfth days, bruises are often yellow.
  - By the fourteenth or fifteenth day, the yellow usually fades and the skin regains its normal color.

TIP:

Yellowing may appear as early as one day after injury. It is not possible to use the coloring of bruises as a definite timetable.

TIP:

Due to gravity shifting extravasated blood, bruises may appear at a location on the body that is remote from the location of the injury.

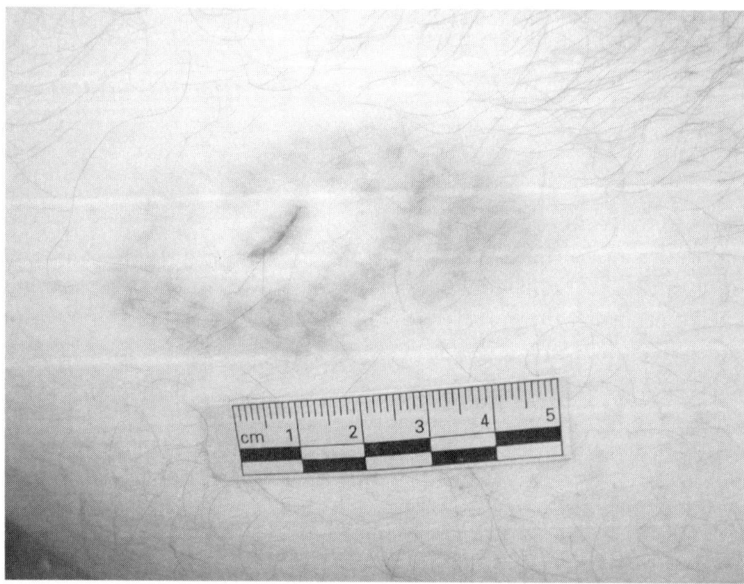

FIGURE 16–13 Bruise, with self-adhesive scale. *Source:* Dodge County, WI, Medical Examiner's Office, P. J. Schoebel.

Guidelines for Photography of Bruises

The photography of deceased victims may cause psychological distress for the photographer. The photography of bruised, living victims may cause distress to the victim and the photographer. This photography should always be performed with a confident, competent, and compassionate demeanor. Some people do not appreciate having their photograph taken on the best of their days. In many cases, when a forensic photographer is documenting an injury or injuries, the victim is experiencing what may be the worst of their days. The bruise injury may be a result of abuse (see Fig. 16–14) or sexual abuse. In such cases, the parts of the victim's body that need to be documented may cause the victim great personal embarrassment. Allow such subjects to keep their private areas covered until those areas become the specific ones that need to be photographed. Explain to the subject what you are doing and why. If a photograph of the face is demanded by protocol, explain that the only people who will see the images and correlate the bruises to the face are the people who need to see them for a case or prosecution. You *can* keep your work from causing distress to everyone involved.

Techniques for Bruise Documentation

The basic method for bruise photography involves the use of a camera with a macro lens and an EFU illuminating the subject from an oblique angle. Always expose at least one image of each bruise with a right-angle reference, such as the ABFO #2. Use of a 2-D scale will allow the rectification of the bruise images to 1:1, life size, for analysis and comparison to objects that may have caused the bruising. Use a color reference for one image in every light source used for the documentation. Use a case identifier if demanded by SOP.

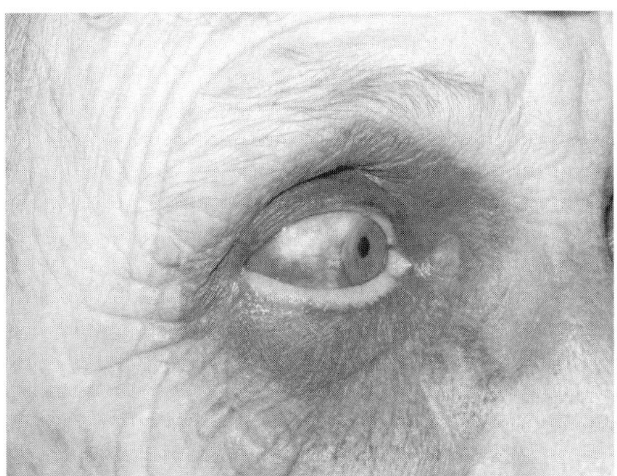

FIGURE 16–14 Bruised eye from elder abuse. *Source:* Dodge County, WI, Medical Examiner's Office, P. J. Schoebel.

Lighting of Bruises

Four distinct types of lighting are used for the digital capture of bruise images:

1. Visible light
2. Red-free visible light
3. Infrared light
4. Reflected ultraviolet light

By using a combination of lighting techniques at different stages, it may be possible to accurately record the size and severity of a bruise at every stage from injury to healed.

Visible Light Visible light photography utilizes the complete range of the visible spectrum. This type of lighting is used for the documentation of any type and size of visible bruising. The techniques are the same as in any other type of forensic macrophotography. Follow all standard SOPs and methods of image recording and analysis.

Red-Free Light Placing a blue or green filter on the front of the camera lens allows only blue or green light to pass and expose the image. Set the camera to capture black-and-white image files. When subjects are predominantly red, the blue-green (red-free) lighting may enhance subject contrast and yield an accurate image of the extent of current bruising. Use a Kodak Wratten No. 44 cyan filter to block all red wavelengths.

Infrared Light Modern digital cameras may contain built-in filters to limit their sensitivity to IR and UV wavelengths. Some methods enable the use of IR and UV wavelengths with any camera.

Infrared light penetrates the outer layers of the skin to a depth of approximately 3 mm.

Visualizing blood under the skin surface may help to image the early stages of bruising. (Refer to Chapter 9 for additional information.)

Reflected Ultraviolet Light UV illumination does not penetrate into the skin. Old surface injuries that are invisible under normal illumination, including scars, bruises, and bite marks, may be revealed under reflected ultraviolet photography. Even old, invisible hammer marks on a victim's head have been made visible by photographing with reflected ultraviolet light.[14]

> **TIP:**
>
> Just because no bruises are visible under any type of lighting does not mean no bruises are present.

> **TIP:**
>
> It is more difficult to document bruises on subjects with darker skin.

Ultraviolet lighting for photographs of pre-bruise bite marks may show more detail than visible light images. In 1994, a five-month-old bite mark photographed with ultraviolet photography became critical evidence at trial.[15]

UV illumination may also be used to photograph indistinct tattoos on skin in any condition.

Lighting for Ultraviolet and Infrared

Modern EFUs have coated flash tubes to minimize UV and IR illumination output. Older EFUs may have extended output in the wavelengths between 300 and 400 nm and between 800 and 900 nm. Older EFUs are recommended for use as a light source for both reflected infrared and ultraviolet image capture.

Filters for UV and IR

- Kodak Wratten No. 87 infrared transmission filter
  - Used to capture infrared images
- Hoya U-340 nearly-black filter
  - Used for reflected ultraviolet capture

Photographing Wounds

An open **wound** is a type of physical trauma that tears, cuts, or punctures the skin (see Fig. 16–15). A closed wound or contusion is caused by blunt-force trauma. Open wounds may lead to death through blood loss or infection.

In criminal cases, photographs of wounds have been uniformly held to be admissible as evidence upon proper identification.[16] In a prosecution for murder, it was held that a photograph of

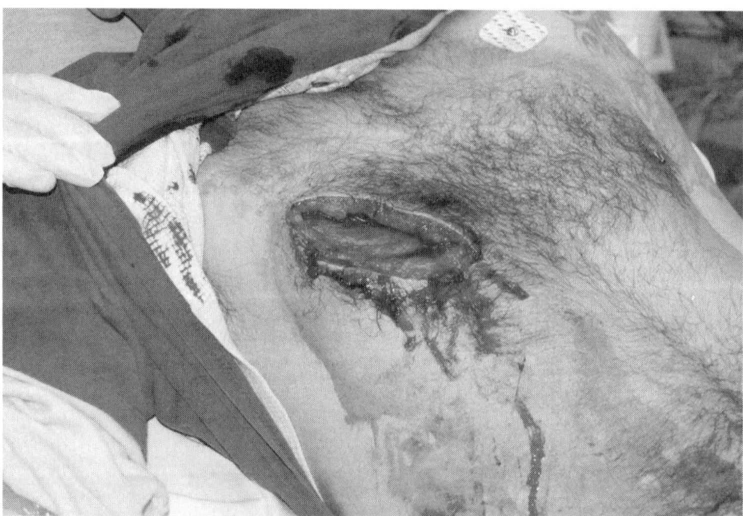

FIGURE 16–15 Lacerated pectoral muscle. *Source:* Aric Dutelle, University of Wisconsin-Platteville.

the deceased was admissible as evidence for the purpose of showing the nature and location of the wounds inflicted upon the murder victim.[17]

Wounds are considered minor under certain circumstances:

- They involve flesh only.
- They are not near bodily orifices.
- Only minor bleeding occurs.
- The wound was not caused by a tool or an animal.

Wounds are considered severe in other cases:

- They involve internal organs.
- They are near bodily orifices.
- Major bleeding occurs.
- They are caused by a tool or an animal.

Open Wounds

Types of open wounds include the following:

- Incisions
    - Cuts caused by clean, sharp-edged objects (see Fig. 16–16)
- Cuts
    - Lacerations that involve only the outer skin
- Lacerations (see Fig. 16–17)
    - Irregular wounds caused by blunt-force trauma to soft tissue
    - Tearing of skin and other tissues
- Abrasions (see Fig. 16–18)
    - Superficial wounds that occur when the skin is scraped off, as in a sliding fall
- Puncture wounds
    - Occur when objects puncture the skin
- Penetration wounds
    - Occur when knifelike objects enter the body.
- Gunshot wounds (see Fig. 16–19)
    - Occur when a bullet or other projectile penetrates into or through the body

Closed Wounds

Types of closed wounds include the following:

- Contusions (bruises)
    - Occur from blunt-force trauma damaging tissue under the skin
- Hematoma
    - Damage to a vessel that causes blood to collect under the skin
- Crushing injuries
    - Caused by force applied over time

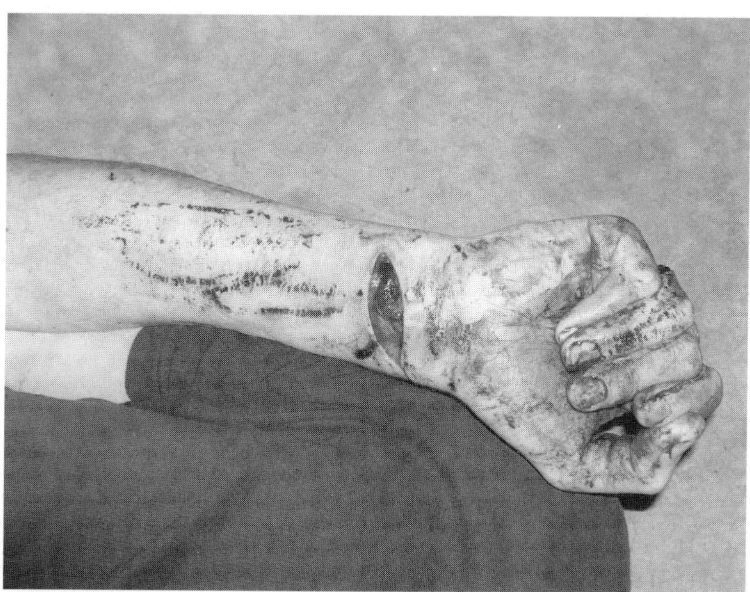

FIGURE 16–16 Incised wound. *Source:* Dodge County, WI, Medical Examiner's Office, P. J. Schoebel.

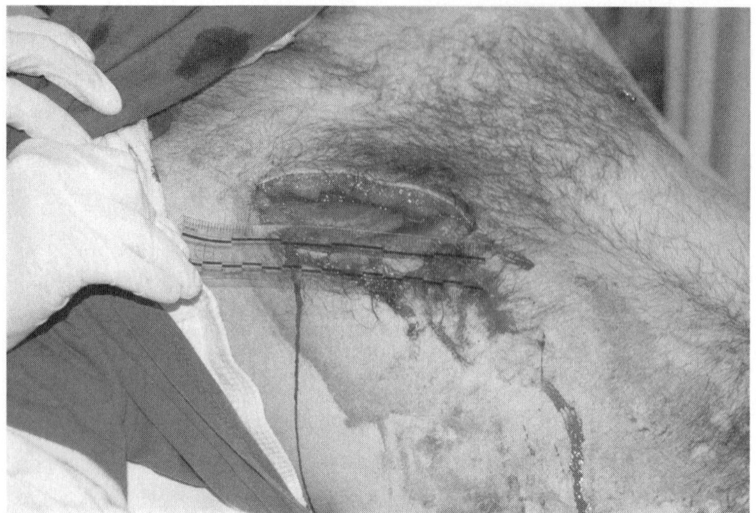

FIGURE 16–17 Laceration, with scale. *Source:* Aric Dutelle, University of Wisconsin-Platteville.

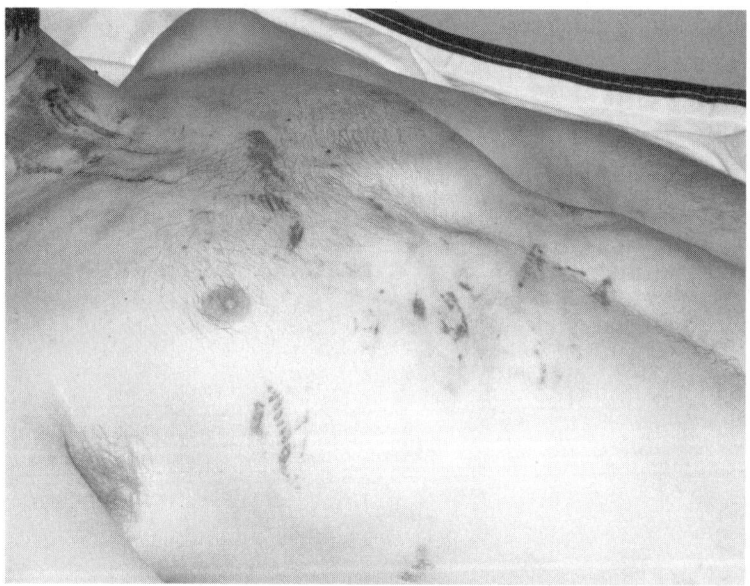

FIGURE 16–18 Abrasion from a motorcycle accident. *Source:* Dodge County, WI, Medical Examiner's Office, P. J. Schoebel.

Proper photography of wounds requires a direct and scientific approach that follows these steps:

- Capture sufficient establishing images to enable the identification of the subject.
- Use a macro lens or other appropriate close-up equipment.
- Use appropriate lighting.
  - EFUs are recommended to ensure the appropriate color of visible lighting and of the image.
- Expose photographs with and without scales.
- Avoid capturing images of extraneous backgrounds and uninvolved body parts.
- Use a color reference when applicable.

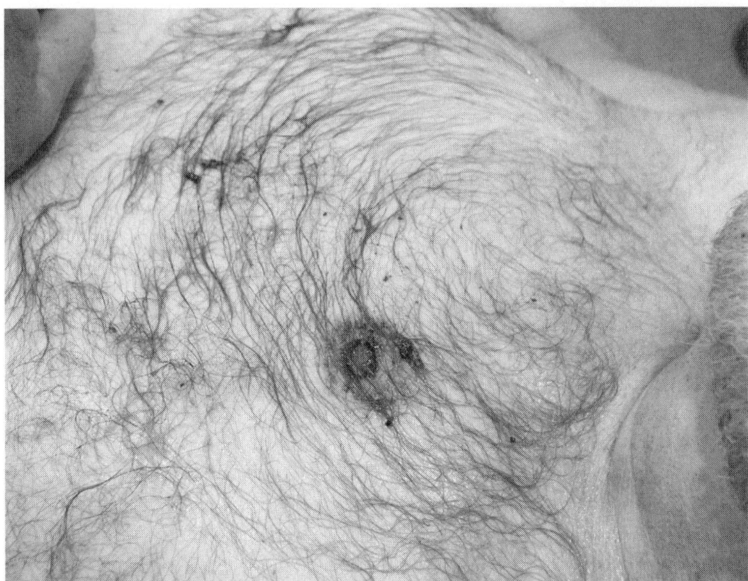

FIGURE 16–19 Gunshot wound. *Source:* Aric Dutelle, University of Wisconsin-Platteville.

> **TIP:**
>
> Skin may be highly reflective. Use oblique flash angles to avoid overexposures.

Photographing Corpses

A crime scene is a location where an illegal act, not necessarily the crime itself, took place. It is an area where physical evidence is retrieved and documented by crime scene investigators and photographers. Some crimes will have only primary scenes. Others will have primary, secondary, and even tertiary crime scenes.

> **TIP:**
>
> The corpse may be the largest source of evidence at the scene of a homicide.

A crime scene investigator performs a range of tasks at the scene of a homicide, including all of the following:

- Locating evidence
- Documenting the evidence
- Collecting the evidence
- Documenting the packaging
- Maintaining a chain of custody
- Securing the evidence

Processing a Homicide Scene

After it has been established that the victim is deceased and a corpse is now evidence, a perimeter should be taped off around the extent of the scene. The perimeter should be placed to include the outer location of any evidence that is likely pertinent to the crime. Until the scene has been properly processed for evidence, the perimeter should not be entered by anyone but the investigator.

At an archaeological site where a corpse has been discovered after an extended period, the scene processing should include the following:

- Identify and mark the perimeter (see Fig. 16–20).
- Wear proper PPE (see Fig. 16–21).
- Photograph the evidence with and without scales and references.
- Work in layers, making photographs at logical intervals (see Fig. 16–22).
- Sift all removed soil for small evidence (see Fig. 16–23).

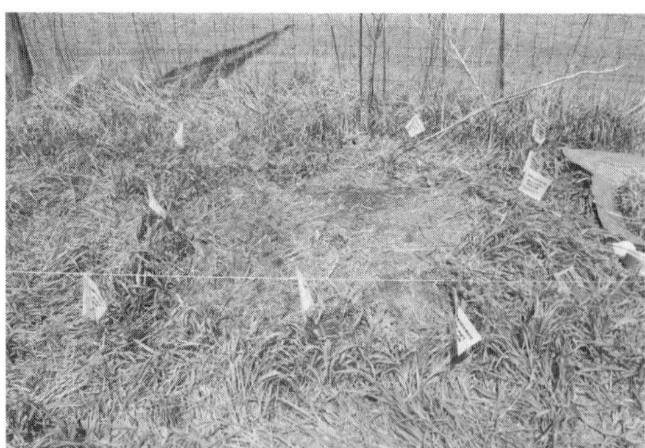

FIGURE 16–20 Gravesite with perimeter locators. *Source:* Aric Dutelle, University of Wisconsin-Platteville.

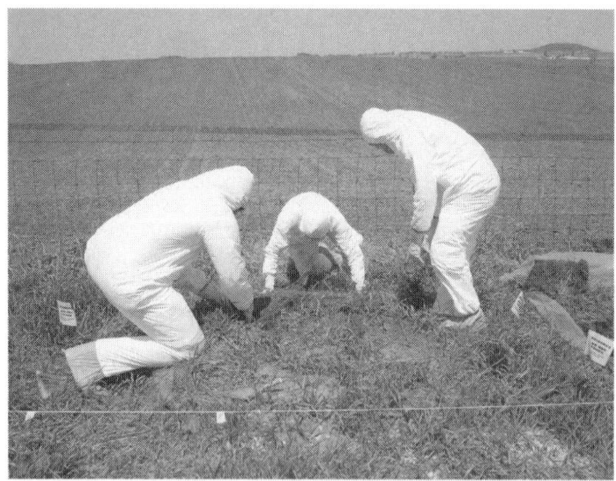

FIGURE 16–21 Investigators in appropriate PPE, excavating a gravesite. *Source:* Aric Dutelle, University of Wisconsin-Platteville.

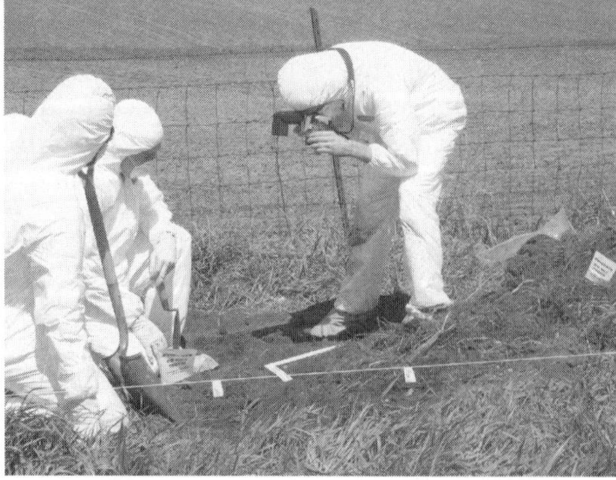

FIGURE 16–22 Photographing the gravesite in logical layers. *Source:* Aric Dutelle, University of Wisconsin-Platteville.

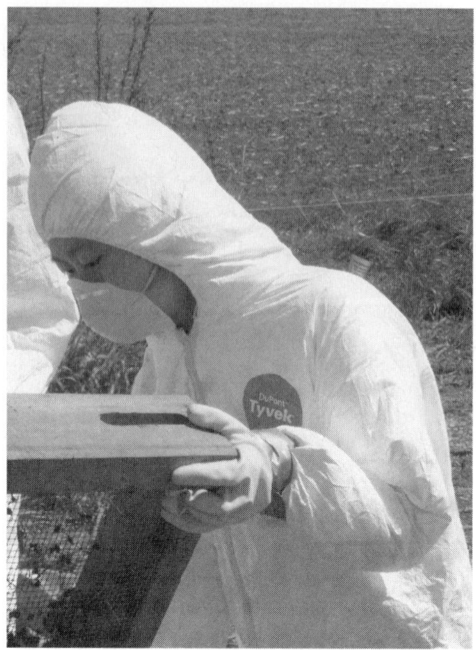

FIGURE 16–23 Sifting the soil at the gravesite. *Source:* Aric Dutelle, University of Wisconsin-Platteville.

- Measure depth and record the three-dimensional location of everything involved in the scene.

Guidelines for Photographing the Corpse

In the field, the corpse should be documented in a systematic and logical manner:

- Locate trauma.
- Document trauma with and without scales and references.
- The series of images should include multiple perspectives.
  - Overalls of the body
    - Head to feet
    - Right side
    - Feet to head (see Fig. 16–24)
    - Left side
    - From above (overall if possible, or in sections)
  - Mid-range, starting at the head and working down
  - Close-ups of all unusual evidence

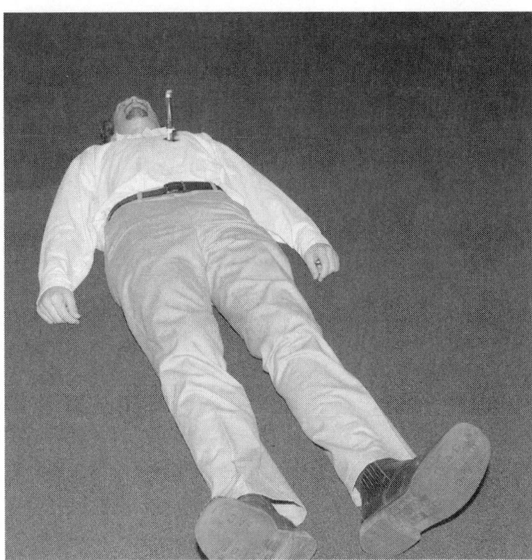

FIGURE 16–24 Overall photograph, feet to head, of deceased, stabbed in the heart. *Source:* Sandy Weiss/Packer Engineering.

EVIDENCE COLLECTION

Trace Evidence

Trace evidence, when found, usually consists of small particles and includes such items as hairs, fibers, fingerprints, and body fluids. Follow specific departmental SOPs or protocols or the FBI's "Trace Evidence Recovery Guidelines" to properly collect and package trace evidence.[18] Always wear gloves and other necessary PPE. The following tools are used for the collection of trace evidence.

Document, collect, and document again:

- Trace evidence
  - Fingerprints
  - Body fluids
  - Hairs (from another source than the victim)
  - Fibers
  - Glass chips and/or flakes
  - Paint chips
  - Soil
  - Grease
  - Oil
  - Botanical material
  - Adhesive
  - Gunshot residue
  - Explosive residue
  - Hydrocarbons

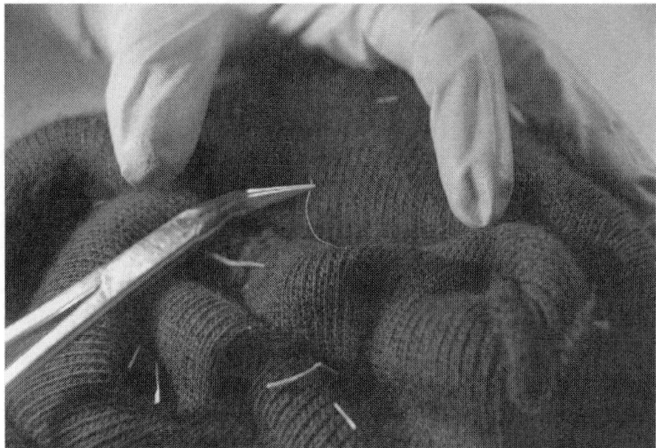

FIGURE 16–25 Using a hemostat to collect a hair from the inside of a knit cap. *Source:* Aric Dutelle, University of Wisconsin-Platteville.

The following tools are used for the collection of trace evidence:

- Tweezers
- Surgical instruments (see Fig. 16–25)
- Pet hair rollers
- Brushes
- Combs
- Vacuum
- And so on

Body Fluids

If areas of the victim are found to have unusual fluids or dried residues, they must be documented and collected. Body fluids are collected by swabbing or scraping (see Fig. 16–26).

Fingerprints

Fingerprints are imprints made by the ridges on the pads of human fingers. The prints are often left on objects at a crime scene and are used in forensic science to identify victims and suspects. Fingerprints are believed to be unique for every person, even identical twins.

Recovered fingerprints serve two purposes;

- The identification of a victim
- The identification of a suspect

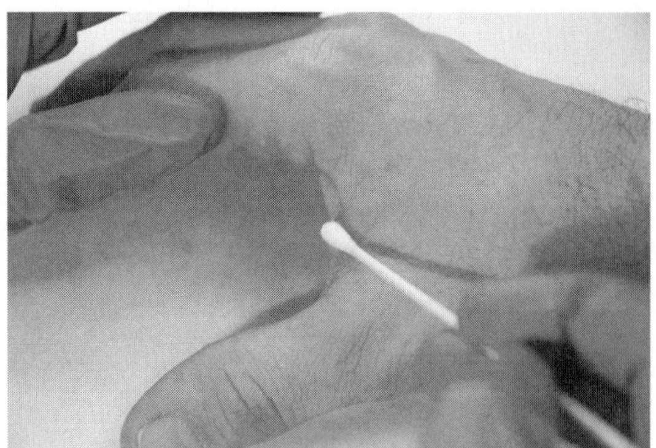

FIGURE 16–26 Collection of body fluid by swabbing. *Source:* Aric Dutelle, University of Wisconsin-Platteville.

The crime scene investigator has the following objectives:

- Search
  - Discovery
  - Recognition
- Development
- Documentation
- Collection

It may be necessary to collect fingerprints of the victim and any that have been left on the corpse by a suspect. Recovering latent prints from human skin is a specialty that should be studied in the course of becoming an experienced investigator. The investigator requires the following in all fingerprint recoveries:

- Information about the surface the print is on
- Information about possible recovery methods
- Instructions for developing and recovering latent prints

Fingerprint Development

- Direct lifting (see Fig. 16–27)
- Super glue fuming
- Direct application of fingerprint powders (see Fig. 16–28)

Experience and study are the best teachers about which method will be most effective. Always document the recovered prints in a logical method for later correlation.

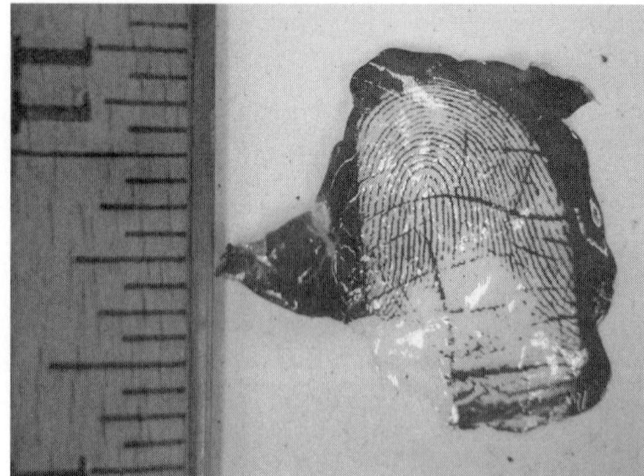

FIGURE 16–27 Fingerprint lifted from a surface with special tape. *Source:* Aric Dutelle, University of Wisconsin-Platteville.

Types of Prints Useful print impressions are made by fingers, palms, toes, feet, and even ears. The types are the same, no matter which body part made the impression. The documentation and collection of any prints are similar to the steps for fingerprints. The databases used for comparison and identification vary in size and source.

Latent fingerprints are impressions left by the friction ridge of fingers on a surface. Latent prints may be visible or invisible. Electronic, chemical, and physical processing techniques

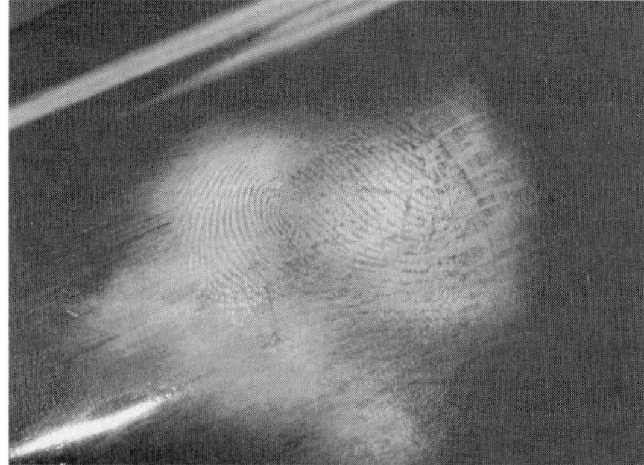

FIGURE 16–28 Fingerprint visualized on a car door by the application of fingerprint powder. *Source:* Aric Dutelle, University of Wisconsin-Platteville.

make it possible to visualize invisible latent prints. The prints may include a complete or partial section of the surface of the finger. They may be smudged, distorted, or both, depending on how they were created. Latent prints are usually less distinct than fingerprints collected under controlled conditions.

Patent prints are friction ridge impressions that are visible to the human eye. They are caused by the transfer of a foreign substance on the finger(s), onto another surface. They may need no enhancement for proper viewing and documentation. They are photographed before collection.

A **plastic print** is an impression made in a material that retains the shape of the ridge detail. This type of prints may be left in wax, window putty, grease, and any type of moldable material. These prints are readily visible and require no enhancement before being photographed.

Search for Prints The search for fingerprint evidence covers all areas of the scene perimeter. The investigator will usually have an SOP for search patterns. Primary and secondary locations will be inspected. Pay special attention to items that logically may have been touched, moved, or look out of place. Alternative light sources and lasers are often utilized in the search, as well as powders.

Print Development Special powders are applied to nonporous surfaces with a soft brush in areas of possible fingerprint locations. The particles of powder will adhere to the substance contained in the print. A variety of chemicals are produced to react with prints deposited on porous and absorbent surfaces, including paper, untreated wood, skin, and so on.

Print Fuming Superglue (cyanoacrylate ester) creates a vapor that forms a residue from the materials contained in latent print deposits. The fumes are dangerous to humans, and PPE must be used. Once any prints are developed, they should be properly documented before collection.

Print Documentation Photography is performed to document the location and material of any prints. Accurate documentation of prints is critical in case the print is damaged or lost during collection. Follow all the basic steps and suggestions for macrophotography in the documentation of any type of fingerprint. Follow all suggested SOPs and protocols.

Print Collection Fingerprint collection differs in SOP and method, depending on the type of print and the type of material on which it is located. Always develop and document the prints before any collection process begins. After collection, place prints on rigid backing cards with a contrasting color background. Note the recovery data on the back of the card, along with all pertinent case information. Closely follow chain-of-custody procedures.

Mobile Fingerprint Scanner Wireless, digital fingerprint scanners and printers are used by law enforcement and security agencies. These devices may be used in any field location to scan, collect, and verify a subject's fingerprints. Scanned fingerprints may be used for database comparison to extract a person's ID profile. Automated Fingerprint Identification (or AFIS) is a system used by law enforcement and governmental agencies for matching unknown fingerprints against a database of known and unknown prints. The system is often used for criminal identification, including the identification of a person or persons suspected of committing a crime. Using the AFIS, the print profile may be sent to wireless devices, including computers, phones, and PDAs. This system may recognize the identity of an individual in real time.

The print images can be collected in a number of ways. The most common method in use today is **optical scanning.** An optical scanner (see Fig. 16–29) uses an imaging sensor, such as a CCD, like those used in digital cameras and camcorders. The scanning process starts when a finger is placed on a glass plate and a charge-coupled device (CCD) camera captures an image. The scanner has a built-in light source, usually an array of LEDs, to illuminate the ridges of the finger. The system generates a negative or **inverted image** of the print. The darker areas (the ridges) reflect more light, and the lighter areas, between the ridges, reflect less.

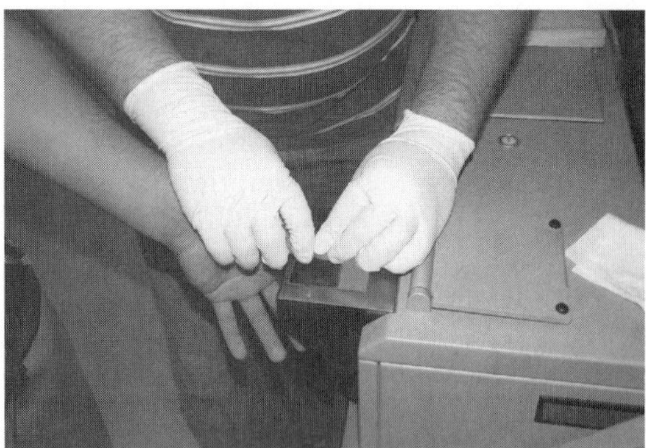

FIGURE 16–29 A fingerprint scanner. *Source:* Constance Rohrer.

If the scanner is satisfied with the quality of the image, it is retained. If the scanner is online with print databases, the print may be compared with others on file. Inked fingerprints may be less prone to optical distortion and contain more information and higher resolution than scanned images, making the older technology worth retaining.

Print Identification The fingerprints from a scene are sent to a fingerprint examiner for identification. It is determined by SOP whether the investigator or the examiner is responsible for the rectification of the image of a print to life size for comparison to prints in established databases.

Blood Evidence

Blood evidence is often essential to the solution of crimes. It is essential to correctly document, collect, and preserve all blood evidence (see Fig. 16–30) DNA analysis is used to characterize bloodstains and may connect the blood to a unique individual or a very small group. Blood evidence may tie suspects and victims together in various ways:

- Finding blood with a victim's genetic markers, ABO blood type, DNA profile
  - On a suspect
  - On something owned by a suspect
  - On something associated to a suspect

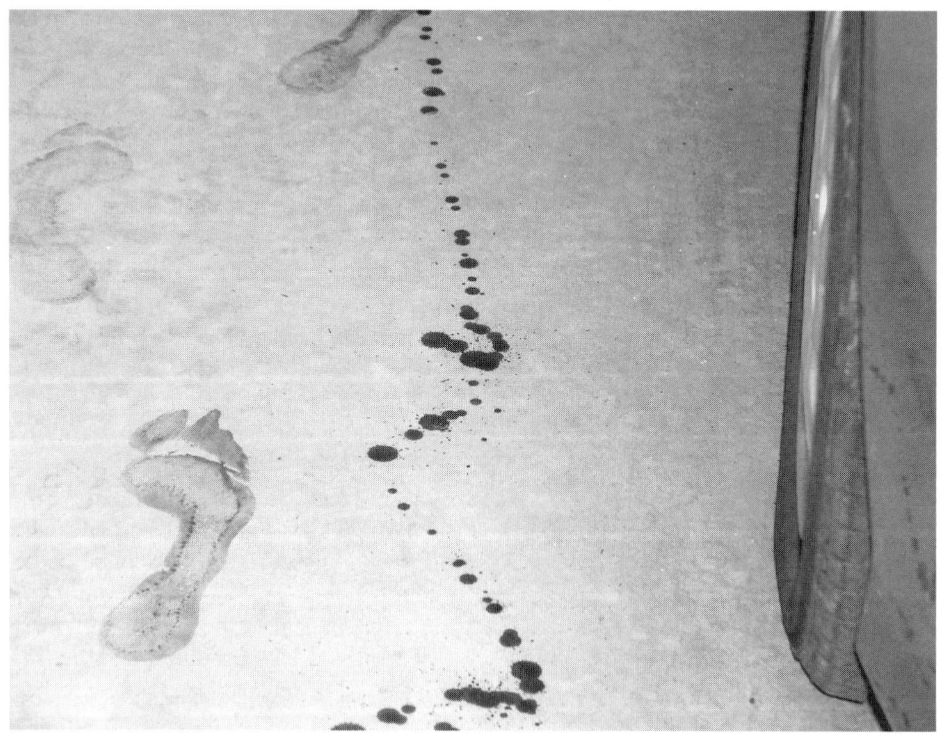

FIGURE 16–30 Blood pattern at scene of a suicide. *Source:* Dodge County, WI. Medical Examiner's Office, P. J. Schoebel.

- Finding blood with a suspect's genetic markers
  - On a victim
  - On something owned by a victim
  - On something associated with a victim
- Blood spatter and/or blood location information

Four types of blood evidence may be found:

- Bloodstains or spatter found at the primary scene
- Bloodstains found away from the primary scene
- Blood spatter patterns that indicate how a crime or a sequence of events occurred
- Blood trails that lead away from a scene

Blood Visualization Certain chemicals are used to enhance the visualization of bloodstains at a scene. **Luminol** will cause bloodstains, old or new, to glow in the dark. It is not a foolproof method but may be useful as a locator for a blood deposit that may then be characterized in other ways. It may react with copper, iron, or cobalt and with some dyes and bleaches to give false-positives for blood. The use of chemicals, including Luminol, may contaminate bloodstains and eliminate the possibilities of further analysis.

A variety of fluids may be found at crime scenes. Presumptive testing may be performed to determine if a fluid or stain is indeed blood.

> **TIP:**
>
> A presumptive test for blood uses chemicals that change color in the presence of blood.

Blood Photography Use high-intensity oblique lighting to search a scene for blood evidence (see Fig. 16–31). This type of lighting will enhance bloodstain visualization. Use the same type of light source for bloodstain and spatter photography. Remember that blood spatter may be very fine and located in unusual places. The suspect of a crime may have attempted to clean the crime scene and may have succeeded in removing the blood from the obvious places. Look behind, under, and above objects. Every scene is three-dimensional, and many suspects forget to look for and remove stains on ceilings.

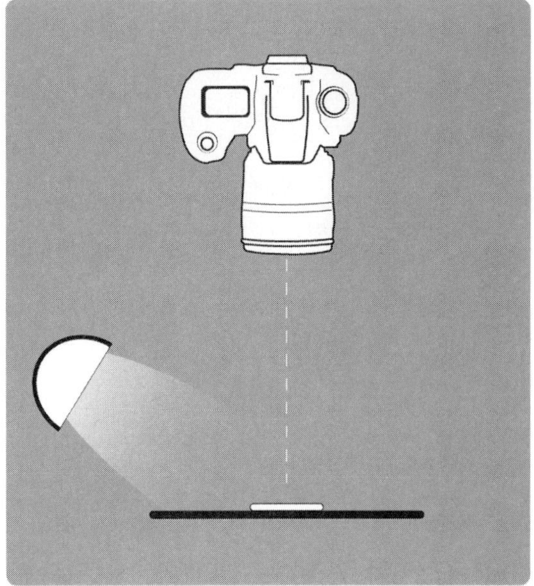

FIGURE 16–31 Oblique lighting for inspection and photography. *Source:* Jessica Weiss.

Photograph the scene in a logical and systematic manner to show the relationship of blood spatters to the various objects and structures at the crime scene. If the crime occurred indoors, the photographs should show how the various areas are connected. This is particularly valuable when recording peripheral bloodstains found in other rooms.

Record overall, mid-range, and close-up images. Use of the proper scale is mandatory. Use a 2-D scale with stains and spatters that cover large areas. Use larger scales, such as yardsticks or pocket rods (see Fig. 16–32) for larger areas. **Pocket rods** are similar to conventional tape measures, except they are made specifically for use during the photographic documentation of evidence and scenes. The rod has no excess material before the first graduation and is classified as a true-zero measure. The graduations are larger and higher in contrast than on conventional tapes to enable recognition in the photographs. The tapes are easily taken out of their plastic case to allow for use in free-standing applications.

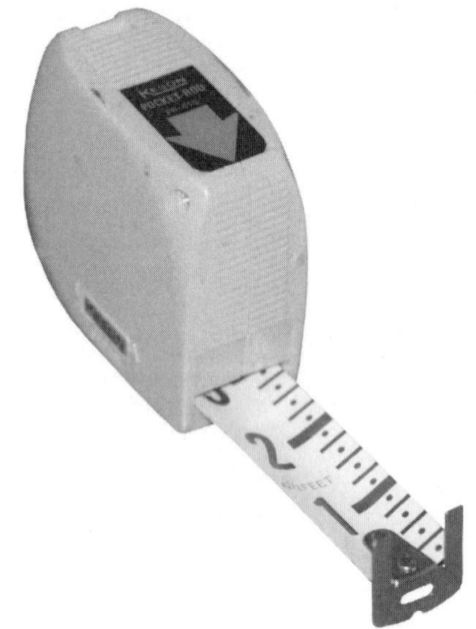

FIGURE 16–32 Pocket rod for high visibility photography of large areas. *Source:* Sandy Weiss/Packer Engineering.

The photographic image of a blood spattered area may later be projected for ease of analysis. During projection, match the scale of the image to an actual scale. This will make the image nearly 1:1 size of the original. The perspective of the image and any optical problems inherent to the camera and projection equipment must be calculated and solved if the stain or spatter analysis is to be exactly 1:1. During the photography of overall images, place the scales parallel and perpendicular to the floor. This enables simpler calculations. If the photograph is exposed oblique to the subject, it will be impossible to match the size of the two scales to the projected image. In the resultant image, one of the yardsticks or rods will be shortened compared to the other. When this occurs, the projector-to-screen angle must be adjusted to bring the dimensions of the image into the same perspective as the subject. Measurements and vectors from projections may be used to determine the direction and points of origin of blood spatter evidence.[19]

One drawback of the analysis of 2-D photographs of 3-D objects is the difficulty inherent in accurate analysis of the information contained in the image. If bloodstain or spatter is on a 3-D object, consider creating 3-D photographs. (Refer to Chapter 8 for application instructions.)

The International Association of Bloodstain Pattern Analysts has created a special glossary of terms used in the description of blood spatters (see Fig. 16–33). This glossary is downloadable from www.iabpa.org/Terminology.pdf.

Collection of Blood Evidence After the locations of blood evidence have been noted, tagged, and documented, the collection process may begin. Collection should be performed using a logical and systematic sequence, following the same route as the walk-through and documentation of the scene. Photographs should be taken of the collection process, and then retaken if layers of evidence that were not previously visible and/or documented are then uncovered.

Follow departmental or FBI protocols for the proper collection and preservation of blood evidence. Always use appropriate safety precautions when handling biological evidence. Be sure to wear PPE, including gloves, masks, or eye protection, as the situation warrants.

Dried Bloodstains If the bloodstained item is small and transportable, package it in a paper bag or envelope.

If the bloodstained item is large or not easily transported, do one of the following:

- Cut out a piece.
- Tape lift a sample.
- Scrape a sample into an envelope.
- Absorb a sample onto a wet, clean, white cotton thread or square.
- Consider the removal and retention of the entire surface, wall, floor, ceiling, and so on.

If possible, the investigator should also collect control samples from unstained areas of the item (**negative controls**) to help correlate a positive result with the variable being tested.

Wet Bloodstains If an item containing a wet bloodstain is small and transportable, package it in a paper bag or envelope, or *very* temporarily in a plastic bag to prevent contamination of other objects. Remove the object from the plastic bag as soon as it arrives at the lab.

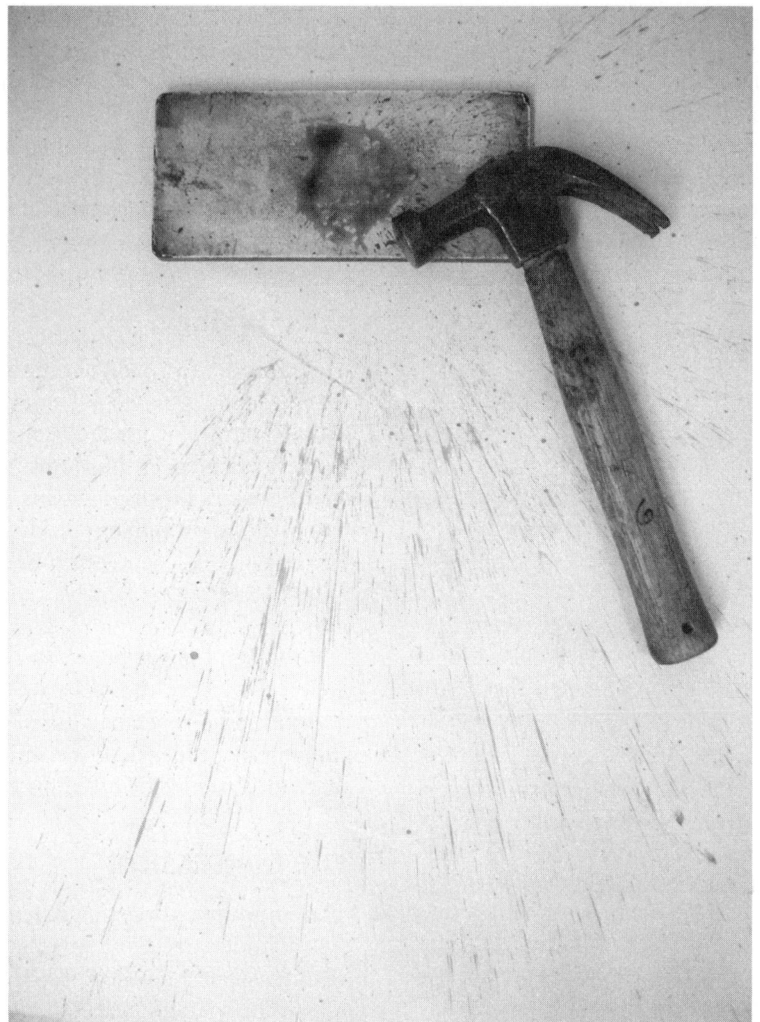

FIGURE 16–33 Blood spatter testing. *Source:* Aric Dutelle, University of Wisconsin-Platteville.

If the wet bloodstained item is large or not easily transported, absorb the stain onto a 1 × 1-inch square of a cotton square (see "Dried Bloodstains").

SUMMARY

Once a crime scene has been thoroughly documented and the locations of evidence marked and documented, the process of collection of evidence may begin. This process should always be prioritized so that the most fragile, transitory, and mobile evidence is collected first. Collection should then continue through the scene, within the established perimeter, in a systematic and logical manner. Photographs should be taken of each piece of evidence, especially if layers of evidence that were previously covered are being revealed.

Crime scene evidence may include firearms, bullets, casings, tool marks, paint chips and/or scrapes, broken objects, fibers, hairs, fingerprints, bite marks, fingernails, blood, and any number of other things needing detailed and accurate documentation. The purpose of the photographs is to provide detailed and accurate documentation for future reference, recognition, identification, and possible individualization of the evidence. If the unique source of the evidence can be found, it may lead to the solution of the crime.

The photographs should always be exposed to yield sufficient sharpness, DoF, and resolution for their final purpose. It is the duty of the photographer to provide images meeting these stipulations.

CASE STUDY

DEATH ROW FOR ARSON AND MURDER

This study is a perfect example of how photographs may mean the difference between life and death in a criminal investigation.

Mr. Madison Hobley (see Fig. 16–34) had been on death row for 15 years before Packer Engineering became involved in his case. The original scene was no longer in a suitable state to be inspected for new evidence. A gasoline can found at the scene was still preserved in evidence and was available, as were all the photographs taken by the officers at the scene. By court order, the photographic exhibits could not be taken from Cook County Jail in Chicago. A portable copy arrangement was assembled, and the exhibits were copied photographically at the jail library, under police supervision. By detailed study of the copied images and the physical evidence, Packer engineers were able to bring forth an opinion that was influential in releasing Mr. Hobley from custody.

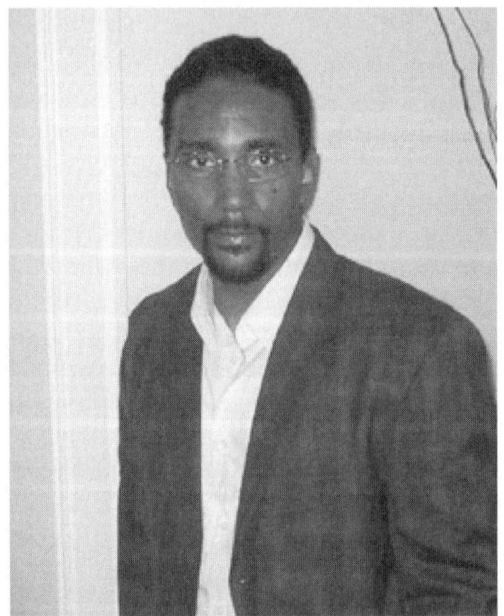

FIGURE 16–34 Mr. Madison Hobley. *Source:* Sandy Weiss/Packer Engineering.

THE CRIME

Mr. Hobley had been sentenced to death, primarily based on alleged confessions obtained by a group of Chicago police officers. Four officers claimed Hobley admitted setting a fire that claimed the lives of his wife, infant son, and five other persons early the morning of January 6, 1987, at an apartment building in the 1100 block of East 82nd Street in Chicago (see Figs. 16–35).

When the fire broke out, Mr. Hobley, then 26, escaped from the scene wearing only his underwear. He repeatedly swore his innocence, alleging that the officers tortured him and, when that failed, they fabricated his confession.

THE CONFESSION

The morning after the fire, Mr. Hobley was placed under arrest and was taken to police headquarters where the alleged confession took place. According to the police, Mr. Hobley said he went to a filling station with a gas can, bought $1 of gasoline, went home, emptied the can into the hallway outside his third-floor apartment and down the stairwell, ignited the gasoline with a match, and threw the can down into the second-floor hallway (see Fig. 16–36). The police said he did this so that he might start a new life with a woman with whom he had recently had an affair.

GASOLINE PURCHASE

Two eyewitnesses identified Mr. Hobley and linked him to the purchase of the gasoline at an Amoco station less than an hour before the fire. The witnesses were also present at the fire scene and testified that they saw the same man who purchased the gasoline watching the fire.

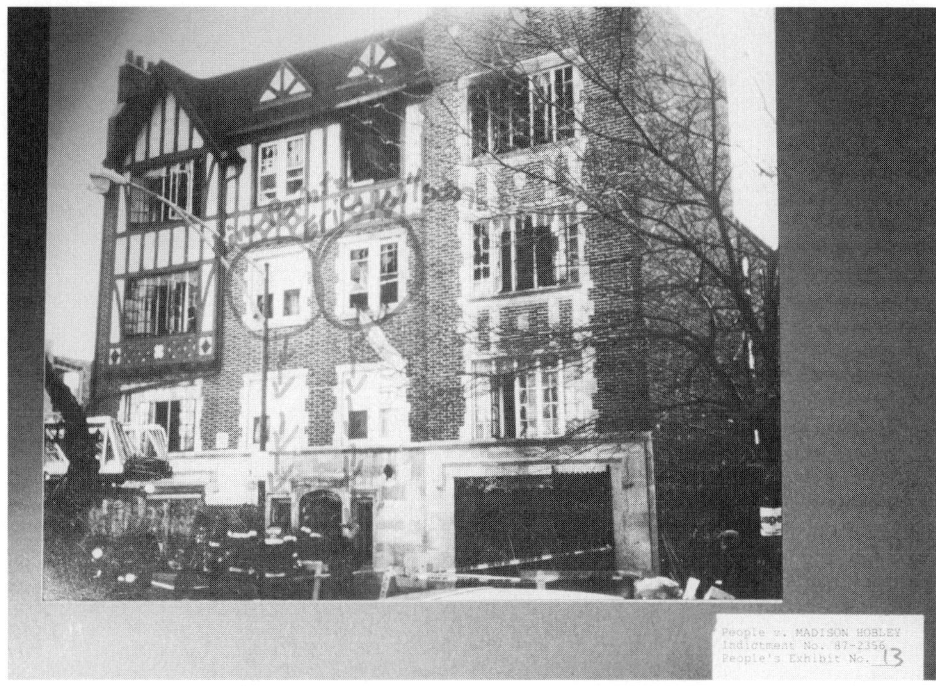

FIGURE 16–35 Outside of arson scene, copy. *Source:* Sandy Weiss/Packer Engineering.

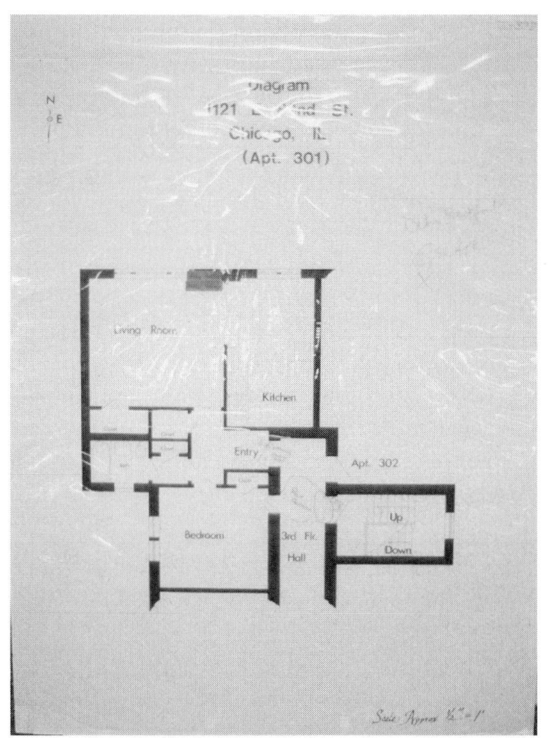

FIGURE 16–36 Plan of structure, copy. *Source:* Sandy Weiss/Packer Engineering.

PHYSICAL EVIDENCE

Police officers introduced a two-gallon gasoline can into evidence that another officer testified he discovered at the fire scene.

A Chicago police detective testified as an arson expert for the prosecution. He told the jury that a burn pattern on the floor in front of the Hobley apartment (see Fig. 16–37) indicated that gasoline had been poured there. He acknowledged that subsequent tests showed no traces of gasoline in the area, but he claimed that it must have been washed away by water the firefighters used to extinguish the fire.

SENTENCE AND APPEALS

The jury found nothing in the evidence and testimony to preclude the imposition of the death penalty. In 1994 the judge sentenced Mr. Hobley to death. The Illinois Supreme Court upheld Mr. Hobley's conviction and death sentence, calling the evidence "overwhelming."[20]

In 1995, Mr. Hobley's appellate attorneys filed a petition for post-conviction relief in the

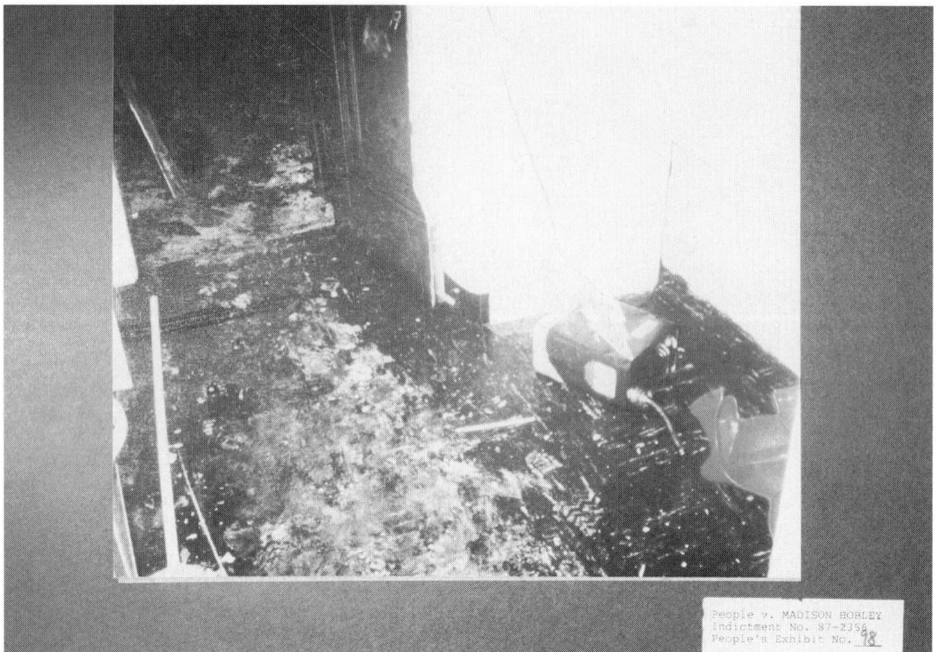

FIGURE 16–37 Floor and gas can, copy. *Source:* Sandy Weiss/Packer Engineering.

circuit court, alleging that the authorities had illegally withheld a forensic report from the trial. The report stated that the gasoline can in evidence had been examined for fingerprints and that Mr. Hobley's prints were not on it.

The report also alleged that authorities had withheld reports showing that the police had recovered a second gasoline can at the scene of the fire and had destroyed it. The implication of these reports was that the fire had been set by someone other than Mr. Hobley and that the can introduced into evidence at the trial had been planted to corroborate Mr. Hobley's confession.

In 1998, the Illinois Supreme Court found the new evidence sufficient to remand the case for an evidentiary hearing. The court stated that "at the defendant's trial, the defense theory was that another person had started the fire. The lack of fingerprints and the existence of a second gasoline can found at the fire scene, would have offered concrete evidentiary support to that defense theory."[21]

THE HEARING

Russell A. Ogle, Ph.D., P.E., CSP, of Packer Engineering, Inc., testified that the gas can (see Fig. 16–38) showed no signs of exposure to the extreme heat that had destroyed other items in the area where the can had been found. He also pointed out that the plastic cap on the can had not been damaged (see Fig. 16–39).

Dr. Ogle also testified, in contradiction to the prosecution expert's contention at Mr. Hobley's trial, that no evidence of burn patterns was found on the third floor of the building. Dr. Ogle said that the fire started in a stairwell lower in the building (see Fig. 16–40).

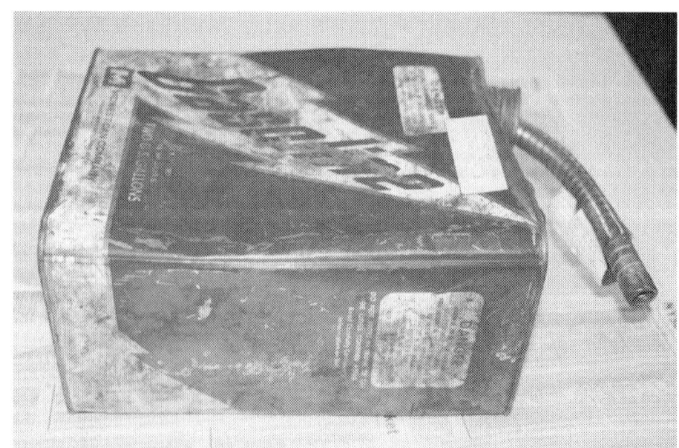

FIGURE 16–38 Gas can in evidence. *Source:* Sandy Weiss/Packer Engineering.

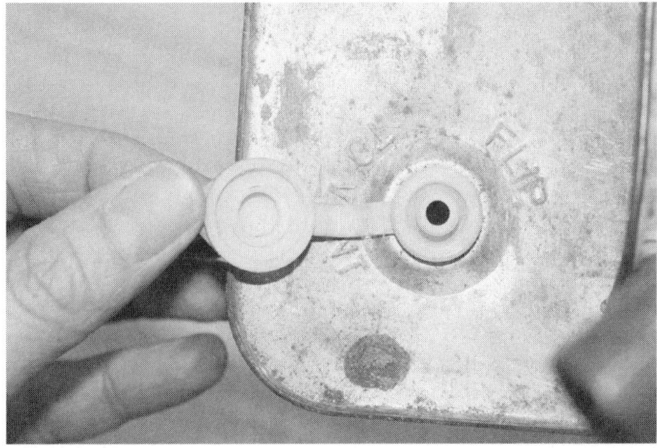

FIGURE 16–39 Undamaged plastic cap on gas can. *Source:* Sandy Weiss/Packer Engineering.

PARDON

On January 9, 2003, then Governor George H. Ryan granted Mr. Hobley a pardon. The governor stated that Mr. Hobley had been convicted on the basis of flawed evidence and that the jury did not have the benefit of all the existing evidence. The photographic and physical evidence from the scene were influential in the pardon of Mr. Hobley.

Some of the details in this summary were prepared by Rob Warden, executive director of the Center on Wrongful Convictions. Northwestern University School of Law, Center on Wrongful Convictions, 357 East Chicago Avenue, Chicago, IL 60611 (312) 503-3100.

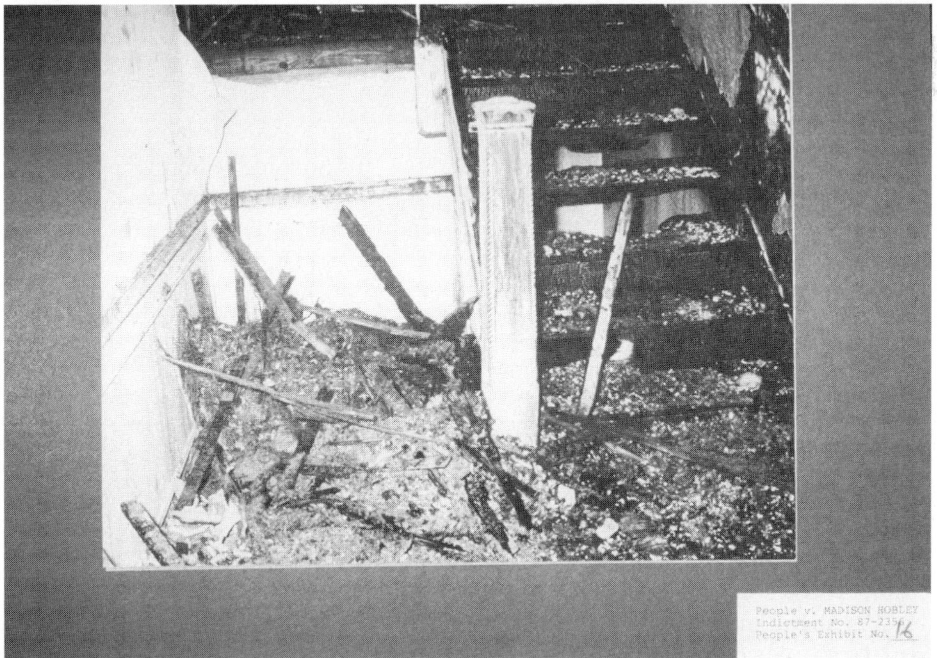

FIGURE 16–40 Lower stairwell, copy. *Source:* Sandy Weiss/Packer Engineering.

KEY TERMS

primary evidence, (p. 462)
secondary or supporting evidence, (p. 462)
metadata, (p. 463)
native format, (p. 463)
case identifier, (p. 464)
crime scene processing, (p. 465)
track width, (p. 470)
wheelbase, (p. 470)
bruise, (p. 470)
extravasation, (p. 470)
ecchymosis, (p. 470)
perimortem, (p. 471)
postmortem, (p. 471)
wound, (p. 474)
trace evidence, (p. 479)
fingerprint, (p. 479)
latent fingerprint, (p. 480)
patent print, (p. 481)
plastic print, (p. 481)
optical scanning, (p. 481)
inverted image, (p. 481)
luminol, (p. 483)
pocket rods, (p. 483)
negative control, (p. 484)

EXERCISES

1. Research legal literature and trial transcripts regarding the concept of deleting unsatisfactory images from digital memory in the field. Write a report and recommendations for the practice.
2. Consider this scenario:
   a. There are 40 acres of land to be searched for the scene of a homicide.
   b. You have 100 people at your disposal for the task. Some are properly trained and some are totally untrained.
   c. You must instruct all of them on technique and coordination.

   What would you tell them to do? When a questionable scene is found, how would you approach the photographic assignment? Be complete in your responses.
3. Using a volunteer subject, have them pose as a corpse in various environments, indoors and outdoors. Add a simulated injury with makeup or a marker. Photograph the corpse completely and document the injury, with and without scales. Pay close attention to any difficulties with the assignment, and design methods to use to alleviate the problems.
4. With a thin sharp knife, create a series of different types of wounds in a melon or squash. Using proper photographic techniques and appropriate scales, make a collection of representative photographs of the wounds.
5. Locate and photograph a collection of shoe prints of different types of surfaces. Photograph the soles of different shoes. Always use the proper technique and scale, if available.

AN ASSIGNMENT FOR THE DARING ONLY

If:

1. Suitable photographic hardware is available, and
2. A suitable and willing subject can be found

Expose a logical and systematic set of images of:

1. New
2. Old/healed
3. Very old

bruises. Use visible, ultraviolet, or infrared lighting and prepare an exhibit of images to demonstrate the differences in the ages of the bruises. If multiple subjects can be found, perform the same exercise with subjects of different skin colors.

APPENDIX 16.1

Digital Imaging Protocol

This is a representative digital imaging protocol, authored and used by law enforcement in Highland Park, Illinois.

TIP:

Use this protocol as a starting point to adapt one for your agency.

CITY OF HIGHLAND PARK, ILLINOIS DEPARTMENT OF POLICE

GENERAL ORDER 143

(Effective 02/12/07)

FROM: THE CHIEF OF POLICE

TO: ALL MEMBERS OF THE POLICE DEPARTMENT

SUBJECT: **CRIME SCENE PROCESSING - DIGITAL PHOTOGRAPHY**

PURPOSE

The purpose of this policy is to provide guidelines in respect to the capture and preservation of digital photographs used for evidentiary purposes.

Capture: The act of gathering images using a digital camera.

Digital Camera: A device that stores images digitally to an internal or external memory device such as a flash card.

Digital Image: Any image stored in a numerical form. For purposes of this general order, the terms Digital Image and Digital Photo are interchangeable.

Identification Officer: A designated Evidence Technician who is trained in downloading and securing digital images.

Evidence Technician: Any Department member who has received specialized training in evidence collection and who has been designated as an evidence technician by the Chief of Police or a designee. Digital photographs may be taken by officers or civilians who are not trained in evidence collection at the direction of a supervisor.

Storage Media: Digital storage devices such as flash cards or other items used to store images captured via a digital camera.

PROCEDURE

A. Evidence Technicians or designated photographers responding to incidents should capture images pertaining to but not limited to the following:
   1. Death Investigation
   2. Sexual Assault
   3. Arson

4. Armed Robbery
5. Battery/Domestic Battery
6. Recovered Stolen Auto
7. Burglary/Theft from Motor Vehicle
8. Criminal Damage to Property
9. Motor vehicle crash involving fatalities or injuries likely to result in fatality
10. Motor vehicle crashes involving City of Highland Park vehicles

B. Digital Camera Settings
1. The Resolution setting on the camera should always be set at the highest resolution.
2. Digital images may be reviewed using the camera, but should not be transferred to any computer or other device that allows for editing of the image.
3. Poor quality images caused by being out of focus, flash failure, blocked lens, blurring due to movement, etc. may be deleted from the camera at the scene, at the discretion of the photographer and re-taken as needed.
4. It is allowable to have multiple cases recorded on one storage media provided that the photo ill card depicting the case number is photographed at the beginning of the series of photographs related to that case.

C. Chain of Evidence for Storage Media
1. Digital images shall be handled and protected with the same care as any item of evidentiary value.
2. When the storage media is full or the photographer decides no additional photographs will be stored on it, the storage media shall be removed from the camera and placed into a protective media case designed for that media. The media case will be placed in an evidence envelope along with a photograph log completed by the photographer and placed in the evidence room for retrieval by the Identification Officer.

D. Long-Term Storage of Images

The Identification Officer or designee will be responsible for the downloading and storage of images. The images shall be stored in the following manner:

1. Images will only be downloaded and stored by the Identification Officer.
2. Images will be written to a write-once CD (CD-R). One CD-R will be used for each case.
3. The serial number of the CD-R will be recorded into the digital photo log database and the CD-R will be maintained in the evidence vault.
4. Once written to a CD-R, the images will also be downloaded into a secured evidence photo directory located on the City computer network.
5. The storage media shall be re-formatted before the media is returned to service.
6. Images will be printed by the Identification Officer when requested.
7. Digital images may be enhanced for investigative purposes or court presentation. The original image will be maintained undisturbed and only a copy of the image will be enhanced.

This General Order is in effect at this time and will remain in effect until further notice.

Reprinted by permission of Detective Jon Lohman and Paul S. Shafer, Chief of Police, City of Highland Park, Illinois.

APPENDIX 16.2

Federal Rules of Evidence

The Federal Rules of Evidence are available online at www.law.cornell.edu/rules/fre.

ARTICLE IX AUTHENTICATION AND IDENTIFICATION

Rule 901 Requirement of Authentication or Identification

a. General provision.

The requirement of authentication or identification as a condition precedent to admissibility is satisfied by evidence sufficient to support a finding that the matter in question is what its proponent claims.

b. Illustrations.

By way of illustration only, and not by way of limitation, the following are examples of authentication or identification conforming with the requirements of this rule:

1. Testimony of witness with knowledge. Testimony that a matter is what it is claimed to be.
2. Non-expert opinion on handwriting. Non-expert opinion as to the genuineness of handwriting, based upon familiarity not acquired for purposes of the litigation.
3. Comparison by trier or expert witness. Comparison by the trier of fact or by expert witnesses with specimens which have been authenticated.
4. Distinctive characteristics and the like. Appearance, contents, substance, internal patterns, or other distinctive characteristics, taken in conjunction with circumstances.
5. Voice identification. Identification of a voice, whether heard firsthand or through mechanical or electronic transmission or recording, by opinion based upon hearing the voice at any time under circumstances connecting it with the alleged speaker.
6. Telephone conversations. Telephone conversations, by evidence that a call was made to the number assigned at the time by the telephone company to a particular person or business, if (A) in the case of a person, circumstances, including self-identification, show the person answering to be the one called, or (B) in the case of a business, the call was made to a place of business and the conversation related to business reasonably transacted over the telephone.
7. Public records or reports. Evidence that a writing authorized by law to be recorded or filed and in fact recorded or filed in a public office, or a purported public record, report, statement, or data compilation, in any form, is from the public office where items of this nature are kept.
8. Ancient documents or data compilation. Evidence that a document or data compilation, in any form, (A) is in such condition as to create no suspicion concerning its authenticity, (B) was in a place where it, if authentic, would likely be, and (C) has been in existence 20 years or more at the time it is offered.
9. Process or system. Evidence describing a process or system used to produce a result and showing that the process or system produces an accurate result.
10. Methods provided by statute or rule. Any method of authentication or identification provided by Act of Congress or by other rules prescribed by the Supreme Court pursuant to statutory authority.

ARTICLE X. CONTENTS OF WRITINGS, RECORDINGS, AND PHOTOGRAPHS

Rule 1001. Definitions

For purposes of this article the following definitions are applicable:

1. Writings and recordings. "Writings" and "recordings" consist of letters, words, or numbers, or their equivalent, set down by handwriting, typewriting, printing, photo-stating, photographing, magnetic impulse, mechanical or electronic recording, or other form of data compilation.
2. Photographs. "Photographs" include still photographs, X-ray films, video tapes, and motion pictures.
3. Original. An "original" of a writing or recording is the writing or recording itself or any counterpart intended to have the same effect by a person executing or issuing it. An "original" of a photograph includes the negative or any print therefrom. If data are stored in a computer or similar device, any printout or other output readable by sight, shown to reflect the data accurately, is an "original."
4. Duplicate. A "duplicate" is a counterpart produced by the same impression as the original, or from the same matrix, or by means of photography, including enlargements and miniatures, or by mechanical or electronic re-recording, or by chemical reproduction, or by other equivalent techniques which accurately reproduces the original.

Rule 1002. Requirement of Original

To prove the content of a writing, recording, or photograph, the original writing, recording, or photograph is required, except as otherwise provided in these rules or by Act of Congress.

Rule 1003. Admissibility of Duplicates

A duplicate is admissible to the same extent as an original unless (1) a genuine question is raised as to the authenticity of the original or (2) in the circumstances it would be unfair to admit the duplicate in lieu of the original.

Rule 1004. Admissibility of Other Evidence of Contents

The original is not required, and other evidence of the contents of a writing, recording, or photograph is admissible if—

1. Originals lost or destroyed. All originals are lost or have been destroyed, unless the proponent lost or destroyed them in bad faith; or
2. Original not obtainable. No original can be obtained by any available judicial process or procedure; or
3. Original in possession of opponent. At a time when an original was under the control of the party against whom offered, that party was put on notice, by the pleadings or otherwise, that the contents would be a subject of proof at the hearing, and that party does not produce the original at the hearing; or
4. Collateral matters. The writing, recording, or photograph is not closely related to a controlling issue.

Chapter **17**

Testifying in the Courtroom

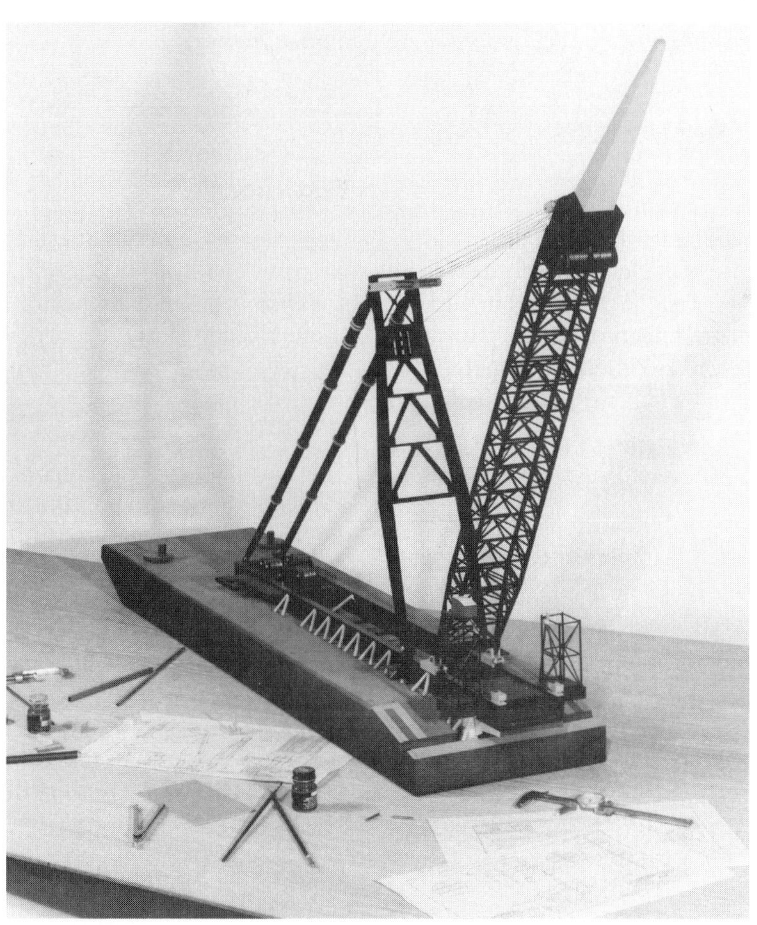

Learning Objectives

AFTER STUDYING THIS CHAPTER, YOU SHOULD BE ABLE TO:

1. Explain the concept, stages, and types of trials
2. Understand the scope of trial testimony
3. Understand the scope of deposition testimony
4. Understand the usefulness of forensic images for the representation of evidence
5. Differentiate the digital formats in which testimony may be offered
6. Comprehend the digital capabilities of the modern courtroom
7. Understand the rules governing the qualifications and title of an expert witness
8. Differentiate the forms of forensic images used for legal proceedings, including physical and computer models
9. Differentiate the uses of animation and simulation in the courtroom
10. Utilize the capabilities of PowerPoint software in digital presentations

TRIALS

A **trial** is a legal event in which parties dispute information, in the form of **evidence**, in a formal setting. The setting is usually a court, and a judge, jury, or other designated finders of fact are present. The goal is to achieve a resolution to a dispute.

Types of Trials

Trials fall into one of two main categories:

1. **Jury trial:** held before a peer group of disinterested members of the community, with a judge presiding
2. **Bench trial:** held before a judge or magistrate, without a jury present

Types of Disputes

Disputes also fall into one of two main categories:

1. **Criminal trial:** to resolve accusations brought by the government against a person accused of a crime
2. **Civil trial:** to resolve a dispute between private parties

Testimony

Legal **testimony** is an attestation under oath of the truth of a matter. Witnesses testify based on personal knowledge or belief, with the purpose of establishing facts.

Evidence

The law establishes the types of evidence that are admissible at trial. **Admissible** evidence includes the following:

- Oral statements
- Written statements
- Exhibits (including photographs)
- Other documentary materials

ADMISSIBILITY OF FORENSIC PHOTOGRAPHS

To be admissible, photographs used for forensic purposes should be an accurate representation of the evidence and conditions existing at the time the photographs were captured. **Forensic**

photography can be defined as the practice of using photographs, admissible in courts of law, to illustrate evidence for the support or refutation of testimony in proceedings where people present **exhibits** (article of tangible evidence) to argue a claim or a person's guilt or innocence.

Misleading photographs, created to demonstrate untrue contentions, should not be admissible. The purpose of this book is to teach the reader the best methods to capture photographs for accurate representations, within the parameters of the existing medium.

Forensic photographs may be used to identify persons, places, and things or to exhibit particular locations or objects of importance to a judge or jury. The photographs may be more easily understood than the oral or written testimony of witnesses. The photographs may also be used to help detect forgeries and to illustrate objects when the original cannot be readily produced or seen. It is permissible to use photographs that are enlarged versions of the evidence, including stereoscopic views.

REPORTS

Reports stating professional opinions about occurrences are common forums for forensic images. In this context, the images are usually small and used for corroboration of statements.

> **TIP:**
>
> If a report is the only eventual use for forensic images, small image files may be sufficient.

Reports may be provided in various ways:

- Printed and sent through the mail or delivered in person
- E-mailed in electronic form
- Posted on Web sites

Report images will usually be up to 4 × 6 inches and need only be 150 to 250 dpi for viewing on a monitor or printing to hard copy. Original image files must remain in their native format and original states. Report images are usually satisfactory in JPEG format. Usage and protocol determine whether or not peer review and multiple signatures are required on a forensic report.

Peer Review

The disposition of large amounts of money and possibly other people's lives may depend on what is written in someone's report. In many cases, before submission the writer should request corroboration from his or her peers about the report. **Peer review** is a process that forces authors to meet the standards of their discipline.

The peer review process often requires higher-resolution images than were contained in the report. These photographs enable the reviewer to visualize the theories and facts contained in the writer's opinion and in the report. For ease of review viewing, 8 × 10-inch or 8.5 × 11-inch images are the normal formats to include when forwarding reports to peers for review. Any enhancement of the images should be noted in a convenient form. JPEG files at 250 to 300 dpi maximum should suffice for the production of the printed images.

Expert Testimony

Discovery is the pre-trial phase in a lawsuit in which each party, through the law of civil procedure, can request documents and other evidence from other parties or can compel the production of evidence by using a subpoena or other discovery devices, such as requests for production and depositions. A **deposition** is the act or fact of taking sworn testimony of a witness outside of court, in certain well-defined legal circumstances. It is a part of the discovery process whereby litigants obtain information from each other in preparation for trial.

Expert Witnesses

A **witness** is an expert, by virtue of education, profession, publication, or experience, and has special knowledge of his or her subject beyond that of the average person. This knowledge should be sufficient for others to rely on the expert's opinion.

Experts may be called on behalf of a plaintiff or the defense. In most cases, the experts will use photographs or other visual exhibits to support their testimony. Experts may hire a photographer, or they may perform the photography themselves. Due to their status as experts, they have a responsibility to present expert-quality images.

When a witness testifies in court, his or her identity and most documents used to prepare his or her opinion, including photographs, are discoverable. Experienced attorneys will advise experts not to expose unnecessary or extraneous photographs, but it is ethical for the expert to disclose during investigation any facts or photographs found damaging to the case.

Exhibits

If an expert uses photographic exhibits during testimony, the images will be either projected or printed. Projected images are more useful if the images were properly exposed and focused. It is legal to include captions, arrows, and any other demonstrative aids on the images to illustrate pertinent findings. It is also necessary to make those additions only on duplicate images, never on the original images.

Exhibit boards taken to court are usually sized around 24 × 30 inches. Smaller photographs are difficult for the whole court to see. To produce 24 × 30-inch prints of reasonable quality, a 6 Mp original image file is required.

> **TIP:**
>
> Captions, arrows, and such may also be added to images as overlays.

Federal Rules of Evidence

Many of the rules governing expert testimony were established in ***Daubert v. Merrell Dow Pharmaceuticals.***[1] According to the Federal Rules of Evidence, the admission of scientific evidence at trials in federal courts is determined by the trial judge. The judge must decide if the evidence offered is scientifically valid and relevant to the case. During cross-examination and the presentation of contrary evidence, the jury decides whether the scientific evidence is credible.

The Standard of Expert Testimony

Rule 702 of the Federal Rules of Evidence governs the admission of expert testimony in court, by the following criteria:

1. The testimony must be scientific in nature, and the testimony must be grounded in generally accepted knowledge, arrived at by the scientific method.
2. The scientific knowledge must assist in understanding the evidence or determining a fact in issue in the case.
3. The Rules provide that the judge will make the initial determination regarding whether the scientific knowledge will assist the trier of fact in the manner contemplated by Rule 702.[2]

Courts have adhered to the standards in *Daubert* and have often been successful in excluding junk science or pseudoscience, as well as experimental and unfounded techniques, from testimony. The scientific method is the proper way to think and investigate, and it is also the standard by which expert evidence is judged in order to be admissible.

> **TIP:**
>
> Keep the scientific method and the Federal Rules of Evidence in mind when producing photographs for court.

Deposition Exhibits

In judicial proceedings in federal court, the procedure for taking depositions in both civil and criminal cases is defined in Rule 30 of the Federal Rules of Civil Procedure and the corresponding provisions in states where the Federal Rules have been adopted.[3]

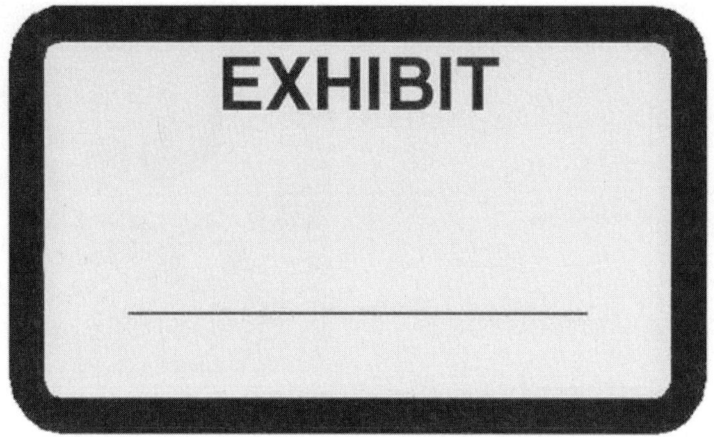

FIGURE 17–1 Exhibit marking tag. *Source:* Sandy Weiss/Packer Engineering.

A court or stenographic reporter must be present at all legal depositions and is empowered to begin the proceedings by administering an oath. The oath that the **deponent** (person being deposed) affirms is the same as if the testimony were being given in court. The reporter is responsible for marking all exhibits used in the deposition (see Fig. 17–1).

Exhibits, including photographs, letters, and other documents, may be introduced into evidence at deposition. Rule 34 of the Federal Rules of Evidence states that any involved party may request the production of any designated documents or electronically stored information for inspection, copying, testing, or sampling. This includes writings, drawings, graphs, charts, photographs, sound recordings, images, and other data or data compilations stored in any medium.

Photographs used at deposition are normally in 8 × 10-inch or 8.5 × 11-inch format. Photographs used in the deposition will have a label affixed directly to their surface by the reporter. The label is for identification and assurance that the images are the same exhibits when presented at trial.

THE DIGITAL COURTROOM

Modern courtrooms may have the capability to utilize multimedia case management systems for the digital presentation of evidence and displays. Such courts are referred to as **digital courtrooms.** Some displays are physical and may be held in the hands of the participants for a tactile experience. Other displays are strictly electronic and provide visual and audio experiences.

Real-time court reporting allows court reporters to convert their stenographic notes into English text, which is then displayed on screens around the courtroom. This technology allows court reporters to deliver transcripts quickly after court adjourns. During trial, participants may review testimony and make notes on their computer screens without interrupting the proceedings. They may perform searches for specific words or phrases.

Witnesses who are testifying can summon evidence through their workstations and annotate or draw on screens, which the system then captures. Some systems also accommodate videoconferencing, enabling people to testify from a distance.

PHYSICAL MODELS

A **physical model** is a 3-D representation of something. To be accurate, the model should be a rescaled version of the original object. A physical model of a large object is usually scaled smaller (see Fig. 17–2), and a model of something small is scaled larger. A physical model of something dynamic may be dynamic or stationary or have parts that are dynamic. A model may show inner parts that are normally not visible.

A model is a 3-D alternative for a 2-D representation, such as a drawing or photograph, and may be used for the re-creation of incidents

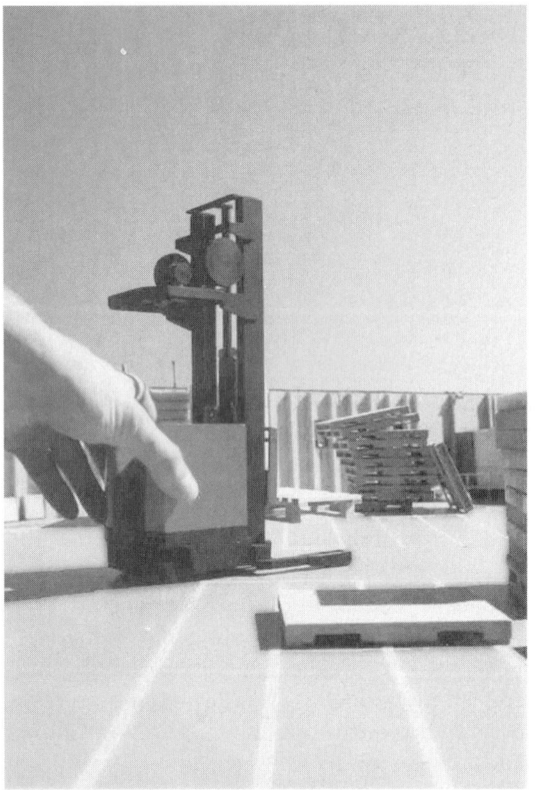

FIGURE 17–2 Physical, scaled-down model of an industrial lift. *Source:* Sandy Weiss/ Packer Engineering.

involving events too catastrophic for actual reconstruction. Such reconstructions are usually limited to the size of the objects, including vehicles (see Fig. 17–3).

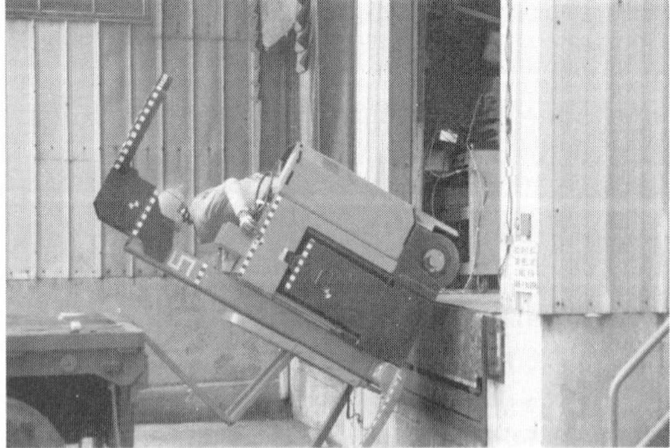

FIGURE 17–3 Forklift accident re-creation. *Source:* Sandy Weiss/Packer Engineering.

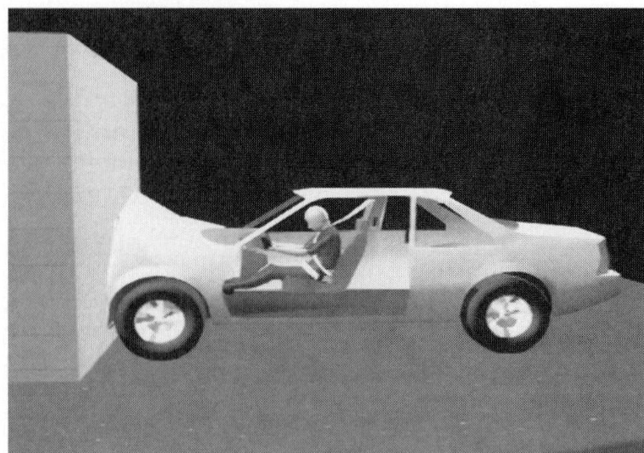

FIGURE 17–4 One frame of a computer animation. *Source:* Sandy Weiss/Packer Engineering.

COMPUTER ANIMATION

Computer animation is a 2-D or 3-D computer graphic, created with moving images to demonstrate an event or sequence of events. The illusion of motion is displayed on computer screens when one image is quickly replaced by another image, similar to the previous image but shifted slightly, in rapid repetition. This is identical to methods for creating the illusion of movement in television and motion pictures.

To create animations, physical models are built in the form of **computer models** using drawing programs such as CAD. The computer model is then programmed to perform a certain sequence of motions. To visualize an object that moves smoothly (see Fig. 17–4) without obvious jumps, image frames must be drawn on the computer at a rate of at least 12 times per second.

Computer animation may have the following characteristics:

- Photorealistic
  - Looks like a true view of a real world
- Non-photorealistic
  - Looks like a cartoon

FORENSIC ANIMATION

Animations are often used in the courtroom to enable the participants to visualize a place, an action, or a situation in court. The animation takes the place of live action in circumstances where it

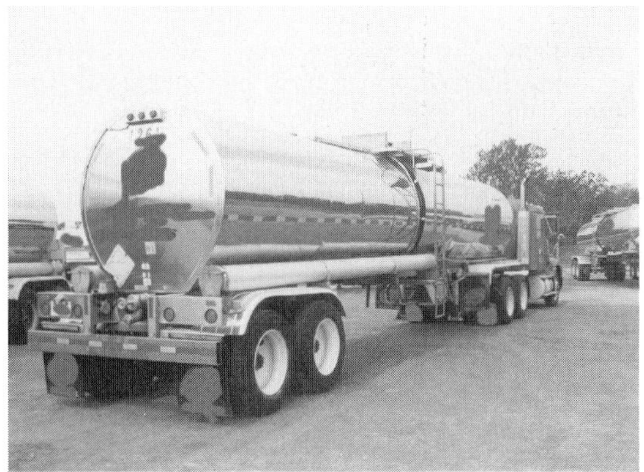

FIGURE 17–5 Tanker truck photograph. *Source:* Sandy Weiss/Packer Engineering.

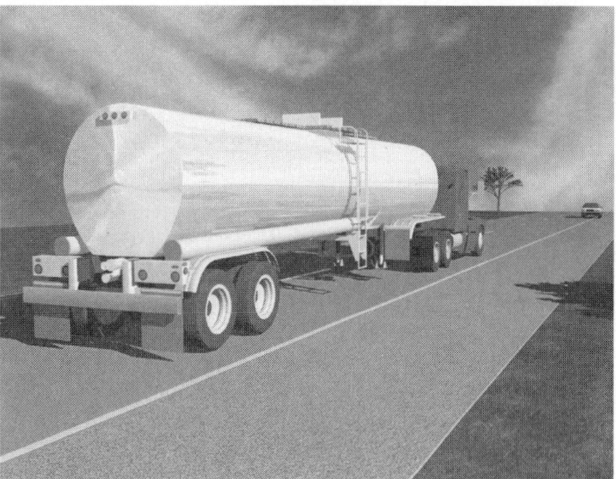

FIGURE 17–6 Computer model of tanker built from the photographic information in Figure 17–5. *Source:* Sandy Weiss/Packer Engineering.

is not possible to bring the action into the courtroom. Animations may be used to explain photos and videos (see Figs. 17–5 and 17–6).

In some situations, it is more logical to make an animation than to make any other form of representation for the courtroom. For example, it is *possible* to take a judge and jury for a ride along a highway with them sitting on top of a tanker truck. A vehicle may approach from the other side of the road, go out of control, crash into the tanker, and explode in a ball of flame. Clearly, this is not a feasible simulation.

Thus, building a computer model of the tanker shown in Figure 17–6 was a better way to present evidence. Measurements were taken of a real subject with scales, and a survey was performed with a total-station. The measurements were plotted into CAD to produce a wire-frame model, and then a 3-D modeling software program was used to complete the computer model and program the action. In this case, it was not necessary to build the tanker to completely (100%) photorealistic parameters.

PHYSICAL AND INTERACTIVE SIMULATION

Physical simulation is a simulation of action where substitute objects represent real objects. The physical objects are used because they are smaller or less expensive than the actual objects. The difference between an animation and a simulation is that an animation is used to approximate an action for ease of demonstration. A simulation reproduces an action to the limits of mathematical and engineering accuracy. In an **interactive simulation**, physical simulations include human operators, like in a flight simulator or a driving simulator.

Animations and simulation are used in courtrooms. Animations are less expensive to produce and require less accuracy.

Computer Simulation

Computer modeling and simulation (see Fig. 17–7) are used for visualizing and analyzing the operation of many types of physical action. Simulations of many kinds of actions are often referred to as synthetic environments.

AUTHENTICATION

Authentication is the validation of a computer or digital file to ensure that it is accurate within the limitations of expectancy.

TIP:

Always be prepared, mentally and physically, to testify to the degree of accuracy of the images or models you are presenting in court.

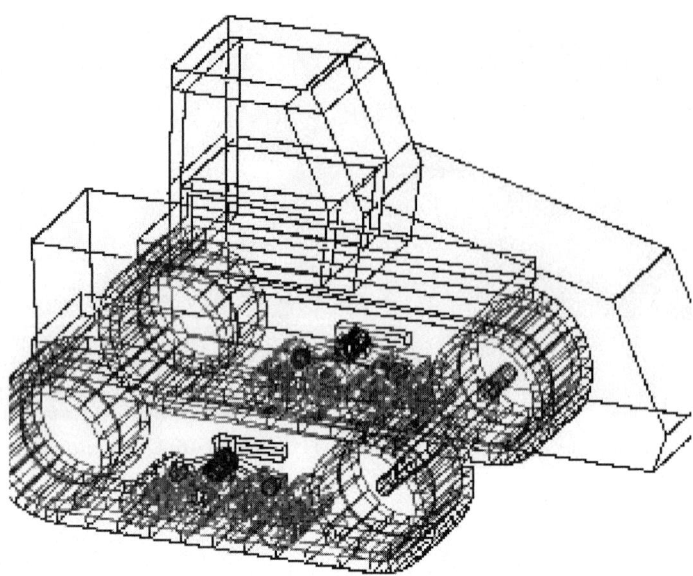

FIGURE 17–7 Tractor wire frame, used as a model to simulate the movement of the treads. *Source:* Sandy Weiss/Packer Engineering.

POWERPOINT

PowerPoint is a presentation software for text, graphics, movies, and other images. Each visual created in PowerPoint is positioned on individual pages or slides and can be connected to create a show. (The term *slide* refers to the archaic use of photographic slide projectors.) PowerPoint slides may be printed or displayed onscreen and navigated at the command of the presenter.

PowerPoint provides many useful presentation possibilities to the experienced user. The overall design of a presentation may be controlled by the use of masters, and the overall structure, including the text, can be easily edited and sequenced.

Most people agree that the use of presentation software may save time and energy for users who may have used other types of visual aids. However, some drawbacks arise from abuse of the features contained in sophisticated presentation software packages. Overuse of sound, animation, entrance and exit "toys," and multiple fonts result in an amateur look and feel that discourages the normal viewer. To look professional, keep presentations simple, yet sophisticated.

Tips for PowerPoint Presentations

- Use a presentation to augment, rather than to replace, the speaker.
- If all the words are on the slides, the audience does not need you.
- Keep the number of words and bullets per slide to a minimum.
- Keep fonts large.
- Use multiple colors minimally.
- *Do not* use sound effects during transitions.
- Do not vary backgrounds or designs within a presentation.
- Learn and take advantage of the capabilities of the software.

Figure 17–8 through 17–13 provide an example of the sophisticated use of the capabilities of PowerPoint for a short presentation. To build useful slides, follow these guidelines:

- Identify the case number in every image (see Fig. 17–8).
- If using the slides to follow a storyline, insert the elapsed time in plain sight (see Fig. 17–9).

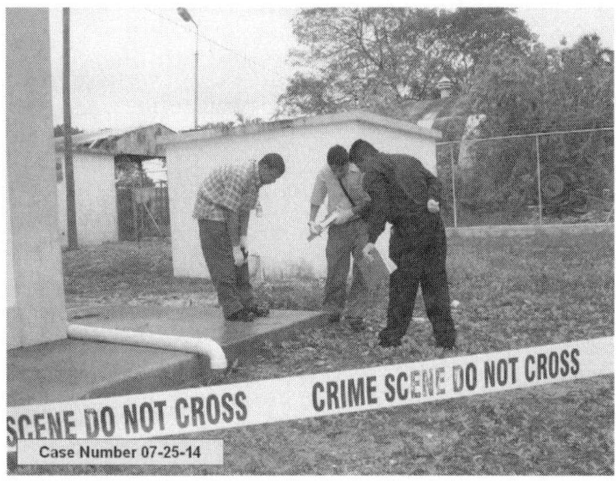

FIGURE 17–8 Show the case number. *Source:* Sandy Weiss/Packer Engineering.

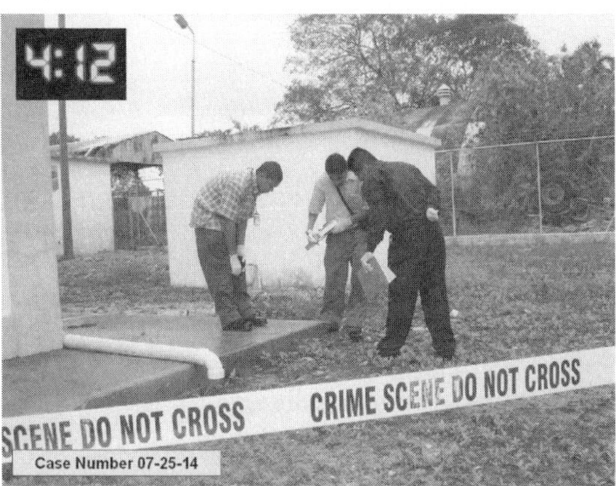

FIGURE 17–9 Add a clock. *Source:* Sandy Weiss/Packer Engineering.

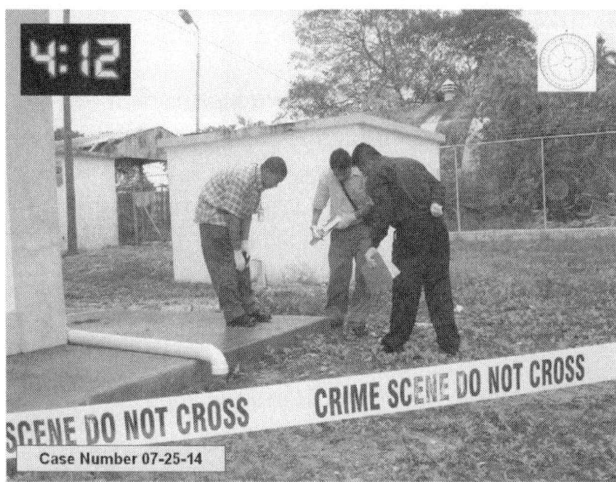

FIGURE 17–10 Include a locator. *Source:* Sandy Weiss/Packer Engineering.

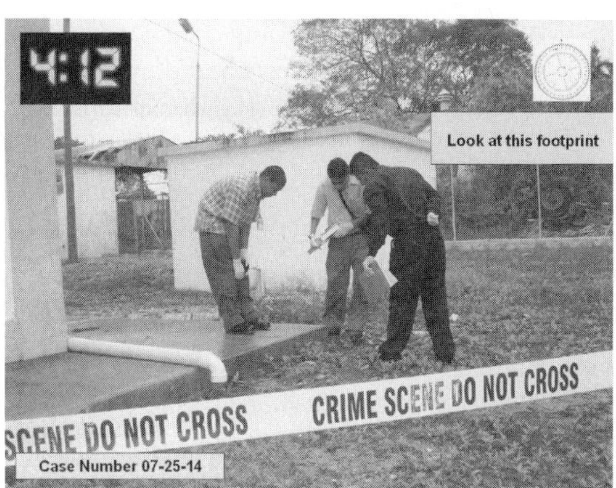

FIGURE 17–11 Add informative text. *Source:* Sandy Weiss/Packer Engineering.

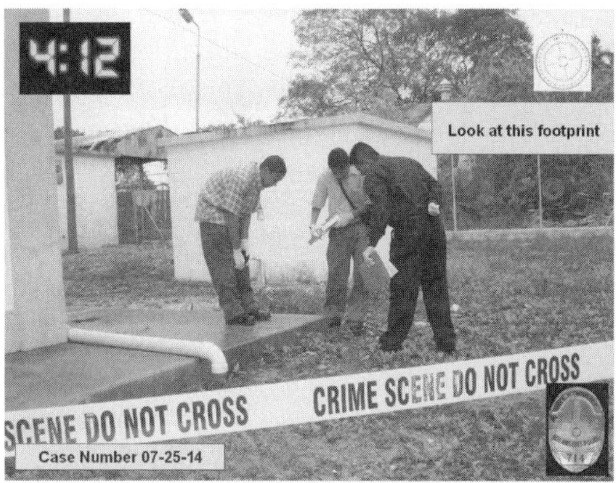

FIGURE 17–12 Add a logo. *Source:* Sandy Weiss/Packer Engineering.

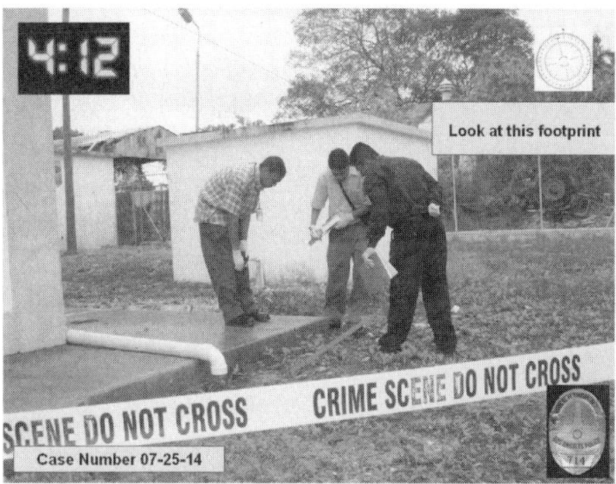

FIGURE 17–13 Add arrows. *Source:* Sandy Weiss/Packer Engineering.

- Use compass headings, GPS numbers, or other references when they will help the audience understand the slide (see Fig. 17–10).
- Insert documented text in the appropriate location (see Fig. 17–11).
- Put a departmental logo and copyright notice on every slide (see Fig. 17–12).
- Indicate directions of travel with broad, bright arrows (see Fig. 17–13).
- Add audio tracks from recordings of the crime, if available.
- Use enough slides to tell the whole story.

It is suitable to include all the background information listed in "Tips for PowerPoint Presentations" on the first slide after the title. It is also suitable to have all these elements enter the slide in sequence, one at a time, during the introduction to the program.

DIGITAL COURTROOM SOFTWARE

Full-service forensic photographers should be prepared to interlace their work with state-of-the-art presentation software, and **courtroom software** allows presenters to take full advantage of the digital courtroom. Numerous brands of courtroom software are available, all with similar features. TrialPro is a good example to consider.

TrialPro Presentation System

TrialPro software is used for the organization, viewing, annotating, and interactive presentation of documents, graphics, and video trial exhibits. It is used by trial attorneys, law firms, and service bureaus. The software is intuitive and designed for ease of data entry during trials and inside the courtroom. It is relatively inexpensive at approximately $600 and a downloadable appraisal package is available online at www.ideaview.com. TrialPro contains a full range of organizational capabilities, including the following:

- Fast, random access to exhibits
- Synchronized deposition transcripts with video
- Use of bar codes for labeling and retrieving documents and exhibits
- Customizable style preferences
- Compatibility with most standard exhibit formats, including
    - PowerPoint
    - Apple QuickTime video
    - Macromedia Director presentations
    - Microsoft Word documents
    - Adobe Acrobat PDF files

Any standard, nonproprietary digital image file format may be displayed using the TrialPro system. Demonstrative exhibits compatible with TrialPro include these:

- Scanned documents
- Graphics
- Charts
- Photographs
- Depositions
- MPEG digital video
- Computer animations

TrialPro for Windows is compatible with any notebook or desktop computer. No special hardware is required. The package supports multiple monitors, or output may be sent to an LCD projector.

SUMMARY

Forensic photographers produce forensic images that are used in court. The images are intended to illustrate ideas, concepts, evidence, and anything else that is too impractical or impossible to bring physically into the courtroom. Due to the significance of the images, it is of utmost importance that they be as accurate as possible within the limitations of their media. To make accurate images, a forensic photographer must comprehend a thorough understanding of the techniques, practices, and protocols of this high-tech vocation.

Modern courtrooms are places where juries of peers are aware of forensics. The impact of forensic television programs, such as *CSI*, have further prepared judges and jurors to understand the concept of forensic evidence and to demand its proper preparation and demonstration. "People who end up on a jury know, or think they know, a great deal about forensic science and the kind of science necessary to solve crimes."[4] In many cases, they think they know more than they actually do. It is critical to be able to educate them to recognize the truth.

CASE STUDY

BARGE CRANE HOOK FAILURE

Immense cast iron hooks are attached to braided cable on specially designed barge cranes and used to lift offshore oil rigs (see Figs. 17–14 and 17–15). In this particular case, the subject hook experienced a failure and lost a tine during a lift. The single tine fell and penetrated multiple levels of the rig, causing extensive physical damages. The manufacturer of the hook was sued for the damages, and the hook was brought to Packer Engineering for failure analysis (see Figs. 17–16 and 17–17).

The failed tine was inspected and sectioned. The smallest pieces were made into micro-specimens, designed for viewing under a metallurgical microscope. The root cause of the failure was a flaw introduced into the metal when the hook was cast at the foundry.

The magnitude of the crane is unimaginable to people who have never seen one in person,

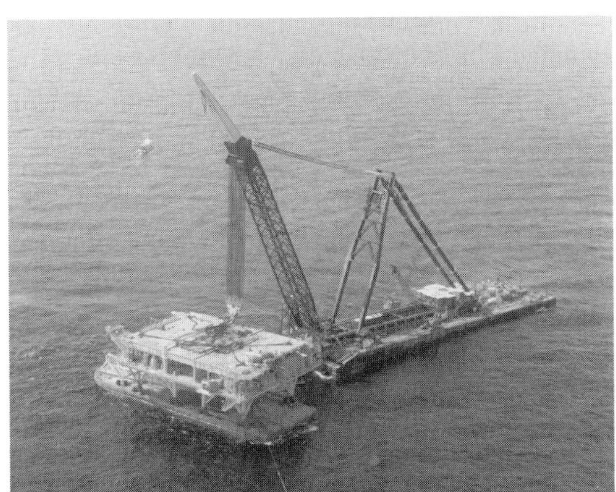

FIGURE 17–14 Barge crane hook lifting offshore rig. *Source:* Sandy Weiss/Packer Engineering.

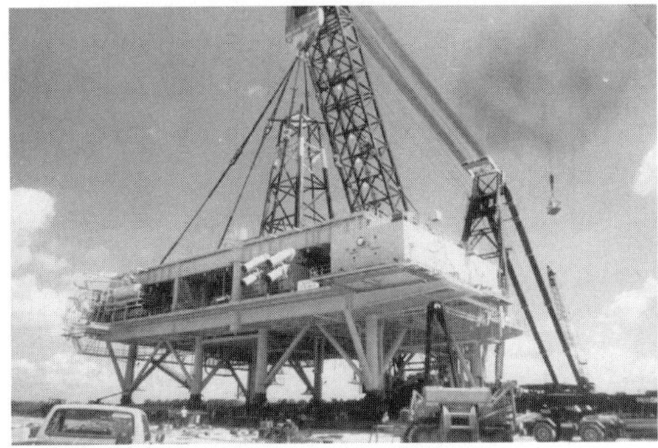

FIGURE 17–15 Barge crane hook lifting offshore rig. The subject hook is at the end of the cable. *Source:* Sandy Weiss/Packer Engineering.

and even the hook was far too large to bring into the courtroom. Large display images were produced for illustrative purposes, but they were insufficient to explain the magnitude of the equipment in court. For this reason, a fully functioning physical model (see Fig. 17–18) of the crane and hook was constructed for use in the courtroom. The model was constructed primarily from data derived from photographs taken of the subject equipment.

The back legs (the tube sections in Fig. 17–18) were collapsible, enabling elevation of the crane. Brass tubing was used for that construction. It was dyed with gun bluing because paint would have been too thick and would have rubbed off as the tubes extended and retracted.

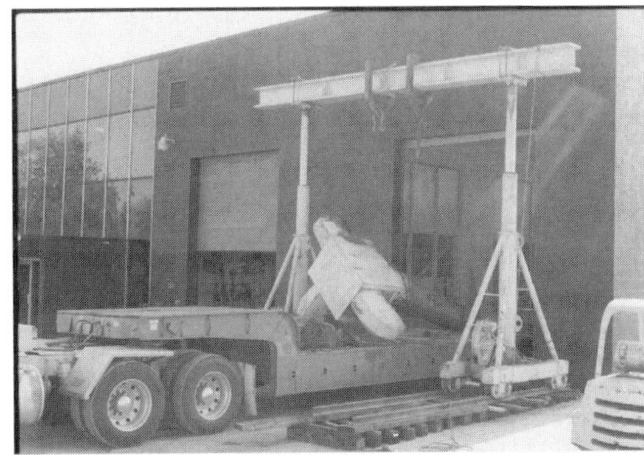

FIGURE 17–16 The hook being delivered to Packer Engineering. *Source:* Sandy Weiss/Packer Engineering.

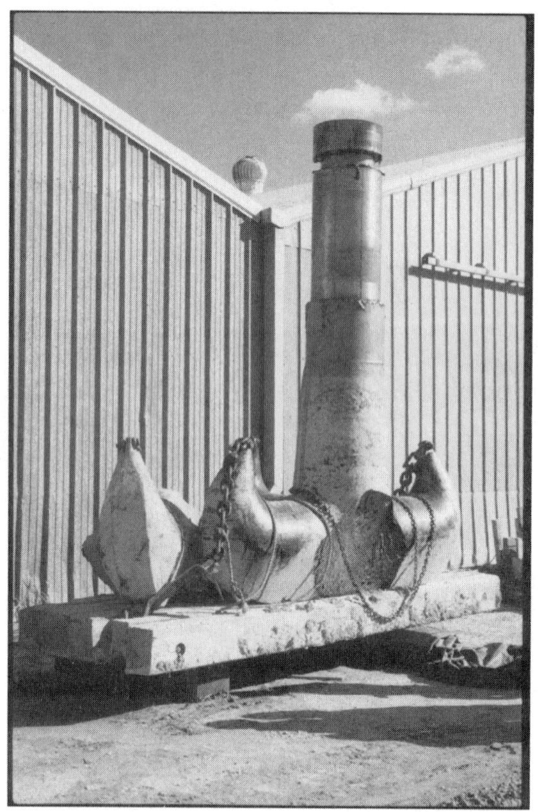

FIGURE 17–17 Barge crane hook in position for inspection. *Source:* Sandy Weiss/Packer Engineering.

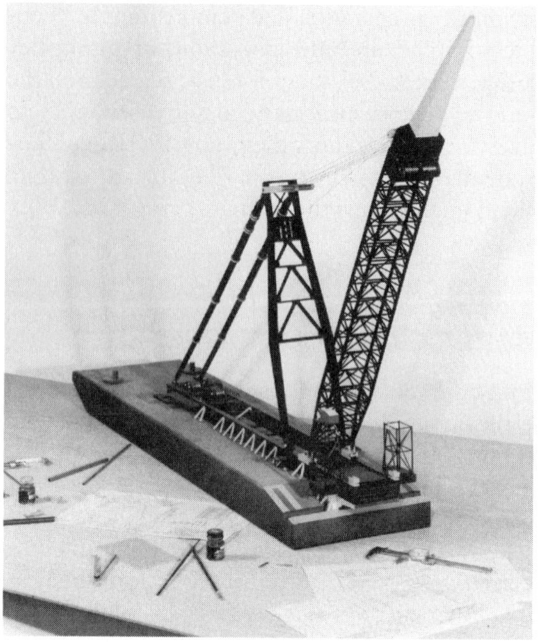

FIGURE 17–18 Physical model of the barge crane. *Source:* Sandy Weiss/Packer Engineering.

The main crane gantry was constructed from soldered brass square and angle stock. The soldering was difficult. Small fixtures were constructed to hold the pieces in place while they were soldered. After the construction was completed, the model was sandblasted and painted.

The real barge crane was sufficiently large for regular, mobile-type construction cranes to drive on the deck, on either side of the main crane. It also was designed for the main gantry to slide back on rails to lower it enough to maneuver under bridges. To accomplish this on the model, plastic rails and slides were attached to the base of the gantry. When the tubes collapsed into themselves, the gantry would slide back between the tubes and the crane would be in its transport position. The model functioned like the real crane.

Originally, the model was intended to be rigged in the same fashion as the real crane so the hook could be raised and lowered and the gantry could also be raised and lowered, using two hand cranks at the back of the model. Sadly, the original project for which the model was commissioned was settled before trial. The rigging was never completed. The model now resides in the offices of the attorney from the project.

KEY TERMS

trial, (p. 496)
evidence, (p. 496)
jury trial, (p. 496)
bench trial, (p. 496)
criminal trial, (p. 496)
civil trial, (p. 496)
testimony, (p. 496)
admissible, (p. 496)
forensic photography, (p. 496)
exhibit, (p. 497)

peer review, (p. 497)
discovery, (p. 497)
deposition, (p. 497)
witness, (p. 497)
Daubert v. Merrell Dow Pharmaceuticals, (p. 498)
deponent, (p. 499)
digital courtroom, (p. 499)
physical model, (p. 499)
computer animation, (p. 500)
computer model, (p. 500)
physical simulation, (p. 501)
interactive simulation, (p. 501)
computer modeling and simulation, (p. 501)
authentication, (p. 501)
PowerPoint, (p. 502)
courtroom software, (p. 504)

EXERCISES

1. Using PowerPoint, create a logical and systematic presentation from a series of images used to document a mock crime or accident scene. Include all major information on the slides, following the examples in this chapter.
2. Attend a legal proceeding at a local courthouse, and write a critique regarding the litigant's use of forensic imaging.
3. Download a sample of courtroom presentation software and plan how you would use it to organize, access, and display all of the documents and images in a trial.
4. Hold a mock trial with your class, and produce the appropriate visual evidence for all aspects of the proceedings.

References

FRONTMATTER

1. Eva Weber, *Pioneers of Photography* (Greenwich, CT: Brompton Books, 1995), 6.
2. M. Jay, *Downcast Eyes: The Denigration of Vision in Twentieth-Century French Thought* (Berkeley: University of California Press, 1993), 125–130.

CHAPTER 1

1. http://www.madwed.com/Quotations/Quotations/Transfer__3/_Mirth___Misanthropy___Mischie/body__oaths___obedience___obligati.html.
2. Sir Arthur Conan Doyle, *The Adventure of The Red Headed League*.
3. Sir Arthur Conan Doyle, *The Boscombe Valley Mystery*.
4. Sir Arthur Conan Doyle, *A Case of Identity*..
5. http://members.aol.com/ELECTRPOW1/POWER1.HTM.
6. http://www.nysut.org/newyorkteacher/2000-2001/010314museum-exercise.html.
7. D.E. Hulick Ph.D., *If the Truth Be Known, Analog vs. Digital in Historic Perspective*, Journal of Evidence Photography, (Spring/Summer 1998), 16–20.
8. Hulick, *If the Truth Be Known, Analog vs. Digital in Historic Perspective*, 16–20.
9. Hulick, *If the Truth Be Known, Analog vs. Digital in Historic Perspective*, 16–20.
10. The American Museum of Photography, www.photographymuseum.com, *A Ghostly Gallery*.
11. The American Museum of Photography, www.photographymuseum.com, *A Ghostly Gallery*.
12. Andre A. Moenssens and Fred E. Inbau, *Scientific Evidence in Criminal Cases*, (The Foundation Press, 1986), 601.
13. Evidence Photographers International Council, Inc., *Standards For Evidence Photography Criminal and Civil*, (1998), 1.
14. Luco *v.* United States, 23 Howard 515 (U.S.1859).
15. Albert Sherman Osborn, *Questioned Documents: A study of questioned documents with an outline of methods by which the facts may be discovered and shown*, (Lawyer's Co-operative Publishing Company, Rochester, NY).
16. Cunningham *v.* Fair Haven & Westville R. Co. (1899) 72 Conn. 244 at 250, 43 A. 1047 at 1049.
17. *Digital Imagery in the Courtroom*, Kodak Professional Imaging, www.kodak.com/global/en/pro.
18. *You Won't Believe Your Eyes: Digital Photography as Legal Evidence*, www.seanet.com.
19. John E. Duckworth, *Forensic Photography*, (Charles C. Thomas, 1983), intro.
20. John Hedgecoe, *Complete Guide to Black & White Photography*, (Sterling Publishing, 1996), 6.
21. *The Focal Encyclopedia of Photography*, Vision, (1957), 1259.
22. Edward S. Bomback, *Manual of Color Photography*, (A.S. Barnes and Co., 1966), 73.
23. *The Focal Encyclopedia of Photography*, Psychology of Vision, (1957), 934.
24. Benjamin J. Cantor, *Photographic Evidence: Establishing Just Verdicts In the Courtroom*, www.expert-pages.com/news/photographic_evidence.htm.
25. Moenssens and Inbau, *Scientific Evidence in Criminal Cases*, 605.
26. VeriPic[tm], www.VeriPic.com, Kwan Software and Engineering, Inc., John Kwan, founder.
27. Richard Kammen and Herbert Blitzer, *The Indiana Lawyer: Insure Admissibility of Digital Images*, Kodak Professional Imaging, 11/95, Vol. 6, No. 15, Computer Technology.
28. Bomback, *Manual of Color Photography*, 73.
29. http://www.ohnonews.com/simpson.html.
30. Bruce Calder, *The Daily Info: O.J. Simpson Watch-Photo Forgery?*, www.calder.net , 12/20/96.
31. CNN, U.S. News Story Page, *Photo Expert Resumes Testimony in Simpson Trial*, 12/20/96, www.cnn.com/US/9612/20/0j.update.
32. Paul Martin Lester, Battle of the Experts, http://commfaculty.fullerton.edu/lester/writings/experts.html.
33. William J. Mitchell, *The Reconfigured Eye: Visual Truth in the Post-Photographic Era*, (1992).

34. Stewart Brand, et al, *Digital Retouching: the End of Photography as Evidence of Anything*, Whole Earth Review, (July 1985), 42.
35. Lee Parker, *Digital Images Still Don't Hold Up in Court*, Claims Magazine, (2/2000), 5.
36. VeriPic[tm].
37. W. V. Quine, *"Truth," in Quiddities*, (The Belknap Press of Harvard University Press, 1987), 212–216.
38. Kodak Professional Imaging, *Forensic Imaging Case Studies*, www.kodak.com/global/en/professional/hub/law/case/forensic.shtml.
39. http://www.epic-photo.org/USA/illinois.htm.
40. http://www.epic-photo.org/epic-certification.htm.
41. http://www.legalvideo.com/abaarticle.html ABA Journal Report, Getting the Money Shot, (4/2005).
42. http://www.legalvideo.com/abaarticle.html ABA Journal Report, Getting the Money Shot, (4/2005).
43 Evidence Photographers International Council, Inc., (Honesdale, PA, 2002).

CHAPTER 2

1. eDiscovery & Digital Evidence, Jay E. Grenig and William C. Gleisner, (Thomson/West Publishing, 2005).
2. Enos, Digital Data Changing Legal Landscape, E-Commerce Times, 5/16/2000, at www.ecommercetimes.com/per/story/3339.html.
3. Lange; *Am I Committing Malpractice by not considering Electronic Data in My Cases?*, Law Practice Today, (July 2004).
4. http://en.wikipedia.org/wiki/Category:Scientific_method.
5. (New York: Farrar Straus & Giroux, 1977).
6. The Focal Encyclopedia of Photography, Psychology of Vision, (1957), 934.
7. Changing Photography, Photographic Vision and the Digital Revolution, School of Photography and Film, Goteborg University, G6teborg, Sweden, page 9, http://www.ckk/pdf/ChaPhotogr.pdf.
8. Moenssens and Inbau, *Scientific Evidence in Criminal Cases*, 601.
9. Moenssens and Inbau, *Scientific Evidence in Criminal Cases*, 601.
10. Paulk *v.* Thomas, No. 42656, Court of Appeals of Georgia, 115 Ga. App. 436; 154 S.E. 2d 872; 1967 Ga. App. Lexis 1132, (Mar 6–17, 1967).
11. Evidence Photographers International Council, for example, in Standards for Evidence Photography, (2004).
12. http://wordnet.princeton.edu/perl/webwn?s=point%20of%20view.
13. Evidence Photographers International Council, for example, in Standards for Evidence Photography, (2004), 1.
14. *The Focal Encyclopedia of Photography*, Psychology of Vision, (1957), 935.
15. Minor White, the "Spring-Tight Line" in Theory of Sequential Photography, Analecta Husserliana, Volume 87, *Human Creation Between Reality and Illusion*, (Springer Netherlands, 2005), 199–229.
16. http://www.mos.org/sln/Leonardo/ExploringLinearPerspective.html.
17. http://wordnet.princeton.edu/perl/webwn?s=point%20of%20view.
18. Moenssens and Inbau, *Scientific Evidence in Criminal Cases*, 618.
19. Moenssens and Inbau, *Scientific Evidence in Criminal Cases*, 618.
20. Moenssens and Inbau, *Scientific Evidence in Criminal Cases*, 618–619.
21. *The Focal Encyclopedia of Photography*, Psychology of Vision, (1957), 935.
22. Andre A. Moenssens and Fred E. Inbau, *Scientific Evidence in Criminal Cases*, (The Foundation Press, 1986).
23. Evidence Photographers International Council, Inc., *Standards for Evidence Photography Criminal and Civil*, (1998), 1.
24. Luco *v.* United States, 23 Howard 515 (U.S. 1859).
25. John Hedgecoe, *Complete Guide to Black & White Photography*, (Sterling Publishing, 1996), 6.
26. Richard T. Kriebel, Stereoscopic Photography section in *The Encyclopedia of Photography*, (Greystone Press, 1964), 3527.
27. http://www.veripic.com.
28. http://www.oregonruleco.com.
29. http://cinemasupplies.stores.yahoo.net/maccol.html.
30. Wiedner & Mcauliffe, Ltd., Attorneys at Law, One North Franklin, Suite 1900 Chicago, IL.
31. http://www.cdpr.ca.gov/docs/county/training/hrngofcr/section2-8.pdf.
32. http://www.fbi.gov/hq/lab/handbook/forensics.pdf.
33. Arnold, N.J. Practice, Criminal Procedure, volume 32, Sec. 1034.
34. http://www.fact-index.com/c/ch/chain_of_custody.html.
35. N.J. Practice, Criminal Procedure by Honorable Leonard, J.S.C. (West Publishing), Volume 32, Chapter 21, Section 1034.
36. Encyclopedia Britannica.

CHAPTER 3

1. *The History of Printmaking* (New York: Scholastic, 1995), 2.
2. Philip B. Meggs, *A History of Graphic Design*, 2nd ed. (New York: Van Nostrand Reinhold, 1992), xiii.
3. Harry Robin, *The Scientific Image: From Cave to Computer* (New York: Abrams, 1992), 9.
4. Meggs, *History of Graphic Design*, 4.
5. Richard H. Wilkinson, *Reading Egyptian Art: A Hieroglyphic Guide to Ancient Egyptian Painting and Sculpture* (New York: Thames and Hudson, 1992), 9.
6. Robin, *Scientific Image*, 9.
7. Robin, *Scientific Image*, 9.
8. Peter Pollack, *The Picture History of Photography from the Earliest Beginnings to the Present Day* (New York: Abrams, 1969), 13.
9. Pollack, *Picture History of Photography*, 14.
10. Pollack, *Picture History of Photography*, 14.
11. Pollack, *Picture History of Photography*, 14.
12. Robin, *Scientific Image*, 9.
13. Robin, *Scientific Image*, 9.
14. Jamie Fenske, Packer Engineering, Inc., Naperville, IL, personal communication.
15. Edward R. Tufte, *Visual Explanations, Images and Quantities, Evidence and Narrative* (Cheshire, CT: Graphic Press, 1997), 50.
16. Robin, *Scientific Image*, 99.
17. Robin, *Scientific Image*, 99.
18. Meggs, *History of Graphic Design*, 4.
19. Robin, *Scientific Image*, 9.
20. Edward R. Tufte, *Envisioning Information* (Cheshire, Connecticut: Graphic Press, 1990), 12.
21. Robin, *Scientific Image*, 9.
22. This section is based on the writings of Steven D. Schafersman, "An Introduction to Science: Scientific Thinking and the Scientific Method," 1994, www.freeinquiry.com/intro-to-sci.html.
23. James E. Starrs, "The C.S.I. Effect," *Scientific Sleuthing Review* (28): 32–34.
24. Starrs, "The C.S.I. Effect," 32–34.
25. Starrs, "The C.S.I. Effect," 32–34.
26. Starrs, "The C.S.I. Effect," 32–34.
27. Starrs, "The C.S.I. Effect," 32–34.
28. John I. Thornton, "The General Assumptions and Rationale of Forensic Identification," in *Modern Scientific Evidence: The Law and Science of Expert Testimony*, eds. David L. Faigman, David H. Kaye, Michael J. Saks, and Joseph Sanders (St. Paul, MN: West Publishing Co., 1997).
29. Paul L. Kirk, *Crime Investigation* (New York: Interscience Publishers, 1953), 4.
30. Robin, *The Scientific Image* 9.
31. H. G. Wells, *The Outline of History*, vol. 3 (New York: Collier, 1922), 860.
32. Robin, *Scientific Image*, 99.
33. Schafersman, "An Introduction to Science."
34. Thomas Kuhn, *The Structure of Scientific Revolutions* (Chicago: University of Chicago Press, 1962), 168.
35. Ronald J. Parrington, "Fractography of Metals and Plastics," *Practical Failure Analysis*, 2(5): 17–19, 44–46, www.asminternational.org/pdf/Fract_PFA.pdf.
36. Paul Duggan, "Bonfire Stack Collapse Kills Nine Texas A&M students," *Washington Post*, November 19, 1999.
37. Duggan, "Bonfire Stack Collapse."
38. Jackie Craven, "Texas Tragedy: Faulty Design?" architecture.about.com/library/weekly/aa111899.htm.
39. Stephen Hawkins, "Texas A&M Tragedy," *Portsmouth Herald*, November 19, 1999, www.seacoastonline.com/1999news/11_19_w1.htm.

CHAPTER 4

1. Paul Wolf, *Elements of Photogrammetry* (New York: McGraw-Hill, 1974), 1.
2. J. Stannard Baker and Lynn B. Fricke, *The Traffic Accident Investigation Manual: At-Scene Investigation and Follow-Up*, 9th ed. (Evanston, IL: Northwestern University Center for Public Safety, 1986), 30–33.

CHAPTER 5

1. David D. Busch, *Nikon D70 Field Guide.* (Hoboken, NJ: Wiley, 2005), 1.
2. Robert Deutsch, "Care and Feeding of Compact Flash Cards," *USA Today*.
3. Daniel Malacara and Zacarias Malacara, *Handbook of Lens Design* (New York: Marcel Dekker, 1994), chap. 12, sec. 4.
4. R. Kingslake, "The Development of the Zoom Lens," *Journal of the SMPTE* 69: 534.
5. Malacara and Malacara, *Handbook of Lens Design*, chap. 12, sec. 4.
6. 3A Committee for the Integrity in Transportation of Imaging Products (ITIP), "Test Results for E-beam Systems Used for Sanitization of the US Mail," www.i3a.org/pdf/i3a_titan_testing_report.pdf.
7. I3A Committee, "Test Results for E-Beam Systems."
8. Information furnished by Robert Wyman, Wyman Enterprises, Inc., 3626 Coral Springs Drive, Coral Springs FL 33065, www.forensicphoto.com.

CHAPTER 6

1. http://www.dpreview.com/news/0011/00111608dynamicrange.asp.

CHAPTER 7

1. Ansel Adams, *The Camera* (Boston: Little, Brown, 1980), 116.
2. Ansel Adams, *The Negative, Exposure and Development* (New York: New York Graphic Society, 1948), 98.

CHAPTER 8

1. Edward S. Bomback, *Manual of Color Photography* (Cranbury, NJ: A. S. Barnes and Company, 1966), 69.
2. Charles E. O'Hara, *Fundamentals of Criminal Investigation*, 5th ed. (Springfield, IL: Charles C Thomas, 1981), 58.
3. Keith Henney and Beverly Dudley, *Handbook of Photography*, 3rd ed. (New York: McGraw Hill, 1939), 572.
4. Bomback, *Manual of Color Photography*, 70.
5. Henney and Dudley, *Handbook of Photography*, 572.
6. Willard D. Morgan and Henry M. Lester, *The Leica Manual* (New York: Morgan and Lester, 1936), 249.
7. Bob Zeller, *The Civil War in Depth* (San Francisco: Chronicle Books, 1997), introduction.
8. Otha C. Spencer, "A Gallery of Stereo Life in the 1890's," *Shutterbug Magazine*, February 1997: 223.
9. Clement Aguila and Michel Rouah, *Exakta Cameras 1933–1978* (Faringdon, UK: Hove Photo Books, 1989), 8.
10. Alfred A Blaker, *Field Photography: Beginning and Advanced Techniques* (San Francisco: W.H. Freeman, 1976), 401.
11. Julian, Brown, ed., *The Chronicle of the Movies* (Avenel, NJ: Crescent Books, 1991), 175.
12. Brown, *The Chronicle of the Movies*, 179.
13. Marilyn B. Rosanes-Berrett, *Do You Really Need Eyeglasses?* (New York: Instant Improvement, 1991), 82–83.
14. John Hedgecoe, *The Art of Color Photography* (New York: Simon & Schuster, 1977), introduction.
15. Bomback, *Manual of Color Photography*, 67.
16. "The Iconoscope Camera Tube," IEEE Virtual Museum, www.ieee-virtual-museum.org/collection/tech.php?id=2345791&lid=1.
17. Derek Winnert, *The Ultimate Encyclopedia of the Movies* (London: Carlton Books, 1995), 43.
18. Susan Pinsky and David Starkman, *The Reel 3-D Catalog*, www.reel3d.com.
19. Suzanne Kantra Kirschner and Frank Vizard, "Everything 3-D," *Popular Science*, January 1998: 34.
20. Marten Ballantyne and Mathews Ballantyne, *The Photo*, vol. I (Tarrytown, NY: Marshall Cavendish, 1983), part 13, 351.
21. Dan McLachlan, Jr., "Extreme Focal Depth in Microscopy," *Applied Optics*, vol. 3: 1009–1013.
22. Nile Root, "Deep-Field Photomacrography," *Biomedical Imaging*, vol. 5: 16–18.
23. Nile Root, "Light Scanning Photomacrography: A Brief History and Its Current Status," *Journal of Biological Photography*, vol. 53: 4.
24. Kenneth Poli, "Ready When You Are E.T.," *Popular Photography*, November 1989: 98–99, 184.
25. George S. Pearl, "Scanning Evidence Photography," *EPIC Journal*, Spring/Summer 1998: 40.
26. Aaron Sussman, *The Amateur Photographer's Handbook*, 6th ed. (New York: Thomas Y. Crowell, 1962), 11.
27. John Hedgecoe, *The Photographer's Handbook* (New York: Knopf, 1979), 301.
28. Pinsky and Starkman, *The Reel 3-D Catalog*, 5.
29. Barry A. J. Fisher, *Techniques of Crime Scene Investigation* (Amsterdam, The Netherlands: Elsevier, 1992), 81–84.

CHAPTER 9

1. Christopher J. Guffey, "Laser Technology: Revolutionizing CSI Work," *Forensic Magazine*, December/January 2007:16.

CHAPTER 11

1. James L. Harris, Sr., and James L. Harris, II, "Forensic Photography and Nighttime Visibility Issues," *Journal of Forensic Sciences*, 37(4): 1084–1095.
2. E. S. Bomback, *Manual of Colour Photography* (New York: A.S. Barnes & Co., 1966), 146.
3. John Duckworth, *Forensic Photography* (Springfield, IL: Charles C Thomas, 1983), 71–73.
4. J. Stannard Baker and Lynn B. Fricke, *The Traffic Accident Investigation Manual*, 9th ed. (Evanston, IL: Northwestern University Traffic Institute, 1986), 36-23 through 36-25.
5. Baker and Fricke, *Traffic Accident Investigation Manual*, 36–25.
6. William G. Hyzer, "An Extinction-Type Photometering Technique for Low-Light Luminance Measurements in Accident Investigations," *Journal of Forensic Sciences*, 33(2): 530–33.

7. Robert D. Holohan, *Nighttime Photography: Show It Like It Is*, SAE paper # 890730, (Warrendale, PA, 1989).
8. Holohan, *Nighttime Photography, Show It Like It Is*, SAE paper # 890730, (Warrendale, PA, 1996).
9. Ernest Klein and Gregory Stephens, *Visibility Study: Methodologies and Reconstruction*, SAE Technical Paper Series #921575 (Warrendale, PA, 1992).
10. Harris and Harris, "Forensic Photography and Nighttime Visibility Issues," 1084–1095.
11. Harris and Harris, "Forensic Photography and Nighttime Visibility Issues." 1084–1095.
12. Harris and Harris, "Forensic Photography and Nighttime Visibility Issues," 1084–1095.
13. Harris and Harris, "Forensic Photography and Nighttime Visibility Issues," 1084–1095.
14. Harris and Harris, "Forensic Photography and Nighttime Visibility Issues," 1084–1095.
15. Harris and Harris, "Forensic Photography and Nighttime Visibility Issues," 1084–1095.
16. W. G. Hyzer, "The Eye, Brain, and Camera in Nighttime Accident Reconstruction," *Photo Electronic Imaging*, February 1993: 8–9.
17. Hyzer, "The Eye, Brain, and Camera," 8–9.
18. Hyzer, "The Eye, Brain, and Camera," 8–9.
19. Hyzer, "The Eye, Brain, and Camera," 8–9.
20. T. J. Ayres, "Psychophysical Validation of Photographic Representation," vol. 6, paper presented at a meeting of American Society of Mechanical Engineers: Safety Engineering and Risk Analysis, (New York, NY, 1996).
21. Ayres, "Psychophysical Validation of Photographic Representation."
22. Ayres, "Psychophysical Validation of Photographic Representation."
23. Baker and Fricke, *Traffic Accident Investigation Manual*, 36–25.
24. Baker and Fricke, *Traffic Accident Investigation Manual*, 36–25.
25. Paul L. Olson, *Forensic Aspects of Driver Perception and Response* (Tucson, AZ: Lawyers & Judges Publishing, 1996), 145–153.
26. Olson, *Forensic Aspects of Driver Perception and Response*, 145–153.
27. Olson, *Forensic Aspects of Driver Perception and Response*, 145–153.
28. Olson, *Forensic Aspects of Driver Perception and Response*, 145–153.
29. Olson, *Forensic Aspects of Driver Perception and Response*, 145–153.
30. J. B. Hyzer, "Photographically Maximizing the Information Recorded in Forensic Images," vol. 8 (paper presented at the Proceedings of the American Academy of Forensic Sciences, Atlanta, 2002).
31. Paul L. Olson, and Eugene Farber, Forensic Aspects of Driver Perception and Response, 2nd ed. (Tucson, AZ: Lawyers & Judges Publishing, 2003), 298.
32. Boyd D. Allin., Kurt W. Isling, and David J. King, "Digital Camera Calibration for Luminance Estimation in Nighttime Visibility Studies," SAE Paper #2007-01-0718 (paper presented at the 2007 World Congress, Detroit, Michigan, 1/7/2007).
33. Harris and Harris, "Forensic Photography and Nighttime Visibility Issue," 1084–1095.
34. 2007 Chicago Building Code and Related Provisions, vol. 1, 10 (13-160-670), Intensity.

CHAPTER 12

1. Andre A. Moenssens, Fred E. Inbau, and James E Starrs, *Scientific Evidence in Criminal Cases*, 3rd ed. (Mineola, NY: The Foundation Press, 1986), 616.
2. Moenssens, et al., *Scientific Evidence in Criminal Cases*, 616.
3. For up-to-the-minute information, consult covert video expert Jimmie Mesis, or Rosemarie Mesis, Publisher of *Professional Investigator Magazine*, at www.PIMagazine.com.
4. Moenssens, et al., *Scientific Evidence*, chap. 11, sec. 13.
5. *Lanford v. People*, 159 Colo. 36, 409 p. 2d 829 (1966); *Carpenter v. State*, 169 Tex. Cr. R. 283, 333 S.W. 2d 391 (1960).
6. All documentation of precedents in this chapter are taken from Moenssens, Inbau, and Starrs, *Scientific Evidence in Criminal Cases*, chap. 11, sec. 13.
7. *Johnson v. United States*, 362 F. 2d 43 (8th Cir. 1966); *People v. Porter*, 105 Cal. App. 2d 324, 233 P 2d 102 (1951).
8. *Kortz v. Guardian Life Ins. Co.*, 144 F 2d 676 (10th Cir. 1944) cert. denied 323 U.S. 728 (1944); *People v. Bowley*, 59 Cal. 2d 855, 31 Cal. Rptr. 471, 382 P. 2d 591 (1963); *Gulf Life Ins. Co. v. Stossel*, 131 Fla 127, 179 So. 163 (1938).
9. *Heiman v. Market St. Railway Co.*, 21 Cal. App 2d 311, 69 P 2d 178 (1937).
10. *Jones v. State*, 151 Tex. Cr. R. 519, 209 S.W. 2d 613 (1948); *State v. Tillinghast*, supra n. 76; *People v. Dabb*, 32 Col. 2d 491, 197 P. 2d 1 (1948); *Sutton v. State*, 237 Ind.305, 145 N.E. 2d 425 (1957); *State v. Perkins*, 355 Mo. 851, 198 S.W. 2d 704 (1946);

Mikus v. United States, 433 F. 2d 719 (2d Cir. 1970); *People v. Dabb*, supra n. 99; *People v. Kendrick*, 56 Cal. 2d 71, 14 Cal. Rptr. 13, 363 P. 2d 13 (1961); *People v. Lindsey*, 56 Cal. 2d 324, 14 Cal. Rptr. 678, 363 P. 2d 910 (1961), cert. denied 368 U.S. 916 (1961); *Lanford v. People*, Colo supra n. 93.

11. *Lanford v. People*, Colo supra n. 93.
12. *People v. Childs*, 67 Ill. App. 3d 473 (1979); *People v. Banks*, 70 Ill, App. 3d 1045 (Ill. 1979); *People v. Techer*, 26 Cr. L. 2251 (NY Sup. Ct., App. Div. 2/21/80).
13. Use of Videotape to Take Deposition for Presentation at Civil Trial in State Court, 66 A.L.R. 3d 637 (1975).
14. U.S. Department of Labor, Occupational Safety & Health Administration (2001). Regulations (Standards - 29 CFR), "Powered Industrial Trucks," 1910.178, Part Number 1910; Occupational Safety and Health Standards, Subpart N, Subpart Title, "Materials Handling and Storage"; Standard Number 1910.178, "Powered Industrial Trucks," Appendix A, 1910.178(a).
15. 11/30/2000, Appendix B, www.osha.gov/pls/oshaweb/owadisp.show_document?p_id=9828&p_table=STANDARDS.
16. Section 5(a)(1) of the OSH Act, www.osha.gov/pls/oshaweb/owadisp.show_document?p_id=3359&p_table=OSHACT.
17. Section 5(a)(1) of the OSH Act, www.osha.gov/pls/oshaweb/owadisp.show_document?p_id=3359&p_table=OSHACT.

CHAPTER 13

1. National Fire Protection Association, *NFPA 921: Guide for Fire and Explosion Investigations* (Quincy, MA: NFPA, 2004).
2. Kristi Mayo, "Editor's Notes," *Evidence Technology Magazine*, November–December 2004: 12–13, 29.
3. *ICD-10: International Statistical Classification of Diseases and Related Health Problems*, 2nd ed. (Geneva, Switzerland: World Health Organization, 2004).
4. Interpol, "Disaster Victim Identification Guide," www.interpol.int/Public/DisasterVictim/guide/default.asp.
5. American Board of Forensic Odontology, "Body Identification Guidelines," *Journal of the American Dental Association, 125*(9): 1244—1246 (also available at www.abfo.org).
6. Bernard Brinkmann, "Harmonization of Medico-Legal Autopsy Rules," *International Journal of Legal Medicine, 113*(1): 1.

CHAPTER 14

1. The full-text version of the National Response Framework may be downloaded for free at http://www.fema.gov/pdf/emergency/nrf/nrf-core.pdf.
2. The missions of the Office of the Armed Forces Medical Examiner (OAFME) include consultation, education, and research, consistent with the missions of the Armed Forces Institute of Pathology (AFIP). OAFME is a component of the AFIP, located at the AFIP Annex, Rockville, Maryland. Regional and Associate Medical Examiners, appointed by the Armed Forces Medical Examiner with concurrence of the respective service Surgeon General, are located at designated military medical treatment facilities within the United States and overseas. The OAFME is staffed 24 hours a day and may be reached at (301) 319-0000; (800) 944-7912; DSN 285-0000; fax (301) 319-0635. The address is AFIP/OAFME, AFIP Annex, 1413 Research Blvd, Bldg 102, Rockville, MD 20850, www.afip.org/Departments/oafme.
3. All images for this study were exposed and furnished by: Mr. Robert Wyman, Wyman Enterprises, Inc., Coral Springs, Florida and Ms. Kathryn McMillan, Evidence Video Investigations, Daytona Beach, Florida. The 3-D CAD model and the conclusions were also furnished by Mr. Wyman.
4. National Transportation Safety Board, Office of Aviation Safety, "Medical/Forensic Group Chairman's Factual Report of Investigation, October 17, 1997," http://www.cnn.com/US/9707/twa.800/reports/forensic.html.

CHAPTER 15

1. R. F. Becker, *Underwater Forensic Investigation* (Upper Saddle River, Pearson Prentice Hall, 2006), 6.
2. A. Dutelle, "Underwater Crime Scene Response," *Evidence Technology Magazine*, 5(4): 24.
3. A. Dutelle, "Underwater Crime Scene Processing," *Law and Order Magazine* March 2007: 68.
4. Professional Association of Diving Instructors (PADI), *Encyclopedia of Recreational Diving*, 3rd ed. (Rancho Santa Margarita, CA: PADI, 2005), 4–18.
5. PADI, *Adventures in Diving Manual*, 3rd ed. (Rancho Santa Margarita, CA: PADI, 2002), 216.
6. M. Edge, *The Underwater Photographer: Digital and Traditional Techniques*, 3rd ed. (Oxford, UK: Focal Press, Jordan Hill, 2006), 212.
7. PADI, *Encyclopedia of Recreational Diving*, 3–87.
8. PADI, *Encyclopedia of Recreational Diving*, 3–88.
9. PADI, *Encyclopedia of Recreational Diving*, 3–89.

10. PADI, *Encyclopedia of Recreational Diving*, 3–89.
11. M. Webster, *The Art & Technique of Underwater Photography* (Surrey, UK: Fountain Press, Ltd., 1998), 8–9.
12. E. M. Robinson, *Crime Scene Photography* (Burlington, MA: Elsevier, 2007), 555.
13. PADI, *Encyclopedia of Recreational Diving*, 4–13.
14. PADI, *Adventures in Diving Manual*, 309.
15. Robinson, *Crime Scene Photography*, 50.
16. Edward M. Robinson, *Crime Scene Photography*, 556.
17. Dutelle, "Underwater Crime Scene Processing," *Law and Order Magazine*, March 2007: 70.
18. D. R. Redsicker, *The Practical Methodology of Forensic Photography*, 2nd ed., (Boca Raton, FL: CRC Press, 2001), 156.
19. PADI, *Encyclopedia of Recreational Diving*, 4–13.
20. Redsicker, *The Practical Methodology of Forensic Photography*, 157.
21. Redsicker, *The Practical Methodology of Forensic Photography*, 157.
22. PADI, *Encyclopedia of Recreational Diving*, 4–14.
23. Webster, *The Art & Technique of Underwater Photography*, 18–19.
24. Robinson, *Crime Scene Photography*, 561.
25. Edge, *The Underwater Photographer*, 215.
26. Redsicker, *The Practical Methodology of Forensic Photography*, 156.
27. Robinson, *Crime Scene Photography*, 564.
28. PADI, *Encyclopedia of Recreational Diving*, 388.
29. Becker, *Underwater Forensic Investigation*, 97.
30. Becker, *Underwater Forensic Investigation*, 53.

CHAPTER 16

1. Technical Working Group on Crime Scene Investigation, *Crime Scene Investigation: A Guide for Law Enforcement* (Washington DC: U.S. Department of Justice, 2000), 1.
2. *State v. Miller*, 43 Oregon 325.
3. *People v. Muller*, 32 Hun 209; *Barnes v. Ingalls*, 39 Ala.
4. Ill. App. 398; 31 Wis. 512; 32 N.Y. Supp. 702.
5. *United States v. Clayton*, 643 F.2d 1071, 1074 (C.A. 5, 1981).
6. *Green v. Terwilliger*, 56 Fed. Rep. 384; *Locke v. Sioux City, etc., R. Co.*, 46 Iowa, 109; *Goldsboro v. Central R. Co.*, 60 N.J. Law, 49; *Crane v. Horton*, 5 Wash. 479, *Bruce v. Beall*, 99 Tenn. 303; 81 Cal. 408; 83 N.Y. 464.
7. *Saturn Manufacturing, Inc. vs. Williams Patent Crusher and Pulverizer Company*, 713 F.2d 1347, 1357 (C.A. 8, 1983).
8. *Riksem v. Hollister*, 96 Idaho 15, 523 P. 2d 1361 (1974) and *Southeastern Engineering & Mfg Co v. Lyda*, 100 Ga.App. 208, 110 S.E.2d 550 (1959).
9. *Keyes vs. State*, 122 Ind. 527; *Blair v. Pelham*, 118 Mass. 420; *Cowley vs. People*, 83 N.Y. 464.
10. C. Swanson, N. C. Chamelin, and L. Territo, *Criminal Investigation*, 5th ed. (New York: McGraw-Hill 1992).
11. *FBI Handbook of Forensic Services*, available online at www.fbi.gov/hq/lab/handbook/intro.htm.revised 2003.
12. *Daubert v. Merrell Dow Pharmaceuticals*, 509 U.S. 579 (1993).
13. California Department of Justice, Documentation of Shoe and Tire Impression Evidence, available online at www.cci.ca.gov/Reference/peb/PEB23.doc.
14. J. Cameron, R. Ruddick, and J. Grant, "Ultraviolet Photography in Medicine," *Forensic Photography*, 2(3): 9–12.
15. T. J. David, "Recapturing a Five Month-Old Bite Mark by Means of Reflective Ultraviolet Photography," *Journal of Forensic Science*, *39*(6): 1560–1567.
16. *Franklin v. State*, 69 Ga. 42, 47 Am. Rep. 748; *People v. Fish*, 125 N. Y. 136.
17. *Franklin v. State*, 69 Ga.
18. Federal Bureau of Investigation, "Trace Evidence Recovery Guidelines" (Washington, DC: U.S. Department of Justice), available online at www.fbi.gov/hq/lab/fsc/backissu/oct1999/trace.htm.
19. S. E. Scott, "Bloodstain Pattern Analysis—Five Years Later" (juried paper presented at the Southern Association of Forensic Scientists, September 18, 1987, Atlanta, Georgia).
20. *People v. Hobley*, 159 Ill. 2d 272 (1994).
21. *People v. Hobley*, 182 Ill. 2d 404 (1998).

CHAPTER 17

1. *Daubert v. Merrell Dow Pharmaceuticals*, 509 U.S. 579 (1993).
2. The Federal Rules of Evidence are available online at www.law.cornell.edu/rules/fre.
3. The Federal Rules of Civil Procedure are available online at www.law.cornell.edu/rules/frcp.
4. A. Dutelle, "The CSI Effect and Your Department," *Law and Order Magazine*, 54(5), 113–114.

Glossary

8-bit: A gray-scale scanned file or scanner setting.
16–bit: The way memory is accessed in Microsoft Windows. All 16–bit applications access memory in 16–bit files.
24-bit: Describes a scanned file or preview image that consists of RGB color information: 256 possible tones for each of three color channels.
Aberration: In the refraction of light by a convex lens, the rays passing through different parts of the lens are brought to a focus at slightly different distances (*spherical aberration*); at the same time, the colored rays are separated by the prismatic action of the lens and likewise brought to a focus at different distances (*chromatic aberration*).
Abstract: Dealing with a subject in the abstract without practical purpose or intention; "abstract reasoning"; "abstract science."
Acceptance angle: The maximum cone half angle for which incident light is captured by and will travel through the optical fiber. If the acceptance angle is q, then the acceptance cone is defined by a solid cone of 2q.
Accidental death: Loss of life that results from bodily injury caused by an accident.
Accommodation: Adjustment of the optics of an eye to keep an object in focus on the retina as its distance from the eye varies.
Accuracy: The degree of conformity of an indicated value to an accepted standard value, or ideal value.
Acuity: Clarity of vision. Acuity is measured as a fraction of normal vision; 20/20 vision indicates an eye that sees at 20 feet what a normal eye should see at 20 feet; 20/400 vision indicates an eye that sees at 20 feet what a normal eye sees at 400 feet.
Adaptation: A change in the sensitivity to light of a photoreceptor or the visual system as a whole to match the average light intensity present. The ability of the eye to adjust to various levels of darkness and light.
Admissible: Pertinent and proper to be considered in reaching a decision. Refers to the evidence considered in determining the issues to be decided in any judicial proceeding.
Adobe: A U.S. software company that created Postscript page description language and the Acrobat portable document system.
Aerial drone: An unmanned aerial vehicle (UAV), among the latest generations of pilot-less aircraft; anything from kites through hobby-size, radio-controlled aircraft, and cruise missiles.
Aesthetic: Having to do with beauty in both form and appearance. An esthetic procedure is one in which the principal purpose is to improve the appearance.
Afterimage: The visual impression that remains after the initial stimulus is removed. Staring at a single intense hue may cause the cones, or color receptors, of the eye to become so fatigued that they perceive only the complement of the original hue when it has been removed.
Airy disc: Due to the wave nature of light, light passing through apertures is diffracted, and the diffraction increases with decreasing aperture size.
Algorithm: A set of ordered steps for solving a problem, such as a mathematical formula or the instructions in a program. The terms *algorithm* and *logic* are synonymous. Both refer to a sequence of steps to solve a problem.
Aliasing: In computer graphics, the process by which smooth curves and other lines become jagged because the resolution of the graphics device or file is not high enough to represent a smooth curve. Smoothing and anti-aliasing techniques can reduce the effect of aliasing.
Ambient light: Available light already existing in an indoor or outdoor setting that is not caused by any illumination created by the photographer.
Anaglyph: A stereoscopic picture consisting of two images of the same object, taken from slightly different angles, in two complementary colors. When viewed through colored spectacles, the images merge to produce a stereoscopic sensation.
Analog signal: A signal that encodes audio, video, or data, transmitted over wire or through the air. The signal is commonly represented as an oscillating wave.

Angle of view: The area of a scene that a lens covers or sees. Determined by the focal length of the lens. A wide-angle lens (short focal length) includes more of the scene—a wider angle of view—than a normal (normal focal length) or telephoto (long focal length) lens.
Angular size: A measurement of how large or small something is using rotational measurement (degrees of arc, arc-minutes, and arc-seconds); useful for measuring things that are so far away they appear two-dimensional.
Animation: The technique in which each frame of a film or movie is produced individually, whether generated as a computer graphic, or by photographing a drawn image, or by repeatedly making small changes to a model unit and then photographing the result with a special animation camera.
Antemortem: Occurring before death.
Anthropomorphic: [ann-thro-pa-more-fik]-attributing human-like characteristics to something that is not human.
Aperture: A small, circular opening inside the lens that can change in diameter to control the amount of light reaching the camera's sensor as a picture is taken. The aperture diameter is expressed in f-stops: the lower the number, the larger the aperture. For instance, the aperture opening when set to f/2.8 is larger than at f/8. The aperture and shutter speed together control the total amount of light reaching the sensor. A larger aperture passes more light through to the sensor. Many cameras have an aperture priority mode that allows you to adjust the aperture to your own liking. shutter speed.
Aperture priority: A mode in which a desired lens opening (f-stop) is manually selected and locked in; the camera then chooses an appropriate shutter speed for proper exposure. Used primarily to control DoF (the range of sharpness) in front of or behind a subject or object.
Application: A computer program, such as an image editor or image browser.
Archival: The ability of a material, including some printing papers and compact discs, to last for many years.
Arson: The willful or malicious burning, or attempt to burn, with or without intent to defraud, a dwelling, house, public building, motor vehicle, aircraft, or personal property of another.
Art: In its broadest meaning, the expression of creativity or imagination, or both.
Art form: An artists' practice or in the development of an artistic genre.
Artwork: Photographs or other visual representations.
ASA: A number set by the American Standards Association, which is placed on film stock to allow calculation of the length and f number of an exposure.
Assault: The crime of violence against another person. In some jurisdictions, assault is used to refer to the actual violence, while in other jurisdictions (in the United States, England and Wales), assault refers only to the threat of violence, while the actual violence is battery. Simple assaults do not involve weapons; aggravated assaults do.
Authentication: The process of determining whether someone or something is, in fact, who or what it is declared to be.
Authenticity: undisputed credibility.
Auto-focus: System by which the camera lens automatically focuses the image of a selected part of the picture.
Autopsy: A surgical procedure after death that involves the examination of body tissues, often to determine cause of death.
Axial: the direction perpendicular to the plane of the top of the object; in a direction along the axis.
Axonometric: A drawing technique devised to represent three-dimensional objects on flat paper. Verticals are drawn to scale, but diagonal dimensions are distorted.
Backscatter: Occurs when flash reflects off suspended underwater particles, resulting in bright spots between the lens and the subject matter. Sometimes referred to as *snow.*
Barrier filter: (or emission filter) The filter that goes in front of your eyes (or camera). Its purpose is to block the intense excitation light that is reflected from your subject and to only allow the fluorescence emission to pass.
Beach marks: Macroscopic progression marks on a fatigue fracture or stress-corrosion cracking surface that indicate successive positions of the advancing crack front. The classic appearance is of irregular elliptical or semielliptical rings, radiating outward from one or more origins. Beach marks (also known as clamshell marks or arrest marks) are typically found on service fractures where the part is loaded randomly, intermittently, or with periodic variations in mean stress or alternating stress.
Beam splitter: An optical component that can split the power contained in one beam of light into two or more beams.
Beautiful: The phenomenon of the experience of pleasure, through the perception of balance and proportion of stimulus. It involves the cognition of a balanced form and structure that elicits attraction and appeal toward a person, animal, inanimate object, scene, music, idea, etc.

Bellows: An accordionlike, light-tight camera accessory that fits between the lens and camera body. Enables closer focus of a subject and may achieve greater-than life-size magnification on a sensor.
Binocular: The simultaneous use of the two eyes in the act of vision to produce one image.
Binocular Vision: blending of the separate images seen by the two eyes. Normal binocular vision produces a stereoscopic image and parallax-induced depth perception.
Biohazard: Infectious agents that present a risk or potential risk to the health of humans or other animals, either directly through infection or indirectly through damage to the environment.
Bit depth: The gray-scale range of an individual pixel. A pixel with 8 bits per color gives a 24-bit image (8 bits×3 colors = 24 bits). CCD sensors are colored in a pixel-by-pixel method. A 30/32-bit color is billions of colors; 24-bit color resolution is 16.7 million colors; 16-bit color is 65,536 colors; 8-bit color is 256 colors; 8-bit gray-scale is 256 shades of gray; 1 bit is black or white.
Bitmap: The method of storing information that maps an image pixel, bit by bit. There are many bitmapped file formats: .bmp, .pcx, .pict, .pict-2, tiff, .tif, .gif, and so on. Most image files are bitmapped. When examined closely, you can see the line of pixels that create edges. Bitmap images are used by all computers. The desktop or screen information for all Windows machines uses .bmp files, while the Macintosh uses .pict files.
Black point: The color that produces color values of 0, 0, 0 for each of the RGB components when scanned or digitized. Normally, the black point is 0% neutral reflectance or transmittance.
Blackbody: A blackbody is an object that absorbs all incident light—neither reflecting it nor allowing it to pass through. A rough analog of blackbody radiation in our day-to-day experience might be in heating a metal or stone: these are said to become "red hot" when they attain one temperature, and then "white hot" for even higher temperatures. Similarly, blackbodies at different temperatures also have varying color temperatures of "white light." Despite its name, light that may appear white does not necessarily contain an even distribution of colors across the visible spectrum.
Bounce flash: Flash illuminating a subject by reflection off a surface, as opposed to direct flash, which is flash light aimed straight at the subject. Sometimes called *bounce lighting*.
Brightness: Attribute of a visual sensation according to which area appears to emit more or less light. The perceived amount of light coming from an area. *Brightness* is often restricted to apply only to lights, and *lightness* is used for the corresponding dimension of the colors of surfaces. One of the three standard elements of color appearance (the other two are hue and saturation). Its colorimetric equivalent is luminance.
Bruise (contusion or ecchymosis): A kind of injury, usually caused by blunt impact, in which the capillaries are damaged, allowing blood to seep into the surrounding tissue. Normally minor but painful, bruises can be serious, leading to hematoma, or can be associated with serious injuries, including fractures and internal bleeding. Minor bruises are recognized by their characteristic blue or purple color in the days following the injury.
Buccal: Pertaining to the surface of a posterior tooth closest to the cheek.
Buffer: Memory in the camera that stores digital photos before they are written to the memory card.
Buoyancy: The upward force exerted on any object placed in a fluid (liquid or gas). Understanding buoyancy principles allows you to predict how changes in your weight, volume, or water density will affect your buoyancy control.
Buoyancy control device (BCD): Inflatable jacket worn by a diver. Holds the scuba system together and allows the diver to control his or her buoyancy by adding or releasing air.
Burn pattern: Fire patterns and their geometry that provide clues about fire spread, area and point of origin, and fuels involved. Helps interpret fire spread with evidence including lines of demarcation, charring, spalling, etc.
CAD: Computer-aided design software that uses a wide range of computer-based tools to assist engineers and architects in their design activities.
Camcorder: A portable electronic device (generally a digital camera) for recording video images and audio onto a storage device; contains both camera and recorder in one unit
Camera: A lightproof box fitted with a lens though which the image of an object is recorded on a material sensitive to light.
Camera Obscura: A dark room (or box) with a small hole in one side, through which an inverted image of the view outside is projected onto the opposite wall, screen, or mirror. The image is then traced. This forerunner of the modern camera was a tool for recording an optically accurate image.
Candela (cd): Standard unit of luminous intensity in the International System of Units (SI) formally defined as the magnitude of an electromagnetic field, in a specified direction, that has a power level of 1/683

watt (1.46×10^{-3} W) per steradian at a frequency of 540 terahertz (540 THz or 5.40×10^{14} Hz).

Candle (standard) : Basic unit of luminous intensity adopted under the International System of Units (SI: Le Système International d'Unité); equal to 1/60 of the luminous intensity per square centimeter of a blackbody radiating at the temperature of 2,046 Kelvin.

Candle power: Luminous intensity of a source of light expressed in candelas.

Capacitor: An electronic device that stores energy and releases it when needed.

Cartesian coordinates: A system of two or three mutually perpendicular axes along which any point may be located in terms of distance and direction from any other point. A mathematical representation of Euclidean space, in which every point can be described by three coordinates (X, Y, and Z) representing the position along the orthogonal X, Y, and Z axes. The point (0, 0, 0) is called the *origin*, which is the global center of the 3-D world.

Cause of death: The one underlying condition (every death is attributed to one), based on information reported on the death certificate and using the international rules for selecting the underlying cause of death from the reported conditions.

CC filter: Color compensating filter. Designed primarily for correcting color bias in color photo printing. CC2OY, for example, indicates a yellow filtration of 0.2 density.

CCD (charge-coupled device) : One of the two main types of image sensors used in digital cameras. When a picture is taken, the CCD is struck by light coming through the camera's lens. Each of the thousands or millions of tiny pixels that make up the CCD convert this light into electrons. The number of electrons, usually described as the pixel's accumulated charge, is measured and then converted to a digital value. This last step occurs outside the CCD, in a camera component called an *analog-to-digital converter.*

CD-R: CD-Recordable: a compact disc that holds either 650 or 700 megabytes of digital information, including digital photos. Creating one is commonly referred to as "burning a CD." A CD-R disc can only be written to once and is an ideal storage medium for original digital photos.

CD-RW: CD-Rewritable: similar in virtually all respects to a CD-R, except that a CD-RW disc can be written to and erased many times. This makes them best suited to many backup tasks, but not long-term storage of original digital photos.

Central perspective: every light ray passing through or bouncing off the subject before reaching the image receptor (film or digital) during exposure, passed through the camera lens, which in this case is mathematically considered to be a single point.

CGS system: System of units of measurement based on the metric system and having the centimeter of length, the gram of mass, and the second of time as its fundamental units. Other cgs units are the dyne of force and the erg of work or energy.

Chain of custody: A method for documenting the history and possession of a sample from the time of collection, through analysis and data reporting, to its final disposition. An item is considered to be in an individual's custody if the item is (1) in the physical possession of that person, (2) within direct view of that person, or (3) placed in a secured area or container by that person.

Character: The properties of a light that distinguish its appearance.

Characteristic curve: A curve (of a film) showing the relationship between the common logarithm of exposure, log K, and the optical density, D; also called the D-log E curve or the H and D curve.

Chevron: A V-shaped pattern.

Chip: Small piece of semiconductor material upon which electronic components and subassemblies are formed.

Chromatic aberration: Color shifts and color artifacts in an image caused by faults in a lens, or by the camera's inability to register all three channels of color information. Single-chip video cameras are especially prone to chromatic aberration.

Chromaticity: Objective measurement of the color of an object or light source.

CIE: Commission Internationale de l'Eclairage, or International Commission on Illumination. International organization that developed a set of universal color standards in 1932.

Circle of confusion: A term in photography relating to the fuzziest a point can be and still be called "in focus" (related to the DoF). Often calculated as the largest circle on the film that will still be seen as a point when enlarged to 8×10 inches and viewed from a normal viewing distance (2 to 3 feet).

Clarity: The property of visual representation using the absolute minimum amount of symbolism necessary for the map user to understand map content without error.

Clipping: A result of oversaturation (too bright) or undersaturation (to dark) in an image. If the video image contains grayscale values outside the image processor's upper and lower limits for the grayscale range, pixels exceeding the limits are set to the highest or lowest values possible.

Close-up lens: An attachment lens that fits on the front of a camera lens, allowing photography at closer distances than normal for that lens.

Closure: In transportation, the process of a unit arriving at a specified location. It begins when the first element arrives at a designated location, and ends when the last element does likewise. For the purposes of studies and command post exercises, a unit is considered essentially closed after 95 percent of its movement requirements for personnel and equipment are completed.

CMOS (complementary metal-oxide semiconductor): One of the two main types of image sensors used in digital cameras. Its basic function is the same as that of a CCD. CMOS sensors are currently found in only a handful of digital cameras.

C-mount: Lenses have 32 threads per inch, and the distance from the rear element to the image plane is 17.52 mm. C-mount lenses are commonly used on motion picture cameras with interchangeable lenses.

CMYK: A color model used when working with print-based images that describes colors as mixtures of cyan, magenta, yellow, and black ink. Some printers use six ink colors to achieve smoother, more photographic prints. The two additional colors are often lighter shades of cyan and magenta. CMYK is contrasted to the RGB (red, green, blue) color model, which is used when working with images intended for electronic presentation, such as on computer monitors, televisions, and LCD screens. CMYK and RGB are also called *color spaces*, because each defines the color gamut or range of colors that it can represent.

Code of Federal Regulations (CFR): The codification of the general and permanent rules published in the *Federal Register* by the executive departments and agencies of the federal government, divided into 50 titles that represent broad areas subject to federal regulation, with each volume of the CFR updated once each calendar year and issued quarterly.

Cognitive: Of, relating to, or being conscious intellectual activity (as thinking, reasoning, remembering, imagining, or learning words).

Colloidal: Condition of matter depicted by its even distribution (solution) of microscopic particles with a diameter of 1 to 100 nanometers in a dispersing substance.

Color: The attribute of visual experience that can be described as having quantitatively specifiable dimensions of hue, saturation, and brightness or lightness. It does not include aspects of extent (e.g., size, shape, texture, etc.) and duration (e.g., movement, flicker, etc.). A color that is seen can be a single wavelength or a combination of many. Most colors are very complex combinations of many wavelengths of various amplitudes.

Color balance: The color balance of a film refers to the kind of light under which it will faithfully render color without the need for filters. Most films are daylight balanced, which means that in daylight, or with a daylight-balanced flash, colors will be true. A tungsten-balanced film can be used under certain types of artificial light to give true colors without filters or special printing techniques.

Color compensation (CC) filter: Filter designed to compensate for the color loss due to depth in various underwater environments.

Color correction: The act of correcting for and eliminating an unwanted color cast. Color correction is performed on an entire image (called *global color correction*) or on just one part (called *local color correction*).

Colorimetry: The science of measuring color and color appearance. Classical colorimetry deals primarily with color matches rather than with color appearance as such. The main focus of colorimetry has been the development of methods for predicting perceptual matches on the basis of physical measurements.

Color management: A technology to calibrate the color of input devices (e.g., scanners or digital cameras), display devices, and output devices (e.g., printers or offset presses). Parts of this technology are implemented in the operating system (OS), the API, or directly in the application.

Color space: A particular variant of a color model with a specific gamut or range of colors, which is one of its chief characteristics. For example, within the color model RGB are a number of color spaces, such as Apple RGB, Adobe RGB (1998), and sRGB. While each of these define color by the same three axes (R, G, and B), they differ in gamut and other specific characteristics.

Color temperature: A characteristic of visible light that has important applications in photography, videography, publishing, and other fields. The color temperature of a light source is determined by comparing its hue with a theoretical, heated blackbody radiator. The Kelvin temperature at which the heated blackbody radiator matches the hue of the light source is that source's color temperature.

Communication: The active process of exchanging information and ideas that involves encoding, transmitting, and decoding intended messages. There are many means of communicating and many different language systems. Speech and language are only a portion of communication. Other aspects of communication may enhance or even eclipse the linguistic code.

CompactFlash(tm): A common type of digital camera memory card, about the size of a matchbook. Two types: Type I and Type II—vary only in their thickness, with Type I being slightly thinner. A CompactFlash memory card can contain either flash memory or a miniature hard drive. The flash memory type is more prevalent.
Competency: A witness's ability to observe, recall and recount under other what happened. Criminal defendants must also be competent to stand trial; they must understand the nature of the proceedings and have the ability to assist their lawyers.
Competitive Intelligence: The process of gathering actionable information on the competitive environment. See SCIP.
Composition: Composition is the plan, placement or arrangement of the elements of art in a work. The general goal is to select and place appropriate elements within the work in order to communicate ideas and feelings with the viewer.
Compressed video: A digital transmission process used to transmit a video signal that compressed information into a fraction of its former bandwidth. Picture quality generally not as good as full-motion video.
Compression artifact: A compression artifact or artifact is a particular type of data error that is typically the result of quantization in lossy data compression.
Computer animation: The art of creating moving images via the use of computers.
Cone: Cone cells, or cones, are cells in the retina which only function in relatively bright light. There are about 6 million in the human eye, concentrated at the fovea and gradually becoming sparser towards the outside of the retina.
Conspicuity: Conspicuity is what makes something stand-out from its surroundings. The more it stands out among other displayed information, the more conspicuous it is said to be.
Constraint: Relationships among objects that are declared once, and then maintained automatically by the system.
Continuous tone: An image in which brightness appears consistent and uninterrupted. Each pixel uses at least 1 byte per red, green, and blue value. This permits 256 density levels per color or more than 16 million mixture colors. Any graphic element that has a gray scale or is not line art originated from a continuous tone image. Examples of continuous tone originals are black-and-white photographs or pencil sketches. Continuous tone originals should be scanned at a minimum of 300 ppi and saved in uncompressed files for use in page layout programs and to preserve tonality.
Contrast: In visual perception, the difference in visual properties that makes an object (or its representation in an image) distinguishable from other objects and the background. The greater the difference, the higher the contrast.
Control points: a system of points with established positions or elevations, or both, which are used as fixed references in positioning map features.
Coroner: The presiding officer of a special court to investigate deaths that occur under unusual circumstances when conventional criminal proceedings are not immediately called for.
Corpse: A dead body, especially a human one.
Creativity: The ability to solve problems; the ability to create knowledge. It is subject-specific: the meta-knowledge of how to solve a specific class of problems. There is no such thing as "raw," undifferentiated creativity.
Credibility: Is the quality of being believable or trustworthy.
Crop factor: The field-of-view reduction on a digital camera when using the same lens focal length from a 35 mm camera. A 25 mm lens on a DSLR camera is no longer a wide-angle lens but corresponds to a 37 mm lens on a 35 mm film body
Dark noise: Image degradation caused by the image sensor's inability to discern detail in low light.
Decoding: A mental activity in which information is deconstructed into understandable or recognizable parts; an element of reading strategies.
Degree of Convergence: The angle of inclination of the two eyes used in depth perception. Inward movement of both eyes toward each other, usually in an effort to maintain single binocular vision as an object approaches.
Densitometer: Densitometers measure the optical, photographic, or area density of a material. They are used in a wide range of applications, from film processing to medical scans.
Density: The degree of tone, weight of darkness, or color within a photo or reproduction; measurable by a densitometer.
Deposition: The act or fact of taking sworn testimony of a witness outside of court, in certain well-defined circumstances. A part of the discovery process whereby litigants obtain information from each other in preparation for trial.
Depth clues (or cues): Images are by and large flat, but they can give the impression of deep or shallow space. The main techniques used for this are making closer objects larger and more strongly colored, and making further objects smaller and paler.
Depth of field (DoF): Zone from the points closest to the camera to the points farthest from the camera

that are in acceptable focus. The range of distance in a scene that appears to be in focus and will be reproduced sharply in an image. DoF is controlled by the lens aperture and extends for a distance in front of and behind the point on which the lens is focused.

Depth of focus: Depends upon the numerical aperture, as well as the magnification, and is inversely proportional to both: the higher the magnification, the shorter the depth of focus for any given numerical aperture.

Depth perception: The ability to recognize three-dimensional objects and their relative position in space.

Developer: In photography, the chemical agent and process used to render photographic images visible after exposure to light. In lithographic platemaking, the material used to remove the unexposed coating.

Diaphragm: A ring or plate with a hole in the center that controls the amount of light entering the camera. An adjustable diaphragm in a lens controls the size of the hole, or aperture, thereby permitting more or less light to pass through the lens to the film.

Diffraction: The tendency of waves to bend around corners. The diffraction of light establishes its nature as a wave.

Diffusion: Refers to the phenomenon in which water scatters and deflects light, thereby reducing the amount of light that penetrates. Also refers to the scattering of light off particles as it travels through the water.

Digital camera: A camera that captures the photo, not on film, but in an electronic imaging sensor that takes the place of film.

Digital courtroom: Technology that gives both attorneys and legal consulting experts the ability to follow trial proceedings in real time from any location in the world with an Internet connection.

Digital photograph: Digital photography, as opposed to film photography, uses an electronic sensor to record the image as a piece of electronic data rather than as chemical changes on film. Since 2005, digital cameras have outsold film cameras, and they include features not found in film cameras, such as the ability to shoot video and record audio. Some other devices, such as mobile phones, now include digital photography features.

Digital video (DV): A type of video recording system that works by using a digital, rather than analog, representation of the video signal.

Digitization: A process of converting an analog image or map into a digital format usable by a computer.

Digitized: A term for information that has been converted into binary digits for computer processing.

Dimensionality: Is the spatial property of having dimensions.

Diopter: A unit of focusing power of a lens. A 2-diopter lens is twice as strong as a 1-diopter lens. While a 1-diopter lens will focus light at 1 meter (39.3 inches), a 2-diopter lens will focus light at .5 meter (19.7 inches).

Disaster: A natural or man-made event that negatively affects life, property, livelihood, or industry, often resulting in permanent changes to human societies, ecosystems, and environment.

Discovery: The pre-trial phase in a lawsuit in which each party through the law of civil procedure can request documents and other evidence from other parties or can compel the production of evidence by using a subpoena or other discovery devices, such as requests for production and depositions.

Disruption: an event that results in a displacement or discontinuity or the act of causing disorder.

Distort: To deliberately exaggerate or manipulate an image to the extreme.

Distortion: Alteration of viewed images caused by variations in glass flatness or in homogeneous portions within the glass; an inherent characteristic of heat-treated glass.

Documentation: Is the written, visual, audio and electronic information about a place or an object.

Download, downloading: The process of moving computer data from one location to another. Though the term is normally used to describe the transfer, or downloading, of data from the Internet, it is also used to describe the transfer of photos from a camera memory card to the computer. *Example:* I downloaded photos to my PC.

DPI (Dots Per Inch): A measurement of the resolution of a digital photo or digital device, including digital cameras and printers. The higher the number, the greater the resolution.

Dynamic: Changeable. Normally used to refer to elements that can change.

Dynamic range: A spread of gray values in an image that are possible to reproduce. An image with a high dynamic range suggests a wide number of gray levels and is normally associated with good contrast levels.

Electromagnetic field: Physical field that is produced by electrically charged objects and that affects the behavior of charged objects in the vicinity of the field.

Electronic flash: Artificial light source produced by an electrical discharge traveling between two electrodes through a gas-filled tube. The light from electronic flash is approximately the same color as daylight.

Electronic shutter: Employed in charge-coupled devices (CCDs) to control integration time (exposure) of

the photodiode array and reduce smear when capturing moving objects.
Elegant: Displaying effortless beauty and simplicity in movement or execution; simple and precise.
Empirical: Relying upon or derived from observation or experiment.
Emulsion: A light-sensitive substance used as a coating for film; made from a silver halide compound. The emulsion side should face the lens when the film is exposed.
Encoding: Conversion of sender's thoughts and ideas into a message, usually in the form of words or signs.
Enhance: To make better or more attractive.
Ethics: The study of fundamental principles that defines values and determines moral duty and obligation.
Evidence: Testimony, records, documents, material objects, or other things presented at a trial to prove the existence or nonexistence of a fact.
Exciter filter (excitation filter): The filter that goes over the light source to convert it from a source of white light to a source of specially filtered light that stimulates (excites) fluorescence.
Exhibit: An article of tangible evidence introduced at a trial.
EXIF (Exchangeable Image File): The file format used by most digital cameras. For example, when a typical camera is set to record a JPEG, it is actually recording an EXIF file that uses JPEG compression to compress the photo data within the file.
Exitance: The total light that comes off a surface; dependent upon the illuminance on and the reflectance of the surface.
Expert: An expert is someone widely recognized as a reliable source of knowledge, technique, or skill whose judgment is accorded authority and status by the public or their peers. Experts have prolonged or intense experience through practice and education in a particular field. The opposite of an expert is generally known as a layperson, while someone who occupies a middle grade of understanding is generally known as a technician and often employed to assist experts.
Expert witness: A witness who, by virtue of education, profession, or experience, is believed to have special knowledge of his or her subject beyond that of the average person, sufficient that others may officially (and legally) rely on his or her opinion.
Exposure: The total amount of light allowed to fall on the film (or electronic sensor in the case of digital photography) during the process of taking a photograph. Measured in exposure value (EV), with higher values denoting more light.
Exposure meter: An instrument (also known as a *light meter*) containing a light-sensitive cell used to measure the amount of light reflected from or falling on a subject. The measurement is usually expressed in shutter speed and aperture combinations that will render an acceptable exposure.
Exposure value (EV): The exposure value (EV) system, which originated in Germany in the 1950s, was created to be a simple-to-use substitute for the shutter speed/aperture combination, using a single number instead of two. Abbreviated EV (always with a plus or minus number attached) indicates the degree of exposure change with exposure compensation or backlight compensation—for example, +1.5 EV, –0.5 EV.
Extension tube: A metal cylinder placed between the camera body and the lens. Shortens the focusing distance. Designated according to the reproduction ratio they afford (image/subject ratio) (e.g., 1:3, 1:2, 1:1, 2:1).
External flash: A supplementary flash unit that connects to the camera with a cable or is triggered by the light from the camera's internal flash. Many fun and creative effects can be created with external flash.
Extinction: Loss of light from an object as a consequence of absorption or scattering by an intervening medium.
Extinction meter: Early type of exposure calculator requiring the use of the human eye for quantification.
Extravasation: Escape of blood from blood vessels and into tissue.
Facsimile: Is an exact copy or reproduction.
Fair: Free from favoritism or self-interest or bias or deception; or conforming to established standards or rules.
Federal Aviation Administration (FAA): The federal agency responsible for the safe and efficient movement of aircraft through the National Airspace System. Has broad legislative authority to create and enforce federal aviation regulations.
Federal Emergency Management Agency (FEMA): An agency of the U.S. Department of Homeland Security (DHS). Coordinates the response to a disaster that has occurred in the United States and overwhelms the resources of local and state authorities.
Fidelity: 1: the accuracy of the representation when compared to the real world. 2: (a) the similarity, both physical and functional, between the simulation and that which it simulates, (b) a measure of the realism of a simulation, or (c) the degree to which the representation within a simulation is similar to a real world object, feature, or condition in a measurable or perceivable manner.
Fiducial marks: Marks placed on aerial camera film during the exposure. Either four or eight fiducial

marks are placed along the edges of the film, and the imaginary lines that connect opposite fiducials intersect at the principal point of a photograph. This is important for recreating the orientation of the film in relationship to the ground.

Field-of-view: The horizontal or vertical scene size at a given length from the camera to the subject.

File: A computer document.

Fill flash: A flash technique used to brighten deep shadow areas, typically outdoors on sunny days. Some digital cameras include a fill flash mode that forces the flash to fire, even in bright light.

Film: A recording medium consisting of thin sheets or strips of transparent or translucent material, such as polyester or acetate, coated with a light-sensitive emulsion. Recording occurs by exposing the film to the light emitted or reflected by the entity being recorded.

Fingerprint: An imprint made by the pattern of ridges on the pad of a human finger. Commonly believed to provide traction for grasping objects. Often left on objects at a crime scene and, therefore, used in forensic science to identify suspects. No two humans have ever been found to have identical fingerprints, thus fingerprints are widely believed to be unique.

Fire investigation: The analysis of fire-related incidents; sometimes referred to as *origin and cause investigation.*

Fire suppression: All activities concerned with controlling and extinguishing a fire following its detection. Synonymous with *fire control.*

FireWire: A type of cabling technology for transferring data to and from digital devices at high speed. Some professional digital cameras and memory card readers connect to the computer over FireWire. FireWire card readers are typically faster than those that connect via USB. Also known as IEEE 1394, FireWire was invented by Apple Computer but is now commonly used with Windows-based PCs as well.

Fixer: A chemical—sodium thiosulfate—used to remove residual silver halides (grain) from films and prints when processing them. Fixer "fixes" the remaining silver halides in place on either film or prints. Also called *hypo.*

Flash bracket: Allows the flash to be positioned directly above or to the side of the camera to help eliminate the harsh shadows often seen in simple snap shots.

Flash duration: The duration of a flash burst from a flash, used to vary flash output, typically from 1/1,000 to 1/20,000 second in contemporary units under auto flash modes.

Flash meter: Device for measuring the light coming from an electronic flash and indicating the appropriate aperture for correct exposure. Some flash meters can also measure the ambient light.

Flash powder: Used in the early days of photography, a mixture of metallic magnesium with an oxidizing agent that, when ignited, produces a bright flash of light.

Flash shoe: Metal fitting on the top of a camera; supports the flash gun and various other accessories, such as a viewfinder or rangefinder.

Flashbulb: A one-time-use glass bulb enclosing a pyrotechnic wire filament that burns out when an electrical current is run through it and generates a bright flash.

Floodlight: Incandescent lighting fixture that emits a broad field of light with a soft edge, such as a border light, scoop light, etc.

Fluorescence: The property of absorbing light of a particular wavelength and then emitting light of a different color and wavelength.

F-Mount: Nikon bayonet mount lenses are F-Mount.

Focal length multiplier: A multiplicative factor that relates the focal length of a digital camera to the focal length of a 35mm camera that produces the same field of view.

Focal length: The distance between the film plane and the focal point (optical center of the lens) when the lens is focused at infinity. The focal length of the lens is marked in millimeters on the lens mount. The principal focal point is the position of best focus for infinity.

Focus: To cause to converge on or toward a central point: "Focus the light on this image." The focus, or focal point of a lens or parabolic mirror, is the point onto which light in a straight line and parallel to the axis is focused. Although the focus is conceptually a point, physically, the focus has a spatial extent, called the *airy disc,* or *blur circle,* due to the width of the aperture of the imaging optics.

Foot-candle: The total intensity of light that falls upon a 1-square-foot surface that is placed 1 foot away from a point source of light that equals 1 candle power.

Foot-Lambert (fL) : The Luma (brightness) resulting from a surface emitting a Luma flux of 1 lumen per square foot. The Luma of a perfectly reflecting surface receiving an illumination of 1 foot-candle.

Force feedback: Feedback that involves a resisting force felt by the user; also see *haptic.*

Forensic: Relating to the use of science or technology in the investigation and establishment of facts or evidence in a court of law.

Forensic archaeology: The application of archaeological techniques and approaches in the legal field, normally the enforcement of criminal law.

Forensic cinematographer: A person who makes motion pictures to be used in the courtroom.

Forensic dentistry/odontology: Forensic odontology is a branch of forensic medicine dealing with the proper examination, handling, and presentation of dental evidence in a court of law. The work of a forensic odontologist includes identification of bite marks on the victims of attack; comparison of bite marks with the teeth of a suspect and presentation of this evidence in court as an expert witness; identification of bite marks in other substances such as wood, leather, and foodstuffs; identification of unknown bodies through dental records; and age estimations of skeletal remains. A forensic odontologist often works with a forensic pathologist or forensic anthropologist.

Forensic entomology: The science and study of insects and other arthropods related to legal investigations; can be divided into three subfields: urban, stored-product, and medicolegal/medicocriminal.

Forensic light source (Alternative light source, ALS): A tool for enhancing observation, photography, and collection of evidence, including latent fingerprints, body fluids, hairs and fibers, bruises, bite marks, wound patterns, shoe and foot imprints, gun shot residues, drug traces, questioned documents, bone fragment detection, and so on. A powerful lamp containing the UV, visible and IR components of light. Filters the light into individual wavelengths that enhance the visualization of evidence by light interaction techniques including fluorescence (evidence glows), absorption (evidence darkens), and oblique lighting (small particle evidence revealed).

Forensic odontology: Deals with proper handling, examination, and evaluation of dental evidence, which will be then presented in the interest of justice; also called *forensic dentistry*.

Format size: The shape or proportions of a picture plane.

Fovea: Central pit in the macula that produces sharpest vision. It contains a high concentration of cones and no retinal blood vessels.

Fractography: Descriptive treatment of fracture, especially in metals, with specific reference to photographs of the fracture surface. Macro-fractography involves photographs at low magnification (25×); micro fractography involves photographs at high magnification (>25×)

Fraud: The act of destroying or damaging any property, personally owned or belonging to another, in order to collect insurance or reward for such loss.

F-stop: The f-number (focal ratio) expresses the diameter of the diaphragm aperture in terms of the effective focal length of the lens. For example, *f*/16 represents a diaphragm aperture diameter that is 1/16 the focal length (or the focal length is 16 times the aperture).

Galvanometer: An instrument that measures small electrical currents by means of deflecting magnetic coils.

Gamma: Curve that describes how the middle tones of images appear. Gamma is a nonlinear function often confused with *brightness* and/or *contrast*. Changing the value of the gamma affects middle tones while leaving the white and black of the image unaltered. Gamma adjustment is often used to compensate for differences between Macintosh and Windows video cards and displays.

Gamut: Every color combination that is possible to produce with a given set of colorants on a given device or system. Refers to the range of available color on a display or printer. A particular color is either in or out of the gamut of the device. If outside, it cannot be accurately shown on that display or printed on that output device. (Each device has its own gamut capabilities.)

Gelatin: A nearly transparent substance, obtained by boiling animal tissue in water, used (1) as the medium for suspending light-sensitive silver halide crystals on photographic film and (2) in the manufacture of gelatin filters.

Geographic Information System (GIS): A computer system capable of capturing, storing, analyzing, and displaying geographically referenced information—that is, data identified according to location.

Gigabyte (Gb) : A unit of storage measurement consisting of one billion bytes (one thousand megabytes).

Go Team: Emergency Response Team, Special Response Team, Special Operations Group, Multi-Disciplinary Investigation Team, the ubiquitous Special Weapons and Tactics (SWAT) team or anything else, this unit represents a focused approach to problem solving and situational response.

Go Kit: Specialized knowledge and equipment are the hallmark of any Go Team. As may be expected, the equipment cache is usually referred to as the "Go Kit." Whether a small belt-pouch, a contractor-size tool box, a wheeled case, a large aircraft-style cargo pallet, or even an entire truck full of equipment.

Graphic: Two-dimensional and three-dimensional works of fine art, graphic art, applied art, photographs, prints and art reproductions, maps, globes, charts, diagrams, models, and technical drawings, including architectural plans.

Grayscale: A photo made up of varying tones of black and white. Synonymous with black and white.

Grid: The pixels of an output device can be regarded as the squares of a grid.

Guide number (GN) : A number that relates the output of electronic flash when used with a particular speed film. The higher the GN, the more the light output. GNs are used to calculate aperture when shooting flash in manual exposure mode. Dividing distance into GN gives the aperture: for example, a flash with a GN of 56 (with ISO 100 film) would give a correct exposure at 10 feet with an aperture of *f*/5.6.
Halation: Blurred effect at the edges of a highlight area of a photograph caused by reflection of light that passed through the film. The light is reflected from either the surface of the film or the camera back.
Haptic: Pertaining to the sense of touch, from the Greek word *haptein*, to grasp.
Haz-Mat (hazardous materials): Chemicals that can harm humans, animals, or the environment. Usually pertains to truck restrictions through tunnels or a heavily populated area where a Haz-Mat related accident or spill would be detrimental to the immediate surroundings.
High-Definition (HD): The output of a high-definition video device or the input of an HD TV receiver or monitor, comprised of (3) primary-color signals: red, green, and blue.
High-Intensity Discharge (HID) light: Produces light by striking an electrical arc across tungsten electrodes housed inside a specially designed tube. Compared with fluorescent and incandescent lamps, HID lamps produce a far higher quantity of light per unit area of lamp package.
Highlights: The brightest parts of a photo.
High-speed camera: A device used for recording action for playback in slow motion.
Histogram: A graph showing the relative distribution of pixels of various densities in an image. The histogram shows the number of pixels, with high density on the left and low density on the right. Its purpose is to show the distribution of tone throughout an image. An image with no shadows will have a histogram with a valley on the left; a histogram with no highlights will have a valley on the right. Some digital cameras include a histogram feature that enables a precise check on the exposure of the photo.
Homicide: The killing of one human being by the act of another. A necessary ingredient of the crimes of murder and manslaughter, but homicide may be committed in some cases without criminal intent and without criminal consequences, as in self-defense.
Horizontal: An orientation relating to, or in parallel with, the horizon; the opposite of vertical. A horizontal line goes from left to right (or vice versa), whereas a vertical line goes from top to bottom (or vice versa).
Hot shoe: The fitting on a camera that holds a small portable flash. Has an electrical contact that aligns with the contact on the flash unit and fires the flash when the shutter release is pressed. Direct flash-to-camera contact eliminates the need for a PC cord.
Hue: The gradation of color within the optical spectrum, or visible spectrum, of light. *Hue* may also refer to a particular color within this spectrum, as defined by its dominant wavelength, or the central tendency of its combined wavelengths. For example, a light wave with a central tendency within 565 to 590 nanometers will be yellow.
Hyperfocal distance: Assuming a permissible circle of confusion, the distance from the lens of the nearest object that is in focus when the lens is focused on infinity. If a lens is focused on the hyperfocal distance, then all points are within the range covered by the DoF, from infinity down to half the hyperfocal distance. The hyperfocal distance depends upon the lens focal length and aperture.
Illuminance: Light arriving at a surface, expressed in lumens per unit area; 1 lumen per square foot equals 1 footcandle, while 1 lumen per square meter equals 1 lux.
Image browser: An application that enables you to view digital photos. Some browsers also allow you to rename files, convert photos from one file format to another, add text descriptions, and more.
Image capture: The use of a device, such as a scanner or digital camera, to create a digital representation of an image. This digital representation can then be stored and used on a computer.
Image editor: A computer program that enables you to adjust a photo to improve its appearance. With image editing software, you can darken or lighten a photo, rotate it, adjust its contrast, crop out extraneous detail, remove red-eye, and more.
Image processing: Manipulation of digitized images that have been scanned, captured by digital cameras, and such to improve the image in some way.
Image resolution: The number of pixels in a digital photo is commonly referred to as its image resolution.
Image sensor: The type of device used in digital camera and camcorders to capture an image. The two most common types are CCD (charge-coupled device) and CMOS (complementary metal-oxide semiconductor). Converts a visual image to an electrical signal. Used chiefly in digital cameras and other imaging devices. Usually an array of CCD or CMOS sensors, such as active pixel sensors.
Image stabilized (IS) lenses: Contain small gyro sensors and servo-actuated optical elements to correct for camera shake, thus stabilizing the image for better

sharpness than nonstabilized optics. Allow a lens to be handheld at shutter speeds two to three stops slower than the minimum required for sharp images with non-IS lenses.

Immediacy: Quickness of action or occurrence; "the immediacy of their response"; "the instancy of modern communication."

Immersive: A story or visual presentation that enables the player to convincingly enter and participate in a virtual world. Refers to the impression that someone has of being somewhere while, in reality, they are physically elsewhere.

Incandescent/tungsten filament: Originally invented by Edison, the most common bulb in use today. Consists of a glowing filament inside a glass bulb. Produces close-to-natural light, has a short life span, and is not very efficient.

Incident light: The light actually falling on a subject, which may not be the same as the amount of light being reflected by the subject.

Infer: To take the results from a small sample and generalize them to the larger population.

Information: A message received and understood; data: a collection of facts from which conclusions may be drawn; statistical data: knowledge acquired through study or experience or instruction (communication theory), a numerical measure of the uncertainty of an outcome.

Infrared light: An area in the electromagnetic spectrum extending beyond red light from 760 nanometers to 1,000 microns (106 nm). The form of radiation used for making non-contact temperature measurements.

Inkjet: A printer that places ink on the paper by spraying droplets through tiny nozzles.

Intensity: The relative purity or saturation of a hue (color), on a scale from bright (pure) to dull (mixed with another hue or a neutral. Also called chroma.

Interlaced video: A method of displaying images on a raster-scanned display device, such as a cathode ray tube (CRT); causes less visible flickering than noninterlaced methods. In the PAL and NTSC standards, the lower (even) field is always drawn first.

Interpol: The International Criminal Police Organization–Interpol (ICPO–Interpol) created in 1923 to assist international criminal police cooperation.

Intra-oral: Inside the mouth.

Inverse Camera: When the focal length, principal point, and format size of a camera are not known, it is necessary to use Inverse Camera to derive measurements with PhotoModeler.

Investigation: A systematic, minute, and thorough attempt to ascertain the facts about something Complex or hidden. It is often formal and official.

ISO (International Standards Organization): Develops standards such as JPEG and MPEG. Digital cameras have an ISO rating that indicates their level of sensitivity to light.

ISO speed: A rating of a film's sensitivity to light. Though digital cameras do not use film, they have adopted the same rating system for describing the sensitivity of the camera's imaging sensor. Digital cameras often include a control for adjusting the ISO speed; some will adjust it automatically, depending on the lighting conditions, adjusting it upward as the available light dims. Generally, as ISO speed climbs, image quality drops.

JPEG: A standard for compressing image data developed by the Joint Photographic Experts Group, hence the name JPEG. Strictly speaking, JPEG is not a file format, it is a compression method that is used within a file format, such as the EXIF–JPEG format common to digital cameras. It is referred to as a lossy format, which means some quality is lost in achieving the high compression rates of JPEGs. Usually, if a high-quality, low-compression JPEG setting is chosen on a digital camera, the loss of quality is not detectable to the eye.

Junk science: A term used to derogate purportedly scientific data, research, analyses, or claims that are driven by political, financial, or other questionable motives.

Kelvin: Base unit of temperature in which absolute zero is 0 K, equal to –273.15 degrees Celsius. Describes the color of the light but not the spectral components. If a light source is described as 5,000 K, it is the same color as a radiating blackbody (a physics term) that is that temperature. Incandescent bulbs are around 2,700 K (reddish), "daylight" is 5,500K (white), and higher temperatures have more blue. Kelvin is referred to as color temperature, the scale used by photographers to measure the warmth or coolness of light. The color of a light source is specified as degrees in Kelvin. The scale is expressed as a range of temperature from about 1,000 K (firelight) to 10,000 K (clear blue afternoon sky) and beyond. In general photographic applications, the most commonly used color temperatures are 3,200 K (tungsten) and 5,500 to 6,000 K (daylight).

Key: An explanatory description or legend to features on a map or chart.

Laser scanner: The process of capturing geometry with a laser. It can be applied to nearly any physical artifact.

Latent: Any chance or accidental impression left by friction ridge skin on a surface, regardless of whether it is visible or invisible at the time of deposition. The invisible image left by the action of light on photographic film or paper. The light changes the photosensitive salts, and when processed, this latent image will become a visible image.

Latitude: The range, in f-stop, that deviates from the optical exposure but will still produce acceptable results on a specific film. Amount by which it is possible to over- or underexpose a light-sensitive material and, with standard processing, still produce acceptable results.

LCD: Liquid Crystal Display: a low-power monitor often used on the top or rear of a digital camera to display settings or the photo itself.

LCD projector: An electronic video/data projector for displaying video and computer images on a large projection screen.

Legend: A key to what the symbols or pictures on a map mean.

Lens mount: An interface—mechanical and often also electrical—between a photographic camera body and a lens. Confined to camera bodies that allow use of interchangeable lenses, most usually SLRs.

Life size: The actual size of a piece of material, as opposed to its size in a representation.

Light: The portion of the electromagnetic spectrum that produces stimulation of the optic nerves and images of everything humans can see. Wavelengths range from 380 to 720 nanometers.

Light-emitting diode (LED) : A semiconductor device that emits incoherent narrow-spectrum light when electrically biased in the forward direction. This effect is a form of electroluminescence. The color of the emitted light depends on the chemical composition of the semiconducting material used and can be near UV, visible, or IR.

Lighting: The devices or techniques used for illumination, usually referring to artificial light sources, such as lamps or flashlights. Creates a real-world environment by allowing the rendering of different grades of darkness and brightness of an object's appearance to make the object look solid.

Light meter: An instrument used to measure the amount of light reflected from or falling on a subject. The measurement is usually expressed in shutter speed and aperture combinations that will render an acceptable exposure (also known as an *exposure meter*).

Light ray: Light is electromagnetic radiation with a wavelength that is visible to the eye, or in a more general sense, any electromagnetic radiation in the range from infrared to ultraviolet.

Line of sight: An imaginary straight line along which an observer looks.

Line pairs: A measurement for resolution. The more line pairs per millimeter, the better the image resolution.

Linear editing: Video editing style where a program is edited together by moving shots from the original source tapes to a master tape, one by one.

Lingual: Pertaining to the side of the tooth toward the tongue.

Linguistic: The broadly conceived scientific study of human language; a linguist is someone who engages in this study.

Literal: Without interpretation or embellishment: "a literal depiction of the scene before him"; limited to the explicit meaning of a word or text: "a literal translation"; avoiding embellishment or exaggeration (used for emphasis): "it's the literal truth."

Lithograph: Prints taken from a drawing done from a polished limestone or zinc or aluminum plates. The drawing is done with greasy crayons, pens, or pencils. A solution containing gum arabic and dilute nitric acid is washed on the stone (or plate). This solution fixes the design in place. The entire plate surface is washed with water and then inked. Print paper is applied and sent through a press, transferring a the image of the stone (or plate) to the paper.

Lossless compression: Refers to a data compression technique in which the file quality is preserved and no data are lost. Commonly used on GIF images, but can only reduce file size to about half of original size.

Lossy: An image that after compression is different from the original image due to lost information. The differences may or may not be noticeable, but a lossy conversion process does not retain all the original information. JPEG is an example of a lossy compression method.

Lossy compression: A scheme that, after decompression, does not produce exactly the same data that were given to the compressor. Due to the nature of image data, the losses are often imperceptible to the human eye. Although image quality may suffer, many experts believe that up to 95% of the data in a typical image may be discarded without a noticeable loss in apparent resolution.

Luma: Short for "luminance"; a value describing the brightness of a video image.

Lumen: The unit of measure for the light energy that flows in air. The total light output from electric sources is expressed in lumens. A uniform source of 1 candlepower placed in a sphere emits 12.57 lumens or mean spherical candela equals to 12.57 lumens.

Luminance: The specific light that comes off the surface, whether off a filament, lightbulb, lens, louver, tabletop, and so on. Varies with both the direction at which the surface is viewed and its gloss characteristics; measured in candela per square foot. Luminance and chromaticity together fully define a perceived color.

Luminol: A chemical used by forensic investigators to detect blood.

Luminosity function: A standard function established by the Commission Internationale de l' Éclairage (CIE) to account for the variable sensitivity of the human eye to radiation at different wavelengths; converts radiant energy into luminous (visible) energy.

Luminous flux: The flux of visible radiation, so weighted as to account for the manner in which the response of the human eye varies with the wavelength of radiation. Basic unit of measurement is the lumen (lm).

Luminous intensity: The intensity (flux per unit solid angle) of visible radiation weighted to take into account the variable response of the human eye as a function of the wavelength of light. Usually expressed in candles.

Lux: The metric level for light level; 1 Lux equals the total intensity of light that falls on a 1-square-meter surface that is placed 1 meter away from a point source of light that equals 1 candle power.

Macro: The ability of a lens to focus just inches away from an object or subject so as to produce big close-ups, sometimes even larger than life size.

Macrophotography: A kind of close-up photography.

Magnification: Measure of the apparent difference in size between the object and the image of the object.

Manipulate: To change the form or picture of a part of a negative.

Manner of death: Five main categories include natural deaths, accidental deaths, homicidal deaths, suicidal deaths, and unexplained deaths.

Mass disaster: Mass fatality incident.

Matrix: A two-dimensional rectangle with row and column values.

Matrix metering: When a digital camera has to set the exposure automatically (the aperture and shutter speed), it often uses matrix metering. A set of areas, or spots, in the picture that the camera looks at and averages to decide on aperture and shutter speed settings—the exposure settings. Sometimes this is "center weighted," meaning that most of the spots are in the center of the frame, and sometimes it is bottom weighted.

Mechanism of death: Physiological or biochemical events that end life; may be gunshot wound, assault, arson, traffic, or other means.

Media: Material on which information is written and stored. Digital photography storage media includes CompactFlash cards and CDs.

Medical examiner (ME): A physician officially authorized by a governmental unit to ascertain the cause of death. Unlike a coroner, the medical examiner is always a physician.

Medicolegal: Pertaining to medicine and law, or to forensic medicine.

Megabyte (Mb) : A unit of measurement equal to one million bytes or 1,024 kilobytes or 1,048,576 bytes.

Megapixel: Equal to one million pixels.

Mesopic vision: Occurs in intermediate lighting (luminance level 10^{-2} to 1 cd/m^2) and is a combination of scotopic and photopic vision.

Metadata: Data about data; more specifically, information (data) about a particular content (data).

Metal: In chemistry, a metal is an element that readily forms ions (cations) and has metallic bonds, and metals are sometimes described as a lattice of positive ions (cations) in a cloud of electrons.

Metering: Metering works in conjunction with the exposure systems of digital cameras. It measures the amount of light, and works out for the photographer the best exposure for you're the image. Some cameras have auto-metering, whereas others offer a metering mode option. A few different metering modes are center-weighted average metering (probably the most common), spot (partial) metering, and matrix or evaluative metering.

Metrology: Metrology is the science and process of ensuring that a measurement meets specified degrees of both accuracy and precision.

Microphotograph: Photographs made using a microscope to capture magnifications much larger than real life.

Minilab: A computer printer that uses traditional chemical photographic processes to make prints of digital images. Photographs are input to the digital minilab using a built-in image scanner, a kiosk that accepts CD-ROMs or memory cards from a digital camera, or a Web site that accepts uploads. The operator can make minor corrections, such as brightness or color saturation.

Mired: A unit of measurement (M) equal to 1,000,000 divided by the given color temperature.

Model: The act of representing something (usually on a smaller scale). A *physical model* is used in various contexts to mean a physical representation of some thing. That thing may be a single item or object (for example, a bolt) or a large system (for example, the solar system).

Modeling light: A light built into a flash unit that remains on while the flash is turned on or in standby mode, permitting the photographer to assess highlight and shadow areas that will be created when exposing the image in the light from the flash.

Modulation transfer function (MTF) : A measure of image quality, in particular how well a repetitive line target is reproduced by a lens in terms of image contrast as compared to object contrast. The MTF value scale goes from 0 to 1, with 1 being the best, though impossible to achieve. One must also specify the frequency of the line target, usually in terms of the number of light/dark stripes or line pairs per millimeter (lp/mm) at the image plane.

Moiré effect: interference patterns caused through the interaction between regular patterns in the subject and the regular array of the image sensor.

Monochromatic: Consisting of a single wavelength or narrow range of wavelengths.

Monochrome: A single color; usually refers to a black-and-white image; also referred to as line art or bitmap mode (Adobe Photoshop)

Monocular: Refers to only one eye.

Motion picture: A term that encompasses motion pictures as individual projects, as well as the field in general.

MPEG (Moving Picture Experts Group): The standard for compression and storage of motion video—for example, videos available though the World Wide Web.

MPEG-2: Offers resolutions of 720 × 480 and 1280 × 720 at 60 fps, with full CD-quality audio. Sufficient for all the major TV standards, including NTSC and HDTV. Can compress a 2-hour video into a few gigabytes.

MPEG-4: A graphics and video compression algorithm standard based on MPEG-1, MPEG-2, and Apple QuickTime technology; designed to transmit video and images over a narrower bandwidth and can mix video with text, graphics, and 2-D and 3-D animation layers.

Multichannel audio: Refers to the use of multiple sound sources to create a richer or live music experience; has become popular with the advent of surround sound, home theater, and DVD systems.

Multimedia: Applications and technologies that manipulate text, data, images, voice, and full-motion video objects.

Murder: The unlawful taking of a human life by another, especially with premeditated malice.

National Incident Management System (NIMS): Developed by the U.S. Secretary of Homeland Security at the request of the president of the United States; integrates effective practices in emergency preparedness and response into a comprehensive national framework for incident management; enables responders at all levels to work together more effectively to manage domestic incidents no matter what the cause, size, or complexity.

National Institute for Occupational Safety and Health (NIOSH): U.S. federal agency responsible for conducting research and making recommendations for the prevention of work-related injury and illness. Part of the Centers for Disease Control and Prevention (CDC) in the Department of Health and Human Services (HHS).

Native format: Proprietary file format of a given application.

Native resolution: The actual number of physical pixels on the display device.

Natural death: Cessation of life in a living organism caused by disease or old age, rather than an accident or act of violence.

Near infrared (NIR): The region of the electromagnetic spectrum between 0.77 and 1.4 microns. Most of the IR solar radiation falls into this region. This near IR (or solar IR) region is transmitted, absorbed, and reflected in a manner similar to visible light by most glazing and nonmetallic building materials. *Short-wave IR* is radiation of the shortest wavelength (i.e., closest to the visible spectrum), about 0.75 to 3.0 mm. *Near IR light* is not visible to human eyes, but many celestial objects shine brightly with this light; typically associated with heat.

Negative: In photography, film containing an image in which the values of the original are reversed so that the dark areas appear light and vice versa.

Negative control: A control sample where a negative result is expected, to help correlate a positive result with the variable being tested.

Neutral color: The colors black, white, and gray. The three light primaries—red, blue, and green—exist in equal amounts in all neutral colors.

Night vision: The ability to see in an environment where the level of ambient illumination is low.

NiMH: Nickel Metal-Hydride: a type of rechargeable battery that can be recharged many times. NiMH batteries provide sufficient power to run digital cameras and flashes.

Noise: Sum of dark and read noises.

Nonlinear editing: Computer-assisted editing of video without the need to assemble it in linear sequence; the video-editing equivalent of word processing. Considered superior to linear editing.

Oblique: Slanting; sculptured other than axially, radially, or concentrically (i.e., other than parallel or perpendicular to a growing edge).

Observation: Any information collected with the senses.

Occlusal: Pertaining to the biting surface of the back teeth.

Occlusion: Any contact between biting or chewing surfaces of upper and lower teeth.

Occupational Safety and Health Administration (OSHA): Branch of the U.S. federal government that sets and enforces occupational health and safety regulations.

Optical center: The point on a lens through which light passes unrefracted; the thickest point of a plus lens or the thinnest point of a minus lens.

Optics: the branch of physics that studies the physical properties of light

Orientation: Orientation is the term used for the cameras position and aiming in space. The orientation of a camera is defined by its coordinates (X,Y,Z) and by its aiming direction (defined by three angles).

Orthogonal: A view that displays a parallel projection along one of the major axes. In an orthogonal view, the camera is oriented so it is perpendicular (orthogonal) to specific planes: the top view faces the XZ plane, the front view faces the XY plane, and the right view faces the YZ plane. An orthogonal view eliminates the effect of distance from a viewpoint, which provides a useful means of locating points and objects in 3-D space and is particularly helpful when modeling objects in wireframe mode.

Output device: Any device by which a computer transforms its information to the outside world. In general, you can think of an output device as a machine that translates machine-readable data into human-readable information. Examples: printers, microform devices, video screens.

Palatal: Pertaining to the surface of the tooth toward the hard palate.

Panchromatic: Designation of films that record all colors in tones of about the same relative brightness as the human eye sees in the original scene; sensitive to all visible wavelengths.

Panorama: A series of photographs taken from a point to cover 360 degrees around that point.

Parallax: As the subject moves closer to the camera, what is seen in the viewfinder is not a precise image of the same area that is captured on film. Some cameras automatically compensate for this by adjusting the frame lines or providing additional lines in the viewfinder. The amount of parallax error differs between cameras and is dependent on the placement of the viewfinder in relation to the lens. Single-lens reflex cameras do not suffer from this problem.

Parallel: Given distinct lines in the plane that are infinite in both directions, the lines are parallel if they never meet. Two distinct lines in the coordinate plane are parallel if and only if they have the same slope.

Paraphenylene diamine: Reducing agent used in some fine grain and color developers.

Patent prints: Prints that are contaminated with foreign matter usually containing dust. Such prints occur when fingers are pressed in a thin layer of dust or powder and some sticks on the friction ridges; when the finger touches something else, a print is identifiable.

Pathologist: A scientist who is skilled in identifying the cause and progress of diseases by examining tissue and fluid from the body, especially one who determines the cause of someone's death by conducting an autopsy.

Peer review: A review of trial reports by scientists who are not involved with the trial. The findings of a trial usually are reviewed before being accepted for publication.

Perception: In psychology and the cognitive sciences, perception is the process of acquiring, interpreting, selecting, and organizing sensory information.

Perimortem: Occurring at the time of death.

Perspective: The appearance of things relative to one another as determined by their distance from the viewer.

Perspective distortion: In photography and cinematography, perspective distortion describes the appearance of a part of the subject appearing abnormally large, relative to the rest of the scene. This is especially noticeable when that part of the scene extends toward the camera. It is affected solely by the distance between the camera and subject; the smaller this distance, the greater the perspective distortion.

Phot: A photometric unit of illuminance, or luminous flux through an area; not a metric (SI) unit; equal to 1 lumen per square centimeter; 10,000 phots equal 1 Lux.

Photogrammetry: The art, science, and technology of obtaining reliable information about physical objects and the environment through processes of recording, measuring and interpreting photographic images.

Photograph: An image (often just called a photo), or a representation of an image, such as one printed on plain paper, created by collecting and focusing reflected electromagnetic radiation. The most common photographs are those created of reflected visible wavelengths, producing permanent records of what the human eye can see.

Photography: Photography is the process of making pictures by means of the action of light. It involves recording light patterns, as reflected from objects, onto a sensitive medium through a timed exposure. The process is done through mechanical, chemical or digital devices commonly known as cameras.

Photometry: Deals with light energy of wavelengths that can cause visual sensation. Human visual range is typically from 380 nanometers to 780 nanometers. Wavelengths outside this range do very little to stimulate the human eye.

Photomontage: The technique of making a picture by assembling pieces of photographs, often in combination with other types of graphic material or the composite picture produced by this technique.
Photon: The quantum of electromagnetic energy, generally regarded as a discrete particle having zero mass, no electric charge, and an indefinitely long lifetime.
Photopic vision: What occurs in normal light (luminance level 1 to 10^6 cd/m^2); color discrimination is optimum.
Photoreceptor: A cell that is specialized for converting the rate at which it absorbs photons to the magnitude of a signal, which can be relayed to and interpreted by the organism's central nervous system.
Photo-sensitivity: The amount to which an object reacts upon receiving photons of light. Devices that are photosensitive include the human retina and photographic film. Film is photosensitive because a chemical reaction occurs on it when struck by light. The same process is used in the electronic device known as a photocathode, which is a surface that emits electrons when struck by light.
Photoshop: Adobe Photoshop, the industry-standard graphics creation and manipulation software package.
Photosite: A single photosensitive element in a CCD that translates to one pixel in the resultant image. Also known as a CCD element.
Photovoltaic (PV): Converting light into electricity. Photo means "light," voltaic means "electric." Commonly referred to as "solar electric."
Picture: In common usage, an artifact that reproduces the likeness of some subject—usually a physical object or a person.
Pixel (Picture Element): Basic unit from which a video or computer picture is made. Essentially a dot with a given color and brightness value. The more pixels, the higher the resolution of the picture.
Plastic print: A print that occurs when the finger touches or presses against a plastic material in such a way that a negative impression of the friction ridge is produced.
Pocket Rod: Similar to conventional tape measures, except they are made specifically for use during the photographic documentation of evidence and scenes. The rod has no excess material before the first graduation and is classified as a true-zero measuring instrument. The graduations are larger and higher in contrast than on conventional tapes to enable recognition in the photographs. The tapes are easily taken out of their plastic case to allow use in free-standing applications.
Point cloud data: The collection of points in 3-D space resulting from scanning an object; represent the surface of the object.
Point-of-view: Angle from which the viewer sees an object.
Postmortem: Occurring after death.
PowerPoint: A popular presentation program developed for the Microsoft Windows and the Macintosh computer operating systems. Being widely used by businesspeople, educators, and trainers, it is among the most prevalent forms of presentation technology.
PPE: Personal protective equipment.
Practice: An activity that is actually routinely performed, regardless of whether it is required in policy or specified in procedure.
Precision: The range in which the best estimates of a true value approximate the true value. Data may be precise but not accurate if an inherent error has been made in the collection. Data may also be accurate but not precise, within the experimental tolerance for error.
Previsualization: The art of concentrating or imagining something very strongly, usually as a visual image.
Primary colors: Those hues that cannot be produced by mixing other hues. Pigment primaries are red, yellow, and blue; light primaries are red, green, and blue. Theoretically, pigment primaries can be mixed together to form all the other hues in the spectrum.
Principal distance: The distance of the projection center from the image plane's principal point (the location in the camera where the optical axis of the lens intersects the image receptor).
Principal point: The position of best focus for infinity.
Professional: Classifications in which the predominant and essential function of the work requires the application of theories, concepts, principles, and methodologies typically acquired through completion of a bachelor's or post-bachelor's degree program. Professional work requires the consistent exercise of discretion to research, analyze, interpret, develop, and apply various criteria to nonroutine and nonmechanical processes.
Program exposure: An exposure mode on an automatic or auto-focus camera that automatically sets both the aperture and the shutter speed for proper exposure.
Progressive scanning: The means by which the picture tubes of computer monitors and newer televisions display images, using a progressive scanning tube to send information to each pixel on a screen sequentially. Offers higher-quality pictures than does interlaced scan.

Pro-sumer: Type of electronic product that straddles the professional and consumer markets, or one who uses such a product. Refers to more expensive semi-professional digital cameras aimed at the consumer market.
Protocol: A document that describes the objective(s), design, methodology, statistical considerations, and organization of a practice. The protocol usually also gives the background and rationale.
Proximity: The property of being close together.
Pseudoscience: Any body of knowledge or practice that purports to be scientific or supported by science but that is judged by the mainstream scientific community to fail to comply with the scientific method.
Qualitative: Referring only to the characteristics of something being described, rather than exact numerical measurement. Indicative only of relative sizes or magnitudes, rather than their numerical values.
Quality: The inherent or distinctive characteristics or properties of a person, object, process or other thing.
Quality of light: Relates to the color of the light sources (color temperature reading in degrees Kelvin). For example, 12:00 noon sun on a clear day would be the ideal condition for photography. The Kelvin reading would be approximately 6,500 k (U.S. broadcast standard).
Quantitative: Involving the measurement of quantity or amount.
Quantity of light: Defined as a measure of a certain light source or area. Can be applied in a variety of ways, from compliance with OSHA safety requirements in a factory to light-level measurement around a bank ATM machine (for security reasons) to a Hollywood studio film set . Light is measured in foot candles (English measurement) or lux (metric measurement).
Radiograph: An image obtained by shining high-energy light or X-rays through a body or object to a detector that records the image on photographic film or a photo-sensitive plate.
Radiometry: The measurement of optical radiation power.
Rape: A crime wherein the victim is forced into sexual activity against his or her will, in particular sexual penetration. It is considered by most societies to be among the most severe crimes.
RAW: Image format in which the data come directly off the CCD, with no in-camera processing performed.
Read noise: Image degradation arising from the limitations of individual pixel amplifiers during signal processing.
Reality: Reality in everyday usage means "everything that exists." The term "Reality," in its most liberal sense, includes everything that is, whether or not it is observable, accessible or understandable by science, philosophy, theology or any other system of analysis.
Reciprocity failure: Occurs when a film's speed cannot be relied upon for proper exposure at slow shutter speed; a shift in the color balance or the darkness of an image caused by very long or very short exposures.
Rectification: The process by which an image or grid is converted from image coordinates to real-world coordinates. Rectification typically involves rotation and scaling of grid cells, and thus requires resampling of values.
Reflectance: Ratio of the radiant energy reflected by a body to the energy incident on it. Spectral reflectance is the reflectance measured within a specific wavelength interval.
Reflected light: Light bounced off a subject, not falling on it.
Reflection: The return of rays of light striking a surface.
Reflector: Any device used to reflect light onto a subject.
Refraction: Property of light that concerns light passing from a medium of one density to a medium of a differing density, such as from air to water or vice versa.
Relief: Any feature of a landmark that is raised above the surface. The opposite of relief is recess.
Replica: A close reproduction of the original.
Report: A type of document written by someone or a group of people. Generally an account of an event, although some reports are simply published findings.
Representation: A presentation to the mind in the form of an idea or image; a visual or tangible rendering of someone or something; a factual statement made by one party to induce another party to enter into a contract; a statement of facts and reasons made to appeal or protest; an activity that stands as an equivalent of something or results in an equivalent.
Reproduce: make a copy or equivalent.
Reproduction Ratio: Indicates the magnification of a subject for macrophotography—specifically, the size of the image recorded on a sensor divided by the actual size of the subject. For example, if the image on film is the same size as the subject, the reproduction ratio is written as 1:1 or 1x.
Resample: To change the number of pixels in an image. Up-sampling uses interpolation to increase the number of pixels, Down-sampling throws away pixels to reduce the size.

Resolution: Measured in pixels per inch (ppi). The number of pixels in the image. The more pixels in the image, the higher the resolution, the sharper the picture, but larger the size of the file. For example, a 1-inch square of an image scanned at 72 ppi contains 5,184 pixels (72×72) and has a file size of 6 K; if the same file is scanned at 144 ppi, it will contain 20,736 pixels (144×144) and a file size of 21 K.
Resolve: make clearly visible; "Can this image be resolved?"
Retina: Light sensitive nerve tissue in the eye that converts images from the eye's optical system into electrical impulses that are sent along the optic nerve to the brain.
RGB (Red, Green, Blue): The color language of computers. Computer monitors and digital cameras use these colors to create all the colors seen on the monitor and saved in files. Green gives the color green but is also used for contrast control.
Ring flash: A circular-shaped electronic flash unit that fits around a lens and provides shadowless, uniform frontal lighting, especially useful in close-up photography.
Robbery: The crime of seizing property through violence or intimidation. A perpetrator of a robbery is a robber. Because most robberies include an ingredient of violence, robberies sometimes result in the harm or murder of their victims. Robbery is generally an urban crime.
Rod: Light-sensitive, specialized retinal receptor cell that works at low light levels (night vision). A normal retina contains 150 million rods.
Root Cause: The real cause or origin of a problem.
RS-232: A standard interface between a computer input/output port and a peripheral device. Signal properties, including time duration, voltage, and current, are specified by the Electronic Industries Association.
Saturation: The intensity of a specific hue, based on the color's purity. A highly saturated hue has a vivid, intense color, while a less saturated hue appears more muted and gray. With no saturation at all, the hue becomes a shade of gray.
Scale: The size or apparent size of an object seen in relation to other objects, people, or its environment or format. In architectural drawings, it is the ratio of the measurements in the drawing to the measurements in the building.
Scanning electron microscope (SEM): An electron-beam-based microscope used to examine, in a three-dimensional screen image, the surface structure of prepared specimens.
Scatter: Refers to light reflected from underwater objects that travels through a medium filled with floating particulates; causes the diffusion and scattering of light.
Scotopic vision: Monochromatic vision of the eye in dim light.
Sealed beam: A type of lamp that includes a reflector and filament as a single assembly, over which a front cover (lens), usually of clear glass, is permanently attached.
Sensitivity: The degree to which a photographic emulsion reacts to light. Fast film, for example, has greater sensitivity than slow film.
Serial: A method for connecting an external device, such as a printer, scanner, or camera, to a computer. It has been all but replaced by USB and FireWire in modern computers.
Shutter priority: A mode in which a desired shutter speed is manually selected and locked in; the camera then chooses an appropriate lens opening (f-stop) for proper exposure. Used primarily to prevent motion blur in fast-moving subjects or objects.
Shutter speed: The camera's shutter speed is a measurement of how long its shutter remains open as the picture is taken. The slower the shutter speed, the longer the exposure time. When the shutter speed is set to 1/125 or simply 125, this means that the shutter will be open for exactly 1/125 of one second. The shutter speed and aperture together control the total amount of light reaching the sensor. Some digital cameras have a shutter priority mode that allows for setting the shutter speed as desired.
SI: The International System of Units is the modern metric system.
Signal-to-noise ratio (SNR): The ratio in decibels (dB) of an audio or video signal, between the signal's maximum peak-to-peak signal voltage and the measured voltage of what remains when the signal is removed (i.e., the ratio of the signal to that of the noise). In video, the higher the ratio, the less snow is visible.
Silver: A chemical element that is a soft white lustrous transition metal, silver has the highest electrical and thermal conductivity of any metal and occurs in minerals and in free form. This metal is used in coins, jewelry, tableware, and photography.
Silver halide: The silver crystals that make up an image on a negative or print. When exposed to light, they create an image. Those that are not exposed are washed off, leaving either a negative (film) or positive (print) image.
Similarity: The quality of being similar.
Simulation: An imitation of some real device or state of affairs. Attempts to represent certain features of the behavior of a physical or abstract system by the behavior of another system.

Single lens reflex (SLR): A camera with one lens only for both viewing and picture taking. The image is reflected onto a viewing screen by a moveable mirror in the camera. The mirror flips out of the way just before the shutter opens, permitting light to strike the film.
Situational Analysis: is an in-depth process to develop understanding of the needs of specific audiences in a specific setting. It involves a combination of data gathering techniques conducted from a variety of perspectives (social, economic, environmental, and political, etc.).
Slave unit: A light-sensitive triggering device that is built in or attached to an electronic flash unit, causing the flash to fire simultaneously with another flash unit. Used to sync strobes and flashes without an electronic sync cord. Also called a *photo slave.*
Slow-speed lens: A lens with a relatively narrow maximum aperture—*f*/8, for example.
Spectral selectivity: A window's ability to transmit visible light while reducing solar heat gain; expressed by a number between 0 and 1. Creation of images using intentionally limited ranges of radiation in the UV, visible, or IR portions of the spectrum.
Spectral sensitivity (of a photoreceptor): Sensitivity of a photoreceptor at each wavelength in the visible spectrum. For a given wavelength, this is equal to the ratio of the photoreceptor response at that wavelength to its response at the most sensitive wavelength. Different photoreceptor types have different spectral sensitivities.
sRGB: Hewlett-Packard and Microsoft proposed the addition of support for a standard color space (sRGB) within the Microsoft operating systems, HP products, the Internet, and all other interested vendors. The aim of this color space is to complement the current color management strategies by enabling a third method of handling color in the operating systems, device drivers, and the Internet that utilizes a simple and robust device independent of color definition.
Standard: A set of criteria (some of which may be mandatory), voluntary guidelines, and best practices. Examples include application development, project management, vendor management, production operation, user support, asset management, technology evaluation, architecture governance, configuration management, problem resolution, etc.
Standard operating procedure (SOP): Written documents that describe in step-by-step detail how a procedure should be done.
Static: Not changeable. The opposite of *dynamic.*
Step wedge: A printed series of density increases, in regular steps from transparent to opaque. A method of making exposure tests when enlarging.
Steradian: The SI unit of solid angle that, having its vertex in the center of a sphere, cuts off an area of the surface of the sphere equal to that of a square with sides of length equal to the radius of the sphere.
Stereo Photography: Stereoscopy, stereoscopic imaging, or three-dimensional (3-D) imaging is a technique to create the illusion of depth in a photograph, movie, or other two-dimensional image, by presenting a slightly different image to each eye.
Stereopsis: Ability to see objects as three-dimensional and to judge their relative distance in space by putting together mental images from both eyes.
Stereoscope: An optical device for creating stereoscopic (or three-dimensional) effects from flat (two-dimensional) images. It is provided with lenses, under which two equal images are placed, so that one is viewed with the right eye and the other with the left. Observed at the same time, the two images merge into a single virtual image which, as a consequence of binocular human vision, appears to be three-dimensional.
Stimulus: Is that which provokes a response, or more generally, the point of interactions of the human system and environment.
Stitching: Combining a series of images to form a larger image or a panoramic photo. Requires special post-editing software.
Stop-down metering: TTL metering in which the light is measured at the picture-taking aperture.
Subcutaneous: Beneath the skin but above the fascia and muscle.
Subject brightness range: The difference in luminance between the darkest and lightest areas of the subject, in both negative and print.
Suicide: From Latin *sui caedere,* to kill oneself. The act of intentionally ending one's own life; sometimes a noun for one who has committed or attempted the act.
Suspended particles: May be organic, such as plankton, or inorganic, as with stirred up sediment (silt).
Symbolism: The systematic or creative use of symbols as abstracted representations of concepts or objects. In a narrow context, symbolism is the applied use of any iconic representations that carry particular conventional meanings.
Symmetric: A figure is symmetric with respect to a line if it can be folded on that line so that every point on one side coincides exactly with a point on the other side. A figure is symmetric with respect to a point O if for each point A on the figure there is a point B on the figure for which O is the midpoint of AB.
Synchronization: Method of synchronizing flash light duration with maximum shutter opening. Usually two settings on a camera: X and M. X is the set-

ting used for electronic flash. M is used for most expendable types of flash (bulbs) that require a delay in shutter opening.

Technical: Of or relating to a practical subject that is organized according to scientific principles.

Technical Pan: Technical Pan was a black-and-white film produced by Kodak. It was generally used as a very slow film, rated at ISO 25 or even 16, although it could be rated up to ISO 320. It was discontinued in 2004. It was *very* fine grained, with variable contrast and high transparency.

Terrestrial: Of the Earth, Earth related.

Testify: Give testimony in a court of law.

Testimony: A solemn attestation as to the truth of a matter. Testifying is the act of providing testimony.

Thermal: Pertaining to high temperatures, direct flames, oxidizing gases, and such.

Three-point perspective: An image with three vanishing points.

Through-the-lens (TTL): Refers both to exposure metering of the light passing through the lens (through-the-lens metering, and TTL flash metering) and to viewing a scene through the same lens that allows light to reach the film (through-the-lens focusing). When TTL flash exposure control is used, a light sensor, positioned inside the camera, measures the amount of light reflected by the film during the actual exposure. Depending upon the film speed and the aperture, the TTL "brain" switches off (quenches) the strobe whenever a sufficient amount of light has produced proper exposure.

Thyristor: Automatic flash gun that cuts off the flash when the exposure is correct. This conserves power, makes recycling quicker, and lengthens battery life.

TIFF (Tagged Image File Format): A file format commonly used for digital scanned images. Images saved in TIFF format can be used on most computers. Developed by Aldus and Microsoft

Timeline: Linear representation of the progress of an animation from the first to the last frame; a chronological display of an edited sequence in a nonlinear editing system.

Tone: Refers to the color quality or color content of the document or parts of the document.

Tooth: Hard, bonelike structures in the jaws of vertebrates; used for biting and chewing or for attack and defense.

Total darkness: Total absence of light.

Total station: A total station is an optical instrument used in modern surveying. It is a combination of an electronic theodolite (transit), an electronic distance measuring device (EDM) and software running on an external computer.

Transcendental: Of or characteristic of a system of philosophy emphasizing the intuitive and spiritual above the empirical and material.

Transmission: The act of sending a message; causing a message to be transmitted.

Transparency: A still, positive image created on a transparent base using photochemical means. The terms *slide* and *reversal film* may also be used. Contrasted with *negative* and *print*.

Triage: The process by which projects or activities are prioritized to determine which should be attempted first, second, and so on, and which projects or activities should never be done at all. Considers the value, complexity, cost, and order in which steps should be accomplished.

Trial: The court proceedings in which the district attorney, or a deputy district attorney, presents the case for the state, attempting to prove beyond a reasonable doubt that the defendant committed the crime as charged.

Triangulation: The method of determining a location on a map by using two or more points through which angles or lines of known directions are drawn; the intersection of these lines is the desired location.

True color: 16.8 million unique color values.

Truth: Primary Principle, means conformity with fact, agreement with reality, accuracy, correctness, verity of a statement or thought, genuineness, reality, conduct following the divine standard, spirituality of life and behavior, that which is true, real, or actual in a general or abstract sense, reality.

Turbidity: The relative concentration of suspended particles found in an underwater environment. May result from healthy and natural phenomena, such as rainwater runoff, or from artificial, unhealthy phenomena, such as pollution.

Two-point perspective: An image with two vanishing points.

Ultraviolet light (UV): The portion of the electromagnetic spectrum with wavelengths from about 100 to 400 nanometers; between ionizing radiation (X-rays) and visible light.

Unsharp masking (USM) : A software feature that selectively sharpens a digital image in areas of high contrast while having little effect on areas of solid color. The effect is to increase the apparent detail and sharpness.

Up-sampling: The process of increasing the sampling rate of a signal. Usually done to increase the bandwidth of a signal.

USB (Universal Serial Bus) : Type of connector for attaching peripherals, such as mice, keyboards, scanners, printers, and disk drives. Offers faster data transfer and easier (plug-and-play) connections than PC parallel port or Mac serial ports. Works with Windows 98/Mac OS 8.5 or above.

Value: Relative darkness or lightness of a color.

Vanishing point: In linear perspective, the point on the horizon line at which lines or edges that are parallel appear to converge.

Vector: In physics and engineering, typically refers to a quantity that has close relationship to the spatial coordinates, informally described as an object with a "magnitude" and a "direction."

Velcro: Registered trade name for a type of hook-and-loop fabric fastener.

Vertical: Perpendicular to the horizon. Up and down.

Video: Having to do with the visual presentation of information, usually on a monitor screen.

Video compression: The process through which a complete video file is reduced in size.

Video editing: A procedure for combining selected portions of video footage to create a new, combined version. During video editing, special effects such as wipes, dissolves, inserts, and so on can be added.

Viewpoint: The position of the camera in relation to the subject.

Virtual reality (VR): A computer simulation of a real three-dimensional world, often supplemented by sound effects. People often associate virtual reality with a body suit and head gear that includes an internal screen. These computerized images can be simulated in any environment, making you feel like you're really there. A more common use for VR is seen in many 3-D computer games.

Virtual tour: A computer-generated tour in which the viewer gets the sense of actually moving in the space.

Visible spectrum: Indefinite range of wavelengths of visible radiation, sometimes taken (for convenience) to lie between 400 and 700 nanometers. Radiation with wavelengths less than 400 nanometers is UV radiation; radiation with wavelengths greater than 700 nanometers is IR radiation. The only part of the electromagnetic spectrum visible to humans, including the colors of the rainbow: red, orange, yellow, green, blue, and violet.

Vision: Visual perception is one of the senses, consisting of the ability to detect light and interpret (see) it as the perception known as sight or naked eye vision. Vision has a specific sensory system.

Vision study: Photographs that are representative of the way the scene looked to the person making the photographs.

Visual acuity: Clarity of vision. Measured as a fraction of normal vision; 20/20 vision indicates an eye that sees at 20 feet what a normal eye should see at 20 feet, and 20/400 vision indicates an eye that sees at 20 feet what a normal eye sees at 400 feet.

Visual communication: The communication of ideas through the visual display of information; primarily associated with two-dimensional images, including alphanumeric, art, signage, and electronic resources. Recent research has focused on Web design and graphically oriented usability.

Visual or visual image: Any concrete image that is visible, including graphics, statuary, architecture, and such. May also refer to the physical or visible aspects of any sign or symbol (apart from its significance).

Visual task: Conventionally designates those details and objects that must be seen for the performance of a given activity and includes the immediate background of the details or objects.

Visualization: The production of two- and three-dimensional pictures; or graphs of the numerical results of computations.

Viz: Short for *visibility*, refers to the distance that a diver can see underwater. Indirectly refers to the turbidity of the water.

Watt/second (WS): Unit of electrical energy equal to the work done when a current of one ampere passes through a resistance of one ohm for one second.

Wavelength: The distance between two successive points of an electromagnetic waveform, usually measured in nanometers (nm).

Weapon of mass destruction/disaster (WMD): A weapon that can kill large numbers of humans, animals, and plants, such as a terrorist attack executed with poisoned gas or an atomic bomb and intended to kill masses of people.

White balance: A way of calibrating a camera's color response to take into account different color temperatures of light (e.g., fluorescent light is greenish; sunlight is more blue; incandescent light is yellowish). This calibration allows the camera to define what the color white is under any of these various lighting conditions. Failure to white balance could result in an unnatural color cast.

White point: In monitor calibration, white point is the color of "pure" white (RGB 255:255:255) on a monitor, expressed as an absolute temperature (in degrees Kelvin). Adjusting the white point of a monitor allows on-screen colors to appear correct, given the lighting in the environment. The color temperature of a white pixel on a computer monitor. Most computer monitors have a white point of 6,500 Kelvin (or higher), which means that white objects on the monitor are actually blue-white, rather than pure white. This in turn means that colors displayed on the monitor are inaccurate.

Witness mark: A punch mark or scratch used to position or locate a part in its proper spot; the mark is made on each half of an assembly so that upon reassembly the marks can be lined up. A scoring or scribing of a line on a machined surface. Something that serves as evidence; a sign. Tool mark examiners perform comparisons of known samples, including projectiles, cartridge cases, and tool marks, etc, to questioned samples, to determine if the questioned samples and known samples can be positively linked.

Workflow: The path and systems used in the linked flow of activities with a specific start and finish that describe a process. The flow defines where inputs are initiated, the location of decision points and the alternatives in output paths, and is used in systems that perform automatic routing.

Working distance: Distance from the front of the lens surface to the subject. The more frequently used term *shooting distance* refers to the distance between the subject and the image plane.

Wound: A physical trauma where the skin is torn, cut, or punctured.

Xenon: Colorless, odorless gas used in a gas discharge lamp to produce white light.

Zone system: Methodology introduced by photographer Ansel Adams for determining optimal exposure and appropriate development for an individual photograph. Based on analysis of subject luminosities in terms of 10 gray tones, labeled zones 0 through X, and previsualization of them as print densities.

Index

G